International Law
Chiefly as Interpreted and Applied in Canada

WITH SUPPORTING WEBSITE AND ONLINE INDEX AT
<http://www.emp.ca/intlaw7>

HUGH M. KINDRED and PHILLIP M. SAUNDERS
General Editors
Faculty of Law
Dalhousie University

JUTTA BRUNNÉE
Faculty of Law
University of Toronto

ROBERT J. CURRIE
Faculty of Law
Dalhousie University

TED L. McDORMAN
Faculty of Law
University of Victoria

ARMAND L.C. deMESTRAL
Faculty of Law
McGill University

KARIN MICKELSON
Faculty of Law
University of British Columbia

RENÉ PROVOST
Faculty of Law
McGill University

LINDA C. REIF
Faculty of Law
University of Alberta

STEPHEN J. TOOPE
Faculty of Law
McGill University

SHARON A. WILLIAMS
Osgoode Hall Law School
York University

SEVENTH EDITION
2006
EMOND MONTGOMERY PUBLICATIONS LIMITED

Emond Montgomery Publications Limited
60 Shaftesbury Avenue
Toronto ON M4T 1A3
http://www.emp.ca

Printed in Canada.

Reprinted in December 2011.

Produced by WordsWorth Communications of Toronto, Canada.

We acknowledge the financial support of the Government of Canada through the Canada Book Fund for our publishing activities.

Library and Archives Canada Cataloguing in Publication

International law, chiefly as interpreted and applied in Canada / Hugh M. Kindred and Phillip M. Saunders, general editors; Jutta Brunée ... [et al.] — 7th ed.

ISBN 978-1-55239-162-4

1. International law — Canada.   2. International law — Sources.
3. International law — Cases.   I. Kindred, Hugh M.   II. Saunders, Phillip Martin

KZ358.A2I57 2006   341'.0971   C2005-906037-9

Preface to the Seventh Edition

Unlike other subjects in the law school curriculum, international law is a whole legal system. In no other field of law is such a broad sweep of ideas, legal concepts, institutions, principles, and rules expected to be digested within the limited span of a single course, now typically three hours per week for one semester. The authors, as teachers of international law, offer this volume of materials for just such an introduction to international law. Inevitably, we have had to make a severe selection not only of legal materials but also of subject matter. We have tried to present the fundamental principles and processes of the international legal system as it has so far evolved, exploring these ideas through as many different areas of its operation as the practical limits of the book allows.

The book is primarily designed for our students, and others like them, who experience the world from a Canadian perspective. Although international law applies globally, it is subject to many different interpretations. Accordingly, we have prepared a volume of materials that, while they include all the principal documents and decisions of whatever origin, also draw extensively on the practice of international law chiefly as interpreted and applied in Canada.

An additional purpose of this book is to provide a reference of first resort for anyone who has need of international legal sources. These users, we imagine, might be members of the legal profession confronted with a legal problem containing international elements, or other persons wishing to discover Canadian practice in a particular area of international law. As fully as the confines of this book permit, we have included comments and citations that we hope will assist our readers to direct their research along the most appropriate lines of enquiry.

The book is also supported by an Internet website. This electronic resource enhances the use of the printed text by the provision of additional international legal sources. In particular, the website provides online access to full copies of the treaties, United Nations documents, and international law case reports partially reproduced in the book. In addition, it offers an electronic index by means of a keyword search of the entire text and footnotes. These online support services are more fully explained in the Notice of Internet Website after this Preface and on the website itself, viewable at <http://www.emp.ca/intlaw7>.

As the 21st century advances, international law is experiencing not only great change but also an increasing rate of change. Indeed, so rapid and extensive have the developments become that international law, it has been suggested, is in a state of flux of transformative proportions not experienced since its evolution, in the time of Grotius, over 350 years ago. The 7th edition of this book carries the subject of international law forward into the 21st century, fully reflective of both the constancy and change at work upon it.

In the course of successive editions the group of co-authors of the book has also altered. The group no longer includes Jean Castel, Don Fleming, Bill Graham, or Ivan Vlasic, but their huge contributions to the development of the book continue to be expressed in its pages and to undergird the revisions of this edition.

Seventh Edition   Hugh Kindred & Phillip Saunders
November 2005   General Editors

Notice of Website

at <http://www.emp.ca/intlaw7>

The Internet website at the above address provides a variety of online support services to enhance the use of this book:

- *Treaty Links* provides access to full copies of the treaties, conventions, and other United Nations' documents that are excerpted in the text.
- *Case Links* affords access to copies of the national and international cases excerpted in the text.

These links are referenced to the book by chapter and page number.

The website also features an *Online Index* that facilitates a Boolean search of the entire text and footnotes of the book by keyword inquiry, and returns page references for the words or phrases that are input.

Once at the website, simply point and click on the service desired for immediate access.

Summary Table of Contents

Detailed Table of Contents

Table of Abbreviations

ACHPR	African Charter of Human and People Rights
ACHR	American Convention on Human Rights
AFN	Assembly of First Nations (Canada)
ANC	African National Congress
A.S.I.L.	American Society of International Law
AU	African Union
B.N.A. Act	British North America Act
Can. T.S.	Canada Treaty Series
CAT	Convention Against Torture
C.C.I.L.	Canadian Council on International Law
CEDAW	Convention on the Elimination of All Forms of Discrimination Against Women
CHM	Common Heritage of Mankind
CIT	Canada Import Tribunal
CLRB	Canadian Labour Relations Board
C.R.C.	Consolidated Regulations of Canada
CRTC	Canadian Radio and Television Commission
CSCE	Conference on Security and Cooperation in Europe
DEA	Drug Enforcement Agency (US)
D.P.P.	Director of Public Prosecutions
DOALOS	Division of Ocean Affairs and the International Law of the Sea (UN)
EC	European Community
E.C.J.	European Court of Justice
ECHR	European Convention for the Protection of Human Rights
ECOSOC	Economic and Social Council (UN)
ECSC	European Coal and Steel Community
EEC	European Economic Community
EEZ	Exclusive Economic Zone
EU	European Union
Eur. T.S.	European Treaty Series
FAO	Food and Agriculture Organization of the United Nations
FCN Treaties	Friendship, Navigation and Commerce Treaties
GATT	General Agreement on Tariffs and Trade

GA. Res.	(UN) General Assembly Resolution
GAOR	(UN) General Assembly Official Records
G.O.Q.	Gazette Officiel du Quebec
GPA	Global Programme of Action
HRC	Human Rights Committee
ICAO	International Civil Aviation Organization
ICC	International Chamber of Commerce
ICCPR	International Covenant on Civil and Political Rights
ICESCR	International Covenant in Economic, Social and Cultural Rights
ICJ	International Court of Justice
ICNAF	International Convention for the Northwest Atlantic Fisheries
ICRC	International Committee of the Red Cross
ICRW	International Convention for the Regulation of Whaling
ICSID	International Centre for the Settlement of Investment Disputes
ICTR	International Criminal Tribunal for Rwanda
ICTY	International Criminal Tribunal for the former Yugoslavia
IGO	Inter-governmental Organization
IMO	International Maritime Organization
IMT	International Military Tribunal
ILC	International Law Commission
I.L.M.	International Legal Materials
ILO	International Labour Organization
INTELSAT	International Telecommunications Satellite Consortium
IOC	International Olympic Committee
IRPA	Immigration and Refugee Protection Act
ITLOS	International Tribunal for the Law of the Sea
ITU	International Telecommunications Union
IWC	International Whaling Commission
MOU	Memorandum of Understanding
MARPOL	International Convention for the Prevention of Pollution from Ships
MFN	Most Favoured Nation
NAFTA	North American Free Trade Agreement
NAFO	North Atlantic Fisheries Organization
NATO	North Atlantic Treat Organization
NGO	Non-Governmental Organization
NLRB	National Labour Relations Board
OAS	Organization of American States
OAU	Organization of African Unity
OECD	Organization for Economic Development
OILPOL	International Convention for the Prevention of Pollution of the Sea by Oil
OSCE	Organization for Security Cooperation in Europe

OSPAR	Convention for the Protection of the Marine Environments of the North-East Atlantic
PCIJ	Permanent Court of International Justice
PSAC	Public Service Alliance of Canada
RFO	Regional Fisheries Organization
SC	(UN) Security Council
SIA	State Immunity Act
SIMA	Special Import Measures Act
S.O.R.	Statutory Orders and Regulations
TAC	Total Allowable Catch
UDHR	Universal Declaration of Human Rights
U.K.T.S.	United Kingdom Treaty Series
UNCED	United Nations Conference on Environment and Development, 1992
UNCLOS	United Nations Conference/Convention on the Law of the Sea
UNCHR	United Nations Commission on Human Rights
UNCITRAL	United Nations Commission on International Trade Law
UNEP	United Nations Environment Programme
UNESCO	United Nations Economic, Social and Cultural Organization
UNGA	United Nations General Assembly
UNHRC	United Nations Human Rights Committee
UNHCR	United Nations High Commissioner for Refugees
U.N.T.S.	United Nations Treaty Series
U.S.C.	United States Code
U.S.T.	United States Treaties and Other International Agreements
U.S. Stat.	United States Statutes at Large
WHO	World Health Organization
Y.B. ILC	Yearbook of the International Law Commission

Table of Cases

This table includes cases referred to by the authors. It does not include cases cited within the reproduced texts and reports. A bold face page number indicates that a (partial) report of the case is reproduced in the text. An "n" after a page number indicates that the case is to be found in footnotes.

Acknowledgments

The general editors are very grateful to the Foundation for Legal Research and to Dalhousie Law School for their financial support toward the preparation of this edition. We are also most thankful to Gillian MacNeil, law student at Dalhousie University, for her cheerful and meticulous bibliographic assistance.

We wish to recognize the generosity of many copyright holders for the use of their works in this book. We have attempted to obtain permission to reproduce all of the extracts from published works that are reprinted here. If we have inadvertently overlooked any acknowledgment, we offer our sincere apologies and will undertake to rectify the omission in any future editions.

American Society of International Law

Myres S. McDougal, "The Hydrogen Bomb Tests and the International Law of the Sea," editorial comment (1955) 49 American Journal of International Law 356 at 356-58. Reproduced with permission from the American Journal of International Law, © American Society of International Law.

Bernard H. Oxman, "Complementary Agreements and Compulsory Jurisdiction" (2001) 95 American Journal of International Law 277 at 281-82. Reproduced with permission from the American Journal of International Law, © American Society of International Law.

The Association of the Bar of the City of New York

Committee on International Human Rights of the Association of the Bar of the City of New York, "The Inter-American Commission: A Promise Unfulfilled" (1993) 48 The Record 589.

Brill Academic Publishers

Jutta Brunnée, "The Stockholm Declaration and the Structure and Processes of International Environmental Law" in M.H. Nordquist, J.N. Moore, & S. Mahmoudi, eds., *The Stockholm Declaration and Law of the Marine Environment* (Leiden: Brill Academic Publishers, 2003) 69.

Brill Academic Publishers (continued)

A. Eide, " 'Law of The Hague' and 'Law of Geneva' Distinguished" from "The Laws of War and Human Rights—Differences and Convergences" in C. Swinarski, ed., *Studies and Essays on International Humanitarian Law and Red Cross Principles, in Honour of Jean Pictet* (Geneva: Martinus Nijhoff, 1984) 675 at 677-78.

Manfred Lachs, "The Development and General Trends of International Law in Our Time" (1980) 169 Hague Recueil 9 at 220, 221.

D. Pharand, "Legal Status of the Arctic Regions" (1979) 163 Hague Recueil 51.

E.D. Brown

E.D. Brown, "Dispute Settlement and the Law of the Sea: The U.N. Convention Regime" (1967) 21 Marine Policy Journal 17, 43.

Cambridge University Press

J.G. Merrills, *International Dispute Settlement* (New York: Cambridge University Press, 1998) 27-28, 42-43. Reprinted with the permission of Cambridge University Press.

Philippe Sands, "Emergence of International Environmental Law" in Philippe Sands, ed., *Principles of International Environmental Law*, 2d ed. (New York: Cambridge University Press, 2003). Reprinted with the permission of Cambridge University Press.

Canadian Bar Association

S. A. Williams, "Conviction After Unlawful Arrest" (1975) 53 Canadian Bar Review 404.

Council on Foreign Relations, Inc.

Lincoln P. Bloomfield, Map from "The Arctic: The Unmanaged Frontier" (1981) 60:1 Foreign Affairs 88. Reprinted by permission of Foreign Affairs. Copyright 1981 by the Council on Foreign Relations, Inc.

Evan Luard, Map from "Who Owns Antarctica?" (1984) 62:5 Foreign Affairs 1176 (part II). Reprinted by permission of Foreign Affairs. Copyright 1984 by the Council on Foreign Relations, Inc.

Dalhousie Law Journal

Dalhousie Law Journal, Maps of Canadian Coastal Baselines (1982-83) 7 Dalhousie Law Journal 32-36.

Department of Foreign Affairs and International Trade

Department of External Affairs, *Canadian Espousal of Claims*, based on J.-G. Castel, Legal Services provided by the Department of External Affairs with respect to International Judical Co-operation and other matters (Ottawa: Department of External Affairs, 1987). Reproduced with the permission of Her Majesty the Queen in Right of Canada, represented by the Minister of Public Works and Government Services, 2005.

Department of External Affairs, *Federalism and International Relations* (Ottawa: Department of External Affairs, 1968) 11-33. Reproduced with the permission of Her Majesty the Queen in Right of Canada, represented by the Minister of Public Works and Government Services, 2005.

Department of External Affairs, Map of the Canadian Arctic, from Statement in the House of Commons by the Secretary of State for External Affairs, Statement 85/49 (10 September 1985) (Ottawa: Department of External Affairs, 1985). Reproduced with the permission of Her Majesty the Queen in Right of Canada, represented by the Minister of Public Works and Government Services, 2005.

Department of External Affairs, Map of fishing zones 1, 2, and 4; 3 and 5, in Communique no. 16 (2 November 1976) (Ottawa: Department of External Affairs, 1976). Reproduced with the permission of Her Majesty the Queen in Right of Canada, represented by the Minister of Foreign Affairs, 2005.

Department of Foreign Affairs and International Trade, "The Responsibility To Protect" in *Report of the International Commission on Intervention and State Sovereignty* (Ottawa: Department of Foreign Affairs and International Trade, 2001) at vii-ix, xi-xii. Reproduced with the permission of Her Majesty the Queen in Right of Canada, represented by the Minister of Foreign Affairs, 2005. Source: <www.iciss.ca/menu-en.asp>.

Encyclopædia Britannica, Inc.

B. Weston, "Human Rights" (© 1992), 20 *Encyclopædia Britannica* 656, 659. Reprinted with permission from Encyclopædia Britannica.

G.H. Hackworth

G.H. Hackworth, Excerpts (1940-44), 5 Digest of International Law 526-27.

International Bar Association

S.A. Williams, "Public International Law Governing Transboundary Pollution" (1984) International Business Lawyer 243 at 246, 248.

The International Centre for Criminal Law Reform and Criminal Justice Policy

S.A. Williams, "The Core Crimes in the Rome Statute on the International Criminal Court" in *The Changing Face of International Criminal Law: Selected Papers* (Vancouver: The International Centre for Criminal Law Reform and Criminal Justice Policy, 2001) 63-72.

International Court of Justice

International Court of Justice, *Response of the International Court of Justice to General Assembly Resolution 52/161* (The Hague: International Court of Justice, 15 December 1997). Source: <www.icj-cij.org/icjwww/igeneralinformation/igeninfvarious/ResponseGA151297.html>.

Stephen M. Schwebel, *Address by the President of the International Court of Justice before the General Assembly of the United Nations* (The Hague: International Court of Justice, 27 October 1998). Source: <www.icj-cij.org/icjwww/ipresscom/SPEECHES/iSpeechPresidentGA98.htm>.

International Joint Commission

International Joint Commission, *The International Joint Commission and the 21st Century: Response of the IJC to a Request by the Governments of Canada and the United States for Proposals on How To Best Assist Them To Meet the Environmental Challenges of the 21st Century* (Ottawa: International Joint Commission, 1997). Source: <www.ijc.org/php/publications/html/21ste.htm>.

Juris Publishing, Inc.

R.R. Churchill & A.V. Lowe, *The Law of the Sea*, 3d ed. (Huntington: Juris Publishing, Inc., 1999). Source: <www.jurispub.com>.

McGill-Queen's University Press

Suzanne Lalonde, *Determining Boundaries in a Conflicted World: The Role of Uti Possidetis* (Montreal: McGill-Queen's University Press, 2002) 202, 233, 240.

Oxford University Press

P. Allott, "The Concept of International Law" in M. Byers, ed., *The Role of Law in International Politics: Essays in International Law and International Relations* (Oxford: Oxford University Press, 2000) at 88. Used by permission of Oxford University Press.

Jutta Brunnée, "Of Sense and Sensibility: Reflections on International Liability Regimes as Tools for Environmental Protection" (2004) 53 International and Comparative Law Quarterly 351 at 353-54. Used by permission of Oxford University Press.

Martti Koskenniemi, "What Is International Law For?" in Malcom D. Evans, ed., *International Law* (Oxford: Oxford University Press, 2001) 89, 102. Used by permission of Oxford University Press.

Daniel Reichert-Facilides, "Down the Danube: The Vienna Convention on the Law of Treaties and the Case Concerning the Gabçíkovo-Nagymaros Project" (1998) 47 *International and Comparative Law Quarterly* 837 at 846. Used by permission of Oxford University Press.

Princeton University Press

Iris M. Young, *Justice and Politics of Difference* (Princeton: Princeton University Press, 1990) 237-38.

Radio the Voice of Vietnam

"Human Rights: A Precious Tree and the Soil to Grow It In" from *Quan Doi Nhan Dan*. Excerpts broadcast on Radio the Voice of Vietnam, Hanoi, in Vietnamese 14:30 GMT, 5 June 1995. (Hanoi: Radio the Voice of Vietnam, 1995).

Simon & Shuster, Inc.

Philip C. Jessup, *A Modern Law of Nations* (New York: The Macmillan Company, 1948) 6-8.

The Royal Institute of International Affairs

G.G. Fitzmaurice, "The Law and Procedure of the International Court of Justice: Treaty Interpretation and Certain Other Treaty Points" (1951) 28 British Year Book of International Law 1.

The Royal Institute of International Affairs (continued)

I.C. MacGibbon, "Customary International Law and Acquiescence" (1957) 33 British
Year Book of International Law 115 at 118-19.

Transnational Publishers

Jutta Brunnée, "Territorial Sovereignty versus Territorial Integrity," in *Acid Rain and
Ozone Layer Depletion: International Law and Regulation* (Ardsley: Transnational Publishers, 1980) at 85-87.

United Nations Publications

The United Nations, *A More Secure World: Our Shared Responsibility*, Report on the
High-level Panel on Threats, Challenges, and Change (U.N. Doc. A/59/565)
(New York: United Nations Publications, 2004) 57-58. The United Nations is the
author of the original material.

The United Nations, *Consideration of Reports Submitted by States Parties Under
Articles 16 and 17 of the Covenant: Concluding Observations of the Committee
on Economic, Social and Cultural Rights: Canada* UN ESCOR (U.N. Doc. E/C
12/1/Add. 31) (New York: United Nations Publications, 1998). The United
Nations is the author of the original material.

The United Nations, "Direct Negotiation" in *Report of the Special Committee on
Principles of International Law Concerning Friendly Relations and Co-
operation Among States* (U.N. Doc. A/5746) (New York: United Nations
Publications, 1964) 65, at 115-17. The United Nations is the author of the
original material.

International Law Commission, "Model Rules on Abitral Procedure" (1958)
Yearbook of International Law Commission 83, article 2. The United Nations is
the author of the original material.

U.N. Office of Public Information, *The Work of the International Law Commission*
(New York: United Nations Publications, 1967) 6, 9, and 12. The United Nations
is the author of the original material.

University of British Columbia Press

C.B. Bourne, ed. (© 1960, 1967, 1971, 1975, 1980, 1988, 1990) 4, 5, 9, 13, 18, 26, 28
The Canadian Yearbook of International Law 510, 277, 276, 372, 301 at 312-15,
324-26, 495. Reprinted with permission of University of British Columbia Press.
All rights reserved by the publisher.

Don McRae, ed. (© 2002) 40 The Canadian Yearbook of International Law 469 at 496-98. Reprinted with permission of University of British Columbia Press. All rights reserved by the publisher.

University of Toronto Press

M. Cohen, "Canada and the International Legal Order: An Inside Perspective," in R. St. J. Macdonald, G.L. Morris & D.M. Johnston, eds., *Canadian Perspectives on International Law and Organization* (Toronto: University of Toronto Press, 1974) 3-8.

R. St. J. Macdonald, "The Relationship Between International Law and Domestic Law in Canada" in R. St. J. Macdonald, G.L. Morris & D.M. Johnston, eds., *Canadian Perspectives on International Law and Organization* (Toronto: University of Toronto Press, 1974) 119.

S.A. Williams

S.A. Williams, "Succession to Treaties," "Succession to Public Property," and "Succession to Public Debts" in *International Legal Effects of Secession by Quebec* (Study No. 8 of the York University Constitutional Reform Project, The Centre for Public Law and Public Policy) (North York: S.A. Williams, 1991) 30-35, 43-44, 44.

S.A. Williams and J.-G. Castel

S.A. Williams and J.-G. Castel, *Canadian Criminal Law, International and Transnational Aspects* (Toronto: Butterworths Canada Inc., 1981) 337-40.

S. A. Williams and A.L.C. de Mestral

S.A. Williams and A.L.C. de Mestral, *An Introduction to International Law*, 2d ed. (Toronto: Butterworths Canada Inc., 1987) 48-50, 53-54, 61, 80-81, 125-26, 161-66, 289-90, 290-92.

The Roles of International Law and International Lawyers

Successive secretaries-general of the United Nations have invoked the "international community" as both the source and object of public international law.[1] The assumptions underlying this phrase are indicative of the dominant historical understanding of how all law is created and at whom public international law is directed. It is a common assumption that law can only emerge from authoritative hierarchies rooted in relatively stable political communities. If there is no community there can be no law because it is only in community that the expectation of compliance with law can be generated. The community that is said to generate public international law is a highly particular one: the community of sovereign states. Traditionally, public international law was regarded purely as a system of principles and rules designed to govern relations between states. The law is produced by that community and imposes obligations upon that community. As a point of departure for a study of international law, this description has the merit of emphasizing the central and still dominant position of states in international affairs. However, in recent times the scope of international law has been steadily expanding so that, in the words of Wilfred Jenks, "it represents the common law of mankind in an early state of development, of which the law governing the relations between states is one, but only one, major division."[2] Perhaps the most significant development is the status newly accorded to individuals in the international legal process. In the field of human rights, for example, individuals now possess international legal rights independently of, and even against, their national state.

Jenks's assertion that public international law can now be regarded as an emergent "common law of mankind" reveals the tensions in the concept of the "international community." For a rich and detailed common law to develop, it is indeed likely that some form of community is required. But how unified must that community be in terms of values and aspirations? In the postmodern era, where pluralism is said to be a defining feature of many national societies, can one expect that global society will be marked by a unity approaching any realistic understanding of community? Is some form of unity

---

1   A. Paulus, "The Influence of the United States on the Concept of the 'International Community'" in M. Byers & G. Nolte, eds., *United States Hegemony and the Foundations of International Law* (2003) at 57.

2   C.W. Jenks, *The Common Law of Mankind* (1958) at 58.

necessary for the development of effective international law? Although the phrasing of the issue is contemporary, the underlying problem is the age-old challenge of international law: is law possible in a global society that is horizontal in organization and that contains no legislature, no executive authority, and only a rudimentary judiciary typically without compulsory jurisdiction?

This challenge has long inspired and frustrated international lawyers. The frustration has prompted some arguments designed to invoke closure. For example, Thomas Franck has argued that

> international law has entered its post-ontological era. Its lawyers need no longer defend the very existence of international law. Thus emancipated from the constraints of defensive ontology, international lawyers are now free to undertake a critical assessment of its content.[3]

Franck's hope was to end the cycle of doubt and introspection that he believed inhibited the possibilities of public international law and that precluded a much-needed critical reflection on its substantive rules. His hope was dashed because it has proven impossible to achieve anything close to consensus on how we should understand the nature of law and the modalities of its social effects in national or global society. What is more, the circumstances surrounding the Iraq invasion in 2003 once again highlighted arguments that when it really matters international law fails to influence, much less constrain, the powerful.[4]

A second defensive posture has been more limited in aspiration, but perhaps more effective. Generations of textbook writers seeking to deflect doubts about the existence and efficacy of international law have simply invited skeptics (and impressionable students) to look at the world around them. On this reading, one can simply declare that international law works because binding norms empirically exist and are complied with. In the ringing words of Philip Jessup:

> Wars, breaches of treaties, oppression of the weak by the strong, are the headlines of the daily press and of the history textbooks. The superficial observer has not noted the steady observance of such treaties as that under which letters are carried all over the world at rates fixed by the Universal Postal Union. He ignores the fact that there is scarcely an instance in two hundred years in which an ambassador has been subjected to suit in courts of the country where he [or she] is stationed. ... The superficial observer has not read the hundreds of decisions handed down by international courts called Mixed Claims Commissions, which have awarded money damages duly paid by the defendant states. ... He may be unfamiliar with the extent to which international law has been incorporated in national law and has thus secured an enforcement agency through the ordinary governmental machinery of the national states. ... The record proves that there is a "law habit" in international relations. It is not immaterial to add that the instances in which judgments of international tribunals have been flouted are so rare that the headline-reader may well place them in the man-bites-dog category.[5]

---

3   T. Franck, *Fairness in International Law and Institutions* (1995) at 6.

4   J. Brunnée & S.J. Toope, "The Use of Force: International Law After Iraq" (2004) 53 I.C.L.Q. 785.

5   P. Jessup, *A Modern Law of Nations* (1948) at 6-8.

The same sense of defensive frustration prompted Louis Henkin to offer up his famous observation that "almost all nations observe almost all principles of international law and almost all of their obligations almost all of the time."[6] The problem with these arguments is that although they are empirically well-grounded, they tend to ignore situations where there is a real public desire for international law to work, but where it often fails to shape state behaviour: where fundamental state interests are at stake and the use of military force is a political option.

The positive inspiration in the challenge to public international law's existence and effectiveness has resulted in a rich, if ultimately incommensurable, body of legal theory. The beginnings of international law as it is known today are usually traced to the 16th and 17th centuries and coincide with the rise of the nation state. Hugo Grotius (1583–1645), a Dutch jurist and diplomat, is widely regarded as the progenitor of international law because his classic treatise[7] was the first systematic account of the field addressed to modern concerns such as the sharing of natural resources. Grotius was very much a product of his era; his work was infused with assumptions rooted in so-called natural law. Although basing himself in a theological tradition originating in Greek thought and developed by Thomas Aquinas (1226–1274), Franciscus de Vitoria (1486–1546), Francisco Suárez (1548–1617), and Alberico Gentilis (1551–1608), Grotius to some extent secularized natural law.[8] Instead of describing the law of nature as derived directly from the will of God, Grotius posited an ideal law grounded in human rationality. In other words, law was to be found in right reason, not created through formal process. The underpinning of all law was the natural principle *pacta sunt servanda* (agreements must be carried out in good faith). This was the fundamental principle of justice, and law was a direct expression of justice. Moreover, specific rules of law emerged from the requirements of nature understood through reason. The natural law tradition waned considerably during the 19th century but re-emerged as a significant inspiration in the 20th. The emergence of international human rights law after World War I, and even more after World War II, cannot be explained without reference to the beneficent influence of natural law thinking over hundreds of years. On the other hand, Emmeric de Vattel (1714–1766) used natural law to construct his fallacious direct analogy between human beings and states, giving rise to the concept of "the fundamental rights of states," impeding the creation of state responsibility for violations of international law for almost a century and a half.

The 19th century saw the development of a theory that directly attacked the concept of natural law: legal positivism. Finding inspiration in the first great positivist theorist, Cornelis van Bynkershoek (1673–1743), most 19th-century international lawyers adopted what would today be called a sociological perspective. Law was to be determined primarily with reference to the actual behaviour of states. Law was created by the exercise of state

---

6   L. Henkin, *How Nations Behave*, 2d ed. (1979) at 47.

7   H. Grotius, *De Jure Belli ac Pacis* (1625).

8   See A. Verdross & H.F. Koeck, "Natural Law: The Tradition of Universal Reason and Authority" in R. St. J. Macdonald & D.M. Johnston, eds., *The Structure and Process of International Law: Essays in Legal Philosophy, Doctrine and Theory* (1984) at 17.

will and was not found in immanent natural principles. As further expounded by Hans Kelsen (1881–1973), law was to be viewed as a normative science, with a rule being rooted in a pre-existing structure of norms in a regression back to a so-called grundnorm or basic rule. Only rules that could be traced back through an authoritative hierarchy to the basic rule could be cast as "legal" rules.[9] Interestingly, one way of phrasing the basic rule for the leading international law positivist, Dionisio Anzilotti (1867–1950), was *pacta sunt servanda*,[10] so this fundamental concept served an equally important role for natural lawyers and positivists, but for completely different reasons. Kelsen and his followers further argued that law was divorced from any moral underpinnings, which were the concern of political science.[11] As later argued by the influential positivist writer H.L.A. Hart (1907–1992), the moral critique of law was necessary, but was external to law itself.[12] Indeed, this separation of law and morals was seen as a virtue because one could never argue that any particular rule was imposed by "nature."

During the 19th century a particular construction of positivism became dominant, one emphasizing "voluntarism."[13] Voluntarism is a direct outgrowth of the preoccupation with sovereignty found in Nicolò Machiavelli (1469–1527), Thomas Hobbes (1588–1679), and John Austin (1790–1859). Voluntarist international legal theory is predicated on the view that states participate in the legal system as a matter of choice. Therefore, any obligations are voluntarily assumed. The implication is that all law is grounded in the consent of states. Even though the role of consent as the basis for all legal obligations has been questioned in the 20th century,[14] voluntarism continues to hold sway in what is sometimes called "statist" thought, the body of analysis that strives to uphold the role of sovereign states in international society. Statism expresses itself in many forms, from an atavistic and traditionalist ease with the state form,[15] to assertions that only state governments can properly express "popular sovereignty,"[16] to defences of the primacy of states in the name of cultural and social diversity, an argument often put forward by

---

9   H. Kelsen, *General Theory of Law and State* (1946).

10 D. Anzilotti, *Corso di Diritto Internazionale*, 3d ed. (1928) vol. 1 in I.A. Shearer, ed., *Starke's International Law*, 11th ed. (1994) at 22, n. 11.

11 H. Kelsen, "Pure Theory of Law" (1934) 50 Law Q. Rev. 474.

12 H.L.A. Hart, *The Concept of Law* (1961).

13 Q.D. Nguyen, *Droit international public*, 7th ed. by P. Dallier & A. Pellet (2002) at 98.

14 See H.A. Smith, *Great Britain and the Law of Nations* (1932) vol. 1 at 12-13; see also B. Simma, "From Bilateralism to Community Interest" (1994) Recueil des cours at 221, 225-27; and S.J. Toope, "Powerful But Unpersuasive? The Role of the United States in the Evolution of Customary International Law" in M. Byers & G. Nolte, eds., *United States Hegemony and the Foundations of International Law* (2003) at 287.

15 S. Ratner & A.-M. Slaughter, "Appraising the Methods of International Law: A Prospectus for Readers" (1999) 93 A.J.I.L. 291.

16 P. Kahn, "American Hegemony and International Law: Speaking to Power: Popular Sovereignty, Human Rights, and the New International Order" (2000) 1 Chicago J. Int'l L. 2. The argument for state-centred popular sovereignty is closely tied to assertions that international law suffers from a "democratic deficit" because its decision-making processes are too removed from the global citizenry. See generally G.H. Fox & B. Roth, eds., *Democratic Governance and International Law* (2000).

scholars from the developing world.[17] Positivism fails to explain the existence and evolution of customary law; it cannot demonstrate why as a matter of logic it is only rules to which a state explicitly consents that are binding; it can lead to anarchy in its assertion that breaches of law may merely be evidence that a norm is changing; and it consistently overemphasizes the role of states in the creation of law. Nonetheless, positivist scholars have made a major contribution to international law by insisting that we should pay attention to the practice of states, that it is not enough for lawyers to posit abstract principles that bear no correspondence to lived reality.

The focus on experience as the grounding of law, rather than on abstract logic or other constructions of the natural, reached its apogee in the American legal realist movement of the 1920s and 1930s. Promoted by such prominent theorists as Roscoe Pound (1870–1964) and Karl Llewelyn (1893–1962), legal realism was based on two central assumptions— first, that the law was completely derived from practice, and particularly from the decisions of courts; and second, that concrete legal decisions were generally taken on the basis of policy considerations. The first assumption connects realism to positivism; the second creates enormous distance between the two theories. For realists, law was to be measured empirically against the social consequences of decisions. Law was therefore instrumental, a handmaiden of political, economic, and social objectives. For this reason, realists are "rule skeptics" who see uncertainty in the very articulation of rules, opening all rules not only to interpretation but to external critique on the basis of policy objectives. This viewpoint has shaped much of 20th century American legal thinking. A clear expression is found in the words of the contemporary theorist and judge, Richard Posner, who describes law as providing

a service to lay communities in the achievement of those communities' self-chosen ends rather than as a norm imposed on those communities in the service of a higher end.[18]

Within public international law American legal realism found its most comprehensive expression in the New Haven School of policy science, founded by Harold Lasswell (1902–1978) and Myers McDougal (1906–1998). These prolific scholars and their innumerable disciples rejected the positivist idea that law could be defined as a body of rules, and they focused instead on the practice of lawyers who were cast as specialists in promoting "authoritative decisions."[19] It is in the process of authoritative decision that the constraining function of law emerges. Not every value choice is supported through law. Legal norms must be assessed against the trends of past decisions and policy goals can only turn into law if the decision is "authoritative" and "controlling":

---

17   See *e.g.* T. Maluwa, *International Law in Post-colonial Africa* (1999). It should be emphasized, however, that support for the state as a bastion of cultural protection does not imply an uncritical acceptance of particular state boundaries. See M. Mutua, "Why Redraw the Map of Africa: A Moral and Legal Inquiry" (1995) 16 Michigan J. Int'l L. 1113.

18   R.A. Posner, *Cardozo: A Study in Reputation* (1990) at 94.

19   See *e.g.* H. Lasswell & M.S. McDougal, "The Identification and Appraisal of Diverse Systems of Public Order" in R. Falk & S. Mendlovitz, eds., *The Strategy of World Order* (1966) at 45 [Lasswell & McDougal, "Identification"]; and H. Lasswell & M.S. McDougal, "Criteria for a Theory about Law" (1971) 44 S. Cal. L. Rev. 362.

Authority is the structure of expectation concerning who, with what qualifications and mode of selection, is competent to make which decisions by what criteria and what procedures. By control we refer to an effective voice in decision, whether authorized or not. The conjunction of common expectations concerning authority with a high degree of corroboration in actual operation is what we understand by law.[20]

Although the processes described by Lasswell and McDougal have been criticized as cumbersome, the sophisticated interdisciplinary analysis and the escape from sterile rule naming has proven so attractive that it is probably fair to describe the New Haven School as the most influential of contemporary theories of international law, at least within the USA.[21] The greatest resistance to the New Haven School is found among those who believe that the theory tends actually to diminish the constraining function of law because the requirement of "control" can slip into a simple recognition of the effects of raw power. In other words, the corroboration of expectation and control may mean that control, read as power, will all too often trump any expectations of authority rooted in substantive criteria or procedure.

Contemporary theoretical alternatives to legal realism and to its New Haven variation arise from a number of sources. In part connecting with the defence of cultural and social diversity put forward by scholars from the developing world, noted on the previous page, and in part deriving from the "critical legal studies" movement that emerged in the United States in the 1970s, a so-called new stream of international law scholarship has sought to reveal the traditionally Eurocentric, and perhaps now Americentric, political underpinnings of international law that reinforce patterns of unjust domination.[22] Within this stream Martti Koskenniemi argues the need for a recommitment to legal formalism, which for a generation at least has been pilloried as an outmoded expression of state positivism:

> The contrast between instrumentalism and formalism is quite fundamental when seeking to answer the question "what is international law for?" From the instrumental perspective, international law exists to realize objectives of some dominant part of the community; from the formalist perspective, it provides a platform to evaluate behaviour, including the behaviour of those in dominant positions. ... The instrumental perspective is typically that of an active and powerful actor in possession of alternative choices; formalism is often the perspective of the weak actor relying on law for protection.[23]

Koskenniemi concludes that international law must be read as both "a repertory of substantive values, preferences, practices that those in dominant positions seek to realize" and as a means of giving "voice to those who have been the objects of other peoples' policies."[24]

---

20   Lasswell & McDougal, "Identification," *ibid.* at 53.

21   R. Falk, "Casting the Spell: The New Haven School of International Law" (1995) 104 Yale L.J. 1991.

22   D. Kennedy, "A New Stream of International Law Scholarship" (1988) 7 Wisconsin Int'l L.J. 6.

23   M. Koskenniemi, "What Is International Law For?" in M. Evans, ed., *International Law*, 1st ed. (2003) at 89, 102 [Koskenniemi, "What Is Law For?"].

24   Koskenniemi, "What Is Law For?," *ibid.* at 110.

The idea that international law challenges social actors in dominant positions, rather than simply cloaking them with power, has informed the work of many other contemporary scholars as well. In asking why states observe rules of international law, Thomas Franck has answered that states are more likely to comply when a rule of international law is viewed as legitimate.[25] For Franck, legitimacy is largely a question of process: who participated in the elaboration of the rule and how was that elaboration accomplished?[26] In other words, if a rule is simply imposed by the powerful, through force, it is unlikely to generate what Franck calls "compliance pull" because the rule will not be widely viewed as legitimate. Franck argues further that legitimacy must then be matched with a sense of justice to generate the "fairness" that is required by the rule of law in international society. Drawing upon a tradition of Kantian cosmopolitanism, Philip Allott describes contemporary international law as an "interstatal unsociety."[27] Like Franck, Allott argues for a value-based construction of international norms that has the capacity to speak truth to power. Bemoaning the essentially private and property-based understandings that dominate international legal discourse, Allott argues for recognition of the social function of law, which he takes to be the promotion of the common interest.[28] Focusing upon the interplay of feminist theory and international law, another influential group of scholars has sought to challenge the powerful by calling upon states and other international actors to reconsider fundamental principles, including sovereignty itself, in the light of women's experience. Hilary Charlesworth and Christine Chinkin have argued, for example, that "[t]raditional international law-making assumes a monolithic state voice that silences individuals and other non-elite groups in the international arena, except insofar as their interests are championed by states."[29] They suggest that the direct effect of international law on individuals demands a more inclusive participation in law making.

These contemporary theoretical debates have been enlivened by another relatively recent development—that is, the increasing interchange between international lawyers and international relations (IR) scholars. There is no single theoretical stream emerging from this interchange. If anything, it has served to reinforce the diverse understandings of the role and possibilities of law manifest within international legal theory. However, the interchange has provided new optics from which to view older debates. As long as realism and neo-realism[30] dominated the IR literature, there was little potential interest in international law. The focus was on the explanation of state behaviour based on

---

25   T. M. Franck, *The Power Of Legitimacy Among Nations* (1990).

26   T. M. Franck, *Fairness In International Law And Institutions* (1995) at 22.

27   P. Allott, *Eunomia: New Order for a New World* (1990) at 244 [Allott, *Eunomia*].

28   P. Allott, "The Concept of International Law" in M. Byers, ed., *The Role of Law in International Politics: Essays in International Law and International Relations* (2000) at 69, 97.

29   H. Charlesworth & C. Chinkin, *The Boundaries of International Law: A Feminist Analysis* (2000) at 69. See also K. Knop, ed., *Gender and Human Rights* (2004).

30   The classical realist position was articulated most forcefully by Hans Morgenthau, perhaps ironically, for he was initially trained as an international lawyer. For classical realists like Morgenthau, the key variable in understanding international politics is material power; "norms" mean very little. See H. Morgenthau, *Politics Among Nations*, 2d ed. (1954) at 8. ("Power covers the domination of man by man, both when it is disciplined by moral ends and controlled by constitutional safeguards as in Western democracies, and when it is that

calculations of state interests and relative power, not on normative considerations. With an important shift in emphasis, various "neo-liberal institutionalist" scholars began to explore the effect of formal and informal institutions in modifying state behaviour. Though they continue to focus on rationalist accounts based on interest analysis,[31] these theorists argue that institutions help progressively to enmesh most states in a world order premised upon shared liberal values. In some of these discussions, the heightened role of state policy networks has been emphasized.[32] Law's role is largely to build institutions and to shape their substantive output. The IR approach with the closest connection to international law is "constructivism." For constructivists, the international order is best viewed as a mutable social structure where law plays a constitutive role through the implicit norms that underlie the entire order. The participation of states in international regimes, including legal regimes, shapes not only the perceived interests of states, but also their very identity. What is more, because law emerges in a continuing dialogue between norm and fact and between means (process) and ends (substance), the participation of a variety of actors, and not just states, is required and validated.[33] After years of mutual incomprehension—with the notable exception of scholars operating in the New Haven School—international lawyers and IR scholars now seem to recognize that they can learn from each other. Many international lawyers recognize that they need better *explanatory* models for the evolution of binding law, and many IR theorists understand that they need more nuanced *normative* models that differentiate among the various types of rules, norms, and principles that help to shape the behaviour of international actors.

Another conceptual way of approaching international law is to focus on its evolution in its historical context. Such work inevitably partakes of all the debates of historiography. Should one focus primarily on the elite individual actor (the "great person" approach to history) or on the minutiae of local changes that cumulatively bring about societal evolution? Is history best understood as "epochal" or as a river of continuous evolutionary change? How does one understand the causal relationship between ideas and social change? The traditional pattern in writing the history of international law was to emphasize a narrative of progress.[34] With the conclusion of the treaties of Westphalia in

---

untamed and barbaric force which finds its laws in nothing but its own strength and its sole justification in its aggrandizement.") Neo-realism is a form of realism that borrows heavily from the methodologies of economics. Its analytic focus is on individual states as homogeneous units that act on the basis of a rationally assessed and pursued self-interest. See K. Waltz, *Theory Of International Politics* (1979).

31   See *e.g.* R.O. Keohane, "Neoliberal Institutionalism: A Perspective on World Politics" in R.O. Keohane, ed., *International Institutions and State Power: Essays in International Relations Theory* (1989) at 1.

32   See *e.g.* A.-M. Slaughter, "Governing the Global Economy through Government Networks" in M. Byers, ed., *The Role of Law in International Politics: Essays in International Law and International Relations* (2000) at 177.

33   See *e.g.* F. Kratochwil, *Rules, Norms and Decisions: On the Conditions of Practical and Legal Reasoning in International Relations and Domestic Affairs* (1989); and J. Brunnée & S.J. Toope, "International Law and Constructivism: Elements of an Interactional Theory of International Law" (2000) 39 Col. J. Trans. L. 19. An instructive introductory text from the international relations perspective is Shirley V. Scott, *International Law in World Politics: An Introduction* (2004).

34   See *e.g.* A. Nussbaum, *A Concise History of the Law of Nations* (1954).

1648, the European wars of religion were ended by the creation of a system of sovereign states, largely based on "nationality," which was itself partly specified through religious affiliation. International law was the product of free interstate diplomatic relations, centred in Europe. It was infused with progressive European social, political, and cultural values, and was enriched by the growing institutions of international politics, notably by the evolution from the League of Nations into the United Nations. German historians, who have dominated the field, tended to favour grand themes and metahistorical assumptions.[35] What was typically absent from this historical scholarship of international law was a critical reflection on the connections between the development of international law and the European colonial project from the 18th to the 20th centuries. This lacuna has been remedied through the efforts of a number of scholars working in the "new stream" of international law, discussed above.[36] They have emphasized that international law formed part of the toolbox of colonial domination and repression.

Entry into the international legal system during the 20th century, and particularly since 1945, of many new states with varied political, cultural, social, and legal backgrounds has had, and is still having, a profound and lasting effect on international law. The original "Concert of Europe" has now been expanded to more than 190 states. The number and diversity of actors in the world arena have exponentially increased the difficulties of administering the decentralized system of nation states. Moreover, the new participants entered the society of states with very different perspectives and soon began to challenge the enduring validity of some of the Eurocentric concepts and principles of international law. The first major challenge to the simple belief in the universal acceptance of classical international law was posed after the Russian Revolution by the emergence of Soviet views[37] on the role of the state, the sources of the law, and the substance of many of its principles. More recently, the developing states of Latin America, Africa, and Asia have urged a reformulation of international law, especially those parts governing foreign investment, development, and other incidents of their former colonial circumstances.[38] As a result, some of the traditional principles of international law have been altogether abandoned (for example, principles governing the acquisition of territory by force) or

[handwritten margin notes: "eurocentric" / "Challenges to the int'l law)"]

---

35   See *e.g.* W. Grewe, *The Epochs of International Law*, trans. and rev. by M. Byers (2000).

36   See *e.g.* A. Carty, *The Decay of International Law? A Reappraisal of the Limits of Legal Imagination in International Affairs* (1986); and A. Anghie, "Finding the Peripheries: Sovereignty and Colonialism in Nineteenth-Century International Law" (1999) 40 Harv. Int'l L.J. 1.

37   See H.W. Baade, ed., *The Soviet Impact on International Law* (1965); K. Grzybowski, *Soviet Public International Law: Doctrines and Diplomatic Practice* (1970); and G.I. Tunkin, *Theory of International Law*, trans. by W.E. Butler (1974). On changes in Soviet approaches to international law in the mid-1980s, see E. McWhinney, "The 'New Thinking' in Soviet International Law: Soviet Doctrines and Practice in the Post-Tunkin Era" (1990) 28 Can. Y.B. Int'l L. 309. Of course, Soviet-Marxist understandings of international law have declined in importance, almost to the point of irrelevance, since the fall of the Berlin Wall and the demise of the U.S.S.R.

38   For relatively early post-colonial accounts, see *e.g.* R.P. Anand, ed., *Asian States and the Development of Universal Law* (1972); R.P. Anand, *New States and International Law* (1972); T.O. Elias, *Africa and the Development of International Law* (1972); and F. Okoye, *International Law and the New African States* (1972).

materially altered (for example, rules relating to the amount of compensation payable upon the expropriation of foreign property). In other instances, wholly new concepts have been introduced (for example, the right of self-determination of peoples and the principle of a state's permanent sovereignty over its natural resources). Yet, even in our seemingly post-colonial world, it is suggested that international law continues sometimes to operate as a lever for cultural and economic domination by the states of the North, and possibly for the single superpower. Martti Koskenniemi has pushed this argument further, inverting the traditional progress narrative of international law by suggesting that what is now described as international law was established not in 1648 at Westphalia but at the meetings of the *Institut de droit international* in the 1870s. According to Koskenniemi, 19th century international lawyers were full participants in the imperial exercise, but their "civilizing" project never recovered from the horrors of World War II. After that time, international law was both "depoliticized and marginalized ... or turned into a technical instrument for the advancement of the agendas of powerful interests or actors in the world scene."[39]

Lest it appear there is little hope for the transformative power of law in international society, one must emphasize the resilience and adaptability of public international law throughout the 20th century. The advent of nuclear energy, mass air travel, space flight, satellite telecommunications, and computer informatics, to mention only a few major new activities, has prompted the creation of new branches of international law, such as space law and environmental law, and great expansion of some traditional ones, most notably the law of the sea. In addition, the revolution in transportation and communications has enormously increased the movement and interaction of people all over the world, resulting in the need for international law to harmonize and accommodate many diverse and competing human interests. One conspicuous consequence has been the emergence of a great number of international organizations covering a wide variety of human activities. Many of these organizations have become associated since 1945 with the United Nations, which has filled the role of a global coordinating organ, and they have been supported by the growth of a whole new body of law regarding international institutions. What is more, the unprecedented growth of world trade, fuelled by the huge energy of the modern multinational enterprise, has given rise to a growing corpus of international economic law to govern transnational commercial transactions. In addition, much greater awareness of the plight of millions of human beings who suffer from poverty, hunger, disease, illiteracy, and the effects of tyranny and war has been made possible by modern media and communications technology. In turn, this awareness has brought about organized efforts, increasingly driven by non-governmental organizations whose power and influence has burgeoned with the information revolution, to improve human well-being and, particularly, to promote economic and social advancement in less developed parts of the world. These concerns have found their legal expression in the further development of humanitarian law, international human rights law, and international

---

39   M. Koskenniemi, *The Gentle Civilizer of Nations: The Rise and Fall of International Law 1870-1960* (2001) at 3 [Koskenniemi, *Gentle Civilizer*].

development law. In sum, international law in the United Nations era has had to adapt to a much changed, multinational, and increasingly interdependent world.[40]

In support of these adaptations, one of the primary goals of 20th century international legal theorists was to promote greater legal responsibility for international actors. Throughout the last century successful efforts were made to establish the doctrine of state responsibility (Chapter 10), to impose responsibility upon individuals for war crimes and crimes against humanity (Chapter 11), to recognize the responsibility of international organizations (Chapter 10), to promote the responsibility of states and private persons for violations of human rights (Chapter 12), and to establish responsibility for failure to protect the environment (Chapter 14). Moving away from the limiting concept that international law is primarily a set of techniques for dispute resolution,[41] and embracing the diverse roles that law can play in institutional design, the promotion of democratic governance, and even in the shaping of identities of international actors,[42] international lawyers have broadened their horizons and reimagined the scope of their field of study and practice. If the result is to view law as purely instrumental, the effect can be to turn the lawyer into a false hero: anything is possible if we just get the law right.[43] But if what has been described as the "invisible college of international lawyers"[44] can imagine itself and its potential role with a modicum of humility, the possibilities for useful engagement are legion.

Koskenniemi argues that international law remains "a terrain of fear and ambition, fantasy and desire, conflict and utopia, and a host of other aspects of the phenomeno-logical lives of its practitioners."[45] In other words, the challenge in promoting greater responsibility under international law is to bolster our own sense of responsibility as international legal practitioners. Our first responsibility may be to dream. In rebutting the inevitable criticism that imagining an escape from our current "interstatal unsociety" is utopian, Philip Allott argues:

> [S]uch human progress as there has been, over the last several thousand years, has been due
> to three strange accidents of evolution, or gifts of God: rationality (the capacity to order our

---

40   See *e.g.* P.E. Corbett, *The Growth of World Law* (1971); R. Falk, *The Status of Law in International Society* (1970); W. Friedmann, *The Changing Structure of International Law* (1964); F.V. Garcia-Amador, *The Emerging International Law of Development* (1990); W. Jenks, *A New World of Law?* (1969); and J. Stone, *Visions of World Order* (1984). For Canadian opinions, see R. St. J. Macdonald, G.L. Morris, & D.M. Johnston, eds., *Canadian Perspectives on International Law and Organisation* (1974).

41   B. Kingsbury, "The International Legal Order" in P. Cane & M. Tushnet, eds., *The Oxford Handbook of Legal Studies* (2003) at 271-72 [Kingsbury, "Legal Order"].

42   See *e.g.* Lon L. Fuller, *The Law in Quest of Itself* (1940); Lon L. Fuller, *The Principles of Social Order: Selected Essays of Lon L. Fuller*, ed. by Kenneth I. Winston (1981) (on institutional design and law's role in democratic governance); and Jutta Brunnée & Stephen J. Toope, "The Changing Nile Basin Regime: Does Law Matter?" (2002) 43 Harv. J. Int'l L. 105 (on law's influence in shaping state identities).

43   Koskenniemi, "What Is Law For?," *supra* note 23 at 98.

44   O. Schachter, "The Invisible College of International Lawyers" (1977) 72 Nw. U.L. Rev. 219, referred to in (2001) 95 A.S.I.L. Proc. at ix.

45   Koskenniemi, *Gentle Civilizer, supra* note 39 at 7.

consciousness); morality (the capacity to take responsibility for our future); and imagination (the capacity to create a reality-for-ourselves). Using these capacities, we found within ourselves another capacity, the capacity to form the idea of the ideal—the idea of a better human future which we can choose to make actual.[46]

Our thoughts are, of course, inevitably conditioned by our experiences, and this returns us to the very foundations of public international law, for it was Grotius who most clearly formulated the inevitable shaping of theory by practice and practice by theory.[47] Butterfield and Wight phrased the point beautifully: Grotian international law "sings a kind of descant over against the movement of diplomacy."[48] It is the interaction of theory and practice that allows us to imagine new futures, what Koskenniemi calls the "promise of justice,"[49] while tempering our hopes with a recognition that, in the muck of real life and real politics, justice will remain an aspiration that can never be fully realized. The interaction of theory and practice builds both hope and modesty, the twin generators of meaningful evolution in international law. Reversing the original natural law formulation that law was imminent in divine justice, it may now be argued that glimpses of justice may be imminent in the practices and theories of law.

The collective practice and theorizing of international law does not support the notion that we live within, or can achieve in any likely future, a true "international community." But this is no cause for despair. In an analogous situation, Iris Young has described the opportune prospects of "city life":

> By "city life" I mean a form of social relations which I define as the being together of strangers. In the city persons and groups interact within spaces and institutions they all experience themselves as belonging to, but without those interactions dissolving into unity or commonness. City dwelling situates one's own identity and activity in relation to a horizon of a vast variety of other activity, and the awareness that this unknown, unfamiliar activity affects the conditions of one's own. … City dwellers are thus together, bound to one another, in what should be and sometimes is a single polity. Their being together entails some common problems and common interests, but they do not create a community of shared final ends, of mutual identification and reciprocity.[50]

Unintentionally, Young here presents a compelling description of world society, and what the much vaunted processes of globalization mean for international law and politics. Our inability to find or create a global community does not preclude practical associations. International lawyers can imagine and seize opportunities to build up the normative framework of international relations, to aspire to justice. Generations of scholar-practitioners have shown the way. Now it is our turn.

---

46   P. Allott, "The Concept of International Law," *supra* note 28 at 88.

47   Kingsbury, "Legal Order," *supra* note 41 at 273.

48   H. Butterfield & M. Wight, eds., *Diplomatic Investigations* (1966) at 29 in Kingsbury, "Legal Order," *supra* note 41 at 273.

49   Koskenniemi, "What Is Law For?," *supra* note 23 at 111.

50   I.M. Young, *Justice and the Politics of Difference* (1990) at 237-38.

CHAPTER TWO

International Legal Persons

A. SUBJECTS OF INTERNATIONAL LAW

International law applies to certain entities as "subjects" of international law. These entities have a legal personality—that is, a capacity similar to that of an individual person in domestic law, to enter into legal relations, and to create the consequent rights and duties attached to that capacity. Without this capacity an entity will be unable to maintain any claims. International law itself determines who shall have legal personality, and not all entities possess the same personality.

Until the 20th century the prevailing view was that only states could possess international legal personality. This was due mainly to the fact that the concept of the state had predominated in the international system and the question of personality had been regarded as belonging exclusively to this domain. Thus, entities other than states could have no standing on the international scene.

As a result of changes in the last century, notably in the areas of human rights, international humanitarian law, and international economic law, non-state actors such as international organizations and even individuals have attained some measure of international legal personality. It must be stressed, however, that they do not possess the same rights and duties as states. Rather, international law has recognized that there are entities other than states that have the capacity to maintain legal relations, to enjoy rights, and possibly to assume obligations in certain given situations set down and regulated by law. These legal relations are severely limited in comparison to those of states. Political realities of the international scene lead to the logical conclusion that states, not individuals, are still the dominant feature of international relations.[1]

The purpose of this chapter is to look at the candidates for legal personality. A number of pertinent questions arise: first, does a particular entity fulfill the prerequisites for "subject" status? Second, what does this capacity for legal personality entail? Third, in

---

1   From S.A. Williams & A.L.C. de Mestral, *An Introduction to International Law*, 2d ed. (1987) at 43. See also I. Brownlie, *Principles of Public International Law*, 6th ed. (2003), cc. 3 and 4; A. Cassese, *International Law in a Divided World* (1986) c. 4; J. Crawford, *The Creation of States in International Law* (1979); L.C. Green, *International Law; A Canadian Perspective*, 2d ed. (1988) at 91-123; C.H. Rousseau, *Droit international public* (1974) vol. 2; M. Shaw, *International Law*, 5th ed. (2003), c. 5; and B. Broms, "Subjects: Entitlement in the International System" in R. St. J. Macdonald & D.M. Johnston, eds., *The Structure and Process of International Law* (1983) at 383.

new candidates, such as peoples seeking self-determination, individuals, international organizations, and multinational corporations, is there or must there be demonstrable legal capacity and, if so, what are its parameters? These questions go to the criteria for becoming a subject of international law.

B. STATES AND STATEHOOD

1. States

States are the principal subjects of the international legal system.[2] The question that confronts international lawyers is how to characterize statehood. What are the relevant criteria to look for? The mechanism of recognition by other states, and its relevance to the establishment of full international personality, will be addressed below in Section B.2.

Montevideo Convention on the Rights and Duties of States
(1936) 165 L.N.T.S. 19; (1934) 28 A.J.I.L. Supp. 75

[The Montevideo Convention, 1933 is the best-known formula for setting out the basic characteristics of statehood. The United States and 15 Latin American states are parties to it. Despite the small number, it is seen as reflecting the classical conditions under customary international law that a prospective state must satisfy. This definition is replicated in § 201 of the 1987 Restatement of the Law (Third), Foreign Relations Law of the United States.]

Article I

The state as a person of international law should possess the following qualifications: (a) a permanent population; (b) a defined territory; (c) government; and (d) capacity to enter into relations with other states.

NOTES

1) It has been suggested that these characteristics outlined in the Montevideo Convention are based on the principle of effectiveness but consideration should also be given to developments in modern international law that suggest that in exceptional cases other criteria either supplement or go against this principle.[3] There is no centralized legal process to assess these factual circumstances. However, consideration must be given to the process under the U.N. Charter for admission of new members and the practice of recognition of new states on a bilateral basis.

---

2   H. Lauterpacht, *International Law: Collected Papers* (1975) vol. 2 at 489 stated that "the orthodox positivist doctrine has been explicit in the affirmation that only states are subjects of international law."

3   See J. Crawford, *supra* note 1 at 77-84 and R. Higgins, *The Development of International Law through the Political Organs of the United Nations* (1963) at 11-57.

2) *Population.* A permanent population is necessary although there is no minimum requirement. Canada recognized Nauru, which in 1982 had a population of 8,421, and the Seychelles, which in 1983 had a population of 69,000. It is not necessary that the population possess the nationality of the new state. This stems from the fact that nationality is dependent on statehood and not vice versa.[4]

3) *Territory.* There is no requirement as to the minimum amount of territory necessary for a prospective state to acquire power over. It may, therefore, be a small area such as Nauru (21 square kilometres). Likewise, there is no requirement that a state have territorial unity. For example, Pakistan was in two parts prior to 1971. A state may also come into being and continue to exist despite border disputes, as was the case with Israel.[5]

4) *Government.* This requirement can be regarded as central to the candidature for statehood. It is a concomitant of independence, the other main criterion, as both indicate a state that is in separate effective control of itself. It is the governmental capacity to exercise power over an area of territory and population that is the key feature. *Quaere* whether the Congo (later Zaire and today the Democratic Republic of the Congo) in 1960 had an effective government. However, its application for membership to the United Nations was approved without a dissenting vote being cast.[6] Perhaps this was a case of premature recognition based on the state gaining independence from a previous sovereign, Belgium. Can it be so justified? Is the precondition of effective government relative to other considerations? Likewise, following the disintegration of the former U.S.S.R., new member states of Armenia, Azerbaijan, Georgia, Kazakhstan, Kyrgyztan, Moldova, Tajikistan, Turkmenistan, and Uzbekistan were admitted to the United Nations in 1992, although strife over governmental authority was ongoing in these countries. The same applied to the former Yugoslavia, in that in 1992 the states of Croatia, Slovenia, and Bosnia-Herzegovina were also admitted to the United Nations, even though fierce struggles for control in some of these countries continued and a United Nations Protection Force (UNPROFOR) was required to supply relief operations in Sarajevo and other parts of Bosnia-Herzegovina.

5) Civil strife can, however, act to obscure an entity's transformation into a state. This was the case in Finland. When the Soviet government decreed that all its peoples had the right of self-determination in 1917, Finland (then part of the Russian empire) declared itself independent. Yet large numbers within Finland opposed independence and, for a time, no organized authority existed. The date of Finland's emergence as a state was an important preliminary matter in the *Aaland Islands Case.* There, the Commission appointed by the League of Nations stated:

> [F]or a considerable time the conditions required for the formation of a sovereign state did not exist. In the midst of revolution and anarchy, certain elements essential to the existence of a state, even some elements of fact, were lacking for a fairly considerable period.

---

4   J. Crawford, *supra* note 1 at 40-42.

5   As to borders not being accurately delimited, see *Deutsche Continental Gas-Gesellschaft v. Polish State* (1929) 5 Ann. Dig. 11 and 15.

6   SC Res. 142 (1960), UN SCOR, 15th year, *Resolutions and Decisions* 12; GA Res. 1480 (XV), UN GAOR, 15th Sess., Supp. No. 16, U.N. Doc. A/4684 (1960) at 64.

Political and social life was disorganized: the authorities were not strong enough to assert themselves; civil war was rife; further, the Diet, the legality of which had been disputed by a large section of the people had been dispersed by the revolutionary party, and the Government had been chased from the capital and forcibly prevented from carrying out its duties: the armed camps and the police were divided into opposing forces, and Russian troops, and after a time Germans also, took part in the civil war between the inhabitants and between Red and White Finnish troops. It is, therefore, difficult to say at what exact date the Finnish Republic, in the legal sense of the term, actually became a definitely constituted sovereign state. This certainly did not take place until a stable political organization had been created, and until the public authorities had become strong enough to assert themselves throughout the territories of the state without the assistance of foreign troops. It would appear that it was in May 1918, that the civil war ended and that the foreign troops began to leave the country, so that from that time onwards it was possible to reestablish order and normal political and social life, little by little.[7]

6) The previous examples are all instances of territories acquiring independent governments and becoming states. Can existing states lose their statehood? Certainly they can do so by agreement to join another country: the Union of Scotland with England and Wales in the United Kingdom is an example. But what is the legal position of a country that devolves into anarchy? Consider the case of Somalia where, in 1992, the government of Siad Barre was overthrown after a long struggle by a combination of opposing forces that then dissolved into a number of warring factions. The country became divided into many territories in which local warlords asserted power by force. Restoration of the semblance of security and basic social services, including food aid, was then attempted by the intervention of the United Nations.

7) *Capacity To Enter into Relations with Other States.* This requirement is both a prerequisite and a consequence of statehood because, until other states accept the existence of the new state, it is prevented from entering into diplomatic relations even if it is capable and willing to do so. Necessarily, such capacity is dependent upon an effective government that is independent. In *Chloride Industrial Batteries v. F & W Freight Ltd.*,[8] it was held that the island of Jersey is not a sovereign state because the United Kingdom is responsible for its external relations. The status of the island is that of a dependent territory. It was not therefore a "country" within the meaning of that term in the Convention on the Contract for the International Carriage of Goods by Road, 1956.

8) Upon certain conditions mentioned in article 4 of the U.N. Charter, reproduced in the Documentary Supplement, membership in the United Nations is open to all states. Affirmation by the Security Council and General Assembly is necessary. As of May 2005, there were 191 member states. If a state is not a member of the United Nations, how should that affect our view of its statehood? In view of article 4, all members of the United Nations may be presumed to be states, but how, for instance, did Somalia and Bosnia-Herzegovina qualify at times when effective government was lacking?

---

7   (1920), L.N.O.J., Special Supp. (No. 3) at 3.

8   (1991), 86 I.L.R. 152 (Eng. C.A.).

9) Independence is also an essential factor for statehood. The claimant to statehood must be able, through its government, to exercise its self-determination, free of the authority, though not necessarily the influence, of any state. Independence is often used interchangeably with the word "sovereignty." However, care should be taken as independence is a necessary component for the attainment of the status, whereas sovereignty is a legal right that flows from it. (See below, the materials on "Sovereignty and Equality.") Note this distinction when considering the case that follows.

Austro-German Customs Union Case
(1931) Advisory Opinion, P.C.I.J. (Ser. A/B) No. 41 at 45-46, 57-58

[This request by the Council of the League of Nations for an advisory opinion from the Permanent Court of International Justice concerned the meaning of the word "independence." The Court was asked to give an opinion as to whether the agreement by Austria and Germany to establish a free-trade customs union was in accordance with the Treaty of Saint-Germain of 1919 and the Protocol No. 1 of Geneva 1922. Article 88 of the Treaty of St. Germain provided that the independence of Austria was inalienable except with the consent of the Council of the League of Nations. In the absence of such consent, Austria undertook to abstain from any act that might compromise its independence either directly or indirectly. The Court held unanimously that there was not an alienation of Austria's independence. However, by eight votes to seven, it advised that the agreement would be incompatible with the Protocol of 1922 and seven of the majority judges found that also to be the case with the Treaty of Saint-Germain.]

THE COURT: ... irrespective of the definition of the independence of States which may be given by legal doctrine or may be adopted in particular instances in the practice of States, the independence of Austria, according to Article 88 of the Treaty of Saint-Germain, must be understood to mean the continued existence of Austria within her present frontiers as a separate State with sole right of decision in all matters economic, political, financial or other with the result that independence is violated, as soon as there is any violation there, either in the economic, political, or any other field, these different aspects of independence being in practice one and indivisible. ... By "alienation," as mentioned in Article 88, must be understood any voluntary act by the Austrian State which would cause it to lose its independence or which would modify its independence in that its sovereign will would be subordinated to the will of another Power or particular group of Powers, or would even be replaced by such will.

Separate opinion of JUDGE ANZILOTTI: ... [T]he independence of Austria within the meaning of Article 88 is nothing else but the existence of Austria, within the frontiers laid down by the Treaty of Saint-Germain, as a separate State and not subject to the authority of any other State or group of States. Independence as thus understood is really no more than the normal condition of States according to international law; it may also be described as sovereignty (suprema potestas), or external sovereignty, by which is meant that the State has over it no other authority than that of international law.

The conception of independence, regarded as the normal characteristic of States as subjects of international law, cannot be better defined than by comparing it with the exceptional and, to some extent abnormal class of States known as "dependent States." These are States subject to the authority of one or more other States. The idea of dependence therefore necessarily implies a relation between a superior State (suzerain, protector, etc.) and an inferior or subject State (vassal, protégé, etc.); the relation between the State which can legally impose its will and the State which is legally compelled to submit to that will. Where there is no such relation of superiority and subordination, it is impossible to speak of dependence within the meaning of international law.

It follows that the legal conception of independence has nothing to do with a State's subordination to international law or with the numerous and constantly increasing states of de facto dependence which characterize the relation of one country to other countries.

It follows that the restrictions upon a State's liberty, whether arising out of ordinary international law or contracted engagements, do not as such in the least affect its independence. As long as these restrictions do not place the State under the legal authority of another State, the former remains an independent State however extensive and burdensome those obligations may be.

This is obviously the standpoint of the Treaty of Saint-Germain when it proclaims the independence of Austria despite the many serious restrictions it imposes upon her freedom in the economic, military and other spheres. These restrictions do not put Austria under the authority of the other contracting States, which means that Austria is an independent State within the meaning of international law.

2. Recognition

The criteria of statehood and of government, discussed above, have to be satisfied by any claimant to international legal personality, but the attainment of these criteria is not by itself sufficient to grant entrance to the society of states. In the current decentralized system of international law, there is no single organ having collective authority to determine claims for admission by new states and governments. The decision is left to the established governments of existing states to exercise their sovereign and independent judgment whether the claims of the new regime should be recognized. The result is a bilateral and reciprocal initiation of full international relations between the existing and the new regimes.

The process of recognition is important in international law because it opens the way to full interstate relations.[9] Both international and internal consequences flow from the act of recognition. From the point of view of a newly recognized regime, the most important effect is that it is acknowledged to hold all the rights at international law of a sovereign equal to other (recognizing) states. This recognition may well be needed to

---

9   For consideration of the degree to which law and legal advisors influence inter-state relations, see L. Henkin, *How Nations Behave*, 2d ed. (1979) and R. St. J. Macdonald, "The Role of the Legal Adviser of Ministries of Foreign Affairs" (1977) 156 Hague Recueil 376.

bolster its recently gained authority. The rights that are acquired are both substantive and procedural. For instance, recognition of a new state typically results in the opening of diplomatic relations and the exchange of ambassadors. Responsibilities, as well as rights, also accompany recognition. Indeed, recognition brings into play a whole body of international rules about the conduct of interstate relations. It is this law that permits governments, through departments of foreign affairs, ambassadors, consuls, trade missions, and other official representatives, to freely transact the daily business of diplomacy.

(a) The Practice of Recognition

Recognition has been described as the "free act by which one or more States acknowledge the existence on a definite territory of a human society politically organized, independent of any other existing State, and capable of observing the obligations of international law, and by which they manifest therefore their intention to consider it a member of the international Community."[10] This description distinguishes two elements in an act of recognition. It confirms first that the claimant to recognition must satisfy the legal criteria for statehood. It goes on to explain that the recognizing state is publicly expressing its decision to respect the claimant as an independent sovereign equal.

Recognition is not limited to states. It is also applied to new governments, to states in a condition of belligerency, to organized and effective insurgents, and more loosely to the territorial claims of states. The distinction between recognition of states and governments is most important. A recognized government cannot exist in the absence of a recognized state. Typically, a new state will be recognized and at the same time the regime that established it will be recognized as the government. In practice, changes to states are not nearly so frequent as changes of governments. Most often the matter of uppermost concern is what to do about a new regime in a recognized state that comes to power by revolutionary means. Unconstitutional changes of government, alterations in the name, and even the limited movement of territorial boundaries do not upset the continuation of recognition of the state itself.

Though the description of recognition clearly acknowledges the power of existing states to recognize others, it does not explain whether this authority is a duty or a discretion. If a claimant fulfills the requirements of statehood, must other states respond with recognition, and when may they react? These questions depend on one's conceptual view of the effect of an act of recognition.

Theories of Recognition
from S. Williams and A.L.C. de Mestral, *An Introduction to International Law*
2d ed. (1987) at 80-81 (footnotes omitted)

There has been much legal argument on the actual effect of recognition. Recognition, it is true, implies not just an attestation that a state or government exists and has the

---

10   Resolution of Institut de Droit International, Brussels (1936) 30 AJ.I.L. Supp. 185.

qualifications to be recognized. This undoubtedly has been evidenced by the delays that can occur before recognition is extended even when a state or government is obviously in existence and effectively functioning. Once recognition has been extended the recognizing state has, in essence, agreed to the formalization of relations between itself and the recognized state or government.

The theories that have been advanced concerning actual effect centre around other, wider, implications of recognition. These theories are basically two in number. First, there is the constitutive theory. According to this theory, recognition has a constitutive effect. It is only through the act of recognition that international personality is conferred. It is recognition that creates the state and gives a new government legal personality and not the process by which they are factually formed. States and governments, according to this theory, are only established as subjects of international law by the will of the international community through recognition. Two striking difficulties arise. Is an unrecognized state bound by international law? What if a state is only recognized by some states and not by others?

Secondly, there is the declaratory theory or evidentiary theory. This theory adopts an opposing approach and in view of state practice may appear to be more in line with reality. It holds that statehood or governmental authority does exist prior to recognition. The recognition is only a formal acceptance of an already existing situation. Thus it is the factual situation that produces the legal constitution of the entities and recognition does not have to be awaited for this purpose.

These two theories are directly in conflict. The first presents the picture of the unrecognized state in a sort of limbo. The second puts emphasis on the facts and belittles the effect of recognition. The difficulty lies in evaluating these two opposites. The correct position probably lies somewhere in between the two. The majority of opinion supports the declaratory theory. Practice points to it. Even when a state refuses to recognize a new state or government, it rarely contends that the new entity has no powers or obligations. The position has in fact been taken that rules of international law are binding upon unrecognized states or governments. The usual reference is made that recognition is being refused not on the grounds of lack of effective control or some such reason but on political grounds. For example the United States approach towards China until 1978 or the Arab world with respect to Israel. If the constitutive approach were to be used perhaps the government of the unrecognized state would not have to abide by any international rules vis-à-vis the non-recognizing state.

It has been suggested that there is a duty on states to recognize where the requisite factors are present. This approach, it is said, would lead the constitutive theory to be modernized. However, the arbitrariness of states' actions in this area does not support this duty. If such a duty were to exist, in what manner could it be enforced? Could a state demand recognition? At the present time each state must decide for itself whether or not to recognize another state or government.

In effect, the truth lies in both theories. Recognition is declaratory in that, for the most part, it is extended to entities that fulfil the factual qualifications; moreover, it is constitutive, in that it enables states or governments to be brought out of a vacuum into the world of diplomacy and international relations as an equal.

NOTES

1) As can be seen from this extract, the constitutive theory places importance on the formal elements of recognition and thus tends to emphasize its legal characteristics. Those who agree with this approach may be expected to be more sympathetic to the view that a new state ought to be recognized by others as soon as it satisfies the minimum criteria.[11] Alternatively, the declaratory theory describes the fact that states often withhold recognition from a new state or government for ulterior political reasons precisely because recognition has such diplomatic as well as legal significance.[12]

2) The United Kingdom used to be one of the few states with a declared recognition policy in accordance with the constitutive theory. The U.K. government was of the opinion that recognition should not depend on whether it approved the regime in question.[13] The statement of policy rightly drew a distinction between recognition and diplomatic relations. Whether ambassadors are exchanged is an entirely discretionary matter. Though it is the normal occurrence upon recognition, there is nothing to prevent the recall of representatives and even the severance of diplomatic relations as a mark of disapproval of the existing government or a new regime. Thus there are many opportunities for the diplomatic display of political opinions other than the process of recognition.

3) The extent to which diplomacy and law are intermingled in decisions about recognition may be judged from the following samples of Canadian statements of practice.

Canadian Practice of Recognition of States
(1972) 10 Can. Y.B. Int'l L. 308-9

[In a letter dated July 23, 1971, the Secretary of State for External Affairs wrote:]

As far as recognition of states is concerned, the Canadian Government must first be satisfied that any entity claiming statehood meets the basic requirements of international law, that is, an independent government wielding effective authority over a definite territory. When these conditions appear to be fulfilled, the timing of recognition is determined in accordance with Canadian national interests, given the political and economic consequences of recognition. Once granted, state recognition survives changes in governments, unless it is explicitly withdrawn.

---

11   For instance, see H. Lauterpacht, *supra* note 2 at 61-63.

12   For instance, see T.C. Chen, *The International Law of Recognition, with Special Reference to Practice in Great Britain and the United States*, edited by L.C. Green (1951) at 77-78.

13   (1951), United Kingdom, House of Commons, *Hansard*, 485 (1951) at 2411.

Approaches to Recognition of Governments
Reported in (1988) 26 Can. Y.B. Int'l L. 324-26

[In a memorandum dated June 30, 1988, the Department of External Affairs wrote:]

There are three principal methods of according recognition to governments: express recognition, tacit recognition and the recognition of states approach. These methods are distinguishable by the degree to which they utilize a statement of recognition when an unconstitutional change in government occurs. Under express recognition, each and every unconstitutional change is the subject of a recognition statement. Under tacit recognition, a recognition statement is not as a general rule issued, though it can be in the event of "exceptional circumstances." The recognition of states approach calls for the recognition of states only, not governments. Accordingly, no statement of recognition is issued in the event of an unconstitutional change of government.

The express method is no longer widely followed. Canada utilized this method until 1973 when we adopted our present policy of tacit recognition. The United States follows in principle the tacit recognition approach. A number of other common law countries are switching to the recognition of states approach. In 1980, the United Kingdom joined a significant number of civil law countries practising the recognition of states approach and earlier this year, Australia announced its intention to recognize states only. ...

Express Recognition

Under this mode, every time an unconstitutional change in government occurs in a foreign state, a review of generally accepted recognition criteria is done, and an express statement according or withholding recognition is made.

Advantages: Its great advantage lies in its clarity and specificity. Once a decision to accord or withhold recognition has been made, that decision is entered into a recognition registry. To determine whether a new government is recognized is simply a matter of consulting the registry.

Disadvantages: The method is cumbersome and time-consuming. Each and every unconstitutional change must be reviewed. While a recognition decision is pending, other states that do not follow this mode will continue normal relations, often to the detriment of the state reviewing its position. Further it leaves the practitioner of this mode open to charges of interference in the internal affairs of other states.

Tacit Recognition

As a general rule, when an unconstitutional change in government occurs, relations are maintained on a business as usual basis. No statement on recognition is issued and Canada's position vis-à-vis the new regime is inferred from the nature of our relations with it. In exceptional circumstances ... it is possible to make an express statement according or withholding recognition. Interests of Canadians in the country is always a major factor.

Advantages: The advantage of tacit recognition is its flexibility in meeting the requirements of most situations that arise. ...

Disadvantages: Tacit recognition is difficult to explain and lacks [clarity in] that our position vis-à-vis the new regime is to be *inferred* from the nature of our relations with it. Further, the reply can cause confusion by asking the layman to draw inferences from acts which have no legal consequences. According to the authors, there are in fact only two acts of government from which recognition may be legitimately inferred: the conclusion of a bilateral treaty; and the appointment and acceptance of diplomatic and consular agents.

Recognition of States Approach

The recognition of states approach was first enunciated by Mexico's foreign minister (Estrada) in the thirties. In a press release of September 29, 1930, Mexico declared that it would no longer issue statements of recognition of governments, because this practice was insulting and offended the sovereignty of nations. Mexico would therefore confine itself to recognizing states only.

Advantages: ... The doctrine is clear and simple and when asked if his country recognizes the new government of country X, a spokesman answers simply that his country recognizes states not governments. Such an approach has considerable benefits because statements on recognition, or inferences to be drawn from our relations with a new government under the policy of tacit recognition, and the likelihood of their being misconstrued are avoided.

Disadvantages: There are inevitably situations in which a government ... may wish to make an express statement either according or withholding recognition. Strict application of the recognition of states approach will not permit a state this freedom to manoeuvre. ...

Express statements according or withholding recognition, which are the hall-mark of the express policy, are popularly linked with the notion of approval, despite explanations to the contrary. A policy such as tacit recognition, which seeks to avoid recognition statements in the majority of cases but preserve them in exceptional situations ... is difficult to explain. A recognition of states approach ... [goes] a long way toward alleviating these misconceptions and difficulties. ...

NOTES

1) Subsequently on November 9, 1988, the Secretary of State for External Affairs announced that Canada would no longer continue the practice of recognizing foreign governments but would follow the so-called Estrada doctrine of recognizing only new or altered states.[14] In making this change in policy, Canada fell into line with the approach

---

14   See (1989) 27 Can. Y.B. Int'l L. 387-88.

of the United States,[15] Britain,[16] France, and many other countries, which either explicitly or tacitly follow the same practice.[17] The Estrada doctrine implies that recognition of governments is at worst harmful and at best unnecessary. Is this true?[18]

2) Why is it advantageous to states to avoid according recognition to foreign governments? Consider the bloody coups d'état that have given rise to new governments in some countries and the despotic regimes of left or right wing persuasion in others. Does the absence of recognition of a government have international legal consequences? Review the previous extract on the theories of recognition.

3) In the absence of recognition of governments, what significance is to be attached to maintaining or breaking diplomatic relations with a state? In a survey of 30 states, Nomura[19] discovered that the factors taken into account for decisions on recognition, where still accorded, and diplomatic relations are the same.

4) If two governments contest authority in the same state, as did Spain or Angola during civil war, what is a state that follows the Estrada doctrine to do?

5) The statement of Canadian practice in recognizing states implies that once the criteria for the physical existence of a new state are satisfied it is only political considerations that determine when and if recognition will be accorded. However, there may also be further legal considerations. If the "new state" is created by a unilateral declaration of independence of a portion of an existing state, the act of recognition may be an unlawful intervention in the affairs of that state contrary to the U.N. Charter article 2(4). For instance, the independence of Rhodesia was never recognized by Canada or any other country, but when it was replaced by the constitutional establishment of Zimbabwe, with the British government's agreement, the new state was quickly recognized by all and admitted to membership in the United Nations. Similarly, consider the world community's negative reaction to the attempted secession of Biafra from Nigeria and the declaration of a Turkish Republic of Northern Cyprus. How should foreign governments respond if Quebec or any other province should proceed unilaterally to secede from Canada? Does the principle of self-determination (discussed below in Section C.4(b) on "Peoples Seeking Self-Determination") affect this issue?

6) The birth or demise of a state in violation of the U.N. Charter, such as by force, is another situation in which recognition should be withheld. When the use of force has occurred, usually the Security Council will become involved and frequently will expressly forbid member states from recognizing the new entity, pursuant to its authority under the Charter article 25, as it did in the cases of Rhodesia and Northern Cyprus. Consider also the U.N. response to Iraq's attempt to annex Kuwait discussed in Chapter 15, Section B.4

---

15   L.T. Galloway, *Recognizing Foreign Governments: The Practice of the United States* (1978).

16   C.R. Symons, "United Kingdom Abolition of the Doctrine of Recognition of Governments: A Rose by Another Name," [1981] Pub. L. 249 and C. Warbrick, "The New British Policy on Recognition of Governments" (1981) 30 I.C.L.Q. 568.

17   L.T. Galloway, *supra* note 15, surveys the practice of many states, as well as tracing the history and evaluating the experience of the United States.

18   See *ibid.* at 148-51; cf. M.J. Peterson, "Recognition of Governments Should Not Be Abolished" (1983) 77 A.J.I.L. 31.

19   I. Nomura, "Recognition of Foreign Governments" (1982) 25 Jap. Ann. Int'l L. 67.

on "Collective Measures Pursuant to the U.N. Charter." As a practical matter, however, the presence of an illegally founded regime that holds effective control over a territory may be difficult to ignore or dislodge, as was shown by the history of Namibia.[20]

The extent of the principle that an illegal regime should not be recognized is equivocal. For instance, the South African government was in the past condemned by the United Nations for its apartheid policies and was prevented from being represented in the General Assembly. Was it unlawful for individual states to recognize the South African government? How bad does a regime's human rights record have to be before it becomes unlawful, as opposed to impolitic, to recognize it? Is the Estrada doctrine of help in these cases?

7) In November 1988, the Palestine Liberation Organization declared the establishment of an independent Palestinian state within the Israeli-occupied territories of the West Bank of the Jordan and the Gaza Strip, with Jerusalem as its capital. What were the legal implications of this declaration for states interested in the Middle East?[21]

8) When all governmental structures and authority in a recognized state break down, as they did in Somalia in 1991-92, what becomes of its legal status?

9) International law does not prescribe any particular form for the act of recognition. Recognition is a matter of the intent of the recognizing government. As such, it may be accorded expressly by way of a diplomatic note, a personal message to the Head of State, or an exchange of communications between foreign ministries; it may even be made by a unilateral public statement, such as a declaration in Parliament. Recognition may also be implied by conduct, such as the opening of diplomatic relations or the signing of a bilateral treaty. But the intention to recognize must be clear and not ambiguous; thus a state that signs a multilateral treaty cannot be assumed without question to recognize all the other signatories, and certainly not when it enters a reservation to this effect.

10) The international community has not yet developed any form of collective recognition, although there is some movement in that direction. Common membership in an international organization does not necessarily signify recognition any more so than common participation in a multilateral treaty. Obviously, the smaller and more integrated the organization is, the stronger is the implication of recognition among the membership. Yet even in a universal organization, it may be argued that election to membership binds all the existing members. See, for example, U.N. Charter article 4,[22] which provides for admission of all "states" who satisfy certain criteria "in the judgment of the Organization." It is consequently very hard to argue that a member of the United Nations is not in fact a state; however, there are members who do not recognize each other as such. For instance, many of the Arab countries do not recognize the state of Israel. In these circumstances, what legal status does admission to the United Nations confer on members? Membership of states certainly does not imply anything about the recognition of their governments.

---

20 See the discussion of the *Namibia Case*, below at Section C.1.

21 See Howley, "Measuring Up: Do the Palestinian Homelands Constitute a Valid State under International Law?" (1989-90), 8 Dick. J. Int'l L. 339 and Prince, "The International Legal Implications of the November 1988 Palestinian Declaration of Statehood" (1989) 25 Stan. J. Int'l L. 681.

22 Reproduced in the Doc. Supp. And see the *Conditions of Admission to the United Nations*, [1948] I.C.J. Rep. 57.

11) In regional organizations that are concerned about the external relations of their member states with non-members, there may be careful consideration given to recognition matters in order to achieve uniformity of action. Thus North Atlantic Treaty Organization (NATO) members consulted over the non-recognition of the Kamal government in Afghanistan. In the case of the European Union, the power to develop a common European position on foreign policy matters has been exercised in recognition questions, such as the decision not to recognize the former "homeland" of Transkei as a separate state distinct from South Africa, and involvement in the creation of new states out of the former Yugoslavia.

Disintegration of Yugoslavia[23]

Prior to 1991 the Socialist Federal Republic of Yugoslavia (SFRY) was composed of six republics—Slovenia, Croatia, Serbia, Bosnia-Herzegovina, Montenegro, and Macedonia. Negotiations among the republics for a looser federation or secession having failed, Yugoslavia politically disintegrated from June 25, 1991 when Slovenia and Croatia unilaterally declared their independence. Subsequently, Bosnia-Herzegovina and Macedonia did the same. The central Yugoslav authorities resisted the dismemberment of the country and called out the armed forces. Fighting began in Slovenia and quickly spread to Croatia and Bosnia-Herzegovina. A ferocious war ensued pitting regular and irregular "national" forces against each other and inflicting horrendous suffering on the mixed Muslim, Croat, and Serbian populations.

In the midst of this chaos, Slovenia, Croatia, Bosnia-Herzegovina, and Macedonia sought international recognition as independent states and admittance to United Nations membership. The European Community (EC) and the wider membership of the Conference on Security and Cooperation in Europe took a communal initiative. The EC issued certain Guidelines on the Recognition of New States in Eastern Europe and in the Soviet Union, as follows:[24]

> The Community and its Member States confirm their attachment to the principles of the Helsinki Act and the Charter of Paris [of the CSCE], in particular the principle of self-determination. They affirm their readiness to recognize, subject to the normal standards of international practice and the political realities in each case, those new States which, following the historic changes in the region, have constituted themselves on a democratic basis, have accepted the appropriate international obligations and have committed themselves in good faith to a peaceful process and to negotiations.
>
> Therefore, they adopt a common position on the process of recognition of these new States, which requires:

---

23   A record of events surrounding the Yugoslav crisis may be read in (1992), 86 A.J.I.L. 568 and 830. A collection of U.N. documents on Yugoslavia is reprinted in (1992), 31 I.L.M. 21; and see R. Rich, "Recognition of States: The Collapse of Yugoslavia and the Soviet Union" (1993), 4 E.J.I.L. 36.

24   Declaration on "Guidelines on the Recognition of New States in Eastern Europe and in the Soviet Union" (Dec. 16, 1991), (1992) 31 I.L.M. 1486.

— respect for the provisions of the Charter of the United Nations and the commitments subscribed to in the Final Act of Helsinki and in the Charter of Paris especially with regard to the rule of law, democracy and human rights;

— guarantees for the rights of ethnic and national groups and minorities in accordance with the commitments subscribed to in the framework of the CSCE;

— respect for the inviolability of all frontiers which can only be changed by peaceful means and by common agreement;

— acceptance of all relevant commitments with regard to disarmament and nuclear non-proliferation as well as to security and regional stability;

— commitment to settle by agreement, including where appropriate by recourse to arbitration, all questions concerning State succession and regional disputes.

The Community and its Member States will not recognize entities which are the result of aggression. They would take account of the effect of recognition on neighbouring States.

The commitment to these principles opens the way to recognition by the Community and its Member States and to the establishment of diplomatic relations. It could be laid down in agreements.

After Slovenia, Croatia, and Bosnia-Herzegovina replied positively to these conditions, member states of the EC granted them recognition, and subsequently the United States and Canada did also. In May 1992 they were admitted to the United Nations. These decisions were taken over strong objections from Serbia about unlawful interference by the EC and from Serbian minorities in Croatia and Bosnia, who sought their own political identity.

Macedonia was not immediately recognized, even though it satisfied the criteria for statehood and accepted the conditions in the EC Guidelines. Greece, a member of the EC, prevented recognition by objecting to the use of the same name as, and implied territorial connections to, its own northernmost province. Eventually a compromise was reached and in April 1993 the new state was recognized under the name of "Former Yugoslav Republic of Macedonia."

In April 1992, Serbia and Montenegro jointly proclaimed themselves the Federal Republic of Yugoslavia (FRY) as successor state to the former Socialist Federal Republic. The proclaimed succession, however, was challenged by the EC, the United States, and Canada as well as by the newly independent states on the former Yugoslav territory. Partly on account of its claims to succession and partly because it has been adjudged an aggressor in the Yugoslav conflict, the FRY was not recognized. Its claims as successor state to occupy Yugoslavia's seat at the United Nations were denied, and in September 1992, the General Assembly resolved[25] that the FRY must apply to the United Nations as a new member. In 2000 the FRY was admitted to membership in the United Nations by resolution of the General Assembly,[26] and in 2003 the official name of the FRY was changed to Serbia and Montenegro.[27]

---

25   G.A. Res. 47/1, U.N. Doc. A/RES/47/1 (1992); and see S.C. Res. 777 (1992) on the demise of the SFRY.

26   G.A. Res. 55/12, U.N. Doc. A/RES/55/12 (2000).

27   See U.N. online at: <www.un.org/Overview/unmember.html>.

What became of the old SFRY? Recognition of its several republics as independent states impliedly extinguished recognition of the former Yugoslavia, but without resolving the problems over dispersion of its assets and obligations.

These events give rise to a number of questions about the developing practice of recognition.

1. What is the impact of the introduction of human rights criteria into the determination of recognition of a state?

2. What was the legal basis for the proclamations of independence by Slovenia, Croatia, and Bosnia-Herzegovina? Could they be claiming to exercise a right of self-determination? Refer to the discussion of self-determination, below. Did the federal authorities have a legal right to try to prevent the destruction of the territorial integrity of Yugoslavia? At what point did it become lawful for the EC and other countries to recognize the new states?

3. Why should recognition initially have been accorded to the units of the former federal republics and not some other territorial configurations? Croatia and Bosnia have large Serbian populations who sought to protect their own identity. Indeed, the Bosnian Serbs declared their own independent Serbian Republic and established a Bosnian Serb legislature. Do the Bosnian Serbs have a right to their own self-determination? Were they entitled to be recognized as constituting an independent state as well? The EC established an Arbitration Commission (commonly called the Badinter Commission after its chairman) to assist its Peace Conference on Yugoslavia. In Opinion No. 2[28] the Commission opined "that international law as it currently stands does not spell out all the implications of the right to self-determination. However, it is well established that, whatever the circumstances, the right to self-determination must not involve changes to existing frontiers at the time of independence (*uti possidetis jure*) except where the States concerned agree otherwise." The Commission gave no reasons for this conclusion. Is it well established?

Much of the horror of the conflict was fuelled by the efforts on all sides to promote their political identity and security. Could it have been relieved by a different recognition policy by the EC?

4. What were the implications of the recognition and admission of the new states in terms of the EC's and the U.N.'s political and legal capacity to intervene in the restructuring of the former Yugoslavia?

(b) International Effects of Recognition

Under international law the effect of recognition is that the state or government that is recognized thereby acquires not only the respect of the recognizing state for all the rights and privileges but also the duties associated with its new-found authority. The principal

---

28   (1992), 92 I.L.R. 167. See also Opinion No. 3 (1992), 92 I.L.R. 170, in which the Commission confirmed that the frontiers of the new states are the same as the boundaries between the former republics of the SFRY. To do so, it again relied on the principle of *uti possidetis*, invoking as authority the opinion of the ICJ in the *Frontier Dispute Case (Burkina Faso v. Mali)*, [1986] I.C.J. Rep. 554, at 565.

measure of this status is admittance to the full range of international processes for the protection of a state's rights and duties. Thus, the recognized state or government can then enter into diplomatic relations with other states by exchanging representatives and may conclude treaties with them. Non-recognition, with its consequent absence of diplomatic relations, may limit an unrecognized regime in pressing its rights, or other states in asserting its responsibilities, under international law. However, non-recognition does not necessarily affect the existence of such rights and duties.

Charter of the Organization of American States
(1948) 119 U.N.T.S. 48, as am. by (1967) 6 I.L.M. 310; Can. T.S. 1990 No. 23

Article 12

The political existence of the State is independent of recognition by other States. Even before being recognized, the State has the right to defend its integrity and independence, to provide for its preservation and prosperity, and consequently to organize itself as it sees fit, to legislate concerning its interests, to administer its services, and to determine the jurisdiction and competence of its courts. The exercise of these rights is limited only by the exercise of the rights of other States in accordance with international law.

Article 13

Recognition implies that the State granting it accepts the personality of the new State, with all the rights and duties that international law prescribes for the two States.

Tinoco Arbitration
Great Britain v. Costa Rica
(1923), 1 R.I.A.A. 375

[In 1914 Tinoco overthrew the government of Costa Rica. He assumed power, called an election, and established a new constitution. In 1919 Tinoco retired on account of ill health and went to Europe. After his government fell a month later, the old constitution was restored and new elections held under it. The new government subsequently passed a law nullifying many of the obligations assumed by the Tinoco regime toward foreigners, including the Royal Bank of Canada and other British nationals. Britain brought this claim on account of the alleged mistreatment of its nationals and, in the course of deciding it, the sole arbitrator, Taft C.J.U.S., considered the status of the Tinoco government.]

TAFT, Arbitrator: ... Great Britain contends, first, that the Tinoco government was the only government of Cost Rica *de facto* and *de jure* for two years and nine months; that during that time there was no other government disputing its sovereignty, that it was in peaceful administration of the whole country, with the acquiescence of its people.

Second, that the succeeding government could not by legislative decree avoid responsibility for acts of that government affecting British subjects, or appropriate or confiscate rights and property by that government except in violation of international law; that the Act of Nullities is as to British interests, therefore itself a nullity, and is to be disregarded, with the consequence that the contracts validly made with the Tinoco government must be performed by the present Costa Rica Government, and that the property which has been invaded or the rights nullified must be restored.

To these contentions the Costa Rican Government answers: First, that the Tinoco government was not a *de facto* or *de jure* government according to the rules of international law. This raises an issue of fact. ...

Third, that Great Britain is stopped by the fact that it did not recognize the Tinoco government during its incumbency, to claim on behalf of its subjects that Tinoco's was a government which could confer rights binding on its successor. ...

First, what are the facts to be gathered from the documents and evidence submitted by the two parties as to the *de facto* character of the Tinoco government?

In January, 1917, Frederico A. Tinoco was Secretary of War under Alfredo Gonzalez, the then President of Costa Rica. On the ground that Gonzalez was seeking reelection as President in violation of a constitutional limitation. Tinoco used the army and navy to seize the government, assume the provisional headship of the Republic and become Commander-in-Chief of the army. Gonzalez took refuge in the American Legation, thence escaping to the United States. Tinoco constituted a provisional government at once and summoned the people to an election for deputies to a constituent assembly on the first of May, 1917. At the same time he directed an election to take place for the Presidency and himself became a candidate. An election was held. Some 61,000 votes were cast for Tinoco and 259 for another candidate. Tinoco then was inaugurated as the President to administer his powers under the former constitution until the creation of a new one. A new constitution was adopted June 8, 1917, supplanting the constitution of 1871. For a full two years Tinoco and the legislative assembly under him peaceably administered the affairs of the Government of Costa Rica, and there was no disorder of a revolutionary character during that interval. No other government of any kind asserted power in the country. The courts sat, Congress legislated, and the government was duly administered. Its power was fully established and peaceably exercised. The people seemed to have accepted Tinoco's government with great good will when it came in, and to have welcomed the change. ...

Though Tinoco came in with popular approval, the result of his two years administration of the law was to rouse opposition to him. Conspiracies outside of the country were projected to organize a force to attack him. But this did not result in any substantial conflict or even a nominal provisional government on the soil until considerably more than two years after the inauguration of his government, and did not result in the establishment of any other real government until September of that year, he having renounced his Presidency in August preceding, on the score of his ill health, and withdrawn to Europe. The truth is that throughout the record as made by the case and counter case, there is no substantial evidence that Tinoco was not in actual peaceable administration without resistance or conflict or contest by anyone until a few months before the time when he retired and resigned. ...

It is not important, however, what were the causes that enabled Tinoco to carry on his government effectively and peaceably. The question is, must his government be considered a link in the continuity of the Government of Costa Rica? I must hold that from the evidence that the Tinoco government was an actual sovereign government.

But it is urged that many leading Powers refused to recognize the Tinoco government, and that recognition by other nations is the chief and best evidence of the birth, existence and continuity of succession of a government. Undoubtedly recognition by other Powers is an important evidential factor in establishing proof of the existence of a government in the society of nations. What are the facts as to this? The Tinoco government was recognized by ... 20 states excluding United States, Great Britain, France and Italy.

The non-recognition by other nations of a government claiming to be a national personality, is usually appropriate evidence that it has not attained the independence and control entitling it by international law to be classed as such. But when recognition *vel non* of a government is by such nations determined by inquiry, not into its *de facto* sovereignty and complete governmental control, but into its illegitimacy or irregularity of origin, their non-recognition loses something of evidential weight on the issue with which those applying the rules of international law are alone concerned. ... Such non-recognition for any reason, however, cannot outweigh the evidence disclosed by this record before me as to the *de facto* character of Tinoco's government, according to the standard set by international law. ...

Third, it is further objected by Costa Rica that Great Britain by her failure to recognize the Tinoco government is estopped now to urge claims of her subjects dependent upon the acts and contracts of the Tinoco government. The evidential weight of such non-recognition against the claim of its *de facto* character I have already considered and admitted. The contention here goes further and precludes a government which did not recognize a *de facto* government from appearing in an international tribunal on behalf of its nationals to claim any rights based on the acts of such government.

To sustain this view a great number of decisions in English and American courts are cited to the point that a municipal court cannot, in litigation before it, recognize or assume the *de facto* character of a foreign government which the executive department of foreign affairs of the government of which the court is a branch has not recognized. This is clearly true ... .

But such cases have no bearing on the point before us. Here the executive of Great Britain takes the position that the Tinoco government which it did not recognize, was nevertheless a *de facto* government that could create rights in British subjects which it now seeks to protect. Of course, as already emphasized, its failure to recognize the *de facto* government can be used against it as evidence to disprove the character it now attributes to that government, but this does not bar it from changing its position. ...

I do not understand the arguments on which an equitable estoppel in such case can rest. The failure to recognize the *de facto* government did not lead the succeeding government to change its position in any way upon the faith of it. Non-recognition may have aided the succeeding government to come into power; but subsequent presentation of claims based on the *de facto* existence of the previous government and its dealings does not work an injury to the succeeding government in the nature of a fraud or breach of faith. An equitable estoppel to prove the truth must rest on previous conduct of the person to be estopped, which has led the person claiming the estoppel into a position in which the truth will injure him. There is no such case here.

There are other estoppels recognized in municipal law than those which rest on equitable considerations. They are based on public policy. It may be urged that it would be in the interest of the stability of governments and the orderly adjustment of international relations, and so a proper rule in international law, that a government in recognizing or refusing to recognize a government claiming admission to the society of nations should thereafter be held to an attitude consistent with its deliberate conclusion in this issue. Arguments for and against such a rule occur to me; but it suffices to say that I have not been cited to text writers of authority or to decisions of significance indicating a general acquiescence of nations in such a rule. Without this, it cannot be applied here as a principle of international law … .

A consideration of the issues before us, therefore, recurs to the merits of the two claims. The decision on them must be governed by the answer to the question whether the claims would have been good against the Tinoco government as a government, unaffected by the Law of Nullities, and unaffected by the Costa Rican Constitution of 1871.

NOTES

1) The British claim was ultimately rejected because the obligations undertaken by the Tinoco government toward the Royal Bank and the other foreigners were held to be invalid under the law in existence at the time—that is, the constitution and laws of Costa Rica under the Tinoco regime.

2) Tinoco's government was an example of an unrecognized regime within a recognized state. How should the case have been decided if Tinoco had led an unrecognized regime in an unrecognized state?

3) Though non-recognition of a government does not affect the rights and responsibilities of the state, their execution is hindered, even incapacitated. Thus, treaties already in force will continue to bind the state but may be, in effect, inoperative during the period of an unrecognized government."[29] Conversely, foreigners travelling, investing, or doing business in a country whose government is unrecognized do so with added risk since their national government has no direct diplomatic channels by which to protect them.

---

29   See, for instance, the *Aaland Islands Case* (1920), L.N.O.J. Special Supp. (No. 3).

3. Sovereignty and Equality

The dual concepts of sovereignty and equality are the cornerstone of public international law.[30] Being sovereign and equal to others, a state has certain rights and corresponding duties. The rights include exclusive control over its territory, its permanent population (with certain provisos today concerning the international protection of human rights), and other aspects of its domestic affairs. The necessary corollary is that there is a duty not to intervene overtly or covertly in the affairs of other states and thus not to interfere with their exclusive domestic jurisdiction. The obligation not to resort to aggression or armed conflict is dealt with later, in Chapter 15 on "Limitation of the Use of Force."

Island of Palmas Case
Netherlands v. United States
(1928), 2 R.I.A.A. 829 at 838-39

[This case is the major authority on title to territory. It concerned the title to the Island of Palmas. In 1898 by the Treaty of Paris, Spain ceded the Philippines to the United States. In 1906 an official of the United States, on a visit to the island, found the Dutch flag flying there. The Netherlands and the United States referred the question of territorial sovereignty over Palmas to arbitration. The award is reported in Chapter 7, Section B.1 on "State Jurisdiction over Territory." It contains the following remarks on state sovereignty:]

Sole arbitrator HUBER: ... Sovereignty in the relation between States signifies independence. Independence in regard to a portion of the globe is the right to exercise therein, to the exclusion of any other State, the functions of a State. The development of the national organization of States during the last few centuries and, as a corollary, the development of international law, have established this principle of the exclusive competence of the State in regard to its own territory in such a way as to make it the point of departure in settling most questions that concern international relations. ... The fact that the functions of a State can be performed by any State within a given zone is ... precisely the characteristic feature of the legal situation pertaining in those parts of the globe which, like the high seas or lands without a master, cannot or do not yet form the territory of a State. ...

---

30 Consider H.J. Morgenthau, *Politics Among Nations*, 6th ed. (1985) at 299-320; and W. Friedmann, *The Changing Structure of International Law* (1964) at 36-37. See L. Wildhaber, "Sovereignty and International Law" and V. Pechota, "Equality: Political Justice in an Unequal World" in Macdonald & Johnston, eds., *supra* note 1 at 425 and 453, respectively. See H. Charlesworth, C. Chinkin, & S. Wright, "Feminist Approaches to International Law" (1991) 85 A.J.I.L. 613 at 622 where they take the view that sovereignty, equality, territorial integrity, and the principle of self-defence of those rights defend the attributes of states as patriarchal structures.

Territorial sovereignty, as has already been said, involves the exclusive right to display the activities of a State. The right has as corollary a duty: the obligation to protect within the territory the rights of other States, in particular their right to integrity and inviolability in peace and in war, together with the rights which each State may claim for its nationals in foreign territory. Without manifesting its territorial sovereignty in a manner corresponding to circumstances, the State cannot fulfil this duty.

Charter of the United Nations
Articles 1 and 2
Reproduced in the Documentary Supplement

NOTES

1) A full discussion of title to territory is contained in Chapter 7 on "State Jurisdiction Over Territory." Arbitrator Huber decided in the *Palmas Case* that the Netherlands had good title as they had continually and peacefully occupied the island since before 1700. Spain could not transfer to the United States more right to the island than it itself possessed.

2) Although independence must be demonstrated in order to acquire statehood, once that status is achieved the state has, as Arbitrator Huber explained, a legal right to its continuance. For example, when Kuwait was overrun by Iraq in 1990, it lost its independence in fact. However, Kuwait's right to independence in the face of the unlawful aggression of Iraq provided legal grounds for the United Nations to authorize measures, including the use of force, to restore the situation *quo ante*.

3) If every state is sovereign and independent, then it follows that each should be free from interference in its affairs. This idea is expressed as both a right to political and territorial integrity and to freedom in the exercise of its domestic jurisdiction, and a duty not to intervene in the affairs of any other state. See U.N. Charter articles 2(4) and (7).

4) The process of gaining statehood, and thus legal personality, in international society involves a mutual and reciprocal recognition of one state by another. As a consequence, each is a sovereign equal of the other. The United Nations, for instance, is founded on the sovereign equality of its member states. See U.N. Charter article 2(1).

5) Hence in law, international society is composed of any number of sovereign, independent, and equal states. But if each state is sovereign in the sense of being free to decide its own destiny independently, how can it be subject to any restraints, especially the rule of international law? What is the source of the legal constraint on a state to mind its own business and not to interfere in the affairs of any other state?

6) Why is a state venerated with sovereignty and its attendant capacities as an international legal person? What is the source of this legal doctrine? Why are some communities denied statehood and legal personality? For instance, what are the legal and political differences between organized communities seeking self-government, like the Basques in Spain and the First Nations in Canada, and the states they find themselves in? Perhaps the answers lie beyond the legal system in the political philosophy that legiti-mated the nation state from the beginnings of modern international law in the 17th century. See the discussion of this issue in Chapter 1.

7) The legal doctrine of independence and equality of states must be distinguished from the political and economic reality of a finite world inhabited by globally interdependent nations. Not even the United States can take a trade policy decision free of the influence of world markets and the economic policies of other governments. Fresh air and water are common resources shared by all people. Global warming and ozone depletion know no state boundaries nor are they susceptible to control by any single state. How can the system of sovereign states take account of these global realities?

8) In modern times the foundational concepts of international law have been encapsulated in the Charter of the United Nations. This document is both the constitution of the United Nations Organization and a constitutional substitute for the international legal system. Articles 1 and 2 express the purposes and principles of this system. Article 1 is a set of objectives agreed among the allied victors of World War II and still reflects the sought after goals in the very different circumstances of world society today. They are more idealistic than normative. Notice how this article recognizes the political, social, cultural, humanitarian, and economic interdependence of international problems and the solidarity of peoples (not states) around the world. Note also that the United Nations (composed of states) is expected to cooperate to solve these human problems. Does this suggest a path to a reconciliation between the system of independent sovereign states and the interdependence of global concerns, raised previously in note 7?

9) Article 2 of the U.N. Charter contains the principles on which the United Nations is founded. Notice how it is constituted of member states that are guaranteed, and in turn must respect, all the customary rights associated with statehood.

10) Article 2(1) provides for legal equality. Must the concept of legal equality be divorced from that of political equality? What is the United Nations trying to do from a legal standpoint in the Charter? Note that article 4(1) of the Charter provides that membership in the United Nations is open to "all ... peace loving states which accept the obligations contained in the present Charter, and in the judgment of the organization are able and willing to carry out these obligations."[31] Article 18(1) provides that each member of the General Assembly of the United Nations shall have one vote. The General Assembly comprises all member states. Does this legal equality in the General Assembly produce political equality? Of what significance is the veto power on all non-procedural matters in the Security Council of the five permanent members (China, France, Russian Federation, United Kingdom, and the United States)? (See article 27(3) of the United Nations Charter.)

11) Note that the International Court of Justice stated in the *Corfu Channel Case*[32] that "between independent states respect for territorial sovereignty is an essential foundation of international relations."

12) In 1993[33] and 1994,[34] the United Nations Security Council established two *Ad Hoc* tribunals to prosecute war crimes and crimes against humanity committed in the territory

31   For an authoritative discussion of this article, see the International Court's advisory opinion in *Conditions of Admission to the United Nations*, [1948] I.C.J. Rep. 57.

32   (*United Kingdom v. Albania*), [1949] I.C.J. Rep. 4 at 35.

33   UN SC Res. 827 (1993), UN SCOR, 48th year, *Resolutions and Decisions* 29.

34   UN SC Res. 955 (1994), UN SCOR, 49th year, *Resolutions and Decisions* 15.

of the former Yugoslavia and genocide in Rwanda. The Security Council in adopting the resolutions with appended statutes based on reports of the Secretary-General of the United Nations, was acting under Chapter VII of the Charter. What was the precondition for these actions not to violate article 2(7) of the Charter? Consider the material presented on the *Ad Hoc* tribunals in Chapter 11, Section B on "Prosecution in the Ad Hoc International Tribunals."

Declaration on Principles of International Law Concerning Friendly Relations and Co-operation among States in Accordance with the Charter of the United Nations
Reproduced in the Documentary Supplement

NOTES

1) The Declaration originated in 1961 as an initiative by the then Soviet Union to codify the "principles of peaceful co-existence" in international law. Many newly independent, developing countries took the opportunity to call for a wholesale rewriting of the principles of international law. Western states resisted these pressures steadfastly. The debate continued for 10 years before the Declaration, in its final form, was adopted. In what respects does it reinforce, elaborate, or modify the principles of the U.N. Charter?

2) What legal force and effect does the Declaration possess? Consider this question from the internal evidence of the document itself, as well as from the external view of the status of General Assembly resolutions. In the decision of the International Court of Justice in *Military Activities In and Against Nicaragua*[35] the Court held that the adoption of the Declaration by states "affords an indication of their *opinio juris* as to customary international law on the question of the less grave forms of the use of force." The Court appears to distinguish grave forms of the use of force (those constituting an armed attack) from other less grave forms. Refer also to Chapter 3, Section E.2 on "Law Making Through International Organizations."

3) There have been other significant attempts to restate the basic principles of the international legal system of states. The regional efforts on the American and European continents are noteworthy. In 1948 the Organization of American States (OAS) was created and became a truly regional organization for the Americas with the accession of Canada in 1989.[36] In bringing together states as politically far apart as the United States and Cuba, the OAS aims to promote collective security and economic and social cooperation. The organization is founded on certain fundamental rights and duties of states expressed in articles 9 to 22 in language similar to that in the U.N. Charter. Thus, article 9 provides: "States have juridically equal rights and equal capacity to exercise these rights, and have equal duties. The rights of each state depend not upon its power to

---

35   [1986] I.C.J. Rep. 14 at 101.

36   (1948) 119 U.N.T.S. 48, as am. by (1967) 6 I.L.M. 310; Can. T.S. 1990 No. 23.

ensure the exercise thereof, but upon the mere fact of its existence as a person under international law."

4) In Europe, the Cold War prevented progress on peace and security issues until 1975 when the long-awaited Conference on Security and Co-operation in Europe (CSCE) was convened. It culminated in the Helsinki Accords,[37] a set of documents signed by 35 states from Eastern and Western Europe and North America, though expressly not creative of legally binding obligations. The many parts were aimed at reducing tensions in Europe through "confidence building measures" affecting security and disarmament and cooperative endeavours in economics, science, technology, environment, industry, trade, transport, tourism, labour, information, culture, education, and humanitarian affairs. The Accords are best known for the relatively brief Declaration on Principles Guiding Relations between Participating States respecting: I. Sovereign equality, respect for the rights inherent in sovereignty; II. Refraining from the threat or use of force; III. Inviolability of frontiers; IV. Territorial integrity of states; V. Peaceful settlement of disputes; VI. Non-intervention in internal affairs; VII. Respect for human rights and fundamental freedoms, including the freedom of thought, conscience, religion or belief; VIII. Equal rights and self-determination of peoples; IX. Co-operation among States; and X. Fulfilment in good faith of obligations under international law.

For the states parties, especially the former U.S.S.R., the Accords were significant for being the first time that West and East blocs had agreed over matters of European security and frontiers. It was also the first time that the United States and the U.S.S.R. ever put their names jointly to a provision about human rights, even though it was expressed in one short principle of a non-binding nature. This was enough, however, for significant public attention to be addressed in subsequent years, especially by non-governmental organizations, at the record of human rights abuses, especially by the Soviet Union.

5) Also in the mid-1970s the states of the developing world, many of which were newly decolonized and politically independent, pressed for economic self-determination. Their efforts culminated in two significant resolutions of the U.N. General Assembly: the Declaration on the Establishment of a New International Economic Order, and the Charter of Economic Rights and Duties of States.[38] The Charter, after listing familiar principles of international relations between sovereign and equal states, went on to elaborate a whole new range of economic rights and duties. These principles were designed to shift the international economy much more toward the needs of the developing world through trade, investment, the transfer of technology, and economic cooperation, with special privileges for developing countries. The Charter also contained a novel chapter on "Common Responsibilities toward the International Community." Unhappily, the Charter is chiefly remembered for an intense struggle between capital exporting states and developing countries about their right to exercise full permanent sovereignty over their

---

37   (1975) 14 I.L.M. 1292. The subsequent development of the CSCE is discussed in Chapter 12, Section B.2(b).

38   GA Res. A/RES/3201, Spec. Sess. S-VI (1974), reprinted in (1974) 13 I.L.M. 715; and GA Res. 3281 (XXIX), UN GAOR, 29th Sess., Supp. No. 31, U.N. Doc. A/9631 (1974) 50, reprinted in (1975) 14 I.L.M. 251, respectively.

natural resources. In particular, the provisions regarding the conditions for expropriation and compensation of foreign property and investments had to be carried by majority vote that did not command the confidence of the industrialized world. See the discussion in Chapter 10, Section B.3 on "Responsibility for Injury to Aliens: Protection of Property."

4. Types of States

The internal organizational arrangements of states are many and varied. They include unitary and confederal states as well as less than sovereign units, such as protectorates, dependencies, and colonies. Apart from the stereotype unitary state, the most significant configuration in international affairs today is the federal state.

Federal States
from S.A. Williams and A.L.C. de Mestral, *An Introduction to International Law* 2d ed. (1987) at 53-54

The most important state today is the federation. This is a union of two or more units comprising a federal political unit and numerous internal political units. No doubt exists that a federal state enjoys international personality in the same manner as a unitary state. Important federal states of the world such as Australia, Brazil, Canada, the Federal Republic of Germany, Nigeria and the United States have always been accorded full international personality despite the fact that the central authorities do not necessarily exercise all the sovereign legislative powers within their respective territories. The problem lies with standing and powers of the constituent units of a federal state on the international level. Some federations such as Australia and the United States vest exclusive authority over the conduct of external affairs in the federal authority and hence appear to preclude any role to the constituent units. Some others such as the Federal Republic of Germany and the Swiss Confederation grant limited treaty making powers to their units. ...

The leading authorities on international law are almost equally divided on this issue and leading textbooks in many countries take different positions. This divergence of views was particularly evident in the debates of the International Law Commission during preparation of the draft on the law of treaties. Powerful arguments exist against according any capacity under international law to the constituent units of federal states. Divergent policies on such questions as recognition of foreign states would lead to insuperable political and legal deadlock, and divergent policies on matters such as cultural or economic relations would create great strains upon any federation. The greatest fear is that direct relations between the constituent units and foreign states could herald the disintegration of the federation itself. On the other hand, if constituent units are to have full exercise of their powers, it appears arbitrary and impractical to deny them any international dimensions. Since today there are few governmental legislative and executive acts that have no international impact in an increasingly interdependent world, any local government which is active in cultural, social and economic issues will resent being forced to go through the central authority for all contacts with foreign governments.

The Vienna Conference meeting to adopt a multilateral Convention on the Law of Treaties failed to resolve this issue. At the behest of many federations, including Canada, the conference rejected a clause which would have granted explicit recognition to the treaty-making capacity of constituent units of federal states. In the absence of a clear treaty rule customary law governs. At present, customary international law does not accept that constituent units can be treated fully as states but does allow them some limited treaty-making capacity.

[For a discussion of the conduct of foreign affairs in Canada, in particular the power to conclude treaties, see Chapter 4, Sections B on "Customary International Law in Canada" and C on "Treaties in Canada." The evolution of Canada into an independent federal state is described in the following essay by Professor Max Cohen.]

Canada and the International Legal Order: An Inside Perspective
by M. Cohen, in R. St. J. Macdonald, G.L. Morris, and D.M. Johnston, eds.,
Canadian Perspectives on International Law and Organization (1974) at 3-8

In a sense Canadian experience with the international legal order is part of the very beginnings of Canada itself. Conquest, war-making, treaty law, and the right of a new subject people related to a grand imperial-colonial design marked the beginnings of the experiment that was to become Canada. In a curious way the "victories" of 1759 and 1760, the proclamations establishing the new imperial government, and the Treaty of Paris of 1763 all laid the foundations for what was then in fact in a united, continental British North America, except for Spanish claims largely in the southern and southwestern territories and the Russian presence on the Alaska mainland for another century. But within less than two decades, in 1783, another Treaty of Paris climaxed the revolution of 1776, and British North America's ambitions now were split between a "loyal" north and the rebellious south—the independent Thirteen— now the United States of America. Revolution, war, and new boundaries had reshaped the British North American remnant, infusing it with a deep and lasting imprint so that, in a sense, the creation of the components that one day were to become an independent Canada had first to be defined by an international legal settlement, itself the product of revolt, war, and dissolution of the first British Empire to be quickly replaced by the second.

Hence it may be said that Canada was sired in warfare, mothered in treaties, and nurtured in the dedicated crèche of both imperial constitutional relations and international law as they were in the latter 18th century. To this day the most urgent and powerful concerns of Canadian policy, for its growth and identity, are an evolutionary reflection of these fractured imperial beginnings. Canada's boundaries were not made final until as late as the Alaska Panhandle dispute of 1903, and a continuing anxiety exists for the management of a society and an economy where the pull of continental integration was always to parallel the stress of searching for national self-definition and political autonomy. No one could have foreseen in 1776 or 1783 that the new, independent English-speaking United States would grow so rapidly as to overshadow quickly the imperial remnant to the north and create by these geopolitical facts the permanent crisis in Canadian life; namely, its development beside an immense neighbour who would outstrip Canada in everything, perhaps, but the determination to achieve an integrity of its own. It is no surprise, therefore, that the long-term Canadian international experience *par excellence*, and the concomitant political–legal preoccupation, should have been the form and substance for managing Canadian relations with the United States; and this remains true to the present day.

Yet side by side with these continental parameters, imposed by geography, politics, and law on an emerging Canada, there was an almost equally important school for that "emergence" in the shift from Empire to Commonwealth. The dominant role played by the opposition of Canada in the evolution of the second British Empire, and its transformation in the latter half of the nineteenth century and the first quarter of the twentieth into the Commonwealth, proved to be a double training ground of paramount significance. For at one and the same time the movement from "colony to nation" required a search for political and "constitutional" solutions within the imperial system which slowly transformed dependence to independence for those British North American communities that remained outside the United States solution of 1783. That process trained Canadians to obtain in peace what their revolutionary cousins in the United States sought and only realized with war: responsible government, representative and essentially independent in the management of local life from a centralized, distant imperial control. ...

If the Commonwealth was the "original" school for Canadian nationhood and for evolving international personality, it was the United States that gave Canada its first taste of learning to live in the severe world of realpolitik where bilateral dealings with an immensely powerful neighbour were the basic geopolitical facts of life for Canada. It is no surprise, therefore, that some of the most important and creative international legal experiences for Canada have emerged from its almost two centuries of dealings with the sometime imperial brothers who went their own national way. Tariffs (and reciprocity agreements), boundaries, boundary waters, fisheries, immigration, and joint obligations to native peoples were all a product of the nineteenth-century process of Canada learning to live successfully with the United States. "Continentalism," no popular word today, was nevertheless destiny for both, and many legal arrangements were mirrors of that shared reality.

The twentieth century multiplied the interpretation of the two societies, accentuated by two world wars and the military–economic–political co-operation to which these led. And so a complex regulatory network evidenced by instruments ranging from a simple exchange of notes to formal treaties marked the era of expanding involvement—in defence production, west coast fisheries, post-World War II military policy for the continent, resource development with the emphasis on mineral, petroleum, forest products, the energy demands from the United States (from the Columbia River Treaty to natural gas exports), and the St-Lawrence Seaway. More recently contradictory trends have emerged such as the new limits on immigration and restrictive economic policies side by side with an immense common obligation to refresh the Great Lakes system from joint pollution over many years. Some interesting case law, through the arbitral process in one form or another, has come out of these relations, albeit infrequently. "Hot pursuit" in the *I'm Alone*, poisonous fumes from the Trail Smelter, and the flooding of recreational shorelines by *Gut Dam* have resulted in doctrines and footnotes uniquely North American in their origin but perhaps universal in their significance. This is certainly true for the *Trail Smelter* case, the first transnational air pollution dispute to invite arbitration and become a precedent. ...

Hence, while it is true that responsible government and essential autonomy were *de facto* true by the third or fourth quarter of the nineteenth century, there were a number of imperial threads still tying the robust Canadian image to the "Mother Country." Good illustrations of this mixture of the imperial-Commonwealth procedures, and their effect on clear international personality as such, may be seen in the powers of the governor general, perhaps until 1947; the pre-World War I appointment of the commander in chief of the Canadian forces from among imperial officers, particularly the royal family; the disputes over the Canadian contribution to and management of its forces in the Boer War; and the controversy over Canadian naval policy in the first years of the twentieth century; and the crucial role for image and fact of sovereignty or independence played by military issues in World War I, since the independence of the Canadian Corps and the determination to have a separate identity for that corps had important psychological and political consequences. They probably influenced the legal–political decision for Canada to be a separate "signatory" (through initials at least) to the Treaty of Versailles. And when to these events are added the Commonwealth conferences of 1926 and 1930 and the Balfour Resolution in 1926, climaxed by the Statute of Westminster in 1931, and the abolition of criminal appeals to the Judicial Committee in the same year—to which should be added the establishment of the Department of External Affairs as a working organism in 1928 (although the department itself was created in 1901), along with the Canadian treaty series—it is obvious how intermixed were the growth lines of a sovereign independent Canada with the evolutionary patterns of the Commonwealth itself.

World War II virtually destroyed any pretensions of "automatic" political or military response to the policies of the United Kingdom or any juridical theories of "subordination." The insistence on a separate Canadian declaration of war on 9 September 1939, the determined position of the government with respect to status and command of Canadian troops, and the special case of the Royal Canadian Air Force, and even the insistent claims to independence for the Royal Canadian Navy were all part of the final erosion of umbilical links to London—as if the reality had not already been forecast by World War I, the Chanak incident over Turkey, and Canadian behaviour generally in the League of Nations and in the multilateral world of the interwar years. What became clear, however, was that the political, military, and legal fading of authority from the United Kingdom, imperial-Commonwealth sources was being replaced by the voluntary alliances of the NATO-NORAD system and this, in effect, provided the primary focus of the new struggle for independence *de facto* if not *de jure*, together with economic questions to be turned now towards the American neighbour and away from the imperial "mother." But unlike the Commonwealth story, there were no historical-juridical anomalies to be resolved. United States–Canadian relations have been a case of bilateral dealings between sovereign equals on a plane of majestic inequality.

NOTES

1) In the Canadian context, even though the external treaty-making power lies in the hands of the federal executive, the treaty implementation competence is divided depending on whether the subject matter falls within section 91 or 92 of the *Constitution Act, 1867*. See the full discussion in Chapter 4, Section C on "Treaties in Canada." This is to be contrasted with the position in Australia where the federal government not only possesses the treaty-making power but also the ability to legislate internally with regard to external affairs, even though ordinarily the subject matter would be within state and not federal jurisdiction.[39]

2) The European Union, composed of 25 member states as of May 2005, is not a federation, but rather a grouping of independent states that have agreed upon limitations of their sovereignty in certain specific areas. However, since the inception of the European Coal and Steel Community (ECSC) in 1951 and the European Economic Community (EEC) in 1957, the aim has been to work toward an ever-increasing degree of integration, including a Europe without internal borders, and with a common currency and political as well as economic policy. As a result, the sovereign member states have conceded an increasing number of powers to supranational institutions such as the Commission and the European Court, and in 2004 signed a further treaty creating a Constitution of the European Union, which as of mid-2005 was not in force.[40]

3) In 1992, the Secretary-General of the United Nations, Dr. Boutros Boutros Ghali, stated in his Report entitled "An Agenda for Peace" that:

> We have entered a time of global tension marked by uniquely contradictory trends. Regional and continental associations of States are evolving ways to deepen cooperation and ease some of the contentious characteristics of sovereign and nationalistic rivalries. National boundaries are blurred by advanced communications and global commerce, and by the decisions of States to yield some sovereign prerogatives to larger, common political associations. At the same time, however,

---

39 See *Koowarta v. Bjelke-Petersen* (1982), 68 I.L.R. 181; 153 C.L.R. 168 (Aust. H.C.); *Commonwealth of Australia v. Tasmania* (1983), 68 I.L.R. 266; 158 C.L.R. 1 (Aust. H.C.); *Richardson v. The Forestry Commission* (1987), 164 C.L.R. 261 (Aust. H.C.); and *Queensland v. The Commonwealth* (1989), 167 C.L.R. 232.

40 See D. O'Keefe & P. Twomey, eds., *Legal Issues of the Maastricht Treaty* (1994); D. McGoldrick, *International Relations Law of the European Union* (1997); I. McLeod, I.D. Hendry, & S. Hyett, *The External Relations of the European Communities* (1996); J. Megret, J.Y. Louis, D. Vignes, & M. Waelbrock, *Le Droit de la Communauté économique européenne* (1973-) vol. 1-15; D. Lasok, *Law and Institutions of European Communities*, 7th ed. (1999); P. Mathijsen, *A Guide to European Community Law*, 7th ed. (1999); and D. Wyatt & A. Dashwood, *European Community Law*, 4th ed. (2000). In 2004 the 25 Member States and 3 candidate States signed the Treaty Establishing A Constitution for Europe, Oct. 29, 2004, 47 Official Journal of the European Union 16/12/2004 C310. This treaty consolidates a number of constitutive agreements in one document, revises and clarifies the roles and interactions of various EU institutions, and for the first time assigns separate legal personality to the EU as an institution (article 7). As of June 2005, the process of ratification was ongoing, but had suffered serious setbacks with referenda in France and the Netherlands rejecting ratification.

fierce new assertions of nationalism and sovereignty spring up, and the cohesion of States is threatened by brutal ethnic, religious, social, cultural or linguistic strife. Social peace is challenged on the one hand by new assertions of discrimination and exclusion, and on the other, by acts of terrorism seeking to undermine evolution and change through democratic means.[41]

In the same Report, in discussing "an integrated approach to human security," he not only talked about the role to be played by the organs of the United Nations but also stressed that the "foundation-stone of this work is and must remain the State." He stated that:

Respect for [a State's] ... fundamental sovereignty and integrity are crucial to any common international progress. The time of absolute and exclusive sovereignty, however, has passed; its theory was never matched by reality. It is the task of leaders of States today to understand this and to find a balance between the needs of internal governance and the requirements of an ever more interdependent world. Commerce, communications and environmental matters transcend administrative borders; but inside those borders is where individuals carry out the first order of their political and social lives. The United Nations has not closed its door. Yet, if every ethnic, religious or linguistic group claimed statehood, there would be no limit to fragmentation, and peace, security and economic well-being for all would become ever more difficult to achieve.

Dr. Boutros Ghali noted that one solution lies in the "commitment to human rights with a special sensitivity to those of minorities, whether ethnic, religious, social or linguistic."

C. OTHER LEGAL PERSONS

Although states are the prototypes of international legal persons, international law does not prevent other candidates from acquiring a measure of personality. In order to do so, a candidate's claim to exercise legal personality must be respected by other international persons—that is, by the existing community of states. The enquiry whether a particular candidate has acquired international personality therefore reduces to a functional question: does the practice of states demonstrate their readiness to permit this candidate to exercise any specific legal capacity on the international plane? If so, it can be said to have attained international personality for that purpose, even though it is very far from having the plenary powers of a state. The chief candidates, which are in the process of developing a degree of international personality, are international organizations, individuals, and "peoples seeking self-determination."

---

41   U.N. Doc. A/47/277-S/24/111, June 17, 1992, paras. 11, 12, 17, and 18. Available online at: <http://www.un.org/Docs/SG/agpeace.html>.

1. International Organizations[42]

Intergovernmental Organizations
from S.A. Williams and A.L.C. de Mestral, *An Introduction to International Law*
2d ed. (1987) at 61

International governmental organizations must be differentiated at the outset from non-governmental organizations. International governmental organizations or institutions are set up by agreement between states. Non-governmental organizations, as the title suggests, are set up by individuals.

The number of both types has multiplied to the extent that their scope encompasses almost every type of activity and interest of humanity. The underlying reason for the development is a realization of the need for international dialogue. Bilateral association was felt to be inadequate, as today's needs necessitate dealings at the international level. The organizations vary from the global such as the United Nations, to the regional, such as the European Union.

What type of legal personality do these subjects of international law enjoy? The answer depends upon the circumstances of the particular arrangement. Thus, it is necessary to look at the institution's constitution to determine its standing. For example article 104 of the U.N. Charter provides that "the organization shall enjoy in the territory of each of its members such legal capacity as may be necessary for the exercise of its functions and the fulfilment of its purposes." This article means that the United Nations has personality under the domestic laws of all its members.

International personality in the context of international organizations is a relative concept. One organization may have certain rights that others do not. Each particular organization has to be examined in detail to determine such factors.

The United Nations[43]

The United Nations is the pre-eminent example amongst international organizations. Before considering its legal personality, it is appropriate to survey, very briefly, its structure, functions, and powers.

---

42   See, generally, P. Sands & P. Klein, *Bowett's Law of International Institutions*, 5th ed. (2001);
H.G. Schermers with N.M Blokker, *International Institutional Law: Unity Within Diversity*, 4th rev. ed.
(2003); M. Rama-Montaldo, "International Legal Personality and Implied Powers of International
Organizations" (1970) 44 Br. Y.B. Int'l L. 111; and D. Vignes, "The Impact of International Organization
on the Development and Application of Public International Law" in Macdonald & Johnston, eds., *supra*
note 1 at 809.

43   Sands & Klein, *Bowett's Law of International Institutions, ibid.* note 30; L.M. Goodrich, E. Hambro &
A.P. Simons, *Charter of the United Nations*, 3d ed. (1969); R. Higgins, *The Development of International
Law Through the Political Organs of the United Nations* (1963); L.B. Sohn, *Cases on United Nations
Law*, 2d ed. (1967); A. Vandenbosch & W.N. Hogan, *United Nations: Background, Organization,
Functions, Activities* (1970); Q. Wright, *International Law and the United Nations* (1960); K.P. Saksena,
Reforming the United Nations (1993); D. Bourantis & J. Weiner, *The United Nations in the New World
Order: The World Organization at Fifty* (1995); B. Urquhart & L. Childers, *A World in Need of Leadership:*

Charter of the United Nations
Read articles 1, 2, 7-32, 55-105
Reproduced in the Documentary Supplement

Consider carefully:

The organization of the United Nations displayed in the chart on the next page.

The purposes of the United Nations, in article 1.

The principles of the United Nations, in article 2, discussed previously.

The composition, powers and voting procedures of the General Assembly compared to the Security Council, in articles 9, 10, 18, 23, 24, 27.

The responsibilities of member states regarding disputes in article 33.

The powers of the Security Council over disputes; compare articles 36 and 39.

The purposes and powers of the Economic and Social Council, in articles 55, 62.

The International Court of Justice is considered in Chapter 6, Section D.

United Nations' Principles and Processes

The high-minded objectives of the Charter have created equally high expectations of the United Nations that have not always been fulfilled. In practice, the United Nations' ability to cope with the world's crises is only as great as the institutional machinery provided to the organization. This machinery maintains a particular balance of authority and powers between the General Assembly and the Security Council as the organs most directly responsible for the maintenance of international peace.

The experience of the General Assembly and the Security Council in 1979-80 in trying to deal simultaneously with Iran's taking of American diplomats as hostages and the former Soviet Union's invasion of Afghanistan is a good demonstration of U.N. principles and processes of operation. The uppermost questions at the time were what the United Nations could and should do in the circumstances. The diary of events set out below provides a brief outline of what the United Nations proceeded to do. It is followed by a series of questions to elucidate the authority that was exercised under the Charter.

Diary of Events:

November 4, 1979	Iranians seized U.S. embassy and staff.
November 9, 17 and December 4, 1979	Security Council resolved unanimously that Iran had to free the American hostages.
December 17, 1979	General Assembly by resolution declared unanimously that the hostage taking was "an offence of grave concern to the international community."
December 24, 1979	Soviet invasion of Afghanistan began.

Tomorrow's United Nations, 2d rev. ed. (1996); and H. von Margoldt et al., *The United Nations System and Its Predecessors* (1997) vol. 1-2; B. Simma, *The Charter of the United Nations: A Commentary*, 2d ed. (2002). Annual surveys of U.N. activities are published in the Yearbooks of the United Nations.

The United Nations System

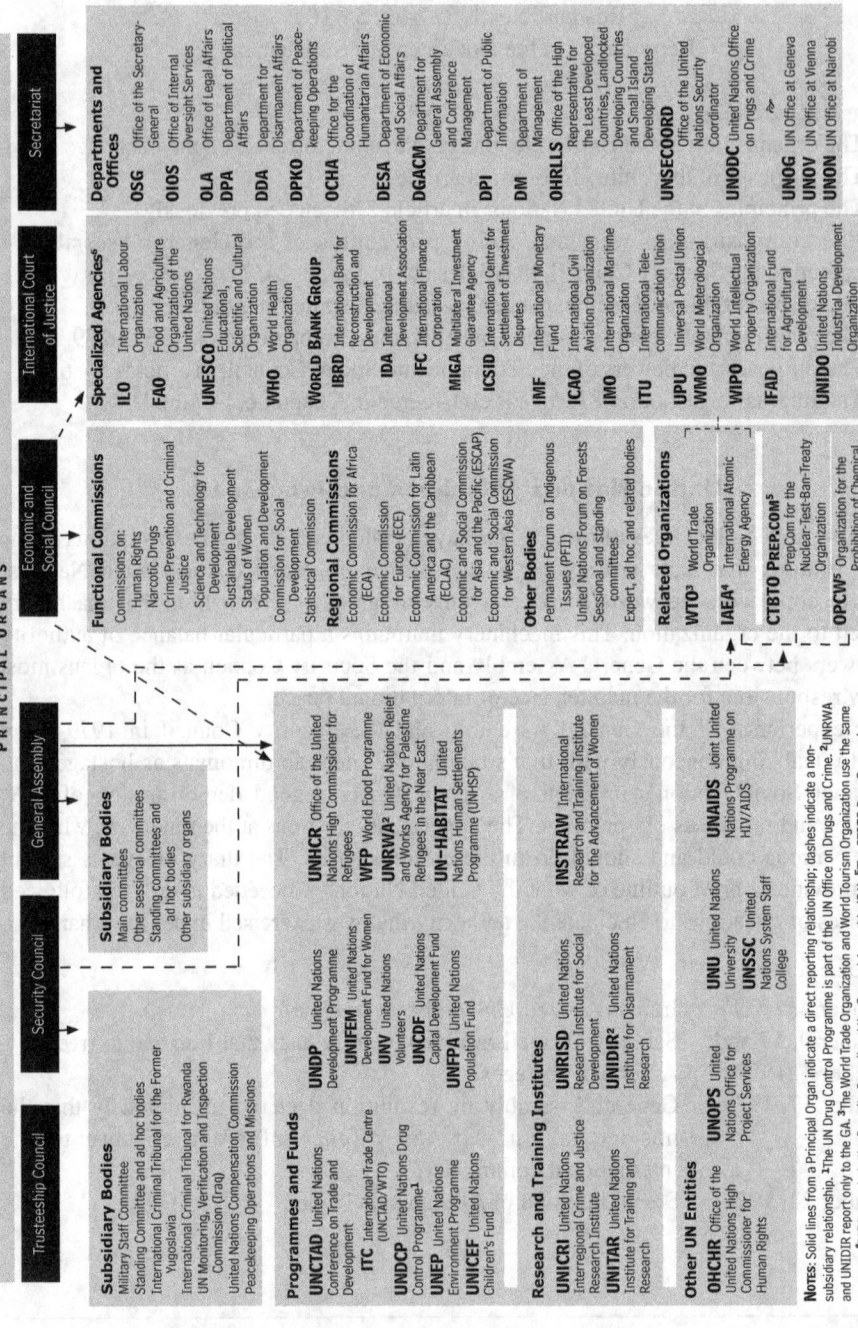

Published by the UN Department of Public Information
DPI/7342—March 2004

PRINCIPAL ORGANS

Trusteeship Council | Security Council | General Assembly | Economic and Social Council | International Court of Justice | Secretariat

Secretariat

Departments and Offices

OSG Office of the Secretary-General
OIOS Office of Internal Oversight Services
OLA Office of Legal Affairs
DPA Department of Political Affairs
DDA Department for Disarmament Affairs
DPKO Department of Peace-keeping Operations
OCHA Office for the Coordination of Humanitarian Affairs
DESA Department of Economic and Social Affairs
DGACM Department for General Assembly and Conference Management
DPI Department of Public Information
DM Department of Management
OHRLLS Office of the High Representative for the Least Developed Countries, Landlocked Developing Countries and Small Island Developing States
UNSECOORD Office of the United Nations Security Coordinator
UNODC United Nations Office on Drugs and Crime
UNOG UN Office at Geneva
UNOV UN Office at Vienna
UNON UN Office at Nairobi

Specialized Agencies[6]

ILO International Labour Organization
FAO Food and Agriculture Organization of the United Nations
UNESCO United Nations Educational, Scientific and Cultural Organization
WHO World Health Organization

World Bank Group
IBRD International Bank for Reconstruction and Development
IDA International Development Association
IFC International Finance Corporation
MIGA Multilateral Investment Guarantee Agency
ICSID International Centre for Settlement of Investment Disputes

IMF International Monetary Fund
ICAO International Civil Aviation Organization
IMO International Maritime Organization
ITU International Tele-communication Union
UPU Universal Postal Union
WMO World Meteorological Organization
WIPO World Intellectual Property Organization
IFAD International Fund for Agricultural Development
UNIDO United Nations Industrial Development Organization
WTO[3] World Tourism Organization

Economic and Social Council

Functional Commissions
Commissions on:
Human Rights
Narcotic Drugs
Crime Prevention and Criminal Justice
Science and Technology for Development
Sustainable Development
Status of Women
Population and Development
Commission for Social Development
Statistical Commission

Regional Commissions
Economic Commission for Africa (ECA)
Economic Commission for Europe (ECE)
Economic Commission for Latin America and the Caribbean (ECLAC)
Economic and Social Commission for Asia and the Pacific (ESCAP)
Economic and Social Commission for Western Asia (ESCWA)

Other Bodies
Permanent Forum on Indigenous Issues (PFII)
United Nations Forum on Forests
Sessional and standing committees
Expert, ad hoc and related bodies

Related Organizations
WTO[3] World Trade Organization
IAEA[4] International Atomic Energy Agency
CTBTO PREP.COM[5] PrepCom for the Nuclear-Test-Ban-Treaty Organization
OPCW[5] Organization for the Prohibition of Chemical Weapons

General Assembly

Subsidiary Bodies
Main committees
Other sessional committees
Standing committees and ad hoc bodies
Other subsidiary organs

Programmes and Funds
UNCTAD United Nations Conference on Trade and Development
ITC International Trade Centre (UNCTAD/WTO)
UNDCP United Nations Drug Control Programme[1]
UNEP United Nations Environment Programme
UNICEF United Nations Children's Fund
UNDP United Nations Development Programme
UNIFEM United Nations Development Fund for Women
UNV United Nations Volunteers
UNCDF United Nations Capital Development Fund
UNFPA United Nations Population Fund
UNHCR Office of the United Nations High Commissioner for Refugees
WFP World Food Programme
UNRWA[2] United Nations Relief and Works Agency for Palestine Refugees in the Near East
UN–HABITAT United Nations Human Settlements Programme (UNHSP)

Research and Training Institutes
UNICRI United Nations Interregional Crime and Justice Research Institute
UNITAR United Nations Institute for Training and Research
UNRISD United Nations Research Institute for Social Development
UNIDIR[2] United Nations Institute for Disarmament Research
INSTRAW International Research and Training Institute for the Advancement of Women

Other UN Entities
OHCHR Office of the United Nations High Commissioner for Human Rights
UNOPS United Nations Office for Project Services
UNU United Nations University
UNSSC United Nations System Staff College
UNAIDS Joint United Nations Programme on HIV/AIDS

Security Council

Subsidiary Bodies
Military Staff Committee
Standing Committee and ad hoc bodies
International Criminal Tribunal for the Former Yugoslavia
International Criminal Tribunal for Rwanda
UN Monitoring, Verification and Inspection Commission (Iraq)
United Nations Compensation Commission
Peacekeeping Operations and Missions

NOTES: Solid lines from a Principal Organ indicate a direct reporting relationship; dashes indicate a non-subsidiary relationship. [1]The UN Drug Control Programme is part of the UN Office on Drugs and Crime. [2]UNRWA and UNIDIR report only to the GA. [3]The World Trade Organization and World Tourism Organization use the same acronym. [4]IAEA reports to the Security Council and the General Assembly (GA). [5]The CTBTO Prep.Com and OPCW report to the GA. [6]Specialized agencies are autonomous organizations working with the UN and each other through the coordinating machinery of the ECOSOC at the intergovernmental level, and through the Chief Executives Board for coordination (CEB) at the inter-secretariat level.

December 31, 1979	Secretary-General Waldheim flew to Tehran for talks with the Iranian authorities. He was not well received.
December 31, 1979	At the same time, the Security Council met again and called on Iran to release the hostages by January 7, 1980 or it would "adopt effective measures." The vote was 11 for to 0 against, with 4 abstentions, including the former U.S.S.R.
January 7, 1980	Security Council met to handle the Afghan crisis. A resolution protesting Soviet military intervention was defeated by a vote of 13 for to 2 against, including the former U.S.S.R.
January 9, 1980	Security Council resolved to call General Assembly into emergency session regarding the Afghan situation. The vote was 12 for to 2 against, including the former U.S.S.R.
January 10, 1980	General Assembly met under the Uniting for Peace Resolution[44] to discuss the Afghan crisis, but was unable to resolve it.
January 13, 1980	Security Council returned to unfinished Iranian business. A resolution to authorize collective sanctions was defeated by a vote of 10 for to 2 against, including the former U.S.S.R.

QUESTIONS

1) By what authority could the Security Council become seized of the Iranian crisis on November 9? See articles 33 to 38.

2) By what authority could the General Assembly become seized of the same matter on December 17, at the same time as the Security Council? See articles 11(2), 12, and 14.

3) What powers did the General Assembly then have in the matter? How much further could it have gone beyond its declaration of "an offence of grave concern"? See articles 2(7) and 10 to 18.

4) On what authority could the Secretary-General take the initiative to intervene personally in the Iranian crisis on December 31? See articles 97 to 101.

5) Also on December 31, the Security Council directed Iran to comply with its earlier resolutions or face effective measures. What was the Council's authority to order a member state such as Iran to do anything? See articles 24 and 25, and the *Namibia* case, reported below.

6) As to the threat of enforcement, what kind of measures might the Security Council have taken? What steps were prerequisite to any Security Council action? See articles 39 to 51. A full discussion of the application of these powers in the context of the Iraq–Kuwait crisis appears in Chapter 15, Section B.4 on "Collective Measures Pursuant to the U.N. Charter."

7) Why were the voting patterns on the three Security Council resolutions of December 31 (on Iran) and January 7 and 9 (on Afghanistan) so consistent, while the results were quite different? See article 27.

8) By what authority could the General Assembly become seized of the Afghan crisis on January 10 when it was no longer in session? See article 20.

---

44   Reported in Chapter 15, Section B.4 on "Collective Measures Pursuant to the U.N. Charter."

9) What powers were available to the General Assembly to deal with the Afghan situation, compared to the Iranian crisis? See articles 2(7) and 10 to 18.

10) The discussions in the General Assembly and the Security Council came to nought. Was the failure of the United Nations to resolve either crisis due more to the lack of legal capacity in the organization or the absence of political capacity in the member states?

NOTE

The powers of the Security Council and the General Assembly, and the legal consequences of United Nations decisions for member and non-member states, were addressed by the I.C.J. in the *Namibia Case*, below.[45] The factual background to this case arose from the League of Nations Mandate System, under which territories of former enemy states in World War I were "given under a mandate to allied states which were to administer them under the guidance of the League of Nations."[46] With the establishment of the United Nations after World War II, remaining Mandate territories were placed under the new "trust territories" system, supervised by the Trusteeship Council of the United Nations. South Africa did not transfer South West Africa (Namibia) to United Nations authority; in 1966 the General Assembly resolved that the Mandate held by South Africa was terminated, and that the United Nations "must discharge those responsibilities with respect to South West Africa."[47] The last Trust Territory (Palau) became independent in 1974, and the Secretary-General has recommended the removal of the Trusteeship Council provisions from the Charter.[48]

Namibia Case
Legal Consequences for States of the Continued Presence of South Africa in Namibia (South-West Africa) Notwithstanding Security Council Resolution 276 (1970)
Advisory Opinion, [1971] I.C.J. Rep. 16

[Following Resolution 2145 (XXI), in which the General Assembly terminated South Africa's mandate, the Security Council called upon South Africa to withdraw from Namibia.[49] South Africa failed to do this and so the Security Council passed Resolution 276 (1970)[50] in which it declared that South Africa's presence in Namibia

---

45   See I. Sagay, *The Legal Aspects of the Namibian Dispute* (1975) and A. Lejeune, *The Case for South West Africa* (1971).

46   S.A. Williams & A.L.C. de Mestral, *An Introduction to International Law*, 2d ed. (1987) at 55.

47   *Question of South West Africa*, GA Res. 2145 (xxi), UN GAOR, 21st Sess., Supp. No. 16, U.N. Doc. A/6316 (1966) at 2.

48   Report of the Secretary-General, *In Larger Freedom: Towards Development, Security, and Human Rights for All*, UN GAOR, 59th Sess., U.N. Doc. A/59/2005 (2005) at 52.

49   South West Africa was renamed Namibia by GA Res. 2372 (XXII), UN GAOR, 22d Sess., Supp. No. 16A (1968).

50   *The Situation in Namibia*, SC Res. 276 (1970), UN SCOR, 25th year, *Resolutions and Decisions* 1.

was illegal and its actions there were invalid. The Security Council further requested an advisory opinion from the International Court on the question: "What are the legal consequences for states of the continued presence of South Africa in Namibia, notwithstanding Security Council resolution 276 (1970)?" The Court first confirmed its earlier opinions that the mandate had survived the collapse of the League of Nations and had been brought into the United Nations system. It then proceeded to discuss the effects of the United Nations' actions, beginning with General Assembly Resolution 2145.]

THE COURT: ...

94. In examining this action of the General Assembly it is appropriate to have regard to the general principles of international law regulating termination of a treaty relationship on account of breach. For even if the mandate is viewed as having the character of an institution, as is maintained, it depends on those international agreements which created the system and regulated its application. As the Court indicated in 1962 "this Mandate, like practically all other similar Mandates" was "a special type of instrument composite in nature and instituting a novel international regime. It incorporates a definite agreement ..." (*I.C.J. Reports 1962*, p. 331). The Court stated conclusively in that Judgment that the Mandate ... "in fact and in law, is an international agreement having the character of a treaty or convention" (*I.C.J. Reports 1962*, p. 330). The rules laid down by the Vienna Convention on the Law of Treaties concerning termination of a treaty relationship on account of breach (adopted without a dissenting vote) may in many respects be considered as a codification of existing customary law on the subject. In the light of these rules, only a material breach of a treaty justifies termination, such breach being defined as:

    a) a repudiation of the treaty not sanctioned by the present Convention; or

    b) the violation of a provision essential to the accomplishment of the object or purpose of the treaty (Art. 60, para. 3)

95. General Assembly resolution 2145 (XXI) determines that both forms of material breach had occurred in this case. By stressing that South Africa "has in fact, disavowed the Mandate," the General Assembly declared in fact that it had repudiated it. The resolution in question is therefore to be viewed as the exercise of the right to terminate a relationship in case of a deliberate and persistent violation of obligations which destroys the very object and purpose of that relationship.

96. It has been contended that the Covenant of the League of Nations did not confer on the Council of the League power to terminate a mandate for misconduct of the mandatory and that no such power could therefore be exercised by the United Nations, since it could not derive from the League greater powers that the latter itself had. For this objection to prevail it would be necessary to show that the mandates system, as established under the League, excluded the application of the general principle of law that a right of termination on account of breach must be presumed to exist in respect of all treaties, except as regards provisions relating to the protection of the human person contained in treaties of a humanitarian character (as indicated in Art. 60, para. 5, of the Vienna Convention). The silence of a treaty as to the existence of such a right cannot be interpreted as implying the exclusion of a right which has its source

outside of the treaty, in general international law, and is dependent on the occurrence of circumstances which are not normally envisaged when a treaty is concluded. ...

102. In a further objection to General Assembly resolution 2145 (XXI) it is contended that it made pronouncements which the Assembly, not being a judicial organ, and not having previously referred the matter to any such organ, was not competent to make. Without dwelling on the conclusions reached in the 1966 Judgment in the South West Africa contentious cases, it is worth recalling that in those cases the applicant States, which complained of material breaches of substantive provisions of the Mandate, were held not to "possess any separate self-contained right which they could assert ... to require the due performance of the Mandate in discharge of the 'sacred trust' " (*I.C.J. Reports 1966*, pp. 29 and 51). On the other hand, the Court declared that: "any divergences of view concerning the conduct of a mandate were regarded as being matters that had their place in the political field, the settlement of which lay between the mandatory and the competent organs of the League" (*ibid.*, p. 45). To deny to a political organ of the United Nations which is a successor of the League in this respect the right to act, on the argument that it lacks competence to render what is described as a judicial decision, would not only be inconsistent but would amount to a complete denial of the remedies available against fundamental breaches of an international undertaking.

103. The Court is unable to appreciate the view that the General Assembly acted unilaterally as party and judge in its own cause. In the 1966 Judgment in the South West Africa Cases, referred to above, it was found that the function to call for the due execution of the relevant provisions of the mandate instruments appertained to the League acting as an entity through its appropriate organs. The right of the League "in the pursuit of its collective, institutional activity, to require the due performance of the Mandate in discharge of the 'sacred trust,' " was specifically recognized (*ibid.*, p. 29). Having regard to this finding, the United Nations as a successor to the League, acting through its competent organs, must be seen above all as the supervisory institution, competent to pronounce, in that capacity, on the conduct of the mandatory with respect to its international obligations, and competent to act accordingly. ...

105. General Assembly resolution 2145 (XXI), after declaring the termination of the Mandate, added in operative paragraph 4 "that South Africa has no other right to administer the Territory." This part of the resolution has been objected to as deciding a transfer of territory. That in fact is not so. The pronouncement made by the General Assembly is based on a conclusion, referred to earlier, reached by the Court in 1950:

> The authority which the Union Government exercises over the Territory is based on the Mandate. If the Mandate lapsed, as the Union Government contends, the latter's authority would equally have lapsed. (*I.C.J. Reports 1950*, p. 133.)

This was confirmed by the Court in its Judgment of 21 December 1962 in the South West Africa Cases (*Ethiopia v. South Africa; Liberia v. South Africa*) (*I.C.J. Reports 1962*, p. 333). Relying on these decisions of the Court, the General Assembly declared that the Mandate having been terminated "South Africa has no other right to administer the Territory." This is not a finding on facts, but the formulation of a legal situation. For it would not be correct to assume that, because the General Assembly is in principle vested with recommendatory powers, it is debarred from adopting, in specific cases within the framework of its competence, resolutions which make determinations or have operative design.

106. By resolution 2145 (XXI) the General Assembly terminated the Mandate. However, lacking the necessary powers to ensure the withdrawal of South Africa from the Territory, it enlisted the co-operation of the Security Council by calling the latter's attention to the resolution, thus acting in accordance with Article 11, paragraph 2, of the Charter. ...

108. Resolution 264 (1969) [of the Security Council], in paragraph 3 of its operative part, calls upon South Africa to withdraw its administration from Namibia immediately. Resolution 269 (1969), in view of South Africa's lack of compliance, after recalling the obligations of Members under Article 25 of the Charter, calls upon the Government of South Africa, in paragraph 5 of its operative part, "to withdraw its administration from the territory immediately and in any case before 4 October 1969." The preamble of resolution 276 (1970) reaffirms General Assembly resolution 2145 (XXI) and espouses it, by referring to the decision, not merely of the General Assembly, but of the United Nations "that the Mandate of South-West Africa was terminated." In the operative part, after condemning the non-compliance by South Africa with General Assembly and Security Council resolutions pertaining to Namibia, the Security Council declares, in paragraph 2, that "the continued presence of the South African authorities in Namibia is illegal" and that consequently all acts taken by the Government of South Africa "on behalf of or concerning Namibia after the termination of the Mandate are illegal and invalid." In paragraph 5 the Security Council "Calls upon all States, particularly those which have economic and other interests in Namibia, to refrain from any dealings with the Government of South Africa which are inconsistent with operative paragraph 2 of this resolution."

109. ... The Security Council, when it adopted these resolutions, was acting in the exercise of what it deemed to be its primary responsibility, the maintenance of peace and security, which, under the Charter, embraces situations which might lead to a breach of the peace. (Art. 1, para. 1.) In the preamble of resolution 264 (1969) the Security Council was "Mindful of the grave consequences of South Africa's continued occupation of Namibia" and in paragraph 4 of that resolution it declared "that the actions of the Government of South Africa designed to destroy the national unity and territorial integrity of Namibia through the establishment of Bantustans are contrary to the provisions of the United Nations Charter." In operative paragraph 3 of resolution 269 (1969) the Security Council decided "that the continued occupation of the territory of Namibia by the South African authorities constitutes an aggressive encroachment on the authority of the United Nations, ..." In operative paragraph 3 of resolution 276 (1970) the Security Council declared further "that the defiant attitude of other Government of South Africa towards the Council's decisions undermines the authority of the United Nations."

110. As to the legal basis of the resolution, Article 24 of the Charter vests in the Security Council the necessary authority to take action such as that taken in the present case. The reference in paragraph 2 of this Article to specific powers of the Security Council under certain chapters of the Charter does not exclude the existence of general

24: Members agree that the security council acts on their behalf in carrying out peace.

powers to discharge the responsibilities conferred in paragraph 1. Reference may be made in this respect to the Secretary-General's Statement, presented to the Security Council on 10 January, 1947, to the effect that "the powers of the Council under Article 24 are not restricted to the specific grants of authority contained in Chapters VI, VII, VIII and XI ... the Members of the United Nations have conferred upon the Security Council powers commensurate with its responsibility for the maintenance of peace and security. The only limitations are the fundamental principles and purposes found in Chapter I of the Charter."

111. As to the effect to be attributed to the declaration contained in paragraph 2 of resolution 276 (1970), the Court considers that the qualification of a situation as illegal does not by itself put an end to it. It can only be the first, necessary step in an endeavour to bring the illegal situation to an end.

112. It would be an untenable interpretation to maintain that, once such a declaration had been made by the Security Council under Article 24 of the Charter, on behalf of all member States, those members would be free to act in disregard of such illegality or even to recognize violations of law resulting from it. When confronted with such an internationally unlawful situation, Members of the United Nations would be expected to act in consequence of the declaration made on their behalf. The question therefore arises as to the effect of this decision of the Security Council for States Members of the United Nations in accordance with Article 25 of the Charter.

113. It has been contended that Article 25 of the Charter applies only to enforcement measures adopted under Chapter VII of the Charter. It is not possible to find in the Charter any support for this view. Article 25 is not confined to decisions in regard to enforcement action but applies to "the decisions of the Security Council" adopted in accordance with the Charter. Moreover, that Article is placed, not in Chapter VII, but immediately after Article 24 in that part of the Charter which deals with the functions and powers of the Security Council. If Article 25 had reference solely to decisions of the Security Council concerning enforcement action under Articles 41 and 42 of the Charter, that is to say, if it were only such decisions which had binding effect, the Article 25 would be superfluous, since this effect is secured by Articles 48 and 49 of the Charter.

114. It has also been contended that the relevant Security Council resolutions are couched in exhortatory rather than mandatory language and that, therefore, they do not purport to impose any legal duty on any State nor to affect legally any right of any State. The language of a resolution of the Security Council should be carefully analyzed before a conclusion can be made as to its binding effect. In view of the nature of the power under Article 25, the question whether they have been in fact exercised is to be determined in each case, having regard to the terms of the resolution to be interpreted, the discussion leading to it, the Charter provisions invoked and, in general, all circumstances that might assist in determining the legal consequences of the resolution of the Security Council.

115. Applying these tests, the Court recalls that in the preamble of resolution 269 (1969), the Security Council was "Mindful of its responsibility to take necessary action to secure strict compliance with the obligations entered into by States Members of the United Nations under the provisions of Article 25 of the Charter of the United

Nations." The Court has therefore reached the conclusion that the decisions made by the Security Council in paragraphs 2 and 5 of resolution 269 (1970), as related to paragraph 3 of resolution 264 (1969) and paragraph 5 of resolution 269 (1969), were adopted in conformity with the purposes and principles of the Charter and in accordance with its Articles 24 and 25. The decisions are consequently binding on all States Members of the United Nations, which are thus under obligation to accept and carry them out.

116. In pronouncing upon the binding nature of the Security Council decisions in question, the Court would recall the following passage in its Advisory Opinion of 11 April 1949 on Reparation for Injuries Suffered in the Service of the United Nations:

> The Charter has not been content to make the Organization created by it merely a center "for harmonizing the actions of nations in the attainment of these common ends" (Article 1, para. 4). It has equipped that centre with organs, and has given it special tasks. It has defined the position of the Members in relation to the Organization by requiring them to give it every assistance in any action undertaken by it (Article 2, para. 5) and to accept and carry out the decisions of the Security Council (*I.C.J. Reports 1949*, p. 178).

Thus when the Security Council adopts a decision under Article 25 in accordance with the Charter, it is for member States to comply with that decision, including those members of the Security Council which voted against it and those Members of the United Nations who are not members of the Council. To hold otherwise would be to deprive this principal organ of its essential functions and powers under the Charter.

117. ... A binding determination made by a competent organ of the United Nations to the effect that a situation is illegal cannot remain without consequence. Once the Court is faced with such a situation, it would be failing in the discharge of its judicial functions if it did not declare that there is an obligation, especially upon Members of the United Nations, to bring that situation to an end. As this Court has held, referring to one of its decisions declaring a situation as contrary to a rule of international law: "This decision entails a legal consequence, namely that of putting an end to the illegal situation" (*I.C.J. Reports 1951*, p. 82).

118. South Africa, being responsible for having created and maintained a situation which the Court has found to have been validly declared illegal, has the obligation to put an end to it. It is therefore under the obligation to withdraw its administration from the Territory of Namibia. By maintaining the present illegal situation, and occupying the Territory without title, South Africa incurs international responsibilities arising from a continuing violation of an international obligation. It also remains accountable for any violations of its international obligations, or of the rights of the people of Namibia. The fact that South Africa no longer has any title to administer the Territory does not release it from its obligations and responsibilities under international law towards other States in respect of the exercise of its powers in relation to this Territory. Physical control of a territory, and not sovereignty or legitimacy of title, is the basis of State liability for acts affecting other States.

119. The member States of the United Nations are, for the reasons given in paragraph 115 above, under obligation to recognize the illegality and invalidity of South Africa's continued presence in Namibia. They are also under obligation to

refrain from lending any support or any form of assistance to South Africa with reference to its occupation of Namibia, subject to paragraph 125 below. ...

125. In general, the non-recognition of South Africa's administration of the Territory should not result in depriving the people of Namibia of any advantages derived from international co-operation. In particular, while official acts performed by the Government of South Africa on behalf of or concerning Namibia after the determination of the Mandate are illegal and invalid, this invalidity cannot be extended to those acts, such as, for instance, the registration of births, deaths and marriages, the effects of which can be ignored only to the detriment of the inhabitants of the Territory.

126. As to non-member States, although not bound by Articles 24 and 25 of the Charter, they have been called upon in paragraphs 2 and 5 of resolution 276 (1970) to give assistance in the action which has been taken by the United Nations with regard to Namibia. In the view of the Court, the termination of the Mandate and the declaration of the illegality of South Africa's presence in Namibia are opposable to all States in the sense of barring *erga omnes* the legality of a situation which is maintained in violation of international law: in particular, no State which enters into relations with South Africa concerning Namibia may expect the United Nations or its Members to recognize the validity or effects of such relationship, or of the consequences thereof. The Mandate having been terminated by decision of the international organization in which the supervisory authority over its administration was vested, and South Africa's continued presence in Namibia having been declared illegal, it is for non-member States to act in accordance with those decisions.

NOTES

1) Who is the guardian of U.N. legality? The authority of the General Assembly and the Security Council is extensive but not unlimited. How is it to be determined whether an action of, say, the Security Council exceeds its powers? May each organ control and interpret its own jurisdiction? Does the International Court of Justice (ICJ) have any role of review? The Charter is deliberately silent on these matters,[51] except to say in article 96 that the General Assembly and the Security Council *may* request the Court to give an advisory opinion on any legal question.[52]

In 1992 in the *Aerial Incident at Lockerbie Case*,[53] Libya applied to the Court for provisional measures against the United States. The application arose out of the assertion by the United States that Libya was harbouring two terrorists indicted for the bombing of Pan Am flight 103 over Lockerbie, Scotland. Under the 1971 Montreal Convention for the Suppression of Unlawful Acts Against the Safety of Civil Aviation, to which both Libya and the United States were parties, Libya was bound to extradite or to prosecute

---

51   Goodrich, Hambro, & Simons, *supra* note 43 at 14.

52   As was done in *Constitution of the Maritime Safety Committee of IMCO*, [1960] I.C.J. Rep. 150; and *Certain Expenses of the United Nations*, [1962] I.C.J. Rep. 151.

53   (1992) 31 I.L.M. 662. The *Montreal Convention* and SC Res. involved in the case are reproduced in Chapter 15, Section B.4 in the materials concerning "Security Council Powers over State-Sponsored Terrorism."

the two accused. The United States demanded their surrender. Libya claimed to be fulfilling its prosecution function. Then the Security Council became seized of the matter. It first urged Libya to comply with the U.S. request and subsequently, acting under Chapter VII, ordered it to do so on pain of economic sanctions. Libya was thus put in the position of being directed to behave one way by the Security Council and having a choice of action under its treaty obligations in the Montreal Convention. By applying for provisional measures, Libya was indirectly asking the Court whether the decision of the Security Council overrode the binding obligations of the treaty, or whether it was made in excess of Security Council authority. Behind this issue was the implied question whether the Court had authority to make such a decision. By a majority of 11:5, the Court determined, in accordance with Charter article 103, that Libya's obligations under the Charter, including the decision of the Security Council rendered binding by article 25, prevailed over the Montreal Convention. The Court therefore declined to order provisional measures to protect Libya's rights under the convention. It did not speak to the question whether it should be reviewing the legal validity of the Security Council resolution, though it adverted to the problem. However, at least one commentator has observed that, in declaring itself on the overriding character of the Security Council resolution, the Court has quietly staked out a claim to be the "ultimate arbiter of institutional legitimacy" in the United Nations.[54] Is this conclusion justified? Is it desirable?[55] Concerning the merits of the case, see the 1998 decision by the International Court of Justice.[56]

2) The United Nations has been criticized in the past for not being capable of resolving conflicts because of political manoeuvring in the General Assembly and, most importantly, in the Security Council. However, the end of the Cold War changed the political dynamic, and consensus among the permanent members of the Security Council seemed possible, as was demonstrated in the Iraq–Kuwait crisis and ensuing first Gulf War in 1991. More generally, there were a number of signs of strength in the early 1990s: the increased consensus in the General Assembly; a world court with a large docket of cases; and an expanded concept and use of peacekeeping. The United Nations was instrumental in facilitating the withdrawal of Soviet troops from Afghanistan; in brokering the ceasefire in the Iran–Iraq war; in mediating the conflicts in Angola and Namibia; in overseeing the disarming of the Nicaraguan rebel force; in establishing the *Ad Hoc* Criminal Tribunals for the former Yugoslavia and Rwanda; and in adopting new conventions on international terrorism.

---

54   T.M. Franck, "The 'Powers of Appreciation': Who Is the Ultimate Guardian of U.N. Legality?" (1992) 86 A.J.I.L. 519.

55   See also E. Lauterpacht, "The Legal Effect of Illegal Acts of International Organisations" in *Cambridge Essays in International Law* (1965) at 88; V. Lowe, "Lockerbie—Changing the Rules During the Game" (1992) 51 Camb. L.J. 408; and W.M. Reisman, "The Constitutional Crisis in the United Nations" (1993) 87 A.J.I.L. 83. This aspect is further discussed in Chapter 6, Section D.4.

56   *Case Concerning Questions of Interpretation and Application of the 1971 Montreal Convention Arising from the Aerial Incident at Lockerbie (Libya v. United States)* (Preliminary Objection) (1998) 37 I.L.M. 587. In 1999, Libya agreed that the two accused might be prosecuted before a special Tribunal composed of Scottish judges, applying Scottish criminal law, sitting at the Hague. In 2001, one of the two accused was convicted, while the other was acquitted. *Her Majesty's Advocate v. Abdelbaset Ali Mohmed Al Megrahi and Al Amin Khalifa Fhimah* (2001) High Court of Justiciary at Camp Zeist (Case No. 1475/99). Available online at: <www.scotcourts.gov.uk/library/lockerbie/index.asp>.

The subsequent track record has been less encouraging. The United Nations was effectively sidelined while NATO engaged in military activities in Kosovo in 1999 (although it assumed an extensive role in the post-hostilities administration of Kosovo). In the events leading up to the invasion of Iraq in 2003, the failure of the United States to obtain Security Council endorsement of its proposed actions led to an intensification of American criticisms of the organization and a willingness to act unilaterally outside the United Nations system: see the discussion of the 2003 invasion of Iraq—Gulf War II—in Chapter 15, Section B.4 on "Collective Measures Pursuant to the U.N. Charter."

3) The difficulties facing the United Nations system in the new millennium have led to repeated calls for reform of the organization, and a process for seeking renewal has been initiated on a number of fronts. In September 2000 the General Assembly adopted the United Nations Millennium Declaration,[57] setting out a number of critical development goals to be attained by 2015.[58] Under the Millennium Project, a group of experts was convened that produced a plan of action for reaching the Millennium Development Goals.[59]

In 2003, the Secretary-General created a 16-member High Level Panel on Threats, Challenges, and Change. Its report, *A More Secure World: Our Shared Responsibility*,[60] made sweeping proposals for new approaches to collective security, the use of force, and terrorism, but also proposed significant alterations to the structure and functioning of the United Nations itself. These included, *inter alia*: creation of a Peacebuilding Commission and Support Office with a mandate to "identify countries which are under stress and risk sliding towards State collapse" and "organize proactive assistance in preventing that process from developing further";[61] enhancing the role of regional organization in peacekeeping and preventive peace operations;[62] making the Economic and Social Council more effective in coordinating the multitude of activities and organizations related to economic and social development, including a focus on the relationship between development and peace and security issues;[63] and improving the functioning of the General Assembly by "a better concepualization and shortening of the agenda, which should reflect the contemporary challenges facing the international community."[64]

---

57   GA Res. 55/2, UN GAOR 55th Sess., Supp. No. 49, U.N. Doc. A/55/49 (2000) 4.

58   *Ibid.* The eight major goals (which have associated concrete targets) have been summarized as follows: eradication of extreme poverty and hunger; achieving universal primary education; promotion of gender equality; reduction of child mortality; improving maternal health; halt and begin to reverse incidence of HIV/AIDS, malaria, and other diseases; achieve environmental sustainability; and develop a global development partnership. See U.N. online at: <www.un.org/millenniumgoals/>.

59   United Nations Development Programme, *Investing in Development: A Practical Plan to Achieve the Millennium Development Goals* (2005). Available online at: <http://www.unmillenniumproject.org/reports/fullreport.htm>.

60   United Nations, *A More Secure World: Our Shared Responsibility. Report of the High Level Panel on Threats, Challenges and Change* (2004). Available online at: <http://www.un.org/secureworld/>.

61   *Ibid.* at 83.

62   *Ibid.* at 84-85.

63   *Ibid.* at 86-87.

64   *Ibid.* at 78-79.

4) The most concrete proposal arising from the Panel report was with respect to reform of the Security Council, a subject of perennial debate. The Panel set out the following principles upon which any reforms should be based:[65]

(a) They should ... increase the involvement in decision-making of those who contribute most to the United Nations financially, militarily and diplomatically—specifically in terms of contributions to United Nations assessed budgets, participation in mandated peace operations, contributions to voluntary activities of the United Nations in the areas of security and development ... . Among developed countries, achieving or making substantial progress towards the internationally agreed level of 0.7 per cent of GNP for ODA should be considered an important criterion of contribution;

(b) They should bring into the decision-making process countries more representative of the broader membership, especially of the developing world;

(c) They should not impair the effectiveness of the Security Council;

(d) They should increase the democratic and accountable nature of the body.

5) Given these principles, the Panel proposed for consideration two models for expansion and reorganization of the Council.[66] Both are based on maintenance of the existing permanent seats, an expansion to 24 seats, and a new distribution of Council Seats among four regional areas: Africa; Asia-Pacific; Europe; and the Americas. Under Model A, there would be 6 new permanent seats, without veto powers, with 2 each for Africa and Asia-Pacific, and 1 each for Europe and the Americas. In addition, 3 new two-year term seats would be created, for a total of 13, and term seats would be distributed on a regional basis (4 for Africa, 6 for Asia-Pacific, 2 for Europe, and 4 for the Americas). Model B would see no new permanent seats, but create 8 four-year renewable-term seats (2 for each region) and 11 two-year non-renewable-term seats (4 for Africa, 3 for Asia-Pacific, 1 for Europe, and 3 for the Americas).

6) The Secretary-General endorsed many of the proposals from the Millennium Project and the High-Level Panel, with respect both to the objectives[67] and the reorganization of the organs of the United Nations,[68] and put them forward as an agenda for consideration at the September 2005 summit of some 150 world leaders. However, the Summit adopted hardly any of the concrete proposals except to resolve to create a Human Rights Council and to recognize the responsibility on all states, individually and through the United Nations, to protect populations from genocide, war crimes, ethnic cleansing, and crimes against humanity.[69]

---

65   *Ibid.* at 80.

66   *Ibid.* at 80-82.

67   Report of the Secretary-General, *In Larger Freedom*, *supra* note 48. The report focuses on the following themes: freedom from want (addressing economic and social development); freedom from fear (dealing with collective security and terrorism); freedom to live in dignity (dealing with human rights, democracy, and the rule of law); and strengthening the United Nations (including the suggested changes to the Security Council as well as other steps).

68   *Ibid.* at 39-52.

69   World Summit documents are available online at: <www.un.org/summit2005/documents.html>.

7) Following this brief survey of the organs and powers of the United Nations, it is necessary to consider its status (and by analogy the legal personality of other international organizations) at international law. This important question was authoritatively determined by the International Court in the following case.

Reparations Case
Advisory Opinion, [1949] I.C.J. Rep. 174

[In 1948, Count Bernadotte, a Swedish national and the U.N. mediator in Palestine, was killed in Jerusalem, which was in Israeli possession. At that time Israel was not yet a member of the United Nations. Before commencing an action for compensation against Israel, the General Assembly asked the I.C.J. for an opinion about the legal capacity of the organization to bring the claim.]

THE COURT: The first question asked of the Court is as follows:

In the event of an agent of the United Nations in the performance of his duties suffering injury in circumstances involving the responsibility of a state, has the United Nations, as an Organization, the capacity to bring an international claim against the responsible *de jure* or *de facto* government with a view to obtaining the reparation due in respect of the damage caused (a) to the United Nations, (b) to the victim or to persons entitled through him? ...

The subjects of law in any legal system are not necessarily identical in their nature or in the extent of their rights, and their nature depends upon the needs of the Community. Throughout its history, the development of international law has been influenced by the requirements of international life, and the progressive increase in the collective action of States has already given rise to instances of action upon the international plane by certain entities which are not States. This development culminated in the establishment in June 1945 of an international organization whose purposes and principles are specified in the Charter of the United Nations. But to achieve these ends the attribution of international personality is indispensable.

The Charter has not been content to make the Organization created by it merely a centre "for harmonizing the actions of nations in the attainment of these common ends" (Article 1, para. 4). It has equipped that centre with organs, and has given it special tasks. It has defined the position of the Members in relation to the Organization by requiring them to give it every assistance in any action undertaken by it (Article 2, para. 5), and to accept and carry out the decisions of the Security Council; by authorizing the General Assembly to make recommendations to the Members; by giving the Organization legal capacity and privileges and immunities in the territory of each of its Members; and by providing for the conclusion of agreements between the Organization and its Members. Practice—in particular the conclusions of conventions to which the Organization is a party—has confirmed the character of the Organization, which occupies a position in certain respects in detachment from its Members, and which is under a duty to remind them, if need be, of certain obligations. It must be added that the Organization is a political body, charged with political tasks of an important character, and covering a wide field namely the maintenance of international peace and security, the development of friendly relations among nations, and the achievement of international co-operation in the solution of problems of an economic, social, cultural or humanitarian character (Article 1); and in dealing with its Members it employs political means. The "Convention on the Privileges and Immunities of the United Nations" of 1946 creates rights and duties between each of the signatories and the Organization (see in particular, Section 35). It is difficult to see how such a convention could operate except upon the international plane and as between parties possessing international personality.

In the opinion of the Court, the Organization was intended to exercise and enjoy, and is in fact exercising and enjoying, functions and rights which can only be explained on the basis of the possession of a large measure of international personality and the capacity to operate upon an international plane. It is at present the supreme type of international organization, and it could not carry out the intentions of its founders if it was devoid of international personality. It must be acknowledged that its Members, by entrusting certain functions to it, with the attendant duties and responsibilities, have clothed it with the competence required to enable those functions to be effectively discharged.

Accordingly, the Court has come to the conclusion that the Organization is an international person. That is not the same thing as saying that it is a State, which it certainly is not, or that its legal personality and rights and duties are the same as those of a State. Still less is it the same thing as saying that it is "a super-State," whatever that expression may mean. It does not even imply that all its rights and duties must be upon the international plane, any more than all the rights and duties of a State must be upon that plane. What it does mean is that it is a subject of international law and capable of possessing international rights and duties, and that it has capacity to maintain its rights by bringing international claims. ...

When the Organization has sustained damage resulting from a breach by a Member of its international obligations, it is impossible to see how it can obtain reparation unless it possesses capacity to bring an international claim. It cannot be supposed that in such an event all the Members of the Organization, save the defendant State must combine to bring a claim against the defendant for the damage suffered by the Organization.

In dealing with the question of law which arises out of Question I(b) ... [t]he only legal question which remains to be considered is whether, in the course of bringing an international claim of this kind, the Organization can recover "the reparation due in respect of the damage caused ... to the victim ... ."

The traditional rule that diplomatic protection is exercised by the national State does not involve the giving of a negative answer to Question I(b).

In the first place, this rule applies to claims brought by a State. But here we have the different and new case of a claim that would be brought by the Organization.

In the second place, even in inter-State relations, there are important exceptions to the rule, for there are cases in which protection may be exercised by a State on behalf of persons not having its nationality.

In the third place, the rule rests on two bases. The first is that the defendant State has broken an obligation towards the national State in respect of its nationals. The second is that only the party to whom an international obligation is due can bring a claim in respect of its breach. This is precisely what happens when the Organization, in bringing a claim for damage suffered by its agent, does so by invoking the breach of an obligation towards itself. Thus, the rule of the nationality of claims affords no reason against recognizing that the Organization has the right to bring a claim for the damage referred to in Question I(b). On the contrary, the principle underlying this rule leads to the recognition of this capacity as belonging to the Organization, when the organization invokes, as the ground of its claim, a breach of an obligation towards itself.

Nor does the analogy of the traditional rule of diplomatic protection of nationals abroad justify in itself an affirmative reply. It is not possible, by a strained use of the concept of allegiance, to assimilate the legal bond which exists, under Article 100 of the Charter, between the Organization on the one hand, and the Secretary-General and the staff on the other, to the bond of nationality existing between a State and its nationals.

The Court is here faced with a new situation. The questions to which it gives rise can only be solved by realizing that the situation is dominated by the provisions of the Charter considered in the light of the principles of international law … .

The question … presupposes that the injury for which the reparation is demanded arises from a breach of an obligation designed to help an agent of the Organization in the performance of his duties. It is not a case in which the wrongful act or omission would merely constitute a breach of the general obligations of a State concerning the position of aliens; claims made under this head would be within the competence of the national State and not, as a general rule, within that of the Organization.

The Charter does not expressly confer upon the Organization the capacity to include, in its claim for reparation, damage caused to the victim or to persons entitled through him. The Court must therefore begin by enquiring whether the provisions of the Charter concerning the functions of the Organization, and the part played by its agents in the performance of those functions, imply for the Organization power to afford its agents the limited protection that would consist in the bringing of a claim on their behalf for reparation for damage suffered in such circumstances. Under international law, the Organization must be deemed to have those powers which, though not expressly provided in the Charter, are conferred upon it by necessary implication as being essential to the performance of its duties. This principle of law was applied by the Permanent Court of International Justice to the International Labour Organization in its Advisory Opinion No. 13 of July 23rd, 1926 (Series B., No. 13, p. 18) and must be applied to the United Nations.

Having regard to its purposes and functions already referred to, the Organization may find it necessary, and has in fact found it necessary, to entrust its agents with important missions to be performed in disturbed parts of the world. Many missions, from their very nature, involve the agents in unusual dangers to which ordinary persons are not exposed. For the same reason, the injuries suffered by its agents in these circumstances will sometimes have occurred in such a manner that their national State would not be justified in bringing a claim for reparation on the ground of diplomatic protection, or, at any rate, would not feel disposed to do so. Both to ensure the efficient and independent performance of these missions and to afford effective support to its agents, the Organization must provide them with adequate protection … .

In order that the agent may perform his duties satisfactorily, he must feel that his protection is assured to him by the Organization, and that he may count on it. To ensure the independence of the agent, and, consequently, the independent action of the Organization itself, it is essential that in performing his duties he need not have to rely on any other protection than that of the Organization (save of course for the direct and immediate protection due from the State in those territory he may be). In particular, he should not have to rely on the protection of his own State. If he had to rely on that State, his independence might well be compromised, contrary to the principle applied by Article 100 of the Charter. And lastly, it is essential that—whether the agent belongs to a powerful or to a weak State; to one more affected or less affected by the complications of international life; to one in sympathy or not in sympathy with the omission of the agent—he should know that in the performance of his duties he is under the protection of the Organization. This assurance is even more necessary when the agent is stateless. ...

The obligations entered into by States to enable the agents of the Organization to perform their duties are undertaken not in the interest of the agents, but in that of the Organization. When it claims redress for a breach of these obligations, the Organization is invoking its own right, the right that the obligations due to it should be respected. On this ground, it asks for reparation of the injury suffered, for "it is a principle of international law that the breach of an engagement involves an obligation to make reparation in an adequate form"; as was stated by the Permanent Court in its Judgment No. 8 of July 26th, 1927 (Series A., No. 9, p. 21). In claiming reparation based on the injury suffered by its agent, the Organization does not represent the agent, but is asserting its own right, the right to secure respect for undertakings entered into towards the Organization.

Having regard to the foregoing considerations, and to the undeniable right of the Organization to demand that its Members shall fulfil the obligations entered into by them in the interest of the good working of the Organization, the Court is of the opinion that in the case of a breach of these obligations, the Organization has the capacity to claim adequate reparation, and that in assessing this reparation it is authorized to include the damage suffered by the victim or by persons entitled through him.

The question remains whether the Organization has "the capacity to bring an international claim against the responsible *de jure* or *de facto* government with a view to obtaining the reparation due in respect of the damage caused (a) to the United Nations, (b) to the victim or to person entitled through him" when the defendant State is not a member of the Organization.

In considering this aspect of Question I(a) and (b), it is necessary to keep in mind the reasons which have led the Court to give an affirmative answer to it when the defendant State is a Member of the Organization. It has now been established that the Organization has capacity to bring claims on the international plane, and that it possessed a right of functional protection in respect of its agents. Here again the Court is authorized to assume that the damage suffered involves the responsibility of a State, and it is not called upon to express an opinion upon the various ways in which that responsibility might be engaged. Accordingly, the question is whether the Organization has capacity to bring a claim against the defendant State to recover reparation in respect of that damage or whether, on the contrary, the defendant State, not being a member, is justified in raising the objection that the Organization lacks the capacity to bring an international claim. On this point, the Court's opinion is that fifty States, representing the vast majority of the members of the international community, had the power, in conformity with international law, to bring into being an entity possessing objective international personality and not merely personality recognized by them alone, together with capacity to bring international claims ... .

Accordingly, the Court arrives at the conclusion that an affirmative answer should be given to Question I (a) and (b) whether or not the dependant state is a Member of the United Nations.

Question II is as follows:

In the event of an affirmative reply on point I(b), how is action by the United Nations to be reconciled with such rights as may be possessed by the State of which the victim is a national?

The affirmative reply given by the Court on point I(b) obliges it now to examine Question II. When the victim has a nationality, cases can clearly occur in which the injury suffered by him may engage the interest both of his national State and of the Organization. In such an event, competition between the State's right of diplomatic protection and the Organization's right of functional protection might arise, and this is the only case with which the Court is invited to deal.

In such a case, there is no rule of law which assigns priority to the one or to the other or which compels either the State or the Organization to refrain from bringing an international claim. The Court sees no reason why the parties concerned should not find solutions inspired by goodwill and common sense, and as between the Organization and its Members it draws attention to their duty to render "every assistance" provided by Article 2, paragraph 5, of the Charter.

Although the bases of the two claims are different that does not mean that the defendant State can be compelled to pay the reparation due in respect of the damage twice over. International tribunals are already familiar with the problem of a claim in which two or more national States are interested and they know how to protect the defendant State in such a case.

NOTES

1) In 1950, Israel paid to the United Nations the sum requested by the Secretary-General for the injuries done on account of Israeli negligence.

2) This case was not only important for the United Nations. It is a landmark decision for all international organizations. It shows that the powers possessed by an organization do not have to be expressly incorporated in its charter or the treaty creating it but can be implied so far as is necessary for the organization to be able to fulfill the functions for which it was set up.

3) The legal status of international organizations and the conduct of their relations with states and other organizations has been the subject of extensive work by the International Law Commission (ILC). Two conventions have been adopted as a result of

the ILC's development of draft conventions: the 1975 Vienna Convention on the Representation of States in their relations with International Organizations of a Universal Character[70] and the 1986 Vienna Convention on the Law of Treaties Between States and International Organizations or Between International Organizations.[71] More recently, the ILC decided in 2000 to include the topic of responsibility of international organizations in its work program. A Special Rapporteur was appointed and a working group established in 2002, and at its 55th session in 2003 the ILC considered the first report of the Special Rapporteur and provisionally adopted three draft articles,[72] dealing with the scope of the draft articles,[73] the use of terms,[74] and the general principles to be applied to attribution of responsibility for wrongful acts. At its 56th session in 2004, the ILC adopted four more draft articles dealing with the following issues: the general rule for attribution of conduct to an organization; conduct of organs placed at the disposal of an international organization by a state or other organization; excess of authority and contravention of instructions; and adoption or acknowledgement of conduct by an international organization.[75] In a summary of the work, the Commission has noted that the work to date, and that projected, is closely connected to the issue of responsibility of states (see the 2001 Draft Articles on Responsibility of States for Internationally Wrongful Acts, which are addressed in detail in Chapter 10, Section A):

> [T]he Commission has followed the general scheme of the articles on responsibility of States for internationally wrongful acts. Broadly continuing with the same scheme, the Special Rapporteur intends to address in his third report, which is due in 2005, the following topics: breach of an international obligation; circumstances precluding wrongfulness; responsibility of an international organization in connection with the wrongful act of a State or another organization.[76]

---

70 U.N. Doc. A/Conf. 67/15, March 14, 1975, reproduced in (1975) 69 A.J.I.L. 730 (not in force).

71 U.N. Doc. A/Conf. 129/14, March 20, 1986, reproduced in (1986) 25 I.L.M. 543 (not in force).

72 *Report of the International Law Commission on the Work of Its Fifty-fifth Session*, UN GAOR, 58th Sess., Supp. No. 10, U.N. Doc. A/58/10 (2003) chp. IV. See also the discussion of this topic, and the continuing work of the ILC, at G. Hafner, "Accountability of International Organizations" (2003) A.S.I.L. Proc. 236 at 237-39.

73 See the text of draft article 1, Report, *ibid.* The draft article refers to the responsibility, not just of international organizations, but also that of states for acts of international organizations.

74 See draft article 2, Report, *ibid.*: "For the purposes of the present draft articles, the term 'international organization' refers to an organization established by a treaty or other instrument governed by international law and possessing its own international legal personality."

75 *Report of the International Law Commission on the Work of Its Fifty-sixth Session*, UN GAOR, 59th Sess., Supp. No. 10, U.N. Doc. A/59/10 (2003) chp. V.

76 See ILC online at: <http://www.un.org/law/ilc/sessions/56/56sess.htm#responsibility_of_intl_organizations>. It should also be noted that a Committee of the International Law Association (ILA) has prepared reports on the broader subject of the "accountability" of international organizations, incorporating such issues as good governance and relationships with non-state actors: International Law Association, *Report of the Seventieth Conference, New Delhi* (2002) 772. See also the discussion at Hafner, *supra* note 72 at 239.

4) Is it possible for a few states to establish by treaty an international organization for a specialized purpose—say to operate a system of telecommunications satellites—and then to demand that other states respect its independent existence and responsibility? For instance, should the organization or the founding states be responsible for an accident, such as the crash landing of a satellite that causes injuries in a foreign territory? What features of the United Nations did the I.C.J. stress in recognizing its objective personality?

5) The *Reparations Case* focuses on the status and capacities of intergovernmental organizations (IGOs) on the international plane. There are also similar issues about their legal personality within national legal systems. For instance, can an IGO sue or be sued, and does it have any immunity in national courts? Is an IGO a separate legal person at national law, like a registered corporation, or may a claimant reach beyond its form and hold the member states responsible for its acts and defaults committed within the domestic legal arena? Being questions about the operation of the national legal system, they are essentially within the domestic jurisdiction of a state and outside of international control. The answers should therefore be sought in domestic constitutional principles, which may disclose different solutions in different states.

In Britain and Canada, a treaty does not affect local rights and law without domestic implementation by legislation. See the discussion on "Treaty Implementation" in Chapter 4, Section C.2. Thus the adhesion of Canada to a convention constituting an IGO, such as the Charter of the Organization of American States (OAS), has no immediate or direct impact on Canadian law. It is as if Canadian law is blind to the legal character of the OAS. To overcome these defects, section 5 of the *Foreign Missions and International Organizations Act*[77] permits the Governor in Council to designate those international organizations that shall have legal capacities as corporate bodies in Canada, and to fix the extent of immunities available to them by reference to the Convention on the Privileges and Immunities of the United Nations.[78]

This mechanism is effective if the Governor in Council makes an order, which is likely at least in those instances where Canada becomes a member of an IGO. But what is the situation if Canada is not a member state and no order has been issued to confer Canadian legal capacity? In *Arab Monetary Fund v. Hashim (No. 3)*,[79] the organization brought a claim in the English courts against its former director general, then resident in London, to recover a large sum of money allegedly stolen by him from the Fund. The organization had been established with international personality by a number of Arab states and had also been constituted as a corporate body in the state of the United Arab Emirates. The defendant sought to stay the action on the grounds the Fund was unknown to English law. In a split decision, the House of Lords decided that by the comity of nations English courts recognize corporate bodies created under the laws of a recognized foreign state and, since the Fund had been so constituted, it should be recognized as entitled to sue.

---

77   S.C. 1991, c. 41.

78   (1946) 1 U.N.T.S. 15 & 90 U.N.T.S. 327, implemented in Canada in S.C. 1991, c. 41, Sch. III. Cf. the experience with a similar system in U.K. in the litigation surrounding the collapse of the International Tin Council, especially *J.H. Rayner (Mincing Lane) Ltd. v. Dept. Trade and Industry*, [1989] 2 A.C. 418 (H.L.); and *Shearson Lehman Bros. Inc. v. MacLaine, Watson & Co. Ltd.*, [1988] 1 W.L.R. (H.L.).

79   [1991] 2 A.C. 114.

Why does recognition of a foreign IGO depend on its incorporation under the domestic law of a member state? Why is the constitution of the IGO as a separate *international* legal person by *recognized* foreign states not sufficient? Should a Canadian court follow the House of Lords' decision? Should it at least accord standing to an IGO that is legally established under foreign law? Or is the permissive power of the Governor in Council under the *Diplomatic Missions* statute to be read as exclusive authority for determining the personality and capacity of IGOs in Canada?[80]

2. Non-Governmental Organizations[81]

Although references to international organizations are commonly to intergovernmental bodies, there are many organizations of a truly international character that are non-governmental in character. These NGOs tend to be overlooked by lawyers as participants in the international system because they do not possess even the limited legal personality of their intergovernmental cousins. In fact, this narrow view excludes a host of actors who exert a major influence on the creation and application of international law, and obscures the practical significance of their roles.

NGOs exist in every field of human activity. They include scientific, medical, professional, sporting, and humanitarian organizations. Although they have not been accorded any official authority by governments,[82] many of the larger structured NGOs also make and apply rules and standards for their fields of concern that are accepted generally as the international norms of conduct in those areas of endeavour. Thus, the International Olympic Committee (IOC) runs international athletics, in conjunction with the international federations of each individual sport, and the International Chamber of Commerce (ICC) regulates the standard terms of international trade and payments. Moreover, the emergence of many interest-based or advocacy NGOs in such fields as human rights has led to a more focused use of the limited legal status that is available.

The status of NGOs at international law has been recognized, to a degree, by the U.N. Charter article 71. It provides that the Economic and Social Council may grant consultative status to NGOs, and several hundred of them have accepted it.[83] Similar arrangements

---

80   Cf. G. Marston, "The Origin of the Personality of International Organizations in United Kingdom Law" (1991) 40 I.C.L.Q. 403.

81   See J.J. Lador-Lederer, *International Non-Governmental Organizations* (1963) and L.C. White, *International Non-Governmental Organizations: Their Purposes, Methods and Accomplishments* (1968); U.N. Department of Public Information, *NGOs: Partners in Social Development* (1995); P.F. Diehl, ed., *The Politics of Global Governance*, 3d ed. (2005); T.G. Weiss, *NGOs, the U.N. and Global Governance* (1996); and L.S. Salamon, *Global Civil Society* (1999).

82   There have been limited attempts at dealing with the legal status of NGOs that focused on recognition of the status of the NGO under the national law of its headquarters. See the discussion of the 1986 European Convention on the Recognition of the Legal Personality of International Non-Governmental Organizations in K. Martens, "Examining the Non-Status of NGOs in International Law" (2003) 10/2 Ind. J. Global Leg. Stud. 1 at 22-23.

83   For a discussion of the categories and process of consultation, see N. Sybesma-Knol, "Non-State Actors in International Organizations: An Attempt at Classification" in T.C. van Boven, et. al., eds., *The Legitimacy of the United Nations: Towards an Enhanced Legal Status of Non-state Actors* (1997) 22 at 33-35.

exist in other organizations in the U.N. family. Consultative status typically permits the NGO to send representatives to meetings as observers, to submit written materials for circulation as U.N. documents, and to use the services provided by the Secretariat. In other words, they have access to participate and influence the work of the body to which they are accredited, but they cannot participate in its decision by voting, though even this deficiency is less significant now that many matters are concluded by consensus.

The lack of legal personality should not detract from the importance of this avenue for participation, by which NGOs contribute as part of the law-making process at the international level, a phenomenon that has existed at least since the development of the International Red Cross in the late 1800s:

> Having succeeded in inspiring several international conventions, the Red Cross can be said to have become the initiator of a treble legislative movement: of a codification of the law of warfare, of priority of humanitarian considerations in hostilities, and of the granting of a status in international law to NGOs.[84]

The contribution of NGOs to law making, and to some extent to monitoring the compliance of states with international law, has flourished noticeably since the UN Conference on Environment and Development (UNCED) in 1992, where hundreds of NGOs staged a complete alternative conference to the formal meetings of government representatives, and contributed to the development of the legal texts. Even more significantly, at the Rome Conference to establish the International Criminal Court in 1998 the coalitions of accredited NGOs had a signal influence on the contents and the conclusion of the Statute, as the U.N. Secretary-General has publicly recognized. It is in the areas of environment[85] and human rights[86] that the influence of NGOs has been most strongly felt.

The remaining question for the future is whether a higher degree of legal status for NGOs at international law, even if still less than full legal personality, is necessary to their effective functioning in the international community.[87] This seems an unlikely prospect. In the 2003 Report of the Panel of Eminent Persons on United Nations–Civil Society Relations,[88] the conclusions and recommendations (endorsed by the Secretary-General[89]) concentrated on improving the integration of NGOs in the work of the United Nations, rather than on the issue of legal personality.

---

84   Lador-Lederer, *supra* note 81 at 84.

85   See *e.g.* the discussion of the role of NGOs in the negotiation of the Kyoto Protocol in M. Betsill, "Environmental NGOs Meet the Sovereign State: The Kyoto Protocol Negotiations on Global Climate Change" (2002) 13/1 Color. J. of Int'l Environ. L. & Pol. 49.

86   See *e.g.* the review of the role of NGOs at the regional level in M. Olz, "Non-Governmental Organizations in Regional Human Rights Systems" (1997) 28 Colum. Human Rights L. Rev. 307.

87   On the need for future evolution of the role of NGOs, see B. Ramcharan "Non-State Actors in the Future United Nations Legal Order" in van Boven et al., *supra* note 83 at 163, and Martens, *supra* note 82 at 24.

88   Report of the Panel of Eminent Persons on United Nations–Civil Society Relations, *We the Peoples: Civil Society, the United Nations and Global Governance*, U.N. Doc. A/58/817 (2004) 6.

89   *In Larger Freedom*, *supra* note 48 at 41.

3. Transnational Corporations[90]

The traditional approach to legal personality would deny transnational corporations full status as subjects of international law. As is the case with NGOs, however, this simple statement is inadequate to explain the actual status of such corporations and their interaction with the institutions and processes of the international community. It should be noted at the outset that the colossal expansion of international trade and commerce brought with it a wide variety of corporate organizational structures. Holder and Brennan have offered a threefold classification. First, *government corporations* include those "wholly or largely government owned and with greater or lesser freedom from direct governmental control." Apart from the implications of this status for such questions as sovereign immunity, there may be occasions on which such entities "engage in international transactions at the behest of government policy."[91] *Intergovernmental corporations* "may bring together a number of governments, and possibly private enterprises also, for functions such as the creation or servicing of public utilities—for example, the building of a tunnel under the English Channel, or the organization of an airline, or for the development of natural resources," and may give rise to international law implications through the agreements that establish them.[92] For *non-governmental corporations*, which are the primary focus of this section, it seems clear that the "importance of private corporate activities to the international legal system is yet to be accommodated in legal theory, which still equates them with the individual."[93]

The multinational involvement of private corporations has been the focus of international attention for many years. Since their activities carry them across state frontiers, yet they are not international in the traditional sense of being intergovernmental, their in-between status has been aptly described by Judge Jessup as "transnational." But as yet there is no certain body of transnational law by which to regulate these corporations. As a result a large number of legal uncertainties surround transnational corporations concerning, for instance, their nationality,[94] the law governing their agreements with foreign governments,[95] and their amenability to the jurisdiction of national authorities extraterritorially.[96] These matters touch issues that are fundamental to the international legal system and generate deeply held opposing views.

With respect to the question of legal personality, the lack of full status as subjects of international law has not prevented transnational corporations from acquiring certain

---

90 See W. Friedmann, *The Changing Structure of International Law* (1964) at 213-31 and D. Wallace Jr., *International Regulation of Multinational Corporations* (1976); N. Jagers, "The Legal Status of the Multinational Corporation Under International Law" in M. Addo, ed., *Human Rights Standards and the Responsibility of Transnational Corporations* (1999) 269.

91 W.E. Holder & G.A. Brennan, *The International Legal System* (1972) at 295.

92 *Ibid.* at 295-96.

93 *Ibid.* at 296.

94 Discussed in Chapter 8, Section B on "Corporations."

95 Discussed in Chapter 10, Section B.3 on "Protection of Property."

96 Discussed in Chapter 9, Section A.4 on "Assertion of Extraterritorial Jurisdiction."

rights and, to a lesser extent, responsibilities, under international law, whatever their formal categorization may be. As one observer put it, in arguing for extension of human rights duties to such corporations, it is not essential that they come with the *full* range of rights and responsibilities:

> It is sufficient, rather, that TNCs [transnational corporations] have limited rights and responsibilities, such as the right to sue and be sued, the ability to assert a right, and the acceptance of legal responsibility in judicial forums, but not have the status of a party to intergovernmental forums and international instruments.[97]

The ability of corporations to bring claims before international tribunals, even though it may be dependent on interstate obligations, nonetheless constitutes a significant example of these entities being accorded some level of legal status under international law:

> TNCs are also empowered to enforce their rights. For example, a treaty created under the World Bank enables corporations to submit disputes to binding arbitration by the International Centre for the Settlement of Investment Disputes, And under NAFTA [North American Free Trade Agreement], corporations are able to seek recompense, spectacularly, from foreign governments for breach of their right to unhindered, cross-border trade through the Agreement's private dispute-settlement mechanism.[98]

There are numerous examples of corporations being granted such rights under international agreements, and even though such measures do not alter the formal status of corporations as equivalent to private individuals, they introduce elements of legal personality that cannot be ignored. Progress has not, however, been as marked with respect to attempts to define corresponding responsibilities of corporations at international law. In the 1970s and 1980s several international initiatives were taken to create a suitable body of rules, particularly with respect to human rights norms, but these resulted in initiatives that were "either unsuccessful or voluntary."[99] The principal thrust of United Nations efforts in this regard was to develop a comprehensive U.N. Code of Conduct on Transnational Corporations,[100] based on the earlier statements of principle by the General

---

97   D. Kinley & J. Tadaki, "From Talk to Walk: The Emergence of Human Rights Responsibilities for Corporations at International Law" (2004) 44 Va. J. Int'l L. 931 at 946.

98   *Ibid.* at 947. The relevant part of the North American Free Trade Agreement, 1992, reproduced at 31 I.L.M. 296, is Chapter 11, which has generated a significant volume of commentary as well as litigation. For a very thorough review of the first 10 years of practice under Chapter 11, see generally J.J. Coe Jr., "Taking Stock Of NAFTA Chapter 11 in Its Tenth Year: An Interim Sketch of Selected Themes, Issues and Methods" (2003) 36 Vand. J. of Transnat'l. L. 1381. See also L. Trakman, *Dispute Settlement Under the NAFTA* (1997) at 41-53.

99   Weissbrodt & M. Kruger, "Norms on the Responsibilities of Transnational Corporations and Other Business Enterprises With Regard To Human Rights" (2003) 97 A.J.I.L. 901 at 902-903. These included the following: International Labour Organization, *Tripartite Declaration of Principles Concerning Multinational Enterprises and Social Policy*, reprinted in (1978) 17 I.L.M. 423; *OECD Guidelines for Multinational Enterprises*, reprinted in (1976) 15 I.L.M. 967, as revised (1979) 18 I.L.M. 986 and 1171. Also see generally, J.-G. Castel *et al.*, *The Canadian Law and Practice of International Trade*, 2d ed. (1997) c. 13.

100 Reprinted in (1984) 23 I.L.M. 626.

Assembly to be found in the Charter of Economic Rights and Duties of States.[101] The Code elaborated standards for the conduct of transnational corporations regarding respect for the sovereignty, the economic and social policies and the laws of the host state, and concerning their ownership, control, financing, taxation, transfer of technology, consumer and environmental protection, and disclosure of corporate information within the foreign state. The Code, which never attained more than draft form,[102] also spelled out the treatment to be accorded to transnational corporations by the host state, including provisions on nationalization, compensation, and jurisdiction.

More recently, in 2003 the United Nations Sub-Commission On the Promotion and Protection of Human Rights approved the Norms on the Responsibilities of Transnational Corporations and Other Business Enterprises with Regard to Human Rights,[103] which in article 1 sets out the following general obligations for states and corporations:

> 1. States have the primary responsibility to promote, secure the fulfilment of, respect, ensure respect of and protect human rights recognized in international as well as national law, including ensuring that transnational corporations and other business enterprises respect human rights. Within their respective spheres of activity and influence, transnational corporations and other business enterprises have the obligation to promote, secure the fulfilment of, respect, ensure respect of and protect human rights recognized in international as well as national law, including the rights and interests of indigenous peoples and other vulnerable groups.

It has been noted, however, that the norms are "unclear as to how corporations could be directly liable under international law for any breaches of these obligations, beyond implying that such a possibility exists."[104] More generally, it seems clear that substantial work on implementation will be required before the imposition of responsibilities on corporations matches their current ability to seek enforcement of rights:

> While the Norms contain rudimentary mechanisms for implementation, the next task for the United Nations, states, businesses and others will be to continue to search for and elaborate more effective methods of implementation.[105]

---

101 UN GA Res. 3281 (XXIX), UN GAOR, 29th Sess., Supp. No. 31, U.N. Doc. A/9631 (1974) 50, reprinted in (1975) 14 I.L.M. 251.

102 Weissbrodt & Kruger, *supra* note 99 at 902. The United Nations has also worked on three other sets of principles that would have complemented and buttressed the more general U.N. Code of Conduct, were they to reach fruition. They are the non-binding Set of Multilaterally Agreed, Equitable Principles and Rules for the Control of Restrictive Business Practices, reprinted in (1980), 19 I.L.M. 813; the draft International Code of Conduct on the Transfer of Technology, UN. Doc. TD/Code TOT/47 (1985); and the draft International Agreement on Illicit Payments: U.N. Doc. E/AC. 67/L.3/Add.1 (1979).

103 U.N. Doc. E/CN.4/Sub.2/2003/12/Rev.2 (2003). For a description of the origins and drafting history, see generally Weissbrodt & Kruger, *supra* note 99.

104 Kinley & Tadaki, *supra* note 97 at 947 (citations omitted).

105 Weissbrodt & Kruger, *supra* note 99 at 922.

4. People

(a) Individuals

Until the 20th century the prevailing view was that states alone possessed true international legal personality.[106] Still today, states alone have standing in contentious proceedings before the International Court of Justice. However, especially in the area of protection of human rights, the individual has attained standing before some international bodies. Early in the 20th century, the procedural capacity of the individual was recognized.[107] For example, under the Polish-German Convention of 1922, which dealt with Upper Silesia, the procedural standing of individuals as claimants was admitted even against their own state.[108] Furthermore, in the *Danzig Railway Officials' Case*[109] the Permanent Court of International Justice held that if by a treaty states parties agree to confer rights on individuals, then an international court should recognize and give effect to them at international law.

These early examples of protection of the rights of individuals have been overtaken by a surge of conventions about human rights and humanitarian laws developed in the second half of the 20th century through the United Nations. The expression of these rights, however, is still not matched by equally effective measures to implement them. As a result, an individual may suffer a violation of an explicit right yet possess no standing to enforce, or no direct access to, a remedy. Refer to Chapter 12 on the "Protection of Human Rights" for a full discussion.

In the area of obligations, individuals have had legal status for a longer period of time. Especially since the war crimes trials after World War II, it is without controversy that individuals can be prosecuted for criminal violations of international customary or conventional law. The offences may take the form of war crimes—that is, violations of the laws of war—and crimes against peace and security—that is, initiating war—crimes against humanity, such as murder, extermination, enslavement, deportation, and genocide, whether in times of peace or war. These international offences may be prosecuted before international tribunals, as was done at Nuremberg and Tokyo in the 1940s and more

---

106 A.A. Norgaard, *The Position of the Individual in International Law* (1962); P.P. Remec, *The Position of the Individual in International Law According to Grotius and Vattel* (1960); W.A. Schabas, *International Human Rights Law and the Canadian Charter*, 2d ed. (1996); H. Lauterpacht, "The Subjects of the Law of Nations" (1947) 63 L.Q.R. 438 and (1948) 64 L.Q.R. 97; and S.A. Williams, "The Role of the Individual in International Law" (1986) Queen's L.J. Spec. Ed. 511.

107 H. Lauterpacht, *Survey of International Law in Relation to the Work of Codification of the International Law Commission*, U.N. Doc. A/CN.4/1/Rev. 1, February 10, 1949 at 19-20, reprinted in E. Lauterpacht, ed., *International Law being the Collected Papers of Hersch Lauterpacht* (1970) vol. 1 at 469-71. See also W.P. Gormley, *The Procedural Status of the Individual before International and Supranational Tribunals* (1966).

108 See, before the Upper Silesia Mixed Tribunal, *Steiner and Gross v. Polish State* (1927-28), 4 Ann. Dig. 291.

109 *Jurisdiction of the Courts of Danzig* (1928), Advisory Opinion, P.C.I.J. (Ser. B) No. 15.

latterly in part by the *Ad Hoc* Criminal Tribunals for the former Yugoslavia and Rwanda. The International Criminal Court, which is addressed in detail in Chapter 11, "International Criminal Law," has jurisdiction over genocide, crimes against humanity, war crimes, and aggression. These crimes may also be tried by national courts, as many states, including Canada, have undertaken.

(b) Peoples Seeking Self-Determination[110]

The interests and identity of people are not limited to individual rights. Groups of people around the world assert collective rights. Constitutional discussions in Canada over the years have made it abundantly clear that First Nations, Métis, and Québécois, for example, consider they have a right to self-determination—that is, a right to choose how they wish to be governed. The ability to assert such a right in law depends on the standing that is accorded to its claimants at international law. In the international context, it must be asked whether the principle of self-determination of peoples has achieved the status of a rule of customary international law or even *jus cogens* and what legal personality pertains to persons seeking to exercise the right. Impetus has been given to its advancement as a legal right in recent times by inclusion in the U.N. Charter, where it is referred to rather than defined and in other resolutions and declarations. Over the past 60 or so years, since the inception of the United Nations, it has been nurtured by the same movement that has supported the development of individual human rights.[111] In U.N. practice, the right to self-determination has been the basis for the decolonization of dependent territories during the 1960s and 1970s, but without settling the claims for its wider application.

Charter of the United Nations
Articles 1(2), 55, and 73
Reproduced in the Documentary Supplement

---

110 See, generally, C. Brölmann, R. Lefeber, & M. Zieck, eds., *Peoples and Minorities in International Law* (1993); A. Cassese, *Self Determination of Peoples* (1995); C. Tomuschat, ed., *Modern Law of Self-Determination* (1993); K. Doehring, "Self-Determination" in B. Simma, ed., *The Charter of the United Nations: A Commentary*, 2d ed. (2002); J. Crawford, ed., *The Rights of Peoples*, 2d ed. (2002); H. Hannun, *Autonomy, Sovereignty and Self-Determination*, rev. ed. (1996); W.J.A. Macartney, ed., *Self-Determination in the Commonwealth* (1988); W. Ofuatey-Kodjoe, *The Principle of Self-Determination in International Law* (1977); M. Pomerance, *Self Determination in Law and Practice* (1982); A. Rigo Sureda, *The Evolution of the Right of Self-Determination* (1973); U.O. Umozurike, *Self Determination in International Law* (1972); P. Thornberry, "Self-Determination, Human Rights: A Review of International Instruments" (1989) 38 I.C.L.Q. 867; and N. Berman, "Sovereignty in Abeyance: Self-Determination and International Law" (1988) 7 Wis. Int'l L.J. 51.

111 See the *International Covenant on Civil and Political Rights*, article I, reproduced in the Doc. Supp. and the discussion of human rights in Chapter 12. The right is reinforced by the Final Act of the Conference on Security and Cooperation in Europe, 1975 reprinted in (1975) 14 I.L.M. 1292.

Declaration on the Granting of Independence to Colonial Countries and Peoples[112]
GA Res. 1514 (XV), UN GAOR, 15th Sess., Supp. No. 16,
U.N. Doc. A/4684 (1960) at 66

The General Assembly ... Declares that

1) The subjection of peoples to alien subjugation, domination and exploitation constitutes a denial of fundamental human rights, is contrary to the Charter of the United Nations and is an impediment to the promotion of world peace and co-operation;

2) All peoples have the right to self-determination; by virtue of that right they freely determine their political status and freely pursue their economic, social and cultural development.

3) Inadequacy of political, economic, social or education preparedness should never serve as a pretext for delaying independence;

4) All armed action or repressive measures of all kinds directed against dependent peoples shall cease in order to enable them to exercise peacefully and freely their right to complete independence, and the integrity of their national territory shall be respected;

5) Immediate steps shall be taken, in Trust and Non-Self-Governing Territories or all other territories which have not yet attained independence, to transfer all powers to the peoples of those territories, without any conditions or reservations, in accordance with their freely expressed will and desire, without any distinction as to race, creed or colour, in order to enable them to enjoy complete independence and freedom.

6) Any attempt aimed at the partial or total disruption of the national unity and the territorial integrity of a country is incompatible with the Purposes and Principles of the Charter of the United Nations;

7) All States shall observe faithfully and strictly the provisions of the Charter of the United Nations, the Universal Declaration of Human Rights and the Present Declaration on the basis of equality, non-interference in the internal affairs of all States, and respect for the sovereign rights of all peoples and their territorial integrity.

Declaration on Principles of International Law Concerning Friendly Relations and Co-operation among States in Accordance with the Charter of the United Nations
See the Fifth Principle, reproduced in the Documentary Supplement

---

112 This resolution was adopted by 80 votes in favour to 0 against with 9 abstentions (Australia, Belgium, Dominican Republic, France, Portugal, South Africa, Spain, the United Kingdom, and the United States). It is commonly known as the Colonial Declaration.

NOTES

1) The U.N. Charter mentions self-determination in articles 1(2) and 55. What do these references mean? Can they reasonably be interpreted in more than one way?[113]

2) In addition to the documents cited here, refer also to article 1 of the International Covenant on Civil and Political Rights, reproduced in the Documentary Supplement, article 7 of the Definition of Aggression, reproduced in Chapter 15, Section A on "Prohibition of the Use of Force," the United Nations General Assembly Declaration on the Occasion of the Fiftieth Anniversary of the United Nations[114] and the 1998 United Nations World Conference on Human Rights, Vienna Declaration and Programme of Action.[115]

Western Sahara Case
Advisory Opinion, [1975] I.C.J. Rep. 12

[Western Sahara had been a colony of Spain since 1884. Its population was mostly nomads. Its assets lie in phosphates. In 1966, the General Assembly of the United Nations invited Spain to decolonize on the basis of Resolution 1514 and asked Spain in Resolution 2229 to consult with neighbouring Mauritania and Morocco to determine procedures for holding a referendum under the auspices of the United Nations. Spain agreed to hold a referendum in 1975. At that time, Morocco under King Hassan claimed the territory based on a "historic title" that predated Spain's acquisition. Mauritania did the same. At the behest of Morocco and Mauritania, the General Assembly sought an advisory opinion in 1974 as to the status of the territory. In the course of doing this, the Court addressed the issue of self-determination.]

THE COURT: ...

54. The Charter of the United Nations, in Article 1, paragraph 2, indicates, as one of the purpose of the United Nations: "To develop friendly relations among nations based on respect for the principle of equal rights and self-determination of peoples. ..." This purpose is further developed in Articles 55 and 56 of the Charter. Those provisions have direct and particular relevance for non-self governing territories, which are dealt with in Chapter XI of the Charter. As the Court stated in its Advisory Opinion of 21 June 1971 on *The Legal Consequences for States of the Continued Presence of South Africa in Namibia (South West Africa) notwithstanding Security Council Resolutions 276* (1970):

> ... the subsequent development of international law in regard to non-self governing territories, as enshrined in the Charter of the United Nations, made the principle of self-determination applicable to all of them (*I.C.J. Reports 1971*, p. 31).

---

113 See J. Crawford, *supra* note 1 at 89-92.

114 GA Res. 50/6, UN GAOR, 50th Sess., Supp. No. 49, U.N. Doc. A/50/49 (1995) 13.

115 A/Conf. 157/24, June 25, 1993, reproduced in (1993) 32 I.L.M. 1663.

55. The principle of self-determination as a right of peoples, and its application for the purpose of bringing all colonial situations to a speedy end, were enunciated in the Declaration on the Granting of Independence to Colonial Countries and Peoples, General Assembly resolution 1514 (XV) … . The above provisions, in particular paragraph 2, thus confirm and emphasize that the application of the right of self-determination requires a free and genuine expression of the will of the peoples concerned.

56. The Court had occasion to refer to this resolution in the above-mentioned Advisory Opinion of 21 June 1971. Speaking of the development of international law in regard to non-self governing territories, the Court there stated:

A further important stage in this development was the Declaration on the Granting of Independence to Colonial Countries and Peoples (General Assembly resolution 1514 (XV) of 14 December 1960), which embraces all peoples and territories which "have not yet attained independence." (*I.C.J. Reports 1971*, p. 31.)

It went on to state:

… the Court must take into consideration the changes which have occurred in the supervening half-century, and its interpretation cannot remain unaffected by the subsequent development of law, through the Charter of the United Nations and by way of customary law (*ibid.*).

The Court concluded:

In the domain to which the present proceedings relate, the last fifty years, as indicated above, have brought important developments. These developments leave little doubt that the ultimate objective of the sacred trust was the self-determination and independence of the peoples concerned. In this domain, as elsewhere, the *corpus iuris gentium* has been considerably enriched, and this the Court, if it is faithfully to discharge its functions, may not ignore. (*Ibid.,* pp. 31 et seq.)

57. General Assembly resolution 1514 (XV) provided the basis for the process of decolonization which has resulted since 1960 in the creation of many States which are today Members of the United Nations. It is complemented in certain of its aspects by General Assembly resolution 1541 (XV), which has been invoked in the present proceedings. The latter resolution contemplates for non-self governing territories more than one possibility, namely:

(a) emergence as a sovereign independent State;
(b) free association with an independent State; or
(c) integration with an independent State.

At the same time, certain of its provisions give effect to the essential feature of the right of self-determination as established in resolution 1514 (XV). Thus principle VII of resolution 1541 (XV) declares that: "Free association should be the result of a free and voluntary choice by the Peoples of the territory concerned expressed through informed and democratic processes." Again, principle IX of resolution 1541 declares that:

Integration should have come about in the following circumstances:

(b) The integration should be the result of the freely expressed wishes of the territory's peoples acting with the full knowledge of the change in their status, their wishes having been expressed through informed and democratic processes, impartially conducted and based on universal adult suffrage. The United Nations could, when it deems it necessary, supervise these processes.

58. General Assembly resolution 2625 (XXV), "Declaration on Principles of International Law concerning Friendly Relations and Co-operation among States in accordance with the Charter of the United Nations" ... mentions other possibilities besides independence, association or integration. But in doing so it reiterates the basic need to take account of the wishes of the people concerned. ...

59. The validity of the principle of self-determination, defined as the need to pay regard to the freely expressed will of peoples, is not affected by the fact that in certain cases the General Assembly has dispensed with the requirement of consulting the inhabitants of a given territory. Those instances were based either on the consideration that a certain population did not constitute a "people" entitled to self-determination or on the conviction that a consultation was totally unnecessary, in view of special circumstances.

Separate opinion of JUDGE DILLARD: At the broadest level there is the problem of determining whether the right of self-determination in the context of non-self governing territories can qualify as a norm of contemporary international law ... .

As is well known [this] ... problem has elicited conflicting views which, in terms of opposing poles, may be described as follows. At one extreme is the contention that even if a particular resolution of the General Assembly is not binding, the cumulative impact of many resolutions when similar in content, voted for by overwhelming majorities and frequently repeated over a period of time may give rise to a general *opinio juris* and thus constitute a norm of customary international law. According to this view, this is the precise situation manifested by the long list of resolutions which, following in the wake of resolution 1514 (XV), have proclaimed the principle of self-determination to be an operative right in the decolonization of non-self governing territories.

At the opposite pole are those who, resisting generally the law-creating powers of the General Assembly, deny that the principle has developed into a "right" with corresponding obligations or that the practice of decolonization has been more than an example of a usage dictated by political expediency or convenience and one which, in addition, has been neither constant nor uniform.

I need not dwell on the theoretical aspects of this broad problem which, as everyone knows, commands an immense literature. Suffice it to call attention to the fact that the present opinion is forthright in proclaiming the existence of the "right" in so far as the present proceedings are concerned.

This is made explicit in paragraph 56 and is fortified by calling into play two dicta in the *Namibia* case (*I.C.J. Reports 1971*, p. 31) to which are added an analysis of the numerous resolutions of the General Assembly dealing in general with its decolonization policy ... .

The pronouncements of the Court thus indicate, in my view, that a norm of international law has emerged applicable to the decolonization of those non-self governing territories which are under the aegis of the United Nations.

It seemed hardly necessary to make more explicit the cardinal restraint which the legal right of self-determination imposes. That restraint may be captured in a single sentence. It is for the people to determine the destiny of the territory and not the territory the destiny of the people. Viewed in this perspective it becomes almost self-evident that the existence of ancient "legal ties" of the kind described in the Opinion, while they may influence some of the projected procedures for decolonization, can have only a tangential effect in the ultimate choices available to the people.

Legal Consequences of the Construction of a Wall in the Occupied Palestinian Territory
Advisory Opinion, [2004] I.C.J. Rep. 136

[The Court was requested by the General Assembly to render an advisory opinion on "the legal consequences arising from the construction of the wall being built by Israel, the occupying Power, in the Occupied Palestinian Territory." The Court found that the construction of the wall was contrary to international law, that Israel was obligated to cease construction and make reparations for damages, and that other states were obligated not to recognize or assist in "maintaining the situation" of illegality. One of the violations of international law identified by the Court related to the principles of self-determination.]

THE COURT ...

88. The Court also notes that the principle of self-determination of peoples has been enshrined in the United Nations Charter and reaffirmed by the General Assembly in resolution 2625 (XXV) cited above, pursuant to which "Every State has the duty to refrain from any forcible action which deprives peoples referred to [in that resolution] ... of their right to self-determination." Article 1 common to the International Covenant on Economic, Social and Cultural Rights and the International Covenant on Civil and Political Rights reaffirms the right of all peoples to self-determination, and lays upon the States parties the obligation to promote the realization of that right and to respect it, in conformity with the provisions of the United Nations Charter.

The Court would recall that in 1971 it emphasized that current developments in "international law in regard to non-self-governing territories, as enshrined in the Charter of the United Nations, made the principle of self-determination applicable to all [such territories]." The Court went on to state that "[t]hese developments leave little doubt that the ultimate objective of the sacred trust" referred to in Article 22, paragraph 1, of the Covenant of the League of Nations "was the self-determination ... of the peoples concerned" (*Legal Consequences for States of the Continued Presence of South Africa in Namibia (South West Africa) notwithstanding Security Council Resolution 276 (1970), Advisory Opinion, I.C.J. Reports 1971*, p. 31, paras. 52-53).

The Court has referred to this principle on a number of occasions in its jurisprudence (*ibid.*; see also *Western Sahara, Advisory Opinion, I.C.J. Reports 1975*, p. 68, para. 162). The Court indeed made it clear that the right of peoples to self-determination is today a right *erga omnes* (see *East Timor (Portugal v. Australia), Judgment, I.C.J. Reports 1995*, p. 102, para. 29). ...

118. As regards the principle of the right of peoples to self-determination, the Court observes that the existence of a "Palestinian people" is no longer in issue. Such existence has moreover been recognized by Israel in the exchange of letters of 9 September 1993 between Mr. Yasser Arafat, President of the Palestine Liberation Organization (PLO) and Mr. Yitzhak Rabin, Israeli Prime Minister. In that correspondence, the President of the PLO recognized "the right of the State of Israel to exist in peace and security" and made various other commitments. In reply, the Israeli Prime Minister informed him that, in the light of those commitments, "the Government of Israel has decided to recognize the PLO as the representative of the Palestinian people." The Israeli–Palestinian Interim Agreement on the West Bank and the Gaza Strip of 28 September 1995 also refers a number of times to the Palestinian people and its "legitimate rights" ... . The Court considers that those rights include the right to self-determination, as the General Assembly has moreover recognized on a number of occasions (see, for example, resolution 58/163 of 22 December 2003). ...

122. In other terms, the route chosen for the wall gives expression in loco to the illegal measures taken by Israel with regard to Jerusalem and the settlements, as deplored by the Security Council. ... That construction, along with measures taken previously, thus severely impedes the exercise by the Palestinian people of its right to self-determination, and is therefore a breach of Israel's obligation to respect that right. ...

155. The Court would observe that the obligations violated by Israel include certain obligations *erga omnes*. As the Court indicated in the *Barcelona Traction* case, such obligations are by their very nature "the concern of all States" and, "[i]n view of the importance of the rights involved, all States can be held to have a legal interest in their protection." (*Barcelona Traction, Light and Power Company, Limited, Second Phase, Judgment, I.C.J. Reports 1970*, p. 32, para. 33.) The obligations *erga omnes* violated by Israel are the obligation to respect the right of the Palestinian people to self-determination, and certain of its obligations under international humanitarian law.

NOTES

1) In the preceding cases the Court was clearly of the view that the right of peoples to self-determination is a firmly established principle of international law, and in the *East Timor Case*[116] the Court referred to the principle of self-determination as "one of the essential principles of international law." What are the sources of law on which the Court could draw in reaching this conclusion? What does this say about the law-making capacity of the General Assembly, and the impact that General Assembly Resolutions have? Are they interpretations of the Charter, or do they go beyond it? See Chapter 3, Section E.2 concerning "Law Making Through International Organizations."

---

116 *East Timor Case (Portugal v. Australia)*, [1995] I.C.J. Rep. 90 at 102.

2) In both *East Timor* and *Legal Consequences of the Construction of a Wall in the Occupied Palestinian Territory* the Court stated that the right to self-determination was an obligation *erga omnes*, thus binding on all states, and one in which all states have a legal interest. In this way an *erga omnes* obligation differs from an ordinary legal obligation whose breach engages only the state that is the direct and immediate victim.[117] On what basis did the Court make such a conclusion?

3) The reference to "peoples" is distinctive. As used in United Nations practice, the term refers to an identifiable group of individuals but is nowhere conclusively defined. Presumably the group must constitute a collectivity of reasonably homogeneous people, such as a cohesive national group. What are the marks of homogeneity? Must the group share a common language or a common ethnic background? Do they have to inhabit an identifiable and separate territory?[118] In the *Legal Consequences of the Construction of a Wall in the Occupied Palestinian Territory*, above, the Court considered the existence of a "Palestinian people" to be "no longer in issue," and referred to actions of both Israel and the General Assembly that recognized the existence and rights of the Palestinian people. Were these appropriate considerations in making this determination? How would the Court approach the problem of determining the existence and status of a "people" in the absence of such facts? See the treatment of this issue by the Supreme Court of Canada in the *Reference re Secession of Quebec*, reproduced below.

4) Does the principle of self-determination refer only to peoples in colonial or neo-colonial situations or under regimes of apartheid, or can it properly be extended to cases of functional domination and discrimination? Consider the comments of Judge Higgins in her separate opinion in *Legal Consequences of the Construction of a Wall in the Occupied Palestinian Territory*:

> 29. There is a substantial body of doctrine and practice on "self-determination beyond colonialism." The United Nations Declaration on Friendly Relations, 1970, (General Assembly resolution 2625 (XXV)) speaks also of self-determination being applicable in circumstances where peoples are subject to "alien subjugation, domination, and exploitation." The General Assembly has passed many resolutions referring to the latter circumstance, having Afghanistan and the Occupied Arab Territories in mind (for example, General Assembly resolution 3236 (XXIX) 1974 (Palestine); General Assembly resolution 2144 (XXV) 1987 (Afghanistan)). The Committee on Human Rights has consistently supported this post-colonial view of self-determination.[119]

---

117 See *Barcelona Traction, Light and Power Co. Case*, [1970] I.C.J. Rep. 3 at paras. 33-34, reproduced in Chapter 8, Section B on "Corporations," and the commentary on this part of the decision by the International Law Commission in "Report of the Commission to the General Assembly on the Work of Its Twenty-Eighth Session" (U.N. Doc. A/31/10) in *Yearbook of the International Law Commission 1976*, vol. 2, part 2 (1976) 99 (U.N. Doc. A/CN.4/SER.4/1976/Add.1).

118 See G. Flack *et al.*, "The International Legal Right of Self-Determination: Four Legal Approaches and Their Textual Foundations" (1992) 1 Dal. J. Leg. Stud. 189. See also A. Cassese, *Self-Determination of Peoples: A Legal Reappraisal* (1995) at 165-66 on the particular issue of criteria in the case of liberation movements.

119 *Legal Consequences of the Construction of a Wall in the Occupied Palestinian Territory*, Advisory Opionion, [2004] I.C.J. Rep. 136, separate opinion of Judge Higgins, at paras. 29-30. Judge Higgins agreed with the extension of the principle to the non-colonial situations, while disputing its applicability on the facts of this case.

5) To what extent does the jurisprudence on self-determination endow peoples with legal personality at international law? The relevant cases have involved claims brought by states (as in *East Timor*) or Advisory Opinions. Is the legal personality of peoples—even assuming they fall within the protected category—restricted to the recognition of their rights, but without any procedural entitlements to bring a legal claim without the intercession of a state, or through the mechanism of an Advisory Opinion?[120]

6) In the Canadian context, based on the preceding materials, does Quebec have a right to self-determination at international law? Do Canada's aboriginal peoples? Review the Supreme Court's opinion below.

Reference re Secession of Quebec[121]
[1998] 2 S.C.R. 217; 161 D.L.R. (4th) 385

[Pursuant to s. 53 of the *Supreme Court Act*, the Governor in Council referred three questions to the Supreme Court of Canada, concerning the possibility of the secession of Quebec. The following extract pertains to the second question, which asked:

    2. Does international law give the National Assembly, legislature or government of Quebec the right to affect the secession of Quebec from Canada unilaterally? In this regard, is there a right to self-determination under international law that would give the National Assembly, legislature or government of Quebec the right to effect the secession of Quebec from Canada unilaterally?]

THE COURT: ...

(1) Secession at International Law

111. It is clear that international law does not specifically grant component parts of sovereign states the legal right to secede unilaterally from their "parent" state. ... Given the lack of specific authorization for unilateral secession, proponents of the existence of such a right at international law are therefore left to attempt to found their argument (i) on the proposition that unilateral secession is not specifically prohibited and that what is not specifically prohibited is inferentially permitted; or (ii) on the implied duty of states to recognize the legitimacy of secession brought about by the exercise of the well-established international law right of "a people" to self-determination. The *amicus curiae* addressed the right of self-determination, but submitted that it was not applicable to the circumstances of Quebec within the Canadian federation, irrespective of the existence or non-existence of a referendum result in favour of secession. We agree on this point with the *amicus curiae*, for reasons that we will briefly develop.

---

120 See Cassese, *supra* note 118 at 165-66, with respect to the nature of the rights conferred and the duties imposed on "peoples" or their representatives, in the form of liberation movements.

121 The pleadings of the federal government contain a comprehensive study, prepared by Professor J. Crawford, of state practice about self-determination from 1945 to 1998.

(a) Absence of a Specific Prohibition

112. International law contains neither a right of unilateral secession nor the explicit denial of such a right, although such a denial is, to some extent, implicit in the exceptional circumstances required for secession to be permitted under the right of a people to self-determination, e.g., the right of secession that arises in the exceptional situation of an oppressed or colonial people, discussed below. As will be seen, international law places great importance on the territorial integrity of nation states and, by and large, leaves the creation of a new state to be determined by the domestic law of the existing state of which the seceding entity presently forms a part (R.Y. Jennings, *The Acquisition of Territory in International Law* (1963) at pp. 8-9). Where, as here, unilateral secession would be incompatible with the domestic Constitution, international law is likely to accept that conclusion subject to the right of peoples to self-determination, a topic to which we now turn.

(b) The Right of a People to Self-Determination

113. While international law generally regulates the conduct of nation states, it does, in some specific circumstances, also recognize the "rights" of entities other than nation states—such as the right of a *people* to self-determination.

114. The existence of the right of a people to self-determination is now so widely recognized in international conventions that the principle has acquired a status beyond "convention" and is considered a general principle of international law. ...

[The Court referred to the U.N. Charter, the two International Covenants, and the 1970 Declaration on Principles of International Law discussed earlier.]

120. In 1993, the U.N. World Conference on Human Rights adopted the *Vienna Declaration and Programme of Action*, A/Conf. 157/24, 25 June 1993, that reaffirmed Article 1 of the two above-mentioned covenants. The U.N. General Assembly's *Declaration on the Occasion of the Fiftieth Anniversary of the United Nations*, GA Res. 50/6, 9 November 1995, also emphasizes the right to self-determination by providing that the U.N.'s member states will:

> 1. ... Continue to reaffirm the right of *self-determination of all peoples*, taking into account the particular situation of peoples under colonial or other forms of alien domination or foreign occupation, and recognize the right of peoples to take legitimate action in accordance with the Charter of the United Nations to realize their inalienable right of self-determination. *This shall not be construed as authorizing* or encouraging any action that would dismember or impair, totally or in part, the *territorial integrity or political unity of sovereign and independent States* conducting themselves in compliance with the principle of equal rights and self-determination of peoples and thus possessed of a Government representing the whole people belonging to the territory without distinction of any kind. [Emphasis added.] ...

122. As will be seen international law expects that the right to self-determination will be exercised by peoples within the framework of existing sovereign states and consistently

with the maintenance of the territorial integrity of those states. Where this is not possible, in the exceptional circumstances discussed below, a right of secession may arise.

(i) Defining "Peoples"

123. International law grants the right to self-determination to "peoples." Accordingly, access to the right requires the threshold step of characterizing as a people the group seeking self-determination. However, as the right to self-determination has developed by virtue of a combination of international agreements and conventions, coupled with state practice, with little formal elaboration of the definition of "peoples," the result has been that the precise meaning of the term "people" remains somewhat uncertain.

124. It is clear that "a people" may include only a portion of the population of an existing state. The right to self-determination has developed largely as a human right, and is generally used in documents that simultaneously contain references to "nation" and "state." The juxtaposition of these terms is indicative that the reference to "people" does not necessarily mean the entirety of a state's population. To restrict the definition of the term to the population of existing states would render the granting of a right to self-determination largely duplicative, given the parallel emphasis within the majority of the source documents on the need to protect the territorial integrity of existing states, and would frustrate its remedial purpose.

125. While much of the Quebec population certainly shares many of the characteristics (such as a common language and culture) that would be considered in determining whether a specific group is a "people," as do other groups within Quebec and/or Canada, it is not necessary to explore this legal characterization to resolve Question 2 appropriately. Similarly, it is not necessary for the Court to determine whether, should a Quebec people exist within the definition of public international law, such a people encompasses the entirety of the provincial population or just a portion thereof. Nor is it necessary to examine the position of the aboriginal population within Quebec. As the following discussion of the scope of the right to self-determination will make clear, whatever be the correct application of the definition of people(s) in this context, their right of self-determination cannot in the present circumstances be said to ground a right to unilateral secession.

(ii) Scope of the Right to Self-Determination

126. The recognized sources of international law establish that the right to self-determination of a people is normally fulfilled through *internal* self-determination— a people's pursuit of its political, economic, social and cultural development within the framework of an existing state. A right to *external* self-determination (which in this case potentially takes the form of the assertion of a right to unilateral secession) arises in only the most extreme of cases and, even then, under carefully defined circumstances. *External* self-determination can be defined as in the following statement from the *Declaration on Friendly Relations, supra*, as

The establishment of a sovereign and independent State, the free association or integration with an independent State or the emergence into any other political status freely determined by a *people* constitute modes of implementing the right of self-determination by *that people*. [Emphasis added.]

127. The international law principle of self-determination has evolved within a framework of respect for the territorial integrity of existing states. The various international documents that support the existence of a people's right to self-determination also contain parallel statements supportive of the conclusion that the exercise of such a right must be sufficiently limited to prevent threats to an existing state's territorial integrity or the stability of relations between sovereign states.

128. *The Declaration on Friendly Relations, supra, Vienna Declaration, supra,* and *Declaration on the Occasion of the Fiftieth Anniversary of the United Nations, supra,* are specific. They state, immediately after affirming a people's right to determine political, economic, social and cultural issues, that such rights are *not* to

> be construed as authorizing or encouraging any action which would dismember or *impair, totally or in part, the territorial integrity or political unity of sovereign and independent States conducting themselves in compliance with the principle of equal rights and self-determination of peoples* as described above and thus possessed of a government representing the whole people belonging to the territory without distinction ... . [Emphasis added.]

129. Similarly, while the concluding document of the Vienna Meeting in 1989 of the Conference on Security and Co-operation in Europe on the follow-up to the *Helsinki Final Act* again refers to peoples having the right to determine "their internal and *external* political status" (emphasis added), that statement is immediately followed by express recognition that the participating states will at all times act, as stated in the *Helsinki Final Act*, "in conformity with the purposes and principles of the Charter of the United Nations and with the relevant norms of international law, *including those relating to territorial integrity of states*" (emphasis added). Principle 5 of the concluding document states that the participating states (including Canada)

> ... confirm their commitment strictly and effectively to observe the principle of the territorial integrity of States. They will refrain from any violation of this principle and thus from any action aimed by direct or indirect means, in contravention of the purposes and principles of the Charter of the United Nations, other obligations under international law or the provisions of the [Helsinki] Final Act, at violating the territorial integrity, political independence or the unity of a State. *No actions or situations in contravention of this principle will be recognized as legal by the participating States.* [Emphasis added.]

Accordingly, the reference in the *Helsinki Final Act* to a people determining its external political status is interpreted to mean the expression of a people's external political status through the government of the existing state, save in the exceptional circumstances discussed below. ...

130. While the *International Covenant on Economic, Social and Cultural Rights, supra,* and the *International Covenant on Civil and Political Rights,* do not specifically refer to the protection of territorial integrity, they both define the ambit of the right to self-determination in terms that are normally attainable within the framework of an

existing state. There is no necessary incompatibility between the maintenance of the territorial integrity of existing states, including Canada, and the right of a "people" to achieve a full measure of self-determination. A state whose government represents the whole of the people or peoples resident within its territory, on a basis of equality and without discrimination, and respects the principles of self-determination in its own internal arrangements, is entitled to the protection under international law of its territorial integrity.

(iii) Colonial and Oppressed Peoples

. . .

132. The right of colonial peoples to exercise their right to self-determination by breaking away from the "imperial" power is now undisputed, but is irrelevant to this Reference.

133. The other clear case where a right to external self-determination accrues is where a people is subject to alien subjugation, domination or exploitation outside a colonial context. This recognition finds its roots in the *Declaration on Friendly Relations*, *supra*: ...

134. A number of commentators have further asserted that the right to self-determination may ground a right to unilateral secession in a third circumstance. ... [T]he underlying proposition is that, when a people is blocked from the meaningful exercise of its right to self-determination internally, it is entitled, as a last resort, to exercise it by secession. The *Vienna Declaration, supra*, requirement that governments represent "the whole people belonging to the territory without distinction of any kind," adds credence to the assertion that such a complete blockage may potentially give rise to a right of secession.

135. Clearly, such a circumstance parallels the other two recognized situations in that the ability of a people to exercise its right to self-determination internally is somehow being totally frustrated. While it remains unclear whether this third proposition actually reflects an established international law standard, it is unnecessary for present purposes to make that determination. Even assuming that the third circumstance is sufficient to create a right to unilateral secession under international law, the current Quebec context cannot be said to approach such a threshold. As stated by the *amicus curiae*, Addendum to the factum of the *amicus curiae*, at paras. 15-16:

[TRANSLATION] 15. The Quebec people is not the victim of attacks on its physical existence or integrity, or of a massive violation of its fundamental rights. The Quebec people is manifestly not, in the opinion of the *amicus curiae*, an oppressed people.

16. For close to 40 of the last 50 years, the Prime Minister of Canada has been a Quebecer. During this period, Quebecers have held from time to time all the most important positions in the federal Cabinet. During the 8 years prior to June 1997, the Prime Minister and the Leader of the Official Opposition in the House of Commons were both Quebecers. At present, the Prime Minister of Canada, the Right Honourable Chief Justice and two other members of the Court, the Chief of Staff of the Canadian Armed Forces and the Canadian ambassador to the United States, not to mention the Deputy Secretary-General of the United Nations, are all Quebecers. The international

achievements of Quebecers in most fields of human endeavour are too numerous to list. Since the dynamism of the Quebec people has been directed toward the business sector, it has been clearly successful in Quebec, the rest of Canada and abroad.

136. The population of Quebec cannot plausibly be said to be denied access to government. Quebecers occupy prominent positions within the government of Canada. Residents of the province freely make political choices and pursue economic, social and cultural development within Quebec, across Canada, and throughout the world. The population of Quebec is equitably represented in legislative, executive and judicial institutions. In short, to reflect the phraseology of the international documents that address the right to self-determination of peoples, Canada is a "sovereign and independent state conducting itself in compliance with the principle of equal rights and self-determination of peoples and thus possessed of a government representing the whole people belonging to the territory without distinction."

137. The continuing failure to reach agreement on amendments to the Constitution, while a matter of concern, does not amount to a denial of self-determination. In the absence of amendments to the Canadian Constitution, we must look at the constitutional arrangements presently in effect, and we cannot conclude under current circumstances that those arrangements place Quebecers in a disadvantaged position within the scope of the international law rule.

138. In summary, the international law right to self-determination only generates, at best, a right to external self-determination in situations of former colonies; where a people is oppressed, as for example under foreign military occupation; or where a definable group is denied meaningful access to government to pursue their political, economic, social and cultural development. In all three situations, the people in question are entitled to a right to external self-determination because they have been denied the ability to exert internally their right to self-determination. Such exceptional circumstances are manifestly inapplicable to Quebec under existing conditions. Accordingly, neither the population of the province of Quebec, even if characterized in terms of "people" or "peoples," nor its representative institutions, the National Assembly, the legislature or government of Quebec, possess a right, under international law, to secede unilaterally from Canada.

139. We would not wish to leave this aspect of our answer to Question 2 without acknowledging the importance of the submissions made to us respecting the rights and concerns of aboriginal peoples in the event of a unilateral secession, as well as the appropriate means of defining the boundaries of a seceding Quebec with particular regard to the northern lands occupied largely by aboriginal peoples. However, the concern of aboriginal peoples is precipitated by the asserted right of Quebec to unilateral secession. In light of our finding that there is no such right applicable to the population of Quebec, either under the Constitution of Canada or at international law, but that on the contrary a clear democratic expression of support for secession would lead under the Constitution to negotiations in which aboriginal interests would be taken into account, it becomes unnecessary to explore further the concerns of the aboriginal peoples in this Reference.

(2) Recognition of a Factual/Political Reality: The "Effectivity" Principle

140. As stated, an argument advanced by the *amicus curiae* on this branch of the Reference was that, while international law may not ground a positive right to unilateral secession in the context of Quebec, international law equally does not prohibit secession and, in fact, international recognition would be conferred on such a political reality if it emerged, for example, via effective control of the territory of what is now the province of Quebec.

141. It is true that international law may well, depending on the circumstances, adapt to recognize a political and/or factual reality, regardless of the legality of the steps leading to its creation. However, as mentioned at the outset, effectivity, as such, does not have any real applicability to Question 2, which asks whether a *right* to unilateral secession exists.

142. No one doubts that legal consequences may flow from political facts, and that "sovereignty is political fact for which no purely legal authority can be constituted ... ," H.W.R. Wade, "The Basis of Legal Sovereignty." [1955] *Camb L.J.* 172, at p. 196. Secession of a province from Canada, if successful in the streets, might well lead to the creation of a new state. Although recognition by other states is not, at least as a matter of theory, necessary to achieve statehood, the viability of a would-be state in the international community depends, as a practical matter, upon recognition by other states. That process of recognition is guided by legal norms. However, international recognition is not alone constitutive of statehood and, critically, does not relate back to the date of secession to serve retroactively as a source of a "legal" right to secede in the first place. Recognition occurs only after a territorial unit has been successful, as a political fact, in achieving secession.

143. As indicated in responding to Question 1, one of the legal norms which may be recognized by states in granting or withholding recognition of emergent states is the legitimacy of the process by which the *de facto* secession is, or was, being pursued. The process of recognition, once considered to be an exercise of pure sovereign discretion, has come to be associated with legal norms. See, e.g., *European Community Declaration on the Guidelines on the Recognition of New States in Eastern Europe and in the Soviet Union*, 31 I.L.M. 1485 (1992), at p. 1487. While national interest and perceived political advantage to the recognizing state obviously play an important role, foreign states may also take into account their view as to the existence of a right to self-determination on the part of the population of the putative state, and a counterpart domestic evaluation, namely, an examination of the legality of the secession according to the law of the state from which the territorial unit purports to have seceded. As we indicated in our answer to Question 1, an emergent state that has disregarded legitimate obligations arising out of its previous situation can potentially expect to be hindered by that disregard in achieving international recognition, at least with respect to the timing of that recognition. On the other hand, compliance by the seceding province with such legitimate obligations would weigh in favour of international recognition. The notion that what is not explicitly prohibited is implicitly permitted has little relevance where (as here) international law refers the legality of secession to the domestic law of the seceding state and the law of that state holds unilateral secession to be unconstitutional.

144. As a court of law, we are ultimately concerned only with legal claims. If the principle of "effectivity" is no more than that "successful revolution begets its own legality" (S.A. de Smith, "Constitutional Lawyers in Revolutionary Situations" (1968), 7 *West. Ont. L. Rev.* 93, at p. 96, it necessarily means that legality follows and does not precede the successful revolution. *Ex hypothesi*, the successful revolution took place outside the constitutional framework of the predecessor state, otherwise it would not be characterized as "a revolution." It may be that a unilateral secession by Quebec would eventually be accorded legal status by Canada and other states, and thus give rise to legal consequences; but this does not support the more radical contention that subsequent recognition of a state of affairs brought about by a unilateral declaration of independence could be taken to mean that secession was achieved under colour of a legal right. ...

154. We have also considered whether a positive legal entitlement to secession exists under international law in the factual circumstances contemplated by Question 1, i.e., a clear democratic expression of support on a clear question for Quebec secession. Some of those who supported an affirmative answer to this question did so on the basis of the recognized right to self-determination that belongs to all "peoples." Although much of the Quebec population certainly shares many of the characteristics of a people, it is not necessary to decide the "people" issue because, whatever may be the correct determination of this issue in the context of Quebec, a right to secession only arises under the principle of self-determination of peoples at international law where "a people" is governed as part of a colonial empire; where "a people" is subject to alien subjugation, domination or exploitation; and possibly where "a people" is denied any meaningful exercise of its right to self-determination within the state of which it forms a part. In other circumstances, peoples are expected to achieve self-determination within the framework of their existing state. A state whose government represents the whole of the people or peoples resident within its territory, on a basis of equality and without discrimination, and respects the principles of self-determination in its internal arrangements, is entitled to maintain its territorial integrity under international law and to have that territorial integrity recognized by other states. Quebec does not meet the threshold of a colonial people or an oppressed people, nor can it be suggested that Quebecers have been denied meaningful access to government to pursue their political, economic, cultural and social development. In the circumstances, the National Assembly, the legislature or the government of Quebec do not enjoy a right at international law to effect the secession of Quebec from Canada unilaterally.

155. Although there is no right, under the Constitution or at international law, to unilateral secession, that is secession without negotiation on the basis just discussed, this does not rule out the possibility of an unconstitutional declaration of secession leading to a *de facto* secession. The ultimate success of such a secession would be dependent on recognition by the international community, which is likely to consider the legality and legitimacy of secession having regard to, amongst other facts, the conduct of Quebec and Canada, in determining whether to grant or withhold recognition. Such recognition, even if granted, would not, however, provide any retroactive justification for the act of secession, either under the Constitution of Canada or at international law.

D. STATE SUCCESSION[122]

There is a definite distinction to be made between state succession and state continuity. State continuity means that a state continues to exist regardless of changes of government, until it is extinguished by absorption into another state or by dissolution. Changes in government, as well as in types of government either by legal or by unconstitutional means, do not affect the continuity of the state in terms of its international legal personality. By the same token, a state is bound by any acts, or engagements of governments that may have become extinct.

State succession, on the other hand, concerns the legal consequences that follow when one state replaces another. Succession can occur in a variety of ways—for example, total absorption of one state by another; partial absorption; independence of one state from another; merger of two existing states; or dismemberment of one state into distinct parts.

In such a circumstance, certain questions of international law must be considered. They can be summed up as follows: to what extent are the existing rights and obligations of the predecessor state extinguished and to what extent does the successor state take up those rights and obligations? As between the two states concerned, the answers are frequently to be found in their Pact of Union or other treaty of succession. In the absence of an agreed solution and vis-à-vis third parties the international rules are by no means settled. The Legal Division of the Department of External Affairs advised in 1968 that

> the question of state succession is highly complex and is one in which the State practice of newly (i.e post-World War II) independent States has departed from the general principles of pre-War international law with the result that present practice is confused and contradictory and the present state of the law highly uncertain.[123]

An event of state succession affects a long list of subject matter. *Ratione materiae* succession usually involves treaty rights and obligations, territorial rights, membership in international organizations, and contractual rights and obligations including concessionary contracts, public debts, claims in tort, public funds and public property, nationality, private and municipal law rights, and the like. *Ratione personae* succession includes rights and obligations (i) between the new State and the predecessor State; (ii) between the new State and third States; and (iii) of the new State with respect to individuals (including legal persons). It is a subject not governed by settled rules.

In the sections that follow, brief consideration will be given to continuity; the rights and duties acquired; and state responsibility for the legal interests of private individuals and changes of their nationality.

---

122 See D.P. O'Connell, *State Succession in Municipal and International Law* (1967) vol. 1-2; I. Brownlie, *supra* note 1 at c. 29; J. Crawford, *supra* note 1 at c. 16; L.C. Green, *supra* note 1 at 153-64; A.D. McNair, *The Law of Treaties* (1961) c. 37; and M. Shaw, *supra* note 1 at c. 17.

123 See J.-G. Castel, *International Law*, 3d ed. (1976) 126.

1. Changes of Government and State Continuity

Matters concerning the recognition of a new government are discussed above, in Section
B.2. But quite apart from its acceptability internationally, the new government inherits
the rights and obligations of the persisting state and its acts bind the state:

Tinoco Arbitration
Great Britain v. Costa Rica
(1923), 1 R.I.A.A. 375

[In 1914 Tinoco overthrew the Government of Costa Rica. He assumed power, called
an election, and established a new constitution. In 1919 Tinoco retired on account of
ill health and went to Europe. After his government fell a month later, the old
constitution was restored and new elections were held under it. The new government
subsequently passed a law nullifying many of the obligations assumed by the Tinoco
regime toward foreigners, including the Royal Bank of Canada and other British
nationals. Britain brought this claim on account of the alleged mistreatment of its
nationals and, in the course of deciding it, the sole arbitrator, Taft C.J.U.S., considered
the status and authority of the Tinoco regime.]

TAFT, Arbitrator: ... Great Britain contends, first, that the Tinoco government was
the only government of Costa Rica *de facto* and *de jure* for two years and nine months;
that during that time there was no other government disputing its sovereignty, that it
was in peaceful administration of the whole country, with the acquiescence of its people.
 Second, that the succeeding government could not by legislative decree avoid
responsibility for acts of that government affecting British subjects, or appropriate or
confiscate rights and property by that government except in violation of international
law; that the Act of Nullities is as to British interests, therefore itself a nullity, and is
to be disregarded, with the consequence that the contracts validly made with the
Tinoco government must be performed by the present Costa Rica government, and
that the property which has been invaded or the rights nullified must be restored.
 To these contentions the Costa Rican Government answers: ... that the contracts
and obligations of the Tinoco government, set up by Great Britain on behalf of its
subjects, are void, and do not create a legal obligation, because the government of
Tinoco and its acts were in violation of the constitution of Costa Rica of 1871.
 ... Dr. John Bassett Moore ... in his *Digest of International Law* ... announces the
general principle which has had such universal acquiescence as to become well-settled
international law:

> Changes in the government or in the internal policy of a State do not as a rule affect its
> position in international law. A monarchy may be transformed into a republic or a
> republic into a monarchy; absolute principles may be substituted for constitutional, or
> the reverse; but, though the government changes, the nation remains, with rights and
> obligations unimpaired. ... The principle of the continuity of States has important

results. The State is bound by engagements entered into by governments that have ceased to exist; the restored government is generally liable for the acts of the usurper ... .

Again Dr. Moore says:

> The origin and organization of government are questions generally of internal discussion and decision. Foreign Powers deal with the existing *de facto* government, when sufficiently established to give reasonable assurance of its permanence, and of the acquiescence of those who constitute the State in its ability to maintain itself, and discharge its internal duties and its external obligations.

The same principle is announced in Professor Borchard's new work on *The Diplomatic Protection of Citizens Abroad*:

> ... [A] general government *de facto* having completely taken the place of the regularly constituted authorities in the State binds the nation. So far as its international obligations are concerned, it represents the State. It succeeds to the debts of the regular government it has displaced and transmits its own obligations to succeeding titular governments. Its loans and contracts bind the State and the State is responsible for the governmental acts of the *de facto* authorities. In general its treaties are valid obligations of the State. It may alienate the national territory and the judgments of its courts are admitted to be effective after its authority has ceased. An exception to these rules has occasionally been noted in the practice of some of the States of Latin America, which declare null and void the acts of an usurping *de facto* intermediary government, when the regular government it has displaced succeeds in restoring its control. Nevertheless, acts validly undertaken in the name of the State and having an international character cannot lightly be repudiated and foreign governments generally insist on their binding force. The legality or constitutional legitimacy of a *de facto* government is without importance internationally so far as the matter of representing the State is concerned.

NOTES

1) The British claim was ultimately rejected because the obligations undertaken by the Tinoco government toward the Royal Bank and the other foreigners were held to be invalid under the law in existence at the time—that is, the constitution and laws of Costa Rica under the Tinoco regime.

2) It is clear from this decision that changes in government do not affect the personality or identity of the state. Thus, the rights and obligations of a state survive such changes in government, whether they be legal or revolutionary.[124] It can even be said that the state continues to exist though there may be a period when there is no effective government, or when the government is in exile because of belligerent occupation of the territory.

---

124 J. Crawford, *supra* note 1 at 28.

2. Succession to Rights and Obligations

Succession to Treaties
from S.A. Williams, "International Legal Effects of Secession by Quebec," Study
No. 8 of the York University Constitutional Reform Project (1991) Centre for
Public Law and Public Policy at 30-35 (text and footnotes altered and updated)

One of the key problems in international law that arises either on the creation of a
new State through decolonization, for example, or the division of an existing State
into two entities, such as would happen to Canada through a unilateral declaration of
independence by Quebec, is that of succession to the treaty of the prior State. It is
naturally a matter of serious political concern. Treaties cover a broad spectrum of
matters and range from exclusively political agreements to multilateral conventions
and through to conveyances of territory between States. The usual method of dealing
with treaties, in relation to succession, has been to decide whether a particular treaty
is classified as "personal" or "real."[125] "Personal" treaties, as the name suggests, are
based on the premise that the parties will continue unchanged. This is an essential
element in the treaty-contract. These treaties are primarily political, concerned with
alliances, mutual defence pacts, dispute settlement, economic, administrative, and
judicial cooperation matters. "Real" treaties, on the other hand, comprise boundary
treaties and other treaties concerning the rights of transit over territory. If it ever was
the case that there was complete devolution of treaty obligations from the predecessor
State to the successor, the practice of the so-called post-colonial era has completely
controverted that position, resulting in the law being far from certain. The most
extreme position put forward by some newly independent States is that, based on the
equality of States upon independence, they should have the absolute right and freedom
to accept or reject any treaty obligation incurred by a former metropolitan power.

Generally speaking, state practice in this post-colonial period took several forms,
including the following: firstly, the assumption of all of the obligations of the former
colonial State for its colony;[126] secondly, the acceptance of all obligations for a short
trial period, which was followed by a declaration specifying those treaties that were
to be accepted;[127] thirdly, the adherence to the rules of customary international law,

---

125 See Williams & de Mestral, *supra* note 1 at 95.

126 Nigeria adopted this approach. See M. Mutiti, *State Succession to Treaties in Respect of Newly
     Independent African States* (1976) at 31. It should be noted that this was the traditional pre-World War II
     approach, and was the position taken by Canada. See *Ex parte O'Dell and Griffen*, [1953] O.R. 190; 105
     C.C.C. 256; [1953] 3 D.L.R. 207 (H.C.). One example would be the many extradition treaties concluded
     by Great Britain on behalf of Canada. These have always been regarded by Canada, and the other state
     parties, as automatically in force after Canada's independence.

127 Malawi adopted this approach. This is also known as the temporizing doctrine or the "Nyerere Doctrine,"
     after President Nyerere of Tanganyika, who used this type of Declaration, having rejected a devolution
     agreement with the United Kingdom. As to the different approaches taken by African States, see Y.
     Makonnen, *International Law and the New States of Africa* (1983).

but the avoidance of adherence to any specific treaties; and, fourthly, the issuance of a general declaration of succession to treaties.[128]

With all of these possibilities, certainty was clearly lacking, and thus the International Law Commission took on the project to codify and progressively develop the international rules in the area. In 1978, the project was completed by the conclusion of the Vienna Convention on Succession of States in Respect of Treaties.[129] It purports to codify customary international law. The general thrust of this Convention is formulated on the basic principle of non-devolution of obligations for "newly independent states" which result from the decolonization process, with the exception of treaties that delimit boundaries, and are said to run with the land and other territorial regimes. However, in the case of Quebec, the pertinent provision is contained in Article 34, which provides that in the case of a new State being formed as a result of separation from an existing independent State, the successor is bound by all the treaties of its predecessor. Two commentators have said that "[t]his somewhat surprising rule was the result of pressure from a number of newly independent states whose interest is now to make separation as difficult a process as possible."[130]

At first sight, this provision would seem to clarify the obligations that would accrue to an independent Quebec. This is not the case on closer analysis. The Convention has, as of May 2005, 18 parties.[131] It entered into force on November 6, 1996. Canada is not a party to it, and it cannot be said to be a complete codification of custom. Certainly, Article 34 is not consistent with State practice. Therefore, as things stand today, the question of succession to treaties is still governed by the rules of customary international law which, based on post-1945 State practice, emphasize non-devolution of obligations, thus allowing new States, however they have emerged,[132] to wipe the slate clean should they wish to do so.

In summary, Quebec would not be bound under customary international law by the treaty obligations entered into by Canada. This stands to reason, as it is a basic principle of treaty-law that treaties bind State parties only,[133] and is analogous to the general principle of privity in domestic contract law. Likewise, even if the new State was prepared to accept the obligations, other existing States it is argued "are not bound to accept a new party, as it were, by operation of law."[134]

---

128 *Ibid.* See also International Law Association, *Helsinki Conference, 52d Report* (1966) 557.

129 (1978) 17 I.L.M. 1488, reproduced below.

130 M. Akehurst, *A Modern Introduction to International Law*, 4th ed. (1982) 370.

131 Not including Canada.

132 See I. Brownlie, *supra* note 1 at 633-34, where he states that the distinctions drawn by the I.L.C. in its drafts, and subsequently in the provisions of the Vienna Convention on Succession of States in Respect of Treaties, adopted in 1978, are not reflected in state practice. He adds further that "the distinction between a secession and the dissolution of federations and unions is unacceptable, both as a proposition of law and as a matter of principle."

133 See the 1969 *Vienna Convention on the Law of Treaties*, art. 34, to which Canada is a party, reproduced in the Documentary Supplement.

134 Brownlie, *supra* note 1 at 633.

This clean slate approach does have exceptions. Quebec would be bound by the rules of customary international law. In this limited circumstance, an existing multilateral convention might be evidence of obligations binding on it, in that the particular convention codifies custom. The second exception would be that of dispositive or localized treaties concerning particular pieces of territory, such as demilitarized zones, navigation, port rights, and fishing rights. Some writers, such as Brownlie, consider that there is insufficient evidence to consider an exception.[135] Others adhere to it as a type of treaty that "impresses a permanent and indefeasible status on the territory."[136] The third exception is for boundary treaties. This differs from the previous category, in that it is based on the need for stability in territorial matters.[137]

Vienna Convention on Succession of States in Respect of Treaties[138]
(1978) 17 I.L.M. 1488

Article 2

1. For the purposes of the present Convention: ...
    (b) "succession of States" means the replacement of one State by another in the responsibility for the international relations of territory; ...

Article 8

1. The obligations or rights of a predecessor State under treaties in force in respect of a territory at the date of a succession of States do not become the obligations or rights of the successor State towards other States parties to those treaties by reason only of the fact that the predecessor State and the successor State have concluded an agreement providing that such obligations or rights shall devolve upon the successor State.

2. Notwithstanding the conclusion of such an agreement, the effects of a succession of States on treaties which, at the date of that succession of States, were in force in respect of the territory in question are governed by the present Convention.

Article 9

1. Obligations or rights under treaties in force in respect of a territory at the date of a succession of States do not become the obligations or rights of the successor State or of other States parties to those treaties by reason only of the fact that the

---

135 *Ibid.* at 634. He is of the view that there is no clear reason why they should be so treated.

136 See the authorities referred to in D.P. O'Connell, *International Law* (1970) vol. 1 at 373 note 26.

137 *Ibid.*

138 See I. Sinclair, "Some Reflections on the Vienna Convention on Succession of States in Respect of Treaties" in *Essays in Honour of Eric Castren* (1979) 149; Caggiano, "The ILC Draft on the Succession of States in Respect of Treaties: A Critical Appraisal" (1975) 1 Ital. Y.B. Int'l L. 69; and P.K. Menon, "Vienna Convention of 1978 on Succession of States in Respect of Treaties" (1981) 59 R.D.I. 19.

successor State has made a unilateral declaration providing for the continuance in force of the treaties in respect of its territory.

2. In such a case, the effects of the succession of States on treaties which, at the date of that succession of States, were in force in respect of the territory in question are governed by the present Convention.

Article 10

1. When a treaty provides that, on the occurrence of a succession of States, a successor State shall have the option to consider itself a party to the treaty, it may notify its succession in respect of the treaty in conformity with the provisions of the treaty or, failing any such provisions, in conformity with the provisions of the present Convention.

2. If a treaty provides that, on the occurrence of a succession of States, a successor State shall be considered as a party to the treaty, that provision takes effect as such only if the successor State expressly accepts in writing to be so considered.

3. In cases falling under paragraph 1 or 2, a successor State which establishes its consent to be a party to the treaty is considered as a party from the date of the succession of States unless the treaty otherwise provides or it is otherwise agreed.

Article 11

A succession of States does not as such affect:

    (a) a boundary established by a treaty; or

    (b) obligations and rights established by a treaty and relating to the régime of a boundary.

Article 12

1. A succession of States does not as such affect:

    (a) obligations relating to the use of any territory, or to restrictions upon its use established by a treaty for the benefit of any territory of a foreign State and considered as attaching to the territories in question;

    (b) rights established by a treaty for the benefit of any territory and relating to the use, or to restrictions upon the use, of any territory of a foreign State and considered as attaching to the territories in question.

2. A succession of States does not as such affect:

    (a) obligations relating to the use of any territory, or to restrictions upon its use, established by a treaty for the benefit of a group of States or of all States and considered as attaching to that territory;

    (b) rights established by a treaty for the benefit of a group of States or of all States and relating to the use of any territory, or to restrictions upon its use, and considered as attaching to that territory.

3. The provisions of the present article do not apply to treaty obligations of the predecessor State providing for the establishment of foreign military bases on the territory to which the succession of States relates. ...

Article 15

When part of the territory of a State, or when any territory for the international relations of which a State is responsible, not being part of the territory of that State, becomes part of the territory of another State:

(a) treaties of the predecessor State cease to be in force in respect of the territory to which the succession of States relates from the date of the succession of States; and

(b) treaties of the successor State are in force in respect of the territory to which the succession of States relates from the date of the succession of States, unless it appears from the treaty or is otherwise established that the application of the treaty to that territory would be incompatible with the object and purpose of the treaty or would radically change the conditions for its operation.

Article 16

A newly independent State is not bound to maintain in force, or to become a party to, any treaty by reason only of the fact that at the date of the succession of States the treaty was in force in respect of the territory to which the succession of States relates.

Article 17

1. Subject to paragraphs 2 and 3, a newly independent State may, by a notification of succession, establish its status as a party to any multilateral treaty which at the date of the succession of States was in force in respect of the territory to which the succession of States relates.

2. Paragraph 1 does not apply if it appears from the treaty or is otherwise established that the application of the treaty in respect of the newly independent State would be incompatible with the object and purpose of the treaty or would radically change the conditions for its operation.

3. When, under the terms of the treaty or by reason of the limited number of the negotiating States and the object and purpose of the treaty, the participation of any other State in the treaty must be considered as requiring the consent of all the parties, the newly independent State may establish its status as a party to the treaty only with such consent. ...

Article 24

1. A bilateral treaty which at the date of a succession of States was in force in respect of the territory to which the succession of States relates is considered as being in force between a newly independent State and the other State party when:

(a) they expressly so agree; or

(b) by reason of their conduct they are to be considered as having so agreed.

2. A treaty considered as being in force under paragraph 1 applied in the relations between the newly independent State and the other State party from the date of the succession of States, unless a different intention appears from their agreement or is otherwise established. ...

Article 34

1. When a part or parts of the territory of a State separate to form one or more States, whether or not the predecessor State continues to exist:

(a) any treaty in force at the date of the succession of States in respect of the entire territory of the predecessor State continues in force in respect of each successor State so formed;

(b) any treaty in force at the date of the succession of States in respect only of that part of the territory of the predecessor State continues in force in respect of that successor State alone.

2. Paragraph 1 does not apply if:

(a) the States concerned otherwise agree; or

(b) it appears from the treaty or is otherwise established that the application of the treaty in respect of the successor State would be incompatible with the object and purpose of the treaty or would radically change the conditions of operation.

NOTES

1) Where territorial changes have occurred, a treaty will likely be terminated either by way of provisions therein concerning denunciation or by the doctrine of fundamental change of circumstances (*rebus sic stantibus*).[139] After the Russian Revolution, the former U.S.S.R. made the claim that a new state had come into being, not simply a new government. It was argued that the new government should not be responsible for the obligations, including debts, of the previous Czarist regime. The doctrine of *rebus sic stantibus* was called in aid of release from such obligations. This argument was rejected by many states. The new government also adopted inconsistent positions with regard to retention of rights belonging to Czarist Russia.[140]

2) Could it be argued that changes to the territory of a state, where secession has occurred, are incompatible with the object and purpose of the treaty? Consider article 62 of the Vienna Convention on the Law of Treaties, reproduced in the Documentary Supplement.

3) Why are boundary and other dispositive treaties not subject to termination based on such a change of circumstances?[141] Consider article 62(2)(a).

4) Within the Commonwealth, it certainly was the traditional view, prior to World War II, that the older British dominions had inherited all the treaty rights and obligations of general application to the United Kingdom at the time they gained separate international status. However much this practice has since changed,[142] so far as Canada is concerned,

---

139 Discussed under "Operation of Treaties" in Chapter 3, Section B.4.

140 See K. Grzybowski, *Soviet Public International Law: Doctrines and Diplomatic Practice* (1970) at 92-95.

141 See M. Shaw, *Title to Territory in Africa* (1986) at 240-44, and J. Brossard, *L'Accession à la souveraineté et le cas de Québec* (1976) at 444-45. Note *Case Concerning the Continental Shelf (Tunisia/Libya)*, [1982] I.C.J. Rep. 65-66; and *Burkina Faso v. Mali*, [1986] I.C.J. Rep. 554 at 556.

142 For cases arising out of the independence of former British or French colonies see, for instance, *Re Westerling*, [1951] Malayan L.R. 288; *Dabrai v. Air India Ltd.*, [1954] Bombay L.R. 944; *Yangtse (London) Ltd. v. Barlas Bros.*, [1961] Pakistani L. Dec. 573; *Trésor Public v. Air Laos et C.A.M.A.T.*

both the Department of Foreign Affairs and the courts[143] adhere to the older view that Canada continues to be bound by the treaties made by the United Kingdom that affect it.

5) In the Canadian context, if Quebec should secede unilaterally, what would happen to the 1951 St. Lawrence Seaway Agreement between Canada and the United States?[144] Note that the distance from the Gulf of the St. Lawrence to Lake Ontario is 2,338 miles, of which 1,000 miles are within the jurisdiction of Quebec. Likewise, what would be the position with respect to the Boundary Waters Treaty of 1909 between Canada and the United States?[145]

6) On August 31, 1990 the former two parts of Germany (FRG and GDR) signed a treaty providing for re-unification on October 3, 1990. On September 12, 1990 the Treaty on the Final Settlement with respect to Germany was signed by the two states and the four allied powers (France, United Kingdom, United States, and the former U.S.S.R.).[146] Article 11 of the bilateral Unification Treaty provided that all the international treaties to which the FRG was a party[147] retain their validity and apply to the whole of unified Germany. Concerning treaties entered into by the former GDR, article 12 provided that discussions with the parties concerned would take place and the newly united Germany would then decide its position. It should be noted that this case was not one of merger of two states creating one new state, but rather of absorption of one state into another.

7) State succession problems in practice are dealt with by devolution agreements, by unilateral declarations, and by original accession to treaties by new states. What is the effect of devolution agreements and unilateral declarations in the light of articles 8 and 9 of the 1978 Vienna Convention?[148]

(1961), 15 Rev. Fr. Droit Aérien 276. See also A.P. Lister, "State Succession to Treaties in the Commonwealth" (1963) 12 I.C.L.Q. 475.

143 See *Ex Parte O'Dell and Griffen*, *supra* note 126, discussed in Chapter 3, Section B.4 on "Operation of Treaties," and D.P. O'Connell, "State Succession and Problems of Treaty Interpretation" (1964) 58 A.J.I.L. 41.

144 Can. T.S. 1952 No. 30.

145 U.S.T. 548; U.K. T.S. 1910 No. 23.

146 (1990) 29 I.L.M. 1186. This confirmed the borders of the new unified Germany as those of the FRG and GDR. All powers held by the allies regarding Berlin and Germany were terminated.

147 Annex I provides for some exceptions.

148 See "Report of the Commission to the General Assembly on the Work of Its Twenty-Sixth Session" (U.N. Doc. A/9610/Rev.1) in *Yearbook of the International Law Commission 1974*, vol. 2, part 1 (1974) 157 at 174 (U.N. Doc. A/CN.4/Ser. A/1974/Add.1), and *Molefi v. Principal Legal Adviser*, [1971] A.C. 182 (P.C.), in which such a declaration by Lesotho was held to be an accession to the *Convention Relating to the Status of Refugees* (1951), 189 U.N.T.S. 137.

Succession to Public Property
from S.A. Williams, "International Legal Effects of Secession by Quebec" (1991)
above at 43-44 (footnotes altered)[149]

In the case where a predecessor State is not extinguished, but merely loses some of its territory to its successor, the seceding State only succeeds to public property situated on the territory that has been transferred, in the absence of an agreement by both parties to the contrary.[150] Article 8 of the 1983 Vienna Convention on Succession of States in Respect of State Property, Archives, and Debts, which is not yet in force, provides that State property comprises property, rights, and interests.[151] Any property that remains under the control of the predecessor State, or on territory retained by it, continues to belong to that State. This is based on well-established rules of customary international law, and is founded, one may say, on the exercise of State sovereignty over territory.[152] This is also in keeping with Article 14 of the 1983 Vienna Convention on Succession of States in Respect of State Property, Archives, and Debts. In this respect, the 1983 Convention serves to the greatest extent as a codification of customary international law. However, it must be emphasized that in general terms, this Convention, another product of the International Law Commission centering around the newly independent States, is very controversial,[153] and, to date, no State has ratified it. Canada, the United States, and nine other States voted against its adoption, and eleven others abstained.

Thus, in the case of Quebec, any public property located on the territory of Quebec would become Quebec State property. This would include public buildings and their contents, federal installations, such as customs offices, post offices, prisons, public transportation systems, such as railways, harbours, airports, educational and artistic establishments maintained at public expense, property of Crown Corporations, and the armed forces' bases and equipment. Property located outside of Canada, such as embassies and consulates, would remain the property of Canada. Only extraterritorial property that could notionally be attributed to Quebec, such as Quebec trade officers in foreign capitals, would fall outside this.

---

149 See also D. Desjardins & C. Gendron, "Legal Issues Concerning the Division of Assets and Debts in State Succession: The Canada-Quebec Debate" in C.D. Howe Institute, *Closing the Books—Dividing Federal Assets and Debts if Canada Breaks Up* (1992) 1 and J. Mennier, "La Convention de Vienne sur la succession d'états en matière de biens, archives et dettes d'état" (1984) 30 Ann. Fr. Dr. Int'l 30.

150 *Halsbury's Laws of England*, 4th ed., vol. 18 (1977), *Foreign Relations Law*, para. 1448; *Restatement of the Law (Third), Foreign Relations Law of the United States*, para. 209; Crawford, *supra* note 1 at 228; I. Brownlie, *supra* note 1 at 624-25 ; Shaw, *supra* note 1 at 891; and M. Shaw, Expert Opinion to the Bélanger-Campeau Commission, Appendix B-1 to the Report at 522, para. 9. See *Peter Pazmany University Case* (1933), P.C.I.J. (Ser. A/B) No. 61 at 237.

151 U.N. Doc. A/Conf.117/14 (1983), reprinted in (1983) 22 I.L.M. 306. Fifteen ratifications or accessions are necessary to bring it into force. As of May 2005 there are only six states parties.

152 M. Arbour, "Secession and International Law—Some Economic Problems in Relation to State Succession" (1978) 19 C. de D. 285 at 293 and 297.

153 J.G. Starke, "International Legal Notes" (1983) 57 Australian L.J. 480 and G. Burdeau, Expert Opinion to the Bélanger-Campeau Commission, Annexe B-3 to the Report, 532 at 549.

NOTE

Clearly, under the rules of customary international law, a successor state acquiring the entire territory of a predecessor state succeeds to all the public property, movable or immovable wherever it is located.[154]

Succession to Public Debts
from S.A. Williams, "International Legal Effects of Secession by Quebec" (1991) above at 44 (footnotes altered)

The question under this heading is to what extent does Quebec have to succeed to the debts of Canada?[155] There is no uniform practice here.[156] Nevertheless, it is suggested that if the particular debt in question was incurred by Canada in order to improve the territory of Quebec, the successor State, then the successor, having benefited from the loan, should be responsible for the debt. Nevertheless, it is suggested that if the particular debt in question was incurred by Canada in order to improve the territory of Quebec, the successor State, then the successor, having benefited from the loan, should be responsible for the debt. The successor must accept the burdens, as well as the benefits, of sovereignty. This type of debt would be classified as a "localized debt." Other debts might be "national," in that they are owed by the State on a national, rather than on a localized, basis, or "local," in that a local autonomous government entity or sub-division in a federal State has contracted them for purposes specific to that area. Customary international law recognizes the obligations of the successor State to take responsibility for "local" debts, as it contracted them itself.[157] With respect to "national" debts and their division, the position is unclear and thus no rule of customary law can be positively identified. Article 37 of the 1983 Vienna Convention [on Succession of States in Respect of State Property, Archives, and Debts[158]] provides for the transfer of what it terms "state debts," defined in Article 33 as "any financial obligation of a predecessor state arising in conformity with international law towards another state, an international organization or any other subject of international law." It therefore excludes debts owed to individual private creditors, a position that has been subjected to criticism.[159] Article 37 states the following:

---

154 See *Haile Selassie v. Cable and Wireless Ltd. (No. 2)*, [1939] Ch. 182, rev'd. at 194 (C.A.).

155 For an analysis of the theoretical underpinnings of this question, albeit not covering the more recent developments, see the classic work of D.P. O'Connell, *supra* note 136, c. 15 and E. Feilchenfeld & H. Wilkinson, *The American Doctrine of State Succession* (1975). For a history of this topic, see M.H. Hoeflich, "Through the Glass Darkly: Reflections Upon the History of Public Debt in Connection with State Succession" (1982) 1 U. Ill. L.R. 39.

156 For an account of the different views, see Arbour, *supra* note 152 at 314-38.

157 See O'Connell, *supra* note 136 at 388, and Shaw, *supra* note 1 at 901.

158 *Supra* note 151.

159 *E.g.* Shaw, Expert Opinion, *supra* note 150 at 524, para. 13; Burdeau, *supra* note 153 at 546; and J.L. Foorman & M.E. Jehle, "Effects of State and Government Succession on Commercial Bank Loans to Foreign Sovereign Borrowers" (1982) 1 U. Ill. L.R. 9.

1. When part of a territory of a State is transferred by that State to another State, the passing of the State debt of the predecessor State to the successor State is to be settled by agreement between them.

2. In the absence of such an agreement, the State debt of the predecessor State shall pass to the successor State in an equitable proportion, taking into account in particular, the property, rights, and interests which pass to the successor State in relation to that State debt.

Article 37 goes beyond the earlier stated position of customary international law, which was restricted to "localized" State debts, and did not cover general "national" State debts. The Convention does not codify custom here.[160] In any event, it is not applicable to the Quebec situation, as Article 37 does not deal with a new successor State, but with transfer between existing States. Article 38 provides for the "newly independent State," and, in summary, provides that no State debt of the predecessor shall pass to its successor. This would not be a codification of custom which allowed for the transfer of "localized debts." Again, it is not referable to the case of Quebec, as Quebec is not a "dependent territory," as that term is defined in Article 2. The 1983 Convention does not deal specifically with secession in a non-colonial situation. It must be remembered that Canada, as a State, has contracted "national" debts on behalf of Canada, as a whole, and on the international plane it is Canada that remains responsible to the creditor.[161] Customary international law indicates that these "national" debts would therefore remain with Canada.[162]

In summary, therefore, the customary international legal position applicable to the Quebec secession would be the transfer of "localized" debts, pertinent to Quebec. Beyond that, there is no set rule. Therefore, in order to settle the issue of the "national debt," there would be a need for successful negotiations between Canada and Quebec. The principles of justice and fairness would seem to this writer to dictate that the debt be divided on the basis of equitable proportionality.[163] Shaw has commented that there are a variety of possibilities for such apportionment, including:

---

160 See Shaw, *ibid.* at 525, para. 15. Generally speaking, Burdeau, *ibid.* at 549, is of the view that, as far as the suggestion that the 1983 Convention codifies custom, "*[i]l est permis d'en douter*." She also mentions that all the authors who have written on the question, including Judge Bedjaoui, the I.L.C. Special Rapporteur, have recognized unanimously that the State practice in the area "était particulièrement confuse et contradictoire et qu'il était par conséquent extrêmement difficile d'en dégager l'existence de règles coutumières précises et unanimement reconnues. *Il est donc hasardeux de considérer que la Convention de 1983 a pu codifier des règles coutumières établies*" (emphasis added).

161 It is for this reason that little, if anything, is said of the possibility of secession in loan agreements between banks and foreign State debtors. See Foorman & Jehle, *supra* note 159 at 9.

162 Shaw, *supra* note 1 at 902. See *Ottoman Public Debt Case* (1925), 1 R.I.A.A. 529; (1925-26) 3 Ann. Dig. 78.

163 See the 1983 *Vienna Convention* article 40, which provides for this in the case where part of a state secedes. However, as much as this would seem to be the most fair solution, it would be difficult to suggest, in this writer's opinion, that this is a codification of, or has subsequently crystallized into, customary international law, and is therefore mandated. See Shaw, *supra* note 1 at 903-4, and Burdeau, *supra* note 153 at 553, where she states that the parties have a great deal of latitude to choose "un critère qui leur paraisse équitable et approprié."

Taxation ratio, extent of territory, population, nationality of creditors, taxable value as distinct from actual revenue contributions, value of assets, and contributions of the territory in question to the central administration.[164]

It would seem unjust to exclude, as does the 1983 Convention, private creditors, whether individual or corporate, from this scheme.[165] Another criterion that might be used is the contribution of the seceding entity to the national revenue, combined with the population figure.[166] Arbour accurately expresses the situation when he comments that once it is admitted that the successor State should assume a part of the public debt then "[t]his point is really the boundary beyond which jurists must give way to economists."[167]

NOTES

1) Should a national debt be determined in whole or in part in proportion to the assets that would be transferred to the successor state? Does this conform to international law?

2) In the Canadian context, if Quebec should secede should the method of division recognize the "historical benefits" that Quebec received within confederation?[168]

3. Respect for Private Rights

Private vested or acquired rights should be respected by the successor state. A change in states of itself does not affect rights, including contracts and concessions made by the former state that were acquired under its laws. But the continuance of those laws is subject to the sovereign authority of the successor state. Yet, even though the successor may change the domestic legal system, it is still under a duty to observe a certain minimum standard of treatment for aliens.[169] The legal context is often expropriation.

---

164   Shaw, Expert Opinion, *supra* note 150 at 526-27 para. 19, citing *Virginia v. West Virginia*, 220 U.S. 1. He suggests that "to be equitable, value over several years ought to be taken."

165   Foorman & Jehle, *supra* note 159 at 15, take the view that as the 1983 Convention (only I.L.C. Draft Articles at the time of their writing) does not cover such private creditors, they "are likely to influence the treatment of such debt."

166   Burdeau, *supra* note 153 at 552, referring to the cases of Jura and Berne.

167   Arbour, *supra* note 152 at 334.

168   Desjardins & Gendron, *supra* note 149 at 22.

169   The existence and content of this standard of treatment of aliens is discussed in Chapter 10, Section B.1. See the *German Settlers Case* (1923), P.C.I.J. (Ser. B.) No. 6; *German Interests in Polish Upper Silesia* (1928), P.C.I.J. (Ser. A.) No. 7 at 21- 22; and *Chorzow Factory Case* (1928), P.C.I.J. (Ser. A.) No. 17 at 46-48.

The Lighthouses Arbitration
France v. Greece
(1956), 12 R.I.A.A. 155; 23 I.L.R. 659

[This case concerned, *inter alia*, claims by France that Greece was responsible for breach of state concessions to its citizens by the autonomous state of Crete. The breaches were committed prior to the extension of Greek sovereignty over Crete.]

THE TRIBUNAL: ... the Tribunal can only come to the conclusion that Greece, having adopted the illegal conduct of Crete in its recent past as an autonomous State, is bound, as successor State, to take upon its charge the financial consequences of the breach of the concession contract. Otherwise, the avowed violation of a contract committed by one of the two States ... with the assent of the other, would, in the event of their merger, have the thoroughly unjust consequence of cancelling a definite financial responsibility and of sacrificing the undoubted rights of a private firm holding a concession to a so-called principle of non-transmission of debts in cases of territorial succession, which in reality does not exist as a general and absolute principle. In this case, the Greek government with good reason commenced by recognizing its own responsibility.

NOTES

1) Questions as to the obligation to pay compensation in cases of nationalization by a predecessor government are discussed in Chapter 10, Section B.3 on "Protection of Property." Should different considerations apply to investments made before the independence of a state as opposed to afterward? Should economic self-determination be one of those considerations?

2) Disregard of these acquired or vested rights must be distinguished from international claims for other personal injuries, which do not devolve upon the successor state. See the following case:

Robert E. Brown Claim
United States–Great Britain Claims Arbitration Tribunal
(1923), 6 R.I.A.A. 120; (1925) 19 A.J.I.L. 193

[The United States sought damages from Great Britain for the denial of rights claimed by Brown, an American citizen, in South Africa prior to its conquest by Great Britain. Brown had staked a large number of gold mining claims at Witfontein even though he had been refused any prospecting licences. The circumstances of this refusal were confused by the actions of the government in Pretoria, which had at first proclaimed the area open to prospecting but had then postponed it. When Brown brought a suit demanding the licences or damages for their denial, the High Court held that since the notice of postponement was not proclaimed in the official Gazette until the day after the opening of prospecting, it was ineffectual and consequently no grounds existed to refuse Brown's application of that day. Brown was issued licences valid for one month but, their renewal being denied, he was forced to return to court on his alternative claim for damages. By the time the case was heard the Chief Justice had been dismissed and the High Court had been reorganized with new justices partial to the government. The decision of this court effectively non-suited Brown.

On these facts, the Claims Tribunal first held Brown had suffered a denial of justice according to the standards of international law at the hands of the government of South Africa. It then turned to the question whether the British Government succeeded to that liability.]

THE TRIBUNAL: ... Passing to the second main question involved, we are equally clear that this liability never passed to or was assumed by the British Government. Neither in the terms of peace granted at the time of the surrender of the Boer forces, nor in the Proclamation of Annexation, can there be found any provision referring to the assumption of liabilities of this nature. It should be borne in mind that this was simply a pending claim for damages against certain officials and had never become a liquidated debt of the former State. Nor is there, properly speaking, any question of State succession here involved. The United States plants itself squarely on two propositions: first, that the British Government, by the acts of its own officials with respect to Brown's case, has become liable to him: and secondly, that in some way a liability was imposed upon the British Government by reason of the peculiar relation of suzerainty which is maintained with respect to the South African Republic.

The first of these contentions is set forth in the Reply as follows:

The United States reaffirms that Brown suffered a denial of justice at the hands of authorities of the South African Republic. Had it not been for this denial of justice, it may be assumed that a diplomatic claim would not have arisen. But it does not follow that, as is contended in His Majesty's Government's Answer, it is incumbent on the United States to show that there is a rule of international law imposing liability on His Majesty's Government for the tortious acts of the South African Republic. Occurrences which took place during the existence of the South African Republic are obviously relevant and important in connection with the case before the Tribunal, but the United States contends that acts of the British Government and of British officials and the general position taken by them with respect to Brown's case have fixed liability on His Majesty's Government.

Again on page 8 of the Reply it said:

The succeeding British authorities to whom Brown applied for the licenses to which he had been declared entitled by the Court also refused to grant the licenses, and therefore refused to carry out the decree of the Court which the United States contends was binding on them. And they have steadfastly refused to make compensation to Brown in lieu of the licenses to which the Court declared Brown to be entitled, failing the granting of the licenses.

The American Agent quoted these passages in his oral argument, and disclaimed any intention of maintaining "that there is any general liability for torts of a defunct State." We have searched the record for any indication that the British authorities did more than leave this matter exactly where it stood when annexation took place. They did not redress the wrong which had been committed, nor did they place any obstacles in Brown's path; they took no action one way or the other. No British official nor any British court undertook to deny Brown justice or to perpetuate the wrong. The Attorney General of the Colony, in his opinion, declared that the courts were still open to the claimant. The contention of the American Agent amounts to an assertion that a succeeding State acquiring a territory by conquest without any undertaking to assume such liabilities is bound to take affirmative steps to right the wrongs done by the former State. We cannot indorse this doctrine ... .

We may grant that a special relation between Great Britain and the South African State, varying considerably in its scope and significance from time to time, existed from the beginning. No doubt Great Britain's position in South Africa imposed upon her a peculiar status and responsibility. She repeatedly declared and asserted her authority as the so-called paramount Power in the region; but the authority which she exerted over the South African Republic certainly at the time of the occurrences here under consideration, in our judgment fell far short of which would be required to make her responsible for the wrong inflicted upon Brown ... . Nowhere is there any clause indicating that Great Britain had any right to interest herself in the internal administration of the country, legislative, executive or judicial; nor is there any evidence that Great Britain ever did undertake to interfere in this way. Indeed the only remedy which Great Britain ever had for maladministration affecting British subjects and those of other Powers, residing in the South African Republic was, as the event proved, to resort to war. If there had been no South African war, we hold that the United States Government would have been obliged to take up Brown's claim with the Government of the Republic and that there would have been no ground for bringing it to the attention of Great Britain. The relation of suzerain did not operate to render Great Britain liable for the acts complained of.

Now therefore: The decision of the Tribunal is that the claim of the United States Government be disallowed.

4. Change of Nationality[170]

When a predecessor state becomes extinct the population takes the nationality of the successor state. However, in other cases leading to succession precision is lacking. There are no uniform rules to apply. It is necessary to look at the treaty between the predecessor and successor state, and their domestic legislation pertaining to nationality in order to determine whether the inhabitants of the territory have taken a new nationality, retained the old, or have both.[171]

---

170 Acquisition of nationality in the absence of state succession is discussed in Chapter 8, Section A on "Individuals" and the importance of nationality for espousal of an international claim is discussed in Chapter 10, Section C.1 on "Espousal and Nationality of Claims."

171 See S.A. Williams, "International Legal Effects of Secession by Quebec," Study No. 8 of the York University Constitutional Reform Project (1991) at 23-29 and D.P. O'Connell, *State Succession in Municipal and International Law* (1967) at 497.

The Providence
(1810) Stewart 186 (N.S. V-Adm.)

[At issue was the effect of the independence of the United States of America upon the allegiance of natural-born subjects to the British Crown.[172]]

DR. CROKE: ... [G]enerally speaking, it is an indisputable maxim of law, that natural allegiance with its duties and the privileges derived from it, is perpetual, unalienable, and indefeasible. But Sir Michael Foster, one of the first authorities in the British law, justly observes, "that though this doctrine of allegiance, founded in birth, may be considered as a good general rule, yet it is not universally true. Cases may be put which will be considered as exceptions to it." It must be admitted to be one of those exceptions, where the tie between the sovereign and the subject is broken; and the connection dissolved by the concurrent acts of the sovereign, to whom it is due, and of the party himself. For all compacts, and the duties and obligations of allegiance are in the nature of a compact, may be dissolved by the mutual consent of all parties interested. A dissolution of this nature took place between the king of Great Britain, and his subjects in the United States, when their independence was acknowledged by the treaty of peace, in the years 1782 and 1783. By the first article of that treaty, His Majesty acknowledged the thirteen States to be free, sovereign, and independent States, and for himself, his heirs, and successors, relinquished all claims to the government, propriety, and territorial rights of the same. This is a complete renunciation of the rights of allegiance, on the part of His Majesty, and a perfect discharge of the inhabitants of that country, from all their obligations as subjects. This treaty was directly authorized by a preceding act of Parliament, 22 Geo. III. c. 46, by which it was enacted, that it should be lawful for His Majesty to conclude a peace with the colonies, any law to the contrary notwithstanding, and was subsequently, though indirectly, confirmed by other acts. There was the sanction therefore of the legislature as well as of the sovereign. On the other hand there was the assent of all the inhabitants of the thirteen colonies, represented and expressed by the ratification of their government, which had been established by their own free choice. From this concurrence of all parties concerned, no act could be more valid, or unexceptionable. The inhabitants of that country, from that time, became aliens to every purpose, and liable to all the disabilities of aliens. As they were no longer bound to any allegiance, so neither were they entitled to any of the privileges of British born subjects.

---

172   See also *Salter v. Hughes* (1864), 5 N.S.R. 409 (C.A.) and *Montgomery v. Graham* (1871), 31 U.C.Q.B. 57 (C.A.).

NOTES

1) In some devolution agreements between former colonial regimes and newly independent states, provision has been made for the inhabitants to choose between the nationalities of the predecessor and successor states. Of specific Canadian interest is the Treaty of Paris, 1763 by which France ceded Canada to Great Britain and made arrangements for French nationals to withdraw or to change their allegiance to the British Crown. The treaty is reported in Chapter 7, Section B.2 on "Territory of Canada."

2) In *Donegani v. Donegani*,[173] it was held that "the cession [of Canada] to Britain involved a change of sovereignty as a result of which the law of England, and not the law of France, would determine the question who were aliens." Note that there was a distinction in English public law between a settled colony and one conquered or ceded. The common law did not automatically apply to the latter. The private law of the former sovereign continued in force until the Crown ordered otherwise.[174] The question as to the extent to which the law of England applied in Canada arose many times until it was settled by the *Quebec Act* of 1774.[175]

3) If the inhabitants of a territory become nationals of the successor state, they are subject to its plenary jurisdiction, apart from international human rights law guarantees.[176] Thus, they will have only that limited recourse to international law.

4) In the face of the growing number of persons dispossessed of their nationality, and thus of the right of access to any country, as a result of so many changes to the states of the world, a Convention on the Reduction of Statelessness was adopted in 1961.[177] This Convention, and the 1999 ILC Draft Articles on the Nationality of Natural Persons in Relation to the Succession of States,[178] are addressed in Chapter 8, Section A.7.

---

173 (1834), 3 Knapp 62; 12 E.R. 571 (P.C.).

174 *Campbell v. Hall* (1774), 1 Cowp. 204; 98 E.R. 1045 (K.B.).

175 14 Geo. III, c. 83, s. 8; R.S.C. 1952, Vol. VI at 6133. In general, see J.-G. Castel, *The Civil Law System of the Province of Quebec* (1962) at 5-35 and especially at 22; also T. Hodgins, "The Law of Allegiance in Canada" (1881) 1 Can. L.T. 1 and *Perlman v. Lieut. Col. Piché* (1918), 54 S.C. 170 (Que.).

176 Shaw, *supra* note 1 at 905.

177 See P. Weis, *Nationality and Statelessness in International Law*, 2d ed. (1979) at 135-60 and D.P. O'Connell, *supra* note 136 at 391-93.

178 *Report of the International Law Commission on the Work of Its 51st Session*, UN GAOR, 54th Sess. Supp. No. 10, U.N. Doc. A/54/10 (1999), chp. IV.

NOTES

CHAPTER THREE

Creation and Ascertainment of International Law

A. SOURCES OF LAW[1]

1. Generally

International law governs relations between independent states. The rules of law binding upon states, therefore, emanate from their own free will as expressed in conventions or by usages generally accepted as expressing principles of law and established in order to regulate the relations between these coexisting independent communities or with a view to the achievement of common aims.

Permanent Court of International Justice, *The Steamship Lotus*[2]

Statute of the International Court of Justice

Article 38

1. The Court, whose function is to decide in accordance with international law such disputes as are submitted to it, shall apply:

(a) international conventions, whether general or particular, establishing rules expressly recognized by the contesting states;

(b) international custom, as evidence of a general practice accepted as law;

(c) the general principles of law recognized by civilized nations;

---

1 See generally Anthony D'Amato, *International Law Sources* (2004); G.M. Danilenko, *Law-Making in the International Community* (1993); George A. Finch, *The Sources of Modern International Law* (1937); Allan E. Gotlieb, *Canadian Treaty-Making* (1968); Anne Marie Jacomy-Millette, *Treaty Law in Canada* (1975); Arnold Duncan McNair, *The Law of Treaties* (1961); Clive Parry, *The Sources and Evidences of International Law* (1965); Max Sorensen, *Les sources du droit international* (1946); G.J.H. van Hoof, *Rethinking the Sources of International Law* (1983); and Hungdah Chiu, "Chinese Views on the Sources of International Law" (1987) 28 Harv. Int'l L.J. 289. See also John H. Currie, *Public International Law* (2001) cc. 3-5; Claude Emanuelli, *Droit international public*, 3d ed. (1998) at 39-127; Pierre-Marie Dupuy, *Droit international public* (1993) at paras. 224-350.

2 From *The Steamship Lotus (France v. Turkey)* (1927), P.C.I.J. (Ser. A) No. 10 at 18.

(d) subject to the provisions of Art. 59, judicial decisions and the teachings of the most highly qualified publicists of the various nations, as subsidiary means for the determination of rules of law.

2. This provision shall not prejudice the power of the Court to decide a case *ex aequo et bono*, if the parties agree thereto.

NOTES

1) Article 59 provides that: "The decision of the Court has no binding force except between the parties and in respect of that particular case."

2) Article 38(1) is considered an authoritative statement of the law-creating processes of international law. In order for the court to apply any asserted rule of positive international law, it must be shown that the rule is the product of one, or more, of the three law-creating processes mentioned in paragraph (a), (b), or (c). These law-creating processes are exclusive for the Court. Under article 38(2), however, the parties to a dispute may request that it be decided *ex aequo et bono* ("in justice and fairness," or "according to what is just and good") rather than on the basis of a strict application of rules of law.

3) Article 38(1)(d), when it refers to "subsidiary means for the determination of rules of law," indicates that decisions of judicial institutions and the teachings of the most highly qualified publicists of the various nations are subsidiary law-determining agencies and not law-creating processes. As Schwarzenberger has pointed out: "Whereas, in the case of the law-creating processes, the emphasis lies on the forms by which any particular rule of international law is created, in the case of the law-determining agencies it is on how an alleged rule is to be verified."[3] In other words, they are evidence by reference to which the existence and contents of the rules of positive international law are determined.

4) Does article 38(1) contain an exhaustive enumeration of the law-creating processes or are there others? For instance, are decisions of international bodies, such as the United Nations, a new law-creating process or manifestations of existing law-creating processes? See Section E.2 on "Law Making through International Organizations."

5) Article 38(1) makes no hierarchical distinction among the three law-creating processes. They are all of equal authority. The potential exists, therefore, for a conflict between rules from different sources. As between the parties, a treaty could possibly override pre-existing custom and a subsequent custom might supplant a treaty. Quite often a conflict between a treaty and custom is more apparent than real; it may be resolved by interpreting the rules so as to avoid conflict. Frequently, the treaty provision is so much more specific than the customary rule that it may be applied without doing harm to the integrity of the more general principle. International tribunals have had few occasions to express themselves on the interplay of several applicable rules. An exceptional instance was the *English Channel Arbitration*[4] concerning the delimitation of

---

3   Georg Schwarzenberger, *International Law*, 3d ed. (1957) vol. 1 at 27.

4   (1977), 18 R.I.A.A. 3 at 36-37. And see Michael B. Akehurst, "The Hierarchy of the Sources of International Law" (1974-75) 47 Brit. Y.B. Int'l L. 273.

the continental shelf between the United Kingdom and France. It took place in 1977 while the U.N. Conference on the Law of the Sea was still in progress. The award states:

47. The Court is directed by Article 2 of the Arbitration Agreement to decide the course of the boundary "in accordance with the rules of international law applicable in the matter as between the Parties"; and, as the Parties agree, the rules of international law to be applied by the Court under this rubric are unquestionably the rules in force today. At the same time, the Court recognises both the importance of the evolution of the law of the sea which is now in progress and the possibility that a development in customary law may, under certain conditions, evidence the assent of the States concerned to the modification, or even termination, of previously existing treaty rights and obligations. But the Continental Shelf Convention of 1958 entered into force as between the Parties little more than a decade ago. Moreover, the information before the Court contains references by the French Republic and the United Kingdom, as well as by other States, to the Convention as an existing treaty in force which are of quite recent date. Consequently, only the most conclusive indications of the intention of the parties to the 1958 Convention to regard it as terminated could warrant this Court in treating it as obsolete and inapplicable as between the French Republic and the United Kingdom in the present matter. In the opinion of the Court, however, neither the records of the Third United Nations Conference on the Law of the Sea nor the practice of States outside the Conference provide any such conclusive indication that the Continental Shelf Convention of 1958 is today considered by its parties to be already obsolete and no longer applicable as a treaty in force.

48. The Court accordingly finds that the Geneva Convention of 1958 on the Continental Shelf is a treaty in force, the provisions of which are applicable as between the Parties to the present proceedings under Article 2 of the Arbitration Agreement. This finding, the Court wishes at the same time to emphasise, does not mean that it regards itself as debarred from taking any account in these proceedings of recent developments in customary law. On the contrary, the Court has no doubt that it should take due account of the evolution of the law of the sea in so far as this may be relevant in the context of the present case.

6) It is possible that the same rule may be derived from more than one of the law-creating processes. For example, law-making treaties often include provisions that are codifications of custom. In such instances, does treaty law supervene over customary law? In *Military Activities In and Against Nicaragua*,[5] the ICJ rejected the view put forward by the United States that the existence of certain principles in the U.N. Charter or other multilateral treaties precluded the possibility that similar rules might exist independently in customary international law either because existing customary rules had been incorporated into the Charter or because the Charter influenced the later adoption of customary rules with a corresponding content. "[E]ven if a treaty norm and a customary norm relevant to the ... dispute were to have exactly the same content, this would not be a reason for the Court to take the view that the operation of the treaty process must

---

5   *Military Activities In and Against Nicaragua (Nicaragua v. United States)*, [1986] I.C.J. Rep. 14. In this case it was decided that the United States had violated its customary international law obligations (a) not to intervene in the affairs of Nicaragua and (b) not to use force against it.

necessarily deprive the customary norm of its separate applicability."[6] Customary international law continues to exist alongside treaty law. The Court elaborated on this point, giving the following example:[7]

> There are a number of reasons for considering that, even if two norms belonging to two sources of international law appear identical in content, and even if the States in question are bound by these rules both on the level of treaty-law and on that of customary international law, these norms retain a separate existence. This is so from the standpoint of their applicability. In a legal dispute affecting two States, one of them may argue that the applicability of a treaty rule to its own conduct depends on the other State's conduct in respect of the application of other rules, on other subjects, also included in the same treaty. For example, if a State exercises its right to terminate or suspend the operation of a treaty on the ground of the violation by the other party of a "provision essential to the accomplishment of the object or purpose of the treaty" (in the words of Art. 60, para. 3(b), of the Vienna Convention on the Law of Treaties), it is exempted, *vis-à-vis* the other State, from a rule of treaty-law because of the breach by that other State of a different rule of treaty law. But if the two rules in question also exist as rules of customary international law, the failure of the one State to apply the one rule does not justify the other State in declining to apply the other rule. Rules which are identical in treaty law and in customary international law are also distinguishable by reference to the methods of interpretation and application. A State may accept a rule contained in a treaty not simply because it favours the application of the rule itself, but also because the treaty establishes what that State regards as desirable institutions or mechanisms to ensure implementation of the rule. Thus, if that rule parallels a rule of customary international law, two rules of the same content are subject to separate treatment as regards the organs competent to verify their implementation, depending on whether they are customary rules or treaty rules. The present dispute illustrates this point.

It will, therefore, be clear that customary international law continues to exist and to apply, separately from international treaty law, even where the two categories of law have an identical content.

7) A distinction is often made between formal sources of law (from which rules of law derive their force, such as in Canada an act of Parliament or a regulation), and material sources of law (those that supply the substance of the rules of law—for instance, the speeches, committee hearings and government reports during the passage of a bill through Parliament, or the departmental materials and Cabinet minutes in the preparation of new regulations). Although law-making treaties may resemble a formal source of law, in the opinion of some writers, it is difficult to maintain the distinction in the field of international law, because there is no constitutional machinery, like a legislature, for the creation of rules of international law.[8]

---

6   *Ibid.* at para. 175. And see para. 177.

7   *Ibid.* at paras. 178-179.

8   See Ian Brownlie, *Principles of Public International Law*, 6th ed. (2003) at 1-4.

2. Soft Law and Jus Cogens

This chapter addresses the law-making sources identified in article 38 (treaties, custom and general principles of law), and then considers other sources of legal norms: first the law-determining mechanisms referred to in article 38(1)(d), and then the potential law-making role of international organizations. However, this fairly traditional survey of the sources of international law should be understood against the backdrop of the tremendous variety and richness of the means by which states, and increasingly also non-state actors, develop norms that affect the functioning of the international system.[9]

The rules that emanate from the law-creating processes listed in article 38 are sometimes referred to as "hard law," or *lex lata*. The term *lex ferenda*, in contrast, refers to norms that have not yet achieved the status of settled law. *Lex ferenda* is sometimes used interchangeably with the term "soft law," but the latter is perhaps more accurately employed to describe instruments that are not legally binding *per se*, though they affect the conduct of international relations by states and may lead to the development of new international law.[10]

The Final Act of the Conference on Security and Cooperation in Europe 1975, better known as the Helsinki Accords,[11] and the OECD Guidelines for Multilateral Enterprises[12] are examples of soft-law instruments, and illustrate that the scope of such instruments is undefined and varied. The Helsinki Accords, for instance, represented an understanding between states how they might be expected to behave—traditional territory for hard-law treaties, in fact—while the OECD Guidelines involved transnational corporations—that is, non-state actors who lack international legal personality to conclude treaties.

These instruments are called "soft law" because they are not directly enforceable in domestic courts or international tribunals. They may, however, be very influential. Consider the influence of the Stockholm Declaration on the Human Environment as the foundation of modern international environmental law even though it is only a declaration of principles and not a treaty.[13] Further, the objectives of hard law, like the umbrella provisions of the U.N. Convention on the Law of the Sea, often cannot be achieved without the secondary means of non-treaty instruments.[14]

---

9   See generally Eibe Riedel, "Standards and Sources: Farewell to the Exclusivity of the Sources Triad in International Law" (1991, II) 2 E.J.I.L. 58.

10   See generally Oscar Schachter, "The Twilight Existence of Nonbinding International Agreements," Editorial Comment (1977) 71 A.J.I.L. 296; Ignaz Seidl-Hohenveldern, "International Economic 'Soft Law' " (1979) 163 Rec. des Cours 165; Tadeusz Gruchalla-Wesierski, "A Framework for Understanding 'Soft Law' " (1984) 30 McGill L.J. 37; C.M. Chinkin, "The Challenge of Soft Law: Development and Change in International Law" (1989) 38 I.C.L.Q. 850; Pierre-Marie Dupuy, "Soft Law and the International Law of the Environment" (1991) 12 Mich. J. Int'l L. 420; and Harmut Hillgenberg, "A Fresh Look at Soft Law" (1999) 10 E.J.I.L. 499. See also Dinah Shelton, ed., *Commitment and Compliance: The Role of Non-Binding Norms in the International Legal System* (2000).

11   (1975) 14 I.L.M. 1292.

12   (1976) 15 I.L.M. 969. See also the discussion of "International Codes of Conduct," in Section E.2 below.

13   Reproduced and discussed in Chapter 14, Section B.2.

14   See van Hoof, *supra* note 1 at 187ff.

A further category of norms not mentioned in article 38 of the ICJ Statute should be mentioned at the outset. The phrase *jus cogens* refers to an open set of peremptory norms of international law.[15] A peremptory norm is defined in article 53 of the Vienna Convention on the Law of Treaties as a "norm accepted and recognized by the international community of States as a whole as a norm from which no derogation is permitted and which can be modified only by a subsequent norm of general international law having the same character." Some principles of international law that have the status of *jus cogens* can be found in treaties, others in custom. Michael Byers has argued that *jus cogens* rules are of a constitutional character: "Nowhere else in the international legal system is the ability of some rules to limit the ability of States to develop, maintain or change other rules, or to prevent them from violating fundamental rules of international public policy, so clear."[16]

There is some uncertainty regarding which norms fall into the *jus cogens* category. A core group of rules can be readily identified, the main characteristic of which is their fundamental importance to social order. On this ground, the pre-eminent example must be the prohibition against the use of force reiterated in article 2 of the U.N. Charter. Others, such as the principle *pacta sunt servanda*, reflect what may be regarded as necessary elements for the existence and operation of the international legal system. Yet others can only be described as norms that have become so widely and deeply imbedded in international law that they are inviolable. For instance, it is unimaginable that any two states could validly agree to divide control of the oceans in violation of the principle of freedom of navigation on the high seas. Finally, and perhaps most importantly, peremptory norms can also derive from elementary considerations of human dignity. Most commentators agree that the prohibitions against genocide, slavery, and torture are *jus cogens* norms. What other rules and principles may also be advanced for inclusion?

---

15   See Ian Sinclair, *The Vienna Convention on the Law of Treaties*, 2d ed. (1984) at 203-26; Lauri Hannikainen, *Peremptory Norms (Jus Cogens) in International Law* (1988); Ronald St. J. MacDonald, "Fundamental Norms in Contemporary International Law" (1987) 25 Can. Y.B. Int'l L. 115; Gennady M. Danilenko, "International Jus Cogens: Issues of Law-Making" (1991) 2 E.J.I.L. 42; Jerzy Sztucki, *Jus Cogens and the Vienna Convention on the Law of Treaties* (1974); Christos L. Rozakis, *The Concept of Jus Cogens in the Law of Treaties* (1976); Georg Schwarzenberger, "International Jus Cogens in International Law" (1964-65) 43 Tex. L. Rev. 455; Gordon A. Christenson, "The World Court and Jus Cogens" (1987) 81 A.J.I.L. 93; Karen Parker & Lyn Beth Neylon, "Jus Cogens: Compelling the Law of Human Rights" (1989) 12 Hastings Int'l & Comp. L. Rev. 411; and F.A. Mann, "The Doctrine of Jus Cogens in International Law" in *Further Studies in International Law* (1990) 84. See also *Barcelona Traction Case (Second Phase) (Belgium v. Spain)*, [1970] I.C.J. Rep. 3 at 32; *Reservations to the Convention on Genocide*, Advisory Opinion, [1951] I.C.J. Rep. 15 at 23; and *Nicaragua v. United States, supra* note 5 at 100, 113.

16   Michael Byers, "Conceptualising the Relationship between Jus Cogens and Erga Omnes Rules" (1997) 66 Nordic J. Int'l L. 211 at 220. This article is a useful consideration of the relationship between *jus cogens* norms and obligations *erga omnes* (obligations owed by a state to the international community as a whole), a topic that has been the subject of considerable academic commentary. Byers argues that *jus cogens* rules are necessarily of an *erga omnes* character, but *erga omnes* obligations need not necessarily be *jus cogens* rules. See also Alfred P. Rubin, "Actio Popularis, Jus Cogens and Offenses Erga Omnes?" (2000-1) 35 New Eng. L. Rev. 265.

B. TREATIES

1. Generally

Although it is generally stated that treaties are a major law-creating process or source of international law, a distinction is sometimes drawn between law-making treaties and treaty-contracts. Law-making treaties are treaties in which a substantial number of states have declared what the law is or should be on a particular topic (one example is the 1961 Vienna Convention on Diplomatic Relations[17]). Such agreements may codify, define, interpret, or abolish existing customary or conventional rules of international law or create new rules for future international conduct. They may also create international institutions. Treaty-contracts, whether bilateral or multilateral, do not create general rules of international law. They create special rights and obligations like private law contracts by virtue of the principle *pacta sunt servanda*, which is a general principle of law (see the discussion in Section B.3 on "Legal Effects of Treaties"). However, in some cases, treaty-contracts may lead to the formation of rules of customary international law or be evidence of the existence of such rules (see Section C on "Custom"). The distinction between law-making treaties and treaty-contracts could be questioned on the ground that both types are of a purely contractual character since they are based on mutual consent.

The basic principles of the law of treaties are set down in the 1969 Vienna Convention on the Law of Treaties, which came into force, including for Canada, in 1980.[18] A memorandum prepared by the Department of External Affairs dated June 4, 1970, expressed this opinion of the Vienna Convention:

> This Convention constitutes a law-making treaty laying down the fundamental principles of contemporary treaty law. Because of the paramount importance of treaties as a source of the international legal obligations binding upon states and the diversity and comprehensiveness of the interlocking network of treaties which today regulate the major part of transactions between states and serve to establish the relationships among them, the Convention must be viewed as virtually the constitutional basis, second in importance only to the U.N. Charter, of the international community of states.

Vienna Convention on the Law of Treaties
Articles 1, 2, 3, 5, and 6
Reproduced in the Documentary Supplement

---

17 500 U.N.T.S. 95, reproduced in the Documentary Supplement.

18 1155 U.N.T.S. 331, reproduced in the Documentary Supplement. See generally Anthony I. Aust, *Modern Treaty Law and Practice* (2000); T.O. Elias, *The Modern Law of Treaties* (1974); Gotlieb, *supra* note 1; James McLeod Hendry, *Treaties and Federal Constitutions* (1955); Peter W. Hogg, *Constitutional Law of Canada*, 4th ed. (1997) c. 11; Jacomy-Millette, *supra* note 1; McNair, *supra* note 1; and Sinclair, *supra* note 15.

NOTES

1) Reading articles 2 and 3 together, there appear to be three essential elements of a treaty. The parties must be subjects of international law, they must intend to create binding obligations under international law, and their agreement must be governed by international law.

In the *Anglo Iranian Oil Company Case*,[19] the ICJ considered the nature and essential elements of a treaty as distinguished from a concession contract:

> The Court cannot accept the view that the contract signed between the Iranian Government and the Anglo-Persian Oil Company has a double character. It is nothing more than a concessionary contract between a government and a foreign corporation. The United Kingdom Government is not a party to the contract; there is no privity of contract between the Government of Iran and the Government of the United Kingdom. Under the contract the Iranian Government cannot claim from the United Kingdom Government any rights which it may claim from the Company, nor can it be called upon to perform towards the United Kingdom Government any rights which it may claim from the Company, nor can it be called upon to perform towards the United Kingdom Government any obligations which it is bound to perform towards the Company. The document bearing the signatures of the representatives of the Iranian Government and the Company has a single purpose: the purpose of regulating the relations between that Government and the Company in regard to the concession. It does not regulate in any way the relations between the two Governments.

2) Do agreements between states always constitute treaties? It is frequently assumed[20] that when two states make an agreement they intend to create binding obligations at international law, *viz.* a treaty. However, that presumption may be rebutted by evidence of the parties' intent that they did not mean their agreement to have legal force. One of the most well-known examples is the Helsinki Accords[21] concluded at the 1975 Conference on Security and Cooperation in Europe, to which both the United States and the former Soviet Union were parties. Low-level intergovernmental arrangements of an administrative character are often concluded as memoranda of understanding that are not intended to have binding legal effect. Though such agreements are not opposable at law against an errant party, they do create standards and expectations of behaviour by which state conduct is measured. They exert an influence on interstate relations as a form of soft law.

3) The Vienna Convention uses the term "treaty," as the generic term, to describe an international agreement. However,

> in addition to "treaty," "convention" and "protocol," one not infrequently finds titles such as "declaration," "charter," "covenant," "pact," "act," "statute," "agreement," "concordat," whilst names like "declaration," "agreement" and "*modus vivendi*" may well be found given

---

19　[1952] I.C.J. Rep. 93 at 112.

20　See F.A. Mann, "Reflections on a Commercial Law of Nations" (1957) 33 Brit. Y.B. Int'l L. 20 at 30-32; cf. J.E.S. Fawcett, "The Legal Character of International Agreements" (1953) 30 Brit. Y.B. Int'l L. 381 at 385; and Kelvin Widdows, "What Is an Agreement in International Law" (1979) 50 Brit. Y.B. Int'l L. 117.

21　(1975) 14 I.L.M. 1292. The Accords stated that they were "not eligible for registration under Article 102" of the U.N. Charter as required of treaties.

both to formal and less formal types of agreements. As to the latter, their nomenclature is almost illimitable, even if some names such as "agreement," "exchange of notes," "exchange of letters," "memorandum of agreement," or "agreed minute" may be more common than others. It is true that some types of instruments are used more frequently for some purposes rather than others; it is also true that some titles are more frequently attached to some types of transaction rather than to others. But there is no exclusive or systematic use of nomenclature for particular types of transaction.[22]

4) Pursuant to article 1, the 1969 Vienna Convention on the Law of Treaties applies to treaties between states. Treaties with or between international organizations are governed by the Convention on the Law of Treaties between States and International Organizations or between International Organizations done at Vienna on March 20, 1986.[23] This Convention parallels the wording of the 1969 Convention with alterations to take account of the extension of its rules to international organizations, and substantive changes where these are essential. It has not yet been adopted by Canada.

5) A treaty is usually written, and the Vienna Convention applies only to treaties in written form (article 2(1)(a)). However, there is nothing to prevent an international engagement being made orally, provided that the representatives of the parties are duly qualified. The obvious danger with such oral agreements is the difficulty of proof of the actual terms when disputes arise under them. In this connection, see the *Legal Status of Eastern Greenland Case*[24] between Denmark and Norway, which involved the question of whether a unilateral oral "declaration" was binding on the party whose minister made it. "Sometimes 'oral' and 'tacit' agreements are equated with each other. Oral agreements may be express or may in some cases be 'tacit.' In a tacit agreement, the fact that an agreement has to come into being may be left to be implied from the actions or statements of the parties rather than made explicit by them."[25]

Nuclear Tests Cases
Australia v. France; New Zealand v. France
[1974] I.C.J. Rep. 253 at 267-70

[France, not being a party to the Nuclear Test Ban Treaty, conducted nuclear tests in the atmosphere in the South Pacific. Australia and New Zealand protested and commenced these cases. Before they were heard, France ended tests and unilaterally announced it would not hold any more in the atmosphere. The Court treated the claims

---

22 "Report of the Commission on the Work of the Second Part of Its Seventeenth Session to the General Assembly" (U.N. Doc. A/6309/Rev.1) in *Yearbook of the International Law Commission 1966*, vol. 2 (1967) at 188 (U.N. Doc. A/CN.4/Ser.A/1966/Add.1).

23 (1986) 25 I.L.M. 543. See P.K. Menon, *The Law of Treaties Between States and International Organizations* (1992).

24 (1933), P.C.I.J. (Ser. A/B) No. 53 at 22, reported in Chapter 7, Section B.1 on "Land Territory: Acquisition of Territory."

25 Gotlieb, *supra* note 1 at 22.

of Australia and New Zealand as moot as a result of its construction of the legal effect of France's announcements, as follows:]

THE COURT: ...

43. It is well recognized that declarations made by way of unilateral acts, concerning legal or factual situations, may have the effect of creating legal obligations. Declarations of this kind may be, and often are, very specific. When it is the intention of the State making the declaration that it should become bound according to its terms, that intention confers on the declaration the character of a legal undertaking, the State being thenceforth legally required to follow a course of conduct consistent with the declaration. An undertaking of this kind, if given publicly, and with an intent to be bound, even though not made within the context of international negotiations, is binding. In these circumstances, nothing in the nature of a *quid pro quo* nor any subsequent acceptance of the declaration, nor even any reply or reaction from other States, is required for the declaration to take effect, since such a requirement would be inconsistent with the strictly unilateral nature of the juridical act by which the pronouncement by the State was made.

44. Of course, not all unilateral acts imply obligation; but a State may choose to take up a certain position in relation to a particular matter with the intention of being bound—the intention is to be ascertained by interpretation of the act. When States make statements by which their freedom of action is to be limited, a restrictive interpretation is called for.

45. With regard to the question of form, it should be observed that this is not a domain in which international law imposes any special or strict requirements. Whether a statement is made orally or in writing makes no essential difference, for such statements made in particular circumstances may create commitments in international law, which does not require that they should be couched in written form ... .

46. One of the basic principles governing the creation and performance of legal obligations, whatever their source, is the principle of good faith. Trust and confidence are inherent in international co-operation, in particular in an age when this co-operation in many fields is becoming increasingly essential. Just as the very rule of *pacta sunt servanda* in the law of treaties is based on good faith, so also is the binding character of an international obligation assumed by unilateral declaration. Thus interested States may take cognizance of unilateral declarations and place confidence in them, and are entitled to require that the obligation thus created be respected ... .

49. Of the statements by the French Government now before the Court, the most essential are clearly those made by the President of the Republic. There can be no doubt, in view of his functions, that his public communications or statements, oral or written, as Head of State, are in international relations acts of the French State. His statements, and those of members of the French Government acting under his authority ... constitute a whole. Thus, in whatever form these statements were expressed, they must be held to constitute an engagement of the State, having regard to their intention and to the circumstances in which they were made ... .

51. In announcing that the 1974 series of atmospheric tests would be the last, the French Government conveyed to the world at large, including the Applicant, its

intention effectively to terminate these tests. It was bound to assume that other States might take note of these statements and rely on their being effective. The validity of these statements and their legal consequences must be considered within the general framework of the security of international intercourse, and the confidence and trust which are so essential in the relations among States. It is from the actual substance of these statements, and from the circumstances attending their making, that the legal implications of the unilateral act must be deduced. The objects of these statements are clear and they were addressed to the international community as a whole, and the Court holds that they constitute an undertaking possessing legal effect. ... It is true that the French Government has consistently maintained, for example in a Note dated 7 February 1973 from the French Ambassador in Canberra to the Prime Minister and Minister for Foreign Affairs of Australia, that it "has the conviction that its nuclear experiments have not violated any rule of international law," nor did France recognize that it was bound by any rule of international law to terminate its tests, but this does not affect the legal consequences of the statements examined above. The Court finds that the unilateral undertaking resulting from these statements cannot be interpreted as having been made in implicit reliance on an arbitrary power of reconsideration. The Court finds further that the French Government has undertaken an obligation with precise nature and limits of which must be understood in accordance with the actual terms in which they have been publicly expressed.

NOTE

Whether legal obligations are created by a unilateral declaration will depend on the intention of the state in making it. No special form for making the declaration is required nor is any *quid pro quo* or acceptance or reaction from other states necessary. The Legal Bureau of the Department of External Affairs expressed the following view in 1980:

We recognize that a State may incur obligations or acquire rights on the plane of international law by unilateral acts, for example, by the acceptance in writing of rights or obligations as a "third State" under the terms of a treaty, or by a declaration under Article 36 (the Optional Clause) of the Statute of the International Court of Justice (a unilateral act by which a State makes an offer to eligible parties).

Unilateral acts of the type discussed in the previous paragraph obviously create obligations in international law which are binding until modified or withdrawn. They should be distinguished from a unilateral declaration of policy or a statement of intention. Declarations of this kind are not normally intended to give rise to obligations which can be relied upon by other States.[26]

---

26 See "Canadian Treaty Practice" (1980) 18 Can. Y.B. Int'l L. 312 at 313. See also Alfred P. Rubin, "The International Legal Effects of Unilateral Declarations" (1977) 71 A.J.I.L. 1.

Canadian Treaty Practice

While international law does not prescribe any specific form or type of international instruments, states are sometimes bound by their constitutional or internal laws to adopt certain patterns for particular agreements. Canadian law has no provision relating to the form or type of agreement, which is therefore largely a matter of convenience to the Canadian Government. In fact, Canadian practice over the years has largely adopted the following types:

(a)   International agreements between heads of states;

(b)   Intergovernmental agreements; and

(c)   Exchanges of notes.

Gotlieb[27] indicates that between 1907 and 1967 Canada has used the following types:

act	general act
additional protocol	instrument
administrative agreement	joint statement
agreed minute	long-term agreement
agreement	long-term arrangement
arrangement	memorandum of agreement
articles of agreement	memorandum of understanding
charter	*modus vivendi*
commercial agreement	payments agreement
constitution	*procès-verbal*
convention	protocol
decision	provisional arrangement
declaration	special protocol
declaration of understanding	statute
exchange of letters	supplementary exchange of notes
exchange of notes	supplementary protocol
executive agreement	treaty
final act	trust agreement
financial agreement	

He also points out that "over seventy per cent of all Canadian bilateral treaties have, since the last war, been in exchange-of-notes form."[28]

The term "treaty" is seldom used by Canada except in relation to peace, neutrality, arms control, and United States–Canada water problems. The term "convention" is far more common. International agreements employing the term "treaty" or "convention" almost invariably require ratification.

A voluntary restraint, memorandum of understanding, or assurance must be distinguished from a treaty, which is binding upon the parties. Thus, the letter from the

27   Gotlieb, *supra* note 1 at 21.

28   Gotlieb, *supra* note 1 at 84.

Japanese Ambassador describing the voluntary restraints that the Japanese government was applying on the export of certain products to Canada in 1965 or the memorandum of understanding between the governments of Canada and Hong Kong respecting the restriction of certain cotton textiles exports to Canada did not create binding obligations at international law. In the case of China, the Chinese Communist State Trading Corporation agreed, as part of the conditions of a long-term wheat agreement, to limit annual exports to Canada of sensitive items. This voluntary restraint was not a treaty obligation.

The distinction between treaties and arrangements or understandings has been described by the Canadian government in the following terms:

> In Canadian practice, arrangements or understandings between the governments of two or more States, no matter what form they take (e.g., a Memorandum of Understanding or an Exchange of Notes or Letters) create commitments of a political and moral character and are not binding in, or governed by, international law. Obviously the mere fact that the instrument is called a Memorandum of Understanding is not decisive in itself, but a conscious effort is made in every instance to ensure that instruments of this kind do not embody clauses of legal obligation. "Will" is used in place of "shall" and the form of the instrument is kept as simple as possible. It is our practice to register these instruments in a Register of Understandings and Arrangements separate from the Treaty Register. They are not published in the Canada Treaty Series but copies are available on request.
>
> Cooperative arrangements at the technical level are frequently concluded between Canadian Government departments or agencies and their counterparts in other countries. Such arrangements, which have multiplied in recent years, constitute an important means of enabling Canadian Government departments and agencies to function more effectively by developing close working-level links with departments and agencies of foreign Governments in fields of common interest.
>
> On occasion, when department-to-department or agency-to-agency arrangements are under negotiation, a need will arise to provide for the settlement of disputes or the handling of claims for personal injury or property damage. Our practice is to embody such clauses in a covering exchange of notes which constitutes an international agreement.
>
> We understand "implementing agreements" as meaning subsidiary arrangements concluded under an umbrella agreement which constitutes a treaty. A typical example would be a development aid or economic cooperation agreement which envisages the need for project agreements. Such subsidiary arrangements are not regarded as treaties and wording is customarily inserted to specify that they shall be considered as administrative arrangements.
>
> The number of government-to-government, department-to-department and agency-to-agency arrangements has increased greatly in recent years. Because of this trend, Canada would welcome the development of some basic ground rules regarding such instruments as Memoranda of Understanding, in particular an understanding that normally they cannot be regarded as creating legal obligations governed by international law.[29]

---

29 "Practice in International Law during 1979 as Reflected in Public Correspondence and Statements of the Department of External Affairs," compiled by H.L. Legault (1980) 18 Can. Y.B. Int'l Law 301 at 312-15.

2. Treaty Making

Conclusion of a Treaty

The conclusion of a treaty is attended by a number of formalities. In the first place, the representative of a state must have "full powers" to give the consent of his or her state (see article 7 of the Vienna Convention reproduced in the Documentary Supplement) and if she or he does not, his or her agreement is without legal effect unless afterward confirmed by that state (article 8). Second, the mode of adoption of the treaty, whether by consensus or voting, has to be agreed upon (article 9). Third, the means to authenticate the definitive text, or texts if the original is in several languages, must be settled (article 10). Finally, the particular steps to express consent to the treaty need to be set down (articles 11-16). Signature is the usual choice, although an exchange of instruments may constitute a bilateral treaty. Multilateral treaties frequently require more than the signature of a representative at the negotiations, demanding the subsequent confirmation by ratification, acceptance, or approval of the state. Typically, a multilateral treaty will also permit a state, which did not sign the agreement, subsequently to accede to it. The process of giving consent is often extended even further by separating the negotiations from the act of signature. A multilateral treaty may state that it will be open for signature at a particular place from a certain future date for a stated time. At the end of the negotiating conference, there may be a signing ceremony but these signatures will only adopt the final act of the conference, which will include the authentic text of the treaty.

Note, however, that even when a treaty requires ratification, acceptance, or approval, signature has some legal effect. Article 18 of the Vienna Convention imposes an obligation on a state that has signed such a treaty "to refrain from acts that would defeat the object and purpose" of the treaty, until it makes its intention clear not to become a party to the treaty.

The Canadian procedure for treaty making on the international plane follows the steps outlined above. However, the constitutional division of powers between the federal and provincial governments complicates Canada's involvement in the conclusion and implementation of many treaties. The problems of treaty making for Canada are fully discussed in Chapter 4, Section C on "Treaties in Canada."

Ratification

Many agreements come into force upon being signed, while others, including most multilateral law-making treaties, become effective only upon subsequent ratification—that is, formal confirmation by the signatory states. In general, important treaties such as peace treaties, alliance treaties, and trade agreements require ratification. Whether a particular treaty requires ratification is determined by the treaty itself. However, in the unusual event that a treaty does not specify whether consent to be bound will be expressed by signature or ratification, the Vienna Convention does not stipulate which will suffice.

Ratification processes are an internal constitutional matter for each country and they may frequently differ from one country to another. In Canada, ratification is part of the royal prerogative and is exercised by the Executive, in this case expressed by means of an Order in Council issued by the Governor General in Council, which authorizes the Minister of Foreign Affairs to sign an instrument of ratification. Ratification is then effected by the delivery to the other party (in the case of a bilateral agreement) of an instrument of ratification signed by the Minister of Foreign Affairs. An instrument called a Protocol of Exchange is customarily signed at the time the exchange of instruments of ratification takes place.

Canadian law and practice does not require parliamentary approval for ratification. For certain important classes of agreements, the Canadian government of the day may decide to seek parliamentary approval prior to ratification. This, it should be appreciated, is not a constitutional requirement but a conscious and deliberate decision by the government. It does not mean that Parliament ratifies the agreements in question but rather that, because of their intrinsic importance, it is thought desirable for Parliament to have an opportunity to consider and approve them, by means of a joint resolution of the Commons and Senate, before the Executive ratifies the particular instruments. The categories for which, in the past, parliamentary approval has been sought prior to ratification fall roughly into four general groups involving:

(1) military or economic sanctions;

(2) large expenditures of public funds or important financial or economic implications;

(3) political considerations of a far-reaching character; and

(4) obligations the performance of which will affect private rights in Canada.

To say that in the past parliamentary approval has been sought for these types of treaties is not to suggest it will be regularly in the future. The practice of different governments has been varied. Cultural agreements have never been considered to fall within the categories enumerated above and no cultural agreement concluded by Canada has been submitted to Parliament for approval prior to ratification.

The Department of Foreign Affairs has adopted a simple one-page format for Canadian instruments of ratification of bilateral treaties, of which the following is an example.

> WHEREAS an Agreement of Social Security was signed at Toronto on November 17, 1977 by duly authorized representatives of the Government of Canada and the Government of Italy,
>
> The Government of Canada, having considered the Agreement, hereby confirms and ratifies it and undertakes to carry out the provisions set forth therein.[30]

Publication and Registration

Once an international agreement has come into force, it is also registered with the Secretariat of the United Nations, as required by article 102 of the U.N. Charter, and article 80 of the Vienna Convention on the Law of Treaties (both of which are reproduced in the Documentary Supplement). International agreements thus registered with the Secretariat are published in the *United Nations Treaty Series* (formerly *League of Nations Treaty Series 1920-1945*).

---

30 On the necessity or absence of ratification, see *Chateau Gai Wines Ltd. v. Institut National des Appellations d'Origine des Vins et Eaux de Vie*, [1975] 1 S.C.R. 190.

In Canada, the Department of Foreign Affairs maintains up-to-date records on the status of all treaties affecting Canada. International agreements governed by international law to which Canada is a signatory or party are indexed in the *Canada Treaty Register*, kept as a file in the Department of Foreign Affairs. The *Treaty Register* contains particulars of the date and place of signature of a treaty, the dates of tabling in, or approval by, Parliament, together with ratifications or accessions, if applicable, and information on entry into force, reservations or declarations, subsequent amendments, and termination. Non-binding arrangements entered into by Canada, such as memoranda of understandings, are indexed in a separate *Register of Understandings and Arrangements*.

Since 1928, international agreements to which Canada is a party are published after they have come into force in an annual treaty series called the *Canada Treaty Series*. The annual report that the Minister of Foreign Affairs is required by statute to make to Parliament contains a list of all international agreements that Canada has entered into during the course of the year covered by the report. Current treaty developments are also brought to Parliament's attention through tabling various international agreements that Canada signs or to which it adheres, or by periodic listing of Orders in Council including those authorizing signature of an agreement or its ratification.

Recent treaty activities of Canada are outlined in an annual digest of practice in the back pages of the *Canadian Yearbook of International Law*.[31] The status of Canada's treaty relations as of January 1988 may be discovered in *Treaties in Force for Canada*. The text of international agreements that require implementation is often found as an appendix to the federal or provincial implementing statute.

International agreements concluded by the United Kingdom that are binding on Canada may be found in the U.K. Treaty Series 1892. Canadian international agreements and instruments of ratification for the period 1875-1939 may also be found in the "Prefix to Statutes" included in the federal statutes for that period. For international agreements concluded with the United States of America, it is also convenient to consult the annual edition of *Treaties in Force* published by the United States Government.

As to the proof of treaties in Canadian courts, the *Canada Evidence Act*,[32] section 21 states that

> 21. evidence of a treaty to which Canada is a party, may be given in all or any of the following ways:
>
> a) by the production of a copy of the *Canada Gazette*, or a volume of the Acts of Parliament purporting to contain a copy of the treaty ... or a notice thereof; ...
>
> c) by the production of a copy of the treaty purporting to be published by the Queen's Printer.

---

31   They are also available online: Canada Treaty Information <http://www.treaty-accord.gc.ca/treaties_clf/>. Earlier Canadian treaties may be located by reference to Christian L. Wiktor, *Canadian Treaty Calendar 1928–1978* (1983) vol. 1-2, supplemented for the period 1979–2003 by Christian L. Wiktor, *Index to Canadian Treaties 1979–2003* (2003). See also Christian L. Wiktor, *Multilateral Treaty Calendar 1648–1995* (1998), which details the location and status of every multilateral treaty since the Treaty of Westphalia in 1648 through 1995.

32   R.S.C. 1985, c. C-5.

Entry into Force

The date an agreement enters into force internationally varies according to the intention of the parties and may be:

(1) On ratification or a given period after that event,[33] or

(2) If ratification is unnecessary, a treaty may come into force immediately or in a given period after signature, or

(3) In the case of Exchange of Notes, normally the date of the second note, or

(4) In the case of a multilateral treaty, it is usually upon ratification by a given number of states as stated in the text of the treaty. For instance, although the U.N. Convention on the Law of the Sea was signed by over 150 states in 1982, by virtue of article 308 it did not enter into force until 12 months after the deposit of the 60th instrument of ratification, which was in 1994. On occasion, a treaty may provide for a more complex formula. For example, article 25 of the Kyoto Protocol to the United Nations Framework Convention on Climate Change required ratification by 55 Parties to the Convention, but added the requirement that the states ratifying must account for at least 55 per cent of the total carbon dioxide emissions for 1990 of the developed country Parties to the Convention. It entered into force on February 16, 2005, 90 days after the deposit of the Russian Federation's instrument of ratification.

The Vienna Convention article 24 reiterates that the manner and time of a treaty's entry into force depends upon the intentions of the parties, but, failing any explicit arrangements, it will take effect as soon as consent to be bound has been given by all the parties. Articles 25 and 28 recognize that exceptionally, if the parties so indicate, a treaty may be applied provisionally pending its entry into force, or it may be made to operate retroactively. By way of contrast, an early Canadian case took a wider view of treaty application. See *In Re Cannon*,[34] where a treaty of extradition was construed to operate retroactively because it did not contain a provision expressly declaring that its stipulations should not apply to crimes committed prior to its conclusion.

Given the potential delay between the conclusion of a treaty and its entry into force, the first few ratifying states may not in fact be bound by the convention *qua* treaty law for some time. They are not, however, without obligations. Article 18 of the Vienna Convention, already mentioned with regard to the legal effect of signature, requires a state that has expressed its consent to be bound by a treaty to refrain from acts that would defeat the object and purpose of the treaty, "pending the entry into force of the treaty and provided that such entry into force is not unduly delayed."

---

33 *Spitz v. Secretary of State of Canada*, [1939] Ex. C.R. 162.

34 (1908), 17 O.L.R. 352 (H.C.J.) and *U.S.A. v. Allard and Charette*, [1991] 1 S.C.R. 861, where the Court again applied the extradition treaty to a crime committed before the treaty was in force, but refused to extradite the fugitives because their acts were not an offence under Canadian law at the time of commission.

Reservations

A reservation is a unilateral statement made by a state when signing, ratifying, accepting, approving, or acceding to a treaty, whereby it purports to exclude or to modify the legal effect of certain provisions of the treaty in their application to that state.

In 1952, the Department of External Affairs commented as follows:

> A state which has previously signed a convention may be unwilling to ratify it as it stands, and may accordingly make a reservation against the operation of one or more of its provisions. The practice of opening conventions for accession by states which have not participated at the drafting stage is conducive to the deposit by such states of instruments of accession which include reservations.
>
> If other states object to such reservations, confusion results—particularly if many states are involved. If the date of entry into force depends on the number of states ratifying or acceding, the confusion is even worse. The problem was considered in the League of Nations, where it was generally agreed that a state could not become a party subject to a reservation unless all other contracting states accepted the reservation. This "classical theory" was based on the view that no state could alter the text of a contract as applied to itself by its own unilateral act unless all other interested states agreed.
>
> Conventions are an important source of international law, and those drafted by international organizations such as the United Nations and its Specialized Agencies are particularly important in this regard. In the past, differences of opinion have arisen as to whether the integrity of the text of such law-making conventions was more or less important than participation of a large number of states.[35]

After World War II, the controversial question of reservations to multilateral conventions was the subject of long debate at the sixth and seventh sessions of the U.N. General Assembly. The question was also considered in 1951 by the ICJ in relation to the Genocide Convention and, in a more general context, by the ILC.

Reservations to the Convention on Genocide Case
Adv. Op. [1951] I.C.J. Rep. 15

[In 1950 the General Assembly of the U.N. asked the ICJ for an advisory opinion on the following questions:

In so far as concerns the Convention on the Prevention and Punishment of the Crime of Genocide in the event of a State ratifying or acceding to the Convention subject to a reservation made either on ratification or on accession, or on signature followed by ratification:

---

35   Department of External Affairs, "Reservations to Multilateral Conventions" (1952) 4 External Affairs 111; Department of External Affairs, "Reservations to Multilateral Conventions" (1960) 12 External Affairs 510.

I. Can the reserving State be regarded as being a party to the Convention while still maintaining its reservation if the reservation is objected to by one or more of the parties to the Convention but not by others?

II. If the answer to Question I is in the affirmative, what is the effect of the reservation as between the reserving State and:

    (a) The parties which object to the reservation?

    (b) Those which accept it?

III. What would be the legal effect as regards the answer to Question I if an objection to a reservation is made:

    (a) By a signatory which has not yet ratified?

    (b) By a State entitled to sign or accede but which has not yet done so?]

THE COURT: All three questions are expressly limited by the terms of the Resolution of the General Assembly to the Convention on the Prevention and Punishment of the Crime of Genocide, and the same Resolution invites the International Law Commission to study the general question of reservations to multilateral conventions both from the point of view of codification and from that of the progressive development of international law. The questions thus having a clearly defined object, the replies which the Court is called upon to give to them are necessarily and strictly limited to that Convention. ...

It is well established that in its treaty relations a State cannot be bound without its consent, and that consequently no reservation can be effective against any State without its agreement thereto. It is also a generally recognized principle that a multilateral convention is the result of an agreement freely concluded upon its clauses and that consequently none of the contracting parties is entitled to frustrate or impair, by means of unilateral decisions or particular agreements, the purpose and *raison d'être* of the convention. To this principle was linked the notion of the integrity of the convention as adopted, a notion which in its traditional concept involved the proposition that no reservation was valid unless it was accepted by all the contracting parties without exception, as would have been the case if it had been stated during the negotiations.

This concept, which is directly inspired by the notion of contract is of undisputed value as a principle. However, as regards the Genocide Convention, it is proper to refer to a variety of circumstances which would lead to a more flexible application of this principle. Among these circumstances may be noted the clearly universal character of the United Nations under whose auspices the Convention was concluded, and the very wide degree of participation envisaged by Article XI of the Convention. Extensive participation in conventions of this type has already given rise to greater flexibility in the international practice concerning multilateral conventions. More general resort to reservations, very great allowance made for tacit assent to reservations, the existence of practices which go so far as to admit that the author of reservations which have been rejected by certain contracting parties is nevertheless to be regarded as a party to the convention, in relation to those contracting parties that have accepted the reservations—all these factors are manifestations of a new need for flexibility in the operation of multilateral conventions.

It must also be pointed out that although the Genocide Convention was finally approved unanimously, it is nevertheless the result of a series of majority votes. The majority principle, while facilitating the conclusion of multilateral conventions, may also make it necessary for certain States to make reservations. This observation is confirmed by the great number of reservations which have been made of recent years to multilateral conventions. ...

The objects of such a convention must also be considered. The Convention was manifestly adopted for a purely humanitarian and civilizing purpose. It is indeed difficult to imagine a convention that might have this dual character to a greater degree, since its object on the one hand is to safeguard the very existence of certain human groups and on the other to confirm and endorse the most elementary principles of morality. In such a convention the contracting States do not have any interests of their own; they merely have, one and all, a common interest, namely, the accomplishment of those high purposes which are the *raison d'être* of the convention. Consequently, in a convention of this type one cannot speak of individual advantages or disadvantages to States, or of the maintenance of a perfect contractual balance between rights and duties. The high ideals which inspired the Convention provide, by virtue of the common will of the parties, the foundation and measure of all its provisions. ...

The object and purpose of the Genocide Convention imply that it was the intention of the General Assembly and of the States which adopted it that as many States as possible should participate. The complete exclusion from the Convention of one or more States would not only restrict the scope of its application, but would detract from the authority of the moral and humanitarian principles which are its basis. It is inconceivable that the contracting parties readily contemplated that an objection to a minor reservation should produce such a result. But even less could the contracting parties have intended to sacrifice the very object of the Convention in favour of a vain desire to secure as many participants as possible. The object and purpose of the Convention thus limit both the freedom of making reservations and that of objecting to them. It follows that it is the compatibility of a reservation with the object and purpose of the Convention that must furnish the criterion for the attitude of a State in making the reservation on accession as well as for the appraisal by a State in objecting to the reservation. ...

On the other hand, it has been argued that there exists a rule of international law subjecting the effect of a reservation to the express or tacit assent of all the contracting parties. This theory rests essentially on a contractual conception of the absolute integrity of the convention as adopted. This view, however, cannot prevail if, having regard to the character of the convention, its purpose and its mode of adoption, it can be established that the parties intended to derogate from that rule by admitting the faculty to make reservations thereto.

It does not appear, moreover, that the conception of the absolute integrity of a convention has been transformed into a rule of international law. The considerable part which tacit assent has always played in estimating the effect which is to be given to reservations scarcely permits one to state that such a rule exists, determining with sufficient precision the effect of objections made to reservations. In fact, the examples of objections made to reservations appear to be too rare in international practice to have given rise to such a rule. It cannot be recognized that the report which was adopted on the subject by the Council of the League of Nations on June 17, 1927, has had this effect. ...

It is inconceivable that a State, even if it has participated in the preparation of the Convention, could, before taking one or the other of the two courses of action provided for becoming a party to the Convention, exclude another State. Possessing no rights which derive from the Convention, that State cannot claim such a right from its status as a Member of the United Nations or from the invitation to sign which has been addressed to it by the General Assembly.

The case of a signatory State is different. Without going into the question of the legal effect of signing an international convention, which necessarily varies in individual cases, the Court considers that signature constitutes a first step to participation in the Convention.

It is evident that without ratification, signature does not make the signatory State a party to the Convention; nevertheless, it establishes a provisional status in favour of that State. This status may decrease in value and importance after the Convention enters into force. But, both before and after the entry into force, this status would justify more favourable treatment being meted out to signatory States in respect of objections than to States which have neither signed nor acceded.

As distinct from the latter States, signatory States have taken certain of the steps necessary for the exercise of the right of being a party. Pending ratification, the provisional status created by signature confers upon the signatory a right to formulate as a precautionary measure objections which have themselves a provisional character. These would disappear if the signature were not followed by ratification, or they would become effective on ratification.

Until this ratification is made, the objection of a signatory State can therefore not have an immediate legal effect in regard to the reserving State. It would merely express and proclaim the eventual attitude of the signatory State when it becomes a party to the Convention.

The legal interest of a signatory State in objecting to a reservation would thus be amply safeguarded. The reserving State would be given notice that as soon as the constitutional or other processes which cause the lapse of time before ratification, have been completed, it would be confronted with a valid objection which carries full legal effect and consequently, it would have to decide, when the objection is stated, whether it wishes to maintain or withdraw its reservation. ...

For these reasons the Court is of opinion,

On Question I, by seven votes to five, that a State which has made and maintained a reservation which has been objected to by one or more of the parties to the Convention but not by others, can be regarded as being a party to the Convention if the reservation is compatible with the object and purpose of the Convention; otherwise, that State cannot be regarded as being a party to the Convention.

On Question II, by seven votes to five, (a) that if a party to the Convention objects to a reservation which it considers to be incompatible with the object and purpose of the Convention, it can in fact consider that the reserving State is not a party to the Convention; (b) that if, on the other hand, a party accepts the reservation as being compatible with the object and purpose of the Convention, it can in fact consider that the reserving State is a party to the Convention.

On Question III, by seven votes to five, (a) that an objection to a reservation made by a signatory State which has not yet ratified the Convention can have the legal effect indicated in the reply to Question I only on ratification. Until that moment it merely serves as a notice to the other State of the eventual attitude of the signatory State; (b) that an objection to a reservation made by a State which is entitled to sign or accede but which has not yet done so, is without legal effect.

NOTES

1) No solution to the fundamental question of the admission of reservations having been reached and all attempts to achieve a compromise having failed, the 1952 General Assembly adopted resolution 598 (VI), requesting the Secretary-General to continue to act as depositary of documents containing reservations or objections without passing on their legal effect. The Secretary-General was asked to communicate the text of such documents to all states concerned, leaving it to each state to draw legal consequences from them. Obviously, this practice could not be considered entirely satisfactory because it meant that the status of the reservations (and, in consequence, the status of the convention itself) remained uncertain.

In 1959, the General Assembly requested the Secretary-General to obtain information from all depositary states and international organizations with respect to depositary practice in relation to reservations, and to prepare a summary of such practices, including his own, for use by the ILC in preparing its reports on the law of treaties and by the General Assembly in considering these reports.

The debate in the U.N. once again revealed a profound divergence of views among delegations on the substantive aspect of reservations. However, it was noticeable that the idea of the absolute integrity of conventions, requiring unanimity of acceptance before a state making a reservation could be admitted as a contracting party, is losing ground, the majority of U.N. members favouring greater flexibility in the obligations of treaties by permitting the contracting parties to enter reservations necessary to make the agreement acceptable, thus making it possible for a larger number of countries to participate.

2) Although the difficulties have not been laid to rest, specific rules curtailing the divergence of views and constraining the practice of making reservations have now been set out in the Vienna Convention articles 2, 19, 20, 21, and 22, reproduced in the Documentary Supplement. To what extent would these provisions resolve the kind of situation presented in the *Genocide Case*? This has not laid to rest the controversy concerning reservations to treaties; lately, the topic has again been on the agenda of the ILC.

3) In recent years the trend in multilateral treaty making has been to control the difficulties that can arise by specifying in the treaty itself which articles may and which may not be the subject of reservations. This practice adds the question of reservations to the negotiations of the substantive matters in the treaty-making process. An example is the Hague Convention on the Civil Aspects of International Child Abduction, which was

signed by Canada on October 25, 1980, and allows the signatory states to enter reservations only with respect to the use of the French or the English language and costs.[36] A number of treaties do not allow any reservations; one example is the Rome Statute of the International Criminal Court.

4) Reservations are important for Canada with regard to the implementation of treaties. Canada frequently strives to have a *federal-state clause* inserted in a multilateral convention or will enter a reservation, both of which have the effect of reserving Canada's obligations at international law concerning matters within the legislative jurisdiction of the Provinces. See the discussion in Chapter 4, Section C.2 on "Treaty Implementation" in Canada.

5) A distinction that must be kept in mind is that between a reservation and an interpretative declaration. The ILC has provided the following definition of the latter: "a unilateral statement, however phrased or named, made by a State ... whereby that State ... purports to specify or clarify the meaning or scope attributed by the declarant to a treaty or to certain of its provisions."[37] The distinction, based on the legal effect that the statement purports to produce, is not always easy to apply in practice. This may account for the fact that the Commission's recent work on reservations has devoted significant attention to interpretative declarations.

3. Legal Effects of Treaties

Pacta Sunt Servanda

Vienna Convention on the Law of Treaties
Articles 26, 27, and 30
Reproduced in the Documentary Supplement

NOTES

1) Every treaty in force is binding upon the parties to it and must be performed by them in good faith. Furthermore, a party may not invoke the provisions of its internal law as justification for its failure to perform a treaty. Thus, as the Permanent Court of International Justice said in the *Polish Nationals in Danzig* case:

[A] State cannot adduce as against another State its own Constitution with a view to eroding obligations incumbent upon it under international law or treaties in force.[38]

2) When successive treaties on the same matter are concluded between the same parties, the later treaty will prevail in the event of incompatible provisions, unless it was clearly made subject to the earlier treaty. If the later treaty does not include all the parties

---

36 See arts. 24, 26, and 42, Hague Conference on Private International Law, 14th Sess., *Actes et documents* (1980) vol. 3 at 413.

37 International Law Commission, *Report on the Work of its Fifty-Sixth Session (Reservations to Treaties: Guide to Practice, Guideline 1.2)* UN GAOR, 59th Sess., Supp. No. 10, U.N. Doc. A/59/10 (2004) 249.

38 (1931), Advisory Opinion, P.C.I.J. (Ser. A/B) No. 42 at 24.

to the earlier one, it will take effect among states who are parties to both agreements, but they are still bound by the earlier treaty vis-à-vis the other states party to it alone.

Third States

Free Zones Case
France v. Switzerland
(1932), P.C.I.J. (Ser. A/B) No. 46 at 96

[Article 435 of the Treaty of Versailles, 1919, provided that France and Switzerland (the latter was not a party to this treaty) should settle between themselves the status of certain territories on their common border. A proposed agreement having been rejected by the Swiss people, France abolished the former status of these territories. The PCIJ was asked whether article 435 had abrogated such status or had created an obligation for Switzerland to abrogate it.]

THE COURT: ... It follows from the foregoing that Article 435, paragraph 2, as such, does not involve the abolition of the free zones. But, even were it otherwise, it is certain that, in any case, Article 435 of the Treaty of Versailles is not binding upon Switzerland, who is not a Party to that Treaty, except to the extent to which that country accepted it. ...

With particular regard to the zone of Gex, the following is to be noted:

Pursuant to Article 6 of the Treaty of Paris of May 30th, 1814, the Powers assembled at the Congress of Vienna addressed to Switzerland, on March 20th, 1815, a "Declaration" to the effect that "as soon as the Helvetic Diet shall have duly and formally acceded to the stipulations in the present instrument, an act shall be prepared containing the acknowledgment and the guarantee, on the part of all the Powers, of the perpetual neutrality of Switzerland, in her new frontiers." The "instrument" which forms part of this Declaration, amongst other territorial clauses, provides that the line of the French customs is to be so placed "that the road which leads from Geneva into Switzerland by Versoy, shall at all times be free."

The proposal thus made to Switzerland by the Powers was accepted by the Federal Diet by means of the "act of acceptance" of May 27th, 1815. ...

On receipt of Switzerland's formal declaration of acceptance, the Powers drew up the instrument promised in their Declaration of March 20th: this instrument is the Declaration of November 20th, 1815.

By this Declaration, signed *inter alios* by France, "the Powers who signed the Declaration of the 20th of March declare ... their formal and authentic acknowledgment of the perpetual neutrality of Switzerland; and they guarantee to that country the integrity and inviolability of its territory in its new limits, such as they are fixed, as well by the Act of the Congress of Vienna as by the Treaty of Paris of this day, and such as they will be hereafter, conformably to the arrangement of the Protocol of November 3rd, extract of which is hereto annexed, which stipulates in favour of the

Helvetic Body a new increase of territory, to be taken from Savoy in order to disengage from enclaves, and complete the circle of the Canton of Geneva. ..."

It follows from all the foregoing that the creation of the Gex zone forms part of a territorial arrangement in favour of Switzerland, made as a result of an agreement between that country and the Powers, including France, which agreement confers on this zone the character of a contract to which Switzerland is a Party.

It also follows that no accession by Switzerland to the Declaration of November 20th was necessary and, in fact, no such accession was sought: it has never been contended that this Declaration is not binding owing to the absence of any accession by Switzerland.

The Court, having reached this conclusion simply on the basis of an examination of the situation of fact in regard to this case, need not consider the legal nature of the Gex zone from the point of view of whether it constitutes a stipulation in favour of a Third Party.

But were the matter also to be envisaged from this aspect, the following observations should be made:

It cannot be lightly presumed that stipulations favourable to a third State have been adopted with the object of creating an actual right in its favour. There is however nothing to prevent the will of sovereign states from having this object and this effect. The question of the existence of a right acquired under an instrument drawn between other states is therefore one to be decided in each particular case: it must be ascertained whether the states which have stipulated in favour of a third state meant to create for that state an actual right which the latter has accepted as such.

All the instruments above mentioned and the circumstances in which they were drawn up establish, in the Court's opinion, that the intention of the Powers was, beside "rounding out" the territory of Geneva and ensuring direct communication between the Canton of Geneva and the rest of Switzerland, to create in favour of Switzerland a right, on which that country could rely, to the withdrawal of the French customs barrier behind the political frontier of the District of Gex, that is to say, of the Gex free zone.

NOTES

1) Now see articles 34 through 38 of the Vienna Convention of the Law of Treaties in the Documentary Supplement. Notice how the Convention distinguishes between rights and obligations extended to third parties. To what extent do these articles reflect the Court's opinion in the *Free Zones Case*?

2) What is the effect of U.N. Charter article 2(6) for non-members?

3) What is the status of a bilateral boundary treaty vis-à-vis a third state?

4) Some of the most common examples of third state rights are Most Favoured Nation (MFN) clauses. These clauses are often included in bilateral treaties governing trade and commerce in order to ensure that each party will automatically acquire all the benefits that may be agreed in any subsequent treaty by the other party with another state. In this way the first state will become the third-party beneficiary of the treatment accorded to the most favoured treaty partners of the other state. The best-known instance of MFN clauses

is the multilateral example found in the General Agreement on Tariffs and Trade article 1, which reads:

> With respect to customs duties and charges of any kind ... in connection with importation or exportation ... , any advantage, favour, privilege or immunity granted by any contracting party [to GATT] to any product originating in or destined for any other country shall be accorded immediately and unconditionally to the like product originating in or destined for the territories of all other contracting parties.

The application of MFN clauses was considered in the *Rights of U.S. Nationals in Morocco Case*,[39] where the Court stated that "the United States, by virtue of this most favoured nation clause, has the right to object to any discrimination in favour of France, in the matter of imports into the French Zone of Morocco."

Interpretation of Treaties

Interpretation of Peace Treaties Case
(Second Phase) Adv. Op. [1950] I.C.J. Rep. 221 at 226

[The 1947 Peace Treaties with Bulgaria, Hungary, and Romania provided for a system of commissions to resolve any disputes concerning their interpretation and execution. When charges were made about the suppression of human rights contrary to the treaties, Bulgaria, Hungary, and Romania refused to participate in the formation of a commission. In an effort to settle the growing dispute, the U.N. General Assembly asked the Court to interpret the treaty provisions respecting the constitution of such commissions.]

THE COURT: ... Having stated, in its Opinion of March 30th, 1950, that the Governments of Bulgaria, Hungary and Romania are obligated to carry out the provisions of those articles of the Peace Treaties which relate to the settlement of disputes, including the provisions for the appointment of their representatives to the Treaty Commissions, and having received information from the Secretary-General of the United Nations that none of those Governments had notified him, within thirty days from the date of the delivery of the Court's Advisory Opinion, of the appointment of its representative to the Treaty Commissions, the Court is now called upon to answer Question III in the Resolution of the General Assembly of October 22nd, 1949, which reads as follows:

> III. If one party fails to appoint a representative to a Treaty Commission under the Treaties of Peace with Bulgaria, Hungary and Romania where that party is obligated to appoint a representative to the Treaty Commission, is the Secretary-General of the United Nations authorized to appoint the third member of the Commission upon the request of the other party to a dispute according to the provisions of the respective Treaties?

---

39   *France v. United States*, [1952] I.C.J. Rep. 176 at 185-86.

Articles 36, 40 and 38, respectively, of the Peace Treaties with Bulgaria, Hungary and Romania, after providing that disputes concerning the interpretation or execution of the Treaties which had not been settled by direct negotiation should be referred to the Three Heads of Mission, continue:

> Any such dispute not resolved by them within a period of two months shall, unless the parties to the dispute mutually agree upon another means of settlement, be referred at the request of either party to the dispute to a Commission composed of one representative of each party and a third member selected by mutual agreement of the two parties from nationals of a third country. Should the two parties fail to agree within a period of one month upon the appointment of the third member, the Secretary-General of the United Nations may be requested by either party to make the appointment.
>
> 2. The decision of the majority of the members of the Commission shall be the decision of the Commission, and shall be accepted by the parties as definitive and binding.

The question at issue is whether the provision empowering the Secretary-General to appoint the third member of the Commission applies to the present case, in which one of the parties refuses to appoint its own representative to the Commission.

It has been contended that the term "third member" is used here simply to distinguish the neutral member from the two Commissioners appointed by the parties without implying that the third member can be appointed only when the two national Commissioners have already been appointed, and that therefore the mere fact of the failure of the parties, within the stipulated period, to select the third member by mutual agreement satisfies the condition required for the appointment of the latter by the Secretary-General.

The Court considers that the text of the Treaties does not admit of this interpretation. While the text in its literal sense does not completely exclude the possibility of the appointment of the third member before the appointment of both national Commissioners, it is nevertheless true that according to the natural and ordinary meaning of the terms it was intended that the appointment of both the national Commissioners should precede that of the third member. This clearly results from the sequence of the events contemplated by the article: appointment of a national Commissioner by each party; selection of a third member by mutual agreement of the parties; failing such agreement within a month, his appointment by the Secretary-General. Moreover, this is the normal order followed in the practice of arbitration, and in the absence of any express provision to the contrary there is no reason to suppose that the parties wished to depart from it.

The Secretary-General's power to appoint a third member is derived solely from the agreement of the parties as expressed in the disputes clause of the Treaties; by its very nature such a clause must be strictly construed and can be applied only in the case expressly provided for therein. The case envisaged in the Treaties is exclusively that of the failure of the parties to agree upon the selection of a third member and by no means the much more serious case of a complete refusal of co-operation by one of them, taking the form of refusing to appoint its own Commissioner. The power conferred upon the Secretary-General to help the parties out of the difficulty of agreeing upon a third member cannot be extended to the situation which now exists. ...

In these circumstances, the appointment of a third member by the Secretary-General, instead of bringing about the constitution of a three-member Commission such as the Treaties provide for, would result only in the constitution of a two-member Commission. A Commission consisting of two members is not the kind of commission for which the Treaties have provided. The opposition of the Commissioner of the only party represented could prevent a Commission so constituted from reaching any decision whatever. Such a Commission could only decide by unanimity, whereas the dispute clause provides that "the decision of the majority of the members of the Commission shall be the decision of the Commission and shall be accepted by the parties as definitive and binding." Nor would the decisions of a Commission of two members, one of whom is appointed by one party only, have the same degree of moral authority as those of a three-member Commission. In every respect, the result would be contrary to the letter as well as the spirit of the Treaties. ...

As the Court has declared in its Opinion of March 30th, 1950, the Governments of Bulgaria, Hungary and Romania are under an obligation to appoint their representatives to the Treaty Commissions, and it is clear that refusal to fulfil a treaty obligation involves international responsibility. Nevertheless, such a refusal cannot alter the conditions contemplated in the Treaties for the exercise by the Secretary-General of his power of appointment. These conditions are not present in this case, and their absence is not made good by the fact that it is due to the breach of a treaty obligation. The failure of machinery for settling disputes by reason of the practical impossibility of creating the Commission provided for in the Treaties is one thing; international responsibility is another. The breach of a treaty obligation cannot be remedied by creating a Commission which is not the kind of Commission contemplated by the Treaties. It is the duty of the Court to interpret the Treaties, not to revise them.

The principle of interpretation expressed in the maxim: *Ut res magis valeat quam pereat*, often referred to as the rule of effectiveness, (see H. Lauterpacht, in 26 British Year Book (1949), at 48) cannot justify the Court in attributing to the provisions for the settlement of disputes in the Peace Treaties a meaning which, as stated above, would be contrary to their letter and spirit. ...

For these reasons, the Court is of opinion, by eleven votes to two, that, if one party fails to appoint a representative to a Treaty Commission under the Peace Treaties with Bulgaria, Hungary and Romania where that party is obligated to appoint a representative to the Treaty Commission, the Secretary-General of the United Nations is not authorized to appoint the third member of the Commission upon the request of the other party to a dispute.

NOTES

1) The World Court has not always been consistent in its approach to treaty interpretation, although the ILC has commented that its jurisprudence "contains many pronouncements from which it is permissible to conclude that the textual [that is, ordinary meaning] approach ... is regarded by it as established by law."[40] Fitzmaurice has ably summed up the difference in approaches in these words:

---

40   *Yearbook of the International Law Commission 1966, supra* note 22 at 220. And see *Competence of the I.L.O.* (1922), Advisory Opinion, P.C.I.J. (Ser. B) Nos. 2 and 3 at 23; *Polish Postal Services in Danzig*

There are today three main schools of thought on the subject, which could conveniently be called the "intentions of the parties" or "founding fathers" school; the "textual" or "ordinary meaning of the words" school; and the "teleological" or "aims and objects" school. The ideas of these three schools are not necessarily exclusive of one another, and theories of treaty interpretation can be constructed (and are indeed normally held) compounded of all three. However, each tends to confer the primacy on one particular aspect of treaty interpretation, if not to the exclusion, certainly to the subordination of the others. Each, in any case, employs a different approach. For the "intentions" school, the prime, indeed the only legitimate, object is to ascertain and give effect to the intentions, or presumed intentions, of the parties: the approach is therefore to discover what these were, or must be taken to have been. For the "meaning of the text" school, the prime object is to establish what the text means according to the ordinary or apparent signification of its terms: the approach is therefore through the study and analysis of the text. For the "aims and objects" school, it is the general purpose of the treaty itself that counts, considered to some extent as having, or as having come to have, an existence of its own, independent of the original intentions of the framers. The main object is to establish this general purpose, and construe the particular clauses in the light of it: hence it is such matters as the general tenor and atmosphere of the treaty, the circumstances in which it was made, the place it has come to have in international life, which for this school indicate the approach to interpretation. It should be added that this last, the teleological, approach has its sphere of operation almost entirely in the field of general multilateral conventions, particularly those of the social, humanitarian, and law-making type. All three approaches are capable, in a given case, of producing the same result in practice; but equally (even though the differences may, on analysis, prove to be more of emphasis and methodology than principle) they are capable of leading to radically divergent results.[41]

He also added in a footnote:

It may be useful to state briefly the main drawback of each method, if employed in isolation or pushed to an extreme. In the case of the "intentions" method, it is the element of unreality or fictitiousness frequently involved. There are so many cases in which the dispute has arisen precisely because the parties had no intentions on the point, or none that were genuinely common. To make the issue dependent on them involves either an abortive search or an artificial construction that does *not* in fact represent their intentions. The "textual" method suffers from the subjective elements involved in the notions of "clear" or "ordinary" meaning, which may be differently understood and applied according to the point of view of the individual judge. There may also be cases where the parties intended a term to be understood in a specialized sense, different from its ordinary one, but failed to make this clear on the face of the text. The teleological method, finally, is always in danger of "spilling over" into judicial legislation: it may amount, not to interpreting but, in effect, to

---

(1925), Advisory Opinion, P.C.I.J. (Ser. B) No. 11 at 39; *The Steamship Lotus (France v. Turkey)* (1927), P.C.I.J. (Ser. A) No. 10 at 16; *Conditions of Admission to the United Nations*, Advisory Opinion, [1948] I.C.J. Rep. 57 at 63; and *Competence of the General Assembly*, Advisory Opinion, [1950] I.C.J. Rep. 4 at 8.

41 G.G. Fitzmaurice, "The Law and Procedure of the International Court of Justice: Treaty Interpretation and Certain Other Treaty Points" (1951) 28 Brit. Y.B. Int'l L. 1.

amending an instrument in order to make it conform better with what the judge regards as its true purposes.

Which school of thought did the World Court follow in the *Interpretation of Peace Treaties Case*?[42] Now review the *Reparations Case*, Adv. Op. [1949] I.C.J. 174, reported in Chapter 2, Section C.1 on "Other Legal Persons: International Organizations." What approach to treaty interpretation was employed there? Does it make any difference that the treaty there in question was the constitutional document of an international organization?

2) Article 31 of the Vienna Convention on the Law of Treaties, reproduced in the Documentary Supplement, lays down the general rule of interpretation that a treaty shall be interpreted in good faith in accordance with the ordinary meaning to be given to its terms in their context and in the light of its object and purpose. Article 32 provides that recourse may be had to supplementary means of interpretation, including the preparatory work of the treaty, in order to confirm the meaning resulting from the application of article 31, or in order to determine the meaning if the interpretation according to article 31 leaves the meaning ambiguous or obscure or leads to a result that is manifestly absurd or unreasonable.

These articles appear at first glance to provide an orderly approach to treaty interpretation, but which of Fitzmaurice's schools of thought do they endorse? On a close reading of article 31, in what circumstances are "the intentions of the parties" relevant? When may preparatory work (*travaux préparatoires*) to the treaty be resorted to? What if it reveals an intended meaning of the parties that differs from the ordinary meaning of the text, or from a subsequent agreement regarding interpretation?

3) In the *Case concerning Border and Transborder Armed Actions*, reference was made to the *travaux préparatoires* in order to confirm the Court's interpretation of article XXXI of the Pact of Bogota as a basis of its jurisdiction.[43]

4) In *Amoco International Finance Corp. v. Iran*, the Iran–United States Claims Tribunal had to apply both a treaty and a customary rule of international law. The Tribunal said:

> As a *lex specialis* in the relations between the two countries, the Treaty supersedes the *lex generalis*, namely customary international law. This does not mean, however, that the latter is irrelevant in the instant case. On the contrary, the rules of customary law may be useful in order to fill in possible *lacunae* of the treaty, to ascertain the meaning of undefined terms in its text or, more generally, to aid interpretation and implementation of its provisions.[44]

5) When a treaty is implemented by national legislation the act will be regarded as the authoritative application of its provisions for internal legal purposes. Yet there is still the question of its interpretation, which has two aspects. On the national plane, should the implemented treaty be interpreted according to domestic rules of statutory interpretation or international principles, if they differ? This question is taken up, as far as Canada is concerned, in Chapter 4, Section C.4 on "Interpretation of Treaties." On the international

---

42   Compare the strong dissent of Judge Read, Advisory Opinion, [1950] I.C.J. Rep. 221 at 231, who made a broad interpretation in order to give effect to the general purposes and objects of the Peace Treaties.

43   *Nicaragua v. Honduras*, [1988] I.C.J. Rep. 69 at 85, 89.

44   (1987), 15 Iran–U.S. C.T.R. 189 at 222.

plane, the national legislation is not a definitive interpretation of the treaty for international purposes. Indeed, it may amount to a breach of the treaty.

In *The David J. Adams*, the arbitral tribunal noted:

> The fundamental principle of the juridical equality of States is opposed to placing one State under the jurisdiction of another State. It is opposed to the subjection of one State to an interpretation of a Treaty asserted by another State. There is no reason why one more than the other should impose such an unilateral interpretation of a contract which is essentially bilateral. The fact that this interpretation is given by the legislative or judicial or any other authority of one of the Parties does not make that interpretation binding upon the other Party.[45]

4. Operation of Treaties

Amendment and Modification

In 1967, the Department of External Affairs sent the following comments in reply to a request for advice on how a multilateral agreement could be amended:

> Although it is always open to the parties to a multilateral agreement to amend it, international law is not yet fixed with respect to how and under what conditions such amendment may take place. A great deal depends on whether or not the parties are all in agreement on what they wish to do. If there is a consensus that an agreement is to be amended, then negotiations can take place to determine the precise nature of the amendments required. Once the definitive form of these amendments has been agreed upon by all the parties, they can be embodied in an amending agreement. ... (a "Protocol of Amendment").
>
> If it were decided that instead of concluding a Protocol of Amendment it would be preferable to terminate the main agreement and replace it with an entirely new agreement, that could be achieved in one of two ways. Firstly, the old agreement could be terminated in accordance with [its] provisions, [or], provided that there was unanimity among all the parties, such notice of termination could be dispensed with and a provision in the new agreement to be concluded would only need to state that it was intended to terminate the previous agreement. The form of the new agreement could be whatever the parties wished.
>
> In this analysis it has also been assumed so far that all parties to the present agreement will in fact be agreed upon the desirability either of amending it or of concluding a new one. If, however, one or more of the parties were unwilling to go along with either of these proposals, the situation would become more complicated. Briefly, in such a case it is generally accepted in international law that those among the parties to an earlier agreement who might wish either to amend that agreement or to conclude a further agreement *inter se* are free to do so. However, the effects of such amendment or new agreement are restricted only to the parties directly concerned, and they continue to be bound by the old agreement in their relations with the other parties who have not agreed to the changes.[46]

---

45 (1921) Nielsen's Reports 524 (U.S.-G.B. Claims Arbitration Tribunal).

46 Reported in (1967) 5 Can. Y.B. Int'l Law 277.

The Vienna Convention article 39 confirms that a treaty may be amended by agreement between the parties. Thus, as concerns a multilateral treaty, a proposal for its amendment may be negotiated and concluded by all or some of the parties, but the amending agreement does not bind parties to the original treaty who do not accept it (article 40(4)), and the amendments may not prejudice their existing treaty rights and obligations (article 41). A state that becomes a party to the treaty after its amendment will be considered a party to the amended treaty, except in relation to a party that has not accepted the amendment (article 40(5)).

Invalidity and Jus Cogens

Vienna Convention on the Law of Treaties
Articles 42, 43, 46, 52, 53, 64, 69, and 71
Reproduced in the Documentary Supplement

NOTES

1) Part V, Section 2 of the Vienna Convention deals with the invalidity of treaties. One potential source of confusion is the use of the term "invalidity" to cover both a situation in which a treaty is voidable and a situation in which it is void *ab initio*. Article 45 recognizes that a state may agree, either expressly or tacitly, to having a treaty that is potentially voidable pursuant to these articles continue in effect. Articles 46-50 address circumstances that a state may invoke as invalidating its consent to be bound by the treaty. Articles 51-53, in contrast, dealing respectively with coercion of a representative of a state, coercion of a state by threat or use of force, and conflicts with *jus cogens*, provide that treaties to which these articles apply are "without legal effect" or "void."

2) Article 46 is an important limitation on a state's ability to escape liability for breach of a treaty by claiming it was never bound because of some technical requirement of its internal law. In this respect, the article complements article 27, which prevents a state from justifying its breach of a treaty to which it is bound by invoking provisions of its internal law. The proviso in article 46 is a legitimate safeguard for a state but of indefinite scope. Suppose, for instance, that the province of British Columbia purported to make a treaty with Japan for the supply of coal. Could the government of Canada set the treaty aside? Could Japan?

3) The provisions on *jus cogens* were some of the most controversial articles in the Vienna Convention.[47] Socialist and developing countries seemed to attach great importance to the idea that there are some imperatives in international law that would override any treaty made in violation of them. Western states were much more skeptical about *jus cogens*, fearing, perhaps, that such an ill-defined concept might invalidate carefully negotiated agreements and jeopardize the stability of the treaty system. There

---

47   Articles 53 and 64. And see the comments on *jus cogens*, *supra* Section A.2 on "Soft Law and Jus Cogens."

was also concern that the concept conflicts with the principle of state sovereignty and the consensual character of international law that it implies.[48]

4) Given the uncertainties surrounding *jus cogens,* the Vienna Convention makes particular provision for disputes about peremptory norms. According to article 66, any one of the parties to a dispute concerning the application or the interpretation of article 53 or 64 may, by a written application, submit it to the ICJ for a decision, unless the parties by common consent agree to go to arbitration.

Termination and Suspension

Vienna Convention on the Law of Treaties
Articles 42, 54–56, 60–63, and 70
Reproduced in the Documentary Supplement

The starting point for a consideration of the termination and suspension of the operation of treaties is article 42(2) of the Vienna Convention, which states, "The termination of a treaty, its denunciation or the withdrawal of a party, may take place only as a result of the application of the provisions of the treaty or of the present Convention. The same rule applies to suspension of the operation of a treaty."[49] The International Law Commission, in its commentary on the draft articles that formed the basis for the Vienna Convention, emphasized that "the validity and continuance in force of a treaty is the normal state of things which may be set aside only on the grounds and under the conditions provided for in the present articles."[50] John Currie categorizes the possible grounds for terminating or suspending treaty obligations as follows: the consent of the parties, material breach, supervening impossibility of performance, and fundamental change of circumstances (*rebus sic stantibus*).[51] Arguments regarding the last three grounds were raised in the following case.

Case Concerning Gabčíkovo-Nagymaros Project (Hungary/Slovakia)
[1997] I.C.J. Rep. 7

[In 1977, Hungary and Czechoslovakia concluded a treaty to build a series of dams in Slovakia and Hungary for the production of electricity, flood control, and improvements to navigation on the River Danube. In 1989, Hungary suspended and later abandoned the project, invoking grave risks to the environment and to the water supply of Budapest. Slovakia, as successor to Czechoslovakia, denied these allegations

---

48   See Danilenko, *supra* note 15.

49   See generally Athanassios Vamvoukos, *Termination of Treaties in International Law* (1985).

50   ILC, *Report, supra* note 22 at 236.

51   Currie, *supra* note 1 at 154-59.

and insisted that Hungary carry out its treaty obligations. It planned and subsequently put into operation an alternative project only on Slovak territory, the operation of which affected Hungary's access to the waters of the Danube.]

THE COURT:

98. The question, as formulated in Article 2, paragraph 1 (c), of the Special Agreement, deals with treaty law since the Court is asked to determine what the legal effects are of the notification of termination of the Treaty. The question is whether Hungary's notification of 19 May 1992 brought the 1977 Treaty to an end, or whether it did not meet the requirements of international law, with the consequence that it did not terminate the Treaty.

99. The Court has referred earlier to the question of the applicability to the present case of the Vienna Convention of 1969 on the Law of Treaties. The Vienna Convention is not directly applicable to the 1977 Treaty inasmuch as both States ratified that Convention only after the Treaty's conclusion. Consequently only those rules which are declaratory of customary law are applicable to the 1977 Treaty. As the Court has already stated above (see paragraph 46), this is the case, in many respects, with Articles 60 to 62 of the Vienna Convention, relating to termination or suspension of the operation of a treaty. On this, the Parties, too, were broadly in agreement.

100. The 1977 Treaty does not contain any provision regarding its termination. Nor is there any indication that the parties intended to admit the possibility of denunciation or withdrawal. On the contrary, the Treaty establishes a long-standing and durable régime of joint investment and joint operation. Consequently, the parties not having agreed otherwise, the Treaty could be terminated only on the limited grounds enumerated in the Vienna Convention.

101. The Court will now turn to the first ground advanced by Hungary, that of the state of necessity. In this respect, the Court will merely observe that, even if a state of necessity is found to exist, it is not a ground for the termination of a treaty. It may only be invoked to exonerate from its responsibility a State which has failed to implement a treaty. Even if found justified, it does not terminate a Treaty; the Treaty may be ineffective as long as the condition of necessity continues to exist; it may in fact be dormant, but—unless the parties by mutual agreement terminate the Treaty— it continues to exist. As soon as the state of necessity ceases to exist, the duty to comply with treaty obligations revives.

102. Hungary also relied on the principle of the impossibility of performance as reflected in Article 61 of the Vienna Convention on the Law of Treaties. Hungary's interpretation of the wording of Article 61 is, however, not in conformity with the terms of that Article, nor with the intentions of the Diplomatic Conference which adopted the Convention. Article 61, paragraph 1, requires the "permanent disappearance or destruction of an object indispensable for the execution" of the treaty to justify the termination of a treaty on grounds of impossibility of performance. During the conference, a proposal was made to extend the scope of the article by including in it cases such as the impossibility to make certain payments because of serious financial difficulties (*Official Records of the United Nations Conference on the Law of Treaties, First Session, Vienna, 26 March-24 May 1968*, Doc. A/CONF.39/

11, Summary records of the plenary meetings and of the meetings of the Committee of the Whole, 62nd Meeting of the Committee of the Whole, pp. 361-365). Although it was recognized that such situations could lead to a preclusion of the wrongfulness of non-performance by a party of its treaty obligations, the participating States were not prepared to consider such situations to be a ground for terminating or suspending a treaty, and preferred to limit themselves to a narrower concept.

103. Hungary contended that the essential object of the Treaty—an economic joint investment which was consistent with environmental protection and which was operated by the two contracting parties jointly—had permanently disappeared and that the Treaty had thus become impossible to perform. It is not necessary for the Court to determine whether the term "object" in Article 61 can also be understood to embrace a legal régime as in any event, even if that were the case, it would have to conclude that in this instance that régime had not definitively ceased to exist. The 1977 Treaty—and in particular its Articles 15, 19 and 20—actually made available to the parties the necessary means to proceed at any time, by negotiation, to the required readjustments between economic imperatives and ecological imperatives. The Court would add that, if the joint exploitation of the investment was no longer possible, this was originally because Hungary did not carry out most of the works for which it was responsible under the 1977 Treaty; Article 61, paragraph 2, of the Vienna Convention expressly provides that impossibility of performance may not be invoked for the termination of a treaty by a party to that treaty when it results from that party's own breach of an obligation flowing from that treaty.

104. Hungary further argued that it was entitled to invoke a number of events which, cumulatively, would have constituted a fundamental change of circumstances. In this respect it specified profound changes of a political nature, the Project's diminishing economic viability, the progress of environmental knowledge and the development of new norms and prescriptions of international environmental law ... .

The Court recalls that, in the *Fisheries Jurisdiction* case (*I.C.J. Reports 1973*, p. 63, para. 36), it stated that,

> Article 62 of the Vienna Convention on the Law of Treaties, ... may in many respects be considered as a codification of existing customary law on the subject of the termination of a treaty relationship on account of change of circumstances.

The prevailing political situation was certainly relevant for the conclusion of the 1977 Treaty. But the Court will recall that the Treaty provided for a joint investment programme for the production of energy, the control of floods and the improvement of navigation on the Danube. In the Court's view, the prevalent political conditions were thus not so closely linked to the object and purpose of the Treaty that they constituted an essential basis of the consent of the parties and, in changing, radically altered the extent of the obligations still to be performed. The same holds good for the economic system in force at the time of the conclusion of the 1977 Treaty. Besides, even though the estimated profitability of the Project might have appeared less in 1992 than in 1977, it does not appear from the record before the Court that it was bound to diminish to such an extent that the treaty obligations of the parties would have been radically transformed as a result.

The Court does not consider that new developments in the state of environmental knowledge and of environmental law can be said to have been completely unforeseen. What is more, the formulation of Articles 15, 19 and 20, designed to accommodate change, made it possible for the parties to take account of such developments and to apply them when implementing those treaty provisions.

The changed circumstances advanced by Hungary are, in the Court's view, not of such a nature, either individually or collectively, that their effect would radically transform the extent of the obligations still to be performed in order to accomplish the Project. A fundamental change of circumstances must have been unforeseen; the existence of the circumstances at the time of the Treaty's conclusion must have constituted an essential basis of the consent of the parties to be bound by the Treaty. The negative and conditional wording of Article 62 of the Vienna Convention on the Law of Treaties is a clear indication moreover that the stability of treaty relations requires that the plea of fundamental change of circumstances be applied only in exceptional cases.

105. The Court will now examine Hungary's argument that it was entitled to terminate the 1977 Treaty on the ground that Czechoslovakia had violated its Articles 15, 19 and 20 (as well as a number of other conventions and rules of general international law); and that the planning, construction and putting into operation of Variant C also amounted to a material breach of the 1977 Treaty.

106. As to that part of Hungary's argument which was based on other treaties and general rules of international law, the Court is of the view that it is only a material breach of the treaty itself, by a State party to that treaty, which entitles the other party to rely on it as a ground for terminating the treaty. The violation of other treaty rules or of rules of general international law may justify the taking of certain measures, including countermeasures, by the injured State, but it does not constitute a ground for termination under the law of treaties.

107. Hungary contended that Czechoslovakia had violated Articles 15, 19 and 20 of the Treaty by refusing to enter into negotiations with Hungary in order to adapt the Joint Contractual Plan to new scientific and legal developments regarding the environment. Articles 15, 19 and 20 oblige the parties jointly to take, on a continuous basis, appropriate measures necessary for the protection of water quality, of nature and of fishing interests.

Articles 15 and 19 expressly provide that the obligations they contain shall be implemented by the means specified in the Joint Contractual Plan. The failure of the parties to agree on those means cannot, on the basis of the record before the Court, be attributed solely to one party. The Court has not found sufficient evidence to conclude that Czechoslovakia had consistently refused to consult with Hungary about the desirability or necessity of measures for the preservation of the environment. The record rather shows that, while both parties indicated, in principle, a willingness to undertake further studies, in practice Czechoslovakia refused to countenance a suspension of the works at Dunakiliti and, later, on Variant C, while Hungary required suspension as a prior condition of environmental investigation because it claimed continuation of the work would prejudice the outcome of negotiations. In this regard it cannot be left out of consideration that Hungary itself, by suspending the works at

Nagymaros and Dunakiliti, contributed to the creation of a situation which was not conducive to the conduct of fruitful negotiations.

108. Hungary's main argument for invoking a material breach of the Treaty was the construction and putting into operation of Variant C. As the Court has found in paragraph 79 above, Czechoslovakia violated the Treaty only when it diverted the waters of the Danube into the bypass canal in October 1992. In constructing the works which would lead to the putting into operation of Variant C, Czechoslovakia did not act unlawfully.

In the Court's view, therefore, the notification of termination by Hungary on 19 May 1992 was premature. No breach of the Treaty by Czechoslovakia had yet taken place and consequently Hungary was not entitled to invoke any such breach of the Treaty as a ground for terminating it when it did.

109. In this regard, it should be noted that, according to Hungary's Declaration of 19 May 1992, the termination of the 1977 Treaty was to take effect as from 25 May 1992, that is only six days later. Both Parties agree that Articles 65 to 67 of the Vienna Convention on the Law of Treaties, if not codifying customary law, at least generally reflect customary international law and contain certain procedural principles which are based on an obligation to act in good faith. As the Court stated in its Advisory Opinion on the *Interpretation of the Agreement of 25 March 1951 between the WHO and Egypt* (in which case the Vienna Convention did not apply):

> Precisely what periods of time may be involved in the observance of the duties to consult and negotiate, and what period of notice of termination should be given, are matters which necessarily vary according to the requirements of the particular case. In principle, therefore, it is for the parties in each case to determine the length of those periods by consultation and negotiation in good faith. (*I.C.J. Reports 1980*, p. 96, para. 49.)

The termination of the Treaty by Hungary was to take effect six days after its notification. On neither of these dates had Hungary suffered injury resulting from acts of Czechoslovakia. The Court must therefore confirm its conclusion that Hungary's termination of the Treaty was premature.

110. Nor can the Court overlook that Czechoslovakia committed the internationally wrongful act of putting into operation Variant C as a result of Hungary's own prior wrongful conduct. As was stated by the Permanent Court of International Justice:

> It is, moreover, a principle generally accepted in the jurisprudence of international arbitration, as well as by municipal courts, that one Party cannot avail himself of the fact that the other has not fulfilled some obligation or has not had recourse to some means of redress, if the former Party has, by some illegal act, prevented the latter from fulfilling the obligation in question, or from having recourse to the tribunal which would have been open, to him. (*Factory at Chorzów, Jurisdiction, Judgment No. 8*, 1927, P.C.I.J., Series A, No. 9, p. 31.)

Hungary, by its own conduct, had prejudiced its right to terminate the Treaty; this would still have been the case even if Czechoslovakia, by the time of the purported termination, had violated a provision essential to the accomplishment of the object or purpose of the Treaty.

111. Finally, the Court will address Hungary's claim that it was entitled to terminate the 1977 Treaty because new requirements of international law for the protection of the environment precluded performance of the Treaty.

112. Neither of the Parties contended that new peremptory norms of environmental law had emerged since the conclusion of the 1977 Treaty, and the Court will consequently not be required to examine the scope of Article 64 of the Vienna Convention on the Law of Treaties. On the other hand, the Court wishes to point out that newly developed norms of environmental law are relevant for the implementation of the Treaty and that the parties could, by agreement, incorporate them through the application of Articles 15, 19 and 20 of the Treaty. These articles do not contain specific obligations of performance but require the parties, in carrying out their obligations to ensure that the quality of water in the Danube is not impaired and that nature is protected, to take new environmental norms into consideration when agreeing upon the means to be specified in the Joint Contractual Plan.

By inserting these evolving provisions in the Treaty, the parties recognized the potential necessity to adapt the Project. Consequently, the Treaty is not static, and is open to adapt to emerging norms of international law. By means of Articles 15 and 19, new environmental norms can be incorporated in the Joint Contractual Plan.

The responsibility to do this was a joint responsibility. The obligations contained in Articles 15, 19 and 20 are, by definition, general and have to be transformed into specific obligations of performance through a process of consultation and negotiation. Their implementation thus requires a mutual willingness to discuss in good faith actual and potential environmental risks.

It is all the more important to do this because as the Court recalled in its *Advisory Opinion on the Legality of the Threat or Use of Nuclear Weapons*, "the environment is not an abstraction but represents the living space, the quality of life and the very health of human beings, including generations unborn" (*I.C.J. Reports 1996*, para. 29 ...) .

The awareness of the vulnerability of the environment and the recognition that environmental risks have to be assessed on a continuous basis have become much stronger in the years since the Treaty's conclusion. These new concerns have enhanced the relevance of Articles 15, 19 and 20.

113. The Court recognizes that both Parties agree on the need to take environmental concerns seriously and to take the required precautionary measures, but they fundamentally disagree on the consequences this has for the joint Project. In such a case, third-party involvement may be helpful and instrumental in finding a solution, provided each of the Parties is flexible in its position.

114. Finally, Hungary maintained that by their conduct both parties had repudiated the Treaty and that a bilateral treaty repudiated by both parties cannot survive. The Court is of the view, however, that although it has found that both Hungary and Czechoslovakia failed to comply with their obligations under the 1977 Treaty, this reciprocal wrongful conduct did not bring the Treaty to an end nor justify its termination. The Court would set a precedent with disturbing implications for treaty relations and the integrity of the rule *pacta sunt servanda* if it were to conclude that a treaty in force between States, which the parties have implemented in considerable

measure and at great cost over a period of years, might be unilaterally set aside on grounds of reciprocal non-compliance. It would be otherwise, of course, if the parties decided to terminate the Treaty by mutual consent. But in this case, while Hungary purported to terminate the Treaty, Czechoslovakia consistently resisted this act and declared it to be without legal effect.

115. In the light of the conclusions it has reached above, the Court, in reply to the question put to it in Article 2, paragraph 1 (c), of the Special Agreement ... , finds that the notification of termination by Hungary of 19 May 1992 did not have the legal effect of terminating the 1977 Treaty and related instruments.

NOTES

1) In paragraph 47 of the judgment, in which the Court discussed the relationship between the law of treaties and the law of state responsibility, it stated that the Vienna Convention "confines itself to defining—in a limitative manner—the conditions in which a treaty may lawfully be denounced or suspended; while the effects of a denunciation or suspension seen as not meeting those conditions are, on the contrary, expressly excluded from the scope of the Convention." Thus, the Court appears to accept the view of the International Law Commission that the grounds for terminating or suspending treaty obligations enumerated in the Convention are exhaustive.

2) One commentator has suggested that with regard to the analysis of fundamental change of circumstances, the Court in *Gabčíkovo* should have added a balancing test, setting the interests of the state calling for termination on the basis of a fundamental change of circumstances against the countervailing interests of the other party. He notes that most domestic legal systems that recognize the doctrine incorporate such a balancing test, but that Article 62 does not include it. He argues as follows:[52]

[T]he Court should have acknowledged the gap in Article 62 and added the balancing test under the heading of interpretation. This would have been all the more justifiable as Article 62 provides only that a fundamental change of circumstances "*may not be invoked unless*" the conditions explicitly set forth are met. The negative wording reflects the widespread skepticism against the reception of *clausula rebus sic stantibus* in international law and was meant to prevent an excessive use of the provision that would corrupt the binding force of treaties. Under these circumstances, it is difficult to see why the introduction of a balancing test as a further *restrictive* element of law should be inconsistent either with the text of the Convention or with the intention of its drafters.

Do you agree that such a balancing test should be read into Article 62? Why or why not?

3) The *rebus sic stantibus* principle has been invoked in a number of cases before the World Court. The ICJ in *Gabčíkovo* referred to its decision in the *Fisheries Jurisdiction Case (Jurisdiction) (United Kingdom v. Iceland)*, in which Iceland unsuccessfully argued that a change of circumstances had terminated a 1961 treaty with the United Kingdom in

---

52   Daniel Reichert-Facilides, "Down the Danube: The Vienna Convention on the Law of Treaties and the Case Concerning the Gabčíkovo-Nagymaros Project" (1998) 47 I.C.L.Q. 837 at 846.

which the parties had agreed that any dispute over fisheries jurisdiction should be referred to the Court.[53] In the *Free Zones Case*,[54] the Permanent Court of International Justice accepted the Swiss government's arguments that the circumstances alleged to have changed were not circumstances on the basis of whose continuance the parties could be said to have entered into the treaty and that France had delayed unreasonably long after the alleged changes of circumstances had manifested themselves. The Court did not address the argument that the *rebus sic stantibus* principle did not apply to treaties creating territorial rights. Arguments regarding *rebus sic stantibus* were also raised in the *Nationality Decrees in Tunis and Morocco Case*.[55]

4) The continuance of a treaty may be affected in two other situations—namely, the *post facto* assertion that the agreement was unequal and imposed, and the outbreak of war.[56] Does article 62 on fundamental change of circumstances cover these situations?

5) It is increasingly common for treaties to contain revision clauses that provide for review after the expiration of a prescribed period of time. Such a clause obliges the signatories to consider amendments requested by one party on account of changed circumstances or for any other reason.

6) As to whether revolutionary changes in Iran in 1978-80 terminated its Treaty of Amity, Economic Relations and Consular Rights with the United States, see *Amoco International Finance Corp. v. Iran*.[57] Amoco claimed the expropriation of its interest in a joint venture in Iran was contrary to the treaty but Iran argued that it was inoperative due to the changed circumstances and to violations of its provisions by the United States. The Tribunal noted that neither change of circumstances nor breach automatically terminates a treaty. If one party concludes that the consequences legally justify termination of a treaty, it may take suitable steps. Neither party had done so in this case. However, the Tribunal also noted that the revolutionary events in Iran "could not be without consequences on the implementation of the treaty." For instance, the part concerning consular relations had to have been suspended upon closure of the consulates and the rupture of diplomatic relations between the United States and Iran. Yet the

---

53   [1973] I.C.J. Rep. 3.

54   *France v. Switzerland* (1932), P.C.I.J. (Ser. A/B) No. 46 at 156-58, reported above in Section B.3 on "Legal Effects of Treaties."

55   *Nationality Decrees in Tunis and Morocco Case* (1923), Advisory Opinion, P.C.I.J. (Ser. B) No. 4 at 12-13, 28-29.

56   As to unequal treaties, see Stuart S. Malawer, *Imposed Treaties and International Law* (1977) and Charles Henry Alexandrowicz, "Treaty and Diplomatic Relations between European and South Asian Powers in the Seventeenth and Eighteenth Centuries" (1960/2) 100 Hague Recueil 203 at 278. As to the effects of war, see *Francis v. The Queen*, [1956] S.C.R. 618. Cf. *Karnuth, Director of Immigration et al. v. United States ex rel. Albro*, 279 U.S. 231 (1929); also, Cecil Hurst, "The Effect of War on Treaties" (1921-22) 2 Brit. Y.B. Int'l L. 37. Hunting rights: *R. v. Syliboy*, [1929] 1 D.L.R. 307 (N.S. Co. Ct.); mutual naturalization: *Re Cimonian* (1915) 23 D.L.R. 363 at 372-73 (Ont. S.C.); and copyright: *Louvigny de Montigny v. Cousineau*, [1950] S.C.R. 297 at 311, which were all dealt with by international agreement, and were held in abeyance during the war at least until the cessation of hostilities and perhaps even until the state of war was formally terminated by a Treaty of Peace: *Spitz v. Secretary of State*, [1939] 2 D.L.R. 546 (Ex. Ct.).

57   (1987), 15 Iran–U.S. C.T.R. 189 at 215-19.

Tribunal did not think the disorder in Iran, though it disrupted the operation of the treaty with respect to the treatment of U.S. nationals, terminated the treaty, nor that the interruption of communications between the two states amounted to an implicit denunciation of the treaty by either party.

7) Article 60 on the termination or suspension of a treaty as a consequence of its breach was applied by the International Court of Justice in the *Namibia Case*[58] in confirming the legitimacy of the U.N. General Assembly's termination of South Africa's mandate over South-West Africa.

8) A number of cases have considered the status of treaties concluded between the United Kingdom and the United States in respect of Canada and the effect of the Statute of Westminster (1931). In *Ex Parte O'Dell and Griffen*,[59] two individuals whose extradition was sought by the United States argued *inter alia* that there was no extradition treaty between Canada and the United States because the Ashburton Treaty of 1842, an imperial treaty, ceased to have validity upon the enactment of the Statute of Westminster. Schroeder J. noted: "Had it been intended that the Ashburton Treaty or any other convention which had been entered into or any other statute which had been enacted by the Imperial Government or Parliament prior to this time, affecting Canada or any of its Provinces, should cease to have validity, one would expect to find express provision for it in The Statute of Westminster or in some other statute. There is nothing to prevent Canada from entering into a new treaty with the United States or substituting some other extradition arrangement for the one which is now embraced within the terms of the Ashburton treaty, but until that is done that treaty remains in full force and effect and is binding upon the signatories thereto, including Canada."[60] In *Regina v. Sikyea*,[61] the Court of Appeal for the Northwest Territories stated that federal statutes that implement treaties made in accordance with section 132 of the *B.N.A. Act* (now the *Constitution Act, 1867*), and before the Statute of Westminster remain valid legislation even when their subject matter falls exclusively under section 92 of that Act, so long as the treaties have not been denounced. It would also appear that such statutes can still be amended by the federal Parliament, if that is necessary to properly carry out the terms of the treaties.

9) Suspension of the operation of a treaty is a possible alternative to denunciation of or withdrawal from it. A treaty may be suspended by consent of all the parties (article 57), or by agreement among some parties only, provided their action does not prejudice the rights and obligations of the other parties or the purposes of the treaty (article 58). Suspension releases the parties from further performance of the treaty but it does not otherwise affect their continuing legal relations. The parties are also bound to refrain from actions that might obstruct resumption of the treaty's operation (article 72).

---

58 Advisory Opinion, [1971] I.C.J. Rep. 16, reported in Chapter 2, Section C on "Other Legal Persons."

59 [1953] O.R. 190 (H.C.).

60 *Ibid.* at 193.

61 (1964), 43 D.L.R. (2d) 150, aff'd. [1964] S.C.R. 642.

Succession to Treaties

The Vienna Convention on the Law of Treaties does "not prejudge any question that may arise in regard to a treaty from a succession of states ..." (article 73). The principles of international law that do govern this matter are discussed in Chapter 2, Section D, on "State Succession."

C. CUSTOM

1. General Customary Law[62]

Customary international law is composed of two elements: (1) there must be a consistent and general international practice among states, and (2) the practice must be accepted as law by the international community. This subjective element of acceptance as law is often known as *opinio juris*.

Three concepts have been advanced to explain why "international custom, as evidence of a general practice accepted as law"[63] is binding on states: consent, estoppel, and reasonableness. Reliance on each of these concepts may lead to different opinions about the existence and contents of an alleged customary rule.

It is easy to make these general propositions about the process of creating customary international law and about the basis for determining its application, but in practice these two different operations are complex and controversial. Part of the controversy stems from the apparent paradox that customary rules binding on all are founded in the unilateral acts of individual states. Here is a statement on this dilemma made in the context of the developing law of the sea. It was delivered in 1970 by the Canadian Representative, Mr. J.A. Beesley, to the First Committee of the U.N. General Assembly:

> Mr. Chairman, there have been a number of references during our debate to the relative merits of unilateralism as compared to multilateralism as methods of developing the Law of the Sea.
>
> The Canadian position on this issue is well-known. In brief, we do not consider multilateral action and unilateral action as mutually exclusive courses; they should not, in our view, be looked on as clear-cut alternatives. The contemporary international law of the sea comprises both conventional and customary law. Conventional or multilateral treaty law must, of course, be developed primarily by multilateral action, drawing as necessary upon principles of customary international law. Thus, multilateral conventions often consist of

---

62   See Anthony A. D'Amato, *The Concept of Custom in International Law* (1971); Michael Byers, *Custom, Power and the Power of Rules: International Relations and Customary International Law* (1999); and H.W.A. Thirlway, *International Customary Law and Codification: An Examination of the Continuing Role of Custom in the Present Period of Codification of International Law* (1972). For a recent overview of some of the main debates, see Jörg Kammerhofer, "Uncertainty in the Formal Sources of International Law: Customary Law and Some of Its Problems" (2004) 15 E.J.I.L. 523. See also Jack L. Goldsmith & Eric A. Posner, "Understanding the Resemblance Between Modern and Traditional Customary International Law" (1999-2000) 40 Va. J. Int'l. L. 639.

63   See art. 38(1)(b) of the Statute of I.C.J., reprinted in the Documentary Supplement.

both a codification of existing principles of international law and progressive development of new principles. Customary international law is, of course, derived primarily from state practice, that is to say, unilateral action by various states, although it frequently draws in turn upon the principles embodied in bilateral and limited multilateral treaties. Law-making treaties often become accepted as such not by virtue of their status as treaties, but through a gradual acceptance by states of the principles they lay down. The complex process of the development of customary international law is still relevant and indeed, in our view, essential to the building of a world order. For these reasons we find it very difficult to be doctrinaire on such questions. The regime of the territorial sea, for example, derives in part from conventional law, including in particular the Geneva Convention on the Territorial Sea (which itself was based in large part upon customary principles) and in part from the very process of the development of customary international law. During the period when it was possible to say, if ever there was such a time, that there existed a rule of law that the breadth of the territorial sea extended to three nautical miles and no further, that principle was created by state practice, and can be altered by state practice, that is to say, by unilateral action on the part of various states, accepted by other states and thus developed into customary international law. How then can we be dogmatic about the merits of either approach to the exclusion of the other? Unilateralism carried to an extreme and based upon differing or conflicting principles could produce complete chaos.

Unilateral action when taken along parallel lines and based upon similar principles can lead to a new regional and perhaps even universal rule of law. Similarly, agreement by the international community reached through a multilateral approach can produce effective rules of law, while doctrinaire insistence upon the multilateral approach as the only legitimate means of developing the law can lead to the situation which has prevailed since the failure of the two Geneva Law of the Sea Conferences to reach agreement upon the breadth of the territorial sea and fishing zones. ... What is required, in our view, is a judicious mix of the two approaches taking into account the complex set of interrelated and sometimes conflicting political, economic and legal considerations, both national and international, and based upon the imperatives of time itself. The seriousness of the problem can determine the urgency of action, which in turn can sometimes dictate the means chosen.[64]

This thesis appears to permit states to act outside the law. Is it acceptable? For instance, in 1970 Canada claimed jurisdiction over a large area of Arctic waters contrary to the principle of the freedom of the high seas. At the time it was a unique unilateral assertion of authority that, however it might have been justified as morally necessary to prevent pollution or politically urgent to protect Canadian sovereignty, was not based on deference to any *opinio juris* in the matter.

One of the best descriptions of the creation of customary international law was provided by Professor Myres McDougal, also in the context of the law of the sea:

[T]he international law of the sea is not a mere static body of rules but is rather a whole decision-making process, a public order which includes a structure of authorized decision-makers as well as a body of highly flexible, inherited prescriptions. It is, in other words, a

---

64   Reported in (1971) 9 Can. Y.B. Int'l Law 276.

process of continuous interaction, of continuous demand and response, in which the decision-makers of particular nation states unilaterally put forward claims of the most diverse and conflicting character to the use of the world's seas, and in which other decision-makers, external to the demanding state and including both national and international officials, weigh and appraise these competing claims in terms of the interests of the world community and of the rival claimants, and ultimately accept or reject them. As such a process, it is a living, growing law, grounded in the practices and sanctioning expectations of nation-state officials, and changing as their demands and expectations are changed by the exigencies of new interests and technology and by other continually evolving conditions in the world arena. ...

The authoritative decision-makers put forward by the public order of the high seas to resolve all these competing claims include, of course, not merely judges of international courts and other international officials, but also those same nation-state officials who on other occasions are themselves claimants. This duality in function ("*dédoublement fonctionnel*"), or fact that the same nation-state officials are alternately, in a process of reciprocal interaction, both claimants and external decision-makers passing upon the claims of others, need not, however, cause confusion: it merely reflects the present lack of specialization and centralization of policy functions in international law generally. Similarly, it may be further observed, without deprecating the authority of international law, that these authoritative decision-makers projected by nation states for creating and applying a common public order, honor each other's unilateral claims to the use of the world's seas not merely by explicit agreements but also by mutual tolerances—expressed in countless decisions in foreign offices, national courts, and national legislatures—which create expectations that effective power will be restrained and exercised in certain uniformities of pattern. This process of reciprocal tolerance of unilateral claim is, too, but that by which in the present state of world organization most decisions about jurisdiction in public and private international law are, and must be, taken. (It is not of course the unilateral claims but rather the reciprocal tolerances of the external decision-makers which create the expectations of pattern and uniformity in decision, of practice in accord with rule, commonly regarded as law.)[65]

While Professor McDougal gives a lucid depiction of the interactive process of creating customary law, he only hints, parenthetically, at how to determine when state practice has passed into law. It is especially difficult to establish whether the general behaviour of states on some particular matter reflects a common practice merely out of convenience or from a sense of legal obligation. Proof of the necessary *opinio juris* is rarely displayed in explicit acceptance of one state's claims by others; rather it is shown by their tolerance of that state's conduct. Professor MacGibbon has analyzed the part played by tolerance and by objection in the creation of customary law:

To determine whether a given practice is being pursued as a matter of right or merely as a matter of convenience may be a task of some difficulty which, however, evidence of either protest or absence of protest may to some extent resolve. In so far as protests are made against refusal to submit to the practice or against aberrations in which the practice takes a

---

65   Myres S. McDougal, "The Hydrogen Bomb Tests and the International Law of the Sea," Editorial Comment (1955) 49 A.J.I.L. 356 at 356-58.

substantially different form, they tend strongly if not conclusively to show the conviction on the part of the protesting States that they were acting in defence of their rights, or, in other words, that the practice was being asserted on the basis of a claim of right. On the other hand, acquiescence in refusals to submit to a given practice, or acquiescence in a contrary practice on the part of other States, affords cogent evidence that the practice is not followed on the basis of a claim of right and that submission to its exercise is not regarded as obligatory—in short, that it is not an international custom. ...

The process of action and reaction which Professor McDougal observed as characteristic of the development of a particular set of customary rules is common to the formation of all rules of customary international law. The fact that claims may conflict to a greater or less degree lends complication to the process of determining what part, if any, of differing claims and practices in respect of a particular matter have crystallized into customary practices with legal sanction. It is probable that only by reference to protest and acquiescence can this question be resolved. Those parts of conflicting claims and practices in respect of a particular matter which are common to all of the claimant States and have encountered no protests are, it is submitted, the acceptable *residuum* of the practice or claim which is apt to attain the status of custom; by contrast, protests maintained against certain parts of the claim suffice to prevent those objectionable features from achieving legal sanction. Finally, it is submitted that the extent to which a general uniform practice has been "accepted as law" may most readily and objectively be gauged by estimating the degree of general consent, or, failing express consent, the degree of general acquiescence which the practice has encountered.[66]

How to weigh the evidence of state practice so as to determine the advent and content of a customary rule of law is considered in the following cases and questions.

The Steamship Lotus
France v. Turkey
(1927), P.C.I.J. (Ser. A) No. 10, reported in Chapter 9, Section A.1 on
"Scope of Jurisdiction Generally"

North Sea Continental Shelf Cases
Federal Republic of Germany v. Denmark and v. Netherlands
[1969] I.C.J. Rep. 3

[In 1964 and 1965 the Federal Republic of Germany entered into agreements with the Netherlands and Denmark for the purpose of delimiting the boundaries of their North Sea continental shelves. These agreements only established a partial dividing line for a short distance from the coast beginning at the point at which the land boundary between the states is located. In order to determine the lateral or median

---

66   I.C. MacGibbon, "Customary International Law and Acquiescence" (1957) 33 Brit. Y.B. Int'l L. 115 at 118-19.

lines with more precision, a matter which proved to be impossible to settle by agreement, the Federal Republic of Germany, the Netherlands, and Denmark agreed to refer the problem to the International Court of Justice.

The question put to the court was as follows: What principles and rules of international law are applicable to the delimitation as between the Parties of the areas of the continental shelf in the North Sea which appertain to each of them beyond the partial boundary [already] determined ... ?

The Netherlands and Denmark argued that the "equidistance-special circumstances principles" in article 6(2) of the 1958 Geneva Convention on the Continental Shelf applied whereas the Federal Republic of Germany relied on the doctrine of the just and equitable share. Article 6 of the Convention reads:

> 1. Where the same continental shelf is adjacent to the territories of two or more States whose coasts are opposite each other, the boundary of the continental shelf appertaining to such States shall be determined by agreement between them. In the absence of agreement, and unless another boundary line is justified by special circumstances, the boundary is the median line, every point of which is equidistant from the nearest points of the baselines from which the breadth of the territorial sea of each State is measured.
>
> 2. Where the same continental shelf is adjacent to the territories of two adjacent States, the boundary of the continental shelf shall be determined by agreement between them. In the absence of agreement, and unless another boundary line is justified by special circumstances, the boundary shall be determined by application of the principle of equidistance from the nearest points of the baselines from which the breadth of the territorial sea of each State is measured.

The Court held that the Federal Republic, which had not ratified the Convention, was not bound by the provisions of article 6. Therefore, the question became: what customary international law existed to delimit the continental shelf between the parties?]

THE COURT: ...

37. It is maintained by Denmark and the Netherlands that the Federal Republic, whatever its position may be in relation to the Geneva Convention, considered as such, is in any event bound to accept delimitation on an equidistance-special circumstances basis, because the use of this method is not in the nature of a merely conventional obligation, but is, or must now be regarded as involving, a rule that is part of the *corpus* of general international law. ... This contention has both a positive law and a more fundamentalist aspect. ... In its fundamentalist aspect, the view put forward derives from what might be called the natural law of the continental shelf, in the sense that the equidistance principle is seen as a necessary expression in the field of delimitation of the accepted doctrine of the exclusive appurtenance of the continental shelf to the nearby coastal State, and therefore as having an *a priori* character of so to speak juristic inevitability. ...

46. The conclusion drawn by the Court is that the notion of equidistance as being logically necessary, in the sense of being an inescapable *a priori* accompaniment of

basic continental shelf doctrine, is incorrect. It is said not to be possible to maintain that there is a rule of law ascribing certain areas to a State as a matter of inherent and original right ... without also admitting the existence of some rule by which those areas can be obligatorily delimited. The Court cannot accept the logic of this view. The problem arises only where there is a dispute and only in respect of the marginal areas involved. The appurtenance of a given area, considered as an entity, in no way governs the precise delimitation of its boundaries, any more than uncertainty as to boundaries can affect territorial rights. ...

60. The conclusions so far reached leave open and still to be considered, the question whether on some basis other than that of an *a priori* logical necessity, i.e. through positive law processes, the equidistance principle has come to be regarded as a rule of customary international law, so that it would be obligatory for the Federal Republic in that way, even though Art. 6 of the Geneva Convention is not, as such, opposable to it. For this purpose it is necessary to examine the status of the principle as it stood when the Convention was drawn up, as it resulted from the effect of the Convention, and in the light of State practice subsequent to the Convention; but it should be clearly understood that in the pronouncements the Court makes on these matters it has in view solely the delimitation provisions (Art. 6) of the Convention, not other parts of it, nor the Convention as such.

61. The first of these questions can conveniently be considered in the form suggested on behalf of Denmark and the Netherlands themselves in the course of the oral hearing, when it was stated that they had not in fact contended that the delimitation article (Art. 6) of the Convention "embodied already received rules of customary law in the sense that the Convention was merely declaratory of existing rules." Their contention was, rather, that although prior to the Conference, continental shelf law was only in the formative stage and State practice lacked uniformity, yet "the process of the definition and consolidation of the emerging customary law took place through the work of the International Law Commission, the reaction of governments to that work and the proceedings of the Geneva Conference"; and this emerging customary law became "crystallized in the adoption of the Continental Shelf Convention by the Conference."

62. Whatever validity this contention may have in respect of at least certain parts of the Convention, the Court cannot accept it as regards the delimitation provision (Art. 6), the relevant parts of which were adopted almost unchanged from the draft of the International Law Commission that formed the basis of discussion at the Conference. The status of the rule in the Convention therefore depends mainly on the processes that led the Commission to propose it. These processes ... [indicate] that the principle of equidistance, as it now figures in Art. 6 of the Convention, was proposed by the Commission with considerable hesitation, somewhat on an experimental basis, at most *de lege ferenda*, and not at all *de lege lata* or as an emerging rule of customary international law. This is clearly not the sort of foundation on which Art. 6 of the Convention could be said to have reflected or crystallized such a rule.

63. The foregoing conclusion receives significant confirmation from the fact that Art. 6 is one of those in respect of which, under the reservations article of the Convention (Art. 12) reservations may be made by any State on signing, ratifying or acceding, for, speaking generally, it is a characteristic of purely conventional rules

and obligations that, in regard to them, some faculty of making unilateral reservations may, within certain limits, be admitted, whereas this cannot be so in the case of general or customary law rules and obligations which, by their very nature, must have equal force for all members of the international community and cannot therefore be the subject of any right of unilateral exclusion exercisable at will by any one of them in its own favour. Consequently, it is to be expected that when, for whatever reason, rules or obligations of this order are embodied, or are intended to be reflected in certain provisions of a convention, such provisions will figure amongst those in respect of which a right of unilateral reservation is not conferred, or is excluded. This expectation is, in principle, fulfilled by Art. 12 of the Geneva Continental Shelf Convention, which permits reservations to be made to all the articles of the Convention "other than to Arts. 1 to 3 inclusive": these three articles being the ones which, it is clear, were then regarded as reflecting, or as crystallizing, or at least as emerging as rules of customary international law relative to the continental shelf, amongst them the question of the seaward extent of the shelf; the juridical character of the coastal State's entitlement; the nature of the rights exercisable; the kind of natural resources to which these relate; and the preservation intact of the legal status as high seas of the waters over the shelf and the legal status of the superjacent air-space.

64. The normal inference would therefore be that any articles that do not figure among those excluded from the faculty of reservation under Art. 12, were not regarded as declaratory of previously existing or emergent rules of law; and this is the inference the Court in fact draws in respect of Art. 6 (delimitation), having regard also to the attitude of the International Law Commission to this provision, as already described in general terms. Naturally this would not of itself prevent this provision from eventually passing into the general *corpus* of customary international law by one of the processes considered in paragraphs 70-81 below. But that is not here the issue. What is now under consideration is whether it originally figured in the Convention as such a rule. ...

70. The Court must now proceed to the last stage in the argument put forward on behalf of Denmark and the Netherlands. This is to the effect that even if there was at the date of the Geneva Convention no rule of customary international law in favour of the equidistance principle and no such rule was crystallized in Art. 6 of the Convention, nevertheless such a rule has come into being since the Convention, partly because of its own impact, partly on the basis of subsequent State practice and that this rule, being now a rule of customary international law binding on all States, including therefore the Federal Republic, should be declared applicable to the delimitation of the boundaries between the Parties' respective continental shelf areas in the North Sea.

71. In so far as this contention is based on the view that Art. 6 of the Convention has had the influence and has produced the effect described, it clearly involves treating that Article as a norm-creating provision which has constituted the foundation of, or has generated a rule which, while only conventional or contractual in its origin, has since passed into the general *corpus* of international law, and is now accepted as such by the *opinio juris*, so as to have become binding even for countries which have never and do not, become parties to the Convention. There is no doubt that this process is a perfectly

possible one and does from time to time occur: it constitutes indeed one of the recognized methods by which new rules of customary international law may be formed. At the same time this result is not lightly to be regarded as having been attained.

72. It would in the first place be necessary that the provision concerned should, at all events potentially, be of a fundamentally norm-creating character such as could be regarded as forming the basis of a general rule of law. Considered *in abstracto* the equidistance principle might be said to fulfill this requirement. Yet in the particular form in which it is embodied in Art. 6 of the Geneva Convention and having regard to the relationship of that Article to other provisions of the Convention, this must be open to some doubt. In the first place, Art. 6 is so framed as to put second the obligation to make use of the equidistance method, causing it to come after a primary obligation to effect delimitation by agreement. Such a primary obligation constitutes an unusual preface to what is claimed to be a potential general rule of law. Without attempting to enter into, still less pronounce upon any question of *jus cogens*, it is well understood that, in practice, rules of international law can, by agreement, be derogated from in particular cases, or as between particular parties, but this is not normally the subject of any express provision, as it is in Art. 6 of the Geneva Convention. Secondly the part played by the notion of special circumstances relative to the principle of equidistance as embodied in Art. 6 and the very considerable, still unresolved, controversies as to the exact meaning and scope of this notion, must raise further doubts as to the potentially norm-creating character of the rule. Finally, the faculty of making reservations to Art. 6, while it might not of itself prevent the equidistance principle being eventually received as general law, does add considerably to the difficulty of regarding this result as having been brought about (or being potentially possible) on the basis of the Convention: for so long as this faculty continues to exist and is not the subject of any revision brought about in consequence of a request made under Art. 13 of the Convention, of which there is at present no official indication, it is the Convention itself which would, for the reasons already indicated, seem to deny to the provisions of Art. 6 the same norm-creating character as, for instance, Arts. 1 and 2 possess.

73. With respect to the other elements usually regarded as necessary before a conventional rule can be considered to have become a general rule of international law, it might be that, even without the passage of any considerable period of time, a very widespread and representative participation in the Convention might suffice of itself, provided it included that of States whose interests were specially affected. In the present case however, the Court notes that, even if allowance is made for the existence of a number of States to whom participation in the Geneva Convention is not open, or which, by reason for instance of being land-locked States, would have no interest in becoming parties to it, the number of ratifications and accessions so far secured is, though respectable, hardly sufficient. That non-ratification may sometimes be due to factors other than active disapproval of the convention concerned can hardly constitute a basis on which positive acceptance of its principles can be implied. The reasons are speculative, but the facts remain.

74. As regards the time element, the Court notes that it is over ten years since the Convention was signed, but that it is even now less than five since it came into force

in June 1964 and that when the present proceedings were brought it was less than three years, while less than one had elapsed at the time when the respective negotiations between the Federal Republic and the other two Parties for a complete delimitation broke down on the question of the application of the equidistance principle. Although the passage of only a short period of time is not necessarily, or of itself, a bar to the formation of a new rule of customary international law on the basis of what was originally a purely conventional rule, an indispensable requirement would be that within the period in question, short though it might be, State practice, including that of States whose interests are specially affected, would have been both extensive and virtually uniform in the sense of the provision invoked; moreover, it should have occurred in such a way as to show a general recognition that a rule of law or legal obligation is involved.

75. The Court must now consider whether State practice in the matter of continental shelf delimitation has, subsequent to the Geneva Convention, been of such a kind as to satisfy this requirement. Leaving aside cases which, for various reasons, the Court does not consider to be reliable guides as precedents, such as delimitations effected between the present Parties themselves, or not relating to international boundaries, some fifteen cases have been cited in the course of the present proceedings, occurring mostly since the signature of the 1958 Geneva Convention, in which continental shelf boundaries have been delimited according to the equidistance principle, in the majority of the cases by agreement, in a few others unilaterally, or else the delimitation was foreshadowed but has not yet been carried out. Amongst these fifteen are the four North Sea delimitations United Kingdom/Norway-Denmark-Netherlands, and Norway/Denmark. ... But even if these various cases constituted more than a very small proportion of those potentially calling for delimitation in the world as a whole, the Court would not think it necessary to enumerate or evaluate them separately, since there are, *a priori*, several grounds which deprive them of weight as precedents in the present context.

76. To begin with, over half the States concerned, whether acting unilaterally or conjointly, were or shortly became parties to the Geneva Convention, and were therefore presumably, so far as they were concerned, acting actually or potentially in the application of the Convention. From their action no inference could legitimately be drawn as to the existence of a rule of customary international law in favour of the equidistance principle. As regards those States, on the other hand, which were not, and have not become parties to the Convention, the basis of their action can only be problematical and must remain entirely speculative. Clearly, they were not applying the Convention. But from that no inference could justifiably be drawn that they believed themselves to be applying a mandatory rule of customary international law. There is not a shred of evidence that they did and ... there is no lack of other reasons for using the equidistance method, so that acting, or agreeing to act in a certain way, does not of itself demonstrate anything of a juridical nature.

77. The essential point in this connection and it seems necessary to stress it, is that even if these instances of action by non-parties to the Convention were much more numerous than they in fact are, they would not, even in the aggregate, suffice in themselves to constitute the *opinio juris*; for, in order to achieve this result, two

conditions must be fulfilled. Not only must the acts concerned amount to a settled practice, but they must also be such, or be carried out in such a way, as to be evidence of a belief that this practice is rendered obligatory by the existence of a rule of law requiring it. The need for such a belief, *i.e.*, the existence of a subjective element, is implicit in the very notion of the *opinio juris sive necessitatis*. The States concerned must therefore feel that they are conforming to what amounts to a legal obligation. The frequency, or even habitual character of the acts is not in itself enough. There are many international acts, *e.g.*, in the field of ceremonial and protocol, which are performed almost invariably, but which are motivated only by considerations of courtesy, convenience or tradition, and not by any sense of legal duty.

78. In this respect the Court follows the view adopted by the Permanent Court of International Justice in the *Lotus* case, as stated in the following passage, the principle of which is, by analogy, applicable almost word for word, *mutatis mutandis*, to the present case (P.C.I.J., Series A., No. 10, 1927, at 28):

> Even if the rarity of the judicial decisions to be found ... were sufficient to prove ... the circumstance alleged ... it would merely show that States had often, in practice, abstained from instituting criminal proceedings, and not that they recognized themselves as being obliged to do so; for only if such abstention were based on their being conscious of having a duty to abstain would it be possible to speak of an international custom. The alleged fact does not allow one to infer that States have been conscious of having such a duty; on the other hand ... there are other circumstances calculated to show that the contrary is true.

Applying this *dictum* to the present case, the position is simply that in certain cases, not a great number, the States concerned agreed to draw or did draw the boundaries concerned according to the principle of equidistance. There is no evidence that they so acted because they felt legally compelled to draw them in this way by reason of a rule of customary law obliging them to do so, especially considering that they might have been motivated by other obvious factors.

79. Finally, it appears that in almost all of the cases cited, the delimitations concerned were median-line delimitations between opposite States, not lateral delimitations between adjacent States. ... [T]he Court regards the case of median-line delimitations between opposite States as different in various respects and as being sufficiently distinct not to constitute a precedent for the delimitation of lateral boundaries. In only one situation discussed by the parties does there appear to have been a geographical configuration which to some extent resembles the present one, in the sense that a number of States on the same coastline are grouped around a sharp curve or bend of it. No complete delimitation in this area has however yet been carried out. But the Court is not concerned to deny to this case, or any other of those cited, all evidential value in favour of the thesis of Denmark and the Netherlands. It simply considers that they are inconclusive, and insufficient to bear the weight sought to be put upon them as evidence of such a settled practice, manifested in such circumstances, as would justify the inference that delimitation according to the principle of equidistance amounts to a mandatory rule of customary international law, more particularly where lateral delimitations are concerned. ...

81. The Court accordingly concludes that if the Geneva Convention was not in its origins or inception declaratory of a mandatory rule of customary international law enjoining the use of the equidistance principle for the delimitation of continental shelf areas between adjacent States neither has its subsequent effect been constitutive of such a rule; and that State practice up-to-date has equally been insufficient for the purpose. ...

[Having thus found that neither of the approaches argued for by the parties was a part of international law, the Court then proceeded to spell out the principles and rules that did apply.]

85. It emerges from the history of the development of the legal régime of the continental shelf ... that the essential reason why the equidistance method is not to be regarded as a rule of law is that, if it were to be compulsorily applied in all situations, this would not be consonant with certain basic legal notions which ... have from the beginning reflected the *opinio juris* in the matter of delimitation; those principles being that delimitation must be the object of agreement between the States concerned, and that such agreement must be arrived at in accordance with equitable principles. ...

88. The Court comes next to the rule of equity. The legal basis of that rule in the particular case of the delimitation of the continental shelf as between adjoining States has already been stated. It must however be noted that the rule rests also on a broader basis. [Whatever the legal reasoning of a court of justice, its decisions must by definition be just, and therefore in that sense equitable. Nevertheless, when mention is made of a court dispensing justice or declaring the law, what is meant is that the decision finds its objective justification in considerations lying not outside but within the rules, and in this field it is precisely a rule of law that calls for the application of equitable principles.] There is consequently no question in this case of any decision *ex aequo et bono*, such as would only be possible under the conditions prescribed by Article 38, paragraph 2, of the Court's Statute. ...

89. It must next be observed that, in certain geographical circumstances which are quite frequently met with, the equidistance method, despite its known advantages, leads unquestionably to inequity, ...

91. Equity does not necessarily imply equality. There can never be any question of completely refashioning nature, and equity does not require that a State without access to the sea should be allotted an area of continental shelf, any more than there could be a question of rendering the situation of a State with an extensive coastline similar to that of a State with a restricted coastline. Equality is to be reckoned within the same plane, and it is not such natural inequalities as these that equity could remedy. But in the present case there are three States whose North Sea coastlines are in fact comparable in length and which, therefore, have been given broadly equal treatment by nature except that the configuration of one of the coastlines would, if the equidistance method is used, deny to one of these States treatment equal or comparable to that given the other two. Here indeed is a case where, in a theoretical situation of equality within the same order, an inequity is created. What is unacceptable in this instance is that a State should enjoy continental shelf rights considerably different from those of its neighbours merely because in the one case the coastline is roughly

convex in form and in the other it is markedly concave, although those coastlines are comparable in length. It is therefore not a question of totally refashioning geography whatever the facts of the situation but, given a geographical situation of quasi-equality as between a number of States, of abating the effects of an incidental special feature from which an unjustifiable difference of treatment could result.

98. A final factor to be taken account of is the element of a reasonable degree of proportionality which a delimitation effected according to equitable principles ought to bring about between the extent of the continental shelf appertaining to the States concerned and the lengths of their respective coastlines—these being measured according to their general direction in order to establish the necessary balance between States with straight, and those with markedly concave or convex coasts, or to reduce very irregular coastlines to their truer proportions. The choice and application of the appropriate technical methods would be a matter for the parties. ...

101. For these reasons, THE COURT, by eleven votes to six, finds that, in each case,

(a) the use of the equidistance method of delimitation not being obligatory as between the Parties; and

(b) there being no other single method of delimitation the use of which is in all circumstances obligatory;

(c) the principles and rules of international law applicable to the delimitation as between the Parties ... are as follows:

1) delimitation is to be effected by agreement in accordance with equitable principles, and taking account of all the relevant circumstances, in such a way as to leave as much as possible to each Party all those parts of the continental shelf that constitute a natural prolongation of its land territory into and under the sea, without encroachment on the natural prolongation of the land territory of the other;

2) if, in the application of the preceding sub-paragraph, the delimitation leaves to the Parties areas that overlap, these are to be divided between them in agreed proportions or, failing agreement, equally, unless they decide on a régime of joint jurisdiction, user, or exploitation for the zones of overlap or any part of them;

(d) in the course of the negotiations, the factors to be taken into account are to include:

1) the general configuration of the coasts of the Parties, as well as the presence of any special or unusual features;

2) so far as known or readily ascertainable, the physical and geological structure, and natural resources, of the continental shelf areas involved;

3) the element of a reasonable degree of proportionality, which a delimitation carried out in accordance with equitable principles ought to bring about between the extent of the continental shelf areas appertaining to the coastal State and the length of its coast measured

in the general direction of the coastline, account being taken for this purpose of the effects, actual or prospective, of any other continental shelf delimitations between adjacent States in the same region.

JUDGE TANAKA dissenting: ... To decide whether these two factors [usage and *opinio juris*] in the formative process of a customary law exist or not, is a delicate and difficult matter. The repetition, the number of examples of State practice, the duration of time required for the generation of customary law cannot be mathematically and uniformly decided. Each fact requires to be evaluated relatively according to the different occasions and circumstances. ... what is important in the matter at issue is not the number or figure of ratifications of and accessions to the Convention or of examples of subsequent State practice, but the meaning which they would imply in the particular circumstances. We cannot evaluate the ratification of the Convention by a large maritime country or the State practice represented by its concluding an agreement on the basis of the equidistance principle, as having exactly the same importance as similar acts by a land-locked country which possessed no particular interest in the delimitation of the continental shelf.

Next, so far as ... *opinio juris sive necessitatis* is concerned, it is extremely difficult to get evidence of its existence in concrete cases. This factor, relating to international motivation and being of a psychological nature, cannot be ascertained very easily, particularly when diverse legislative and executive organs of a government participate in an internal process of decision-making in respect of ratification or other State acts. There is no other way than to ascertain the existence of *opinio juris* from the fact of the external existence of a certain custom and its necessity felt in the international community, rather than to seek evidence as to the subjective motives for each example of State practice, which is something which is impossible of achievement. ...

JUDGE LACHS dissenting: ... Delay in the ratification of and accession to multilateral treaties is a well-known phenomenon in contemporary treaty practice ... experience indicates that in most cases [it is] caused by factors extraneous to the substance and objective of the instrument in question. ... [This] indicates that the number of ratifications and accessions cannot, in itself, be considered conclusive with regard to the general acceptance of a given instrument.

In the case of the Convention on the Continental Shelf, there are other elements that must be given their due weight. In particular, 31 States came into existence during the period between its signature (28 June, 1958) and its entry into force (10 June, 1964) while 13 other nations have since acceded to independence. Thus, the time during which these 44 States could have completed the necessary procedure enabling them to become parties to the Convention has been rather limited, in some cases very limited. Taking into account the great and urgent problems each of them had to face, one cannot be surprised that many of them did not consider it a matter of priority. This notwithstanding, nine of those States have acceded to the Convention. Twenty-six of the total number of States in existence are moreover land-locked and cannot be considered as having a special and immediate interest in speedy accession to the Convention (only five of them in fact acceded).

Finally, it is noteworthy that about 70 States are at present engaged in the exploration and exploitation of continental shelf areas.

It is the above analysis which is relevant, not the straight comparison between the total number of States in existence and the number of parties to the Convention. It reveals in fact that the number of parties to the Convention on the Continental Shelf is very impressive, including as it does the majority of States actively engaged in the exploration of continental shelves.

... [I]n the world today an essential factor in the formation of a new rule of general international law is to be taken into account: namely that States with different political, economic and legal systems, States of all continents, participate in the process. No more can a general rule of international law be established by the *fiat* of one or of a few or, as it was once claimed, by the consensus of European States only. ...

All this leads to the conclusion that the principles and rules enshrined in the Convention and in particular the equidistance rule, have been accepted not only by those States which are parties to the Convention on the Continental Shelf, but also by those which have subsequently followed it in agreements, or in their legislation, or have acquiesced in it when faced with legislative acts of other States affecting them. This can be viewed as evidence of a practice widespread enough to satisfy the criteria for a general rule of law.

For to become binding, a rule or principle of international law need not pass the test of universal acceptance. This is reflected in several statements of the Court, *e.g.*: "generally ... adopted in the practice of States" (*Fisheries Judgment, I.C.J.R. 1951*, p. 128). Not all States have ... an opportunity or possibility of applying a given rule. The evidence should be sought in the behaviour of a great number of States, possibly the majority of States, in any case the great majority of the interested States. ...

JUDGE AD HOC SORENSEN dissenting: ... I agree, of course, that one should not lightly reach the conclusion that a convention is binding upon a non-contracting State. But I find it necessary to take account of the fact, to which the Court does not give specific weight, that the Geneva Convention belongs to a particular category of multilateral conventions, namely those which result from the work of the United Nations in the field of codification and progressive development of international law, under Art. 13 of the Charter. ...

According to classic doctrine ... [the] practice [necessary to establish a rule of customary international law] must have been pursued over a certain length of time. There have even been those who have maintained the necessity of "immemorial usage." In its previous jurisprudence, however, the Court does not seem to have laid down strict requirements as to the duration of the usage or practice which may be accepted as law. In particular, it does not seem to have drawn any conclusion in this respect from the ordinary meaning of the word "custom" when used in other contexts. ... The possibility has thus been reserved for recognizing the rapid emergence of a new rule of customary law based on the recent practice of States. This is particularly important in view of the extremely dynamic process of evolution in which the international community is engaged at the present stage of history. Whether the mainspring of this evolution is to be found in the development of ideas, in social and economic factors, or in new technology, it is characteristic of our time that new problems and circumstances incessantly arise and imperatively call for legal regulation. In situations of this nature, a convention adopted as part of the combined process of codification and progressive development of international law may well constitute, or come to constitute, the decisive evidence of generally accepted new rules of international law. The fact that it does not purport simply to be declaratory of existing customary law is immaterial in this context. The convention may serve as an authoritative guide for the practice of States faced with the relevant new legal problems and its provisions thus become the nucleus around which a new set of generally recognized legal rules may crystallize. The word "custom," with its traditional time connotation, may not even be an adequate expression for the purpose of describing this particular source of law. ...

In my opinion, the conclusion may therefore safely be drawn that as a result of a continuous process over a quarter of a century, the rules embodied in the Geneva Convention on the Continental Shelf have now attained the status of generally accepted rules of international law.

That being so, it is nevertheless necessary to examine in particular the attitude of the Federal Republic of Germany with regard to the Convention. In the *Fisheries* case, the Court said that the ten-mile rule would in any event "appear to be inapplicable as against Norway inasmuch as she has always opposed any attempt to apply it to the Norwegian coast" (*I.C.J.R. 1951*, p. 131). Similarly, it might be argued in the present cases that the Convention on the Continental Shelf would be inapplicable as against the Federal Republic, if she had consistently refused to recognize it as an expression of generally accepted rules of international law and had objected to its applicability as against her. But far from adopting such an attitude, the Federal Republic has gone quite a long way towards recognizing the Convention. It is part of the whole picture, though not decisive in itself, that the Federal Republic signed the Convention in 1958, immediately before the time-limit for signature under Art. 8. More significant is the fact that the Federal Republic has relied on the Convention for the purpose of asserting her own rights in the continental shelf. ... This attitude is relevant, not so much in the context of the traditional legal concepts of recognition, acquiescence or estoppel, as in the context of the general process of creating international legal rules of universal applicability. At a decisive stage of this formative process, an interested State, which was not a party to the Convention, formally recorded its view that the Convention was an expression of generally applicable international law. This view being perfectly well founded, that State is not now in a position to escape the authority of the Convention.

It has been asserted that the possibility, made available by Art. 12, of entering reservations to certain articles of the Convention, makes it difficult to understand the articles in question as embodying generally accepted rules of international law. ... [I]n my view, the faculty of making reservations to a treaty provision has no necessary connection with the question whether or not the provision can be considered as expressing a generally recognized rule of law. To substantiate this opinion it may be sufficient to point out that a number of reservations have been made to provisions of the Convention on the High Seas, although this Convention, according to its preamble, is "generally declaratory of established principles of international law." Some of these reservations have been objected to by other contracting States, while other reservations have been tacitly accepted. The acceptance, whether tacit or express, of a reservation made by a contracting party does not have the effect of depriving the Convention as a whole, or the relevant article in particular, of its declaratory character. It only has the effect of establishing a special contractual relationship between the parties concerned within the general framework of the customary law embodied in the Convention. Provided the customary rule does not belong to the category of *jus cogens*, a special contractual relationship of this nature is not invalid as such. Consequently, there is no incompatibility between the faculty of making reservations to certain articles of the Convention on the Continental Shelf and the recognition of that Convention or the particular articles as an expression of generally accepted rules of international law.

NOTES

Use this decision[67] to answer the following questions:

1) What constitutes state practice? For instance, do the judgments of municipal courts constitute state practice?[68]

2) How much state practice is required? Is a single act sufficient to constitute general practice or must there be several acts over a certain period of time? How many states are needed? For instance, would Chad, a landlocked state, have to concur with the practice of the states having a continental shelf?

3) How much consistency in state practice is required? In the case of *Military Activities In and Against Nicaragua*, the ICJ observed:

It is not to be expected that in the practice of States the application of the rules in question should have been perfect, in the sense that States should have refrained, with complete consistency, from the use of force or from intervention in each other's internal affairs. The Court does not consider that, for a rule to be established as customary, the corresponding practice must be in absolutely rigorous conformity with the rule. In order to deduce the existence of customary rules, the Court deems it sufficient that the conduct of States should, in general, be consistent with such rules, and that instances of State conduct inconsistent with a given rule, should generally have been treated as breaches of that rule, not as indications of the recognition of a new rule. If a State acts in a way prima facie incompatible with a recognized rule, but defends its conduct by appealing to exceptions or justifications contained within the rule itself, then whether or not the State's conduct is in fact justifiable on that basis, the significance of that attitude is to confirm rather than to weaken the rule.[69]

---

67   For a critique of this decision, see Wolfgang Friedmann, "The North Sea Continental Shelf Cases—A Critique" (1970) 64 A.J.I.L. 229.

68   See also "Nationality of Women" (U.N. Doc. A/CN.4/33) in *Yearbook of the International Law Commission 1950*, vol. 2 (1957) at 368-72 (U.N. Doc. A/CN.4/Ser.A/1950/Add.1); and *Anglo-Norwegian Fisheries Case (United Kingdom v. Norway)*, [1951] I.C.J. Rep. 116 at 191.

69   *Nicaragua v. United States*, *supra* note 5.

4) Are dissenting and non-participating states bound by custom?[70] This is a very important question with respect to new states.[71] Does the absence of protest mean acquiescence?[72]

5) How is *opinio juris* proved? Can it be presumed from consistent practice in regard to matters normally treated as involving rights and obligations or is it necessary that the practice be accompanied by assertions of legal duty or right?

6) How do states change a custom? Can the dissent of one state bring down a custom or is that state still bound by it?

7) Can treaties that contain provisions that are declaratory of customary law be invoked as evidence of such law? Should it make a difference that reservations are allowed to a particular treaty rule? Note that in the *Continental Shelf (Libya v. Malta) Case* the ICJ stated:

> It is of course axiomatic that the material of customary international law is to be looked for primarily in the actual practice and *opinio juris* of States, even though multilateral conventions may have an important role to play in recording and defining rules deriving from custom, or indeed in developing them.[73]

Thus, where two states agree to incorporate a particular rule derived from custom in a treaty, their agreement suffices to make that rule binding upon them. But in the field of customary international law, the shared view of the parties as to the content of what they regard as the rule is not enough. The court must satisfy itself that the existence of the rule is confirmed by state practice.[74]

8) Note how the formation of customary rules is concerned with unilateral acts of states, rather than their multilateral agreement as in law-making treaties. What is the significance of this difference? Consider the commentary by Beesley in the introduction to this section.

2. Regional or Special Customary Law

Can there be local, as opposed to universal, customary law? If so, are the criteria for its creation the same as those for general customary law? These questions were explored by the ICJ in the following cases.

---

70   See Ted L. Stein, "The Approach of the Different Drummer: The Principle of the Persistent Objector in International Law" (1985) 26 Harv. Int'l L.J. 457; Jonathan I. Charney, "The Persistent Objector Rule and the Development of Customary International Law" (1985) 56 Brit. Y.B. Int'l L. 1.

71   See Hanna Bokor-Szegö, *New States and International Law,* rev. by Ottó Bihari & György Haraszti, trans. by Sándor Simon (1970).

72   See also *Fisheries Jurisdiction Case (Merits) (United Kingdom v. Iceland)*, [1974] I.C.J. Rep. 3 (read separate opinion of Judge Dillard at 58); *Anglo-Norwegian Fisheries Case, supra* note 68; *South West Africa Case (Second Phase) (Ethiopia v. South Africa; Liberia v. Africa)*, [1966] I.C.J. Rep. 6 (read Tanaka J. dissenting at 291).

73   [1985] I.C.J. Rep. 13 at 29-30.

74   See *Nicaragua v. United States, supra* note 5 at 97-98.

Right of Passage over Indian Territory Case
Portugal v. India
[1960] I.C.J. Rep. 6

[Portugal held several small enclaves of territory within India. One, Daman, was on the coast, but the others were inland. Portugal claimed a right of passage to its inland enclaves and alleged that India had interfered with the exercise of this right.]

THE COURT: ... Portugal claims a right of passage between Daman and the enclaves, and between the enclaves, across intervening Indian territory, to the extent necessary for the exercise of its sovereignty over the enclaves, subject to India's right of regulation and control of the passage claimed, and without any immunity in Portugal's favour. It claims further that India is under obligation so to exercise its power of regulation and control as not to prevent the passage necessary for the exercise of Portugal's sovereignty over the enclaves. ...

With regard to Portugal's claim of a right of passage as formulated by it on the basis of local custom, it is objected on behalf of India that no local custom could be established between only two States. It is difficult to see why the number of States between which a local custom may be established on the basis of long practice must necessarily be larger than two. The Court sees no reason why long continued practice between two States accepted by them as regulating their relations should not form the basis of mutual rights and obligations between the two States. ...

The Court, therefore, concludes that, with regard to private persons, civil officials and goods in general there existed during the British and post-British periods a constant and uniform practice allowing free passage between Daman and the enclaves. This practice having continued over a period extending beyond a century and a quarter unaffected by the change in regime in respect of the intervening territory which occurred when India became independent, the Court is, in view of all the circumstances of the case, satisfied that that practice was accepted as law by the Parties and has given rise to a right and a correlative obligation. ...

The Court is here dealing with a concrete case having special features. Historically the case goes back to a period when, and relates to a region in which, the relations between neighbouring States were not regulated by precisely formulated rules but were governed largely by practice. Where therefore the Court finds a practice clearly established between two States which was accepted by the Parties as governing the relations between them, the Court must attribute decisive effect to that practice for the purpose of determining their specific rights and obligations. Such a particular practice must prevail over any general rules.

Asylum Case
Colombia v. Peru
[1950] I.C.J. Rep. 266 at 276-78

[The Colombian government claimed that it had the right to give asylum to the Peruvian Haya de la Torre, who had sought refuge in the Colombian Embassy in Peru. It relied not only on the rules arising from agreements, but on an alleged regional or local custom peculiar to Latin American States.]

THE COURT: ... The Party which relies on a custom of this kind must prove that this custom is established in such a manner that it has become binding on the other Party. The Colombian Government must prove that the rule invoked by it is in accordance with a constant and uniform usage practised by the States in question, and that this usage is the expression of a right appertaining to the State granting asylum and a duty incumbent on the territorial State. This follows from Art. 38 of the Statute of the Court, which refers to international custom "as evidence of a general practice accepted as law."

In support of its contention concerning the existence of such a custom, the Colombian Government has referred to a large number of extradition treaties which, as already explained, can have no bearing on the question now under consideration. It has cited conventions and agreements which do not contain any provision concerning the alleged rule of unilateral and definitive qualification such as the Montevideo Convention of 1889 on international penal law, the Bolivian Agreement of 1911 and the Havana Convention of 1928. It has invoked conventions which have not been ratified by Peru, such as the Montevideo Conventions of 1933 and 1939. The Convention of 1933 has, in fact, been ratified by not more than eleven States and the Convention of 1939 by two States only. ...

It is particularly the Montevideo Convention of 1933 which Counsel for the Colombian Government has also relied on in this connexion. It is contended that this Convention has merely codified principles which were already recognized by Latin-American custom and that it is valid against Peru as a proof of customary law. The limited number of States which have ratified this Convention reveals the weakness of this argument and furthermore, it is invalidated by the preamble which states that this Convention modifies the Havana Convention.

Finally, the Colombian Government has referred to a large number of particular cases in which diplomatic asylum was in fact granted and respected. But it has not shown that the alleged rule of unilateral and definitive qualification was invoked or if in some cases it was in fact invoked—that it was, apart from conventional stipulations, exercised by the States granting asylum as a right appertaining to them and respected by the territorial States as a duty incumbent on them and not merely for reasons of political expediency. The facts brought to the knowledge of the Court disclose so much uncertainty and contradiction, so much fluctuation and discrepancy in the exercise of diplomatic asylum and in the official views expressed on various occasions, there has been so much inconsistency in the rapid succession of conventions on asylum, ratified by some States and rejected by others and the practice has been so much influenced by considerations of political expediency in the various cases, that it is not possible to discern in all this any constant and uniform usage, accepted as law, with regard to the alleged rule of unilateral and definitive qualification of the offence.

The Court cannot therefore find that the Colombian Government has proved the existence of such custom. But even if it could be supposed that such a custom existed between certain Latin-American States only, it could not be invoked against Peru which, far from having by its attitude adhered to it, has on the contrary, repudiated it by refraining from ratifying the Montevideo Convention of 1933 and 1939, which were the first to include a rule concerning the qualification of the offence in matters of diplomatic asylum.

NOTES

1) In the *Right of Passage* case the Court, while accepting the customary law right claimed by Portugal, held that India had not violated it. Subsequently, India absorbed the Portuguese territories.

2) Regional or local customs may vary from general customary international law by adding or detracting from it. However, they must not violate existing rules of *jus cogens*.

3) Does a special or particular custom require a higher degree of proof than a general custom?[75]

D. GENERAL PRINCIPLES OF LAW

There is still some disagreement about the meaning of "the general principles of law recognized by civilized nations," found in article 38(1)(c) of the Statute of the International Court.[76] Most commonly, these general principles are accepted as those that exist in all municipal systems of law that have reached a comparable stage of development. They are primarily principles of private law or procedure. On the other hand, former socialist states were of the opinion that general principles of law could mean only general principles of *international* law. In other words, general principles of municipal law are part of international law to the extent that they have been adopted by states as a custom or in a treaty. Therefore, where a principle originally borrowed from municipal law has acquired the status of a custom, there is no need to resort to paragraph (c) of article 38(1).[77] But what about general principles that are not already part of international customary or conventional law? Judge Tanaka, for instance, considered general principles of law a primary source of international law because they have the character of *jus rationale* and are "valid through all kinds of human societies."[78]

---

75 In addition to the cases in the text, see *Rights of U.S. Nationals in Morocco Case (United States v. France)*, [1952] I.C.J. Rep. 176.

76 See Bin Cheng, *General Principles of Law as Applied by International Courts and Tribunals* (1953, reprinted 1987). See also M. Cherif Bassiouni, "A Functional Approach to 'General Principles of International Law'" (1989-90) 11 Mich. J. Int'l L. 768.

77 See G.I. Tunkin, *Das Völkerrecht der Gegenwart: Theorie und Praxis*, trans. by Klaus Wolf (1963) at 125-27.

78 *South West Africa Case (Second Phase) (Ethiopia v. South Africa; Liberia v. South Africa)*, [1966] I.C.J. Rep. 6 at 296, dissenting opinion.

On several occasions the International Court of Justice has applied principles of municipal law that are generally recognized. These principles constitute a reservoir of law that the court is authorized to apply. For instance, in the *Chorzow Factory Case*,[79] the Permanent Court said: "it is ... a general conception of law that any breach of an engagement involves an obligation to make reparation" and in the *Temple of Preah Vihear Case*,[80] the International Court stated: "It is an established rule of law that the plea of error cannot be allowed as an element vitiating consent if the party advancing it contributed by its own conduct to the error." See also the *Effect of Awards of U.N. Administrative Tribunal Case*,[81] where the Court said: "According to a well-established and generally recognized principle of law, a judgment rendered by a judicial body is *res judicata* and has binding force between the parties to the dispute." As to whether the doctrine of estoppel is a general principle of law, see the *Gulf of Maine Case*,[82] where the Chamber observed that "in any case the concepts of acquiescence and estoppel, irrespective of the status accorded to them by international law, both follow from the fundamental principles of good faith and equity," and, therefore, took both concepts into its consideration. Furthermore, in *Sea-Land Service, Inc. v. Iran*,[83] the Iran–U.S. Claims Tribunal held that the concept of unjust enrichment is "widely accepted as having been assimilated into the catalogue of general principles of law available to be applied by international tribunals."

Note that section 11(g) of the *Canadian Charter of Rights and Freedoms*[84] provides that:

> Any person charged with an offence has the right ... not to be found guilty on account of any act or omission unless, at the time of the act or omission, it constituted an offence under Canadian or international law or was criminal according to the general principles of law recognized by the community of nations.

This provision is thought to have been included in order to preserve Canada's authority to prosecute war criminals and others who may have committed "offences against the peace and security of mankind."

The process by which general principles of law are found and applied by the ICJ is demonstrated in the following case.

---

79   *Germany v. Polish Republic* (1928), P.C.I.J. (Ser. A) No. 17 at 29.

80   *Cambodia v. Thailand*, [1962] I.C.J. Rep. 6 at 26.

81   Advisory Opinion, [1954] I.C.J. Rep. 47 at 53.

82   *Canada v. United States*, [1984] I.C.J. Rep. 246 at paras. 129-48.

83   (1984), 6 Iran–U.S. C.T.R. 149 at 168-69.

84   Part I of the *Constitution Act, 1982*, being Schedule B of the *Canada Act 1982* (U.K.), 1982, c. 11.

International Status of South West Africa Case
Adv. Op. [1950] I.C.J. Rep. 128

[In 1949, the U.N. General Assembly asked the International Court to advise on the international status of South West Africa (now Namibia). This request caused the Court to interpret the terms of the Mandate of that territory to South Africa. In the course of his separate opinion, Sir Arnold McNair drew upon general principles of law in order to determine the meaning of the "sacred trust of civilization" accepted by South Africa under the Mandate.]

JUDGE McNAIR: ... What is the duty of an international tribunal when confronted with a new legal institution the object and terminology of which are reminiscent of the rules and institutions of private law? To what extent is it useful or necessary to examine what may at first sight appear to be relevant analogies in private law systems and draw help and inspiration from them? International law has recruited and continues to recruit many of its rules and institutions from private systems of law. Article 38(I)(c) of the Statute of the Court bears witness that this process is still active, and it will be noted that this article authorizes the Court to "apply ... (c) the general principles of law recognized by civilized nations." The way in which international law borrows from this source is not by means of importing private law institutions "lock, stock and barrel," ready-made and fully equipped with a set of rules. It would be difficult to reconcile such a process with the application of "the general principles of law." In my opinion, the true view of the duty of international tribunals in this matter is to regard any features or terminology which are reminiscent of the rules and institutions of private law as an indication of policy and principles rather than as directly importing these rules and institutions. ...

Let us then seek to discover the underlying policy and principles of Article 22 and of the Mandate. No technical significance can be attached to the words "sacred trust of civilization," but they are an apt description of the policy of the authors of the Mandates System, and the words "sacred trust" were not used here for the first time in relation to dependent peoples (see Duncan Hall, *Mandates, Dependencies and Trusteeships*, at 97-100). Any English lawyer who was instructed to prepare the legal instruments required to give effect to the policy of Article 22 would inevitably be reminded of, and influenced by, the trust of English and American law, though he would soon realize the need of much adaptation for the purposes of the new international institution. Professor Brierly's opinion, stated in the *British Year Book of International Law*, 1929, at 217-19, that the governing principle of the Mandates System is to be found in the trust, and his quotation from an article by M. Lepaulle, are here very much in point, and it is worth noting that the historical basis of the legal enforcement of the English trust is that it was something which was binding upon the conscience of the trustee; that is why it was legally enforced. It also seems probable that the conception of the Mandates System owes something to the French *tutelle*.

Nearly every legal system possesses some institution whereby the property (and sometimes the persons) of those who are not *sui juris*, such as a minor or a lunatic, can be entrusted to some responsible person as a trustee or *tuteur* or *curateur*. The

Anglo-American trust serves this purpose, and another purpose even more closely akin to the Mandates System, namely, the vesting of property in trustees, and its management by them in order that the public or some class of the public may derive benefit or that some public purpose may be served. The trust has frequently been used to protect the weak and the dependent, in cases where there is "great might on the one side and unmight on the other," and the English courts have for many centuries pursued a vigorous policy in the administration and enforcement of trusts.

There are three general principles which are common to all these institutions:

(a) that the control of the trustee, *tuteur* or *curateur* over the property is limited in one way or another; he is not in the position of the normal complete owner, who can do what he likes with his own, because he is precluded from administering the property for his own personal benefit;

(b) that the trustee, *tuteur* or *curateur* is under some kind of legal obligation, based on confidence and conscience, to carry out the trust or mission confided to him for the benefit of some other person or for some public purpose;

(c) that any attempt by one of these persons to absorb the property entrusted to him into his own patrimony would be illegal and would be prevented by the law.

These are some of the general principles of private law which throw light upon this new institution, and I am convinced that in its future development the law governing the trust is a source from which much can be derived.

Equity in International Law

The expression "equity" has at least three different legal senses. Equity may be used to adapt the law to the facts of individual cases (equity *intra legem*); it may be used to fill gaps in the law (equity *praeter legem*); and it may be used as a reason for refusing to apply unjust laws (equity *contra legem*). International tribunals can apply equity *intra legem*. It is more doubtful whether they can apply equity *praeter legem*; although, on occasion, they have claimed such power. They cannot apply equity *contra legem* in the absence of an express authorization.[85]

In the *Norwegian Shipowners Claims*,[86] the tribunal expressed the view that "law and equity" are to be understood to mean "general principles of justice as distinguished from any particular system of jurisprudence or the municipal law of any State." Be careful to distinguish equity in this international sense from the technical use of the same term in common law jurisdictions. Note too that the World Court's power under its Statute article 38(2), in the Appendix, to decide a case "*ex aequo et bono*" is not to be equated to equity in this legal sense either. The following case explains the difference.

---

85   See Michael Akehurst, "Equity and General Principles of Law" (1976) 25 I.C.L.Q. 801. See generally Thomas M. Franck & Dennis Sughrue, "The International Role of Equity-as-Fairness" (1992-93) 81 Geo. L.J. 563; Vaughan Lowe, "The Role of Equity in International Law" (1988-89) 12 Austl. Y.B. Int'l L. 54.

86   (1922) 17 A.J.I.L. 362 at 384. See also the *Cayuga Indians Claim* (1926), Nielsen's Rep. 203 at 307 *et seq.*

Diversion of Water from the Meuse Case
Netherlands v. Belgium
(1937), P.C.I.J. (Ser. A/B) No. 70 at 76-77

Separate opinion of JUDGE HUDSON: ... What are widely known as principles of equity have long been considered to constitute a part of international law, and as such they have often been applied by international tribunals. ... A sharp division between law and equity, such as prevails in the administration of justice in some States, should find no place in international jurisprudence; even in some national legal systems, there has been a strong tendency towards the fusion of law and equity. Some international tribunals are expressly directed by the *compromis* which control them to apply "law and equity." See the *Cayuga Indians Case*, Nielsen's Report of the United States— British Claims Arbitration (1926), at 307. Of such a provision, a special tribunal of the Permanent Court of Arbitration said in 1922 that "the majority of international lawyers seem to agree that these words are to be understood to mean general principles of justice as distinguished from any particular systems of jurisprudence." Proceedings of the United States—Norwegian Tribunal (1922), at 141. Numerous arbitration treaties have been concluded in recent years which apply to differences "which are justiciable in their nature by reason of being susceptible of decision by the application of the principles of law or equity." Whether the reference in an arbitration treaty is to the application of "law and equity," or to justiciability dependent on the possibility of applying "law or equity," it would seem to envisage equity as a part of law.

The Court has not been expressly authorised by its Statute to apply equity as distinguished from law. ... Article 38 of the Statute expressly directs the application of "general principles of law recognised by civilised nations," and in more than one nation principles of equity have an established place in the legal system. The Court's recognition of equity as a part of international law is in no way restricted by the special power conferred upon it "to decide a case *ex aequo et bono*, if the parties agree thereto." ... It must be concluded, therefore, that under Article 38 of the Statute, if not independently of that Article, the Court has some freedom to consider principles of equity as part of the international law which it must apply.

It would seem to be an important principle of equity that where two parties have assumed an identical or a reciprocal obligation, one party which is engaged in a continuing non-performance of that obligation should not be permitted to take advantage of a similar non-performance of that obligation by the other party. The principle finds expression in the so-called maxims of equity which exercised great influence in the creative period of the development of the Anglo-American law. Some of these maxims are, "Equality is equity"; "He who seeks equity must do equity." It is in line with such maxims that "a court of equity refuses relief to a plaintiff whose conduct in regard to the subject-matter of the litigation has been improper." ... A very similar principle was received into Roman Law. ... This conception was the basis of Articles 320 and 322 of the German Civil Code, and even where a code is silent on the point Planiol states the general principle that "*dans tout rapport synallagmatique, chacune des deux parties ne peut exiger la prestation qui lui est due que si elle offre elle-même d'exécuter son obligation.*"

North Sea Continental Shelf Cases
Federal Republic of Germany v. Denmark and v. Netherlands
[1969] I.C.J. Rep. 3, reported above in Section C.1 on "General Customary Law"

Read particularly paragraphs 88, 89, 91, and 98.

NOTES

1) In the award made in the *English Channel Arbitration* in 1977, the tribunal applied principles of equity as part of the relevant international law.[87] In the *Continental Shelf (Tunisia v. Libya) Case*,[88] the ICJ also applied principles of equity to reach an equitable solution. The majority of the Court stated:

71. Equity as a legal concept is a direct emanation of the idea of justice. The Court whose task is by definition to administer justice is bound to apply it. In the course of the history of legal systems the term "equity" has been used to define various legal concepts. It was often contrasted with the rigid rules of positive law, the severity of which had to be mitigated in order to do justice. In general, this contrast has no parallel in the development of international law; the legal concept of equity is a general principle directly applicable as law. Moreover, when applying positive international law, a court may choose among several possible interpretations of the law the one which appears, in the light of the circumstances of the case, to be closest to the requirements of justice. Application of equitable principles is to be distinguished from a decision *ex aequo et bono*. The Court can take such a decision only on condition that the Parties agree (Art. 38, para. 2, of the Statute), and the Court is then freed from the strict application of legal rules in order to bring about an appropriate settlement. The task of the Court in the present case is quite different: it is bound to apply equitable principles as part of international law, and to balance up the various considerations which it regards as relevant in order to produce an equitable result. While it is clear that no rigid rules exist as to the exact weight to be attached to each element in the case, this is very far from being an exercise of discretion or conciliation; nor is it an operation of distributive justice.

Compare the dissenting opinion of Judge Gros:

19. Much more is here involved than a difference of opinion as to how equity should be conceived: what is at issue is the decision dividing a continental shelf between two States which requested that it be delivered in accordance with the law. If a State claiming a right to an area of continental shelf really possesses that right such as it describes it, it is not equity to deprive it of it but an error of law, and therein lies a far-reaching complaint since the judgments of the Court are irreversible as between the Parties. Equity is not a sort of independent and subjective vision that takes the place of law. The Judgment states that there can be no question in the instant case of applying *ex aequo et bono*. Statements are one thing, the effective pronouncements of the Judgment are another. For the foregoing reasons,

---

87   *United Kingdom v. France* (1979) 18 I.L.M. 397 at paras. 70, 103, 195-99. And see M.D. Blecher, "Equitable Delimitation of the Continental Shelf" (1979) 73 A.J.I.L. 60.

88   [1982] I.C.J. Rep. 18.

E. Other Sources of Law?

and those I give below, it is not equity which has struck me as
of the Judgment.

2) See also the decision in the *Gulf of Maine Case.*[89]
the opinion that customary international law cannot be ex
criteria to be applied. Having drawn the single maritime
parties, the Chamber then verified whether the result of
intrinsically equitable in the light of all the circumstances

3) Equity in the sense of humanitarian considerations
has a role to play in the creation of rules of international law.[90]

E. OTHER SOURCES OF LAW?

1. Subsidiary Means for the Determination of Rules of Law

Refer to the Statute of the International Court of Justice article 38(1)(d) in the
Documentary Supplement and the distinction between law-creating and law-determining
at the very beginning of this chapter. Note how subparagraph (d) speaks only of subsidiary
means of determining international law, thereby implying that they are secondary to the
primary sources noted in subparagraphs (a), (b), and (c).

Judicial Decisions

Although article 59 of the Statute of the International Court of Justice provides that "[t]he
decision of the Court has no binding force except between the parties and in respect of
that particular case," the Court uses its judgments for guidance in later cases,[91] and they
are widely relied on by other tribunals and by states as persuasive opinions as to the state
of international law.

Legal Commentaries

Many years before the Statute of the World Court referred inelegantly to the "teachings of
the most highly qualified publicists"[92] as a means of determining international law, the
status of legal commentaries was fully explained in *R. v. Keyn* by Cockburn C.J.:

---

89 *Canada v. United States, supra* note 82 at paras. 79-81, 111-12, 129-48, 157-58, 230-41.

90 See I.I. Lukashuk, "Morality and International Law" (1974) 14 Indian J. Int'l L. 321 and *Corfu Channel
    Case (United Kingdom v. Albania),* [1949] I.C.J. Rep. 4 at 22.

91 See *e.g. France v. United States, supra* note 39 at 200; *Effect of Awards of U.N. Administrative Tribunal
    Case,* Advisory Opinion, [1954] I.C.J. Rep. 47 at 53, 56; and H. Lauterpacht, *The Development of
    International Law by the International Court,* rev. ed. (1958). As to the role of international tribunals in
    the development of international law, see Patrick M. Norton, "A Law of the Future or a Law of the Past?
    Modern Tribunals and the International Law of Expropriation" (1991) 85 A.J.I.L. 474 at 497.

92 A historical survey of the role and influence of teachings in the development of international law is
    provided by Manfred Lachs, a former President of the Court, in *The Teacher in International Law:
    Teachings and Teaching,* 2d ed. (1987).

n international law, however valuable their labours may be in elucidating and ng the principles and rules of law, cannot make the law. To be binding, the law ave received the assent of the nations who are to be bound by it. This assent may be press, as by treaty or the acknowledged concurrence of governments, or may be implied from established usage,—an instance of which is to be found in the fact that merchant vessels on the high seas are held to be subject only to the law of the nation under whose flag they sail, while in the ports of a foreign state they are subject to the local law as well as to that of their own country. In the absence of proof of assent, as derived from one or other of these sources, no unanimity on the part of theoretical writers would warrant the judicial application of the law on the sole authority of their views or statements. ... It is said that we are to take the statements of the publicists as conclusive proof of the assent in question and much has been said to impress on us the respect which is due to their authority and that they are to be looked upon as witnesses of the facts to which they speak, witnesses whose statements, or the foundation on which those statements rest, we are scarcely at liberty to question. I demur altogether to this position. I entertain a profound respect for the opinion of jurists when dealing with the matters of juridical principle and opinion, but we are here dealing with a question not of opinion but of fact and I must assert my entire liberty to examine the evidence and see upon what foundation these statements are based. The question is not one of theoretical opinion, but of fact, and fortunately, the writers upon whose statements we are called upon to act have afforded us the means of testing those statements by reference to facts. They refer us to two things, and to these alone—treaties and usage.[93]

2. Law Making through International Organizations

Codification and Progressive Development

Codification is one of the methods used for clarifying and developing international law although it is more likely to succeed when law and practice are already reasonably clear, extensive, and accepted. The attempts at codification are the result of efforts by private organizations such as the Institut de Droit International and the International Law Association or by international organizations such as the U.N. and its subsidiary organs.

In 1967, the General Assembly of the U.N., pursuant to the Charter article 13(1), established the International Law Commission. Composed of 34 members elected by the General Assembly for at least a five-year term, who sit as individuals and not as representatives of their governments, it has for objects the promotion of the progressive development and codification of international law. Article 15 of the Statute of the International Law Commission makes a distinction between progressive development, meaning "the preparation of draft conventions on subjects which have not yet been regulated by international law or in regard to which the law has not yet been sufficiently developed in the practice of States," and codification, meaning "the more precise formulation and systematization of rules of international law in fields where there already has been extensive State practice, precedent and doctrine." According to the U.N.'s own commentary:

---

93   (1876), 2 Ex. D. 63 at 202-3.

The drafters of the Statute conceived progressive development as a conscious effort towards the creation of new rules of international law, whether by means of the regulation of a new topic or by means of the comprehensive revision of existing rules. Accordingly, they considered that when the Commission is engaged in the progressive development of any branch of law, the consummation of the work could be achieved only by means of an international convention. Thus, the Statute contemplates that the Commission prepares a draft convention, and the General Assembly then decides whether steps should be taken to bring about the conclusion of an international convention.

On the other hand, when the Commission's task is one of codification (namely, the more precise formulation and systematization of existing customary law), the Statute envisages two other possible conclusions to its work: (a) simple publication of its report; and (b) a resolution of the General Assembly, taking note of or adopting the report (article 23, paragraph 1). The Statute also lays down the specific steps to be taken by the Commission in the course of its work on progressive development (articles 16 and 17) and on codification (articles 18 to 23).

The Commission follows essentially the same method for both types of work. A Special Rapporteur is appointed for each topic; an appropriate plan of work is formulated; where desirable, Governments are requested to furnish the texts of relevant laws, decrees, judicial decisions, treaties and diplomatic correspondence; the Special Rapporteur submits a report, on the basis of which a provisional draft is approved by the Commission, normally in the form of articles, with a commentary setting forth precedents, any divergencies of views expressed in the Commission, and alternative solutions considered. ... Governments under current procedure are normally given more than one year in which to study these provisional drafts and present their written observations. The Special Rapporteur studies the replies received, together with any comments made in the debates of the Sixth Committee, and submits a further report, recommending the changes in the provisional draft that seem appropriate. The Commission, then, on the basis of that report and the comments, adopts a final draft, which it submits to the General Assembly with a recommendation regarding further action.[94]

In practice, codification and progressive development of the law become intermingled. In his dissenting opinion in the *North Sea Continental Shelf Cases*, Judge *Ad Hoc* Sorenson[95] had this to say:

It has come to be generally recognised, however, that this distinction between codification and progressive development may be difficult to apply rigorously to the facts of international legal relations. Although theoretically clear and distinguishable, the two notions tend in practice to overlap or to leave between them an intermediate area in which it is not possible to indicate precisely where codification ends and progressive development begins. The very act of formulating or restating an existing customary rule may have the effect of defining its contents more precisely and removing such doubts as may have existed as to its exact scope

---

94   U.N. Office of Public Information, *The Work of the International Law Commission* (1967) at 6, 9, and 12. See also J.S. Morton, *The International Law Commission of the United Nations* (2000).

95   *Federal Republic of Germany v. Denmark; Federal Republic of Germany v. Netherlands*, [1969] I.C.J. Rep. 4 at 242-43.

or the modalities of its application. The opportunity may also be taken of adapting the rule to contemporary conditions, whether factual or legal, in the international community. On the other hand, a treaty purporting to create new law may be based on a certain amount of State practice and doctrinal opinion which has not yet crystallised into customary law.

The reports, documents, and summary records of discussions of the Commission are published by the United Nations in *Yearbooks of the International Law Commission*, and they provide a fertile source of evidence and opinion on the state of customary international law as well as the thinking of the Commissioners. The Commission has been responsible for the preparation of a number of multilateral conventions that are now in force. Two examples included in this book are the 1961 Vienna Convention on Diplomatic Relations discussed in Chapter 5, Section D on "Diplomatic Immunities" and the 1969 Vienna Convention on the Law of Treaties considered in Section B on "Treaties" in this chapter.

Resolutions of the United Nations

The legal effect of General Assembly resolutions has proved a fertile subject of continuing discussion.[96] Under the Charter, the General Assembly has clear authority to make binding decisions only with respect to budgetary and administrative matters of the U.N. (See article 17 in the Documentary Supplement.) For all its other work, the General Assembly is empowered to make "recommendations" (articles 10-16) that are not considered binding *per se* but can have value as means for the determination of international law.

In the *South West Africa, Voting Procedure Case*, Judge Lauterpacht observed:

> A Resolution recommending to an Administering State a specific course of action creates some legal obligation which, however rudimentary, elastic and imperfect, is nevertheless a legal obligation and constitutes a measure of supervision. The State in question, while not bound to accept the recommendation, is bound to give it due consideration in good faith.[97]

---

96   See Obed Y. Asamoah, *The Legal Significance of the Declarations of the General Assembly of the United Nations* (1966); Hanna Bokor-Szego, *The Role of the United Nations in International Legislation*, trans. by Sandor Simon (1978); Bin Cheng, "United Nations Resolutions on Outer Space: 'Instant' International Customary Law?" (1965) 5 Indian J. Int'l L. 23; D.H.N. Johnson, "The Effect of Resolutions of the General Assembly of the United Nations" (1955-56) 32 Brit. Y.B. Int'l L. 97; Roy Lee, "Rule-Making in the United Nations: Opinio Communitatis" (1994-95) 27 N.Y.U.J. Int'l. L. & Pol. 571; Maurice Mendelson, "The Legal Character of General Assembly Resolutions: Some Considerations of Principle" in Kamal Hossain, ed., *Legal Aspects of the New International Economic Order* (1980) 95; Stephen M. Schwebel, "The Effect of Resolutions of the U.N. General Assembly on Customary International Law" (1979) 3 A.S.I.L. 301; F. Blaine Sloan, "The Binding Force of a 'Recommendation' of the General Assembly of the United Nations" (1948) 25 Brit. Y.B. Int'l L. 1 and "General Assembly Resolutions Revisited (Forty Years Later)" (1987) 58 Brit. Y.B. Int'l L. 39; Blaine Sloan, *United Nations General Assembly Resolutions In Our Changing World* (1991); and Rosalyn Higgins, "The Role of Resolutions of International Organizations in the Process of Creating Norms in the International System" in W.E. Butler, ed., *International Law and the International System* (1987) 21.

97   Advisory Opinion, [1955] I.C.J. Rep. 67 at 118-19.

In truth, General Assembly resolutions are so varied in purpose, content, and support that their legal value is very individual, depending upon the circumstances under which they are adopted and the principles that they state. The *Western Sahara Case*, reported in Chapter 2, Section C.4(b), is an example where the ICJ made extensive use of General Assembly resolutions in the course of establishing and applying the principle of self-determination of peoples.

Security Council resolutions are more straightforward in the light of the mandatory language of the Charter article 25, which has been authoritatively interpreted by the Court in the *Namibia Case*.[98]

Namibia Case
Adv. Op. [1971] I.C.J. Rep. 16, reported in Chapter 2, Section C.1 on
"Other Legal Persons: International Organizations"

Texaco v. Libya
(1978), 17 I.L.M. 1, reported in Chapter 10, Section B.3(a) on "Basic Principles"
and B.3(d) on "Breach of Contract"

Read paragraphs 83-87 and 90 concerning the status of U.N. resolutions on permanent sovereignty over natural resources.

Legality of the Threat or Use of Nuclear Weapons Case
[1996] I.C.J. Rep. 226

[The U.N. General Assembly asked the Court for an advisory opinion on the question: "Is the threat or use of nuclear weapons in any circumstances permitted under international law?" In the course of its opinion, reproduced in Chapter 6, Section D.3, the Court considered the significance of U.N. General Assembly resolutions for the formation of customary international law.]

THE COURT: ...
   64. The Court will now turn to an examination of customary international law to determine whether a prohibition of the threat or use of nuclear weapons as such flows from that source of law. As the Court has stated, the substance of that law must be "looked for primarily in the actual practice and *opinio juris* of States" (*Continental Shelf (Libyan Arab Jamahirya/Malta), Judgment, I.C.J. Reports 1985*, p. 29, para. 27).
   65. States which hold the view that the use of nuclear weapons is illegal have endeavoured to demonstrate the existence of a customary rule prohibiting this use. They refer to a consistent practice of non-utilization of nuclear weapons by States

---

98   Rosalyn Higgins, "The Advisory Opinion on Namibia: Which U.N. Resolutions Are Binding under Article 25 of the Charter?" (1972) 21 I.C.L.Q. 270.

since 1945 and they would see in that practice the expression of an *opinio juris* on the part of those who possess such weapons.

66. Some other States, which assert the legality of the threat and use of nuclear weapons in certain circumstances, invoked the doctrine and practice of deterrence in support of their argument. They recall that they have always, in concert with certain other States, reserved the right to use those weapons in the exercise of the right to self-defence against an armed attack threatening their vital security interests. In their view, if nuclear weapons have not been used since 1945, it is not on account of an existing or nascent custom but merely because circumstances that might justify their use have fortunately not arisen.

67. The Court does not intend to pronounce here upon the practice known as the "policy of deterrence." It notes that it is a fact that a number of States adhered to that practice during the greater part of the Cold War and continue to adhere to it. Furthermore, the members of the international community are profoundly divided on the matter of whether non-recourse to nuclear weapons over the past 50 years constitutes the expression of an *opinio juris*. Under these circumstances the Court does not consider itself able to find that there is such an *opinio juris*.

68. According to certain States, the important series of General Assembly resolutions, beginning with resolution 1653 (XVI) of 24 November 1961, that deal with nuclear weapons and that affirm, with consistent regularity, the illegality of nuclear weapons, signify the existence of a rule of international customary law which prohibits recourse to those weapons. According to other States, however, the resolutions in question have no binding character on their own account and are not declaratory of any customary rule of prohibition of nuclear weapons; some of these States have also pointed out that this series of resolutions not only did not meet with the approval of all of the nuclear-weapon States but of many other States as well.

69. States which consider that the use of nuclear weapons is illegal indicated that those resolutions did not claim to create any new rules, but were confined to a confirmation of customary law relating to the prohibition of means or methods of warfare which, by their use, overstepped the bounds of what is permissible in the conduct of hostilities. In their view, the resolutions in question did no more than apply to nuclear weapons the existing rules of international law applicable in armed conflict; they were no more than the "envelope" or *instrumentum* containing certain pre-existing customary rules of international law. For those States it is accordingly of little importance that the *instrumentum* should have occasioned negative votes, which cannot have the effect of obliterating those customary rules which have been confirmed by treaty law.

70. The Court notes that General Assembly resolutions, even if they are not binding, may sometimes have normative value. They can, in certain circumstances, provide evidence important for establishing the existence of a rule or the emergence of an *opinio juris*. To establish whether this is true of a given General Assembly resolution, it is necessary to look at its content and the conditions of its adoption; it is also necessary to see whether an *opinio juris* exists as to its normative character. Or a series of resolutions may show the gradual evolution of the *opinio juris* required for the establishment of a new rule.

71. Examined in their totality, the General Assembly resolutions put before the Court declare that the use of nuclear weapons would be "a direct violation of the Charter of the United Nations"; and in certain formulations that such use "should be prohibited." The focus of these resolutions has sometimes shifted to diverse related matters; however, several of the resolutions under consideration in the present case have been adopted with substantial numbers of negative votes and abstentions; thus, although those resolutions are a clear sign of deep concern regarding the problem of nuclear weapons, they still fall short of establishing the existence of an *opinio juris* on the illegality of the use of such weapons.

72. The Court further notes that the first of the resolutions of the General Assembly expressly proclaiming the illegality of the use of nuclear weapons, resolution 1653 (XVI) of 24 November 1961 (mentioned in subsequent resolutions), after referring to certain international declarations and binding agreements, from the Declaration of St. Petersburg of 1868 to the Geneva Protocol of 1925, proceeded to qualify the legal nature of nuclear weapons, determine their effects, and apply general rules of customary law to nuclear weapons in particular. That application by the General Assembly of general rules of customary law to the particular case of nuclear weapons indicates that, in its view, there was no specific rule of customary law which prohibited the use of nuclear weapons; if such a rule had existed, the General Assembly could simply have referred to it and would not have needed to undertake such an exercise of legal qualification.

73. Having said this, the Court points out that the adoption each year by the General Assembly, by a large majority, of resolutions recalling the content of resolution 1653 (XVI), and requesting the member States to conclude a convention prohibiting the use of nuclear weapons in any circumstance, reveals the desire of a very large section of the international community to take, by a specific and express prohibition of the use of nuclear weapons, a significant step forward along the road to complete nuclear disarmament. The emergence, as *lex lata*, of a customary rule specifically prohibiting the use of nuclear weapons as such is hampered by the continuing tensions between the nascent *opinio juris* on the one hand, and the still strong adherence to the practice of deterrence on the other.

NOTES

1) In *Libyan American Oil Company v. Libya*,[99] the arbitrator commented on the same resolutions regarding permanent sovereignty over natural resources as those discussed in *Texaco v. Libya*. He observed: "[T]he said Resolutions, if not a unanimous source of law, are evidence of the recent dominant trend of international opinion concerning the sovereign right of states over their natural resources." What is the legal significance of a "dominant trend of international opinion"?

2) In a memorandum dated August 28, 1974, the Legal Bureau of the Department of External Affairs stated the Canadian position with respect to declarations and resolutions of the U.N. General Assembly:

---

99   (1981) 20 I.L.M. 1 at 53.

Declarations and resolutions of the General Assembly, while they may contribute to the evolution of norms of international law, do not create legal rights or obligations for any state. A vote for a resolution, or acquiescence in its adoption without a vote (which need not be, and in the case of the 6th UNGA Special Session was not in fact, the same as adoption by "consensus," which implies the full support of virtually all participants), simply expresses a government's policy and intentions on the subject matter. Statements made in explanation of vote serve to clarify this expression of policy. This is particularly true of statements of interpretation and of reservations. If the government in question wishes to change its policy and announce this fact, it will do so in an appropriate way. Until it has done so the earlier statement of policy, including any interpretations and reservations, remains valid.

Some developed countries have proposed that, wherever one resolution is referred to in a later resolution, the latter should refer to the former resolution "as adopted." The intention is that the words "as adopted" would incorporate by inference interpretations, reservations and objections expressed to the former resolution at the time it was adopted. The developing countries, because they consider such reservations, etc., of no significance, oppose the "as adopted" formulation. Canada takes the position that such reservations, etc. remain valid whether or not the "as adopted" formula is used; and that they need not be repeated every time the resolution in question is referred to in a subsequent resolution.[100]

3) From the evidence of these cases and comments, what matters should be taken into account in weighing the legal consequences of a particular U.N. resolution?

4) The ICJ has commented on the use that may be made of General Assembly resolutions in *Military Activities In and Against Nicaragua* in these words:

> The Court has however to be satisfied that there exists in customary international law an *opinio juris* as to the binding character of such abstention [from the use of force]. This *opinio juris* may, though with all due caution, be deduced from, *inter alia*, the attitude of the Parties and the attitude of States towards certain General Assembly resolutions, and particularly resolution 2625 (XXV) entitled "Declaration on Principles of International Law concerning Friendly Relations and Co-operation among States in accordance with the Charter of the United Nations." The effect of consent to the text of such resolutions cannot be understood as merely that of a "reiteration or elucidation" of the treaty commitment undertaken in the Charter. On the contrary, it may be understood as an acceptance of the validity of the rule or set of rules declared by the resolution by themselves. The principle of non-use of force, for example, may thus be regarded as a principle of customary international law.[101]

How does this statement compare with the traditional western view as expressed by Canada in note 2 above?

5) Although General Assembly resolutions rarely establish binding obligations, in what ways do they contribute to the creation and ascertainment of international law? Consider this question in the light of such other important resolutions as the Declaration

---

100 Reprinted in (1975) 13 Can. Y.B. Int'l Law 372.

101 *Nicaragua v. United States, supra* note 5 at 99-100.

on Principles of International Law, the Definition of Aggression, the Universal Declaration of Human Rights, and the Seabed Declaration.[102]

International Codes of Conduct
from a memorandum of the Legal Bureau of the Department of External Affairs
reported in (1990) 28 Can. Y.B. Int'l L. 495

International "codes of conduct" have been agreed upon in different legal forms: treaties, legally binding decisions of treaty organs, recommendations of intergovernmental organizations, "declarations" and "guidelines" adopted in the exercise of national competencies but coordinated in international organizations (e.g., in the OECD and the EEC), and "guidelines" and "company codes" of private organizations. While, from the point of view of legal terminology, it would seem preferable to distinguish codes from the recognized formal law-creating processes by confining the term to legally non-binding "voluntary codes," State practice uses the term for sets of international rules negotiated for transnational business activities irrespective of whether the codes are legally binding or not. As international law neither stipulates rules of form for codes nor recognizes them as an independent formal source of law, the legal effects of each code provision thus have to be determined separately.

The legal effects of "voluntary codes" depend on the intentions and competencies of the declarant States and organizations as well as on the content, acceptance and actual application of code provisions. They may become effective in four ways:

(a) The adoption of a code as a "recommendation" does not invest its provisions with international law status; the presumption is against interpreting recommendations as constituting informal agreement or "instant customary law." However, even express disclaimers, such as to the effect that "observance of the Guidelines is voluntary and not legally enforceable," cannot preclude the possibility of an *opinio juris sive necessitatis* gradually coming into being and resulting in code provisions evolving through the recognized law-creating processes into international agreements, customary international law or general principles of law. The capability and "normative force" of code provisions to develop into future international law is contingent on the generality or specificity of their content, their respective addressees, their acceptance as an expression of consensus, and their actual application, which is enhanced and reviewed by the implementation mechanisms provided for in the various codes.

(b) The acquiescence in recommendation, recognition or application of code provisions can estop consenting States and organizations from contesting the existence of principles and rules of international law and may result in *bona fide* obligations distinguishable only in degree and scope from obligations under the rules of international law. Codes recommending their implementation through enforceable rules can have a "legitimate effect" and demonstrate

---

102   See the Documentary Supplement; Chapter 15, Section A; and Chapter 13, Section C, respectively.

that "voluntary codes" are not intended to shield their addressees from the legal enforcement of code provisions. As expression of consensus on "standards of public policy," codes can contribute to the development of an international *ordre public*. The judicial determination of "public policy" and *boni mores* by reference to voluntary codes again illustrates the difficulty of drawing a sharp dividing line between "soft" and "hard" law.

(c) In addition, legally non-binding codes often contain restatements and persuasive evidence of the existence, meaning and scope of principles and rules of law. Codes are often aimed at regulating areas which are subject to divergent legislation and conflicting jurisdictional claims, such as antitrust, tax evasion, transfer-pricing, disclosure of information, technology transfer and illicit payments. In such areas, code provisions can serve as subsidiary means for the determination of rules of law on, for example, the scope of jurisdiction, the reasonable link requirement for extraterritorial enforcement jurisdiction, and rules of non-intervention and comity.

(d) The development of code provisions into international law requires evidence of effectiveness which only State practice can provide. The objective of regulating transnational entities, the separate entities of which are legally organized under the respective national laws of home and host States and without legal status under international law, often requires national implementing laws, thus possibly contributing to the harmonization of domestic legislation for which codes set out common standards or provide model laws. The case law in this area also illustrates the potential influence of code provisions on the interpretation of company law and of their possible evolution into trade usages, *boni mores* or general principles of business law.

NOTE

In 2000, the U.N. launched a new initiative, the Global Compact, following a 1999 address by Secretary-General Kofi Annan at the World Economic Forum. The Compact brings companies together with U.N. agencies, labour, and civil society to support ten (originally nine) principles in the areas of human rights, labour, the environment, and anti-corruption, and is described by the U.N. in the following terms: "The Global Compact is not a regulatory instrument—it does not 'police,' enforce or measure the behavior or actions of companies. Rather, the Global Compact relies on public accountability, transparency and the enlightened self-interest of companies, labour and civil society to initiate and share substantive action in pursuing the principles upon which the Global Compact is based."[103]

---

103 On-line: The Global Compact, online: <http://www.unglobalcompact.org/Portal/Default.asp?>. For commentary, see Symposium (United Nations Global Compact) (2001) 34 Cornell Int'l L.J. 481-521. See generally John J. Kirton & Michael J. Trebilcock, eds., *Hard Choices, Soft Law: Voluntary Standards in Global Trade, Environment, and Social Governance* (2004).

CHAPTER FOUR

National Application of International Law

A. NATIONAL APPLICATION IN CANADA[1]

International law has internal as well as intergovernmental applications. The degree of its integration and execution within the national legal system depends on the nature of the relationship between domestic law and international law. This in turn can be seen as being controlled either by the domestic or by the international legal order. The ultimate question to be answered is, to what extent may international legal principles be relied upon as imposing legally enforceable obligations, or conferring legally enforceable rights, on individuals in their domestic system? This question is, in some contexts, referred to as the "direct applicability" or "direct effect" of international law in the domestic legal

---

1　On international law as applied in domestic systems, generally, see I. Brownlie, *Principles of Public International Law*, 6th ed. (2003) c. 2; P.-M. Dupuy, *Droit International Public*, 7th ed. (2004) partie 3.; D. Nguyen Quoc, Daillier & Pellet, *Droit International Public*, 7th ed. (2002). For Canada, see J.M. Arbour, *Droit international public*, 4th ed. (2002) c. 4; J. Currie, *Public International Law* (2001) c. 6; G. van Ert, *Using International Law in Canadian Courts* (2002); S. Beaulac, "National Application of International Law: The Statutory Interpretation Perspective" (2003) 51 Can. Y.B. Int'l Law 225; J. Brunnée & S. Toope, "A Hesitant Embrace: The Application of International Law by Canadian Courts" (2002) 40 Can.Y.B. Int'l L. 3; M. Cohen & A.F. Bayefsky, "The Canadian Charter of Rights and Freedoms and Public International Law" (1983) 61 Can. Bar Rev. 265; L. Lebel & G. Chao, "The Rise of International Law in Canadian Constitutional Litigation: Fugue or Fusion? Recent Developments and Challenges in Internationalizing International Law" (2002) 16 Sup. Ct. L. Rev. 23; H. Kindred, "The Use of Unimplemented Treaties in Canada: Practice and Prospects in the Supreme Court" in Carmody, Iwasawa & Rhodes, eds., *Trilateral Perspectives on International Legal Issues: Conflict and Coherence* (2003) at 3; K. Knop, "Here and There: International Law in Domestic Courts" (2000) 32 N.Y.U.J. Int'l L. & Pol. 501; R. St. J. Macdonald, "The Relationship between International Law and Domestic Law in Canada" in Macdonald, Morris, & Johnston, eds., *Canadian Perspectives on International Law and Organization* (1974) at 88; A. de Mestral "L'évolution des rapports entre le droit Canadien et le droit international un demi siècle après l'affaire des conventions internationales du travail" (1987) 25 Can.Y.B. Int'l L. 301; R. Provost, "Le juge mondialisé : légitimité judiciaire et le droit international au Canada" in Belleau & Lacasse, eds., *Claire L'Heureux-Dubé à la Cour suprême du Canada 1987–2002* (2004) at 569; C. Vanek, "Is International Law a Part of the Law of Canada?" (1949-50) 8 U.T.L.J. 251.

system. Different states are more or less receptive to international law as a part of their domestic legal structure.[2]

The Canadian approach appears to be undergoing major changes. Canadian courts are under increasing pressure to show more openness to public international law and have begun to respond. However, the legacy of the past is not a solid one and much ambiguity remains.

Doctrinal analysis of this issue is generally presented in terms of the "adoptionist" or "transformationist" approach to the relationship of international and domestic law. Unfortunately, there is little agreement in doctrine on these issues and the cases, which reflect different approaches in different jurisdictions (and are sometimes decided by judges unfamiliar with the international legal process), often do not articulate the theory that underlies the result arrived at by the bench. From the point of view of comparative law, the matter is further complicated by the diversity of approaches to this issue in different states with different legal traditions. The approaches adopted by Canadian courts over the last hundred years share this ambiguity. In Canada, as in many jurisdictions, it is the domestic constitutional framework of the state that determines the degree to which international law is applied in any given circumstance. The importance of an understanding of this relationship in any given legal system cannot be over-emphasized, for it is the degree to which international law is a part of the domestic legal system that determines to what extent international legal principles will be relevant for individual citizens as well as for nation states and their governments.

In Canada, certain trends may be observed. A good argument may be made from the cases that follow that Canada is adoptionist in respect of customary international law and transformationist in respect of conventional law—the latter clearly springing from following the British public law tradition that treaties must be enacted into law by Parliament before they can affect private rights. The extent to which the interpretation of such laws will be informed by a judicial examination of the international obligations that gave rise to them illustrates just how receptive the domestic legal system is to international law. It may also give scope to applying international norms in a way that goes well beyond the intent of the legislature.

The need to "transform" treaty obligations by way of statute gives rise to important constitutional considerations in the Canadian context, governed as it is by a federal constitution. It becomes important to determine which level of government has legislative competence in respect of Canada's international obligations. The federal government is generally regarded as having exclusive international personality in the sense that only it may bind Canada to an international agreement. The question is whether it may enact legislation giving internal effect to all or only some international agreements. This issue is one of considerable practical significance as international undertakings become increasingly important as a source of domestic law (tax treaties, labour conventions, law of the sea, public health, environmental concerns, trade relations, international commercial arbitration, and so forth). There may also be a question as to what extent the division of

---

2   For an extensive review of the policy considerations underlying the "transformation" of treaty provisions into domestic law, see J. Jackson, "Status of Treaties in Domestic Legal Systems: A Policy Analysis" (1992) 86 Am. J. Int'l L. 310.

legislative powers contained in sections 91 and 92 of the *Constitution Act* is influenced by Canada's expanding international obligations, particularly in the commercial field.[3]

Another issue that often arises is the question of the consequence of a conflict between international law, either customary or conventional, and domestic law. In Canada, this matter also has a constitutional dimension in that a different approach may be taken depending on whether one is concerned with federal or provincial statutes.[4]

Finally, there is the question of the increasingly dynamic role of the *Charter of Rights and Freedoms*.[5] To what extent is international law in general applicable both in interpreting the terms contained in the Charter and in ascertaining the scope of its provisions? In this respect, internationally accepted human rights norms are of particular importance[6] and interpretations of similar language contained in other international human rights instruments, the International Covenant on Civil and Political Rights,[7] or the European Convention on Human Rights,[8] for example, may be of considerable value to a court in applying the Charter. An understanding of the relationship between international legal norms and the domestic legal system is becoming increasingly important to lawyers in an interdependent world characterized by complex transnational transactions. A comparison of how other jurisdictions treat such issues is thus helpful both in comprehending the effectiveness of international legal obligations in such jurisdictions and in providing a measure of how the Canadian system functions.

In recent years, Canadian law appears to be in the process of change in this field as the courts are becoming more sensitive to the pressures created by international law as well as the responses to these pressures adopted by other states. Lately, Canadian courts have shown remarkable willingness to consider arguments based on international law, but they also show great caution in their responses. The courts are concerned, even confused, about how they should deal with the different sources of law that exist in the international legal system, which they continue to view as constituting a different legal order from the Canadian legal system. It is not clear whether Canadian judges consider that they have any duty to enforce international legal rules. In this respect the Canadian judiciary maintains a profoundly "dualist" position at a time when many other legal systems are moving toward a more "monist" position.

Apart from their difficulty in knowing the content of international law, Canadian courts appear to be concerned by the fact that this body of law is not made by Parliament or the provincial legislatures but rather appears to be executive-made law. It is therefore

---

3   S.M. Beck & I. Bernier, eds., *Canada and the New Constitution: The Unfinished Agenda* (1983).

4   See G.V. LaForest, "May the Provinces Legislate in Violation of International Law?" (1961) 39 Can. Bar Rev. 78.

5   *Constitution Act, 1982*, being Schedule B to the *Canada Act 1982* (U.K.), 1982, c. 11.

6   See *e.g. Singh et al. v. Minister of Employment and Immigration*, [1985] 1 S.C.R. 177 and *Re Service Employees' International Union, Local 204 and Broadway Manor Nursing Home* (1984), 44 O.R. (2d) 392 (Div. Ct.); *Slaight Communications Inc. v. Davidson*, [1989] 1 S.C.R. 1038.

7   Reproduced in the Documentary Supplement and discussed in Chapter 12, Section B.2(a) on "Universal Norms."

8   Reported in Chapter 12, Section B.2(b) on "Regional Norms."

distrusted as having inherently less democratic justification than law made by democratically elected legislatures. While these are serious concerns, they do not respond to the fact that the executive does in fact play a vital role in law making in Canada and in many other democracies. Furthermore, this position leads to the logical conclusion that international law has no legal force unless Canada accepts it. Taken to its logical extreme this position suggests that only domestic law is genuine law.

Canadian courts also continue to struggle with the difference between customary international law and treaty law. Many, but not all, judges appear to be willing to treat customary international law as creating rights and duties in the Canadian legal order as part of the body of common law. The courts have always taken the position that treaties require transformation to produce legal effect in the Canadian legal order: this is entirely appropriate in the light of the constitutional considerations listed above, but there is considerable divergence of views as to the nature of the legal intervention required to ensure that a treaty has been implemented. What is meant by "implementation" is anything but clear. Most dicta suggest the need for a specific legislative act relating to the particular treaty and do not take account of the situation arising when the *Constitution of Canada* or pre-existing legislation or prerogative powers already provide a legal basis for implementation. This terminological uncertainty can give rise to very different outcomes in particular cases. Although the various issues mentioned above naturally entwine, they have been divided for the purposes of analysis into two sections—customary international law and treaty law—for the convenience of analysis.

B. CUSTOMARY INTERNATIONAL LAW IN CANADA

The way the courts approach international law affects the scope and force of its application internally in Canada. Following British public law, whose principles were received into Canada, Canadian courts in varying degrees have entertained two approaches—the doctrines of adoption and of transformation. In *Trendtex Trading Corp. Ltd. v. Central Bank of Nigeria*,[9] Lord Denning described, with characteristic pungency, the attributes and the significance of these two doctrines (where he writes "incorporation" read "adoption" in Canadian parlance):

> One school of thought holds to the doctrine of *incorporation*. It says that the rules of international law are incorporated into English law automatically and considered to be part of English law unless they are in conflict with an Act of Parliament. The other school of thought holds to the doctrine of *transformation*. It says that the rules of international law are not to be considered as part of English law except in so far as they have been already adopted and made part of our law by the decisions of the judges, or by Act of Parliament, or long established custom. The difference is vital when you are faced with a change in the rules of international law. Under the doctrine of incorporation, when the rules of international law change, our English law changes with them. But, under the doctrine of transformation, the English law does not change. It is bound by precedent. It is bound down to those rules of

---

9   [1977] 1 Q.B. 529 at 553-54 (C.A.).

international law which have been accepted and adopted in the past. It cannot develop as international law develops.

(i) *The doctrine of incorporation.* The doctrine of incorporation goes back to 1737 in *Buvot v. Barbut* (1736) 3 Burr. 1481; 4 Burr. 2016; sub nom. *Barbuit's Case in Chancery* (1737) Forr. 280, in which Lord Talbot L.C. (who was highly esteemed) made a declaration which was taken down by young William Murray (who was of counsel in the case) and adopted by him in 1764 when he was Lord Mansfield C.J. in *Triquet v. Bath* (1764) 3 Burr. 1478:

> Lord Talbot declared a clear opinion—"That the law of nations in its full extent was part of the law of England, ... that the law of nations was to be collected from the practice of different nations and the authority of writers." Accordingly, he argued and determined from such instances, and the authorities of Grotius, Barbeyrac, Binkershoek, Wiquefort, etc., there being no English writer of eminence on the subject.

That doctrine was accepted, not only by Lord Mansfield himself, but also by Sir William Blackstone, and other great names, too numerous to mention. In 1853 Lord Lyndhurst in the House of Lords, with the concurrence of all his colleagues there, declared that ... "the law of nations, according to the decision of our greatest judges, is part of the law of England": see Sir George Cornewall Lewis's book, *Lewis on Foreign Jurisdiction* (1859), pp. 66-67.

(ii) *The doctrine of transformation.* The doctrine of transformation only goes back to 1876 in the judgment of Cockburn C.J. in *Reg. v. Keyn* (1876) 2 Ex. D. 63, 202-203:

> For writers on international law, however valuable their labours may be in elucidating and ascertaining the principles and rules of law, cannot make the law. To be binding, the law must have received the assent of the nations who are to be bound by it ... .
> Nor, in my opinion, would the clearest proof of unanimous assent on the part of other nations be sufficient to authorize the tribunals of this country to apply, without an Act of Parliament, what would practically amount to a new law. In so doing, we should be unjustifiably usurping the province of the legislature.

To this I may add the saying of Lord Atkin in *Chung Chi Cheung v. The King* [1939] A.C. 160, 167-68:

> So far, at any rate, as the courts of this country are concerned, international law has no validity save in so far as its principles are accepted and adopted by our own domestic law.

Lord Denning was speaking in that case of a customary international law norm—the rule of sovereign immunity. He left no doubt that he thought the doctrine of incorporation (adoption) was the correct one for English law in respect of customary international law.[10] The question is whether the same can be said for Canada. After a careful review of the Canadian cases, Professor Macdonald reached the guarded conclusion "there is room for the view that the law on the relationship of customary international law to domestic

---

10   In recent years the courts of the United Kingdom have consistently held to this position; see *Campaign for Nuclear Disarmament v. Prime Minister*, [2002] E.W.H.C. 2759 (Q.B.) at para. 23.

law in Canada is the same as it is in England."[11] Consider the following selection of cases as means to elaborate upon this general expression of opinion.

Foreign Legations Case
In the Matter of a Reference as to the Powers of the Corporation of the City of Ottawa and the Corporation of the Village of Rockcliffe Park To Levy Rates on Foreign Legations and High Commissioners' Residences, [1943] S.C.R. 208

[In this reference, the Court was asked to advise whether the *Ontario Assessment Act*, which declared in section 4 that "All real property in Ontario ... shall be liable to taxation," rendered the property of foreign states assessable and exigible to municipal taxation. The basic question was whether Ottawa city council had the power to levy rates on a number of foreign legations.]

DUFF C.J.: ... There are some general principles touching the position of the property of a foreign state and the minister of a foreign state that have been accepted and adopted by the law of England (which, except as modified by statute, is the law of Ontario) as part of the law of nations. It should, however, be observed at the outset that we are only concerned here with such rules as applied in normal times and in normal circumstances. We are not in any way concerned with the qualifications of these rules that may be necessary in order to meet special circumstances in which the interest of the state in relation to public safety, or public order, may be affected. What I have to say as to general principles must, therefore, be taken to be subject to that observation. ...

It is probable that the privileges attributed to foreign representatives by the law in England, as part of the law of nations, are at least as liberal as those recognized by the law of any other country. In *Heathfield v. Chilton* [(1767) 4 Burrow 2015], Lord Mansfield said;—

The law of nations will be carried as far in England, as anywhere.

[The Chief Justice then proceeded to ascertain the existence and scope of a foreign state's immunities, including immunity from taxation of its property, under international law. These immunities are discussed in detail in Chapter 5, Section C on "State Immunities."]

The principles governing the immunities of a foreign sovereign and his diplomatic agents and his property do not, of course, limit the legislative authority of the legislature having jurisdiction in the particular matter affected by any immunity claimed, or alleged. It is not necessary, in the view I take, to consider the respective jurisdictions of the Parliament of Canada and the local legislatures in this matter of taxation in respect of real estate owned, or occupied, by a foreign state, or a diplomatic

---

11   R. St. J. Macdonald, *supra* note 1 at 111; and see there (at 94) comments as to the authority of *R. v. Keyn* and *Chung Chi Cheung v. The King* as establishing the doctrine of transformation.

agent in his character of representative of a foreign state. The general language of the enactments imposing the taxation in question must be construed as saving to the privileges of foreign states. The general principle is put with great clearness and force in the judgment of Marshall C.J., from which I have quoted so freely. These are the words [*Schooner Exchange v. McFaddon* (1812), 7 Cranch 116, at 146 (U.S.S.C.)]:

> Without doubt, the sovereign of the place is capable of destroying this implication. He may claim and exercise jurisdiction either by employing force, or by subjecting such vessels to the ordinary tribunals. ... Those general statutory provisions ... which are descriptive of the ordinary jurisdiction ... ought not, in the opinion of this Court, to be so construed as to give them jurisdiction in a case, in which the sovereign power has impliedly consented to waive its jurisdiction.

The questions referred should all be answered in the negative.

· · ·

TASCHEREAU J.: ... Of course, the rapid expansion of international relations between Canada and the other countries of the world, could not be foreseen in 1867, but it is common ground that external affairs is a matter which is exclusively under Federal control, and it is in pursuance of these rights that the Canadian Government have exchanged ministers with foreign countries.

I quite agree, that if the Federal authorities contract obligations with foreign countries, their competence does not "become enlarged to keep pace with enlarged functions," and as Lord Atkin said in *Attorney General for Canada v. Attorney General for Ontario* ([1937] A.C. 326, at 352):

> In other words, the Dominion cannot, merely by making promises to foreign countries, clothe itself with legislative authority inconsistent with the constitution which gave it birth. ...

The question is whether under International Law, a property belonging to a foreign State may be assessed for municipal purposes. A negative answer would in no way clothe the Dominion with any "enlarged competence," and the denial to the Province and the Municipal authorities of the right to levy such rates, would not extend the field of federal legislative powers.

I have come to the conclusion that practically in all the leading countries of the world, it is a settled and accepted rule of International Law, that property belonging to a foreign Government, occupied by its accredited representative, cannot be assessed and taxed for state or municipal purposes.

The Minister himself, is not, as a rule, subject to the authority of a foreign power, and cannot be impleaded in the courts of the country where he is sent. His immunity from legal process extends to the property of the State, which is exempt from all forms of taxation. It is with this in mind that must be read the *Assessment Act* of Ontario.

I had the advantage of reading the reasons for judgment of the Chief Justice. He has made a thorough review of the jurisprudence and of the opinions of the text-writers on the subject, and with what he has said, I entirely concur.

I would answer ... [the basic question] in the negative.

[Separate and somewhat different opinions were rendered by Justices Kerwin, Hudson, and Rinfret.]

NOTES

1) Are the judges in this case adoptionist or transformationist in their approach?[12]

2) As a general maxim, a statute will be interpreted in such a way that it will not violate principles of public international law unless its clear meaning will admit of no other interpretation.[13] Do the judges in this case apply the maxim or do they go further?

3) In the United States, by comparison, the Supreme Court has clearly established the status of customary international law in the case of *The Paquete Habana*, involving the seizure of a foreign ship. The Court stated:

International law is part of our law, and must be ascertained and administered by the courts of justice of appropriate jurisdiction, as often as questions of right depending upon it are duly presented for their determination. For this purpose, where there is no treaty, and no controlling executive or legislative act or judicial decision, resort must be had to the customs and usages of civilised nations.[14]

It is also clear that federal legislation may violate international law, if that is the intent of Congress,[15] and that U.S. officials may act contrary to it if so authorized by a controlling executive act.[16]

4) The *Foreign Legations Case* concerned a conflict between a customary international law rule and a provincial statute. If customary international law is adopted into Canadian law, does it overreach prior case law? Consider the following case.

Saint John v. Fraser-Brace Overseas Corp.
[1958] S.C.R. 263

[Pursuant to an agreement between the governments of Canada and the United States for the construction of a radar defence system, certain contractors in Saint John carried out work on sites located in that city. The materials used in the work were either the property of the United States government or held by the contractors on its behalf. Saint John imposed municipal taxes both on certain leasehold interests in the lands and on personal property situated there. The contractors paid the taxes "under protest" and brought an action to recover them.]

---

12   See also *Reference re Exemption of U.S. Forces from Canadian Criminal Law*, [1943] S.C.R. 483; [1943] 4 D.L.R. 11.

13   See *Re Arrow River and Tributaries Slide and Boom Co. Ltd.*, [1932] 2 D.L.R. 250 (S.C.C.), reported below in Section C.3 on "Conflicts Between International Law and Canadian Statutes."

14   175 U.S. 677 at 700 (1900).

15   *Head Money Cases: Edye v. Robertson*, 112 U.S. 580 (1884).

16   See *Garcia-Mir v. Meese*, 788 F.2d 1446 (11th Cir. 1986), which involved the restraint of Cuban refugees in a manner contrary to international law.

RAND J.: This appeal raises a question of liability to taxation by the appellants of property used by the respondents as contractors with the Government of the United States in the construction of what is described as the "extension and co-ordination of a continental radar defence system within Canada," to serve as an agency of defence for both countries against possible air attacks. ...

Enough has been said to indicate the precise obligation of the contractors to the United States Government. It was essentially one to furnish services, with all property, materials, tools, equipment and other means used or employed in or for the work of construction, supplied by the United States. The fact that this field station was at some distance from the scene of the permanent works does not affect its relation to them or its derivative character. If the works would be exempt, then all property used in or for their construction, including that in field operations, regardless of situs, is necessarily identified with the ultimate purpose. All that was done within the municipality is to be taken as one with the final accomplishment, and the purpose of that accomplishment will determine that of the property used by these subsidiary agencies.

The general principle of immunity from legal processes in the broadest sense in what may be called the host country of public property of a foreign state has been given its authoritative statement for Canada by Duff C.J. in the *Foreign Legations Reference*, [above]. There, as here, he was dealing with taxation under general language in which only the interpretation of the statute was in question. The significant aspect of the matter examined by him was that of the theory on which the immunity is to be placed. ...

It is obvious that the life of every state is, under the swift transformation of these days, becoming deeply implicated with that of the others in a *de facto* society of nations. If in 1767 Lord Mansfield, as in *Heathfield v. Chilton*, could say, "The law of nations will be carried as far in England, as any where," in this country, in the 20th century, in the presence of the United Nations and the multiplicity of impacts with which technical developments have entwined the entire globe, we cannot say anything less.

In the language of Sir Alexander Cockburn quoted by Lord Atkin in *Chung Chi Cheung*, ... in the absence of precise precedent we must seek the rule which "reason and good sense ... would prescribe." In this we are not to disregard the practical consideration, if not the necessity, of that "general assent and reciprocity," of which Lord Macmillan speaks in *Compania Naviera Vascongardo v. The "Cristina" et al.*, cited in the reasons of McNair C.J. But to say that precedent is now required for every proposed application to matter which differs only in accidentals, that new concrete instances must be left to legislation or convention, would be a virtual repudiation of the concept of inherent adaptability which has maintained the life of the common law, and a retrograde step in evolving the rules of international intercourse. However slowly and meticulously they are to be fashioned they must be permitted to meet the necessities of increasing international involvements. It is the essence of the principle of precedent that new applications are to be determined according to their total elements including assumptions and attitudes, and in the international sphere the whole field of the behaviour of states, whether exhibited in actual conduct, conventions, arbitrations or adjudications, is pertinent to the determination of each issue. ...

Public works of this sort are not ordinarily considered subjects of taxation. Their object is to preserve the agencies that produce national wealth, the source of taxes. So to tax Government is simply to remit locally what has been exacted nationally. The work carried on by either Government in its own land would be untaxable, and that principle must carry over to the territory of the joint work.

I am unable, then, to infer that with an identity of purpose, status and rule in each country, either the invitation or its acceptance proceeded upon any other basis than that of the rule of exemption from taxation. Why should we deny to property designed for common national preservation a sovereign character and purpose equal at least to that of an ambassador's furniture? Works of this sort are not to be looked upon, in principle, as furnishing a source of taxation for municipalities nor state necessities an object of revenue; any other view would be a strange commentary upon our conception of the role of Government in these days. Public works may, at times, impose upon local resources burdens of municipal responsibility; but the exemption here does not touch services for which payment is ordinarily made, as water, electricity, etc. These the foreign invitees must, as their food-supply and property generally, acquire as purchasers. If strictly general municipal services providing fire-protection, repair of streets, etc., are excessively affected, the appeal must be to the domestic Government as participant in the work; and adjustment between the two countries becomes a political matter.

NOTES

1) Is Rand J.'s approach in the *Saint John* case adoptionist or transformationist?

2) Is there any suggestion in the case that there is a hierarchical relationship between public international law and domestic law? Which would prevail in the event of a conflict?

3) In *Re Newfoundland Continental Shelf*[17] the Supreme Court impliedly confirmed the doctrine of adoption. Both Canada and Newfoundland claimed the rights of the coastal state recognized by international law. The Supreme Court did not pause to consider whether or how international principles might resolve national legal problems, but instead it went straight to the usual sources of international law expressed in the Statute of the International Court article 38. Having dismissed treaty sources and general principles as having no application, it framed the question thus:

> The critical issue then is whether the sovereign right, arising *ipso jure*, to explore and exploit in the continental shelf was a matter of customary international law by 1949.

The Court then made an extensive survey of state claims to the continental shelf beginning in 1942. It took note of the International Law Commission's work, in particular observing that the matter involved the progressive development of international law, and it discussed such subsidiary case law and scholarly commentary as was made available on the subject. It was then stated:

> We conclude that international law had not sufficiently developed by 1949 to confer, *ipso jure*, the right of the coastal state to explore and exploit the continental shelf. We think that in 1949 state practice was neither sufficiently widespread to constitute a general practice

---

17   [1984] 1 S.C.R. 86, reported in Chapter 13, Section B.5.

nor sufficiently consistent to constitute settled law. Furthermore, several of the early state claims exceeded that which international law subsequently recognized in the 1958 Geneva Convention. International Law on the continental shelf developed relatively quickly, but it had not attained concrete form by 1949.[18]

Thus the Supreme Court provided an unusual but admirable demonstration of how a court should canvass the existence of customary international law. Furthermore, it considered the evolution of customary international law in a manner that indicated that it was a source of law in Canada.

4) More recently, in answering the second question in *Reference re Secession of Quebec*,[19] "does international law give ... Quebec the right to effect the secession of Quebec from Canada unilaterally?," the Supreme Court once again was required to apply international legal principles. Unfortunately, in making use of a great range of international legal materials both customary and conventional, it did not consider their variable legal status and did not explain how international law operates within the Canadian legal system. The Supreme Court did, however, reach the following conclusion, which is part of the reasons for its opinion:

In summary, the international law right to self-determination only generates, at best, a right to external self-determination in situations of former colonies; where a people is oppressed, as for example under foreign military occupation; or where a definite group is denied meaningful access to government to pursue their political, economic, social and cultural development. In all three situations, the people in question are entitled to a right to external self-determination because they have been denied the ability to exert internally their right to self-determination. Such exceptional circumstances are manifestly inapplicable to Québec under existing conditions. Accordingly, neither the population of the province of Québec, even if characterized in terms of "people" or "peoples," nor its representative institutions, the National Assembly, the legislature or government of Québec, possess a right, under international law, to secede unilaterally from Canada.[20]

Thus the Supreme Court in this reference, as in *Re Newfoundland Continental Shelf*, has treated international law as granting important public rights to Canadians and Canadian governments as well as setting limits to the exercise of these rights. If this statement is true, is there not sufficient evidence that the rules of customary international law form part of Canadian law?

5) In addition to the limited statements of the Supreme Court regarding the status and effect of customary international law in Canada, the Court of Appeal for Ontario has more recently rendered several decisions[21] that help to clarify the situation, including the following opinion.

---

18   *Ibid.* at 117 and 124.

19   [1998] 2 S.C.R. 217, 161 D.L.R. (4th) 385, reproduced in Chapter 2, Section C.4(b). See the case comment of S.J. Toope in (1999) 93 Am. J. Int'l L. 519.

20   S.C.R. *ibid.* at 287.

21   See also *Re Regina and Palacios* (1984), 45 O.R. (2nd) 269.

Bouzari v. Islamic Republic of Iran
(2004), 243 D.L.R. (4th) 406, 71 O.R. (3d) 675 (C.A.);
leave to appeal to S.C.C. refused, January 27, 2005
Reproduced in Chapter 5, Section C.4 on "State Immunities: Personal Injury
Exception to Immunity." Read paragraphs 64 and 65 especially.[22]

Judicial Notice of International Law

Even when a court is prepared to adopt customary international law as relevant to the disposition of a case, it still has to discover the contents of the applicable rule. This raises the perennial question, how do judges determine the international law to be applied? Professor R. St. J. Macdonald[23] has commented:

> Throughout our discussion of both the English and Canadian courts' handling of customary international rules, the concept of judicial notice has played a silent but fundamental role; for without it, the entry of these customary rules into our domestic law would be much more complicated. ...
>
> According to *Black's Law Dictionary*, judicial notice is the act by which a court, in conducting a trial, or framing its decision, will, of its own motion, and without the production of evidence, recognize the existence and truth of certain facts, having a bearing on the controversy at bar, which, from their nature, are not properly the subject of testimony, or which are universally regarded as established by common notoriety, e.g. the laws of the state, international law, historical events, the constitution and course of nature, main geographical features, etc. ...
>
> Fortunately, it is true, as Lauterpacht pointed out, that "international law need not be proved in the same way as foreign law or any other fact must be proved—apparently for the reason that it is not foreign law." He continued: "Judicial notice is taken of it as of Acts of Parliament or of any branch of the unwritten law, although having regard to the frequent absence of direct authority the range of judicial inquiry is wider and, on occasions, more laborious than in the case of ordinary rules of municipal law." ...
>
> In Canada, also, the standard practice has been to notice judicially international law, although, as in England, the Canadian courts have not usually seen fit to comment on this point directly. There have, however, been several judicial comments which make clear that international law is judicially noticed in the same way that domestic law is. In *The North*,[24] Davies J., in upholding the lower court finding, said that the hot pursuit doctrine "being part of the law of nations was properly judicially taken notice of and acted upon." This statement can only mean that customary rules which are part of international law are to be judicially noticed. In the *Armed Forces Reference*,[25] Taschereau J. saw his task as, first, "to seek if there exists" the customary rule in question. The implication in this statement is that it is the judge who must do the seeking, just as he does in domestic law; in fact, in domestic law, the

---

22   See also the portion of the judgment reproduced below in Section D on "Jus Cogens in Canadian Law."

23   *Supra* note 1 at 111.

24   *The King v. The Ship North* (1906), 37 S.C.R. 385.

25   *Reference re Exemption of U.S. Forces from Canadian Criminal Law, supra* note 12.

task could be described using exactly the same words: to seek if there exists the domestic rule in question. The conclusion that international law is being treated as part of domestic law in this regard is inescapable.

The most explicit statement about the use of international law by Canadian courts was made by Rand J. in *Saint John v. Fraser-Brace Overseas Corp.*, reproduced above.[26] Rand J. admonished the courts to "seek the rule which reason and good sense would prescribe." This directive, he interpreted, required courts to take judicial notice of contemporary international rules without too much regard for previous domestic precedents. How could Rand J. ignore the doctrine of *stare decisis*?[27]

C. TREATIES IN CANADA

Treaties raise different considerations from customary law. Since Canada is a federal country, the constitutional authority to negotiate and make a treaty may differ from the locus of power to apply it. Consequently, this section first addresses the exercise of treaty-making powers in Canada before discussing the process of treaty implementation. The section next addresses an issue that parallels a difficulty with customary law: what is the consequence of a conflict between a statute (federal or provincial) and an international obligation of Canada? Then consideration is given to the methods of interpreting implemented treaties and the relevance of unimplemented treaties in Canadian law.

1. Treaty Making

Federal Position[28]
from Canada, Department of External Affairs,
Federalism and International Relations (1968), 11-33

The exclusive responsibility of the Federal Government in the field of treaty-making rests upon three considerations: the principles of international law relating to the power of component parts of federal states to make treaties; the constitutions and constitutional practices of federal states; and, finally, the Canadian Constitution and constitutional practice. These three aspects are examined below.

---

26 And see Rand J.'s opinion in *Reference re Exemption of U.S. Forces*, *supra* note 12 at 524. In *Pan American World Airways Inc. v. The Queen* (1979), 96 D.L.R. (3d) 267 (F.C.T.D.), Mahoney J. confirmed that international law need not be proved like foreign law, and therefore expert opinion as to the construction of a treaty is inadmissible as evidence but may be adopted as argument. See also G. van Ert, "The Admissibility of International Legal Evidence" (2005) 84 Can. Bar Rev. 31.

27 See Denning L.J. in *Trendtex Trading*, *supra* in text at note 9.

28 See also T.A. Levy, "Provincial International Status Revisited" (1976-77) 3 Dal. L.J. 70; R. St. J. Macdonald, "International Treaty Law and the Domestic Law of Canada" (1975) 2 Dal. L.J. 307; and E. McWhinney, "The Constitutional Competence Within Federal Systems as to International Agreements" (1964-68) 1 Can. Legal Studies 145.

(i) The Principles of International Law

The question whether the members of a federal union can make treaties or international agreements has been studied at length by the International Law Commission, a subsidiary organ of the United Nations General Assembly, and by various experts on the law of treaties who have prepared reports for the Commission. The Commission has taken the view that the question whether a member of a federal union can have a treaty-making capacity depends upon the constitution of the country concerned. In other words, the Commission is of the view that international law cannot by itself decide whether or not a member of a federal union can make a treaty. International law looks, in the first instance, to the constitution of the state in question to determine the treaty-making capacity. ...

(ii) The Constitutions of Federal States

The constitutions of the great majority of states reserve to the federal government the responsibility for the conclusion of international agreements and make it clear that the constituent parts do not possess this right. There are, however, some federal states (Switzerland, the United States, the Federal Republic of Germany and the U.S.S.R.) whose constitutional practice apparently allows the constituent parts to enter into certain types of agreements with foreign states. However, the experience of these states cannot be treated as common because their constitutional practices differ materially one from another: under the Swiss Constitution the Federal Government is authorized to make international agreements on behalf of the constituent parts; the United States Constitution provides that the Congress may authorize "compacts" between the states of the union and foreign sovereign states, but as of this time no such agreements have been concluded; finally although the Constitutions of the Federal Republic of Germany and the Soviet Union authorize the constituent parts to make international agreements in some areas, they are subject to federal direction or control.

... In summary, however, it may be concluded that even in the case of constitutions which authorize the constituent members to enter into international agreements in certain fields, all provide that this authority must be exercised either under federal control or through the intermediary of the federal government. Moreover, it has been pointed out by constitutional experts that powers of this nature which may be exercised by members of federal unions have been used with diminishing frequency in recent years.

No federal constitution authorizes the constituent parts to enter freely and independently into international agreements.

(iii) The Canadian Constitution

Having examined the constitutions of a number of federal states, it remains to be considered where the treaty-making power resides under the Canadian Constitution.

The assumption in 1867 was that the treaty-making power would remain part of the prerogative powers with respect to the conduct of external affairs, which rested with the Sovereign and were exercised on the advice of Her British Ministers. For this reason, the *British North America Act*[29] is silent on this question, although it is provided in s. 132 that the Canadian Parliament and Government

> shall have all powers necessary or proper for performing [that is, implementing] the Obligations of Canada or of any Provinces thereof, as part of the British Empire, towards Foreign Countries arising under Treaties between the Empire and such Foreign Countries.

Thus, in 1867 and for approximately the next half-century, the treaty-making capacity in respect of Canada was vested exclusively in the Imperial Government. However, in the period 1871-1923, procedures slowly evolved by which Canadian Government representatives at first participated in negotiations leading to an imperial treaty affecting Canada (Washington Treaty of 1871), then later came to sign such agreements as a member of the Empire (Treaty of Versailles, 1919), and finally signed such agreements on behalf of Canada (Halibut Fisheries Treaty, 1923). As noted above, this new procedure was confirmed at the Imperial Conference of 1926; Canada and other dominions were henceforth to be able to negotiate and enter into treaties affecting their own interests and ratification was to be effected at the instance of the dominion concerned. The dominions were also accorded the right to establish direct diplomatic relations with foreign powers.

The prerogative powers of the Crown, initially reserved for the Queen under s. 9 of the *British North America Act*, are now exercised by the Governor-General. In the colonial period, the extent of the delegation of the prerogative power was limited by the subordinate position occupied by the colony, but it may be assumed that, upon the achievement of independence those prerogative powers remaining in the Crown passed to the Governor-General, and all such prerogatives are implicitly held by the Governor-General even in the absence of specific delegation. In other words, it is reasonable to conclude that the powers required by an independent state in fact reside in that state, and, further, that, when Canada achieved autonomy, only one entity became independent and was recognized as such by the international community. In addition, the new Letters Patent issued by the Governor-General in 1947 declare:

> 2. And We do hereby authorize and empower Our Governor-General, with the advice of Our Privy Council for Canada or of any members thereof or individually, as the case requires, to exercise all powers and authorities lawfully belonging to Us in respect of Canada. …
> 3. And We do hereby authorize and empower Our Governor-General to keep and use Our Great Seal of Canada for sealing all things whatsoever that may be passed under Our Great Seal of Canada.

From the terms of the Letters Patent, read in conjunction with the 1939 provision for a Great Seal for Canada, it may be concluded that the foreign affairs prerogative is now exercised by the Governor-General.

---

29   Now the *Constitution Act, 1867*, as renamed by the *Canada Act, 1982* (U.K.), 1982, c.11.

Further, the burden of judicial opinion, particularly in the *Labour Conventions Case*, 1937,[30] is that the authority to enter into international agreements resides exclusively with the federal authority. Chief Justice Duff's opinion in that case includes the following observation:

> As regards all such international arrangements, it is a necessary consequence of the respective positions of the Dominion Executive and the Provincial Executives that this authority (to enter into international agreements) resides in the Parliament of Canada. The Lieutenant-Governors represent the Crown for certain purposes. But, in no respect does the Lieutenant-Governor of a Province represent the Crown in respect to relations with foreign Governments. The Canadian Executive, again, constitutionally acts under responsibility to the Parliament of Canada and it is that Parliament alone which can constitutionally control its conduct of external affairs.[31]

It was also his opinion that the documents of the Imperial Conferences of 1923 and 1926 constituted authoritative evidence of constitutional usage, including the assertion that "agreements between Great Britain and a foreign country or a dominion and a foreign country shall take the form of treaties between heads of state (except in the case of agreements between governments) ... ." Chief Justice Duff and Justices Davis and Kerwin concluded that Canada had the power to enter into agreements on matters falling within the provincial legislative competence by the "crystallization of constitutional usage and constitutional law."

Proponents of a provincial capacity at international law have suggested that the prerogative powers of the Lieutenant-Governor include the power to carry on foreign affairs or at least to enter into treaties in areas of provincial legislative jurisdiction. Historically the powers of the Lieutenant-Governors have been the source of considerable dispute, but two decisions of the Judicial Committee (*Liquidators of the Maritime Bank of Canada v. The Receiver-General of New Brunswick*, 1892,[32] and *Bonanza Creek Mining Company Limited v. The King*, 1916)[33] have been cited as establishing both that the government of each province represents the Queen in the exercise of her prerogative regarding all matters affecting the rights of the province, and, more particularly, that external prerogatives are among those which have devolved upon the Lieutenant-Governors in legislative fields assigned to the provinces. This conclusion is open to doubt on various grounds. The Privy Council could not have had in mind the devolution of the Crown's external prerogatives because at the time these cases were decided they had not devolved to Canada. Moreover, the *Bonanza Creek* case had no foreign aspects to it and dealt exclusively with internal questions. In any event, provincial legislative competence is restricted to matters of an essentially local nature and therefore any parallel executive powers would also be so limited, and not applicable to the foreign affairs field.

---

30   [1937] A.C. 326 (P.C.).

31   [1936] S.C.R. 461 at 488.

32   [1892] A.C. 437.

33   [1916] 1 A.C. 566.

Further, the powers of the Federal Government as set forth in the *British North America Act* are not such as to support the view that the Queen's external prerogatives developed [sic] upon the Lieutenant-Governors of the provinces. In particular, the Federal Executive is empowered to disallow acts passed by provincial legislatures whether or not such acts deal with matters within the legislative competence of the provinces. Thus, if the provincial governments possessed treaty-making powers under the BNA Act, they would be in a position in which the Federal Government could prevent them from implementing any such agreements. Although these powers have not been used for many years, they are nonetheless historically significant in determining the nature of Canadian federalism. Seen in this way, they create a strong presumption that under the Constitution the provinces could not have been intended to enjoy independent status in their own right.

The following conclusions may be drawn from the above analysis:

1. In Canada the constitutional authority to conclude international agreements is a part of the royal prerogative and, with respect to treaties, is exercised in the name of Canada by the Governor-General, usually on the advice of the Secretary of State for External Affairs. The prerogative powers in respect of foreign affairs and treaty-making devolved upon the Federal executive at the time when Canada became an autonomous member of the British Commonwealth of Nations. In addition, the delegation of the prerogative powers of the Crown in right of Canada to the Governor-General were clearly confirmed by the Letters Patent of 1947.

2. There has never been any delegation of such prerogative powers to the Lieutenant-Governors of the provinces. Nor is there any authority for the assertion that the provinces received any part of the royal prerogative with respect to foreign affairs and the power to make treaties.

3. That such a situation was not created by the *British North America Act* may also be seen from the fact that the Federal Government, through the exercise of the power of disallowance, could make it impossible for the provinces to perform any treaty which required legislation. ...

Provincial Practice in Respect of Arrangements with Foreign States

A review of the material available reveals that provinces have long shown a desire to enter into agreements of a local nature with foreign jurisdictions, affecting, for example, roads, bridges, electric power, and similar enterprises. More recently, a desire has also been expressed to enter into agreements of a broader nature covering, for example, co-operation in the cultural and technological fields. In addition, certain provinces maintain representation abroad in the form of commercial or trade offices, information and travel bureaux, and offices of agents general or delegates general, which lead both to a variety of dealings with foreign governments and their agents and to certain arrangements of a contractual nature with the authorities of the countries concerned.

Dealings between the provinces or their agents and foreign jurisdictions may take a variety of forms.

Agreements between Provincial or Local Jurisdictions and Foreign Entities,
Not Regarded as Subject to the Provisions of International Law

It has been the practice for Canadian provinces to enter into various kinds of
administrative arrangements of an informal character with foreign jurisdictions which,
as they are not subject to international law, are generally not regarded by it as binding.
Arrangements of this type often involve the reciprocal recognition of legislation
between two jurisdictions, for example, legislation concerning automobile licensing
as between Ontario and other jurisdictions, or arrangements (upheld judicially in the
Scott case, 1952) regarding maintenance orders between provinces and other
jurisdictions in the Commonwealth.

Arrangements between the Provinces and Foreign Governments Which Are
Subsumed under Agreements between Canada and the
Foreign Government Concerned

Arrangements of this sort are fewer in number and more recent in time. ...

Contracts Subject to Private Law

It appears that the Canadian provinces have entered into and continue to enter into a
variety of contracts of a private law character. For example, many Canadian provinces
maintain offices in the United States or Europe and it may be assumed that they have
entered into contracts with governmental agencies in the jurisdictions within which
their offices are located relating to leases, fuel and power supply, telephones and a
variety of other matters. These contracts, it should be noted, are exclusively of a private
or commercial nature. ...

Co-operation in Treaty-Making and Implementation

For some time the Federal Government has followed the practice of consulting with
the provinces on various questions related to treaty-making and treaty-
implementation. This procedure provides a means for harmonizing the interests of
the federal and provincial governments and, in addition, offers an opportunity to give
effect to the wishes of the provinces with respect to treaties in areas in which they
have legislative responsibility. In the latter field, it is also a necessary component of
the process leading to the implementation of international agreements.

     Consultation may take a number of forms, including direct discussions between
the federal and provincial authorities, and may be initiated prior to or during
negotiations on a proposed treaty, as well as in the stages subsequent to signature
when questions regarding implementation may require federal–provincial co-
operation. Although they have not followed a fixed pattern, the procedures which
have been devised thus far have proved successful in many cases, and have resulted
in a substantial Canadian achievement in respect of ratification and implementation.
... Nevertheless, it is a record which the Government recognizes could be improved
through more effective means of consultation.

As suggested [above], the provinces may enter into a variety of administrative arrangements which are not binding in international law. In addition, various means for giving international validity to agreements involving the provinces have been employed or contemplated. Certain of these techniques are instructive as an indication of the means which are open for more extensive co-operation. Most prominent among them are indemnity agreements, ad hoc covering agreements and general framework agreements (accords cadres).

Indemnity Agreements

According to this procedure the Federal Government, after consultation with a province or provinces, enters into an agreement with the government of a foreign state on a matter of interest to a province. The agreement is supplemented, on the Canadian side, by an agreement between the Federal Government and the province concerned, under which the province undertakes to provide such legislative authority as might be necessary to enable the discharge within its territory of its obligations under the agreement. The province also indemnifies the Federal Government in respect of any liability that might arise by reason of the default of the province in implementing the obligations of Canada under its international agreement with the foreign state. An example of this technique is the Columbia River Treaty and Protocol. The procedure adopted was that, after extensive consultations with the British Columbia government, a federal delegation including representatives from the province negotiated a bilateral agreement with the United States. An arrangement was worked out with the Province of British Columbia whereby the province undertook to execute the terms of the treaty and to indemnify the Federal Government in the event of its failure to do so. Another example is the procedure worked out in the case of the St. Lawrence Seaway, involving the Province of Ontario.

As the examples cited above suggest, this technique may have particular merit in cases in which a province wishes to conclude an agreement with a U.S. state on a local matter of joint concern. An added advantage of this type of arrangement is that a province can be directly involved in the consultations leading to the bilateral agreement which forms the basis of Canada's international obligation.

Ad Hoc Covering Agreements

This technique allows the provincial authorities a direct way of achieving international arrangements in matters affecting their interests. It would normally take the form of an exchange of notes between the Federal Government and the foreign state concerned, which gives assent to arrangements between the provincial authorities and a foreign governmental agency. The exchange of notes gives international legal effect to the arrangements between the province and the foreign entity, but does not involve the province itself acquiring international rights or accepting international obligations. Only the Canadian Government is bound internationally by the agreement, but the province participates fully in treaty-making through co-operation with the federal authorities.

An example of this procedure is the "education entente" ... [signed February 27, 1965] in which an understanding in the field of education between Quebec and France

was given international status by an exchange of notes between the French Ambassador in Ottawa and the Secretary of State for External Affairs.

General Framework Agreements or Accords Cadres

This technique is similar to the ad hoc procedure described above except that it is not
intended to be restricted in its application to a specific agreement between a province
and a foreign entity, but rather to allow for future agreements in a given field by any
province which may be interested. As in the case of the ad hoc procedure, the Federal
Government remains responsible in international law for such arrangements. At the
same time, the provinces are provided with an open-ended opportunity to provide for
their interests in a given field, for example, educational or cultural exchanges,
whenever they wish to take advantage of the framework agreement to conclude
appropriate arrangements with the foreign government in question.

The best known example of this type is the cultural agreement and accompanying
exchange of letters signed by the Canadian and French Governments on November
17, 1965. ... [T]his agreement provides for the possibility of collaboration in the
cultural field between France and any of the Canadian provinces, and was
accompanied by an exchange of letters which specified that the authority for the
provinces to enter into ententes with France could be derived in the future, if they so
wished, from the cultural agreement and an exchange of letters or through a further
exchange of notes by the Governments of Canada and France.

The above methods provide a broad and flexible range of techniques which, when
employed in conjunction with close consultation and co-operation between the federal
and provincial authorities, are capable of allowing for the full expression of provincial
interests in treaty-making. At the same time, they give validity in international law to
provincial arrangements with foreign jurisdictions, thereby avoiding confusion as to
the rights and responsibilities of the members of the Canadian federation on the
international plane. ...

Québec Position[34]

Article 6 of the Vienna Convention on the Law of Treaties (reproduced in the
Documentary Supplement) does not deal with the power of a member of a federal union
to make treaties because, in its preparatory work, the International Law Commission took
the view that this issue depends upon the constitution of the country concerned. In
Canada, since the *Constitution Act* is silent on treaty making, the Québec government, on
several occasions, especially between 1964 and 1969, has maintained that the Province

---

34   See C. Emanuelli, *Droit International Public*, 3d ed. (1998) at 73; J.-Y. Morin, F. Rigaldes & D. Turp,
     Droit International Public, Notes et Documents, 3d ed. (1997) vol. 2, Doc. Nos. 75, 76, 77; J.-Y. Morin,
     "La conclusion d'accords internationaux par les provinces canadiennes à la lumière du droit comparé"
     (1965) 3 Can. Y.B. Int'l L. 127; J.-Y. Morin, "La Personalité Internationale du Québec" (1984) 1
     R.Q.D.I. 163; J.-Y. Morin, "Le Québec et le pouvoir de conclure des accords internationaux" (1966) 1
     Etudes Jur. Can. 136; and A.L.C. de Mestral, "Le Québec et les relations internationales" in P. Patenaude,
     ed., *Québec—Communauté Française de Belgique* (1991) at 209.

has the capacity to enter into treaties with respect to matters that are within its exclusive legislative jurisdiction. The Québec government, as well as Québec constitutional experts, specifically have rejected the arguments advanced by the federal government in *Federalism and International Relations*, reproduced above, to support its claim to exclusive responsibility in the field of treaty making. Analysis of the Letters Patent of 1947 leads them to conclude that with respect to the exercise of the Royal Prerogative, the Letters Patent cannot prevail over the *Constitution Act*. Thus, the exercise of the Royal Prerogative must be shared and correspond to the division of legislative powers between the federal and provincial governments. With respect to matters that fall within their exclusive jurisdiction, the provinces possess both executive and legislative power, which means that the prerogative powers of the Lieutenant-Governor include the power to enter into treaties with respect to these matters.

In Canada, the negotiation and signature of a treaty, it is argued, cannot be separated from its implementation. However, the provinces should not act in a way that is contrary to the foreign policy of the federal government. Therefore, each province, before signing a treaty, should communicate its contents to the federal government. Where the subject matter of the treaty falls within the exclusive jurisdiction of the provinces, the federal government might reject the treaty, but only if it is incompatible with Canada's foreign policy. If, on the other hand, the subject matter of the treaty does not fall within the exclusive jurisdiction of the provinces, the federal government could reject the treaty if it is incompatible either with Canada's foreign policy or federal domestic policy. Assent to the treaty given by the federal government should be communicated to the foreign state involved. Conversely, if the federal government decided to negotiate a treaty touching upon matters within the jurisdiction of the provinces, it should notify them and associate them with its negotiation, conclusion, and ratification. Some Québec authors go as far as maintaining that the only control over the constitutionality of a treaty should be judicial (that is, whether the treaty is *ultra vires*). On the political level, they assert that Québec should be free to enter into any type of treaty without having to consult the federal government.[35]

In furtherance of its position, Québec has enacted the following provision.

An Act Respecting the Ministère des Relations Internationales
R.S.Q. c. M-25.1.1

International Commitments

Administration of Programs

19. The Minister shall see to the negotiation and implementation of international agreements and shall administer the programs created under such agreements. He may, in writing, entrust the administration of certain of such programs to another minister. ...

---

35   See J.-Y. Morin, "Le Québec et le pouvoir de conclure des accords internationaux," *supra* note 34.

"International Agreement"

The expression "international agreement" means an accord, whatever its particular designation, reached between the Government or one of its departments or agencies, on the one part, and a foreign government or one of its departments, an international organization, or an agency of such a government or organization, on the other part.

Approval

20. Notwithstanding any contrary legislative provision, international agreements must be signed by the Minister and endorsed by the Government in order to be valid. ...

Signature, Approval, Ratification

Subject to section 22.5, international agreements referred to in section 22.2 must, to be valid, be signed by the Minister, approved by the National Assembly and ratified by the Government. ...

Interests of Québec

22.1. The Minister shall see to the interests of Québec during the negotiation of any international accord, whatever its particular designation, between the Government of Canada and a foreign government or an international organization, which pertains to any matter within the constitutional jurisdiction of Québec. The Minister shall ensure and coordinate the implementation of any such accord in Québec.

Agreement

The Minister may agree to the signing of such an accord by Canada.

Order

The Government must, in order to be bound by an international accord pertaining to any matter within the constitutional jurisdiction of Québec and to give its assent to Canada's expressing its consent to be bound by such an accord, make an order to that effect. The same applies in respect of the termination of such an accord.

Reservations by Québec

The Minister and the Government may subject their respective agreement and assent to the formulation by Canada, when it expresses its consent to be bound, of the reservations expressed by Québec. ...

Tabling in the National Assembly

22.2. Every important international commitment, including the reservations relating thereto, if any, shall be tabled in the National Assembly by the Minister at the time deemed proper by the Minister. The tabled text of an international commitment shall be accompanied with an explanatory note on the content and effects of the commitment.

"Important International Commitment"

The expression "important international commitment" means an international agreement referred to in section 19 or an international accord referred to in section 22.1 and any instrument relating to either of them, which, in the opinion of the Minister,

1) requires, for its implementation by Québec, the passing of an Act or the making of a regulation, the imposition of a tax or the acceptance of an important financial obligation;

2) concerns human rights and freedoms;

3) concerns international trade; or

4) should be tabled in the National Assembly. …

Motion by the Minister

22.3. The Minister may present a motion proposing that an important international commitment tabled in the National Assembly be approved or rejected by the Assembly. No prior notice is required if the motion is presented immediately after the tabling of the commitment. Unless the Assembly, with the unanimous consent of its members, decides otherwise, the motion shall be the subject of a two-hour debate that may not begin before the lapse of 10 days after the tabling of the commitment. The only amendment that may be received is an amendment proposing to defer the approval or rejection of the commitment by the Assembly. …

Approval by the National Assembly

22.4. The ratification of an international agreement or the making of an order referred to in the third paragraph of section 22.1 shall not take place, where it concerns an important international commitment, until the commitment is approved by the National Assembly.

NOTES

1) How well-founded constitutionally is either the Federal or the Québec position?

2) What practical effects and problems for the administration of foreign policy are created by each position? Which position is preferable?

3) Note how the provisions of the Québec statute deal both with the conclusion of agreements directly negotiated by the government of Québec and also international treaties negotiated by the government of Canada pertaining to matters within provincial legislative jurisdiction.

4) Does the provision requiring approval by the National Assembly constitute a precedent that might usefully be followed by the federal Parliament?

2. Treaty Implementation

Implementation is the process of giving effect to the provisions of a treaty within the national legal system. Implementation is a complex concept and can be used in a number of different senses. Implementation can mean giving the very words of the treaty the force of law to be invoked before domestic courts. This is captured in the law of the European Union by the concepts of direct application or direct effect. In American constitutional law it is captured by the concept of the self-executing treaty. That such a result is possible in public international law is revealed by the *Danzig Railway Officials Case*.[36] In monist jurisdictions or in states such as France or Mexico where the constitutions give treaties a status equivalent to ordinary statutes this is also possible. However, in a profoundly dualist jurisdiction such as Canada, the matter becomes more complex and sometimes confused.

In Canada, the term "implementation" appears to be used to mean several different things. It can mean giving the very words of the treaty the force of law to be invoked before the courts. It can also mean transposing the treaty into domestic statutory language. Arguably it should also cover the situation where pre-existing legal authority to perform the obligations of the treaty exists under the Constitution, a statute, authority to make a regulation, a regulation, the prerogative or private law, and thus no formal change in the law is required. Why should a treaty that is encompassed by pre-existing law be any less implemented than one that is incorporated by new and special legislation? But it is not clear that all judges understand this proposition: many seem to consider that in such circumstances they are dealing with an unimplemented treaty.

In Canadian practice, most important law-making treaties need legislative implementation. This requirement is the result of the constitutional separation of powers. Although the executive in exercise of the royal prerogative may conclude a treaty, it cannot change or make new law without being authorized to do so. That is the responsibility of the legislature. As a result, a treaty made by the federal government will bind Canada as a country, but its provisions cannot affect internal law until they have been implemented by legislation or unless appropriate legislation exists at the time of ratification to ensure that the commitments of the treaty can be carried out under domestic law.

The process of treaty implementation in Canada clearly follows the doctrine of transformation, in sharp distinction to the Canadian courts' adoptionist approach toward customary law. The issue is complicated by the fact that there are many different types of treaties, ranging from major codification and law-making treaties to the simple exchange of notes between governments on administrative issues. Some treaties raise novel regulatory issues such as the Kyoto Protocol, while others, such as maritime navigation treaties, exist in areas already covered by complex pre-existing regulatory schemes. Arguably some treaties need no legislative action at all to be implemented. It is often said that defence pacts and peace treaties are of this character because they do not affect internal law, but only bind the government in the manner in which it conducts Canada's external relations. Some other treaty provisions require only administrative enforcement by Cabinet, government officials, or administrative tribunals; this may be done without

---

36   *Jurisdiction of the Courts of Danzig* (1928), Advisory Opinion, P.C.I.J. (Ser. B) No. 15.

changes to Canadian statute law.[37] However, these treaties still have to be transformed by executive acts of the government to have any internal effect and such administrative acts require the authority of statute or prerogative power. There may be yet other situations in which treaties have effects within Canadian law: consider Section C.5 below on the "Impact of Unimplemented Treaties."

Several methods of statutory implementation are available. The first one is to incorporate the actual text of the treaty into the domestic law, either *in toto*, as in the case of the four 1949 Geneva Conventions and of the Warsaw Convention of 1929, or in part, as with the Vienna Convention on Diplomatic Relations. The treaty having thus become a Canadian law, its text is a direct source of rights and obligations. A second method is to incorporate the substance of the treaty into Canadian law. In this case, the text of the treaty does not become a part of the domestic law; it confers no direct rights and imposes no direct obligations. The source of rights and obligations is that part of the domestic law that reflects the treaty's substance.[38] Occasionally legislation may be enacted to give effect to a whole class of treaties as each one is concluded. For example, the *Extradition Act* authorizes extradition "in accordance with this Act and a relevant extradition agreement."[39] Frequently, Law Officers of the Crown will deem it unnecessary to initiate new legislation because the substance of the treaty can be found in pre-existing common or statute law, or in statutory authority that can be used to make the necessary regulations in order to ensure implementation.

When any method other than explicit new implementing legislation is adopted, there may be some difficulty in determining whether the treaty in question has actually been implemented. This problem becomes significant where the subject matter of the treaty could affect the rights of individuals. For instance, in *Capital Cities Communications Inc. v. Canadian Radio-Television Commission*, discussed below in Section C.5 on "Impact of Unimplemented Treaties," the plaintiffs sought to protect their commercial interests in certain television programs, which they supplied, by reliance upon the Inter-American Radio Communications Convention, which Canada had ratified. However, the Supreme Court of the day refused to accept the contentions that the treaty had been implemented impliedly by the *Radio Act*, or that it could be used to interpret the *Broadcasting Act*. This kind of case poses a question about how to tell whether a particular act implements a particular treaty. The answer, according to Laskin C.J.C., is that implementation must be manifest, not inferred. "The courts should be able to say, on the basis of the expression of the legislation, that it is implementing legislation."[40] It is quite possible that the Chief

---

37 See *e.g. Rousseau Metal Inc. v. Canada* (1988), 80 N.R. 74 (F.C.A.) (federal government's application of GATT Agreement on Government Procurement).

38 A good example of such legislation is the *Special Import Measures Act*, R.S.C. 1985, c. S-15, which implemented various GATT trade agreements, discussed below in *National Corn Growers Assn. v. Canada (Import Tribunal)*, [1990] 2 S.C.R. 1324.

39 S.C. 1999, c. 18, s. 3. Section 8 requires courts to take judicial notice of extradition treaties published in the *Canada Gazette* or the *Canada Treaty Series*.

40 *MacDonald and Railquip Enterprises Ltd. v. Vapor Canada Ltd.*, [1977] 2 S.C.R. 134 at 171. Laskin C.J.C.'s opinion has since been applied in a quite literal way in *R. v. Crown Zellerbach Canada Ltd.* (1984), 7 D.L.R. (4th) 449 (B.C.C.A).

Justice of Canada took this position because he believed, contrary to the *Labour Conventions Case*, reproduced below, that Parliament actually did possess legislative jurisdiction to implement all treaties regardless of the division of powers, but that this power could only be invoked in an explicit fashion. Hence his concern that the intention to implement be manifest. Much, quite possibly unintended, confusion has resulted from this position.

When the issue of implementing legislation arises, the federal character of Canada again creates difficulties. The *Constitution Acts* have very little to say about international treaties. Section 132 of the 1867 Act vested the federal Parliament with powers for "performing the Obligations of Canada or of any Province thereof as part of the British Empire toward Foreign Countries, arising under Treaties between the Empire and such Foreign Countries." However, since Canada achieved independent status and "Empire treaties" are no longer concluded, section 132 seems to have become a vestige of the past. Furthermore, Parliament has no special jurisdiction under the residuary clause of section 91 to implement treaties concerning matters within provincial legislative jurisdiction. As a result, jurisdiction to adopt laws for the purpose of implementing treaties is determined by the ordinary rules governing the division of legislative powers under the constitution. This was the conclusion of the Privy Council in the well-known *Labour Conventions Case*, which continues to cloud the performance of treaty obligations by Canada with the uncertainties considered in the following materials.

Labour Conventions Case
Attorney General for Canada v. Attorney General for Ontario
[1937] A.C. 326; [1937] 1 D.L.R. 673 (J.C.P.C.)

[In 1935, Canada ratified three conventions prepared by the International Labour Conference. Parliament then proceeded to pass legislation in accordance with the provisions of the conventions. On appeal from the Supreme Court of Canada, the Judicial Committee advised that the legislation was *ultra vires* the federal Parliament; that legislative competence on the subject concerned was vested in the legislatures of the provinces.]

LORD ATKIN: ... It will be essential to keep in mind the distinction between the formation and the performance, of the obligations constituted by a treaty, using that word as comprising any agreement between two or more sovereign States. Within the British Empire there is a well-established rule that the making of a treaty is an executive act, while the performance of its obligations, if they entail alteration of the existing domestic law, requires legislative action. Unlike some other countries, the stipulations of a treaty duly ratified do not within the Empire, by virtue of the treaty alone, have the force of law. If the national executive, the government of the day, decide to incur the obligations of a treaty which involved alteration of law they have to run the risk of obtaining the assent of Parliament to the necessary statute or statutes. To make themselves as secure as possible they will often in such cases before final ratification seek to obtain from Parliament an expression of approval. But it has never been suggested, and it is not the law, that such an expression of approval operates as law, or that in law it precludes the assenting Parliament, or any subsequent Parliament, from refusing to give its sanction to any legislative proposals that may subsequently be brought before it. Parliament, no doubt, as the Chief Justice points out, has a constitutional control over the executive: but it cannot be disputed that the creation of the obligations undertaken in treaties and the assent to their form and quality are the function of the executive alone. Once they are created, while they bind the State as against the other contracting parties, Parliament may refuse to perform them and so leave the State in default. In a unitary State whose Legislature possesses unlimited powers the problem is simple. Parliament will either fulfil or not treaty obligations imposed upon the State by its executive. The nature of the obligations does not affect the complete authority of the Legislature to make them law if it so chooses. But in a State where the Legislature does not possess absolute authority, in a federal State where legislative authority is limited by a constitutional document, or is divided up between different Legislatures in accordance with the classes of subject-matter submitted for legislation, the problem is complex. The obligations imposed by treaty may have to be performed, if at all, by several Legislatures; and the executive have the task of obtaining the legislative assent not of the one Parliament to whom they may be responsible, but possibly of several Parliaments to whom they stand in no direct relation. The question is not how is the obligation formed, that is the function of the executive; but how is the obligation to be performed, and that depends upon the authority of the competent Legislature or Legislatures. ...

For the purposes of ss. 91 and 92, i.e., the distribution of legislative powers between the Dominion and the Provinces, there is no such thing as treaty legislation as such. The distribution is based on classes of subjects; and as a treaty deals with a particular class of subjects so will the legislative power of performing it be ascertained. No one can doubt that this distribution is one of the most essential conditions, probably the most essential condition, in the inter-provincial compact to which the *British North America Act* gives effect.

NOTES

1) Lord Atkin refused to decide whether the federal executive has independent authority to enter into a treaty or convention relating to a matter that, apart from the treaty or convention, is within provincial legislative authority. At the Supreme Court level, however, Duff C.J. stated that it did.[41]

---

41 *Supra* note 31. Generally on the case, see A. de Mestral "L'évolution des rapports entre le droit canadien et le droit international un demi siècle après l'affaire des conventions internationales du travail" (1987) 25 Can.Y.B. Int'l L. 301; C.C. Hyde, "Canada's 'Water-Tight Compartments'" (1937) 31 Am. J. Int'l L. 466; G. LaForest, "The Labour Conventions Case Revisited" (1974) 12 Can. Y.B. Int. L. 137; W. Lederman, "Legislative Power to Implement Treaty Obligations in Canada" in J.H. Aitchison, ed., *The Political Process in Canada* (1963) at 171; N. MacKenzie, "Canada and the Treaty-Making Power" (1937) 15 Can. Bar Rev. 436; W.G. Rice, "Can Canada Ratify International Labour Conventions?" (1937) 12 Wis. L. Rev. 185; F.R. Scott, "The Consequences of the Privy Council Decisions" (1937) 15 Can. Bar Rev. 485; and R. Stewart, "Canada and International Labour Conventions" (1938) 32 Am. J. Int'l L. 36.

2) Article 46 of the Vienna Convention on the Law of Treaties (reproduced in the Documentary Supplement) establishes a rule of international law by which there is a presumption of competence to conclude treaties. To avoid the consequences of this provision, Canada, from time to time, seeks to include a federal state clause when negotiating a treaty that requires implementation by the provinces. Such a clause permits Canada to ratify the treaty with respect to one or more of the provinces that signify their agreement. The effect is to commit Canada to the treaty only on a phased basis as individual provinces agree to be bound. When no federal state clause is included in the text of a treaty, Canada may deposit a reservation to the same effect with its signature.[42] However, this kind of fractional or fragmentary ratification of a treaty in order to avoid Canadian complexities of implementation is not very satisfactory and is increasingly unpopular internationally. In the field of human rights, for instance, there is a growing conviction that states should not be able to limit the scope of their obligations under treaties that have a *jus cogens*[43] character—that is, treaties whose purpose is to codify basic law from which the parties may not derogate. Thus the International Convention on the Elimination of All Forms of Racial Discrimination makes no allowance in the form of a federal-state clause for the position of federal states. Similarly, the World Trade Organization agreements[44] admit of no reservations.

3) Given the increasingly interdependent nature of world society, should the federal Parliament have the power to implement treaties even when they touch on areas of domestic competence of the provinces? Would this authority ensure that Canada carries out its international obligations under a treaty? The courts have given a few indefinite hints that the *Labour Conventions Case* might be reconsidered. See *MacDonald and Railquip Enterprises Ltd. v. Vapor Canada Ltd.* where the late Chief Justice Laskin in an *obiter dictum* said:

> Although the foregoing references would support a reconsideration of the *Labour Conventions* case, I find it unnecessary to do so here.[45]

4) If the *Labour Conventions Case* were to be reconsidered, would it be destructive of federalism as we know it? What types of checks and balances in the federal legislative

---

42   *E.g.* Canada's reservation to the U.N. Convention on the Political Rights of Women, Can. T.S. 1957 No. 3. An example of a federal state clause is article 11 of the U.N. Convention on the Recovery Abroad of Maintenance, (1957) 268 U.N.T.S. 32. And see H.A. Leal, "Federal State Clauses and the Conventions of the Hague Conference on Private International Law" (1984) 8 Dal. L.J. 257.

43   Discussed above in Chapter 3, Section B.4 on "Operation of Treaties."

44   See the Marrakesh Agreement Establishing the World Trade Organisation, Article XVI.5, (1994) 33 I.L.M. 1144.

45   [1977] 2 S.C.R. 134 at 169. See also the discussion of Laskin C.J.C.'s views in *Capital Cities Communications Inc. v. Canadian Radio-Television Commission* discussed in the introduction to Section C.5 on "Impact of Unimplemented Treaties." See also *Schneider v. The Queen*, [1982] 2 S.C.R. 112; 139 D.L.R. (3d) 417 and *Wetmore v. A.G. Ont.* (1983), 49 N.R. 286 (S.C.C.) for other *obiter dicta* concerning the treaty power. Note also A.L.C. de Mestral, "Comment" (1983) 61 Can. Bar Rev. 856 and P. Hogg, *Constitutional Law of Canada*, 4th ed. (1997) at 300.

process would be necessary?[46] Would an expanded role for the Senate with provincial appointment procedures be one solution? Would the solution be to give treaty-making authority to the provinces?[47] This problem may be particularly acute in regard to the multilateral and bilateral arrangements that are necessary in consequence of global economic interdependence.[48]

5) The practice of the United States provides an interesting comparison with the situation in Canada. The United States Constitution vests the power to make treaties in the President, with the advice and consent of the Senate.[49] When the power is not circumscribed by an Act of Congress, the President may also enter into executive agreements. By and large, these agreements are analogous to treaties in U.S. domestic law and are far more numerous than formal treaties adopted with the advice and consent of the Senate.[50]

Regarding the issue of the transformation of a treaty into domestic law, it may be said that the United States stands somewhere in between the "monist" position of the Netherlands and the "dualist" position of the United Kingdom.[51] This is because a treaty adopted by a two-thirds majority vote of the Senate has the effect of a statute by virtue of article VI of the Constitution and becomes a part of "the supreme law of the land."[52] This constitutional provision resolves the problems of conflicts between treaties and statutes that are so much trouble in Canada. Since a treaty ratified by the Senate is analogous to a statute, it may be annulled by a subsequent statute if such is the clear intent of Congress.[53] Conversely, a

---

46 See G.L. Morris, "Canadian Federalism and International Law" and A. Dufour, "Fédéralisme Canadien et droit international" in Macdonald, Morris, & Johnston, *supra* note 1 at 55 and 72 respectively.

47 Some authors argue that the provinces do possess an international personality concomitant with their legislative jurisdiction. See the previous subsection on "Treaty-Making, Quebec Position."

48 See R. Howse, "The Labour Conventions Doctrine in an Era of Global Interdependence: Rethinking the Constitutional Dimensions of Canada's Economic Relations" (1990) 16 Can. Bus. L.J. 160; I. Bernier,"Le Concept d'union économique dans la constitution canadienne: de l'intégration commerciale à l'intégration des facteurs de production" (1979) 20 C. de D. 177; I. Bernier, "La constitution canadienne et la réglementation des relations économiques internationales au sortir du 'Tokyo Round'" (1979) 20 C. de D. 673; and A.L.C. de Mestral, "The implementation of Canada's International Economic Obligations" in Queen's Law Journal, *International Law; Critical Choices for Canada 1985-2000* (Special Issue, 1986) at 192.

49 U.S. Const. art. II, §2, cl. 2.

50 See *U.S. v. Pink*, 315 U.S. 203 (1942). However, an executive agreement, unlike a treaty, cannot override a prior act of Congress: *U.S. v. Guy W. Capps Inc.*, 204 F.2d 655 (4th Cir. 1953). On executive agreements, see P.M. Shane & H.H. Bruff, *The Law of Presidential Power* (1988); L. Margolis, *Executive Agreements and Presidential Power in Foreign Policy* (1986); and *Restatement of the Law (Third), Foreign Relations Law of the United States* §303.

51 J. Jackson, *supra* note 2 at 320.

52 However this simple controlling principle is in practice complicated by a distinction drawn between self-executing and non-self-executing treaties and agreements: see the *Head Money Cases, supra* note 15; J. Jackson *supra* note 2; and *Restatement, supra* note 50 at §111.

53 *Ex parte Lum Poy*, 23 F.2d 690 (W.D. Wash. 1928); *Cook v. U.S.*, 288 U.S. 102 (1933); and *Fong Yue Ting v. U.S.*, 149 U.S. 698 (1893).

treaty subsequent in time will prevail over a prior inconsistent federal statute. Furthermore, the obligation of a treaty adopted by the Senate always prevails over inconsistent provisions in state constitutions[54] and state statutes.[55] In practice, both state and federal laws will, where possible, be construed in such a way as not to conflict with such provisions.

The priority of executive agreements over federal statutes or state law is by no means as clearly ensured. In the field of foreign trade, for example, most trade agreements are concluded by the President pursuant to general legislative authority to make trade agreements, and are subject to a subsequent affirmative vote of both Houses of Congress approving the agreement as well as the implementing legislation and regulations.

6) Recent Canadian cases have opened the door to the possibility that the "watertight compartment" concept adumbrated by Lord Atkin in the *Labour Conventions Case* may yet be respected while giving the federal government more flexibility through an enlarged concept of its traditional sources of competence. The peace, order, and good government power (P.O.G.G.) and the general trade and commerce power, contained in section 91 of the *Constitution Act, 1867* are two sources of possible authority. It may be said that in *General Motors of Canada Ltd. v. City National Leasing*[56] the Supreme Court breathed new vigour into the trade and commerce power, clearly establishing federal legislative jurisdiction to regulate trade in general in cases where the economy is being treated as a single national unit, where the provinces acting either jointly or severally would be incapable of passing such legislation, and where the failure to include one or more provinces would jeopardize the application of the legislation elsewhere in the country.[57] Can this head of power justify federal implementation of general trade agreements such as the North American Free Trade Agreement (which extends into such provincial areas of jurisdiction as services),[58] and even more narrowly focused international treaties such as the Vienna Convention on the International Sale of Goods?[59] Or does the enactment of legislation by the provinces to implement the Vienna Sales Convention contradict the view of an expanded federal power in this area?[60]

7) The *Labour Conventions Case* also put a more restrictive interpretation on the P.O.G.G. power than earlier cases.[61] Recently the Supreme Court had cause to reconsider the P.O.G.G. power. In what circumstances does the following case also provide support for federal authority to implement treaties? In which of the following areas might it permit federal implementation of international regulations: radio, television, and Internet communications; atmospheric environmental controls; human rights; health services; or

---

54   *U.S. v. Rockefeller*, 260 F. 346 (D.M. 1919).

55   *Clark v. Allen*, 331 U.S. 503 (1947).

56   [1989] 1 S.C.R. 641; 58 D.L.R. (4th) 255.

57   H.S. Fairley, "Developments in Constitutional Law: The 1983-84 Term" (1985) 7 Sup. Ct. L. Rev. 63.

58   See discussions by H.S. Fairley, W. Lederman, & P. Monahan, in D. McRae & D. Steger, eds., *Understanding the Free Trade Agreement* (1988) at c. VII; and Howse, *supra* note 48 at 180.

59   See Howse, *supra* note 48 at 178.

60   See the note by M.L. Jewitt (1987) 26 I.L.M. 714.

61   *Re Regulation and Control of Aeronautics in Canada*, [1932] A.C. 54; [1932] 1 D.L.R. 58 (J.C.P.C.) and *Re Regulation and Control of Radio Communications in Canada*, [1932] A.C. 304; [1932] 2 D.L.R. 81 (J.C.P.C.).

education? Did the decision confirming the validity of the federal statute in this case turn on the fact that it implemented a treaty or on the characterization of the matter involved?

R. v. Crown Zellerbach Canada Ltd.
[1988] 1 S.C.R. 401; 49 D.L.R. (4th) 161

[The defendant was charged with dumping waste into the waters of British Columbia contrary to the provisions of the *Ocean Dumping Control Act*,[62] which implements Canada's obligations under the London Convention on the Prevention of Marine Pollution by Dumping of Wastes and Other Matter.[63] The site of the dumping was within the internal waters of B.C. At trial and on appeal in B.C. it was held that, insofar as the internal waters of B.C. were concerned, the Act was *ultra vires* Parliament. In the Supreme Court, the validity of the Act was upheld. Le Dain J., speaking for the majority, agreed with the lower courts that the Act could not be justified in its application to the internal waters of a province under the navigation or fisheries jurisdictions of the federal government, but he considered it operable under the P.O.G.G. power.]

Le DAIN J.: ... Marine pollution, because of its predominantly extra-provincial as well as international character and implications, is clearly a matter of concern to Canada as a whole. The question is whether the control of pollution by the dumping of substances in marine waters, including provincial marine waters, is a single, indivisible matter, distinct from the control of pollution by the dumping of substances in other provincial waters. The *Ocean Dumping Control Act* reflects a distinction between the pollution of salt water and the pollution of fresh water. The question, as I conceive it, is whether that distinction is sufficient to make the control of marine pollution by the dumping of substances a single, indivisible matter falling within the national concern doctrine of the peace, order and good government power.

Marine pollution by the dumping of substances is clearly treated by the Convention on the Prevention of Marine Pollution by Dumping of Waters and other Matter as a distinct and separate form of water pollution having its own characteristics and scientific considerations. This impression is reinforced by the United Nations Report of the Joint Group of Experts on the Scientific Aspects of Marine Pollution, Reports and Studies No. 15, The Review of the Health of the Oceans (UNESCO 1982) (hereinafter referred to as the "U.N. Report"), which forms part of the materials placed before the Court in the argument. It is to be noted, however, that, unlike the *Ocean Dumping Control Act*, the Convention does not require regulation of pollution by the dumping of waste in the internal marine waters of a state. Article III, para. 3, of the Convention defines the "sea" as "all marine waters other than the internal waters of the States." The internal marine waters of a state are those which lie landward of the

---

62   R.S.C. 1985, c. O-2.

63   Can. T.S. 1979 No. 36; (1972) 11 I.L.M. 1291.

baseline of the territorial sea, which is determined in accordance with the rules laid
down in the United Nations Convention on the Law of the Sea (1982). The limitation
of the undertaking in the Convention, presumably for reasons of state policy, to the
control of dumping in the territorial sea and the open sea cannot, in my opinion,
obscure the obviously close relationship, which is emphasized in the U.N. Report,
between pollution in coastal waters, including the internal marine waters of a state,
and pollution in the territorial sea. Moreover, there is much force, in my opinion, in
the appellant's contention that the difficulty of ascertaining by visual observation the
boundary between the territorial sea and the internal marine waters of a state creates
an unacceptable degree of uncertainty for the application of regulatory and penal
provisions. This, and not simply the possibility or likelihood of the movement of
pollutants across that line, is what constitutes the essential indivisibility of the matter
of marine pollution by the dumping of substances.

For these reasons I am of the opinion that s. 4(1) of the *Ocean Dumping Control
Act* is constitutionally valid as enacted in relation to a matter falling within the national
concern doctrine of the peace, order and good government power of the Parliament of
Canada, and, in particular, that it is constitutional in its application to the dumping of
waste in the waters of Beaver Cove. I would accordingly allow the appeal.

3. Conflicts Between International Law and Canadian Statutes

Re Arrow River and Tributaries Slide and Boom Co. Ltd.
(1931), 66 O.L.R. 577 (C.A.); rev'd. [1932] 2 D.L.R. 250 (S.C.C.)

[Pursuant to a provincial statute, the *Lakes and Rivers Improvements Act*,[64] the Arrow
River Co. was incorporated to construct facilities for the movement of timber down
the Arrow River and its tributaries, including the Pigeon River, which serves as a part
of the border between Canada (Ontario) and the United States. After completion of
the work, the Arrow River Co. applied under the Act to the court to fix the tolls to
which it was entitled. The appellant, the Pigeon Timber Co., objected to paying any
tolls when floating their logs down the Pigeon River, claiming an exemption under
the Webster-Ashburton Treaty of 1842, which provided "that all the water
communications and all the usual portages along the line ... [including] the Pigeon
River, as now actually used, shall be free and open to the use of the subjects and
citizens of both countries."]

For the Ontario Court of Appeal, RIDDELL J.A.: ... The objection of the appellant is
substantially that, owing to the Ashburton Treaty of 1842, this river was to be "free
and open" for the nationals of the two contracting parties, Britain and the United States.

The real argument based upon this Treaty has been misapprehended, the learned
Judge disposing of the matter on the proposition, which is undoubted law, namely,
that, in British countries, treaties to which Britain is a party are not as such binding

---

64   R.S.O. 1927, c. 43.

upon the individual subjects, but are only contracts binding in honour upon the contracting States. He consequently held that the Arrow company need not pay any attention to the Treaty.

The real argument is that the Treaty was made with her Majesty, and is binding in honour upon her Majesty's successor, his present Majesty, as it was upon his predecessor. Consequently, the Sovereign will not be considered as enacting anything that will conflict with his plain duty, unless the language employed in the statute is perfectly clear and explicit, admitting of no other interpretation. I speak of his Majesty enacting, because, although, by reason of our system of Responsible Government, statutes are approved by the representatives of the people, nevertheless every Ontario Act begins, "His Majesty, by and with the advice and consent of the Legislative Assembly of the Province of Ontario, enacts … ." The statutes are all enacted by his Majesty, though the advice and consent of the Legislature is necessary under our Constitution.

The King cannot be thought of as violating his agreement with the other contracting Power; and, if the legislation can fairly be read in such a way as to reject any imputation of breaking faith, it must be so read.

That the works placed on the bed of the Pigeon River must necessarily interfere with the free navigation of the Pigeon River on the Ontario side is not disputed; consequently, the terms of the Treaty are set at naught.

The company to be incorporated under the Act in question was to be so incorporated for the purpose of "acquiring or constructing and maintaining and operating works upon any lake or river in Ontario": sec. 32. This may well be read as meaning what I think it says, i.e., the lake or river is to be "in Ontario," not "partly in Ontario." That it cannot be interpreted as intended to cover such a river as the Pigeon River, is, I think, indicated by sec. 42, giving the company the right to expropriate any land requisite for the undertaking.

To put it simply, placing his Majesty in the position of an honourable man, who had agreed that another should have the right to pass over his land under the water, could it be even imagined that he would either himself build such structures as are in question here or authorise another to do so? To my mind, to ask this question is to answer it.

I think that the statute was not intended to and does not confer upon this company the right to build upon the bed of the Pigeon River anything which may interfere with the enjoyment of free and open use of it by the citizens of the United States. That what the Arrow Company has done has such effect is perfectly obvious from the evidence.

I would … prohibit the fixing of tolls for any part of the Pigeon River.

In the Supreme Court of Canada, SMITH J.: … It seems to me, … that looking at the statute as a whole, s. 32 has not the restricted application assigned to it by the Appellate Division. So interpreted, the section would also have no application to boundary streams between Provinces, such as the Ottawa River, and all works in that and other boundary rivers and streams, unless otherwise authorized, would, in consequence, be without legal sanction.

Moreover, s. 14 of the Act has special provisions in relation to works in international streams, and the works there referred to are, I think, unquestionably works authorized by the Act itself, that is by s. 32.

I am, therefore, of opinion that s. 32 has application to the Pigeon River and ... am further of opinion that it is not in conflict with the terms of the treaty. ...

The part of the Pigeon River, in which the works in question are situated, is not stated in the affidavit, filed by respondent, to have been in actual use at the time of the treaty for water communication and the map filed as an exhibit to the affidavit indicates, as the terms of the treaty also indicate, that what was in actual use at that time was the Grand Portage which carried traffic round and past the obstruction of the high falls and rapids that rendered the part of the Pigeon River in question non-navigable for traffic then carried on.

It appears that some of these falls are 120 ft. in height, and that the total drop in this part of the river is 620 ft. All the waters of these streams that were navigable were in use for transportation at the time of the treaty, and at the parts of the river not navigable the portages were used. In my opinion the right preserved by the passage of the treaty quoted was the right to continue to use the water communication and portages then in use. ... What was being dealt with, and what was in the contemplation of the parties, was travel and transportation over the water communications and portages as then used, and there was in my opinion no thought or intention of dealing with the use of these non-navigable rapids and falls that were not in use and could not be used, the passing of which was provided for by the portages. ...

In my opinion the passage of the Ashburton Treaty quoted above does not apply to the non-navigable part of Pigeon River in which the works in question are situated.

The appeal should be allowed ... .

LAMONT J.: ... The first question requiring consideration is: Does the imposition of tolls by the appellants, under s. 52 ... [of the Act] for the use of improvements made by them on Pigeon River, conflict with the provisions of ... the Ashburton-Webster Treaty. ...

1. ... [W]hat is the meaning to be given to "water communications" in ... [the Treaty]? These are to be kept "free and open" for the use of the subjects of both countries, as are also the usual portages "along the line" ... .

In construing the treaty we have to determine the intentions of the framers thereof as expressed in the words used. Did they intend that the whole river should come within the term "water communications," or only those parts of it between portages over which boats could pass at the date of the treaty? In order to understand these words it is material to inquire what was the subject-matter with respect to which they were used, and the object the framers of the treaty had in view? The subject-matter to which they were applied was the waters of the Pigeon River, and other rivers, streams and lakes up which the boundary line from Lake Superior to the Lake of the Woods was being run. The object of the provision was to secure to the subjects of both countries the free and untrammeled right to use these water stretches irrespective of whether they were on one side of the boundary line or the other.

Although at the date of the treaty the chief purpose for which these water communications were being used was the transportation by boat or canoe of persons and goods, the clause in question places no limit on the purposes for which they might be used. They are to be "free and open" to the people of both countries for whatever purpose they may desire to use them as a water communication. If, therefore, they could be used for any purpose which did not necessitate the making of a portage to get past a point of danger, I see nothing in the clause, or in any other part of the treaty, which would compel the use of the portage in order to have a free passage. To hold that water communications should be limited to those portions of the river navigable by boats at the time the treaty was signed, would, in my opinion, be to give too narrow a construction to the language used, and to impute a want of vision to the framers of the treaty.

Furthermore such a construction would lead to the result that certain portions of the river around which portages had to be made at the date of the treaty owing to low water, would not constitute a water communication at another season when boats could pass over them with ease and safety. ...

If a river may properly be called navigable notwithstanding that it is necessary to make use of portages at certain points, it would seem equally appropriate to designate it as a "water communication ... ."

2. I cannot agree with the appellants' contention that the words "free and open" in the last clause of art. 2, are consistent with the imposition of tolls for the use of improvements erected in the river. In my opinion the meaning of these words in the clause is that the citizens of both countries are to be at liberty, as a matter of right, to travel these waters on both sides of the fixed boundary line without let or hindrance from anyone, or having to pay anything for so doing. This seems to me to be the natural and ordinary meaning of the words and the meaning which, at the time of the treaty, the subjects of both countries would place upon them. That this is the meaning the words were intended to bear seems to me to be indicated also by art. 7 of the treaty, which reads:

> VII. It is further agreed that the channels in the River St. Lawrence on both sides of the Long Sault Island and of Barnhart Island, the channels in the River Detroit, on both sides of the Island Bois Blanc, and between that island and both the Canadian and American shores, and all the several channels and passages between the various islands lying near the junction of the River St. Clair with the lake of that name, shall be equally free and open to the ships, vessels, and boats of both Parties.

If we give effect to the appellants' interpretation of the words "free and open" it would entitle either of the contracting parties who improved the navigation of any of the channels on its own side of these waters to levy a toll on every vessel making use of such channel. I cannot believe such to have been the intention of the parties. As Riddell J.A. pointed out in his judgment below, ... at 578-79, the appellants here by building upon the bed of the river have interfered with the enjoyment of the free and open use of it by the citizens of the United States. This, as I read it, is contrary to the treaty. The result, therefore is, that in my opinion, s. 52 of the *Lakes and Rivers Improvement Act*, insofar as it authorizes the imposition of tolls for the use of improvements erected in the Pigeon River, is at variance with the provisions of the treaty.

The next question is: Does the fact that s. 52 is repugnant to the provisions of the treaty make the section invalid as a legislative enactment?

The Second Divisional Court thought that because a former Sovereign had been a party to the treaty and His Majesty was in honour bound to uphold it, and, as the Act in question was passed in His Majesty's name, it should not be given a construction inconsistent with the terms of the treaty if it could fairly be otherwise interpreted. The Court referred to s. 32 of the Act for the purpose of showing that the company was incorporated only for "acquiring or constructing and maintaining and operating works upon any lake or river in Ontario," and held that, as Pigeon River was only partly in Ontario, the Act was not intended to apply to that river.

That Pigeon River is only in part in the Province of Ontario, does not, in my opinion, render the Act inapplicable to that part, for provincial legislative enactments, unless restricted as to the area to which they shall apply, effectively operate throughout the whole Province.

Had the Legislature intended to exclude international boundary rivers from the operation of the Act, I think it would have said so in express terms and not have left the matter to inference, particularly when the inference can only be drawn by giving an unusual construction to the language used. The view that the Act was intended to apply to international boundary waters in so far as they were in Ontario is, I think, supported by the reference to such waters in s. 14. The Act, being applicable to boundary waters, was it, in other respects, within the competence of the Legislature to enact.

It has long been well settled by the Privy Council that within the provincial area and the ambit of the classes of subjects enumerated in s. 92 of the *B.N.A. Act, 1867*, the legislative competence of a provincial Legislature is as plenary and as ample as the Imperial Parliament in the plenitude of its power possessed, and could bestow. That the subject-matter of the Act in question falls within the enumerated heads of s. 92 is not disputed nor indeed could it well be. ... The Act must, therefore, be held to be valid unless the existence of the treaty of itself imposes a limitation upon the provincial legislative power. In my opinion the treaty alone cannot be considered as having that effect. The treaty in itself is not equivalent to an Imperial Act and, without the sanction of Parliament, the Crown cannot alter the existing law by entering into a contract with a foreign power. For a breach of a treaty a nation is responsible only to the other contracting nation and its own sense of right and justice. Where, as here, a treaty provides that certain rights or privileges are to be enjoyed by the subjects of both contracting parties, these rights and privileges are, under our law, enforceable by the Courts only where the treaty has been implemented or sanctioned by legislation rendering it binding upon the subject. Upon this point I agree with the view expressed by both Courts below, "that in British countries treaties to which Great Britain is a party are not as such binding upon the individual subject but are only contracts binding in honour upon the contracting states." ...

In the case before us it is not suggested that any legislation, Imperial or Canadian, was ever passed implementing or sanctioning the provision of the treaty that the water communications above referred to should be free and open to the subjects of both countries. That provision, therefore, has only the force of a contract between Great Britain and the United States which is ineffectual to impose any limitation upon the legislative power exclusively bestowed by the Imperial Parliament upon the Legislature of a Province. In the absence of affirming legislation this provision of the treaty cannot be enforced by any of our Courts whose authority is derived from municipal law.

I am, therefore, of opinion that s. 52, in question in this appeal, must be considered to be a valid enactment until the treaty is implemented by Imperial or Dominion legislation.

The appeal should be allowed. ...

ANGLIN C.J.C.: ... I agree in the allowance of this appeal largely for the reasons stated by my brothers Lamont and Smith. I should, however, have preferred it had the majority of the Court seen its way clear to base its decision upon a holding that, upon the true construction of the clause of the Ashburton Treaty ... ', it was merely meant to ensure to the citizens of both countries equality of rights in regard to the water communications, portages, etc., and that it never was intended thereby to provide that in no event should either party to the treaty be at liberty, as regards citizens of its own nationality, to impose tolls for the use of improvements lawfully to be made thereon.

In other words, where either party to the treaty saw fit to impose tolls upon its own citizens, in regard to such improvements, it should be at liberty to impose like tolls (but none greater) on citizens of the other country for the use of the improvements so made. Otherwise, it would follow that neither country could impose any tolls whatsoever upon its own citizens, because that would interfere with the water communications, portages, etc., being "free and open" to the use of the subjects and citizens of both countries.

[Rinfret J. concurred with Smith J., while Cannon J. concurred with Lamont J.]

NOTES

1) In this case the judges made subtle attempts to construe away the apparent conflict between the treaty and the statute. They obviously accepted that it was their obligation to make sense of both, if possible, but each judge went about the task in a different way. The following questions seek to elicit the different approaches and underlying principles of international and Canadian law that may have motivated them.

2) Notice how each judge emphasized a different phrase in the treaty in giving his opinion. What were the different effects on its interpretation?

3) Does Riddell J.A.'s judgment in *Re Arrow River* at the level of the Ontario Court of Appeal support the proposition that a provincial statute may not violate an international obligation?

4) Riddell J.A. and Smith J., in the Supreme Court, both resolved the apparent conflict between the treaty and the statute by construing it away, but they reached contradictory solutions. In taking this interpretative approach, the judgments implicitly admit to a conflict between certain fundamental principles of Canadian constitutional law and of international law. What are those principles? Which judgment provides the more persuasive resolution of this conflict?

5) Smith J. and Lamont J. were both aware of the tension between the international responsibilities of Canada and the legislative supremacy of the provincial legislature, but they had very different views about the way in which Canada's obligations under the treaty were to be treated. Which is preferable?

6) Was Lamont J.'s resort to traditional theory adequate for this case? This was a boundary treaty: should it be approached differently from other treaties? Could an alternative argument have been made on the basis that the treaty had attained the status of local customary international law?

7) In recent years the Supreme Court of Canada has shown a renewed willingness to seek to interpret Canadian law in a manner that is compatible with Canada's international

obligations. This was most succinctly put by Chief Justice McLachlin in 2004 in the case of *Canadian Foundation for Children, Youth and the Law v. A.G. Can.*[65] The Chief Justice stated the principle that "[s]tatutes should be construed to comply with Canada's international obligations." In doing so she followed a previous decision of the Court, *Ordon Estate v. Grail*,[66] where it was stated by Justices Iacobucci and Major that: "[a]lthough international law is not binding upon Parliament or the provincial legislatures, a court must presume that legislation is intended to comply with Canada's obligations under international instruments and as a member of the international community." The practice of construing statutes and international obligations compatibly whenever possible can be traced back through cases such as *National Corn Growers Assn. v. Canada (Import Tribunal)* in 1990 and *Daniels v. White and the Queen*[67] in 1968 to the evident efforts of the justices in *Re Arrow River* in 1931, and even earlier. Gibran van Ert, in the leading study on the subject,[68] has argued convincingly for the acceptance of a presumption of compatibility of Canadian and international law. Is Mr. van Ert's thesis *lex lata* or still *lex ferenda*?

Power To Legislate Contrary to International Law?

One author, Vanek, has contended that in Canada neither the provincial legislatures nor Parliament have the power to legislate contrary to international law,[69] while Professor LaForest (as he then was) in one article queried the ability of the provinces to so legislate.[70]

Vanek's argument for the restraint on Parliament and the legislatures was built on two premises. Putting the presumption in note 7, that the legislature does not intend to enact statutes contrary to international law, together with the fact that the *Constitution Act, 1867* is silent about the matter, he asserted that Parliament has not been given the power to do so. He concluded:

> [A]lthough Canadian legislative authorities may refrain from enacting legislation for the purpose of implementing treaties binding upon Canada, at all events they have not the power, affirmatively, to enact legislation in contravention of the obligations of Canada under such treaties. Neither have Canadian legislative authorities the power to enact legislation in contravention of customary international law, for the same constitutional restriction on the legislative power applies both with regard to customary and conventional international law.[71]

What are the strengths and weaknesses of this argument?

---

65   [2004] 1 S.C.R. 76 at 100.

66   [1998] 3 S.C.R. 437 at para. 137.

67   [1990] 2 S.C.R. 1324 at 1371 and [1968] S.C.R. 517 at 541 respectively.

68   *Supra* note 1.

69   C. Vanek, *supra* note 1.

70   G.V. LaForest, *supra* note 4.

71   C. Vanek, *supra* note 1 at 292.

In contrast, Professor Macdonald[72] disagrees with the conclusions of both writers:

It is submitted, with respect, that both these positions are incorrect, at least under present law. First, the dominion and provincial governments enjoy equal and plenary powers within their individual spheres of competence; thus if one may violate international law, so may the other. Second, it is clear that if the English parliament legislates in unambiguous terms contrary to customary international law that legislation is valid. Third, there is no reason to believe that the English rule of the supremacy of parliament does not apply in Canada. Indeed the passage from *Chung*, which sets out the English rule has been cited with approval several times by the Supreme Court of Canada. ... Fourth, the English parliament can override treaty obligations with clear legislation. Fifth, the supremacy of Canadian federal statutes over treaties, that is, conventional international law, was recognized in the *Swait* case where Hyde J. of the Quebec Court of Queen's Bench, in rejecting an argument that the *Trustee Act* violated Canada's international obligations, said that "whatever may have been the case before the Statute of Westminster, 1931-32 (U.K.), c. 4, the laws of Canada are supreme within the framework of the B.N.A. Act and where Parliament has clearly legislated on some matter within its jurisdiction, the validity of that legislation cannot be affected by external treaties."[73] Sixth, the only two judges on the Supreme Court who decided the point held that the province of Ontario could legislate in violation of the Webster-Ashburton Treaty in the *Arrow River*[74] case itself. Thus, it follows that both federal and provincial legislatures, in exercise of their supremacy, may legislate in violation of any form of international law.

It would seem that Professor Macdonald has stronger grounds of argument than Vanek. Do you agree?

4. Interpretation of Treaties

When a treaty fails to be applied by a national court, should it be interpreted according to the ordinary rules of statutory interpretation or according to international principles? In Canada, this question is particularly pertinent because a treaty is typically given internal effect by legislation. Furthermore, Canadian public law principles of statutory interpretation may be different from their international counterparts. For many years Canadian courts were frequently restrictive in their approach to interpreting statutes related to treaties. They often applied domestic principles of statutory interpretation rather than the international rules found in the Vienna Convention on the Law of Treaties, articles 31-32, reproduced in the Documentary Supplement, and they employed an ordinary or plain-meaning approach that excluded extrinsic evidence such as a relevant treaty unless there was some evident ambiguity on the face of the act. For instance, in *R. v. Sikyea* the court stated:

---

72   *Supra* note 1 at 119.

73   *Swait v. Board of Trustees of Maritime Transportation Unions* (1967), 61 D.L.R. (2d) 317 at 322 (Que. C.A.).

74   [1932] 2 D.L.R. 250 (S.C.C.), reproduced at the beginning of this subsection.

We were invited by counsel for the respondent to apply to the *Migratory Birds Convention Act* those rules which have been laid down for the interpretation of treaties in international law and we have been referred to many authorities on how these treaties should be interpreted. We are not, however, concerned with interpreting the Convention, but only the legislation by which it is implemented. To that statute the ordinary rules of interpretation are applicable and the authorities referred to have no application.[75]

Estey J., speaking for the Supreme Court in *Schavernoch v. Foreign Claims Commission*,[76] was hardly less adamant. The case concerned the meaning of regulations passed to distribute the proceeds of a lump sum settlement of Canadian claims against Czechoslovakia. He said:

Extensive references were laid before the court concerning the negotiation of rights by countries for compensation of their nationals by reason of expropriations or confiscation by other countries. These conventions or customs may find some validity in proceedings in specified international tribunals or perhaps even in domestic tribunals where specific legislative authority has made them operative. Here the regulations fall to be interpreted according to the maxims of interpretation applicable to Canadian law generally. The only rule of interpretation which seems to have any bearing in these proceedings is the plain meaning rule because no ambiguity can be found either in the Order in Council or indeed in the agreement therein referred to if the latter step may be validly taken.[77]

The recent tendency of Canadian courts is to be more sensitive to the provisions of treaties when interpreting statutes that implement them. The Supreme Court of Canada has now firmly adopted the use of the international rules of interpretation of the Vienna Convention.[78] This seems to be the wisest approach in the face of a statute whose purpose is to give effect to the provisions of a treaty. In addition, in a line of cases since 1988, the Supreme Court of Canada has consistently affirmed that the modern approach is to interpret the words of a statute in their context.[79] Such an approach grants courts much greater freedom to consider extrinsic aids to statutory interpretation. Even so, judges remain concerned as to how far a court should go in referring to the treaty when interpreting a statute; they are even more concerned as to how widely a court should range beyond the treaty itself into its material sources and the surrounding customary international law. This appears to be an area where the law is in process of major change.

75   (1964), 46 W.W.R. 65 at 79 (N.W.T.C.A.); aff'd. (1964), 49 W.W.R. 306 (S.C.C.).

76   [1982] 1 S.C.R. 1092. Strictly speaking, this case did not involve a statute, but raised an analogous problem about regulations made to implement an international agreement. Compare *Albany Packing Co. Inc. v. The Registrar of Trade Marks*, [1940] Ex.C.R. 256 at 265; *R. v. Wedge*, [1939] 4 D.L.R. 323 (B.C.S.C); *R. v. Oakes*, [1986] 1 S.C.R. 103 at 120-21; and *Ref. Re Public Service Employee Relations Act (Alta.)*, [1987] 1 S.C.R. 313 at 348-59.

77   *Ibid.* at 1100.

78   In addition to the cases reproduced below, see *R. v. Ward* (1994), 103 D.L.R. (4th) 1 (S.C.C.); and *Thomson v. Thomson*, [1994] 3 S.C.R. 551.

79   See H. Kindred, *supra* note 1 at 12-16; S. Beaulac, "National Application of International Law: The Statutory Interpretation Perspective" (2003) 41 Can. Y.B. Int'l L. 225.

National Corn Growers Assn. v. Canada (Import Tribunal)
[1990] 2 S.C.R. 1324

[The Supreme Court of Canada had to decide, *inter alia*, whether it was acceptable for the Canadian Import Tribunal to have referred to the General Agreement on Tariffs and Trade (GATT) and its Code on Subsidies and Countervailing Measures for the purpose of interpreting section 42 of the *Special Import Measures Act* (SIMA).[80]]

GONTHIER J. for the majority: The first issue to be decided is whether it was patently unreasonable for the tribunal to make reference to the GATT for the purpose of interpreting SIMA. In turning to that issue, I note that it was not disputed in either of the courts below that the Canadian legislation was designed to implement Canada's GATT obligations. Since I am prepared to accept that such is the case, the only issue that really needs to be discussed concerns the exact use which may be made of the GATT in interpreting s. 42. My comments on this issue will be brief since no party to these appeals suggested that the tribunal acted unreasonably in referring to the international agreement.

The first comment I wish to make is that I share the appellants' view that in circumstances where the domestic legislation is unclear it is reasonable to examine any underlying international agreement. In interpreting legislation which has been enacted with a view towards implementing international obligations, as is the case here, it is reasonable for a tribunal to examine the domestic law in the context of the relevant agreement to clarify any uncertainty. Indeed where the text of the domestic law lends itself to it, one should also strive to expound an interpretation which is consonant with the relevant international obligations.

Second, and more specifically, it is reasonable to make reference to an international agreement at the very outset of the inquiry to determine if there is any ambiguity, even latent, in the domestic legislation. The Court of Appeal's suggestion that recourse to an international treaty is only available where the provision of the domestic legislation is ambiguous on its face is to be rejected. As I. Brownlie has stated at p. 51 of *Principles of Public International Law*, 3rd ed. (Oxford: Clarendon Press, 1979):

> If the convention may be used on the correct principle that the statute is intended to implement the convention then, it follows, the latter becomes a proper aid to interpretation, and, more especially, may reveal a latent ambiguity in the text of the statute even if this was "clear in itself." Moreover, the principle or presumption that the Crown does not intend to break an international treaty must have the corollary that the text of the international instrument is a primary source of meaning or "interpretation." The courts have lately accepted the need to refer to the relevant treaty even in the absence of ambiguity in the legislative text when taken in isolation.

In *Schavernoch v. Foreign Claims Comm'n* ... this court had occasion to comment upon the circumstances in which it is proper for the courts to consult an underlying international agreement. Though the language used by Estey J. is perhaps not explicit,

---

80   *Supra* note 38.

I do not understand his remarks to mean that consultation of the treaty is proper only where it appears that the text to be interpreted is ambiguous on its face. At pp. 451-2 of his decision, he writes:

> If one could assert an ambiguity, either patent *or latent*, in the regulations it might be that a court could find support for making reference to matters external to the regulations in order to interpret its terms. Because, however, there is in my view no ambiguity arising from the above-quoted excerpt from these regulations, there is no authority and none was drawn to our attention in argument entitling a court to take recourse either to an underlying international agreement or to textbooks on international law with reference to the negotiation of agreements or to take recourse to reports made to the Government of Canada by persons engaged in the negotiation referred to in the regulations. (Emphasis added.)

The suggestion that recourse can be had to an underlying international agreement where a latent ambiguity can be asserted implies that there is no need to find a patent ambiguity *before* consultation of the agreement is possible. As a latent ambiguity must arise out of matters external to the text to be interpreted, such an international agreement may be used, as I have just suggested, at the preliminary stage of determining if an ambiguity exists.

Pushpanathan v. Canada (Minister of Citizenship and Immigration)
(1998), 160 D.L.R. (4th) 193 (S.C.C.)

[Pushpanathan claimed refugee status in Canada under the Convention Relating to the Status of Refugees as implemented by the Immigration Act. His claim was denied by virtue of article 1F(c) of the Convention, which excludes individuals "guilty of acts contrary to the purposes and principles of the United Nations." In reversing this decision, the Supreme Court discussed the interpretation of the Convention incorporated in the Statute.]

BASTARACHE J. (L'Heureux-Dubé, Gonthier, and McLachlin J.J. concurring): ...

B. Principles of Treaty Interpretation: Determining the Purpose of Article 1F(c)

[51] Although some non-governmental organizations advocated the determination of exclusion under Article 1F(c) of the Convention by the United Nations High Commissioner for Refugees, it was ultimately decided that each contracting state would decide for itself when a refugee claimant is within the scope of the exclusion clause. ... Since the purpose of the Act incorporating Article 1F(c) is to implement the underlying Convention, the Court must adopt an interpretation consistent with Canada's obligations under the Convention. The wording of the Convention and the rules of treaty interpretation will therefore be applied to determine the meaning of Article 1F(c) in domestic law (*Ward, supra,* at pp. 713-16).

[52] Those rules are succinctly articulated in the *Vienna Convention on the Law of Treaties,* Can. T.S. 1980 No, 37 ("Vienna Convention"), which states:

ARTICLE 31
General Rule of Interpretation

1. A treaty shall be interpreted in good faith in accordance with the ordinary meaning to be given to the terms of the treaty in their context and in light of its object and purpose.

2. The context for the purpose of the interpretation of a treaty shall comprise, in addition to the text, including its preamble and annexes:

(a) any agreement relating to the treaty which was made between all the parties in connexion with the conclusion of the treaty;

(b) any instrument which was made by one or more parties in connexion with the conclusion of the treaty and accepted by the other parties as an instrument related to the treaty.

3. There shall be taken into account, together with the context:

(a) any subsequent agreement between the parties regarding the interpretation of the treaty or the application of its provisions;

(b) any subsequent practice in the application of the treaty which establishes the agreement of the parties regarding its interpretation;

(c) any relevant rules of international law applicable in the relations between the parties.

4. A special meaning shall be give to a term if it is established that the parties so intended.

ARTICLE 32
Supplementary Means of Interpretation

Recourse may be had to supplementary means of interpretation, including the preparatory work of the treaty and the circumstances of its conclusion, in order to confirm the meaning resulting from the application of article 31, or to determine the meaning when the interpretation according to article 31:

(a) leaves the meaning ambiguous or obscure; or

(b) leads to a result which is manifestly absurd or unreasonable.

[53] These rules have been applied by this Court in two recent cases, one involving direct incorporation of treaty provisions (*Thomson v. Thomson*, [1994] 3 S.C.R. 551, 119 D.L.R. (4th) 253) and another involving a section of the *Immigration Act* intended to implement Canada's obligations under the Convention (*Ward, supra*). In the latter case, LaForest J. makes use of several interpretative devices: the drafting history of, and preparatory work on the provision in question; the United Nations High Commissioner for Refugees' Handbook on Procedures and Criteria for Determining Refugee Status ("UNHCR Handbook"), and previous judicial comment on the purpose and object of the treaty. Indeed, at p. 713, LaForest J. was willing to consider submissions of individual delegations in the *travaux préparatoires*, although he recognized that, depending on their content and on the context, such statements "may not go far" in supporting one interpretation over another.

Canadian Foundation for Children, Youth, and the Law v. A.G. Canada
[2004] 1 S.C.R. 76

[The Supreme Court had to decide whether s. 43 of the *Criminal Code*, which allows parents and teachers to use minor physical force to discipline children under their care, violated s. 7 or 15 of the Charter or was otherwise void as being constitutionally vague. In the course of deciding that the provision was constitutionally valid, the Court referred to a variety of international instruments.]

McLACHLIN C.J.: ...

[31] Within this limited area of application, further precision on what is reasonable under the circumstances may be derived from international treaty obligations. Statutes should be construed to comply with Canada's international obligations: *Ordon Estate v. Grail*, [1998] 3 S.C.R. 437, at para. 137. Canada's international commitments confirm that physical correction that either harms or degrades a child is unreasonable.

[32] Canada is a party to the United Nations *Convention on the Rights of the Child*. Article 5 of the Convention requires state parties to

> respect the responsibilities, rights and duties of parents or ... other persons legally responsible for the child, to provide, in a manner consistent with the evolving capacities of the child, appropriate direction and guidance in the exercise by the child of the rights recognized in the present Convention.

Article 19(1) requires the state party to

> protect the child from all forms of physical or mental violence, injury or abuse, neglect or negligent treatment, maltreatment or exploitation, including sexual abuse, while in the care of parent(s), legal guardian(s) or any other person who has the care of the child. [Emphasis added.]

Finally, Article 37(a) requires state parties to ensure that "*[n]o child shall be subjected to torture or other cruel, inhuman or degrading treatment or punishment*" (emphasis added). This language is also found in the *International Covenant on Civil and Political Rights*, Can. T.S. 1976 No. 47, to which Canada is a party. Article 7 of the Covenant states that "[n]o one shall be subjected to torture or to cruel, inhuman or degrading treatment or punishment." The preamble to the *International Covenant on Civil and Political Rights* makes it clear that its provisions apply to "all members of the human family." From these international obligations, it follows that what is "reasonable under the circumstances" will seek to avoid harm to the child and will never include cruel, inhuman or degrading treatment.

[33] Neither the *Convention on the Rights of the Child* nor the *International Covenant on Civil and Political Rights* explicitly require state parties to ban all corporal punishment of children. In the process of monitoring compliance with the *International Covenant on Civil and Political Rights*, however, the Human Rights Committee of the United Nations has expressed the view that corporal punishment of children in schools engages Article 7's prohibition of degrading treatment or punishment: see for example, *Report of the Human Rights Committee*, vol. I, UN GAOR, Fiftieth Session,

Supp. No. 40 (A/50/40) (1995), at paras. 426 and 434; *Report of the Human Rights Committee*, vol. I, UN GAOR, Fifty-fourth Session, Supp. No. 40 (A/54/40) (1999), at para. 358; *Report of the Human Rights Committee*, vol. I, UN GAOR, Fifty-fifth Session, Supp. No. 40 (A/55/40) (2000), at paras. 306 and 429. The Committee has not expressed a similar opinion regarding parental use of mild corporal punishment.

[34] Section 43's ambit is further defined by the direction to consider the circumstances under which corrective force is used. National and international precedents have set out factors to be considered. Article 3 of the *European Convention on Human Rights*, 213 U.N.T.S. 221, forbids inhuman and degrading treatment. The European Court of Human Rights, in determining whether parental treatment of a child was severe enough to fall within the scope of Article 3, held that assessment must take account of "all the circumstances of the case, such as the nature and context of the treatment, its duration, its physical and mental effects and, in some instances, the sex, age and state of health of the victim": Eur. Court H.R., *A. v. United Kingdom*, judgment of 23 September 1998, *Reports of Judgments and Decisions* 1998-VI, p. 2699. These factors properly focus on the prospective effect of the corrective force upon the child, as required by s. 43.

NOTES

1) In addition to establishing that the international rules of treaty interpretation found in the Vienna Convention will be employed in construing a statute that implements a convention, these cases indicate that Canadian courts may also seek the purpose and meaning of the convention from its *travaux préparatoires*.[81] What other materials might a court use as an interpretive aid?[82]

2) In the passage quoted above from *Canadian Foundation for Children, Youth and the Law*, the Chief Justice used the U.N. Covenant and decisions of an appropriate international judicial organ to assist with the interpretation of the *Criminal Code* and the limits that the Charter might set upon its application. This approach reflects a sound invocation of international law in the domestic context. Do you agree?

3) In *Suresh v. Canada (Minister of Citizenship and Immigration)*, reproduced below in Section D on "Jus Cogens in Canadian Law," the Supreme Court employed two treaties—the Convention Against Torture and the International Covenant on Civil and Political Rights, to which Canada is a party—to assist it in interpreting the *Immigration Act* as it implements the Refugee Convention. Why is it appropriate to refer to treaties that have not been explicitly implemented by legislation to read down the impact of a treaty that has been specifically incorporated in Canadian law?

---

81   Compare to British practice in *Salomon v. Com'rs. of Customs and Excise*, [1967] 2 Q.B. 116 (C.A.); *Buchanan v. Babco*, [1978] A.C. 141 at 152 (H.L.); *Fothergill v. Monarch Airlines*, [1981] A.C. 251 (H.L.); and *R. v. Sec. State for the Home Dept., ex parte Sivakumaran*, [1988] 2 W.L.R. 92 (H.L.).

82   Cf. the references to U.N. reports by Le Dain J. in *R. v. Crown Zellerbach Canada Ltd.*, [1988] 1 S.C.R. 401, reproduced above in Section C.2 on "Treaty Implementation," and references to other international sources by Justice LaForest in *Thomson v. Thomson*, [1994] 3 S.C.R. 551; and by Esson C.J.S.C. in *Quintette Coal Ltd. v. Nippon Steel Corp.* (1990), 47 B.C.L.R. (2d) 201; aff'd. (1991), 50 B.C.L.R. (2d) 207 (C.A.).

4) How should a court go about interpreting a statute that gives effect to customary international law, such as the *State Immunity Act* reproduced in Chapter 5, Section C.1 on "Immunity Generally." May it look beyond the words of the statute? If so, where? How appropriate was LaForest J.'s review of foreign jurisprudence in *Re Canada Labour Code*, reproduced in Chapter 5, Section C.3.

5) In *R. v. Parisien*,[83] the Supreme Court, citing article 31 of the Vienna convention on the Law of Treaties,[84] stated that in interpreting Canada's undertaking to Brazil the extradition treaty must, as in the case of terms in other international agreements, be read in context and in the light of its object and purpose as well as in the light of general principles of international law.

6) In *Re Arrow River*, reproduced in the previous subsection, differences in the judgments heavily depended upon the different interpretative approaches of the judges. Which school of treaty interpretation did each belong to? Consider the discussion of treaty interpretation in Chapter 3, Section B.3 on "Legal Effects of Treaties." Notice also that different portions of the treaty text were given particular emphasis by the judges. How did the selection of different phrases for emphasis affect the individual judgments?

7) All the judges in *Re Arrow River* impliedly accepted that their task was to read and interpret the treaty in the light of the situation at the time it was concluded. They thus confirmed as part of Canadian practice what is known internationally as the intertemporal principle of interpretation.[85]

8) Some treaty-implementing legislation recognizes the need to refer to international sources in order to understand concepts that may be unfamiliar to Canadian lawyers. Thus section 13 of the *International Commercial Arbitrations Act* of Ontario[86] provides:

> 13. For the purpose of interpreting the Model Law [on arbitration, being implemented by this Act], recourse may be had, in addition to aids to interpretation ordinarily available under the law of Ontario, to,
>
> (a) the Report of the United Nations Commission on International Trade Law on the work of its eighteenth session (June 3-21, 1985); and
>
> (b) the Analytical Commentary contained in the Report of the Secretary General to the eighteenth session of the United Nations Commission on International Trade Law, as published in The Canada Gazette, Par I, Vol. 120, No. 40, October 4, 1986, Supplement.[87]

These references are useful because the UNCITRAL Model Law, incorporated in the Act, introduces some vague concepts that represent an amalgam of ideas from civil and common law jurisdictions, state planned and free market economies, and developed and

---

83   [1988] 1 S.C.R. 950 at 958.

84   Reproduced in the Documentary Supplement and discussed *supra* in Chapter 3, Section B.3 on "Legal Effects of Treaties."

85   See also *Samson v. The Queen*, [1957] S.C.R. 832 at 837; and *Atty.-Gen. of Quebec v. Sioui*, [1990] 1 S.C.R. 1025.

86   S.O. 1988, c. 30.

87   For a similar example in the U.K., see *Civil Jurisdiction and Judgments Act, 1982* (U.K.), 1982, c. 27, s. 3(2).

developing countries.[88] The *International Sale of Goods Act* of Ontario,[89] which has similar characteristics, has no similar provision. Does this mean that it should be interpreted exclusively by domestic rules of statutory construction?

What is the significance for the Canadian court of article 7 of the Convention on the International Sale of Goods, implemented by this statute, which refers judges to international decisions to promote uniformity in its application?

9) In the process of applying a statute implementing a treaty, what cognizance should a court have for foreign state actions toward, and judicial interpretations of, the same treaty? In granting leave to appeal in *Rio Algom Limited v. Sammi Steel Co.*, Henry J. said:

> There can be no doubt that the proposed appeal involves matters of considerable importance to the development of consistency in the application of the Model Law throughout the nations that have adopted it. As I understand it, the purpose and spirit of the ... [*International Commercial Arbitration Act*] in adopting the Model Law, was to make Ontario commercial arbitration law consistent with the law of other international trading countries so as to enhance and encourage international commerce in Ontario and the resolution of disputes by rules of international commercial arbitration; for this it is important that appellate courts address the issues emerging in this case.[90]

Is there a rule of comity governing the interpretation of multilateral treaties that requires reference to the case law of other state signatories? Some treaties admonish the states parties to seek a uniform interpretation.[91] If Canadian courts are to harmonize domestic statutes with their international counterparts (as suggested in this case and by Lord Macmillan in the *Stag Line Case*, cited in *Re Regina and Palacios*[92]), to what extent should they conduct a comparative analysis of foreign jurisprudence? What problems of multilateral treaty interpretation might be raised by this approach?

10) The official version of a treaty may be expressed in several languages. Sometimes the legislative draftsman may make a mistake when transcribing the treaty into statutory language, either in English or in French. Which should prevail? In *Composers, Authors and Publishers Assoc. of Canada Ltd. v. CTV Television Network Ltd.*, Pigeon J. said:

> Once it is ascertained that interpretation has to be resorted to, the intention must be gathered from the statute as a whole and this certainly includes the Schedule that is referred to in the body of the Act and is printed with it. Upon such consideration it becomes apparent that sub-para. (f) is intended to achieve the results contemplated in paragraph 1 of article 11 bis.

---

88 See W. Graham, "The Internationalization of Commercial Arbitration in Canada: A Preliminary Reaction" (1987-88) 13 Can. Bus. L.J. 1 at 11. Jackson, *supra* note 2 at 338 makes the point that inclusion of the treaty in the legislation is an effective way for dualist states to make the treaty text easily accessible to domestic lawyers. This technique also preserves a legislative check against the problems that are associated with recognizing a higher status for the treaty or giving its terms direct applicability.

89 S.O. 1988, c. 45.

90 (1991), 47 C.P.C. (2d) 251 (Ont. Gen. Div.). See also the *Quintette Coal* case, *supra* note 82.

91 *E.g.* the U.N. *Convention on the Carriage of Goods by Sea*, 1978, article 3, implemented in Canada by the *Marine Liability Act*, S.C. 2001, c. 6, s. 41 & Sched 4.

92 (1984), 45 O.R. (2d) 289 (C.A.) See also *Corocraft v. Pan American Airways*, [1969] 1 Q.B. 616 (C.A.)

Bearing in mind that the Rome Convention is in French no other conclusion is possible but that the intent is to provide that copyright includes the exclusive right of public performance or representation by radio broadcasting ("communication au public par la radio diffusion").[93]

11) In addition to implementation of a specific treaty by legislation, an international agreement may also come into play domestically by the way a statute directs the courts or administrative bodies to comply with international legal obligations in fulfilling their functions. The following two cases from Australia and the United Kingdom demonstrate the legal impact of such directory legislation in those jurisdictions. Would Canadian courts in similar situations rule in the same manner?[94]

Project Blue Sky v. Australian Broadcasting Authority
[1998] H.C.A. 28; 194 C.L.R. 355 (footnotes omitted)

McHUGH, Gummow, Kirby, and Hayne JJ.: ...

[44] The question in this appeal is whether a program standard, ... known as the Australian Content Standard, made by the respondent, the Australian Broadcasting Authority (ABA), is invalid. The appellants contend that it is invalid because it gives preference to Australian television programmes contrary to Australia's obligations under the Australia New Zealand Closer Economic Relations Trade Agreement (the Trade Agreement) and the Trade in Services Protocol to the Trade Agreement (the Protocol).

[45] The appeal is brought against an order of the Full Court of the Federal Court of Australia (Wilcox and Finn JJ., Northrop J. dissenting) which set aside an order made by Davies J. in the Federal Court. The order made by Davies J. declared that the Australian Content Standard was invalid to the extent that it was inconsistent with the Trade Agreement and the Protocol.

[46] The appellants are companies involved in the New Zealand film industry. The ABA was established by the *Broadcasting Services Act* (Cth) (the Act) ... to supervise and control television and radio broadcasting in Australia. Section 158 sets out its primary functions. They include:

> (j) to develop program standards relating to broadcasting in Australia; and
>
> (k) to monitor compliance with those standards.

---

93   [1968] S.C.R. 676 at 681-82. See also, *Corocraft v. Pan American Airways, ibid.*, and R.M. Beaupré, *Interpreting Bilingual Legislation*, 2d ed. (1986) at 33.

94   Consider the model of the Canadian *Extradition Act*, noticed *supra* at note 39, the presumption that the legislature acts in compliance with Canada's international obligations, discussed *supra* at note 65, and the observations of Pigeon J. on the role of federal administrative bodies vis-à-vis binding treaties, reported *infra* at note 101.

The Legislation

[47] Section 4(1) of the Act declares that Parliament "intends that different levels of regulatory control be applied across the range of broadcasting services according to the degree of influence that different types of broadcasting services are able to exert in shaping community views in Australia."

[48] Three of the objects of the Act are ... :

(d) to ensure that Australians have effective control of the more influential broadcasting services; and

(e) to promote the role of broadcasting services in developing and reflecting a sense of Australian identity, character and cultural diversity; and ...

(g) to encourage providers of commercial and community broadcasting services to be responsive to the need for a fair and accurate coverage of matters of public interest and for an appropriate coverage of matters of local significance.

[49] Section 160 declares that:

The ABA is to perform its functions in a manner consistent with:

(a) the objects of this Act and the regulatory policy described in section 4; and

(b) any general policies of the Government notified by the Minister under section 161; and

(c) any directions given by the Minister in accordance with this Act; and

(d) Australia's obligations under any convention to which Australia is a party or any agreement between Australia and a foreign country. ...

[60] The objects specified in s. 3 of the Act make it clear that a primary purpose of the Act is to ensure that Australian television is controlled by Australians for the benefit of Australians. The objects require that the Act should be administered so that broadcastings reflect a sense of Australian identity, character and cultural diversity, that Australians will effectively control important broadcasting services and that those services will provide an appropriate coverage of matters of local significance. However, the direction in s. 160(d) contains the potential for conflict with the objects of the Act because it requires the ABA to perform its functions in a manner consistent with Australia's obligations under any convention to which Australia is a party or under any agreement between Australia and a foreign country. It is not difficult to imagine treaties entered into between Australia and a foreign country which may be utterly inconsistent with those objects. ...

The Trade Agreement and the Protocol

[63] The Trade Agreement came into force on 1 January 1983. Its object was the expansion of free trade between Australia and New Zealand. In August 1988, the Protocol was signed. It came into effect on 1 January 1989.

[64] Article 4 of the Protocol states:

Each Member State shall grant to persons of the other Member State and services provided by them access rights in its market no less favourable than those allowed to its own persons and services provided by them.

[65] Article 5 states:

Each Member State shall accord to persons of the other Member State and services provided by them treatment no less favourable than that accorded in like circumstances to its persons and services provided by them.

[66] It was common ground between the parties that the provisions of cl 9 of the Australian Content Standard are in conflict with the provisions of Arts. 4 and 5 of the Protocol. That being so, two questions arise: (1) is cl 9 of the Australian Content Standard in breach of s. 160(d) of the Act; (2) if it is, is cl 9 invalid? ...

An Australian Content Standard Must Be Consistent with the Trade Agreement and the Protocol

[82] The Trade Agreement and the Protocol are agreements "between Australia and a foreign country" within the meaning of s. 160(d). They fall within the ordinary grammatical meaning of that paragraph. Moreover, the Explanatory Memorandum that accompanied the Bill that became the Act stated that clause 160 ... :

Requires the ABA to perform its functions in a manner consistent with various matters, including Australia's international obligations or agreements such as Closer Economic Relations with New Zealand. ...

[84] Clause 9 of the Australian Content Standard published in December 1995 is plainly in breach of Australia's obligations under Arts. 4 and 5 of the Protocol. That is because cl 9 requires Australian programs to constitute 50 per cent (rising to 55 per cent) of programming broadcasts made between 6 am and midnight. Consequently, Australian programs have an assured market of at least 50 per cent of broadcasting time while New Zealand programs have to compete with all other programs including Australian programs for the balance of broadcasting time. New Zealand programs therefore have less favourable access rights to the market for television programs than Australian programs have. As a result, cl 9 of the Australian Content Standard is in breach of Art. 4 (access rights of persons and services to a market to be no less favourable) and Art. 5 (treatment of persons and services to be no less favourable) of the Protocol and was therefore made in contravention of s. 122(4).

[85] It would seem to follow from the conclusion that cl 9 is in breach of the Act that other provisions of the Standard such as cll 10-16, which have a similar effect to cl 9, were also made in breach of s. 122(4). However, the Court heard no detailed submissions on the validity of cll 10-16. For the purpose of the present case, it is unnecessary to come to any fixed view about the validity of these clauses. It is sufficient to hold that cl 9 was made in breach of the Act. ...

[100] In a case like the present, however, the difference between holding an act done in breach of s. 160 is invalid and holding it is valid is likely to be of significance only in respect of actions already carried out by, or done in reliance on the conduct of, the ABA. Although an act done in contravention of s. 160 is not invalid, it is a breach of the Act and therefore unlawful. Failure to comply with a directory provision "may in particular cases be punishable" ... . That being so, a person with sufficient

interest is entitled to sue for a declaration that the ABA has acted in breach of the Act and, in an appropriate case, obtain an injunction restraining that body from taking any further action based on its unlawful action.

[In a separate opinion, Brennan C.J.A. found that clause 9 was invalid.]

H.P. Bulmer Ltd. v. J. Bollinger SA
[1974] Ch. 401 at 418 (C.A.)

[This case involved the relationship between European Community Law and English Law.]

LORD DENNING: ... The first and fundamental point is that the Treaty concerns only those matters which have a European element, that is to say, matters which affect people or property in the nine countries of the Common Market besides ourselves. The Treaty does not touch any of the matters which concern solely England and the people in it. These are still governed by English law. They are not affected by the Treaty. But when we come to matters with a European element, the Treaty is like an incoming tide. It flows into the estuaries and up the rivers. It cannot be held back, Parliament has decreed that the Treaty is henceforward to be part of our law. It is equal in force to any statute. The governing provision is section 2(1) of the *European Communities Act* 1972. It says: "All such rights, powers, liabilities, obligations and restrictions from time to time created or arising by or under the Treaties, and all such remedies and procedures from time to time provided for by or under the Treaties, as in accordance with the Treaties are without further enactment to be given legal effect or used in the United Kingdom shall be recognized and available in law, and be enforced, allowed and followed accordingly; and the expression 'enforceable community right' and similar expressions shall be read as referring to one to which this sub-section applies." ...

The statute is expressed in forthright terms which are absolute and all-embracing. Any rights or obligations created by the Treaty are to be given legal effect in England without more ado. Any remedies or procedures provided by the Treaty are to be made available here without being open to question. In future, in transactions which cross the frontiers, we must no longer speak or think of English law as something on its own. We must speak and think of community law, of community rights and obligations, and we must give effect to them. This means a great effort for the lawyers. We have to learn a new system. The Treaty, with the regulations and directives, covers many volumes. The case law is contained in hundreds of reported cases both in the European Court of Justice and in the national courts of the nine. Many must be studied before the right result can be reached. We must get down to it.

5. Impact of Unimplemented Treaties

Although the courts have said often enough that a treaty must be implemented by legislation in order to change existing Canadian law, they do not exclude the influence of unimplemented conventions. As demonstrated above in subsection 3, the courts will do their best to avoid interpretations of internal law that would violate Canada's treaty obligations. But the question remains: how far may these best efforts be taken?

In thinking about this question, it is important to know what the judges have in mind when they refer to an "unimplemented" treaty. Some dicta appear to suggest that in order to be fully implemented the treaty must be the object of a specific law implementing it. If this is the case, what is the difference between a law that incorporates the actual language of the treaty or incorporates it in an appendix (for example, the *Foreign Missions and International Organisations Act*[95] and an act that transposes the treaty into Canadian statutory language (for instance, the *Special Import Measures Act*[96])? Is an act that grants statutory authority to make regulations in order to implement a treaty a genuine implementing act? Do the many human rights acts existing at the federal and provincial level implement Canada's international obligations under the U.N. Covenants and other human rights treaties or should there be an act for each treaty? In other words, are there not many situations where pre-existing legislation covers the subject matter of a treaty? In such circumstances, what are the consequences when the federal and provincial governments act as though they had full legislative authorization to give effect to the treaty and do not adopt any special new legislation? What of the Charter, which deals with broad issues of human rights and sets the basic standard of conduct for the federal and provincial governments? Does the Charter not constitute an act of implementation in a great many cases? Unfortunately the answer to these questions when one looks at many recent judicial dicta is best summed up in the Roman maxim *tot homines tot sententiae* (to each his own opinion).

The practice of the Federal Department of Justice when called upon to determine whether Canada can ratify a treaty is to consider issues of legislative jurisdiction first and, if they are clear, to consider also whether existing substantive law or authority to adopt regulations is sufficient to authorize actions required by the treaty. If the answer is positive no legislation is recommended. Is the Department of Justice mistaken in its approach? Should it always recommend the adoption of a new law to ensure genuine implementation as understood by some judges?

In the 1970s and 1980s the Supreme Court of Canada was led by Chief Justice Laskin, who was firmly of the view that implementation of a treaty by legislation should be manifest and not inferred. He enunciated this position most clearly in *Macdonald and Railquip Enterprises Ltd. v. Vapor Canada Ltd.*,[97] where he stated that "[t]he courts should be able to say, on the basis of the expression of the legislation, that it is implementing legislation."[98] This view has had a profound influence on judicial thinking

---

95   S.C. 1991, c.41.

96   *Supra* note 38.

97   [1977] 2 S.C.R. 134 .

98   *Ibid.* at 171.

about implementation. Courts tend to look for an explicit statement of the intention to implement the treaty before they are prepared to give it legal effect in Canadian law. The result is that, failing the most explicit statement of the intention to implement, courts have tended to treat many treaties as being unimplemented. What most judges and commentators have failed to notice is that Chief Justice Laskin adopted this position in *Vapor Canada* essentially for constitutional reasons relating to the peace, order, and good government power and not for reasons of treaty law. Chief Justice Laskin was of the view, contrary to the *Labour Conventions Case*, that Parliament possessed the jurisdiction to legislate to implement any treaty, by virtue of the general power in the *Constitution Act, 1867*, s. 91, but that this power could only be triggered by a clear statement of Parliament's intention to implement a treaty. His concern was with the exercise of the general power, not with treaty law as such, but this has led many to believe that implementation can only be effected by an explicit statement of the intention to do so. The unfortunate implication is that judges may take the view that a treaty that does not require special implementing legislation, because there already exists a constitutional provision, a law, or a regulatory power providing for its operation, is not genuinely implemented. This also suggests that government lawyers charged with implementing many treaties are negligent if they do not propose the adoption of specific implementing legislation, or even that legislation that does not give effect to the actual words of the treaty is not genuine implementing legislation.

The result of the situation described above has been a series of judgments on allegedly unimplemented treaties. A notable example in point, decided by Chief Justice Laskin, but subject to a strong dissent by Justice Pigeon is the case of *Capital Cities Communications Inc. v. C.R.T.C.*[99] In this case, Chief Justice Laskin decided that the Canadian Radio-television and Telecommunications Commission was free to authorize changes to broadcasting signals coming from the United States by Canadian cable providers in violation of the Inter-American Radio Communications Convention of 1937. Canada had ratified this convention in 1941 but no explicit act of Parliament required that its provisions be applied by Canadian regulators or by regulated companies. According to Chief Justice Laskin:

> There is nothing in the *Broadcasting Act*, nor was our attention directed to any other legislation which would give the Commission any other status than that of a federal regulatory agency established with defined statutory powers. There is nothing to show that it derives any authority from the Convention or that the Convention, *per se*, qualifies the regulatory authority conferred upon the Commission by the *Broadcasting Act*.[100]

For this reason Laskin C.J. held that the Convention could not be invoked before him to restrain a decision by the CRTC.

In dissent, Justice Pigeon stated:

> I cannot agree that the Commission may properly issue authorizations in violation of Canada's treaty obligations. Its duty is to implement the policy established by Parliament. While this

---

99   [1978] 2 S.C.R. 141.

100 *Ibid.* at 172-73.

policy makes no reference to Canada's treaty obligations, it is an integral part of the national structure that external affairs are the responsibility of the federal Government. It is an over-simplification to say that treaties are of no legal effect unless implemented by legislation.[101]

Clearly not all judges shared the views of Chief Justice Laskin; however, they have been influential and many judges have been reluctant to place great weight on what they deem to be unimplemented treaties. The following extracts from the decisions of the Federal Court of Appeal and the Supreme Court in the case of *National Corn Growers Assn. v. Canada (Import Tribunal)* display the difficulty judges may have in characterizing a treaty as implemented or unimplemented. *Baker v. Canada*, reproduced immediately afterward, indicates the important impact of a treaty on domestic law even if it is regarded as unimplemented.

National Corn Growers Assn. v. Canada (Import Tribunal)
(1989), 58 D.L.R. (4th) 642 (F.C.A.); aff'd. [1990] 2 S.C.R. 1324

[The courts had to decide, *inter alia*, whether it was acceptable for the Canadian Import Tribunal to have referred to the General Agreement on Tariffs and Trade (GATT) and its Code on Subsidies and Countervailing Duties for the purpose of interpreting section 42 of the *Special Import Measures Act* (SIMA).[102]]

In the Federal Court of Appeal, IACOBUCCI C.J. for the majority: ... [I]ntention to implement treaty obligations is different from saying that the treaty provisions should, in effect, be a substitute for the words and meaning that are employed in the specific provisions of s. 42 of the Act. It should be remembered that treaties in the Canadian context require implementing legislation to have any force and effect under Canadian law and it is the wording of the implementing legislation which is of paramount importance.

I acknowledge that a court should, as a general matter, interpret statutes so as to be in conformity with international obligations. As was said by Lord Denning M.R. in *Salomon v. Com'rs of Customs and Excise, supra* [[1966] 3 All E.R. 871 (C.A.)] (at p. 874):

> I think that we are entitled to look at [the international convention], because it is an instrument which is binding in international law; and we ought always to interpret our statutes so as to be in conformity with international law. [The statute under consideration] does not in terms incorporate the convention, nor refer to it; but that does not matter. We can look at it.

In the same case Diplock L.J., as he then was, expressed the general principles applicable to the instant case in this way (at pp. 875-76):

> ... If the terms of the legislation are clear and unambiguous, they must be given effect to whether or not they carry out Her Majesty's treaty obligations, for the sovereign

---

101 *Ibid.* at 188.

102 *Special Import Measures Act, supra* note 38.

power of the Queen in Parliament extends to breaking treaties ... and any remedy for such a breach of an international obligation lies in a forum other than Her Majesty's own courts. If the terms of the legislation are not clear, however, but are reasonably capable of more than one meaning, the treaty itself becomes relevant, for there is a prima facie presumption that Parliament does not intend to act in breach of international law, including therein specific treaty obligations. ...

... In my view s. 42 is clear and unambiguous; although other sections of the Act refer to the GATT and Subsidies and Countervailing Duties Agreement which in turn use the term subsidized imports, s. 42 refers only to subsidizing of goods or subsidizing and makes no reference to subsidized imports as being the cause of material injury to producers.

[The Chief Justice then went on to cite a number of specific references in SIMA:]

In my mind these specific references by Parliament to the GATT and Subsidies and Countervailing Duties Agreement show a pattern of Parliament's intention, that is, when it wishes to incorporate a concept from the GATT or Subsidies and Countervailing Duties Agreement, it has done so deliberately and precisely and we should not therefore incorporate terms or concepts from the underlying international agreements or treaties when clear language has been used by Parliament and when it has not expressly directed reference to the underlying international agreements.

... To my mind the adoption of the interpretation advocated by the applicants is tantamount to concluding that Canada should and must implement every aspect of the relevant treaty provisions and I do not believe it is proper for a court to embrace such an approach. At all times the question must be what has been said by Parliament in the language of the legislation.

MacGUIGAN J. dissenting: ... In the case at bar it is not merely a comparison of the subject matter of the statute and the convention that leads to the conclusion that SIMA was enacted to implement the Code. It is, most particularly, the quantity and the quality of the incorporation of the Code by SIMA to the point that principal concepts of the Code (i.e., subsidized imports, subsidized imports causing injury to the domestic producers, tolerance of subsidies other than export subsidies) have been adopted. In sum, the Act is so enmeshed with the Code that it must be taken to be an implementation and reflection of it. It must therefore be presumed that Parliament intended that SIMA should be interpreted in accordance with the Code. Consequently, to the extent that the majority decision of CIT depended upon an interpretation of SIMA contrary to the Code it was vitiated by error of law.

[In the Supreme Court of Canada all the judges affirmed the Federal Court's decision. GONTHIER J., writing for the majority, treated SIMA as giving effect to Canada's obligations under the GATT. Whether the CIT should have had recourse to the GATT Code was for him, it seems, a question about the appropriate methods of interpretation of an implementing statute. See his judgment reported in the previous subsection of materials on "Interpretation of Treaties."]

Wilson J., concurring, said: ... Similarly, I do not think that it is this court's role on an application for judicial review to look beyond the tribunal's statute to determine whether the tribunal's interpretation of that statute is consistent with Canada's international obligations. If the interpretation is not consistent with Canada's obligations under the GATT, then it is for the legislature to address this matter. Until such time as the courts in this country are given the responsibility of enforcing the GATT, I do not think that they should begin to analyze the merits of a tribunal's interpretation of the Act in light of the GATT. Courts have no particular expertise in the interpretation of international trade agreements and, in my view, they should not get into the business of trying to explain the significance of the Kennedy and Tokyo Rounds of negotiations (or the ongoing Uruguay Round of talks) for the GATT, let alone for the "proper" interpretation of the Act.

Baker v. Canada (Minister of Citizenship and Immigration)
[1999] 2 S.C.R. 817

[Ms Baker, a Jamaican citizen, entered Canada in 1981 but never acquired permanent resident status. She had four Canadian-born children. She was ordered deported in 1992 but she sought to apply for permanent residency based on humanitarian and compassionate grounds (H & C), pursuant to the *Immigration Act* section 114(2). The Immigration Officer denied her application, stating there were insufficient H & C considerations. Ms Baker appealed on several grounds, including the argument that the Minister's discretion under section 114(2) had been improperly exercised. Part of this argument depended on the International Convention on the Rights of the Child, to which Canada is a party.]

L'Heureux-Dubé J., Gonthier, McLachlin, Bastarache, and Binnie JJ. concurring: ...

[50] The appellant argues that ... principles of administrative law require this discretion to be exercised in accordance with the Convention, and that the Minister should apply the best interests of the child as a primary consideration in H & C decisions. The respondent submits that the Convention has not been implemented in Canadian law, and that to require that s. 114(2) and the regulations made under it be interpreted in accordance with the Convention would be improper, since it would interfere with the broad discretion granted by Parliament, and with the division of powers between the federal and provincial governments. ...

[66] The wording of s. 114(2) and of regulation 2.1 requires that a decision-maker exercise the power based upon "*compassionate* or *humanitarian* considerations" (emphasis added). These words and their meaning must be central in determining whether an individual H & C decision was a reasonable exercise of the power conferred by Parliament. The legislation and regulations direct the Minister to determine whether the person's admission should be facilitated owing to the existence of such considerations. They show Parliament's intention that those exercising the discretion conferred by the statute act in a humanitarian and compassionate manner. This Court

has found that it is necessary for the Minister to *consider* an H & C request when an application is made: ... [*Minister of Employment and Immigration v. Jiminez-Perez*, [1984] 2 S.C.R. 565]. Similarly, when considering it, the request must be evaluated in a manner that is respectful of humanitarian and compassionate considerations.

[67] Determining whether the approach taken by the immigration officer was within the boundaries set out by the words of the statute and the values of administrative law requires a contextual approach, as is taken to statutory interpretation generally: see *R. v. Gladue*, [1999] 1 S.C.R. 688; *Rizzo v. Rizzo Shoes Ltd. (Re)*, [1998] 1 S.C.R. 27, at paras. 20-23. In my opinion, a reasonable exercise of the power conferred by the section requires close attention to the interests and needs of children. Children's rights, and attention to their interests, are central humanitarian and compassionate values in Canadian society. Indications of children's interests as important considerations governing the manner in which H & C powers should be exercised may be found, for example, in the purposes of the Act, in international instruments, and in the guidelines for making H & C decisions published by the Minister herself.

(a) The Objectives of the Act

[68] The objectives of the Act include, in s. 3(c):

to facilitate the reunion in Canada of Canadian citizens and permanent residents with their close relatives from abroad;

Although this provision speaks of Parliament's objective of reuniting citizens and permanent residents with their close relatives from abroad, it is consistent, in my opinion, with a large and liberal interpretation of the values underlying this legislation and its purposes to presume that Parliament also placed a high value on keeping citizens and permanent residents together with their close relatives who are already in Canada. The obligation to take seriously and place important weight on keeping children in contact with both parents, if possible, and maintaining connections between close family members is suggested by the objective articulated in s. 3(c).

(b) International Law

[69] Another indicator of the importance of considering the interests of children when making a compassionate and humanitarian decision is the ratification by Canada of the Convention on the Rights of the Child, and the recognition of the importance of children's rights and the best interests of children in other international instruments ratified by Canada. International treaties and conventions are not part of Canadian law unless they have been implemented by statute: *Francis v. The Queen*, [1956] S.C.R. 618, at p. 621; *Capital Cities Communications Inc. v. Canadian Radio-Television Commission*, [1978] 2 S.C.R. 141, at pp. 172-73. I agree with the respondent and the Court of Appeal that the Convention has not been implemented by Parliament. Its provisions therefore have no direct application within Canadian law.

[70] Nevertheless, the values reflected in international human rights law may help inform the contextual approach to statutory interpretation and judicial review. As stated in R. Sullivan, Driedger on the Construction of Statutes (3rd ed. 1994), at p. 330:

[T]he legislature is presumed to respect the values and principles contained in international law, both customary and conventional. These constitute a part of the legal context in which legislation is enacted and read. *In so far as possible, therefore, interpretations that reflect these values and principles are preferred.* [Emphasis added.]

The important role of international human rights law as an aid in interpreting domestic law has also been emphasized in other common law countries: see, for example, *Tavita v. Minister of Immigration*, [1994] 2 N.Z.L.R. 257 (C.A.), at p. 266; *Vishaka v. Rajasthan*, [1997] 3 L.R.C. 361 (S.C. India), at p. 367. It is also a critical influence on the interpretation of the scope of the rights included in the Charter: *Slaight Communications*. ... ; *R. v. Keegstra*, [1990] 3 S.C.R. 697.

[71] The values and principles of the Convention recognize the importance of being attentive to the rights and best interests of children when decisions are made that relate to and affect their future. In addition, the preamble, recalling the Universal Declaration of Human Rights, recognizes that "childhood is entitled to special care and assistance." A similar emphasis on the importance of placing considerable value on the protection of children and their needs and interests is also contained in other international instruments. The United Nations Declaration of the Rights of the Child (1959), in its preamble, states that the child "needs special safeguards and care." The principles of the Convention and other international instruments place special importance on protections for children and childhood, and on particular consideration of their interests, needs, and rights. They help show the values that are central in determining whether this decision was a reasonable exercise of the H & C power. ...

[74] It follows that I disagree with the Federal Court of Appeal's holding in *Shah*, ... [(1994), 170 N.R. 4] at p. 239, that a s. 114(2) decision is "wholly a matter of judgment and discretion" (emphasis added). The wording of s. 114(2) and of the regulations shows that the discretion granted is confined within certain boundaries. While I agree with the Court of Appeal that the Act gives the applicant no right to a particular outcome or to the application of a particular legal test, and that the doctrine of legitimate expectations does not mandate a result consistent with the wording of any international instruments, the decision must be made following an approach that respects humanitarian and compassionate values. Therefore, attentiveness and sensitivity to the importance of the rights of children, to their best interests, and to the hardship that may be caused to them by a negative decision is essential for an H & C decision to be made in a reasonable manner. While deference should be given to immigration officers on s. 114(2) judicial review applications, decisions cannot stand when the manner in which the decision was made and the approach taken are in conflict with humanitarian and compassionate values. The Minister's guidelines themselves reflect this approach. However, the decision here was inconsistent with it.

[75] The certified question asks whether the best interests of children must be a primary consideration when assessing an applicant under s. 114(2) and the regulations. The principles discussed above indicate that, for the exercise of the discretion to fall within the standard of reasonableness, the decision-maker should consider children's best interests as an important factor, give them substantial weight, and be alert, alive and sensitive to them. That is not to say that children's best interests must always

outweigh other considerations, or that there will not be other reasons for denying an H & C claim even when children's interests are given this consideration. However, where the interests of children are minimized, in a manner inconsistent with Canada's humanitarian and compassionate tradition and the Minister's guidelines, the decision will be unreasonable.

(e) Conclusions and Disposition

[76] Therefore, ... because the exercise of the H & C discretion was unreasonable, I would allow this appeal.

IACOBUCCI J., Cory J. concurring: ...

[78] I agree with L'Heureux-Dubé J.'s reasons and disposition of this appeal, except to the extent that my colleague addresses the effect of international law on the exercise of Ministerial discretion pursuant to s. 114(2) of the Immigration Act, R.S.C., 1985, c. I-2. The certified question at issue in this appeal concerns whether federal immigration authorities must treat the best interests of the child as a primary consideration in assessing an application for humanitarian and compassionate consideration under s. 114(2) of the Act, given that the legislation does not implement the provisions contained in the Convention of the Rights of the Child, Can. T.S. 1992 No. 3, a multilateral convention to which Canada is party. In my opinion, the certified question should be answered in the negative.

[79] It is a matter of well-settled law that an international convention ratified by the executive branch of government is of no force or effect within the Canadian legal system until such time as its provisions have been incorporated into domestic law by way of implementing legislation: *Capital Cities Communications Inc. v. Canadian Radio-Television Commission*, [1978] 2 S.C.R. 141. I do not agree with the approach adopted by my colleague, wherein reference is made to the underlying values of an unimplemented international treaty in the course of the contextual approach to statutory interpretation and administrative law, because such an approach is not in accordance with the Court's jurisprudence concerning the status of international law within the domestic legal system.

[80] In my view, one should proceed with caution in deciding matters of this nature, lest we adversely affect the balance maintained by our Parliamentary tradition, or inadvertently grant the executive the power to bind citizens without the necessity of involving the legislative branch. I do not share my colleague's confidence that the Court's precedent in *Capital Cities*, *supra*, survives intact following the adoption of a principle of law which permits reference to an unincorporated convention during the process of statutory interpretation. Instead, the result will be that the appellant is able to achieve indirectly what cannot be achieved directly, namely, to give force and effect within the domestic legal system to international obligations undertaken by the executive alone that have yet to be subject to the democratic will of Parliament.

[81] The primacy accorded to the rights of children in the Convention, assuming for the sake of argument that the factual circumstances of this appeal are included within the scope of the relevant provisions, is irrelevant unless and until such

provisions are the subject of legislation enacted by Parliament. In answering the certified question in the negative, I am mindful that the result may well have been different had my colleague concluded that the appellant's claim fell within the ambit of rights protected by the Canadian Charter of Rights and Freedoms. Had this been the case, the Court would have had an opportunity to consider the application of the interpretive presumption, established by the Court's decision in *Slaight Communications Inc. v. Davidson*, [1989] 1 S.C.R. 1038, and confirmed in subsequent jurisprudence, that administrative discretion involving Charter rights be exercised in accordance with similar international human rights norms.

Appeal allowed with costs.

NOTES

1) In the light of the above decisions, what does it take for a treaty to be implemented by a statute? Is full incorporation of the text of the treaty by reference required or will an explicit statement that the statute implements the treaty suffice? Is transposition of the treaty into statutory language sufficient? Is it sufficient that the implementation be performed under a power to make regulations? Is it sufficient if the law allows the executive to fulfill the treaty's obligations or must it require such action explicitly? Does it suffice if the Charter requires an outcome consonant with the treaty? Given the presumption that the legislature does not intend to enact laws in violation of Canada's treaty obligations,[103] should it be assumed that a statute implements a treaty unless a contrary intention is clearly indicated?

2) The decision in *National Corn Growers* turned to some extent on a disagreement between the various justices in the two Courts as to whether the Canadian Import Tribunal had, in fact, misinterpreted the relevant GATT Code provisions. The majority were clearly of the view that the Tribunal was a specialized one that should be allowed to make its own interpretation of the facts and law, that SIMA contained a privative clause, and that therefore the Tribunal's decision should only be interfered with where it could not be sustained on any reasonable interpretation of the facts or the law.

3) In the *Capital Cities* case Laskin C.J. and Pigeon J. differed radically over the status and authority of the CRTC to consider the international obligations of Canada. Which is the preferable approach toward administrative agencies? Should public officials and subordinate tribunals not be required to respect treaty commitments made by the Crown?

4) Wilson J. in *National Corn Growers* seemed to think it definitely wrong for the court to refer to the treaty. How does her attitude compare with the approach of the Supreme Court justices in *Re Arrow River* reported previously in Section C.3 on "Conflicts between International Law and Canadian Statutes"?[104] Is Gonthier J.'s view in *National Corn Growers* a better one?

---

103   As discussed *supra* at note 65.

104   And see *Re Mitchell and The Queen* (1983), 42 O.R. (2d) 481 at 482 (H.C.) and M. Cohen & A.F. Bayefsky, *supra* note 1 at 298.

5) *Baker v. Canada* contains an important contribution by the Supreme Court on the use of what the justices considered to be an unimplemented treaty. What does it add to the continuing debate? Was the treaty really unimplemented? How could it come about that the Federal Government would ratify a treaty and yet not take the necessary steps to implement it? Is there perhaps a disagreement between the courts and the executive as to what is required to implement treaty provisions?[105]

6) Should it make a difference whether the court is asked to refer to an unimplemented treaty in order (a) to determine the outcome of the case directly by using it as the relevant decisional law, (b) to remedy gaps and ambiguities in domestic rules, or (c) to overturn a rule otherwise enforceable by a domestic court?[106]

7) Does the more liberal view of Gonthier J. represent judicial recognition of the more interdependent world in which we live? How will the courts approach the interpretation of such obligations as those arising out of the GATT, which, in order to be understood, may require reference to dozens of international agreements as well as an understanding of how they have been applied by the parties in practice and interpreted by the WTO's dispute resolution mechanism. Might this complexity explain Wilson J.'s reluctance in this respect?

8) An early suggestion regarding the status that might be accorded to unimplemented treaties was made by Professor Macdonald, as follows:

> To the separation of powers between the Crown and parliament, it is submitted that this could be preserved while still enabling (and forcing) Canada to fulfill her international obligations by according ratified but unimplemented treaties a status superior to common law but inferior to statute. Thus, if a ratified treaty changed domestic law which was not covered by statute, the treaty would be effective even without legislation. If the treaty changed domestic law governed by statute, the statute and the treaty would be interpreted to avoid conflict, but if that were impossible then the statute would rule until and unless the treaty were implemented by legislation. Thus parliament would still have the final word, yet Canada's solemn international commitments would have some meaning.[107]

Would this suggestion be worth adopting? Could the courts do so without a constitutional amendment?

9) Has the time come to require that public officials, including ministers and administrative tribunals, make their decisions in conformity with all duly ratified treaties, regardless of whether they have been implemented by express legislation? Other constructive but less radical suggestions have been made in recent years by a number of authors. Professors Brunnée and Toope in an important article have called on the judiciary to consider that treaties have been implemented when "Canadian law is in conformity with a treaty due to prior statutory, common law, or even administrative policy."[108]

---

105 See also *Suresh v. Canada*, reproduced below in Section D on "Jus Cogens in Canadian Law." Compare *Ahani v. Canada (Minister of Citizenship and Immigration)*, [2002] 1 S.C.R. 72.

106 See J. Claydon, "The Application of Human Rights Law by Canadian Courts" (1981) 30 Buff. L. Rev. 727.

107 R. St. J. Macdonald, *supra* note 1 at 127.

108 J. Brunnée & S. Toope, *supra* note 1 at 26.

Professor Kindred has argued that the result of recent jurisprudence "places a heavy duty on a court to find an interpretation of a statute that conforms with Canada's obligations under an unimplemented treaty after a thorough consideration of all international, as well as domestic, legal sources relevant to the context of the statute."[109] Professor Provost has suggested that the same result can be achieved by conceiving the judicial function as having been globalized and hence responsible to both the domestic and the international legal spheres.[110] Gibran van Ert, in the most extensive study of the question to date, argues for the acceptance of a broad presumption of compatibility between Canadian domestic law and Canada's treaty commitments:

> For the treaty presumption to apply equally to implemented and unimplemented treaties makes sense, for a primary purpose of the presumption is to prevent breaches of Canada's international obligations. A treaty commitment is no less binding on Canada internationally for being unimplemented in Canadian law.[111]

10) The Australian and English courts have also made important contributions to the resolution of this issue in recent years. In the case of the *Minister of Immigration and Ethnic Affairs v. Teoh*[112] the High Court of Australia ruled that the ratification of the Convention on the Rights of the Child 1989 raised the legitimate expectation that the Minister, exercising his discretion under the law, would act in conformity with the treaty and required the Minister to do so. This decision has been followed in England by the Court of Appeal in the case of *R. v. Secretary of State for the Home Department, ex parte Ahmed*.[113]

D. JUS COGENS IN CANADIAN LAW

Jus cogens, a peremptory norm of international law that cannot be contradicted,[114] is a very special manifestation of customary international law. It raises similar issues to other customary rules, but at a deeper level because *jus cogens* commands obedience by all levels of government whether legislative, executive, or judicial. To their credit, Canadian courts, led by the Supreme Court of Canada, have been open to arguments based on *jus cogens*. These arguments have been made in conjunction with other arguments founded on both treaty and customary law. One of the most remarkable recent decisions dealing with *jus cogens* was delivered by the Supreme Court in the following case.

---

109 H. Kindred, *supra* note 1 at 26.

110 R. Provost, *supra* note 1 at 569.

111 G. van Ert, *supra* note 1 at 208.

112 (1994-95), 183 C.L.R. 273 (H.C.A.).

113 [1999] Imm. L.R. 22 at 36 (C.A.).

114 See the explanation of *jus cogens* in Chapter 3 Section B.4 on "Operation of Treaties: Invalidity and Jus Cogens."

Suresh v. Canada (Minister of Citizenship and Immigration)
[2002] 1 S.C.R. 3

[Suresh, a member of the Tamil Tigers, considered to be a terrorist group by the Canadian government, appealed a deportation order on the ground that he risked torture if returned to Sri Lanka. The Supreme Court ultimately decided on constitutional and administrative grounds that Suresh could not be deported without a further and fairer hearing, but, in its reasons for judgment, a unanimous bench considered arguments based on *jus cogens* as well as submissions about conflicts among relevant treaties and between those treaties and Canadian legislation.]

THE COURT: ...

[59] We have examined the argument that from the perspective of Canadian law to deport a Convention refugee to torture violates the principles of fundamental justice. However, that does not end the inquiry. The provisions of the *Immigration Act* dealing with deportation must be considered in their international context: *Pushpanathan* ... [[1998] 1 S.C.R. 982, reproduced above in Section C.4]. Similarly, the principles of fundamental justice expressed in s. 7 of the Charter and the limits on rights that may be justified under s. 1 of the Charter cannot be considered in isolation from the international norms which they reflect. A complete understanding of the Act and the Charter requires consideration of the international perspective.

[60] International treaty norms are not, strictly speaking, binding in Canada unless they have been incorporated into Canadian law by enactment. However, in seeking the meaning of the Canadian Constitution, the courts may be informed by international law. Our concern is not with Canada's international obligations *qua* obligations; rather, our concern is with the principles of fundamental justice. We look to international law as evidence of these principles and not as controlling in itself.

[61] It has been submitted by the intervener, Amnesty International, that the absolute prohibition on torture is a peremptory norm of customary international law, or *jus cogens*. Articles 53 and 64 of the *Vienna Convention on the Law of Treaties*, Can. T.S. 1980 No. 37, provide that existing or new peremptory norms prevail over treaties. Article 53 defines a peremptory norm as

> a norm accepted and recognized by the international community of States as a whole as a norm from which no derogation is permitted and which can be modified only by a subsequent norm of general international law having the same character.

This raises the question of whether the prohibition on torture is a peremptory norm. Peremptory norms develop over time and by general consensus of the international community. This is the difficulty in interpreting international law; it is often impossible to pinpoint when a norm is generally accepted and to identify who makes up the international community. As noted by L. Hannikainen, *Peremptory Norms (Jus Cogens) in International Law: Historical Development, Criteria, Present Status* (1988), at pp. 723-24:

> The clarification of the notion of *jus cogens* in international law is advancing, but is still far from being completed.

On the other hand, the international community of States has been *inactive in stating expressly* which norms it recognizes as peremptory in the present-day international law. In the opinion of the present writer, this inactivity, and the consequent uncertainty as to which norms are peremptory, constitute at present *the main problem of the viability of jus cogens*. [Emphasis in original.]

[62] In the case at bar, there are three compelling indicia that the prohibition of torture is a peremptory norm. First, there is the great number of multilateral instruments that explicitly prohibit torture: see *Geneva Convention Relative to the Treatment of Prisoners of War* (1949), Can. T.S. 1965 No. 20, p. 84, Article 3; *Geneva Convention for the Amelioration of the Condition of the Wounded and Sick in Armed Forces in the Field* (1949), Can. T.S. 1965 No. 20, p. 25, Article 3; *Geneva Convention for the Amelioration of the Condition of Wounded, Sick and Shipwrecked Members of Armed Forces at Sea* (1949), Can. T.S. 1965 No. 20, p. 55, Article 3; *Geneva Convention Relative to the Protection of Civilian Persons in Time of War* (1949), Can. T.S. 1965 No. 20, p. 163, Article 3; *Universal Declaration of Human Rights*, GA Res. 217 A (III), UN Doc. A/810, at 71 (1948), Article 5; *Declaration on the Protection of All Persons from Being Subjected to Torture and Other Cruel, Inhuman or Degrading Treatment or Punishment*, GA Res. 3452 (XXX), UN Doc. A/10034 (1975); *International Covenant on Civil and Political Rights* (1966), Can. T.S. 1976 No. 47 ("ICCPR"), Article 7; *European Convention for the Protection of Human Rights and Fundamental Freedoms* (1950), 213 U.N.T.S. 221, Article 3; *American Convention on Human Rights* (1969), 1144 U.N.T.S. 123, Article 5; *African Charter on Human and Peoples' Rights* (1981), 21 I.L.M. 58, Article 5; *Universal Islamic Declaration of Human Rights* (1981), 9:2 *The Muslim World League Journal* 25, Article VII.

[63] Second, Amnesty International submitted that no state has ever legalized torture or admitted to its deliberate practice and that governments accused of practising torture regularly deny their involvement, placing responsibility on individual state agents or groups outside the government's control. Therefore, it argues that the weight of these domestic practices is further evidence of a universal acceptance of the prohibition on torture. Counsel for the respondents, while not conceding this point, did not refer this Court to any evidence of state practice to contradict this submission. However, it is noted in most academic writings that most, if not all states have officially prohibited the use of torture as part of their administrative practices, see : Hannikainen, *supra*, at p. 503.

[64] Last, a number of international authorities state that the prohibition on torture is an established peremptory norm: see Hannikainen, *supra*, at p. 509; M. N. Shaw, *International Law* (4th ed. 1997), at pp. 203-4; *Prosecutor v. Furundzija*, 38 I.L.M. 317 (1999) (International Criminal Tribunal for the Former Yugoslavia, Trial Chamber, No. IT-95-17/1-T, December 10, 1998); *R. v. Bow Street Metropolitan Stipendiary Magistrate, Ex parte Pinochet Ugarte (No. 3)*, [1999] 2 W.L.R. 827 (H.L.). Others do not explicitly set it out as a peremptory norm; however, they do generally accept that the protection of human rights or humanitarian rights is a peremptory norm: see I. Brownlie, *Principles of Public International Law* (5th ed. 1998), at p. 515, and C. Emanuelli, *Droit international public: Contribution à l'étude du droit international selon une perspective canadienne* (1998), at sections 251, 1394 and 1396.

[65] Although this Court is not being asked to pronounce on the status of the prohibition on torture in international law, the fact that such a principle is included in numerous multilateral instruments, that it does not form part of any known domestic administrative practice, and that it is considered by many academics to be an emerging, if not established peremptory norm, suggests that it cannot be easily derogated from. With this in mind, we now turn to the interpretation of the conflicting instruments at issue in this case.

[66] Deportation to torture is prohibited by both the ICCPR, which Canada ratified in 1976, and the CAT, which Canada ratified in 1987. The relevant provisions of the ICCPR read:

ARTICLE 4

1. In time of public emergency which threatens the life of the nation and the existence of which is officially proclaimed, the States Parties to the present Covenant may take measures derogating from their obligations under the present Covenant to the extent strictly required by the exigencies of the situation, provided that such measures are not inconsistent with their other obligations under international law ... .

2. No derogation from articles 6, 7, 8 (paragraphs 1 and 2), 11, 15, 16 and 18 may be made under this provision.

ARTICLE 7

No one shall be subjected to torture or to cruel, inhuman or degrading treatment or punishment ... .

While the provisions of the ICCPR do not themselves specifically address the permissibility of a state's expelling a person to face torture elsewhere, *General Comment 20* to the ICCPR makes clear that Article 7 is intended to cover that scenario, explaining that "[s]tates parties must not expose individuals to the danger of torture ... upon return to another country by way of their extradition, expulsion or refoulement" (para. 9).

[67] We do not share Robertson J.A.'s view that *General Comment 20* should be disregarded because it "contradicts" the clear language of Article 7. In our view, there is no contradiction between the two provisions. *General Comment 20* does not run counter to Article 7; rather, it explains it. Nothing would prevent a state from adhering both to Article 7 and to *General Comment 20*, and *General Comment 20* does not detract from rights preserved or provided by Article 7. The clear import of the ICCPR, read together with the *General Comment 20*, is to foreclose a state from expelling a person to face torture elsewhere.

[68] The CAT takes the same stand. The relevant provisions of that document read:

ARTICLE 1

1. For the purposes of this Convention, the term "torture" means any act by which severe pain or suffering, whether physical or mental, is intentionally inflicted on a person for such purposes as obtaining from him or a third person information or a confession, punishing him for an act he or a third person has committed or is suspected of having committed, or intimidating or coercing him or a third person, or for any reason based on discrimination of any kind, when such pain or suffering is inflicted by or at the instigation of or with the consent or acquiescence of a public official or other person

acting in an official capacity. It does not include pain or suffering arising only from, inherent in or incidental to lawful sanctions.

2. This article is without prejudice to any international instrument or national legislation which does or may contain provisions of wider application.

ARTICLE 2

1. Each State Party shall take effective legislative, administrative, judicial or other measures to prevent acts of torture in any territory under its jurisdiction.

2. No exceptional circumstances whatsoever ... may be invoked as a justification of torture.

ARTICLE 3

1. *No State Party shall expel, return ("refouler") or extradite a person to another State where there are substantial grounds for believing that he would be in danger of being subjected to torture.* [Emphasis added.]

ARTICLE 16

2. The provisions of this Convention are without prejudice to the provisions of any other international instrument or national law which prohibits cruel, inhuman or degrading treatment or punishment or which relates to extradition or expulsion.

The CAT's import is clear: a state is not to expel a person to face torture, which includes both the physical and mental infliction of pain and suffering, elsewhere.

[69] Robertson J.A., however, held that the CAT's clear proscription of deportation to torture must defer to Article 33(2) of the *Refugee Convention*, which permits a country to return (*refouler*) a refugee who is a danger to the country's security. The relevant provisions of the *Refugee Convention* state:

ARTICLE 33

1. No Contracting State shall expel or return ("refouler") a refugee in any manner whatsoever to the frontiers of territories where his life or freedom would be threatened on account of his race, religion, nationality, membership or a particular social group or political opinion.

2. The benefit of the present provision may not, however, be claimed by a refugee whom there are reasonable grounds for regarding as a danger to the security of the country in which he is, or who, having been convicted by a final judgment of a particularly serious crime, constitutes a danger to the community of that country.

[70] Article 33 of the *Refugee Convention* appears on its face to stand in opposition to the categorical rejection of deportation to torture in the CAT. Robertson J.A., faced with this apparent contradiction, attempted to read the two conventions in a way that minimized the contradiction, holding that the anti-deportation provisions of the CAT were not binding, but derogable.

[71] We are not convinced that the contradiction can be resolved in this way. It is not apparent to us that the clear prohibitions on torture in the CAT were intended to be derogable. First, the absence of an express prohibition against derogation in Article 3 of the CAT together with the "without prejudice" language of Article 16 do not seem to permit derogation. Nor does it follow from the assertion in Article 2(2) of

CAT that "[n]o exceptional circumstances ... may be invoked as a justification of torture," that the absence of such a clause in the Article 3 *refoulement* provision permits acts leading to torture in exceptional circumstances. Moreover, the history of Article 16 of the CAT suggests that it was intended to leave the door open to other legal instruments providing greater protection, not to serve as the means for reducing protection. During the deliberations of the Working Group that drafted the CAT, Article 16 was characterized as a "saving clause affirming the continued validity of other instruments prohibiting punishments or cruel, inhuman, or degrading treatment": Convention against Torture, *travaux préparatoires*, UN Doc. E/CN.4/1408, at p. 66. This undermines the suggestion that Article 16 can be used as a means of narrowing the scope of protection that the CAT was intended to provide.

[72] In our view, the prohibition in the ICCPR and the CAT on returning a refugee to face a risk of torture reflects the prevailing international norm. Article 33 of the *Refugee Convention* protects, in a limited way, refugees from threats to life and freedom from all sources. By contrast, the CAT protects everyone, without derogation, from state-sponsored torture. Moreover, the *Refugee Convention* itself expresses a "profound concern for refugees" and its principal purpose is to "assure refugees the widest possible exercise of ... fundamental rights and freedoms" (Preamble). This negates the suggestion that the provisions of the *Refugee Convention* should be used to deny rights that other legal instruments make universally available to everyone.

[73] Recognition of the dominant status of the CAT in international law is consistent with the position taken by the UN Committee against Torture, which has applied Article 3(1) even to individuals who have terrorist associations. (The CAT provides for the creation of a Committee against Torture to monitor compliance with the treaty: see CAT, Part II, Articles 17-24.) More particularly, the Committee against Torture has advised that Canada should "[c]omply fully with article 3(1) ... whether or not the individual is a serious criminal or security risk": see Committee against Torture, *Conclusions and Recommendations of the Committee against Torture: Canada*, UN Doc. CAT/C/XXV/Concl.4, at para. 6(a).

[74] Finally, we note that the Supreme Court of Israel sitting as the High Court of Justice and the House of Lords have rejected torture as a legitimate tool to use in combatting terrorism and protecting national security: H.C. 6536/95, *Hat'm Abu Zayda v. Israel General Security Service*, 38 I.L.M. 1471 (1999); *Rehman*, [2001] 3 W.L.R. 877 (H.L.) at para. 54, *per* Lord Hoffmann.

[75] We conclude that the better view is that international law rejects deportation to torture, even where national security interests are at stake. This is the norm which best informs the content of the principles of fundamental justice under s. 7 of the Charter.

(iii) Application to Section 53(1)(b) of the Immigration Act

[76] The Canadian rejection of torture is reflected in the international conventions to which Canada is a party. The Canadian and international perspectives in turn inform our constitutional norms. The rejection of state action leading to torture generally, and deportation to torture specifically, is virtually categoric. Indeed, both domestic and international jurisprudence suggest that torture is so abhorrent that it will almost

always be disproportionate to interests on the other side of the balance, even security interests. This suggests that, barring extraordinary circumstances, deportation to torture will generally violate the principles of fundamental justice protected by s. 7 of the Charter. To paraphrase Lord Hoffmann in *Rehman, supra*, at para. 54, states must find some other way of ensuring national security.

[77] The Minister is obliged to exercise the discretion conferred upon her by the *Immigration Act* in accordance with the Constitution. This requires the Minister to balance the relevant factors in the case before her. As stated in *Rehman, supra*, at para. 56, *per* Lord Hoffmann:

> The question of whether the risk to national security is sufficient to justify the appellant's deportation cannot be answered by taking each allegation seriatim and deciding whether it has been established to some standard of proof. It is a question of evaluation and judgment, in which it is necessary to take into account not only the degree of probability of prejudice to national security but also the importance of the security interest at stake and the serious consequences of deportation for the deportee.

Similarly, Lord Slynn of Hadley stated, at para. 16:

> Whether there is ... a real possibility [of an adverse effect on the U.K. even if it is not direct or immediate] is a matter which has to be weighed up by the Secretary of State and balanced against the possible injustice to th[e] individual if a deportation order is made.

In Canada, the balance struck by the Minister must conform to the principles of fundamental justice under s. 7 of the Charter. It follows that insofar as the *Immigration Act* leaves open the possibility of deportation to torture, the Minister should generally decline to deport refugees where on the evidence there is a substantial risk of torture.

[78] We do not exclude the possibility that in exceptional circumstances, deportation to face torture might be justified, either as a consequence of the balancing process mandated by s. 7 of the Charter or under s. 1. (A violation of s. 7 will be saved by s. 1 "only in cases arising out of exceptional conditions, such as natural disasters, the outbreak of war, epidemics and the like": see *Re B.C. Motor Vehicle Act*, [[1985] 2 S.C.R. 779] at p. 518; and *New Brunswick (Minister of Health and Community Services) v. G. (J.)*, [1999] 3 S.C.R. 46, at para. 99.) Insofar as Canada is unable to deport a person where there are substantial grounds to believe he or she would be tortured on return, this is not because Article 3 of the CAT directly constrains the actions of the Canadian government, but because the fundamental justice balance under s. 7 of the Charter generally precludes deportation to torture when applied on a case-by-case basis. We may predict that it will rarely be struck in favour of expulsion where there is a serious risk of torture. However, as the matter is one of balance, precise prediction is elusive. The ambit of an exceptional discretion to deport to torture, if any, must await future cases.

[79] In these circumstances, s. 53(1)(b) does not violate s. 7 of the Charter. What is at issue is not the legislation, but the Minister's obligation to exercise the discretion s. 53 confers in a constitutional manner.

NOTES

1) What did the Supreme Court decide in this passage? Is it possible to hold that there is a *jus cogens* rule of law and yet not give it effect in Canadian law? Does this reflect a view that there is no rule of *jus cogens*, that even *jus cogens* serves only to assist with the interpretation of Canadian constitutional and administrative law rules, or that the rule in question was not duly implemented?

2) Notice how the Supreme Court relied on two binding but not legislatively implemented treaties, which it read as prohibiting deportation to torture, to interpret a statute that clearly implements a treaty that admits the possibility of deportation to torture. What are the implications of the Court's reasoning for the principles of treaty implementation? Does this passage simply reflect the difficulty that Canadian courts experience in determining the precise nature and legal effect of various rules of international law?

3) The case of *Bouzari v. Islamic Republic of Iran*, referred to in Section B above on "Customary International Law in Canada," is also of interest for its additional comments on peremptory norms in Canadian law.

Bouzari v. Islamic Republic of Iran
(2004), 243 D.L.R. (4th) 406, 71 O.R. (3d) 675 (C.A.);
leave to appeal to S.C.C. refused, January 27, 2005

[Bouzari sought to sue Iran for damages as a result of his abduction and torture by agents of Iran prior to coming to Canada as a landed immigrant. The trial judge held his action was barred because Iran was entitled to state immunity from suit. The Appeal Court affirmed this decision in a judgment that is reproduced in Chapter 5, Section C.4 on "State Immunities: Personal Injury Exception to Immunity." It also discussed the impact of *jus cogens* within Canadian law.]

GOUDGE J.A.: ...

[84] The appellant also argues that Canada is bound by peremptory norms of customary international law to permit a civil claim against a foreign state for torture committed abroad.

[85] As Professor Greenwood put it, customary international law is generally defined as widespread and consistent state practice accepted as law. The immunity of states from civil proceedings in the courts of foreign jurisdictions is an example of a principle of customary international law. The enactment of the *SIA* [*State Immunity Act*, reproduced in Chapter 5, Section C.1] confirms that state immunity is a part of Canada's domestic law.

[86] A peremptory norm of customary international law or rule of *jus cogens* is a higher form of customary law. It is one accepted and recognized by the international community of states as a norm from which no derogation is permitted. Not only does the rule of *jus cogens* override other rules of customary international law in conflict

with it, but, by the *Vienna Convention on the Law of Treaties*, a treaty obligation
which conflicts with a rule of *jus cogens* is of no force or effect in international law.

[87] The motion judge found that prohibition of torture is a rule of *jus cogens*. For
the purpose of this appeal, no one, including the Attorney General of Canada,
questions this conclusion. Rather the question is the scope of that norm. In particular,
does it extend to a requirement to provide the right to a civil remedy for torture
committed abroad by a foreign state?

[88] The motion judge conducted a careful review of the decisions of domestic
and international tribunals and state immunity legislation and concluded that the
peremptory norm prohibiting torture does not carry with it such an obligation. She
put her conclusion succinctly at para. 63 of her reasons:

> An examination of the decisions of national courts and international tribunals, as well
> as state legislation with respect to sovereign immunity, indicates that there is no principle
> of customary international law which provides an exception from state immunity where
> an act of torture has been committed outside the forum, even for acts contrary to *jus
> cogens*. Indeed, the evidence of state practice, as reflected in these and other sources,
> leads to the conclusion that there is an ongoing rule of customary international law
> providing state immunity for acts of torture committed outside the forum state.

[89] The appellant attacks this conclusion primarily on two bases. First, he says
that if the prohibition against torture is to be respected, torture cannot be considered a
state function and therefore cannot be accorded state immunity. In this he relies on
R. v. Bow Street Metropolitan Stipendiary Magistrate, ex parte Pinochet (No. 3),
[2000] 1 A.C. 147.

[90] I do not agree. As I have discussed, the SIA simply does not include a civil
action for damages for torture in any of the specifically drawn exceptions to the
encompassing state immunity provided in s. 3(1). Moreover, the extent of the
prohibition against torture as a rule of *jus cogens* is determined not by any particular
view of what is required if it is to be meaningful, but rather by the widespread and
consistent practice of states. As the motion judge found, that practice reflects the
customary international law principle that state immunity is provided for acts of torture
committed outside the forum state, not the obligation contended for by the appellant.

[91] Finally, nothing in *Pinochet* is inconsistent with this. As the motion judge
points out, *Pinochet* concerned criminal proceedings against an individual, not civil
proceedings against the state of Chile. It is in that context that one of the law lords,
Lord Browne-Wilkinson (at 203) offered the view that the commission by an
individual of the international crime of torture cannot be considered to be an act done
in an official capacity on behalf of the state and therefore is not a state function.
However, three of the law lords: Lord Hutton (at 254 and 264), Lord Millett (at 278)
and Lord Phillips of Worth Matravers (at 280) expressly discussed the immunity of
the state from civil proceedings for torture committed in that state and all accepted
that it would apply. Thus, the opinions in *Pinochet* clearly reflect the distinction for
state immunity purposes between proceedings seeking a criminal sanction against an
individual for acts of torture committed abroad and proceedings seeking a civil remedy
against a foreign state for the same acts. In the former case, the sanction can be

imposed on the individual without subjecting one state to the jurisdiction of another. That is not so in the latter case.

[92] This distinction is relevant for the appellant's second point. The appellant argues that the prohibition against torture constitutes a right to be free from torture and where there is a right there must be a remedy.

[93] There are two answers to this. The first reflects the distinction drawn in *Pinochet*. As a matter of principle, providing a civil remedy for breach of the prohibition of torture is not the only way to give effect to that prohibition. The criminal prosecution of individual torturers who commit their acts abroad (which is expressly sanctioned by the *Convention Against Torture*) gives some effect to the prohibition without damaging the principle of state sovereignty on which relations between nations are based.

[94] The second answer is that as a matter of practice, states do not accord a civil remedy for torture committed abroad by foreign states. The peremptory norm of prohibition against torture does not encompass the civil remedy contended for by the appellant.

[95] Thus, I see no basis to depart from the conclusion of the motion judge. Just as Canada's treaty obligations do not do so, the rules of customary international law binding Canada do not accord to the appellant the civil remedy he seeks. Both under customary international law and international treaty there is today a balance struck between the condemnation of torture as an international crime against humanity and the principle that states must treat each other as equals not to be subjected to each other's jurisdiction. It would be inconsistent with this balance to provide a civil remedy against a foreign state for torture committed abroad. In the future, perhaps as the international human rights movement gathers greater force, this balance may change, either through the domestic legislation of states or by international treaty. However, this is not a change to be effected by a domestic court adding an exception to the *SIA* that is not there, or seeing a widespread state practice that does not exist today.

E. "INDIAN TREATIES"

Canada is a party to a large number of so-called Indian treaties. The term reflects the fact that the agreements with the indigenous peoples living in Canada are so referred to in the *Indian Act*,[115] section 88. These agreements with the First Nations raise all the same questions of application as international treaties but in special circumstances. The first question is whether they are international treaties, or domestic agreements internal to the Canadian legal system, or *sui generis*. The answer will affect whether they need to be implemented, what impact they have on conflicting legislation, and how they should be interpreted. The following Supreme Court judgment is one of a growing number of decisions[116] that deal with these issues.

---

115 R.S.C. 1985, c. I-6, as am. They are also recognized in the *Constitution Act, 1982*, s. 35(1), found in Schedule B of the *Canada Act 1982* (U.K.), 1982, c. 11.

116 See, in addition to the cases cited in the judgment, *Ontario (Attorney General) v. Bear Island Foundation* (1989), 68 O.R. (2d) 394 (C.A.) and *R. v. Ireland* (1991), 1 O.R. (3d) 577 at 585 (Gen. Div.).

R. v. Sioui
[1990] 1 S.C.R. 1025

[The defendants, members of a Huron band in Quebec, were charged with the offence of cutting down trees, camping, and making fires in non-designated places in a provincial park, contrary to regulations under the Quebec *Parks Act*.[117] The defendants relied upon the rights granted to them by Governor Murray in the following agreement:

> THESE are to certify that the CHIEF of the HURON tribe of Indians, having come to me in the name of His Nation, to submit to His Nation, to submit to His BRITANNICK MAJESTY, to make Peace, has been received under my Protection, with his whole Tribe; and henceforth no English Officer or party is to molest, or interrupt them in returning to their Settlement at LORETTE; and they are received upon the same terms with the Canadians, being allowed the free Exercise of their Religion, their Customs, and Liberty of trading with the English:—recommending it to the Officers commanding the Posts, to treat them kindly.
>
> Given under my hand at Longueil, this 5th day of September, 1760.

In the Courts below there was a difference of opinion as to whether this document constituted a "treaty" within the meaning of s. 88 of the *Indian Act*, which states: "Subject to the terms of any treaty ... all laws of general application from time to time in force in any province are applicable to and in respect of Indians in the province. ..."[118] The majority of the Québec Court of Appeal thought it was such a treaty, which consequently provided the defendants with immunity from prosecution. Affirming this view, Lamer J. spoke for the Supreme Court when he said:]

LAMER J.: Our courts and those of our neighbours to the south have already considered what distinguishes a treaty with the Indians from other agreements affecting them. The task is not an easy one. In *Simon v. The Queen*, [1985] 2 S.C.R. 387, this Court adopted the comment of Norris J.A. in *R. v. White and Bob* (1964), 50 D.L.R. (2d) 613 (B.C.C.A.) (affirmed in the Supreme Court (1965), 52 D.L.R. (2d) 481), that the courts should show flexibility in determining the legal nature of a document recording a transaction with the Indians. In particular, they must take into account the historical context and perception each party might have as to the nature of the undertaking contained in the document under consideration. To the question of whether the document at issue in *White and Bob* was a treaty within the meaning of the *Indian Act*, Norris J.A. replied (at pp. 648-49):

> The question is, in my respectful opinion, to be resolved not by the application of rigid rules of construction without regard to the circumstances existing when the document

---

117 R.S.Q. c. P-9; Regulation respecting the Parc de la Jacques Cartier, O.C. 3108-81, 11 November 1981, G.O.Q. 1981.II.3518.

118 R.S.C. 1985, c.I-6.

was completed nor by the tests of modern day draftsmanship. In determining what the intention of Parliament was at the time of the enactment of s. 87 [now s. 88] of the *Indian Act*, Parliament is to be taken to have had in mind the common understanding of the parties to the document at the time it was executed.

As the Chief Justice said in *Simon*, *supra*, treaties and statutes relating to Indians should be liberally construed and uncertainties resolved in favour of the Indians (at p. 410). In our quest for the legal nature of the document of September 5, 1760, therefore, we should adopt a broad and generous interpretation of what constitutes a treaty.

In my opinion, this liberal and generous attitude, heedful of historical fact, should also guide us in examining the preliminary question of the capacity to sign a treaty, as illustrated by *Simon* and *White and Bob*.

Finally, once a valid treaty is found to exist, that treaty must in turn be given a just, broad and liberal construction. This principle, for which there is ample precedent, was recently reaffirmed in *Simon*. The factors underlying this rule were eloquently stated in *Jones v. Meehan*, 175 U.S. 1 (1899), a judgment of the United States Supreme Court, and are I think just as relevant to questions involving the existence of a treaty and the capacity of the parties as they are to the interpretation of a treaty (at pp. 10-11):

> In construing any treaty between the United States and an Indian tribe, it must always ... be borne in mind that the negotiations for the treaty are conducted, on the part of the United States, an enlightened and powerful nation, by representatives skilled in diplomacy, masters of a written language, understanding the modes and forms of creating the various technical estates known to their law, and assisted by an interpreter employed by themselves; that the treaty is drawn up by them and in their own language; that the Indians, on the other hand, are a weak and dependent people, who have no written language and are wholly unfamiliar with all the forms of legal expression, and whose only knowledge of the terms in which the treaty is framed is that imparted to them by the interpreter employed by the United States; and that the treaty must therefore be construed, not according to the technical meaning of its words to learned lawyers, but in the sense in which they would naturally be understood by the Indians.

The Indian people are today much better versed in the art of negotiation with public authorities than they were when the United States Supreme Court handed down its decision in *Jones*. As the document in question was signed over a hundred years before that decision, these considerations argue all the more strongly for the courts to adopt a generous and liberal approach.

[Lamer J. next considered the capacity of the various parties, General Murray, Great Britain, and the Hurons to enter into this agreement, given the fact that it predates the Treaty of Paris of 1763. In that context he quoted the following passage from *R. v. White and Bob*:]

In the section [88] "Treaty" is not a word of art and in my respectful opinion, it embraces all such engagements made by persons in authority as may be brought within the term "the word of the white man" the sanctity of which was, at the time of British

exploration and settlement, the most important means of obtaining the goodwill and
co-operation of the native tribes and ensuring that the colonists would be protected
from death and destruction. On such assurance the Indians relied.

[In analyzing the agreement itself, Lamer J. recognized that there were aspects of it
that did not conform to it being a treaty, while there were others that were consistent
with it being one. He then turned to the use of extrinsic evidence to establish the
nature of the document:]

As this Court recently noted in *R. v. Horse*, [1988] 1 S.C.R. 187, at p. 201, extrinsic
evidence is not to be used as an aid to interpreting a treaty in the absence of ambiguity
or where the result would be to alter its terms by adding words to or subtracting
words from the written agreement. This rule also applies in determining the legal
nature of a document relating to the Indians. However, a more flexible approach is
necessary as the question of the existence of a treaty within the meaning of s. 88 of
the *Indian Act* is generally closely bound up with the circumstances existing when
the document was prepared (*White and Bob*, *supra*, at pp. 648-49, and *Simon*, *supra*,
at pp. 409-10). In any case, the wording alone will not suffice to determine the legal
nature of the document before the Court. On the one hand, we have before us a
document the form of which and some of whose subject-matter suggest that it is not a
treaty, and on the other, we find it to contain protection of fundamental rights which
supports the opposite conclusion. The ambiguity arising from this document thus
means that the Court must look at extrinsic evidence to determine its legal nature. ...

It was suggested that the Court examine three types of extrinsic evidence to assist
it in determining whether the document of September 5 is a treaty. First, to indicate
the parties' intent to enter into a treaty, the Court was offered evidence to present a
picture of the historical context of the period. Then, evidence was presented of certain
facts closely associated with the signing of the document and relating to the existence
of the various constituent elements of a treaty. Finally still with a view to determine
whether the parties intended to enter into a treaty, the Court was told of the subsequent
conduct of the parties in respect of the document of September 5, 1760.

I should first mention that the admissibility of certain documents submitted by the
intervener the National Indian Brotherhood/Assembly of First Nations in support of its
arguments was contested. The intervener was relying on documents that were not part
of the record in the lower courts. The appellant agreed that certain of these documents,
namely Murray's Journal, letters and instructions, should be included in the record
provided this Court considered that their admissibility was justified by the concept of
judicial notice. I am of the view that all the documents to which I will refer, whether
my attention was drawn to them by the intervener or as a result of my personal
research, are documents of a historical nature which I am entitled to rely on pursuant
to the concept of judicial knowledge. As Norris J.A. said in *White and Bob* (at p. 629):

> The Court is entitled "to take judicial notice of the facts of history whether past or
> contemporaneous" as Lord du Parcq said in *Monarch Steamship Co. Ltd. v. Karlshamns
> Oljefabriker (A/B)*, [1949] A.C. 196 at p. 234, [1949] 1 All E.R. 1 at p. 20, and it is

entitled to rely on its own historical knowledge and researches, *Real v. Bishop of Lincoln*, [1892] A.C. 644, Lord Halsbury, L.C., at pp. 652-4.

The documents I cite all enable the Court, in my view, to identify more accurately the historical context essential to the resolution of this case.

[After an extensive examination of the historical context, and of the desire of the British to conclude agreements with the native peoples, Lamer J. observed:]

From the historical situation I have just briefly outlined the appellant deduced that the document at issue is only a capitulation and that the legal nature of such a document should not be construed differently depending on whether it relates to the Indians or to the French. The Court has before it, he submitted, only a capitulation comparable to a capitulation of French soldiers or Canadians, which cannot be elevated to the category of a treaty within the meaning of s. 88 of the *Indian Act* simply because an Indian tribe was a party to it. In other words, as Murray signed the same kind of document with respect to the Indians, the French or the Canadians his intent could not have been any different. The appellant also maintains that, like the capitulations of the Canadians and the French soldiers, this document was only temporary in nature in that its consequences would cease when the fate of Canada was finally settled at the end of the war.

I consider that, instead, we can conclude from the historical documents that both Great Britain and France felt that the Indian nations had sufficient independence and played a large enough role in North America for it to be good policy to maintain relations with them very close to those maintained between sovereign nations.

[Lamer J. then considered, *inter alia*, the journals of General Murray, the conduct of Great Britain and France, the consequences of the Treaty of Paris of 1763 and the Royal Proclamation of 1763, none of which extinguished the rights granted by the agreement in question. He continued:]

Legislative and administrative history also provides no basis for concluding that the treaty was extinguished. In 1853, 9,600 acres of land located outside the territory at issue were ceded to the Hurons by the Government of Lower Canada. These lands were within the boundaries of the lands frequented by the Hurons when the treaty of September 5 was concluded. In 1903 the Hurons again ceded these 9,600 acres, without reserving the rights that had been granted to them under the treaty of September 5. The Attorney General of Quebec considers that by making this cession without reservation, the Hurons indicated beyond all doubt that this document was not a source of rights so far as they were concerned. This argument cannot stand. Assuming that the 9,600 acres ceded were initially the subject of the treaty, the absence of any reservation in the deed ceding this territory clearly cannot be interpreted as a waiver of the benefits of the treaty in the territory which was not the subject of the cession, whatever the effect of the absence of such a reservation may be with respect to the territory ceded.

The appellant further argues that by adopting the *Act to establish the Laurentides National Park*, S.Q. 1895, 58 Vict., c. 22, and by making the territory in question a park, the Quebec legislator clearly expressed his intention to prohibit the carrying on of certain activities in this territory, whether or not such activities are protected by an Indian treaty.

Section 88 of the *Indian Act* is designed specifically to protect the Indians from provincial legislation that might attempt to deprive them of rights protected by a treaty. A legislated change in the use of the territory thus does not extinguish rights otherwise protected by a treaty. If the treaty gives the Hurons the right to carry on their customs and religion in the territory of Jacques-Cartier park, the existence of a provincial statute and subordinate legislation will not ordinarily affect that right.

Finally, the appellant argues that non-use of the treaty over a long period of time may extinguish its effect. He cites no authority for this. I do not think that this argument carries much weight: a solemn agreement cannot lose its validity merely because it has not been invoked to, which in any case is disputed by the respondents, who maintain that it was relied on in a seignorial claim in 1824. Such a proposition would mean that a treaty could be extinguished merely because it had not been relied on in litigation, which is untenable.

In view of the liberal and generous approach that must be adopted towards Indians' rights and the evidence in the record, I cannot conclude that the treaty of September 5 no longer had any legal effect on May 29, 1982.

The question that arises at this point is as to whether the treaty is capable of rendering ss. 9 and 37 of the Regulations inoperative. To answer this it will now be necessary to consider the territorial scope of the rights guaranteed by the treaty, since the appellant recognizes that the activities with which the respondents are charged are customary or religious in nature. ...

Although the document of September 5 is a treaty within the meaning of s. 88 of the *Indian Act*, that does not necessarily mean that the respondents are exempt from the application of the Regulation respecting the Parc de la Jacques-Cartier. It is still necessary that the treaty protecting activities of the kind with which the respondents are charged cover the territory of Jacques-Cartier park. The appellant argues that the territorial scope of the treaty does not extend to the territory of the park. The respondents, on the other hand, argue that the treaty confers personal rights on them and that they are in no way seeking to assert rights of a territorial nature.

Although this case does not involve a territorial claim as such, in that the Hurons are not claiming control over territory, I am of the view that exercise of the right they are claiming has an essential territorial aspect. The respondents argue that they have a right to carry on their customs and religious rites in a specific territory, namely that of the park. The substantive content of the right cannot be considered apart from its territorial content. Just as it would distort the nature of a right of way to consider it while ignoring its territorial aspect, one cannot logically disregard the territorial aspect of the substantive rights guaranteed by the treaty of September 5, 1760. The respondents must therefore show that the treaty guaranteed their right to carry on their customs and religious rites in the territory of Jacques-Cartier park.

The treaty gives the Hurons the freedom to carry on their customs and their religion. No mention is made in the treaty itself of the territory over which these rights may be exercised There is also no indication that the territory of what is now Jacques-Cartier park was contemplated. However, for a freedom to have real value and meaning, it must be possible to exercise it somewhere. That does not mean, despite the importance of the rights concerned, that the Indians can exercise it anywhere. Our analysis will be confined to setting the limits of the promise made in the treaty, since the respondents have at no time based their argument on the existence of aboriginal rights protecting the activities with which they are charged.

... I conclude that in view of the absence of any express mention of the territorial scope of the treaty, it has to be assumed that the parties to the treaty of September 5 intended to reconcile the Hurons' need to protect the exercise of their customs and the desire of the British conquerors to expand. Protecting the exercise of the customs in all parts of the territory frequented when it is not incompatible with its occupancy is in my opinion the most reasonable way of reconciling the competing interests. This, in my view, is the definition of the common intent of the parties which best reflects the actual intent of the Hurons and of Murray on September 5, 1760. Defining the common intent of the parties on the question of territory in this way makes it possible to give full effect to the spirit of conciliation, while respecting the practical requirements of the British. This gave the English the necessary flexibility to be able to respond in due course to the increasing need to use Canada's resources, in the event that Canada remained under British suzerainty. The Hurons, for their part, were protecting their customs wherever their exercise would not be prejudicial to the use to which the territory concerned would be put. The Hurons could not reasonably expect that the use would forever remain what it was in 1760. Before the treaty was signed, they had carried on their customs in accordance with restrictions already imposed by an occupancy incompatible with such exercise. The Hurons were only asking to be permitted to continue to carry on their customs on the lands frequented to the extent that those customs did not interfere with enjoyment of the lands by their occupier. I readily accept that the Hurons were probably not aware of the legal consequences, and in particular of the right to occupy to the exclusion of others, which the main European legal systems attached to the concept of private ownership. Nonetheless I cannot believe that the Hurons ever believed that the treaty gave them the right to cut down trees in the garden of a house as part of their right to carry on their customs.

Jacques-Cartier park falls into the category of land occupied by the Crown, since the province has set it aside for a specific use. What is important is not so much that the province has legislated with respect to this territory but that it is using it, is in fact occupying the space. As occupancy has been established, the question is whether the type of occupancy to which the park is subject is incompatible with the exercise of the activities with which the respondents were charged, as these undoubtedly constitute religious customs or rites. Since, in view of the situation in 1760, we must assume some limitation on the exercise of rights protected by the treaty, it is up to the Crown to prove that its occupancy of the territory cannot be accommodated to reasonable exercise of the Hurons' rights.

The Crown presented evidence on such compatibility but that evidence did not persuade me that exercise of the rites and customs at issue here is incompatible with the occupancy.

NOTES

1) The Court held that the treaty with the Huron was an enforceable agreement in Canadian law. Is it a treaty in the international sense? Compare what the Court said with the criteria for an international treaty set out in Chapter 3, Section B.1 on "Treaties: Generally." Or is the treaty, by virtue of the *Constitution Act, 1982* section 35 and the *Indian Act* section 88, a discrete part of Canadian law?[119]

In *Simon v. The Queen*, in the course of determining the status of the Treaty of 1752 between the Mi'kmaq of Maritime Canada and the British Crown, the Supreme Court observed: "While it may be helpful in some instances to analogize the principles of international treaty law to Indian treaties, these principles are not determinative. An Indian treaty is unique; it is an agreement *sui generis* that is neither created nor terminated according to the rules of international law." While the Supreme Court's opinion may be definitive from a Canadian constitutional viewpoint, would an international tribunal reach the same conclusion?

2) Why is the Huron treaty enforceable over the Québec *Parks Act*? Has it been implemented? Does it need to be? Compare the Supreme Court's approach to international treaties in *Re Arrow River*, reported previously in Section C.3.

3) Does the Court's approach to treaty interpretation in this case conform to the rules generally applied in Canada to international agreements? Refer to Section C.4 on "Interpretation of Treaties." What motivates any different treatment?[120]

---

119 Schedule B of the *Canada Act, 1982, supra* note 115, and R.S.C. 1985, c. I-6, respectively. See *Simon v. The Queen*, [1985] 2 S.C.R. 381.

120 On the use of extrinsic evidence to interpret Indian treaties, the courts have reinforced their view that they should make generous allowance for the context of the treaties' oral negotiations; see *R. v. Badger*, [1996] 1 S.C.R. 771; *Delgamuukw v. British Columbia*, [1997] 3 S.C.R. 1010; and *R. v. Marshall* (1999), 177 D.L.R. (4th) 513.

CHAPTER FIVE

Interstate Relations

A. INTRODUCTION

As long as international society is organized, as a matter of law, around the existence of states that exercise independent sovereign authority, there is a need for a mechanism of admission to that society. The concept of recognition fulfills this need and opens the way to full interstate relations. This legal concept is discussed in Chapter 2, Section B.2 on "States and Statehood: Recognition" where its international application is emphasized. In fact, both international and internal consequences flow from the act of recognition. From the point of view of a newly recognized regime, the most important international effect is that the regime is acknowledged to hold all the rights at international law of a sovereign equal to other (recognizing) states. This recognition may well be needed to bolster its recently gained authority. The rights that are acquired are both substantive and procedural. For instance, recognition of a new state typically results in the opening of diplomatic relations and the exchange of ambassadors.

Responsibilities, as well as rights, also accompany recognition. Indeed, recognition brings into play a whole body of international rules about the conduct of interstate relations. It is this law that permits governments, through departments of foreign affairs, ambassadors, consuls, trade missions, and other official representatives, to freely transact the daily business of diplomacy. There has long been universal appreciation of the mutual necessity of rules and procedures to facilitate these diplomatic contacts. Yet every state, as a legally independent sovereign, has territorial authority to control the entry, movement, and activities of foreigners and foreign influences. Hence foreign state representatives would risk the wrath of receiving governments every time they transmitted displeasing communiqués were there not also rules to protect the channels of diplomacy. Thus much of the law of interstate relations consists of rules that grant immunity from the jurisdiction of the territorial sovereign to the foreign head of state, the government, its representatives, and property.

This chapter explains the law of interstate relations as it affects the national legal system. It begins with a consideration of the way an act of recognition is communicated internally between the government and the courts; it then proceeds to discuss some of the domestic consequences of an act of recognition. Because by far the most important effects of recognition are the accrual of certain state immunities and diplomatic and consular immunities, these matters are taken up separately in later sections of the chapter.

B. RECOGNITION[1]

Internationally, recognition is a mutual matter between the governments of two states; it also creates consequences internally for the other organs of the states. Hence the operation of domestic laws and procedures must be adjusted to take account of the rights and privileges of recognized states and their governments.

1. Executive Certificates

Within the recognizing state, the act of recognition by its government is a signal to all its other organs, including the courts, that they must now respect the international rights of the new foreign regime. Consequently, the first matter to consider is how the courts are to be informed about acts of recognition by the government.

In the case of diplomatic representatives accredited to Canada, when their credentials have been accepted by the Governor in Council their names are added to the diplomatic list published in the Royal Gazette. However, recognition of the foreign regimes themselves are not formally published. The courts, therefore, have to ask the government whether it has granted recognition or not. This is typically done by addressing the Minister of Foreign Affairs with a request for an Executive Certificate.

Re Chateau-Gai Wines Ltd. and A.-G. for Can.
[1970] Ex. C.R. 366 at 382-84

[In the course of a trademark dispute over the use of the appellation "champagne," the court had to consider the effect of the Canada–France Trade Agreement of 1933. One of the uncertainties was whether the signed treaty ever entered into force between the two countries.]

JACKETT P.: ... In principle, as it seems to me, a question whether of fact or law or both, as to whether an international agreement between Canada and another country has come into force between Canada and another sovereign power so as to create international rights and obligations, must be determined, in case of doubt, in the same way as

---

1   See, generally, H.M. Blix, "Contemporary Aspects of Recognition" (1970) 130 Hague Recueil 587; I. Brownlie, *Principles of Public International Law*, 6th ed. (2003) c. 5; T.C. Chen, *The International Law of Recognition* (1951); J. Dugard, *Recognition and the United Nations* (1987); H. Lauterpacht, *Recognition in International Law* (1947); D.P. O'Connell, *International Law*, 2d ed. (1970) vol. 1 at cc. 5, 6; P.K. Menon, *The Law of Recognition in International Law* (1994); M.J. Peterson, *Recognition of Governments* (1997); S. Talmon, *Recognition of Governments in International Law* (1998); T.D. Grant, *The Recognition of States* (1999); and from a Canadian viewpoint, see J.M. Arbour, *Droit International Public*, 4th ed. (2002) at 241-53; E. Binavince, "Canadian Practice in Matters of Recognition," in R. St. J. Macdonald, G. Morris & D.M. Johnston, eds., *Canadian Perspectives on International Law and Organization* (1974) at 153; and L.C. Green, *International Law: A Canadian Perspective*, 2d ed. (1988) at 123.

(a) a question as to whether a person is a foreign sovereign power,

(b) a question as to what persons must be regarded as constituting the effective government of a foreign territory,

(c) a question as to whether a particular place must be regarded as being in Canada or as being under the authority of a foreign sovereign authority,

(d) a question as to whether Canada is at peace or at war with a foreign power, or

(e) a question as to whether a person in Canada is entitled to diplomatic privileges as being an ambassador of a foreign power or a member of the entourage of such an ambassador.

All such questions are questions within the realm of responsibility of the executive arm of government and, being questions on which the state should speak with one voice, they are questions with regard to which the courts should accept from the appropriate minister of the Crown a certificate as to Canada's position. In my opinion, this view of the law is well settled.

NOTES

1) The practice of seeking executive certificates is well settled indeed. President Jackett could cite cases going back to *Taylor v. Barclay*[2] in 1828. His enumeration of topics is an accurate statement of the matters on which the courts regularly request ministerial certificates. The courts decide for themselves a number of similar matters, such as the representative status of foreign government agencies and trading enterprises,[3] or the status of alleged foreign state property.[4] Are these not also "questions within the realm of responsibility of the executive arm of government"?

2) One of the cases relied upon by Jackett P. was *The Arantzazu Mendi*, which involved a request for a certificate concerning the status of the Nationalist Government of Spain during the Spanish Civil War. Lord Atkin remarked:

I pause here to say that not only is this the correct procedure, but that it is the only procedure by which the Court can inform itself of the material fact whether the party sought to be impleaded or whose property is sought to be affected, is a foreign sovereign state.[5]

Should Canadian courts follow Lord Atkin's dictum?[6] Why would the courts want to limit their sources of evidence of a "material fact"? For instance, what is the court to do

---

2   2 Sim. 213; 57 E.R. 769 (H.C. Ch.).

3   *E.g. Compania Mercantil Argentina v. U.S. Shipping Board* (1924), 93 Sol. J. 816 (C.A.); *Krajina v. Tass Agency*, [1949] 2 All E.R. 274 (C.A.); and *Baccus S.R.L. v. Servicio National del Trigo*, [1957] 1 Q.B. 438 (C.A.).

4   *E.g. Haile Selassie v. Cable and Wireless Ltd. (No. 2)*, [1939] Ch. 182 (C.A.).

5   [1939] A.C. 256 at 264. See also the majority view in *Duff Development v. Kelantan*, [1924] A.C. 797 (H.L.), on which Lord Atkin relied.

6   The issue is now affected by statute. See the *State Immunity Act*, R.S.C. 1985, c. S-18, s. 14, reported *infra*, in Section C on "State Immunities," and the *Foreign Missions and International Organizations Act*, S.C. 1991, c. 41, reported *infra*, in Section D on "Diplomatic Immunities."

if, because of the diplomatic delicacy of the situation, the government issues an insufficient or ambiguous certificate? See, for example, the certificate issued in *Luther v. Sagor*.[7] In *Duff Development v. Kelantan*, Lord Sumner said:

> [T]he Courts are bound … to act on the best evidence and, if the question is whether some new State or some older State, whose sovereignty is not notorious, is a sovereign state or not, the best evidence is a statement, which the Crown condescends to permit the appropriate Secretary of State to give on its behalf.[8]

3) The use of executive certificates is said to have a deeper purpose than merely being the means to inform the courts of the government's opinion. They fulfill that function, but the function itself is thought essential because, as Jackett P. said, "the State should speak with one voice." Lord Atkin stated this principle most clearly in *The Arantzazu Mendi*:

> Our State cannot speak with two voices on such a matter, the judiciary saying one thing, the executive another. Our Sovereign has to decide whom he will recognize as a fellow sovereign in the family of States; and the relations of the foreign State with ours in the matter of State immunities must flow from that decision alone.[9]

Though the principle is frequently reiterated, the reasons for it have never been made plain by the courts. Do you consider the principle necessary on account of the constitutional separation of powers between the executive government and the judiciary, or out of a fear of embarrassing the government in the conduct of its foreign policy, or for any other reason? As a consequence of the principle, the courts defer to the government and abnegate a part of their adjudicative function. Although the courts have never attempted to define the range of matters over which they will accept the decision of the government, they have included all the situations itemized by Jackett P. and also questions concerning the boundaries of a foreign state, the authority of foreign acts of state, the extent of national territory, and the protection of national sovereignty from foreign extra-territorial jurisdiction.[10]

4) Jackett P. said that executive certificates should be sought whether the question was "of fact or law or both," but Lord Atkin, in the quotation from *The Arantzazu Mendi* in note 2 above, spoke only of "material fact." Which opinion is correct? Harrison Moore coined the apt phrase "facts of state"[11] to cover all those matters that are decisions of policy for the government and thereafter become facts in the courts' determinations at law. Consider the situation faced by Jackett P.: what was the force and effect of a certain treaty? Although it was undoubtedly right to ask the secretary of state what had been done by Canada, does it necessarily follow that in law the intended result had been achieved? Whose job is it to interpret the effect of the treaty?

---

7   Reported after these notes. See A.B. Lyons, "Judicial Application of International Law and the 'Temporizing' Certificate of the Executive" (1952) 29 Br. Y.B. Int'l L. 227.

8   *Duff Development, supra* note 5 at 824. This view was criticized by Lord Atkin in the *The Arantzazu Mendi, supra* note 5.

9   *Supra* note 5 at 264.

10   For a critical view of the principle and its consequences, see H.M. Kindred, "Foreign Governments Before the Courts" (1980) 58 Can. Bar Rev. 602.

11   In his *Act of State in English Law* (1906) at 33.

2. National Effects of Recognition

The newly recognized state or government may expect to have its sovereign authority respected in the recognizing state by all organs of government. This respect is usually said to include the right:

1) to sue in the courts of the recognizing state;

2) to take control of state property located in the recognizing state;

3) to have effect accorded to its legislative and executive acts of state; and

4) to claim immunity from suit in the courts of the recognizing state for itself, its property, and its representatives.

Since these rights exist at international law, a failure of the recognizing government to accord them to the new authorities creates international responsibility. In Canada's case, this means that the courts, the police, the civil service, the legislatures, and all the other parts of the federal and provincial governments are bound to respect these foreign states' rights.

The following case of *Luther v. Sagor* is the leading authority[12] on which all the legal consequences of recognition and non-recognition have been erected in the United Kingdom and Canada.

Luther v. Sagor
[1921] 1 K.B. 456, rev'd. [1921] 3 K.B. 532 (C.A.)

[The plaintiff's saw mill and business was confiscated by decree of the Soviet Government following the Russian Revolution. Later, agents of the government sold some of the stock of plywood from the mill to the defendant company. When it imported the plywood into Britain, the plaintiff brought suit, claiming to be the true owner.]

ROCHE J.: … [I]t is clear that the defendants' claim to defeat the plaintiff's title depends in the first instance upon the decree … being a valid legislative act which can be recognized as such in the Courts of this country.

Whether the decree in question is a valid legislative act which can be recognized as such by the Courts of this country must, in my judgment, depend upon whether the power from which it purports to emanate is what it apparently claims to be, a sovereign power, in this case the sovereign power of the Russian Federative Republic. The proper source of information as to a foreign power, its status and sovereignty, is the Sovereign of this country through the Government.

I therefore propose to deal with the case upon the information furnished by His Majesty's Secretary of State for Foreign Affairs. The attitude proper to be adopted by a Court of this country with regard to foreign governments or powers I understand to be as follows: (1) If a foreign government is recognized by the Government of this country

---

12   See also *Princess Paley Olga v. Weisz*, [1929] 1 K.B. 718 (C.A.) and *Williams & Humbert Ltd. v. W & H Trade Marks (Jersey) Ltd.*, [1986] 1 All E.R. 129 (H.L.).

the Courts of this country may and must recognize the sovereignty of that foreign government and the validity of its acts: see *Republic of Peru v. Dreyfus* [38 Ch.D. 348], and the cases there cited. (2) If a foreign government, or its sovereignty, is not recognized by the Government of this country the Courts of this country either cannot, or at least need not, or ought not, to take notice of, or recognize such foreign government or its sovereignty. This negative proposition is, I think, also established and recognized by the judgment of Kay J. in *Republic of Peru v. Dreyfus* [38 Ch.D. at 357, 358, and 359].

This being the law which must guide and direct my decision, I have to consider whether and in what sense the Government represented by M. Krassin in this matter is recognized by His Majesty's Government. The materials for a decision have been provided for me by the parties who have each by their solicitors asked for information from His Majesty's Secretary of State for Foreign Affairs.

[Roche J. first read the letter to the defendants, then the following letter to the plaintiffs.]

FOREIGN OFFICE
27th November, 1920

Gentlemen,

I am directed by Earl Curzon of Kedleston to acknowledge the receipt of your letter FT/A of November 19th, requesting certain information concerning the Russian Trade Delegation in this Country, and the Esthonian-Russian Peace Treaty. I am to inform you that for a certain limited purpose His Majesty's Government has regarded Monsieur Krassin as exempt from the process of the Courts, and also for the like limited purpose His Majesty's Government has assented to the claim that that which Monsieur Krassin represents in this Country is a State Government of Russia, but that beyond these propositions the Foreign Office has not gone, nor moreover do these expressions of opinion purport to decide difficult, and it may be very special questions of law upon which it may become necessary for the Courts to pronounce. I am to add that His Majesty's Government have never officially recognized the Soviet Government in any way.

It was said on behalf of the defendants that these communications were vague and ambiguous. I should rather say that they were guarded, but as clear as the indeterminate position of affairs in connection with the subject-matter of the communications enabled them to be; ... On these materials I am not satisfied that His Majesty's Government has recognized the Soviet Government as the Government of a Russian Federative Republic or of any sovereign state or power. I therefore am unable to recognize it, or to hold it has sovereignty, or is able by decree to deprive the plaintiff company of its property. Accordingly I decide this point against the defendants ... .

Judgment for plaintiffs.

On Appeal, BANKES L.J.: ... Upon the evidence which was before the learned judge I think that his decision was quite right.

In this Court the appellants asked leave to adduce further evidence, and as the respondents raised no objection, the evidence was given. It consisted of two letters from the Foreign Office dated respectively April 20 and 22, 1921. The first is in reply to a letter dated April 12, which the appellants' solicitors wrote to the Under Secretary of State for Foreign Affairs, asking for a "Certificate for production to the Court of Appeal that the Government of the Russian Socialist Federal Soviet Republic is recognized by His Majesty's Government as the de facto Government of Russia." To this request a reply was received dated April 20, 1921, in these terms: "I am directed by Earl Curzon of Kedleston to refer to your letter of April 12, asking for information as to the relations between His Majesty's Government and the Soviet Government of Russia. (2.) I am to inform you that His Majesty's Government recognize the Soviet Government as the de facto Government of Russia." The letter of April 22 is in reply to a request for information whether His Majesty's Government recognized the Provisional Government of Russia, and as to the period of its duration, and the extent of its jurisdiction. The answer contains (inter alia) the statement that the Provisional Government came into power on March 14, 1917, that it was recognized by His Majesty's Government as the then existing Government of Russia, and that the Constituent Assembly remained in session until December 13, 1917, when it was dispersed by the Soviet authorities. The statement contained in the letter of April 20 is accepted by the respondents' counsel as the proper and sufficient proof of the recognition of the Soviet Government as the de facto Government of Russia.

Under these circumstances the whole aspect of the case is changed, and it becomes necessary to consider matters which were not material in the Court below. The first is a question of law of very considerable importance, namely, what is the effect of the recognition by His Majesty's Government in April, 1921, of the Soviet Government as the de facto Government of Russia upon the past acts of that Government, and how far back, if at all, does that recognition extend. ...

On the first point counsel have been unable to refer the Court to any English authority. Attention has been called to three cases decided in the Supreme Court of the United States: *Williams v. Bruffy* [96 U.S. 176]; *Underhill v. Hernandez* [168 U.S. 250]; and *Oetjen v. Central Leather Co.* [246 U.S. 297]. In none of these cases is any distinction attempted to be drawn in argument between the effect of a recognition of a government as a de facto government and a recognition of a government as a government de jure, nor is any decision given upon that point; nor, except incidentally, is any mention made as to the effect of the recognition of a government upon its past acts. The mention occurs in two passages. ...

The second mention of the point occurs in the judgment of Fuller C.J. in *Underhill v. Hernandez* [168 U.S. 253]. He says, in speaking of civil wars: "If the party seeking to dislodge the existing government succeeds, and the independence of the government it has set up is recognized, then the acts of such government from the commencement of its existence are regarded as those of an independent nation." These are weighty expressions of opinion on a question of international law. Neither learned judge cites any authority for his proposition. Each appears to treat the matter as one resting on principle. On principle the views put forward by these learned judges appear to me to be sound. ...

An attempt was made by the respondents' counsel to draw a distinction between the effect of a recognition of a government as a de facto government and the effect of a recognition of a government as a government de jure, and to say that the latter form of recognition might relate back to acts of state of a date earlier than the date of recognition, whereas the former could not. Wheaton quoting from Mountague Bernard states the distinction between a de jure and a de facto government thus: "A de jure government is one which, in the opinion of the person using the phrase, ought to possess the powers of sovereignty, though at the time it may be deprived of them. A de facto government is one which is really in possession of them, although the possession may be wrongful or precarious." For some purposes no doubt a distinction can be drawn between the effect of the recognition by a sovereign state of the one form of government or of the other, but for the present purpose in my opinion no distinction can be drawn. The Government of this country having, to use the language just quoted, recognized the Soviet Government as the Government really in possession of the powers of sovereignty in Russia, the acts of that Government must be treated by the Courts of this country with all the respect due to the acts of a duly recognized foreign sovereign state.

SCRUTTON L.J.: ... What the Court cannot do directly it cannot in my view do indirectly. If it could not question the title of the Government of Russia to goods brought by that Government to England, it cannot indirectly question it in the hands of a purchaser from that Government by denying that the Government could confer any good title to the property. This immunity follows from recognition as a sovereign state. Should there be any government which appropriates other people's property without compensation, the remedy appears to be to refuse to recognize it as a sovereign state. Then the Courts could investigate the title without infringing the comity of nations. But it is impossible to recognize a government and yet claim to exercise jurisdiction over its person or property against its will. Further, the Courts in questions whether a particular person or institution is a sovereign must be guided only by the statement of the sovereign on whose behalf they exercise jurisdiction. ... In the present case we have from the Foreign Office a recognition of the Soviet Republic in 1921 as the de facto Government, and a statement that in 1917 the Soviet authorities expelled the previous Government recognized by His Majesty. It appears to me that this binds us to recognize the decree of 1918 by a department of the Soviet Republic, and the sale in 1920 by the Soviet Republic of property claimed by them to be theirs under that decree, as acts of a sovereign state the validity of which cannot be questioned by the Courts of this country.

[Warrington L.J. delivered a concurring judgment.]

Appeal allowed.

NOTES

1) This case shows how sharply the courts draw the distinction between the effects of recognition and non-recognition even though their difference depends upon nothing more than the attitude of the government of the day at the time of the case. Do you find the results persuasive? Consider the problems surrounding claims to state property and retroactivity of recognition discussed in the following notes.

2) A foreign state has a right to control and dispose of its own property as it wishes. But where there are two contending governments in the state, whether because of invasion or civil war, which has the better right to the state property? The issue was squarely presented in a series of cases arising out of the conquest of Ethiopia, or Abyssinia, by Italy in 1935.[13] Emperor Haile Selassie went into exile in London but he was still recognized by Great Britain as the legal sovereign of Ethiopia. At the same time the Italian authorities were recognized as exercising governmental power *de facto*. The English courts were faced with competing claims for state property both within and without Ethiopia. Application of the principle in *Luther v. Sagor* that the recognized government had the right to state property provided no obvious remedy, since the British government had granted a degree of recognition to both claimants.

3) In *Haile Selassie v. Cable and Wireless Ltd. (No. 2)*,[14] the property in issue was a debt payable in London by the defendant company on its contract with the Director-General of Posts, Telegraphs and Telephones of Ethiopia for the transmission of wireless messages. Haile Selassie, as the recognized *de jure* Emperor of Ethiopia, claimed payment over the Italian Government as the recognized *de facto* government within Ethiopia. The trial judge determined the matter according to the notional location of the property. Although acknowledging the recognized authority of the Italian Government over state property within Ethiopia, the court found nothing had divested the Emperor of his title to sue for the debt collectable outside Ethiopia. The decision was reversed on appeal because, by that time, the Italian Government had been recognized as exercising sole *de jure* authority over Ethiopia. Why should rights to state property turn on the recognition policy of a foreign government? What will be the effect on this kind of dispute of the revised Canadian approach not to recognize new governments?

4) A problem also arises where the acts and events surrounding an action in the courts occurred before recognition was accorded. Are they to be ignored because the foreign state or government was then unrecognized, or should the grant of recognition be given retroactive effect?[15] *Luther v. Sagor* is the leading English authority on this aspect of recognition as well. It decided not only that recognition is retroactive but that it extends back in time to validate all the public acts of the recognized government since it came to power. This decision raises two further issues. The first is a question of fact to determine in each case when a newly recognized government acquired power. In the case of a palace *coup*, the moment is usually clear. But in the event of a protracted civil war, it may be most uncertain.

---

13   As well as cases involving the Spanish civil war at approximately the same time. See *Banco de Bilbao v. Sancha and Rey*, [1938] 2 K.B. 176 (C.A.).

14   *Supra* note 4.

15   See D.P. O'Connell, *supra* note 1 at 185-92.

The courts have traditionally asked the government to state in its executive certificate the date of inception of the regime, but even the government cannot always supply a firm reply, and now, under the changed recognition policy, it may be unwilling to do so.

5) The second problem is a question of law as to the effect of the acts of the previously recognized government committed after the inception of the new regime but before it is in turn recognized. There may be an interim period when the old and the new governments both have some effective power in the territory, or over the assets, of the state. How are the courts to handle a clash of authority between the acts of the then recognized government and the retroactively effective acts of the subsequently recognized government? Does the retroactive recognition of one regime and its actions impliedly invalidate retroactively the acts of the other? In *Gdynia Amerika Linie Zeglugowe Spolka Akcyjna v. Boguslawski*,[16] the House of Lords decided that the recognition "enables and requires the courts ... to regard as valid not only acts done by the new government after its recognition but also acts done by it before its recognition insofar as those acts related to matters under its control at the time when the acts were done." Their Lordships did not accept the argument that this "necessarily or logically involves antedating for all purposes the withdrawal of the recognition of the old government." They did not think it inconsistent to say that "the recognition of the new government has certain retroactive effects, but that the recognition of the old government remains effective down to the date when it was in fact withdrawn."

6) The crucial element in the decision that the recognition of two successive governments may overlap is the limitation of the authority of each of them to "acts related to matters under its control at the time when the acts were done." In *Boguslawski*'s case, it was relatively easy to respect retroactively the acts of the new government committed in Poland since it had effective control there at the time, while at the same time to enforce the decrees of the old government in exile over extraterritorial affairs that the new authorities had not yet moved against. Greater difficulties arise when both governments take action with respect to the same subject matter. In *Civil Air Transport Inc. v. Central Air Transport Corp.*,[17] 40 aircraft belonging to the Nationalist government of China were flown to Hong Kong shortly before the advancing Communist forces took full control of the mainland. The Nationalist government, having withdrawn to Taiwan, sold the aircraft but the individuals who flew them to Hong Kong seized control of them in the name of the new Communist government. Shortly afterward the British government recognized the Communist authorities as the government of China in place of the Nationalist regime. The purchaser of the aircraft sued for their possession and succeeded because the Nationalist government was their owner and controller at the time of sale while their subsequent seizure was illegal under Hong Kong law. Viscount Simon stated on behalf of the Privy Council that "[p]rimarily, at any rate, retroactivity of recognition operates to validate acts of a *de facto* government which has subsequently become the new *de jure* government, and not to invalidate acts of the previous *de jure* government."[18] But he also observed:

16   [1953] A.C. 11 at 44-45 (H.L.).

17   [1953] A.C. 70 (J.C.P.C.).

18   *Ibid.* at 93.

Subsequent recognition de jure of a new government as the result of a successful insurrection can in certain cases annul a sale of goods by a previous government. If the previous government sells goods which belong to it but are situated in territory effectively occupied at the time by insurgent forces acting on behalf of what is already a de facto new government, the sale may be valid if the insurgents are afterwards defeated and possession of the goods is regained by the old government. But if the old government never regains the goods and the de facto new government becomes recognized by H.M. Government as the de jure government, purchasers from the old government will not be held in her Majesty's courts to have a good title after that recognition.

7) Compare the solicitude given to the acts of recognized governments with the harsh consequences that befall the actions of an unrecognized regime. The lack of recognition results in a failure by the courts to acknowledge that any legal consequences flow from legislative, executive, or judicial actions in the foreign state. In *Carl-Zeiss-Stiftung v. Rayner & Keeler Ltd. (No. 2)*,[19] in which the absence of recognition of East Germany was at stake, Lord Reid stated:

> We must not only disregard all new laws and decrees made by the Democratic Republic or its Government, but we must also disregard all executive and judicial acts done by persons appointed by that Government because we must regard their appointments as invalid. The result of that would be far-reaching. Trade with the Eastern Zone of Germany is not discouraged. But the incorporation of every company in East Germany under any new law made by the Democratic Republic or by the official act of an official appointed by its Government would have to be regarded as a nullity, so that any such company could neither sue nor be sued in this country. And any civil marriage under any such new law, or owing its validity to the act of any such official, would also have to be treated as a nullity, so that we should have to regard the children as illegitimate. And the same would apply to divorces and all manner of judicial decisions, whether in family or commercial questions. And that would affect not only status of persons formerly domiciled in East Germany but property in this country the devolution of which depended on East German law.

Notwithstanding this devastating catalogue of disorder, the House of Lords in substance confirmed the principle established in *Luther v. Sagor*. Thus, for instance, divorce decrees granted in Rhodesia during the unrecognized regime of Mr. Ian Smith after his unilateral declaration of independence have since been declared ineffective.[20]

3. National Impact of the Estrada Doctrine on Recognition

In 1988 the Canadian government changed its practice on recognition to follow the so-called Estrada Doctrine. Under current Canadian policy, as discussed in Chapter 2, Section B.2 on "Recognition," the government confines itself to the recognition of states

---

[19] [1967] 1 A.C. 853 at 907. Cf. the judgment of Lord Wilberforce at 954, which left some opening for reconsideration. And see D.W. Greig, "The Carl-Zeiss Case and the Position of an Unrecognized Government in English Law" (1967) 83 L.Q. Rev. 96.

[20] *Adams v. Adams*, [1970] 3 All. E.R. 572 (P.D.A.).

and no longer pronounces publicly about the status of governments. Such a policy presents a dilemma for the courts regarding their practice of applying for and relying upon executive certificates. What purpose will executive certificates serve? What form is the Canadian government's answer to a request likely to take?

One practical problem involves the right of a foreign government to sue in the Canadian courts. Since only recognized governments may bring actions, how are the courts to determine the standing of a claimant regime now that the Canadian government will not award recognition? If the courts are compelled to make their own determinations, what criteria should they use?

The English case of *Republic of Somalia v. Woodhouse Drake and Carey Suisse S.A.*[21] confronted this issue in 1993. This case arose over the proceeds of sale of a cargo of rice owned by the Republic of Somalia. In light of the internal conflict in Somalia after the overthrow of President Siad Barre, it was very uncertain who, if anyone, governed the country and therefore had the right to receive the proceeds of sale. The British Government responded by letter to three requests with information about the confused situation but would not express a view on the recognition of any regime. The court accepted the responsibility for determining the government of Somalia for itself, using the British Government's letters as the best evidence of its dealings with Somalia. Hobhouse J. stated that the factors to be taken into account in deciding whether a government exists are: (a) whether it is the constitutional government of the state; (b) the degree, nature, and stability of administrative control that it exercises in the state; (c) whether the British Government has dealings with it and, if so, the nature of those dealings; and (d) in marginal cases, the extent of international recognition it has achieved.

American courts have long made their own determinations about foreign regimes, unfettered by compulsory certificates concerning recognition.[22] Should Canadian courts do likewise? Should they apply Hobhouse J.'s criteria? How would the Canadian court obtain the necessary evidence?

The Canadian government still practises the recognition of states and so the judicial practice of requesting executive certificates is still appropriate when the status of some territory is uncertain. But it may be that the government, out of sensitivity for its diplomatic relations, does not wish to express its views publicly. Review the very temporizing certificate issued to the trial court in *Luthor v. Sagor*, reproduced in the previous subsection, and note the difficulty Roche J. had in interpreting its meaning. A prominent example of a sensitive diplomatic situation is the continuing uncertainty over

---

21   [1993] Q.B. 54. Cf. *Gur Corp. v. Trust Bank of Africa Ltd.*, [1986] 3 W.L.R. 583 (C.A.) and *National Petrochemical Co. of Iran v. The M/T Stolt Sheaf*, 860 F.2d 551 (2d Cir. 1989). And see J.E. Herbsman, "Unrecognized Foreign Sovereign Court Access After National Petrochemical Company of Iran v. The M/T Stolt Sheaf" (1989) 12 Ford. Int'l L.J. 790.

22   *E.g. Wulfsohn v. Russian Socialist Federated Soviet Republic*, 234 N.Y. 372; 138 N.E. 24 (N.Y.C.A. 1923); *Salimoff & Co. v. Standard Oil of New York*, 262 N.Y. 220; 186 N.E. 679 (N.Y.C.A. 1933); and *Upright v. Mercury Business Machines Co.*, 13 App. Div. 2d 36, 213 N.Y.S. 2d 417 (1st Dept. 1961). See S. Lubman, "The Unrecognized Government in American Courts: Upright v. Mercury Business Machines" (1962) 62 Col. L.R. 275. The practice has not been completely uniform. See *The Maret*, 145 F.2d 231 (3d Cir. 1944); and D.P. O'Connell, *supra* note 1 at 172-80.

the international status of Taiwan. In the face of insistent assertions by Beijing that it is the government of the whole of China, including the Taiwanese islands, other states, including Canada, have studiously avoided official recognition of Taiwan even as they maintain trade and other contacts with the authorities in Taipei. Faced with such a situation of non-recognition of a state, what should a Canadian court do? Is the solution in the following case a satisfactory one?[23]

Parent v. Singapore Airlines Ltd.
[2003] J.Q. no. 18068 (Q.S.C.) (in translation) (footnotes omitted)

[François Parent, while a passenger on Singapore Airlines (SAL) from Singapore to Montreal via Taipei, Los Angeles, and Toronto, was injured in an accident at takeoff from Taipei. He sued SAL for damages, but SAL asserted that responsibility lay on Taipei airport's Taiwanese governmental administrator. SAL sought indemnity from the Civil Aeronautics Administration (CAA) of Taiwan, but the CAA claimed immunity from suit under the *State Immunity Act*, reproduced below in Section C.1.]

MARIE ST-PIERRE J.: ...
[31] [T]he issue in this litigation is the following: Does the CAA enjoy immunity from jurisdiction under the terms of the *State Immunity Act*?

[32] It is not disputed that the CAA is a department of the Ministry of Transportation and Communication of the Government of Taiwan without judicial existence separate from that Ministry. It remains to be determined whether the Ministry of Transportation and Communication of the Government of Taiwan is a "Ministry of a Foreign State" within the meaning of the *State Immunity Act*, or otherwise stated, if the Republic of China (Taiwan) is a "foreign state" within the meaning of that Act.

[33] Counsel for SAL submit that the absence of a certificate and the refusal of the Department of Foreign Affairs and International Trade to issue a certificate are conclusive: the CAA is not entitled to claim immunity from the jurisdiction of the court in circumstances where the Department refuses to officially recognize it by issuing a certificate pursuant to the provisions of the Act, the statute which gives it that right.

[34] Counsel for CAA do not share this point of view. According to them, the certificate constitutes at the very most a means of proof. While admittedly preferred, this means of proof is not the only admissible evidence. The analysis of the Department's letter has to be made bearing in mind the diplomatic context in which the Department must act. This letter is not a certificate within the meaning of section

---

[23]   See also *Luigi Monta of Genoa v. Cechofract Co. Ltd.*, [1956] 2 Q.B. 552; *Re Al-Fin Corporations' Patent*, [1970] Ch. 160; *Gur Corp.*, *supra* note 21; *Hesperides Hotels Ltd. v. Aegean Turkish Holidays Ltd.*, [1978] 1 Q.B. 205 (C.A.); H.M. Kindred, *supra* note 10; and J.G. Merrills, "Law, Politics and the Legislation of the Unrecognized Government" (1968-69) 3 Ott. L. Rev. 1. But consider *Loizidou v. Turkey* (1995), 103 I.L.R. 622 (Eur. Ct. H.R.).

14 of the Act and its content cannot be interpreted as equivalent to a rejection of the legal position of CAA as to the applicability of the immunity that it claims. In all cases, it is up to the Court to apply the State Immunity Act in light of the evidence provided, and that being the case, to determine if Taiwan is a "foreign state" within the meaning of this Act.

[35] Two sub-questions arise from the positions presented by the parties:

[35.1] What is the effect of the absence of a certificate issued pursuant to section 14 of the Act?

[35.2] Is Taiwan a "foreign state" within the meaning of the Act?

What is the effect of the absence of a certificate issued pursuant to section 14 of the Act?

[36] The terms used by Parliament in section 14 of the Act are the following:

> *French Version:* Le certificat délivré ... est *admissible en preuve* et fait foi pour toute question touchant ... .

> *English Version:* A certificate issued ... is *admissible* in evidence as conclusive proof of any matter stated in the certificate ... ." (Our [emphasis])

[37] In section 14 of the Canadian legislation, Parliament provides that it is not necessary to have witnesses testify where a certificate has been issued because, in that case, that which is stated in the certificate is simply proven by its admission into evidence. However, it does not say that the admission into evidence of a certificate issued by the Department is required. Furthermore, it does not say that the status of "foreign state" within the meaning of the Act is established by admission of the certificate into evidence of the certificate under section 14. ...

[39] [T]he absence of a certificate issued pursuant to section 14 of the Act does not necessarily mean the absence of the right to state immunity. Indeed, Parliament does not say "whether a state is a foreign state for the purposes of the Act is established by the production into evidence of a certificate issued by the Department"; Parliament says "a certificate is admissible" to establish whether a state is a foreign state. To say that a certificate is admissible does not mean that the certificate is the only means of proof available to interested parties. If Parliament had wished that to be the case, it would have been necessary to draft the provisions of the Act differently. ...

[42] The issuance of a certificate does not present any difficulties when the position of Canada with respect to the recognition of the foreign state is clear, accepted and not susceptible of causing or provoking any political or diplomatic difficulties.

[43] It may be otherwise when that is not the case. In such circumstances, nothing prevents the Department of Foreign Affairs and International Trade from giving the task to the Court of determining whether immunity applies in the absence of an issued certificate, but in light of the evidence submitted. ...

[46] Furthermore, the Act obliges the Court to do all that is necessary on its own to ensure proper application of immunity: it relates to a matter of public order.

[47] Hence, in the absence of a certificate, the Court must analyse the proof presented including, in the present matter, the exchange of letters between counsel for SAL and the Department and then, in light of all of this evidence, determine if "Taiwan" is a "foreign state" within the meaning of the Act.

[48] In leaving the power to the Courts to determine if a party litigant is a "foreign state" within the meaning of the Act in light of the proof submitted (which may or may not include a certificate), the Canadian Parliament keeps the law separate from political and diplomatic concerns.

[49] In those instances where political and diplomatic persons can or wish to officially recognize the situation, or when they wish to exercise control over it, the Department has the power to issue a certificate pursuant to section 14 of the Act. This proof is conclusive and the Court is bound by its contents, subject of course to its interpretation.

[50] On the other hand, where political and diplomatic persons cannot officially recognize the situation or the Department abstains from issuing a certificate, the task of determining the facts, and arriving at conclusions about them, is given to the Court that is seized of the application.

[51] Interpreted in this manner, the Act achieves its purpose (to integrate into Canadian law the principle of state immunity arising out of customary international law) having regard for the principles of public international law on which this immunity is based (sovereignty, independence, dignity and equality of states). Is Taiwan a "foreign state" for the purposes of this Act?

[52] The Act does not define the term "foreign state."

[53] The Act having integrated into Canadian law the principle of state immunity arising out of customary international law, it is there that one must look to international public law to find the definition to apply. As Mr. Justice Pigeon wrote in the decision of *Daniel v. White*:

> [T]his was a case for the application of the rule of construction that Parliament is not presumed to legislate in breach of a treaty or in any manner inconsistent with the comity of nations or the established rules of international law. [(1968), S.C.R. 517 at 541]

[54] The existence of a state implies the presence of four elements:

> According to international law, the existence of a State implies the presence of four elements: These elements are identified in Section 1 of the Convention of Montevideo on the rights and duties of States, and are:
>
> — the presence of a defined territory;
> — the presence of a permanent population;
> — the presence of an effective government;
> — the capacity to enter in relations with other States.
>
> Furthermore, to have the greatest effect in the international community, the existence of a State must be recognized by other States. This recognition is principally, but not exclusively, linked to the presence of the constituent elements of the State. [Claude Emanuelli, *Droit international public* (1998) at 262-63]

[55] The recognition of a State by other States does not create the State: the birth and existence of a State is a question of fact.

> The declaratory theory, on the contrary, sees the act of recognition as the simple acknowledgement of an established fact. This theory is inspired by judicial sociology.

The birth of a State is a question of fact; it does not depend on the acquiescence of other States. This theory is confirmed by international practice. [Claude Emanuelli, *Droit international public* (1998) at 189]

[56] The evidence in the present matter is conclusive with respect to the four constituent elements of the State: (1) the island of Taiwan constitutes a defined territory; (2) the island of Taiwan is occupied by a permanent population; (3) a government exercising effective control exists in Taiwan; and (4) the government of Taiwan enters into relations with other states.

[57] Moreover this reality is clearly confirmed:

[57.1] On the occasion of a statement made by the Canadian Minister of External Affairs, the Honourable Paul Martin, during a speech in Banff entitled Canada and the Pacific and reproduced in *The Canadian Yearbook of International Law*, volume VI, 1968:

We consider that the isolation of Communist China from a large part of normal international relations is dangerous. We are prepared to accept the reality of the victory in mainland China in 1949 ... . We consider, however, that the effective political independence of Taiwan is a political reality too. ...

[58] The Court concludes, therefore, with respect to the present matter, that CAA has the right to immunity pursuant to the Act.

[59] That being the case, and in conclusion, the Court adopts the remarks of the author Hugh M. Kindred:

In pursuing this course, the courts may find themselves granting a degree of respect or even immunity for a foreign regime that superficially may seem wholly out of accord with the government's declarations of diplomatic distance. But the illusion will be in the denials of recognition by the government for diplomacy's sake and no longer in the fictions of the courts. [Hugh Kindred, "Foreign Governments Before the Courts" (1980) 58 Can. Bar Rev. 602 at 620]

FOR THESE REASONS, the Court:

ALLOWS the application of CAA for dismissal of the claim for indemnity;

DISMISSES the claim for indemnity by SAL against CAA; All with costs.

4. Foreign Acts of State

The phrase "act of state" is not a term of art in international law. It is best known as a doctrine of American law but it is widely and variously used. It is employed here simply to refer to an official public act, whether legislative, executive, or judicial, of a recognized foreign government.

A common predicament faces the legal system of every country. Since all states are sovereign equals, each state must respect the public acts of every other state it recognizes. The problem is to determine how, and how far, to give effect to such acts of the foreign state in the recognizing state. As this problem is a matter for each national legal system to resolve, it is not surprising that different solutions have been reached, and that they reflect the various arrangements for the separation of governmental powers to be found in different countries.

The American act of state doctrine has had a great influence well beyond the United States for several reasons. The United States courts were among the first to face the problem and so their judgments have provided a source of opinion for others. More recently, in the course of elaborating the doctrine to cope with the American division of constitutional authority over foreign affairs, the United States courts have exerted a certain international jurisdiction, which has inevitably collided with the sovereign powers of foreign governments. In sum, the American act of state doctrine offers a rich comparative experience for other countries like Canada, as well as raising important questions about judicial responsibility internationally. In these materials some comparative sources are used, but the emphasis is placed upon the way Canadian courts[24] have handled foreign acts of state in the few cases in which they have been considered.

Laane and Baltser v. The Estonian State Cargo & Passenger Steamship Line
[1949] S.C.R. 530

[The case concerned the distribution of the proceeds of a judicial sale of the S.S. *Elise* after its arrest in Saint John. Although registered in Estonia by her Estonian owners, the appellants Laane and Baltser, the *Elise* had left Estonia in July 1939 and had sailed exclusively between the United Kingdom and Canada until its arrest. During this time Estonia became a part of the U.S.S.R. and Canada recognized this change. By several decrees, the new Soviet government of the Estonian Republic purported to nationalize the Estonian shipping industry, including the appellants' business, and to fix compensation for expropriated ships at 25 percent of their value. Shortly afterward, the respondent state corporation was established to run the nationalized ships. The court was asked: "(1) Were the Decrees and Statutes herein recited effective in nationalizing the Steamship ELISE and transferring ownership to the plaintiff herein [the Estonian Steamship Line]? (2) Is the plaintiff entitled to maintain the action and receive the proceeds?"]

RINFRET C.J.: ... The decrees relied on by it were declared illegal and unconstitutional by the English Court of Appeal in the *Talinna case*. It may be doubted whether their language was sufficient to vest the steamship *Elise* in the respondent. In the *Talinna case* it was held that they lacked the necessary wording to make them effective in that respect; and, further, that they were incomplete in the sense that the last stage to give them force of law had not been proceeded with. At the material time the *Elise* was in the Port of Saint John, Canada, a foreign country. She was then in possession of the appellants and the respondent never got possession of the ship, nor any control of her,

---

24   See H.M. Kindred, "Acts of State and the Application of International Law in Canadian Courts" (1979) 10 Rev. Droit Sherbrooke 271.

before the ship was sold by the Marshal. The proceedings herein were instituted after the sale and were not directed against the ship herself, but against the proceeds of the sale, then deposited in a Canadian Admiralty Court.

Moreover, the decrees are of an evident confiscatory nature and, even if they purport to have extra-territorial effect, they cannot be recognized by a foreign country, under the well-established principles of international law. Quite independent of their illegality and unconstitutionality, they are not of such a character that they could be recognized in a British Court of Law.

For these reasons, the appeal should be maintained and the proceedings of the respondent dismissed. There should be an order that the proceeds of the sale of the *Elise* in Court should be paid out to Laane and Baltser.

RAND J.: ... [T]here can be no doubt that once a private ship is voluntarily brought within a country's territory it is submitted to the laws of that country. The jurisdiction arising is primary and fundamental; but the particular law to be applied to determine legal relations in respect of the vessel is quite another matter. But, whether viewed as recognition of legal effects of foreign law or as affirmative enforcement of foreign law, that its application is through the act and authority of the territorial state follows from the language of Chief Justice Marshall in *Schooner Exchange v. M'Fadden* (1812), 7 Cranch 116, at 136:

> All exceptions, therefore, to the full and complete power of a nation within its own territories, must be traced up to the consent of the nation itself. They can flow from no other legitimate source.

... [T]he application [of foreign law] is by the territorial power and jurisdictionally with such modifications of a foreign rule as it pleases. It is what we should expect, therefore, that there are certain rules, more or less clearly defined, by which the enforcement in the domestic forum of a foreign law is refused.

It is now established that a common law jurisdiction will not enforce directly or indirectly the penal or the revenue laws of another state, to which Dicey in Rule 54, 5th Ed., adds, political law; and there is the general principle that no state will apply a law of another which offends against some fundamental morality or public policy. The first question then is whether there is some such policy of New Brunswick with which the confirmation of the attempted acquisition of this vessel by Estonia would conflict. The taking of property for public purposes without compensation certainly clashes with our notions of the conditions which should attend the exercise of that power, and I should not view the proposed award of 25 per cent of the value as avoiding that conflict. The provincial law is invoked to effect the transfer of the appellant's property on those terms: and we must ask whether the considerations of international expediency so far transcend normal policy as to overcome the repugnance of our political conceptions toward such an act. I do not think they do.

The effect of the decrees bears elements also of analogy to the operation of a revenue law. A state imposes a tax as a small fraction of the property of its citizens, and it is taken for a public purpose. But whether the fraction is five or seventy-five per cent and even though limited to certain classes of property, coercion and public object are common to both cases. We refuse to aid a neighbour state in collecting the lesser exaction even though taxation is universally accepted as a proper state faculty; on what ground should we enforce the greater?

But there is what I think a still more important aspect in which the question is to be viewed. The acquisition of property here is not to be dissociated from the larger political policy of which it is in reality an incident. The matters before us evidence the fundamental change effected in the constitution of the Estonian state, of which that acquisition is only one, though an important, particular. What has been set up is a social organization in which the dominant position of the individual, as recognized in our polity, has been repudiated and in which the institution of private property, so far as that has to do with producing goods and services, has been abolished; and those functions, together with the existing means, taken over by the state. If at the time of the decrees every Estonian ship had been sunk, their principal purpose would still have been realized in vesting in the state, apart from ports and immoveable works in Estonia, the monopoly of carrying on shipping services.

What is asked of the foreign territorial law is, therefore, to aid in the execution of a fundamental political law of Estonia which serves no interest of the foreign state. The law of conflicts is concerned with the determination of rights in property and personal relations which are conceived as distinct from the law under which they arise; but, laws of the class in question are not migratory and are deemed to be operative only within their own territories. If the transfer of property by such a law of Estonia has been satisfied by the condition of territorial jurisdiction, the title will be recognized and enforced, as in England the similar decrees of Russia: *Luther v. Sagor* ... But where that legislative basis is absent there is no warrant in international accommodation to call upon another state to exercise its sovereign power to supply the jurisdictional deficiency in completing such a political program: ... .

I would, therefore, allow the appeal and direct judgment in favour of the appellants with costs in both courts.

[Concurring opinions were delivered by Kerwin J. (Estey J. concurring) and Kellock J.]

NOTES

1) In *Luther v. Sagor* Bankes and Scrutton L.JJ. said that the acts of a recognized government must be respected and may not be questioned by the courts.[25] In so saying they were repeating a principle founded in *Blad's Case*[26] in 1673 and *Duke of Brunswick v. King of Hanover*[27] in 1848 and already well established in United States courts. In 1897 in *Underhill v. Hernandez*, Fuller C.J. declared:

---

[25] Reported above in Section B.2 on "National Effects of Recognition," and stated even more forcefully by Warrington J. at 548.

[26] 3 Swan 602; 36 E.R. 991 (P.C.).

[27] 2 H.L. Cas. 1; 9 E.R. 993 (H.L.).

Every sovereign state is bound to respect the independence of every other sovereign state, and the courts of one country will not sit in judgment on the acts of the government of another done within its own territory. Redress of grievances, by reason of such acts must be obtained through the means open to be availed of by sovereign powers as between themselves.[28]

French courts have also said they lack jurisdiction to hear a claim arising from the acts of a foreign sovereign government.[29] What fact distinguished *Laane and Baltser* from *Luther v. Sagor* and allowed the court to disregard the Estonian decree?

2) Did the Supreme Court in fact sit in judgment on the acts of the government of Estonia? Rand J. pointed out that although Estonian law governed the issue, it could only operate in a Canadian court through the authority of Canadian law. This is a principle of conflicts of law, not international law. By characterizing the problem this way, Rand J. was able to apply well-accepted controls of the forum state against unwanted intrusions of the foreign state. This degree of disrespect or disregard of the acts of a foreign state is acceptable in international law on account of its reciprocal character. Foreign states must have equal regard for Canadian sovereignty, particularly within its own territory and courts. The inclination is strong for Canadian courts to resolve act of state problems through conflicts of law principles.[30]

3) Suppose the *Elise* had been in an Estonian port and was beneficially owned by a Canadian company just prior to nationalization. How might the court then have decided the issue?

4) For a Canadian case in which the courts were prepared to sit in judgment of foreign laws without regard either to the presence or absence of recognition of the government, or to respect for foreign acts of state, see *Juelle v. Trudeau*.[31] The case was a classic example of title to moveable property, having been confiscated abroad, being refought within the Canadian jurisdiction. The plaintiffs alleged they were the true owners of seven horses bred from the stock of their stud farm in Cuba, which was violently and illegally confiscated by Castro forces. The defendants pleaded that, having received an offer to sell the animals from a representative of the Cuban government, they purchased them in good faith from the registered owners in Cuba and had since peaceably possessed them and raced them in Canada. On the evidence, the trial court held the seizure contrary to Cuban law and of null effect upon the plaintiff's title. On appeal, the court regarded the confiscation as fully in compliance with Cuban law and hence effective to transfer ownership to the defendants' vendors. The cause for reversal was the sharply different reading of Cuban law between the two courts. The trial judge appears to have applied the pre-revolutionary law, while the justices of appeal referred to the decrees and

---

28   168 U.S. 250 at 252. See likewise, *Oetjen v. Central Leather Co.*, 246 U.S. 297 at 303 (1918).

29   See *Société Internationale de Plantations d'Hévéas v. Lao Import Export Co.* (1988), 80 I.L.R. 688 (Court of Cassation).

30   See also *Brown, Gow, Wilson v. Beleggings-Societeit N.V.*, [1961] O.R. 815. But compare Hall J.'s dissent in *Calder v. British Columbia (Attorney General)*, [1973] S.C.R. 313.

31   (1970), 7 D.L.R. (3d) 82 (Q.S.C.), rev'd. (1972), C.A. 870 (Que.).

constitutional amendments of Castro's government. Unfortunately at neither level did the court provide reasons for its particular assessment of Cuban controls on property.

5) Recognition principles in *Luther v. Sagor* and conflicts principles in *Laane and Baltser* led the courts away from their ordinary adjudicative function and the application of the usual Canadian sources of law. One of those sources is international law.[32] Although it is undoubtedly correct that the courts of one country should not judge the acts of another by their own national laws, for that would be an abuse of the other's sovereignty, why should they not determine the validity of those acts by international law? Is a Canadian court obliged to respect an act of a foreign state that is contrary to international law? Consider the following experience of American and English courts.

Banco Nacional de Cuba v. Sabbatino[33]
376 U.S. 398 (1964)

[The Cuban government in effect confiscated and then resold for its own account to the same purchaser a cargo of sugar lying in a Cuban port. A Cuban state bank later brought this action in New York to recover the purchase price but its title to the sugar and its interest in the monies held in a U.S. bank were challenged by the original owner of the sugar, a corporation registered in Cuba but principally owned by American residents. It succeeded at trial and on appeal because the courts refused to apply the act of state doctrine in the face of a violation of international law, which they so found on the evidence that the Cuban acts were retaliatory, discriminatory, and without adequate compensation.

In reversing these decisions, the Supreme Court reasserted the force of the act of state doctrine even in the face of breaches of international law. It said of the doctrine:][34]

[I]ts continuing vitality depends on its capacity to reflect the proper distribution of functions between the judicial and political branches of the Government on matters bearing upon foreign affairs. It should be apparent that the greater the degree of codification or consensus concerning a particular area of international law, the more appropriate it is for the judiciary to render decisions regarding it, since the courts can then focus on the application of an agreed principle to circumstances of fact rather than on the sensitive task of establishing a principle not inconsistent with the national interest or with international justice. It is also evident that some aspects of international law touch more sharply on national nerves than do others; the less important the implications of an issue are for our foreign relations, the weaker the justification for exclusivity in the political branches.

---

32   Chapter 4, Section A on "National Application in Canada."

33   See R. Falk, *The Role of Domestic Courts in the International Legal Order* (1964); Mooney, *Foreign Seizures: Sabbatino and the Act of State Doctrine* (1967); and a deluge of articles on this celebrated case.

34   At 427-28.

[The actual decision in the case was a narrow one:]³⁵

Therefore, rather than laying down or reaffirming an inflexible and all-encompassing rule in this case, we decide only that the Judicial Branch will not examine the validity of a taking of property within its own territory by a foreign sovereign government, extant and recognized by this country at the time of suit, ... even if the complaint alleges that the taking violates customary international law.

[And so the U.S. Supreme Court ordered the U.S. bank to pay money owed by a U.S. citizen over to a foreign government pursuant to a decree made in retaliation against the United States and in violation of international law.]

NOTES

1) Although the Supreme Court applied the act of state doctrine, it did not consider that international law required it to do so. Probably the more pertinent question is whether international law forbids a court from enforcing an illegal act of state. Instead, the Supreme Court acted in the light of its position in the American legal system. In that context, clearly some balance has to be struck by the courts between upholding the constitutional division of national authority over foreign affairs and enforcing international law. Do you consider the criteria put forth by the U.S. Supreme Court suitable for Canada? How should Canadian courts accommodate the government's policy toward a foreign regime when a Canadian corporation challenges the international legality of an act of expropriation of its property by that regime?

2) As a result of the flexible case-by-case approach to the act of state doctrine encouraged by *Sabbatino*, the U.S. Secretary of State has quite often intervened in subsequent cases by way of an *amicus* brief. The brief typically explains the government's foreign policy interests in the dispute and declares its view of the merits, including whether it regards the application of the act of state doctrine as desirable or not. Do you think a similar practice would be appropriate in Canada?

3) When is the conduct complained of an act of state? Consider the request of the Philippines government for an injunction to prevent the former President Marcos from disposing of assets in New York because, it was alleged, they had been obtained by the President while in office through fraud on the Philippines. One court said the act of state doctrine was no bar to an injunction because the acts of the deposed President should not be regarded as acts of state.³⁶ Might the former ruler of Panama, Manuel Noriega, have pleaded the act of state doctrine in his trial in the United States for drug smuggling while he held power?³⁷

---

35   At 428.

36   See *Philippines v. Marcos*, 806 F.2d 344 (2d Cir. 1986), cert. denied, 481 U.S. 1048 (1987). Cf. *Philippines v. Marcos*, 818 F.2d 1473 (9th Cir. 1987), rev'd., 862 F.2d 1355 (9th Cir., *en banc*, 1988), cert. denied, 109 S.Ct. 1933 (1989).

37   See *United States v. Noriega*, 746 F. Supp. 1506 (S.D. Fla. 1990). See also *Liu v. Republic of China*, 892 F.2d 1419 (9th. Cir. 1989).

4) Such was the furor over *Sabbatino* that Congress quickly passed the "Hickenlooper Amendment" to the *Foreign Assistance Act of 1961*.[38] This reversed the particular decision in *Sabbatino* and thus rescued the possibility of an application of international law by the U.S. courts to foreign state acts of expropriation. There has since been a plentiful supply of cases about the scope of the Hickenlooper Amendment and the life of the American act of state doctrine outside of it,[39] which has not been resolved finally by the U.S. Supreme Court.[40]

5) In Britain,[41] so great has been the influence of *Luther v. Sagor* on the courts that the House of Lords did not have the opportunity to consider whether it would "examine the validity" at international law of a foreign act of state until 1976. In 1953 in *The Rose Mary*,[42] a British court in Aden had held that Iranian legislative acts of nationalization were contrary to international law but the decision has been overshadowed by criticisms that the court applied erroneous views of international law.[43] When the House of Lords considered the matter in *Oppenheimer v. Cattermole*, Lord Cross, speaking for the majority, said:

> A judge should, of course, be very slow to refuse to give effect to the legislation of a foreign state in any sphere in which, according to accepted principles of international law, the foreign state has jurisdiction. He may well have an inadequate understanding of the circumstances in which the legislation was passed and his refusal to recognize it may be embarrassing to the branch of the executive which is concerned to maintain friendly relations between this country and the foreign country in question. But I think ... that it is part of the public policy of this country that our courts should give effect to clearly established rules of international law ... . [W]hat we are concerned with here is legislation [of Nazi Germany] which takes away without compensation from [the Jewish] section of the citizen body singled out on racial grounds all their property on which the state passing the legislation can lay its hands and, in addition, deprives them of their citizenship. To my mind a law of this

---

[38] 22 U.S.C., §2370. See also 9 U.S.C., §15 added in 1988 to prevent the doctrine interfering in arbitrations with foreign states.

[39] And an equally plentiful supply of learned opinions. For reviews of the progress of *Sabbatino* in the context of "restatement of the law," see M. Halberstrom, "Sabbatino Resurrected: The Act of State Doctrine in the Revised Restatement of U.S. Foreign Relations Law" (1985) 79 A.J.I.L. 68; M. Leigh, "Sabbatino's Silver Anniversary and the Restatement: No Cause for Celebration" (1990) 24 Int'l Lawyer 1; and *Restatement of the Law (Third), Foreign Relations Law of the United States*, sections 443, 444. For an account of the doctrine's development see J.W. Dellapenna, "Deciphering the Act of State Doctrine" (1990) 35 Vill. L.R. 1.

[40] See *W.S. Kirkpatrick & Co. v. Environmental Tectonics Corp., International* 493 U.S. 400 (1990). For a concise exploration of the development and operation of the doctrine see M.W. Janis, *An Introduction to International Law*, 4th ed. (2003) at 353-60.

[41] See D.L. Jones, "Act of Foreign State in English Law: The Ghost Goes East" (1981-82) 22 Va. J. Int'l L. 433; H.M. Kindred, "Acts of State and the Application of International Law in English Courts" (1981) 19 Can. Y.B. Int'l L. 271; and M. Singer, "The Act of State Doctrine of the United Kingdom: An Analysis, with Comparisons to United States Practice" (1981) 75 A.J.I.L. 283.

[42] [1953] 1 W.L.R. 246. See also *In re Claim by Helbert Wagg & Co. Ltd.*, [1956] Ch. 323.

[43] K. Lipstein, [1956] Camb. L.J. 138 at 140; D.W. Greig, *International Law*, 2d ed. (1976) at 62-63; and D.P. O'Connell, "A Critique of the Iranian Oil Litigation" (1955) 4 I.C.L.Q. 267.

sort constitutes so grave an infringement of human rights that the courts of this country ought to refuse to recognise it as a law at all.[44]

Lord Cross was concerned, like the U.S. Supreme Court in *Sabbatino*, to point out the need to balance the courts' responsibilities in the face of international law and the executive government's authority over foreign affairs by national law. But he established *prima facie* a centre of balance that was quite different from *Sabbatino*. What was it? Which approach would you consider more appropriate to a Canadian court faced with the same kind of issues, such as *Juelle v. Trudeau*?[45]

6) Subsequently, in *Buttes Gas and Oil Co. v. Hammer and Occidental Petroleum Corp.* Lord Wilberforce spoke for the House of Lords, saying:

It is one thing to assert that effect will not be given to a foreign municipal law or executive act if it is contrary to public policy, or to international law ... and quite another to claim that the courts may examine the validity, under international law, or some doctrine of public policy, of an act or acts operating in the area of transactions between states ... .

So I think that the essential question is whether ... there exists in English law a more general principle that the courts will not adjudicate on transactions of foreign sovereign states. Though I would prefer to avoid argument on terminology, it seems desirable to consider this principle, if existing, not as a variety of act of state but one for judicial restraint or abstention ... .

In my opinion there is, and for long has been, such a general principle, starting in English law, adopted and generalized in the law of the USA, which is effective and compelling in English courts. This principle is not one of discretion, but is inherent in the very nature of the judicial process.[46]

Lord Wilberforce then traced the general principle from *Blad's Case* through *Underhill*, *Oetjen*, *Luther v. Sagor*, and *Sabbatino* to the U.S. decisions in similar suits between the immediate litigants and concluded:

Leaving aside all possibility of embarrassment in our foreign relations (which it can be said have not been drawn to the attention of the court by the executive), there are, to follow the Fifth Circuit Court of Appeals, no judicial or manageable standards by which to judge these issues.[47]

Lord Wilberforce here asserted a general principle, wider than the act of state doctrine, that interstate issues are not justiciable in the absence of judicial or manageable standards by which to judge them. Perhaps the issues in the case were unmanageable but it is difficult to appreciate why international law is not an adequate, not to say appropriate, standard of adjudication.

7) The non-justiciability of interstate issues on the ground of public policy, as presented by Lord Wilberforce, is a more diffuse concept than the act of state doctrine. It

---

44   [1976] A.C. 249 at 277-78. Cf. *Williams & Humbert Ltd. v. W & H Trade Marks (Jersey) Ltd.*, [1986] 1 All E.R. 129 at 138 (H.L.).

45   Reported *supra* note 31.

46   [1981] 3 All E.R. 616 at 628.

47   *Ibid.* at 633.

encompasses the doctrine, but it has not smothered the courts' power to adjudge foreign state acts, as more recent decisions of the House of Lords indicate. In particular, in *Kuwait Airways Corp. v. Iraqi Airways Co.*[48] the Law Lords developed the circumstances in which the act of state doctrine will not be applied and the courts will adjudicate upon the lawfulness of foreign state actions. The case arose out of the invasion and annexation of Kuwait by Iraq in 1990. By a resolution of the Iraqi Revolutionary Command Council, Kuwait Airlines was dissolved and all its assets, including the 10 aircraft involved in this case, were transferred to the state-owned Iraqi Airways. Kuwait Airlines then sued Iraqi Airways in the English courts for return of the aircraft or compensation. Hence the authority of the Iraqi Council's resolution was put in issue. Had the act of state doctrine been applied, the courts would simply have acknowledged the legislative act of the Iraqi government and rejected the plaintiff's claim. Instead, they refused to recognize the effect of the Iraqi resolution. Recounting Iraq's flagrant violation of international law and the Security Council's condemnation of its annexation of Kuwait, the House of Lords readily developed another restriction on the operation of the act of state doctrine. To the exception for grave abuses of internationally protected human rights, applied by the House of Lords in *Oppenheimer v. Cattermole*, the Law Lords now added violations of the international prohibition against the use of force. More important, they made clear that the scope of exceptions to the act of state doctrine is not fixed, but may potentially include any clear violation of a well-established rule of international law.

Does this approach answer Lord Wilberforce's concern in *Buttes* that there are no judicial or manageable standards by which to judge foreign state acts? How does it redress the balance struck by the act of state doctrine between interest in supporting the rule of international law and concern to respect foreign sovereign acts? Does it achieve an appropriate balance? One commentator has called the decision "deft and defensively progressive, reflective of the English courts' commendable move in recent times towards a more direct engagement … with the United Kingdom's international engagements."[49] Should Canadian courts follow the House of Lords?

C. STATE IMMUNITIES

1. Immunity Generally[50]

A recognized state is entitled by international law to immunity from the jurisdiction of the courts of other states. The basic reason behind the law is that, all states being sovereign equals, one cannot exercise authority over another. The old phrase "sovereign

---

[48] [2002] 2 A.C. 883. And see Li-ann Thio, "English Public Policy, the Act of State Doctrine and Flagrant Violations of Fundamental International Law: Kuwait Airways Corp. v. Iraqi Airways Co. (2002)" (2002-3) 18 Conn. J. Int'l L. 585. See also *Pinochet (No. 1)*, [2000] 1 A.C. 61, [1998] 3 W.L.R. 1456 and *Pinochet (No. 3)*, [2000] 1 A.C. 147, [1999] 2 W.L.R. 827 and the symposium of articles on these cases in (1999) 48 I.C.L.Q. 937 especially E. Denza 949 at 956.

[49] (2002) 73 Br. Y.B. Int'l L. 400 at 403.

[50] See G.M. Badr, *State Immunity: An Analytical and Prognostic View* (1984); C. Schreuer, *State Immunity: Some Recent Developments* (1988); I. Sinclair, "The Law of Sovereign Immunity: Recent Developments"

immunity" reflects the origin of the principle as a personal attribute of the foreign head of state. The sovereign head may use the courts to sue if she or he wishes, but she or he cannot be compelled to submit to their authority. The sovereign head has this freedom as the personification of the state, and therefrom flows all the immunities allowed to officials, governmental agencies, and state property nationally operating or held in her or his name. This principle applies whether a private person begins a civil action against the head of state or, even more strongly, if a local state official should initiate criminal proceedings for an offence under national law.[51]

The effect of granting immunity is to stay the action of the plaintiff and thus to prevent the trial and possible remedy of an alleged wrong. *Congo v. Venne*[52] was a typical case. M. Venne, a Quebec architect, sued the Republic of the Congo for the cost of his professional services in preparing studies and sketches for a national pavilion that the Congo had proposed to build in Montreal at Expo '67 but never did. In respecting the Congo's assertion of immunity, the Supreme Court denied a private Canadian citizen his ordinary right of access to justice. The resulting ouster of the rights of a claimant poses two questions: (1) is there a sufficient justification for state immunity and, if so, (2) how far should that immunity extend? The old case of *The Schooner Exchange* still provides an instructive discussion on these questions.

The Schooner Exchange v. M'Faddon
11 U.S. 116 (1812)

[Two Americans claimed the *Schooner Exchange* belonged to them when she arrived in the port of Philadelphia. They alleged that two years previously the vessel had been seized at sea by French forces and wrongfully taken from them. The U.S. Attorney stated that a French public ship named the *Balaou* had been driven into Philadelphia by bad weather and, being owned by the Emperor of France, she ought to be released from the arrest of the claimants.]

MARSHALL C.J.: ... The jurisdiction of the nation within its own territory is necessarily exclusive and absolute. It is susceptible of no limitation not imposed by itself.

All exceptions, therefore, to the full and complete power of a nation within its own territories, must be traced up to the consent of the nation itself. They can flow from no other legitimate source ... .

(1980) 167 Hague Recueil 133; S. Sucharitkul, "Immunities of Foreign States Before National Authorities" (1976) 149 Hague Recueil 87; the Australian Law Reform Commission, Report No. 24, *Foreign State Immunity* (1984); *UN Convention on the Jurisdictional Immunities of States and Their Property*, U.N. GA Res. 59/38 (2004); Institut de Droit International (I. Brownlie), *Contemporary Problems Concerning the Jurisdictional Immunity of States* (1991) available online at: <http://www.idi-iil.org/idiE/resolutionsE/1991_bal_03_en.PDF>; J. Bröhmer, *State Immunity and the Violation of Human Rights* (1997); and E. Morgan, *International Law and the Canadian Courts* (1990) c. 1.

51   In some circumstances a foreign head of state is not immune from prosecution before national courts for heinous international offences; see Chapter 11, Section A.

52   [1971] S.C.R. 997.

The world being composed of distinct sovereignties, possessing equal rights and equal independence, whose mutual benefit is promoted by intercourse with each other, and by an interchange of those good offices which humanity dictates and its wants require, all sovereigns have consented to a relaxation in practice, in cases under certain peculiar circumstances, of that absolute and complete jurisdiction within their respective territories which sovereignty confers. ...

This full and absolute territorial jurisdiction being alike the attribute of every sovereign, and being incapable of conferring extra-territorial power, would not seem to contemplate foreign sovereigns nor their sovereign rights as its objects. One sovereign being in no respect amenable to another; and being bound by obligations of the highest character not to degrade the dignity of his nation, by placing himself or its sovereign rights within the jurisdiction of another, can be supposed to enter a foreign territory only under an express license, or in the confidence that the immunities belonging to his independent sovereign station, though not expressly stipulated, are reserved by implication, and will be extended to him.

This perfect equality and absolute independence of sovereigns, and this common interest impelling them to mutual intercourse, and an interchange of good offices with each other, have given rise to a class of cases in which every sovereign is understood to waive the exercise of a part of that complete exclusive territorial jurisdiction, which has been stated to be the attribute of every nation.

1st. One of these is admitted to be the exemption of the person of the sovereign from arrest or detention within a foreign territory. ...

Why has the whole civilized world concurred in this construction? The answer cannot be mistaken. A foreign sovereign is not understood as intending to subject himself to a jurisdiction incompatible with his dignity, and the dignity of his nation, and it is to avoid this subjection that the license has been obtained. The character to whom it is given, and the object for which it is granted, equally require that it should be construed to impart full security to the person who has obtained it. This security, however, need not be expressed; it is implied from the circumstances of the case. ...

2d. A second case, standing on the same principles with the first, is the immunity which all civilized nations allow to foreign ministers. ...

3d. A third case in which a sovereign is understood to cede a portion of his territorial jurisdiction is, where he allows the troops of a foreign prince to pass through his dominions. ...

But the rule which is applicable to armies, does not appear to be equally applicable to ships of war entering the ports of a friendly power. The injury inseparable from the march of an army through an inhabited country, and the dangers often, indeed generally, attending it, do not ensue from admitting a ship of war, without special license, into a friendly port. ...

If there be no prohibition, the ports of a friendly nation are considered as open to the public ships of all powers with whom it is at peace, and they are supposed to enter such ports and to remain in them while allowed to remain, under the protection of the government of the place. ...

Are there reasons for denying the application of this principle to ships of war? ...

To the Court, it appears, that where, without treaty, the ports of a nation are open to the private and public ships of a friendly power, whose subjects have also liberty without special license, to enter the country for business or amusement, a clear distinction is to be drawn between the rights accorded to private individuals or private trading vessels, and those accorded to public armed ships which constitute a part of the military force of the nation.

The preceding reasoning, has maintained the propositions that all exemptions from territorial jurisdiction, must be derived from the consent of the sovereign of the territory; that this consent may be implied or expressed; and that when implied, its extent must be regulated by the nature of the case, and the views under which the parties requiring and conceding it must be supposed to act.

When private individuals of one nation spread themselves through another as business or caprice may direct, mingling indiscriminately with the inhabitants of that other, or when merchant vessels enter for the purposes of trade, it would be obviously inconvenient and dangerous to society, and would subject the laws to continual infraction, and the government to degradation, if such individuals or merchants did not owe temporary and local allegiance, and were not amenable to the jurisdiction of the country. Nor can the foreign sovereign have any motive for wishing such exemption. His subjects thus passing into foreign countries, are not employed by him, nor are they engaged in national pursuits. Consequently there are powerful motives for not exempting persons of this description from the jurisdiction of the country in which they are found, and no one motive for requiring it. The implied license, therefore, under which they enter can never be construed to grant such exemption.

But in all respects different is the situation of a public armed ship. She constitutes a part of the military force of her nation; acts under the immediate and direct command of the sovereign; is employed by him in national objects. He has many and powerful motives for preventing those objects from being defeated by the interference of a foreign state. Such interference cannot take place without affecting his power and his dignity. The implied license therefore under which such vessel enters a friendly port, may reasonably be construed, and it seems to the Court, ought to be construed, as containing an exemption from the jurisdiction of the sovereign, within whose territory she claims the rites of hospitality.

Upon these principles, by the unanimous consent of nations, a foreigner is amenable to the laws of the place; but certainly in practice, nations have not yet asserted their jurisdiction over the public armed ships of a foreign sovereign entering a port open for their reception. ...

[T]here is a manifest distinction between the private property of the person who happens to be a prince, and that military force which supports the sovereign power, and maintains the dignity and the independence of a nation. A prince, by acquiring private property in a foreign country, may possibly be considered as subjecting that property to the territorial jurisdiction; he may be considered as so far laying down the prince, and assuming the character of a private individual; but this he cannot be presumed to do with respect to any portion of that armed force, which upholds his crown, and the nation he is entrusted to govern. ...

It seems then to the Court, to be a principle of public law, that national ships of war, entering the port of a friendly power open for their reception, are to be considered as exempted by the consent of that power from its jurisdiction.

Without doubt, the sovereign of the place is capable of destroying this implication. He may claim and exercise jurisdiction either by employing force, or by subjecting such vessels to the ordinary tribunals. But until such power be exerted in a manner not to be misunderstood, the sovereign cannot be considered as having imparted to the ordinary tribunals a jurisdiction, which it would be a breach of faith to exercise. Those general statutory provisions therefore which are descriptive of the ordinary jurisdiction of the judicial tribunals, which give an individual whose property has been wrested from him, a right to claim that property in the courts of the country, in which it is found, ought not, in the opinion of this Court, to be so construed as to give them jurisdiction in a case, in which the sovereign power has impliedly consented to wave its jurisdiction.

The arguments in favour of this opinion which have been drawn from the general inability of the judicial power to enforce its decisions in cases of this description, from the consideration, that the sovereign power of the nation is alone competent to avenge wrongs committed by a sovereign, that the questions to which such wrongs give birth are rather questions of policy than of law, that they are for diplomatic, rather than legal discussion, are of great weight, and merit serious attention. ...

If the preceding reasoning be correct, the [*Schooner*] *Exchange*, being a public armed ship, in the service of a foreign sovereign, with whom the government of the United States is at peace, and having entered an American port open for her reception, on the terms on which ships of war are generally permitted to enter the ports of a friendly power, must be considered as having come into the American territory, under an implied promise, that while necessarily within it, and demeaning herself in a friendly manner, she should be exempt from the jurisdiction of the country. ...

NOTES

1) Chief Justice Marshall justified state immunity on the traditional grounds of sovereign equality and the dignity of states. But notice that he also gave a functional reason concerning the mutual benefit of diplomatic and other foreign relations. Are these reasons convincing?

2) Sovereign equality of states is a reciprocal doctrine. If a foreign head of state cannot be expected to submit to the jurisdiction of the local courts, why should the local sovereign be expected to subjugate its jurisdiction to foreign authority? Did Marshall C.J. provide any answer? Is it more in keeping, nowadays, with the dignity of a foreign sovereign to submit to the rule of law than to claim to be above it?[53]

3) Did Marshall C.J. grant blanket immunity to foreign sovereigns, their ministers, and their property in accordance with the so-called absolute theory discussed below, or

---

53   Cf. Lord Denning's opinion in *Rahimtoola v. Nizam of Hyderabad*, [1958] A.C. 379 at 418 (H.L.).

did he draw distinctions among the sovereign's acts and possessions, thus foreshadowing a more restrictive approach to state immunity?

Scope of Immunity

The immunity of a foreign state is generally regarded as extending beyond the state itself and the head of state to:

— the government and all governmental organs,

— the leader of the government, the foreign minister and other ministers, officials, and agents of the state with respect to their official acts,

— public corporations independently created but operating in effect as government organs, and

— state-owned property.

Diplomatic, consular, and other representatives abroad are excluded from this list because they are subject to separate privileges and immunities now fixed by multilateral treaty. These immunities are considered in the next section.

Immunity is granted from all phases of judicial process. It is not limited to jurisdiction over the merits but is available against attachment before suit and against execution after judgment. For instance, submission by a state to the local jurisdiction in the merits of a case does not mean that its property may be subjected to execution to enforce a subsequent judgment against it. The property of the state is entitled to immunity from attachment and execution, unless the state submits further to the jurisdiction.

Even though a sovereign state may claim immunity in these kinds of situations, does it have a right to immunity on all such occasions? A positive answer was developed by the British courts and a doctrine of absolute immunity was laid down in *The Parlement Belge*.[54] This position was reiterated over and over on both sides of the Atlantic for many years. See, for instance, the clear statement of support for absolute immunity made by the Supreme Court of Canada in *Dessaulles v. Republic of Poland*.[55] But the growing interdependence of states and the increasing involvement of governments in commercial ventures in the 20th century forced many countries to the conclusion that the absolute theory is impractical and unreasonable. If a government department chooses to participate in the marketplace of a foreign state, why should it expect any different treatment or regulation than private trading parties? On this basis, a theory of restrictive immunity was founded and has flourished. The restrictive approach to state immunity is now almost universally practised as a matter of customary international law. However, uncertainties remain, not least about the basic distinction between a sovereign act (*jure imperii*) that attracts immunity and a commercial act (*jure gestionis*) that no longer does so.

---

[54]   (1880), L.R. 5 P.D. 197.

[55]   [1944] 4 D.L.R. 1.

Although diplomatic immunity has long been the subject of treaty definition, first bilaterally and now multilaterally, state immunity is *par excellence* a matter of customary international law. Nevertheless, in an effort to provide some order in times of changing practices, the states of Western Europe have adopted a Convention on State Immunity.[56] Its approach to the application of the restrictive theory of immunity is to include a list of particular situations where no immunity will be granted because the acts in question are acts *jure gestionis* or because the foreign state has consented to the court's jurisdiction. The United Kingdom signed this convention and implemented it by the *State Immunity Act 1978*.[57] The United States has also followed the restrictive theory since 1952. For reasons chiefly concerning the constitutional interrelation between the Department of State and the American judiciary, the U.S. application of the restrictive theory has been clarified and confirmed by the *Foreign Sovereign Immunities Act of 1976*.[58]

Canada remained for some time in splendid isolation in the western world by continuing to apply the absolute theory of immunity. Notwithstanding a strong dissent by Laskin J. in *Congo v. Venne*,[59] the Supreme Court failed to take a firm position for change. This uncertainty at the top did not hinder several provincial courts from adopting a restrictive approach.[60] Toward the straightening out of these judicial dilemmas, Parliament passed the following *State Immunity Act*. It was desired by government officials in part because it had become impossible to explain simply to foreign states and their representatives what sovereign immunities they might expect to receive in Canada. Even so, such parliamentary action is singularly remarkable for attempting to legislate customary international law. The source of this law is beyond Canada alone, yet the principle of supremacy of Parliament ensures that the courts will apply the international law crystallized in the Act even as the community of nation states changes and develops it. See the case of *Bouzari v. Islamic Republic of Iran* reproduced in subsection 4 below. The risk of such a development is increased by the fact that through the 1990s several United Nations bodies worked to develop a multilateral treaty on the subject. By the fall of 2004 the draft of the UN Convention on the Jurisdictional Immunities of States and Their Property was finalized. It was subsequently adopted by the General Assembly on December 2nd and was opened for signature through January 17, 2007.[61] It is reproduced below, after the *State Immunity Act*.

---

56   Reprinted in (1972) 11 I.L.M. 470.

57   (U.K.) 1978, c. 33.

58   28 U.S.C. §§. 1602-11, reprinted in (1976) 15 I.L.M. 1388.

59   *Supra* note 52.

60   See, for instance, *Zodiak International Products Inc. v. Polish People's Republic* (1977), 81 D.L.R. (3d) 656 (Que. C.A.); *Smith v. Canadian Javelin* (1976), 68 D.L.R. (3d) 428 (Ont. H.C.); J.L. Marasinghe, "A Reassessment of Sovereign Immunity" (1977) 9 Ott. L.R. 474; and H.M. Kindred, *supra* note 10.

61   *UN Convention on the Jurisdictional Immunities of States and Their Property, supra* note 50.

State Immunity Act[62]
R.S.C. 1985, c. S-18, as am.

Interpretation

2. In this Act, "agency of a foreign state" means any legal entity that is an organ of the foreign state but that is separate from the foreign state;

"commercial activity" means any particular transaction, act or conduct or any regular course of conduct that by reason of its nature is of a commercial character;

"foreign state" includes

(a) any sovereign or other head of the foreign state or of any political subdivision of the foreign state while acting as such in a public capacity,

(b) any government of the foreign state or of any political subdivision of the foreign state, including any of its departments, and any agency of the foreign state, and

(c) any political subdivision of the foreign state;

"political subdivision" means a province, state or other like political subdivision of a foreign state that is a federal state.

State Immunity

3.(1) Except as provided by this Act, a foreign state is immune from the jurisdiction of any court in Canada.

(2) In any proceedings before a court, the court shall give effect to the immunity conferred on a foreign state by subsection (1) notwithstanding that the state has failed to take any step in the proceedings.

4.(1) A foreign state is not immune from the jurisdiction of a court if the state waives the immunity conferred by subsection 3(1) by submitting to the jurisdiction of the court in accordance with subsection (2) or (4).

(2) In any proceedings before a court, a foreign state submits to the jurisdiction of the court where it

(a) explicitly submits to the jurisdiction of the court by written agreement or otherwise either before or after the proceedings commence;

(b) initiates the proceedings in the court; or

(c) intervenes or takes any step in the proceedings before the court.

(3) Paragraph (2)(c) does not apply to

(a) any intervention or step taken by a foreign state in proceedings before a court for the purpose of claiming immunity from the jurisdiction of the court; or

(b) any step taken by a foreign state in ignorance of facts entitling it to immunity if those facts could not reasonably have been ascertained before the step was taken and immunity is claimed as soon as reasonably practicable after they are ascertained.

---

[62]   For commentary on the Act, see B.D. Coad, "The Canadian State Immunity Act" (1983) 14 L. & Pol. Int. Bus. 1197; H.L. Molot & M.L. Jewitt, "The State Immunity Act of Canada" (1982) 20 Can. Y.B. Int'l L. 79; and D. Turp, "Commentaire relatif a la Loi sur l'immunité des États étrangers devant les tribunaux" (1983) 17 Rev. Jur. Themis 175.

(4) A foreign state that initiates proceedings in a court or that intervenes or takes any step in proceedings before a court, other than an intervention or step to which paragraph (2)(c) does not apply, submits to the jurisdiction of the court in respect of any third party proceedings that arise, or counter-claim that arises, out of the subject-matter of the proceedings initiated by the state or in which the state has so intervened or taken a step.

(5) Where, in any proceedings before a court, a foreign state submits to the jurisdiction of the court in accordance with subsection (2) or (4), that submission is deemed to be a submission by the state to the jurisdiction of such one or more courts by which those proceedings may, in whole or in part, subsequently be considered on appeal or in the exercise of supervisory jurisdiction.

5. A foreign state is not immune from the jurisdiction of a court in any proceedings that relate to any commercial activity of the foreign state.

6. A foreign state is not immune from the jurisdiction of a court in any proceedings that relate to

(a) any death or personal or bodily injury, or

(b) any damage to or loss of property

that occurs in Canada.

7.(1) A foreign state is not immune from the jurisdiction of a court in any proceedings that relate to

(a) an action *in rem* against a ship owned or operated by the state, or

(b) an action *in personam* for enforcing a claim in connection with a ship owned or operated by the state,

if, at the time the claim arose or the proceedings were commenced, the ship was being used or was intended for use in a commercial activity.

(2) A foreign state is not immune from the jurisdiction of a court in any proceedings that relate to

(a) an action *in rem* against any cargo owned by the state if, at the time the claim arose or the proceedings were commenced, the cargo and the ship carrying the cargo were being used or were intended for use in a commercial activity; or

(b) an action *in personam* for enforcing a claim in connection with any cargo owned by the state if, at the time the claim arose or the proceedings were commenced, the ship carrying the cargo was being used or was intended for use in a commercial activity.

(3) For the purpose of subsections (1) and (2), a ship or cargo owned by a foreign state includes any ship or cargo in the possession or control of the state and any ship or cargo in which the state claims an interest.

8. A foreign state is not immune from the jurisdiction of a court in any proceedings that relate to an interest or, in the Province of Quebec, a right of the state in property that arises by way of succession, gift or *bona vacantia*.

Procedure and Relief

9.(1) Service of an originating document on a foreign state, other than on an agency of the foreign state, may be made

(a) in any manner agreed on by the state;

(b) in accordance with any international Convention to which the state is a party; or

(c) in the manner provided in subsection (2).

(2) For the purposes of paragraph (1)(c), anyone wishing to serve an originating document on a foreign state may deliver a copy of the document, in person or by registered mail, to the Deputy Minister of Foreign Affairs or a person designated by him for the purpose, who shall transmit it to the foreign state.

(3) Service of an originating document on an agency of a foreign state may be made

(a) in any manner agreed on by the agency;

(b) in accordance with any international Convention applicable to the agency; or

(c) in accordance with any applicable rules of court.

(4) Where service on an agency of a foreign state cannot be made under subsection (3), a court may, by order, direct how service is to be made.

(5) Where service of an originating document is made in the manner provided in subsection (2), service of the document shall be deemed to have been made on the day that the Deputy Minister of Foreign Affairs or a person designated by him pursuant to subsection (2) certifies to the relevant court that the copy of the document has been transmitted to the foreign state.

10.(1) Where, in any proceedings in a court, service of an originating document has been made on a foreign state in accordance with subsection 9(1), (3) or (4) and the state has failed to take, within the time limited therefor by the rules of the court or otherwise by law, the initial step required of a defendant or respondent in those proceedings in that court, no further step toward judgment may be taken in the proceedings except after the expiration of at least sixty days following the date of service of the originating document.

(2) Where judgment is signed against a foreign state in any proceedings in which the state has failed to take the initial step referred to in subsection (1), a certified copy of the judgment shall be served on the foreign state

(a) where service of the document that originated the proceedings was made on an agency of the foreign state, in such manner as is ordered by the court; or

(b) in any other case, in the manner specified in paragraph 9(1)(c) as though the judgment were an originating document.

(3) Where, by reason of subsection (2), a certified copy of a judgment is required to be served in the manner specified in paragraph 9(1)(c), subsections 9(2) and (5) apply with such modifications as the circumstances require.

(4) A foreign state may, within sixty days after service on it of a certified copy of a judgment pursuant to subsection (2), apply to have the judgment set aside.

11.(1) Subject to subsection (3), no relief by way of an injunction, specific performance or the recovery of land or other property may be granted against a foreign state unless the state consents in writing to that relief and, where the state so consents, the relief granted shall not be greater than that consented to by the state.

(2) Submission by a foreign state to the jurisdiction of a court is not consent for the purposes of subsection (1).

(3) This section does not apply to an agency of a foreign state.

12.(1) Subject to subsections (2) and (3), property of a foreign state that is located in Canada is immune from attachment and execution and, in the case of an action *in rem*, from arrest, detention, seizure and forfeiture except where

(a) the state has, either explicitly or by implication, waived its immunity from attachment, execution, arrest, detention, seizure or forfeiture, unless the foreign state has withdrawn the waiver of immunity in accordance with any term thereof that permits such withdrawal;

(b) the property is used or is intended for a commercial activity; or

(c) the execution relates to a judgment establishing rights in property that has been acquired by succession or gift or in immovable property located in Canada.

(2) Subject to subsection (3), property of an agency of a foreign state is not immune from attachment and execution and, in the case of an action *in rem*, from arrest, detention, seizure and forfeiture, for the purpose of satisfying a judgment of a court in any proceedings in respect of which the agency is not immune from the jurisdiction of the court by reason of any provision of this Act.

(3) Property of a foreign state

(a) that is used or is intended to be used in connection with a military activity, and

(b) that is military in nature or is under the control of a military authority or defence agency

is immune from attachment and execution and, in the case of an action *in rem*, from arrest, detention, seizure and forfeiture.

(4) Subject to subsection (5), property of a foreign central bank or monetary authority that is held for its own account and is not used or intended for a commercial activity is immune from attachment and execution.

(5) The immunity conferred on property of a foreign central bank or monetary authority by subsection (4) does not apply where the bank, authority or its parent foreign government has explicitly waived the immunity, unless the bank, authority or government has withdrawn the waiver of immunity in accordance with any term thereof that permits such withdrawal.

13.(1) No penalty or fine may be imposed by a court against a foreign state for any failure or refusal by the state to produce any document or other information in the course of proceedings before the court.

(2) Subsection (1) does not apply to an agency of a foreign state.

General

14.(1) A certificate issued by the Minister of Foreign Affairs, or on his behalf by a person authorized by him, with respect to any of the following questions, namely,

(a) whether a country is a foreign state for the purposes of this Act,

(b) whether a particular area or territory of a foreign state is a political subdivision of that state, or

(c) whether a person or persons are to be regarded as the head or government of a foreign state or of a political subdivision of the foreign state,

is admissible in evidence as conclusive proof of any matter stated in the certificate with respect to that question, without proof of the signature of the Minister of Foreign

Affairs or other person or of that other person's authorization by the Minister of Foreign Affairs.

(2) A certificate issued by the Deputy Minister of Foreign Affairs, or on his behalf by a person designated by him pursuant to subsection 9(2), with respect to service of an originating or other document on a foreign state in accordance with that subsection is admissible in evidence as conclusive proof of any matter stated in the certificate with respect to that service, without proof of the signature of the Deputy Minister of Foreign Affairs or other person or of that other person's authorization by the Deputy Minister of Foreign Affairs.

15. The Governor in Council may, on the recommendation of the Minister of Foreign Affairs, by order restrict any immunity or privileges under this Act in relation to a foreign state where, in the opinion of the Governor in Council, the immunity or privileges exceed those accorded by the law of that state.

16. Where, in any proceeding or other matter to which a provision of this Act and a provision of the *Visiting Forces Act* or the *Foreign Missions and International Organizations Act* apply, there is a conflict between those provisions, the provision of this Act ceases to apply in the proceeding or other matter to the extent of the conflict.

17. Except to the extent required to give effect to this Act, nothing in this Act shall be construed or applied so as to negate or affect any rules of a court, including rules of a court relating to service of a document out of the jurisdiction of the court.

18. This Act does not apply to criminal proceedings or proceedings in the nature of criminal proceedings.

United Nations Convention on the Jurisdictional Immunities
of States and Their Property
UN GA Res. 59/38 (2004)

Article 1
Scope of the Present Convention

The present Convention applies to the immunity of a State and its property from the jurisdiction of the courts of another State.

Article 2
Use of Terms

1. For the purposes of the present Convention:

(a) "court" means any organ of a State, however named, entitled to exercise judicial functions;

(b) "State" means:

(i) the State and its various organs of government;

(ii) constituent units of a federal State or political subdivisions of the State, which are entitled to perform acts in the exercise of the sovereign authority, and are acting in that capacity;

      (iii) agencies or instrumentalities of the State or other entities, to the extent that they are entitled to perform and are actually performing acts in the exercise of sovereign authority of the State;

      (iv) representatives of the State acting in that capacity;

  (c) "commercial transaction" means

      (i) any commercial contract or transaction for the sale of goods or supply of services;

      (ii) any contract for a loan or other transaction of a financial nature, including any obligation of guarantee or of indemnity in respect of any such loan or transaction;

      (iii) any other contract or transaction of a commercial, industrial, trading or professional nature, but not including a contract of employment of persons.

2. In determining whether a contract or transaction is a "commercial transaction" under paragraph 1(c), reference should be made primarily to the nature of the contract or transaction, but its purpose should also be taken into account if the parties to the contract or transaction have so agreed, or if, in the practice of the State of the forum, that purpose is relevant to determining the non-commercial character of the contract or transaction.

3. The provisions of paragraphs 1 and 2 regarding the use of terms in the present Convention are without prejudice to the use of those terms or to the meanings which may be given to them in other international instruments or in the internal law of any State. ...

Article 5
State Immunity

A State enjoys immunity, in respect of itself and its property, from the jurisdiction of the courts of another State subject to the provisions of the present Convention. ...

Article 7
Express Consent to Exercise of Jurisdiction

1. A State cannot invoke immunity from jurisdiction in a proceeding before a court of another State with regard to a matter or case if it has expressly consented to the exercise of jurisdiction by the court with regard to the matter or case:

  (a) by international agreement;

  (b) in a written contract; or

  (c) by a declaration before the court or by a written communication in a specific proceeding.

2. Agreement by a State for the application of the law of another State shall not be interpreted as consent to the exercise of jurisdiction by the courts of that other State. ...

Article 10
Commercial Transactions

1. If a State engages in a commercial transaction with a foreign natural or juridicial person and, by virtue of the applicable rules of private international law, differences

relating to the commercial transaction fall within the jurisdiction of a court of another State, the State cannot invoke immunity from that jurisdiction in a proceeding arising out of that commercial transaction.

2. Paragraph 1 does not apply:

(a) in the case of a commercial transaction between States; or

(b) if the parties to the commercial transaction have expressly agreed otherwise.

3. Where a State enterprise or other entity established by a State which has an independent legal personality and is capable of:

(a) suing or being sued; and

(b) acquiring, owning or possessing and disposing of property, including property which that State has authorized it to operate or manage,

is involved in a proceeding which relates to a commercial transaction in which that entity is engaged, the immunity from jurisdiction enjoyed by that State shall not be affected.

[The Annex to the Convention, which, by article 25, forms an integral part of the Convention, contains interpretive understandings of several provisions of the Convention. With respect to article 10(3), its understood application "does not prejudice the question of 'piercing the corporate veil,' questions relating to a situation where a State entity has deliberately misrepresented its financial position or subsequently reduced its assets to avoid satisfying a claim, or other related issues."]

Article 11
Contracts of Employment

1. Unless otherwise agreed between the States concerned, a State cannot invoke immunity from jurisdiction before a court of another State which is otherwise competent in a proceeding which relates to a contract of employment between the State and an individual for work performed or to be performed, in whole or in part, in the territory of that other State.

2. Paragraph 1 does not apply if:

(a) the employee has been recruited to perform particular functions in the exercise of governmental authority;

(b) the employee is:

(i) a diplomatic agent, as defined in the Vienna Convention on Diplomatic Relations of 1961;

(ii) a consular officer, as defined in the Vienna Convention on Consular Relations of 1963;

(iii) a member of the diplomatic staff of a permanent mission to an international organization, or of a special mission, or is recruited to represent a State at an international conference; or

(iv) any other person enjoying diplomatic immunity;

(c) the subject matter of the proceeding is the recruitment, renewal of employment or reinstatement of an individual;

(d) the subject matter of the proceeding is the dismissal or termination of employment of an individual and, as determined by the head of State, the head of

Government or the Minister for Foreign Affairs of the employer State, such a proceeding would interfere with the security interests of that State;

(e) the employee is a national of the employer State at the time when the proceeding is instituted, unless this person has the permanent residence in the State of the forum; or

(f) the employer State and the employee have otherwise agreed in writing, subject to any considerations of public policy conferring on the courts of the State of the forum exclusive jurisdiction by reason of the subject matter of the proceeding.

Article 12
Personal Injuries and Damage to Property

Unless otherwise agreed between the States concerned, a State cannot invoke immunity from jurisdiction before a court of another State which is otherwise competent in a proceeding which relates to pecuniary compensation for death or injury to the person, or damage to or loss of tangible property, caused by an act or omission which is alleged to be attributable to the State, if the act or omission occurred in whole or in part in the territory of that other State and if the author of the act or omission was present in that territory at the time of the act or omission.

Article 13
Ownership, Possession, and Use of Property

Unless otherwise agreed between the States concerned, a State cannot invoke immunity from jurisdiction before a court of another State which is otherwise competent in a proceeding which relates to the determination of:

(a) any right or interest of the State in, or its possession or use of, or any obligation of the State arising out of its interest in, or its possession or use of, immovable property situated in the State of the forum;

(b) any right or interest of the State in movable or immovable property arising by way of succession, gift or *bona vacantia*; or

(c) any right or interest of the State in the administration of property, such as trust property, the estate of a bankrupt or the property of a company in the event of its winding up. ...

Article 18
State Immunity from Pre-judgment Measures of Constraint

No pre-judgment measures of constraint, such as attachment or arrest, against property of a State may be taken in connection with a proceeding before a court of another State unless and except to the extent that:

(a) the State has expressly consented to the taking of such measures as indicated:

(i) by international agreement;

(ii) by an arbitration agreement or in a written contract;

(iii) by a declaration before the court or by a written communication after a dispute between the parties has arisen; or

(b) the State has allocated or earmarked property for the satisfaction of the claim which is the object of that proceeding.

Article 19
State Immunity from Post-judgment Measures of Constraint

No post-judgment measures of constraint, such as attachment, arrest or execution, against property of a State may be taken in connection with a proceeding before a court of another State unless and except to the extent that:

(a) the State has expressly consented to the taking of such measures as indicated:

(i) by international agreement;

(ii) by an arbitration agreement or in a written contract; or

(iii) by a declaration before the court or by a written communication after a dispute between the parties has arisen; or

(b) the State has allocated or earmarked property for the satisfaction of the claim which is the object of that proceeding; or

(c) it has been established that the property is specifically in use or intended for use by the State for other than government non-commercial purposes and is in the territory of the State of the forum, provided that post-judgment measures of constraint may only be taken against property that has a connection with the entity against which the proceeding was directed.

[The Annex to the Convention expresses an interpretive understanding that "entity," as used in article 19(c), "means the State as an independent legal personality, a constituent unit of a federal State, a subdivision of a State, agency or instrumentality of a State or other entity, which enjoys independent legal personality."]

Article 21
Specific Categories of Property

1. The following categories, in particular, of property of a State shall not be considered as property specifically in use or intended for use by the State for other than government non-commercial purposes under article 19, subparagraph (c):

(a) property, including any bank account, which is used or intended for use in the performance of the functions of the diplomatic mission of the State or its consular posts, special missions, missions to international organizations or delegations to organs of international organizations or to international conferences;

(b) property of a military character or used or intended for use in the performance of military functions;

(c) property of the central bank or other monetary authority of the State;

(d) property forming part of the cultural heritage of the State or part of its archives and not placed or intended to be placed on sale;

(e) property forming part of an exhibition of objects of scientific, cultural or historical interest and not placed or intended to be placed on sale.

2. Paragraph 1 is without prejudice to articles 18 and 19, subparagraphs (a) and (b).

NOTES

1) The UN Convention was developed from a set of Draft Articles on Jurisdictional Immunities of States and Their Property prepared by the International Law Commission and recommended to the U.N. General Assembly in 1991.[63]

2) Waiver of immunity: articles 8 and 9 of the U.N. Convention complement article 7 in addressing the concept of waiver of immunity. Article 8 notes that a state cannot invoke immunity from jurisdiction in a proceeding before a court of another state if it has instituted the proceeding or intervened in the proceeding. Similarly, article 9 inhibits a state that has instituted a proceeding or intervened in an action from invoking immunity from the jurisdiction of the court in respect of any counterclaim arising out of the same legal relationship or facts as the principal claim.

3) Immunity of property: article 13 of the UN Convention notes that states cannot invoke immunity from jurisdiction before a court of another state in a proceeding relating to the determination of certain property interests, particularly real estate and trust property. Articles 14, 15, and 16 extend the classes of property or ownership interests for which a state may not invoke immunity—article 14 adds intellectual and industrial property; article 15 covers a state's participation in companies or other collective enterprises; and article 16 includes ships owned or operated by a state, other than warships.

2. Waiver of Immunity

Even under the restrictive theory, the basic principle remains that states are generally immune from suit. As the *State Immunity Act* states in section 3(1): "Except as provided by this Act, a foreign state is immune from the jurisdiction of any court in Canada."[64] But, a foreign state may choose to submit to the local jurisdiction and then it will be treated as having waived its immunity. See the *State Immunity Act* section 4. However, a submission to the court purely for the purpose of claiming immunity will not amount to a waiver: see section 4(3).

The most obvious instance of waiver of immunity occurs when a foreign state initiates an action as the plaintiff, but there are many other situations mentioned in section 4 of the Act.[65]

---

[63]   (1991) 30 I.L.M. 1554. See G. Triggs, "An International Convention on Sovereign Immunity? Some Problems in Application of the Restrictive Theory" (1982) 9 Monash U.L.R. 74; D.W. Greig, "Forum State Jurisdiction and Sovereign Immunity under the International Law Commission's Draft Articles" (1989) 38 I.C.L.Q. 243 and 560; L.W. Lowe, "The International Law Commission's Draft Articles on the Jurisdictional Immunities of States and Their Property: The Commercial Contract Exception" (1989) 27 Colum. J. Transnat. L. 657; and V. Morris, "The International Law Commission's Draft Convention on the Jurisdictional Immunities of States and their Property" (1988-89) 17 Denver J. Int'l L. & Pol. 345.

[64]   See also the *UN Convention* art. 5, reproduced above.

[65]   See also the *UN Convention* art. 7, reproduced above.

Formerly, a waiver was only effective if it was made in the face of the court.[66] In the light of section 4(2)(a), however, it seems that a foreign state may waive its immunity before any proceedings are begun. Thus an appropriately worded jurisdiction clause in a contract with a foreign state should now suffice as a waiver of its immunity in any subsequent litigation about the agreement. Unfortunately, the statutory alteration of procedure in Canada is not as clear as in the U.K. *State Immunity Act 1978*, which expressly declares that a state may submit to the jurisdiction "by a prior written agreement."[67]

In waiving its immunity, a state gives up its rights and privileges by choice and so the courts are careful to ensure it has clearly and deliberately consented. The scope of the waiver when a foreign state sues and the defendant counterclaims is an instance of particular difficulty, as the following case shows.[68]

United States of America v. Friedland
(1999), 182 D.L.R. (4th) 614 (O.C.A.)

[The United States, through the Environmental Protection Agency (E.P.A.), sued Friedland in Colorado for environmental cleanup costs in the amount of $152,000,000. Having obtained an *ex parte* garnishment order against Friedland in Colorado, the United States used it to acquire an *ex parte* Mareva injunction in Ontario to inhibit Friedland from disposing of his INCO share certificates pending the outcome of the suit. The United States relied on affidavits sworn by Nancy Mangone, the lead E.P.A. lawyer, in one of which paragraph 81 stated, "The United States will undertake at the hearing on the motion herein ... to pay any damages assessed by this Court that Friedland may suffer should an injunction turn out to have been wrongly given or if the United States does not prevail on the merits." However, the order of Borins J. granting the Mareva injunction to the United States contained the undertaking to "abide by an Order this court may make as to damages in case this Court should hereafter determine that the Defendant has sustained damages by reason of this Order which the Plaintiff ought to pay." The Mareva injunction was subsequently dissolved and Friedland, instead of seeking an inquiry on the undertaking of the United States, filed a defence and a counterclaim for damages. The United States then brought a motion to dismiss Friedland's counterclaim on the basis of state immunity. The motions judge, Lederman J., dismissed the motion and the United States appealed.]

BY THE COURT: ...

[11] Section 4(2)(a) of the SIA creates an exception to the general principle of sovereign immunity where a foreign state waives its immunity. That section provides:

---

66   See *Mighell v. Sultan of Johore*, [1894] 1 Q.B. 149 (C.A.); *Duff Development Co.*, *supra* note 5; and *Kahan v. Pakistan Federation*, [1951] 2 K.B. 1003 (C.A.).

67   *Supra* note 57, s. 2(2). See E. Kwaw, "Sovereign Immunity and Jurisdiction Clauses in International Lending: The Canadian Perspective" (1995-96) 11 B.F.L.R. 27.

68   See also *Schreiber v. Canada (Attorney General)*, [2002] 3 S.C.R. 269.

4(2) In any proceedings before a court, a foreign state submits to the jurisdiction of the court where it

(a) Explicitly submits to the jurisdiction of the court by written agreement or otherwise either before or after the proceedings commence;

[12] Lederman J. found that the USA had explicitly submitted to the court's jurisdiction within the meaning of s. 4(2)(a). He held that the statement in para. 81 of the Mangone affidavit constituted an explicit waiver of immunity which was "not limited to the possibly narrow scope that a court, on an inquiry, may give to an undertaking as to damages" and which did not contain words of limitation that excluded tort claims. As such, Friedland could properly assert by way of counterclaim reasonable and viable claims extending from the natural meaning of the undertaking.

[13] The appellants submitted that Lederman J. erred in finding that the USA had explicitly submitted to the jurisdiction of the courts within the meaning of s. 4(2)(a) of the SIA. The argued that the exception in s. 4(2)(a) must be applied strictly; that the mere fact that the statement did not exclude tort claims is not sufficient to establish a waiver of immunity to tort claims and is, at most, a waiver of immunity to the court's jurisdiction to inquire under the undertaking; and that the Mangone affidavit does not constitute an undertaking but is, at best, merely confirmation that counsel for the USA had authority to provide an undertaking at a future hearing.

[14] In our view, this ground of appeal must succeed. On its plain language, the statement in para. 81 is a statement of intention to provide an undertaking in the future. The actual undertaking provided by the USA was that given pursuant to the Mareva injunction granted by Borins J. One must look to that undertaking to determine whether there was an explicit submission to the jurisdiction of the courts, and if so, the extent of the submission.

[15] The language of the undertaking in the order of Borins J. clearly constitutes an explicit submission to the jurisdiction of the courts. But any waiver of immunity must be clear and unequivocal; it cannot be presumed: [citing *Re Canada Labour Code*, reproduced in the next subsection]. Nothing in the language of the undertaking indicates that the scope of that submission extended to tort claims. By its wording, the submission is limited to the extent undertaken—*viz.*, a submission to the jurisdiction of the court to inquire under the undertaking—and goes no further. The undertaking does not constitute an explicit waiver for the purposes of Friedland's counterclaim within the meaning of s. 4(2)(a) of the SIA.

3. Sections 4(2) and (4) of the SIA

[16] Section 4(4) creates an exception to the general principle of sovereign immunity where a foreign state initiates or intervenes in any proceedings before a court. The relevant portions of s. 4 provide:

4(2) In any proceedings before a court, a foreign state submits to the jurisdiction of the court where it …

(a) initiates proceedings in the court; …

(4) A foreign state that initiates proceedings in a court or that intervenes or takes any step in proceedings before a court, other than an intervention or step to which

paragraph (2)(c) does not apply, submits to the jurisdiction of the court in respect of any third party proceedings that arise, or counter-claim that arises, out of the subject-matter of the proceedings initiated by the state or in which the state has so intervened or taken a step.

[17] Lederman J. held that the USA had waived its immunity within the meaning of s. 4(4) when it initiated *ex parte* proceedings seeking a Mareva injunction. He found that s. 4(4) was not simply a codification of the common law and that there was no requirement that a counterclaim against a foreign state be merely "defensive" in nature. He rejected the USA's argument that there was no claim left to which Friedland could respond, observing that "the action though barely alive, is 'still breathing' " and could properly serve as the basis for a counterclaim. He then considered the degree of nexus required between the counterclaim and the proceeding initiated by the foreign sovereign. Noting the lack of a clear statement of the degree of nexus required, he applied a "reasonable and contextual approach" and found that the claims asserted in Friedland's counterclaim had a sufficient nexus to the subject-matter of the proceeding.

[18] The appellants submitted that Lederman J. erred in finding that the USA implicitly waived its immunity within the meaning of s. 4(4). In our view, this ground of appeal must also succeed. The requirement in s. 4(4) that a counterclaim against a foreign sovereign arise "out of the subject-matter of the proceedings initiated by the state" indicates an intention to exclude counterclaims that are independent of the state's claim. At common law, the "subject-matter" requirement was understood as precluding counterclaims that were not merely defensive in nature ... . Thus, a defendant could raise any counterclaim that allowed him or her to answer the claim brought by the state, but could not raise any counterclaim that was outside or independent of the state's claim.

[19] Counsel for Friedland argued that s. 4(4) contains no words of limitation apart from the "subject-matter" requirement. He contrasted s. 4(4) with the equivalent provision in the U.S. and U.K. acts providing for sovereign immunity, which expressly limit the amount and kind of relief which may be sought, and noted that Parliament could have similarly limited s. 4(4) if it had wished to do so. We find this argument unpersuasive. The SIA was enacted in the context of common law principles governing sovereign immunity. One such principle was the subject-matter requirement for counterclaims against a foreign sovereign. Nothing in s. 4(4) indicates Parliament's intention to alter this common law "subject-matter" requirement. While the SIA contains no limitation respecting the amount and kind of relief that may be sought by way of counterclaim, the requirement that a counterclaim be defensive in nature is distinct from a limitation respecting the amount and kind of relief sought by way of counterclaim. As such, s. 4(4) must be understood as allowing a counterclaim against a foreign sovereign only to the extent that it allows the defendant to answer the claim initiated by the state.

[20] The Ontario proceeding was initiated by the USA by way of a statement of claim seeking an injunction restraining Friedland from dealing with $152,000,000 (U.S.) in INCO shares pending disposition of the CERCLA proceedings brought in Colorado. After the injunction was lifted by Sharpe J., Friedland filed a statement of

defence and counterclaim, seeking damages for conspiracy, abuse of process, libel, breach of disclosure duties, loss of business opportunity and damage to reputation. The counterclaim does not merely answer the claim brought by the USA; it asserts tort claims that are independent of the proceeding initiated by the USA. Friedland does not simply respond to the USA's claim; rather, he seeks damages for conduct that both preceded and followed the *ex parte* motion for a Mareva injunction. His counterclaim cannot be said to arise out of the subject-matter of the proceeding brought by the USA within the meaning of s. 4(4) of the SIA.

3. Commercial Activity Exception to Immunity

The most common situation in which a state loses its immunity from suit is when it has engaged in a commercial activity. In Canada the exception is expressed in the *State Immunity Act* section 5. The adoption of the restrictive theory requires the courts to distinguish between sovereign acts (*jure imperii*) and commercial acts (*jure gestionis*). Their decisions have not been consistent for the reason that it is extremely difficult to draw a line between public and commercial activities. It is an ironic paradox that the restrictive approach has been introduced in an attempt to cope with government intervention in commercial affairs, when such involvement is itself a deliberate act of state policy.

The two seemingly most popular yet contending tests to distinguish commercial activities are to enquire into the purpose of the transaction (a public act has a public object), or to scrutinize the nature of the action (a commercial deal is a commercial act whoever transacts it). In truth, a precise distinction may be impossible.[69] The problem persists after the passage of the *State Immunity Act* because the statutory definition of "commercial activity" in section 2 is so broad. The courts have had difficulty applying the definition, so it may be useful to seek further guidance from the UN Convention articles 2 and 10, reproduced above, and its *travaux préparatoires*, as well as from foreign cases and comparable legislation.

U.K. State Immunity Act 1978[70]
U.K. 1978, c. 33

1.(1) A State is immune from the jurisdiction of the courts of the United Kingdom except as provided in the following provisions of this Part of this Act. ...

3.(1) A State is not immune as respects proceedings relating to—

(a) a commercial transaction entered into by the State; or

(b) an obligation of the State which by virtue of a contract (whether a commercial transaction or not) falls to be performed wholly or partly in the United Kingdom.

---

69   See J. Crawford, "International Law and Foreign Sovereigns: Distinguishing Immune Transactions" (1983) 54 Br. Y.B. Int'l L. 75.

70   See C. Lewis, *State and Diplomatic Immunity*, 3d ed. (1990) and F.A. Mann, "The State Immunity Act 1978" (1979) 50 Br. Y.B. Int'l L. 43.

(2) This section does not apply if the parties to the dispute are States or have otherwise agreed in writing; and subsection (1)(b) above does not apply if the contract (not being a commercial transaction) was made in the territory of the State concerned and the obligation in question is governed by its administrative law.

(3) In this section "commercial transaction" means

(a) any contract for the supply of goods or services;

(b) any loan or other transaction for the provision of finance and any guarantee or indemnity in respect of any such transaction or of any other financial obligation; and

(c) any other transaction or activity (whether of a commercial, industrial, financial, professional or other similar character) into which a State enters or in which it engages otherwise than in the exercise of sovereign authority;

but neither paragraph of subsection (1) above applies to a contract of employment between a State and an individual.

U.S. Foreign Sovereign Immunities Act of 1976[71]
28 U.S.C. 1602-11; (1976) 15 I.L.M. 1388

Section 1603 Definitions

For the purposes of this chapter ...

(d) A "commercial activity" means either a regular course of commercial conduct or a particular commercial transaction or act. The commercial character of an activity shall be determined by reference to the nature of the course of conduct or particular transaction or act, rather than by reference to its purpose.

(e) A "commercial activity carried on in the United States by a foreign state" means commercial activity carried on by such state and having substantial contact with the United States.

Section 1604 Immunity of a Foreign State from Jurisdiction

Subject to existing international agreements to which the United States is a party at the time of enactment of this Act a foreign state shall be immune from the jurisdiction of the courts of the United States and of the States except as provided in sections 1605 to 1607 of this chapter.

Section 1605 General Exceptions to the Jurisdictional Immunity of a Foreign State

(a) A foreign state shall not be immune from the jurisdiction of courts of the United States or of the States in any case ...

(2) in which the action is based upon a commercial activity carried on in the United States by the foreign state; or upon an act performed in the United States in connection

---

[71] See R.B. von Mehren, "The Foreign Sovereign Immunity Act of 1976" (1978) 17 Colum. J. Transnat. L. 33; K.P. Simmons, "The Foreign Sovereign Immunity Act of 1976: Giving the Plaintiff His Day in Court" (1977-78) 46 Ford. L. Rev. 543; and a "Special Issue: The Foreign Sovereign Immunities Act Ten Years Later" (1986) 19 Vanderbilt J. Transnat. L. 1-179.

with a commercial activity of the foreign state elsewhere; or upon an act outside the territory of the United States in connection with a commercial activity of the foreign state elsewhere and that act causes a direct effect in the United States.

Trendtex Trading Corp. Ltd. v. Central Bank of Nigeria
[1977] 1 Q.B. 529 (C.A.)

[The plaintiff sold cement that was destined for Nigeria to the use of the government of the day in its many building projects. The Central Bank of Nigeria issued a letter of credit for the price of the cement. A very large number of similar contracts were also made. On becoming inundated with arriving shipments of cement, the succeeding Nigerian government had to take emergency action, which included ordering the Central Bank not to honour the letter of credit in this case. The plaintiff sued the Bank for payment.]

LORD DENNING M.R.: ... The Central Bank of Nigeria claim that they cannot be sued in this country on the letter of credit: because they are entitled to sovereign immunity. The plaintiff, Trendtex Trading Corporation, disputes this on the ground that this is an ordinary commercial transaction to which sovereign immunity does not apply. ...

The General Picture

The doctrine of sovereign immunity is based on international law. It is one of the rules of international law that a sovereign state should not be impleaded in the courts of another sovereign state against its will. Like all rules of international law, this rule is said to arise out of the consensus of the civilized nations of the world. All nations agree upon it. So it is part of the law of nations.

To my mind this notion of a consensus is a fiction. The nations are not in the least agreed upon the doctrine of sovereign immunity. The courts of every country differ in their application of it. Some grant absolute immunity. Others grant limited immunity, with each defining the limits differently. There is no consensus whatever. Yet this does not mean that there is no rule of international law upon the subject. It only means that we differ as to what that rule is. Each country delimits for itself the bounds of sovereign immunity. Each creates for itself the exceptions from it. It is, I think, for the courts of this country to define the rule as best they can, seeking guidance from the decisions of the courts of other countries, from the jurists who have studied the problem, from treaties and conventions and, above all, defining the rule in terms which are consonant with justice rather than adverse to it. ...

(i) *The doctrine of absolute immunity.* A century ago no sovereign state engaged in commercial activities. It kept to the traditional functions of a sovereign—to maintain law and order—to conduct foreign affairs—and to see to the defence of the country. It was in those days that England—with most other countries—adopted the rule of absolute immunity. It was adopted because it was considered to be the rule of international law at that time. In *The Parlement Belge* (1880), 5 P.D. 197, at 205, Brett L.J. said:

> The exemption of the person of every sovereign from adverse suit is admitted to be a part of the law of nations … [so also] of some property … The universal agreement which has made these propositions part of the law of nations has been an implied agreement.

The rule was stated by Dicey in his work on *Conflict of Laws*, and repeated religiously by the judges thereafter. The classic restatement of it was made by Lord Atkin in *Compania Naviera Vascongado v. S.S. Cristina (The Cristina)*, [1938] A.C. 485, at 490:

> The courts of a country will not implead a foreign sovereign, that is, they will not by their process make him against his will a party to legal proceedings whether the proceedings involve process against his person or seek to recover from him specific property or damages.

That doctrine was repeated by Viscount Simonds in *Rahimtoola v. Nizam of Hyderabad*, [1958] A.C. 379, at 394. He treated it as if it was a rule of English law, fixed and immutable, not to be departed from, even by the House of Lords itself.

(ii) *The doctrine of restrictive immunity*. In the last 50 years there has been a complete transformation in the functions of a sovereign state. Nearly every country now engages in commercial activities. It has its departments of state—or creates its own legal entities—which go into the market places of the world. They charter ships. They buy commodities. They issue letters of credit. This transformation has changed the rules of international law relating to sovereign immunity. Many countries have now departed from the rule of absolute immunity. So many have departed from it that it can no longer be considered a rule of international law. It has been replaced by a doctrine of restrictive immunity. This doctrine gives immunity to acts of a governmental nature, described in Latin as *jure imperii*, but no immunity to acts of a commercial nature, *jure gestionis*. In 1951 Sir Hersch Lauterpacht showed that, even at that date, many European countries had abandoned the doctrine of absolute immunity and adopted that of restrictive immunity—see his important article, "The Problem of Jurisdictional Immunities of Foreign States" in *The British Year Book of International Law, 1951*, vol. 28, at 220-272. Since that date there have been important conversions to the same view. Great impetus was given to it in 1952 in the famous "Tate letter" in the United States. Many countries have now adopted it. We have been given a valuable collection of recent decisions in which the courts of Belgium, Holland, the German Federal Republic, the United States of America and others have abandoned absolute immunity and granted only restrictive immunity. Most authoritative of all is the opinion of the Supreme Court of the United States in *Alfred Dunhill of London Inc. v. Republic of Cuba*. It was delivered on May 24, 1976, by White J. with the concurrence of the Chief Justice, Powell J. and Rehnquist J.:

> Although it had other views in years gone by, in 1952, as evidenced by … (the Tate letter) … the United States abandoned the absolute theory of sovereign immunity and embraced the restrictive view under which immunity in our courts should be granted only with respect to causes of action arising out of a foreign state's public or governmental actions and not with respect to those arising out of its commercial or proprietary actions. This has been the official policy of our government since that time,

as the attached letter of November 25, 1975, confirms ... "Such adjudications are consistent with international law on sovereign immunity."

To this I would add the European Convention on State Immunity (Basle, 1972), article 4, paragraph 1, which has been signed by most of the European countries.

[In the light of these changes, Lord Denning then adopted the restrictive approach to immunity.]

The Application to This Case

So I turn to see whether the transaction here was such as to attract sovereign immunity, or not. It was suggested that the original contracts for cement were made by the Ministry of Defence of Nigeria: and that the cement was for the building of barracks for the army. On this account it was said that the contracts of purchase were acts of a governmental nature, *jure imperii*, and not of a commercial nature, *jure gestionis*. They were like a contract of purchase of boots for the army. But I do not think this should affect the question of immunity. If a government department goes into the market places of the world and buys boots or cement—as a commercial transaction—that government department should be subject to all the rules of the market place. The seller is not concerned with the purpose to which the purchaser intends to put the goods.

There is another answer. Trendtex here are not suing on the contracts of purchase. They are claiming on the letter of credit which is an entirely separate contract. It was a straightforward commercial transaction. The letter of credit was issued in London through a London bank in the ordinary course of commercial dealings. It is completely within the territorial jurisdiction of our courts. I do not think it is open to the Government of Nigeria to claim sovereign immunity in respect of it. ...

Alter Ego or Organ of Government

If we are still bound to apply the doctrine of absolute immunity, there is, even so, an important question arising upon it. The doctrine grants immunity to a foreign government or its department of state, or any body which can be regarded as an "alter ego or organ" of the government. But how are we to discover whether a body is an "alter ego or organ" of the government?

The cases on this subject are difficult to follow, even in this country: let alone those in other countries. And yet, we have to find what is the rule of international law for all of them. It is particularly difficult because different countries have different ways of arranging internal affairs. In some countries the government departments conduct all their business through their own offices—even ordinary commercial dealings—without setting up separate corporations or legal entities. In other countries they set up separate corporations or legal entities which are under the complete control of the department, but which enter into commercial transactions, buying and selling goods, owning and chartering ships, just like any ordinary trading concern. This difference in internal arrangements ought not to affect the availability of immunity in international law. A foreign department of state ought not to lose its immunity simply because it conducts some of its activities by means of a separate legal entity. It was so held by this court in *Baccus S.R.L. v. Servicio Nacional Del Trigo*, [1957] 1 Q.B. 438.

Another problem arises because of the internal laws of many countries which grant immunities and privileges to its own organizations. Some organizations can sue, or be sued, in their courts. Others cannot. In England we have had for centuries special immunities and privileges for "the Crown"—a phrase which has been held to cover many governmental departments and many emanations of government departments—but not nationalized commercial undertakings: see *Tamlin v. Hannaford*, [1950] 1 K.B. 18. The phrase "the Crown" is so elastic that under the Crown Proceedings Act 1947 the Treasury have issued a list of government departments covered by the Act. It includes even the Forestry Commission. It cannot be right that international law should grant or refuse absolute immunity, according to the immunities granted internally. I would put on one side, therefore, our cases about the privileges, prerogatives and exceptions of the "Crown."

It is often said that a certificate by the ambassador, saying whether or not an organization is a department of state, is of much weight, though not decisive: see *Krajina v. Tass Agency*, [1949] 2 All E.R. 274. But even this is not to my mind satisfactory. What is the test which the ambassador is to apply? In the absence of any test, an ambassador may apply the test of control, asking himself: is the organization under the control of a minister of state? On such a test, he might certify any nationalized undertaking to be a department of state. He might certify that a press agency or an agricultural corporation (which carried out ordinary commercial dealings) was a department of state, simply because it was under the complete control of the government.

I confess that I can think of no satisfactory test except that of looking to the functions and control of the organization. I do not think that it should depend on the foreign law alone. I would look to all the evidence to see whether the organization was under government control and exercised governmental functions. ...

With these considerations in mind, I turn to our problem.

Central Bank of Nigeria

At the hearing we were taken through the Act of 1958 under which the Central Bank of Nigeria was established, and of the amendments to it by later decrees. All the relevant provisions were closely examined: and we had the benefit of expert evidence on affidavit which was most helpful. The upshot of it all may be summarized as follows. (i) The Central Bank of Nigeria is a central bank modelled on the Bank of England. (ii) It has governmental functions in that it issues legal tender; it safeguards the international value of the currency; and it acts as banker and financial adviser to the government. (iii) Its affairs are under a great deal of government control in that the Federal Executive Council may overrule the board on monetary and banking policy and on internal administrative policy. (iv) It acts as banker for other banks in Nigeria and abroad, and maintains accounts with other banks. It acts as banker for the states within the federation: but has few, if any, private customers.

In these circumstances I have found it difficult to decide whether or not the Central Bank of Nigeria should be considered in international law a department of the

Federation of Nigeria, even though it is a separate legal entity. But, on the whole, I do not think it should be.

This conclusion would be enough to decide the case, but I find it so difficult that I prefer to rest my decision on the ground that there is no immunity in respect of commercial transactions, even for a government department.

[Stephenson and Shaw L.JJ. concurred in separate opinions.]

Re Canada Labour Code
(United States of America v. Public Service Alliance of Canada)
[1992] 2 S.C.R. 50

[Sixty Canadian civilian employees on the U.S. naval base at Argentia, Newfoundland, sought union certification before the Canada Labour Relations Board. The Canadians were employed as firefighters and tradespeople to do maintenance work on the two-square-mile base, which supported anti-submarine warfare command and tactical forces through the operation of a high security communications centre. When maintenance was required in the communications centre, the Canadian employees had to have a special pass and a military escort, and the work area was sealed off. The United States claimed immunity from the certification proceedings pursuant to the *State Immunity Act* sections 2 and 5, but the Board held it had jurisdiction and the Federal Court of Appeal affirmed the decision.]

LaFOREST J. (L'Heureux-Dubé and Gonthier JJ. concurring): ... First, what is the "nature" of the activity in question—*i.e.*, does employment at the base constitute commercial activity? Second, are the proceedings in this case—a union certification application—"related" to that activity? The two questions are, of course, interrelated, and neither can be answered in absolute terms. Certain aspects of employment at the base are commercial, but in other respects the employment relationship is infused with sovereign attributes. Accordingly, the certification proceeding affects both the commercial and sovereign aspects of employment at the base. The issue then becomes whether the effect on the commercial realm is sufficiently strong as to form a "nexus" so that it can truly be said that the proceedings "relate" to commercial activity. In my view, a nexus exists only between the certification proceedings and the *sovereign* attributes of labour relations at the base. The effect on commercial activity is merely incidental, and cannot trigger the application of s. 5 of the *State Immunity Act*.

In the courts below and on the hearing of this appeal, considerable importance was attached to the distinction between the nature of the employment relationship (a valid consideration under the statute) and the purpose of that relationship (purportedly an invalid consideration). I find it difficult if not impossible to distinguish in a principled manner between the nature and purpose of employment relationships, and I would thus decline to follow this approach. Nature and purpose are interrelated, and it is impossible to determine the former without considering the latter. I do not accept that the definition of "commercial activity" in the Act precludes consideration of its purpose. That definition, in circuitous fashion, defines "commercial activity" as conduct that "by reason of its nature is of a commercial character." In many cases, it may be unnecessary to delve into metaphysical distinctions between the ontology and teleology of the activity in question. However, if consideration of purpose is helpful in determining the nature of an activity, then such considerations should be and are allowed under the Act. Further, when an activity is multifaceted in nature (as in the instant case) consideration of its purpose will assist in determining which facets are truly "related" to the proceedings in issue. ...

The Nature of the Activity

In determining the nature of the activity in question, it is useful to begin by acknowledging that employment at a military base is a multi-faceted relationship. It is simply not valid to isolate one aspect of this activity and label it as either "sovereign" or "commercial" in nature. A better approach is to determine which aspects of the activity are relevant to the proceedings in issue, and then to assess the impact of the proceedings on these attributes as a whole.

The United States argues that the work performed by the Canadian civilian personnel is an integral and indispensable part of its stated defence mission and that it takes place within the context of an international agreement—the Lease—which gives the United States the right of management and control over the base. The Board, on the other hand, argues that this Court should only consider the threshold nature of the activity, namely a contract of employment, and ignore its context or purpose. PSAC is prepared to go a little further and characterizes the relevant activity as employment to provide maintenance services to a military base in return for remuneration. The Canadian personnel involved are essentially tradesmen who "fix water pipes, run boilers, perform new construction, and generally maintain the physical buildings on the base." The nature of the contract of employment is similar to an employment contract in the private sector, because the employees are using the same trade skills as they would use in the employ of a private contractor.

One aspect of employment at the base is this bare contract of service entered into by each employee. This aspect carries with it a range of rights and obligations that normally attach to such a contract. For the employee, these include the right to be paid, the right not to be wrongfully terminated, etc. Obligations of the employee include diligence, obedience and honesty. These attributes of the employment relationship will fall at various points along a spectrum between purely "sovereign" and "commercial" activities. For example, the right to be paid is for the most part a commercial aspect of the employment relationship. On the other hand, the right to dismiss an employee without notice for security reasons is a sovereign attribute of the relationship.

Another aspect of the employment relationship is the structuring of work at the base. This entails decisions about what work will be done, when and by whom. Traditionally, decisions regarding this aspect of employment are reserved for management—in this case, the base commander. This aspect of the employment relationship will, in most instances, be "sovereign" in character since it goes to the heart of the operation of the base.

It is impossible to ignore the sovereign purpose of this latter aspect of the employment relationship. Argentia is a military post, conceived in times of war as an air and naval base. In peacetime it has served as a highly sensitive communications and surveillance post. In another war the base could play a crucial role in American military activities in the North Atlantic. I can think of no activity of a foreign state that is more inherently sovereign than the operation of such a base. As such, the United States government must be granted the unfettered authority to manage and control employment activity at the base. ...

In the result, the "activity" at Argentia has a double aspect. It is at once sovereign and commercial. The question becomes, do the certification proceedings "relate" to the commercial aspect of this activity? To this issue I now turn.

Relationship between the Certification Proceedings and the Employment Activity

Section 5 of the *State Immunity Act* requires that the proceedings in question *relate* to the activity at issue. For me, it is not enough that the proceedings merely "touch on" or "incidentally affect" the hiring of civilian labour at the base. Acceptance of such a minimal requirement would broaden the "commercial activity" exception to the point of depriving sovereign immunity of any meaning. Such an approach is equivalent to the "once a trader, always a trader" approach rejected by Lord Wilberforce in *1º Congreso* [*del Partido*, [1983] A.C. 244 (H.L.)]. Instead, the entire context of the activity at Argentia must be considered. In this regard, it is not enough to take the employment contracts in isolation, and decide that bargaining unit certification proceedings will have some bearing on these contracts. A more substantial connection is needed. Of relevance is the competing nexus between the proceedings and the sovereign aspects of the employment activity at the base. Also of importance is the breadth of scope of the proceedings of the Board ... Finally, at this stage of the analysis, it will again be useful to consider the purpose of the activity in question. ...

What the Board is seeking to do is assert its jurisdiction and regulatory control over labour relations on the base, and I agree with counsel for the Attorney General of Canada that there is too tenuous a connection between the U.S. Navy's entering the local labour market for the purpose of hiring individual employees, and non-consensual labour management relations imposed under the *Canada Labour Code*, to create the requisite nexus for commercial activity to be brought into play in this case.

I also agree with the Attorney General of Canada that the objective of the Board's proceedings is the imposition of collective bargaining by the Canadian state, and under the control of a Canadian court. The nexus between this objective and the management of the base constitutes an unacceptable interference with American sovereignty. This is more than just a theoretical concern, as becomes apparent upon consideration of the consequences of submission to the Board's jurisdiction.

Collective bargaining carries with it the right of employees to strike to enforce their contract demands. A strike at the Argentia base would, at a minimum, disrupt its military mission. It is true that the employees' services are not directly required to achieve this mission. However, the indirect effect of the loss of 60 full-time employees cannot be lightly dismissed. I am not prepared to concede that a boiler plant operator or an engineer at the base does not contribute in some important way to the successful operation of the base. In oral argument, PSAC submitted that the military could fly in additional military personnel to replace the striking workers. This may be a feasible solution in peacetime, but in a war every day of down time at the base would be critical. Simply put, the United States is entitled to absolute control of the base and so over the availability of its labour force, particularly in times of war. At all events, it can hardly be said not to interfere seriously with the control of the base, which is expressly conferred upon the United States by the Lease. ...

PSAC argued that the presence of a union must not be a real threat to the military mission of the base, because the base commander had agreed to bargain collectively in the 1982 Memorandum of Understanding. However, it is not the presence of a union or the process of collective bargaining *per se* to which the U.S. Navy objects. Rather, it is the required submission to a foreign labour tribunal and to a foreign labour relations regime that is the problem. The U.S. Navy's concerns are legitimate. Collective bargaining under the Memorandum was acceptable because it would be governed by American legislation. As such, ultimate control over the labour force would remain with the United States. If, for example, a strike occurred during wartime, the United States could pass legislation requiring the employees to return to work. If instead the *Canada Labour Code* is to govern the relationship, then the United States would be powerless to compel the Argentia employees to end a strike. This is the reason that comparisons between the Argentia employees and civilian workers at Canadian military bases are misleading. While the latter have the right to strike, Parliament can pass legislation to force these workers back to their jobs in times of national crisis. Such an option would not be available to American legislators with regard to Argentia, if the *Canada Labour Code* were to govern.

Beyond the possibility of a strike, collective bargaining curtails the U.S. Navy's control of the base in many other ways. The Board's mandate under the *Canada Labour Code* allows it to intrude in a variety of ways into internal base affairs. The Board can impose terms in a collective agreement, reinstate employees and rescind disciplinary actions taken by the Base commander; it could order the military to provide information on its operations, and it has a broad right of inquiry into those operations. In my view, these would be unacceptable intrusions into the sovereign realm of the Argentia base.

Case law in other jurisdictions has recognized an immunity for foreign instrumentalities from domestic labour relations tribunals. ...

[LaForest J. referred to *Libyan Arab Jamahiriya v. Trobbiani* (1990), 73 Riv. Dir. Int. 403 (Italy), in which the court declined jurisdiction to hear a Libyan embassy employee's wage classification claim because it would have required an inquiry into the organizational activities of the foreign embassy. He also quoted the case of *Italian Trade Union for Embassy and Consular Staff v. United States* (1981) 65 I.L.R. 338 (Italy) in which the court refrained from considering a claim of anti-union activity brought against an American consulate because to have intervened, and especially to have made an order, would have infringed on the foreign state's power to organize its own offices and act *jure imperii*.]

In the United States, only the case of *Goethe House New York, German Cultural Center v. N.L.R.B.* [(1988), 685 F.Supp. 427, rev'd. 869 F.2d 75] deals directly with labour relations at a non-commercial instrumentality of a foreign state. ... In *Goethe House*, the West German government petitioned for a preliminary injunction enjoining the National Labour Relations Board from processing a representation application on behalf of non-German employees at a non-profit cultural centre sponsored by the Foreign Office of the Federal Republic of Germany. In the District Court, Owen J. granted the injunction, ruling that the cultural centre could claim sovereign immunity from the jurisdiction of the N.L.R.B. In so doing, he distinguished certification proceedings from a simple action in contract damages, the former constituting intervention "into the underlying employment structure of a conceded arm of a foreign state that is not involved in commercial activity" (at p. 430).

A majority of the Court of Appeals overturned this decision, ruling that the petition was premature. The Court of Appeals, in *obiter*, expressed doubt over the ultimate success of the immunity claim, at p. 79:

> To justify its assertion of jurisdiction, the district court wrote that requiring Goethe House to submit to N.L.R.B. jurisdiction might interfere with the West German government's "employment objectives in implementing cultural foreign policy" and might cause disturbances and embarrassment in international relations. In our view, the district court's concerns were largely unfounded and did not warrant the court's intervention in the case. Even if the Union were certified as the bargaining agent of Goethe House's non-German employees, we fail to see how the presence of the Union would interfere with Goethe House's implementation of West German cultural foreign policy. Under the N.L.R.A., Goethe House would have a duty to bargain with the Union over wages, hours and other terms and conditions of employment, ... Goethe House would have no duty to bargain over how it performed its mission of promoting German culture. ... Moreover, the fact that the German employees at Goethe House presently are unionized belies the prospect that the presence of a union for the non-German employees would hamper Goethe House's operations.

In dissent, Lumbard J. took a different view of the impact of the Board's assertion of jurisdiction, at p. 81:

> The Board has not brought to our attention any case in which any United States agency has successfully asserted its jurisdiction over Goethe House or any similar establishment of a foreign government that engages in what so patently are foreign relations activities. I find it inappropriate to force so indelicate a result in this case, with its extensive foreign relations ramifications. ...
>
> The Board's proposition that the mere hiring of seven non-German employees (among up to 40 German employees) itself manifests commercial activity is not persuasive. It strains logic to suggest that any time a foreign sovereign employs a messenger, a bookkeeper or a custodian, it becomes thereby a commercial enterprise and is subject to the jurisdiction of American administrative agencies.

I am not persuaded by the reasoning of the majority of the Court of Appeals in *Goethe House*, nor am I convinced of the factual comparability of a cultural centre to a military base. The majority decision reasons that the presence of a union would not interfere with the successful completion of the cultural centre's mission. I disagree on two counts. First, it is not the presence of a union, *per se*, nor collective bargaining by workers, that is in issue. I note that the Argentia base was willing to bargain with PSAC, and entered into an agreement to that effect. What the base objects to is subjection to the jurisdiction of a domestic court. The majority decision in *Goethe House* fails to appreciate this distinction. If the only effect of union certification proceedings was, as the majority suggests, a duty to bargain over terms of employment, then I would agree with the result in *Goethe House*. However, as we have seen, the impact is much greater.

The factual distinction between a cultural centre and a military base must also be emphasized. Again, this is a matter of comparing the sovereign purposes of these two institutions. It may be that the sovereign mission of a cultural centre would not be impaired by subjection to a foreign labour relations regime. I note that the mission of the cultural centre was described in the NLRB decision as "like those of a library and also similar to a foundation or educational institution contributing to the cultural and educational values of the community." However, a military base is of a completely different order. As we have seen, the current mission of the Argentia base is to collect military data in an environment of secrecy, discipline and security. A library may succeed despite the imposition of collective bargaining by a foreign state; a military base may not.

In short, *Goethe House* must be viewed in its factual context. The case does not stand for the broad proposition that domestic employees of all foreign entities operating the United States will be entitled to the protection of American labour relations legislation. Moreover, the case certainly does not suggest that American courts would refuse to recognize the immunity of a Canadian embassy based in the United States. I thus do not agree with the view of my colleague, Justice Cory, that courts of the United States would consider labour relations on a foreign military base to constitute a mere commercial activity. ...

Although the contracts of employment at the Argentia base might (in the loosest sense of the word) be "related" to the certification proceedings, in that they serve as a condition precedent to the certification application, they do not lie at the heart of the matter. Rather, the application seeks to supplant the private contractual relationship between the employees and employer with a statutory scheme of collective bargaining which by definition regulates the management of the base. The union certification procedure relates most obviously and directly to the sovereign attributes of a foreign state, which must remain immune from such proceedings.

CORY J. (Sopinka J. concurring) dissenting: ... The Canadian definition of commercial activity differs from the American in that it does not explicitly bar a consideration of the purpose of an activity as does the American statute. Nonetheless, the CLRB and the Federal Court of Appeal both found that a bar against the consideration of the purpose of an activity was implicit in the Canadian version although not explicit. I cannot accept that conclusion. The material shows that the drafters of the Canadian Act were aware of the particular wording of the American legislation. I would infer that they departed from it intentionally. By not prohibiting the consideration of the purpose of an activity, the drafters avoided an overly narrow interpretation of the definition. ...

How then should the Canadian definition be construed? Clearly, it places paramount importance on the nature of the activity. To identify this "nature" or quality of an activity, a Court should have regard to the context in which the activity took place. In order to do that, it will often be necessary to consider the immediate purpose of the actions taken by the foreign state. This approach fosters the goal of reasonably restricting state immunity. It does so by looking beyond the ultimate purpose of the foreign state's action, which will almost always be public, while continuing to protect by immunity the truly sovereign acts of states from domestic court proceedings. It does not unduly restrict the courts in classifying an activity according to its nature by unnecessarily narrowing the scope of the inquiry. This contextual approach complies with the definition of commercial activity contained in the Canadian statute by retaining the nature of the activity as the focus of the decision. On the other hand, it avoids the problems caused by attempting to treat the nature and purpose of an activity as completely separate and discrete inquiries.

Application to the Case at Bar

The United States claims immunity from the certification of a union by the CLRB. The issue as to whether or not the U.S. is entitled to immunity depends, in this context, on the answer to two questions. (1) What is the task for which the workers were hired? (2) Is the activity of hiring a person to perform that task one in which a private party could engage?

What was the task for which the workers were hired? The certification process was invoked by employees who worked as firefighters, plumbers and mechanics on the base. These are support workers for the military personnel. The U.S. Navy required that these workers obtain security passes in order to enter the base. The essential military activity is carried out in the communications buildings. The ordinary security pass, which maintenance workers require to enter the base, is not sufficient to gain access to the communication building. The security regime set up for entrance to the communications building makes it clear that not only are the workers not privy to any sensitive information, but also that the U.S. Navy does not regard them as secure personnel.

The United States argues that the essential task of the base is national defence. As a result, it is said that the hiring of workers for the base falls within the scope of public acts of sovereign states. I cannot accept that contention. A state may not rely on the ultimate purpose of an activity to qualify its acts. Here the employees serve merely as support staff. In carrying out their tasks they often work alongside the employees of local private contractors who are engaged to carry out maintenance work at the base. Apart from their support role, they serve no purpose that is critical to the operation of the communications centre. It would offend common sense to characterize the direct employment of workers by a state as a public act, when that same work is on occasion performed by workers hired by, and working for, a private sub-contractor called in to perform the task.

Is the hiring of workers as support staff an activity in which a private person could engage? The employment of maintenance workers with very restricted access to a secure site is certainly an activity in which private parties could engage. The hiring of these workers, therefore, must fall into the category of a private act which by its nature is a commercial activity.

Even If a Contract of Employment Relationship Is Characterized as a Private Act, Can a Collective Bargaining Relationship Be Characterized in the Same Way?

The intervener, the Attorney General of Canada, contended that a distinction should be drawn between individual contracts of employment and certification proceedings which initiate a collective bargaining relationship. It was argued that even if the contract of employment relationship could be considered to be a private act, falling within the category of a commercial transaction, the collective bargaining relationship is not. A collective bargaining relationship, it was said, would affect the management of a sovereign state's undertaking. Further, it is a relationship that was legally distinct from the common law relationship of employment. I cannot agree. ...

The view that entry into a collective bargaining relationship differs in some significant way from an individual contract of employment perhaps arises from an underlying concern that once the Board certifies a union, it would have broad authority to supervise labour-management relations at the base. The appellant raised the prospect of potential strike action by Canadian civilian employees which might disrupt the operation of the base. In response, the union observed that the U.S. Navy would have the option of bringing in replacement workers in such an event. It must be remembered that there is no bar to the hiring of replacement workers in the *Canada Labour Code*. As well, it can be, I think, readily assumed that the vast military organization of the United States has easy access to replacement employees.

No doubt, as a result of certification the CLRB will have other powers including the hearing of grievances. However, this cannot be of any real concern to the respondent since the U.S. Navy was readily prepared to accept an American collective bargaining regime operating under the applicable American statute. Thus the U.S. government has demonstrated that it is not adverse to the certification of a union in general terms and that it is prepared to accept the consequences which arise from certification. Rather, the U.S. government claims state immunity from the processes of a Canadian tribunal. That claim must be rejected. The act of hiring support service employees was one which a private person could undertake. It was in the nature of a commercial activity. Once it has been demonstrated that a foreign state does not fall within the ambit of immunity protected by the Canadian statute it should not receive any special dispensation from Canadian law. A Canadian worker, working on Canadian soil, should not be deprived of the benefits of Canadian law unless the foreign state is acting in a context which warrants immunity.

Notably, American courts have held that a foreign state is not entitled to immunity from the proceedings of the National Labour Relations Board when the actions of that state fall within the legislated definition of commercial activity. See, for example, *State Bank of India v. N.L.R.B.*, 808 F.2d 526 (1986), at p. 535. Similarly, in *Goethe House New York, German Cultural Center v. N.L.R.B.*, 869 F.2d 75 (1989), cert. denied 110 S. Ct. 52 (1989), the Court of Appeals considered *in obiter* the effect of certifying a union in the workplace of a foreign state. Pierce J.A. observed that the presence of a union would not have any impact on the state function of implementing German cultural policy. It would merely impose duties on the German government to bargain over conditions of employment for its non-German staff. Similarly, in the case at bar the certification of maintenance workers will not compromise the security of the surveillance functions of the base.

In summary, state immunity only exists with respect to court proceedings. There is no principle of state immunity which exempts a foreign government from the application of Canadian laws when the questioned actions are commercial in nature, as defined by the *State Immunity Act*. The U.S.A. cannot claim immunity from the jurisdiction of the CLRB. There is no valid reason, disclosed by the facts of this case, why Canadians working in Canada should not have the benefit and protection of Canadian law. Particularly is this so when it is apparent that Americans working in the United States for a foreign state would, in similar circumstances, have the benefit of American law.

NOTES

1) Notice how the majority and dissenting opinions both concluded that the U.S. claim to immunity in this case turned on the nature of the action involved *and* that the definition of "commercial activity" in the *State Immunity Act* section 2, reproduced above, though referring to its nature, does not exclude its purpose. However, LaForest J. and Cory J. each said the issue of state immunity depended on the answers to two questions. Were those questions the same for both judges?

2) To what extent did their answers to their own questions reflect the viewpoint of the U.S. government or the Canadian workers? Which side's view should a state immunity decision respect?

3) Before a characterization as commercial can be made, the activity in question must be identified. In answering their own questions, what did the judges consider to be the relevant activities in this case? Did they justify their identification of the activities to be considered? How much did this identification affect each judge's decision?[72]

4) Many activities of governments and their agents have a double aspect—they are at once both commercial and sovereign in nature. The problem for the courts is not so much how to distinguish in the abstract between the two, but, as LaForest J. and Cory J. demonstrated by their disagreement, how to weigh the relative importance of each contributing element in the activity in issue. In *Butcher v. Saint Lucia*[73] Aitken J. considered LaForest J.'s majority judgment as follows:

15. In regard to the question of how the proceedings relate to the activity in question, LaForest J. cautioned that it is not enough for the proceedings to merely "touch on" or "incidentally affect" the commercial aspect of the activity for the commercial exception

---

72   For a commentary on the case see R. Hornby, "State Immunity Re Canada Labour Code: A Common Sense Solution to the Commercial Activity Exception" (1992) 30 Can. Y.B. Int'l L. 301.

73   (1998), 21 C.P.C. (4th) 236 (O.C.J.).

under the *State Immunity Act* to be triggered. Rather an analysis is required as to where the stronger connection or the real nexus lies between the proceedings and the activity. If the greatest impact of the proceedings is on the sovereign aspect of the activity, then the commercial activity exception under the Act is inapplicable. LaForest J. decided that the most significant impact of the certification proceedings in *Canada Labour Code, Re* was on the management and operation of the base, and not on the individual employment contracts between the U.S. Government and the civilian employees. He found that the objective of the certification proceedings was the imposition of collective bargaining under Canadian legislation and under the purview of Canadian courts on the management of an American military base, something that was "an unacceptable interference with American sovereignty."

In *Butcher*'s case, the government of Saint Lucia offered him the position of Consul General to Canada but shortly afterward suspended the appointment as a result of negative media coverage around his criminal conviction in Canada. Butcher instituted proceedings against the Prime Minister of Saint Lucia for breach of their agreement, but Saint Lucia claimed state immunity under the *State Immunity Act* section 5. In the light of his view of the approach to section 5 taken by LaForest J. in *Re Canada Labour Code*, Aitken J. had no difficulty in upholding Saint Lucia's right to immunity:

> 16. Retaining the services of the plaintiff to act as its Consul General in Toronto was an activity by the Government of Saint Lucia which had both a commercial and a sovereign aspect. The act of entering a contract for the provision of identified services over a fixed period of time with stipulated compensation is commercial in nature. However, the appointment of a Consul General to establish a Consulate for Saint Lucia in Toronto, to be Saint Lucia's principal representative in Toronto and to be responsible for carrying on all normal Consular activities in Toronto is an activity of a sovereign nature. The significance of this aspect of the activity far outweighs in importance the commercial aspect of the activity. ...

> 19. The Government of Saint Lucia should not have to justify to a Canadian court how it makes its decisions regarding the appointment of its representatives, such as consuls, or how it decides to suspend the services of anyone in such a position.

5) What legal value are references to English and American statutes and precedents in a Canadian case under the *State Immunity Act*? How did the judges in *Re Canada Labour Code* employ the U.S. precedent in the *Goethe House* case cited within it? Would the definition of "commercial transaction" in the Draft UN Convention article 2(c), reproduced above, have been of any assistance?

6) It seems, following *Re Canada Labour Code* and *Butcher v. Saint Lucia*, that Canadian courts will read the purpose of a state's actions quite broadly in determining the nature of its activities. If so, the effect will be to restrict the commercial exception to state immunity. Is this what the restrictive theory of immunity means or what the Canadian Parliament intended?

7) In *Congo v. Venne*,[74] prior to the *State Immunity Act*, the Congo successfully claimed immunity from a suit by M. Venne for unpaid architectural services. He had

---

74   *Supra* note 52.

prepared studies for a national pavilion for the Congo at Expo '67 in Montreal. Should the case be decided the same way under the Act?

8) How should construction work on an ambassador's residence be regarded? Should it attract immunity under the *State Immunity Act*?[75]

9) The particular issue in *Trendtex* about the status and immunity of a national central bank is now governed expressly in Canada by the *State Immunity Act* sections 12(4) and (5). Do these provisions resolve all the problems posed by a central bank that engages in both government and private banking?[76] Do the UN Convention articles 19(c) and 21(1)(c) provide a satisfactory solution?

10) In *1º Congreso del Partido*,[77] a Cuban state trading enterprise was delivering a cargo of sugar aboard a Cuban state-owned vessel to a Chilean company. While discharging in Valparaiso, Chile, a revolution occurred in which the socialist government of Allende was replaced by the right-wing regime of Pinochet. The Cuban government so strongly disapproved that it ordered the Cuban ship to stop delivery and leave Chile. When the Chilean buyers brought an action to recover the cargo of sugar or its value, Cuba claimed immunity from suit. This leading House of Lords case sharply exposes the difficulties in characterizing a state's actions. Obviously, the sale and delivery of sugar is a commercial transaction but was that the critical activity in the case? How should one regard the order of the Cuban government to stop the delivery? Cuba claimed that the breach of the sugar contract was the result of a foreign policy decision. What acts should the court focus on? Is the broken transaction divisible into several parts, or should it be treated all as one? Lord Wilberforce eventually denied the claim to immunity because he judged that everything done by Cuba in performing and breaking the contract was done as a shipowner, and not as an exercise of sovereign powers. Should the case be decided the same way under the Canadian *State Immunity Act*?

11) There has been much argument about the characterization of an act according to its nature and/or its purpose. As Lord Denning pointed out in *Trendtex*, state practice, both legislative and judicial, has been quite varied. Much of that diversity may stem from the fact that the attempted distinction between the nature and the purpose of an act is unreal. As the Australian Law Reform Commission has commented:

> It is not possible to classify the nature of any human activity without reference to its purpose. The nature of an activity is not some abstract idea (certainly not for legal purposes), but rather the focused, or relevant, or "central" purpose (according to some criterion). The classifications "governmental" and "commercial" are themselves purposive.[78]

---

75   Cf. *Claim against the Empire of Iran* (1963), 45 I.L.R. 57 (Ger.) and *Planmount Ltd. v. Republic of Zaire*, [1981] 1 All E.R. 1110 (Q.B.).

76   See D. Asiedu-Akrofi, "Central Bank Immunity and the Inadequacy of the Restrictive Immunity Approach" (1990) 28 Can. Y.B. Int'l L. 261.

77   [1983] 1 A.C. 244 (H.L.). And see H. Fox, "State Immunity: The House of Lords' Decision in *1º Congreso del Partido*" (1982) 98 L.Q.R. 94.

78   *Supra* note 50 at 28. Under the Canadian Act s. 5 it is sufficient if the suit relates to any commercial activity of the foreign state. Thus a personal injury action by an employee against a foreign commercial state agency may be brought. See *Ferguson v. Arctic Transport Ltd.*, [1995] 3 F.C. 656.

The difficulty in discriminating between different kinds of acts is compounded by the fact that the ambit of commercial activities has never been agreed. There is no international consensus on the limits of governmental involvement in trade and commerce. Some countries maintain relatively free market economies while others pursue distinctly interventionist economic policies. A few countries operate totally state-directed economic systems. Moreover, the term "commercial," as a single criterion for characterizing state acts that are not immune, is an overworked concept. As the Australian Law Reform Commission has also stated in connection with "commercial":

> It is too narrow in its coverage, since there are many relatively routine acts which are neither distinctive to states (i.e. "governmental") nor, in the absence of some special feature, commercial. And particular acts may be at the same time "commercial" and "governmental" (e.g. the letting of a contract for major public works), or they may have "commercial" and "governmental" elements inextricably mixed (e.g. an embassy car may be driving a diplomat to a meeting and the diplomat's spouse to a shopping centre). The problem of inextricably mixed activities is particularly acute in the area of execution of judgments against mixed funds. And finally, even when an act is itself apparently "governmental" (by whatever criteria) the aspect of the act which causes damage may have nothing in particular to do with its governmental character. For example, a car driving a diplomat to a meeting may simply be involved in an accident.[79]

12) The overburdened category of "commercial activity" may be relieved by breaking down the circumstances in which immunity is denied into a number of discrete situations, each specifically defined and regulated. This has been done to a limited extent by the *State Immunity Act*: see sections 6, 7, and 8. A much longer list of acts and events for which a state has no immunity is set down in the U.K. statute and the UN Convention.

13) The immunities granted by the Act may be lifted by the Governor in Council under section 15 for any state that does not accord Canada reciprocal equivalent immunities. This power has been exercised against the United States. Since the United States does not accord immunity to foreign state agencies unless the foreign government has majority ownership of it, Canada has restricted the immunity of American governmental agencies on similar terms.[80]

4. Personal Injury Exception to Immunity

In addition to losing its immunity from suit when it engages in commercial activity in Canada, a foreign state may also be subjected to the jurisdiction of the courts in proceedings involving death, personal or bodily injury, or damage or loss of property: see the *State Immunity Act* section 6. The phrasing of this exception has presented some difficulty in determining the scope of personal injuries that are intended to be protected. Do they include mental distress and loss of liberty consequent upon arrest and detention as asserted by Karlheinz Schreiber in the case reproduced below? Further, might the

[79]   *Ibid.* at 27.
[80]   See SOR/97-121.

exception be an avenue for the protection of international human rights? Could a victim of torture or other physical abuse at the instance of a foreign state bring a suit in Canada, as Houshang Bouzari attempted to do in the case reproduced after *Schreiber*?

Schreiber v. Canada (Attorney General)
[2002] 3 S.C.R. 269

[Germany requested Canada to arrest and extradite Schreiber to answer criminal charges of tax evasion. Schreiber was detained in jail for eight days before being released on bail. He then sued Germany for damages for personal injuries suffered through his arrest and detention. Germany claimed state immunity from this suit.]

LEBEL J.: ...

[28] The appellant submits that the mental distress, denial of liberty and damage to reputation he suffered due to his wrongful arrest and imprisonment was a "personal injury" under the exception in s. 6(a) of the *State Immunity Act*, and that it therefore limits Germany's immunity. ...

2. *Whether Wrongful Arrest and Imprisonment Constitute "Personal Injury"*

[38] The main issue raised by the appellant is whether the Court of Appeal for Ontario erred in holding that the term "personal injury" in s. 6(a) of the *State Immunity Act* applies only to claims of physical injury, and does not apply to wrongful arrest and imprisonment. The decision from the Court of Appeal followed its earlier decision in *Friedland* [reproduced in subsection 12 above], which was under appeal in this Court at the time *Schreiber* was being heard in the Court of Appeal. It should be noted that the appeal in *Friedland* was subsequently discontinued: [2001] 2 S.C.R. ix. Doherty J.A. found that the *Friedland* case was dispositive of the appellant's submission that his claim fell within the s. 6(a) exemption to state immunity and found no basis for departing from this earlier decision.

[39] The appellant argues that the Court of Appeal for Ontario has rendered conflicting judgements on the meaning of "personal injury" in s. 6(a) of the *State Immunity Act*. In *Walker* [(1994), 16 O.R. (3d) 504], McKinlay J.A. of the Court of Appeal for Ontario wrote at p. 510 that:

> We agree with the position of counsel for the respondent that the scope of personal injury covered by s. 6 is not merely physical, but could include mental distress, emotional upset, and restriction of liberty. However, we do not accept his position that the alleged injuries in this case occurred in Canada, as required by s. 6.

On the other hand, in *Friedland, supra,* the same court stated at para. 25 that:

> In our view, s. 6(a) does not assist Friedland. The *obiter* statement of McKinlay J.A. in *Walker,* at p. 510, that "the scope of personal injury covered by s. 6 ... could include mental distress, emotional upset, and restriction of liberty" does not mean that s. 6 extends to mental distress or emotional upset in all cases. Otherwise, a party could

invoke s. 6(a) merely by claiming damages for alleged mental distress or emotional upset, an interpretation that would expand the exception far beyond its intended scope and render the doctrine of sovereign immunity ineffective. *We agree with counsel for the appellants that the "personal injury" exception refers primarily to physical injury that s. 6(a) extends to mental distress and emotional upset only insofar as such harm arises from or is linked to a physical injury.* This interpretation is consistent with the generally accepted international understanding of the "personal injury" exception to sovereign immunity. [Emphasis added.]

[40] According to the appellant, Canadian law recognizes that imprisonment is an injury to the person. In criminal law, wrongful imprisonment is regarded as a serious offence. In tort law, false imprisonment is actionable. In constitutional law, imprisonment is recognized as a deprivation of a person's s. 7 Charter right to liberty. While imprisoned, a person's freedom of movement is restricted and his or her privacy violated. The appellant submits that Canadian law also recognizes that the suffering of mental distress and damage to his reputation are injuries to a person. As such, he concludes that clear wording in s. 6(a) would be required to offset the recognition that the causing of mental distress and injury to reputation through wrongful imprisonment are injuries to the person. Since s. 6(a) has no such clear wording, mental distress and injury to reputation through wrongful imprisonment must be included in the exception to foreign state immunity in s. 6(a).

[41] The respondents counter that the appellant did not suffer personal injury within the meaning of s. 6(a). They submit that the only "injury" suffered by the appellant was a lawful, peaceful arrest, which, they assert, was made pursuant to a purported error of law. In their view, such an error of law cannot be "personal injury" for the purposes of s. 6(a).

[42] I agree with the submission of the respondent Germany that *Friedland* established that the scope of the exception in s. 6(a) is limited to instances where mental distress and emotional upset were linked to a physical injury. For example, psychological distress may fall within the exception where such distress is manifested physically, such as in the case of nervous shock. It seems clear that McKinlay J.A.'s statement in *Walker* was made in *obiter* and that such finding had no bearing on the case before that court. I further agree that Doherty J.A. was correct when he chose to rely on *Friedland* in reaching his decision to dismiss the appellant's appeal as it seems consistent with the position taken in academic writings and international law sources. ...

(c) Application of International Human Rights Law

[48] In support of a broad interpretation of the personal injury exception, the intervener Amnesty International advanced the proposition that the right to the protection of mental integrity and to compensation for its violation has risen to the level of a peremptory norm of international law which prevails over the doctrine of sovereign immunity.

[49] I agree with the intervener that some forms of incarceration may conceivably constitute international human rights violations, such as an inordinately long sentence, or abusive conditions. However, incarceration is a lawful part of the Canadian justice

system. Without evidence of physical harm, to find that lawful incarceration amounts to compensable mental injury would be to find that every prisoner who is incarcerated by the Canadian penal system is entitled to receive damages from the state. Although I agree with some of the submissions of the intervener with respect to the fact that mental injury may be compensable in some form at international law, neither the intervener nor any other party has established that a peremptory norm of international law has now come into existence which would completely oust the doctrine of state immunity and allow domestic courts to entertain claims in the circumstances of this case.

Bouzari v. Islamic Republic of Iran
(2004), 243 D.L.R. (4th) 406, 71 O.R. (3d) 675 (C.A.);
leave to appeal to S.C.C. refused, January 27, 2005

GOUDGE J.A.:

[1] From June 1993 to January 1994 Houshang Bouzari was abducted, imprisoned and brutally tortured by agents of the Islamic Republic of Iran. Shortly after his release, he escaped from Iran and eventually came to Canada as a landed immigrant in 1998. He now seeks to sue Iran for the damages he suffered.

[2] Swinton J. found that his action is barred by the *State Immunity Act*, R.S.C. 1985, c. S-18 (the "SIA") and that neither the limited exceptions in the SIA, nor public international law nor the *Canadian Charter of Rights and Freedoms* could relieve against this conclusion. She therefore dismissed the action. For the reasons that follow, I agree and would therefore dismiss the appeal.

[3] This appeal engages two important principles: the prohibition of torture, which is widely acknowledged as vital to international human rights, and the requirement that sovereign states not be subjected to each other's jurisdiction, which is widely acknowledged as vital to the relations between nations. The balance struck today between these two principles by both Canada's domestic legislation and public international law prohibits a civil claim (though not a criminal prosecution) from being brought in Canada for the torture suffered in Iran by Mr. Bouzari. Hence, Mr. Bouzari's civil action was properly dismissed. ...

The State Immunity Act Issue

[39] The appellant brings this action against a foreign state. The action therefore necessarily engages the principle of sovereign immunity or state immunity.

[40] Founded on the concepts of the sovereign equality of states and the non-interference of states in the internal affairs of each other, the principle is rooted in customary international law.

[41] Historically, it provided foreign states with absolute immunity from proceedings in the courts of other states. However, over the years, the dictates of justice have led to some attenuation in the absolute immunity of states, through the evolution of certain specified exceptions to the general rule. Nevertheless, the doctrine of restrictive immunity which has emerged continues to have the general principle of

state immunity as its foundation. In *Schreiber v. Canada (Attorney General)* (2002), 216 D.L.R. (4th) 513 (S.C.C.) LeBel J. put it this way at para. 17:

> Despite the increasing number of emerging exceptions, the general principle of sovereign immunity remains an important part of the international legal order, except when expressly stated otherwise, and there is no evidence that an international peremptory norm has been established to suggest otherwise. Indeed, Brownlie [*Principles of Public International Law*, 5th ed. (Oxford: Clarendon Press, 1998)], *supra*, notes at pp. 332-33 that:
>
>> It is far from easy to state the current legal position in terms of customary or general international law. Recent writers emphasize that there is a *trend* in the practice of states towards the restrictive doctrine of immunity but avoid firm and precise prescriptions as to the present state of the law. [Emphasis in original.]

As observed at the outset of these reasons, this principle of international law has been incorporated into the Canadian domestic legal order through the enactment of the federal *State Immunity Act*.

[42] The SIA reflects this approach. It was passed by Parliament in 1982 and makes foreign states immune from civil suits in Canadian courts unless one of the exceptions in the Act applies. Section 3 is its cornerstone:

> 3(1) Except as provided by this Act, a foreign state is immune from the jurisdiction of any court in Canada.
>
> (2) In any proceedings before a court, the court shall give effect to the immunity conferred on a foreign state by subsection (1) notwithstanding that the state has failed to take any step in the proceedings.

[43] The appellant relies on three exceptions. The first is found in s. 18 of the Act:

> 18. This Act does not apply to criminal proceedings or proceedings in the nature of criminal proceedings.

[44] The appellant argues that this proceeding is in the nature of a criminal proceeding because he is seeking punitive damages which are in the nature of a fine. The motion judge rejected this argument, concluding that this relief is available only in a civil proceeding after a finding of civil liability and an award of compensatory damages. She found that while the purpose of punitive damages is to deter, they remain a remedy in a civil proceeding. I agree.

[45] Second, the appellant relies on the tort exception found in s. 6 of the Act:

> 6. A foreign state is not immune from the jurisdiction of a court in any proceedings that relate to
>
>> (a) any death or personal or bodily injury, or
>>
>> (b) any damage to or loss of property
>
> that occurs in Canada.

[46] The appellant argues that his suffering continues in Canada and that this constitutes injury occurring in Canada. The motion judge rejected this argument as

well, finding that the appellant continues to suffer from physical and psychological injuries inflicted on him not in Canada, but in Iran, because of the acts of torture committed there.

[47] Again I agree. This reasoning conforms with LeBel J.'s discussion of this exception in *Schreiber, supra*. At para. 80 he describes it as reflecting "a legislative intent to create an exception to state immunity which would be restricted to a class of claims arising out of a physical breach of personal integrity." Viewing the exception in this light, the SIA requires that the physical breach of personal integrity giving rise to the claim take place in Canada. The appellant cannot meet that condition. He was tortured in Iran.

[48] The third exception cited by the appellant, and the one he relies on most heavily, is that relating to commercial activity. It is found in s. 5 of the Act:

> 5. A foreign state is not immune from the jurisdiction of a court in any proceedings that relate to any commercial activity of the foreign state.

[49] The Act also contains the following definition of "commercial activity":

> "commercial activity" means any particular transaction, act or conduct or any regular course of conduct that by reason of its nature is of a commercial character[.]

[50] The appellant argues that this exception applies because the acts of torture on which his claim is based are related to the appellant's commercial activity in connection with the South Pars oil and gas field. The motion judge disagreed, finding that regardless of their purpose, these acts were exercises of the state policing, security and imprisonment powers and therefore were inherently sovereign and not commercial in nature.

[51] I agree with her conclusion that the commercial activity exception does not apply here. Section 5 of the Act requires that the acts to which the proceedings relate (namely the acts of torture) be commercial in nature. It is not enough that the proceedings relate to acts which, in turn, relate to commercial activity of the foreign state. To interpret the exception in this way, as the appellant contends, would broaden the exception beyond the clear language of the SIA.

[52] The issue, then, is whether the acts of torture for which the appellant sues can be said to be commercial in nature. *Re Canada Labour Code*, [1992] 2 S.C.R. 50 is the leading authority on this question. Writing for the majority at 69, LaForest J. set out the two basic questions raised by s. 5: first, whether the acts in question constitute commercial activity and second, whether the proceedings are related to that activity.

[53] LaForest J. found that a consideration of the purpose of the acts is of some, although limited, use in determining both their nature and which facets of the acts in question are truly "related" to the proceedings in issue. Here, apart from their purpose, the acts of torture underpinning the appellant's action cannot be said to have anything to do with commerce. They are nothing more than unilaterally imposed acts of brutality. The appellant believes that they were committed with a purpose of affecting his involvement in the commercial activity of the South Pars project. Even if this is taken to include an intention to affect the commercial activity of Iran, that is not enough to turn the acts of torture themselves into the commercial activity of Iran. The acts of torture are related only by intention to the commercial activity of the South Pars project.

[54] Moreover, the proceedings here are not truly "related" to this aspect of the acts of torture. If the appellant's claim proceeds, the purpose of these acts is of little if any relevance to the appellant's ability to recover damages for them. Damages would flow regardless of the purpose of the acts. In other words, the only aspect of the acts of torture that can be linked in any way to the commercial activity of Iran is their alleged purpose. Since this proceeding is not "related" to this aspect of the acts in question, it cannot be said that these acts relate to any commercial activity of Iran for the purposes of s. 5 of the SIA.

[55] Hence, I conclude that the commercial activity exception in s. 5 of the Act has no application to this case.

[56] The final argument related to the SIA issue is raised by the intervener CLAIHR. It argues that the enactment of the SIA has not displaced the common law of state immunity and that, under that common law, torture cannot be legitimized as a government act and cannot therefore attract immunity.

[57] In my view, the wording of the SIA must be taken as a complete answer to this argument. Section 3(1) could not be clearer. To reiterate, it says:

> 3(1) *Except as provided by this Act*, a foreign state is immune from the jurisdiction of any court in Canada [emphasis added].

[58] The plain and ordinary meaning of these words is that they codify the law of sovereign immunity. Indeed in *Re Canada Labour Code, supra*, LaForest J. says exactly that at 69:

> This appeal raises the issue of sovereign immunity, *as codified in the State Immunity Act* [emphasis added].

[59] Thus, the appellant is left with the exceptions in the Act, and, as I have indicated, none of the three he advances applies to this case.

The Public International Law Issue

• • •

[60] This issue takes the appellant beyond the exceptions to state immunity which are expressly enacted in the SIA. He argues that the SIA must be read in conformity with Canada's public international law obligations and that both by treaty and by peremptory norms of customary international law, Canada is bound to permit a civil remedy against a foreign state for torture committed abroad. He says that Canada's obligations under international law require that the SIA be interpreted to provide an exception to state immunity for such a claim.

[61] The motion judge dismissed this argument. She carefully analyzed both Canada's treaty obligations and its obligations under customary public international law and found that neither extends to the obligation contended for by the appellant.

[62] I agree with her analysis and will return to it in more detail. First, however, it is useful to turn to a preliminary point about the interplay between Canada's obligations at public international law and its domestic legislation.

[63] Canada's international law obligations can arise as a matter of conventional international law or customary international law.

[64] Where Canada has undertaken treaty obligations, it is bound by them as a matter of conventional international law. Parliament is then presumed to legislate consistently with those obligations. See *Schreiber*, *supra*, at para. 50. Thus, so far as possible, courts should interpret domestic legislation consistently with these treaty obligations.

[65] The same is true when Canada's obligations arise as a matter of customary international law. As acknowledged by the Attorney General in this case, customary rules of international law are directly incorporated into Canadian domestic law unless explicitly ousted by contrary legislation. So far as possible, domestic legislation should be interpreted consistently with those obligations. This is even more so where the obligation is a peremptory norm of customary international law, or *jus cogens*. ...[81]

[66] However, ... whether Canada's obligations arise pursuant to treaty or to customary international law, it is open to Canada to legislate contrary to them. Such legislation would determine Canada's domestic law although it would put Canada in breach of its international obligations.

[67] This discussion is important in this case because the SIA so clearly provides the code for according state immunity as a matter of Canadian domestic law. Even if Canada's international law obligations required that Canada permit a civil remedy for torture abroad by a foreign state, Canada has legislated in a way that does not do so. Section 3 of the SIA accords complete state immunity except as provided by the SIA. And, as we have seen, none of the relevant exceptions in the SIA permits a civil claim against a foreign state for torture committed abroad. Canada has clearly legislated so as not to create this exception to state immunity whether it has an international law obligation to do so or not.

NOTES

1) The original English version of section 6 of the *State Immunity Act* referred only to "death or personal injury." While the *Schreiber* case was proceeding to the Supreme Court, the *Harmonization Act, No. 1*[82] extended the phrase to read "death or personal or bodily injury." Schreiber argued that consequently "personal injury" must mean something more than "bodily injury"; otherwise its inclusion would be redundant. He asserted it covered mental integrity, dignity, and reputation, but the Supreme Court disagreed. It accepted Canada's submission that the amendment was only made to harmonize the English and French versions of the text.

2) In the *Bouzari* case the court held that the *State Immunity Act* section 3 overrode all Canada's international obligations both customary and conventional. The section certainly may be read this way, but such an interpretation overlooks the fact that the Act itself is intended to be a legislative expression of the customary international law of restrictive immunity. Should the court have engaged in an analysis of how the development of

---

[81]   The concept of *jus cogens* is explained in Chapter 3, Section B.4 on "Operation of Treaties: Invalidity and Jus Cogens" and the discussion of its impact in this case is reproduced in Chapter 4, Section D on "Jus Cogens in Canadian Law."

[82]   S.C. 2001, c. 4, s. 121.

international human rights obligations may have affected the international practice of state immunity behind the *State Immunity Act*?

3) Although Bouzari's suit against the state of Iran was dismissed, might he have brought an action against his torturers? Immunity is granted for the protection of the state, not for the personal benefit of the officials who act on the state's behalf. Nevertheless, immunity attaches to the head of state, the prime minister, and other ministers of state because they personify the state in varying degrees. Refer to the definition of "foreign state" in section 2 of the Act. Ordinarily lower state officials are also immune from suit in respect of their conduct on behalf of the state because the state is entitled to immunity for its acts, which, inevitably, are performed for it by its agents. See *Jaffe v. Miller*.[83] But in 2004 the English Court of Appeal entertained a suit against foreign state agents by their torture victims. *Jones v. Ministry of Interior of the Kingdom of Saudi Arabia* combined the various claims of four plaintiffs, Jones, Mitchell, Walker, and Sampson (a Canadian), arising from their systematic torture while in custody in Saudi Arabia. Jones's claim against the Saudi Interior Ministry was struck out because Saudi Arabia was entitled to immunity *ratione personae* (by reason of the person). However, the claims of all four plaintiffs against several named officials of Saudi Arabia were allowed to go forward—that is to say, the Court of Appeal remitted them to the Master to determine whether service out of the jurisdiction against the foreign defendants was appropriate. After a careful analysis of the trend of restrictive immunity, as practised by courts in several jurisdictions, around such an egregious abuse of human rights as torture, Mance L.J. concluded:

> [W]hatever the position may be apart from article 6 of the European Convention [on Human Rights], it can no longer be appropriate to give blanket immunity to a foreign state's claim, to state immunity *ratione materiae* [by reason of the subject matter] in respect of a state official alleged to have committed acts of systematic torture. To do so could deprive the right of access to a court under article 6 of real meaning in a case where a victim of torture had no prospect of recourse in the state whose officials committed the torture. But a proportionate approach in pursuit of a legitimate aim is, by definition, not the same as an approach requiring all states either to assume universal civil jurisdiction or ... to forego all discretionary qualifications on the breadth of their technical jurisdictional rules. In order to determine whether a claim for systematic torture should be allowed to proceed in the English courts, it would thus, on my view, be necessary for the court to consider and balance all relevant factors, including any evidence before it as to the availability or otherwise of an effective remedy for the torture in the state responsible for it. This exercise would have to be undertaken at the same time as considering any other jurisdictional issues which arise (including thereby issues of discretion and forum non conveniens). Only on that basis could it be possible to arrive at appropriate conclusion, balancing all potentially relevant factors.

---

83   (1993), 13 O.R. (3d) 745; 103 D.L.R. (4th) 315 (O.C.A.). Jaffe's suit against officials of the state of Florida, for conspiracy to kidnap him in Toronto and convey him to Florida for criminal prosecution, was dismissed on account of the officials' immunity while acting within the scope of their duties. See also *Tritt v. United States of America* (1989), 68 O.R. (2d) 284 (H.C.).

The considerations underlying state immunity would continue to be relevant as factors to be weighed, especially in cases which had on their face little to do with England.[84]

Should Canadian courts adopt this approach? Would it have assisted Bouzari? Compare the American case of *Filartiga v. Peña-Irala* under the unique U.S. *Alien Tort Claims Act*, reproduced at the end of Chapter 12, Section C.2 on "Non-Treaty Mechanisms."

4) Bouzari brought a civil action against his torturers. What about their criminal responsibility? May heads of state and other senior officials who commit or authorize torture and other grave human rights violations claim immunity from criminal prosecution? See the *State Immunity Act* section 18. Do they have immunity under customary international law? Review *The Schooner Exchange* case and see Chapter 11, Section D on "National Prosecution of International Crimes."

5. Immunity of State Organs and Property

Immunity of Governmental Organs and Agencies

State authority is exercised through a great variety of governmental organs and agencies. Section 2 of the *State Immunity Act* distinguishes between the state itself and its political subdivisions (such as the provinces of a federal state), government departments, and agencies, which are separate organs of the state. The Act respects the immunities of all these emanations of the state, although some are subject to special rules. However, before immunity may be asserted in a particular case, it has to be shown that the foreign defendant has the status of a state organ or agency within the meaning of section 2. The Act itself provides little guidance on what constitutes an organ or an agency of a state, perhaps because the way that states arrange their governmental affairs is so varied. The courts, however, have wrestled with this issue both before and after the enactment of the *State Immunity Act*. The *Trendtex* case, reproduced above in subsection 3, is a leading decision on the question of the qualifying status of an entity that claims immunity. *Mellenger* and *Ferguson*, reproduced below, provide instructive examples of the *Tendtrex* approach.

Mellenger v. New Brunswick Development Corporation
[1971] 1 W.L.R. 604 (C.A.)

LORD DENNING M.R.: In this case Mr. Mellenger and Mr. Levin, both Canadian citizens, seek to sue the New Brunswick Development Corporation. They claim a sum of a quarter of a million pounds. They say that it is commission which has been earned by them for introducing an important commercial enterprise into New Brunswick. ...

[Counsel for the defendant] says that the New Brunswick Development Corporation is an arm of the Government of the Province of New Brunswick, and cannot be sued in this country. It is entitled to sovereign immunity. He produced two affidavits, one

---

84   [2004] EWCA Civ. 1394 at para. 92.

sworn by Mr. Paterson, the Agent-General in London of the Province of New Brunswick, the other by Mr. Hoyt, the solicitor for the corporation, who has come over from Canada. They produced the statute under which the corporation is established, which showed, they say, that it is an arm of the government.

... The British North America Act 1867 gave Canada a federal constitution. Under it the powers of government were divided between the dominion government and the provincial governments. Some of those powers were vested in the dominion government. The rest remained with the provincial governments. Each provincial government, within its own sphere, retained its independence and autonomy directly under the Crown. The Crown is sovereign in New Brunswick for provincial powers, just as it is sovereign in Canada for dominion powers: see *Liquidators of the Maritime Bank of Canada v. Receiver-General of New Brunswick*, [1892] A.C. 437. It follows that the Province of New Brunswick is a sovereign state in its own right, and entitled, if it so wishes, to claim sovereign immunity.

The next point is whether the New Brunswick Development Corporation can avail itself of the doctrine of sovereign immunity. If the corporation is part and parcel of the Government of New Brunswick—so much so as to be identified with it like a government department—it can clearly claim immunity. For this purpose we must turn to the statute which set it up. It was established by the New Brunswick Development Corporation Act of April 11, 1959. Section 1 says:

There is hereby constituted on *behalf of Her Majesty in right of New Brunswick* a body corporate under the name of The New Brunswick Development Corporation, ...

Then follow sections which show the close connection of the corporation with the government. The Minister of Industry is an ex officio director. The other directors are appointed by the Lieutenant-Governor in Council. There is no issued capital. The corporation has no stocks or shares. Its principal power is (under section 3(1)(a)) to "... assist, promote, encourage and advance the industrial development, prosperity and economic welfare of the province."

It is true that there is a later subsection [section 3(2)(a)] which gives the corporation power, subject to the approval of the Lieutenant-Governor in Council, to "carry on any business of an industrial, commercial or of any agricultural nature." But the evidence shows that the corporation has never exercised this later power. It has never pursued any ordinary trade or commerce. All that it has done is to promote the industrial development of the province in the way that a government department does, such as the Board of Trade in England. In the circumstances it seems to me that the corporation is really part and parcel of the Government of New Brunswick. The very words that it is constituted "on behalf of Her Majesty in right of New Brunswick" bring it within the words which were used [per Denning L.J.] in *Tamlin v. Hannaford*, [1950] 1 K.B. 18, at 25:

When Parliament intends that a new corporation should act on behalf of the Crown, it as a rule says so expressly, ...

On this ground alone, I would hold that the corporation is in the same position as a government department, and is entitled to plead sovereign immunity.

Apart, however, from the statute, the functions of the corporation, as carried out in practice, show that it is carrying out the policy of the Government of New Brunswick itself. It is its alter ego. If and in so far as the corporation played any part in this case, it was identified with the government. The evidence shows that the Premier of the province played a leading part. The corporation itself has never been legally involved in the transaction. It was not the owner of the land on which the factory is being built. The Airscrew Weyroc people bought it from some private owner. The corporation has made no contract with anyone about these transactions. But the Government of New Brunswick itself has done so. It agreed to guarantee a bond issue if required. There is no single point in which the corporation itself has been involved. It was just the alter ego of the government, and can claim sovereign immunity: see *Rahimtoola v. Nizam of Hyderabad*, [1958] A.C. 379, at 393, by Lord Simonds. ...

Seeing that the corporation is in the same position as a government department, it cannot be sued here. The Crown Proceedings Act 1947, does not authorize proceedings to be taken here against the Crown in respect of New Brunswick: see section 40(2)(b) of the Act. But I expect that New Brunswick has a statute similar to our 1947 statute, enabling the Crown to be sued there. This may enure, in the long run, to the benefit of the plaintiffs because they will be able to sue the corporation and the government there as defendants: and thus avoid any difficulty as to who is the proper defendant.

But this plea of sovereign immunity must, I think, succeed. The appeal should be allowed and the action dismissed.

[Phillimore L.J. concurred. Salmond L.J. concurred in a separate opinion.]

Ferguson v. Arctic Transportation Ltd.
[1995] 3 F.C. 656 (T.D.)

[Ferguson began a suit for damages for injuries suffered while piloting a barge owned by Arctic Transportation Ltd. through the Panama Canal. The defendants sought to add the Panama Canal Commission as a third party to the action, but it claimed state immunity.]

REED J.: ... The *State Immunity Act*, R.S.C. 1985, c. S-18, section 3, provides that a foreign state is immune from the jurisdiction of all courts in Canada, except as otherwise provided by the Act. Section 5 of the Act provides that a foreign state is not immune "in any proceedings that relate to any commercial activity of the foreign state."

I have no doubt that the activities of the Panama Canal Commission, as they are relevant for the purposes of this case, are commercial in nature. The Commission is responsible for the operation, management and maintenance of the Panama Canal. The Commission provides for the movement of vessels through the canal. It is paid significant amounts of money for this service. The Commission did not seriously dispute that it was engaged, at least, in part, in commercial activities. The burden is on the Commission to demonstrate its entitlement to immunity, if it wishes to rely on such.

This is not a situation similar to that which existed in *Re Canada Labour Code*, [1992] 2 S.C.R. 50. In that case, the alleged commercial activity (the employment of civilian staff) was peripheral to the main foreign state activity (the operation of a military base). State immunity was therefore not lost. In the present case, the commercial activity (the charging of tolls for and the movement of vessels through the canal) is central to the Commission's functions and to the transaction between the defendants and the Commission. ...

Secondly, although the Commission referred to itself as "an agency in the executive branch of the United States government," it is the definition of agency in the *State Immunity Act*, R.S.C., 1985, c. S-18, that governs, not the Commission's self description. Section 2 of that Act states: ...

"agency of a foreign state" means any legal entity that is an organ of the foreign state but that is separate from the foreign state;

Most of the jurisprudence which was cited above involves attempts, prior to the enactment of the *State Immunity Act*, to determine whether an entity was separate from a foreign state for the purpose of making it answerable to suit in the particular Court in question. In this context, in *Ferranti-Packard Ltd. v. Cushman Rentals Ltd. et. al.* (1980), 30 O.R. (2d) 194 [at 196], the Ontario High Court referred to the reasoning of Lord Denning M.R. in *Trendtex Trading Corpn. v. Central Bank of Nigeria*, [1977] 1 Q.B. 529, at page 560:

I confess that I can think of no satisfactory test except that of looking to the functions and control of the organisation. I do not think that it should depend on the foreign law alone. I would look to all the evidence to see whether the organisation was under government control and exercised governmental functions.

The Court, then, went on to examine the constitutive legislation for the New York Thruway Authority. It was that organization whose status was under consideration. Factors which were assessed as relevant to the issue of separateness were: the amount of state control over the organization; whether it could sue or be sued in its own name; whether it was a separate legal (corporate) entity. This same approach was followed in *Ogdensburg Bridge & Port Authority v. Twp. Of Edwardsburg*, [1967] 1 O.R. 87 (C.A.).

In the present case, the defendants rely on a number of features of the *Panama Canal Treaty between the United States of America and the Republic of Panama, 1977* and on the *Panama Canal Act*, 22 U.S.C.S. 3601-3872 (1993), in support of their contention that the Commission is an organ of the foreign state "that is separate from the foreign state."

With respect to the Treaty, reference is made to those provisions which require the appointment of Panamanian nationals to the Board of the Commission and that, after January 1, 1990, the Administrator of the Commission is to be a Panamanian. These appointments, however, are to be made by "the United States of America." ...

Reference is made to the nature of the activities being carried on by the Commission. It is argued that these are not normal state functions. Yet article III(4) of the Treaty provides that the activities of the Commission will be performed in "carrying out the responsibilities and rights of the United States of America." The provisions of the Treaty do not support an argument that the Commission is to be a separate entity.

With respect to the *Panama Canal Act*, reference is made to the fact that the Commission has authority to enter into contracts to lease office space and to borrow funds. But authority to lease office space is a very limited power and the authority to borrow funds is limited to borrowing from the United States Treasury (3712a, 3714). The borrowing cannot exceed $400,000,000.

In so far as the right to sue and be sued is concerned, the Commission's authority, under the *Panama Canal Act*, cannot properly be characterized as such. The Commission is given authority to settle claims up to an amount of $50,000 and any such settlement "shall constitute a complete release *by the claimant* of his claim against the United States *and against any employee of the United States acting in the course of his employment who is involved in the matter giving rise to the claim*" (3761(c)) [emphasis added]. The Commission is authorized to pay damages in certain circumstances: "when the injury was proximately caused by negligence or fault on the part of an officer or employee of the United States" (3771(a), 3775). And, the acceptance by a claimant of an amount awarded to him shall be deemed to be, "in full settlement of such claim against the Government of the United States." There is a provision that if an individual does not agree with a claim settlement offered by the Commission that person may "bring an action on the claim against the Commission in the United States District Court for the Eastern District of Louisiana" and that such action shall proceed according to the principles of law which apply "in like cases between a private party and a department or agency of the United States" (3776). ...

It is the President of the United States, not the Commission, who sets tolls and makes the rules respecting the measurements of vessels that can transit the canal (3791). Commission employees are governed by "the laws of the United States regarding duties and responsibilities of Federal employees" (3622(a)). And the section establishing the Commission (3611) states:

3611. Panama Canal Commission: Establishment
There is established in the executive branch of the United States Government an agency to be known as the Panama Canal Commission ... . The Commission shall, under the general supervision of the Board ... be responsible for the maintenance and operation of the Panama Canal and the facilities and appurtenances related thereto. The authority of the President with respect to the Commission shall be exercised through the Secretary of Defence.

As noted, the provisions of the Treaty are of little assistance. They contemplate the creation of a Commission but do not provide an indication as to whether it will be a part of or separate from the Government of the United States. The provisions of the *Panama Canal Act*, similarly, do not evidence a separate entity, as envisaged by the definition found in section 2 of the *State Immunity Act*. There is no separate legal corporate entity. There is no general right to sue and be sued. There is a limited right to settle claims on behalf of the United States Government and to pay out awards from appropriations. There is no general right to borrow money. Employees are subject to the duties and responsibilities imposed on federal employees. The President retains extensive control. The activity being undertaken is pursuant to an international treaty under which responsibilities devolve on the United States Government. I cannot conclude that the Commission is "an organ of the foreign state ... that is separate from the foreign state."

NOTES

1) In the *Ferguson* case, the court took care to determine that the Panama Canal Commission was an organ, and not an agency, of the United States because of the difference in the process of service of originating documents on a state and on an agency of a state, as detailed in the *State Immunity Act* section 9. Would it have made any difference whether the Commission was an organ or an agency of the United States for the substantive issue of its lack of immunity under section 5?

2) Some Crown corporations and state agencies are set up to be independent of governmental policies and influence. Would they have the status to claim immunity? In *Ferranti-Packard Ltd. v. Cushman Rentals Ltd.*,[85] the New York State Thruway, whose function is to construct and operate the highway system in New York State, was denied immunity in the Ontario Courts on account of its independence in establishing its policies and executing its responsibilities. But is not the administration of a public road transportation system an exercise of governmental authority even when it is executed through a separately constituted body? On this basis, even the courts might not be regarded as governmental organs.

3) What criteria and evidence are used to determine the status of a state-owned corporation or other separate legal entity? Consider how the courts in *Trendtex*, *Mellenger*, and *Ferguson* looked to the enabling legislation, the organization of the enterprise, its functions, and the degree of political control.[86]

4) The entity seeking immunity does not have to be constituted as a government agency: it seems that it is sufficient if an entity is authorized to act on behalf of the government for the activities impugned in the case. In *Walker v. Bank of New York*,[87] the court treated the bank and its employees, who were requested to assist U.S. law enforcement officers in their criminal investigation of Walker, as agents of the United States for this purpose and thus entitled to immunity.

The Appeal Court rejected the trial judge's opinion that the *State Immunity Act* required the entity claiming immunity to have an ongoing institutionalized relationship with the state in order to qualify as a state agency. Instead, it said:

---

85   (1980), 30 O.R. (2d) 194 (Div. Ct.), aff'd. (1981), 31 O.R. (2d) 799 (C.A.).

86   See also *Krajina, supra* note 3; *Baccus S.R.L. v. Servicio Nacional del Trigo, supra* note 3, noting that both were decided under the absolute theory of immunity; *Czarnikow v. Rolimpex*, [1978] Q.B. 176 (C.A.), aff'd. [1979] A.C. 351 (H.L.); *Lorac Transport Ltd. v. The Ship "Atra"* (1984), 9 D.L.R. (4th) 129 (F.C.); *Bouchard v. J.L. Le Saux Ltée* (1984), 45 O.R. (2d) 792 (Mast. Ch.); *First National City Bank v. Banco Para el Comercio Exterior de Cuba* (1983), 462 U.S. 611; 103 S.Ct. 2591; P.J. Kincaid, "Sovereign Immunity of Foreign State-Owned Corporations" (1976) 10 Jo. World Tr. L. 110; and W.C. Hoffman, "The Separate Entity Rule in International Perspective" (1991) 65 Tul. L. Rev. 535. The burden of proof that a body claiming immunity is an agency of a foreign state rests on the claimant: *D. and J. Coustas Shipping Co. S.A. v. Cia de Navegnçao Lloyd Brasileiro* (1990), 48 F.T.R. 161.

87   (1994), 16 O.R. (3d) 504 (C.A.). See J. Walker, "Immunity for Extraterritorial Enforcement Measures in Canada: The Supreme Court Declines to Decide" (1994) 1 Can. Int'l Law. 17.

Applying the definition [of "agency of a foreign state" in section 2] to the Bank and its employees, it is clear that each is a "legal entity," and that each is "separate from the foreign state." The only question remaining is whether each is an "organ of the foreign state." The word "organ" is a very broad one. The Oxford English Dictionary defines it as "a means of action or operation, an instrument, a 'tool'; a person, body of persons, or thing by which some purpose is carried out or some function performed." In this case the bank employees involved did not act on their own initiative. They acted at the request of U.S. government law enforcement officers for the purpose of assisting them in their investigation of possible criminal activities. To acknowledge sovereign immunity for the U.S. Government and its employees in such a situation, and to expose persons providing them with requested assistance is, on the surface, grossly unfair. But, as has been pointed out in many cases, the doctrine of sovereign immunity is not a doctrine of fairness but, rather, one of necessity developed in the interest of international comity. However, we are of the view that the use of the broad word "organ" in the Act, which was promulgated to codify the application of the doctrine in Canada, indicates the intention of parliament to protect individuals and institutions who act at the request of a foreign state in situations where that state would enjoy sovereign immunity.[88]

Is the approach taken by the Appeal Court in *Walker* consistent with the enquiry into the institutional arrangements and practices of the claimants to immunity in the three cases reproduced above? Is the Appeal Court's approach appropriate, or is it stretching the scope of immunity too far?

5) Once the status of an agency of the foreign state is established so that a claim to immunity may be laid, it still has to be determined whether the kinds of activities of the agency preclude its immunity. In the *Mellenger* case there was no difficulty because the N.B. Development Corporation never engaged in trade or commerce but only promoted industrial development. Is it likely that the Canadian Wheat Board, which has a monopoly on the sale and export of wheat from Canada, would qualify for immunity? Consider section 5 of the Act. Notice that in some parts of the Act distinctions are expressly drawn between the degree of immunity of the foreign state and an agency of that state. Immunity of state property is one area: see sections 11 and 12, discussed below.

6) While the *Mellenger* case shows that a province, such as New Brunswick, is a sovereign state entitled to immunity in foreign courts, does it follow that there is inter-provincial immunity before Canadian courts? In *Western Surety Co. v. Elk Valley Logging Ltd.*,[89] the Court followed *Mellenger* in deciding that Alberta is a sovereign state vis-à-vis British Columbia and thus granted immunity, on a restrictive basis, to Alberta in the B.C. court action. However, an Ontario Court in *R. v. Eldorado Nuclear Ltd.*[90] held that restricted sovereign immunity did not apply in the relations between Canada and the provinces. Should the *State Immunity Act* now govern interprovincial immunities? The court in the *Western Surety* case said it did not apply to Alberta because it refers to foreign states, meaning countries and provinces outside of Canada. See section 2 of the Act.

---

88 *Ibid.* at 508.

89 (1986), 31 B.L.R. 193 (B.C.S.C.).

90 (1981), 121 D.L.R. (3d) 392 (Ont. Co. Ct.), aff'd. (1981), 128 D.L.R. (3d) 82 (Ont. Div. Ct.).

Immunity of State Property

The property of a foreign state is generally immune from attachment, judgment, and execution under the *State Immunity Act*. See sections 11 and 12. However, immunity cannot be claimed for land, buildings, goods, chattels, money, and other intangible assets unless they are "property of a foreign state." No guidance is provided by the Act about the meaning in this statute of the very technical word "property," except in the cases of ships and cargo in section 7(3) and interests that arise "by way of succession, gift or *bona vacantia*" in section 8. Consequently, there must be doubt, where the foreign state's interest is less than ownership, whether the property, for which it claims immunity, has sufficient sovereign status to qualify for immunity. For instance:

1) Is a house, which is leased to a foreign government for use as a private residence by one of its representatives, the property of a foreign state?[91]

2) Are the Ottawa bank accounts of a foreign diplomatic mission open to attachment?[92]

There seems to be a further difficulty in these uncertain situations as to how any right to immunity shall be established, seeing that section 3 of the Act directs a court "to give effect to the immunity conferred on a foreign state ... notwithstanding that the state has failed to take any steps in the proceedings."

A particularly acute problem occurs when the plaintiff's claim is that his or her property has been wrongly taken or used by the foreign state defendant. Is the assertion of ownership of the property by the state sufficient to found its immunity and so to stay the action? The difficulty is that any investigation of the state's title to the property would appear to breach its right to immunity. Consider the situation in *The Schooner Exchange*, reported at the beginning of this section, and the following case.[93]

Juan Ismael and Co. Inc. v. Government of Indonesia
[1955] A.C. 72 (J.C.P.C.)

[The plaintiff had previously chartered a ship to the Indonesian government, who still retained it after the charter party was ended. The plaintiff claimed repossession but the government asserted that it had bought the vessel through an agent of the plaintiff's and claimed immunity for its property.]

EARL JOWITT: ... Where the foreign sovereign State is directly impleaded the writ will be set aside, but where the foreign sovereign State is not a party to the

---

91   Cf. *Re Royal Bank of Canada and Corriveau and Cuba* (1980), 30 O.R. (2d) 653 (H.C.).

92   Cf. *Alcom Ltd. v. Republic of Colombia*, [1984] 2 All E.R. 6 (H.L.), and see *UN Convention on the Jurisdictional Immunities of States and Their Property*, *supra* note 50, articles 18 and 19.

93   See also *Shearson Lehman Brothers Inc. v. MacLaine, Watson & Co. Ltd.*, [1988] 1 W.L.R. 16 (H.L.).

proceedings, but claims that it is interested in the property to which the action relates and is therefore indirectly impleaded, a difficult question arises as to how far the foreign sovereign government must go in establishing its right to the interest claimed. Plainly if the foreign government is required as a condition of obtaining immunity to prove its title to the property in question the immunity ceases to be of any practical effect. The difficulty was cogently expressed by Lord Radcliffe in the case of the *Dollfus Mieg*, [1952] A.C. 582, at 616 where he said: "A stay of proceedings on the ground of immunity has normally to be granted or refused at a stage in the action when interests are claimed but not established, and indeed to require him [i.e., the foreign sovereign] to establish his interest before the court (which may involve the court's denial of his claim) is to do the very thing which the general principle requires that our courts should not do."

In the case of *The Jupiter*, [1924] P. 236, where the writ was in rem against the ship, Scrutton L.J. based his judgment on the view that an assertion by a foreign sovereign that he claimed a right in property must be accepted by the court as conclusive without investigating whether the claim be good or bad. ... The view that a bare assertion by a foreign government of its claim is sufficient has the advantage of being logical, and simple in application, but it may lead to a very grave injustice if the claim asserted by the foreign government is in fact not maintainable, and the view of Scrutton L.J. has not found favour in subsequent cases. ...

In their Lordships' opinion a foreign government claiming that its interest in property will be affected by the judgment in an action to which it is not a party, is not bound as a condition of obtaining immunity to prove its title to the interest claimed, but it must produce evidence to satisfy the court that its claim is not merely illusory, nor founded on a title manifestly defective. The court must be satisfied that conflicting rights have to be decided in relation to the foreign government's claim. When the court reaches that point it must decline to decide the rights and must stay the action, but it ought not to stay the action before that point is reached.

[In the event, the Privy Council found the Indonesian government's assertion "manifestly defective" and rejected the claim to immunity.]

NOTES

1) Is this the procedure anticipated by the *State Immunity Act* for dealing with claims of immunity for foreign state property?

2) Special rules are contained in section 7 of the Act regarding foreign state ships. Do they help to resolve the kind of dilemma that arose in the *Juan Ismael* case?[94]

3) While sections 11 and 12 of the Act protect the property of the foreign state, section 6 restricts its immunity where it is connected to the death, personal injury, or loss of property of others. If a receiver, appointed by an American court, unlawfully seized

---

[94]   See also the similar provisions in the *Federal Courts Act*, R.S.C. 1985, c. F-7, s. 43(7)(c).

property in Canada and an action in trespass is brought, can the United States claim immunity under customary international law?[95] Under the *State Immunity Act*?

6. Execution of Judgments

If a foreign state that is not immune from jurisdiction is held liable in the action, it is expected to fulfill in good faith the compensatory order of the court. If it does not, the plaintiffs likely will want to execute their judgment against any property of the foreign state that can be discovered within the jurisdiction. May they do so, or is the state's property protected from execution by its own immunity? Indeed, even before trial and judgment, the plaintiffs may wish to secure the assets of the defendant state from dissipation or removal from the jurisdiction pending the outcome of their suit. May they attach the foreign state's property as security, or is it immune both before and after judgment?

The answers to these questions are to be found in sections 11 and 12 of the *State Immunity Act*. In the first place, waiver of immunity by the foreign state to the jurisdiction of the court over the case, under section 4, does not incur the loss of immunity from a court order for remedies or relief such as an injunction or a direction for specific performance or recovery of property: see sections 11(1) and (2). Nor does it defeat the immunity of the foreign state's property from attachment or execution, unless the property is for use in a commercial activity: see section 12. Hence, plaintiffs seeking pre-judgment attachment or post-judgment execution against the foreign state's property may not be successful unless the foreign state owner makes a separate waiver of immunity: see section 12(1)(a). The details of sections 11 and 12 make finer distinctions still; in particular they distinguish the position of agencies of the foreign state from the state itself. Curial orders against a state agency under section 11 are permitted, and attachment and execution against a state agency's property under section 12 is allowed when the agency is itself subject to the court's jurisdiction.

Should there be immunity from execution or is the practice a hangover from the absolute theory of state immunity? Why must the foreign state waive its immunity at every stage of the proceedings? Would it be appropriate to apply to foreign states the rule governing state agencies—that in the absence of immunity from jurisdiction over the merits of the case, their property is not immune from attachment or execution either?

In the pre-Act case of *Re Royal Bank of Canada and Corriveau and Cuba*,[96] Mr. Corriveau obtained a default judgment against Cuba for breach of a lease of property as its chancellory. Shortly before the end of the lease, Cuba allowed the water pipes in the building to freeze, causing extensive damage. Mr. Corriveau tried to execute his judgment for this damage against the funds in the Cuban account at the Royal Bank but Cuba objected. Cromarty J., after reviewing most of the principal authorities, remarked:

> International law appears to provide a protection against execution even if a judgment has been obtained. The *Diplomatic and Consular Privileges and Immunities Act* [now replaced by the *Foreign Missions and International Organizations Act*, S.C. 1991, c. 41], by analogy,

---

[95]   See *Carrato v. U.S.A.* (1982), 141 D.L.R. (3d) 456 (Ont. H.C.).

[96]   (1980), 30 O.R. (2d) 653 (H.C.).

contemplates the present situation. Article 31, s. 3 in a paragraph separate from that which deals with immunity from the civil jurisdiction forbids execution. There is some support for this inference in the comment of Rand J. in the *City and County of St. John et al. v. Fraser-Brace Overseas Corp. et al.*, [[1957] S.C.R. 263, at 268].[97]

He went on to hold:

The only record before me shows that the leased premises were for governmental use and that the moneys in the bank were in the "possession" of the foreign Sovereign State.[98]

If the use of the leased premises was a public act by Cuba, as Cromarty J. seems to imply, perhaps there should not have been a judgment against Cuba at all. In any event, should immunity from execution depend upon the character of the original transaction or upon the status of the property being seized?[99]

D. DIPLOMATIC IMMUNITIES

The rules and principles of diplomatic privileges and immunities are some of the oldest parts of international law. The present ones date from the beginnings of modern international law in the 16th century. The emergence of the nation state with the attendant development of communications, growth of trade and industry, and expansion of political alignments confronted heads of state with the need to maintain continuous official contact with each other. Thus the appointment of ambassadors and the maintenance of permanent legations early became commonplace.

The accreditation of diplomats necessitated some system to ensure the appropriate recognition of their status as foreign state representatives. Thus there developed an increasingly refined set of practices about diplomatic precedence, protocol, privilege, and immunity. Supplemented by national laws, such as the English *Diplomatic Privileges Act, 1708*,[100] and numerous bilateral treaties, these practices had developed by the 20th century into a large body of detailed rules of customary international law. This customary law has been codified since 1961 in the Vienna Convention on Diplomatic Relations, which was ratified by Canada in 1966 and is now implemented by the *Foreign Missions and International Organizations Act*.[101]

There are two principal theories put forward as bases for the privileges and immunities of diplomats. One is the so-called functional theory that diplomats ought to be at liberty to devote themselves fully to the service of their state. The second basis is that diplomats

---

[97]   *Ibid.* at 658.

[98]   *Ibid.* at 659.

[99]   And see *Philippine Embassy Bank Account Case* (1977), 65 I.L.R. 146 (Ger.); *Iran v. Sociétés Eurodif and Sofidif* (1982), 65 I.L.R. 93 (Fr.); L.C.R. di Brozolo, "Italian Case Note" (1990) 84 A.J.I.L. 573; H. Fox, "Enforcement Jurisdiction, Foreign State Property and Diplomatic Immunity" (1985) 34 I.C.L.Q. 115; J. Crawford, "Execution of Judgments and Foreign Sovereign Immunity" (1982) 75 A.J.I.L. 820; and the Australian Law Reform Commission, *supra* note 50 at 73-74.

[100]   7 Ann., c. 12.

[101]   S.C. 1991, c. 41.

owe no allegiance to the receiving state and consequently are not subject to its laws. The former theory seems preferable as a description of the historical development of diplomatic relations and is affirmed by the Vienna Convention in its preamble as the purpose of the privileges and immunities.

This section of materials concentrates on the law regarding diplomats,[102] although there are other bodies of rules respecting other state representatives and international persons. These include consuls, international organizations, and their staff as well as the accredited representatives of the member states, judges of the International Court of Justice and of the International Criminal Court, special missions, and visiting forces, all of which are mentioned briefly at the end of this section.

Vienna Convention on Diplomatic Relations
Articles 1-3, 9, 22-27, 29-32, 34, 36, 37-41, 43, and 44
Reproduced in the Documentary Supplement

Foreign Missions and International Organizations Act
S.C. 1991, c. 41

3.(1) Articles 1, 22 to 24 and 27 to 40 of the Vienna Convention on Diplomatic Relations ... have the force of law in Canada in respect of all foreign states, regardless of whether those states are parties to those Conventions. ...

4.(1) For the purpose of according to the diplomatic mission and consular posts of any foreign state, and persons connected therewith, treatment that is comparable to the treatment accorded to the Canadian diplomatic mission and Canadian consular posts in that foreign state, and persons connected therewith, the Minister of Foreign Affairs may, by order, with respect to that state's diplomatic mission and any of its consular posts, and any person connected therewith,

   (a) extend any of the privileges and immunities accorded thereto under section 3, other than duty and tax relief privileges;

   (b) grant thereto any of the benefits set out in the regulations;

   (c) withdraw any of the privileges, immunities and benefits accorded or granted thereto; and

   (d) restore any privilege, immunity or benefit withdrawn pursuant to para-graph (c). ...

---

102   See M. Hardy, *Modern Diplomatic Law* (1968); Ld. Gore-Booth, ed., *Satow's Guide to Diplomatic Practice*, 5th ed. (1979); F. Przetacznik, *Protection of Officials of Foreign States According to International Law* (1983); L. Dembinski, *The Modern Law of Diplomacy* (1988); B.S. Murty, *The International Law of Diplomacy* (1989); C. Lewis, *supra* note 70; B. Sen, *A Diplomat's Handbook of International Law and Practice*, 3d rev. ed. (1988); J.C. Barker, *The Abuse of Diplomatic Privileges and Immunities* (1996); E. Denza, *Diplomatic Law*, 2d ed. (1998, re-released with a new preface 2004); J. Salmon & S. Sucharitkul, "Les missions diplomatiques entre deux chaises: Immunité diplomatique ou immunité d'état?" (1987) 33 Ann. Fr. Dr. Int. 163; and A. Dufour, "La protection des immunités diplomatique et consulaires au Canada" (1973) 11 Can. Y.B. Int'l L. 123 and (1974) 12 Can. Y.B. Int'l L. 3.

11. A certificate purporting to be issued by or under the authority of the Minister of Foreign Affairs and containing any statement of fact relevant to any of the following questions shall be received in evidence in any action or proceeding as proof of the fact stated in the certificate without proof of the signature or official character of the person appearing to have sighed the certificate:

(a) whether a diplomatic mission, a consular post or an office of a political subdivision of a foreign state has been established with the consent of the Government of Canada;

(b) whether an organization or conference is the subject of an order under section 5;

(c) whether a mission is accredited to an international organization;

(d) whether any premises or archives are the premises or archives of an office of a political subdivision of a foreign state; or

(e) whether any person, diplomatic mission, consular post, office of a political subdivision of a foreign state, international organization or accredited mission has privileges, immunities or benefits under this Act.

12.(1) The Governor in Council may make such regulations and orders as are necessary for the purpose of giving effect to any of the provisions that have the force of law pursuant to section 3.

(2) The Governor in Council may make regulations

(a) setting out the benefits that may be granted for the purposes of subsection 4(1).

NOTES

1) This Act consolidates two previous pieces of legislation implementing in Canada the Vienna Convention on Diplomatic Relations, the Vienna Convention on Consular Relations, and the Convention on the Privileges and Immunities of the United Nations, which now appear in Schedules I, II, and III, respectively.

2) Section 6 authorizes the Minister for External Affairs to grant consular privileges in Canada to the office and representatives of a political subdivision of a foreign state where its duties are substantially the same as those of a consul, provided reciprocal treatment is afforded to the agents of Canadian provinces in that state.

1. Diplomatic Asylum

The premises of a diplomatic mission are, by article 22 of the Vienna Convention, both immune and inviolable. These terms overlap in some degree. Immunity mainly conveys freedom from legal process and duties, while inviolability chiefly suggests freedom from physical interference. The legal process, if allowed to run its course, could result in an order that would disturb the possession of the mission.

Although the premises of and the personnel accredited to the mission are secured from interference by the Convention, it makes no reference to the practice of granting asylum to others who enter there. Diplomatic asylum is contentious enough that it was purposefully avoided at the Vienna Conference. Its practice is most common in, but not limited to, Latin America where it is observed by treaties but is not part of customary international law. See the *Asylum Case* reported in Chapter 3, Section C.2.

If diplomatic asylum is not condoned by international law, nevertheless there is very little that host states can do about it. If a foreign mission provides asylum to a political refugee, its immunity and inviolability prevents the host state from interfering. The wrath of the local government toward the individual in asylum is usually not so great as to risk endangering its foreign policy interests by intervening in the mission in breach of the law or by breaking diplomatic relations with the protecting state.

2. Legal Character and Duration of Immunity

Dickinson v. Del Solar
[1930] 1 K.B. 376

[Dickinson sued Del Solar in negligence for injuries suffered in a motor car accident. The third party, Del Solar's insurance company, asserted he had no legal liability because he was at the time First Secretary to the Peruvian Legation. But the Minister of the Legation forbade Del Solar from relying upon diplomatic immunity because the accident occurred when the car was being used for private purposes.]

LORD HEWART C.J.: ... Diplomatic agents are not, in virtue of their privileges as such, immune from legal liability for any wrongful acts. The accurate statement is that they are not liable to be sued in the English Courts unless they submit to the jurisdiction. Diplomatic privilege does not import immunity from legal liability, but only exemption from local jurisdiction. The privilege is the privilege of the Sovereign by whom the diplomatic agent is accredited, and it may be waived with the sanction of the Sovereign or of the official superior of the agent: ... In the present case the privilege was waived and jurisdiction was submitted to by the entry of appearance: ... and as Mr. Del Solar had so submitted to the jurisdiction it was no longer open to him to set up privilege. If privilege had been pleaded as a defence, the defence could, in the circumstances, have been struck out. Mr. Del Solar was bound to obey the direction of his Minister in the matter. In these circumstances ... the judgment clearly creates a legal liability against which the insurance company have agreed to indemnify him. ... I hold therefore that the third parties here are liable.

Ghosh v. D'Rozario
[1963] 1 Q.B. 106 (C.A.)

[Ghosh alleged that he had been slandered in 1956 by D'Rozario, who, at the time, was a staff member of the High Commission for India in the United Kingdom. In 1957 D'Rozario went to India but he returned to England as a private citizen in 1959, when he was served with a writ for the slander. In 1960 D'Rozario went back to India and returned once more to England as a diplomat at the High Commission. He then claimed immunity and sought a stay of the action.]

HOLROYD PEARCE L.J.: ... The real point in the case is whether, as a matter of principle, a defendant's diplomatic immunity which comes into existence after an action has been started, and while it is pending, necessitates a stay of those proceedings. It is conceded that had the defendant's diplomatic immunity existed when the writ was issued, the proceedings would not be maintainable. It is conceded further that the steps taken by the defendant earlier in the action when he had no diplomatic immunity cannot constitute any waiver or voluntary acceptance of jurisdiction by the defendant, for he had then no right of immunity which he could waive and, having been duly served, he was bound to submit to the jurisdiction. It is argued, however, that once this court has taken jurisdiction between the litigants, it will not relax its grasp even though facts occur thereafter which would create diplomatic immunity. ...

Diplomatic immunity is likely to create individual hardship. But this hardship must bow to a general overriding principle of comity between conflicting jurisdictions. An ambassador must live in a foreign land, and if he could be summoned before the tribunals of that foreign land, or coerced by its legal process, it would be an affront to his sovereign, and an interference with his work. For the same reasons it is necessary that the embassy staff as well as the ambassador should be immune. The immunity belongs to the State, and not to its representatives individually. There is no difference in principle between the ambassador and the humbler members of his staff providing that they are properly accredited, and on the necessary list. ...

But I prefer to decide the matter on a broader ground. It would be no less an affront and an interference to subject an ambassador to actions that were in existence before he acquired his diplomatic status and immunity than it would be to allow a writ to be served on him. Moreover, if a pre-existing action were allowed to proceed against an ambassador, it would create undesirable practical difficulties. The court could not order him or impose any sanction on his conduct. He could with impunity be a most unruly litigant. The mischief which the general rule is intended to avoid at the cost of some individual hardship would inevitably arise. In my judgment the general principles that confer diplomatic immunity against the initiation of proceedings confer an equal immunity against the continuation of pre-existing and hitherto properly constituted proceedings. I would, therefore, dismiss the appeal.

[Davies L.J. and Wilberforce J. concurred in separate opinions.]

NOTES

1) In the reverse situation, if a writ were to be issued against a defendant during his or her diplomatic posting and, rather than have it struck out, if the diplomat were to allow the case to come to trial after the end of his or her term of service, would the suit be upheld?[103]

2) If immunity is granted only from process and not from liability, it may be important to know when that immunity ends. Consider the situation that arose in Ottawa in 1983.[104]

---

[103]   See *Empson v. Smith*, [1966] 1 Q.B. 426 (C.A.) and *Shaw v. Shaw*, [1979] 3 All E.R. 1 (Fam. Div.).

[104]   See *Re Regina and Palacios* (1984), 45 O.R. (2d) 269 (C.A.).

Palacios was the first secretary at the Nicaraguan embassy until early in July. He was charged later in the month with illegal possession of weapons and possession of cocaine for the purpose of trafficking. The Nicaraguan embassy stated that Palacios finished his official duties on July 12, nearly two weeks before he was charged, but he argued that his immunity continued until he left the country either for another post or for home. In fact Palacios went to the United States for a brief visit on July 16 and he was charged on his return to Canada. Was Palacios entitled to invoke immunity? See the Vienna Convention article 39. Would it make any difference whether the alleged activities for which he was charged may have occurred before July 12 or afterward?

3) If the act complained of is committed by a diplomat in the exercise of his or her duties, does he or she lose immunity for it when the posting ends and he or she leaves the receiving state? See article 39(2).

4) The privileges and immunities of diplomats do not come without responsibilities to the host state. By article 41, they have a duty to respect the laws of the receiving state and not to interfere in its internal affairs. Since, by article 29, diplomats are inviolable, if they do break the local law, they cannot be arrested or detained, unless the sending state waives their immunity, as discussed below. This is of serious concern given the number of offences committed each year:

> Foreign diplomats escaped prosecution on 246 violations of Canadian law by invoking privileges of diplomatic immunity in 1982, up from 174 a year earlier, the Commons was told yesterday. The majority were traffic offences. Parking tickets accounted for 220 of the 1982 offences while 14 involved speeding, four seatbelt infractions, one impaired driving and one illegal use of studded tires. Four shoplifting incidents, one cheque fraud case and one charge of illegal marijuana possession rounded out the list.[105]

In any of these situations, the only recourse of the receiving state is to declare the offending diplomat *persona non grata* and request his or her recall by the sending state: see article 9. Is this an appropriate resolution for serious crimes like drug trafficking or dangerous driving causing death?

5) In fact, the receiving state may cut short a diplomat's tenure at any time by declaring him or her *persona non grata* without giving an explanation at all: see article 9. This is common practice when the receiving state suspects that a diplomat has engaged in espionage, and the sending state frequently takes reciprocal action. But any kind of behaviour unacceptable to the receiving state may found its decision to request a diplomat's recall. In the case of *Copello v. Canada (Minister of Foreign Affairs)*,[106] the Italian diplomat, Dr. Copello, did not commit any offence but reportedly behaved inappropriately, uncooperatively, and perhaps aggressively in two incidents in Whitehorse and Vancouver. The Minister of Foreign Affairs, by diplomatic note to Italy, requested

---

[105]   Reply by the Minister of External Affairs to a written question in the House of Commons, as reported in *The Globe and Mail*, September 17, 1983. And see J.T. Southwick, "Abuse of Diplomatic Privilege and Immunity: Compensatory and Restrictive Reforms" (1988) 15 Syracuse J. Int'l L. & Com. 82.

[106]   2003 F.C.A. 295; 308 N.R. 175; (2003), 3 Admin. L.R. (4th) 214.

that Dr. Copello leave Canada. In a most unusual move, Dr. Copello then applied to the Federal Court for judicial review of the Minister's decision. However, the courts had little difficulty in determining that the expulsion of diplomats is a matter of Crown prerogative over foreign affairs, which is not a justiciable legal issue.

3. Waiver of Diplomatic Immunity

The Vienna Convention declares that diplomatic immunity may be waived. See article 32 reproduced in the Documentary Supplement. Its provisions have clarified the rules about waiver. In particular, a waiver must be express and does not extend beyond immunity from suit unless a separate waiver of immunity from execution is also made. Where the Vienna Convention is not certain, customary law still applies. Thus, where article 32(1) provides that diplomatic immunity "may be waived by the sending state" but says no more, the question who may act for the sending state has to be answered by resort to prior practice. In *R. v. Madan* it was said:

> [I]t is clear that that waiver must be a waiver by a person with full knowledge of his rights and a waiver by or on behalf of the chief representative of the state in question. In other words, it is not the person entitled to a privilege who may waive it unless he does so as agent or on behalf of the representative of the country concerned; it must be the waiver of the representative of the state.[107]

The immunity is the privilege of the state, not of the individual, and so members of the administrative and technical staff of the mission or of the service staff, or members of the family of a diplomatic agent entitled to diplomatic immunity cannot themselves waive their immunity: waiver, to be valid, can be done only by their superior—that is, the head of the mission. But it is not so clear as the *Madan* case may suggest that the head of the mission can waive his own immunity. Schwarzenberger has argued that the head of the mission cannot do so because the right to immunity is enjoyed by the state, and is not granted to any diplomat in a personal capacity. He asserted that the immunity of the head of the mission can be waived only by or with the permission of his own government.[108]

Although the Convention allows for waiver of immunity, the practical question is whether foreign diplomats will waive their immunity for ordinary matters of their personal lives not connected with or prejudicial to their official functions. The Vienna Conference adopted a resolution recommending that sending states should waive diplomatic immunity in civil actions with local citizens wherever the mission is unimpeded.

---

107 [1961] 1 All E.R. 588 at 591 (C.C.A.).

108 G. Schwarzenberger & E.D. Brown, *A Manual of International Law*, 6th ed. (1976) at 80.

U.S. Diplomatic and Consular Staff in Tehran Case
United States v. Iran
[1980] I.C.J. Rep. 3

[In November 1979 the U.S. embassy in Tehran was overrun by an armed group of several hundred "militants." The premises were occupied, the documents and archives were ransacked, and the diplomatic personnel together with two other American nationals were taken hostage. Iran did not participate in the case brought by the United States, but the International Court was able to exercise jurisdiction because both states were parties to the Vienna Convention on Diplomatic Relations including its Optional Protocol, which provides for the compulsory jurisdiction of the Court in disputes about the Convention.]

THE COURT: ...

[56] ... The events which are the subject of the United States' claims fall into two phases which it will be convenient to examine separately.

[57] The first of these phases covers the armed attack on the United States Embassy by militants on 4 November 1979, the overrunning of its premises, the seizure of its inmates as hostages, the appropriation of its property and archives and the conduct of the Iranian authorities in the face of those occurrences. ...

[58] No suggestion has been made that the militants, when they executed their attack on the Embassy, had any form of official status as recognized "agents" or organs of the Iranian State. Their conduct in mounting the attack, overrunning the Embassy and seizing its inmates as hostages cannot, therefore, be regarded as imputable to that State on that basis. ...

[61] The conclusion just reached ... does not mean that Iran is, in consequence, free of any responsibility in regard to those attacks; for its own conduct was in conflict with its international obligations. By a number of provisions of the Vienna Conventions of 1961 and 1963, Iran was placed under the most categorical obligations, as a receiving State, to take appropriate steps to ensure the protection of the United States Embassy and Consulates, their staffs, their archives, their means of communication and the freedom of movement of the members of their staffs. ...

[63] The facts ... establish to the satisfaction of the Court that on 4 November 1979 the Iranian Government failed altogether to take any "appropriate steps" to protect the premises, staff and archives of the United States' mission against attack by the militants, and to take any steps either to prevent this attack or to stop it before it reached its completion. ...

[66] As to the actual conduct of the Iranian authorities when faced with the events of 4 November 1979, the information before the Court establishes that, despite assurances previously given by them to the United States Government and despite repeated and urgent calls for help, they took no apparent steps either to prevent the militants from invading the Embassy or to persuade or to compel them to withdraw. Furthermore, after the militants had forced an entry into the premises of the Embassy, the Iranian authorities made no effort to compel or even to persuade them to withdraw from the Embassy and to free the diplomatic and consular staff whom they had made prisoner.

[67] This inaction of the Iranian Government by itself constituted clear and serious violation of Iran's obligations to the United States under the provisions of Article 22, paragraph 2, and Articles 24, 25, 26, 27 and 29 of the 1961 Vienna Convention on Diplomatic Relations. ...

[69] The second phase of the events which are the subject of the United States' claims comprises the whole series of facts which occurred following the completion of the occupation of the United States Embassy by the militants. ... The occupation having taken place and the diplomatic and consular personnel of the United States' mission having been taken hostage, the action required of the Iranian Government by the Vienna Conventions and by general international law was manifest. Its plain duty was at once to make every effort, and to take every appropriate step, to bring these flagrant infringements of the inviolability of the premises, archives and diplomatic and consular staff of the United States Embassy to a speedy end, ... and in general to re-establish the status quo and to offer reparation for the damage.

[70] No such step was, however, taken by the Iranian authorities. ...

[71] In any event expressions of approval of the take-over of the Embassy ... by militants came immediately from numerous Iranian authorities, including religious, judicial, executive, police and broadcasting authorities. Above all, the Ayatollah Khomeini himself made crystal clear the endorsement by the State both of the take-over of the Embassy ... and of the detention of the Embassy staff as hostages. At a reception in Qom on 5 November, the Ayatollah Khomeini left his audience in no doubt as to his approval of the action of the militants in occupying the Embassy, to which he said they had resorted "because they saw that the shah was allowed in America." ...

[73] The seal of official government approval was finally set on this situation by a decree issued on 17 November 1979 by the Ayatollah Khomeini. His decree began with the assertion that the American Embassy was "a centre of espionage and conspiracy" and that "those people who hatched plots against our Islamic movement in that place do not enjoy international diplomatic respect." He went on expressly to declare that the premises of the Embassy and the hostages would remain as they were until the United States had handed over the former Shah for trial and returned his property to Iran. ...

[74] The policy thus announced by the Ayatollah Khomeini, ... was complied with by other Iranian authorities and endorsed by them repeatedly in statements made in various contexts. The result of that policy was fundamentally to transform the legal nature of the situation created by the occupation of the Embassy and the detention of its diplomatic and consular staff as hostages. The approval given to these facts by the Ayatollah Khomeini and other organs of the Iranian State, and the decision to perpetuate them, translated continuing occupation of the Embassy and detention of the hostages into acts of that State. The militants, authors of the invasion and jailers of the hostages, had now become agents of the Iranian State for whose acts the State itself was internationally responsible. ...

[76] The Iranian authorities' decision to continue the subjection of the premises of the United States Embassy to occupation by militants and of the Embassy staff to detention as hostages, clearly gave rise to repeated and multiple breaches of the applicable provisions of the Vienna Conventions even more serious than those which

arose from their failure to take any steps to prevent the attacks on the inviolability of these premises and staff.

[77] In the first place, these facts constituted breaches additional to those already committed of paragraph 2 of Article 22 of the 1961 Vienna Convention on Diplomatic Relations which requires Iran to protect the premises of the mission against any intrusion or damage and to prevent any disturbance of its peace or impairment of its dignity. Paragraphs 1 and 3 of that Article have also been infringed, and continue to be infringed, since they forbid agents of a receiving State to enter the premises of a mission without consent or to undertake any search, requisition, attachment or like measure on the premises. Secondly, they constitute continuing breaches of Article 29 of the same Convention which forbids any arrest or detention of a diplomatic agent and any attack on his person, freedom or dignity. Thirdly, the Iranian authorities are without doubt in continuing breach of the provisions of Articles 25, 26 and 27 of the 1961 Vienna Convention ... concerning facilities for the performance of functions, freedom of movement and communications for diplomatic and consular staff, as well as of Article 24 of the former Convention ... which provide for the absolute inviolability of the archives and documents of diplomatic missions and consulates. This particular violation has been made manifest to the world by repeated statements by the militants occupying the Embassy, who claim to be in possession of documents from the archives, and by various government authorities, purporting to specify the contents thereof. ...

[86] The rules of diplomatic law, in short, constitute a self-contained regime which, on the one hand, lays down the receiving State's obligations regarding the facilities, privileges and immunities to be accorded to diplomatic missions and, on the other, foresees their possible abuse by members of the mission and specifies the means at the disposal of the receiving State to counter any such abuse. These means are, by their nature, entirely efficacious, for unless the sending State recalls the member of the mission objected to forthwith, the prospect of the almost immediate loss of his privileges and immunities, because of the withdrawal by the receiving State of his recognition as a member of the mission, will in practice compel that person, in his own interest, to depart at once. But the principle of the inviolability of the persons of diplomatic agents and the premises of diplomatic missions is one of the very foundations of this long-established régime, to the evolution of which the traditions of Islam made a substantial contribution. The fundamental character of the principle of inviolability is, moreover, strongly underlined by the provisions of Article 44 and 45 of the Convention of 1961 ...

Even in the case of armed conflict or in the case of a breach in diplomatic relations those provisions require that both the inviolability of the members of a diplomatic mission and of the premises, property and archives of the mission must be respected by the receiving State.

NOTES

1) The Court held, by 13 votes to 2, that Iran had violated and was still violating its obligations toward the United States. It also decided, unanimously, that Iran must immediately release the hostages and, by 12 votes to 3, that Iran was under an obligation

to make reparation. Iran did not comply with the Court's judgment but released the hostages in January 1981 as a result of a negotiated settlement with the United States.[109]

2) If Iran had appeared in the case and brought evidence that the American diplomats were spies who had engaged in espionage from the haven of the U.S. embassy, as was alleged, would such proof constitute a defence to Iranian wrongdoing? A valid counterclaim? Consider the Vienna Convention articles 9 and 41.[110]

3) During the course of the litigation, the United States took a number of actions against Iran that in Judge Morozov's opinion, at least, created a situation surrounding the litigation that "has no precedent in the whole history of the administration of international justice. ..." In particular, the United States froze $12 billion worth of Iranian assets, it introduced legislation to pay American nationals for outstanding claims against Iran out of Iranian assets, and it made a military incursion into Iran in an attempt to rescue the hostages. How do you think these events should affect the Court's decision on Iran's liability? On Iran's duty to make reparations?[111]

4) This case involved abuse of foreign diplomats by the host state. If the issue is breach of diplomatic privileges by the foreign representatives, what can the host state do in response? Consider articles 9, 29, and 41 reproduced in the Documentary Supplement. Are the provisions of the Convention sufficient in the face of serious offences? Consider two incidents in Britain in which (1) a police officer on the street was fatally shot by someone from inside the Libyan mission, and (2) a Nigerian citizen was rescued at Heathrow Airport as he was about to be abducted to Nigeria in the diplomatic bag. Can the host state take countermeasures outside of the Convention? Refer to the discussion of "Countermeasures" in Chapter 10, Section D.2.[112]

Consular and Other Immunities

from S.A. Williams and A.L.C. de Mestral, *An Introduction to International Law* 2d ed. (1987), 161-66 (most footnotes omitted)

B. The Vienna Convention on Consular Relations, 1963[113]

Consular relations, like diplomatic relations, are established by mutual consent between the sending and receiving states. In effect, consent to diplomatic relations,

---

109 For opinions on the case, see M.W. Janis, "The Role of the International Court in the Hostages Crisis" and E. Gordon & P.J. Youngblood, "... A Rejoinder" (1980-81) 13 Conn. L.R. 263, 429, and 459; and T.L. Stein, "Contempt, Crisis and the Court: The World Court and the Hostage Rescue Attempt" (1982) 76 A.J.I.L. 499.

110 And see the judgment, [1980] I.C.J. Rep. 3 at 38-40.

111 See *ibid.* at 43-44, and Judge Morozov's dissent at 53-57.

112 See R. Higgins, "The Abuse of Diplomatic Privileges and Immunities: Recent United Kingdom Experience" (1985) 79 A.J.I.L. 641 and M. Herdegen, "The Abuse of Diplomatic Privileges and Countermeasures not Covered by Vienna Convention on Diplomatic Relations" (1986) 46 Zeit. Aus. Off. Recht & Volkerrecht 734.

113 Can. T.S. 1947 No. 25. Canada acceded to this Convention on July 18, 1974. And see L.T. Lee, *Consular Law and Practice*, 2d ed. (1991).

unless otherwise stated, implies consent to consular relations. The Vienna Convention on Consular Relations of 1963 was influenced by the adoption of the Convention on Diplomatic Relations in 1961. However, it does not codify all pre-existing rules of customary international law.

Consuls, although they represent their state, do so in a different way from diplomats. They are not concerned with political relations between the two states but with administrative matters. Their functions consist in, *inter alia*, issuing of visas and passports, assisting nationals of their state and furthering the commercial, economic, cultural and scientific relations of their state with the host state. Consulates exist in many provincial cities as well as the capital cities of the host states.

Many of the provisions concerning the inviolability of consular premises, are similar to those found in the Diplomatic Relations Convention although the wording is more restrictive. Archives and documents belonging to the consulate are inviolable. As with diplomatic agents, consular officers must be treated with due respect and shall not be liable to arrest or detention pending trial except in the case of a grave crime and pursuant to a decision by the competent judicial authority. Canada has implemented this Convention in the same Act of 1977.[114] Section 2(3) of that Act stipulates that the reference in article 41(1) of the Vienna Convention on Consular Relations to a "grave crime" shall be construed in Canada as a reference to any offence created by an Act of Parliament for which an offender may be sentenced to imprisonment for five years or more.

Consular officers and employees enjoy a more limited immunity from jurisdiction than diplomats. In both criminal and civil matters immunity is restricted by article 43(1) to acts performed in the course of their consular functions. The provisions as to waiver are the same as in the earlier Convention.

Where diplomatic agents are assigned to the consular section of a mission they continue to enjoy the privileges and immunities recognized by the rules of international law on diplomatic relations.

C. Special Missions

Special missions or ad hoc missions are sent to certain countries for a specific and limited purpose. They supplement the diplomatic and consular missions in this regard. The use of such temporary missions has become more prevalent since the development of faster transportation.

As a result, no rules of customary international law can be said to have developed on this subject. Thus, the Convention of 1969 dealing with Special Missions[115] is not a codification of existing law and is not binding on non-parties. It is not certain yet whether the law will develop into customary rules by non-parties adhering to them. ...

---

114   *Diplomatic and Consular Privileges and Immunities Act*, S.C. 1976-77, c. 31 [now replaced by the *Foreign Missions and International Organizations Act*, S.C. 1991, c. 41].

115   GA Res. 2530 (XXIV), UN GAOR, 24th Sess., Supp. No. 30, U.N. Doc. A/7630 (1969) 99, reprinted in (1969) 8 I.L.M. 73 [in force since June 21, 1985]. Canada has not signed or ratified the Convention.

The model for the Convention on Special Missions was the Vienna Convention on Diplomatic Relations of 1961. The only difference is that under article 8 the sending state must inform the host state of both the size and the composition of the mission. Article 17 provides that the mission must be located in a place agreed upon by the states concerned or be located in the Foreign Ministry of the host state. ...

D. Privileges and Immunities of the United Nations

Article 105 of the U.N. Charter provides in general terms that the United Nations should enjoy in the territory of each member state such privileges and immunities as are necessary for the fulfillment of its purposes. It further provides that the representatives of the member states at the United Nations and officials of the United Nations itself shall likewise enjoy the privileges and immunities that are necessary for the independent exercise of their functions.

The General Assembly is authorized by article 105 of the Charter to make recommendations with a view to determining the details of these privileges and immunities, or to propose conventions for this purpose.

In relation to this authorization in 1946 the General Assembly of the United Nations adopted the Convention on the Privileges and Immunities of the United Nations.[116] Canada ratified this Convention on June 22, 1948, with a reservation relating to taxation. This convention provides, *inter alia*, for the following: immunity of United Nations property and assets from legal process unless such immunity is waived; inviolability of premises and archives and special privileges for its representatives including immunity from criminal jurisdiction.

A number of special agreements have also been concluded with those states in those territories the United Nations or one of its subsidiary organs meets or has its headquarters. For example, the agreement between the United States and the United Nations regarding the headquarters of the United Nations in New York.[117]

In 1947, the General Assembly adopted another Convention for the co-ordination of privileges and immunities of the specialized agencies with those of the United Nations itself.[118] Canada acceded to this Convention on the Privileges and Immunities of the Specialized Agencies on March 29, 1966. Again a reservation was made regarding taxes. The United Nations did not accept the Canadian instrument of accession deposited with the said reservation and Canada is not therefore listed among the parties to the Convention. ...

---

[116] Otherwise known as the General Convention (1949) 43 A.J.I.L. Supp. 1. This [now] forms Schedule III to the *Foreign Missions and International Organizations Act*, S.C. 1991, c. 41.

[117] (1949) 43 A.J.I.L. Supp. 8.

[118] 33 U.N.T.S. 261 & 290.

E. The International Court of Justice

Under the provisions of article 19 of the Statute of the Court, the judges of the International Court of Justice enjoy diplomatic privileges and immunities when acting in their official capacity.

F. Visiting Forces

Opinions have differed as to how far immunity should be extended to foreign visiting forces. United States practice generally favoured absolute immunity. Today it is not looked upon in such an exclusive manner. The remedy to avoid controversy from the United States viewpoint has been to conclude numerous special agreements with the host state. ...

The *Visiting Forces Act, 1970,*[119] applies today in respect of a state designated by the Governor in Council. Under s. 5(1), the Canadian courts have jurisdiction in respect of acts or omissions constituting an offence against any Canadian laws committed by a member of a visiting force or a dependant, subject to s. 6(2). Sections 6(1) and 6(2) provide that the service authorities and service courts of a visiting force may exercise within Canada in relation to members of the force and their dependants criminal and disciplinary jurisdiction conferred upon them by the sending state, with respect to alleged offences concerning the property or security of the sending state, the person or property of another member of the visiting force or dependant, or an act done or an omission in the performance of official duty.

NOTES

1) The United Nations has expanded its work on the privileges and immunities of intergovernmental organizations beyond the U.N. itself and the specialized agencies. In 1975 it adopted the Vienna Convention on the Representation of States in their Relations with International Organizations of a Universal Character.[120]

2) Canada is not a party to the 1975 convention, but arranges for appropriate privileges and immunities for international organizations under the *Foreign Missions and International Organizations Act.*[121] Section 5 permits the Governor in Council to

---

119   [Now R.S.C. 1985, c. V-2.] Note that when Canadian forces are visiting other countries they are subject to Canadian criminal law and the local criminal law under ... the *National Defence Act,* [now R.S.C. 1985, c. N-5, ss. 130-32]. Therefore, they are subject to the concurrent jurisdiction of Canadian service tribunals and the local courts. Immunity from the local jurisdiction in the absence of specific agreement would be based on customary international law. See Law Reform Commission Working Paper 37, *Extraterritorial Jurisdiction* (1984) at 129. See also the North Atlantic Treaty Status of Forces Agreement, Can. T.S. 1951 & 1953 No. 13, which is a multilateral treaty governing the exercise of jurisdiction between the sending and receiving states relating to visiting forces from a NATO state. For the jurisdictional immunities of United Nations forces see *e.g.* the agreement between the United Nations and Cyprus (1964) 492 U.N.T.S. 57.

120   U.N. Doc. A/CONF. 67/16 (1975), not yet in force.

121   S.C. 1991, c. 41. And see the litigation surrounding the collapse of the International Tin Council, especially *J.H. Rayner (Mincing Lane) Ltd. v. Dept. Trade and Industry,* [1989] 3 W.L.R. 969 (H.L.) and

designate those international organizations that shall have legal capacities as corporate bodies in Canada and to fix the extent of immunities available to them under the Convention on the Privileges and Immunities of the United Nations. The Governor in Council also has authority to apply the Convention on U.N. Privileges or the Vienna Convention on Diplomatic Relations, as suitable, to foreign state representatives to, and foreign staff members of, international organizations meeting or headquartered in Canada.

3) As host to the International Civil Aviation Organisation (ICAO) in Montreal, Canada has direct responsibilities and special arrangements for its premises and personnel. These are set out in the Headquarters Agreement between Canada and the ICAO[122] and include inviolability of its premises, immunity of its property, and functional immunities and privileges for its personnel to fulfill their duties.

4) The rapid increase in the number and complexity of United Nations peacekeeping operations, both civilian and military, since 1990 has given rise to serious questions about the participants' safety, status, and immunities in the territory of operations. The United Nations tried to resolve the problems by adopting a Convention on the Safety of United Nations and Associated Personnel that prohibits attacks on personnel engaged in humanitarian missions, as well as against their equipment and premises.[123]

5) Under the Rome Statute of the International Criminal Court both the Court and its judges are granted privileges and immunities in the territory of states parties.[124]

Shearson Lehman Brothers Inc. v. MacLaine, Watson & Co. Ltd., *supra* note 93. See also *Canada (Attorney General) v. Lavigne* (1997), 145 D.L.R. (4th) 252, in which the prosecution of a Canadian importer of alcohol on behalf of the International Civil Aviation Organisation in Montreal was stopped because the organization, as a specialized agency of the U.N., had been accorded all the benefits of the Convention on the Privileges and Immunities of the United Nations by order of the Governor in Council under the *Foreign Missions and International Organizations Act*: SOR/94-563.

[122] Can. T.S. 1992 No. 7 and the Supplementary Agreement between Canada and ICAO, Can. T.S. 1999 No. 20. On the interface of these treaty arrangements with the Canadian legal system, see *Miller v. Canada*, [2001] 1 S.C.R. 407. See also P. Dai, "The Headquarters Agreement between Canada and the International Civil Aviation Organization" (1964) 2 Can. Y.B. Int'l L. 205. A Headquarters Agreement was also signed between Canada and the United Nations concerning the United Nations Audio-Visual Information Centre on Human Settlements, Can. T.S. 1977 No. 27.

[123] *Convention on the Safety of United Nations and Associated Personnel (Annex)*, GA res. 49/59, UN GAOR, 49th Sess., Supp. No. 49, U.N. Doc. A/49/49 (1994) 299. See H. Kindred, "The Protection of Peacekeepers" (1995) 33 Can. Y.B. Int'l L. 257; P. Kirsch, "Convention on the Safety of United Nations and Associated Personnel" (1994) 23 C.C.I.L. Proc. 182. The Convention entered into force 15 January, 1999. Canada ratified the Convention 3 March, 2002.

[124] U.N. Doc. A/CONF.183/9 (17 July 1998) as corrected, art. 48. *Agreement on the Privileges and Immunities of the International Criminal Court*, ICC-ASP/1/3 printed in *Assembly of States Parties to the Rome Statute of the International Criminal Court*, Official Records, Sess. 1, 3-10 September 2002, at 215.

CHAPTER SIX

International Dispute Settlement

A. INTRODUCTION: THE RANGE OF DISPUTE RESOLUTION MECHANISMS

The international legal system, like any other legal system, requires some means of settling disputes that may arise among its various actors. Over the course of its history, but particularly over the past century, the international system has developed a complex array of mechanisms and institutions for the settlement of disputes. The choice of the means of resolution is generally left to the parties; however, in the U.N. era, the settlement of disputes by peaceful means has come to be viewed as a requirement of international law. Arguably, this means a great deal more than merely refraining from the use of force; it may be said to require an active commitment on the part of States to resolve their differences and minimize the potential for threats to international peace and security.[1]

This obligation is reflected in various provisions of the U.N. Charter. Article 1(1)[2] declares the pacific settlement of disputes to be a purpose of the organization, in order to further the maintenance of international peace and security. Article 2(3) obliges member states to settle their disputes by peaceful means. Chapter 6 of the U.N. Charter on the Pacific Settlement of Disputes elaborates on these objectives and obligations. In particular, article 33 lists a number of alternative means of peaceful dispute settlement: "negotiation, enquiry, mediation, conciliation, arbitration, judicial settlement, resort to regional agencies or arrangements, or other peaceful means of [the parties'] own choice." This was clearly not intended to be an exhaustive enumeration of the choices available. The Security Council is given the power, under article 34, to investigate any situation that might give rise to a dispute and, by article 36, to recommend any appropriate method of adjustment of the differences between states, and the extension of the good offices of an intermediary, such as the Secretary-General under article 99. These provisions were further elaborated in the Declaration on Principles of International Law Concerning Friendly Relations and Co-operation among States in Accordance with the Charter of the United Nations.[3] More recently, the heads of state and government, gathered in the General

---

1   See the discussion of the various interpretations of this obligation in Nii Lante Wallace-Bruce, *The Settlement of International Disputes: The Contribution of Australia and New Zealand* (1998) at 28-37.

2   Reproduced in the Documentary Supplement.

3   Reproduced in the Documentary Supplement.

Assembly for the World Summit in September 2005, "emphasize[d] the obligation of states to settle their disputes by peaceful means in accordance with Chapter VI of the Charter, including when appropriate, by the use of the International Court of Justice."[4]

Dispute resolution mechanisms can be seen as lying at different points along a continuum of third-party involvement and binding character. A distinction can be drawn between "diplomatic" means of peaceful settlement of disputes, which include negotiation, good offices, mediation, inquiry, and conciliation, on the one hand, and "adjudicative" means of dispute settlement, which include arbitration and judicial settlement, on the other. Such a distinction should not be overstated, however, as all forms of international dispute settlement involve a significant legal component, and all take place within a broader political context that tends to influence the legal outcome. As Robert Y. Jennings, a distinguished international lawyer and former president of the International Court of Justice (ICJ), has noted:

> It is a besetting weakness of lawyers—and not only of international lawyers—to think of law, and even sometimes to attempt to define law, as if it consisted only of rules suitable to be applied by courts in adversary proceedings between two parties. This distorted view of the role of the law in a society is singularly inapt for international law which throughout its history has been employed much more as an instrument of diplomacy than of formal forensic confrontation. Naturally, courts and court-law are of great importance in international law; yet so also is that law which provides the frameworks, procedures and standards for international political decision; and it is certainly the further development of this latter kind of international law which presents the most urgent problem today.[5]

In many international disputes several methods of settlement are employed together or consecutively, or elements of them are integrated to meet the needs of the particular situation. Typically, the parties will at least initially give pre-eminence to the political elements of their dispute and will try to seek a settlement by diplomacy. Some differences can be distinguished among the "diplomatic means." Negotiation only involves the parties themselves and is aimed at achieving a mutually acceptable outcome, while good offices, mediation, inquiry, and conciliation all involve third-party intervention aimed not at deciding the dispute, but at inducing or assisting the parties to settle it for themselves. By selecting adjudicative means, the parties treat the dispute as "justiciable"—that is, capable of solution by law. These mechanisms also have significant differences between them. While arbitration leads to a binding settlement of a dispute on the basis of law, it differs from judicial settlement in that, as a rule, parties have the competence to appoint arbitrators, determine the procedure, and indicate the applicable law as they see fit. Judicial settlement is probably the least commonly applied process of conflict resolution in the international community, though not necessarily the least significant.

The materials that follow in this chapter discuss each of the dispute settlement techniques mentioned above, beginning with *inter partes* negotiation and proceeding

---

4   *2005 World Summit Outcome*, U.N. Doc. A/60/L.1 (2005) at para. 73.

5   Robert Y. Jennings, "General Course on Principles of International Law" (1967) 121 Rec. des Cours 323 at 327-28. See also Jauquin Tacsan, *The Dynamics of International Law in Conflict Resolution* (1992).

through methods of third-party intervention of increasingly authoritative character. The primary purpose is to provide an overview of the general framework for dispute settlement in international law. However, it is important to recognize that the range of peaceful means of dispute settlement is growing as new techniques and institutional mechanisms to verify and enforce compliance with international law are devised and agreed on. These are typically established by treaty and moulded to the particular subject matter of the convention. Thus, they are specific to the parties and to the subject of the treaty and are chiefly discussed in the relevant chapters dealing with those particular fields of international law. The concluding section of this chapter is therefore limited to a brief survey of some of these more specialized agencies for dispute settlement.

B. DIPLOMATIC MEANS OF DISPUTE SETTLEMENT[6]

Diplomatic means tend not to be sharply differentiated and separately institutionalized procedures. Yet each method has a distinct characteristic that makes it worthy of separate consideration. Most international disputes are dealt with through direct negotiations between the parties in conflict. However, when the parties fail to settle their differences by negotiation between themselves, the introduction of a trusted stranger may help them.[7] The intervention of a third party can occur in several ways, all of which are intended to facilitate the resolution of a dispute by the parties themselves. The intervening third party does not decide the matter for them, but advises them. The differences between these processes are largely a matter of the intervenor's degree of initiative in securing a settlement. While good offices connote little more than a third party (frequently an influential individual) encouraging the parties to negotiate and acting as a conduit for the parties' proposals to each other, conciliation is likely to involve an investigation of the dispute and the presentation of a formal, albeit non-binding, proposal for its solution. Mediation and inquiry lie somewhere in between. Generally an inquiry is set up only to determine the facts of the dispute. A mediator assists the parties' negotiations and makes independent proposals for the resolution of a dispute, but usually on the basis of information the parties have made available.

---

6   Marcel M.T.A. Brus, *Third Party Dispute Settlement in an Interdependent World: Developing a Theoretical Framework* (1995); John Collier & Vaughan Lowe, *The Settlement of Disputes in International Law: Institutions and Procedures* (1999); David Davies Memorial Institute of International Studies, *International Disputes: The Legal Aspects* (1972); Hersch Lauterpacht, *The Function of Law in the International Community* (1933); J.G. Merrills, *International Dispute Settlement*, 3d ed. (1998); K. Venkata Raman, ed., *International Dispute Settlement Through the United Nations* (1977); Wallace-Bruce, *supra* note 1; Connie Peck, *The United Nations as a Dispute Settlement System: Improving the Mechanism for the Prevention and Resolution of Conflict* (1996); and Malcom D. Evans, ed., *Remedies in International Law: The Institutional Dilemma* (1998). For a comprehensive set of documents relating to dispute settlement, see Karin Oellers-Frahm & Andreas Zimmerman, eds., *Dispute Settlement in Public International Law: Texts and Materials* (2001). See also *Peaceful Settlement of Disputes Between States: A Selective Bibliography* (1991).

7   See Thomas Princen, *Intermediaries in International Conflict* (1992).

1. Negotiation[8]

Article 33 of the U.N. Charter does not state the various peaceful means of dispute settlement in any particular order of priority, but by far the most important method is direct negotiation between the parties in conflict. The primary advantage of negotiation is obvious: it offers each party complete control over its vital interests in the dispute at all stages along the way to resolution.

In the process of drafting the Declaration on Principles of International Law Concerning Friendly Relations and Co-operation Among States,[9] there was considerable debate over whether negotiation should be accorded formal priority among the various mechanisms for peaceful settlement of disputes.[10] Several Special Committee representatives, entrusted by the General Assembly with studying the relevant principles of international law, insisted that direct negotiation was the fundamental means of resolving international disputes, and should be recognized as such:

> [I]f direct negotiation was the means by which most international disputes were settled, that was due to the fact that by its very nature it most adequately met the need for the prompt and flexible settlement of international disputes, that it better preserved the equality of the parties, that it could be used for the settlement of both political and legal disputes, and that it offered the most effective means for the peaceful settlement of disputes. Moreover, direct negotiations best promoted compromise, and prevented disputes from acquiring proportions which made them a threat to international peace and security, since they made it possible for conflicts to be dealt with as soon as they arose. Furthermore, direct negotiation was a means that did not oblige third States to take up a specific position on disputes which did not affect their interests or threaten international peace and security .... In addition, the means of direct negotiation, while it brought about the settlement of disputes, could at the same time bring into being rules regulating future relations between the States concerned, thus promoting the development of international law.[11]

Those who felt that negotiation should not be given priority over other means of dispute settlement insisted that "the constant trend in the development of international law in this regard since the 19th century had been to transcend the stage of negotiation and to establish and improve more institutional means of settlement based on recourse to third parties or organs."[12] They also pointed out various disadvantages of negotiation:

---

8   See Gilbert R. Winham, "International Negotiation in an Age of Transition" (1979-80) 35 Int'l J. 1; P. Terrence Hopmann, *The Negotiation Process and the Resolution of International Conflicts* (1996); Victor A. Kremenjuk, ed., *International Negotiation: Analysis, Approaches, Issues*, 2d ed. (2002); and Janice Gross Stein, ed., *Getting to the Table: The Processes of International Prenegotiation* (1989).

9   Reproduced in the Documentary Supplement.

10 See *Report of the Special Committee on Principles of International Law Concerning Friendly Relations and Co-operation Among States*, U.N. Doc. A/5746 "Direct Negotiation," paras. 155-63, [1964] U.N. Jur. Y. B. 65 at 115-17.

11 *Ibid.*, para. 156 at 115.

12 *Ibid.*, para. 158 at 116.

[D]irect negotiation did not allow the facts to be established objectively and impartially, nor enable third parties to exercise a moderating influence on the dispute, nor prevent the putting forward of exaggerated claims which might aggravate the dispute, nor ensure equal terms, since usually one of the parties was in a weaker position than the other; nor could it be used for the solution of certain types of disputes, nor guarantee the solution of a dispute since either party could choose to be intransigent at any moment.[13]

In the final result, the Declaration followed the Charter in not according priority to any one method of dispute settlement, but the debate illustrates many of the ongoing issues surrounding the importance and efficacy of negotiation.

Negotiation can take many different forms. Merrills identifies four possibilities: normal diplomatic channels, the most common form, in which negotiations are carried out by foreign offices or diplomatic representatives; competent authorities, in which negotiations are conducted by representatives of a specialized ministry or department; institutionalized negotiation, in which the parties set up a "mixed" or "joint" commission in order to address a "recurrent problem or a situation requiring continuous supervision"; and summit discussions, meetings between heads of state or foreign ministers, which tend to be resorted to when other forms of negotiation have been unproductive.[14]

In Canadian practice, informal contacts with foreign governments may be made by senior officials of the federal government, as well as locally stationed diplomatic staff, on their own initiative and authority. Such contacts are likely to be preliminary to opening negotiations or to sound out opinion. Whether formal or informal, negotiations of any importance usually require ministerial, and even Cabinet, authorization. Even so, the actual negotiating is likely to be undertaken by a delegation of mostly middle-rank officials. A senior officer or a Minister will be the nominal leader but he or she may not be much involved until the final stages of agreement and signature are reached, unless the matter is of a high political character.

A number of factors may influence the conduct of intergovernmental negotiations.[15] To achieve a negotiated settlement, each party must believe that the benefits to be gained from an agreement will be outweighed by the compromises it must make. In particular, domestic and international public opinion may have considerable impact. "The element of give and take which is usually an essential part of a successful negotiation is likely to be inhibited if every step is being monitored by interested pressure groups at home, while the suspicion that the other side may simply be interested in eliciting a favourable audience reaction may lead serious proposals to be dismissed as mere propaganda."[16] The

---

13   *Ibid.*

14   See Merrills, *supra* note 6 at 8-12. Merrills points out, however, that "summit diplomacy is usually the culmination of a great deal of conventional negotiation and in some cases at least reflects nothing more than a desire to make political capital out of an agreement that is already assured."

15   See *e.g.* the discussion of the cultural dimension of negotiation tactics in Guy Olivier Faure & Jeffrey Z. Rubin, eds., *Culture and Negotiation: The Resolution of Water Disputes* (1993) and Paul R. Kimmel, "Cultural Perspectives on International Negotiations" (1994) 50 J. of Social Issues 179.

16   Merrills, *supra* note 6 at 15.

unprecedented level of scrutiny by the media is another factor that has changed the nature of international negotiations, though states frequently use it to their advantage by using the media to send diplomatic messages to each other under the guise of public announcements and press conferences.

An entirely new level of scrutiny is introduced in the conduct of multilateral negotiations. At the present time, many international conferences take place under intense scrutiny by the media and representatives of civil society, which in some instances extends to a day-by-day account of activities. While the media may be denied access to some of the more delicate diplomatic issues, the speculation that surrounds them may in and of itself exert considerable pressure. Multilateral negotiations introduce a host of other considerations as well; to some extent they represent a significant departure from bilateral negotiation tactics.[17]

2. Good Offices[18]

As noted previously, a third party providing good offices has a fairly limited role and tends to act mainly as a conduit for the parties' proposals to one another. However, the importance of this role and of the particular individual or entity chosen to undertake it should not be underestimated. As Lachs has pointed out, "[T]he provision of good offices— what has been called 'quiet diplomacy'—is an important function which may be entrusted to personalities with special qualifications on whom both parties agree."[19] Well-known individuals or heads of state might be called on, and in the U.N. era the Secretary-General of the United Nations has played a particularly prominent role. According to Lachs:

> In quite a number of cases, the Secretary-General has in fact been able to assist in resolving disputes or has succeeded in arresting the deterioration of a situation by his actions conducted in time. As has been demonstrated in several concrete cases, it is especially his "quiet diplomacy" which may be fruitful in situations with a humanitarian background.[20]

The potentially thankless nature of the task involved was explained by Secretary-General U Thant as follows:

---

17   See generally Johan Kaufmann, *Conference Diplomacy: An Introductory Analysis,* 3d ed. (1996) and Johan Kaufmann, ed., *Effective Negotiation: Case Studies in Conference Diplomacy* (1989). The conduct of negotiations by Canada in the largest multilateral conference to date—the Third U.N. Conference on the Law of the Sea—is analyzed in A.L.C. de Mestral & L.H.J. Legault, "Multilateral Negotiation— Canada and the Law of the Sea Conference" (1979-80) 35 Int'l J. 47. See also Barry Buzan, "Negotiating by Consensus: Developments in Technique at the United Nations Conference on the Law of the Sea" (1981) 75 A.J.I.L. 324.

18   See B.G. Ramcharan, "Good Offices, Preventive Action, and Peacemaking by the United Nations Secretary-General" (1996) C.C.I.L. Proc. 112. See also Raymond R. Probst, *"Good Offices" in the Light of Swiss International Practice and Experience* (1989) and B.G. Ramcharan, *Humanitarian Good Offices in International Law* (1983).

19   Manfred Lachs, "The Development and General Trends of International Law in Our Time" (1980) 169 Hague Recueil 9 at 220.

20   *Ibid.*

The kind of problem involved is invariably delicate and difficult and usually involves the prestige and public position of the governments concerned. If a way out is to be found, it must, therefore, be through mutual confidence, mutual respect and absolute discretion. Any hint that an action of the Secretary-General might serve to score political points for one party or another, or, indeed, that credit might be claimed publicly on his behalf for this or that development, would almost invariably and instantly render his efforts useless. Thus, it is often the case that while the Secretary-General is working privately with the parties in an attempt to resolve a delicate situation, he is criticized publicly for his inaction or even for lack of interest.[21]

A separate issue that arises is whether such a role is an appropriate one for the Secretary-General who, after all, is an international civil servant and the chief *administrative* officer of the United Nations. His or her position and power are defined by the Charter articles 97 to 101, reproduced in the Documentary Supplement. Where in those articles is authority granted to him or her to intervene in disputes between member states? That successive Secretaries-General have intervened in international disputes, frequently to advantage, has not prevented questions being raised about their authority to do so by states that consider their actions an interference in sovereign or domestic affairs. The usual reply is that the Secretary-General is entitled under article 99 "to bring to the attention of the Security Council any matter that in his opinion may threaten the maintenance of international peace and security" and, to do so, he has a right to take whatever steps he considers necessary to inform himself about a pending dispute.[22] Is this a legitimate interpretation of article 99? In fact, the increasing involvement of the United Nations in conflict situations around the world has already required the Secretary-General to take even greater initiatives. These certainly involve a significant departure from the mere provision of good offices. See the subsequent discussion in Section E on "Other Agencies of Peaceful Settlement of Disputes."

3. Mediation[23]

As noted above, mediation occupies a "middle ground" among the various diplomatic methods of dispute settlement. Merrills describes the process thus:

---

21 *Ibid.* at 221.

22 Vratislav Pechota, "The Quiet Approach: A Study of the Good Offices Exercised by the United Nations Secretary-General in the Cause of Peace" in Raman, *supra* note 6 at 585. See also Tom Boudreau, *Sheathing the Sword: The UN Secretary-General and the Prevention of International Conflict* (1991); B.G. Ramcharan, *The International Law and Practice of Early-Warning and Preventive Diplomacy: The Emerging Global Watch* (1991) c. 2; Stephen M. Schwebel, *The Secretary-General of the United Nations: His Political Powers and Practice* (1952); and Alan James, "The Secretary-General: A Comparative Analysis," in G.R. Berridge & A. Jennings, eds., *Diplomacy at the U.N.* (1985) at 31.

23 See also Jacob Bercovich & Jeffrey Z. Rubin, *Mediation in International Relations: Multiple Approaches to Conflict Management* (1992); Chester A. Crocker, Fen Osler Hampson, & Pamela Aall, eds., *Herding Cats: Multiparty Mediation in a Complex World* (1999); Marieke Kleiboer, *The Multiple Realities of International Mediation* (1998); C.R. Mitchell & K. Webb, *New Approaches to International Mediation* (1988); and Saadia Touval & I. William Zartman, eds., *International Mediation in Theory and Practice* (1985).

Like good offices, mediation is essentially an adjunct of negotiation, but with the mediator as an active participant, authorised, and indeed expected, to advance his own proposals and to interpret, as well as to transmit, each party's proposals to the other. What distinguishes this kind of assistance from conciliation is that a mediator generally makes his proposals informally and on the basis of information supplied by the parties, rather than his own investigations, although in practice such distinctions tend to be blurred. In a given case it may be difficult to draw the line between mediation and conciliation, or to say exactly when good offices ended and mediation began.[24]

The parties themselves may seek to involve a mediator, whether an individual, a state, or an international organization, whether governmental or non-governmental;[25] alternatively, any one of these entities may offer to mediate. In any event, recourse to mediation depends on the consent of the parties in conflict. There may be a certain reluctance to involve a third party in any capacity. However, mediation offers clear benefits to the parties, as Merrills notes:

> Once under way it provides the governments in dispute with the possibility of a solution, but without any prior commitment to accept the mediator's suggestions. Consequently, it has the advantage of allowing them to retain control of the dispute, probably an essential requirement if negotiations are deadlocked on a matter of vital interest. On the other hand, if a face-saving compromise is what is needed, it may be politically easier to make the necessary concessions in the course of mediation than in direct negotiation. If a dispute concerns sensitive issues, the fact that the proceedings can be completely confidential is an advantage in any case.[26]

The success of the mediation, equally, depends largely on the parties.[27] The "non-bindingness" of the mediator's proposals is well established. For example, article 6 of the 1899 Hague Convention for the Pacific Settlement of International Disputes provided that mediation, "either at the request of the parties at variance, or on the initiative of Powers strangers to the dispute, [has] exclusively the character of advice and never [has] binding force."[28] Nevertheless, this aspect should not be overemphasized. According to Merrills:

> It would be quite wrong to think that a mediator is merely someone who lends his authority to an agreement that is already virtually made. On the contrary, by facilitating the parties' dialogue, providing them with information and suggestions, identifying and exploring their aims and canvassing a range of possible solutions, he can play a vital role in moving them towards agreement. Although success will often be incomplete and failure sometimes inevitable, the mediator's job is to do his best for the parties, and trust that they will reciprocate.[29]

---

24   Merrills, *supra* note 6 at 27.

25   See the discussion in Merrills of the role of the International Committee of the Red Cross, *supra* note 6 at 28.

26   Merrills, *supra* note 6 at 27-28.

27   For a discussion of some of the factors that may affect the success of mediation, such as exhaustion or the risks of escalation, see Merrills, *supra* note 6 at 39-43.

28   Article 6 also refers to good offices.

29   Merrills, *supra* note 6 at 42-43.

4. Commissions of Inquiry

Investigation of the events giving rise to a dispute is a necessary part of all the processes of peaceful settlement. Commissions of inquiry, however, are institutional arrangements for the ascertainment of facts, separate and apart from efforts at settlement. They were introduced into international law by the Hague Conventions for the Pacific Settlement of International Disputes, 1899 and 1907. They are intended to provide a service of independent and objective fact-finding in the hope that clarification of the situation in dispute may help to dissolve contentious issues and to change favourably the attitudes and negotiating positions of the parties. The report of a commission is not binding or determinative, for the parties are free to decide what use and effect it shall have. Although the Hague Conventions created the process, a commission of inquiry has to be constituted on each occasion by agreement of the parties.

Commissions of inquiry under the Hague Conventions have not been frequent,[30] but the process of inquiry is a flexible addition to the battery of means to resolve international disputes and so it has been picked up by other organizations. For example, the ICJ, under its Rules of Court article 66, permits a fact-finding inquiry in the course of a case.[31] The International Civil Aviation Organization (ICAO) Council ordered an investigation in the case of the *Destruction of Korean Airlines Flight 007*,[32] and the U.N. Convention on the Law of the Sea provides for the constitution of special arbitral tribunals empowered to undertake inquiries.[33] Recently, commissions of inquiry have been set up to deal with certain particularly thorny political and humanitarian problems,[34] thus demonstrating the ongoing importance of this particular mechanism.

---

30 For a discussion see Merrills, *supra* note 6, c. 3.

31 As in the *Corfu Channel Case*, [1949] I.C.J. Rep. 4 at 142, 152, 258. See also W.F. Foster, "Fact Finding in the World Court" (1969) 7 Can. Y.B. Int'l L. 150.

32 See report of the incident in Chapter 7, Section D.1 on "Airspace."

33 (1982) 21 I.L.M. 1261, Annex VIII, art. 5.

34 See *e.g.* the description of the establishment of an International Humanitarian Fact-Finding Commission under article 90 of the Protocol Additional to the Geneva Convention of 12 August 1949 and Relating to the Protection of Victims of International Armed Conflicts (Protocol I), in Erich Kussbach, "The International Humanitarian Fact-Finding Commission" (1994) 43 I.C.L.Q. 174. The Commission's website is online: International Humanitarian Fact-Finding Commission <http://www.ihffc.org/>. Article 90 required that the Commission could only be established when 20 parties had agreed to accept its competence; thus, its establishment was delayed until after Canada, the 20th state to do so, made its declaration on November 20, 1990. In 1999, a Commission of Inquiry was set up by the U.N. in order to compile information on possible violations of human rights and breaches of international humanitarian law occurring in East Timor following the results of a popular consultation in which the majority voted in favour of independence from Indonesia. The report of the Commission is available online: United Nations <http://www.unhchr.ch/huridocda/huridoca.nsf/(Symbol)/A.54.726,+S.2000.59.En>. In 2004, the Security Council requested that the Secretary-General establish an international commission of inquiry in order to investigate reports of violations of international humanitarian law and human rights law in Darfur. The report of the Commission was released in early 2005; see Report of the International Commission of Inquiry on Darfur to the United Nations Secretary-General, online: Office of the United Nations High Commissioner for Human Rights <http://www.ohchr.org/english/darfur.htm>.

5. Conciliation[35]

The historical origins of conciliation are usually traced to the so-called Bryan treaties, under which parties agreed to refer "all disputes whatsoever" that could not be settled by other means to standing "Peace Commissions" for investigation and report, and also agreed not to go to war until the Commission issued its report. The inspiration for the mechanism was said to be the commission of inquiry mechanism established by the Hague Conventions.[36]

Conciliation has been defined as "the process of settling a dispute by referring it to a commission of persons whose task it is to elucidate the facts and ... to make a report containing proposals for a settlement, but not having the binding character of an award or judgment."[37] There has been some debate about the exact nature of conciliation. Merrills notes that it can be seen as a form of "institutionalised negotiation," in that "the task of the commission is to encourage and structure the parties' dialogue, while providing them with whatever assistance may be necessary to bring it to a successful conclusion."[38] This aspect of conciliation emphasizes its similarities with mediation. However, as Merrills also notes, "Another view is that conciliation is closer to inquiry or arbitration; that the commission's function is to provide information and advice as to the merits of the parties' positions and to suggest a settlement that corresponds to what they deserve, not what they claim."[39] This gives rise to certain distinctive problems. For example, because a commission's report consists of a set of proposals rather than a decision, commissions are faced with "something of a dilemma. On the one hand they wish to make their proposals as persuasive as possible by supporting them with reasons; on the other they are unwilling to provide the parties with legal arguments or findings of fact that may be cited in subsequent litigation."[40]

Conciliation has been included in the dispute settlement procedures of a number of multilateral treaties, including the Vienna Convention on the Law of Treaties,[41] the International Covenant on Civil and Political Rights,[42] the U.N. Convention on the Law of the Sea,[43] and the Organization for Security and Co-operation in Europe's Convention on Conciliation and Arbitration within the OSCE.[44] In addition, in 1981 the U.N.

---

35   See Jean-Pierre Cot, *International Conciliation*, trans. by R. Myers (1972).

36   See J.L. Brierly, *The Law of Nations: An Introduction to the International Law of Peace*, 6th ed. (1955) at 374.

37   Oppenheim, quoted in Brierly, *ibid*.

38   Merrills, *supra* note 6 at 70.

39   *Ibid.*

40   *Ibid.* at 73. Merrills goes on to discuss how some commissions have dealt with this problem.

41   (1969) 1155 U.N.T.S. 331, art. 66, Annex. See T.O. Elias, *The Modern Laws of Treaties* (1974) c. 13.

42   (1966) 999 U.N.T.S. 171, art. 42.

43   (1982) 21 I.L.M. 1261 art. 284, Annex V.

44   (1993) 32 I.L.M. 551. The Court of Conciliation and Arbitration was set up under the Convention to settle disputes submitted to it by states parties; it provides for the establishment of ad hoc Conciliation Commissions from a roster of conciliators appointed by all states parties. See also the *U.N. Draft Rules for the Conciliation of Disputes Between States* (1991) 30 I.L.M. 229.

Commission on International Trade Law (UNCITRAL) published a set of conciliation rules, including a model contract clause by which to invoke the rules.[45] Belief in the possibilities of conciliation has demonstrably not abated. However, although upward of 200 treaties providing for conciliation have been concluded, few cases have actually been heard. Thus, the process has not fulfilled expectations. In theory, conciliation serves a large variety of useful purposes. Lauterpacht has enumerated these advantages as follows:[46] it brings the parties together; through a moratorium on their actions it prevents sudden breaches of the peace; it replaces rigid law with reasonable discourse about the controversy; it is marked by simplicity; it may have the advantages of the services of experts; and, as its findings are not binding in any case, it eases the conclusion of treaties on the pacific settlement of disputes. Conciliation is most useful in practice, Merrills suggests,[47] in disputes where legal issues are foremost but the parties want an equitable compromise. Perhaps the major obstacle to its use, then, is that such a combination of circumstances is not common.

C. ARBITRATION[48]

In turning to arbitration, the line is crossed from diplomatic methods of settling disputes to adjudication. The contrast is sharpened by the fact that an arbitral award is a binding decision. In choosing arbitration, the parties to a dispute invite others to resolve it for them.

Arbitration has a long history. In modern times, its practice is usually traced to the series of arbitrations that arose from the Jay Treaty of 1794 between the United Kingdom and the United States. The popularity of arbitration as a means of resolving international disputes in the 19th century culminated in the establishment of the Permanent Court of Arbitration (PCA)[49] through the Hague Conventions for the Pacific Settlement of International Disputes, 1899 and 1907. The effect of its creation was to institutionalize the process of arbitration. Each state party to the Hague Conventions appoints four persons to the panel of arbitrators. When two states parties are in conflict and seek arbitration, they each select two arbitrators from the panel, only one of whom may be a national. The four arbitrators then choose an umpire.

The name "Permanent Court of Arbitration" is somewhat misleading. As can be seen from the process, it is not a court in the sense that the World Court is, and it is not permanent. On each occasion the arbitral tribunal has to be constituted by the parties. Yet

---

45   Available online: United Nations Commission on International Trade Law <http://www.uncitral.org/en-index.htm>. See Linda C. Reif, "Conciliation as a Mechanism for the Resolution of International Economic and Business Disputes" (1990-91) 14 Fordham Int'l L.J. 578 at 615-19.

46   Lauterpacht, *supra* note 6 at 261.

47   Merrills, *supra* note 6 at 85.

48   See Sam Muller & Wim Mijs, eds., *The Flame Rekindled: New Hopes for International Arbitration* (1994); Thomas Oehmke, *International Arbitration* (1990); Mauro Rubino-Sammartano, *International Arbitration: Law and Practice*, 2d ed. (2001); Stephen J. Toope, *Mixed International Arbitration: Studies in Arbitration Between States and Private Persons* (1990); and J. Gillis Wetter, ed., *The International Arbitral Process: Public and Private* (1979) 5 vols. of materials and opinions.

49   Online: Permanent Court of Arbitration <http://www.pca-cpa.org>.

the idea of a stable panel of arbitrators paved the way for the creation of a truly permanent organ of adjudication in the form of the World Court. The Permanent Court of Arbitration itself, though not the process of arbitration, had fallen into relative disuse, but it has apparently experienced a revitalization since the celebration of its 100th anniversary in 1999.[50] The PCA is also used to assist in the selection of the judges for the ICJ. The national groups of persons on the panel of arbitrators make the initial nominations of candidates for election as judges.[51]

In essence, arbitration is a form of adjudication that permits the parties to constitute and to operate their own court. Consequently, it has the attractions for states in disputes that they can select individuals as arbitrators in whom they have confidence and they can control the procedure that will be employed to resolve their conflict. The parties may also determine what law, national or international, shall be applied to their dispute. Indeed, they may also direct the tribunal to temper law with equitable considerations. The parties might go so far as to invite the tribunal to decide *ex aequo et bono*; in effect, to legislate a solution for them.

It must be appreciated that arbitration is only possible between states in dispute if, notwithstanding the depth of their differences over the substantive conflict, they genuinely desire a decision about it and are mutually trusting enough to negotiate an agreement about the procedure to obtain it. These difficulties may be reduced in connection with disputes over matters that are the subject of a treaty between states if arbitral arrangements are written into their original agreement. It is obviously easier to establish a tribunal to decide possible future disputes, such as the interpretation of the treaty, at the time the parties are in full agreement. The most significant recent example is the elaborate machinery for dispute settlement that was negotiated and included in the 1982 U.N. Convention on the Law of the Sea.[52] Arbitral arrangements are also frequently included in concession agreements and other contracts between governments and multinational corporations. The investing corporation cannot appear as a party to a case before the World Court, yet it may not be willing to subject its claims to the jurisdiction of the courts and the law of the state with whose government it is contracting. The obvious

---

50   The PCA's annual report for 2003 notes that "[o]ver the course of 2003, the PCA's registry caseload reached an all-time high of eleven pending cases, and twenty-two requests for designation of an appointing authority or services as appointing authority." PCA, 103rd Annual Report (2003), Executive Summary, para. 1, online: Permanent Court of Arbitration <http://www.pca-cpa.org/ENGLISH/AR/ Report%202003/2003%20Summary%20Report.pdf>. See International Bureau of the Permanent Court of Arbitration, ed., *International Alternative Dispute Resolution: Past, Present and Future—The Permanent Court of Arbitration Centennial Papers* (2000); P. Hamilton et al., *The Permanent Court of Arbitration: International Arbitration and Dispute Settlement Summaries of Awards, Settlement Agreements and Reports* (1999). See also the description of efforts to revitalize the PCA in J.L. Bleich, "A New Direction for the PCA: The Work of the Expert Group" in Muller & Mijs, *supra* note 48 at 17.

51   See *infra*, under the heading "Judges of the Court," Section D.1 on "Organization of the Court."

52   (1982) 21 I.L.M. 1261 arts. 279-99 (reproduced in the Documentary Supplement), Annexes VII, VIII, discussed *infra*, in Section E under the heading "Selected Specialized Agencies." See also Merrills, *supra* note 6 c. 8; and Louis B. Sohn, "The Role of Arbitration in Recent International Multilateral Treaties" (1982-83) 23 Va. J. Int'l L. 171.

choice of an adjudicative process is arbitration. Two instances, involving breach of petroleum concessions, were *Texaco v. Libya* and *LIAMCO v. Libya*.[53]

In the absence of any prior agreement to arbitrate, the parties must take care of all the details in their *compromis d'arbitrage* or agreement for submission of a dispute to arbitration. A great many details of procedure must be addressed. Any omission may mean that the tribunal is not granted the necessary authority to complete the arbitration, and the expectations of the parties, or one of them, will be frustrated. Moreover, unless the *compromis* is tightly drawn, one side may find it easy at a later stage, when feelings may be exacerbated or confidence in the process may have dissolved, to withdraw from or otherwise frustrate the arbitration. For the purpose of creating an *ad hoc* tribunal, the work of the International Law Commission (ILC) may be helpful. Building on the experience of the Permanent Court of Arbitration, the *General Act for the Pacific Settlement of International Disputes* (1928)[54] and a host of bilateral treaties, the ILC prepared a set of Model Rules on Arbitral Procedure.

International Law Commission, Model Rules on Arbitral Procedure, Article 2
[1958] Y.B.I.L.C. 83

1. Unless there are earlier agreements which suffice for the purpose, for example in the undertaking to arbitrate itself, the parties having recourse to arbitration shall conclude a *compromis* which shall specify, as a minimum:

(a) The undertaking to arbitrate according to which the dispute is to be submitted to the arbitrators;

(b) The subject-matter of the dispute and, if possible, the points on which the parties are or are not agreed;

(c) The method of constituting the tribunal and the number of arbitrators;

2. In addition, the *compromis* shall include any other provisions deemed desirable by the parties, in particular:

(i) The rules of law and the principles to be applied by the tribunal, and the right, if any, conferred on it to decide *ex aequo et bono* as though it had legislative functions in the matter;

(ii) The power, if any, of the tribunal to make recommendations to the parties;

(iii) Such power as may be conferred on the tribunal to make its own rules of procedure;

(iv) The procedure to be followed by the tribunal; provided that, once constituted, the tribunal shall be free to override any provisions of the *compromis* which may prevent it from rendering its award;

(v) The number of members required for the constitution of a *quorum* for the conduct of the hearings;

---

53   (1977) 53 I.L.R. 389; (1978) 17 I.L.M. 1 reported in Chapter 10, Sections B.3(a) and (d); and (1981) 20 I.L.M. 1, respectively.

54   92 L.N.T.S. 343.

     (vi) The majority required for the award;

     (vii) The time limit within which the award shall be rendered;

     (viii) The right of the members of the tribunal to attach dissenting or individual opinions to the award, or any prohibition of such opinions;

     (ix) The languages to be employed in the course of the proceedings;

     (x) The manner in which the costs and disbursements shall be apportioned;

     (xi) The services which the International Court of Justice may be asked to render.

NOTES

1) As their name suggests, these rules are not obligatory but are a set of standards for the constitution and conduct of an arbitral tribunal that can be adopted by the disputing parties if they wish. They offer the opportunity to streamline part of the process of arranging an arbitration. They also serve as a reminder of what needs to be agreed. This list is not exhaustive but it does indicate the extensive range of matters that have to be addressed.

2) An arbitral award is final and binding on the parties. Nevertheless, there may still be difficulties at the next stage of execution of the award. One side may assert the award is a nullity because the arbitrators exceeded their powers. The other side may complain that the award has not been complied with. Unfortunately, international law does not appear to provide any procedure to overcome these difficulties between states, should they arise. Resort to the ICJ is not available unless the parties expressly agree. This situation underscores the consensual basis of the arbitral process, and has to be resolved diplomatically.

The Iran–U.S. Claims Tribunal, which has dealt with thousands of state and private claims since its commencement in 1981, should be mentioned in this regard. Commentators are still assessing its innovations and to what degree they will have lasting effects on the practice of international arbitration.[55] One has remarked that the Tribunal's major contribution may be the advance made in enforcement of awards.[56] A unique Security Account was established along with the Tribunal. It is constituted of Iranian funds released from U.S. freeze orders and attachments and is used to pay the awards as ordered by the Tribunal. Since subjection to jurisdiction on the merits of a dispute does not entail execution against state assets of any subsequent award, the creation of a mechanism to ensure payment is a significant novel feature.

---

55 See George H. Aldrich, *The Jurisprudence of the Iran-United States Claims Tribunal* (1996); David D. Caron, "The Nature of the Iran-United States Claims Tribunal and the Evolving Structure of International Dispute Resolution" (1990) 84 A.J.I.L. 104; David D. Caron & John R. Crook, eds., *The Iran-United States Claims Tribunal and the Process of International Claims Resolution* (2000); Rahmatullah Khan, *The Iran-United States Claims Tribunal: Controversies, Cases, and Contribution* (1990); R.B. Lillich & D.J. Bederman, "Jurisprudence of the Foreign Claims Settlement Commission: Iran Claims" (1997) 91 A.J.I.L. 436; Wayne Mapp, *The Iran-United States Claims Tribunal, The First Ten Years, 1981-1991: An Assessment of the Tribunal's Jurisprudence and its Contribution to International Arbitration* (1993); Mauro Rubino-Sammartano, *International Arbitration Law* (1990) c. 5; Toope, *supra* note 48 cc. 8, 9; and John A. Westberg, *International Transactions and Claims Involving Government Parties, Case Law of the Iran-United States Claims Tribunal* (1991).

56 Toope, *supra* note 48 at 361.

3) International commercial arbitration is an area of growing importance. For international commercial arbitrations, several well-known sets of rules are available. The parties may choose from procedures established, for instance, by the International Chamber of Commerce (ICC),[57] the International Centre for Settlement of Investment Disputes (ICSID),[58] or the U.N. Commission on International Trade Law (UNCITRAL).[59] The Model Law on International Commercial Arbitration produced by UNCITRAL in 1985 has already been implemented by Canada[60] and several of the provinces.[61] The recent, rapid growth of international commercial arbitration is also contributing to the development of a special body of transnational law made up eclectically from the rules of international law, common principles of national legal systems, and the usages of international trade, and increasingly referred to as *lex mercatoria*.[62] This body of law has also had a considerable influence on the law relating to interstate arbitration. For example, in 1992 the Permanent Court of Arbitration adopted the "Optional Rules for Arbitrating Disputes between Two States," which were patterned after the UNCITRAL Arbitration Rules.[63]

An award in a transnational commercial arbitration between a corporation and a government may be enforceable in a state where assets of the losing party can be found if the New York Convention on Recognition and Enforcement of Foreign Arbitral Awards,[64] or some similar bilateral treaty, can be brought into operation. Although Canada has

---

57   See W. Lawrence Craig, William W. Park, & Jan Paulsson, *International Commercial Arbitration: International Chamber of Commerce Arbitration*, 3d ed. (2000); Mark Huleatt-James & Nicholas Gould, *International Commercial Arbitration: A Handbook*, 2d ed. (1999); and Alan Redfern & Martin Hunter, *Law and Practice of International Commercial Arbitration*, 4th ed. (2004).

58   See generally Moshe Hirsch, *The Arbitration Mechanism of the International Centre for the Settlement of Investment Disputes* (1993).

59   Online: United Nations Commission on International Trade Law <http://www.uncitral.org/en-index.htm>.

60   *Commercial Arbitration Act*, R.S.C. 1985 (2d Supp.), c. 17.

61   See, generally, Ljiljana Biukovic, "Impact of the Adoption of the Model Law in Canada: Creating a New Environment for International Arbitration" (1998) 30 Can. Bus. L.J. 376.

62   See Thomas E. Carbonneau, ed., *Lex Mercatoria and Arbitration: A Discussion of the New Law Merchant*, 2d ed. (1998).

63   Online: Permanent Court of Arbitration <http://www.pca-cpa.org/ENGLISH/BD/2stateng.htm>. The website notes that "[e]xperience in arbitrations since 1981 suggests that the UNCITRAL Arbitration Rules provide fair and effective procedures for the peaceful resolution of disputes between States concerning the interpretation, application and performance of treaties and other agreements, although they were designed for commercial arbitration." See generally Jan Paulsson, "Cross-Enrichment of Public and Private Law Dispute Resolution Mechanisms in the International Arena" (1992) 9 J. Int'l Arb. 60. In relation to the Iran-U.S. Claims Tribunal, see Stewart Abercrombie Baker & Mark David Davis, *The UNCITRAL Arbitration Rules in Practice: The Experience of the Iran-United States Claims Tribunal* (1992) and Matti Pellonpää & David D. Caron, *The UNCITRAL Arbitration Rules as Interpreted and Applied: Selected Problems in Light of the Practice of the Iran-United States Claims Tribunal* (1994).

64   (1958) 330 U.N.T.S. 3. See Albert Jan van den Berg, *The New York Arbitration Convention of 1958: Towards a Uniform Judicial Interpretation* (1981) and Giorgio Gaja, *International Commercial Arbitration: New York Convention* (1985) binders 1, 2.

ratified and implemented the New York Convention,[65] the prospects of enforcing awards against foreign governments may still be surrounded with legal uncertainties.[66]

4) Since the awards of international arbitral tribunals are a subsidiary source for the determination of international law,[67] their publication is significant. Many have been collected and reprinted by the United Nations in a series of volumes entitled Reports of International Arbitral Awards (UNRIAA). Current awards of importance appear in International Legal Materials and the International Law Reports. There are a number of collections of international commercial arbitral awards, including the International Chamber of Commerce's Collection of ICC Arbitral Awards.

D. THE WORLD COURT[68]

1. Organization of the Court

The "World Court" is a phrase that is used to refer collectively to the Permanent Court of International Justice (PCIJ) and its successor, the present International Court of Justice (ICJ). The PCIJ was created in 1921 by treaty, known generally as the Statute of the Court. It was not part of the League of Nations strictly speaking and so its continued existence was not affected by the failure of the League. When the United Nations was set up, however, a fresh start was preferred, and the ICJ replaced the PCIJ. However, the Statute of the ICJ

65   *United Nations Foreign Arbitral Awards Convention Act*, R.S.C. 1985 (2d Supp.), c. 16.

66   See Georges R. Delaume, "Arbitration with Governments: 'Domestic' v. 'International' Awards" (1983) 17 Int'l Law. 687 and Toope, *supra* note 48 c. 4.

67   I.C.J. Statute, article 38(1)(d), reproduced in the Documentary Supplement.

68   See, generally, Mohammed Sameh M. Amr, *The Role of the International Court of Justice as the Principal Judicial Organ of the United Nations* (2003); Max Planck Institute for Comparative Public Law and International Law, *Judicial Settlement of International Disputes* (1974); Lori F. Damrosch, ed., *The International Court of Justice at a Crossroads* (1987); Arthur Eyffinger & Arthur Witteveen, *The International Court of Justice, 1946-1996* (1996); T.O. Elias, *The International Court of Justice and Some Contemporary Problems* (1983); Richard Falk, *Reviving the World Court* (1986); Thomas M. Franck, *Judging the World Court* (1986); Terry D. Gill, *Litigation Strategy at the International Court* (1989); Terry D. Gill, ed., *Rosenne's The World Court: What It Is and How It Works*, 6th ed. (2003); Leo Gross, ed., *The Future of the International Court of Justice* (1976) vols. 1-2; C. Wilfred Jenks, *The Prospects of International Adjudication* (1964); Robert Jennings, *International Courts and International Politics* (1986); Vaughan Lowe & Malgosia Fitzmaurice, eds., *Fifty Years of the International Court of Justice: Essays in Honour of Sir Robert Jennings* (1996); Edward McWhinney, *Judicial Settlement of International Disputes: Jurisdiction, Justiciability, and Judicial Law-making on the Contemporary International Court* (1991); A.S. Muller, David Raic & J.M. Thuransky, eds., *The International Court of Justice: Its Future Role after Fifty Years* (1997); Shabtai Rosenne, *The Law and Practice of the International Court*, 3d ed. (1997); Shabtai Rosenne, *Procedure in the International Court: A Commentary on the 1978 Rules of the International Court of Justice* (1983); and Nagendra Singh, *The Role and Record of the International Court of Justice* (1989). An annual record of the Court's administration and activities may be found in its Yearbooks. The Court's website is <http://www.icj-cij.org>. See also the very useful United Nations, *Summaries of Judgments, Advisory Opinions and Orders of the International Court of Justice 1948-1991* (1992-95); and United Nations *Summaries of Judgments, Advisory Opinions and Orders of the International Court of Justice 1992-1996* (1998).

is practically identical with the old Statute of the PCIJ. The jurisdiction of the PCIJ was also carried over without interruption by article 37 of the Statute, at least for parties to the present Statute. The materials that follow focus upon the experience of the current court.

The ICJ is one of the six principal organs of the United Nations (Charter article 7), and the principal judicial organ (Charter article 92). It functions according to the U.N. Charter articles 92 to 96 and its own Statute, which is annexed to the Charter. All members of the United Nations are *ipso facto* parties to the Statute.

The following notes and questions are designed to introduce the salient features of the ICJ, emphasizing those characteristics that differ from the usual arrangements and procedures of national courts. The Statute is reproduced in the Documentary Supplement.

Judges of the Court

1) The Court is composed of 15 members (Statute article 3) elected by the General Assembly and the Security Council (Statute articles 4-8 and 10-12). A president and vice-president are elected for three years by the Court from among its membership (Statute article 21). Judges must be "persons of high moral character, who possess the qualifications required in their respective countries for appointment to the highest judicial offices, or are jurisconsults of recognized competence in international law" (Statute article 2). Individual qualifications aside, the body as a whole is expected to represent "the main forms of civilization and ... the principal legal systems of the world" (Statute article 9).

2) While article 2 provides that the judges are to be elected "regardless of nationality," nationality plays an obvious role in the makeup in the Court and is mentioned in several places in the Statute (articles 3, 5(2), and 10(3)). Moreover, the overall composition of the Court has changed over the years to reflect the development of regional representation within the U.N. system more generally. By informal understanding, the permanent members of the Security Council each have a national as a judge on the Court. The distribution of seats on the Court is usually 5 from Western Europe and North America, 2 from Eastern Europe, 3 from Africa and the Middle East, 3 from Asia, and 2 from Latin America. Only one Canadian has been elected a regular member of the Court. He was Judge John E. Read, who served from 1946 to 1958. Some say that this geographical distribution, which is not provided for in the Statute, has politicized elections to the Court. Do you think it is damaging to the Court's legitimacy?[69]

3) Nationality also comes into play when cases are being heard. Parties to a case may appoint a judge *ad hoc* if no member of the Court has their nationality (Statute article 31). (When several parties have the same interest, they are deemed to be only one party for the purposes of this provision, pursuant to article 31(5).) This right exists even where neither side has a national on the Court, so the provision is not merely a matter of evening out the balance between the opposing parties. Compared with national courts, which

---

69   For considerations of the election process, see Christopher Harland, "International Court of Justice Elections: A Report on the First Fifty Years" (1996) 34 Can. Y.B. Int'l L. 303 and Niels Blokker & Sam Muller, "The 1996 Elections to the International Court of Justice: New Tendencies in the Post Cold War Era?" (1998) 47 I.C.L.Q. 211. See also Edward McWhinney, "Law, Politics and 'Regionalism' in the Nomination and Election of World Court Judges" (1986) 13 Syracuse J. Int'l L. & Com. 1.

operate on the principle that one shall not judge one's own cause, this appears problematic, particularly in the light of the predictable experience that almost invariably the *ad hoc* judges side with the party appointing them. Why should a member of the Court who is the national of a party be allowed to sit on the case at all? The heterogeneous and plural character of international society is said to falsify the analogy to national courts. Do you agree? Do you consider that the nationality of the judges is relevant to an impartial and independent court?[70]

4) In relation to judicial impartiality, however, it should also be noted that article 17(2) of the Statute provides that no member of the Court may participate in the decision of any case in which he or she has previously taken part "as agent, counsel or advocate for one of the parties, or as a member of a national or international court, or of a commission of enquiry, or in any other capacity." Thus, in the *Lockerbie Case*, discussed below in Section D.4 on "A Judicial Review Power for the Court?" Judge Higgins asked to be excused from participation since she had acted as Counsel for the United Kingdom prior to her election to the Court. In this regard see also article 24.

5) Judges serve for nine years and are eligible for re-election. Five seats come up for election every three years (Statute article 13).

6) The Court is permanently in session except during judicial vacations (Statute article 23), and the judges are not allowed to exercise "any political or administrative function, or engage in any other occupation of a professional nature" (Statute article 16). The seat of the Court is in the Peace Palace at The Hague, Netherlands (Statute article 22).

Parties Before the Court

Only states may be parties in contentious cases before the Court, pursuant to Statute article 34(1). Moreover, the Court is not open to every state automatically. A state must become a party to the Statute and may qualify in any one of three ways (Statute article 35 and Charter article 93):

(1) As noted above, members of the United Nations are *ipso facto* parties to the Statute. This includes the great majority of states.

(2) Non-members of the United Nations may become parties to the Statute by accepting the conditions laid down by the General Assembly. Switzerland has taken this route, as did Liechtenstein and Japan prior to becoming U.N. members. The General Assembly required each of them to accept the provisions of the ICJ Statute, to accept the obligations of compliance with a decision of the Court in Charter article 94, and to pay an equitable proportion of the expenses of the Court.

(3) Any other state may appear before the Court in a particular case provided it accepts the conditions laid down by the Security Council in 1946 that provide in part as follows:

---

70   See Manfred Lachs, "Some Reflections on the Nationality of Judges of the International Court of Justice" (1992) 4 Pace Y.B. Int'l L. 49. See also Lyndel V. Prott, *The Latent Power of Culture and the International Judge* (1979).

[S]uch state shall previously have deposited with the Registrar of the Court a declaration by which it accepts the jurisdiction of the Court, in accordance with the Charter of the United Nations and with the terms and subject to the conditions of the Statute and Rules of the Court, and undertakes to comply in good faith with the decision or decisions of the Court and to accept all the obligations of a Member of the United Nations under Article 94 of the Charter.

This process has been resorted to by several states, including Albania, Cambodia, Ceylon, Finland, West Germany, Italy, Japan, Laos, and Vietnam. All are now members of the United Nations and thus automatically parties to the Statute.

International organizations cannot be parties in contentious cases, but may be asked for information or may provide it on their own initiative pursuant to article 34(2). In addition, the General Assembly and certain other U.N. bodies may request advisory opinions (discussed later in this section under the heading "Advisory Opinions"). Some commentators have suggested that international organizations be granted standing before the Court;[71] others have argued that the Court be opened up to communications from individuals.[72] Would you support such a proposal? Why or why not? Who would be the most logical candidates for standing before the Court?

2. Jurisdiction of the Court[73]

The ICJ is different from national courts in that it does not automatically have jurisdiction over all disputes between parties with standing. The jurisdiction of the ICJ, like that of its predecessor, is unlimited as to subject matter according to article 36(1) of its Statute. However, its jurisdiction over states is based on voluntary acceptance by the parties. In other words, the Court cannot hear a contentious case, even though the litigant states are parties to the Statute, unless they all consent. This restriction severely limits the number of cases that can be brought before the Court. What do you suppose is the reason for it?

Three methods by which States can accept the jurisdiction of the International Court are the following:[74]

---

71   See *e.g.* P.C. Szasz, "Granting International Organizations Ius Standi in the International Court of Justice" in Muller, Raic & Thuransky, *supra* note 68 at 169.

72   See *e.g.* Mark W. Janis, "Individuals and the International Court" in Muller, Raic & Thuransky, *supra* note 68 at 205.

73   The website of the ICJ includes a listing of "Treaties and Other Documents" that contain clauses relating to the jurisdiction of the Court and of "Declarations Recognizing as Compulsory the Jurisdiction of the Court." "Treaties and Other Documents," online: International Court of Justice <http://www.icj-cij.org/icjwww/ibasicdocuments/ibasictext/ibasictreatiesandotherdocs.htm>. "Declarations Recognizing as Compulsory the Jurisdiction of the Court," online: International Court of Justice <http://www.icj-cij.org/icjwww/ibasicdocuments/ibasictext/ibasicdeclarations.htm>.

74   Wallace-Bruce mentions a fourth possible basis of jurisdiction in contentious cases, *forum prorogatum*, by which a respondent "consents to the jurisdiction subsequent to the commencement of proceedings against it" (*supra* note 1 at 124). However, he notes, "the Court does not apply the doctrine lightly. There is a strong onus on the applicant invoking it to demonstrate that the other party has given an unequivocal indication of its voluntary and indisputable acceptance of the Court's jurisdiction" (at 125). Article 38, paragraph 5 of the Rules of Court provides as follows: "When the applicant State proposes to found the

By special agreement: parties agree to submit a particular dispute to the Court (Statute Article 36(1)).

By compromissory clause: parties to a treaty agree to submit disputes arising out of the treaty, or parts of it, to the Court (Statute Article 36(1)).

By way of a declaration under Article 36(2): a state accepts the compulsory jurisdiction of the Court in relation to any other state accepting the same obligation. This is frequently referred to as the "Optional Clause." It provides the option or opportunity for a state to declare its acceptance of the Court's jurisdiction generally and in advance, and subject to certain conditions if it so chooses.

Article 40 of the Statute provides that cases may be brought before the Court either by the notification of a special agreement or by a written application where jurisdiction arises by way of a compromissory clause or article 36(2). A special agreement has the advantage of conferring jurisdiction without question, and therefore may be used even though alternative bases of jurisdiction exist. A written application is made when a state commences a case unilaterally. Since one party cannot seize the Court with jurisdiction without the consent of the other, it must have good reason to believe that the other party is obliged to submit to the Court.

Pursuant to article 36(6) of its Statute, the Court has power to determine whether or not it has jurisdiction. This is sometimes referred to as "la compétence de la compétence." Nevertheless, over the years of the Court's existence several States have failed to appear to answer cases brought by unilateral application.[75] The Statute article 53 makes plain that the Court may give default judgment provided it is satisfied that it has jurisdiction over the case and that the claim is well founded in fact and in law. Non-appearance of the respondent, however, is a clear indication that it will also ignore any decision. This regrettable practice has been used to the advantage of the errant state. In refusing to appear, the respondent often makes sometimes lengthy communications to the Court from the wings.[76] These statements, which typically outline the case the state would make were it to appear, cannot be ignored by the Court. So the respondent state has the advantage of having its arguments aired and considered even while it refrains from appearing.

---

jurisdiction of the Court upon a consent thereto yet to be given or manifested by the State against which such application is made, the application shall be transmitted to that State. It shall not however be entered in the General List, nor any action be taken in the proceedings, unless and until the State against which such application is made consents to the Court's jurisdiction for the purposes of the case." This was employed in one case currently on the Court's docket, the *Case Concerning Certain Criminal Procedures in France (Republic of the Congo v. France)*, online: International Court of Justice <http://www.icj-cij.org/icjwww/idocket/icof/icofframe.htm>.

75　The U.S. withdrawal from the *Military Activities In and Against Nicaragua Case* was a notable example. See, generally, Stanimir A. Alexandrov, "Non-Appearance before the International Court of Justice" (1995) 33 Colum. J. Transnat'l L. 41; Jerome B. Elkind, *Non-Appearance Before the International Court of Justice: Functional and Comparative Analysis* (1984); Gerald Fitzmaurice, "The Problem of the 'Non-Appearing' Defendant Government" (1980) 51 Brit. Y.B. Int'l L. 89; and H.W.A. Thirlway, *Non-Appearance Before the International Court of Justice* (1985).

76　See *e.g.* Iran's communications in the *U.S. Diplomatic Staff in Tehran Case*, [1979] I.C.J. Rep. 7 and 23; [1980] I.C.J. Rep. 3, reported in Chapter 5, Section D on "Diplomatic Immunities."

In addition to the original parties to a case, other states may intervene[77] (Statute articles 62 and 63). What is the difference between these two articles? Experience with these articles was slight but positive[78] until three cases in the 1980s, where the Court refused each would-be intervenor.[79] In the 1990 case *Land, Island and Maritime Frontier Dispute (El Salvador v. Honduras)*,[80] however, Nicaragua was allowed to intervene because its interest might have been affected by the Chamber's decision. Moreover, as an intervenor, as opposed to becoming a party by mutual consent, it was not required to establish any jurisdictional link to the parties. In 1999, the full Court took this same approach to jurisdiction in allowing Equatorial Guinea to intervene in the *Case Concerning Land and Maritime Boundary Between Cameroon and Nigeria*.[81] In 2001, the Court refused an application by the Philippines to intervene in the *Case Concerning Sovereignty over Pulau Ligitan and Pulau Sipadan (Indonesia/Malaysia)*.[82] The Court accepted that a State may intervene not only when the operative part of a judgment is capable of affecting its legal interests, but also where those interests relate to the reasoning constituting the underpinning of that operative decision. In the particular circumstances of the case, however, the Philippines had not established that it had such an interest. It remains unclear what "interest of a legal nature" of the intervenor must be at stake.[83] Rosenne has implied that such lack of clarity is inherent in the nature of this type of determination, noting, "Each decision of the Court must ... be situated within the material and temporal context of the case, itself situated within the parameters established by the parties to that case."[84] Is there an argument to be made that the right to intervene should be interpreted expansively? What would be the appropriate stance on intervention if a case involved *erga omnes* obligations?[85]

In certain circumstances the Court may be precluded from exercising jurisdiction over a dispute in which two parties have accepted its jurisdiction because of the effect on third

---

77   See generally Shabtai Rosenne, *Intervention in the International Court of Justice* (1993).

78   See *The Steamship Wimbledon* (1923), P.C.I.J. (Ser. A) No. 1 at 11 (Poland intervening); *Haya de la Torre Case*, [1951] I.C.J. Rep. 71 at 76 (Cuba intervening); and *Nuclear Tests Cases*, [1974] I.C.J. Rep. 530 and 535 (Fiji's request lapsed with the cases).

79   *Continental Shelf (Tunisia v. Libya) Case*, [1981] I.C.J. Rep. 3 (Malta refused); *Continental Shelf (Libya v. Malta) Case*, [1984] I.C.J. Rep. 3 (Italy refused); and *Military Activities In and Against Nicaragua*, [1984] I.C.J. Rep. 215 (El Salvador refused). For commentary, see C.M. Chinkin, "Third Party Intervention Before the International Court of Justice" (1986) 80 A.J.I.L. 495; Gerald P. McGinley, "Intervention in the International Court: The Libya/Malta Continental Shelf Case" (1985) 34 I.C.L.Q. 671; Jerzy Sztucki, "Intervention under Article 63 of the I.C.J. Statute in the Phase of Preliminary Proceedings: The 'Salvadorean Incident' " (1985) 79 A.J.I.L. 1005.

80   [1990] I.C.J. Rep. 92.

81   Order of October 21, 1999, [1999] I.C.J. Rep. 1029.

82   *Application by the Philippines for Permission to Intervene*, [2001] I.C.J. Rep. 575.

83   For commentary see J.G. Merrills, "Sovereignty over Pulau Ligitan and Pulau Sipadan (Indonesia/ Malaysia): The Philippines' Intervention" (2002) 51:3 I.C.L.Q. 709 at 718-22.

84   Rosenne, *supra* note 77 at 189. He also indicates, however, that the Court's approach might be explained by reference to the purpose of particular attempts at intervention (at 189-90).

85   See the discussion in Sean D. Murphy, "Amplifying the World Court's Jurisdiction Through Counter-Claims and Third-Party Intervention" (2000) 33 Geo. Wash. J. Int'l L. & Econ. 5.

parties that have not accepted the Court's jurisdiction. In the *Case Concerning East Timor*,[86] Portugal attempted to bring a claim against Australia with regard to a treaty that the latter had concluded with Indonesia in relation to the "Timor Gap," alleging infringements both of the right of the people of East Timor to self-determination and of the rights of Portugal as the administering Power. Both Portugal and Australia had made declarations under article 36(2). Australia's principal objection was that "the decision sought from the Court by Portugal would inevitably require the Court to rule on the lawfulness of the conduct of a third State, namely Indonesia, in the absence of that State's consent."[87] The Court emphasized that "it is not necessarily prevented from adjudicating when the judgment it is asked to give might affect the legal interests of a State which is not a party to the case."[88] However, recalling its judgment in the *Case Concerning Monetary Gold Removed from Rome in 1943*,[89] the Court concluded that "the effect of the judgment requested by Portugal would amount to a determination that Indonesia's entry into and continued presence in East Timor are unlawful and that, as a consequence, it does not have the treaty-making power in matters relating to the continental shelf resources of East Timor. Indonesia's rights and obligations would thus constitute the very subject matter of such a judgment made in the absence of that State's consent."[90] Thus, the Court refused to exercise the jurisdiction it had by virtue of the optional clause declarations made by Portugal and Australia.[91]

Jurisdiction by Special Agreement

Throughout its history, the Court has frequently been granted jurisdiction by special agreement. Recently, such agreements were concluded by Benin and Niger in 2002 with regard to a frontier dispute[92] and by Malaysia and Singapore in 2003 with regard to a dispute concerning sovereignty over Pedra Branca/Pulau Batu Puteh, Middle Rocks and South Ledge.[93] Whether a document constitutes a special agreement may be a matter of interpretation. In the *Case Concerning Maritime Delimitation and Territorial Questions between Qatar and Bahrain (Qatar v. Bahrain),* the Court was called upon to determine whether a series of documents (an exchange of letters between the King of Saudi Arabia and the Amir of Qatar; an exchange of letters between the King of Saudi Arabia and the

---

86   [1995] I.C.J. Rep. 90. For critical commentary, see Natalie S. Klein, "Multilateral Disputes and the Doctrine of Necessary Parties in the East Timor Case" (1996) 21 Yale J. Int'l L. 305. For background to the case before the judgment, see Gerry J. Simpson, "Judging the East Timor Dispute: Self-Determination at the International Court of Justice" (1994) 17 Hastings Int'l & Comp. L. Rev. 323.

87   *Case Concerning East Timor, ibid.* at 100.

88   *Ibid.* at 104.

89   (Preliminary Question), [1954] I.C.J. Rep. 19.

90   *Case Concerning East Timor, supra* note 86 at 105.

91   Judge Weeramantry wrote a lengthy and strongly worded dissenting opinion; *Case Concerning East Timor, supra* note 86 at 139.

92   Online: International Court of Justice <http://www.icj-cij.org/icjwww/idocket/ibn/ibnframe.htm>.

93   Online: International Court of Justice <http://www.icj-cij.org/icjwww/idocket/imasi/imasiframe.htm>.

Amir of Bahrain; and a document signed by the Ministers of Foreign Affairs of Bahrain, Qatar, and Saudi Arabia) constituted an agreement to submit the dispute to the Court. By its judgment of July 1, 1994, the Court found that these were international agreements creating rights and obligations for the parties and that, by the terms of those agreements, the parties had undertaken to submit to the Court the whole of the dispute between them. However, given that the Court only had before it an application from Qatar, it allowed the parties the opportunity to submit the whole of the dispute jointly. By its judgment of February 15, 1995, the Court confirmed its earlier decision that it had jurisdiction over the dispute.[94]

Article 40 merely provides that the subject of the dispute and the parties shall be indicated. However, special agreements may also include a general description of the background to the dispute, the specific issue(s) to be determined by the Court, particular treaties that may be applicable, and certain procedural stipulations.[95]

Jurisdiction by Treaty

Literally hundreds of treaties provide for recourse to the Court in case of disputes arising out of the interpretation or application of the treaty or particular provisions thereof.[96]

On the docket in July 2004, among the cases brought under compromissory clauses, the Court's jurisdiction arose under the Genocide Convention in the *Case Concerning Application of the Convention on the Prevention and Punishment of the Crime of Genocide (Bosnia and Herzegovina v. Serbia and Montenegro)*[97] and the *Case Concerning Application of the Convention on the Prevention and Punishment of the Crime of Genocide (Croatia v. Serbia and Montenegro)*,[98] and under the European Convention for the Peaceful Settlement of Disputes in the *Case Concerning Certain Property (Liechtenstein v. Germany).*[99]

Compulsory Jurisdiction Under ICJ Statute Article 36(2)[100]

A relatively small number of states have accepted the compulsory jurisdiction of the International Court. As of early 2005, 59 states had made declarations under article 36(2) of the Court's Statute: Australia, Austria, Barbados, Belgium, Botswana, Bulgaria, Cambodia, Cameroon, Canada, Costa Rica, Cyprus, Democratic Republic of the Congo,

---

94   [1995] I.C.J. Rep. 6.

95   See *e.g.* the special agreement for the dispute concerning Kasiliki/Sedudu Island, between Botswana and Namibia; online: International Court of Justice <http://www.icj-cij.org/icjwww/idocket/ibona/ibonaframe.htm>. The case was decided by the Court in 1999.

96   The website of the ICJ includes a listing of "Treaties and Other Documents" that contain clauses relating to the jurisdiction of the Court; "Treaties and Other Documents," *supra* note 73. It is clearly indicated that "[t]he fact that a treaty is or is not included in this section is without prejudice to its possible application by the Court in a particular case." Such agreements are also listed in the Yearbook of the ICJ.

97   Online: International Court of Justice <http://www.icj-cij.org/icjwww/idocket/ibhy/ibhyframe.htm>.

98   Online: International Court of Justice <http://www.icj-cij.org/icjwww/idocket/icry/icryframe.htm>.

99   Online: International Court of Justice <http://www.icj-cij.org/icjwww/idocket/ila/ilaframe.htm>.

100 See generally Renata Szafarz, *The Compulsory Jurisdiction of the International Court of Justice* (1993).

Denmark, Egypt, Estonia, Finland, Gambia, Georgia, Greece, Guinea, Guinea-Bissau, Honduras, Hungary, India, Ivory Coast, Japan, Kenya, Lesotho, Liberia, Liechtenstein, Madagascar, Malawi, Malta, Mauritius, Mexico, Nauru, Netherlands, New Zealand, Nigeria, Norway, Pakistan, Paraguay, Peru, Philippines, Poland, Portugal, Senegal, Serbia and Montenegro, Slovakia, Somalia, Spain, Sudan, Surinam, Swaziland, Sweden, Switzerland, Togo, Uganda, and the United Kingdom.[101] A further 6 states had made declarations under article 36(2) of the Statute of the PCIJ, which are deemed to be acceptances of the compulsory jurisdiction of the ICJ pursuant to article 36(5) of its Statute: Dominican Republic, Haiti, Luxembourg, Nicaragua, Panama, and Uruguay. Five states, including France and the United States (both permanent members of the Security Council), have terminated their declarations under article 36(2).[102] The declaration made by the Republic of China in 1946 was not recognized by the People's Republic, as was communicated to the Secretary-General in 1972. In addition, 6 declarations (those of Bolivia, Brazil, El Salvador, Guatemala, Thailand, and Turkey) were made for specified periods of time that expired.

The total of 65 states accepting the compulsory jurisdiction of the Court must be compared against the membership of the United Nations, which is over 190. Nonetheless, a slight upward trend may be detected. Eleven states filed article 36(2) declarations in the 1990s: Poland and Spain in 1990; Estonia in 1991; Bulgaria, Hungary, and Madagascar in 1992; Cameroon and Greece in 1994; Georgia in 1995; Paraguay in 1996; Guinea in 1998; and Serbia and Montenegro (formerly Yugoslavia) in 1999. A further four declarations have been filed since 2000: by Lesotho in 2000, Ivory Coast in 2001, Peru in 2003, and Slovakia in 2004. It is noteworthy (and heartening) that these states represent a diversity of regions.

Many of those declarations are subject to reservations, involving limitations ranging from subject matter to time frame. Consider the following examples.

101 "Declarations Recognizing as Compulsory the Jurisdiction of the Court," online: International Court of Justice <http://www.icj-cij.org/icjwww/ibasicdocuments/ibasictext/ibasicdeclarations.htm>.

102 The other states are South Africa, in 1967, and Israel in 1985; Colombia terminated its declaration under Article 36(2) of the Statute of the PCIJ in 2001. For the reasons for U.S. withdrawal, see U.S. Department of State's statement reprinted in (1985) 24 I.L.M. at 1743. For commentary, see the editorial remarks of Thomas M. Franck, "Icy Day at the ICJ" (1985) 79 A.J.I.L. 379; and W. Michael Reisman, "Has the International Court Exceeded Its Jurisdiction?" (1986) 80 A.J.I.L. 128. The former U.S.S.R. (the other permanent member) never made a declaration, but in 1989 then-President Gorbachev unilaterally accepted the compulsory jurisdiction of the Court in matters concerning six U.N. human rights conventions; see U.N. Doc. A/44/171 (1989) and Y.K. Tyagi, "The World Court After the Cold War" in R.S. Pathak & R.P. Dhokalia, eds., International Law in Transition (1992) at 231.

Sample Declarations Recognizing Jurisdiction

Canada

On behalf of the Government of Canada,

(1) I give notice that I hereby terminate the acceptance by Canada of the compulsory jurisdiction of the International Court of Justice hitherto effective by virtue of the declaration made on 10 September 1985 in conformity with paragraph 2 of Article 36 of the Statute of the Court.

(2) I declare that the Government of Canada accepts as compulsory *ipso facto* and without special convention, on condition of reciprocity, the jurisdiction of the International Court of Justice, in conformity with paragraph 2 of Article 36 of the Statute of the Court, until such time as notice may be given to terminate the acceptance, over all disputes arising after the present declaration with regard to situations or facts subsequent to this declaration, other than:

(a) disputes in regard to which parties have agreed or shall agree to have recourse to some other method of peaceful settlement;

(b) disputes with the Government of any other country which is a member of the Commonwealth, all of which disputes shall be settled in such manner as the parties have agreed or shall agree;

(c) disputes with regard to questions which by international law fall exclusively within the jurisdiction of Canada; and

(d) disputes arising out of or concerning conservation and management measures taken by Canada with respect to vessels fishing in the NAFO Regulatory Area, as defined in the Convention on Future Multilateral Co-operation in the Northwest Atlantic Fisheries, 1978, and the enforcement of such measures.

(3) The Government of Canada also reserves the right at any time, by means of a notification addressed to the Secretary-General of the United Nations, and with effect as from the moment of such notification, either to add to, amend or withdraw any of the foregoing reservations, or any that may hereafter be added.

New York, May 10, 1994

(Signed) Louise Fréchette
Ambassador and Permanent Representative

India

I have the honour to declare, on behalf of the Government of the Republic of India, that they accept, in conformity with paragraph 2 of Article 36 of the Statute of the Court, until such time as notice may be given to terminate such acceptance, as compulsory ipso facto and without special agreement, and on the basis and condition of reciprocity, the jurisdiction of the International Court of Justice over all disputes other than:

(1) disputes in regard to which the parties to the dispute have agreed or shall agree to have recourse to some other method or methods of settlement;

(2) disputes with the Government of any State which is or has been a Member of the Commonwealth of Nations;

(3) disputes in regard to matters which are essentially within the domestic jurisdiction of the Republic of India;

(4) disputes relating to or connected with facts or situations of hostilities, armed conflicts, individual or collective actions taken in self-defence, resistance to aggression, fulfilment of obligations imposed by international bodies, and other similar or related acts, measures or situations in which India is, has been or may in future be involved;

(5) disputes with regard to which any other party to a dispute has accepted the compulsory jurisdiction of the International Court of Justice exclusively for or in relation to the purposes of such dispute; or where the acceptance of the Court's compulsory jurisdiction on behalf of a party to the dispute was deposited or ratified less than 12 months prior to the filing of the application bringing the dispute before the Court;

(6) disputes where the jurisdiction of the Court is or may be founded on the basis of a treaty concluded under the auspices of the League of Nations, unless the Government of India specially agree to jurisdiction in each case;

(7) disputes concerning the interpretation or application of a multilateral treaty unless all the parties to the treaty are also parties to the case before the Court or Government of India specially agree to jurisdiction;

(8) disputes with the government of any State with which, on the date of an application to bring a dispute before the Court, the Government of India has no diplomatic relations or which has not been recognized by the Government of India;

(9) disputes with non-sovereign States or territories;

(10) disputes with India concerning or relating to:

(a) The status of its territory or the modification or delimitation on of its frontiers or any other matter concerning boundaries;

(b) the territorial sea, the continental shelf and the margins, the exclusive fishery zone, the exclusive economic zone, and other zones of national maritime jurisdiction including for the regulation and control of marine pollution and the conduct of scientific research by foreign vessels;

(c) the condition and status of its islands, bays and gulfs and that of the bays and gulfs that for historical reasons belong to it;

(d) the airspace superjacent to its land and maritime territory; and

(e) the determination and delimitation of its maritime boundaries.

(11) disputes prior to the date of this declaration, including any dispute the foundations, reasons, facts, causes, origins, definitions, allegations or bases of which existed prior to this date, even if they are submitted or brought to the knowledge of the Court hereafter.

This declaration revokes and replaces the previous declaration made by the Government of India on 14th September 1959.

(Signed) Swaran Singh
Minister of External Affairs

Paraguay

I HEREBY ACCEPT on behalf of the Government of Paraguay the compulsory jurisdiction of the International Court of Justice, with headquarters at The Hague, reciprocally in relation to other States accepting the same obligation in respect of all disputes as provided for in Article 36, paragraph 2, of the Statute of the Court. The present declaration shall apply only to disputes arising subsequent to the date of this declaration.

25 September 1996

(Signed) Rubén MELGAREJO LANZONI
Minister for Foreign Affairs

(Signed) Juan Carlos WASMOSY
President

NOTES

1) As can be seen from these examples, many article 36(2) declarations contain extensive reservations.[103] States frequently exclude certain substantive areas—for example, many declarations exclude disputes with regard to territory or state boundaries, as in paragraph 10 of the Indian declaration. Poland's declaration excludes, *inter alia*, "disputes with regard to environmental protection" and "disputes with regard to foreign liabilities or debts." Are these kinds of reservations permissible (Statute article 36(3))?

Another fairly common form of reservation excludes the Court's jurisdiction with regard to matters falling within domestic jurisdiction.[104] However, there are a number of different versions of such a reservation. Consider, for example, the restrictions to this effect found in both paragraph 2(c) of the Canadian declaration and paragraph (3) of the Indian declaration. How do they differ and what are the potential implications of this difference? A somewhat notorious version of this type of reservation was found in the U.S. declaration before withdrawal of its acceptance of the International Court's jurisdiction. This so-called Connally clause (named after the Secretary of State at the time the declaration was originally made) precluded the Court from taking jurisdiction over anything essentially within U.S. jurisdiction "as determined by the United States." This is sometimes referred to as a "self-judging" or "automatic" reservation. It is not unique to the United States; Mexico, for example, also has such a condition in its acceptance. What is the scope of the jurisdiction granted to the Court by a declaration that includes such a reservation? Is such a reservation valid in light of Statute article 36(6)?[105] The Court has not pronounced upon this matter. Although this was the form of

---

103 See Stanimir A. Alexandrov, *Reservations in Unilateral Declarations Accepting the Compulsory Jurisdiction of the International Court of Justice* (1995).

104 See *ibid.* at 67-95.

105 James Crawford, "The Legal Effect of Automatic Reservations to the Jurisdiction of the International Court" (1979) 50 Brit. Y. B. Int'l L. 63.

France's declaration in the *Norwegian Loans Case*,[106] the majority of the Court declined to rule on the automatic reservation since neither side had questioned its validity.[107] However, in a separate opinion in that case,[108] Judge Lauterpacht said that it was contrary to the Statute and, since the declarant government retained control, it had not effected a legal obligation. Do you agree?

2) A significant feature of reservations under article 36(2) is that they may be invoked by the other party to a dispute before the Court. By Statute article 36(3), a state may expressly make its declaration subject to a condition of reciprocity, but reciprocity is already built in by reason of the language of article 36(2). It takes the unilateral declaration of each of the opposing states to establish the Court's jurisdiction to hear their case, and the Court only has jurisdiction over matters that are common ground between them.[109] In the *Anglo-Iranian Oil Case*, the Court noted that jurisdiction is conferred upon it "only to the extent to which the two declarations coincide in conferring it."[110] The *Norwegian Loans Case* mentioned above displayed the ultimate irony. The claimant state, France, reserved all matters within its domestic jurisdiction as it understood that phrase. This reservation was successfully invoked against France by the defendant state, Norway. Thus, the Court was without jurisdiction to hear the case. What accounts for the importance of reciprocity within the Optional Clause system?

3) Restrictions regarding procedural matters are also quite common. See, for example, Canada's assertion of a right to "add to, amend or withdraw any of the foregoing reservations" with immediate effect. Unlike substantive restrictions on the Court's jurisdiction, procedural restrictions have been interpreted by the Court not to be subject to the condition of reciprocity. For example, the Court had occasion to consider the effects of time limits in optional declarations in the case of *Military Activities In and Against Nicaragua*.[111] Shortly before Nicaragua commenced the action, the United States deposited an amendment to its declaration by which it expected to forestall the jurisdiction of the Court. It declared it was to take effect immediately even though the then standing U.S. declaration provided for six months' notice of termination. Should the United States have been allowed to rely on its amendment or should Nicaragua have been permitted to depend upon the standing declaration? The critical date for establishing commonality of obligations between two declarant states was held in the *Right of Passage Over Indian Territory Case*[112] to be the moment of the filing of an application to commence a case. The United States contended it had a right to amend its unilateral declaration in any event and could take advantage reciprocally of the lack of any provision for notice of

---

106 [1957] I.C.J. Rep. 9.

107 *Ibid.* at 27.

108 *Ibid.* at 44.

109 For a consideration of some of the scholarly debate about the proper interpretation of reciprocity see Alexandrov, *supra* note 103 at 33-39.

110 (Jurisdiction), [1952] I.C.J. Rep. 89 at 103.

111 (Jurisdiction and Admissibility), [1984] I.C.J. Rep. 392.

112 (Preliminary Objections), [1957] I.C.J. Rep. 125.

termination in the Nicaraguan declaration. Although three judges accepted this argument, the majority of the Court did not, finding as follows:

> The notion of reciprocity is concerned with the scope and substance of the commitments entered into, including reservations, and not with the formal conditions of their creation, duration or extinction. It appears clearly that reciprocity cannot be invoked in order to excuse departure from the terms of a State's own declaration, whatever its scope, limitations or conditions.[113]

The Court decided by 11 votes to 5 that it had jurisdiction on the basis of article 36(2); given that some judges were prepared to find jurisdiction on other grounds, the Court decided by 15 votes to 1 (Judge Schwebel of the U.S. dissenting) that it had jurisdiction in the case. The United States thereafter withdrew from further participation.[114]

4) In the *Case Concerning Land and Maritime Boundary Between Cameroon and Nigeria (Cameroon v. Nigeria)*,[115] Cameroon, which had deposited a declaration under article 36(2) with the U.N. Secretary-General on March 3, 1994, filed a unilateral application with the Registry of the Court on March 29. Nigeria, among its preliminary objections, noted that on the date of the filing of the application it had no way of knowing, and did not actually know, that Cameroon had deposited a declaration. Recalling its judgment in the *Right of Passage Over Indian Territory Case*, the Court noted:

> Any State party to the Statute, in adhering to the jurisdiction of the Court in accordance with Article 36, paragraph 2, accepts jurisdiction in its relations with States previously having adhered to that clause. At the same time, it makes a standing offer to the other States party to the Statute which have not yet deposited a declaration of acceptance. The day one of those States accepts that offer by depositing in its turn its declaration of acceptance, the consensual bond is established and no further condition needs to be fulfilled.[116]

The Court rejected Nigeria's objections and found that it had jurisdiction to adjudicate upon the dispute. Nigeria subsequently amended its declaration under article 36(2).

On December 30, 1998, Guinea, which had deposited a declaration under article 36(2) earlier that month, brought a claim against the Congo: *Case Concerning Ahmadou Diallo (Republic of Guinea v. Democratic Republic of the Congo)*.[117]

5) The scope of a state's optional clause declaration, and especially any reservations of jurisdiction within it, is often disputed and thus the Court is required to provide an interpretation. The Court's approach to this task is well explained in the *Fisheries Jurisdiction Case* between Spain and Canada. The factual context of the "Turbot War" that gave rise to this case is discussed in Chapter 13, Section E.1 on "Fisheries" under the heading "East Coast Fisheries and the Estai."

---

113   *Supra* note 111 at 419. The Court also relied on its previous decision in the *Interhandel Case*, [1959] I.C.J. Rep. 6. For a discussion of the case, see Editorial Comments (1985) 79 A.J.I.L. 373.

114   See the statements of the United States, reprinted in (1985) 24 I.L.M. at 246 & 249.

115   Online: International Court of Justice <http://www.icj-cij.org/icjwww/idocket/icn/icnframe.htm>.

116   Judgment of June 11, 1998 (Preliminary Objections), [1998] I.C.J. Rep. 275 at para. 25.

117   Online: International Court of Justice <http://www.icj-cij.org/icjwww/idocket/igc/igcframe.htm>.

Fisheries Jurisdiction Case
Spain v. Canada
[1998] I.C.J. Rep. 432

[In March 1995, Canada arrested the Spanish fishing trawler, the *Estai*, found fishing on the Nose of the Newfoundland Grand Banks 245 nautical miles from the Canadian shore. The vessel was brought to St. John's where its master was charged with violation of the *Coastal Fisheries Protection Act*. This Act had been amended the previous year to permit enforcement of Canadian fish conservation and management measures beyond Canada's 200 nautical mile fishing zone into the "NAFO Regulatory Area." Spain filed an application with the ICJ on the basis of the optional clause declarations that each state had made, alleging that Canada had violated the principle of the freedom of the high seas and infringed the sovereign rights of Spain. Canada denied that its declaration gave jurisdiction to the Court.]

THE COURT: ...

[61] The Court recalls that subparagraph 2(d) of the Canadian declaration excludes the Court's jurisdiction in the following terms:

> disputes arising out of or concerning conservation and management measures taken by Canada with respect to vessels fishing in the NAFO Regulatory Area, as defined in the Convention on Future Multilateral Co-operation in the Northwest Atlantic Fisheries, 1978, and the enforcement of such measures. ...

Canada contends that the dispute submitted to the Court is precisely of the kind envisaged by the cited text; it falls entirely within the terms of the subparagraph and the Court accordingly has no jurisdiction to entertain it.

For Spain, on the other hand, whatever Canada's intentions, they were not achieved by the words of the reservation, which does not cover the dispute; thus the Court has jurisdiction. In support of this view Spain relies on four main arguments: first, the dispute which it has brought before the Court falls outside the terms of the Canadian reservation by reason of its subject-matter; secondly, the amended Coastal Fisheries Protection Act and its implementing regulations cannot, in international law, constitute "conservation and management measures"; thirdly, the reservation covers only "vessels" which are stateless or flying a flag of convenience, and fourthly, the pursuit, boarding the seizure of the *Estai* cannot be regarded in international law as "the enforcement of ..." conservation and management "measures." ...

[At paragraph 54, the Court explained the nature of optional clause declarations by quoting an earlier decision:]

Declarations of acceptance of the compulsory jurisdiction of the Court are facultative, unilateral engagements, that States are absolutely free to make or not to make. In making the declaration a State is equally free either to do so unconditionally and without limit of time for its duration, or to qualify it with conditions or reservations. (*Military and Paramilitary Activities in and against Nicaragua (Nicaragua v. United*

States of America), Jurisdiction and Admissibility, Judgment, I.C.J. Reports 1984, p. 418, para. 59.)

[The Court also addressed the purpose of declarations, and from that purpose expounded the proper approach to their interpretation.]

[44] The Court recalls that the interpretation of declarations made under Article 36, paragraph 2, of the Stature, and of any reservations they contain, is directed to establishing whether mutual consent has been given to the jurisdiction of the Court. It is for each State, in formulating its declaration, to decide upon the limits it places upon its acceptance of the jurisdiction of the Court: "This jurisdiction only exists within the limits within which it has been accepted" (Phosphates in Morocco, Judgment, 1938, P.C.I.J., Series A/B, No. 74, p. 23). Conditions or reservations thus do not by their terms derogate from a wider acceptance already given. Rather, they operate to define the parameters of the State's acceptance of the compulsory jurisdiction of the Court. There is thus no reason to interpret them restrictively. All elements in a declaration under Article 36, paragraph 2, of the Statute which, read together, comprise the acceptance by the declarant State of the Court's jurisdiction, are to be interpreted as a unity, applying the same legal principles of interpretation throughout. ...

[46] A declaration of acceptance of the compulsory jurisdiction of the Court, whether there are specified limits set to that acceptance or not, is a unilateral act of State sovereignty. At the same time, it establishes a consensual bond and the potential for a jurisdictional link with the other States which have made declarations pursuant to Article 36, paragraph 2, of the Statute, and "makes a standing offer to the other States party to the Statute which have not yet deposited a declaration of acceptance" (*Land and Maritime Boundary between Cameroon and Nigeria (Cameroon v. Nigeria)*, Preliminary Objections, I.C.J. Reports 1998, para. 25). The regime relating to the interpretation of declarations made under Article 36 of the Statute is not identical with that established for the interpretation of treaties by the Vienna Convention on the Law of Treaties (ibid., para. 30). Spain has suggested in its pleadings that "[t]his does not mean that the legal rules and the art of interpreting declarations (and reservations) do not coincide with those governing the interpretation of treaties." The Court observes that the provisions of that Convention may only apply analogously to the extent compatible with the *sui generis* character of the unilateral acceptance of the Court's jurisdiction.

[47] In the event, the Court has in earlier cases elaborated the appropriate rules for the interpretation of declarations and reservations. Every declaration "must be interpreted as it stands, having regard to the words actually used" (Anglo-Iranian Oil Co., Preliminary Objection, Judgment, I.C.J. Reports 1952, p. 105). Every reservation must be given effect "as it stands" (Certain Norwegian Loans, Judgment, I.C.J. Reports 1957, p. 27). Therefore, declarations and reservations are to be read as a whole. Moreover, "the Court cannot base itself on a purely grammatical interpretation of the text. It must seek the interpretation which is in harmony with a natural and reasonable way of reading the text." (Anglo-Iranian Oil Co., Preliminary Objection, Judgment, I.C.J. Reports 1952, p. 104.)

[48] At the same time, since a declaration under Article 36, paragraph 2, of the Statute, is a unilaterally drafted instrument, the Court has not hesitated to place a certain emphasis on the intention of the depositing State. Indeed, in the case concerning Anglo-Iranian Oil Co., the Court found that the limiting words chosen in Iran's declaration were "a decisive confirmation of the intention of the Government of Iran at the time when it accepted the compulsory jurisdiction of the Court" (ibid., p. 107).

[49] The Court will thus interpret the relevant words of a declaration including a reservation contained therein in a natural and reasonable way, having due regard to the intention of the State concerned at the time when it accepted the compulsory jurisdiction of the Court. The intention of a reserving State may be deduced not only from the text of the relevant clause, but also from the context in which the clause is to be read, and an examination of evidence regarding the circumstances of its preparation and the purposes intended to be served …

[The Court examined each of Spain's contentions in turn but, applying these principles of interpretation, it decided that the dispute came within the terms of the reservation in Canada's declaration and therefore it did not have jurisdiction. Five judges, including Vice-President Weeramantry, dissented.]

VICE-PRESIDENT WEERAMANTRY dissenting: … [footnotes omitted]

[24] Where, as in this case, there is a general submission to the Court's jurisdiction, followed by particular exceptions, the general part states the principle underlying the declaration, namely, the principle of submission. That general part sets the framework within which the Court's jurisdiction is accepted. It constitutes, inter alia, a submission to the general corpus of international law and, in particular, to its ruling principles. The reservations constitute exceptions—in this case *ratione materiae*—to that jurisdiction. They do not constitute exceptions to the ruling principles of the corpus of international law … .

[47] … The principle that a document must, as far as possible, be given validity applies not merely to the reservations clause, taken in isolation, but to the document taken as a whole. The purpose of the entire document is to subscribe to the jurisdiction of the Court, in accordance with the principle of reciprocity, in all matters, other than those which are specifically excepted. The application of this principle to the document read as a whole means that effect should be given to this general intention as far as is reasonable. To hold that vast areas of possible international wrongdoing are withdrawn from the Court's jurisdiction merely because they occur in the context of an operation which can be described as a conservation or enforcement measure is to denude the consensual document of a vital part of its meaning … . I do not think it would be reasonable to give to reservations clauses such an extended and all-comprehensive meaning … .

[52] It is in the nature of things impossible to define where the reach of a reservation clause ends, but it is clear that there will be cases which are manifestly so far beyond its ambit that one can be in no doubt that its applicability has yielded to the applicability of the general part of the Declaration. The present case, provided the allegations of Spain are substantiated, is one such. …

[53] Much was made in argument of the negative effects that would ensue to the optional jurisdictional system if the Court were to hold that the reservations clause does not exclude the matter in question from the jurisdiction of the Court. It seems to me, however, that apart from the non-judicial nature of this argument, it is the Court's mission to uphold the integrity of its jurisdiction so far as has been entrusted to it by the optional clause system. I have referred earlier to this area of judicial jurisdiction as a haven of legality within the international system. Within that protected area, it is important that the rule of law should prevail, irrespective of such considerations as the favourable or unfavourable reception of the Court's determinations in relation to its jurisdiction.

[54] It may indeed be argued, on the contrary, that the preservation of legality within the system would strengthen rather than undermine its integrity. I do not think it is open to the Court, if a violation of a bedrock principle of international law is brought to its attention, to pass by this illegality on the basis that it is subsumed within the reservations clause. Such an approach could well weaken not only the authority of the Court, but also the integrity of the entire system of international law, which is a seamless web, and cannot be applied in bits and pieces. It is within this seamless fabric of international law that the entire optional clause system functions, and that consent to the Court's jurisdiction must be construed.

[55] I am fortified in reaching this conclusion by the circumstance that it accords with the philosophy underlying the creation of the optional clause. A brief historical excursus into this area will help to place the present problem in its overall context.

[56] The optional clause system, it will be remembered, was the international community's answer, after the agonies of World War I, to the hitherto intractable problem of carving out an area for the judicial settlement of international disputes, amidst the welter of conflicting claims of State sovereignty. These interests had for several centuries of recorded thought in many cultures eluded all attempts at the creation of such a jurisdiction. At long last a working formula was devised, in terms suggested by the Brazilian delegation to the Peace Conference (and in particular Mr. Raoul Fernandes), so as to create, in the midst of the clash of opposing sovereign interests, a comparatively small haven in which disputes would be resolved by a supranational judiciary in accordance with international law. ...

[58] In this area, a panel of regular judges—as opposed to ad hoc arbitrators—would administer justice among the nations, as domestic tribunals had traditionally administered justice among the subjects of a State. This totally unprecedented creation of a system of truly international adjudication was described on the same occasion as "the most remarkable step forward that humanity in its upward struggle has accomplished in the realm of law." Though now upwards of 70 years in operation, it is still of tender growth when compared with the thousands of years of domestic adjudication which had preceded it.

[59] [I]n the administration of this hard-won jurisdiction the high idealism that attended its birth needs to be kept in constant view. As this jurisdiction gathers strength through its continued exercise, the tendency is to be resisted of limiting it within the confines of circumscribed interpretations, when other interpretations more consistent with its spirit and purpose are equally available within its governing Statute. That interpretation should, in my view, be preferred which tends to strengthen that

jurisdiction, provided such interpretation is available within the parameters of the consenting State's declaration.

[60] It is also to be recalled in this context that the universal expectation of the time was that the creation of this jurisdiction was only the first step towards the gradual enlargement of that jurisdiction in the light of the experience of its administration. ...

[62] I appreciate that two views are possible as to how an increasing confidence in the system of international adjudication can be fostered.

[63] One view is the use of extreme caution in the assumption of jurisdiction, striking down every situation where, upon the literal meaning of the declaration, there is room for the interpretation that the State in question has not expressly granted its consent. This approach, while quite rightly basing itself on the principle of consent, can apply that principle somewhat too literally, thus resulting in a progressive diminution of that hard-won area of international jurisdiction that has been entrusted to the custody of the Court.

[64] Another view is that the jurisdiction granted to the Court must be exercised in the context of the broader responsibility of developing that jurisdiction in the light of the right of both States to seek from the one international court that is in existence a resolution of their dispute in accordance with the overall scheme of international justice—based always, of course, on the presence of consent.

[65] There could well be a range of possible interpretations of a declaration, and it seems to me that the interests of justice are best served by taking a broader view where that is consistent with the terms of the declaration. Thus construed, these submissions to the jurisdiction can afford the Court the basis for building up a growing body of jurisprudence, as well as for increasing the confidence of States in the reach and the value of international adjudication. Decisions which tend to diminish that jurisdiction in its formative stage may well inhibit the growth of the potentially vigorous sapling of international adjudication, and deter parties, who might otherwise approach the Court for a resolution of their disputes, from doing so.

[66] All of these principles make no encroachments whatsoever on the undoubted right of every sovereign State in its own unfettered discretion to determine whether it will or will not enter the judicial enclave created by the Statute. The discussions attending the acceptance of this clause show how careful the drafters were to ensure the preservation of State autonomy in this regard, for the imposition of compulsory jurisdiction, in however small a measure, was seen as a significant encroachment upon State autonomy.

[67] The entire architecture of the scheme points, however, to the preservation of the international rule of law within that judicial haven once entered. It was important to ensure that those who so entered had the assurance of the unimpeded reign of international law within that haven. Least was it under contemplation that a State could, while being within the system, disengage itself from the operation of Charter rules or basic principles of international law.

[68] Such disengagement from the ruling principles of international law is different in quality from the exclusion of Court jurisdiction in respect of specified categories of cases or areas of activity. Disengagement of jurisdiction from the latter is just as manifestly within the power of a State as disengagement from the former is not.

[69] Fundamental breaches of international law, if committed in the course of a particular activity, could clearly fall into the area over which the Court has been granted a general jurisdiction by a State's declaration. All the more would they tend to attract jurisdiction where, as in the present declaration, the general part submits all disputes arising after the declaration to the jurisdiction of the Court. Acceptance of the proposition that actions diverging fundamentally from the basics of international law can escape Court scrutiny, because they also fall literally within a reservations clause, could amount to an abdication of a portion of that hard-won jurisdiction which the Court was designed to exercise.

[70] The progressive contraction of that jurisdiction which could result could weaken the prospects for its continuing development, which were envisaged when it was launched. As Justice Cardozo has so eloquently reminded us in regard to the judicial process, "the inn that shelters for the night is not the journey's end" and, if the long and difficult road towards the goal of judicial settlement of international disputes is to be made easier, each stop along the way must offer the maximum judicial shelter it can provide.

[71] Upon the interpretation of the reservations clause which is indicated above, the Court is not in a position to reject the Spanish Application *in limine* on the basis of manifest lack of jurisdiction. There may well be no jurisdiction, and there may just as well be jurisdiction. The issue can only be determined once it is known whether the facts bring the case within the general submission to jurisdiction, or within the reservations clause. Until these are known, the Court is not entitled to reject Spain's Application.

NOTES

1) Consider the strikingly different views of article 36(2) expressed in the majority decision and the dissenting opinion of Vice-President Weeramantry. Which do you find more persuasive and why? Will the result in this case encourage states to accept the compulsory jurisdiction of the Court?

2) The Optional Clause has been the subject of considerable controversy over the years,[118] and many question its efficacy, given the extensive use of reservations and, perhaps more important, the limited degree of participation by states. Despite the increase mentioned above, only approximately one-third of the U.N. members have made declarations. There are few Asian participants, and the absence of four out of five of the permanent members of the Security Council is also noticeable. On the other hand, strong proponents of the compulsory jurisdiction system remain. For example, in the U.N. Secretary-General's 1992 report entitled "An Agenda for Peace," the following recommendation appeared:

---

118 See generally Alexandrov, *supra* note 103. A careful survey of the state practice surrounding the Optional Clause was provided in the dissenting judgment of Judge Oda in *Military Activities In and Against Nicaragua (Jurisdiction),* [1984] I.C.J. Rep. 392 at 471. See also C.H.M. Waldock, "Decline of the Optional Clause" (1955-56) 32 Brit. Y. B. Int'l L. 244.

All Member States should accept the general jurisdiction of the International Court under Article 36 of its Statute, without any reservation, before the end of the United Nations Decade of International Law in the year 2000.[119]

How would you respond to this recommendation given the somewhat slim support for the Optional Clause to this point, and based on your understanding of the role of the ICJ within the international legal system?

3. Decisions of the Court

Contentious Cases

1) The Court decides cases according to international law as found in the sources listed in its Statute article 38.[120] It has control over its own procedure, and it has established Rules of Court. The current set, dating from 1978, was amended in 2000.[121]

2) Ordinarily all 15 Members of the Court will sit to hear a case, although the quorum is only 9 (Statute article 25). However, the Statute also provides for the formation of chambers of as few as three judges (Statute articles 26 to 29). Chambers may be formed for particular categories of disputes (article 26(1)). The sole example of this type to date is the establishment in July 1993 of the "Chamber for Environmental Matters." Chambers can also be formed at the request of the parties (article 26(2) and (3)). The revision of the Rules of Court in 1978 granted prospective parties an element of influence over the composition of a chamber as well as its size. Canada and the United States exercised this new procedure for the first time in the *Gulf of Maine Case*[122] and requested a chamber of five judges from western countries. They thereby demonstrated how important it is to states who decides their case.[123] Do you think this precedent, if followed, will enhance or diminish the work and standing of the Court or the judicial development of international law?[124] Although some commentators had concerns about a possible trend in this direction, chambers of the Court have not been used all that often. The most recent example is the *Case Concerning the Frontier Dispute (Benin/Niger).*[125]

---

119 U.N. Doc. A/47/277-S/24111 (1992), online: United Nations <http://www.un.org/docs/SG/agpeace.html>.

120 Reproduced in the Documentary Supplement and discussed *supra* in Chapter 3, Section A.

121 "Basic Documents," online: International Court of Justice <http://www.icj-cij.org/icjwww/ ibasicdocuments/ibasictext/ibasicrulesofcourt_20001205.html>. For a discussion, see Shabtai Rosenne, *Procedure in the International Court, supra* note 68 and Hugh Thirlway, "The Law and Procedure of the International Court of Justice 1960-1989" (1996) 67 Brit. Y. B. Int'l L. 1.

122 [1982] I.C.J. Rep. 3.

123 This has led some commentators to note that the ICJ becomes much like an arbitral panel. See *e.g.* J.C. Guilds, "'If It Quacks Like a Duck': Comparing the ICJ Chambers to International Arbitration for a Mechanism of Enforcement" (1992) 16 Md. J. Int'l L. & Trade 43.

124 See Edward McWhinney, *Supreme Courts and Judicial Law-Making: Constitutional Tribunals and Constitutional Review* (1986) at 30-34 and D.M. McRae, "Adjudication of the Maritime Boundary in the Gulf of Maine" (1979) 17 Can. Y.B. Int'l L. 292.

125 See the Order on the formation of the chamber; online: International Court of Justice <http://www.icj-cij.org/icjwww/idocket/ibn/ibn_orders/ibn_iorder_20021127.pdf>.

3) A case is decided by a majority of the judges. In the event of a tie, the President has a casting vote, as occurred in the *Steamship Lotus*.[126] The judgment must contain the reasons of the majority, but there are frequently separate opinions by concurring judges, as well as dissenting opinions[127] (Statute articles 55 to 58).

4) What is the force of a decision of the Court (Statute article 59)? The judgment is final and without appeal, and is subject to revision only in limited circumstances (Statute articles 60 and 61). In the light of these articles, what subsequent impact do you think a judgment has on international law? Refer to Statute article 38(1)(d). While all the decisions of the PCIJ were complied with, the record for the ICJ is not as consistent.[128] For instance, the judgments in the *Corfu Channel Case*,[129] the *Fisheries Jurisdiction Case*,[130] the *U.S. Diplomatic Staff in Tehran Case*,[131] and the *Military Activities In and Against Nicaragua Case*[132] were not observed. How may a decision be enforced (Charter article 94)? Involvement of the Security Council is bound to politicize the judicial resolution of the dispute in question. Why is it necessary to turn to the Security Council for enforcement? Is the process likely to be used? Might it be possible to enforce an ICJ decision in a national court?

5) "Provisional measures"[133] may be taken by the Court in the course of a case when necessary "to preserve the respective rights of either party" (Statute article 41). What is the force of such interim measures? Compare the language of Statute articles 41 and 59. Interim measures have been pronounced in a number of cases, in at least five of which, the *Anglo-Iranian Oil Case*,[134] the *Fisheries Jurisdiction Case*,[135] the *Nuclear Tests Cases*,[136] the *U.S. Diplomatic Staff in Tehran Case*,[137] and the *Military Activities In and Against Nicaragua Case*,[138] they were not honoured at all. In recent years, such orders have been made in three cases brought against the United States under the Vienna Convention on Consular Relations, by Paraguay, Germany, and Mexico respectively.[139]

---

126 *The Steamship Lotus* (1927), P.C.I.J. (Ser. A) No. 10, reported in Chapter 9, Section A.1 on "Scope of Jurisdiction."

127 See Ijaz Hussain, *Dissenting and Separate Opinions at the World Court* (1984).

128 See generally Constanze Schulte, *Compliance with Decisions of the International Court of Justice* (2004).

129 [1949] I.C.J. Rep. 4, reported in Chapter 13, Section B.3 on "International Straits."

130 [1974] I.C.J. Rep. 3 at 175.

131 *Supra* note 76.

132 [1986] I.C.J. Rep. 14.

133 See Elias, *supra* note 68 c. 3; Jerome B. Elkind, *Interim Protection: A Functional Approach* (1981); and Jerzy Sztucki, *Interim Measures in the Hague Court* (1983).

134 [1951] I.C.J. Rep. 89.

135 [1972] I.C.J. Rep. 12 at 30.

136 [1973] I.C.J. Rep. 99 at 135.

137 [1979] I.C.J. Rep. 23.

138 [1984] I.C.J. Rep. 169.

139 *Case Concerning the Vienna Convention on Consular Relations (Paraguay v. United States)*, [1998] I.C.J. Rep. 426; *LaGrand Case (Germany v. United States)*, online: International Court of Justice <http://www.icj-cij.org/icjwww/idocket/igus/igusframe.htm>; *Case Concerning Avena and other Mexican*

All three cases involved the imposition of the death penalty and, in all three, the ICJ indicated that the United States must take measures to prevent executions pending its final judgment in the case. In the first, despite appeals by the U.S. State Department, the Governor of Virginia refused to grant a stay of execution and the Paraguayan national in question was executed as scheduled. The case was later withdrawn by Paraguay. In the second, the *LaGrand* case, the execution again went ahead. In its judgment, the ICJ found that its orders indicating provisional measures have binding effect and that the United States had not complied with the order in that case.[140]

What should be the criteria to determine whether the circumstances warrant provisional measures? In the *Aegean Sea Continental Shelf Case*,[141] the Court required proof of "irreparable prejudice to the rights in issue," which, in that situation, it did not find. This is a stiff standard but it is unclear whether it excludes all situations that are compensable by money. The Court applied the same standard in the *U.S. Diplomatic Staff in Tehran Case*[142] and held in favour of the United States, ordering Iran to release the hostages and restore the U.S. embassy. This was clearly an appropriate case for provisional measures, notwithstanding Iran's assertion that the Court would in effect judge the merits. Although the Court had refused to indicate provisional measures in the *Chorzow Factory (Indemnity) Case*[143] because the request was "designed to obtain an interim judgment in favour of a part of the claim" for a sum of money, the U.S. request regarding the hostages was to protect the lives of its nationals and its property pending adjudication of Iran's responsibility for its actions toward them. The cases arising under the Vienna Convention on Consular Relations, mentioned above, were relatively clear examples of situations of "irreparable prejudice." In the case brought by Mexico, however, the Court took a fairly cautious approach. Mexico had requested *inter alia* that the United States should take all measures necessary to ensure that no Mexican national be executed. In fact, no execution dates had been set for any of the 54 Mexican nationals. The Court indicated that the lack of set dates for the executions did not preclude it from indicating provisional measures. However, it went through each case to determine which individuals were at risk of execution in the coming months or weeks, and indicated provisional measures with regard to 3 individuals. The Court found that the other 51, although on death row, were not in the same position, although it left open the possibility of indicating further provisional measures prior to rendering its final judgment.

6) May the Court indicate provisional measures under Statute article 41 at the request of one party, if the other party has not yet consented to the Court's jurisdiction to entertain the merits of the case under Statute article 36?[144] In the *Aegean Sea Continental*

   Nationals (Mexico v. United States), online: International Court of Justice <http://www.icj-cij.org/icjwww/idocket/imus/imusframe.htm>.

140 *LaGrand Case (Germany v. United States)*, Judgment of June 27, 2001, [2001] I.C.J. Rep. 466.

141 [1976] I.C.J. Rep. 3 at 11.

142 [1979] I.C.J. Rep. 7 at 19 and 16.

143 (1927), P.C.I.J. (Ser. A) No. 12 at 10.

144 See J. Peter A. Bernhardt, "The Provisional Measures Procedure of the International Court of Justice through U.S. Staff in Tehran: Fiat Justitia, Pereat Curia?" (1980) 20 Va. J. Int'l L. 557; Elkind, *supra* note 133 c. 7; D.M. McRae, Note (1973) 8 U.B.C.L. Rev. 375; and Sztucki, *supra* note 133 c. 5.

Shelf Case, the majority of 12 did not consider it necessary to decide the question; however, 7 concurring judges wrote separate opinions expressing views that a finding of jurisdiction, with varying degrees of certainty, was an essential prerequisite to pronouncing interim measures. Judge Jimenez de Aréchaga considered article 41 to be an autonomous grant of jurisdiction, but jurisdiction over the merits was a relevant circumstance in the determination of provisional measures. Three other judges thought the Court must reach a provisional conviction that it has jurisdiction under article 36. Judges Morozov and Tarazi said a full finding on jurisdiction is necessary. What would be the practical effect if the views of Judges Morozov and Tarazi prevail? What would be the effect of indicating provisional measures without enquiring into jurisdiction? Consider this question in the light of the Court's judgment in the *LaGrand* case, mentioned above in Note 5, that its orders indicating provisional measures have binding effect.

Advisory Opinions[145]

The Court is empowered to give advisory opinions on legal questions put to it by the General Assembly, the Security Council, and such other organs and specialized agencies of the United Nations as are authorized by the General Assembly "on legal questions arising within the scope of their activities" (Charter article 96 and Statute article 65). Some of the authorized organs and agencies are the International Labour Organization (ILO), Food and Agriculture Organization (FAO), United Nations Educational, Scientific and Cultural Organization (UNESCO), World Health Organization (WHO), World Bank, International Finance Corporation (IFC), International Development Association (IDA), International Monetary Fund (IMF), International Civil Aviation Organization (ICAO), International Telecommunications Union (ITU), International Maritime Organization (IMO), and World Intellectual Property Organization (WIPO).[146] Some of the Court's most significant and influential decisions have been rendered in this format, including: the *Reparations Case*,[147] dealing with powers of United Nations; the *Western Sahara Case*,[148] dealing with the concept of *terra nullius* and the right of self-determination; and, most recently, the two advisory opinions on the legality of the use of nuclear weapons.

The request by the World Health Organization (WHO) for an advisory opinion on the *Legality of the Use by a State of Nuclear Weapons in Armed Conflict*[149] was in fact turned down by the Court. WHO had submitted the following question:

---

145 See Kenneth James Keith, *The Extent of the Advisory Jurisdiction of the International Court of Justice* (1971); Michla Pomerance, *The Advisory Function of the International Court in the League and U.N. Eras* (1973); Dharma Pratap, *The Advisory Jurisdiction of the International Court* (1972); and P.C. Szasz, "Enhancing the Advisory Competence of the World Court" in Gross, *supra* note 68 at 499.

146 "Organs and Specialized Agencies of the United Nations Authorized to Request Advisory Opinions," online: International Court of Justice <http://www.icj-cij.org/icjwww/ibasicdocuments/ibasictext/ibasicorgansandspecialized.html>.

147 [1949] I.C.J. Rep. 174, reported in Chapter 2, Section C.1 on "International Organizations."

148 [1975] I.C.J. Rep. 12.

149 Adv. Op. [1996] I.C.J. Rep. 66.

In view of the health and environmental effects, would the use of nuclear weapons by a State in war or other armed conflict be a breach of its obligations under international law including the WHO Constitution?

Unusually but, perhaps, not surprisingly, several states argued before the Court that this was a political, not a legal, question, and went beyond the scope of WHO's proper activities. The Court stated at paragraph 10 that "three conditions must be satisfied in order to found the jurisdiction of the Court when a request for an advisory opinion is submitted to it by a specialized agency: the agency requesting the opinion must be duly authorized, under the Charter, to request opinions from the Court; the opinion requested must be on a legal question; and this question must be one arising within the scope of the activities of the requesting agency."

It was clear that WHO had been authorized to request advisory opinions and the Court had little difficulty in satisfying itself that the question asked was a legal one:

15. ... The Court has already had occasion to indicate that questions

Framed in terms of law and rais[ing] problems of international law ... are by their very nature susceptible of a reply based on law ... [and] appear ... to be questions of a legal character (Western Sahara, Advisory Opinion, I.C.J. Reports 1975, p. 18, para. 15).

16. The question put to the Court by the World Health Assembly does in fact constitute a legal question. ... [To address the question] the Court must identify the obligations of States under the rules of law invoked, and assess whether the behaviour in question conforms to those obligations, thus giving an answer to the question posed based on law. ... The fact that this question also has political aspects, as, in the nature of things, is the case with so many questions which arise in international life, does not suffice to deprive it of its character as a "legal question" and to "deprive the Court of a competence expressly conferred on it by its Statute." ... Whatever its political aspects, the Court cannot refuse to admit the legal character of a question which invites it to discharge an essentially judicial task, namely, an assessment of the legality of the possible conduct of States with regard to the obligations imposed upon them by international law ... .

17. The Court also finds that the political nature of the motives which may be said to have inspired the request and the political implications that the opinion given might have are of no relevance in the establishment of its jurisdiction to give such an opinion.

However, the third condition, that the question had to be within the scope of activities of WHO, posed problems. The Court determined that the question asked related "not to the effects of the use of nuclear weapons on health, but to the legality of the use of such weapons in view of their health and environmental effects. Whatever these effects might be, the competence of the WHO to deal with them ... [was, in the Court's view,] not dependent on the legality of the acts that caused them." The Court concluded that the WHO's Constitution did not give it competence over the legality of nuclear weapons so it had no authority to ask such a question.

Similar arguments to persuade the Court not to give an advisory opinion in the other case, brought by the U.N. General Assembly, were not successful. The Court delivered the following opinion.

Legality of the Threat or Use of Nuclear Weapons
Adv. Op. [1996] I.C.J. Rep. 226

[The General Assembly submitted the following question to the Court for an advisory opinion: is the threat or use of nuclear weapons in any circumstance permitted under international law? After determining that it had jurisdiction to give a reply to the General Assembly's request for an advisory opinion, the Court considered the question of whether it should decline to exercise such jurisdiction.]

THE COURT: ...

[14] Article 65, paragraph 1, of the Statute provides: "The Court *may* give an advisory opinion ..." This is more than an enabling provision. As the Court has repeatedly emphasized, the Statute leaves a discretion as to whether or not it will give an advisory opinion that has been requested of it, once it has established its competence to do so. In this context, the Court has previously noted as follows:

> The Court's Opinion is given not to the States, but to the organ which is entitled to request it; the reply of the Court, itself an "organ of the United Nations," represents its participation in the activities of the Organization, and, in principle, should not be refused. (Interpretation of Peace Treaties with Bulgaria, Hungary and Romania, First Phase, Advisory Opinion, I.C.J. Reports 1950, p. 71 ...)

The Court has constantly been mindful of its responsibilities as "the principal judicial organ of the United Nations" (Charter, Art. 92). When considering each request, it is mindful that it should not, in principle, refuse to give an advisory opinion. In accordance with the consistent jurisprudence of the Court, only "compelling reasons" could lead it to such a refusal ... There has been no refusal, based on the discretionary power of the Court, to act upon a request for advisory opinion in the history of the present Court; in the case concerning the Legality of the Use by a State of Nuclear Weapons in Armed Conflict, the refusal to give the World Health Organization the advisory opinion requested by it was justified by the Court's lack of jurisdiction in that case. The Permanent Court of International Justice took the view on only one occasion that it could not reply to a question put to it, having regard to the very particular circumstances of the case, among which were that the question directly concerned an already existing dispute, one of the States parties to which was neither a party to the Statute of the Permanent Court nor a Member of the League of Nations, objected to the proceedings, and refused to take part in any way (Status of Eastern Carelia, P.C.I.J., Series B, No. 5).

[15] Most of the reasons adduced in these proceedings in order to persuade the Court that in the exercise of its discretionary power it should decline to render the opinion requested by General Assembly resolution 49/75K were summarized in the following statement made by one State in the written proceedings:

> The question presented is vague and abstract, addressing complex issues which are the subject of consideration among interested States and within other bodies of the United Nations which have an express mandate to address these matters. An opinion by the

Court in regard to the question presented would provide no practical assistance to the General Assembly in carrying out its functions under the Charter. Such an opinion has the potential of undermining progress already made or being made on this sensitive subject and, therefore, is contrary to the interest of the United Nations Organization. (United States of America, Written Statement, pp. 1-2; cf. pp. 3-7, II. See also United Kingdom, Written Statement, pp. 9-20, paras. 2.23-2.45; France, Written Statement, pp. 13-20, paras. 5-9; Finland, Written Statement, pp. 1-2; Netherlands, Written Statement, pp. 3-4, paras. 6-13; Germany, Written Statement, pp. 3-6, para. 2(b).))

In contending that the question put to the Court is vague and abstract, some States appeared to mean by this that there exists no specific dispute on the subject-matter of the question. In order to respond to this argument, it is necessary to distinguish between requirements governing contentious procedure and those applicable to advisory opinions. The purpose of the advisory function is not to settle—at least directly— disputes between States, but to offer legal advice to the organs and institutions requesting the opinion (cf. Interpretation of Peace Treaties I.C.J. Reports 1950, p. 71). The fact that the question put to the Court does not relate to a specific dispute should consequently not lead the Court to decline to give the opinion requested.

Moreover, it is the clear position of the Court that to contend that it should not deal with a question couched in abstract terms is "a mere affirmation devoid of any justification," and that "the Court may give an advisory opinion on any legal question, abstract or otherwise" (Conditions of Admission of a State to Membership in the United Nations (Article 4 of the Charter), Advisory Opinion, 1948, I.C.J. Reports 1947-1948, p. 61. ....)

Certain States have however expressed the fear that the abstract nature of the question might lead the Court to make hypothetical or speculative declarations outside the scope of its judicial function. The Court does not consider that, in giving an advisory opinion in the present case, it would necessarily have to write "scenarios," to study various types of nuclear weapons and to evaluate highly complex and controversial technological, strategic and scientific information. The Court will simply address the issues arising in all their aspects by applying the legal rules relevant to the situation.

[16] Certain States have observed that the General Assembly has not explained to the Court for what precise purposes it seeks the advisory opinion. Nevertheless, it is not for the Court itself to purport to decide whether or not an advisory opinion is needed by the Assembly for the performance of its functions. The General Assembly has the right to decide for itself on the usefulness of an opinion in the light of its own needs.

Equally, once the Assembly has asked, by adopting a resolution, for an advisory opinion on a legal question, the Court, in determining whether there are any compelling reasons for it to refuse to give such an opinion, will not have regard to the origins or to the political history of the request, or to the distribution of votes in respect of the adopted resolution.

[17] It has also been submitted that a reply from the Court in this case might adversely affect disarmament negotiations and would, therefore, be contrary to the interest of the United Nations. The Court is aware that, no matter what might be its conclusions in any opinion it might give, they would have relevance for the continuing

debate on the matter in the General Assembly and would present an additional element in the negotiations on the matter. Beyond that, the effect of the opinion is a matter of appreciation. The Court has heard contrary positions advanced and there are no evident criteria by which it can prefer one assessment to another. That being so, the Court cannot regard this factor as a compelling reason to decline to exercise its jurisdiction.

[18] Finally, it has been contended by some States that in answering the question posed, the Court would be going beyond its judicial role and would be taking upon itself a law-making capacity. It is clear that the Court cannot legislate, and, in the circumstances of the present case, it is not called upon to do so. Rather its task is to engage in its normal judicial function of ascertaining the existence or otherwise of legal principles and rules applicable to the threat or use of nuclear weapons. The contention that the giving of an answer to the question posed would require the Court to legislate is based on a supposition that the present *corpus juris* is devoid of relevant rules in this matter. The Court could not accede to this argument; it states the existing law and does not legislate. This is so even if, in stating and applying the law, the Court necessarily has to specify its scope and sometimes note its general trend.

[19] In view of what is stated above, the Court concludes that it has the authority to deliver an opinion on the question posed by the General Assembly, and that there exist no "compelling reasons" which would lead the Court to exercise its discretion not to do so.

An entirely different question is whether the Court, under the constraints placed upon it as a judicial organ, will be able to give a complete answer to the question asked of it. However, that is a different matter from a refusal to answer at all.

NOTES

1) The Court held: unanimously, that there is in neither customary nor conventional international law any specific authorization of the threat or use of nuclear weapons; by 11 votes to 3, that there is in neither customary nor conventional international law any comprehensive and universal prohibition of the threat or use of nuclear weapons as such; unanimously, that a threat or use of force by means of nuclear weapons that is contrary to article 2, paragraph 4, of the U.N. Charter and that fails to meet all the requirements of article 51, is unlawful; unanimously, that a threat or use of nuclear weapons should also be compatible with the requirements of the international law applicable in armed conflict, particularly the principles and rules of international humanitarian law, as well as with specific obligations under treaties and other undertakings that expressly deal with nuclear weapons.[150] As a consequence, by the President casting his vote to break a 7 to 7 tie, the Court held (at para. 105(D)):

> It follows from the above-mentioned requirements that the threat or use of nuclear weapons would generally be contrary to the rules of international law applicable in armed conflict, and in particular the principles and rules of humanitarian law; However, in view of the

---

150 *Legality of the Threat or Use of Nuclear Weapons* (Adv. Op.), [1996] I.C.J. Rep. 226.

current state of international law, and of the elements of fact at its disposal, the Court cannot conclude definitively whether the threat or use of nuclear weapons would be lawful or unlawful in an extreme circumstance of self-defence, in which the very survival of a State would be at stake.

The Court also held unanimously that there exists an obligation to pursue in good faith and bring to a conclusion negotiations leading to nuclear disarmament in all its aspects under strict and effective international control.

2) Although somewhat ambiguous in its outcome, this decision has been heralded by many commentators.[151] It is also noteworthy because of the "grassroots" process by which it came before the court in the first place.[152] Would you consider this to be a positive trend? What other areas might be ripe for judicial consideration through this mechanism?

3) The advisory opinion might be said to allow the Court to step outside its arguably rather narrow dispute resolution function and instead look to the future development of international law. At the same time, there has been a marked reluctance on the part of the Court to step too far outside the bounds of its judicial role, as reflected in paragraph 18 of the opinion above. Do you view such restraint as justified, or would you prefer to see the Court take a more activist stance?

4) On several occasions states involved in a situation that was the subject of the request for an advisory opinion objected on the basis that they had not consented to the Court's jurisdiction. This was at issue in the recent advisory opinion on the Legal Consequences of the Construction of a Wall in the Occupied Palestinian Territory.

Legal Consequences of the Construction of a Wall in the Occupied Palestinian Territory
[2004] I.C.J. Rep. 136

[On December 8, 2003, the General Assembly adopted resolution A/RES/ES-10/14 (A/ES-10/L.16) in which it requested that the International Court of Justice "urgently render an advisory opinion on the following question: What are the legal consequences arising from the construction of the wall being built by Israel, the occupying Power, in the Occupied Palestinian Territory, including in and around East Jerusalem, as described in the report of the Secretary-General, considering the rules and principles of international law, including the Fourth Geneva Convention of 1949, and relevant

---

151 For commentary on the decision and its significance, see Michael J. Matheson, "The Opinions of the International Court of Justice on the Threat or Use of Nuclear Weapons" (1997) 91 A.J.I.L. 417 and Richard A. Falk, "Nuclear Weapons, International Law and the World Court: A Historic Encounter (Editorial Comment)" (1997) 91 A.J.I.L. 64. See also "Symposium: Nuclear Weapons, the World Court, and Global Security" (1997) 7 Transnat'l L. & Contemp. Probs. No. 2.

152 H.J. Evans, "The World Court Project on Nuclear Weapons and International Law" (1993) New Zealand L. J. 249 and R. Falk, "The Nuclear Weapons Advisory Opinion and the New Jurisprudence of Global Civil Society" (1997) 7 Transnat'l L. & Contemp. Probs. 333.

Security Council and General Assembly resolutions?" Having concluded that it had jurisdiction to render the advisory opinion, the Court proceeded to address the contention that it should decline to exercise its jurisdiction because of the presence of specific aspects of the General Assembly's request that would render the exercise of the Court's jurisdiction improper and inconsistent with the Court's judicial function. The Court began by reiterating many of the points set out in the Advisory Opinion on the Legality of the Threat or Use of Nuclear Weapons, noting that while the Court has a discretionary power to decline to give an advisory opinion even if the conditions of jurisdiction are met, only compelling reasons should lead the Court to refuse its opinion, and that the present Court has never declined to respond to a request for an advisory opinion. It also noted the "very particular circumstances" under which the Permanent Court of International Justice took the view that it should not reply to a question put to it in the *Status of Eastern Carelia, Advisory Opinion* (1923), P.C.I.J. (Ser. B) (No. 5), as set out in para. 14 of the Advisory Opinion on the *Legality of the Threat or Use of Nuclear Weapons*, excerpted above.]

[45] These considerations do not release the Court from the duty to satisfy itself, each time it is seised of a request for an opinion, as to the propriety of the exercise of its judicial function, by reference to the criterion of "compelling reasons." ... The Court will accordingly examine in detail and in the light of its jurisprudence each of the arguments presented to it in this regard.

[46] The first such argument is to the effect that the Court should not exercise its jurisdiction in the present case because the request concerns a contentious matter between Israel and Palestine, in respect of which Israel has not consented to the exercise of that jurisdiction. According to this view, the subject-matter of the question posed by the General Assembly "is an integral part of the wider Israeli–Palestinian dispute concerning questions of terrorism, security, borders, settlements, Jerusalem and other related matters." Israel has emphasized that it has never consented to the settlement of this wider dispute by the Court or by any other means of compulsory adjudication; on the contrary, it contends that the parties repeatedly agreed that these issues are to be settled by negotiation, with the possibility of an agreement that recourse could be had to arbitration. It is accordingly contended that the Court should decline to give the present Opinion, on the basis *inter alia* of the precedent of the decision of the Permanent Court of International Justice on the *Status of Eastern Carelia*.

[47] The Court observes that the lack of consent to the Court's contentious jurisdiction by interested States has no bearing on the Court's jurisdiction to give an advisory opinion. In an Advisory Opinion of 1950, the Court explained that:

> The consent of States, parties to a dispute, is the basis of the Court's jurisdiction in contentious cases. The situation is different in regard to advisory proceedings even where the Request for an Opinion relates to a legal question actually pending between States. The Court's reply is only of an advisory character: as such, it has no binding force. It follows that no State, whether a Member of the United Nations or not, can prevent the giving of an Advisory Opinion which the United Nations considers to be desirable in order to obtain enlightenment as to the course of action it should take. The

Court's Opinion is given not to the States, but to the organ which is entitled to request it; the reply of the Court, itself an "organ of the United Nations," represents its participation in the activities of the Organization, and, in principle, should not be refused. (*Interpretation of Peace Treaties with Bulgaria, Hungary and Romania, First Phase, Advisory Opinion, I.C.J. Reports 1950*, p. 71; see also *Western Sahara, I.C.J. Reports 1975*, p. 24, para. 31.)

It followed from this that, in those proceedings, the Court did not refuse to respond to the request for an advisory opinion on the ground that, in the particular circumstances, it lacked jurisdiction. The Court did however examine the opposition of certain interested States to the request by the General Assembly in the context of issues of judicial propriety. Commenting on its 1950 decision, the Court explained in its Advisory Opinion on *Western Sahara* that it had "[t]hus ... recognized that lack of consent might constitute a ground for declining to give the opinion requested if, in the circumstances of a given case, considerations of judicial propriety should oblige the Court to refuse an opinion." The Court continued:

In certain circumstances ... the lack of consent of an interested State may render the giving of an advisory opinion incompatible with the Court's judicial character. An instance of this would be when the circumstances disclose that to give a reply would have the effect of circumventing the principle that a State is not obliged to allow its disputes to be submitted to judicial settlement without its consent. (*Western Sahara, I.C.J. Reports 1975*, p. 25, paras. 32-33.)

In applying that principle to the request concerning *Western Sahara*, the Court found that a legal controversy did indeed exist, but one which had arisen during the proceedings of the General Assembly and in relation to matters with which the Assembly was dealing. It had not arisen independently in bilateral relations (*ibid.*, p. 25, para. 34).

[48] As regards the request for an advisory opinion now before it, the Court acknowledges that Israel and Palestine have expressed radically divergent views on the legal consequences of Israel's construction of the wall, on which the Court has been asked to pronounce. However, as the Court has itself noted, "Differences of views ... on legal issues have existed in practically every advisory proceeding" (*Legal Consequences for States of the Continued Presence of South Africa in Namibia (South West Africa) notwithstanding Security Council Resolution 276 (1970), Advisory Opinion, I.C.J. Reports 1971*, p. 24, para. 34).

[49] Furthermore, the Court does not consider that the subject-matter of the General Assembly's request can be regarded as only a bilateral matter between Israel and Palestine. Given the powers and responsibilities of the United Nations in questions relating to international peace and security, it is the Court's view that the construction of the wall must be deemed to be directly of concern to the United Nations. The responsibility of the United Nations in this matter also has its origin in the Mandate and the Partition Resolution concerning Palestine. ... This responsibility has been described by the General Assembly as "a permanent responsibility towards the question of Palestine until the question is resolved in all its aspects in a satisfactory

manner in accordance with international legitimacy" (General Assembly resolution 57/107 of 3 December 2002). Within the institutional framework of the Organization, this responsibility has been manifested by the adoption of many Security Council and General Assembly resolutions, and by the creation of several subsidiary bodies specifically established to assist in the realization of the inalienable rights of the Palestinian people.

[50] The object of the request before the Court is to obtain from the Court an opinion which the General Assembly deems of assistance to it for the proper exercise of its functions. The opinion is requested on a question which is of particularly acute concern to the United Nations, and one which is located in a much broader frame of reference than a bilateral dispute. In the circumstances, the Court does not consider that to give an opinion would have the effect of circumventing the principle of consent to judicial settlement, and the Court accordingly cannot, in the exercise of its discretion, decline to give an opinion on that ground.

NOTES

1) The Court went on to deal with several other arguments regarding the propriety of rendering an advisory opinion in these circumstances. It rejected the contention that it should decline to give the opinion because its opinion could impede a political, negotiated solution to the Israeli–Palestinian conflict, noting that it was not clear what influence its opinion might have on those negotiations and that participants in the present proceedings had expressed differing views in this regard. The Court found that it had before it sufficient information and evidence to enable it to give the opinion requested by the General Assembly. Finally, the Court rejected the argument that it should decline to give the requested opinion because the opinion would lack any useful purpose given that the General Assembly had already declared the construction of the wall to be illegal and had already determined the legal consequences by demanding that Israel stop and reverse its construction; the Court cannot substitute its assessment of the usefulness of the opinion requested for that of the organ that seeks the opinion. The Court concluded that there was no compelling reason precluding it from giving the requested opinion.

2) On the substantive question before it, the Court found, *inter alia*, that the construction of the wall being built by Israel, the occupying Power, in the Occupied Palestinian Territory, including in and around East Jerusalem, and its associated regime, is contrary to international law; that Israel is under an obligation to terminate its breaches of international law, to cease the works of construction of the wall being built in the Occupied Palestinian Territory, to dismantle the structure already situated there, and to repeal or render ineffective all legislative and regulatory acts relating thereto; that Israel is under an obligation to make reparation for all damage caused by the construction of the wall in the Occupied Palestinian Territory; that all States are under an obligation not to recognize the illegal situation resulting from the construction of the wall and not to render aid or assistance in maintaining the situation created by such construction; and that the United Nations, and especially the General Assembly and the Security Council, should consider what further action is required to bring to an end the illegal situation

resulting from the construction of the wall and the associated regime, taking due account of the present Advisory Opinion. The penultimate paragraph of the opinion contains the following statement:

[162] The Court has reached the conclusion that the construction of the wall by Israel in the Occupied Palestinian Territory is contrary to international law and has stated the legal consequences that are to be drawn from that illegality. The Court considers itself bound to add that this construction must be placed in a more general context. Since 1947, the year when General Assembly resolution 181 (II) was adopted and the Mandate for Palestine was terminated, there has been a succession of armed conflicts, acts of indiscriminate violence and repressive measures on the former mandated territory. The Court would emphasize that both Israel and Palestine are under an obligation scrupulously to observe the rules of international humanitarian law, one of the paramount purposes of which is to protect civilian life. Illegal actions and unilateral decisions have been taken on all sides, whereas, in the Court's view, this tragic situation can be brought to an end only through implementation in good faith of all relevant Security Council resolutions ... . The Court considers that it has a duty to draw the attention of the General Assembly, to which the present Opinion is addressed, to the need for these efforts to be encouraged with a view to achieving as soon as possible, on the basis of international law, a negotiated solution to the outstanding problems and the establishment of a Palestinian State, existing side by side with Israel and its other neighbours, with peace and security for all in the region.

3) As noted previously, U.N. organs and agencies do not ordinarily have standing before the Court. Can they use the process of an advisory opinion to litigate their own disputes? Consider the *Reparations Case*.[153] While advisory opinions are very useful for resolving uncertain legal issues of general concern, such as points of interpretation of the U.N. Charter of the kind raised in that case, is there something problematic about the Court, as the chief judicial organ of the United Nations, pronouncing upon such issues? Was this concern at issue in the advisory opinion excerpted above?

4) Along these same lines, why are states denied the right to ask for advisory opinions? Are there other kinds of authorities or organizations that might usefully be given the right to ask for advisory opinions directly?[154] Would it be useful to enhance the capacity of the ICJ to give advisory opinions? In what way might this be done that would be acceptable to states parties to the Statute?

4. A Judicial Review Power for the Court?

The U.N. Charter declares in article 92 that the ICJ is "the principal judicial organ" of the organization but does not explain the relationship between the Court and the other organs

---

153   *Supra* note 147. See also *Difference Relating to Immunity from Legal Process of a Special Rapporteur of the Commission on Human Rights (Advisory Opinion)*, online: International Court of Justice <http://www.icj-cij.org/icjwww/idocket/inuma/inumaframe.htm>.

154   Louis B. Sohn, "Broadening the Advisory Jurisdiction of the International Court of Justice" (1983) 77 A.J.I.L. 124 and Stephen M. Schwebel, "Preliminary Rulings by the I.C.J. at the Instance of National Courts" (1987-88) 28 Va. J. Int'l L. 495.

of the United Nations. Of foremost concern from a legal point of view is whether the Court has any power to review the legality of the acts and decisions of the other organs. It cannot be assumed that the Court does or does not have the power of judicial review, and the silence of the Charter on the point does not help. While the question has arisen in a number of cases, it has perhaps never been so prominent as in the Lockerbie dispute between Libya and the United States and United Kingdom. The Court did not express a view, yet an avalanche of commentary on the case has revolved around its implications for a power of judicial review.[155]

The case arose out of the explosion of a Pan American aircraft over Lockerbie, Scotland, on December 21, 1988, which resulted in the deaths of all 259 people on board as well as 11 residents of Lockerbie. In late 1991, the conclusions of a wide-ranging criminal investigation were announced, and it was alleged that two Libyan nationals (reportedly members of the Libyan intelligence service) had caused a bomb to be placed aboard the flight. An account of the evidence against the accused was transmitted to the Libyan Government, together with a request for the surrender of the two accused to stand trial either in Scotland or in the United States. On November 27, 1991, citing Libya's lack of response to the earlier request, the United States and the United Kingdom made a joint declaration demanding that Libya surrender the individuals accused of the bombing, acknowledge its involvement, and make reparation. The declaration ended by stating, "We expect Libya to comply promptly and in full." The declaration was circulated to the General Assembly and the Security Council. The matter was brought before the Security Council by the United States and the United Kingdom, resulting in the adoption on January 21, 1992 of resolution 731 (1992), which, *inter alia*, urged "the Libyan government immediately to provide a full and effective response to [the United States and the United Kingdom] requests so as to contribute to the elimination of international terrorism." On March 3, 1992, Libya brought a claim before the ICJ against the United States and the United Kingdom under the 1971 Montreal Convention for the Suppression of Unlawful Acts against the Safety of Civil Aviation, to which all three States are parties. Libya argued that there was no extradition treaty between itself and the United Kingdom or the United States, and that according to the Convention it was entitled to take measures

---

155 For a sampling of the huge amounts of commentary that the case has generated, see Dapo Akande, "The International Court of Justice and the Security Council: Is There Room for Judicial Control of Decisions of the Political Organs of the United Nations?" (1997) 46 I.C.L.Q. 309; Jose E. Alvarez, "Judging the Security Council" (1996) 90 A.J.I.L. 1; Thomas M. Franck, "The 'Powers of Appreciation': Who Is the Ultimate Guardian of UN Legality?" (1992) 86 A.J.I.L. 519; Vera Gowlland-Debbas, "The Relationship Between the International Court of Justice and the Security Council in the Light of the Lockerbie Case" (1994) 88 A.J.I.L. 643; Angus M. Gunn, "Council and Court: Prospects in Lockerbie for an International Rule of Law" (1993) 52 U. T. Fac. L. Rev. 206; R. St. J. MacDonald, "Changing Relations Between the International Court of Justice and the Security Council of the United Nations" (1993) 31 Can. Y. B. Int'l L. 3; Bernd Martenczuk, "The Security Council, the International Court and Judicial Review: What Lessons from Lockerbie?" (1999) 10 E.J.I.L. 517; Edward McWhinney, "The International Court as Emerging Constitutional Court and the Co-ordinate UN Institutions (especially the Security Council): Implications of the Aerial Incident at Lockerbie" (1992) 30 Can. Y.B. Int'l L. 261; W. Michael Reisman, "The Constitutional Crisis in the United Nations" (1993) 87 A.J.I.L. 83; and Geoffrey R. Watson, "Constitutionalism, Judicial Review, and the World Court" (1993) 34 Harv. Int'l L. J. 1. See also the discussion of the case under "Responses to State-Sponsored Terrorism" in Chapter 15, Section B.4.

to exercise its criminal jurisdiction and to prosecute the accused. Libya also requested provisional measures to prevent further action by the United Kingdom and the United States, including action in the Security Council. On March 31, 1992, three days after the conclusion of the oral hearings regarding the request for provisional measures, the Security Council adopted resolution 748 (1992), in which it specifically referred to the suppression of acts of international terrorism as being "essential for the maintenance of international peace and security," invoked its Chapter VII powers, and imposed sanctions against Libya. On April 14, 1992, the ICJ denied Libya's request for provisional measures. On November 11, 1993, the Security Council adopted resolution 883 (1993) in which it referred to Libya's failure to comply with its earlier resolutions and Libya's continued failure to demonstrate its renunciation of terrorism as constituting a "threat to international peace and security," and extended the scope of the sanctions against Libya. On February 27, 1998, the Court delivered a judgment on the preliminary questions of jurisdiction and admissibility. In finding that it did have jurisdiction under the Montreal Convention, the majority sidestepped the "judicial review" issue by focusing on the date upon which Libya had brought its original application, at which time no binding Security Council resolution existed. In a strong dissent, President Schwebel specifically addressed the question of judicial review.

Case Concerning Questions of Interpretation and Application of the 1971 Montreal Convention Arising from the Aerial Incident at Lockerbie (Preliminary Objections) (Libyan Arab Jamahiriya v. United Kingdom), [1998] I.C.J. Rep. 115, reprinted in (1998) 37 I.L.M. 587

PRESIDENT SCHWEBEL dissenting: ...

The Court's decision in effect to join the preliminary objections to the merits ... has regrettable if unintended results, the least of which is requiring the Parties to argue, and the Court to hear, arguments on those objections, or some of those objections, for a third time. It will prolong a challenge to the integrity and authority of the Security Council. It may be taken as providing excuse for continued defiance of the Council's binding resolutions. It may be seen as prejudicing an important contemporary aspect of the Council's efforts to maintain international peace and security by combating State-sponsored international terrorism. Justice for the victims of an appalling atrocity may be further delayed and denied. The Court may have opened itself, not only in this but in future cases, to appearing to offer to recalcitrant States a means to parry and frustrate decisions of the Security Council by way of appeal to the Court.

Judicial Review

That last spectre raises the question of whether the Court is empowered to exercise judicial review of the decisions of the Security Council, a question as to which I think it right to express my current views. The Court is not generally so empowered, and it is particularly without power to overrule or undercut decisions of the Security Council made by it in pursuance of its authority under Articles 39, 41 and 42 of the Charter to determine the existence of any threat to the peace, breach of the peace, or act of aggression and to decide upon responsive measures to be taken to maintain or restore international peace and security.

The Court more than once has disclaimed possessing a power of judicial review. In its Advisory Opinion in the case concerning *Certain Expenses of the United Nations* (Article 17, paragraph 2, of the Charter), the Court declared:

> In the legal systems of States, there is often some procedure for determining the validity of even a legislative or governmental act, but no analogous procedure is to be found in the structure of the United Nations. Proposals made during the drafting of the Charter to place the ultimate authority to interpret the Charter in the International Court of Justice were not accepted; the opinion which the Court is in course of rendering is an advisory opinion. As anticipated in 1945, therefore, each organ must, in the first place at least, determine its own jurisdiction. If the Security Council, for example, adopts a resolution purportedly for the maintenance of international peace and security and if, in accordance with a mandate or authorization in such resolution, the Secretary-General incurs financial obligations, these amounts must be presumed to constitute "expenses of the Organization." (I.C.J. Reports 1962, p. 168.)

In its Advisory Opinion on *Legal Consequences for States of the Continued Presence of South Africa in Namibia (South West Africa) notwithstanding Security Council Resolution 276 (1970),* the Court reiterated that:

> Undoubtedly, the Court does not possess powers of judicial review or appeal in respect of the decisions taken by the United Nations organs concerned. (I.C.J. Reports 1971, p. 45.)

It should be noted that the Court made these holdings in advisory proceedings, in which the Security Council and the General Assembly are entitled to request the Court's opinion "on any legal question." The authority of the Court to respond to such questions, and, in the course of so doing, to pass upon relevant resolutions of the Security Council and General Assembly, is not disputed. Nevertheless, if the Court could hold as it did in advisory proceedings, a fortiori in contentious proceedings the Court can hardly be entitled to invent, assert and apply powers of judicial review.

While the Court so far has not had occasion in contentious proceedings to pass upon an alleged authority to judicially review decisions of the Security Council, it may be recalled that, in *Military and Paramilitary Activities in and against Nicaragua (Nicaragua v. United States of America),* Jurisdiction and Admissibility, Judgment, the Court observed that:

> The Court is not asked to say that the Security Council was wrong in its decision, nor that there was anything inconsistent with law in the way in which the members of the Council employed their right to vote. The Court is asked to pass judgment on certain legal aspects of a situation which has also been considered by the Security Council, a procedure which is entirely consonant with its position as the principal judicial organ of the United Nations. (I.C.J. Reports 1984, p. 436.)

The implication of this statement is that, if the Court had been asked by the Applicant to say that the Security Council had been wrong in its decision, the Court would have reached another conclusion.

The texts of the Charter of the United Nations and of the Statute of the Court furnish no shred of support for a conclusion that the Court possesses a power of judicial review in general, or a power to supervene the decisions of the Security Council in particular. On the contrary, by the absence of any such provision, and by according the Security Council "primary responsibility for the maintenance of international peace and security," the Charter and the Statute import the contrary. So extraordinary a power as that of judicial review is not ordinarily to be implied and never has been on the international plane. If the Court were to generate such a power, the Security Council would no longer be primary in its assigned responsibilities, because if the Court could overrule, negate, modify—or, as in this case, hold as proposed that decisions of the Security Council are not "opposable" to the principal object State of those decisions and to the object of its sanctions—it would be the Court and not the Council that would exercise, or purport to exercise, the dispositive and hence primary authority.

The drafters of the Charter above all resolved to accord the Security Council alone extraordinary powers. They did so in order to further realization of the first Purpose of the United Nations. ...

[Articles 24 and 25]—the very heart of the Charter's design for the maintenance of international peace—manifest the plenitude of the powers of the Security Council, which are elaborated by the provisions of Chapters VI, VII, and VIII of the Charter. They also demonstrate that the Security Council is subject to the rule of law; it shall act in accordance with the Purposes and Principles of the United Nations and its decisions must be adopted in accordance with the Charter. At the same time, as Article 103 imports, it may lawfully decide upon measures which may in the interests of the maintenance or restoration of international peace and security derogate from the rights of a State under international law. The first Purpose of the United Nations quoted above also so indicates, for the reference to the principles of justice and international law designedly relates only to adjustment or settlement by peaceful means, and not to the taking of effective collective measures for the prevention and removal of threats to and breaches of the peace. It was deliberately so provided to ensure that the vital duty of preventing and removing threats to and breaches of the peace would not be limited by existing law. ...

It does not follow from the facts that the decisions of the Security Council must be in accordance with the Charter, and that the International Court of Justice is the principal judicial organ of the United Nations, that the Court is empowered to ensure that the Council's decisions do accord with the Charter. To hold that it does so follow is a monumental non sequitur, which overlooks the truth that, in many legal systems, national and international, the subjection of the acts of an organ to law by no means entails subjection of the legality of its actions to judicial review. In many cases, the system relies not upon judicial review but on self-censorship by the organ concerned or by its members or on review by another political organ.

Judicial review could have been provided for at San Francisco, in full or lesser measure, directly or indirectly, but both directly and indirectly it was not in any measure contemplated or enacted. Not only was the Court not authorized to be the ultimate interpreter of the Charter, as the Court acknowledged in the case concerning *Certain Expenses of the United Nations*. Proposals which in restricted measure would have accorded the Court a degree of authority, by way of advisory proceedings, to pass upon the legality of proposed resolutions of the Security Council in the sphere of peaceful settlement—what came to be Chapter VI of the Charter—were not accepted. What was never proposed, considered, or, so far as the records reveal, even imagined, was that the International Court of Justice would be entrusted with, or would develop, a power of judicial review at large, or a power to supervene, modify, negate or confine the applicability of resolutions of the Security Council whether directly or in the guise of interpretation.

That this is understandable, indeed obvious, is the clearer in the light of the conjunction of political circumstances at the time that the Charter was conceived, drafted and adopted. The Charter was largely a concept and draft of the United States, and secondarily of the United Kingdom; the other most influential State concerned was the USSR. The United States was cautious about the endowments of the Court. Recalling the rejection by the Senate of the United States a decade earlier of adherence to the Statute of the Permanent Court of International Justice, the Department of State was concerned to assure that nothing in the Charter concerning the Court, and nothing in the Statute which was to be an integral part of the Charter, could prejudice the giving of advice and consent by the Senate to the ratification of the Charter. Thus the Report of the Senate Committee on Foreign Relations on the United Nations Charter of 16 July 1945 to the Senate recommending ratification of the Charter specified:

> The Charter does not permit the Security Council or the General Assembly to force states to bring cases to the Court, nor does it or the Statute permit the Court to interfere with the functions of the Security Council or the General Assembly ...

> The British Government which, together with the United States, was the principal proponent of the creation of the Permanent Court of International Justice and which had played a large and constructive part in respect of that Court, was hardly less cautious in its approach to the powers of the International Court of Justice. ...

> As for the Government of the Union of Soviet Socialist Republics—a Government which had been ideologically hostile to the Court since its creation (as a reading of the *Eastern Carelia* case so vividly illustrates)—can it be thought that Stalin, whose preoccupation in the days of San Francisco was giving the veto power the widest possible reach, could have assented to the establishment of a Court authorized to possess or develop the authority to review and vary the application of resolutions adopted by the Security Council under Chapter VII of the Charter?

At San Francisco, Belgium proposed the following amendment:

> Any State, party to a dispute brought before the Security Council, shall have the right to ask the Permanent Court of International Justice whether a recommendation or a decision made by the Council or proposed in it infringes on its essential rights. If the Court considers that such rights have been disregarded or are threatened, it is for the Council either to reconsider the question or to refer the dispute to the Assembly for decision. (UNCIO, Vol. 3, p. 336.)

The purpose of the amendment, the Belgian delegate explained, was to allow the State concerned to seek an advisory opinion from the Court if that State believed that a Security Council recommendation infringed upon its essential rights. It was not in any sense the purpose of the amendment to limit the legitimate powers of the Security Council (ibid., Vol. 12, pp. 48-49).

The Belgian proposal gave rise to a mixed reaction, support from States such as Ecuador and Colombia, and opposition from Great Power Sponsors of the Conference. ...

[T]he delegate of Belgium [later] stated that, since it was now clearly understood that a recommendation under what was to become Chapter VI did not possess obligatory effect, he wished to withdraw his amendment. ...

Subsequently, the Conference rejected a proposal by Belgium to refer disagreements between organs of the United Nations on interpretation of the Charter to the Court. The pertinent report concludes:

> Under unitary forms of national government the final determination of such a question may be vested in the highest court or in some other national authority. However, the nature of the Organization and of its operation would not seem to be such as to invite the inclusion in the Charter of any provision of this nature. If two member states are at variance concerning the correct interpretation of the Charter, they are of course free to submit the dispute to the International Court of Justice as in the case of any other treaty. Similarly, it would also be open to the General Assembly or to the Security Council, in appropriate circumstances, to ask the International Court of Justice for an advisory opinion concerning the meaning of a provision of the Charter. (Ibid., Vol. 13, pp. 668-669.)

It may finally be recalled that, at San Francisco, it was resolved "to leave to the Council the entire decision, and also the entire responsibility for that decision, as to what constitutes a threat to peace, a breach of the peace, or an act of aggression" (Ibid., Vol. 11, p. 17).

The conclusions to which the *travaux préparatoires* and text of the Charter lead are that the Court was not and was not meant to be invested with a power of judicial review of the legality or effects of decisions of the Security Council. Only the Security Council can determine what is a threat to or breach of the peace or act of aggression under Article 39, and under Article 39 only it can "decide what measures shall be taken ... to maintain or restore international peace and security." Two States at variance in the interpretation of the Charter may submit a dispute to the Court, but that facility does not empower the Court to set aside or second-guess the determinations of the Security Council under Article 39. Contentious cases may come before the Court that call for its passing upon questions of law raised by Council decisions and for interpreting pertinent Council resolutions. But that power cannot be equated with an authority to review and confute the decisions of the Security Council.

It may of course be maintained that the Charter is a living instrument; that the present-day interpreters of the Charter are not bound by the intentions of its drafters of 50 years ago; that the Court has interpreted the powers of the United Nations constructively in other respects, and could take a constructive view of its own powers in respect of judicial review or some variation of it. The difficulty with this approach is that for the Court to engraft upon the Charter régime a power to review, and revise the reach of, resolutions of the Security Council would not be evolutionary but revolutionary. It would be not a development but a departure, and a great and grave departure. It would not be a development even arguably derived from the terms or structure of the Charter and Statute. It would not be a development arising out of customary international law, which has no principle of or provision for judicial review. It would not be a development drawn from the general principles of law. Judicial review, in varying forms, is found in a number of democratic polities, most famously that of the United States, where it was developed by the Supreme Court itself. But it is by no means a universal or even general principle of government or law. It is hardly found outside the democratic world and is not uniformly found in it. Where it exists internationally, as in the European Union, it is expressly provided for by treaty in specific terms. The United Nations is far from being a government, or an international organization comparable in its integration to the European Union, and it is not democratic.

The conclusion that the Court cannot judicially review or revise the resolutions of the Security Council is buttressed by the fact that only States may be parties in cases before the Court. The Security Council cannot be a party. For the Court to adjudge the legality of the Council's decisions in a proceeding brought by one State against another would be for the Court to adjudicate the Council's rights without giving the Council a hearing, which would run counter to fundamental judicial principles. It would run counter as well to the jurisprudence of the Court. (Cf. *East Timor (Portugal v. Australia)*, Judgment, I.C.J. Reports 1995, pp. 100-105; *Monetary Gold Removed from Rome in 1943*, Judgment, I.C.J. Reports 1954, pp. 32-33.) Any such judgment could not bind the Council, because, by the terms of Article 59 of the Statute, the decision of the Court has no binding force except between the parties and in respect of that particular case.

At the same time, a judgment of the Court which held resolutions of the Security Council adopted under Chapter VII of the Charter not to bind or to be "opposable" to a State, despite the terms of Article 25 of the Charter, would seriously prejudice the effectiveness of the Council's resolutions and subvert the integrity of the Charter. Such a holding would be tantamount to a judgment that the resolutions of the Security Council were *ultra vires*, at any rate in relation to that State. That could set the stage for an extraordinary confrontation between the Court and the Security Council. It could give rise to the question, is a holding by the Court that the Council has acted *ultra vires* a holding which of itself is *ultra vires*?

For some 45 years, the world rightly criticized stalemate in the Security Council. With the end of the Cold War, the Security Council has taken great strides towards performing as it was empowered to perform. That in turn has given rise to the complaint by some Members of the United Nations that they lack influence over the Council's decision-making. However understandable that complaint may be, it cannot furnish the Court with the legal authority to supervene the resolutions of the Security Council. The argument that it does is a purely political argument; the complaints that give rise to it should be addressed to and by the United Nations in its consideration of the reform of the Security Council. It is not an argument that can be heard in a court of law.

NOTES

1) Do you agree with President Schwebel's conclusion that to "read in" a power of judicial review on the part of the ICJ would "subvert the integrity of the Charter"? In your view, should the Court be bound by the intentions of the Charter's drafters?

2) One concern that is frequently raised regarding judicial review in the domestic context is that of the legitimacy of having an unelected judiciary review the decisions of a democratically elected government. Does the fact that the United Nations is not democratic, as President Schwebel notes, strengthen the argument in favour of judicial review? Why or why not?

3) Following the Court's judgment on jurisdiction and admissibility in 1998, diplomatic negotiations resulted in an agreement among the three states that the suspects would be tried by a panel of Scottish judges, applying Scottish law, but sitting at The Hague. After the arrival of the suspects in the Netherlands in April 1999, Security Council sanctions were suspended. In January 2001, one defendant was found guilty and sentenced to life imprisonment; the other was acquitted. In response to further U.S. and U.K. demands, Libya made arrangements to compensate the families of the victims, and, in August 2003, made an official admission of responsibility for the bombing. On September 10, 2003, the case was discontinued at the joint request of the parties. On September 12, 2003, the Security Council formally lifted sanctions against Libya.

5. Significance of the International Court of Justice

The significance of the Court has been a question much debated among international lawyers and other commentators. Some of the concerns raised in this section—such as those regarding the limited acceptance of the Court's compulsory jurisdiction and the phenomenon of "non-appearing" states—have at times given rise to the concern that the Court is a marginal institution in interstate relations.

Perhaps the most significant concern has focused on the limited number of disputes brought before the Court. Many factors account for the ebb and flow in the size of the Court's docket. Yet the question remains why states do not take more of their many conflicts to the World Court. Three factors are frequently cited.

First, governments are reluctant to surrender control over their affairs. There is a risk of loss in court both of face and merits. While a cynical explanation would be that too many states are uninterested in an international rule of law, Akehurst has suggested that the main reason that states are unwilling to turn their disputes over to the Court is because they believe that judicial decisions are unpredictable.[156] The fact that a dispute cannot be settled by negotiation often indicates that the relevant law or the facts of the case are uncertain. Yet it is these uncertain cases that are ripe for adjudication, and present the most unpredictable results. The risks associated with unpredictability increase according to the degree that a government regards its vital national interests as being at stake. When high matters of state are involved, the desire for straightforward settlement may not be as great as the risk of losing in court, or risks associated with no settlement, at least for the time being.

---

156   Michael Akehurst, *A Modern Introduction to International Law*, 6th ed. (1987) at 250.

Second, many states have not seemed to have much confidence in judicial settlement in general and the ICJ in particular. It takes an act of faith for states to remove their dispute from its natural arena of diplomacy into a judicial forum, where they lose control of it to third parties—the judges—and that move is not encouraged by any suspicion about the Court. At one time, the centre of concern was the composition of the Court, focusing not so much on the personal qualifications of individual judges as the aggregate balance of their backgrounds and viewpoints. As Anand has noted,[157] African and Asian nations in particular did not think the make up of the Court kept pace with the increasingly universal composition of the international community. Changes have been wrought, however, so that the geographical distribution of judges now reflects the Security Council,[158] and a much more representative and plural range of voices is heard.

Third, one party to a dispute often considers the international law inadequate to meet its situation. It essentially demands a change in the law, yet it anticipates the Court would only condemn it by existing law. The Canadian declaration accepting the compulsory jurisdiction of the Court is a striking example. See the discussion in regard to the *Fisheries Jurisdiction Case*, above in Section D.2 on "Jurisdiction of the Court" under the heading "Parties Before the Court." Although courts do develop the law,[159] they tend to be careful and conservative in approach. This tendency is even stronger in the ICJ because it does not have compulsory jurisdiction.

In the mid-1980s, concern about the Court's role was particularly pronounced, due largely to the United States' failure to participate at the merits stage of the case concerning *Military Activities In and Against Nicaragua*, and its subsequent retraction of its acceptance of the compulsory jurisdiction of the Court in 1986. However, the disengagement of the United States did not appear to cause an undermining of the credibility of the ICJ, which many feared. In fact, the number of cases brought before the Court has increased since that time and it is now as busy as at any time in its history.[160] The United States itself has been actively involved, albeit as respondent, most recently in the *Lockerbie Case*, the *Oil Platforms Case*,[161] and three cases concerning the Vienna Convention on Consular Relations brought to the Court by Paraguay, Germany, and Mexico, referred to above.

Many of the more recent cases have been instituted by developing countries, especially African and Asian states, against both Western nations and their neighbours in the developing world. This experience demonstrates a great change in attitudes toward the ICJ from the previous suspicion of it as hostage to western states, with a membership unrepresentative of the plurality of the world, that applied a legal status quo. This has

157 R.P. Anand, "Role of International Adjudication" in Gross, *supra* note 68 vol. 1 at 9.

158 As explained above in Section D.1 on "Organization of the Court" under the heading "Judges of the Court."

159 For an assessment of the ICJ in this respect, see Manfred Lachs, "Some Reflections on the Contribution of the International Court of Justice to the Development of International Law" (1983) 10 Syracuse J. Int'l L. & Com. 239.

160 For a discussion of the situation at the end of the Cold War see R.P. Anand, "The World Court on Trial" in R.S. Pathak & R.P. Dhokalia, eds., *International Law in Transition, supra* note 102 at 245 & Keith Highet, "The Peace Palace Heats Up: The World Court in Business Again?" (1991) 85 A.J.I.L. 646.

161 *Case Concerning Oil Platforms (Islamic Republic of Iran v. United States of America)*, online: International Court of Justice <http://www.icj-cij.org/icjwww/idocket/iop/iopjudgment/iop_ijudgment_20031106.PDF>.

resulted in increased confidence in the Court and a great boost to its docket. Nevertheless, significant problems remain. In a 1998 address to the General Assembly, the then President of the Court raised many of the hopes and concerns surrounding the Court at this time.

Address by the President of the International Court of Justice
Judge Stephen M. Schwebel before the General Assembly of the United Nations
(October 27, 1998), online: <http://www.icj-cij.org/icjwww/ipresscom/
SPEECHES/iSpeechPresidentGA98.htm>

[T]his year the international community took an extraordinary step towards the creation of an International Criminal Court, a court to try individuals for grave, specified international crimes. When that Court is established, it will make its contribution to the development and application of a more effective international law. It will join the family of international judicial bodies created in past decades and more recently, a family whose father is the World Court—the popular name for the Permanent Court of International Justice and the International Court of Justice— which has successfully operated for more than 70 years. This year is notable in the life of international courts for another reason as well, for it marks the first case before the International Tribunal for the Law of the Sea.

A measure of the achievement of the World Court is that today it is taken for granted that permanent international tribunals can function effectively. What was the untested ideal of the peace movement at the dawn of the 20th century has become a reality at its sunset, insofar as it has been demonstrated and accepted that the World Court and other international tribunals can contribute significantly to the peaceful and just settlement of international disputes.

Yet the treasured ideal of the early peace movement—that international judicial settlement would be the substitute for war—has been shown to have been unrealistic. International judicial settlement does not produce peace in the large; rather it is peace that is conducive to the settlement of inevitable international disputes by international adjudication. In times of high international tension, States avoid judicial recourse; in times of low international tension, States are more inclined to settle their disputes judicially.

That at any rate may be one important reason why today the International Court of Justice is as busy as it and its predecessor have been since 1922.

In so far as their jurisdiction does not duplicate that of pre-existing courts, the creation of specialized and regional international courts is to be welcomed. It reflects the vitality and complexity of international life. It evidences the understanding that the effectiveness of international law can be increased by equipping legal obligations with means of their determination and enforcement.

The proliferation of international courts at the same time raises the question of the role of the International Court of Justice, and of problems proliferation may pose.

The Charter of the United Nations provides that the International Court of Justice shall be "the principal judicial organ of the United Nations." The Court has thus been endowed with a special, and the most senior, judicial position within the United Nations system. As domestic legal systems have a supreme court, the international community has its principal judicial organ. But the International Court of Justice is not, or at any rate is not now, a supreme court of appeal from other international judicial bodies, and still less a court of appeal from national courts.

While not acting as a court of appeal, the International Court of Justice has acted as the principal judicial organ of the United Nations in more than one way.

First of all, the Court contributes to the peaceful settlement of international disputes in furtherance of the first Purpose of the United Nations, "to bring about by peaceful means, and in conformity with the principles of justice and international law, adjustment or settlement of international disputes which might lead to a breach of the peace."

On occasion the Court may deal with disputes which, if unsettled, might lead to a breach of the peace. Indeed, the Court has dealt with cases which did lead to hostilities. Despite that fact, those disputes were submitted to the Court, sometimes by bilateral agreement, other times by unilateral application; and they were resolved without further hostilities, and remain resolved to this day.

Thus a primary way in which the Court performs as the principal judicial organ of the United Nations is as a factor and actor in the maintenance of international peace and security. Today the Court is integrated into the United Nations system of the peaceful settlement of international disputes. The Court is no longer seen solely as "the last resort" in the resolution of disputes. States rather may have recourse to the Court in parallel with other methods of dispute resolution, appreciating that such recourse may complement the work of the Security Council and the General Assembly as well as bilateral negotiations.

In this combined process of dispute resolution, judicial recourse has helped parties to a dispute to clarify their positions. Parties are led to reduce and transform their sometimes overstated political assertions into factual and legal claims. This process may moderate tensions and lead to a better and fuller understanding of opposing claims. The result is that, in some cases, political negotiations have resumed and succeeded before the Court rendered judgment. In other cases, the Court's decision has provided the parties with legal conclusions which they may use in framing further negotiations and in achieving settlement of the dispute ... .

To turn to the second way in which the Court acts as the principal judicial organ of the United Nations—and of the world community as a whole—it is the most authoritative interpreter of the legal obligations of States in disputes between them. This indeed is its paramount function, and it antedates the establishment of the United Nations. This central role of the Court as the adjudicator of contentious differences between States represents over 70 years of achievement in settling international legal disputes.

In the third place, the Court as the Organization's principal judicial organ has acted as the supreme interpreter of the United Nations Charter (and of associated instruments such as the General Convention on Privileges and Immunities of the United Nations, which is the focus of an advisory proceeding now in progress in the Court). It has been the authoritative interpreter of the legal obligations of States under the Charter. This the Court has done in a number of advisory and contentious proceedings.

In furtherance of the Charter's Purposes and Principles, the Court has progressively interpreted the Charter and so strengthened the United Nations and through it the international community as a whole. ...

I said earlier that international adjudication is not the substitute for war; that peace conduces to international adjudication rather than that international adjudication produces peace. Largely speaking, that is true. The Permanent Court of International Justice did not prevent, and could not reasonably have been expected to prevent, World War II. But as noted the International Court of Justice does work as a significant element in the peace-promoting machinery of the United Nations.

While the Court and other principal organs of the United Nations may work together, it is vital that the judicial independence of the Court is maintained. That is a matter of some delicacy. The Court is bound to give due weight to the powers, practice and positions of other United Nations organs, and particular weight to decisions of the Security Council taken under Chapter VII of the Charter. But in deciding on the law, the Court is and must remain free of the political influence of the United Nations as it is bound to remain free of the political influence of any of its Members.

Finally, there is another characteristic that distinguishes the International Court of Justice from specialized and regional international tribunals. The Court is the only truly universal judicial body of general jurisdiction. Unlike specialized judicial and arbitral bodies, the Court enjoys comprehensive jurisdiction in inter-State disputes. Unlike bilateral or regional bodies, the Court is available to all States of the international community, on all aspects of international law.

The Court's decisions, large and small, general and particular, may have an influence beyond the parties in dispute and beyond the issues in dispute. The Court has contributed to the growth of international law, to a universal system of international law. Over the years, the Court has interpreted, refined and advanced principles of international law that govern the whole of international society.

It is inevitable that other international tribunals will apply the law whose content has been influenced by the Court, and that the Court will apply the law as it may be influenced by other international tribunals. At the same time, it is possible that various courts may arrive at different interpretations of the law. Proliferation risks conflict.

But the risk should not be exaggerated. While in principle there is a single system of international law, in practice there are various views on issues of the law, and not only between international tribunals and among other authoritative interpreters of the law. There are differences within the International Court of Justice itself. That is marked not only by separate and dissenting opinions, but in adjustments of the holdings of the Court over the years.

In practice international courts may be expected to demonstrate due respect for the opinions of other international courts. The International Court of Justice looks forward to working harmoniously with other international tribunals. But the fabric of international law and life is, it is believed, resilient enough to sustain such occasional differences as may arise.

NOTES

1) Is there a tension between seeing the Court as the "most authoritative interpreter of the legal obligations of States in disputes between them," on the one hand, and also

emphasizing that States "may have recourse to the Court in parallel with other methods of dispute resolution," on the other?

2) In your view, what challenges might the proliferation of international tribunals pose to the Court?[162]

3) In his address, President Schwebel went on to emphasize that one major challenge faced by the ICJ is lack of resources. The budget of the Court for 2002-3 was approximately US$26 million. In contrast, the budget for the International Criminal Tribunal (ICT) for the former Yugoslavia was US$223,169,800 in 2002-3.[163] Similarly, the International Criminal Tribunal for Rwanda received US$177,739,400 for its work during the same period.[164] The ICJ itself has attempted to draw this to the attention of the General Assembly, sometimes in the strongest possible terms. In 1997, in response to a request from the General Assembly for comments on the implications of its increased caseload, the Court noted:

> The time has come for the General Assembly to provide the necessary increase in resources to match the internal efforts already made by the Court itself, so that a major organ of the United Nations can carry out the single task allocated to it under the Charter—the settlement of disputes between States and the provision of advisory opinions in accordance with international law. The truth is that in failing to provide the necessary resources, notwithstanding all the efforts made by the Court itself, the General Assembly is diminishing the importance it attaches to the peaceful resolution of international disputes through law.[165]

4) Another issue in relation to resources concerns States who may wish to access the Court, particularly developing nations. In 1989, the Secretary-General's Trust Fund to Assist States in the Settlement of Disputes through the ICJ was set up to facilitate access to the Court by states that might otherwise find the costs involved prohibitive.[166] The Fund can provide "financial assistance to States for expenses incurred in connexion with: (i) a dispute submitted to the International Court of Justice by way of a special agreement,

---

162 See *e.g.* "The Proliferation of International Tribunals: Piecing Together the Puzzle," a Special Issue of the New York University Journal of International Law & Politics, (1999) 31 N.Y.U. J. Int'l L. & Pol. 679; Thomas Buergenthal, "Proliferation of International Courts & Tribunals: Is It Good or Bad" (2001) 14 Leiden J. Int'l L. 267-275; Shane Spelliscy, "The Proliferation of International Tribunals: A Chink in the Armor" (2001) 40 Colum. J. Transnat'l L. 143.

163 Online: International Criminal Tribunal for the former Yugoslavia <http://www.un.org/icty/glance/index.htm>.

164 Online: International Criminal Tribunal for Rwanda <http://www.ictr.org>.

165 *Response of the International Court of Justice to General Assembly Resolution 52/161 of 15 December 1997*, online: International Court of Justice <http://www.icj-cij.org/icjwww/igeneralinformation/igeninfvarious/ResponseGA151297.html>.

166 Online: United Nations <http://www.un.org/law/trustfund/trustfund.htm>. See Peter H.F. Bekker, "Current Developments—International Legal Aid in Practice: The ICJ Trust Fund" (1993) 87 A.J.I.L. 659. See also the description of the Permanent Court of Arbitration's "Financial Assistance Fund for the Settlement of International Disputes," online: Permanent Court of Arbitration <http://www.pca-cpa.org/ENGLISH/BD/torfundenglish.htm>.

or (ii) the execution of a Judgment of the Court resulting from such special agreement."[167] Sir Robert Jennings has noted that since the administrative costs of the Court itself are built into the U.N. budget, the fund "is in a position to help with the costs of counsel, secretarial assistance, accommodations and translation."[168] The Fund has been used on relatively few occasions; most recently, in 2004, Benin and Niger were each awarded $350,000 for the settlement of a boundary dispute.[169] What other practical steps might be taken to make the Court more accessible and appealing to States?[170]

E. OTHER AGENCIES OF PEACEFUL SETTLEMENT OF DISPUTES

The emphasis in this chapter has been upon the means of settling disputes, but the range of agencies by which these means may be effected should not be ignored. The growing richness in number, variety, and method of these agencies for dispute settlement is one of the most noteworthy features of the international system at present. Their proliferation in the late 20th century counters the pessimistic view that states are not much interested in third-party settlement processes, particularly compulsory ones. The new agencies have been created to meet specific needs in an increasingly interdependent world. Thus, they tend to have a specialized jurisdiction by geographical area or subject matter, or both.

The various organs of the United Nations provide the greatest opportunity for, and pre-eminent example of, dispute settlement machinery. In addition to the ICJ, the General Assembly and the Security Council each has its own specific responsibilities for composing the peace.[171] The United Nations is so often involved in disputes between States because, in Pechota's estimation,[172] the organization "seems to meet best the three essential conditions for a reasonably successful third-party intervention in the settlement." He notes that the United Nations has a standing that member states cannot ignore, offers methods and procedures known and generally agreeable to them, and disposes of resources that can be turned to positive effect.[173] While only the Security Council has compulsory powers (under Chapter VII) to make decisions and give orders having

---

167 "Terms of Reference, Guidelines & Rules of the Secretary-General's Trust Fund to Assist States in the Settlement of Disputes through the International Court of Justice" (1989) 28 I.L.M. 1590 at 1592 para. 6, online: United Nations <http://www.un.org/law/trustfund/eterms.pdf>.

168 Robert Y. Jennings, "The International Court of Justice After Fifty Years" (1995) 89 A.J.I.L. 493 at 501.

169 United Nations, Press Release, SG/2087 L/3070 (04/06/2004) online: <http://www.un.org/law/trustfund/press_release/English.htm>.

170 See *e.g.* the suggestions made in the speech by H.E. Judge Gilbert Guillaume, President of the ICJ, to the General Assembly on October 29, 2002, "Statement of the President of the Court" online: International Court of Justice <http://www.icj-cij.org/icjwww/ipresscom/SPEECHES/iSpeechPresident_Guillaume_GA57_20021029.htm>.

171 Discussed in Chapter 15, "Limitation of the Use of Force."

172 V. Pechota, "Complementary Structures of Third-Party Settlement of International Disputes" in Raman, ed., *supra* note 6 at 153-54.

173 For a consideration of the U.N.'s impact in the area of boundary disputes, see Victor Prescott, "Contributions of the United Nations To Solving Boundary & Territorial Disputes, 1945-1995" (1996) 15 Political Geography 287.

supranational authority over the members to whom they are directed, there are many indications of an overall trend in the U.N. system involving a move from reacting to situations that might be said to constitute potential threats to peace and security to proactively anticipating and containing such situations.[174] It should also be noted that many specialized agencies within the U.N. system provide organs for dispute settlement in their own fields. Some major ones include the IMO[175] and the ICAO.[176]

The U.N. Charter articles 52 to 54 also provide support for regional agencies that administer the means of pacific settlement of local disputes. There are many regional organizations that make extensive dispute settlement machinery available to member states.[177] Some obvious examples, which offer widely different procedures, are the African Union (AU),[178] the Organization of American States (OAS),[179] the North Atlantic Treaty Organization (NATO),[180] and the Organization for Security and Co-operation in Europe (OSCE).[181] The European Union offers perhaps the premier, albeit unique, example of a regional institution for the settlement of disputes in the European Court of Justice (ECJ).[182] Its competence comprises, *inter alia*, the authority to hear and determine cases alleging the failure of Member States to fulfill treaty obligations, to review the legality of acts or omissions by treaty institutions, and to rule on proposed agreements between the EU and third states or other international organizations. It has supranational

---

174 See *An Agenda for Peace*, U.N. Doc. A/47/277-S/24111 (1992) online: United Nations <http://www.un.org/docs/SG/agpeace.html> and *An Agenda for Peace, Supplement*, U.N. Doc. A/50/60-S/1995/1 (1995), online: United Nations <http://www.un.org/docs/SG/agsupp.html>. See also Connie Peck, *The United Nations as a Dispute Settlement System: Improving Mechanisms for the Prevention & Resolution of Conflict* (1996).

175 Online: International Maritime Organization <http://www.imo.org>.

176 Online: International Civil Aviation Organization <http://www.icao.org>. For an overview of the mechanisms available in this area, see Dimitri Maniatis, "Conflict in the Skies: The Settlement of International Aviation Disputes" (1995) 20 Ann. Air & Sp. L. (Part II) 167.

177 For a general discussion of the range & role of regional organizations, see Merrills, *supra* note 6 c. 11.

178 Formerly the Organization of African Unity (OAU). The African Court of Justice is one of the organs of the AU. Online: African Union <http://www.africa-union.org/>.

179 Online: Organization of American States <http://www.oas.org>.

180 Online: North Atlantic Treaty Organization <http://www.nato.int>.

181 Formerly the Conference on Security & Cooperation in Europe; online: Organization for Security & Co-operation in Europe <http://www.osce.org>.

182 Online: Court of Justice of the European Communities <http://www.curia.eu.int>. For a discussion see J.W. Bridge, "The Court of Justice of the European Communities & the Prospects for International Adjudication" in Mark W. Janis, ed., *International Courts for the Twenty-First Century* (1992) at 87. See also Joxerramon Bengoetxea, *The Legal Reasoning of the European Court of Justice: Towards a European Jurisprudence* (1993); L. Neville Brown & Francis G. Jacobs, *The Court of Justice of the European Communities*, 5th ed. (2000); Gráinne de Búrca & J.H.H. Weiler, eds., *The European Court of Justice* (2001); K.P.E. Lasok, *The European Court of Justice: Practice and Procedure*, 2d ed. (1994); Jean-Victor Louis, *The Community Legal Order*, 3d ed. (1995); P.S.R.F. Mathijsen, *A Guide to European Union Law*, 8th ed. (2004) c. 3 Part 4; P.J.G. Kapteyn & P.V. van Themaat, *Introduction to the Law of the European Communities*, 2d ed. 1989 by Laurence W. Gormley cc. 4, 6; Gordon Slynn, *Introducing a European Legal Order: The Hamlyn Lectures* (1992); Henry G. Schermers & Denis F. Waelbroeck, *Judicial Protection in the European Union*, 6th ed. (2001); and Josephine Steiner, *Textbook on EC Law*, 4th ed. (1994) Part III.

authority over member states and its decisions have direct applicability within them. In pronouncing the meaning and effect of EU law, the ECJ may overrule the legislative and judicial acts of a Member State; its only limitation is that it shall not interfere in the domestic jurisdiction of a member state in the absence of conflict with EU law. Thus, the ECJ occupies a unique position. On the one hand, it "is a specialist court which operates within a narrow treaty-defined field of international law to serve the specific interests of the Member States within the European [Union]."[183] On the other hand, as the "supreme court" of the EU, the ECJ is also "endowed with competences which are not traditionally characteristic of international courts."[184] As noted by one author, the member states of the European Union "have committed themselves to a programme of socio-economic integration which is implemented and enforced through the instrumentality of the law set out in and made under the authority of the Treaties ... that law alone is the focus of the jurisdiction of the ECJ; a jurisdiction which both *ratione personae* and *ratione materiae* the Member States have unequivocally accepted in advance, permanently, exclusively and compulsorily."[185] Thus, what is perhaps the most notable characteristic of the ECJ is the role that it has played in driving the integration of the EU.[186]

The International Joint Commission

Canada has had resort to a wide range of international dispute settlement mechanisms in its relations with other states.[187] It also has a long-standing involvement with a unique example of bilateral dispute settlement. The Canada–United States International Joint Commission (IJC)[188] has responsibilities with respect to the waters that mark the

---

183 Bridge, *supra* note 182 at 88.

184 *Ibid.*

185 *Ibid.* at 89.

186 See the debate on this issue between Geoffrey Garrett, on the one hand, and Anne-Marie Slaughter and Walter Mattli, on the other, beginning with Anne-Marie Burley & Walter Mattli, "Europe Before the Court: A Political Theory of Legal Integration" (1993) 47 Int'l Organization 41; Geoffrey Garrett, "The Politics of Legal Integration in the European Union" (1995) 49 Int'l Organization 171; and Walter Mattli & Anne-Marie Slaughter, "Law and Politics in the European Union: A Reply to Garrett" (1995) 49 Int'l Organization 183. See also Karen J. Alter, "The European Court's Political Power" (1996) 19 West European Politics 458; James L. Gibson & Gregory A. Caldeira, "The Legitimacy of Transnational Legal Institutions: Compliance, Support, and the European Court of Justice" (1995) 39 Am. J. Pol. Sci. 459; and Donna Starr-Deelen & Bart Deelen, "The European Court of Justice as a Federator" (1996) 26 Publius 81.

187 See *e.g.* the East Coast "Turbot War" and the resulting *Fisheries Jurisdiction Case* considered in Chapter 13, Section E.1 on "Fisheries" under the heading "East Coast Fisheries and the Estai" and in this chapter in Section D.2 on "Jurisdiction of the Court"; the dispute with France over the maritime boundary of Saint-Pierre and Miquelon discussed in Chapter 13, Section D on "Boundary Delimitation Problems"; and the Pacific Salmon dispute explored in Chapter 13, Section E.1 on "Fisheries" under the heading "West Coast Fisheries."

188 See Maxwell Cohen, *The Regime of Boundary Waters: The Canadian-United States Experience* (1977); David LeMarquand, "The International Joint Commission and Changing Canada-United States Boundary Relations" (1993) 33 Nat. Res. J. 59; L.H. Legault, "The Role of Law and Diplomacy in Dispute Resolution: The IJC as a Possible Model" (2000) 26 Can.-U.S.L.J. 47; Robert Spencer et al., eds., *The International Joint Commission Seventy Years On* (1981); and Stephen J. Toope & Jutta Brunnée, "Freshwater Regimes:

international boundary between these two countries. Established under the 1909 Boundary Waters Treaty[189] between the United States and the United Kingdom, on behalf of Canada, and composed of three commissioners from each side, the Commission has a broad mandate that includes investigative and monitoring powers in some situations and quasi-judicial authority in others. The work of the Commission has been a successful demonstration of bilateral means to reach peaceful accommodations over a shared resource. Consider the following document prepared by the IJC for the governments of Canada and the United States.

The International Joint Commission and the 21st Century: Response of the IJC to a Request by the Governments of Canada and the United States for Proposals on How To Best Assist Them To Meet the Environmental Challenges of the 21st Century
Online: <http://www.ijc.org/php/publications/html/21ste.htm>

B. The IJC's Role in a Successful Transboundary Environmental Relationship

From the beginning, the Commission's fundamental role has been to prevent and resolve transboundary environmental and water-resource disputes between the U.S. and Canada through processes that seek the common interest of both countries. What has developed over time is a kind of institution that does not exist elsewhere. This institution not only offers the two countries a flexible set of mechanisms to help them manage their relationship in the boundary region, but also provides them with the assurance that it will reflect the shared system of principles and values recognized in the Boundary Waters Treaty.

The Commission has two primary responsibilities under the treaty. First, the IJC acts as a quasi-judicial body to consider applications for approval to build and operate certain works in boundary waters and in rivers that flow across the boundary. Secondly, at the request of the parties, the Commission examines and provides non-binding recommendations on transboundary issues (the so-called "reference" function).

In its quasi-judicial role, the Commission is responsible for approving projects that affect boundary waters and, in some cases, transboundary rivers, unless the project is authorized by a special agreement between the two countries. The Commission's independent, quasi-judicial decisions must be based on the rules and principles set forth in the treaty. Because the principles are expressed in general terms, the Commission can take account of new values and activities in the management of transboundary waterways, such as the environment and recreational boating, which were not viewed in the same way in 1909. The Commission retains jurisdiction over

---

The Mandate of the International Joint Commission" (1998) 15 Ariz. J. Int'l & Comp. L. 273. See also "Symposium: The North American Experience Managing International Transboundary Water Resources: The International Joint Commission and the International Boundary and Water Commission" (1993) 33 Nat. Res. J. 1-200. See online: International Joint Commission <http://www.ijc.org/>.

189 (1909) U.K.T.S. 1910 No. 23, T.S. No. 548, 12 Bevans 319.

projects it has approved, so that it can oversee their operation and adapt the terms of its approval to changing circumstances.

Under its reference function and at the request of governments, the Commission investigates and reports on issues of concern along the boundary. These reports are advisory in nature and not binding on the governments. There are few restrictions on the issues or responsibilities that can be given to the IJC in this way. Thus, the Commission has undertaken such diverse roles as investigating and reporting on transboundary water and air pollution or recommending principles for developing resources, all with a view to preventing and resolving transboundary conflicts.

The Commission also has critical duties under the Great Lakes Water Quality Agreement. The parties have made the Commission responsible for the monitoring of progress and coordination of activities associated with the Great Lakes Water Quality Agreement. The agreement authorized the Commission to establish permanent binational advisory boards and a binational regional office in Windsor, Ontario to support the work of assuring cleanup of the Great Lakes. The Commission's recommendations, including the establishment of areas of concern and remedial action plans, a more vigorous effort to combat toxic contamination, the establishment of a "zero discharge" demonstration project in Lake Superior, and perhaps most important of all, the implementation of an ecosystem approach to stewardship of the resource, have contributed much to the joint mission of Great Lakes restoration.

The Commission's inherent responsibility for preventing and resolving transboundary disputes requires it to alert governments to situations along the border which have the potential for transboundary conflict so that early action can be taken to avoid or resolve such conflict. This is one of the Commission's most valuable functions. It is also an area in which there is opportunity for a more active Commission role.

The Commission is a binational rather than a bilateral institution. There is parity between the U.S. and Canada within the Commission and there is equality between the two countries in the Boundary Waters Treaty. Commissioners do not act as members of national delegations seeking national advantage under instructions from their governments. Instead, they are members of a single body seeking solutions to common problems in the common interest.

The Boundary Waters Treaty established a framework for the Commission's role. Within this framework, the IJC has developed a process that has provided the basis for much of the success of the bilateral environmental relationship. This process is characterized by six main elements.

Consultation and Consensus Building.

The treaty and the Commission's Rules of Procedure call for the concurrence of at least four Commissioners to ensure that decisions can be reached only if at least one Commissioner from each country agrees. The Commission and its network of advisory and regulatory boards, in any case, strive for consensus as a means of reflecting the common interest. In practice, most Commission decisions are taken in this way and the Commission requires some key boards to refer matters to the Commission for decision if board members are unable to achieve consensus.

Providing a Forum for Public Participation.

Article XII of the Boundary Waters Treaty requires the Commission, in any proceeding, inquiry or matter within its jurisdiction, to assure that "all parties interested therein shall be given convenient opportunity to be heard." In practice, the Commission has always emphasized the importance of public participation and advice.

The Commission provides a forum for the public to participate with governments in developing means of addressing environmental issues. Government officials can meet on neutral ground to discuss and coordinate policies and programs. In much the same way, opportunities are created for exchanges of views, knowledge and information among all those interested in an issue, which again furthers the development of understanding and consensus.

Engagement of Local Governments.

The Commission invites and facilitates the engagement of state, provincial and municipal governments and other authorities in transboundary environmental issues. At the same time, the IJC brings binational and national resources and considerations to bear on the resolution of local and regional matters.

Joint Fact-Finding.

This is a cornerstone of Commission practice. The Commission recognizes that binational joint fact-finding builds an important and often essential foundation for the achievement of consensus on appropriate actions. Joint fact-finding normally takes place within the Commission's advisory and regulatory boards, whose members are drawn equally from both countries and who are recognized as having the range of expertise required to address an issue.

Objectivity and Independence.

The authors of the Boundary Waters Treaty built into the Commission an expectation that its members would seek to find solutions in the common interest of the two nations. To that end, Commissioners "make and subscribe a solemn declaration in writing" that they "will faithfully and impartially perform the duties imposed" under the treaty. Similarly, members of IJC boards are expected to serve the Commission in their personal and professional capacities. This allows board members to explore all options, which helps promote the development of novel solutions and consensus.

Flexibility.

One of the most important features of the Commission's work has been the flexibility, inherent in its mandate and process, to be able to adapt to the circumstances of particular transboundary issues or conditions. The terms of the Boundary Waters Treaty have allowed the Commission, in practice, to develop innovative mechanisms for soliciting public participation, for problem-solving, and for working with the governments themselves.

The Commission finds that all six of these elements of the Commission's approach have become a fundamental part of the relationship between the parties in boundary areas. They have kept difficult issues from the diplomatic agenda of the governments. They have helped to ensure the continued health of the environmental relationship. Looking ahead to the unparalleled challenges of the 21st century, the Commission believes these practices will increase in importance as the basis for a successful transboundary relationship.

NOTES

1) In the context of his discussion of forms of negotiation, Merrills cites the IJC as "an outstanding example" of a commission entrusted with a broad mandate of indefinite duration.[190] However, the IJC is in many ways *sui generis*. Consider the fact that, as noted in the above report, the "Commissioners do not act as members of national delegations seeking national advantage under instructions from their governments. Instead, they are members of a single body seeking solutions to common problems in the common interest." How does this differ from the classic model of interstate negotiation? What factors might account for the success of a consensus-building approach in this context?

2) Another notable aspect of the IJC is the emphasis on public participation and local involvement.[191] Do you see this as a model that other forms of interstate dispute settlement might follow? Why or why not?

3) Compare the experience of Canada and the United States in managing their shared resources,

   i) in the waters of the Great Lakes, through the IJC, discussed in Chapter 14, Section G.2 on "Canada–United States Great Lakes Water Regimes," and

   ii) in the salmon of the Pacific waters, discussed in Chapter 13, Section E.1 on "Fisheries" under the heading "West Coast Fisheries."

What lessons does each experience provide about how to, or how not to, achieve joint regulatory schemes over shared resources? Might it be useful to extend the jurisdiction of the IJC, or create another standing commission with similar kinds of powers, over the shared fisheries of the east and west coasts of North America?

Selected Specialized Agencies

An ever-increasing number of institutions serve the purpose of promoting peaceful solutions to international disputes in particular subject areas. To provide perspective on the scope and variety of these dispute settlement agencies, the following notes comment

---

190   Merrills, *supra* note 6 at 9.

191   See *e.g.* David J. Allee, "Subnational Governance and the International Joint Commission: Local Management of United States and Canadian Boundary Waters" (1993) 33 Nat. Res. J. 133; Mimi Larsen Becker, "The International Joint Commission and Public Participation: Past Experiences, Present Challenges, Future Tasks" (1993) 33 Nat. Res. J. 235; and E. Richmond Olson & Geoffrey Thornburn, "The Estate of the Citizen and Its Manifestation in an International Institution: The International Joint Commission" (1984) 4 Windsor Y. B. Access Just. 371.

on a selection of specialized institutions, most of which are individually examined more fully elsewhere in this book.

1) Law of the Sea: Part XV of the U.N. Convention on the Law of the Sea establishes an elaborate scheme for the settlement of disputes concerning the oceans and the seabed.[192] It is discussed in Chapter 13, Section F on "Dispute Settlement in the Law of the Sea." UNCLOS contains a general restatement and elaboration of the obligation to settle disputes peacefully (article 279) by any means of their choice (article 280) or in accordance with the terms of other agreements to which they may be party. However, if the Parties are unable to reach a settlement, they are obligated to submit their dispute to a court or tribunal (article 286). Generally, states parties will have made a written declaration of their forum of choice from among the following: (1) the International Tribunal for the Law of the Sea, (2) the ICJ, (3) an arbitral tribunal as constituted under Annex VII of the U.N. Convention, or (4) a special tribunal as constituted under Annex VIII of the U.N. Convention (article 287). If the parties have not declared their forum of choice, the dispute will be arbitrated under the Annex VII procedure (article 287(3)). However, there are both general and optional exceptions to the obligation of states parties to submit disputes to compulsory procedures entailing binding decisions. Parties may exclude "certain disputes relating to marine scientific research, fisheries, maritime boundaries, military activities and enforcement activities and disputes where the Security Council is acting."[193]

The International Tribunal for the Law of the Sea is an institution established by the Convention. Composed of 21 independent members "elected by States Parties to the Convention from among persons with recognized competence in the field of law of the sea and representing the principal legal systems of the world" (Annex VI), it has been in operation since 1996. Although it is characterized by the United Nations as "the central forum established by the U.N. Convention on the Law of the Sea for the peaceful settlement of disputes,"[194] a number of the states parties that have declared their choice of procedure under article 287 have made the ICJ their forum of choice, while others have chosen Annex VII arbitration.[195]

The complex dispute resolution system set up by the Convention has been both praised and criticized. One author captures the ambivalence in the following passage:

---

192 See E.D. Brown, "Dispute Settlement and the Law of the Sea: The U.N. Convention Regime" (1997) 21 Marine Pol'y 17 and Jonathan I. Charney, "The Implications of Expanding International Dispute Settlement Systems: The 1982 Convention on the Law of the Sea (Editorial Comment)" (1996) 90 A.J.I.L. 69. For background on the development of Part XV, see also R.R. Churchill & A.V. Lowe, *The Law of the Sea*, 3d ed. (1999) c. 19; Myron H. Nordquist, Shabtai Rosenne, & Louis B. Sohn, *United Nations Convention on the Law of the Sea 1982: A Commentary* (1989) vol. 5; David Anderson, "International Tribunal for the Law of the Sea" in Malcom D. Evans, ed., *Remedies in International Law: The Institutional Dilemma* (1998) 71; and Robin Churchill, "Dispute Settlement in the Law of the Sea: The Context of the International Tribunal for the Law of the Sea and Alternatives to It" in Evans, *ibid.* at 85.

193 Brown, *supra* note 192 at 42.

194 Online: United Nations <http://www.un.org/Depts/los/settlement_of_disputes/settlement_of_disputes.htm>. The members of the ITLOS were elected in August 1996.

195 Online: United Nations <http://www.un.org/Depts/los/settlement_of_disputes/choice_procedure.htm>.

In one sense, the scheme for settlement of disputes embodied in Part XV of the UN Convention has already been successful. The fact is that States, by ratifying or acceding to the Convention, are demonstrating that they are prepared to accept a conventional obligation to comply with a dispute settlement system which includes compulsory procedures entailing binding decisions. ... However, this advance has been gained at a cost ... . [T]he obligation to accept such compulsory procedures is subject to a variety of important exceptions. Moreover, the very feature which may have persuaded some States to accept Part XV—the proliferation of dispute-settlement mechanisms on offer—may lead to a fragmented system in which uniformity and consistency of jurisprudence will be seen to have been sacrificed to the primary objective of ensuring that disputes arising from the Convention may be finally and peacefully settled.[196]

2) International Trade: The increasingly transnational nature of many business transactions has given rise to various kinds of dispute resolution agencies. For example, the ICSID, discussed in Chapter 10, Section B.3(c) on "Standard of Compensation and Method of Valuation" conducts mixed arbitrations of disputes between private enterprise investors and host states.[197] Perhaps the most significant occurrence in this context, however, has been the development of dispute resolution mechanisms in the area of international trade.[198] Originally, the GATT was the only institution to offer any compulsory machinery to handle trade disputes.[199] It obliged states that were in dispute to consult with each other and then, if no settlement was reached, with the body of Contracting Parties, who might then appoint a working group or panel of experts to hear the matter. The Contracting Parties remained the ultimate (political) decision makers in the system, although it became increasingly judicialized in operation over the years.

The Final Act of the Uruguay Round of GATT negotiations resulted in the establishment of the World Trade Organization (WTO).[200] According to many commentators, the most important structural innovation of the Uruguay Round was the "formalization of a system of adjudication."[201] The Dispute Settlement Body (DSB),

---

196 Brown, *supra* note 192 at 43.

197 See Rubino-Sammartano, *supra* note 55 c. 4 and Toope, *supra* note 48 c. 7.

198 In the North American context, the trade dispute machinery of the North American Free Trade Agreement (NAFTA) is worth noting. See David Lopez, "Dispute Resolution Under NAFTA: Lessons from the Early Experience" (1997) 32 Tex. Int'l L. J. 163; Sidney Picker, "The NAFTA Chapter 20 Dispute Resolution Process: A View From the Inside" (1997) 23 Can.-U.S.L.J. 525; and Rex J. Zedalis, "Claims by Individuals in International Economic Law: NAFTA Developments" (1996) 7 Am. Rev. Int'l Arb. 115. See also Jon R. Johnson, *The North American Free Trade Agreement: A Comprehensive Guide* (1994).

199 See Kenneth W. Dam, *The GATT: Law and International Economic Organization* (1970) c. 20; Robert E. Hudec, *The GATT Legal System and the World Trade Diplomacy*, 2d ed. (1990); John H. Jackson, *World Trade and the Law of GATT: A Legal Analysis of the General Agreement on Tariffs and Trade* (1969) c. 8; Pierre Pescatore, William J. Davey, & Andreas F. Lowenfeld, *Handbook of GATT Dispute Settlement* (1991); and Kenneth R. Simmonds & Brian H.W. Hill, eds., *Law and Practice Under the GATT* (1988) at Part II: Conciliations.

200 For an outline of the evolution from the original GATT system of 1947 to the WTO system, see Alec Stone Sweet, "The New GATT: Dispute Resolution and the Judicialization of the Trade Regime" in Mary L. Volcansek, ed., *Law Above Nations: Supranational Courts and the Legalization of Politics* (1997) at 118.

201 Sweet, *ibid.* at 135.

which in essence is the General Council under another name, and thus includes all members of the WTO, was created, as was the Standing Appellate Body.[202] The new dispute resolution system under the WTO can be characterized as more efficient than that which existed previously under GATT for several reasons. The GATT dispute settlement system did not employ fixed timetables, and panel recommendations could only be adopted by consensus. This resulted in cases that frequently dragged on without resolution. Under the new WTO system, however, the process is more structured and involves fixed deadlines whereby a dispute should be settled within one year's time and within 15 months if the panel's report is appealed. Further strengthening the new system is the requirement for consensus to overturn a panel decision, in contrast to the GATT requirement of consensus to adopt a panel decision.

Despite the compulsory nature of WTO dispute resolution mechanisms, it is important to keep in mind that the priority of the WTO is not to produce rulings, but rather to promote the timely settlement of trade disputes among its members. Thus, the first stage in a dispute is always one of consultation between the disputing parties, and even after the dispute resolution mechanism is in motion and a panel has been constituted, consultation and mediation are available. Similarly, once a dispute is decided it is not inevitable that trade sanctions will be applied. Generally, the "losing" party will state its intention to follow the panel's recommendations within 30 days or some other "reasonable amount of time" following the adoption of the panel's report by the DSB. If the "losing" party fails to adopt the panel's recommendations it is then obligated to negotiate with the complainant party in order to determine some mutually acceptable compensation. If the matter of compensation cannot be agreed on between the disputing parties, the complainant may ask the DSB to impose sanctions on the losing party. The DSB will usually grant authorization for sanctions within 30 days unless there is consensus among member states against such sanctions. The set time frame and clear consequences stand in marked contrast to the open-ended nature of most international dispute settlement. While the WTO dispute resolution scheme has not escaped criticism, focusing in particular on the closed nature of the panel proceedings, it remains a significant development in international dispute settlement.

---

202 A more detailed account of the procedure may be found on the WTO's website, online: World Trade Organization <http://www.wto.org>. See, generally, Steven P. Croley & John H. Jackson, "WTO Dispute Procedures, Standard of Review, and Deference to National Governments" (1996) 90 A.J.I.L. 193; Norio Komuro, "The WTO Dispute Settlement Mechanism: Coverage and Procedures of the WTO Under-standing" (1995) 12 J. Int'l Arb. 81; David Palmeter & Petros. C. Mavroidis, *Dispute Settlement in the World Trade Organization*, 2d ed. (2004); Ernst-Ulrich Petersmann, *The GATT/WTO Dispute Settlement System: International Law, International Organizations, and Dispute Settlement* (1997); Ernst-Ulrich Petersmann, ed., *International Trade Law and the GATT/WTO Dispute Settlement System* (1997); and Frank Warren Swacker, Kenneth Robert Redden & Larry B. Wenger, *World Trade Without Barriers: The World Trade Organization (WTO) and Dispute Resolution* (1995). For a debate about the nature of WTO dispute settlement, see Judith H. Bello, "The WTO Dispute Settlement Understanding: Less Is More" (1996) 90 A.J.I.L. 416 and John H. Jackson, "The WTO Dispute Settlement Understanding— Misunderstandings on the Nature of Legal Obligation" (1997) 91 A.J.I.L. 60. For general information on the WTO, see Joseph F. Dennin, general ed., *Law and Practice of the World Trade Organization* (1995).

3) Human Rights and Criminal Responsibilities: In the human rights area the European Court of Human Rights,[203] the Inter-American Court of Human Rights,[204] and the U.N. Petition System all determine human rights claims.[205] These and other mechanisms are discussed in Chapter 12, Section B.2. They differ from most international dispute settlement in that rather than focusing on state-to-state processes, they allow individuals access to international machinery in order to ensure compliance with human rights norms. Perhaps the single most visible development in this area in recent years has been the establishment of institutions to prosecute and punish violations of humanitarian law,[206] such as the International Criminal Tribunal for the former Yugoslavia,[207] the International Criminal Tribunal for Rwanda,[208] and, most recently, the International Criminal Court.[209] The work of these Tribunals and Court are discussed in Chapter 11, Sections B and C.

4) Protection of the Environment: Some of the most innovative techniques to encourage compliance and prevent disputes have occurred in the area of international environmental law. The emphasis on protection of the environment has encouraged new legal principles respecting precaution and the need for impact assessment before undertaking projects with transboundary effects, along with obligations to notify and consult with neighbouring states. All of these duties tend to reduce surprises, injuries, and, consequently, disputes between states. They are backed up by subject-specific treaty provisions on dispute resolution and compliance, among which the best known is the Non-Compliance Procedure (NCP) set up under the Montreal Protocol on Substances that Deplete the Ozone Layer.[210] Under this procedure an Implementation Committee has been established and empowered to monitor the performance of the states parties. The aim is to secure "an amicable solution of the matter on the basis of respect for the provisions of the Protocol" (NCP para. 8). The Committee reports to the Meeting of the Parties, which may "decide upon and call for steps to bring about full compliance with

203 Online: European Court of Human Rights <http://www.echr.coe.int/>. See, generally, M.W. Janis, "The European Court of Human Rights" in Mark W. Janis, *International Courts for the Twenty-First Century, supra* note 182 at 105-16.

204 See generally Christina M. Cerna, "The Inter-American Court of Human Rights" in Janis, *International Courts for the Twenty-First Century*, *supra* note 182 at 117-58. Online: Inter-American Court of Human Rights <http://www.corteidh.or.cr/index_ing.html> (the English language website appears to be in progress; the Spanish version, at <http://www.corteidh.or.cr/index.htm>, is much more complete). Online: Inter-American Commission on Human Rights <http://www.oas.org/main/main.asp?sLang=E&sLink=http://www.oas.org/OASpage/humanrights.htm>.

205 See generally Emmanuel Spiry, "Le reglement pacifique des differends relatifs aux droits de l'homme: synthese, developpements recents et bilan" (1996) 74 R.D.I.S.D.P. 81.

206 See generally David J. Scheffer, "International Judicial Intervention" (1996) 102 Foreign Policy 34.

207 See International Criminal Tribunal for the former Yugoslavia, *supra* note 163.

208 See International Criminal Tribunal for Rwanda, *supra* note 164.

209 Online: International Criminal Court <http://www.icc-cpi.int/>.

210 See Jeff Trask, "Montreal Protocol Noncompliance Procedure: The Best Approach to Resolving International Environmental Disputes?" (1992) 80 Georgetown L.J. 1973. See generally Edith Brown Weiss & Harold K. Jacobson, eds., *Engaging Countries: Strengthening Compliance with International Environmental Accords* (1998).

the Protocol, including measures to assist the Parties' compliance with the Protocol, and to further the Protocol's objectives" (NCP para. 9). The Kyoto Protocol to the Framework Convention on Climate Change also includes a compliance regime. There is a Compliance Committee made up of two branches, a Facilitative Branch and an Enforcement Branch. The former will provide advice and assistance to Parties in order to promote compliance, whereas the latter will have the power to determine consequences for Parties failing to meet their commitments under the Protocol.[211] These environmental principles and procedures are more fully discussed in Chapter 14, Sections B.3 on "Selected Contemporary Developments" and D on "Protection of the Ozone Layer."

5) The multiplicity of dispute settlement options can give rise to issues respecting conflicts or overlaps of jurisdiction. This arose in the *Southern Bluefin Tuna Case*,[212] an Annex VII Arbitral Tribunal under the U.N. Convention on the Law of the Sea (see above, Note 1). The Tribunal found that it had no jurisdiction to rule on the merits of the case, given the existence of a regional treaty, binding on the parties to the dispute, which incorporated a dispute settlement mechanism.[213] The rather cautious approach of the Tribunal on this issue has been described in the following terms by Bernard Oxman:[214]

> The pivotal issue identified by the arbitral tribunal was the effect of an agreement concluded by the three parties to the arbitration, the 1993 Convention for the Conservation of Southern Bluefin Tuna (CSBT Convention). Its dispute settlement clauses provide for binding third-party settlement only with the consent in each case of all parties to the dispute. The tribunal's conclusions might be summarized as follows:
>
> (1) the dispute between the parties concerning the interpretation and application of the LOS Convention with which the tribunal was seized, and their dispute concerning the interpretation or implementation of the CSBT Convention, are the same dispute;
>
> (2) the provisions of the CSBT Convention regarding settlement of disputes, notwithstanding the fact that they expressly refer only to a dispute concerning the interpretation or implementation of this Convention," constitute an agreement for the settlement of the same dispute concerning the interpretation or application of the LOS Convention; and

---

211 See Jutta Brunnée, "A Fine Balance: Facilitation and Enforcement in the Design of a Compliance Regime for the Kyoto Protocol" (2000) 13 Tul. Envtl. L.J. 223; Xueman Wang & Glenn Wiser, "The Implementation and Compliance Regimes Under the Climate Change Convention and Its Kyoto Protocol" (2002) 11 R.E.C.I.E.L. 181.

212 (*Australia and New Zealand v. Japan*) Jurisdiction and Admissibility (2000) 39 I.L.M. 1359. Available online at <http://www.oceanlaw.net/cases/tuna2a.htm>.

213 Article 281 (1) of the U.N. Convention on the Law of the Sea provides that where parties to a dispute "concerning the interpretation or application of this Convention have agreed to seek settlement of the dispute by a peaceful means of their own choice" the compulsory procedures would "apply only where no settlement has been reached by recourse to such means and the agreement between the parties does not exclude any further procedure."

214 Bernard H. Oxman, "Complementary Agreements and Compulsory Jurisdiction" (2001) 95 A.J.I.L. 277 at 281-82.

(3) the effect of the provisions of the CSBT Convention regarding settlement of disputes, notwithstanding the absence of an express reference to dispute settlement obligations under other treaties in general or the LOS Convention in particular, is to exclude compulsory jurisdiction under both Conventions.

6) All these modern examples of agencies for dispute settlement are encouraging developments in the application of international law. Their growing number and forms are advancing the rule of international law in many directions. While many applaud what they see as a trend to subject the sovereign authority of the state to compulsory adjudicative agencies operating in a transnational legal context, it is also important to bear in mind that a lack of compulsory dispute settlement mechanisms in any particular area does not in and of itself signify a lack of willingness of states to uphold international standards.[215] Instead, attention must be paid to the range of means by which states both resolve and attempt to avoid disputes, through consensus-building mechanisms, frameworks for exchanging information, and the like. As the authors of a book dealing with compliance with regulatory standards have noted:

> Traditionally, sovereignty has signified the complete autonomy of the state to act as it chooses, without legal limitation by any superior entity. The state realized and expressed its sovereignty through independent action to achieve its goals. If sovereignty in such terms ever existed outside books on international law and international relations, however, it no longer has any real world meaning. ... [F]or all but a few self-isolated nations, sovereignty no longer consists in the freedom of states to act independently, in their perceived self-interest, but in membership in reasonably good standing in the regimes that make up the substance of international life.[216]

---

215 See generally Abram Chayes & Antonia Handler Chayes, *The New Sovereignty: Compliance with International Regulatory Agreements* (1995).

216 *Ibid.* at 26, 27.

CHAPTER SEVEN

State Jurisdiction Over Territory

A. INTRODUCTION

The terms "sovereignty" and "jurisdiction"[1] are often used interchangeably in relation to the territory of a state. It is important to stress that "sovereignty" always implies jurisdiction, whereas the reverse is not the case. The term "jurisdiction" is used to describe many different things, including the competence of a court ("civil" or "criminal" jurisdiction), the scope of authority of a particular state organ (jurisdiction over immigration) or of an organ of an international organization (jurisdiction of the U.N. Security Council), or the scope of authority of a state over its territory. In the last sense, "territorial jurisdiction" in international law means the competence of a state to prescribe and enforce rules of domestic law governing conduct within its territory (prescriptive and enforcement jurisdiction). The authority of a state to regulate conduct within its territory is supreme and is subject only to specific limitations set by customary international law or by treaty (for example, concerning diplomatic immunities described previously in Chapter 5, and certain basic human rights, considered later in Chapter 12).

In traditional international law the surface of the earth and the regions above and below may be subject to one of three possible regimes.[2] An area may be under the *sovereignty* of a state—for example, the land territory of states; or it may be *res communis*—for example, the high seas and outer space—shared by all nations and incapable of lawful appropriation by any state; or it may be *res nullius*—for example, a piece of land unclaimed by any state—capable of lawful national appropriation. Apart from an unclaimed portion of Antarctica, there is no area of the planet earth that can today be characterized as *res nullius*. In recent years, beginning with the UNGA Seabed resolution of 1970,[3] a new legal category of territory has been added to the traditional ones—territory designated as the "Common Heritage of Mankind" (CHM)[4]—which is

---

1   I. Brownlie, *Principles of Public International Law*, 6th ed. (2003) at 105-6 and 297 and S.A. Williams & J.-G. Castel, *Canadian Criminal Law; International and Transnational Aspects* (1981) at 3.

2   S.P. Sharma, *Territorial Acquisition, Disputes and International Law* (1997); J. Crawford, *The Creation of States in International Law* (1979); R. Y. Jennings, *The Acquisition of Territory in International Law* (1963); K. Baslar, *The Concept of the Common Heritage of Mankind in International Law* (1998).

3   *Seabed Declaration* GA Res. 2749 (XXV), UN GAOR, 25th Sess., Supp. No. 28, UN Doc. A/8028 (1970) 24, reported in Chapter 13, Section C.

4   Humankind or humanity is sometimes substituted for mankind. See P. B. Payoyo, *Cries of the Sea: World Inequality, Sustainable Development and the Common Heritage of Humanity* (1997).

governed by special rules. The areas subject to the regime of the CHM are the mineral resources of the seabed, the ocean floor and the subsoil thereof, lying beyond the limits of national jurisdiction, as well as the moon and other celestial bodies. Although in some respects similar to the concept of *res communis*, the concept of the CHM differs from the former. Thus according to B. Cheng, in peacetime, under the regime of *res communis*, "as long as a State respects the exclusive quasi-territorial jurisdiction of other States over their own ships, aircraft and spacecraft, general international law allows it to use the area or even to abuse it more or less as it wishes, including the appropriation of its natural resources."[5] By contrast, the concept of the CHM, notes this author, incorporates "the idea that the management, exploitation and distribution of the natural resources of the area in question are matters to be decided by the international community … and are not to be left to the initiative and discretion of individual States or their nationals." Although the subject of lengthy debates during the Third U.N. Conference on the Law of the Sea (1973-82), the CHM concept was for the first time incorporated in an international treaty in the 1979 Agreement Governing the Activities of States on the Moon and Other Celestial Bodies (article 11). The legal status and content of CHM is a subject of controversy.[6]

Under the Montevideo Convention on the Rights and Duties of States (1933),[7] a "defined territory" is one of the indispensable attributes of statehood. The Convention is generally regarded as reflecting customary international law in the matter. The territory of each state, regardless of its size, is tri-dimensional; it consists of the surface (land and, if a coastal state, a portion of the sea), subsurface (*usque ad inferos*), and a column of air to an as yet undetermined altitude coinciding with that state's land and sea boundaries. The territory of coastal states, in contrast with the territory of landlocked states, extends seaward to the outer limit of their territorial seas (maximum of 12 nautical miles). The territory of states endowed with so-called historic bays may also extend over a large maritime area, such as Hudson Bay in the case of Canada. Questions concerning a state's maritime domain are explored in Chapter 13 on the "Law of the Sea."

Possession of territory is so fundamental to statehood that a state would cease to exist if all of its territory were annexed to another state, and the act of annexation did not violate the U.N. Charter. However, in the exercise of its sovereignty, which includes full and exclusive authority over its territory, each state is free to transfer by agreement a part of that territory to another state (for example, Russia's sale in 1867 of Alaska and France's sale in 1803 of Louisiana, both to the United States), or to form a territorial union with another state (for example, the short-lived merger of Egypt and Syria in 1958 into the "United Arab Republic").

---

5   B. Cheng, "The Legal Regime of Airspace and Outer Space: The Boundary Problem, Functionalism versus Spatialism: The Major Premises" (1980) 5 Annals Air & Space L. 323 at 337; see also Baslar, *supra* note 2 at 38.

6   See Baslar, *supra* note 2 at 335; and Payoyo, *supra* note 4 at 227. In contrast to these writers, see C.C. Joyner, *Governing the Frozen Commons: The Antarctic Regime and Environmental Protection* (1998) at 220, who states, at 234: "Put bluntly, the common heritage concept has not been openly or tacitly embraced as a binding principle of international law by those governments having the technology to make exploitation of the commons possible for the benefit of all mankind."

7   (1936) 165 L.N.T.S. 19; (1934) 28 A.J.I.L. Supp. 75; reported in Chapter 2, Section B on "States and Statehood."

B. LAND TERRITORY

1. Acquisition of Territory[8]

Traditional international law recognizes five different modalities for the acquisition of territory: occupation, cession, prescription, conquest, and accretion. A state may acquire territory through *occupation* only if two conditions are satisfied: (1) the territory thus acquired must have been *res nullius*—that is, belonging to no other state or to the international community as a whole and (2) the occupying state exercises effective control over such territory. The criteria for effective occupation vary from place to place and from time to time (see *Island of Palmas* arbitration following these comments).

Cession indicates the transfer of territory from one state to another by a treaty of cession. Thus in 1763, by the Treaty of Paris, France ceded Upper and Lower Canada to Britain and in 1898, by another Treaty of Paris, Spain ceded the Philippines to the United States. Similar to cession would be the acquisition of territory by a new state through the grant of independence by a former colonial power. Under international law, before the U.N. Charter, it was immaterial that a treaty of cession was imposed by force or a threat of force. However, following the adoption of the Charter and the Vienna Convention on the Law of Treaties, discussed in Chapter 3, Section B on "Treaties," a treaty of cession obtained through the unlawful use of force can no longer be regarded as valid. Thus, article 2(4) of the Charter prohibits "the threat or use of force against the territorial integrity ... of any state" and article 52 of the Vienna Convention declares any treaty "void if its conclusion has been procured by the threat or use of force in violation of the principles of international law embodied in the Charter of the United Nations."

A state that has peaceably occupied a certain territory with the knowledge of and without protest by the original sovereign (or claimant) may, after a period of time (probably measured in decades), acquire title to that territory through *prescription*.

Conquest denotes the acquisition of territory achieved through war and subsequent annexation of all or a part of the territory of the defeated enemy state. This mode of acquisition can no longer be reconciled with the principles of modern international law, for the same reasons as given above in regard to cession extracted by force.

Accretion—the least important among the modalities of acquisition—refers to the enlargement of a state's territory through natural forces, for example, through the change of course of a river or the recession of the sea. It should be pointed out that, in territorial disputes between states, more than one modality of acquisition will usually be invoked.

I. Brownlie provides the following warning about the traditional modalities of territorial acquisition: "Labels are never a substitute for analysis."[9] He goes on as follows:

> The issue of territorial sovereignty, or title, is often complex, and involves the application of various principles of the law to the material facts. The result of this process cannot always be ascribed to any single dominant rule or "mode of acquisition." The orthodox analysis does not prepare the student for the interaction of principles of acquiescence and recognition with

---

8   Brownlie, *supra* note 1 c. 7; Sharma, *supra* note 2 at 35; Crawford, *supra* note 2 at 173; Jennings, *supra* note 2; and Malcolm N. Shaw, *Title to Territory in Africa* (1986).

9   Brownlie, *supra* note 1 at 127.

the other rules. … Lastly, the importance of showing a better right to possess in contentious cases, i.e. of relative title, is obscured if too much credit is given to the five "models."

Almost all of the land territorial disputes in the last decades have either been respecting islands (often uninhabited and of concern for the marine jurisdiction associated with them) or as land boundary disputes usually arising from uncertain treaties or other documents. It is important to note that these sovereignty disputes can engage states in very intense ways. For example, the United Kingdom and Argentina engaged in a war regarding the Falkland/Malvinas Islands.[10] The invasion of Kuwait by Iraq in 1990 was also the result of a land territorial dispute.[11]

One of the most complicated sovereignty disputes involves the small islets in the middle of the South China Sea referred to as the Spratly Islands.[12] China and Vietnam claim all of the islands. Malaysia, Philippines, and Brunei claim some of them. Taiwan also occupies at least one of the islands. These disputed islands have been the source of conflict among the claiming states, although in recent years a degree of calm has existed as a result of improved international relations. The Spratly Islands are also of interest because of the various proposals that have been made and processes that have been undertaken to manage the disputes.

Interestingly, courts and tribunals have been playing an increasingly important role in resolving land territorial disputes. In late 2002, the ICJ issued judgments respecting island sovereignty disputed between Malaysia and Indonesia[13] and the land boundary between Cameroon and Nigeria.[14] There are a number of similar cases before the ICJ.

There are two "Canadian" islands that are subject to sovereignty claims by other states. One is Machias Seal Island, inhabited by a lighthouse keeper, located at the mouth of the Bay of Fundy where the opposing claimant is the United States. Canada and the United States agreed in the *Gulf of Maine Case* (discussed in Chapter 13, Section D) to avoid the sovereignty dispute over the island by asking the court to determine the maritime boundary from a point well seaward of the island. The second dispute concerns the uninhabited island of Hans, which is located in the high Arctic between Ellesmere Island and Greenland. Denmark claims this one kilometre wide island.[15]

---

10   Sharma, *supra* note 2 at 301-4.

11   See generally Sharma, *supra* note 2 at 271-79.

12   See Sharma, *supra* note 2 at 282-90; M.J. Valencia, J.M. Van Dyke, & N.A. Ludwig, *Sharing the Resources of the South China Sea* (1997); I. Townsend-Gault, "Preventative Diplomacy and Pro-Activity in the South China Sea" (1998) 20 Contemporary Southeast Asia 171; and Nguyen Hong Thao, "The 2002 Declaration on the Conduct of Parties in the South China Seas: A Note" (2003) 34 Ocean Dev. & Int. L. 279.

13   *Case Concerning the Sovereignty over Pulau Ligitan and Pulau Sipadan (Indonesia/Malaysia)*, [2002] I.C.J. Rep. 625. The ICJ determined that the islands belonged to Malaysia.

14   *Case Concerning the Land and Maritime Boundary between Cameroon and Nigeria*, [2002] I.C.J. Rep. 303.

15   Regarding Canada's two contested islands, see David H. Gray, "Canada's Unresolved Maritime Boundaries" (1994) 48 GEOMATICA 131 at 138-40 and 142-43.

Island of Palmas Case
Netherlands v. United States
(1928), 2 R.I.A.A. 829

[Palmas (or Miangas) is a small isolated island situated about 50 miles southeast from the Island of Mindanao (the Philippines). The dispute had its origin in the visit to Palmas by U.S. General Leonard Wood, on January 21, 1906. In the course of his visit the U.S. official discovered that the island was considered by the Netherlands to be a part of the Dutch East Indies. In the ensuing diplomatic controversy, the United States contended that the island of Palmas was included in the Philippine Archipelago ceded by Spain to the United States in 1898 by the Treaty of Paris. The Netherlands claimed sovereignty by virtue of its continuous and undisputed display of authority over the island during a long period of time. Eventually, the two countries agreed to submit their differences to arbitration.]

MAX HUBER, Arbitrator: ... In the first place the Arbitrator deems it necessary to make some general remarks on *sovereignty in its relation to territory*. ...

Sovereignty in the relation between States signifies independence. Independence in regard to a portion of the globe is the right to exercise therein, to the exclusion of any other State, the functions of a State. The development of the national organisation of States during the last few centuries and, as a corollary, the development of international law, have established this principle of the exclusive competence of the State in regard to its own territory in such a way as to make it the point of departure in settling most questions that concern international relations. The special cases of the composite State, of collective sovereignty, etc. do not fall to be considered here and do not, for that matter, throw any doubt upon the principle which has just been enunciated. Under this reservation it may be stated that territorial sovereignty belongs always to one, or in exceptional circumstances to several States, to the exclusion of all others. The fact that the functions of a State can be performed by any State within a given zone is, on the other hand, precisely the characteristic feature of the legal situation pertaining in those parts of the globe, which, like the high seas or lands without a master, cannot or do not yet form the territory of a State.

Territorial sovereignty is, in general, a situation recognised and delimited in space, either by so-called natural frontiers as recognised by international law or by outward signs of delimitation that are undisputed, or else by legal engagements entered into between interested neighbours, such as frontier conventions, or by acts of recognition of States within fixed boundaries. If a dispute arises as to the sovereignty over a portion of territory, it is customary to examine which of the States claiming sovereignty possesses a title—cession, conquest, occupation, etc.—superior to that which the other State might possibly bring forward against it. However, if the contestation is based on the fact that the other Party has actually displayed sovereignty, it cannot be sufficient to establish the title by which territorial sovereignty was validly acquired at a certain moment; it must also be shown that the territorial sovereignty has continued to exist and did exist at the moment which for the decision of the dispute must be considered as critical. This demonstration consists in the actual display of State activities, such as belongs only to the territorial sovereign.

Titles of acquisition of territorial sovereignty in present-day international law are either based on an act of effective apprehension, such as occupation or conquest, or, like cession, presuppose that the ceding and the cessionary Power or at least one of them, have the faculty of effectively disposing of the ceded territory. In the same way natural accretion can only be conceived of as an accretion to a portion of territory where there exists an actual sovereignty capable of extending to a spot which falls within its sphere of activity. It seems therefore natural that an element which is essential for the constitution of sovereignty should not be lacking in its continuation. So true is this, that practice, as well as doctrine, recognizes—though under different legal formulae and with certain differences as to the conditions required—that the continuous and peaceful display of territorial sovereignty (peaceful in relation to other States) is as good as a title. The growing insistence with which international law, ever since the middle of the 18th century, has demanded that the occupation shall be effective would be inconceivable, if effectiveness were required only for the act of acquisition and not equally for the maintenance of the right. If the effectiveness has above all been insisted on in regard to occupation, this is because the question rarely arises in connection with territories in which there is already an established order of things. Just as before the rise of international law, boundaries of lands were necessarily determined by the fact that the power of a State was exercised within them, so too, under the reign of international law, the fact of peaceful and continuous display is still one of the most important considerations in establishing boundaries between States.

Territorial sovereignty, as has already been said, involves the exclusive right to display the activities of a State. This right has as corollary a duty: the obligation to protect within the territory the rights of other States, in particular their right to integrity and inviolability in peace and in war, together with the rights which each State may claim for its nationals in foreign territory. Without manifesting its territorial sovereignty in a manner corresponding to circumstances, the State cannot fulfil this duty. Territorial sovereignty cannot limit itself to its negative side, i.e. to excluding the activities of other States; for it serves to divide between nations the space upon which human activities are employed, in order to assure them at all points the minimum of protection of which international law is the guardian. ...

Manifestations of territorial sovereignty assume, it is true, different forms, according to conditions of time and place. Although continuous in principle, sovereignty cannot be exercised in fact at every moment on every point of a territory. The intermittence and discontinuity compatible with the maintenance of the right necessarily differ according as inhabited or uninhabited regions are involved, or regions enclosed within territories in which sovereignty is incontestably displayed or again regions accessible from, for instance, the high seas.

... The *title alleged by the United States of America* as constituting the immediate foundation of its claim is that of *cession*, brought about by the Treaty of Paris, which cession transferred all rights of sovereignty which Spain may have possessed in the region indicated in Article III of the said Treaty and therefore also those concerning the Island of Palmas (or Miangas).

It is evident that Spain could not transfer more rights than she herself possessed. ...

The essential point is therefore whether the Island of Palmas (or Miangas) at the moment of the conclusion and coming into force of the Treaty of Paris formed a part of the Spanish or Netherlands territory. The United States declares that Palmas (or Miangas) was Spanish territory and denies the existence of Dutch sovereignty; the Netherlands maintain the existence of their sovereignty and deny that of Spain. ...

In the last place there remains to be considered *title arising out of contiguity*. Although States have in certain circumstances maintained that islands relatively close to their shores belonged to them in virtue of their geographical situation, it is impossible to show the existence of a rule of positive international law to the effect that islands situated outside territorial waters should belong to a State from the mere fact that its territory forms the *terra firma* (nearest continent or island of considerable size). Not only would it seem that there are no precedents sufficiently frequent and sufficiently precise in their bearing to establish such a rule of international law, but the alleged principle itself is by its very nature so uncertain and contested that even Governments of the same State have on different occasions maintained contradictory opinions as to its soundness. The principle of contiguity, in regard to islands, may not be out of place when it is a question of allotting them to one State rather than another, either by agreement between the Parties, or by a decision not necessarily based on law; but as a rule establishing *ipso jure* the presumption of sovereignty in favour of a particular State, this principle would be in conflict with what has been said as to territorial sovereignty and as to the necessary relation between the right to exclude other States from a region and the duty to display therein the activities of a State. Nor is this principle of contiguity admissible as a legal method of deciding questions of territorial sovereignty; for it is wholly lacking in precision and would in its application lead to arbitrary results. This would be especially true in a case such as that of the island in question, which is not relatively close to one single continent, but forms part of a large archipelago in which strict delimitations between the different parts are not naturally obvious. ...

The conclusions to be derived from the above examination of the arguments of the Parties are the following:

The claim of the United States to sovereignty over the Island of Palmas (or Miangas) is derived from Spain by way of cession under the Treaty of Paris. The latter Treaty, though it comprises the island in dispute within the limits of cession, and in spite of the absence of any reserves or protest by the Netherlands as to these limits, has not created in favour of the United States any title of sovereignty such as was not already vested in Spain. The essential point is therefore to decide whether Spain had sovereignty over Palmas (or Miangas) at the time of the coming into force of the Treaty of Paris.

The United States base their claim on the titles of discovery, of recognition by treaty and of contiguity, i.e. titles relating to acts or circumstances leading to the acquisition of sovereignty; they have however not established the fact that sovereignty so acquired was effectively displayed at any time. The Netherlands on the contrary found their claim to sovereignty essentially on the title of the peaceful and continuous display of state authority over the island. Since this title would in international law prevail over a title of acquisition of sovereignty not followed by actual display of state authority, it is necessary to ascertain in the first place, whether the contention of the Netherlands is sufficiently established by evidence, and, if so, for what period of time. ...

The acts of indirect or direct display of Netherlands sovereignty at Palmas (or Miangas), especially in the 18th and early 19th centuries are not numerous, and there are considerable gaps in the evidence of continuous display. But apart from the consideration that the manifestations of sovereignty over a small and distant island, inhabited only by natives, cannot be expected to be frequent, it is not necessary that the display of sovereignty should go back to a very far distant period. It may suffice that such display existed in 1898, and had already existed as continuous and peaceful before that date long enough to enable any Power who might have considered herself as possessing sovereignty over the island, or having a claim to sovereignty, to have, according to local conditions, a reasonable possibility for ascertaining the existence of a state of things contrary to her real or alleged rights. ...

Since the moment when the Spaniards, in withdrawing from the Moluccas in 1666, made express reservations as to the maintenance of their sovereign rights, up to the contestation made by the United States in 1906, no contestation or other action whatever or protest against the exercise of territorial rights by the Netherlands over the Talautse (Sangi) Isles and their dependencies (Miangas included) has been recorded. The peaceful character of the display of Netherlands sovereignty for the entire period to which the evidence concerning acts of display relates (1700–1906) must be admitted.

There is moreover no evidence which would establish any act of display of sovereignty over the island by Spain or another Power, such as might counter-balance or annihilate the manifestations of Netherlands sovereignty. As to third Powers, the evidence submitted to the Tribunal does not disclose any trace of such action, at least from the middle of the 17th century onwards. These circumstances, together with the absence of any evidence of a conflict between Spanish and Netherlands authorities during more than two centuries as regards Palmas (or Miangas), are an indirect proof of the exclusive display of Netherlands sovereignty.

This being so, it remains to be considered first whether the display of state authority might not be legally defective and therefore unable to create a valid title of sovereignty, and secondly whether the United States may not put forward a better title to that of the Netherlands.

As to the conditions of acquisition of sovereignty by way of continuous and peaceful display of state authority (so-called prescription), some of which have been discussed in the United States Counter Memorandum, the following must be said:

The display has been open and public, that is to say that it was in conformity with usages as to exercise of sovereignty over colonial states. A clandestine exercise of state authority over an inhabited territory during a considerable length of time would seem to be impossible. An obligation for the Netherlands to notify to other Powers the establishment of suzerainty over the Sangi States or of the display of sovereignty in these territories did not exist. ...

The conditions of acquisition of sovereignty by the Netherlands are therefore to be considered as fulfilled. It remains now to be seen whether the United States as successors of Spain are in a position to bring forward an equivalent or stronger title. This is to be answered in the negative.

The title of discovery, if it had not been already disposed of by the Treaties of Münster and Utrecht would, under the most favourable and most extensive interpretation, exist only as an inchoate title, as a claim to establish sovereignty by effective occupation. An inchoate title however cannot prevail over a definite title founded on continuous and peaceful display of sovereignty.

The title of contiguity, understood as a basis of territorial sovereignty, has no foundation in international law.

The title of recognition by treaty does not apply, because even if the Sangi States, with the dependency of Miangas, are to be considered as "held and possessed" by Spain in 1648, the rights of Spain to be derived from the Treaty of Münster would have been superseded by those which were acquired by the Treaty of Utrecht. Now if there is evidence of a state of possession in 1714 concerning the island of Palmas (or Miangas), such evidence is exclusively in favour of the Netherlands. But even if the Treaty of Utrecht could not be taken into consideration, the acquiescence of Spain in the situation created after 1677 would deprive her and her successors of the possibility of still invoking conventional rights at the present time.

The Netherlands title of sovereignty, acquired by continuous and peaceful display of state authority during a long period of time going probably back beyond the year 1700, therefore holds good. ...

NOTES

1) In the *Clipperton Island Case*,[16] the Arbitrator, King Victor Emmanuel III of Italy, stated:

It is beyond doubt that by immemorial usage having the force of law, besides the *animus occupandi*, the actual, and not the nominal, taking of possession is a necessary condition of occupation. This taking of possession consists of the act, or series of acts, by which the occupying state reduces to its possession the territory in question and takes steps to exercise exclusive authority there. Strictly speaking, and in ordinary cases, that only takes place when the state establishes in the territory itself an organization capable of making its laws respected. But this step is, properly speaking, but a means of procedure to the taking of possession, and, therefore, is not identical with the latter. There may also be cases where it is unnecessary to have recourse to this method. Thus, if a territory, by virtue of the fact that it was completely uninhabited, is, from the first moment when the occupying state makes its appearance there, at the absolute and undisputed disposition of that state, from that moment the taking of possession must be considered as accomplished, and the occupation is thereby completed.

2) As to acquisition of territory by cession, see the *St. Catherines Milling and Lumber Co. v. The Queen*, reported in the following subsection.

---

16   *Mexico v. France* (1931), 2 R.I.A.A. 1105.

Legal Status of Eastern Greenland Case
Denmark v. Norway
(1933) P.C.I.J. (Ser. A/B) No. 53

[The dispute was triggered by Norway's proclamation of sovereignty over Eastern Greenland, an uncolonized part of the island. Denmark, which claimed sovereignty over the whole island, instituted proceedings against Norway in the Permanent Court of International Justice asking the Court to declare the Norwegian Act invalid.]

THE COURT: ... The Danish submission ... that the Norwegian occupation of July 10, 1931, is invalid, is founded upon the contention that the area occupied was at the time of the occupation subject to Danish sovereignty; that the area is part of Greenland, and at the time of the occupation Danish sovereignty existed over all Greenland; consequently it could not be occupied by another Power.

In support of this contention, the Danish Government advances two propositions. The first is that the sovereignty which Denmark now enjoys over Greenland has existed for a long time, has been continuously and peacefully exercised, and, until the present dispute has not been contested by any Power. This proposition Denmark sets out to establish as a fact. The second proposition is that Norway has by treaty or otherwise herself recognized Danish sovereignty over Greenland as a whole and therefore cannot now dispute it.

The Norwegian submissions are that Denmark possessed no sovereignty over the area which Norway occupied on July 10, 1931, and that at the time of the occupation the area was *terra nullius*. Her contention is that the area lay outside the limits of the Danish colonies in Greenland and that Danish sovereignty extended no further than the limits of these colonies.

... On the Danish side it was maintained that the promise which in 1919 the Norwegian Minister for Foreign Affairs, speaking on behalf of his Government, gave to the diplomatic representative of the Danish Government ... debarred Norway from proceeding to any occupation of territory in Greenland, even if she had not by other acts recognized an existing Danish sovereignty there. ...

The Danish claim is not founded upon any particular act of occupation, but alleges—to use the phrase employed in the *Palmas Island* decision of the Permanent Court of Arbitration, April 4, 1928—a title "founded on the peaceful and continuous display of State authority over the island." It is based upon the view that Denmark now enjoys all the rights which the King of Denmark and Norway enjoyed up till 1814. Both the existence and the extent of these rights must therefore be considered, as well as the Danish claim to sovereignty since that date.

It must be borne in mind, however, that as the critical date is July 10, 1931, it is not necessary that sovereignty over Greenland should have existed throughout the period during which the Danish Government maintains that it was in being. Even if the material submitted to the Court might be thought insufficient to establish the existence of that sovereignty during the earlier periods, this would not exclude a finding that it is sufficient to establish a valid title in the period immediately preceding the occupation. ...

It is impossible to read the records of the decisions in cases as to territorial sovereignty without observing that in many cases the tribunal has been satisfied with very little in the way of actual exercise of sovereign rights, provided that the other State could not make out a superior claim. This is particularly true in the case of claims to sovereignty over areas in thinly populated or unsettled countries. ...

In order to establish the contention that Denmark has exercised in fact sovereignty over all Greenland for a long time, Counsel for Denmark have laid stress on the long series of conventions—mostly commercial in character—which have been concluded by Denmark and in which, with the concurrence of the other contracting Party, a stipulation has been inserted to the effect that the convention shall not apply to Greenland.

... The importance of these treaties is that they show a willingness on the part of the States with which Denmark has contracted to admit her right to exclude Greenland. To some of these treaties, Norway has herself been a party.

... These treaties may also be regarded as demonstrating sufficiently Denmark's will and intention to exercise sovereignty over Greenland ...

In view of the above facts, when taken in conjunction with the legislation she had enacted applicable to Greenland generally, the numerous treaties in which Denmark, with the concurrence of the other contracting party, provided for the non-application of the treaty to Greenland in general, and the absence of all claim to sovereignty over Greenland by any other Power, Denmark must be regarded as having displayed during this period of 1814 to 1915 her authority over the uncolonized part of the country to a degree sufficient to confer valid title to the sovereignty.

... Nevertheless, the conclusion which the Court has reached is that the view upheld by the Danish Government in the present case is right, and that the object which that Government was endeavouring to secure was an assurance from each of the foreign governments concerned that it accepted the Danish point of view that all Greenland was already subject to Danish sovereignty and was therefore content to see an extension of Denmark's activities to the uncolonized parts of Greenland. ...

The next government to be approached was the Norwegian. That Government had already manifested a desire to acquire Spitzbergen, and in April, 1919, the Danish Government had given the Norwegian Government to understand that, as there were no Danish interests in Spitzbergen which ran counter to those of Norway, Denmark would not oppose the Norwegian aspirations.

Early in July, 1919, the Danish Minister for Foreign Affairs learned ... that the Spitzbergen question was to come before a Committee of the Peace Conference.

Instructions were thereupon issued, on July 12, 1919, to the Danish Minister at Christiania to make to the Norwegian Minister for Foreign Affairs a communication to the effect that a Committee had just been constituted at the Peace Conference "for the purpose of considering the claims that may be put forward by different countries to Spitzbergen," and that the Danish Government would be prepared to renew before this Committee, the unofficial assurance already given to the Norwegian Government, according to which Denmark ... would raise no objection to Norway's claim. ... In making this statement to the Norwegian Minister for Foreign Affairs, the Danish Minister was to point out "that the Danish Government had been anxious for some years past to obtain the recognition by all the interested Powers of Denmark's sovereignty over the whole of Greenland and that it intended to place that question before the above-mentioned Committee"; that the Government of the United States of America had made a declaration that that Government would not oppose the extension of Danish political and economic interests over all Greenland; and further that the Danish Government counted on the Norwegian Government not making any difficulties with regard to such an extension.

When, on July 14, 1919, the Danish Minister saw the Norwegian Minister of Foreign Affairs, M. Ihlen, the latter merely replied "that the question would be considered."... On July 22 following, the Minister for Foreign Affairs, after informing his colleagues of the Norwegian Cabinet, made a statement to the Danish Minister to the effect "that the Norwegian Government would not make any difficulties in the settlement of this question" (i.e., the question raised on July 14 by the Danish Government). These are the words recorded in the minute by M. Ihlen himself. According to the report made by the Danish Minister to his own Government, M. Ihlen's words were that "the plans of the Royal (Danish) Government respecting Danish sovereignty over the whole of Greenland ... would meet with no difficulty on the part of Norway." ...

The period subsequent to ... 1921 witnessed a considerable increase in the activity of the Danish Government on the eastern coast of Greenland. ...

These were all cases in which the Danish Government was exercising governmental functions in connection with the territory now under dispute.

The character of these Danish acts is not altered by the protests or reserves which, from time to time, were made by the Norwegian Government. ...

It follows from the above that the Court is satisfied that Denmark has succeeded in establishing her contention that at the critical date, namely, July 10, 1931, she possessed a valid title to the sovereignty over all Greenland.

This finding constitutes by itself sufficient reason for holding that the occupation of July 10, 1931, and any steps taken in this connection by the Norwegian Government, were illegal and invalid.

The Court will now consider the second Danish proposition that Norway had given certain undertakings which recognized Danish sovereignty over all Greenland. ...

What Denmark desired to obtain from Norway was that the latter should do nothing to obstruct the Danish plans in regard to Greenland. The declaration which the Minister of Foreign Affairs gave on July 22, 1919, on behalf of the Norwegian Government, was definitely affirmative: "I told the Danish Minister today that the Norwegian Government would not make any difficulty in the settlement of this question."

The Court considers it beyond all dispute that a reply of this nature given by the Minister for Foreign Affairs on behalf of his Government in response to a request by the diplomatic representative of a foreign Power, in regard to a question falling within his province, is binding upon the country to which the Minister belongs.

... The Court is unable to regard the Ihlen declaration of July 22, 1919, otherwise than as unconditional and definitive.

... The Court is unable to read into the words of the Ihlen declaration "in the settlement of this question"—i.e., the Greenland question—a condition which would render the promise to refrain from making any difficulties inoperative should a settlement not be reached. The promise was unconditional and definitive. ...

It follows that, as a result of the undertaking involved in the Ihlen declaration of July 22, 1919, Norway is under an obligation to refrain from contesting Danish sovereignty over Greenland as a whole, and *a fortiori* to refrain from occupying a part of Greenland.

NOTES

1) Dissenting judgments were delivered by Judge Anzilotti and by Norwegian Judge Ad Hoc Vogt.

2) In *Minquiers and Ecrehos Case*[17] the International Court of Justice was called upon to determine whether France or the United Kingdom had sovereignty over a number of islets and rocks in the English Channel. By Special Agreement, the parties agreed to exclude the concept of *terra nullius* as a basis for resolving the competing claims. Both countries asserted in the course of the proceedings an ancient title to the disputed islets and rocks. On weighing the evidence submitted, the Court unanimously found for the United Kingdom. The decisive factor in the Court's decision was the more recent evidence of the exercise of "State functions" over the disputed territory by the United Kingdom.

3) The dispute between Thailand and Cambodia concerning the sovereignty over the Temple of Preah Vihear[18] was described by the International Court of Justice as follows: "Cambodia alleges a violation on the part of Thailand of Cambodia's territorial sovereignty over the region of the Temple of Preah Vihear and its precincts. Thailand replies by affirming that the area in question lies on the Thai side of the common frontier between the two countries and is under the sovereignty of Thailand." The Temple is an ancient sanctuary and, although partially in ruins, of great artistic and archeological interest. The Court examined the evidence presented by the parties in support of their claims and concluded that:

> the most significant episode consisted of the visit paid to the Temple in 1930 by Prince Damrong, formerly Minister of the Interior, and at this time President of the Royal Institute of Siam, charged with duties in connection with the National Library and with archaeological monuments. The visit was part of an archaeological tour made by the Prince with the permission of the King of Siam, and it clearly had a quasi-official character. When the Prince arrived at Preah Vihear, he was officially received there by the French Resident for the adjoining Cambodian province, on behalf of the Resident Superior, with the French flag flying. The Prince could not possibly have failed to see the implications of a reception of this character. A clearer affirmation of title on the French Indo-Chinese side can scarcely be imagined. It demanded a reaction. Thailand did nothing. Furthermore, when Prince Damrong on his return to Bangkok sent the French Resident some photographs of the occasion, he used language which seems to admit that France, through her Resident, had acted as the host country.

---

17 *France v. United Kingdom*, [1953] I.C.J. Rep. 47. See R. St. J. Macdonald, "The Minquiers and Ecrehos Case" (1954-55) 1 McGill L.J. 277.

18 *Temple of Preah Vihear Case (Cambodia v. Thailand)*, [1962] I.C.J. Rep. 6 at 12 & 30.

The explanations regarding Prince Damrong's visit given on behalf of Thailand have not been found convincing by the Court. Looking at the incident as a whole, it appears to have amounted to a tacit recognition by Siam of the sovereignty of Cambodia (under French Protectorate) over Preah Vihear, through a failure to react in any way, on an occasion that called for a reaction in order to affirm or preserve title in the face of an obvious rival claim. What seems clear is that either Siam did not in fact believe she had any title—and this would be wholly consistent with her attitude all along, and thereafter, to the Annex I map and line or else she decided not to assert it, which again means that she accepted the French claim, or accepted the frontier at Preah Vihear as it was drawn on the map.

By a 9 to 3 vote the Court found that the Temple is situated in territory under the sovereignty of Cambodia; and by 7 votes to 5 that Thailand was under an obligation to restore to Cambodia any archeological objects that had been removed from the Temple by the Thai authorities after the occupation of the Temple by Thailand in 1954.

4) In the *Western Sahara Case*[19] (reproduced in Chapter 2, Section C.2), the U.N. General Assembly asked the ICJ to answer the question: Was Western Sahara at the time of colonization by Spain a territory belonging to no one (*terra nullius*)? The Court responded as follows:

[79] ... In the view of the Court, therefore, a determination that Western Sahara was a "*terra nullius*" at the time of colonization by Spain would be possible only if it were established that at that time the territory belonged to no-one in the sense that it was then open to acquisition through the legal process of "occupation."

[80] Whatever differences of opinion there may have been among jurists, the State practice of the relevant period indicates that territories inhabited by tribes or peoples having a social and political organization were not regarded as *terrae nullius*. It shows that in the case of such territories the acquisition of sovereignty was not generally considered as effected unilaterally through "occupation" of *terra nullius* by original title but through agreements concluded with local rulers. On occasion, it is true, the word "occupation" was used in a non-technical sense denoting simply acquisition of sovereignty; but that did not signify that the acquisition of sovereignty through such agreements with authorities of the country was regarded as an "occupation" of a "*terra nullius*" in the proper sense of these terms. On the contrary, such agreements with local rulers, whether or not considered as an actual "cession" of the territory, were regarded as derivative roots of title, and not original titles obtained by occupation of *terrae nullius*.

[81] In the present instance, the information furnished to the Court shows that at the time of colonization Western Sahara was inhabited by peoples which, if nomadic, were socially and politically organized in tribes and under chiefs competent to represent them.

---

19   [1975] I.C.J. Rep. 12.

Sovereignty over Pulau Ligitan and Pulau Sipadan Case
(Indonesia/Malaysia)
[2002] I.C.J. Rep. 625

[The dispute involved two small islands in the Celebes Sea. Before the 1980s neither was inhabited. The Court rejected the argument of the two states, which suggested that the basis of title flowed from an 1891 Treaty or by succession, and instead focused on "*effectivités*" (effective occupation).[20] The Court decided that the "critical date"[21] respecting State acts was 1969, commenting at para. 135 that "it cannot take into consideration acts having taken place after the date on which the dispute between the Parties crystallized unless such acts are a normal continuation of prior acts and are not undertaken for the purpose of improving the legal position of the Party which relies on them."]

THE COURT: ...

[143] As evidence of ... effective administration over the islands, Malaysia cites the measures taken by the North Borneo authorities to regulate and control the collecting of turtle eggs on Ligitan and Sipadan, an activity of some economic significance in the area at the time. It refers in particular to the Turtle Preservation ordinance of 1917, the purpose of which was to limit the capture of turtles and the collection of turtle eggs "within the State [of North Borneo] or the territorial waters thereof." The Court notes that the Ordinance provided in this respect for a licensing system and for the creation of native reserves for the collection of turtle eggs and listed Sipadan among the islands included in one of those reserves.

Malaysia adduces several documents showing that the 1917 Turtle Preservation Ordinance was applied until the 1950s at least. In this regard, it cites, for example, the licence issued on 28 April 1954 by the District Officer of Tawau permitting the capture of turtles pursuant to Section 2 of the Ordinance. The Court observes that this licence covered an area including "the islands of Sipadan, Ligitan, Kapalat, Mabul, Dinawan and Si-Amil."

Further, Malaysia mentions certain cases both before and after 1930 in which it has been shown that administrative authorities settled disputes about the collection of turtle eggs on Sipadan.

[144] Malaysia also refers to the fact that in 1933 Sipadan, under Section 28 of the Land Ordinance, 1930, was declared to be "a reserve for the purpose of bird sanctuaries."

[145] The Court is of the opinion that both the measures taken to regulate and control the collecting of turtle eggs and the establishment of a bird reserve must be seen as regulatory and administrative assertions of authority over territory which is specified by name.

---

20   See Brownlie, *supra* note 1 at 133-38 and Sharma, *supra* note 2 at 61-66 and 180-82.

21   Brownlie, *supra* note 1 at 126 cautions: "There are several types of critical date, and it is difficult and probably misleading to formulate general definitions."

[146] Malaysia further invokes the fact that the authorities of the colony of North Borneo constructed a lighthouse on Sipadan in 1962 and another on Ligitan in 1963, that those lighthouses exist to this day and that they have been maintained by Malaysian authorities since its independence. It contends that the construction and maintenance of such lighthouses is "part of a pattern of exercise of State authority appropriate in kind and degree to the character of the places involved."

[147] The Court observes that the construction and operation of lighthouses and navigational aids are not normally considered manifestations of State authority (*Minquiers and Ecrehos, Judgment, I.C.J. Reports 1953*, p. 71). The Court, however, recalls that in its Judgment in the case concerning *Maritime Delimitation and Territorial Questions between Qatar and Bahrain (Qatar v. Bahrain)* it stated as follows:

> Certain types of activities invoked by Bahrain such as the drilling of artesian wells would, taken by themselves, be considered controversial as acts performed *à titre de souverain*. The construction of navigational aids, on the other hand, can be legally relevant in the case of very small islands. In the present case, taking into account the size of Qit'at Jaradah, the activities carried out by Bahrain on that island must be considered sufficient to support Bahrain's claim that it has sovereignty over it." (*Judgment, Merits, I.C.J. Reports 2001*, para. 197)

The Court is of the view that the same considerations apply in the present case.

[148] The Court notes that the activities relied upon by Malaysia, both in its own name and as successor State of Great Britain, are modest in number but that they are diverse in character and include legislative, administrative and quasi-judicial acts. They cover a considerable period of time and show a pattern revealing an intention to exercise State functions in respect of the two islands in the context of the administration of a wider range of islands.

The Court moreover cannot disregard the fact that at the time when these activities were carried out, neither Indonesia nor its predecessor, the Netherlands, ever expressed its disagreement or protest. In this regard, the Court notes that in 1962 and 1963 the Indonesian authorities did not even remind the authorities of the colony of North Borneo, or Malaysia after its independence, that the construction of the lighthouses at those times had taken place on territory which they considered Indonesian; even if they regarded these lighthouses as merely destined for safe navigation in an area which was of particular importance for navigation in the waters off North Borneo, such behaviour is unusual.

[149] Given the circumstances of the case, and in particular in view of the evidence furnished by the Parties, the Court concludes that Malaysia has title to Ligitan and Sipadan on the basis of the *effectivités* referred to above.

NOTE

The facts and findings in the above case may be of particular interest in the Canada–United States dispute respecting Machias Seal Island where Canadian actions regarding a bird sanctuary and the lighthouse appear to be part of an argument for effective occupation that may be raised by Canada.

Boundary Disputes[22]

S.P. Sharma argues that there is a distinction between a boundary dispute and a territorial dispute, although it is acknowledged that the problems, policies, and legal arguments are similar.[23] Sharma posits that a boundary dispute is an exercise of dividing territory whereas a territorial dispute is one where the goal is the exclusive sovereignty over a particular area.

Among the changes that have taken place in Central and Eastern Europe since the demise of the Soviet Union, special mention should be made of the conclusion of a "Treaty on the Final Settlement with Respect to Germany," signed in Moscow on September 12, 1990. Article I of the Treaty explicitly addresses the question of boundaries after the reunification of Germany: "(1) The United Germany shall comprise the territory of the Federal Republic of Germany, the German Democratic Republic and the whole of Berlin. Its external borders shall be the borders of the Federal Republic of Germany and the Democratic Republic of Germany and shall be definitive from the date on which the present Treaty comes into force. The confirmation of the definitive nature of the borders of the United Germany is an essential element of the peaceful order in Europe. (2) The United Germany and the Republic of Poland shall confirm the existing border between them in a treaty that is binding under international law. (3) The United Germany has no territorial claims whatsoever against other states and shall not assert any in the future."[24]

Agreements are the manner by which most disputes regarding land boundaries are resolved. In recent years, the ICJ has been called upon to resolve three land boundary disputes all of which engaged the interpretation of treaties and other documents.

In 1994 the ICJ decided the *Case Concerning the Territorial Dispute (Libya/Chad)*.[25] Chad argued that the boundary was set out in a 1955 Libya–France treaty. Libya took the view that the 1955 treaty did not establish the specific boundary. The Court found that the 1955 treaty did define the boundary between Libya and Chad.

In the *Case Concerning Kasikili/Sedudu Island (Botswana/Namibia)*,[26] the ICJ was faced with determining a river boundary as well as the legal status of an island in the river. The principal dispute was over the application of the reference to the "main channel" in an 1890 Germany–Great Britain treaty. The Court looked at the depth and width of the channel in the River Chobe as well as the profile of the riverbed and the navigable channel, and determined the main channel followed the deepest soundings. The result favoured Botswana. Regarding the island, the Court determined that since Namibia was not able to make its case on prescription, and since the island was on the Botswana side of the main channel, it belonged to Botswana. What is interesting about the case is

---

22   Various aspects of boundary disputes are extensively explored in S. Boggs, *International Boundaries* (1940); M. M. Whiteman, *Digest of International Law* (1963) vol. 2 at 1028 ff (1964) vol. 3 at 1-871; A.O. Cukwurah, *The Settlement of Boundary Disputes in International Law* (1967); A. J. Day, ed., *Border and Territorial Disputes* (1982); and Societe francaise pour le droit international, *La frontiere: Collogue de Poitiers* (1980).

23   Sharma, *supra* note 2 at 21.

24   (1990) 29 I.L.M. 1187.

25   [1994] I.C.J. Rep. 1.

26   [1999] I.C.J. Rep. 1045.

that the Court made note of undertakings by the two states in 1992 that the nationals and vessels of both States are to enjoy unimpeded navigation.

The *Land and Maritime Boundary between Cameroon and Nigeria Case*,[27] decided in 2002, is not like the above cases. As regards the land boundary issue, there were documents that the Court reviewed in interpreting the existence of a boundary. The complicating factor was Nigeria's assertion that its effective occupation of various land areas should determine the land boundary or, in some situations, that, regardless of the old documents, its effective occupation had displaced the established title. The latter argument was particularly made regarding the Bakassi Peninsula in the Gulf of Guinea, which is a potentially oil rich area under Nigerian control. The Court supported the boundary arising from the relevant documents and did not give effect to Nigerian arguments regarding its occupation. Prior to the decision, the governments of the two states had assured the U.N. Secretary-General that they would abide by the decision. However, the initial Nigerian reaction to the ICJ decision was to dispute it. A mixed commission brokered by and involving the U.N. was established to help resolve the dispute between the two states. Reports from Nigeria indicate the floating of the idea of holding a referendum within Bakassi regarding sovereignty. The Mixed Commission had set September 15, 2004 as the date for withdrawal by Nigeria. Nigeria failed to withdraw. Meanwhile, there has been some success in discussions regarding the land and ocean boundary, with some areas having been swapped and with Nigeria withdrawing certain claims and accepting the Court's decision.

Case Concerning the Frontier Dispute
Burkina Faso v. Republic of Mali
[1986] I.C.J. Rep. 554

[In 1960 Burkina Faso and Mali achieved independence from France. The territory of the two new states had been part of French West Africa. The question before the Chamber of the ICJ was the location of the boundary. The Chamber was required to determine the administrative boundary dividing the French colonies prior to independence. The details of the decision are not relevant, although the preliminary comments of the Court are important.]

THE CHAMBER: ...

[17] The Parties have argued at length over how the present dispute is to be classified in terms of a distinction sometimes made by legal writers between "frontier disputes" or "delimitation disputes," and "disputes as to attribution of territory." According to this distinction, the former refer to delimitation operations affecting what has been described as "a portion of land which is not geographically autonomous" whereas the object of the latter is the attribution of sovereignty over the whole of a geographical entity. Both Parties seem ultimately to have accepted that the

---

27   *Cameroon v. Nigeria, supra* note 14.

present dispute belongs rather to the category of delimitation disputes, even though they fail to agree on the conclusions to be drawn from this. In fact, however, in the great majority of cases, including this one, the distinction outlined above is not so much a difference in kind but rather a difference of degree as to the way the operation in question is carried out. The effect of any delimitation, no matter how small the disputed area crossed by the line, is an apportionment of the areas of land lying on either side of the line. ...

[20] Since the two Parties have, as noted above, expressly requested the Chamber to resolve their dispute on the basis, in particular, of the "principle of the intangibility of frontiers inherited from colonization," the Chamber cannot disregard the principle of *uti possidetis juris*, the application of which gives rise to this respect for intangibility of frontiers. Although there is no need, for the purposes of the present case, to show that this is a firmly established principle of international law where decolonization is concerned, the Chamber nonetheless wishes to emphasize its general scope, in view of its exceptional importance for the African continent and for the two Parties. In this connection it should be noted that the principle of *uti possidetis* seems to have been first invoked and applied in Spanish America, inasmuch as this was the continent which first witnessed the phenomenon of decolonization involving the formation of a number of sovereign States on territory formerly belonging to a single metropolitan State. Nevertheless the principle is not a special rule which pertains solely to one specific system of international law. It is a general principle, which is logically connected with the phenomenon of the obtaining of independence, wherever it occurs. Its obvious purpose is to prevent the independence and stability of new States being endangered by fratricidal struggles provoked by the challenging of frontiers following the withdrawal of the administering power. ...

[23] There are several different aspects to this principle, in its well-known application in Spanish America. The first aspect, emphasized by the Latin genitive *juris*, is found in the pre-eminence accorded to legal title over effective possession as a basis of sovereignty. Its purpose, at the time of the achievement of independence by the former Spanish colonies of America, was to scotch any designs which non-American colonizing powers might have on regions which had been assigned by the former metropolitan State to one division or another, but which were still uninhabited or unexplored. However, there is more to the principle of *uti possidetis* than this particular aspect. The essence of the principle lies in its primary aim of securing respect for the territorial boundaries at the moment when independence is achieved. Such territorial boundaries might be no more than delimitations between different administrative divisions or colonies all subject to the same sovereign. In that case, the application of the principle of *uti possidetis* resulted in administrative boundaries being transformed into international frontiers in the full sense of the term. This is true both of the States which took shape in the regions of South America which were dependent on the Spanish Crown, and of the States Parties to the present case, which took shape within the vast territories of French West Africa. *Uti possidetis*, as a principle which upgraded former administrative delimitations, established during the colonial period, to international frontiers, is therefore a principle of a general kind which is logically connected with this form of decolonization wherever it occurs.

[24] The territorial boundaries which have to be respected may also derive from international frontiers, which previously divided a colony of one State from a colony of another, or indeed a colonial territory from the territory of an independent State, or one which was under protectorate, but had retained its international personality. There is no doubt that the obligation to respect pre-existing international frontiers in the event of a State succession derives from a general rule of international law, whether or not the rule is expressed in the formula *uti possidetis*. Hence the numerous solemn affirmations of the intangibility of the frontiers existing at the time of the independence of African States, whether made by senior African statesmen or by organs of the Organization of African Unity itself, are evidently declaratory rather than constitutive: they recognize and confirm an existing principle, and do not seek to consecrate a new principle or the extension to Africa of a rule previously applied only in another continent.

[25] However, it may be wondered how the time-hallowed principle has been able to withstand the new approaches to international law as expressed in Africa, where the successive attainment of independence and the emergence of new States have been accompanied by a certain questioning of traditional international law. At first sight this principle conflicts outright with another one, the right of peoples to self-determination. In fact, however, the maintenance of the territorial status quo in Africa is often seen as the wisest course, to preserve what has been achieved by peoples who have struggled for their independence, and to avoid a disruption which would deprive the continent of the gains achieved by much sacrifice. The essential requirement of stability in order to survive, to develop and gradually to consolidate their independence in all fields, has induced African States judiciously to consent to the respecting of colonial frontiers, and to take account of it in the interpretation of the principle of self-determination of peoples.

[26] Thus the principle of *uti possidetis* has kept its place among the most important legal principles, despite the apparent contradiction which explained its coexistence alongside the new norms. Indeed it was by deliberate choice that African States selected, among all the classic principles, that of *uti possidetis*. This remains an undeniable fact. In the light of the foregoing remarks, it is clear that the applicability of *uti possidetis* in the present case cannot be challenged merely because in 1960, the year when Mali and Burkina Faso achieved independence, the Organization of African Unity which was to proclaim this principle did not yet exist, and the above-mentioned resolution calling for respect for the pre-existing frontiers dates only from 1964. ...

[29] The determination of a frontier line between two States is obviously a matter of international law, but the Parties both recognize also that the question has here to be appraised in the light of French colonial law, "*droit d'outre-mer.*" Since the territories of the two States had been part of French West Africa, the former boundary between them became an international frontier only at the moment when they became independent. The line which the Chamber is required to determine as being that which existed in 1959-1960 was at that time merely the administrative boundary dividing two former French colonies, called *Territoires d'outre-mer* from 1946; as such it had to be defined not according to international law, but according to the French legislation which was applicable to such *territoires*.

[30] One clarification is, however, necessary as concerns the application of French *droit d'outre-mer*. By becoming independent, a new State acquires sovereignty with the territorial base and boundaries left to it by the colonial power. This is part of the ordinary operation of the machinery of State succession. International law—and consequently the principle of *uti possidetis*—applies to the new State (as a State) not with retroactive effect, but immediately and from that moment onwards. It applies to the State *as it is*, i.e., to the "photograph" of the territorial situation then existing.

NOTES

1) The *uti possidetis juris* principle[28] was applied with some clarification by the Chamber of the ICJ in the *Case Concerning the Land, Island and Maritime Frontier (El Salvador/Honduras)*.[29] How would you articulate the meaning of *uti possidetis juris*? Is it, or should it be, restricted to colonial situations? Is it, or should it be, restricted only to situations where new states have a common colonial past? It was the legal opinion of the Arbitration Commission of the Conference on Yugoslavia that *uti possidetis* was the governing principle of international law respecting the boundaries between Croatia and Serbia and between Bosnia-Herzegovina and Serbia.[30]

2) Professor Lalonde, in a detailed examination of *uti possidetis*, directly challenges the conclusions of the Yugoslavia Arbitration Commission. She states:

[T]here appears to be no legal basis for the Arbitration Commission's characterization of *uti posseditis* as a general principle of international law. Not only did the Commission transpose a colonial principle of uncertain status to a radically different situation—the dissolution of a sovereign state—but it also radically transformed the principle.[31]

More generally, Lalonde takes the view that "state practice does not appear to support the claim that it now enjoys the status of a customary rule of international law."[32] She concluded:

If the "colonial *uti possidetis* principle" is to be a guiding principle in resolving current and future territorial disputes, then the basis for its application in such situations must be clarified. *Uti posseditis* represents a valid option, not a binding solution imposed under the mantle of custom.[33]

---

28   See S. Lalonde, *Determining Boundaries in a Conflicted World; The Role of Uti Possidetis* (2002); and Malcolm N. Shaw, "The Heritage of States: The Principle of Uti Possidetis Juris Today" (1996) 67 Brit. Y.B. Int'l L. 75.

29   [1992] I.C.J. Rep. 351.

30   *Opinion No. 3* (1992), 92 I.L.R. 170 (Conference of Yugoslavia, Arbitration Commission, January 11, 1992). See Shaw, *supra* note 28 at 106 and Mathew C. Craven, "The European Community Arbitration Commission on Yugoslavia" (1995) 66 Brit. Y.B. Int'l L. 333.

31   Lalonde, *supra* note 28 at 202.

32   *Ibid.* at 233.

33   *Ibid.* at 240.

2. Territory of Canada

St. Catherines Milling and Lumber Co. v. The Queen
(1887), 13 S.C.R. 577 at 643

[The question before the Court was whether under the *BNA Act, 1867* (now the *Constitution Act, 1867*) some 50,000 square miles of timberland in Ontario belonged to the Province of Ontario or the Dominion of Canada. The lands in question formed part of lands surrendered by an Indian tribe by a treaty to Canada. The excerpt that follows deals with the legal effects of the conquest of Canada by Great Britain and the subsequent cession by France by the Treaty of Paris, 1763.]

TASCHEREAU J.: ... There is no doubt of the correctness of the proposition laid down by the Supreme Court of Louisiana, in *Breaux v. Johns*, "that on the discovery of the American continent the principle was asserted or acknowledged by all European nations, that discovery followed by actual possession gave title to the soil to the Government by whose subjects, or by whose authority, it was made, not only against other European Governments but against the natives themselves. While the different nations of Europe respected the rights (I would say the claims) of the natives as occupants, they all asserted the ultimate dominion and title to the soil to be in the Sovereign." 4 La. An. 141.

That such was the case with the French Government in Canada, during its occupancy thereof, is an incontrovertible fact. The King was vested with the ownership of all the ungranted lands in the colony as part of the crown domain, and royal grant conveyed the full estate and entitled the grantee to possession. The contention, that the royal grants and charters merely asserted a title in the grantees against Europeans or white men, but that they were nothing but blank papers so far as the rights of the natives were concerned, was certainly not then thought of, either in France or in Canada. Neither in the commission or letters patent to the Marquis de la Roche in 1578 and 1598, nor in the charter to the Cent Associés in 1627, nor in the retrocession of the same in 1663, nor in the charter to the West Indies Company in 1664 nor in the retrocession of the same in 1674, by which proprietary Government in Canada came to an end, nor in the six hundred concessions of seigniories extending from the Atlantic to Lake Superior, made by these companies, or by the Kings themselves, nor in any grant of land whatever during the 225 years of the French domination, can be found even an allusion to, or a mention of, the Indian title.

On the contrary, in express terms, de la Roche was authorized to take possession of, and hold as his own property, all lands whatsoever that he might conquer from any one but the allies and confederates of the crown, and, likewise, the charter of the West Indies Company granted them the full ownership of all lands whatsoever, in Canada, which they would conquer, or from which they would drive away the Indians by force of arms. Such was the spirit of all the royal grants of the period. The King granted lands, seigniories, territories, with the understanding that if any of these lands, seigniories, or territories proved to be occupied by aborigines, on the grantees rested

or enter into an agreement

the onus to get rid of them, either by chasing them away by force, or by a more conciliatory policy, as they would think proper. In many instances, no doubt, the grantees, or the King himself, deemed it cheaper or wiser to buy them than to fight them, but that was never construed as a recognition of their right to any legal title whatsoever. The fee and the legal possession were in the King or his grantees.

Now when by the treaty of 1763, France ceded to Great Britain all her rights of sovereignty, property and possession over Canada, and its islands, lands, places and coasts, including, as admitted at the argument, the lands now in controversy, it is unquestionable that the full title to the territory ceded became vested in the new sovereign, and that he thereafter owned it in allodium as part of the crown domain, in as full and ample a manner as the King of France had previously owned it. That it should be otherwise for the lands now in dispute, I cannot see on what principle. To exclude from the full operation of the cession by France all the lands then occupied by the Indians, would be to declare that not an inch of land thereby passed to the King of England, as, at that time, the whole of the unpatented lands of Canada were in their possession in as full and ample a manner as the 57,000 square miles of the territory in dispute can be said to be in possession of the 26,000 Indians who roam over it.

NOTES

1) The assertion, accepted in the above case by the Supreme Court of Canada, that the native peoples of North America possess no stronger right over the lands they inhabit than that of an "occupant" has since undergone significant changes. This is most evident in the Supreme Court of Canada's decision in *Delgamuukw v. British Columbia*.[34] The precise legal status in international law of native lands remains ambiguous. See the discussion of "Agreements with Indigenous Peoples" in Chapter 4, Section A.2(f).

2) The Treaty of Paris, 1763,[35] provided in article IV as follows:

His Most Christian Majesty renounces all pretensions which he has heretofore formed or might have formed to Nova Scotia or Acadia in all its parts, and guaranties the whole of it, and with all its dependencies, to the King of Great Britain: Moreover, his Most Christian Majesty cedes and guaranties to his said Britannick Majesty, in full right, Canada, with all its dependencies, as well as the island of Cape Breton and all the other islands and coasts in the gulph and river of St. Lawrence, and in general, every thing that depends on the said countries, lands, islands, and coasts, with the sovereignty, property, possession, and all rights acquired by treaty, or otherwise, which the Most Christian King and the Crown of France have had till now over the said countries, lands, islands, places, coasts, and their inhabitants, so that the Most Christian King cedes and makes over the whole to the said King, and to the Crown of Great Britain, and that in the most ample manner and form, without restriction, and without any liberty to depart from the said cession and guaranty

---

34 [1997] 3 S.C.R. 1010.

35 Canada, Parliament, "Documents Relating to the Constitutional History of Canada" by Adam Shortt & Arthur G. Doughty in *Sessional Papers*, No. 7 (1906-7) 73 at 85.

under any pretence, or to disturb Great Britain in the possessions above mentioned. His Britannick Majesty, on his side, agrees to grant the liberty of the Catholick religion to the inhabitants of Canada: he will, in consequence, give the most precise and most effectual orders, that his new Roman Catholic subjects may profess the worship of their religion according to the rites of the Romish church, as far as the laws of Great Britain permit. His Britannick Majesty farther agrees, that the French inhabitants, or others who had been subjects of the Most Christian King in Canada, may retire with all safety and freedom wherever they shall think proper, and may sell their estates, provided it be to the subjects of his Britannick Majesty, and bring away their effects as well as their persons, without being restrained in their emigration, under any pretence whatsoever, except that of debts or of criminal prosecutions: The term limited for this emigration shal be fixed to the space of eighteen months, to be computed from the day of the exchange of the ratification of the present treaty.

3) In the absence of treaty arrangements between the predecessor and the successor states, the effects on nationality of succession to territory are uncertain. Questions of state succession, including change of nationality, are considered in Chapter 2, Section D.

Newfoundland[36]

The problems involved in the union of Newfoundland to Canada have had a long history. Delegates from Newfoundland participated in the conference at Quebec in 1864 when the broad outlines of Confederation were laid, but Newfoundland declined to enter union some five years later when the Confederation Party was defeated at the polls. The door, however, always remained open, section 146 of the *BNA Act, 1867* (now the *Constitution Act, 1867*) providing for the entry at any time of Newfoundland, as well as of Prince Edward Island and British Columbia, on such terms and conditions as might mutually be agreed. Canadian policy throughout the years always was that the first move must come from Newfoundland. Following a financial collapse in 1894, overtures for union were made by Newfoundland, but negotiations broke down over financial terms, and no further formal moves toward union were made till 1947.

On March 20, 1947, the Governor of Newfoundland, on behalf of the Newfoundland National Convention, asked the Government of Canada whether it would receive a delegation to ascertain what fair and equitable basis might exist for the federal union of Newfoundland with Canada. The Canadian Government agreed and in June 1947 a delegation from the Convention came to Ottawa. Meetings with a Committee of the Cabinet continued till September. On October 29, 1947, the Prime Minister of Canada sent to the Governor of Newfoundland, for transmission to the National Convention, a statement of terms believed to constitute a fair and equitable basis of union, should the people of Newfoundland desire to enter into Confederation.

---

36   (1949) 1 *External Affairs* at 3-8 and *Terms of Union of Newfoundland with Canada*, Schedule to the *Newfoundland Act (U.K.)*, 12 & 13 Geo. VI, 1949, c. 22. See also Department of External Affairs, *Report and Documents Relating to the Negotiations for the Union of Newfoundland with Canada* (1949) (Conference Series 1948, No. 2).

The statement of terms submitted by the Canadian Government was debated at length in the Newfoundland National Convention and during the campaigns for the two referenda that followed.

In the first referendum, held on June 3, 1948, three options were before the people: continuation of commission of government, confederation, and restoration of responsible government. In round numbers, the vote was about 22,000 for commission of government, about 64,000 for Confederation, and about 69,400 for responsible government. In accordance with the conditions announced in advance, no proposed form of government having received a majority, a second referendum was required on the two leading forms.

In the second referendum, held on July 22, 1948, Confederation received a majority of about 7,000 votes and a majority of 18 of the 25 electoral districts. In a statement issued on July 30, the Prime Minister of Canada said the result was "clear beyond all possibility of misunderstanding" and that the Government would be glad to receive with the least possible delay authorized representatives of Newfoundland "to negotiate the terms of union" on the basis of his letter of October 29, 1947 to the Governor of Newfoundland, and the document transmitted with it. A delegation was shortly thereafter appointed by the Governor of Newfoundland, and arrived in Ottawa on October 6, 1948, where negotiations were begun with a committee of the Cabinet.

On December 11, 1948, A Memorandum of Agreement was entered into between Canada and Newfoundland. The signature took place in the Senate Chamber in Ottawa. The terms of union were approved by the Canadian Parliament and the Newfoundland Commission of Government, and confirmed by the United Kingdom Parliament. Formal Union took place on March 31, 1949.

Arctic Islands

There is no debate that the islands of the Arctic archipelago are Canadian. With the exception of the minuscule Hans Island between Ellesmere Island and Greenland contested by Denmark,[37] there is no challenge by any other state that the Arctic Islands are unquestionably under the sovereignty of Canada. Canadian sovereignty over the Arctic Islands is not subject to being lost or diminished by any action or inaction on the part of the government of Canada or the three northern territories.

In 1870 Canada acquired from the Hudson's Bay Company "Rupert's Land and the North-Western Territory," which includes part of Baffin Island and areas adjacent to the now northern boundaries of Manitoba and Saskatchewan.[38] In 1880, through a U.K. Order-in-Council, confirmed by the 1895 *Imperial Colonial Boundaries Act*, "all British possessions on the American continent not hitherto annexed to any colony" that were British (primarily the Arctic islands) were transferred to Canada.[39] Throughout this

---

37   See text *supra* at note 15.

38   Item 3 of the Schedule to the *Constitution Act, 1982*, being Schedule B to the *Canada Act 1982* (U.K.), 1982, c. 11 is the "Order of Her Majesty in Council admitting Rupert's Land and the North-Western Territory into the union, dated the 23rd day of June, 1870."

39   Item 8, *ibid.* is the " Order of Her Majesty in Council admitting all British possessions and Territories in North America and islands adjacent thereto into the Union, dated the 31st day of July, 1880."

period and during the next few decades there were a number of Canadian expeditions to the Arctic. As well there were expeditions by the United States and Norway. A Norwegian expedition headed by Otto Sverdup from 1898 to 1902 resulted in Norwegian territorial claims to all or part of Cornwallis Island, Devon Island, and other areas (approximately 100,000 square miles). "The Norwegian claim was not withdrawn until 1930, when it was abandoned on Canada's agreeing to pay the costs of the Sverdrup expedition."[40]

Other issues regarding Canada's Arctic are discussed below.

Frontiers of Canada[41]

Since Newfoundland joined the Union in 1949, all of Canada's land frontiers are with the United States of America. From Passamaquoddy Bay, bordered by New Brunswick and Maine, to the Straits of Juan de Fuca, bordered by British Columbia and Washington, the Canada–United States boundary runs for 3,987 miles, over half of which (2,198 miles) is water boundary. The Alaska–Canada boundary of 1,540 miles runs from Portland Canal on the Pacific Ocean to the Arctic Ocean near the mouth of the Mackenzie River. Difficulties have naturally arisen over boundaries between the two countries, but have always been settled by peaceful means in accord with the spirit of the Treaty of Ghent of December 24, 1814 that "there shall be a firm and universal peace between His Britannic Majesty and the United States."

Several maritime boundaries of Canada remain unsettled—for example, in the Beaufort Sea and the Dixon Entrance. These matters are examined in Chapter 13, Section D on the "Law of the Sea." Canada's Arctic frontiers are discussed below.

In the course of the constitutional debate about the relationship between the Province of Quebec and Canada, the question of boundaries was raised should Quebec acquire the status of a sovereign independent state. The representatives of the Quebec government have on many occasions asserted the right of Quebec to its present boundaries.

A contrary opinion with respect to an independent Quebec has been advanced by some commentators and by speakers for the native peoples of the Province. According to their view, the territories in the north, attached to Quebec by federal Acts of 1898 and 1912 (representing approximately two-thirds of Quebec's land mass) and populated largely by aboriginals, should remain part of Canada in the event of Quebec's separation. An additional possibility of altering the boundaries of an independent Quebec could be based on the right to self-determination for the identifiable minorities living in Quebec.

International law, in particular the *uti possidetis juris* concept, appears to support the position of the Province of Quebec. Professor Lalonde, in her detailed study of *uti possidetis*, is not supportive of the principle being applicable to Quebec. She takes the view that expert opinion given to the Commission on the Future of Quebec on *uti*

---

40   N. L. Nicholson, *The Boundaries of the Canadian Confederation* (1979) at 66.

41   For a more detailed account of the treaties relevant to Canada's land frontiers, see J.-G. Castel, *International Law: Chiefly as Interpreted and Applied in Canada*, 3d ed. (1976) at 217 ff. See also P. E. Corbett, *The Settlement of Canadian-American Disputes* (1937, reprinted 1970); A. Poole, "The Boundaries of Canada" (1964) 42 Can. Bar. Rev. 100; and Nicholson, *supra* note 40.

possidetis was flawed.[42] Note that the international law of state secession is also relevant. Regarding the self-determination argument by identifiable minorities living in Quebec, it is debatable how strong their international law claim is, given the Supreme Court of Canada's determination that Quebec has no right at international law to exercise self-determination.[43]

C. ARCTIC AND ANTARCTIC AREAS

1. The Arctic[44]

Beyond the superficial commonality of climate, there is very little in common between the Arctic and Antarctic areas. Antarctica is a continent with a surrounding ocean area. The Arctic area is dominated by the Arctic Ocean with surrounding land areas (Canada, Greenland (Denmark), Norway, the Russian Federation, and the United States). The international law applicable to the Arctic area is primarily that of the law of the sea (see generally Chapter 13). The international law applicable to Antarctica is based primarily in the Antarctic Treaty of December 1, 1959[45] and related agreements. While the Antarctic Treaty creates the framework for state interaction in Antarctica, there is no such arrangement in the Arctic. The only pan-Arctic body is the Arctic Council created pursuant to the 1996 Declaration on the Establishment of the Arctic Council.[46] The Arctic Council, a non-treaty based international organization, is a consulting mechanism for environmental and other Arctic matters.

Legal Status of the Arctic Regions
by D. Pharand (1979) 163 Hague Recueil 51

[While sovereignty over the land territory in the Arctic is no longer in dispute, potentially controversial issues remain unresolved. They include the limits of the continental shelf of Arctic states; the scope of Canada's jurisdiction over the waters of its archipelago; and the nature of control Canada is entitled to exercise over the straits constituting the Northwest Passage. Professor Pharand surveys these and other issues:[47]]

---

42   Lalonde, *supra* note 28 at 222 and generally at 203-22.

43   *Reference Re Secession of Quebec*, [1998] 2 S.C.R. 217; 161 D.L.R. (4th) 385, reproduced in Chapter 2, Section D.4(b).

44   D. Pharand, *The Law of the Sea and the Arctic* (1973); D. Pharand (with L. H. Legault), *The Northwest Passage: Arctic Straits* (1984); D. Pharand, *Canada's Arctic Waters in International Law* (1988); E. Francks, *Maritime Claims in the Arctic* (1993); and D. R. Rothwell, *The Polar Regions and the Development of International Law* (1996).

45   402 U.N.T.S. 71 (in force since 1961) and see next subsection.

46   See the Arctic Council website at <http://www.arctic-council.org>. Note also the comments in Chapter 13, Section E, under subheading "Pollution Prevention in Arctic Waters."

47   See also D. Pharand, "The Legal Regime of the Arctic: Some Outstanding Issues" (1984) 39 Int'l J. 742.

There is no longer any question as to territorial sovereignty in the Arctic, but since jurisdiction on the continental shelf depends on territorial sovereignty, it is necessary to know exactly who owns what before attacking the problems relating to the continental shelf. ... There can be no doubt today that the Soviet Union has complete sovereignty over all of the islands north of its wide-ranging coast. ...

Legal Status of the Arctic Ocean

Except for the presence of ice floes on top of its waters, the Arctic Ocean is like any other ocean. The possibility of exercising the freedom of the seas, particularly the freedom of navigation, exists to a considerable degree already. Most of the other freedoms of the seas are also exercised, namely, the freedom of overflight, the freedom of fishing and the freedom of scientific research. The freedom to lay submarine cables and pipelines has not yet been exercised, but with the improved knowledge of the sea floor and of technology, that possibility certainly exists. In these circumstances, the waters of the Arctic Ocean must be considered as high seas, as in any other ocean.

The attitude of virtually all Arctic States has been in accord with the above conclusion. American submarines, icebreakers, aircraft and scientists on drifting ice stations, are all evidence that the United States considers the Arctic Ocean as high seas and open to all nations. As for the Soviet Union, it has been engaged in similar activities (especially marine scientific research) all over the Arctic Ocean for more than 25 years and, in spite of the opinion of some of its jurists to the contrary, it must be taken to subscribe to the freedom of the seas in the Arctic Ocean.

Canada has occasionally expressed doubt as to the status of the Arctic Ocean as high seas, particularly the Beaufort Sea, when discussing the status of the Northwest Passage. However, Canada's recent exploration of the Lomonosov Ridge by a group of scientists, installed on an ice floe floating across different sectors of the Arctic Ocean, would seem to indicate that it no longer believes, if it ever did, that the freedom of the seas is not applicable. ...

Legal Status of Ice Islands

Considering the extensive use being made of ice islands for marine scientific research, as well as a limited use for the exploration of the continental shelf, it would be preferable that they be submitted to some legal régime. This preference becomes apparent when ice islands, such as those of the Soviet Union, drift close to the coasts of other States. In such a case, the activities carried on aboard the ice island might understandably become of concern to the coastal State. More specifically, the latter might wish to verify the exact nature of the activities carried on, to ensure that its security and other national interests are not being affected.

The question of the legal status of ice islands is of comparatively recent origin, and no customary international law has yet developed through the practice of States. ...

Air Space over Arctic Lands and Islands

Since territorial sovereignty is now well established in the Arctic, the five Arctic States have complete and exclusive sovereignty over the air space above their respective territories. This includes sovereignty over Svalbard in favour of Norway, in spite of the limitations contained in the 1920 Treaty, since those limitations do not affect Norwegian sovereignty as such and, therefore, it extends to the air space above the archipelago. In other words, there is no more freedom of overflight over the Arctic territories and territorial waters than there is over territories situated anywhere else. ...

Air Space over the Arctic Ocean

It follows logically from what has been said already about the air space over the lands and islands, the shelf and the economic zone, that freedom of overflight exists all over the waters of the Arctic Ocean beyond the territorial sea. It was suggested by a few jurists, back in the 1930s, in particular by the Soviet writer, Lakhtine, that because of the presence of the ice cover, Arctic States should have complete sovereignty over their respective sectors, including the air space. With the advance in technology and knowledge of the precise physical character of the Arctic Ocean, this has not been suggested in recent years. And, indeed, the attitude of the various Arctic States has been to respect the freedom of overflight. This freedom has been respected, not only over the Arctic Ocean generally, but over the ice islands as well, even when they were occupied. For instance, American aircraft have flown over ice islands occupied by Soviet scientists and vice versa.

Air Space over the Northeast and Northwest Passages

Since those Passages are not used presently for international navigation, there would be no freedom of overflight where there is an overlap of territorial waters in those straits. In the Northeast Passage, this would apply to the Vilkitsky Straits, south of Severnaya Zemlya, linking the Kara and Laptev Seas. Those straits are approximately 22½ and 11 miles wide. ... As for the Northwest Passage, there would be no freedom of overflight in Barrow Strait, where a small group of islands narrows the Passage to about 15 miles wide.

Canada and Arctic Waters

As already noted, there is no question of Canada's sovereignty over the islands of the Canadian Arctic. The central legal question for Canada is the nature of its claim respecting both the waters interlocking the Arctic Islands and the ocean area seaward of the Arctic archipelago.

Seaward of Canada's Arctic archipelago into the Arctic Ocean, Canada has put in place a 200 nautical mile exclusive economic zone[48] (see Chapter 13, Section B.4). There is also the 1970 *Arctic Waters Pollution Prevention Act*[49] that applies to vessel traffic in the waters interlocking the Arctic Islands and within a zone to a distance from land of 100 nautical miles (see Chapter 13, Section E.2).

---

48 *Oceans Act*, S.C. 1996, c. 31, s. 13.

49 R.S.C. 1985, c. A-12.

As regards the continental shelf beyond the EEZ in the Arctic Ocean, there is reason to believe that Canada may make use of the Law of the Sea Convention, article 76, and set the outer limit of the continental shelf well beyond 200 nautical miles in some places (see Chapter 13, Section B.5). It is also reasonable to expect that Greenland (Denmark) will be able to establish its outer limit of the continental shelf well beyond 200 nautical miles. Whether the continental shelf under the North Pole would come under Canadian or Greenland (Denmark) jurisdiction is yet to be established.

The so-called sector theory of allocation of the Arctic Ocean based on meridians of longitude extending from the North Pole south to the most easterly and westerly points on the Arctic Circle of a state, first propounded in 1907 by a Canadian Senator, has long been fixated in the Canadian imagination. However, it is hard to track official government of Canada use of the Sector Theory as a basis for claimed authority over land or water in the Arctic. The unquestioned application of the international law of the sea to the Arctic Ocean by all Arctic states, including Canada, renders the Sector Theory legally defunct.[50]

The legal status of the waters within the Arctic Island archipelago engages numerous law of the sea matters: historic waters (see Chapter 13, Section B.2); straight baselines (see Chapter 13, Section B.1(a)); innocent passage rights (see Chapter 13, Section B.1(c)); and whether the Northwest Passage constitutes a strait used for international navigation (see Chapter 13, Section B.3).

In the aftermath of the controversial voyage of the U.S. Coast Guard icebreaker *Polar Sea* through the Canadian Arctic waters, in August 1985, Prime Minister Brian Mulroney unequivocally asserted Canada's sovereignty over the Northwest Passage and the waters of the Arctic archipelago: "There is no doubt that the Northwest Passage and that part of the world belongs to Canada. It is ours. We assert our sovereignty over it should there be a suggestion to the contrary by anyone, that would be an unfriendly act, and so construed by the government of Canada."[51]

While the U.S. authorities informed the Government of Canada that the voyage would be undertaken, they did not request Canadian permission. The reason lies in the U.S. view that the Northwest Passage is a "strait used for international navigation" and, as a consequence, vessel passage does not require the permission of the adjacent state (here Canada). The United States did not deny that the waters of the Canadian Arctic are Canadian; rather, it asserted that the jurisdiction Canada could exercise over those waters was limited by the fact that the Northwest Passage was an international strait.

Shortly thereafter, Joe Clark, Secretary of State for External Affairs, speaking in the House of Commons on September 10, 1985, announced a new policy of Canada for its Arctic waters. He said, *inter alia*:[52]

> The voyage of the *Polar Sea* demonstrated that Canada, in the past, had not developed the means to ensure our sovereignty over time. ... I wish to declare to the House the policy of this government in respect of Canadian sovereignty in Arctic waters, ... Canada's

---

50   On the sector theory, see Pharand, *Canada's Arctic Waters, supra* note 44 at 1-87.

51   "Our Arctic Claim Not in Doubt: PM" *The Montreal Gazette* (23 August 1985), B.1.

52   External Affairs Canada, *Statements and Speeches* (1985) No. 85/7. See T.L. McDorman, "In the Wake of the 'Polar Sea': Canadian Jurisdiction and the Northwest Passage" (1986) 27 C. de D. 623.

sovereignty in the Arctic is indivisible. It embraces land, sea, and ice. It extends without interruption to the seaward-facing coasts of the Arctic islands. These islands are joined and not divided by the waters between them. They are bridged for most of the year by ice. From time immemorial Canada's Inuit people have used and occupied the ice as they have used and occupied the land. The policy of this government is to maintain the natural unity of the Canadian Arctic archipelago, and to preserve Canada's sovereignty over land, sea, and ice undiminished and undivided. That sovereignty has long been upheld by Canada. No previous government, however, has defined its precise limits or delineated Canada's internal waters and territorial sea in the Arctic. This government proposes to do so.

The Minister for External Affairs announced a number of measures designed to implement the new policy, including (1) immediate adoption of an Order-in-Council establishing straight baselines around the Arctic archipelago, with effect from January 1, 1986 (see following map), and (2) enactment of a *Canadian Laws Offshore Application Act* designed to extend the application of federal and provincial laws to offshore areas around all the coasts of Canada to the full extent permitted under international law. The intended act was eventually passed in 1990 and subsequently was incorporated in the *Oceans Act*.[53]

On January 11, 1988, Canada and the United States concluded an agreement on "Arctic Cooperation." The United States pledged that "all navigation by United States icebreakers within waters claimed by Canada to be internal will be undertaken with the consent of the Government of Canada." However, the two parties agreed that "[n]othing in this agreement ... nor any practice thereunder affects the respective positions of the Governments of the United States and of Canada on the Law of the Sea in this or other maritime areas or their respective positions regarding third parties."[54]

In 2002 Canada's jurisdiction in Arctic waters was publicly summarized by two members of the Department of Foreign Affairs as follows.[55]

It is Canada's position that straight baselines drawn around the perimeter of the Arctic archipelago constitute the outer limits of its internal waters. Canada's full sovereignty over these waters, including the Northwest Passage, is based on historic title and no right of passage is therefore recognized. Further strengthening Canada's sovereignty position is the ongoing use and occupation of the covering ice by its Inuit people "*from time immemorial*."

... Assuming for a moment that Canada's position is not supportable on grounds of historic title alone, the question then arises whether the Northwest Passage constitutes a strait used for international navigation and by extension a right of transit passage exists. Determining whether a waterway constitutes a strait used for international navigation is a complicated question of fact dependent, among other things, on whether the waterway has been used for international shipping. Most observers would be hard-pressed to make such

---

53 *Territorial Sea Geographical Coordinates (Area 7) Order*, S.O.R./1985-872, originally made pursuant to the *Territorial Sea and Fishing Zones Act*, R.S.C. 1985, c. T-8, s. 5(1), but now subsumed under the *Oceans Act*, S.C. 1996, c. 31, reported in Chapter 13, Section B.1(e) on "Exercise of Jurisdiction by Canada."

54 (1989) 28 I.L.M. 142. See F. Mathys, "Accord de cooperation dans l'Arctique entre le Canada et les Etas-Unis d'Amerique" (1987) 25 Can. Y.B. Int'l L. 345.

55 Reproduced in "Canadian Practice at the Department of Foreign Affairs in 2001-2" (2002) 40 Can. Y.B. Int'l L. 469 at 496-98 (footnotes deleted).

The Canadian Arctic

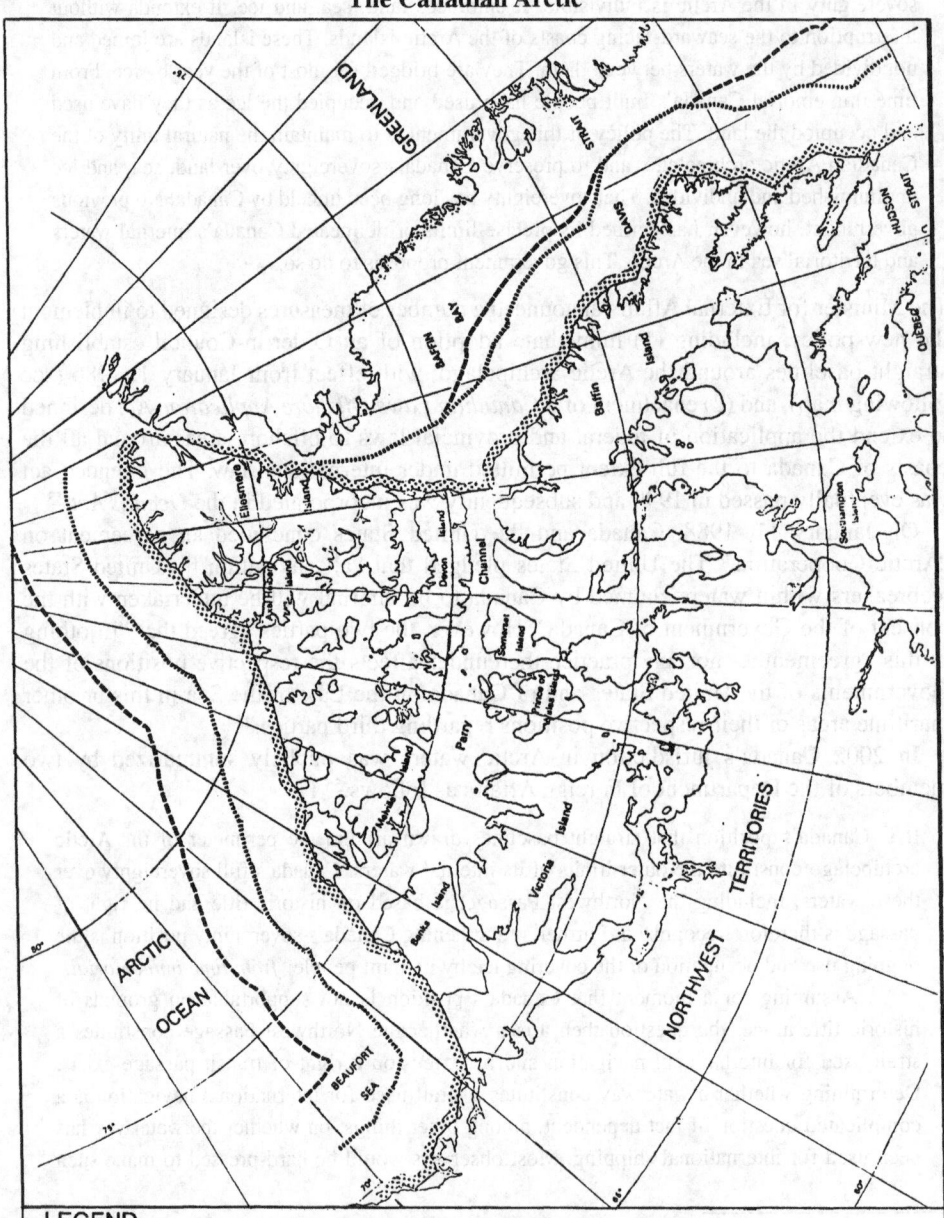

LEGEND
▪▪▪▪▪▪ 200-mile Fishing Zone
░░░░░░░ 100-mile Pollution Prevention Zone
▩▩▩▩▩▩ 12-mile Territorial Sea
———— Straight Baselines
NOTE: All waters within the straight baselines are internal waters of Canada.
Reproduced from the Government of Canada.

an assertion, notwithstanding sporadic voyages by United States vessels through the Passage. In this regard, the controversial 1969-1970 passage of the American tanker *Manhattan* and the 1985 voyage of the United States Coast Guard icebreaker *Polar Sea* sparked a public debate over whether the federal government was doing enough to prevent internationalization of the Northwest Passage and preserve Canada's sovereignty in the Canadian Arctic.

The Agreement reached between the Canadian and United States governments in the aftermath of the *Polar Sea*'s transit seeks to preserve each side's position on the status of the Northwest Passage—namely the Canadian position that it is not a strait used for international navigation and the United States' position that it is—while providing a practical way for United States ship traffic to utilize the Passage." ...

Beyond the issue of sovereignty, the most obvious practical significance of whether the Passage is internal waters or a strait used for international navigation is what means are employed to protect the Arctic marine environment. As internal waters, there is no question that Canadian environmental law, including the *Arctic Waters Pollution Prevention Act* and associated regulations, would apply to vessels utilizing the Passage, whether or not it is ice covered. As a strait used for international navigation, it is quite likely that this legislation and consequential regulations would govern vessel traffic transiting the Passage as long as ice cover remains most of the year. Article 234 of the *United Nations Law of the Sea Convention* gives coastal states the right to protect areas within their exclusive economic zones that are ice covered for most of the year, where the climactic conditions are particularly severe, there are navigational hazards created by the ice, and pollution would cause irreversible environmental damage.

NOTES

1) How strong is Canada's case that the waters of the Arctic archipelago are historic internal waters?[56]

2) The United States has protested Canada's proclaimed Arctic straight baselines.[57] The complaint is with the alleged excessive length of some of the straight line segments and that the baselines are not congruent with the general direction of the coastline. Reviewing the international law on straight baselines set out in Chapter 13, Section B.1(a), are the baselines legally valid?

3) Is the Northwest Passage a "strait used for international navigation"? Refer to Chapter 13, Section B.3.

4) Concerns about the thinning Arctic ice cap and the possibility of increased international vessel passage through the Northwest Passage has raised questions about the sustainability of Canada's legal claims regarding its Arctic waters. Some of the debate has been in terms of reduced or lost sovereignty, thus raising fears that the Arctic waters (and to some uninformed commentators even the Arctic islands) may somehow be lost by

---

56 See Pharand, *Canada's Arctic Waters*, *supra* note 44 at 91-125.

57 See J.A. Roach & R. W. Smith, *United States Responses to Excessive Maritime Claims*, 2d ed. (1996) at 117-21.

Canada.[58] The discussants really question whether the increase in traffic will affect Canada's legal claims respecting jurisdiction over the Arctic waters. What effect might increased international vessel passage through the Northwest Passage have on Canada's jurisdiction over the waters of the Arctic archipelago?

2. Antarctica[59]

The present legal regime of the vast, ice-covered continent of Antarctica is based on the Antarctic Treaty of December 1, 1959.[60] From the original 12 signatories,[61] designated in the Treaty as Consultative Parties, the number of states parties had grown to 45 (including Canada since 1988). Seventeen of these parties, in addition to the original signatories, have been accorded the privileged status of Consultative Parties, who are the only ones under the Treaty allowed to vote on policy matters. Seven of the original parties— Argentina, Australia, Chile, France, New Zealand, Norway, and the United Kingdom— have territorial claims in Antarctica (see following map). Australia's claim is the largest, covering approximately two-fifths of the continent (2,300,000 square miles). The shape of the territorial claims is influenced by the so-called sector theory, once popular in the Arctic, with pie-shaped slices of sectors following longitudinal coordinates from the South Pole to a line near 60 degrees south latitude. The legal basis of the claims of the various state claimants differs: some rely on a combination of discovery, exploration, and even "effective occupation," and others on the principles of contiguity and the sector theory. Belgium, Japan, South Africa, Russia, and the United States, all original Consultative Parties, have no territorial claims of their own and have consistently refused to recognize such claims advanced by other states. The claims of Argentina, Chile, and the United Kingdom overlap (in regard to Graham Land and neighbouring islands), while a relatively large sector of the continent remains unclaimed. In view of their pre-eminent role in the exploration of Antarctica, the position of the United States and Russia is bound to have a significant bearing on the future legal regime of the region.

---

58   See Rob Huebert, "The Shipping News Part II: How Canada's Arctic Sovereignty is on Thinning Ice" (2003) 58 Int. J. 295; Franklyn Griffiths, "The Shipping News: Canada's Arctic Sovereignty Not on Thinning Ice" (2003) 58 Int. J. 257; C. Anderson, "Global Warming and Canada's Shipping Lanes: An Oceanographer's View" (2003) 17 Ocean Yrbk 563; H. Hengeveld, "Climate Change and Canada's Shipping Lanes: The Background Science" (2003) 17 Ocean Y.B. 580; and D. M. Johnson, "The Future of the Arctic Ocean: Competing Domains of International Public Policy" (2003) 17 Ocean Y.B. 596.

59   See generally Rothwell, *supra* note 44; E.J. Sahurie, *The International Law of Antarctica* (1992); A. Watts, *International Law and the Antarctic Treaty System* (1992); Joyner, *supra* note 6. See also the website maintained by the Antarctic Treaty Secretariat at <http://www.ats.org.ar.>.

60   402 U.N.T.S. 71 (in force since 1961). See F.M. Auburn, *Antarctic Law and Politics* (1982); W.M. Bush, *Antarctica and International Law: A Collection of Inter-State and National Documents* (1991) 4 vols. A continuation of bound volumes published 1982-1988; C.C. Joyner & S.K. Chopra, eds., *The Antarctic Legal Regime* (1988); Sahurie, *ibid.*; D. Pharand, "L'Arctique et l'Antarctique: Patrimonie Commun de l'Humanite?" (1982) 7 Annals Air & Space L. 415; and K.M. Shusterich, "The Antarctic Treaty System: History, Substance, and Speculation" (1984) 39 Int. J. 800.

61   The original signatories are Argentina, Australia, Belgium, Chile, France, Japan, New Zealand, Norway, South Africa, U.S.S.R. (now the Russian Federation), United Kingdom, and the United States.

Antarctica

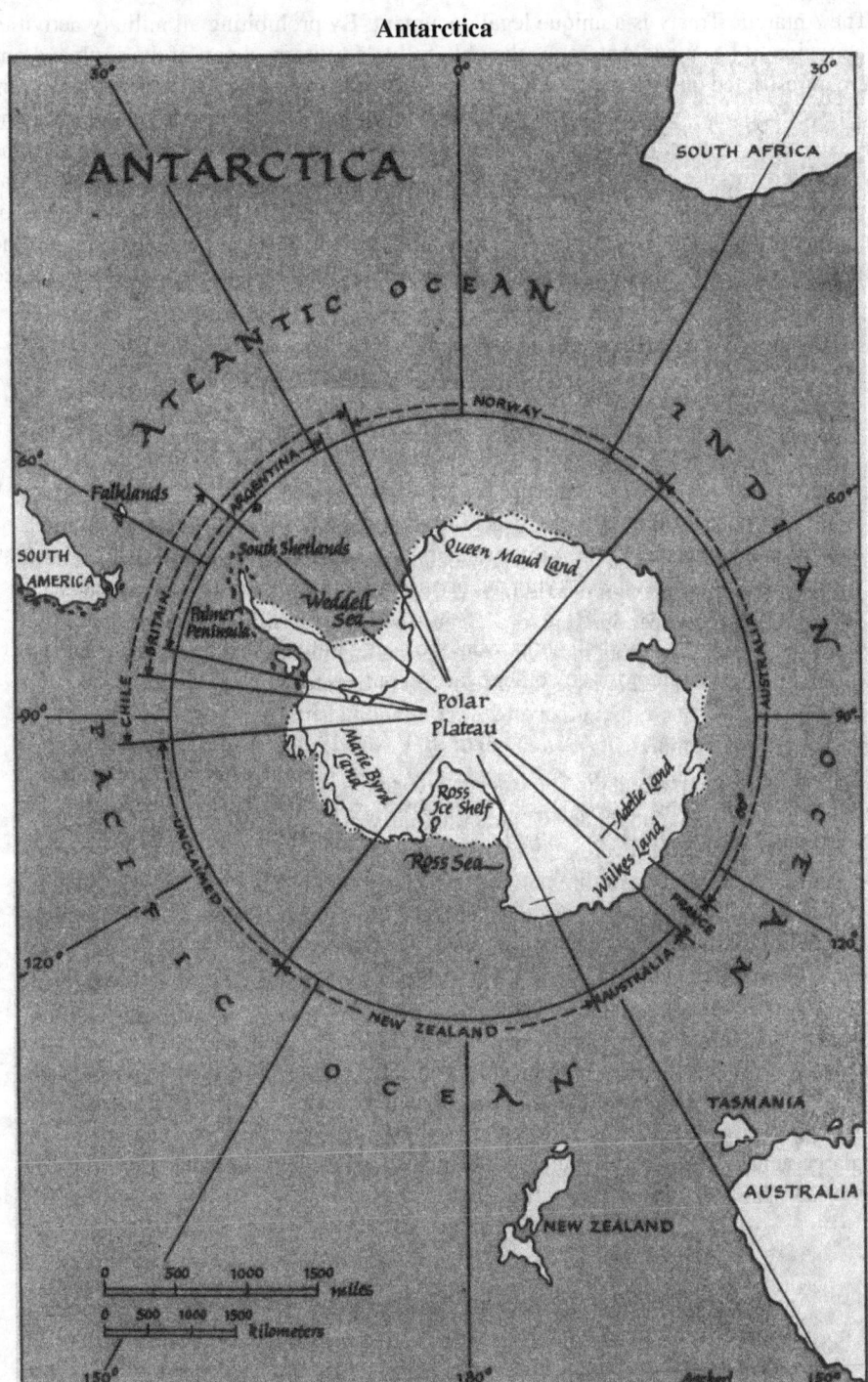

Reproduced from (1984), 62 *Foreign Affairs* 1176 (Part II).

The Antarctic Treaty is a unique legal document. By prohibiting all military activities in the region, it has made Antarctica the only fully demilitarized part of the earth and one where unrestricted on-site inspection is in force. It is also the only multilateral agreement that has effectively suspended, for an indefinite period, the final determination of the legal status of national claims to sovereignty over an entire continent. Despite the unsettled territorial claims, no significant conflict involving the contracting parties has occurred during the years since the signing of the Treaty. In the 1980s, the issue of changing the legal status of Antarctica by a new treaty to make the whole continent the common heritage of mankind was mooted. However, the original treaty was extended unchanged at a review conference in 1991.

The Antarctic Treaty
(1959) 402 U.N.T.S. 71

Article I

1. Antarctica shall be used for peaceful purposes only. There shall be prohibited, *inter alia*, any measures of a military nature, such as the establishment of military bases and fortifications, the carrying out of military manoeuvres, as well as the testing of any type of weapons.

2. The present Treaty shall not prevent the use of military personnel or equipment for scientific research or for any other peaceful purpose. ...

Article IV

1. Nothing contained in the present Treaty shall be interpreted as:

(a) a renunciation by any Contracting Party of previously asserted rights of or claims to territorial sovereignty in Antarctica;

(b) a renunciation or diminution by any Contracting Party of any basis of claim to territorial sovereignty in Antarctica which it may have whether as a result of its activities or those of its nationals in Antarctica, or otherwise;

(c) prejudicing the position of any Contracting Party as regards its recognition or non-recognition of any other State's right of or claim or basis of claim to territorial sovereignty in Antarctica.

2. No acts or activities taking place while the present Treaty is in force shall constitute a basis for asserting, supporting or denying a claim to territorial sovereignty in Antarctica or create any rights of sovereignty in Antarctica. No new claim, or enlargement of an existing claim, to territorial sovereignty in Antarctica shall be asserted while the present Treaty is in force.

Article V

1. Any nuclear explosions in Antarctica and the disposal there of radioactive waste material shall be prohibited.

2. In the event of the conclusion of international agreements concerning the use of nuclear energy, including nuclear explosions and the disposal of radioactive waste material, to which all the Contracting Parties whose representatives are entitled to

participate in the meetings provided for under Article IX are parties, the rules established under such agreements shall apply in Antarctica.

Article VI

The provisions of the present Treaty shall apply to the area south of 60° South Latitude, including all ice shelves, but nothing in the present Treaty shall prejudice or in any way affect the rights, or the exercise of the rights of any State under international law with regard to the high seas within that area.

Article VII

1. In order to promote the objectives and ensure the observance of the provisions of the present Treaty, each Contracting Party whose representatives are entitled to participate in the meetings referred to in Article IX of the Treaty shall have the right to designate observers to carry out any inspection provided for by the present Article. Observers shall be nationals of the Contracting Parties which designate them. The names of observers shall be communicated to every other Contracting Party having the right to designate observers; and like notice shall be given of the termination of their appointment.

2. Each observer designated in accordance with the provisions of paragraph 1 of this Article shall have complete freedom of access at any time to any or all areas of Antarctica.

3. All areas of Antarctica, including all stations, installations and equipment within those areas, and all ships and aircraft at points of discharging or embarking cargoes or personnel in Antarctica, shall be open at all times to inspection by any observers designated in accordance with paragraph 1 of this Article.

4. Aerial observation may be carried out at any time over any or all areas of Antarctica by any of the Contracting Parties having the right to designate observers. ...

Article IX

1. Representatives of the Contracting Parties named in the preamble to the present Treaty shall meet at the City of Canberra within two months after the date of entry into force of the Treaty, and thereafter at suitable intervals, and places, for the purpose of exchanging information, consulting together on matters of common interest pertaining to Antarctica, and formulating and considering, and recommending to their Governments, measures in furtherance of the principles and objectives of the Treaty. ...

2. Each Contracting Party which has become a party to the present Treaty by accession under Article XIII shall be entitled to appoint representatives to participate in the meetings referred to in paragraph 1 of the present Article, during such time as that Contracting Party demonstrates its interest in Antarctica by conducting substantial scientific research activity there, such as the establishment of a scientific station or the despatch of a scientific expedition. ...

Article XII

1.(a) The present Treaty may be modified or amended at any time by unanimous agreement of the Contracting Parties whose representatives are entitled to participate in the meetings provided for under Article IX. Any such modification or amendment shall enter into force when the depositary Government has received notice from all such Contracting Parties that they have ratified it.

(b) Such modification or amendment shall thereafter enter into force as to any other Contracting Party when notice of ratification by it has been received by the depositary Government. Any such Contracting Party from which no notice of ratification is received within a period of two years from the date of entry into force of the modification or amendment in accordance with the provisions of subparagraph 1(a) of this Article shall be deemed to have withdrawn from the present Treaty on the date of the expiration of such period.

2.(a) If after the expiration of thirty years from the date of entry into force of the present Treaty, any of the Contracting Parties whose representatives are entitled to participate in the meetings provided for under Article IX so requests by a communication addressed to the depositary Government, a Conference of all the Contracting Parties shall be held as soon as practicable to review the operation of the Treaty.

(b) Any modification or amendment to the present Treaty which is approved at such a Conference by a majority of the Contracting Parties there represented, including a majority of those whose representatives are entitled to participate in the meetings provided for under Article IX, shall be communicated by the depositary Government to all the Contracting Parties immediately after the termination of the Conference and shall enter into force in accordance with the provisions of paragraph 1 of the present Article.

NOTES

1) Subsequent to the conclusion of the Antarctic Treaty, three additional multilateral agreements regulating the activities within the region have been opened for signature— the Convention for the Conservation of Antarctic Seals (June 1, 1972),[62] the Convention on the Conservation of Antarctic Marine Living Resources (May 20, 1980),[63] and the Protocol on Environmental Protection to the Antarctic Treaty (October 4, 1991), with five Annexes, which form an integral part of the Protocol.[64] The Protocol and its Annexes are a most elaborate and demanding international multilateral agreement for the protection of the environment. The key article 7 provides that "[a]ny activity relating to mineral resources, other than scientific research, shall be prohibited." The prohibition is to last at least 50 years, following the entry into force of the Protocol (article 25). This Protocol can be modified or amended at any time, provided all Consultative Parties agree. No reservations are permitted to the Protocol (article 24). The four Annexes cover virtually every aspect of environmental protection: Environmental Impact Assessment (Annex I);

---

62   In force 1978. Reprinted in (1972) 11 I.L.M. 251.

63   In force 1982. Reprinted in (1980) 19 I.L.M. 837.

64   In force 1998. Reprinted in (1991) 30 I.L.M. 1460. Canada became a party in 2003. The fifth Annex came into force only in 2002. For an account of the genesis of the Protocol and its significant features, see S.K.N. Blay, "New Trends in the Protection of the Antarctic Environment: The 1991 Madrid Protocol" (1992) 86 A.J.I.L. 377. See also D.H. Overholt, "Environmental Protection in the Antarctic: Past, Present and Future" (1990) 28 Can. Y.B. Int'l L. 227.

"Conservation of Antarctic Fauna and Flora" (Annex II); "Waste Disposal and Waste Management" (Annex III); and "Prevention of Marine Pollution" (Annex IV). In addition, a Schedule to the Protocol provides for the establishment of a special Arbitral Tribunal. The Protocol entered into legal force on January 14, 1998.

2) D. Rothwell has summarized the effects of the Antarctic Treaty system as follows:[65]

> By adopting innovative approaches to solving sovereignty disputes, rejecting traditional notions of territorial jurisdiction, creating a regime in which emphasis is given to freedom of scientific research, establishing protective measures for the flora and fauna of a whole continent and region, implementing an ecosystem approach to marine living resource management, prohibiting all mining activities in order to protect the environment and implementing a legal system that seeks to protect the dependent and associated environment of the region from the impact of all human activities, the ATS has made substantial contributions to international law.

D. AIRSPACE AND OUTER SPACE

1. Airspace[66]

Chicago Convention on International Civil Aviation
(1944) 15 U.N.T.S. 295

PREAMBLE

Whereas the future development of international civil aviation can greatly help to create and preserve friendship and understanding among the nations and peoples of the world, yet its abuse can become a threat to the general security; and

Whereas it is desirable to avoid friction and to promote that cooperation between nations and peoples upon which the peace of the world depends;

Therefore, the undersigned governments having agreed on certain principles and arrangements in order that international civil aviation may be developed in a safe and

---

65   Rothwell, *supra* note 44 at 154.

66   See T. Buergenthal, *Law-Making in the International Civil Aviation Organization* (1969); J. C. Cooper, *Explorations in Aerospace Law*, ed. by I. A. Vlasic (1968); D. H. N. Johnson, *Rights in Airspace* (1965); A.F. Lowenfeld, *Aviation Law; Cases and Materials*, 2d ed. (1981); E. McWhinney & M.A. Bradley, eds., *The Freedom of the Air* (1968/1969); N. Mateesco-Matte, *Treatise on Air-Aeronautical Law* (1981); P. Martin *et al.*, eds., *Shawcross & Beaumont on Air Law*, 4th ed. (1977); I. H. Ph. Diederiks-Verschoor, *An Introduction to Air Law*, 7th ed. (2001); and J. Naveau, *International Air Transport in a Changing World* (1989). The International Civil Aviation Organization (ICAO), located in Montreal, is the UN body with principal concern for international air law. The ICAO website is <http://www.icao.int>. The McGill Institute of Air and Space Law is the world's leading centre regarding both air and space law. The annual publication of the McGill Institute, *Annals of Air and Space Law*, is the leading source on commentary regarding international air law as well as the work of the ICAO. In particular (2002) 27 Annals Air & Space L. provides a collection of articles and papers from the 50th anniversary conference of the McGill Institute.

orderly manner and that international air transport services may be established on the basis of equality of opportunity and operated soundly and economically;

Have accordingly concluded this Convention to that end.

Article 1

The contracting States recognize that every State has complete and exclusive sovereignty over the airspace above its territory.

Article 2

For the purpose of this Convention the territory of a State shall be deemed to be the land areas and territorial waters adjacent thereto under the sovereignty, suzerainty, protection or mandate of such State.

Article 3

(a) This Convention shall be applicable only to civil aircraft and shall not be applicable to state aircraft.

(b) Aircraft used in military, customs and police services shall be deemed to be state aircraft.

(c) No state aircraft of a contracting State shall fly over the territory of another State or land thereon without authorization by special agreement or otherwise, and in accordance with the terms thereof.

(d) The contracting States undertake, when issuing regulations for their state aircraft, that they will have due regard for the safety of navigation of civil aircraft.

Article 4

Each contracting State agrees not to use civil aviation for any purpose inconsistent with the aims of this Convention.

Chapter II

FLIGHT OVER TERRITORY OF CONTRACTING STATES

Article 5

Each contracting State agrees that all aircraft of the other contracting States, being aircraft not engaged in scheduled international air services shall have the right, subject to the observance of the terms of this Convention, to make flights into or in transit non-stop across its territory and to make stops for non-traffic purposes without the necessity of obtaining prior permission, and subject to the right of the State flown over to require landing. Each contracting State nevertheless reserves the right, for reasons of safety of flight, to require aircraft desiring to proceed over regions which are inaccessible or without adequate air navigation facilities to follow prescribed routes, or to obtain special permission for such flights.

Such aircraft, if engaged in the carriage of passengers, cargo, or mail for remuneration or hire on other than scheduled international air services, shall also, subject to the provisions of Article 7, have the privilege of taking on or discharging passengers, cargo, or mail, subject to the right of any State where such embarkation or discharge takes place to impose such regulations, conditions or limitations as it may consider desirable.

Article 6

No scheduled international air service may be operated over or into the territory of a contracting State, except with the special permission or other authorization of that State, and in accordance with the terms of such permission or authorization. ...

Article 8

No aircraft capable of being flown without a pilot shall be flown without a pilot over the territory of a contracting State without special authorization by that State and in accordance with the terms of such authorization. Each contracting State undertakes to insure that the flight of such aircraft without a pilot in regions open to civil aircraft shall be so controlled as to obviate danger to civil aircraft.

Article 9

(a) Each contracting State may, for reasons of military necessity or public safety, restrict or prohibit uniformly the aircraft of other States from flying over certain areas of its territory, provided that no distinction in this respect is made between the aircraft of the State whose territory is involved, engaged in international scheduled airline services, and the aircraft of the other contracting States likewise engaged. Such prohibited areas shall be of reasonable extent and location so as not to interfere unnecessarily with air navigation. Descriptions of such prohibited areas in the territory of a contracting State, as well as any subsequent alterations therein, shall be communicated as soon as possible to the other contracting States and to the International Civil Aviation Organization.

(b) Each contracting State reserves also the right, in exceptional circumstances or during a period of emergency, or in the interest of public safety, and with immediate effect, temporarily to restrict or prohibit flying over the whole or any part of its territory, on condition that such restriction or prohibition shall be applicable without distinction of nationality to aircraft of all other States.

(c) Each contracting State, under such regulations as it may prescribe, may require any aircraft entering the area contemplated in subparagraphs (a) or (b) above to effect a landing as soon as practicable thereafter at some designated airport within its territory.

Destruction of Korean Airlines Flight 007

The seriousness with which certain states view violations of their air sovereignty was illustrated by the incident involving the destruction of Korean Airlines Flight 007 in

September 1983. The following excerpts from the debates in the U.N. Security Council and the diplomatic notes addressed to the Soviet Union by the United States and Canada provide an illustration of the contradictory assertions regarding the circumstances of the incident (quite common to disputes involving aerial intrusions). The same excerpts also offer an indication of what states regard as the rules of international law governing the treatment of civilian aerial intruders.

Mrs. J. KIRKPATRICK (U.S. Ambassador to the United Nations):[67]
Most of the world outside the Soviet Union has heard by now of the Korean Air Lines flight 007 carrying 269 persons between New York and Seoul, which strayed off course into Soviet air space, was tracked by Soviet radar, was targeted by a Soviet SU-15, whose pilot coolly, and after careful consideration, fired two air-launched missiles which destroyed the Korean airliner and apparently its 269 passengers and crew. ...
There are internationally agreed upon standards for intercepting unwelcome aircraft. Those internationally agreed upon standards call for serious efforts at identification, verification and warning and—if the case is serious—for intercepting the intruder and forcing it to land or to leave one's airspace. Sovereignty neither requires nor permits shooting down airliners in peacetime.
Recently the Soviets have implied that KAL 007 may have been mistaken for a United States aerial reconnaissance flight, but that is no more persuasive. The Korean Air Lines Boeing 747 was on a routine, scheduled flight. At the time it was shot down the United States reconnaissance plane referred to by the Soviets had been on the ground for more than one hour, more than 1,500 miles away. Moreover, the United States does not fly reconnaissance missions in Soviet airspace. We do regularly operate aircraft in international airspace to monitor Soviet compliance with SALT and other arms control agreements. The Soviet government knows what our usual flight patterns are and can readily identify these missions.

Mr. O. TROYANOVSKY (U.S.S.R. Ambassador to the United Nations):[68]
... [I]t is an irrefutable fact—and indeed, it has not been denied by American representatives—that the intruder plane had been in Soviet air space for some considerable time. It penetrated 500 kilometres inside Soviet territory. It ignored every attempt made by the Soviet ground services and air forces to identify it. It was unwilling to land at the nearest Soviet airfield. ...
Something further should be said about the general circumstances in which this gross violation of Soviet air space by the South Korean airliner occurred. Contrary to what has been suggested here by the representative of the United States, there have recently been deliberate violations of Soviet State borders by American planes. Such violations, committed with assumed impunity, have become more and more systematic: such violations occurred in 1982 on 22 February, 13 March and 4 and 7

67   UN SCOR, 37th Year, 2471st Mtg., U.N. Doc. S/PV.2471 (1983). Reprinted in (1983) 22 I.L.M. 1121.
68   I.L.M., *ibid.* at 1125.

May. There have been 12 similar violations so far this year—including one on 4 April by planes from the aircraft carriers *Midway* and *Enterprise*. In those instances the Soviet Union made official protests. There was, however no response from the United States. On the contrary, the activities of American reconnaissance planes near the air borders of the Soviet Union have increased: on 31 August of this year, on the eve of the South Korean plane's invasion of the air space of the Soviet Union, and in that same area, seven flights by American reconnaissance planes of the RC-135 type were recorded. On 31 August, from 1745 to 2049 hours, Moscow time, in an area directly contiguous to the point at which the South Korean plane entered Soviet air space and at a height of 8,000 metres, a reconnaissance plane of that type was observed carrying out manoeuvres.

At the same time three United States warships appeared very close to Soviet waters. On 31 August at 2000 hours, 800 kilometres south-east of the town of Petropavlovsky-on-Kamchatka, a Soviet radar station discovered an unknown plane with radar characteristics similar to those of the RC-135 that was on course towards the Kamchatka Peninsula also at the height of 8,000-9,000 metres. Subsequently the Soviet ground stations tried to establish communication with it regarding the violation. However, the aircraft did not reply and continued on the same course, going even deeper into the Soviet air space. So as to identify the aircraft and give it assistance, air defence planes were launched to meet it. There was no reaction by the intruder to their commands. It continued on its flight with its navigational lights turned off, which was characteristic of flights by American reconnaissance planes. The intruder flew over the Kamchatka territory and in fact directly over the Soviet naval base and other military sites. When the intruder approached Sakhalin Island, another group of air defence planes was sent aloft to meet it which once again tried to establish contact with it and to conduct it to the nearest Soviet airport. However, the intruder not only continued on the same course without responding to the warning manoeuvre carried out by the Soviet planes, but also changed its course entering the airspace directly over the southern part of Sakhalin Island and flew over the Soviet naval base while at the same time altering its altitude. It was only thereafter that a warning shot was fired with tracers from the Soviet plane.

All these facts in aggregate suggest strongly that the course and nature of the flight carried out by the South Korean airliner was not fortuitous, but rather a scenario that had been prepared for this tragic event long before.

Mr. AMNEUS (Representative of Sweden to the United Nations):[69]

It is a well known fact that the Soviet Union has severe rules of its own for the protection of the State boundary, enabling Soviet units to use force even against civilian aircraft. Such rules and instructions are not in accordance with generally accepted norms of international law relevant to civilian transportation.

All countries having air traffic to and from the Soviet Union have a right to demand that Soviet authorities do not use force against their aircraft in cases of navigational

---

69   *Ibid.* at 1127.

faults. All civilian aircraft must be treated in a manner that eliminates risks to the safety of the aircraft and its passengers. Interception routines must be applied in such a strict way as to eliminate any risk for mistake with regard to the identity of intercepted aircraft.

DIPLOMATIC NOTE submitted to the U.S.S.R. on September 8, 1983 by Canada's Department of External Affairs (excerpt):[70]

The Department is of the opinion that the actions of the Soviet military in destroying a civilian airliner constitute a flagrant breach of general principles of international law as well as of well-established rules and procedures of international civil aviation and cannot be justified on legal, moral or other grounds.

DIPLOMATIC NOTE submitted to the U.S.S.R. on September 16, 1983 by the U.S. Department of State (excerpt):[71]

The United States refers to the Soviet Union's action of September 1, 1983 in firing upon and destroying an unarmed civil airliner, Korean Air Lines Flight No. 007, in the vicinity of Sakhalin Island, thereby causing the deaths of 269 innocent persons. The United States considers this action as a flagrant and unjustifiable breach of applicable principles of international law and as a direct violation of internationally agreed procedures to be followed when an aircraft inadvertently intrudes on a state's territorial airspace. The United States submits that the Soviet Union's action was wrongful and gives rise to responsibility under international law to make reparation.

The United States Government therefore demands that the Soviet Union provide prompt, adequate, and effective compensation to the United States Government for the lives of United States nationals aboard Korean Air Lines Flight No. 007 and for any other compensable loss incurred by any United States national as a result of the Soviet Union's wrongful actions. The United States will advise the Soviet Union at a later date of the specific losses for which the United States considers the Soviet Union responsible under international law.

---

70   Reprinted in (1983) 22 I.L.M. 1190.

71   *Ibid.* at 1198. And see, "Destruction of Korean Air Lines Boeing 747 Over Sea of Japan, 31 August 1983; Report of ICAO Fact-Finding Investigation" (1983), reproduced in part in (1984) 23 I.L.M. 865. For a discussion of the legal issues involved in this incident, see B. Cheng, "The Destruction of KAL Flight KE 007, and Article 3 Bis of the Chicago Convention," in J. van Gravesande & A. van der Veen Vonk, eds., *Air Worthy Liber Amicorum Honouring Professor Dr. I.H. Ph. Diederiks-Verschoor* (1985) 49; G. Guillaume, "La destruction, le 1er Septembre 1983, de l'avion des Korean Airlines (vol KE 007)" (1984) Rev. Fr. D.A. 215; F. Hassan, "The Shooting Down of Korean Airlines Flight 007 by the USSR and the Future of Air Safety for Passengers" (1984) 33 I.C.L.Q. 712; and P. Martin, "Destruction of Korean Airlines Boeing 747 over Sea of Japan, 31 August 1983" (1984) 9 Air L. 138.

Downing of Iran Air Flight 655[72]

On July 3, 1988, an Iran Air passenger aircraft on a scheduled flight from Bandar Abbas (Iran) to Dubai (United Arab Emirates) was shot down by two missiles launched from the U.S. guided missile cruiser *Vincennes*, which was on duty in the Persian Gulf. The downing of the A300 Airbus took place over international waters of the Strait of Hormuz. All 290 persons aboard the aircraft perished. The incident occurred during the Iran–Iraq war, which was fought on land, in the air, and over the waters of the Persian Gulf.

In the course of hostilities Iraq was carrying out air strikes against Iranian oil facilities and ships, while fast Iranian gunboats were harassing merchant vessels approaching the Strait of Hormuz. Shortly before firing its missiles, the American warship attempted to establish radio contact with the Iranian airliner but was unsuccessful, as the airliner was not equipped to receive communications on the military radio frequency used by the *Vincennes*. Believing that the Iranian airliner was a military aircraft with hostile intentions, the captain of the *Vincennes* ordered missiles to be fired. The very next day, upon learning of the tragic mistake, President Reagan issued a statement of sympathy and condolences for the victims and their families. On July 11, 1988, the President announced that the United States would offer compensation to the families of those killed in the crash on an *ex gratia* basis, that is, not out of a sense of legal obligation. In the debate held at the request of Iran in the UN Security Council on July 14, 1988, Vice-President George Bush stated *inter alia*: "The U.S.S. *Vincennes* acted in self-defense. This tragic accident occurred against the backdrop of repeated, unjustified, unprovoked, and unlawful Iranian attacks against U.S. merchant shipping and armed forces ... . Despite these hostilities, Iranian authorities failed to divert Iran Air #655 from the area."

The Report of the International Civil Aviation Organization (ICAO) fact-finding investigation, conducted pursuant to the decision of the ICAO Council of July 14, 1988, concluded, without apportioning blame, that the incident was caused by misidentification of Flight 655. Subsequent to the submission of this report, Iran sought from the ICAO Council condemnation of the United States for its commission of "a crime of international character" and explicit recognition of the obligation on the part of the United States to pay compensation for the harm done. The ICAO Council refused to endorse either of these requests and in its resolution of March 17, 1989, limited itself to stating, *inter alia*, that it "deeply deplores the tragic incident which occurred as a consequence of events and errors in identification of the aircraft which resulted in the accidental destruction of an Iran Air airliner" and reaffirmed "again the fundamental principle of general international law that States must refrain from resorting to the use of weapons against civil aircraft."

---

72   For a comprehensive account of the incident, see "Destruction of Iran Airbus A300 in the Vicinity of Qesham Island, Islamic Republic of Iran on July 3, 1988; Report of the ICAO Fact-Finding Investigation" (1989) 28 I.L.M. 900. The Resolution of the ICAO Council, adopted March 17, 1989, is reproduced (*ibid.* at 898). The official position of the U.S. and several commentaries appear in H.G. Maier, "Agora: The Downing of Iran Air Flight 655" (1989) 83 A.J.I.L. 318.

Dissatisfied with this decision of the Council as well as with the U.S. responses to the Iranian claims, on May 17, 1989, Iran instituted proceedings in the International Court of Justice against the United States. The Iranian application asked the Court to adjudge and declare that: (a) the ICAO Council decision was erroneous; (b) the United States violated the Chicago Convention and the Montreal Convention; and (c) the Government of the United States should pay compensation to the Islamic Republic. In 1996, the *Case Concerning the Aerial Incident of 3 July 1988 (Iran v. United States)* was discontinued on notification to the ICJ that the parties had entered into "an agreement in full and final settlement" of the dispute.[73] The United States agreed to pay Iran compensation of US$61.8 million.

NOTES

1) In 2001 military aircraft from China and the United States collided in the airspace over China's 200 nautical mile zone. Subsequent to the collision, the American airplane (an EP-3E surveillance plane) landed at an airstrip on China's Hainan Island. China was of the view that the U.S. airplane's overflight of China's exclusive economic zone and landing without authorization or notification was inconsistent with international law. The United States disagreed, adding that the U.S. airplane's need to make an emergency landing was not its fault. The U.S. air crew were eventually allowed to leave China. The United States sought to repair the plane and fly it off of Hainan Island. In fact, China dismantled the plane and returned it to the United States.[74]

2) The Chicago Convention does not explicitly prohibit the use of force against intruding civil aircraft. Neither the Convention nor customary law accords absolute immunity to civil aircraft entering foreign airspace without authorization.[75] A strong argument can be made, however, that the use of force against a civilian airliner in peacetime is justified only in the most exceptional circumstances, when the vital security interests of the overflown state are at stake. Brownlie comments that "[a]erial trespass may be met with appropriate measures of prevention, but does not normally justify instant attack with the object of destroying the trespasser."[76] This conclusion finds support in the virtually universal condemnation of the Soviet attack on the Korean airliner and, especially, in the resolution of the ICAO Council adopted on September 16, 1983 by a vote 26 in favour to 2 against, with 3 abstentions. In addition to "deeply deploring" the Soviet action, the Council asserted that "such use of armed force against international

---

73   [1996] I.C.J. Rep. 9.

74   See "Aerial Incident of the Coast of China," Note (2001) 95 A.J.I.L. 630-33 and I. Shearer, "Military Activities in the Exclusive Economic Zone: The Case of Aerial Surveillance" (2003) 17 Ocean Y.B. 548.

75   For an overview of law and state practice, see K.-G. Park, *La protection de la souverainete aerienne* (1991); W. Hughes, "Aerial Intrusions by Civil Airliners and the Use of Force" (1980) 45 J. Air L. & Com. 595; O.J. Lissitzyn, "The Treatment of Arial Intruders in Recent Practice and International Law" (1953) 47 A.J.I.L. 559 and "Some Legal Implications of the U-2 and RB-47 Incidents" (1962) 56 A.J.I.L. 135; J. Sundberg, "Legitimate Responses to Aerial Intruders: The View from a Neutral State" (1985) 10 Annals Air & Space L. 251; and Q. Wright, "Legal Aspects of the U-2 Incident" (1960) 54 A.J.I.L. 836.

76   Brownlie, *supra* note 1 at 115-16.

civil aviation is incompatible with the norms governing international behaviour and elementary considerations of humanity and with the rules, Standards and Recommended Practices enshrined in the Chicago Convention and its Annexes and invokes generally recognized legal consequences."[77]

3) States parties to the Chicago Convention are obliged to comply with the "Standards" adopted by ICAO and included in annexes to the Convention. However, in the event of impossibility of compliance, notification to the ICAO Council is mandatory under article 38 of the Convention. "Recommended practices," also included in annexes, are non-obligatory; member states are merely expected to "endeavour to conform in accordance with the Convention." The "Standards" in force include the Rules of the Air appended to the Convention as Annex 2, which contain provisions relevant to the interception of civil aircraft. In 1986, the Council of ICAO adopted Amendment 27 to the Rules of the Air, of which the key provision reads in part:[78]

3.8.1 Interception of civil aircraft shall be governed by appropriate regulations and administrative directives issued by contracting States in compliance with the Convention on International Civil Aviation, and in particular Article 3(d) under which contracting States undertake, when issuing regulations for their State aircraft, to have due regard for the safety of navigation of civil aircraft.

4) Compare the downing of Korean Airline Flight 007 with the downing of Iran Air Flight 655. In what respects are these incidents similar and how do they differ in law? Should they have been treated differently by ICAO?

Protocol to the Chicago Convention
(1984) 23 I.L.M. 705

[In the aftermath of the destruction by a Soviet fighter aircraft of Korean Airlines Flight 007, on September 1, 1983, the ICAO Assembly adopted unanimously on May 10, 1984 an amendment to the Chicago Convention—article 3 *bis*—designed to prevent such incidents in the future. The amendment entered into force in October 1998. Interestingly, the United States has not ratified the amendment.]

Article 3 bis

(a) The contracting States recognize that every State must refrain from resorting to the use of weapons against civil aircraft in flight and that, in case of interception, the lives of persons on board and the safety of aircraft must not be endangered. This provision shall not be interpreted as modifying in any way the rights and obligations of States set forth in the Charter of the United Nations.

---

77 *Resolution of the Extraordinary Session of the Council—Appendix A*, reprinted in (1983) 22 I.L.M. 1150.

78 *Convention on International Civil Aviation, Annex 2—Rules of the Air*, ICAO, Doc. 7300/9 (July 1990). And see M. Milde, "Interception of Civil Aircraft vs. Misuse of Civil Aviation" (1986) 11 Annals Air & Space L. 105 for background information concerning this amendment.

(b) The contracting States recognize that every State, in the exercise of its sovereignty, is entitled to require the landing at some designated airport of a civil aircraft flying above its territory without authority or if there are reasonable grounds to conclude that it is being used for any purpose inconsistent with the aims of this Convention; it may also give such aircraft any other instructions to put an end to such violations. For this purpose, the contracting States may resort to any appropriate means consistent with relevant rules of international law, including the relevant provisions of this Convention, specifically paragraph (a) of this Article. Each contracting State agrees to publish its regulations in force regarding the interception of civil aircraft.

(c) Every civil aircraft shall comply with an order given in conformity with paragraph (b) of this Article. To this end each contracting State shall establish all necessary provisions in its national laws or regulations to make such compliance mandatory for any civil aircraft registered in that State or operated by as person having his principal place of business or permanent residence in that State. Each contracting State shall make any violation of such applicable laws or regulations punishable by severe penalties and shall submit the case to its competent authorities in accordance with its laws or regulations.

(d) Each contracting State shall take appropriate measures to prohibit the deliberate use of any civil aircraft registered in that State or operated by an operator who has his principal place of business or permanent residence in that State for any purpose inconsistent with the aims of this Convention. This provision shall not affect paragraph (a) or derogate from paragraphs (b) and (c) of this Article.

NOTES

1) In the opinion of many observers, article 3 *bis* poses a number of problems. For instance, Professor B. Cheng asks: "Is Article 3 bis declaratory of general international law?"; "What is the meaning of the phrase 'to refrain'?"; "Is, under Article 3 bis, the duty not to endanger the safety of civil aircraft in flight and the lives of persons on board absolute?"[79]

2) Pursuant to the obligations regarding interception of civil aircraft imposed by article 3 *bis* (b) and by the Rules of the Air as quoted above, ICAO has adopted the following "principles to be observed by States" in formulating and publishing the necessary regulations:[80]

1.1 To achieve the uniformity in regulations which is necessary for the safety of navigation of civil aircraft due regard shall be had by Contracting States to the following principles when developing regulations and administrative directives:

a) interception of civil aircraft will be undertaken only as a last resort;

b) if undertaken, an interception will be limited to determining the identity of the aircraft, unless it is necessary to return the aircraft to its planned track, direct it beyond the boundaries of national airspace, guide it away from a prohibited, restricted or danger area or instruct it to effect a landing at a designated aerodrome;

---

79   Cheng, *supra* note 71 at 59.

80   *Rules of the Air, supra* note 78.

c) practice interception of civil aircraft will not be undertaken;

d) navigational guidance and related information will be given to an intercepted aircraft by radiotelephony, whenever radio contact can be established; and

e) in the case where an intercepted civil aircraft is required to land in the territory overflown, the aerodrome designated for the landing is to be suitable for the safe landing of the aircraft type concerned.

1.2 Contracting States shall publish a standard method that has been established for the manoeuvring of aircraft intercepting a civil aircraft. Such method shall be designed to avoid any hazard for the intercepted aircraft.

Air Defence Identification Zones[81]

In December 1950, during the Korean war, the United States promulgated a set of rules establishing "Air Defense Identification Zones" (ADIZ) around its territory. The ADIZ rules were designed to control all air traffic in the airspace adjacent to the U.S. territory and extended hundreds of miles over the high seas. The declared purpose of the rules was to protect the United States against hostile aircraft. The rules required all aircraft intending to enter an ADIZ to file a flight plan with the appropriate U.S. aeronautical authority. In addition, the pilot in command of a foreign civil aircraft would not be admitted to the U.S. territory without making position reports when not less than one hour and not more than two hours average direct cruising distance from the United States.

Five months later, Canada adopted similar regulations. The Security Control of Air Traffic Order[82] under the *Aeronautics Act*[83] sets out the Coastal Canadian Air Defence Identification Zone (coastal CADIZ) and the Domestic Canadian Air Defence Identification Zone (domestic CADIZ) and the requirements respecting these zones. Reference should also be made to the April 2000 Emergency Security Control of Air Traffic (ESCAT) Plan.

> The ... Plan provides the roles, responsibilities and procedures of Transport Canada, NAV CANADA and the Department of National Defence authorities to regulate the movements, within Canadian airspace, of friendly non-tactical aircraft; facilitate identification, tracking and engagement of hostile aircraft; and ensure the preservation of civil and military aircraft for employment in national survival operations.[84]

---

81 J. Denaro, "States' Jurisdiction in Airspace under International Law" (1970) 36 J. Air L. & Comm. 688; I. Head, "ADIZ, International Law and Contiguous Airspace" (1964) 3 Alta. L. Rev. 182; J. T. Murchison, *The Contiguous Air Space Zone in International Law*, rev. ed. (1957); and "Air Defense Identification Zones: Creeping Jurisdiction in the Airspace," Note (1978) 18 Va. J. Int'l L. 485. See also M. Milde, "United Nations Convention in the Law of the Sea; Possible Implications for International Air Law" (1983) 8 Annals Air & Space L. 167.

82 C.R.C., c. 63 (1978).

83 R.S.C. 1985, c. A-2.

84 Transport Canada website, "Emergency Security Control of Air Traffic (ESCAT) (TP 1258E)" at <http://www.tc.gc.ca/CivilAviation/systemSafety/CACO/escat.htm>.

This practice of unilateral extension of jurisdiction by coastal states, initiated by the United States, was subsequently emulated by a number of other states, with virtually no protest. The tacit acquiescence accorded by the international community to a practice not in conformity with the freedom of the high seas is most likely due to three factors: (1) the slight inconvenience caused by the tolerant application of these rules in practice; (2) improved safety for all users of the airspace in question; and (3) improved security of coastal states through timely identification of aircraft in the vicinity of their territory. Although ADIZ rules remain in force to this day, they have never been formally authorized either through an official act of ICAO or through an international treaty such as the 1982 Convention on the Law of the Sea.

Military Aircraft in Foreign Airspace[85]

Military aircraft lawfully within the territory of a foreign state enjoy virtually the same immunity from local jurisdiction as do visiting warships. There might be a difference in the treatment accorded foreign aircraft and foreign warships when the entry is due to distress— that is, without prior authorization by the receiving state. States might view with suspicion a foreign military aircraft penetrating their airspace by claiming distress. Simulated distress and fraudulent entry is much more likely to involve an aircraft than a warship.

States very strictly regulate the admission of foreign aircraft to their airspace. Unauthorized entry into the national airspace by a foreign military aircraft is often treated as being made with hostile intentions. Some states, as we have seen, assert the right to employ force not only against military aerial intruders but also against intruding civil aircraft.

2. Outer Space[86]

Outer Space Treaty
Treaty on Principles Governing the Activities of States in the Exploration and Use
of Outer Space, including the Moon and Other Celestial Bodies
Can. T.S. 1967 No. 19; 610 U.N.T.S. 205, in force 1967

Article I

The exploration and use of outer space, including the moon and other celestial bodies, shall be carried out for the benefit and in the interests of all countries, irrespective of their degree of economic or scientific development, and shall be the province of all mankind.

---

85   See M. Peng, *Le Statut Juridique de l'Aeronef Militaire* (1957).

86   See C.Q. Christol, *The Modern International Law of Outer Space* (1982); J. Fawcett, *Outer Space; New Challenges to Law and Policy* (1984); N. Jasentuliyana & R.S.K. Lee, eds., *Manual on Space Law* (1979); M. Lachs, *The Law of Outer Space; An Experience in Contemporary Law-Making* (1972); M.S. McDougal, H.D. Lasswell & I.A. Vlasic, *Law and Public Order in Space* (1963); N. Mateesco-Matte, ed., *Space Activities and Emerging International Law* (1984); G.H. Reynolds & R.P. Merges, *Outer Space; Problems of Law and Policy*, 2d ed. (1997); H.A. Wassenbergh, *Principles of Outer Space Law in Hindsight* (1991); N. Jasentuliyana, ed., *Space Law; Development and Scope* (1992); I.H.

Outer space, including the moon and other celestial bodies, shall be free for exploration and use by all States without discrimination of any kind, on a basis of equality and in accordance with international law, and there shall be free access to all areas of celestial bodies.

There shall be freedom of scientific investigation in outer space, including the moon and other celestial bodies, and States shall facilitate and encourage international co-operation in such investigation.

Article II

Outer space, including the moon and other celestial bodies, is not subject to national appropriation by claim of sovereignty, by means of use or occupation, or by any other means.

Article III

States Parties to the Treaty shall carry on activities in the exploration and use of outer space, including the moon and other celestial bodies, in accordance with international law, including the Charter of the United Nations, in the interest of maintaining international peace and security and promoting international co-operation and understanding.

Article IV

States Parties to the Treaty undertake not to place in orbit around the earth any objects carrying nuclear weapons or any other kinds of weapons of mass destruction, install such weapons on celestial bodies, or station such weapons in outer space in any other manner.

The moon and other celestial bodies shall be used by all States Parties to the Treaty exclusively for peaceful purposes. The establishment of military bases, installations and fortifications, the testing of any type of weapons and the conduct of military manoeuvres on celestial bodies shall be forbidden. The use of military personnel for scientific research or for any other peaceful purposes shall not be prohibited. The use of any equipment or facility necessary for peaceful exploration of the moon and other celestial bodies shall also not be prohibited.

Ph. Diederiks-Verschoor, *An Introduction to Space Law* (1993); and P. Fauteux, "Canada's Participation in the Development of Space Law: How Well Does the Recent Past Bode for the Future?" in *Proceedings of the Conference on International Law: Critical Choices for Canada 1985-2000* (1986) Queen's L.J. Spec. Ed. 415. For an extensive collection of national and international official space law documents, see K.-H. Bockstiegel & M. Benko, *Space Law: Basic Legal Documents* (1991) 2 vols. Note should also be made of the articles and commentaries in the *Annals of Air and Space Law* and the *Journal of Space Law*. Reference should also be made to the United Nations General Assembly Committee on the Peaceful Uses of Outer Space and the Office for Outer Space Affairs that serves as the secretariat to the Committee. The website for the Office of Outer Space Affairs is <http://www.oosa.unvienna.org>. *The Report of the Third U.N. Conference on the Exploration and Peaceful Uses of Outer Space (Unispace III Report)*, U.N. Doc. A/Conf.184/6 (1999), available on the above website, provides a helpful overview of many of the Space issues currently being discussed. The summary of Space Law is at pages 65-68.

Article V

States Parties to the Treaty shall regard astronauts as envoys of mankind in outer space and shall render to them all possible assistance in the event of accident, distress, or emergency landing on the territory of another State Party or on the high seas. When astronauts make such a landing, they shall be safely and promptly returned to the State of registry of their space vehicle.

In carrying on activities in outer space and on celestial bodies, the astronauts of one State Party shall render all possible assistance to the astronauts of other States Parties.

States Parties to the Treaty shall immediately inform the other States Parties to the Treaty or the Secretary-General of the United Nations of any phenomena they discover in outer space, including the moon and other celestial bodies, which could constitute a danger to the life or health of astronauts.

Article VI

States Parties to the Treaty shall bear international responsibility for national activities in outer space, including the moon and other celestial bodies, whether such activities are carried on by governmental agencies or by non-governmental entities, and for assuring that national activities are carried out in conformity with the provisions set forth in the present Treaty. The activities of non-governmental entities in outer space, including the moon and other celestial bodies, shall require authorization and continuing supervision by the appropriate State Party to the Treaty. When activities are carried on in outer space, including the moon and other celestial bodies, by an international organization, responsibility for compliance with this Treaty shall be borne both by the international organization and by the States Parties to the Treaty participating in such organization.

Article VII

Each State Party to the Treaty that launches or procures the launching of an object into outer space, including the moon and other celestial bodies, and each State Party from whose territory or facility an object is launched, is internationally liable for damage to another State Party to the Treaty or to its natural or juridical persons by such object or its component parts on the Earth, in air space or in outer space, including the moon and other celestial bodies.

Article VIII

A State Party to the Treaty on whose registry an object launched into outer space is carried shall retain jurisdiction and control over such object, and over any personnel thereof, while in outer space or on a celestial body. Ownership of objects launched into outer space, including objects landed or constructed on a celestial body, and of their component parts, is not affected by their presence in outer space or on a celestial body or by their return to the Earth. Such objects or component parts found beyond the limits of the State Party to the Treaty on whose registry they are carried shall be returned to that State Party, which shall, upon request, furnish identifying data prior to their return. ...

Article XI

In order to promote international co-operation in the peaceful exploration and use of outer space, States Parties to the Treaty conducting activities in outer space, including the moon and other celestial bodies, agree to inform the Secretary-General of the United Nations as well as the public and the international scientific community, to the greatest extent feasible and practicable, of the nature, conduct, locations and results of such activities. On receiving the said information, the Secretary-General of the United Nations should be prepared to disseminate it immediately and effectively.

Moon Treaty[87]
Agreement Governing the Activities of States on the Moon and
Other Celestial Bodies
U.N. Doc. A/34/664, reprinted in (1979) 18 I.L.M. 1434, in force 1984

[The most important provisions of the Moon Treaty and the only ones that materially expand the principles of the Outer Space Treaty deal with the legal regime of lunar resources. This was the first multilateral treaty to incorporate the concept of the common heritage of mankind, and is the main reason for the refusal of a number of countries to ratify it.]

Article 1

1. The provisions of this Agreement relating to the moon shall also apply to other celestial bodies within the solar system, other than the earth, except in so far as specific legal norms enter into force with respect to any of these celestial bodies.

2. For the purposes of this Agreement reference to the moon shall include orbits around or other trajectories to or around it. ...

Article 6

1. There shall be freedom of scientific investigation on the moon by all States Parties without discrimination of any kind, on the basis of equality and in accordance with international law.

2. In carrying out scientific investigations and in furtherance of the provisions of this Agreement, the States Parties shall have the right to collect on and remove from

---

87   C.Q. Christol, "The Moon Treaty Enters Into Force" (1985) 79 A.J.I.L. 163; E. Galloway, "Agreement Governing the Activities of States on the Moon and Other Celestial Bodies" (1980) 5 Annals Air & Space L. 481; and C.Q. Christol, "The Moon Treaty and the Allocation of Resources" (1997) 22/2 Annals Air & Space L. 31.

the moon samples of its mineral and other substances. Such samples shall remain at the disposal of those States Parties which caused them to be collected and may be used by them for scientific purposes. States Parties shall have regard to the desirability of making a portion of such samples available to other interested States Parties and the international scientific community for scientific investigation. States Parties may in the course of scientific investigations also use mineral and other substances of the moon in quantities appropriate for the support of their missions. ...

Article 11

1. The moon and its natural resources are the common heritage of mankind, which finds its expression in the provision of this Agreement, in particular in paragraph 5 of this article.

2. The moon is not subject to national appropriation by any claim of sovereignty, by means of use or occupation, or by any other means.

3. Neither the surface nor the subsurface of the moon, nor any part thereof or natural resources in place, shall become the property of any State, international intergovernmental or non-governmental organization, national organization or non-governmental entity or of any natural person. The placement of personnel, space vehicles, equipment, facilities, stations and installations on or below the surface of the moon, including structures connected with its surface or subsurface, shall not create a right of ownership over the surface or the subsurface of the moon or any areas thereof. The foregoing provisions are without prejudice to the international régime referred to in paragraph 5 of this article.

4. States Parties have the right to exploration and use of the moon without discrimination of any kind, on the basis of equality and in accordance with international law and the provisions of this Agreement.

5. States Parties to this Agreement hereby undertake to establish an international régime, including appropriate procedures, to govern the exploitation of the natural resources of the moon as such exploitation is about to become feasible. This provision shall be implemented in accordance with article 18 of this Agreement.

6. In order to facilitate the establishment of the international régime referred to in paragraph 5 of this article, States Parties shall inform the Secretary-General of the United Nations as well as the public and the international scientific community, to the greatest extent feasible and practicable, of any natural resources they may discover on the moon.

7. The main purposes of the international régime to be established shall include:

    (a) The orderly and safe development of the natural resources of the moon;

    (b) The rational management of those resources;

    (c) The expansion of opportunities in the use of those resources;

    (d) An equitable sharing by all States Parties in the benefits derived from those resources, whereby the interests and needs of the developing countries, as well as the efforts of those countries which have contributed either directly or indirectly to the exploration of the moon, shall be given special consideration.

8. All the activities with respect to the natural resources of the moon shall be carried out in a manner compatible with the purposes specified in paragraph 7 of this article and the provisions of article 6, paragraph 2, of this Agreement.

Convention on International Liability for Damage Caused by Space Objects[88]
Can. T.S. 1975 No. 7; 961 U.N.T.S. 187, in force 1972

[Next to the Outer Space Treaty, the Space Liability Convention is the most important international agreement relating to space activities. It provides that a launching state is liable for damage caused on the surface of the earth or to aircraft in flight by objects it sent into space. The Convention is one of the rare multilateral treaties that provide for absolute liability of states for damages.]

Article I

For the purposes of this Convention:
(a) The term "damage" means loss of life, personal injury or other impairment of health; or loss of or damage to property of States or of persons, natural or juridical, or property of international intergovernmental organizations;
(b) The term "launching" includes attempted launching;
(c) The term "launching State" means:
   (i) A State which launches or procures the launching of a space object;
   (ii) A State from whose territory or facility a space object is launched;
(d) The term "space object" includes component parts of a space object as well as its launch vehicle and parts thereof.

Article II

A launching State shall be absolutely liable to pay compensation for damage caused by its space object on the surface of the earth or to aircraft in flight.

Article III

In the event of damage being caused elsewhere than on the surface of the earth to a space object of one launching State or to persons or property on board such a space object by a space object of another launching State, the latter shall be liable only if the damage is due to its fault or the fault of persons for whom it is responsible.

---

88 C.Q. Christol, "International Liability for Damage Caused by Space Objects" (1980) 74 A.J.I.L. 346; W. Foster, "The Convention on International Liability for Damage Caused by Space Objects" (1972) 10 Can. Y.B. Int. L. 137; and S. Gorove, "Liability in Space Law: An Overview" (1983) 8 Annals Air & Space L. 373.

Article IV

1. In the event of damage being caused elsewhere than on the surface of the earth to a space object of one launching State or to persons or property on board such a space object by a space object of another launching State, and of damage thereby being caused to a third State or to its natural or juridical persons, the first two States shall be jointly and severally liable to the third State, to the extent indicated by the following:

(a) If the damage has been caused to the third State on the surface of the earth or to aircraft in flight, their liability to the third State shall be absolute;

(b) If the damage has been caused to a space object of the third State or to persons or property on board that space object elsewhere than on the surface of the earth, their liability to the third State shall be based on the fault of either of the first two States or on the fault of persons for whom either is responsible.

2. In all cases of joint and several liability referred to in paragraph 1 of this article, the burden of compensation for the damage shall be apportioned between the first two States in accordance with the extent to which they were at fault; if the extent of the fault of each of these States cannot be established, the burden of compensation shall be apportioned equally between them. Such apportionment shall be without prejudice to the right of the third State to seek the entire compensation due under this Convention from any or all of the launching States which are jointly and severally liable.

Article V

1. Whenever two or more States jointly launch a space object, they shall be jointly and severally liable for any damage caused.

2. A launching State which has paid compensation for damage shall have the right to present a claim for indemnification to other participants in the joint launching. The participants in a joint launching may conclude agreements regarding the apportioning among themselves of the financial obligation in respect of which they are jointly and severally liable. Such agreements shall be without prejudice to the right of a State sustaining damage to seek the entire compensation due under this Convention from any or all of the launching States which are jointly and severally liable.

3. A State from whose territory or facility a space object is launched shall be regarded as a participant in joint launching.

Article VI

1. Subject to the provisions of paragraph 2 of this article, exoneration from absolute liability shall be granted to the extent that a launching State establishes that the damage has resulted either wholly or partially from gross negligence or from an act or omission done with intent to cause damage on the part of a claimant State or of natural or juridical persons it represents.

2. No exoneration whatever shall be granted in cases where the damage has resulted from activities conducted by a launching State which are not in conformity with international law including, in particular, the Charter of the United Nations and the Treaty on Principles Governing the Activities of States in the Exploration and Use of Outer Space, including the Moon and Other Celestial Bodies. ...

Article VIII

1. A State which suffers damage, or whose natural or juridical persons suffer damage, may present to a launching State a claim for compensation for such damage.

2. If the State of nationality has not presented a claim, another State may, in respect of damage sustained in its territory by any natural or juridical person, present a claim to a launching State.

3. If neither the State of nationality nor the State in whose territory the damage was sustained has presented a claim or notified its intention of presenting a claim, another State may, in respect of damage sustained by its permanent residents, present a claim to a launching State. ...

Article XI

1. Presentation of a claim to a launching State for compensation for damage under this Convention shall not require the prior exhaustion of any local remedies which may be available to a claimant State or to natural or juridical persons it represents. ...

Article XII

The compensation which the launching State shall be liable to pay for damage under this Convention shall be determined in accordance with international law and the principles of justice and equity, in order to provide such reparation in respect of the damage as will restore the person, natural or juridical, State or international organization on whose behalf the claim is presented to the condition which would have existed if the damage had not occurred.

Article XIII

Unless the claimant State and the State from which compensation is due under this Convention agree on another form of compensation, the compensation shall be paid in the currency of the claimant State or, if that State so requests, in the currency of the State from which compensation is due.

Article XIV

If no settlement of a claim is arrived at through diplomatic negotiations as provided for in article IX, within one year from the date on which the claimant State notifies the launching State that it has submitted the documentation of its claim, the parties concerned shall establish a Claims Commission at the request of either party.

Article XV

1. The Claims Commission shall be composed of three members: one appointed by the claimant State, one appointed by the launching State and the third member, the Chairman, to be chosen by both parties jointly. Each party shall make its appointment within two months of the request for the establishment of the Claims Commission. ...

Article XVIII

The Claims Commission shall decide the merits of the claim for compensation and determine the amount of compensation payable, if any.

Article XIX

1. The Claims Commission shall act in accordance with the provisions of article XII.

2. The decision of the Commission shall be final and binding if the parties have so agreed; otherwise the Commission shall render a final and recommendatory award, which the parties shall consider in good faith. The Commission shall state the reasons for its decision or award.

3. The Commission shall give its decision or award as promptly as possible and no later than one year from the date of its establishment, unless an extension of this period is found necessary by the Commission.

NOTES

1) The Space Liability Convention was invoked by the Canadian Government in its claim for compensation for damage caused by the disintegration of Soviet satellite *Cosmos 954* over northern Canada in 1978. The claim is discussed in the context of "State Responsibility" in Chapter 10, Section A.2.

2) In anticipation of the first manned landing on the Moon, on the initiative of the United States, in 1968 the Agreement on the Rescue of Astronauts, the Return of Astronauts and the Return of Objects launched into Outer Space was concluded.[89] The Agreement provides for procedures for aiding and repatriating astronauts in the event of accident or emergency landing. The parties also agreed to recover and return space objects that fall on their territory to the state of registry. However, the party on whose territory such space object is found may withhold its return until the launching state furnishes data identifying the object as belonging to it.

The Geostationary Satellite Orbit

The so-called geostationary orbit is located above the equator, 35,871 kilometres from the surface of the Earth. It is the ideal location for communication satellites; when placed in that orbit a satellite viewed from the Earth appears to be stationary, remaining at all times in the same position. It was early realized that the geostationary orbit is a limited natural resource that can accommodate only a limited number of communication satellites. The location of the orbit and its rapid saturation with satellites belonging to a handful of developed nations has led several equatorial states to adopt in Bogota, Colombia on December 3, 1976 a declaration on the legal status of that part of outer space.[90] The

---

89   (1968) 72 U.N.T.S. 119; Can. T.S. 1975 No. 6.

90   The full text of the *Bogotá Declaration* is reprinted in N. Jasentuliyana and R.S.K. Lee eds., *Manual on Space Law* (1979) vol. 2 at 383.

Declaration proclaimed the segments of geostationary synchronous orbit coinciding with the boundaries of the subjacent states to be "part of the territory over which Equatorial states exercise their national sovereignty."

The issue of the legal regime for the geostationary orbit has been on the agenda of the Legal Subcommittee of the U.N. Committee on the Peaceful Uses of Outer Space since 1978 (on the recommendation of the U.N.G.A. resolution 196(XXXII), of December 1977).[91] The International Telecommunication Union, through its World Administrative Radio Conferences, has also been actively seeking a solution to the problem. A substantial number of states, including most of the leading users of space telecommunications, maintain that geostationary orbits are inseparable from outer space and therefore are fully subject to the relevant provisions of the 1967 Outer Space Treaty. Whereas the Outer Space Treaty contains no specific rules with respect to such orbits, it does prohibit national appropriation by claim of sovereignty, by means of use or occupation, or by any other means. Thus, on both legal and practical grounds, major users of the orbit refuse to accept the view that by reason of their geographical position the equatorial countries should be considered as having special rights to segments of the geostationary orbit superjacent to their territories. No serious technical problems in the use of the orbit have been encountered to date. A temporary solution, not affecting the future legal status of this orbit, has been achieved under the auspices of the International Telecommunication Union (ITU).

NOTE

The question of where the sovereign airspace ends and free outer space begins, also known as the question of the definition and delimitation of outer space, continues to defy all attempts at resolution. The question was originally raised at the time of the first satellite launching, in 1957, and since 1967, it has been regularly on the agenda of the U.N. Outer Space Committee. Some states, led by the United States, insist that there is no need at this time to establish by treaty the boundary between sovereign airspace and free outer space. A definition or delimitation of outer space should be undertaken, these states argue, only when a practical need for one arises. The former Soviet Union, supported by a number of other States, proposed to draw the boundary at an altitude between 100 kilometres and 110 kilometres above sea level. Included in the proposal was a provision allowing "innocent passage" through the airspace of one state of a space object of another state for the purpose of reaching orbit or returning to Earth. It is safe to predict that when a consensus is eventually reached, the upper boundary of sovereign airspace will not be higher than 100 kilometres above sea level.

---

91   Fawcett, *supra* note 86 at 51-79; R. Jakhu, "The Legal Status of the Geostationary Orbit" (1982) 7 Annals Air & Space L. 333; and "The Evolution of the ITU's Regulatory Regime Governing Space Radiocommunication Services and the Geostationary Satellite Orbit" (1983) 8 Annals Air & Space L. 381.

Nuclear Power Sources in Outer Space

Shortly after the accident of the Soviet *Cosmos 954*, on the initiative of Canada, the question of satellites with nuclear power sources (NPS) on board was placed on the agenda of the U.N. Outer Space Committee. Both the United States and the Soviet Union have been operating nuclear-powered spacecraft since the 1960s. With the building of bigger space structures, it is likely that much more powerful, and therefore much more hazardous, NPS will be stationed in outer space, in the relative vicinity of the Earth. Satellites carrying NPS do not operate in a legal vacuum; they are subject to the provisions of the Space Liability Convention, the Outer Space Treaty, and general international law as well. Nonetheless, in the aftermath of the *Cosmos 954* accident Canada, supported by a number of other countries, submitted to the Legal Sub-Committee of the U.N. Outer Space Committee a comprehensive survey of relevant rules of space law and concluded that there was an urgent need for supplementing that body of law with special provisions concerning the use of NPS. Canada proposed that new principles be elaborated and eventually incorporated in an international treaty.

In 1992, the U.N. General Assembly adopted as a resolution the "Principles Relevant to the Use of Nuclear Power Sources in Outer Space."[92] The text contains 11 "principles." This important document recognizes that for some outer space missions NPS are well suited or even essential due to their compactness and long life (preamble). However, the use of NPS in space should be limited to those missions that cannot be operated reasonably by non-nuclear energy sources (principle 3). These principles apply only to NPS designed to generate electric power on board spare vehicles for non-propulsive purposes (preamble). To assure appropriate levels of safety, nuclear reactors may be operated on interplanetary missions; in sufficiently high orbits to allow for the decay of the fission materials and to minimize the risks of collision with other space objects; and in low-Earth orbits if they can be propelled to sufficiently high orbit after the completion of their mission (principles 3.2.1 and 3.2.2). Nuclear reactors on board spacecraft may use only highly enriched uranium 235 as fuel and must not be made critical before they have reached their operating orbit or interplanetary trajectory (principles 3.2.3 and 3.2.4). The design and construction of the nuclear reactor must ensure that it cannot become critical before reaching the operating orbit during all possible events, including rocket explosion, unplanned re-entry, and impact on ground or water (principle 3.2.5). Radioisotope generators may also be used for space missions provided that at the conclusion of their mission, if in Earth orbit, they can be transferred to a safe high orbit (principle 3.1). When a malfunctioning spacecraft with NPS on board poses a risk of re-entry to the Earth, the launching state must give timely warning to the states concerned (principle 5). All states possessing monitoring facilities are obliged to communicate the relevant information concerning the malfunctioning spacecraft to the U.N. Secretary-General and the states at risk (principle 7). The Legal Subcommittee of the U.N. Outer Space Committee is currently reviewing these principles.

---

92   GA Res. 47/68, UN GAOR, 47th Sess., Supp. No. 49, UN Doc. A/47/49 (1992) 88.

Military Activities in Space

Almost from the beginning of the space age, there have been military-related activities in space. A recent paper on the military uses of outer space, identified the following types of activities existing or contemplated: reconnaissance satellites; meteorological satellites; communication satellites; navigation satellites; anti-satellite weapons; ballistic missile defence and, more generally, space weapons.[93] The Outer Space Treaty prohibits the stationing of nuclear weapons or other weapons of mass destruction in space (Article IV). Beyond this limitation, at least in the view of one commentator, "international law at present imposes relatively few restrictions on military space activities overall, and virtually no limits on space weaponry in particular."[94] This conclusion is supported by unsuccessful attempts to negotiate a banning of space weapons together with a view that "peaceful" uses of outer space are to be understood in the context of activities taking place when the wording was adopted and that such activities included military uses of space. While there is a clear appetite on the part of many (states and commentators) for "weapons-free space" and a limitation or banishment of military uses of space, international legal developments in this area can be expected to be incremental or non-existent in the foreseeable future.

---

93   Bhupendra Jasani, "Military Use of Outer Space" (2002) 27 Annals Air & Space L. 347.

94   Christopher M. Petras, "The Debate over the Weaponization of Space: A Military–Legal Conspectus" (2003) 28 Annals Air & Space L. 171 at 196.

CHAPTER EIGHT

Nationality

A. INDIVIDUALS

Nationality is the basic link between an individual and the state. An individual has the nationality of the state that confers it and domestic law controls its acquisition and loss.[1] However, there must be a genuine link between the state granting the nationality and the individual. In *Re Lynch* it was stated that:

> A man's nationality forms a continuing state of things and not a physical fact which occurs at a particular moment. A man's nationality is a continuing relationship between the sovereign State on the one hand and the citizen on the other. The fundamental basis of a man's nationality is his membership of an independent political community. This legal relationship involves rights and corresponding duties on both—on the part of the citizen no less than on the part of the State.[2]

The link of nationality is so important in international law because it is the basis of a state's jurisdiction over persons, both human and juridical, beyond its territory. Nationality is a two-way relationship. Rights and obligations are implicit in a conferral of nationality by a state upon an individual. An individual owes allegiance to her or his state of nationality and may seek its protection. A state may, if it so wishes, formally espouse through diplomatic channels the claims of its nationals in cases of injury done by another state; a state will be responsible for acts of its nationals undertaken on behalf of the state with the state's consent or when done privately if the state has not been duly diligent in preventing the wrongful acts or in prosecuting and punishing them; states may only impose military service on their nationals unless an exemption has been granted by the national state of the alien;[3] some states refuse to extradite their own nationals and correlatively have provisions in their penal laws for jurisdiction over criminal offences

---

1   See the *Nationality Decrees in Tunis and Morocco Case* (1923) P.C.I.J. (Ser. B.) No. 4. See, generally, R. Donner, *The Regulation of Nationality in International Law*, 2d ed. (1994); P. Weis, *Nationality and Statelessness in International Law*, 2d ed. (1978); H.F. van Panhuys, *The Role of Nationality in International Law* (1959); and A.P. Mutharika, *The Regulation of Statelessness under International and National Law* (1977) 2 vols. (looseleaf).

2   (1929-30), 5 Ann. Dig. 221 at 222 (United States–Mexico General Claims Commission).

3   Some states have imposed this duty on permanent residents: see *Polites v. The Commonwealth* (1945) 70 C.L.R. 60 (H.C.).

based on nationality. This chapter explores the rules of nationality itself, starting with the individual's acquisition of nationality.

1. Acquisition of Nationality

Acquisition of Nationality
from S.A. Williams and A.L.C. de Mestral, *An Introduction to International Law*, 2d ed. (1987) at 290, 292

It is important to realize at the outset that although in referring to the status of an individual the terms citizen and national are used synonymously, in fact nationality is wider in scope. The term "citizen" refers to a person who is endowed with full political and civil rights in the state concerned. The term "national" although it includes a citizen also refers to a person who is not a citizen but yet has a right to the protection of the state and in turn owes allegiance to it. A national may be denied the rights of citizenship but will not lose the nationality itself on this basis. Thus, for example in *Kahane v. Parisi and the Austrian State*[4] it was held that although Jewish persons in Romania were denied the privileges of citizenship in many cases, they were still nationals of that state. ... Although it is up to the domestic law of each state to set down its own requirements, nevertheless the practice of states shows that most nationality laws have certain features in common.

(a) Jus Soli and Jus Sanguinis
Nationality may be acquired by birth. This may result from birth in the territory of the state (*jus soli*) or from birth outside the territory of the state, but to parents who are nationals of the state (*jus sanguinis*). Some states have adopted one or the other of these principles. Others such as the United Kingdom and Canada have utilized both. ...

(b) Naturalization
This term is used in its widest sense to cover the acquisition of nationality after birth. Technically, it refers to an alien receiving a foreign nationality upon an application made by him. In general, nationality by naturalization may be acquired by one of several different methods: direct naturalization of a person under general naturalization laws, which in some countries is a judicial process, in others a legislative process and in still others an executive process; derivative naturalization, where for example a child who is minor becomes naturalized because of the naturalization of either or both his parents, where a spouse becomes naturalized through the other spouse's naturalization, or where an alien becomes naturalized through marriage to a citizen; adoption of an alien minor; group or collective naturalization, which occurs through the transfer of territory from one state to another, or where a state passes

---

4   (1929-30), 5 Ann. Dig. 213.

legislation with special reference to a certain class of persons and special legislation in individual cases.

Citizenship Act
R.S.C. 1985, c. C-29, as amended

[A new Canadian *Citizenship Act* was proposed in Bill C-16 of 1999 (which progressed as far as second reading in the Senate), and again in Bill C-19 of 2002 (reaching second reading in the House of Commons).[5] Acquisition of Canadian citizenship by birth is regulated by section 3(1) of the current Act, as follows:]

Subject to this Act, a person is a citizen if

(a) the person was born in Canada after February 14, 1977;

(b) the person was born outside Canada after February 14, 1977 and at the time of his birth one of his parents, other than a parent who adopted him, was a citizen;

(c) the person has been granted or acquired citizenship pursuant to section 5 or 11 and, in the case of a person who is fourteen years of age or over on the day that he is granted citizenship, he has taken the oath of citizenship;

(d) the person was a citizen immediately before February 15, 1977; or

(e) the person was entitled, immediately before February 15, 1977, to become a citizen under paragraph 5(1)(b) of the former Act.

[The Canadian Act is restrictive in its approach to the *jus soli* principle as illustrated by section 3(2), which provides:]

Paragraph (1)(a) does not apply to a person if, at the time of his birth, neither of his parents was a citizen or lawfully admitted to Canada for permanent residence and either of his parents was

(a) a diplomatic or consular officer or other representative or employee in Canada of a foreign government;

(b) an employee in the service of a person referred to in paragraph (a); or

(c) an officer or employee in Canada of a specialized agency of the United Nations or an officer or employee in Canada of any other international organization to whom there is granted, by or under any Act of the Parliament of Canada, diplomatic privileges and immunities certified by the Minister of Foreign Affairs to be equivalent to those granted to a person or persons referred to in paragraph (a).

[Naturalization in Canada is governed by section 5 of the *Citizenship Act*, which provides in part:]

---

5   Bill C-16, *An Act Respecting Canadian Citizenship*, 2d Sess., 36th Parl., 1999 (2d reading, Senate, 27 June 2000); Bill C-18, *The Citizenship of Canada Act*, 2d Sess., 37th Parl. 2002 (2d reading, 8 November, 2002).

(1) The Minister shall grant citizenship to any person who

(a) makes application for citizenship;

(b) is eighteen years of age or over;

(c) is a permanent resident within the meaning of subsection 2(1) of the *Immigration and Refugee Protection Act*, and has, within the four years immediately preceding the date of his or her application, accumulated at least three years of residence in Canada calculated in the following manner: ...

(d) has an adequate knowledge of one of the official languages of Canada;

(e) has an adequate knowledge of Canada and of the responsibilities and privileges of citizenship; and

(f) is not under a removal order and is not the subject of a declaration by the Governor in Council made pursuant to section 20.

(1.1) Any day during which an applicant for citizenship resided with the applicant's spouse or common-law partner who at the time was a Canadian citizen and was employed outside of Canada in or with the Canadian armed forces or the public service of Canada or of a province, otherwise than as a locally engaged person, shall be treated as equivalent to one day of residence in Canada for the purposes of paragraph (1)(c) and subsection 11(1).

(2) The Minister shall grant citizenship to any person who

(a) is a permanent resident within the meaning of subsection 2(1) of the *Immigration and Refugee Protection Act*, and is the minor child of a citizen if an application for citizenship is made to the Minister by a person authorized by regulation to make the application on behalf of the minor child; ...

(3) The Minister may, in his discretion, waive on compassionate grounds,

(a) in the case of any person, the requirements of paragraph (1)(d) or (e);

(b) in the case of a minor, the requirement respecting age set out in paragraph (1)(b), the requirement respecting length of residence in Canada set out in paragraph (1)(c) or the requirement to take the oath of citizenship; and

(c) in the case of any person who is prevented from understanding the significance of taking the oath of citizenship by reason of a mental disability, the requirement to take the oath.

(4) In order to alleviate cases of special and unusual hardship or to reward services of an exceptional value to Canada, and notwithstanding any other provisions of this Act, the Governor in Council may, in his discretion, direct the Minister to grant citizenship to any person and, where such a direction is made, the Minister shall forthwith grant citizenship to the person named in the direction.

6. A citizen, whether or not born in Canada, is entitled to all rights, powers and privileges and is subject to all obligations, duties and liabilities to which a person who is a citizen under paragraph 3(1)(a) is entitled or subject and has a like status to that of such person.

NOTES

1) Many countries still confer citizenship only if the father was a citizen. Canada's *Citizenship Act* states in section 3(1)(b) that a child born outside of Canada will be a

Canadian if either one of the parents was a Canadian citizen at the time. Also under the Canadian Act, citizenship is not automatically imposed upon a woman who marries a Canadian citizen, whereas this is still the case in some other countries. The Canadian position is in keeping with the 1957 Convention on the Nationality of Married Women,[6] which provides that a woman who marries a citizen of another state should not automatically lose her original nationality. Article 9 of the 1979 Convention on the Elimination of All Forms of Discrimination Against Women,[7] to which Canada is a contracting party, provides that in nationality issues women should have equal rights with men to acquire, change, or retain nationality. Marriage should not automatically change a woman's nationality, render her stateless, or force her to assume her husband's nationality. The article states that women shall have equal rights with men with respect to the nationality of their children.

2) In fact marriage is not a ground for acquiring Canadian citizenship at all. Residence is what matters: see section 5(1) of the *Citizenship Act*. Marriage may however make it easier for a foreign spouse to take up residence in Canada and thus qualify for citizenship.

3) Article 24(3) of the 1966 International Covenant on Civil and Political Rights, reproduced in the Documentary Supplement, provides that every child has the right to acquire a nationality. This has been reaffirmed in the 1989 Convention on the Rights of the Child.[8]

4) Is the national state bound to admit or to receive its citizen?[9] In Canada, section 6(1) of the *Canadian Charter of Rights and Freedoms*[10] provides that every Canadian citizen has "the right to enter, to remain in and to leave Canada."

5) In the European Community, there is freedom of movement of persons for citizens of the 25 member states as well as freedom of establishment.[11] Furthermore, the Maastricht Treaty on European Union,[12] in article 8, provides for a citizenship of the Union. Every national of the member states is a citizen of the Union and enjoys the rights conferred by the treaty as well as being subject to the duties imposed thereby. These rights include the ability to vote and stand as a candidate in municipal elections in a member state of which he or she is not a national but resides. The same applies to elections for the European Parliament. The treaty also makes provisions with respect to

---

6   309 U.N.T.S. 65; Can. T.S. 1960 No. 2.

7   Can. T.S. 1982 No. 31. See R.J. Cook, "Reservations to the Convention on the Elimination of All Forms of Discrimination Against Women" (1990) 30 Va. J. Int'l L. 643 at 693-96.

8   Adopted without a vote in the United Nations General Assembly on November 20, 1989. See U.N. GA Res. 44/25, UN GAOR, 44th Sess., Supp. No. 49, U.N. Doc. A/44/49 (1989) 166 that introduced the Convention. See (1989) 28 I.L.M. 1448. For an interesting discussion of the Convention see (1991) 62 Rev. I.D.P. 723-975.

9   See Weis, *supra* note 1 at 45-46 and Van Panhuys, *supra* note 1 at 55-56. Note *R. v. Secretary of State for the Home Dept., ex parte Thakrar*, [1974] 2 W.L.R. 593 (C.A.).

10   *Constitution Act, 1982*, being Schedule B to the *Canada Act, 1982* (U.K.) 1982, c. 11.

11   See *Treaty Establishing the European Economic Community* (1957) 298 U.N.T.S. 11, article 48 (freedom of movement of workers) and article 52 (freedom of establishment).

12   (1992) 31 I.L.M. 253.

the right of diplomatic protection, addressed below in the materials dealing with the International Law Commission (ILC) Draft Articles on Diplomatic Protection.

2. Recognition of Nationality at International Law

Notteböhm Case
Liechtenstein v. Guatemala
[1955] I.C.J. Rep. 4

[This case was submitted on December 17, 1951, by an application filed by Liechtenstein against Guatemala, claiming damages in respect of various war measures that Guatemala had taken against the person and property of Friedrich Notteböhm, who was born a German national but who was alleged to have become a citizen of Liechtenstein. Guatemala objected that Liechtenstein's claim was inadmissible: it thus put in issue the nationality of Notteböhm.]

THE COURT: ... In order to decide upon the admissibility of the Application, the Court must ascertain whether the nationality conferred on Notteböhm by Liechtenstein by means of a naturalization ... can be validly invoked as against Guatemala, whether it bestows upon Liechtenstein a sufficient title to the exercise of protection in respect of Notteböhm as against Guatemala and therefore entitles it to seize the Court of a claim relating to him. In this connection, Counsel for Liechtenstein said: "the essential question is whether Mr. Notteböhm, having acquired the nationality of Liechtenstein, that acquisition of nationality is one which must be recognized by other States." This formulation is accurate, subject to the twofold reservation that, in the first place, what is involved is not recognition for all purposes but merely for the purposes of the admissibility of the Application, and, secondly, that what is involved is not recognition by all States but only by Guatemala.

The Court does not propose to go beyond the limited scope of the question which it has to decide, namely whether the nationality conferred on Notteböhm can be relied upon as against Guatemala in justification of the proceedings instituted before the Court. It must decide this question on the basis of international law; to do so is consistent with the nature of the question and with the nature of the Court's own function. ...

Since no proof has been adduced that Guatemala has recognized the title to the exercise of protection relied upon by Liechtenstein as being derived from the naturalization which it granted to Notteböhm, the Court must consider whether such an act of granting nationality by Liechtenstein directly entails an obligation on the part of Guatemala to recognize its effect, namely, Liechtenstein's right to exercise its protection. In other words, it must be determined whether that unilateral act by Liechtenstein is one which can be relied upon against Guatemala in regard to the exercise of protection. The Court will deal with this question without considering that of the validity of Notteböhm's naturalization according to the law of Liechtenstein.

It is for Liechtenstein, as it is for every sovereign State, to settle by its own legislation the rules relating to the acquisition of its nationality, and to confer that nationality by naturalization granted by its own organs in accordance with that legislation. It is not necessary to determine whether international law imposes any limitation on its freedom of decision in this domain. Furthermore, nationality has its most immediate, its most far-reaching and, for most people, its only effects within the legal system of the State conferring it. Nationality serves above all to determine that the person upon whom it is conferred enjoys the rights and is bound by the obligations which the law of the state in question grants to or imposes on its nationals. This is implied in the wider concept that nationality is within the domestic jurisdiction of the State.

But the issue which the Court must decide is not one which pertains to the legal system of Liechtenstein. It does not depend on the law or on the decision of Liechtenstein whether that State is entitled to exercise its protection, in the case under consideration. To exercise protection, to apply to the Court, is to place oneself on the plane of international law. It is international law which determines whether a State is entitled to exercise protection and to seise the Court.

The naturalization of Nottebõhm was an act performed by Liechtenstein in the exercise of its domestic jurisdiction. The question to be decided is whether that act has the international effect here under consideration.

International practice provides many examples of acts performed by States in the exercise of domestic jurisdiction which do not necessarily or automatically have international effect, which are not necessarily and automatically binding on other States or which are binding on them only subject to certain conditions: this is the case, for instance, of a judgement given by the competent court of a State which it sought to invoke in another State.

... In most cases arbitrators have not strictly speaking had to decide a conflict of nationality as between States, but rather to determine whether the nationality invoked by the applicant State was one which could be relied upon as against the respondent State, that is to say, whether it entitled the applicant State to exercise protection. International arbitrators, having before them allegations of nationality by the Applicant State which were contested by the respondent State, have sought to ascertain whether nationality had been conferred by the applicant State in circumstances such as to give rise to an obligation on the part of the respondent State to recognize the effect of that nationality. In order to decide this question arbitrators have evolved certain principles for determining whether full international effect was attributed to the nationality invoked. The same issue is now before the Court: it must be resolved by applying the same principles.

... International arbitrators have decided in the same way numerous cases of dual nationality, where the question arose with regard to the exercise of protection. They have given their preference to the real and effective nationality, that which accorded with the facts, that based on stronger factual ties between the person concerned and one of the States whose nationality is involved. Different factors are taken into consideration, and their importance will vary from one case to the next: the habitual residence of the individual concerned is an important factor, but there are other factors such as the centre of his interests, his family ties, his participation in public life, attachment shown by him for a given country and inculcated in his children, etc.

Similarly, the courts of third States, when they have before them an individual whom two other States hold to be their national, seek to resolve the conflict by having recourse to international criteria and their prevailing tendency is to prefer the real and effective nationality.

The same tendency prevails in the writings of publicists and in practice. This notion is inherent in the provisions of Article 3, paragraph 2, of the Statute of the Court. National laws reflect this tendency when, *inter alia*, they make naturalization dependent on conditions indicating the existence of a link, which may vary in their nature but which are essentially concerned with this idea. The Liechtenstein Law of January 4th, 1934, is a good example.

The practice of certain States which refrain from exercising protection in favour of a naturalised person when the latter has in fact, by his prolonged absence, severed his links with what is no longer for him anything but his nominal country, manifests the view of these States that, in order to be capable of being invoked against another State, nationality must correspond with the factual situation. A similar view is manifested in the relevant provisions of the bilateral nationality treaties concluded between the United States of America and other States since 1868, such as those sometimes referred to as the Bancroft Treaties, and in the Pan-American Convention, signed at Rio de Janeiro on August 13th, 1906, on the status of naturalized citizens who resume residence in their country of origin.

The character thus recognized on the international level as pertaining to nationality is in no way inconsistent with the fact that international law leaves it to each State to lay down the rules governing the grant of its own nationality. The reason for this is that the diversity of demographic conditions has thus far made it impossible for any general agreement to be reached on the rules relating to nationality, although the latter by its very nature affects international relations. It has been considered that the best way of making such rules accord with the varying demographic conditions in different countries is to leave the fixing of such rules to the competence of each State. On the other hand, a State cannot claim that the rules it has thus laid down are entitled to recognition by another State unless it has acted in conformity with this general aim of making the legal bond of nationality accord with the individual's genuine connection with the State which assumes the defence of its citizens by means of protection as against other States. The requirement that such a concordance must exist is found in the studies carried on in the course of the last thirty years upon the initiative and under the auspices of the League of Nations and the United Nations. It explains the provision which the Conference for the Codification of International Law, held at The Hague in 1930, inserted in Article I of the Convention relating to the Conflict of Nationality Laws, laying down that the law enacted by a State for the purpose of determining who are its nationals "shall be recognized by other States in so far as it is consistent with ... international custom, and the principles of law generally recognized with regard to nationality." In the same spirit, Article 5 of the Convention refers to criteria of the individual's genuine connections for the purpose of resolving questions of dual nationality which arise in third States.

According to the practice of States, to arbitral and judicial decisions and to the opinions of writers, nationality is a legal bond having as its basis a social fact of attachment, a genuine connection of existence, interests and sentiments, together with the existence of reciprocal rights and duties. It may be said to constitute the juridical expression of the fact that the individual upon whom it is conferred, either directly by the law or as the result of an act of the authorities, is in fact more closely connected with the population of the State conferring nationality than with that of any other State. Conferred by a State, it only entitles that State to exercise protection vis-à-vis another State, if it constitutes a translation into juridical terms of the individual's connection with the State which has made him its national. ...

Since this is the character which nationality must present when it is invoked to furnish the State which has granted it with a title to the exercise of protection and to the institution of international judicial proceedings, the Court must ascertain whether the nationality granted to Notteböhm by means of naturalization is of this character or, in other words, whether the factual connection between Notteböhm and Liechtenstein in the period preceding, contemporaneous with and following his naturalization appears to be sufficiently close, so preponderant in relation to any connection which may have existed between him and any other State, that it is possible to regard the nationality conferred upon him as real and effective as the exact juridical expression of a social fact of a connection which existed previously or came into existence thereafter.

Naturalization is not a matter to be taken lightly. To seek and to obtain it is not something that happens frequently in the life of a human being. It involves his breaking of a bond of allegiance and his establishment of a new bond of allegiance. It may have far-reaching consequences and involve profound changes in the destiny of the individual who obtains it. It concerns him personally, and to consider it only from the point of view of its repercussions with regard to his property would be to misunderstand its profound significance. In order to appraise its international effect, it is impossible to disregard the circumstances in which it was conferred, the serious character which attaches to it, the real and effective, and not merely the verbal preference of the individual seeking it for the country which grants it to him.

At the time of his naturalization does Notteböhm appear to have been more closely attached by his tradition, his establishment, his interests, his activities, his family ties, his intentions for the near future to Liechtenstein than to any other State? ...

The essential facts are as follows:

At the date when he applied for naturalization Notteböhm had been a German national from the time of birth. He had always retained his connections with members of his family who had remained in Germany and he had always had business connections with that country. His country had been at war for more than a month, and there is nothing to indicate that the application for naturalization then made by Notteböhm was motivated by any desire to dissociate himself from the Government of his country.

He had been settled in Guatemala for 34 years. He had carried on his activities there. It was the main seat of his interests. He returned there shortly after his naturalization, and it remained the centre of his interests and of his business activities. He stayed there until his removal as a result of war measures in 1943. He subsequently attempted to return there, and he now complains of Guatemala's refusal to admit him. There, too, were several members of his family who sought to safeguard his interests.

In contrast, his actual connections with Liechtenstein were extremely tenuous. No settled abode, no prolonged residence in that country at the time of his application for naturalization: the application indicates that he was paying a visit there and confirms the transient character of this visit by its request that the naturalization proceedings should be initiated and concluded without delay. No intention of settling there was shown at that time or realized in the ensuing weeks, months or years—on the contrary, he returned to Guatemala very shortly after his naturalization and showed every intention of remaining there. If Notteböhm went to Liechtenstein in 1946, this was because of the refusal of Guatemala to admit him. No indication is given of the grounds warranting the waiver to the condition of residence, required by the 1934 Nationality Law, which waiver was implicitly granted to him. There is no allegation of any economic interests or of any activities exercised or to be exercised in Liechtenstein, and no manifestation of any intention whatsoever to transfer all or some of his interests and his business activities to Liechtenstein. It is unnecessary in this connection to attribute much importance to the promise to pay the taxes levied at the time of his naturalization. The only links to be discovered between the Principality and Notteböhm are the short sojourns already referred to and the presence in Vaduz of one of his brothers: but his brother's presence is referred to in his application for naturalization only as a reference to his good conduct. Furthermore, other members of his family have asserted Notteböhm's desire to spend his old age in Guatemala.

These facts clearly establish, on the one hand, the absence of any bond of attachment between Notteböhm and Liechtenstein and, on the other hand, the existence of a long standing and close connection between him and Guatemala, a link which his naturalization in no way weakened. That naturalization was not based on any real prior connection with Liechtenstein, nor did it in any way alter the manner of life of the person upon whom it was conferred in exceptional circumstances of speed and accommodation. In both respects, it was lacking in the genuineness requisite to an act of such importance, if it is to be entitled to be respected by a State in the position of Guatemala. It was granted without regard to the concept of nationality adopted in international relations.

Naturalization was asked for not so much for the purpose of obtaining a legal recognition of Notteböhm's membership in fact in the population of Liechtenstein, as it was to enable him to substitute for his status as a national of a belligerent State that of a neutral State, with the sole aim of thus coming within the protection of Liechtenstein but not becoming wedded to its traditions, its interests, its way of life or of assuming the obligations—other than fiscal obligations—and exercising the rights pertaining to the status thus acquired.

Guatemala is under no obligation to recognize a nationality granted in such circumstances. Liechtenstein consequently is not entitled to extend its protection to Notteböhm vis-à-vis Guatemala. ...

For these reasons,

The Court,

by eleven votes to three,

Holds that the claim submitted by the Government of the Principality of Liechtenstein is inadmissible.

NOTES

1) Is there a definition of nationality in international law? If not, does it pose a problem that there are divergent national definitions?

2) Is there a general principle of international law requiring a genuine link for the conferment of nationality? Is "genuine" the same as "effective"?[13] Why should a state not be able to espouse the claims of any of its nationals? Note that the 1985 Rules regarding International Claims issued by the British Foreign and Commonwealth office[14] simply state in Rule I that: "Her Majesty's Government will not take up the claim unless the claimant is a United Kingdom national and was so at the date of the injury."

3) Why was it not relevant that Liechtenstein's law provided for loss of any prior nationality and Germany's law provided for loss of German nationality on acquisition of another nationality?

4) Could Liechtenstein have espoused a claim on behalf of Notteböhm against Germany? Could Guatemala have protected him against any state? If Notteböhm had in fact been born in Liechtenstein, and had become a permanent resident of Guatemala, could Liechtenstein have espoused a claim against Guatemala? Should Germany alone have been able to contest Notteböhm's naturalization? Note the importance in the eyes of the Court of the comparative ties of Notteböhm to Liechtenstein and Guatemala.[15] The Court stated that Notteböhm had a "long standing and close connection" with Guatemala. Suppose Notteböhm alleged that he had been injured by Canada. Could Liechtenstein espouse a claim on his behalf against Canada?

5) Other cases may result in dual nationality, such as when the act of naturalization does not revoke the person's original nationality. Supposing this to have been the law in Germany, what then would Notteböhm's position have been?

6) In *Flegenheimer*, which follows, the Italian–United States Conciliation Commission distinguished *Notteböhm*, noting that different considerations apply in a case involving only one nationality.

Flegenheimer Claim
Italian–United States Conciliation Commission
(1958), 14 R.I.A.A. 327; 25 I.L.R. 91

[Flegenheimer had lost his United States nationality in 1894 when he acquired German nationality. In 1940, under German law, he lost his German nationality and was

---

13 See I. Brownlie, *Principles of Public International Law*, 6th ed. (2003) at 387-88, 395-406.

14 (1988) 37 I.C.L.Q. 1006.

15 See Chapter 10, Section C.1 on "Espousal and Nationality of Claims" for an analysis of the nationality of claims issue. See also the *Flegenheimer Claim* (1958), 14 R.I.A.A. 327; 25 I.L.R. 91 (Italian–United States Conciliation Commission); the *Canevaro Case (Italy v. Peru)* (1912), 11 R.I.A.A. 397, translated in (1912) 6 A.J.I.L. 746 and reported later in this section together with the *Hague Convention on Certain Questions Relating to the Conflict of Nationality Laws* (1930) 179 L.N.T.S. 89.

rendered stateless. The United States espoused his claim before the Commission for property damage in World War II. The Commission dismissed his claim but still addressed the Italian argument that even assuming he had retained his United States nationality, it lacked the genuine connection required by *Notteböhm*.]

THE COMMISSION: ...

The Commission is of the opinion that it is doubtful that the International Court of Justice intended to establish a rule of general international law in requiring, in the Notteböhm Case, that there must exist an effective link between the person and the State in order that the latter may exercise its right of diplomatic protection on behalf of the former. ...

The theory of effective or active nationality was established, in the Law of Nations, and above all in international private law, for the purpose of settling conflicts between two national states, or two national laws, regarding persons simultaneously vested with both nationalities, in order to decide which of them is to be dominant, whether that described as nominal, based on legal provisions of a given legal system, or that described as effective or active, equally based on legal provisions of another legal system, but confirmed by elements of fact (domicile, participation in the political life, the center of family business interests, etc.). It must allow one to make a distinction, between two bonds of nationality equally founded in law, which is the stronger and hence the effective one. ...

But when a person is vested with only one nationality, which is attributed to him or her either *jure sanguinis* or *jure soli*, or by a valid naturalization entailing the positive loss of the former nationality, the theory of effective nationality cannot be applied without the risk of causing confusion. It lacks a sufficiently positive basis to be applied to a nationality which finds support in a state law. There does not in fact exist any criterion of proven effectiveness for disclosing the effectiveness of a bond with a political collectivity, and the persons by the thousands who, because of the facility of travel in the modern world, possess the positive legal nationality of a State, but live in foreign States where they are domiciled and where their family and business center is located, would be exposed to non-recognition, at the international level, of the nationality with which they are undeniably vested by virtue of the laws of their national State, if this doctrine were to be generalized.

3. The Right of Diplomatic Protection

Both *Notteböhm* and *Flegenheimer* deal with the right of states to extend diplomatic protection to their nationals. In 1996, the ILC identified this topic as one "appropriate for codification and progressive development," and in December 1996 the General Assembly requested that the Commission pursue the issue. A Working Group was established, and a Special Rapporteur appointed in 1997. At its 56th session, in 2004, the ILC adopted, on first reading, the text of 19 draft articles, including a number dealing with the question of nationality as it relates to diplomatic protection (issues arising from nationality of corporations and ships are dealt with below in sections B and C, respectively). The Draft

Articles on Diplomatic Protection were transmitted to the Secretary-General, to be distributed to governments for comments (to be submitted by January 2006).[16]

International Law Commission, Draft Articles on Diplomatic Protection
Report of the International Law Commission on the Work of Its 56th Session,
UN GAOR, 59th Sess., Supp. No 10, U.N. Doc. A/59/10 (2004) chp. IV

PART I: GENERAL PROVISIONS

Article 1
Definition and Scope

Diplomatic protection consists of resort to diplomatic action or other means of peaceful settlement by a State adopting in its own right the cause of its national in respect of an injury to that national arising from an internationally wrongful act of another State.

. . .

PART II: NATIONALITY

Chapter I: General Principles

Article 3
Protection by the State of Nationality

   1. The State entitled to exercise diplomatic protection is the State of nationality.

   2. Notwithstanding paragraph 1, diplomatic protection may be exercised in respect of a non-national in accordance with draft article 8.

Chapter II: Natural Persons

Article 4
State of Nationality of a Natural Person

For the purposes of diplomatic protection of natural persons, a State of nationality means a State whose nationality the individual sought to be protected has acquired by

---

16 *Report of the International Law Commission on the Work of Its 56th Session,* UN GAOR, 59th Sess., Supp. No. 10, U.N. Doc. A/59/10 (2004) chp. IV. For a summary of the work conducted, and the consideration at various sessions of the Commission, see the Report at 14-16. In 1999 the first Special Rapporteur, Mr. Mohamed Bennouna, was elected a Judge of the International Criminal Tribunal for the Former Yugoslavia, and Mr. Christopher John R. Dugard was appinted as Special Rapporteur for the topic.

birth, descent, succession of States, naturalization or in any other manner, not inconsistent with international law.

· · ·

Article 6
Multiple Nationality and Claim Against a Third State

1. Any State of which a dual or multiple national is a national may exercise diplomatic protection in respect of that national against a State of which that individual is not a national.

2. Two or more States of nationality may jointly exercise diplomatic protection in respect of a dual or multiple national.

Article 7
Multiple Nationality and Claim Against a State of Nationality

A State of nationality may not exercise diplomatic protection in respect of a person against a State of which that person is also a national unless the nationality of the former State is predominant, both at the time of the injury and at the date of the official presentation of the claim.

Article 8
Stateless Persons and Refugees

1. A State may exercise diplomatic protection in respect of a stateless person who, at the time of the injury and at the date of the official presentation of the claim, is lawfully and habitually resident in that State.

2. A State may exercise diplomatic protection in respect of a person who is recognized as a refugee by that State when that person, at the time of the injury and at the date of the official presentation of the claim, is lawfully and habitually resident in that State.

3. Paragraph 2 does not apply in respect of an injury caused by an internationally wrongful act of the State of nationality of the refugee.

NOTE

Article 8(c) of the Maastricht Treaty on European Union provides as follows:

Every citizen of the Union shall, in the territory of a third country in which the Member State of which he is a national is not represented, be entitled to protection by the diplomatic or consular authorities of any Member State, on the same conditions as the nationals of that State. Before 31 December 1993, Member States shall establish the necessary rules among themselves and start the international negotiations required to secure this protection.[17]

---

17   *Supra* note 12 at article 8(c).

Is this article consistent with the approach adopted by the ILC in the draft articles reproduced above? Does it establish or claim any right for EU member states to provide diplomatic protection for non-nationals in the territories of non-members?

4. Dual and Multiple Nationality

By application of the *jus sanguinis* and *jus soli* principles, coupled with naturalization, an individual may have more than one nationality.

1930 Hague Convention on Conflict of Nationality Laws
179 L.N.T.S. 89; Can. T.S. 1930 No. 7

Article 1

It is for each state to determine under its own law who are its nationals. This law shall be recognized by other States in so far as it is consistent with international conventions, international custom and the principles of law generally recognized with regard to nationality.

Article 2

Any question as to whether a person possesses the nationality of a particular State shall be determined in accordance with the laws of that State.

Article 3

Subject to the provisions of the present convention, a person having two or more nationalities may be regarded as its national by each of the States whose nationality he possesses.

Article 4

A State may not afford diplomatic protection to one of its nationals against a State whose nationality such person also possesses.

Article 5

Within a third State, a person having more than one nationality shall be treated as if he had only one. Without prejudice to the application of its law in matters of personal status and of any conventions in force, a third State shall, of the nationalities which any such person possesses, recognize exclusively in its territory either the nationality of the country in which he is habitually and principally resident, or the nationality of the country with which the circumstances he appears to be most closely connected.

Article 6

Without prejudice to the liberty of a State to accord wider rights to renounce its nationality, a person possessing two nationalities acquired without any voluntary act on his part may renounce one of them with the authorization of the State whose nationality he desires to surrender.

This authorization may not be refused in the case of a person who has his habitual and permanent residence abroad, if the conditions laid down in the law of the State whose nationality he desires to surrender are satisfied.

Canevaro Case
Italy v. Peru
(1912), 11 R.I.A.A. 397; 6 A.J.I.L. 746
Permanent Court of Arbitration, The Hague

[This case concerned a claim made by Italy against Peru for a debt owed by that government to the Canevaro brothers. Concerning the status of Raphael Canevaro, the Court held that he was a Peruvian by birth and an Italian under article 4 of the Italian Civil Code, which assigned him that nationality because his father was Italian.]

THE COURT: … And whereas, as a matter of fact, Raphael Canevaro has on several occasions acted as a Peruvian citizen, both by running as a candidate for the Senate, where none are admitted except Peruvian citizens and where he went to defend his election, and also especially by accepting the office of Consul General of the Netherlands, after soliciting the authorization of the Peruvian Government and the Peruvian Congress;

And whereas, under these circumstances, whatever Raphael Canevaro's status may be in Italy with respect to his nationality, the Government of Peru has a right to consider him as a Peruvian citizen and to deny his status as an Italian claimant;

And whereas, the claim of 1880 belongs at present to the three Canevaro brothers, two of whom are certainly Italians;

And one is justified in wondering whether this circumstance renders the law of 1889 inapplicable;

And whereas, the tribunal need not inquire what decision should be reached if the claim had belonged to Italians at the time the law was enacted which reduced to so large an extent the rights of the creditors of Peru, and whether the same sacrifices could be imposed on foreigners as on natives;

But at present it is solely a question of ascertaining whether the situation in which natives are placed, and which they have to accept, will be radically modified because foreigners are substituted for natives in one form or another.

NOTES

1) The Court held that Raphael Canevaro could not succeed against Peru. His two brothers who were solely Italians were successful in their claim.

2) Rule III of the 1985 British Rules regarding International Claims[18] state that where the claimant has dual nationality the British government may take up the claim although it may be appropriate in certain circumstances to do so jointly with the other state of nationality's government. With respect to the type of scenario presented above in the Canevaro case the same rule states:

> Her Majesty's Government will not normally take up his claim as a United Kingdom national if the respondent state is the state of his second nationality, but may do so if the respondent state has, in the circumstances which gave rise to the injury, treated the claimant as a United Kingdom national.

3) See also articles 6 and 7 of the ILC Draft Articles on Diplomatic Protection, reproduced above. Article 6 provides that, in the case of multiple nationality, diplomatic protection may be exercised by any of the states of nationality or may be exercised jointly. Article 7 restricts the claim of protection by one state of nationality against another to those cases in which the nationality of the claiming state is "predominant" over the other.

Iran–United States Case No. A/18
Iran–United States Claims Tribunal
(1984), 5 Iran–U.S.C.T.R. 251; (1984) 23 I.L.M. 489

[On account of a great many claims being brought against Iran by dual United States–Iranian citizens, the Full Tribunal was requested to decide whether it had jurisdiction to hear the merits of such claims. The Tribunal turned to customary international law, finding the Iranian–U.S. Claims Settlement Declaration not sufficiently clear.]

THE TRIBUNAL: ...

Article 4 of the [1930 Hague] Convention ... must be interpreted very cautiously. Not only is it more than fifty years old and found in a treaty to which only 20 states are parties, but great changes have occurred since then in the concept of diplomatic protection ... . This concept continues to be in a process of transformation ... .

Moreover, the negotiating history of Article 4 ... suggests that its application is doubtful in a case, such as the present one, where a dual national, by himself, brings before an international tribunal his own claim against one of the States whose nationality he possesses. Such a proposal was made during the Conference, but it was rejected ... .

Another reason why the applicability of Article 4 to the claims of dual nationals before this Tribunal is debatable is that it applies by its own terms solely to "diplomatic protection" by a State. While this Tribunal is clearly an international tribunal

---

18 *Supra* note 14 at 1007.

established by treaty and while some of its cases involve disputes between the two
governments and involve the interpretation and application of public international
law, most disputes (including all those by dual nationals) involve a private party on
the one side and a government or government-controlled entity on the other, and many
involve primarily issues of municipal law and general principles of law. In such cases
it is the rights of the claimant, not of his nation, that are to be determined by the
Tribunal. This should be contrasted with the situation of espousal of claims in
international law ... .

... [T]he Parties in the present case have acknowledged that the law prior to 1930
was uncertain ... . The Tribunal ... is satisfied that, whatever the state of the law prior
to 1945, the better rule at the time [the Settlement Declaration was] concluded and
today is the Rule of dominant and effective nationality. ...

While *Notteböhm* itself did not involve a claim against a State of which Notteböhm
was a national, it demonstrated the acceptance and approval by the International Court
of Justice of the search for the real and effective nationality based on the facts of a
case, instead of an approach relying on more formalistic criteria. ...

A few months later ... the Italian–United States Conciliation Commission ...
decided in the *Mergé Case*[19] that the principle "... based on the sovereign equality of
States, which excludes diplomatic protection in the case of dual nationality, must
yield before the principle of effective nationality whenever such nationality is that of
the claiming State." ...

This trend toward modification of the Hague Convention rule of non-responsibility
by search for the dominant and effective nationality is scarcely surprising as it is
consistent with the contemporaneous development of international law to accord legal
protections to individuals, even against the state of which they are nationals. ...

For the reasons stated above, the Tribunal holds that it has jurisdiction over claims
against Iran by dual Iran–United States nationals when the dominant and effective
nationality of the claimant during the relevant period from the date the claim arose
until 19 January 1981 was that of the United States. In determining the dominant and
effective nationality, the Tribunal will consider all relevant factors, including habitual
residence, centre of interests, family ties, participation in public life and other evidence
of attachment.

NOTES

1) The Iran–United States Claims Tribunal was established in 1981 and sits at The
Hague. It was set up as part of the package for the release of the U.S. hostages held in the
U.S. Embassy in Tehran. As seen in the extract above, it is of special interest that private
claims are asserted by the individual claimant and not grounded on state espousal.[20]

---

19   (1955), 22 I.L.R. 443 (Italian–United States Conciliation Commission).

20   See D. Caron, "The Nature of the Iran–United States Claims Tribunal and the Evolving Structure of
     International Dispute Resolution" (1990) 84 A.J.I.L. 104.

2) Nationality laws may provide the individual with an option to retain or renounce nationality. Section 9 of the Canadian *Citizenship Act*[21] provides:

(1) A citizen may, on application, renounce his citizenship if he
(a) is a citizen of a country other than Canada or, if his application is accepted, will become a citizen of a country other than Canada;
(b) is not the subject of a declaration by the Governor in Council made pursuant to section 20;
(c) is not a minor;
(d) is not prevented from understanding the significance of renouncing citizenship by reason of the person having a mental disability; and
(e) does not reside in Canada.
(2) The Minister may, in the Minister's discretion, waive on compassionate grounds the requirements of paragraph (1)(d) or (e).
(3) Where an application for renunciation is approved, the Minister shall issue a certificate of renunciation to the applicant and the applicant ceases to be a citizen after the expiration of the day on which the certificate is issued or such later day as the certificate may specify.

3) In reply to an enquiry about the possibility of a Canadian holding dual nationality becoming liable to foreign military service, the Department of External Affairs wrote in March 1968:

Many countries do not recognize the acquisition of another nationality by their citizens as affecting in any way the citizenship they already possess and are not prepared to relieve such persons of the responsibilities and obligations which devolve upon their citizens. Since this practice has the sanction of international law the authorities of the countries concerned are entitled in their territory to require all their citizens, whether dual nationals or otherwise, to comply with the stipulations of their laws, just as Canada insists that Canadian citizens who are also nationals of another country must be treated in Canada as having the same rights, privileges and responsibilities as all other Canadian citizens. It is considerations of this sort that have prompted us to issue a relevant caveat to Canadians with dual nationality in the pamphlet "Information for Canadians Travelling Overseas."[22]

5. Allegiance

The corollary to a state's protection of its nationals is the duty of allegiance that nationals owe to their state while at home or abroad. A state may prosecute those persons owing allegiance to it for treasonous activities against the state committed abroad. As well, reference should be made more generally to the active and passive nationality bases of jurisdiction contained in Chapter 9, Section A on "Subject Matter Jurisdiction." In Canada, the *Criminal Code*, section 46(3) provides that a Canadian citizen or "a person who owes

---

21   R.S.C. 1985, c. C-29, as amended. S.C. 1992, c. 21.

22   Quoted in J.-G. Castel, *International Law*, 3d ed. (1976) at 464.

allegiance to Her Majesty in Right of Canada" commits treason if he or she performs the acts in question "while in or out of Canada." The same acts are treason if committed in Canada by any person.[23]

In 1946, the British House of Lords had before them the appeal from William Joyce in *Joyce v. Director of Public Prosecutions*.[24] Joyce was not a British citizen; he had been born in 1906 in the United States. However, after living in England from 1921 until 1939, he fraudulently obtained a British passport, which he was not entitled to, and went to Berlin where during World War II he was an employee of the German Radio Company as a propaganda news broadcaster. He was arrested in 1945 and was prosecuted in Britain for treason. He was found guilty. The issue on appeal was whether as a foreigner he owed allegiance to Britain. The House of Lords held that if he had been a natural born or a naturalized British citizen he clearly would have owed allegiance. Generally, aliens only owe allegiance when resident or if abroad when they have maintained a connection with the state of residence, such as leaving family or effects behind them. In Joyce's case he had not. Nevertheless, the majority held that by his own volition he had maintained his ties with Britain. It made no difference that he had lied to get the passport. The effect of obtaining the passport was that he was entitled to British protection abroad, and he extended his duty of allegiance beyond the time when he left Britain for Germany. He had not, according to the House of Lords, surrendered the passport or taken any other overt step to withdraw from his allegiance. The Court held that the act of treason itself could not be so viewed. In fact Joyce's special value to Nazi Germany was that he represented himself as a British subject and his German workbook in his possession when arrested indicated this. The passport itself was never found.

6. Proof of Nationality

A duly authorized passport is only *prima facie* evidence of nationality.[25] States usually only issue passports to their nationals. However, such issuance does not create nationality. Eligibility in Canada depends on whether the applicant is a Canadian citizen as defined in the *Citizenship Act*.

Canadian passports are issued by the Minister of Foreign Affairs in the exercise of the Royal Prerogative. There is no statute governing the issuance of Canadian passports and no person has a legal entitlement to one. In Canada the legal position is that the Minister of Foreign Affairs has discretionary power to issue or withhold a passport.

The Canadian government issues passports to Canadian citizens so that they may possess evidence of their identity and national status when entering another country. Three types of passports are issued—ordinary, special, and diplomatic. Any Canadian citizen may normally receive an ordinary passport. However, in certain instances,

---

23   R.S.C. 1985, c. C-46, as am., s. 46(3)(a), (b).

24   [1946] A.C. 347 (H.L.). For a similar case concerning the broadcaster known as "Tokyo Rose" see *D'Aquino v. United States*, 192 F.2d 338 (U.S.C.A. 9th Cir. 1951).

25   *Re Gur* (1971), 1 I.A.C. 384.

depending on the nature of their governmental or parliamentary duties and purposes of travel abroad, some Canadians are entitled to receive either a special or diplomatic passport.

Passports are rarely withheld except when the applicant is indebted to the Government for repatriation expenses. At the request of the police or judicial authorities, they may be withheld from a person who is charged with a serious criminal offence and is on bail while awaiting trial. In addition, it is sometimes necessary to withhold passport facilities for children under the age of 16 years when there is a marital dispute involving legal custody and it appears that the parent applying for the passport does not have a clear right to take the child out of Canada.

Endorsements are placed in passports when the bearers have urgent reasons for travel and it has been decided to provide them with interim passport facilities even though they have not met all departmental requirements: for example, they have not repaid the department for financial assistance provided while they were abroad or they have failed to satisfy the department that their last passports are not recoverable. Also, when financial assistance is given to Canadian citizens at a post abroad, unless they are issued emergency passports for return to Canada, their ordinary passports are endorsed as being valid only for travel to Canada and countries en route.

7. Loss of Nationality and Statelessness

Loss of Nationality

Nationality may be renounced. A child with two nationalities because of the dual principles of *jus solis* and *jus sanguinis* may be allowed to renounce one upon coming to majority.

Section 7 of the *Citizenship Act*[26] provides:

> Where a person who was born outside Canada after the coming into force of this Act is a citizen because at the time of his birth one of his parents was a citizen by virtue of paragraph 3(1)(b) or 3(1)(e), that person ceases to be a citizen upon attaining the age of twenty-eight years unless he
>
> (a) makes application to retain his citizenship; and
>
> (b) registers as a citizen and either resides in Canada for a period of at least one year immediately preceding the date of his application or establishes a substantial connection with Canada.

Some states do not allow a citizen to remain as such if he or she acquires a new nationality. This is not the case in Canada.

Denationalization or denaturalization may also occur by way of legislation. It may be used as a penalty for the commission of serious crimes such as treason, espionage, or war crimes under international law. Section 10 of the *Citizenship Act* provides as follows:

---

26   R.S.C. 1985, c. C-29, as amended. See also section 9, reported *supra* at note 21. See *Canada (Secretary of State) v. Luitjens* (1991), 46 F.T.R. 267 (T.D.), appeal quashed 54 F.T.R. 237 (C.A.), leave to appeal to S.C.C. refused 10 C.R.R. (4th) 384n.

(1) Subject to section 17 but notwithstanding any other section of this Act, where the Governor in Council, upon a report from the Minister, is satisfied that any person has obtained, retained, renounced or resumed citizenship under this Act by false representation or fraud or by knowingly concealing material circumstances,

(a) the person ceases to be a citizen, or

(b) the renunciation of citizenship by the person shall be deemed to have no effect, as of such date as, may be fixed by order of the Governor in Council with respect thereto.

(2) A person shall be deemed to have obtained citizenship by false representation or fraud or by knowingly concealing material circumstances if

(a) he was lawfully admitted to Canada for permanent residence by false representation or fraud or by knowingly concealing material circumstances; and

(b) he subsequently obtained citizenship because he had been admitted to Canada for permanent residence.

Statelessness

Statelessness can arise through a variety of circumstances: conflicts of nationality laws, changes of sovereignty over territory,[27] or denationalization by the state.

Stoeck v. Public Trustee
[1921] 2 Ch. 67

RUSSELL J.: The plaintiff sues the Public Trustee and the Attorney-General for a declaration that he was not on January 10, 1920 (the date when the Treaty of Peace with Germany came into force), and is not, a German national within the meaning of the Treaty of Peace Order, 1919, or the Treaty of Peace; and he also asks for other relief. The object of his action is to ascertain whether certain property in this country—namely, (i) a sum of 2722 pounds 11s. 6d.; (ii) a balance at the bank of 172 pounds 9s. 4d.; and (iii) some furniture in store—are subject to the charge created by s. 1, sub-s. XVI, of the Treaty of Peace Order, and whether he can deal with such property without incurring the pains and penalties prescribed by sub-s. XVII of the same section. ...

The relevant personal history of the plaintiff is as follows: He was born in 1872 at Kreuznach in Rhenish Prussia. In October, 1895, he left Prussia and went to reside in Belgium. On June 26, 1896, he obtained his discharge from Prussian Nationality. He never subsequently applied for, or obtained the nationality of any German state. In November, 1896, he came to England, and made this country his permanent home. He was never naturalized here. In May, 1916, he was interned. In 1918 he was deported to Holland; thence he went to Germany and has resided there ever since. ...

---

27   See Chapter 2, Section D on "State Succession."

The relevant question affecting the plaintiff is this: Is his property here property belonging to a German national and, therefore, property which is charged by the Treaty of Peace Order, and which he may not deal with except with the consent of the custodian or at the risk of fine and imprisonment? ...

The question for me to decide in this connection is whether the plaintiff on the evidence before me has satisfied me that he has lost his German nationality for all purposes. ...

This evidence satisfies me that the plaintiff has lost his German nationality for all purposes. It is not suggested that he has acquired any other nationality. If then such a condition is possible in law the plaintiff is a person of no nationality; he is a stateless person. Is such a condition possible in law? So far as international law is concerned, opinions appear to differ. ... After all the question of what State a person belongs to must ultimately be decided by the municipal law of the State to which he claims that he belongs; and if no state exists according to the municipal law of which a given individual is its national, it is difficult to see to what State he can belong, how he can be other than a stateless person, or why an international lawyer or any one else should close his eyes to such a possibility.

How does the matter stand as regards German municipal law? It is clear on the evidence before me that German municipal law recognized the condition of a stateless person. ...

How does the matter stand in regard to English municipal law? ... The dearth of direct authority in English law upon this point is not to be wondered at. In truth the question of statelessness can have seldom arisen as an important or practical question. The division into subjects and aliens is clear and sufficient for the ordinary purposes of the common law; and the stateless person would be one of the aliens. But the present case has raised the question, and, upon consideration of the arguments addressed to me and the statutory enactments before referred to, I hold that the condition of a stateless person is not a condition unrecognized by the municipal law of this country.

There remains for consideration the contention that the words "German national" in the Treaty of Peace Order, and s. iv. of Part X of the Treaty of Peace, mean or include a German national according to English law. I confess I have difficulty in following this. Whether a person is a national of a country must be determined by the municipal law of that country. Upon this I think all text writers are agreed. It would be strange were it otherwise. How could the municipal law of England determine that a person *is* a national of Germany? It might determine that for the purposes of English municipal law a person shall be deemed to be a national of Germany, or shall be treated as if he were a national of Germany; but that would not constitute him a national of Germany, if he were not such according to the municipal law of Germany. In truth there is not and cannot be such an individual as a German national according to English law; and there could be no justification for interpreting or expanding the words "German national" in the manner suggested.

[A declaration for the plaintiff was granted.]

Problems of the Stateless Individual
from S.A. Williams and A.L.C. de Mestral, *An Introduction to International Law*,
2d ed. (1987) at 289-90 (footnotes omitted)

The problem is a serious one, as persons without a nationality are under an extreme disability. Article 15 of the Universal Declaration of Human Rights, 1948 which was adopted by the General Assembly of the United Nations, lays down as a common standard to be achieved by states that "everyone has the right to a nationality."

The questions to be answered are how does such a condition arise and what can be done to prevent it? Answering the first is the simpler task. There are thousands of individuals who suffer this condition or whose nationality is a matter of dispute. At the present time, it is the prerogative of states to adopt their own nationality laws and there is no restriction on their liberty to adopt rules which may result in statelessness. For example, James Brown is born in state A of parents whose nationality is that of state B, while they are on holiday in state A. Under the law of state B, nationality is only given on the basis of birth on the territory of state B according to the *jus soli* principle. The law of state A provides that its nationality is only acquired at birth by individuals whose parents are nationals of state A. In this situation, James Brown would have neither the nationality of state A nor of state B. Statelessness may also result if nationality is taken away as a penalty or otherwise. Statelessness shows clearly that through the application of domestic laws in several states, a serious lacuna is left which threatens the application of the principles of international law.

What measures has the international community taken to reduce statelessness? Conventions have been signed that deal with the subject, but it must be remembered that the stumbling block to a solution is that it is the domestic law that deals with the subject at the state and individual levels. The 1948 Universal Declaration of Human Rights states that besides the fact that everyone should possess a nationality, no one should be arbitrarily deprived of nationality. This principle of possession is one that has been easily accepted by states but, as mentioned above, uniform practice has been hard to come by as each state has its own nationality laws which often can be at variance with those of another state. The United Nations Convention on the Reduction of Statelessness of 1961 ... achieved a limited measure of headway. It provides, *inter alia*, that persons who would otherwise be stateless should acquire the nationality of the state of birth. [It also prohibits deprivation of nationality on "racial, ethnic, religious, or political grounds."]

The only way to prevent this disabling condition is to ensure that states take a flexible approach and do in fact allow for both the use of the *jus soli* and *jus sanguinis* theories, to oblige states not to adopt legislation that has the effect of denationalization, to encourage a liberal approach on the conferment of nationality on stateless persons and lastly to grant relief through international conventions which allow the use of identity or travel documents and to ensure the admission of such persons to states and employment within those states, thus leading to eventual nationalization.

NOTES

1) The League of Nations in 1922 issued to stateless persons the so-called Nansen passport.[28] This was, however, simply an identity document and permitted the person to travel and a right of re-entry to the state that had issued it.[29]

2) The United Nations has two relevant multilateral conventions, the 1954 Convention on the Status of Stateless Persons,[30] and the 1961 Convention on the Reduction of Statelessness,[31] which came into force in 1975 and has applied to Canada since its accession in 1978.

Convention on the Reduction of Statelessness
U.N. Doc. A/CONF. 9/15 (1961)

Article 10

1. Every treaty between Contracting States providing for the transfer of territory shall include provisions designed to secure that no person shall become stateless as a result of the transfer. A Contracting State shall use its best endeavours to secure that any such treaty made by it with a State which is not a party to this Convention includes such provisions.

2. In the absence of such provisions a Contracting State to which territory is transferred or which otherwise acquires territory shall confer its nationality on such persons as would otherwise become stateless as a result of the transfer or acquisition.

NOTE

Since 1993, the International Law Commission (ILC) has included in its agenda the topic of "state succession and its impact on the nationality of natural and legal persons." At its 51st session in 1999 the Commission adopted, on second reading, the text of the Draft Articles on Nationality of Natural Persons in Relation to the Succession of States.[32]

---

28 *Agreement on the Issue of Certificates of Identity to Russian Refugees* (1922) 13 L.N.T.S. 237.

29 See L.C. Green, "Is World Citizenship a Legal Practicality?" (1987) 25 Can. Y. B. Int'l L. 151 at 181.

30 360 U.N.T.S. 117. Some 57 states are parties.

31 989 U.N.T.S. 175. Only 29 states, including Canada, are parties.

32 *Report of the International Law Commission on the Work of Its 51st Session*, U.N. GAOR, 54th Sess. Supp. No. 10, U.N. Doc. A/54/10 (1999) chp. IV.

International Law Commission, Draft Articles on Nationality of Natural Persons in Relation to the Succession of States

Report of the International Law Commission on the Work of Its 51st Session,
UN GAOR, 54th Sess., Supp. No 10, U.N. Doc. A/54/10 (1999) chp. IV

PART I: GENERAL PROVISIONS

Article 1
Right to a Nationality

Every individual who, on the date of the succession of States, had the nationality of the predecessor State, irrespective of the mode of acquisition of that nationality, has the right to the nationality of at least one of the States concerned, in accordance with the present draft articles. ...

Article 4
Prevention of Statelessness

States concerned shall take all appropriate measures to prevent persons who, on the date of the succession of States, had the nationality of the predecessor State from becoming stateless as a result of such succession.

Article 5
Presumption of Nationality

Subject to the provisions of the present draft articles, persons concerned having their habitual residence in the territory affected by the succession of States are presumed to acquire the nationality of the successor State on the date of such succession.

Article 6
Legislation Concerning Nationality and Other Connected Issues

Each State concerned should, without undue delay, enact legislation on nationality and other connected issues arising in relation to the succession of States consistent with the provisions of the present draft articles. It should take all appropriate measures to ensure that persons concerned will be apprised, within a reasonable time period, of the effect of its legislation on their nationality, of any choices they may have thereunder, as well as of the consequences that the exercise of such choices will have on their status. ...

Article 10
Loss of Nationality upon the Voluntary Acquisition of the
Nationality of Another State

1. A predecessor State may provide that persons concerned who, in relation to the succession of States, voluntarily acquire the nationality of a successor State shall lose its nationality.

2. A successor State may provide that persons concerned who, in relation to the succession of States, voluntarily acquire the nationality of another successor State or, as the case may be, retain the nationality of the predecessor State shall lose its nationality acquired in relation to such succession.

Article 11
Respect for the Will of Persons Concerned

1. States concerned shall give consideration to the will of persons concerned whenever those persons are qualified to acquire the nationality of two or more States concerned. ...

Article 15
Non-discrimination

States concerned shall not deny persons concerned the right to retain or acquire a nationality or the right of option upon the succession of States by discriminating on any ground.

Article 16
Prohibition of Arbitrary Decisions Concerning Nationality Issues

Persons concerned shall not be arbitrarily deprived of the nationality of the predecessor State, or arbitrarily denied the right to acquire the nationality of the successor State or any right of option, to which they are entitled in relation to the succession of States. ...

PART II: PROVISIONS RELATING TO SPECIFIC CATEGORIES OF
SUCCESSION OF STATES

Section 4, Separation of Part or Parts of the Territory

Article 24
Attribution of the Nationality of the Successor State

When part or parts of the territory of a State separate from that State and form one or more successor States while the predecessor State continues to exist, a successor State shall, unless otherwise indicated by the exercise of a right of option, attribute its nationality to:

  (a) persons concerned having their habitual residence in its territory; and
  (b) subject to the provisions of article 8:

  (i) persons concerned not covered by subparagraph (a) having an appropriate legal connection with a constituent unit of the predecessor State that has become part of that successor State;

  (ii) persons concerned not entitled to a nationality of any State concerned under subparagraphs (a) and (b)(i) having their habitual residence in a third State, who were born in or, before leaving the predecessor State, had their last habitual residence in what has become the territory of that successor State or having any other appropriate connection with that successor State.

Article 25
Withdrawal of the Nationality of the Predecessor State

1. The predecessor State shall withdraw its nationality from persons concerned qualified to acquire the nationality of the successor State in accordance with article 24. It shall not, however, withdraw its nationality before such persons acquire the nationality of the successor State.

2. Unless otherwise indicated by the exercise of a right of option, the predecessor State shall not, however, withdraw its nationality from persons referred to in paragraph 1 who:

(a) have their habitual residence in its territory;

(b) are not covered by subparagraph (a) and have an appropriate legal connection with a constituent unit of the predecessor State that has remained part of the predecessor State;

(c) have their habitual residence in a third State, and were born in or, before leaving the predecessor State, had their last habitual residence in what has remained part of the territory of the predecessor State or have any other appropriate connection with that State.

Article 26
Granting of the Right of Option by the Predecessor and the Successor States

Predecessor and successor States shall grant a right of option to all persons concerned covered by the provisions of articles 24 and 25, paragraph 2, who are qualified to have the nationality of both the predecessor and successor States or of two or more successor States.

NOTES

1) Article 1 provides for a right to a nationality. Which state is to be presented with the claim? Does it depend upon the type of succession of state and the nature of the links that the person has with the one or more states involved?

2) In 1997, the Council of Europe adopted the European Convention on Nationality.[33] It contains general principles on nationality, its acquisition and loss, and the interrelationship between state succession and nationality.

3) The problem of dual nationality and statelessness in the context of state succession becomes particularly acute in cases of the dissolution of states amid armed conflict. Various manifestations of the nationality issue were addressed by the Eritrea–Ethiopia Claims Commission in its *Partial Award on Civilian Claims*, in which Eritrea had claimed *inter alia* for "deprivation of nationality" of certain persons by Ethiopia.

---

33   Eur. Doc. DIR/JUR(97)6, Eur. T.S. 166; (1998) 37 I.L.M. 44.

**Partial Award, Civilians Claims, Eritrea's Claims 15, 16, 23, and 27–32
Between the State of Eritrea and the Federal Democratic Republic of
Ethiopia (December 17, 2004)**
Eritrea–Ethiopia Claims Commission (2005) 44 I.L.M. 601; PCA online:
http://www.pca-cpa.org/ENGLISH/RPC/ (footnotes omitted)

THE COMMISSION ...

6. ... Eritrea's main claims and Ethiopia's defenses have their origins in the unusual circumstances leading to the emergence of Eritrea as a separate State during the early 1990s. ... In 1991, following the success of their long and bitter struggle against the Mengistu regime in Ethiopia, the successful revolutionary movements that had assumed power in Addis Ababa and Asmara agreed that "the people of Eritrea have the right to determine their own future by themselves and ... that the future status of Eritrea should be decided by the Eritrean people in a referendum ... ."

7. Organizing the Referendum was a large and complex task undertaken by the Referendum Commission of Eritrea ("RCE") appointed in April 1992. A Referendum Proclamation issued on April 7, 1992 established detailed procedures and limited participation to persons over 18 "having Eritrean citizenship." ... The Referendum was successfully held on 23–25 April 1993, with extremely high participation and almost 99% of voters voting for Eritrea's independence. ...

8. During the decades when Eritrea did not exist as a separate political entity, there was extensive movement of population both into and out of the area of present-day Eritrea. ... Many Ethiopians of Eritrean ancestry knew only Ethiopia as their home. Many thousands of persons who were born or whose parents were born within the present-day boundaries of Eritrea came to reside as Ethiopian citizens in Addis Ababa and elsewhere in Ethiopia. ...

10. The heart of Eritrea's case is its contention that beginning soon after the outbreak of war in May 1998, Ethiopia wrongfully denationalized, expelled, mistreated and deprived of property tens of thousands of Ethiopian citizens of Eritrean origin in violation of multiple international legal obligations. ...

57. Neither international humanitarian law nor any treaty applicable between the Parties during the war addresses the loss of nationality or the situation of dual nationals in wartime. With respect to customary international law, Ethiopia contended that customary international law gives a State discretion to deprive its nationals of its nationality if they acquire a second nationality. For its part, Eritrea emphasized everyone's right to a nationality, as expressed in Article 15 of the Universal Declaration of Human Rights, particularly the right not to be arbitrarily deprived of one's nationality. Eritrea maintained that those expelled had not acquired Eritrean nationality, and so were unlawfully rendered stateless by Ethiopia's actions.

58. The Commission agrees with both Parties regarding the relevance of the customary law rules they cited. The problem remains, however, to apply them in the circumstances here. The question before the Commission is whether Ethiopia's actions were unlawful in the unusual circumstances of the creation of the new State of Eritrea followed by the outbreak of war between Eritrea and Ethiopia. ...

60. With respect to Eritrea's contention, the Commission also recognizes that international law limits States' power to deprive persons of their nationality. ... In assessing whether deprivation of nationality was arbitrary, the Commission considered several factors, including whether the action had a basis in law; whether it resulted in persons being rendered stateless; and whether there were legitimate reasons for it to be taken given the totality of the circumstances. ...

62. If Ethiopia's nationality law were properly implemented in accordance with its terms, only dual nationals could be affected, and that law, by itself, could not result in making any person stateless. Given the fact, however, that Ethiopia did not implement that law until sometime in 1998 with respect to its nationals who had acquired Eritrean nationality between 1993 and 1998, the possibility could not be excluded that some persons who had acquired Eritrean nationality had subsequently lost it and thus were made stateless by Ethiopia's action. ...

64. The Commission will examine separately Eritrea's claims regarding several groups deprived of their Ethiopian nationality.

65. *Dual Nationals Deprived of Their Ethiopian Nationality and Expelled for Security Reasons.* Ethiopia contended that when the war broke out, its duration and extent could not be foreseen. Ethiopian security officials were said to be deeply concerned about the potential security threats posed by over 66,000 Ethiopian residents who had shown a significant attachment to the now-enemy State by acquiring Eritrean nationality in order to register for the Referendum or otherwise.

66. Ethiopia insisted that it did not view Eritrean nationality alone as sufficient to deem anyone a security threat subject to loss of nationality and expulsion. For that, additional ties or actions indicating a possible threat to Ethiopia's security were required. The principal indicators were raising money on behalf of Eritrea or participating in organizations promoting Eritrean Government interests or encouraging closer links between expatriate Eritreans and Eritrea. ...

70. Persons identified through this process were then individually detained, brought to collection centers and then expelled, usually within a few days. Expellees' passports and other documents indicating Ethiopian nationality were confiscated, and Ethiopia subsequently treated them as having lost their Ethiopian nationality. ...

71. Deprivation of nationality is a serious matter with important and lasting consequences for those affected. In principle, it should follow procedures in which affected persons are adequately informed regarding the proceedings, can present their cases to an objective decision maker, and can seek objective outside review. Ethiopia's process often fell short of this. The process was hurried. Detainees received no written notification, and some claimed they were never told what was happening. ...

72. Notwithstanding the limitations of the process, the record also shows that Ethiopia faced an exceptional situation. It was at war with Eritrea. Thousands of Ethiopians with personal and ethnic ties to Eritrea had taken steps to acquire Eritrean nationality. Some of these participated in groups that supported the Eritrean Government and often acted on its behalf. In response, Ethiopia devised and implemented a system applying reasonable criteria to identify individual dual nationals thought to pose threats to its wartime security. Given the exceptional wartime circumstances, the Commission finds that the loss of Ethiopian nationality after being

identified through this process was not arbitrary and contrary to international law. Eritrea's claims in this regard are rejected.

73. *Dual Nationals Who Chose To Leave Ethiopia and Go to Eritrea.* There were many dual nationals who decided to leave Ethiopia during the war and go to Eritrea. The total number is uncertain. ... While many, but not all, of these were relatives of those who were expelled for security reasons, the Commission recognizes that, whatever their individual motives may have been, it was a serious act that could not be without consequences for any dual national of two hostile belligerents to choose to leave one for the other while they were at war with each other. The Commission decides that the termination of the Ethiopian nationality of these persons was not arbitrary and was not in violation of international law.

74. *Dual Nationals Remaining in Ethiopia: "Yellow-Card People."* It is undisputed that a considerable number of other dual nationals remained in Ethiopia during the war, that Ethiopia deprived them of their Ethiopian nationality and, in August 1999, required them to present themselves and register as aliens and obtain a residence permit. ... Those who did not comply "will be considered an illegal person who has unlawfully entered the country and shall be treated as such according to the law."

75. Those who registered received distinctive yellow alien identity cards, and were referred to at the hearing as "yellow-card people." The numbers affected were disputed. ... Whatever the numbers affected, there was no evidence indicating that the dual nationals in this group threatened Ethiopian security or suggesting other reasons for taking away their Ethiopian nationality. There was no process to identify individuals warranting special consideration and no apparent possibility of review or appeal. Considering that rights to such benefits as land ownership and business licenses, as well as passports and other travel documents, were at stake, the Commission finds that this wide-scale deprivation of Ethiopian nationality of persons remaining in Ethiopia was, under the circumstances, arbitrary and contrary to international law.

76. *Dual Nationals Who Were in Third Countries or Who Left Ethiopia To Go to Third Countries.* Eritrea also contended that an undetermined number of the persons found by the Commission to have been dual nationals were present in other countries when Ethiopia determined that they would no longer be accepted as Ethiopian nationals. As with the "yellow-card people," there is no evidence indicating that these people, by their mere presence in third countries, could reasonably be presumed to be security threats or that they were found to be potential threats through any individualized assessment process. Moreover, the only means by which they could contest their treatment was to approach Ethiopian diplomatic or consular establishments abroad, and the evidence showed that those who did so to seek clarification or assistance were sent away. The Commission finds that the members of this group were also arbitrarily deprived of their Ethiopian citizenship in violation of international law.

77. *Dual Nationals Who Were in Eritrea.* The record does not indicate how many dual nationals were in Eritrea when the war began in May 1998 and soon thereafter, when Ethiopia terminated the Ethiopian nationality of Eritrea–Ethiopia dual nationals, but the Commission must assume that some were there. While it could not fairly be

assumed that mere presence in Eritrea was proof that such dual nationals were security risks, the Commission finds that the evident risks and the inability to contact them under wartime conditions made such termination not arbitrary or otherwise unlawful.

78. *Dual Nationals Expelled for Other Reasons.* While Ethiopia asserted that no one was expelled except for holders of Eritrean nationality found to be security risks through the process previously described, the evidence shows that an unknown, but considerable, number of dual nationals were expelled without having been subject to this process. ... The Commission holds that the termination of the Ethiopian nationality of all such persons was arbitrary and unlawful.

B. CORPORATIONS

Determining the nationality of corporations[34] is complicated by two features of their character. First, like individuals, they may have a variety of contacts with different countries. Thus a company, established and registered in one country, for tax purposes perhaps, may have its head office in another country and its main place of business in a third. Such a multinational enterprise is likely to have branch plants and offices in several other countries and to be owned by shareholders of many nationalities in constantly changing proportions as its shares are traded. How are these national connections significant in international law? Second, unlike individuals, corporations are juridical persons by virtue of national legislation. How should international law regard such entities of purely national origin and status? Furthermore, the company laws of different countries are not the same, in particular in the way they ascribe nationality. Thus the laws of one country may grant nationality to a corporation because it was created and registered there, while the legal system of another attaches nationality to the same corporation because its centre of business activities is within the jurisdiction.[35] What cognizance should international law take of these differences in company laws? These difficult questions came before the World Court in the following case.

---

34   See, generally: G.A. Ban Hecke, "Nationality of Companies Analysed" (1961) 8 Ned. Tijdshrift Int. Recht 223; R.E.L.V. Williams & M. Chrussachi, "The Nationality of Corporations" (1933) 49 L.Q. Rev. 334; E.M. Krishna, "Nationality and Subsidiary Ownership Patterns in Multinational Corporations" (1996) 27 J. Int'l Bus. Stud. 225; I. Seidl-Hohenveldern, *Corporations in and under International Law* (1987); P. Muchlinski, *Multinational Enterprises and the Law* (1995); Y. Hadari, "The Choice of National Law Applicable to the Multinational Enterprise and the Nationality of Such Enterprise," [1974] Duke L.J. 1; T. Vogelaar, "Multinational Corporations and International Law" (1980) 27 Ned. Tijdshrift Int. Recht 69; and C. Staker, "Diplomatic Protection of Private Business Companies: Determining Corporate Personality for International Law Purposes" (1990) 61 Brit. Y.B. Int'l L. 155.

35   For a review of the type of problems posed when there is an interface between these two differing concepts, see W.F. Ebke, "The Limited Partnership and Transnational Combinations of Business Forms: 'Delaware Syndrome' Versus European Community Law" (1988) 22 Int. Lawyer 191; on the consequences of the difference between domicile and nationality on the one hand and residence (for tax purposes) on the other, see *R. v. H.M. Treasury and Commissioners of Inland Revenue ex parte Daily Mail and General Trust plc*, [1988] 3 C.M.L.R. 713 (Eur. Ct. J.). For the European attempt to resolve these and other problems of the harmonization of European company law by the creation of a supranational company, a Societas Europaea, see EC, European Parliament Committee of Legal Affairs, *Draft Report on the Proposal for a Regulation in the Statute for a European Company*, Doc. EN/PR/84056, June 27, 1990.

Barcelona Traction, Light and Power Co. Case[36]
Belgium v. Spain
[1970] I.C.J. Rep. 3

[The Barcelona Traction Co. had been formed under Canadian law. Its business involved the exploitation of hydroelectric facilities in Spain, where it had many operating subsidiaries. When the company was declared bankrupt in Spain, a very high percentage of its shares had been beneficially owned for more than 25 years by two large Belgian corporations. Belgium claimed compensation from Spain on account of the manner in which the Spanish authorities had permitted the bankruptcy of the company and the disposal of its assets. Spain raised several preliminary objections, in one of which it asserted that since the alleged injury was to the company, not the shareholders, Belgium had no standing to bring the claim. The Court ultimately dealt with this issue in its judgment on the merits.]

THE COURT: ...

[33] When a State admits into its territory foreign investments or foreign nationals, whether natural or juristic persons, it is bound to extend to them the protection of the law and assumes obligations concerning the treatment to be afforded them. These obligations, however, are neither absolute nor unqualified. In particular, an essential distinction should be drawn between the obligations of a State towards the international community as a whole, and those arising *vis-à-vis* another State in the field of diplomatic protection. By their very nature the former are the concern of all States. In view of the importance of the rights involved, all States can be held to have a legal interest in their protection; they are obligations *erga omnes*.

[34] Such obligations derive, for example, in contemporary international law, from the outlawing of acts of aggression, and of genocide, as also from the principles and rules concerning basic rights of the human person including protection from slavery and racial discrimination. Some of the corresponding rights of protection have entered into the body of general international law (*Reservations to the Convention on the Prevention and Punishment of the Crime of Genocide, Advisory Opinion, I.C.J. Reports 1951*, p. 23); others are conferred by international instruments of a universal or quasi-universal character.

[35] Obligations the performance of which is the subject of diplomatic protection are not of the same category. It cannot be held, when one such obligation in particular is in question, in a specific case, that all States have a legal interest in its observance. In order to bring a claim in respect of the breach of such an obligation, a State must first establish its right to do so, for the rules on the subject rest on two suppositions:

The first is that the defendant State had broken an obligation towards the national State in respect of its nationals. The second is that only the party to whom an international obligation is due can bring a claim in respect of its breach. (*Reparation*

---

36   See H.W. Briggs, "Barcelona Traction: The 'Jus Standi' of Belgium" (1971) 65 A.J.I.L. 327; R. Higgins, "Aspects of the Case Concerning the Barcelona Traction, Light and Power Company Ltd." (1970) 11 Va. J. Int. L. 327; and R.B. Lillich, "The Rigidity of Barcelona" (1971) 65 A.J.I.L. 522.

for Injuries Suffered in the Service of the United Nations, Advisory Opinion, I.C.J. Reports 1949, pp. 181-182).

In the present case it is therefore essential to establish whether the losses allegedly suffered by Belgian shareholders in Barcelona Traction were the consequence of the violation of obligations of which they were the beneficiaries. In other words: has a right of Belgium been violated on account of its nationals' having suffered infringement of their rights as shareholders in a company not of Belgian nationality?

[36] Thus it is the existence or absence of a right, belonging to Belgium and recognized as such by international law, which is decisive for the problem of Belgium's capacity. ...

[38] In this field international law is called upon to recognize institutions of municipal law that have an important and extensive role in the international field. This does not necessarily imply drawing any analogy between its own institutions and those of municipal law, nor does it amount to making rules of international law dependent upon categories of municipal law. All it means is that international law has had to recognize the corporate entity as an institution created by States in a domain essentially within their domestic jurisdiction. This in turn requires that, whenever legal issues arise concerning the shareholders, as to which rights international law has not established its own rules, it has to refer to the relevant rules of municipal law. ...

[41] Municipal law determines the legal situation not only of such limited liability companies but also of those persons who hold shares in them. ... The concept and structure of the company are founded on and determined by a firm distinction between the separate entity of the company and that of the shareholder, each with a distinct set of rights. The separation of property rights as between company and shareholder is an important manifestation of this distinction. So long as the company is in existence the shareholder has no right to the corporate assets. ...

[44] Notwithstanding the separate corporate personality, a wrong done to the company frequently causes prejudice to its shareholders. But the mere fact that damage is sustained by both company and shareholder does not imply that both are entitled to claim compensation. ... Thus whenever a shareholder's interests are harmed by an act done to the company, it is to the latter that he must look to institute appropriate action; for although two separate entities may have suffered from the same wrong, it is only one entity whose rights have been infringed. ...

[47] The situation is different if the act complained of is aimed at the direct rights of the shareholder as such. It is well known that there are rights which municipal law confers upon the latter distinct from those of the company, including the right to any declared dividend, the right to attend and vote at general meetings, the right to share in the residual assets of the company on liquidation. Whenever one of his direct rights is infringed, the shareholder has an independent right of action. ...

[48] The Belgian Government claims that shareholders of Belgian nationality suffered damage in consequence of unlawful acts of the Spanish authorities and, in particular, that the Barcelona Traction shares, though they did not cease to exist, were emptied of all real economic content. It accordingly contends that the shareholders had an independent right to redress, notwithstanding the fact that the acts complained of were directed against the company as such. Thus the legal issue is reducible to the

question of whether it is legitimate to identify an attack on company rights, resulting in damage to shareholders, with the violation of their direct rights. ...

[50] In turning now to the international legal aspects of the case, the Court must, as already indicated, start from the fact that the present case essentially involves factors derived from municipal law the distinction and the community between the company and the shareholder which the Parties, however widely their interpretations may differ, each take as the point of departure of their reasoning. If the Court were to decide the case in disregard of the relevant institutions of municipal law it would, without justification, invite serious legal difficulties. It would lose touch with reality, for there are no corresponding institutions of international law to which the Court could resort. Thus the Court has, as indicated, not only to take cognizance of municipal law but also to refer to it. It is to rules generally accepted by municipal legal systems which recognize the limited company whose capital is represented by shares, and not to the municipal law of a particular State, that international law refers. In referring to such rules, the Court cannot modify, still less deform them.

[51] On the international plane, the Belgian Government has advanced the proposition that it is inadmissible to deny the shareholders' national State a right of diplomatic protection merely on the ground that another State possesses a corresponding right in respect of the company itself. In strict logic and law this formulation of the Belgian claim to *jus standi* assumes the existence of the very right that requires demonstration. In fact the Belgian Government has repeatedly stressed that there exists no rule of international law which would deny the national State of the shareholders the right of diplomatic protection for the purpose of seeking redress pursuant to unlawful acts committed by another State against the company in which they hold shares. This, by emphasizing the absence of any express denial of the right, conversely implies the admission that there is no rule of international law which expressly confers such a right on the shareholders' national State.

[52] International law may not, in some fields, provide specific rules in particular cases. In the concrete situation, the company against which allegedly unlawful acts were directed is expressly vested with a right, whereas no such right is specifically provided for the shareholder in respect of those acts. Thus the position of the company rests on a positive rule of both municipal and international law. As to the shareholder, while he has certain rights expressly provided for him by municipal law ... , appeal can, in the circumstances of the present case, only be made to the silence of international law. Such silence scarcely admits of interpretation in favour of the shareholder.

[53] It is quite true, as was recalled in the course of oral argument in the present case, that concurrent claims are not excluded in the case of a person who, having entered the service of an international organization and retained his nationality, enjoys simultaneously the right to be protected by his national State and the right to be protected by the organization to which he belongs. This however is a case of one person in possession of two separate bases of protection, each of which is valid (*Reparation for Injuries Suffered in the Service of the United Nations*, Advisory Opinion, I.C.J. Reports 1949, at 185). There is no analogy between such a situation and that of foreign shareholders in a company which has been the victim of a violation of international law which has caused them damage. ...

[55] The Court will now examine other grounds on which it is conceivable that the submission by the Belgian Government of a claim on behalf of shareholders in Barcelona Traction may be justified. ...

[The Court then took note of the municipal law practice of "lifting the veil" of incorporation in exceptional cases, and acknowledged that there may be special circumstances for doing likewise internationally in the interest of protecting shareholders.]

[64] In this connection two particular situations must be studied: the case of the company having ceased to exist and the case of the company's national State lacking capacity to take action on its behalf.

[65] As regards the first of these possibilities ... [t]here can, however, be no question but that Barcelona Traction has lost all its assets in Spain, and was placed in receivership in Canada, a receiver and manager having been appointed. It is common ground that from the economic viewpoint the company has been entirely paralyzed. ...

[66] It cannot however, be contended that the corporate entity of the company has ceased to exist, or that it has lost its capacity to take corporate action. ... It has not become incapable in law of defending its own rights and the interests of the shareholders. In particular, a precarious financial situation cannot be equated with the demise of the corporate entity, which is the hypothesis under consideration: the company's status in law is alone relevant, and not its economic condition, nor even the possibility of its being "practically defunct" a description on which argument has been based but which lacks all legal precision. Only in the event of the legal demise of the company are the shareholders deprived of the possibility of a remedy available through the company: it is only if they became deprived of all such possibility that an independent right of action for them and their government could arise.

[67] In the present case, Barcelona Traction is in receivership in the country of incorporation. Far from implying the demise of the entity or of its rights, this much rather denotes that those rights are preserved for so long as no liquidation has ensued. Though in receivership, the company continues to exist. Moreover, it is a matter of public record that the company's shares were quoted on the stock-market at a recent date.

[68] ... The Court is thus not confronted with the first hypothesis contemplated in paragraph 64, and need not pronounce upon it.

[69] The Court will now turn to the second possibility, that of the lack of capacity of the company's national State to act on its behalf. The first question which must be asked here is whether Canada—the third apex of the triangular relationship—is, in law, the national State of Barcelona Traction.

[70] In allocating corporate entities to States for purposes of diplomatic protection, international law is based, but only to a limited extent, on an analogy with the rules governing the nationality of individuals. The traditional rule attributes the right of diplomatic protection of a corporate entity to the State under the laws of which it is incorporated and in whose territory it has its registered office. These two criteria have been confirmed by long practice and by numerous international instruments. This notwithstanding, further or different links are at times said to be required in order that a right of diplomatic protection should exist.

Indeed, it has been the practice of some States to give a company incorporated under their law diplomatic protection solely when it has its seat (*siège social*) or management or centre of control in their territory, or when a majority or a substantial proportion of the shares has been owned by nationals of the State concerned. Only then, it has been held, does there exist between the corporation and the State in question a genuine connection of the kind familiar from other branches of international law. However, in the particular field of the diplomatic protection of corporate entities, no absolute test of the "genuine connection" has found general acceptance. Such tests as have been applied are of a relative nature, and sometimes links with one State have had to be weighed against those with another. In this connection reference has been made to the *Notteböhm Case* ... . However, given both the legal and factual aspects of protection in the present case the Court is of the opinion that there can be no analogy with the issues raised or the decision given in that case.

[71] In the present case, it is not disputed that the company was incorporated in Canada and has its registered office in that country. The incorporation of the company under the law of Canada was an act of free choice. Not only did the founders of the company seek its incorporation under Canadian law but it has remained under that law for a period of over 50 years. It has maintained in Canada its registered office, its accounts and its share registers. Board meetings were held there for many years; it has been listed in the records of the Canadian tax authorities. Thus a close and permanent connection has been established, fortified by the passage of over half a century. This connection is in no way weakened by the fact that the company engaged from the very outset in commercial activities outside Canada, for that was its declared object. Barcelona Traction's links with Canada are thus manifold.

[72] Furthermore, the Canadian nationality of the company has received general recognition. Prior to the institution of proceedings before the Court, three other governments apart from that of Canada (those of the United Kingdom, the United States and Belgium) made representations concerning the treatment accorded to Barcelona Traction by the Spanish authorities. The United Kingdom Government intervened on behalf of bondholders and of shareholders. Several representations were also made by the United States Government, but not on behalf of the Barcelona Traction company as such.

[73] Both Governments acted at certain stages in close co-operation with the Canadian Government. ...

[74] As to the Belgian Government, its earlier action was also undertaken in close co-operation with the Canadian Government. The Belgian Government admitted the Canadian character of the company in the course of the present proceedings. It explicitly stated that Barcelona Traction was a company of neither Spanish nor Belgian nationality but a Canadian company incorporated in Canada. The Belgian Government has even conceded that it was not concerned with the injury suffered by Barcelona Traction itself, since that was Canada's affair. ...

[76] In sum, the record shows that from 1948 onwards the Canadian Government made to the Spanish Government numerous representations which cannot be viewed otherwise than as the exercise of diplomatic protection in respect of the Barcelona Traction company. Therefore this was not a case where diplomatic protection was

refused or remained in the sphere of fiction. It is also clear that over the whole period of its diplomatic activity the Canadian Government proceeded in full knowledge of the Belgian attitude and activity.

[77] It is true that at a certain point the Canadian Government ceased to act on behalf of Barcelona Traction, for reasons which have not been fully revealed, though a statement made in a letter of 19 July 1955 by the Canadian Secretary of State for External Affairs suggests that it felt the matter should be settled by means of private negotiations. The Canadian Government has nonetheless retained its capacity to exercise diplomatic protection; no legal impediment has prevented it from doing so: no fact has arisen to render this protection impossible. It has discontinued its action of its own free will.

[78] The Court would here observe that, within the limits prescribed by international law, a State may exercise diplomatic protection by whatever means and to whatever extent it thinks fit, for it is its own right that the State is asserting. Should the natural or legal persons on whose behalf it is acting consider that their rights are not adequately protected, they have no remedy in international law. All they can do is to resort to municipal law, if means are available, with a view to furthering their cause or obtaining redress. The municipal legislator may lay upon the State an obligation to protect its citizens abroad, and may also confer upon the national a right to demand the performance of that obligation, and clothe the right with corresponding sanctions. However, all these questions remain within the province of municipal law and do not affect the position internationally.

[79] The State must be viewed as the sole judge to decide whether its protection will be granted, to what extent it is granted, and when it will cease. It remains in this respect a discretionary power the exercise of which may be determined by considerations of a political or other nature, unrelated to the particular case. Since the claim of the State is not identical with that of the individual or corporate person whose cause is espoused, the State enjoys complete freedom of action. Whatever the reasons for any change of attitude, the fact cannot in itself constitute a justification for the exercise of diplomatic protection by another government, unless there is some independent and otherwise valid ground for that. ...

[81] The cessation by the Canadian Government of the diplomatic protection of Barcelona Traction cannot, then, be interpreted to mean that there is no remedy against the Spanish Government for the damage done by the allegedly unlawful acts of the Spanish authorities. ... Therefore there is no substance in the argument that for the Belgian Government to bring a claim before the Court represented the only possibility of obtaining redress for the damage suffered by Barcelona Traction and, through it, by its shareholders. ...

[83] The Canadian Government's right of protection in respect of the Barcelona Traction company remains unaffected by the present proceedings. The Spanish Government has never challenged the Canadian nationality of the company, either in the diplomatic correspondence with the Canadian Government or before the Court. Moreover it has unreservedly recognized Canada as the national State of Barcelona Traction in both written pleadings and oral statements made in the course of the present proceedings. Consequently, the Court considers that the Spanish Government has not questioned Canada's right to protect the company. ...

[88] It follows from what has already been stated above that, where it is a question of an unlawful act committed against a company representing foreign capital, the general rule of international law authorizes the national State of the company alone to make a claim.

[89] Considering the important developments of the last half-century, the growth of foreign investments and the expansion of the international activities of corporations, in particular of holding companies, which are often multinational, and considering the way in which the economic interests of States have proliferated, it may at first sight appear surprising that the evolution of law has not gone further and that no generally accepted rules in the matter have crystallized on the international plane. Nevertheless, a more thorough examination of the facts shows that the law on the subject has been formed in a period characterized by an intense conflict of systems and interests. It is essentially bilateral relations which have been concerned, relations in which the rights of both the State exercising diplomatic protection and the State in respect of which protection is sought have had to be safeguarded. Here as elsewhere, a body of rules could only have developed with the consent of those concerned. The difficulties encountered have been reflected in the evolution of the law on the subject.

[90] Thus, in the present state of the law, the protection of shareholders requires that recourse be had to treaty stipulations or special agreements directly concluded between the private investor and the State in which the investment is placed. States ever more frequently provide for such protection, in both bilateral and multilateral relations, either by means of special instruments or within the framework of wider economic arrangements. Indeed, whether in the form of multilateral or bilateral treaties between States, or in that of agreements between States and companies, there has since the second world war been considerable development in the protection of foreign investments. The instruments in question contain provisions as to jurisdiction and procedure in case of disputes concerning the treatment of investing companies by the States in which they invest capital. Sometimes companies are themselves vested with a direct right to defend their interests against States through prescribed procedures. No such instrument is in force between the Parties to the present case. ...

[92] Since the general rule on the subject does not entitle the Belgian government to put forward a claim in this case, the question remains to be considered whether nonetheless, as the Belgian Government has contended during the proceedings, considerations of equity do not require that it be held to possess a right of protection ... a theory has been developed to the effect that the State of the shareholders has a right of diplomatic protection when the State whose responsibility is invoked is the national State of the company. Whatever the validity of this theory may be, it is certainly not applicable to the present case, since Spain is not the national State of Barcelona Traction.

[93] On the other hand, the Court considers that, in the field of diplomatic protection as in all other fields of international law, it is necessary that the law be applied reasonably. It has been suggested that if in a given case it is not possible to apply the general rule that the right of diplomatic protection of a company belongs to its national State, considerations of equity might call for the possibility of protection of the shareholders in question by their own national State. This hypothesis does not correspond to the circumstances of the present case.

[94] In view, however, of the discretionary nature of diplomatic protection, considerations of equity cannot require more than the possibility for some protector State to intervene, whether it be the national State of the company, by virtue of the general rule mentioned above, or, in a secondary capacity, the national State of the shareholders who claim protection. In this connection, account should also be taken of the practical effects of deducing from considerations of equity any broader right of protection for the national State of the shareholders. It must first of all be observed that it would be difficult on an equitable basis to make distinctions according to any quantitative test: it would seem that the owner of 1 per cent, and the owner of 90 per cent, of the share-capital should have the same possibility of enjoying the benefit of diplomatic protection. The protector State may, of course, be disinclined to take up the case of the single small shareholder, but it could scarcely be denied the right to do so in the name of equitable considerations. In that field, protection by the national State of the shareholders can hardly be graduated according to the absolute or relative size of the shareholding involved. ...

[96] The Court considers that the adoption of the theory of diplomatic protection of shareholders as such, by opening the door to competing diplomatic claims, could create an atmosphere of confusion and insecurity in international economic relations. The danger would be all the greater inasmuch as the shares of companies whose activity is international are widely scattered and frequently change hands. It might perhaps be claimed that, if the right of protection belonging to the national States of the shareholders were considered as only secondary to that of the national State of the company, there would be less danger of difficulties of the kind contemplated. However, the Court must state that the essence of a secondary right is that it only comes into existence at the time when the original right ceases to exist. As the right of protection vested in the national State of the company cannot be regarded as extinguished because it is not exercised, it is not possible to accept the proposition that in case of its non-exercise the national State of the shareholders have a right of protection secondary to that of the national State of the company. Furthermore, study of factual situations in which this theory might possibly be applied gives rise to the following observations.

[97] The situations in which foreign shareholders in a company wish to have recourse to diplomatic protection by their own national State may vary. It may happen that the national State of the company simply refuses to grant it its diplomatic protection, or that it begins to exercise it (as in the present case) but does not pursue its action to the end. It may also happen that the national State of the company and the State which has committed a violation of international law with regard to the company arrive at a settlement of the matter, by agreeing on compensation for the company, but that the foreign shareholders find the compensation insufficient. Now, as a matter of principle, it would be difficult to draw a distinction between these three cases so far as the protection of foreign shareholders by their national State is concerned, since in each case they may have suffered real damage. Furthermore, the national State of the company is perfectly free to decide how far it is appropriate for it to protect the company, and is not bound to make public the reasons for its decision. To reconcile this discretionary power of the company's national State with a right of protection falling to the shareholders' national State would be particularly difficult

when the former State has concluded, with the State which has contravened international law with regard to the company, an agreement granting the company compensation which the foreign shareholders find inadequate. If, after such a settlement, the national State of the foreign shareholders could in its turn put forward a claim based on the same facts, this would be likely to introduce into the negotiation of this kind of agreement a lack of security which would be contrary to the stability which it is the object of international law to establish in international relations.

[98] It is quite true, as recalled in paragraph 53, that international law recognizes parallel rights of protection in the case of a person in the service of an international organization. Nor is the possibility excluded of concurrent claims being made on behalf of persons having dual nationality, although in that case lack of a genuine link with one of the two States may be set up against the exercise by that State of the right of protection. It must be observed, however, that in these two types of situation the number of possible protectors is necessarily very small, and their identity normally not difficult to determine. In this respect such cases of dual protection are markedly different from the claims to which recognition of a general right of protection of foreign shareholders by their various national States might give rise.

[99] It should also be observed that the promoters of a company whose operations will be international must take into account the fact that States have, with regard to their nationals, a discretionary power to grant diplomatic protection or to refuse it. When establishing a company in a foreign country, its promoters are normally impelled by particular considerations; it is often a question of tax or other advantages offered by the host State. It does not seem to be in any way inequitable that the advantages thus obtained should be balanced by the risks arising from the fact that the protection of the company and hence of its shareholders is thus entrusted to a State other than the national State of the shareholders.

[100] In the present case, it is clear from what has been said above that Barcelona Traction was never reduced to a position of impotence such that it could not have approached its national State, Canada, to ask for its diplomatic protection, and that, as far as appeared to the Court, there was nothing to prevent Canada from continuing to grant its diplomatic protection to Barcelona Traction if it had considered that it should do so.

[101] For the above reasons, the Court is not of the opinion that, in the particular circumstances of the present case, *jus standi* is conferred in the Belgian government by considerations of equity. ...

[103] Accordingly, the Court rejects the Belgian government's claim by fifteen votes to one, twelve votes of the majority being based on the reasons set out in the present judgment.

NOTES

1) In considering the nationality of a corporation, the Court said that the *Nottebōhm* case, reported in the previous section, was not a suitable analogy. Why not? If a genuine link in the sense of that case is inappropriate, what is the rationale for ascribing a

nationality to a company?[37] Consider the formula adopted in article 9 of the ILC Draft Articles on Diplomatic Protection in 2004:

> 9. For the purposes of diplomatic protection of corporations, the State of nationality means the State under whose law the corporation was formed and in whose territory it has its registered office or the seat of its management or some similar connection.[38]

2) Since Canada did not choose to espouse the claim of the Barcelona Traction Company, why should not Belgium be allowed to exercise "a secondary capacity" (paragraph 94) as a closely affected state whose shareholding nationals, as owners of the corporation, had a central interest in the outcome?

3) Although Belgium was refused standing in this case, the Court would have allowed the national state of the shareholders to bring a claim in certain circumstances. What are they? Review paragraphs 64-77 and 92-93. The Canadian company was wound up in 1980. How might this event have affected any outstanding claims of the shareholders?

4) The conservative opinion of the Court in this case may not be surprising in view of the control of states over the nationality of corporations in a double sense. Not only was the Court bound to apply the customary law on the subject as derived from the practice of nation states, but also, as the Court noted in paragraph 38, corporations are juristic persons of national/municipal law creation. The Court, however, was well aware of the complexities accompanying "the expansion of the international activities of corporations" (paragraph 89) when it delivered its opinion in 1970.

5) Belgium based its argument for standing in this case on the fact that two Belgian corporations owned virtually all of the equity in Barcelona Traction. If the Court had accepted this argument should it then have "lifted the corporate veil" of those corporations to determine the nationality of the actual providers of capital?

6) In paragraph 92 of its judgment, the Court referred to the case of the expropriation of the assets of a local corporation that is beneficially owned by foreigners. In some cases, particularly for sensitive industries such as banking or communications, local incorporation is required by host states. In such cases capital exporting states have argued that they may exercise diplomatic protection to protect the interests of their nationals who are the shareholders.[39] In the ILC Draft Articles on Diplomatic Protection, article 11, the following approach was adopted with respect to protection of shareholders in the case of injury to the corporation:

> 11. The State of nationality of the shareholders in a corporation shall not be entitled to exercise diplomatic protection on behalf of such shareholders in the case of an injury to the corporation unless:
>
> (a) The corporation has ceased to exist according to the law of the State of incorporation for a reason unrelated to the injury; or

---

37   See D. Harris, "The Protection of Companies in International Law in the Light of the Notteböhm Case" (1969) 18 Int. & Comp. L.Q. 275 at 302.

38   *Supra* note 16, article 9.

39   See *The Mexican Eagle Co. Case*, Cmd. 5758 at 9.

(b) The corporation had, at the time of the injury, the nationality of the State alleged to be responsible for causing injury, and incorporation under the law of the latter State was required by it as a precondition for doing business there.[40]

7) The majority judgment denied there had been any infringement of the direct rights of the shareholders. If there had been, do the shareholders have interests independent of the corporation? If so, might the national state of the shareholders exercise its diplomatic protection over these interests? Consider the formula adopted in article 12 of the ILC Draft Articles:

12. To the extent that an internationally wrongful act of a State causes direct injury to the rights of shareholders as such, as distinct from those of the corporation itself, the State of nationality of any such shareholders is entitled to exercise diplomatic protection in respect of its nationals.[41]

8) The United Kingdom Rules regarding international claims state that the United Kingdom may intervene to protect its nationals who have interests in a corporation that has been injured by its state of incorporation.[42] The practice of the United States is generally as follows:

(a) The United States will generally consider a claim on behalf of corporations organized in the United States if 50% or more of their stock is owned by United States citizens.

(b) The United States will consider a claim on behalf of domestic shareholders if a significant portion of the foreign corporation's stock is owned by Americans, foreign American stock ownership being usually regarded as significant if it is 25% or more.[43]

9) What degree of ownership should be required of shareholders before their national state has a right that would be recognized by an international tribunal? As to wholly owned foreign subsidiaries, consider the *ELSI Case* reproduced below. What about widely held multinational corporations?

10) Should a liquidation of the company by the host state be required before recognizing any right of the national state of the shareholders to espouse a claim for direct injury to shareholders?[44]

11) Bilateral and unilateral treaties to protect foreign investments are increasingly common. Usually these agreements expressly include the right of a country to exercise diplomatic protection of its nationals who are shareholders in a foreign corporation. An example of such an agreement may be seen in the *ELSI Case*.

---

40 Draft Articles on Diplomatic Protections, *supra* note 16, article 11.

41 *Ibid.*, article 12.

42 See D.J. Harris, *Cases and Materials on International Law*, 5th ed. (1998) at 615.

43 See H.J. Steiner & D.F. Vagts, *Transnational Legal Problems: Materials and Text*, 4th ed. (1994) at 222.

44 See the *Delagoa Bay Case* (1888-89), 81 B.F.S.P. 691.

Elettronica Sicula S.p.A. (ELSI Case)[45]
United States v. Italy
[1989] I.C.J. Rep. 15

[A chamber of the Court had to consider whether the requisitioning of the assets of an Italian company (ELSI), which was the wholly owned subsidiary of two American Companies (Raytheon and Machlett), constituted a violation of Italian international obligations to the United States. The status of the United States to advance the claims of Raytheon to be compensated for the damage done to its Italian subsidiary was based upon the provisions of the Treaty of Friendship, Navigation and Commerce between Italy and the United States, which specifically provided in article III(2) that each country's corporations could "control and manage corporations ... of such other high contracting party."[46] The seizure in question was alleged to be an interference with the American Company's right to control and manage its Italian subsidiary. Furthermore, article V(2), in providing protection from expropriation, referred to interests held "directly or indirectly" by either party.

The Chamber held that the requisitioning did not give rise to any liability for Italy as it was not guilty of any internationally illegal conduct. The Chamber as a whole did not specifically consider the status of the United States to maintain the action, seemingly accepting it as obvious that for the treaty to make sense the United States would have to be able to espouse its nationals' interests *qua* shareholder in the Italian company. However, some judges, including Judge Oda, addressed this issue in individual judgments:]

JUDGE ODA, separate opinion: ... The action of the United States Government in bringing the present case against the Italian Government before the International Court of Justice resulted from its espousal of the cause of Raytheon and Machlett, the shareholders ... .

It did not espouse the cause of ELSI.

The very concept of a joint-stock company embodies a distinction between the corporate entity and the assemblage of shareholders. The fundamental character of the company, particularly with regard to the shareholders' status, was so clearly expounded in the Court's Judgment in the case concerning the *Barcelona Traction, Light and Power Company, Limited* (New Application) that it is relevant to quote certain passages from that decision ... [see the extracts from that case reproduced above].

Raytheon and Machlett certainly could, in Italy, "organize, control and manage" corporations in which they held 100 per cent of the shares—as in the case of ELSI— but this cannot be taken to mean that those United States corporations, as shareholders of ELSI, can lay claim to any rights other than those rights of shareholders guaranteed to them under Italian law as well as under the general principles of law concerning

---

45   See T. Gill (1990) 84 A.J.I.L. 249 and F.A. Mann, "Foreign Investment in the International Court of Justice: The ELSI Case" (1992) 86 A.J.I.L. 92.

46   (1948) 79 U.N.T.S. 171, TIAS No. 1965, 63 U.S. Stat. 2255.

companies. The rights of Raytheon and Machlett as shareholders of ELSI remained the same and were not augmented by the FCN Treaty. Those rights which Raytheon and Machlett could have enjoyed under the FCN Treaty were not breached by the requisition order, because that order did not affect the "direct rights" of those United States corporations, as shareholders of an Italian company, but was directed at the Italian company of which they remained shareholders ... .

It is a great privilege to be able to engage in business in a country other than one's own. By being permitted to undertake commercial or manufacturing activities or transactions through businesses incorporated in another country, nationals of a foreign country will obtain further benefits. Yet these local companies, as legal entities of that country, are subject to local laws and regulations; so that foreigners may have to accept a number of restrictions in return for the advantages of doing business through such local companies.[47]

NOTES

1) The consequence of this judgment is, in the words of one commentator, to render the language of the FCN treaties of the U.S. effective to extend diplomatic protection to American shareholders who control foreign local subsidiaries.[48] Since ELSI was a 100 percent owned subsidiary, the case does not deal with the more difficult question of a local company owned by a variety of foreign interests.

2) The Convention on the Settlement of Investment Disputes Between States and Nationals of Other States[49] establishes an international centre at Washington for the resolution of such disputes: the International Centre for the Settlement of Investment Disputes, or ICSID. The machinery of ICSID is discussed in Chapter 10, Section B.3(d) on "Breach of Contract" but it is necessary to note here that its work is to settle disputes between host states and foreign private investors. Whether an investor has a foreign or local nationality is therefore an important enquiry, especially since the Convention recognizes that a host state may require foreign investors to be locally incorporated. However, in addition, article 25(2) of the Convention allows the parties to agree that, because of its foreign control, such a corporation is a national of another contracting state for the purpose of conferring jurisdiction on the Centre. When a host state enters into an ICSID Arbitration Agreement with a locally incorporated company, that agreement constitutes a recognition that the company is a foreign national for the purposes of article 25(2) and there is a presumption that the foreign control aspect required by the article is present.[50] Even so, for such a corporation to be considered a national of another contracting state for the purposes of the Convention, there must be a "genuine link" between the

---

47   [1989] I.C.J. Rep. 15 at 130, 138-39, 140-41, 144. F.A. Mann, *supra* note 45, criticized Judge Oda's position as "curious" and guilty of "dogmatism."

48   T. Gill, *supra* note 45 at 257-58.

49   (1965) 575 U.N.T.S. 159. Canada is not yet a party.

50   *Liberian Timber Corporation (Letco) v. Republic of Liberia* (1988) 26 I.L.M. 647 at 653, 654.

corporation and the other state party to the convention.[51] Whether such a link needs to be as strong as that required to exercise diplomatic protection is open to question.[52]

3) A related question concerns the nationality of corporations for the purpose of benefiting from international agreements or being able to carry out certain domestic activities. Some international agreements recognize "a place of establishment" or a "beneficial ownership" test as establishing a right to benefit under the agreement.

The North American Free Trade Agreement (NAFTA), for instance, states that a "person" of a Party means a natural person or an enterprise, which is defined as "any entity constituted or organized under applicable law, whether or not for profit, and whether privately owned or governmentally owned, including any corporation, trust, partnership, sole proprietorship, joint venture or other association."[53] This definition is refined in its application in specific chapters in NAFTA. Thus, under the Services Chapter, a Party may deny the benefits of NAFTA to a service provider if the services involved are offered by an enterprise of another Party, when it is in fact controlled by nationals of a non-Party, and it has no substantial business activities in the territory of any Party.[54]

How far should such agreements go in tracing back the beneficial owners of the capital employed in the enterprise? How practicable is such an inquiry?

4) The fact of incorporation in a given country may make that corporation a national of that country for some international law purposes but domestic law may require varying degrees of local beneficial ownership before it will be permitted to carry on certain specific activities.[55]

5) In addition to local beneficial ownership, corporations that seek the advantages of trade arrangements typically also have to demonstrate the local origin or added value of their products. Thus the benefits of market access under NAFTA are only available to goods that qualify under NAFTA's rules of origin as being from one of the states parties. Now that goods are increasingly assembled in one country from components made in several other countries, the rules of origin for the finished products have also become very complex to establish and to administer,[56] and the identification of "national" interests may be a complicated issue:

51 C.F. Amerasinghe, "Jurisdiction Ratione Personae Under the Convention on the Settlement of Investment Disputes Between States and Nationals of Other States" (1974-75) 47 Brit. Y.B. Int'l L. 227 at 267.

52 C.F. Amerasinghe, "Dispute Settlement Machinery in Relations between States and Multinational Enterprises with particular reference to the ICSID" (1977) 11 Int. Lawyer 45 at 52.

53 (1993) 32 I.L.M. 296; S.C. 1993, c. 44, art. 201.

54 Ibid., article 1211.

55 For example, the provisions of NAFTA outlined above in text note 3. See also the Factortame Case, [1990] 2 C.E.C. 189 (E.C.J.); [1990] 3 C.M.L.R. 375 (H.L.), where a similar provision in British law (involving the beneficial ownership of shares in a company operating U.K. registered fishing vessels in U.K. territorial waters) was held to be contrary to EC legal provisions that ensure the freedom of establishment in the community.

56 See T.T. Shimazaki, "North American Free Trade Agreement: Rules of Origin—Free Trade or Trade Barrier?" (1997) 25 West. State U. L. Rev. 1 and J.A. LaNasa, "Rules of Origin and the Uruguay Round's Effectiveness in Harmonizing and Regulating Them" (1996) 90 A.J.I.L. 625.

Through their international networks, global companies move inputs and outputs among geographically dispersed facilities. ... In many instances, "imported" products contain a higher proportion of local content (tangible and intangible) than competing "domestic" products. Determining the nationality of corporations has also become more difficult in the wake of far-reaching investment and capital market liberalization. Hence the relative economic importance for the host country of national versus foreign firms—the "who is us?" debate—... is also much less clear-cut than in the past.[57]

6) The operations of transnational enterprises may also result in the extraterritorial assertion of jurisdiction by the state of incorporation, whether with respect to the corporation itself or a subsidiary incorporated under another state's laws. This practice, which is one manifestation of the extraterritoriality issue (discussed more generally in Chapter 9, Section A.4), is particularly associated with the United States:

> The United States increasingly has broadened the definition of nationality of corporations to establish prescriptive jurisdiction over entities organized under the laws of other nations whether they are subsidiaries of U.S. corporations, parent companies of subsidiaries within the United States, or corporations otherwise under control of U.S. citizens through investment ownership.[58]

C. SHIPS[59]

A ship carries the nationality of the state whose flag it flies, and nationality is a status granted by that state, the conditions for which are within the control of that state. Nationality provides the legal basis for the rights and duties pertaining to the ship. By virtue of the grant of nationality, a ship exercises a state's rights for its vessels to navigate the world's oceans, to engage in fishing and maritime commerce, and to enjoy the benefits deriving from treaties concluded by its state of nationality (known as the "flag state" or the "state of registry"). Nationality also imposes burdens upon the ship. The ship remains subject to the laws and treaty commitments of the flag state for the duration of its operating life or until it lawfully changes its national character. In time of national

---

57   P. Sauvé & A. Zampetti, "Subsidiarity Perspectives on the New Trade Agenda" (2000) 3 J. Int'l Econ. L. 83 at 88.

58   See *e.g.* T. Dunning, "D'Amato in a China Shop: Problems of Extraterritoriality with the Iran and Libya Sanctions Act of 1996" (1998) 19 U. Pa. J. Int'l Econ. L. 169 at 177. On the implications of recent developments in corporate governance in the United States, and their application on an extraterritorial basis, see D. Vagts, "Extraterritoriality and Corporate Governance Law" (2003) 97 A.J.I.L. 289.

59   See *e.g.* E. Anderson, "The Nationality of Ships and Flags of Convenience: Economics, Politics, and Alternatives" (1996) 21 Tulane Maritime L.J. 139; B. Boczek, *Flags of Convenience: An International Legal Study* (1962); M. McDougal, W. Burke, & I. Vlasic, "The Maintenance of Public Order at Sea and the Nationality of Ships" (1960) 54 A.J.I.L. 25; H. Meyers, *The Nationality of Ships* (1967); and M.R. Rienow, *The Test of the Nationality of a Merchant Vessel* (1937). For a review of the implications of vessel nationality for maritime security, with particular reference to terrorism, see J. Mellor, "Missing the Boat: The Legal and Practical Problems of the Prevention of Maritime Terrorism" (2002-3) 18 Am. U. Int'l L. Rev. 341.

emergency or war, it may be pressed into the service of the government of the flag state. These issues, and that of the ill-defined requirement for a "genuine link" between the flag state and the vessel, are addressed in Chapter 13, Section B.6. In Canada, the process and requirements for registration of ships, and thus the grant of nationality, are found in the *Canada Shipping Act*, Part I, which requires the registration of all ships over 15 gross tons, and permits the registration of other vessels. Vessels may be registered by "qualified persons," which for the purposes of the Act include Canadian citizens or permanent residents, and corporations incorporated under federal or provincial law.[60] In addition, foreign corporations may also register ships in Canada under certain conditions:

> 17. Unless they are registered in a foreign country, the following ships may be registered under this Part: ...
>
>> (b) a ship that is owned by a corporation incorporated under the laws of a country other than Canada if one of the following is acting with respect to all matters relating to the ship, namely,
>>
>>> (i) a subsidiary of the corporation that is incorporated under the laws of Canada or a province,
>>>
>>> (ii) an employee or director in Canada of any branch office of the corporation that is carrying on business in Canada, or
>>>
>>> (iii) a ship management company incorporated under the laws of Canada or a province; and
>>
>> (c) a ship that is in the exclusive possession of a qualified person under a financing agreement under which the person will acquire ownership on completion of the agreement.[61]

NOTES

1) In *United States v. Marino-Garcia*, the court summarized the status of stateless vessels in modern international law very precisely:

> Vessels without nationality are international pariahs. They have no internationally recognized right to navigate freely on the high seas. ... Moreover, flagless vessels are frequently not subject to the laws of a flag-state. As such, they represent "floating sanctuaries from authority" and constitute a potential threat to the order and stability of navigation on the high seas. ...
>
> The absence of any right to navigate freely on the high seas coupled with the potential threat to order on international waterways has led various courts to conclude that international law places no restrictions upon a nation's right to subject stateless vessels to its jurisdiction. ... Thus, the assertion of jurisdiction over stateless vessels on the high seas in no way transgresses recognized principles of international law.[62]

---

60   R.S.C. 1985, c. S-9, as amended, s. 2 and Part I.6.

61   *Ibid.* at s. 17.

62   679 F.2d 1373 at 1382 (11th Cir. 1982). See also *United States v. Pinto-Mejia*, 720 F.2d 248 (2d Cir. 1983) where the court quoted with approval the above summary.

2) The facts surrounding the Canadian court case of *Romania (State) v. Cheng*[63] raised an unusual problem respecting vessel nationality. Romania sought extradition of the Taiwanese captain and officers of the Taiwan registered ship, *M.V. Maersk Dubai*, for allegedly throwing three Romanian stowaways overboard during a voyage across the Atlantic to Canada. Captain Cheng and the officers were detained by Canadian authorities in the port of Halifax upon information laid by four crew members. Penal jurisdiction on board a vessel on the high seas falls to the flag state, but in this instance the application of that principle was complicated by the fact that Canada does not recognize Taiwan as an independent state. The court eventually decided that the extradition request was technically faulty and the detainees, on their release, returned to Taiwan. What alternative actions might the Canadian government have taken in these circumstances, either upon detention or release of the captain and officers of the *M.V. Maersk Dubai*?

3) Warships are not subject to the rules of international law governing the nationality of ships. A warship is commonly registered in the naval list of a state to which it belongs, but such a list does not have to be made public. All that international law requires is that in time of peace the nationality of warships must be easily verifiable. That is effected by the naval flag that every warship must fly. In peacetime the flag alone will almost always be sufficient evidence of the national character of a warship. In addition "warships on the high seas have complete immunity from the jurisdiction of any States other than the flag State" (U.N. Convention on the Law of the Sea, article 95).

4) Where crew members hold a nationality other than that of the ship, the state of nationality may offer diplomatic protection in addition to the right of the flag state to "seek redress" for injuries sustained in the "course of an injury to the vessel." This issue was addressed in draft article 19 of the 2004 ILC Draft Articles on Diplomatic Protection:

> 19. The right of the State of nationality of the members of the crew of a ship to exercise diplomatic protection on their behalf is not affected by the right of the State of nationality of a ship to seek redress on behalf of such crew members, irrespective of their nationality, when they have been injured in the course of an injury to the vessel resulting from an internationally wrongful act.[64]

---

63   (1997), 114 C.C.C. 289 (N.S.S.C.). See also the commentary of M. McConnell, "Forward This Cargo to Taiwan: Canadian Extradition Law and Practice Relating to Crime on the High Seas" (1997) 8 Crim. L. Forum 335.

64   *Supra* note 16, article 19. The ILC Commentary on this draft article notes the distinction between the right of diplomatic protection exercised by the state of nationality and the right of the flag state to seek redress for injuries connected to injury to the vessel. The latter is not truly "diplomatic protection," although the Commentary acknowledges the "close resemblance between this type of protection and diplomatic protection." See the Report, *supra* note 16 at 90-91.

D. AIRCRAFT AND SPACECRAFT

Nationality of Aircraft[65]

Aircraft, like sea-going vessels, have the nationality of the country of their registry. The nationality of an aircraft connotes the legal link between the state of registry (alias the "flag state") and the aircraft. No unregistered aircraft is allowed to fly in the national airspace of any country, including the country of its origin, or in international airspace (that is, over the high seas). The state of nationality is responsible for the conduct of the aircraft when it operates beyond its national boundaries and the laws of that state apply to events aboard,[66] except when the aircraft is within the territorial jurisdiction of another state. For purposes of easy identification, all civil aircraft registered in member states of the International Civil Aviation Organization (ICAO) are required to display externally their nationality and registration marks.[67] The nationality mark consists of one or more letters or a combination of letters and numbers (Canada's nationality mark is "CF"), followed by the registration mark that may also consist of letters, numbers, or a combination of both.

It should be pointed out that the right to carry traffic in scheduled international air services, granted through bilateral air transport agreements, is based on the nationality of the airlines of the states parties rather than the nationality of aircraft.

The Convention on International Civil Aviation of 1944 (the Chicago Convention), the principal treaty governing civil aviation activities throughout the world, distinguishes between "civil" aircraft and "state" aircraft.[68] The Convention explicitly exempts state aircraft (that is, military, customs, and police aircraft) from its application. Thus neither the Convention (apart from its provisions relating to air sovereignty) nor the standards, practices, and procedures established by ICAO and included in the annexes to the Convention, apply to state aircraft. Military aircraft are commonly registered in a special registry kept by the defence authorities of the state to which they belong. That registry, as a rule, is not open to the public. As with warships, international law requires military aircraft to display external marks of their national character, effected by painting on the aircraft a special symbol characteristic of a particular air force.

---

65   See J.C. Cooper, *Explorations in Aerospace Law*, ed. by I. Vlasic (1968) 205; J. Honig, *The Legal Status of Aircraft* (1956); M. McDougal, H. Lasswell, & I. Vlasic, *Law and Public Order in Space* (1963) 513; and M. Peng, *Le Statut Juridique de l'Aeronef Militaire* (1957).

66   See the *Tokyo Convention on Offences and Certain Other Acts Committed on Board Aircraft*, article 3 (1963) 704 U.N.T.S. 219.

67   Annex 7 to the *Convention on International Civil Aviation (the Chicago Convention)* (1944) 15 U.N.T.S. 295.

68   *Ibid.*, article 3.

Chicago Convention on International Civil Aviation
(1944) 15 U.N.T.S. 295

NATIONALITY OF AIRCRAFT

Article 17

Aircraft have the nationality of the State in which they are registered.

Article 18

An aircraft cannot be validly registered in more than one State, but its registration may be changed from one State to another.

Article 19

The registration or transfer of registration of aircraft in any contracting State shall be made in accordance with its laws and regulations.

Article 20

Every aircraft engaged in international air navigation shall bear its appropriate nationality and registration marks.

RULES OF THE AIR

Article 12

Each contracting State undertakes to adopt measures to insure that every aircraft flying over or manoeuvring within its territory and that every aircraft carrying its nationality mark, wherever such aircraft may be, shall comply with the rules and regulations relating to the flight and manoeuver of aircraft there in force. ... Over the high seas, the rules in force shall be those established under this Convention. Each contracting State undertakes to insure the prosecution of all persons violating the regulations applicable.

Registration of Spacecraft[69]

The need for the registration of spacecraft was noted by member states of the United Nations as early as 1959 when the U.N. *Ad Hoc* Committee on the Peaceful Uses of Outer Space prepared the first comprehensive study of the legal issues arising out of space activities. Since 1961, the United Nations maintained a voluntary registry until a

---

69 See A. Cocca, "Registration of Space Objects," in N. Jasentuliyana & R. Lee, eds., *Manual on Space Law* (1979) vol. 1 at 173; N. Matte, "The Convention on Registration of Objects Launched into Outer Space" (1976) 1 Annals Air & Space L. 231; and A. Young, "A Decennial Review of the Registration Convention" (1986) 11 Annals Air & Space L. 287. It may be of some interest to note that no state has ever registered one of its satellites as serving military objectives.

new Registration Convention was done in 1975, which makes registration mandatory for the contracting parties. The registration regime for spacecraft differs from those applicable to ships and aircraft in several important respects. The Convention prescribes that, in addition to a national registry, there shall also be an international registry kept by the U.N. Secretary-General; no distinction is made between military and non-military spacecraft, both being subject to dual registration; and external marks of nationality are not obligatory for spacecraft.

The principal purposes of the Registration Convention are to secure greater safety in the uses of outer space and to facilitate the identification of the state responsible for damage caused by its spacecraft. Canada is a party to this Convention.

Convention on Registration of Objects Launched into Outer Space
Can. T.S. 1976 No. 36; (1975) 14 I.L.M. 43

Article I

For the purposes of this Convention:
   a. The term "launching State" means:
       i. A State which launches or procures the launching of a space object;
       ii. A State from whose territory or facility a space object is launched;
   b. The term "space object" includes component parts of a space object as well as its launch vehicle and parts thereof;
   c. The term "State of registry" means a launching State on whose registry a space object is carried in accordance with article II.

Article II

1. When a space object is launched into earth orbit or beyond, the launching State shall register the space object by means of an entry in an appropriate registry which it shall maintain. Each launching State shall inform the Secretary-General of the United Nations of the establishment of such a registry.

2. Where there are two or more launching States in respect of any such space object, they shall jointly determine which one of them shall register the object in accordance with paragraph 1 of this article, bearing in mind the provisions of article VIII of the Treaty on Principles Governing the Activities of States in the Exploration and Use of Outer Space, including the Moon and Other Celestial Bodies, and without prejudice to appropriate agreements concluded or to be concluded among the launching States on jurisdiction and control over the space object and over any personnel thereof.

3. The contents of each registry and the conditions under which it is maintained shall be determined by the State of registry concerned.

Article III

1. The Secretary-General of the United Nations shall maintain a Register in which the information furnished in accordance with article IV shall be recorded.

2. There shall be full and open access to the information in this Register.

Article IV

1. Each State of registry shall furnish to the Secretary-General of the United Nations, as soon as practicable, the following information concerning each space object carried on its registry:

    a. Name of launching State or States;

    b. An appropriate designator of the space object or its registration number;

    c. Date and territory or location of launch;

    d. Basic orbital parameters, including:

        i. Nodal period,

        ii. Inclination,

        iii. Apogee,

        iv. Perigee;

    e. General function of the space object.

2. Each State of registry may, from time to time, provide the Secretary-General of the United Nations with additional information concerning a space object carried on its registry.

3. Each State of registry shall notify the Secretary-General of the United Nations, to the greatest extent feasible and as soon as practicable, of space objects concerning which it has previously transmitted information, and which have been but no longer are in earth orbit.

Article V

Whenever a space object launched into earth orbit or beyond is marked with the designator or registration number referred to in article IV, paragraph 1(b), or both, the State of registry shall notify the Secretary-General of this fact when submitting the information regarding the space object in accordance with article IV. In such case, the Secretary-General of the United Nations shall record this notification in the Register.

Article VI

Where the application of the provisions of this Convention has not enabled a State Party to identify a space object which has caused damage to it or to any of its natural or juridical persons, or which may be of a hazardous or deleterious nature, other States Parties, including in particular States possessing space monitoring and tracking facilities, shall respond to the greatest extent feasible to a request by that State Party, or transmitted through the Secretary-General on its behalf, for assistance under equitable and reasonable conditions in the identification of the object. A State Party making such a request shall, to the greatest extent feasible, submit information as to the time, nature and circumstances of the events giving rise to the request. Arrangements under which such assistance shall be rendered shall be the subject of agreement between the parties concerned.

CHAPTER NINE

State Jurisdiction Over Persons

In international law the term "jurisdiction" is used in a number of different ways to denote the exercise of powers by a state over events, persons, and property.[1] Within its own territory a state has plenary authority,[2] and its jurisdiction is "a vital and indeed central feature of state sovereignty, for it is an exercise of authority which may alter or create or terminate legal relationships and obligations."[3] But since states are sovereign and equal, it follows that one state may not exercise jurisdiction in a way that interferes with the rights of other states. Thus, it can be questioned whether states that enact legislation having an extraterritorial effect are complying with their duty not to interfere in the domestic affairs of another state. There must be limits to a state's jurisdiction over persons from a legislative and enforcement perspective, if those powers are to co-exist with another state's jurisdiction over its territory. It is the scope of these limits that are considered in this chapter.[4]

At the outset an important distinction must be made between a state's ability to prescribe a rule of law and its capacity to enforce that rule. In the language of international law, this distinction may be referred to as "prescriptive" and "enforcement" jurisdiction. The exercise of a state's jurisdiction may be legislative, executive, or judicial, according to its internal constitutional arrangement of powers. In Canada, for instance, Parliament and the provincial legislatures prescribe laws that the courts by their decisions apply. The governments have executive authority to enforce both the legislation and the courts' decisions. On the international plane, however, a state's legal authority to act is not

---

1   See the Introduction to Chapter 7 on "State Jurisdiction Over Territory."

2   As discussed in Chapter 2, Section B on "States and Statehood."

3   M. Shaw, *International Law*, 5th ed. (2003) 572.

4   See I. Brownlie, *Principles of Public International Law*, 6th ed. (2003) cc. 14, 15, and 18; L.C. Green, *International Law: A Canadian Perspective*, 2d ed. (1988) 125-37 and 173-87; S.A. Williams & J.-G. Castel, *Canadian Criminal Law: International and Transnational Aspects* (1981) cc. 1-8; S.A. Williams & A.L.C. de Mestral, *An Introduction to International Law*, 2d ed. (1987) c. 9; M. Akehurst, "Jurisdiction in International Law" (1972-73) 46 Brit. Y.B. Int'l L. 145; C. Blakesley, "United States Jurisdiction Over Extraterritorial Crime" (1982) 73 J. of Crim. L. & Criminol. 1109 and "A Conceptual Framework for Extradition and Jurisdiction over Extraterritorial Crimes" (1984) 4 Utah L. Rev. 685; F.A. Mann, "The Doctrine of International Jurisdiction Revisited After Twenty Years" (1984) 186 Hague Receuil 9; Law Reform Commission of Canada, Working Paper 37, *Extraterritorial Jurisdiction* (1984); and American Law Institute, *Restatement of the Law (Third), Foreign Relations Law of the United States* (1987) and Council of Europe, Committee on Crime Problems, *Extraterritorial Criminal Jurisdiction* (1990).

always so complete. On occasion, the state may have the jurisdiction to make a rule of law but lack the jurisdiction to enforce it.

It is also necessary to keep in mind the difference between control of the objects, acts, and events that may be complained of—that is, the subject matter over which jurisdiction is asserted—and power over the actors, human or legal, who perpetrate the alleged wrongs. In order to validly prescribe and enforce its laws, whether civil or criminal, a state must have jurisdiction over both the subject matter and the person involved. Bearing in mind that either or both the subject matter and the actor may be beyond the territory of the state seeking to assert jurisdiction, this chapter has been divided into two parts, treating "subject-matter jurisdiction" and "jurisdiction over the person" separately only for explanatory purposes.

It should be noted that the issue of the criminal jurisdiction of international tribunals, as opposed to national courts, is considered later in Chapter 11 on "International Criminal Law."

A. SUBJECT-MATTER JURISDICTION

1. Scope of Jurisdiction Generally

Since a state has sovereign authority within its borders, its power to legislate cannot be denied.[5] Thus, in principle, a state may exercise jurisdiction over the subject matter of anything within its territory. However, a state may not legislate in violation of its international obligations without being liable under the principles of state responsibility.[6] International law does prohibit the exercise of prescriptive jurisdiction in certain cases. Also, in both civil and criminal matters, several bases of jurisdiction are recognized and, consequently, it is possible for more than one state to claim jurisdiction over the subject matter at the same time. Then such rules as exist to limit jurisdiction may help to prevent a potential conflict. Should a national authority, such as a court, disregard a prohibition and continue to assert jurisdiction, an international claim may ensue. As Beale has stated:

> [T]he sovereign cannot confer legal jurisdiction on his courts or his legislature when he has no such jurisdiction according to the principles of international law.[7]

Civil Jurisdiction

Customary and conventional international law do not set down any general rules placing restrictions on the jurisdiction of domestic courts in civil matters. The exceptions are in the areas of state and diplomatic immunities considered in Chapter 5 on "Interstate Relations."

---

5   M. Shaw, *supra* note 3 at 576.

6   Discussed in Chapter 10 on "State Responsibility."

7   J.H. Beale, "The Jurisdiction of a Sovereign State" (1922-23) 36 Harv. L. Rev. 241 at 243. Note that the same author in his *Conflict of Laws* (1935) at 274-75 inexplicably recanted and stated the opposite: "jurisdiction ... is with us a question of our own common law and not of a generally accepted doctrine of the law of nations" and is "fixed by the common law."

The only other standard imposed by international law is that a state must maintain an adequate system of adjudication in civil cases and must apply the rules of private international law (or conflicts of law) where appropriate.[8] The failure to do so may incur state responsibility for the mistreatment of an alien, discussed in Chapter 10, Section B on "Responsibility for Injury to Aliens" or for the breach of his or her human rights, considered in Chapter 12 on "Protection of Human Rights."

Criminal Jurisdiction
from S.A. Williams and A.L.C. de Mestral, *An Introduction to International Law*,
2d ed. (1987) 125-26 (footnotes omitted)

Traditionally, jurisdiction *in personam* or *in rem* refers to the power of the courts to enter judgments binding on particular persons or things. Although Canada may define the criminal character and consequences of conduct taking place entirely within Canada, this does not always mean that Canadian courts can enter judgment against a person found guilty of such conduct and sentence him if he is physically outside of Canada. In this situation even though the courts may have jurisdiction over the offence, they do not have jurisdiction over the person. Both are necessary. Correlatively, while Canadian authorities have the right to arrest a person while he is in Canada and although the Canadian courts would then have jurisdiction *in personam* over him, it does not follow that under international law Canada has the right to prosecute such a person under a Canadian statute when the unlawful acts were committed entirely abroad. This proposition is reinforced where the accused is an alien and the acts which were committed outside of Canada had no effects within Canada.

In this section we shall consider two questions: the reach of the legislative power of a state (jurisdiction over the crime) and the reach of the processes of its courts (jurisdiction over the person).

In international criminal law, judicial jurisdiction is subservient to legislative jurisdiction. The choice of law must precede the choice of court. Particular behaviour is only prohibited if there is some law that declares that it is. When a prosecution is initiated, this means that a law has already been chosen and the accused will be proceeded against pursuant to that law. This will determine which court has jurisdiction. For example, if the *Criminal Code* of Canada is applicable to the alleged offence, Canadian courts will have jurisdiction. If, on the other hand, the alleged offence is subject to some foreign law, Canadian courts will have no jurisdiction.

Domestic penal systems fix their own jurisdictional rules. Canadian law gives Canadian courts their rules of jurisdiction. Domestic systems do not take into account foreign laws. Canadian criminal courts are only interested in applying Canadian law. Thus, even though for example, Canadian rules of criminal law may be international

---

8   Brownlie, *supra* note 4 at 298; M. Akehurst, *supra* note 4 at 177; and D. Bowett, "Jurisdiction: Changing Problems of Authority over Activities and Resources" (1982) 53 Brit. Y.B. Int'l L. 1 at 3-4. On the subject of private international law, see J.-G. Castel, *Canadian Conflict of Laws*, 5th ed. (c. 2002-2003).

by their object in that they may reach international activities, they are by their nature domestic rules.

... The practice of individual states with respect to the exercise of jurisdiction over persons, property, acts or events, is not uniform. This lack of uniformity has a historical and geographical origin. The Anglo-American tradition tends to follow the territorial principle of jurisdiction according to which a state may exercise jurisdiction over persons and property or acts occurring within its territory. This preference can be explained by the fact that the territories under Anglo-American control were dominated by sea-frontiers. Individuals could not move as quickly or easily between these states as they could between states with land boundaries. The Western European states take a much broader view of jurisdictional principles precisely because of the geographical layout of a multiplicity of land or river frontiers. Movement between states has always been easier and to prevent fugitives from justice being able to escape trial, the nationality principle was established.

NOTES

1) It is useful to distinguish among "international" crimes that are prescribed by customary international law, such as genocide, war crimes, and crimes against humanity; "transnational crimes of international concern," which are crimes that are prescribed through domestic implementation of international treaties, such as acts of international terrorism and narcotics trafficking; and "transnational crimes of domestic concern," which are common crimes with constituent elements occurring in more than one state. A good example is the *Libman* case, reproduced in this chapter under Section A.3 on "Scope of Territorial Jurisdiction."

2) Where an international tribunal, either *ad hoc* or permanent, considered in Chapter 11 on "International Criminal Law," does not have jurisdiction over the particular offence, then an indirect scheme of enforcement must be employed. In many instances, states are obligated by multilateral conventions either to extradite or prosecute international offenders such as terrorist bombers. See article 8(1) of the 1998 International Convention for the Suppression of Terrorist Bombings[9] later in this chapter under Section A.6 on "Suppression of Transnational Crime."

The Steamship Lotus
France v. Turkey
(1927) P.C.I.J. Ser. A., No. 10

[By a special agreement, France and Turkey submitted to the Permanent Court of International Justice two questions, the first of which read:

(1) Has Turkey, contrary to Article 15 of the Convention of Lausanne of July 24th, 1923, respecting conditions of residence and business and jurisdiction, acted in conflict

---

9   U.N. Doc. A/RES/52/164, January 9, 1998.

with the principles of international law—and if so, what principles—by instituting following the collision which occurred on August 2nd, 1926, on the high seas between the French steamer *Lotus* and the Turkish steamer *Boz-Kourt* and upon the arrival of the French steamer at Constantinople—as well as against the captain of the Turkish steamship—joint criminal proceedings in pursuance of Turkish law against M. Demons, officer of the watch on board the *Lotus* at the time of the collision, in consequence of the loss of the *Boz-Kourt* having involved the death of eight Turkish sailors and passengers?

This question arose because Turkish authorities had arrested M. Demons on his arrival in Constantinople and tried and convicted him to a term of imprisonment.]

THE COURT: ... The prosecution was instituted in pursuance of Turkish legislation. ... Article 6 of the Turkish Penal Code, Law No. 765 of March 1st, 1926 (Official Gazette No. 320 of March 13th, 1926), runs as follows:

[Translation:] Any foreigner who, apart from the cases contemplated by Article 4, commits an offence abroad to the prejudice of Turkey or of a Turkish subject, for which offence Turkish law prescribes a penalty involving loss of freedom for a minimum period of not less than one year, shall be punished in accordance with the Turkish Penal Code provided that he is arrested in Turkey. The penalty shall however be reduced by one third and instead of the death penalty, twenty years of penal servitude shall be awarded. ...

... [T]he question submitted to the Court is not whether that article is compatible with the principles of international law; it is more general. The Court is asked to state whether or not the principles of international law prevent Turkey from instituting criminal proceedings against Lieutenant Demons under Turkish law. ...

It is Article 15 of the Convention of Lausanne of July 24th, 1923, respecting conditions of residence and business and jurisdiction, which refers the Contracting Parties to the principles of international law as regards the delimitation of their respective jurisdiction. This clause is as follows:

Subject to the provisions of Article 16, all questions of jurisdiction shall, as between Turkey and the other contracting Powers, be decided in accordance with the principles of international law.

... The Court, having to consider whether there are any rules of international law which may have been violated by the prosecution in pursuance of Turkish law of Lieutenant Demons, is confronted in the first place by a question of principle which, in the written and oral arguments of the two Parties, has proved to be a fundamental one. The French Government contends that the Turkish Courts, in order to have jurisdiction, should be able to point to some title to jurisdiction recognized by international law in favour of Turkey. On the other hand, the Turkish Government takes the view that Article 15 allows Turkey jurisdiction whenever such jurisdiction does not come into conflict with a principle of international law. ...

This way of stating the question is also dictated by the very nature and existing conditions of international law.

International law governs relations between independent states. The rules of law binding upon States therefore emanate from their own free will as expressed in conventions or by usages generally accepted as expressing principles of law and established in order to regulate the relations between co-existing independent communities or with a view to the achievement of common aims. Restrictions upon the independence of States cannot therefore be presumed.

Now the first and foremost restriction imposed by international law upon a State is that—failing the existence of a permissive rule to the contrary—it may not exercise its power in any form in the territory of another State. In this sense jurisdiction is certainly territorial; it cannot be exercised by a State outside its territory except by virtue of a permissive rule derived from international custom or from a convention.

It does not, however, follow that international law prohibits a State from exercising jurisdiction in its own territory, in respect of any case which relates to acts which have taken place abroad, and in which it cannot rely on some permissive rule of international law. Such a view would only be tenable if international law contained a general prohibition to States to extend the application of their laws and the jurisdiction of their courts to persons, property and acts outside their territory, and if, as an exception to this general prohibition, it allowed States to do so in certain specific cases. But this is certainly not the case under international law as it stands at present. Far from laying down a general prohibition to the effect that States may not extend the application of their laws and the jurisdiction of their courts to persons, property and acts outside their territory, it leaves them in this respect a wide measure of discretion which is only limited in certain cases by prohibitive rules; as regards other cases, every State remains free to adopt the principles which it regards as best and most suitable. ...

In these circumstances, all that can be required of a State is that it should not overstep the limits which international law places upon its jurisdiction; within these limits, its title to exercise jurisdiction rests in its sovereignty.

It follows from the foregoing that the contention of the French Government to the effect that Turkey must in each case be able to cite a rule of international law authorizing her to exercise jurisdiction, is opposed to the generally accepted international law to which Article 15 of the Convention of Lausanne refers. Having regard to the terms of Article 15 and to the construction which the Court has just placed upon it, this contention would apply in regard to civil as well as to criminal cases, and would be applicable on conditions of absolute reciprocity as between Turkey and the other contracting Parties; in practice, it would therefore in many cases result in paralysing the action of the courts, owing to the impossibility of citing a universally accepted rule on which to support the exercise of their jurisdiction. ...

The Court therefore must ... ascertain whether or not there exists a rule of international law limiting the freedom of States to extend the criminal jurisdiction of their courts to a situation uniting the circumstances of the present case.

... The Court will not proceed to ascertain whether general international law, to which Article 15 of the Convention of Lausanne refers, contains a rule prohibiting Turkey from prosecuting Lieutenant Demons.

For this purpose, it will in the first place examine the value of the arguments advanced by the French Government, without however omitting to take into account other possible aspects of the problem, which might show the existence of a restrictive rule applicable in this case.

The arguments advanced by the French Government, other than those concerned above, are, in substance, the three following: *French Arguments ↓*

(1) International law does not allow a State to take proceedings with regard to offenses committed by foreigners abroad, simply by reason of the nationality of the victim; and such is the situation in the present case because the offence must be regarded as having been committed on board the French vessel.

(2) International law recognizes the exclusive jurisdiction of the State whose flag is flown as regards everything which occurs on board a ship on the high seas.

(3) Lastly, this principle is especially applicable in a collision case.

As regards the first argument, the Court feels obliged in the first place to recall that its examination is strictly confined to the specific situation in the present case, for it is only in regard to this situation that its decision is asked for.

As has already been observed, the characteristic features of the situation of fact are as follows: there has been a collision on the high seas between two vessels flying different flags, on one of which was one of the persons alleged to be guilty of the offence, whilst the victims were on board the other.

This being so, the Court does not think it necessary to consider the contention that a State cannot punish offences committed abroad by a foreigner simply by reason of the nationality of the victim. For this contention only relates to the case where the nationality of the victim is the only criterion on which the criminal jurisdiction of the State is based. Even if that argument were correct generally speaking—and in regard to this the Court reserves its opinion—it could only be used in the present case if international law forbade Turkey to take into consideration the fact that the offence produced its effects on the Turkish vessel and consequently in a place assimilated to Turkish territory in which the application of Turkish criminal law cannot be challenged, even in regard to offences committed there by foreigners. But no such rule of international law exists. No argument has come to the knowledge of the Court from which it could be deduced that States recognize themselves to be under an obligation towards each other only to have regard to the place where the author of the offence happens to be at the time of the offence. On the contrary, it is certain that the courts of many countries, even of countries which have given their criminal legislation a strictly territorial character, interpret criminal law in the sense that offences, the authors of which at the moment of commission are in the territory of another State, are nevertheless to be regarded as having been committed in the national territory, if one of the constituent elements of the offence, and more especially its effects, have taken place there. French courts have, in regard to a variety of situations, given decisions sanctioning this way of interpreting the territorial principle. Again, the Court does not know of any cases in which governments have protested against the fact that the criminal law of some country contained a rule to this effect or that the courts of a country construed their criminal law in this sense. Consequently, once it is admitted that the effects of the offence were produced on the Turkish vessel, it becomes impossible to hold that there is a rule of international law which prohibits Turkey from prosecuting Lieutenant Demons because of the fact that the author of the offence was on board the French ship. ...

The second argument put forward by the French Government is the principle that the State whose flag is flown has exclusive jurisdiction over everything which occurs on board a merchant ship on the high seas.

It is certainly true that—apart from certain special cases which are defined by international law—vessels on the high seas are subject to no authority except that of the State whose flag they fly. In virtue of the principle of the freedom of the seas, that is to say, the absence of any territorial sovereignty upon the high seas, no State may exercise any kind of jurisdiction over foreign vessels upon them. Thus, if a war vessel, happening to be at the spot where a collision occurs between a vessel flying its flag and a foreign vessel, were to send on board the latter an officer to make investigations or to take evidence such an act would undoubtedly be contrary to international law.

But it by no means follows that a State can never in its own territory exercise jurisdiction over acts which have occurred on board a foreign ship on the high seas. A corollary of the principle of the freedom of the seas is that a ship on the high seas is assimilated to the territory of the State the flag of which it flies, for, just as in its own territory, that State exercises its authority upon it, and no other State may do so. All that can be said is that by virtue of the principle of the freedom of the seas, a ship is placed in the same position as national territory; but there is nothing to support the claim according to which the rights of the State under whose flag the vessel sails may go farther than the rights which it exercises within its territory properly so called. It follows that what occurs on board a vessel on the high seas must be regarded as if it occurred on the territory of the State whose flag the ship flies. If, therefore, a guilty act committed on the high seas produces its effects on a vessel flying another flag or in foreign territory, the same principles must be applied as if the territories of two different States were concerned, and the conclusion must therefore be drawn that there is no rule of international law prohibiting the State to which the ship on which the effects of the offence have taken place belongs, from regarding the offence as having been committed in its territory and prosecuting, accordingly, the delinquent.

This conclusion could only be overcome if it were shown that there was a rule of customary international law which, going further than the principle stated above, established the exclusive jurisdiction of the State whose flag was flown. ...

In the Court's opinion the existence of such a rule has not been conclusively proved. ...

The Court therefore has arrived at the conclusion that the second argument put forward by the French Government does not, any more than the first, establish the existence of a rule of international law prohibiting Turkey from prosecuting Lieutenant Demons.

It only remains to examine the third argument advanced by the French Government and to ascertain whether a rule specially applying to collision cases has grown up, according to which criminal proceedings regarding such cases come exclusively within the jurisdiction of the State whose flag is flown. ...

So far as the Court is aware there are no decisions of international tribunals on this matter; but some decisions of municipal courts have been cited. Without pausing to consider the value to be attributed to the judgments of municipal courts in connection

→ referring to a general principle rather than Int'l custom.

with the establishment of the existence of a rule of international law, it will suffice to observe that the decisions quoted sometimes support one view and sometimes the other.

... It will suffice to observe that, as municipal jurisprudence is thus divided, it is hardly possible to see in it an indication of the existence of the restrictive rule of international law which alone could serve as a basis for the contention of the French Government. ...

The conclusion at which the Court has therefore arrived is that there is no rule of international law in regard to collision cases to the effect that criminal proceedings are exclusively within the jurisdiction of the State whose flag is flown.

This conclusion moreover is easily explained if the manner in which the collision brings the jurisdiction of two different countries into play be considered.

The offence for which Lieutenant Demons appears to have been prosecuted was an act—of negligence or imprudence—having its origin on board the *Lotus*, whilst its effects made themselves felt on board the *Boz-Kourt*. These two elements are, legally, entirely inseparable, so much so that their separation renders the offence non-existent. Neither the exclusive jurisdiction of either State nor the limitations of the jurisdiction of each to the occurrences which took place on the respective ships would appear calculated to satisfy the requirements of justice and effectively to protect the interests of the two States. It is only natural that each should be able to exercise jurisdiction and to do so in respect of the incident as a whole. It is therefore a case of concurrent jurisdiction. ...

For these reasons, the Court, having heard both Parties, gives, by the President's casting vote—the votes being equally divided—judgment to the effect: [that Turkey had "not acted in conflict with the principles of international law."]

NOTES

1) As this case shows, few rigid limits on jurisdiction over the offence are set down by customary international law. The practical limitation, however, is that no state will generally attempt to exercise jurisdiction over matters in which it has no substantial interest or concern.

2) The discrete ruling that in collisions on the high seas jurisdiction is not limited to the flag state has since been overtaken by the 1958 Geneva Convention on the High Seas article 11, which is reiterated in the 1982 U.N. Convention on the Law of the Sea, article 97, reproduced in the Documentary Supplement and discussed in Chapter 13, Section B.6 on the "High Seas."

2. Bases of Criminal Jurisdiction

There are at least six bases upon which claims to prescriptive or enforcement jurisdiction may be founded.[10] International law does not place them in a hierarchical order. However, some are universally recognized while others are not. On account of the fact that several bases may operate for the same criminal action, concurrent jurisdiction will result and

---

10   Remember that jurisdiction over the offence (prescriptive jurisdiction) and over the person (enforcement jurisdiction) are both necessary in most states before a criminal prosecution may proceed. A state may have the one but not necessarily the other. See S.A. Williams & J.-G. Castel, *supra* note 4 at 7.

depending upon the law in the forum state double jeopardy could result. For example, suppose a Portuguese crew member of a French merchant ship stabs a Spanish crew member on board the ship when it is docked in the Canadian port of Halifax. Which of the states has jurisdiction over the stabbing offence? Does more than one? The role of international law here is to determine which domestic law or laws are to apply. Mann has aptly suggested:

> Jurisdiction ... is concerned with what has been described as one of the fundamental functions of public international law, viz., the function of regulating and delivering the respective competencies of states, "de conférer, de repartir et de réglementer les compétences."[11]

The six bases[12] that have been used by states are as follows:

Territorial Principle

The state in whose territory a crime was committed has jurisdiction over the offence. This is the primary working rule. Territory includes the land mass, internal waters and their beds, territorial sea and its subsoil, and air space above all of the former.[13] Territory has also been extended for certain functional ends to a 200 nautical mile exclusive economic zone and to the continental shelf.[14]

It is a manifestation of state sovereignty that a state should have jurisdiction over all persons, citizens and aliens alike, and things within its territory.[15] Canada's position is basically a territorial one. Section 6(2) of the Canadian *Criminal Code* provides that:

> Subject to this Act or any other Act of Parliament, no person shall be convicted or discharged under section 736 of an offence committed outside Canada.

In complicated situations there are five possible different applications of this principle. First, an act may be deemed to have been committed in the place where it is commenced. This is the subjective or initiatory principle. Second, the objective or terminatory principle provides that the state where the act is consummated or where the last constituent element of the offence occurs has jurisdiction. Third is the injured forum theory, whereby the state that has felt detrimental effects takes jurisdiction over the offence. Fourth is the approach taken by Lord Diplock in *Treacy v. D.P.P.*,[16] where he suggested the theory that

---

11   F.A. Mann, *supra* note 4 at 15.

12   See "Harvard Research Draft Convention on Jurisdiction with Respect to Crime" (1935) 29 A.J.I.L. Supp. 439; S.A. Williams & J.-G. Castel, *supra* note 4 at cc. 1-5; I. Brownlie, *supra* note 4 at 299-305; C. Blakesley, *supra* note 4; *Restatement, supra* note 4.

13   See further Chapter 7 on "State Jurisdiction Over Territory."

14   See Chapter 13, Section B on "Law of the Sea: Marine Zones" for discussion on how these maritime zones are delimited. Jurisdiction is asserted by Canada through the *Oceans Act*, S.C. 1996, c. 31, as amended, reproduced in Chapter 13, Section B.1(a).

15   See *Compania Naviera Vascongado v. Steamship Cristina*, [1938] A.C. 485 at 496, per Lord MacMillan.

16   [1971] A.C. 537 (H.L.).

a state may take jurisdiction when any element of the offence occurs within its borders. Fifth, a state may take jurisdiction where it has a reasonable and legitimate interest in doing so, compared with other involved states. In *Libman v. The Queen*,[17] the Supreme Court of Canada held that Canadian courts will take jurisdiction where a significant portion of the activities have taken place in Canada. This real and substantial link test is discussed below in Section A.3 on "Scope of Territorial Jurisdiction."

Nationality Principle[18]

The nationality of the offender is accepted as a basis of jurisdiction and is used extensively by civil law countries. Common law countries, however, have been reticent in their use of this principle. Historically, states such as Canada have claimed jurisdiction on this ground for only a few serious crimes, though they have not challenged its wider use by other states. The nationality principle is the corollary to the reluctance to extradite citizens or nationals that most civil law states display. Common law states have allowed the extradition of nationals to take place, as has been demonstrated by Canada in *Federal Republic of Germany v. Rauca*;[19] *United States v. Cotroni*; *United States v. El Zein*.[20]

In recent years, Canada has begun to make more use of this principle toward combating various kinds of international and transnational crimes of international concern, and the *Criminal Code* now provides for nationality-based jurisdiction for crimes such as treason (section 46(3)); certain crimes related to the International Space Station (section 7(2.3)); the various international terrorist offences prescribed by multilateral conventions to which Canada is a party, as well as crimes committed against internationally protected persons and U.N. personnel (sections 7(3) and (3.74)); and certain sexual offences taking place outside Canada (section 7(4.1)).[21]

The combination of the use of the territorial and nationality principles may create parallel concurrent jurisdiction over an offence and hence potential double jeopardy.[22] Therefore, the use of the nationality principle would be better confined to the most serious offences.

Passive Personality Principle

By this principle a state may claim jurisdiction over crimes committed abroad, even by aliens, against its nationals. Opposition has been expressed to the use of this principle. It

---

17　[1985] 2 S.C.R. 178, reproduced below in Section A.3 on "Scope of Territorial Jurisdiction."

18　Acquisition and loss of nationality are discussed in Chapter 8 on "Nationality."

19　See also the *Crimes Against Humanity and War Crimes Act*, S.C. 2000, c. 24, section 8(a)(i), reproduced in Chapter 11, Section D; the *Foreign Enlistment Act*, R.S.C. 1985, c. F-28, as amended; the *Security of Information Act*, R.S.C. 1985, c. O-5; S.C. 2001, c. 41, as amended.

20　(1983), 41 O.R. (2d) 225 (C.A.).

21　[1989] 1 S.C.R. 1469.

22　Though in this regard, see section 7(6) of the *Criminal Code*, allowing for the special pleas of *autrefois acquit, autrefois convict*, and pardon.

was contested by France in *The Steamship Lotus* but the Court reserved its opinion as it was not the sole basis of Turkish jurisdiction. However, Judge Moore expressed a strong dissenting opinion, which included this condemnation of the passive personality principle:

> [T]he countries by which the claim [based on the passive personality principle] has been espoused are said to have adopted the "system of protection."
>
> What, we may ask, is this system? In substance, it means that the citizen of one country, when he visits another country, takes with him for his "protection" the law of his own country and subjects those with whom he comes into contact to the operation of that law. In this way the inhabitant of a great commercial city, in which foreigners congregate, may in the course of an hour unconsciously fall under the operation of a number of foreign criminal codes. This is by no means a fanciful supposition; it is merely an illustration of what is daily occurring, if the "protective principle" is admissible. It is evident that this claim is at variance not only with the principle of exclusive jurisdiction of a state over its own territory, but also with the equally well-settled principle that a person visiting a foreign country, far from radiating for his protection the jurisdiction of his own country, falls under the dominion of the local law, and except so far as his government may diplomatically intervene in case of a denial of justice, must look to that law for his protection.
>
> No one disputes the right of a state to subject its citizens abroad to the operations of its own penal laws, if it sees fit to do so. This concerns simply the citizen and his own government, and no other government can properly interfere. But the case is fundamentally different where a country claims either that its penal laws apply to other countries and to what takes place wholly within such countries, or, if it does not claim this, that it may punish foreigners for alleged violations, even in their own country, of laws to which they were not subject.[23]

There are a limited number of examples of this principle in the Canadian *Criminal Code*, such as sections 7(3)(d)(i) and (ii), which give jurisdiction to a Canadian court where acts or omissions take place abroad against persons who are internationally protected persons representing Canada or members of their families;[24] and section 7(3.1)(e) dealing with hostage taking.[25] See also section 8(a)(iii) of the *Crimes Against Humanity and War Crimes Act*[26] concerning victims of genocide, war crimes, and crimes against humanity. These provisions reflect the acceptance by the international community of wide bases of criminal jurisdiction to combat international crime.[27]

---

23   (1927), P.C.I.J. (Ser. A.) No. 10 at 65. The judgment of the majority is reported in the previous subsection. See also the *Cutting Case* (1906), 2 Moore Dig. Int. L. 228.

24   This section implements Canada's obligations under the 1973 *Convention on the Prevention and Punishment of Crimes against Internationally Protected Persons*, Can. T.S. 1977 No. 43, reprinted in (1974) 13 I.L.M. 41.

25   This implements Canada's obligations under the 1979 *Convention Against the Taking of Hostages*, U.N. Doc. A/C.6/34/L23, reprinted in (1979) 18 I.L.M. 1456.

26   *Supra* note 19.

27   In *United States v. Yunis (No. 2)*, 681 F.Supp. 909 (D.D.C. 1988), the accused was charged with hijacking a Jordanian airline in Beirut. There were three U.S. citizens on board. The Court held that the passive personality principle together with the universal principle provided an appropriate basis for jurisdiction.

Protective Principle[28]

Under this principle a state may exercise jurisdiction over acts committed abroad that are prejudicial to its security, territorial integrity, and political independence. For example, the types of crime covered could include treason, espionage, and counterfeiting of currency, postage stamps, seals, passports, and other public documents.

Canada and other countries such as the United Kingdom have not favoured this principle when unaccompanied by other factors such as nationality or other forms of allegiance tying the accused to the forum.[29]

Universal Principle

Generally speaking, three interpretations of this principle have been put forward by states. First, that a state may exercise jurisdiction over all crimes, committed by anyone, wherever they may occur. This is seldom, if ever, used.[30] The second applies the principle to serious crimes where the international nature of the offence justifies its universal repression and the perpetrators are considered *hostes humani generis* or enemies of humankind. Any state may, as a matter of customary international law,[31] prosecute any individual for these crimes, regardless of where they were committed or the individual's nationality. This applies to such crimes as piracy, slavery, genocide, war crimes, crimes against humanity, and torture.

The third interpretation is more common, and is something of a subset of the second. It emerges from treaties in which states agree that any of them may[32] "universally" try individuals who commit the crimes dealt with in the treaties themselves. This is imperative in areas such as hostage taking, hijacking, and other international terrorist offences covered by these multilateral conventions, where the states, to whom the other bases of jurisdiction are applicable, are unwilling to prosecute or where extradition is not possible for whatever reason. This application of the universal principle is based on the presence of the accused on the territory of the forum state. It enables the obligation in many conventions—namely, to extradite or to submit the case to a state's own authorities for the purposes of prosecution—to be fulfilled.

Canada uses the latter two bases, though in a limited fashion, in the *Criminal Code*. Section 74 provides for piracy; section 7(2) concerns hijacking and other offences against civil aviation and, in section 7(2.1)(e)-(g), against fixed platforms at sea or international

---

The U.S. makes fairly extensive use of the passive personality principle; see, for example, the "Special maritime and territorial jurisdiction of the United States" under 18 U.S.C. § 7(7).

28 See generally I. Cameron, *The Protective Principle of International Criminal Jurisdiction* (1994).

29 See *Joyce v. D.P.P.*, [1946] A.C. 347 (H.L.) for analysis of what constitutes allegiance. See also *R. v. Casement*, [1917] 1 K.B. 98 and *R. v. Neumann* (1949), 3 S.A. 1238 (Sp. Cr. Ct. Transvaal).

30 See *Universal Jurisdiction Case* (1958), 28 I.L.R. 341 (Austrian S.C.) and the *Hungarian Deserter Case* (1959), 28 I.L.R. 343 (Austrian S.C.).

31 See A. Cassese, *International Criminal Law* (2003) at 293-95.

32 And in some cases, "shall" rather than "may"; see the discussion of *aut dedere, aut judicare* in subsection 6 below.

shipping; sections 7(3)(c) and 7(3.1)(f) proscribe attacks on internationally protected persons and hostage taking, respectively; section 7(3.71)(d) controls crimes against United Nations officers and associated personnel; section 7(3.5)(c) involves offences against nuclear material; and section 269.1 deals with torture by government officials. Section 8(b) of the *Crimes Against Humanity and War Crimes Act* operates with respect to genocide, war crimes, and crimes against humanity. The practice of universal jurisdiction is considered more fully below in Section A.5 on "Scope of Universal Jurisdiction."

By Agreement

Jurisdiction of one state within the territory of another state may always be granted by agreement. An example is the 1951 North Atlantic Treaty Status of Forces Agreement[33] implemented by the *Visiting Forces Act*.[34] Following the arrangements between the North Atlantic Treaty Organization (NATO) partners, the Canada–United States Agreement grants rights of entry into Canada for U.S. military personnel, and permits, within generous limits, American criminal laws and courts to operate inside Canada on U.S. military bases. The Agreement also makes special arrangements for civil claims by Canadians against visiting U.S. personnel.

3. Scope of Territorial Jurisdiction

To apply territorial jurisdiction it is first necessary to consider what is meant by a crime being "committed" in a certain locale. If A standing inside the border of state X shoots across the frontier and kills B who is standing in state Y, which state has the jurisdiction over the criminal offence? What if A stabs B in state X, and B then crosses the frontier to state Y where she dies from the wounds so inflicted?

Does "commission" mean initiated, consummated, or carried out completely within the territory of one state? Could it be interpreted to mean that jurisdiction over the offence may be assumed if any element of the offence occurs within a state or if any detrimental effect results there? Should "any" element or effect be sufficient, or must there be a substantial connection with the forum? The Law Reform Commission of Canada addressed the above question as follows:

> It should be noted that nothing is said in subsection 5(2) [now 6(2)] about offenses committed "partly" outside Canada; and unfortunately the *Criminal Code* is also silent as to what constitutes "committing" an offence *in* Canada. And so the question arises: Need all the elements of an offence occur in Canada to constitute *under Canadian law* the commission of an offence here?
>
> ... We believe there is room in, and reason for, Canadian law to utilize both the constituent element doctrine and the effects doctrine, or to put it another way, to implement both the subjective territorial principle and the objective territorial principle in Canadian criminal law. An offence would then be triable in Canada if it were committed in whole or

---

33   Can. T.S. 1953 No. 13.

34   R.S.C. 1985, c. V-2, as amended.

in part in Canada, or wholly outside Canada where the offender knowingly caused direct and substantial harmful effects to occur in Canada.[35]

The Supreme Court of Canada has since spoken on the matter in the *Libman* case, below.

Libman v. The Queen   *Genuine Link*
[1985] 2 S.C.R. 178   *Principle*

[Libman employed sales personnel in Toronto to telemarket to U.S. residents shares in two companies purportedly engaged in gold mining in Costa Rica. The purchasers were induced to buy the shares by deliberate misrepresentations, and were told to send their payments to offices operated by Libman's associates in Costa Rica and Panama, where he collected his share. Libman was charged with fraud and conspiracy to commit fraud. In defence he argued that the gist of the offence of fraud is the deprivation of the victims, which occurred in this case either in the United States, where the purchase monies were mailed, or in Costa Rica or Panama, where they were received. Either way, the deprivation was completed outside of Canada and so there was no jurisdiction to prosecute him in Canada.]

LaFOREST J.: ... I find it unnecessary to enter these niceties because my difficulties with the gist of the offence and the completion of the offence tests arise on a much broader plane. To begin with, these tests seem to me to involve a large measure of unreality. It requires, for example, that one hold that what happens to money obtained abroad when it is in fact brought to Canada in accordance with a carefully concocted fraudulent scheme originating here, is ... neither here nor there. This kind of thinking has, perhaps not altogether fairly, given rise to the kind of reproach that a lawyer is a person who can look at a thing connected with another as not being so connected. For everyone knows that the transaction in the present case is both here and there.

This is not the only example of the rather special kind of thinking required to apply the tests proposed. We saw from *R. v. Harden*, [1962] 1 All E.R. 286, for instance, that a criminal can locate a fraudulent scheme where it is most convenient to himself simply by arranging with the person whom he proposes to defraud where the agreement is to be completed. Such absurdities obviously invite a return to first principles.

As noted earlier, the territorial principle in criminal law was developed by the courts to respond to two practical considerations, first, that a country has generally little direct concern for the actions of malefactors abroad, and secondly, that other States may legitimately take umbrage if a country attempts to regulate matters taking place wholly or substantially within their territories. For these reasons the courts adopted a presumption against the application of laws beyond the realm, a presumption later codified in this country in s. 5(2) [now 6(2)] of the Criminal Code.

While we saw there were occasional strong expressions of the territorial doctrine, particularly in earlier times, the fact is that the courts never applied the doctrine rigidly.

---

35   *Supra* note 4 at 103 and 105.

To have done so, as Cockburn C.J. noted in *R. v. Keyn* (1876), L.R. 2 Ex. D. 63 at p. 233, would have meant that a State could not apply its laws to offenses whose elements occurred in several countries. This would have provided an easy escape for international criminals. What the courts sought to do, albeit in ways that were sometimes rather unsophisticated and at times inconsistent with the expressed rationales in earlier cases, was to give the principle an interpretation consistent with its underlying rationale. They did not, and indeed were not really invited to deal with transactions in other countries that had no domestic impact. But Canadian courts (like those in England and other countries for that matter) frequently took jurisdiction over transnational offenses that occurred partly in Canada where they felt this country had a legitimate interest in doing so. Interestingly, s. 5(2) [now 6(2)] of the Code expresses the territorial principle in a manner that rather reflects its purpose. That provision does not say that criminal law is confined to Canadian territory; it says rather that no person "shall be convicted ... for an offence committed outside Canada."

This country has a legitimate interest in prosecuting persons for activities that take place abroad but have an unlawful consequence here. ... Indeed, from an early period the English courts have recognized such an interest in other countries: see *R. v. Jacobi and Hiller* (1881), 46 L.R. 595; *R. v. Nillins* (1884), 53 L.J.M.C. 157, and *R. v. Godfrey*, [1923] 1 K.B. 24. The protection of the public in this country is widely acknowledged to be a legitimate purpose of criminal law, and one moreover that another nation could not easily say offended the dictates of comity.

But the courts did not confine themselves to taking jurisdiction over transnational offenses whose impact was felt within the country. As early as 1883 (*R. v. Holmes* (1883), 12 Q.B.D. 23) they also took jurisdiction in cases where the victim and hence the impact was abroad. In the early cases, there was a tendency to justify this in terms of the links that connected the act to the jurisdiction. In doing so they foreshadowed modern academic writing on the subject, which points out that a similar approach prevails in both public and private international law: see Sharon A. Williams and J.-G. Castel, *Canadian Criminal Law, International and Transnational Aspects* (1981), c. 2, p. 71 et seq.; see also Lynden Hall, " 'Territorial' Jurisdiction and the Criminal Law," [1972] *Crim. L.R.* 276.

Starting with *R. v. Ellis*, [1899] 1 Q.B. 230, in England, the courts began to use another test: that an offence takes place where its gist or gravamen occurs. This approach was particularly prevalent in Canada. It is possible to explain many of the cases on this basis which, at the superficial level, may seem rational. The location of the offence according to this approach also corresponds to the place where the fruits of the wrongful scheme are obtained, so one can easily be led into thinking that is where the wrongful act takes place. But whatever value the notion of the gist of an offence may have for other purposes, it has little relevance in this context. The offence of fraud, for example, consists not only of obtaining money, goods or other property; it also requires that they have been obtained by fraud. Both elements must be proved. Similarly, in the offence of obtaining property by false pretences, no matter how much one insists that the gist of the offence is the obtaining, the offence can only take place if the property is obtained by false pretences. What is more, I see no overriding policy reason that would favour the place of obtaining the goods. There are many cases, it is true, where this is also the place where the impact is felt, but that is not necessarily so (see *Holmes*, for example). Nor will it necessarily be the place where the harm is felt (see *Ellis*).

Sometimes the gist or gravamen test is associated (though the two may be looked at separately) with the "completion of the offence" or terminatory test, as in the present case, for example. This seems more prevalent in England, at least in the eyes of some academics: see, for example, Glanville Williams, *ibid.* That test may have the advantage of removing criminal liability for acts that take place after the offence as defined is completed, but it also has the result of removing from consideration earlier acts constituting the offence, here the fraudulent activities alleged to have occurred in Toronto.

It also ignores the fact that the fruits of the transaction were obtained in Canada as contemplated by the scheme. Their delivery here was not accidental or irrelevant. It was an integral part of the scheme. While it may not in strictness constitute part of the offence, it is, I think, relevant in considering whether a transaction falls outside Canadian territory. For in considering that question we must, in my view, take into account all relevant facts that take place in Canada that may legitimately give this country an interest in prosecuting the offence. One must then consider whether there is anything in those facts that offends international comity. If I may borrow the expression of Meredith J.A., in *R. v. Backrack* (1913), 21 C.C.C. 257, 11 D.L.R. 522, 28 O.L.R. 32, the law would be lame indeed if its strictures could be avoided by the simple artifice of going outside the country to obtain the fruits of a scheme that was hatched in and largely put into effect in Canada. In this case, the whole operation of obtaining the proceeds of the fraud outside the country was a mere sham and should be treated as such.

Indeed, I would agree with Osler J., who heard the application to quash, that the preparatory activities to perpetrate the fraudulent scheme were in themselves sufficient to warrant a holding that the offence took place in Canada. The scheme was devised here, the whole operation that made it function, the directing minds, the boiler-room— all were situate in Toronto. The fact that this approach would catch cases where the victims of the scheme were harmed outside the country makes no difference. That would also occur under the gist of the offence test when the moneys were obtained in Canada, as it would under the completion of the crime test when the crime was completed here. Apart from this, though the criminal law is undoubtedly intended for the protection of the public, it does not do so solely by the simple expedient of directly protecting the public from harm. Rather, in conformity with its major purposes, it attempts to underline the fundamental values of our society; see the Law Reform Commission of Canada, Report No. 3, Our Criminal Law (1979). In doing so, it reinforces the law-abiding sentiments in society. Walsh J., in *Shulman v. the King* (1946), 2 C.R. 153 [at 156], caught the essence of this when, after noting that "there is more to [a] (criminal offence) than its successful culmination," he added: "Its preparation and evolution, even in the case of failure, is reprehensible." It would be a sad commentary on our law if it was limited to underlining society's values by the prosecution of minor offenders while permitting more seasoned practitioners to operate on a world-wide scale from a Canadian base by the simple manipulation of a technicality of the law's own making. What would be underlined in the public's mind by allowing criminals to go free simply because their operations have grown to international proportions, I shall not attempt to expound.

I am also aware that the view I have taken leaves open the possibility that a person could be prosecuted for the same offence in more than one country, but any injustice that might result from this eventuality could be avoided by resort to the pleas of *autrefois acquit and autrefois convict*, which have been applied to persons tried in other countries: see *Burrows v. Jemino* (1726), 2 Str. 733, 93 E.R. 815; *R. v. Roche* (1775), 1 Leach 134, 168 E.R. 169; *R. v. Azzopardi* (1843), 2 Mood. 289, 169 E.R. 115; *R. v. Aughet* (1918), 13 Cr. App. R. 101; see also *Treacy v. Director of Public Prosecutions* [1971] A.C. 537.

I might summarize my approach to the limits of territoriality in this way. As I see it, all that is necessary to make an offence subject to the jurisdiction of our courts is that a significant portion of the activities constituting that offence took place in Canada. As it is put by modern academics, it is sufficient that there be a "real and substantial link" between an offence and this country, a test well known in public and private international law: see Williams and Castel, *ibid.*; Hall, *ibid.* As Professor Hall notes (p. 277), this does not require legislation. It was the courts after all that defined the manner in which the doctrine of territoriality applied, and the test proposed simply amounts to a revival of the earlier way of formulating the principle. It is in fact the test that best reconciles all cases. ...

That this approach is attuned to modern times is evident from the fact that some variant of it has been recommended by numerous law reform bodies or adopted in legislation: see, *inter alia*, the English Law Commission's Report on the *Territorial and Extraterritorial Extent of the Criminal Law* (Law Com. 91, 1978); the American Law Institute's *Model Penal Code* (Proposed Official Draft, 1962), s. 1.03; the *New Zealand Crimes Act*, 1961 (N.Z.), c. 43, s. 7, and the recent Law Reform Commission of Canada Working Paper No. 37, *Extraterritorial Jurisdiction*, Part III.

Just what may contribute a real and substantial link in a particular case, I need not explore. There were ample links here. The outer limits of the test may, however, well be coterminous with the requirements of international comity.

As I have already noted, in some of the early cases the English courts tended to express a narrow view of the territorial application of English law so as to ensure that they did not unduly infringe on the jurisdiction of other States. However, even as early as the late 19th century, following the invention and development of modern means of communication, they began to exercise criminal jurisdiction over transnational transactions as long as a significant part of the chain of action occurred in England. Since then, means of communications have proliferated at an accelerating pace and the common interests of States have grown proportionately. Under these circumstances, the notion of comity, which means no more nor less than "kindly and considerate behaviour towards each other," has also evolved. How considerate is it of the interests of the United States in this case to permit criminals based in this country to prey on its citizens? How does it conform to its interests or to ours for us to permit such activities when law enforcement agencies in both countries have developed co-operative schemes to prevent and prosecute those engaged in such activities? To ask these questions is to answer them. No issue of comity is involved here. In this regard, I make mine the words of Lord Diplock in *Treacy v. D.P.P.*, cited earlier. I also agree with the sentiments expressed by Lord Salmon in *Director of Public Prosecutions v.*

Doot et. al., [1973] A.C. 807, that we should not be indifferent to the protection of the public in other countries. In a shrinking world, we are all our brothers' keepers. In the criminal arena this is underlined by the international co-operative schemes that have been developed among national law enforcement bodies.

For these reasons, I have no difficulty in holding, on the facts agreed upon for the purposes of this appeal, that the counts of fraud with which the appellant is charged may properly be prosecuted in Canada, and I see nothing in the requirements of international comity that would dictate that this country refrain from exercising its jurisdiction. Since these fraudulent activities took place is Canada, it follows from the reasons set forth in *Re Chapman*, [1970] 5 C.C.C. 46, [1970] 3 O.R. 344, 11 C.R.N.S. 1, that the conspiracy count may also be proceeded with in Canada.

For these reasons, I would dismiss the appeal.

NOTES

1) Under sections 465(3) and (4) of the Canadian *Criminal Code* it is an offence to conspire in Canada to commit an act outside of Canada that is an offence in that place, and to conspire outside of Canada to commit an offence in Canada.[36]

2) In the *Libman* case the court used as a jurisdictional test a "real and substantial link" between the offence and Canada. How significant was it that Libman's fraudulent gains, though paid abroad, were brought back to Canada? Could the sales personnel, for instance, also be subjected to prosecution in Canada?

3) What other states might have wanted to prosecute Libman? In what circumstances would they have jurisdiction to do so?

4) In 1996 a case came before the Canadian courts concerning allegations that three Romanian stowaways had been thrown overboard into the Atlantic ocean from the Taiwanese flagged vessel, the *M.V. Maersk Dubai*, by the Captain and several of the officers.[37] Captain Cheng and the other officers, who were Taiwanese nationals, were detained on arrival of the vessel in Halifax, Nova Scotia, on information laid by four Filipino crew members. On the basis of the 1893 Treaty between Great Britain and Romania for the Mutual Surrender of Fugitive Criminals, Romania requested the extradition of Captain Cheng and the other officers on charges of murder. This request raised a number of interesting international legal questions concerning international criminal law but also, on another level, the status of Taiwan. Key to the case was the issue of jurisdiction over the offence. Article 1 of the 1893 Treaty provided that:

> The High Contracting Parties engage to deliver up to each other those persons who, being accused or convicted of a crime or offence committed in the territory of the one party, shall be found in the territory of the other party, under the circumstances and conditions stated in the present treaty.

---

36   See S.A. Williams & J.-G. Castel, *supra* note 4 at 88-90 and M. Goode, *Criminal Conspiracy in Canada* (1975).

37   *Romania (State) v. Cheng* (1997), 114 C.C.C. (3d) 289 (N.S.S.C.). The extradition treaty may be found at U.K.T.S. 1894 No. 14. For a case comment, see M. McConnell (1997) 8 Crim. L.F. 335.

Extradition requests are confined by the language of the *Extradition Act* and the pertinent treaty. Bearing in mind the language of article 1, on what principle of jurisdiction could the Romanian request have been based? The Court denied the request for extradition to Romania because of a lack of jurisdiction under the terms of the Treaty. Captain Cheng and the other officers returned to Taiwan, where Captain Cheng was subsequently charged with manslaughter.

What were Canada's other options? Did Taiwan have jurisdiction over the offences? Refer to the *Lotus* case, above, and articles 91-97 of the 1982 U.N. Convention on the Law of the Sea, reproduced in the Documentary Supplement, concerning nationality of ships and penal jurisdiction. Note should be taken of the fact, however, that Canada does not recognize Taiwan as a sovereign state and consequently does not have official diplomatic relations with Taiwan. As a result, Canada and Taiwan have no extradition treaty. Neither does Canada have an extradition treaty with the People's Republic of China, which claims Taiwan as a part of the State of China.

Could Canada have prosecuted the alleged offenders in Canada? Refer to sections 6(2) and 7 of the Canadian *Criminal Code* and the *Libman* case.

4. Assertion of Extraterritorial Jurisdiction

Introduction[38]

Few topics have generated more disagreement and controversy between states and jurists than the extraterritorial application of national laws. Defining what is meant by the phrase "extraterritorial application of national laws" gives rise to problems in itself: here, it is taken to mean the asserted rights of a state to impose its laws on conduct engaged in by persons who are not its residents or nationals and that occurs outside of its territory. In short, it covers the assertions of jurisdiction over the activities of foreigners abroad.[39]

The classic example follows: a citizen in state A sells a product to a citizen in state B. This is a legal activity both in state A and state B. In state C, however, it is illegal to sell that product to citizens in state B. When the citizen from state A visits or goes to do business in state C, he or she is prosecuted or sued for the activity of selling to a citizen in state B. The usual argument of state C is that the activity outside its borders had an effect within its territory. There are, of course, many permutations on this scenario.

---

38   Generally see J.-G. Castel, *Extraterritoriality in International Trade: Canada and United States of America Practices Compared* (1988); K.M. Meessen, ed., *Extraterritorial Jurisdiction in Theory and Practice* (1996); D. Rosenthal & W. Knighton, *National Laws and International Commerce: The Problem of Extraterritoriality* (1982); M. Akehurst, "Jurisdiction in International Law" (1972-73) 46 Brit. Y.B. Int'l L. 145; D.W. Bowett, "Jurisdiction: Changing Patterns of Authority over Activities and Resources," in R. St. J. Macdonald & D.M. Johnston, *The Structure and Process of International Law* (1983) at 555; H. Scott Fairley, "Exceeding the Limits of Territorial Bounds: The Helms-Burton Act" (1996) Can. Y.B. Int'l L. 161; P.M. Roth, "Reasonable Extraterritoriality: Correcting the 'Balance of Interests' " (1992) 41 I.C.L.Q. 245; and *Restatement, supra* note 4, ss. 401-3.

39   The leading international case concerning the limits that international law imposes on the exercise of state jurisdiction is *The Steamship Lotus, supra* note 23.

Respecting extraterritorial assertions of jurisdiction three trends are noticeable. The first is a growing recognition of the increasing interdependence of states. As a result of modern technology, particularly in the area of communications, many events that formerly would not have taken place in more than one jurisdiction now may take place in several and may have therefore a transnational nature. This is true of activities governed both by civil and criminal law. Many governments have recognized that they need to extend their jurisdiction beyond traditional territorial notions in order to ensure that their publics, or indeed, perhaps even the interests of a foreign public, are protected against injurious acts that occur beyond their borders and thus also within the jurisdiction of another state. The resulting problem is a conflict of concurrent jurisdiction over transnational events. Sorting out which law or policy should govern these events sometimes requires balancing the competing claims of two states having possibly different contacts with the event. Solutions on the merits will depend, to a large degree, on whose rules determine the threshold issues of what factors will justify the assertion of jurisdiction and therefore which forum will rule on the substance.

A second trend is the advocacy of national legislation to penalize foreign individuals and companies for undertaking legal activities in foreign jurisdictions that are considered by the legislating state to be environmentally destructive or inconsistent with worker, children's, or human rights. The scenario occurs when state C seeks to penalize a company from state A for environmental practices in state B that do not meet the standards of state C, although they do meet the standards of state B. Few examples of this type of legislation yet exist.

A third and somewhat contradictory trend is the defensive measures that states are taking to protect their interests from the exercise of extraterritorial jurisdiction by other states. Certain countries have extended their jurisdiction beyond the limits that others are willing to accept as being reasonable in international law. There have been reactions to these "excessive" jurisdictional claims by other states. As occasion suits, however, the objectors may themselves be guilty of the very conduct they condemn.

Examples of Canadian law applying extraterritorially were, until recently, infrequent. Canadian criminal law, for example, that traditionally, as set out in section 6(2) of the Code, is not to be interpreted as applying outside of Canada, now applies to a variety of events beyond its borders. Under the pressure of recent events, Canada has been required to extend its jurisdiction in such matters as aircraft hijacking, for the protection of its diplomats abroad and in the event of hostage taking. As early as the *Arctic Waters Pollution Protection Act of 1970*, Canada had indicated its willingness to extend the application of Canadian laws beyond its borders where special national needs required it. Pursuant to the *Coastal Fisheries Protection Act*, in 1995 Canada seized a Spanish fishing trawler, the *Estai*, beyond Canada's borders, in this case on the high seas, for breaching Canadian law that applied to the high seas.[40] Changes to the *Competition Act*

---

40   The incident over the *Estai* is discussed in Chapter 13, Section E.1 under "East Coast Fisheries and the Estai." The International Court's decision in the case brought against Canada is reproduced in Chapter 6, Section D.2 on "Jurisdiction of the Court." Reference may also be made to the domestic case that arose from the arrest of the *Estai: Jose Pereira E. Hijos v. Canada*, [1997] 2 F.C. 84. Usually a state asserting extraterritorial jurisdiction is trying to apply its laws against an offender. The reverse arose in *R. v. Cook*,

and the introduction of the *Foreign Extraterritorial Measures Act of 1984* and the *Special Economic Measures Act of 1992* indicate a much more aggressive approach to this issue.

Reaction to the perceived exorbitant assertion of jurisdiction usually occurs where a foreign state applies its laws, not only to events that have their primary links with it, but also to other events of limited connection, that in other respects are perfectly licit under their local law. Similarly, objection is likely to be raised when a state tries to impose its legal process, not only on its own nationals while abroad, but also on foreigners who may be associated with them in lawful ways according to the law of their own countries. The range of the irritants has greatly increased in recent years. Initially American anti-trust laws were the primary cause for alarm but lately extraterritorial jurisdiction has also been asserted in other subject areas, such as export controls, taxation, securities, asset controls, corrupt practices, and bankruptcy and insolvency. The exercise of procedural authority extraterritorially by courts or administrative organs also occurs. Attempts have been made against completely foreign companies to subject them to jurisdiction and courts have ordered the subpoena of witnesses and the production of documents located abroad in the aid of lawsuits that may have only a tenuous connection with the jurisdiction where they have been commenced.

While extraterritorial assertions of jurisdiction have most frequently been viewed as irritants to international relations and have called forth both diplomatic and legal reactions from affected states, another perspective also has to be recognized. The modern global economy is as yet regulated by the decentralized legal system that is international law. Hence, it is only nation states that can exercise any authority over multinational enterprises in their transnational operations. Thus, at times, extraterritorial applications of jurisdiction may be essential in order to reach international drug trafficking, organized crime, corrupt business practices, and other illicit activities.

The international legal issues involved in questions of extraterritoriality are complex, particularly since the right to exercise jurisdiction may vary, depending on whether one is concerned with the jurisdiction to legislate, to adjudicate, or to enforce. The exercise of jurisdiction in each of these three areas depends upon a different basis. Indeed different subject areas, whether civil or criminal, raise different problems and may have to be approached from individual perspectives. This section provides a few examples of different assertions of, and reactions to, extraterritorial authority.

Clash of Economic Policies: Anti-Trust Actions[41]

Anti-trust legislation, an American name for competition laws, poses particular problems when applied to activities beyond the borders of the state exercising jurisdiction. Implicit in such legislation are states' concepts concerning the relative advantages or disadvantages

---

[1998] 2 S.C.R. 597. The Supreme Court held that the accused, when interviewed by two Canadian detectives in the United States, was entitled to extraterritorial application of the Canadian *Charter of Rights* for his protection.

41   J.-G. Castel, *supra* note 38 at 27; J.-G. Castel, "The Extraterritorial Effects of Anti-trust Laws" (1983) 179 Hague Recueil 21; and Yoshio Ohara, "New US Policy on the Extraterritorial Application of Antitrust Law and Foreign Responses," in Meessen, *supra* note 38 at 166.

of minimizing competition, decentralizing economic decision-making, fixing prices, allocating national human and other resources to achieve certain national goals, and other economic policies that are designed to respond to that state's levels of economic development. Such policies are a reflection of basic political notions that undergird a state's economic structure. The application of such policies to activities carried on in other states risks interfering with their pursuit of similar goals within their own territory.

In the United States, the *Sherman Act*[42] renders illegal every contract or conspiracy in restraint of interstate or foreign trade or commerce of the United States. In *Alcoa*, an early case under the legislation,[43] the Court of Appeal was faced with a conflict between the clearly extraterritorial ambit of the *Sherman Act*, on the one hand, and the presumption that Congress intended to legislate in a manner consistent with the principles of international law governing jurisdiction, on the other. Judge Learned Hand found that the Act did have extraterritorial reach, by invoking effects-based territorial jurisdiction:

> Two situations are possible. There may be agreements made beyond our borders not intended to affect imports, which do affect them, or which affect exports. Almost any limitation of the supply of goods in Europe, for example, or in South America, may have repercussions in the United States if there is trade between the two. Yet when one considers the international complications likely to arise from an effort in this country to treat such agreements as unlawful, it is safe to assume that Congress certainly did not intend the Act to cover them. Such agreements may on the other hand intend to include imports into the United States, and yet it may appear that they have had no effect upon them. That situation might be thought to fall within the doctrine that intent may be a substitute for performance in the case of a contract made within the United States; or it might be thought to fall within the doctrine that a statute should not be interpreted to cover acts abroad which have no consequence here. We shall not choose between these alternatives; but for argument we shall assume that the Act does not cover agreements, even though intended to affect imports or exports, unless its performance is shown actually to have had some effect upon them.

In the result, the Court concluded that the defendant foreign companies, who had struck agreements in Switzerland to fix world prices in aluminum, had violated the *Sherman Act* because the agreements were intended to affect, and did affect, U.S. imports.

While Judge Hand characterized the effects-based test as resting on "settled law," the finding in *Alcoa* was criticized as being inconsistent with international law and interstate comity, and was even questioned by subsequent court decisions.[44] However, the *Foreign Trade Antitrust Improvements Act of 1982* directed that the *Sherman Act* does not apply to foreign business conduct unless "such conduct has a direct, substantial and reasonably foreseeable effect" on U.S. commerce. In *Hartford Fire Insurance v. California*,[45] the U.S. Supreme Court applied this approach in finding that certain U.K. companies had violated the *Sherman Act*, notwithstanding that their conduct was legal in the U.K. Souter

---

42 *Sherman Antitrust Act*, 15 U.S.C. § 1-7.

43 *United States v. Aluminum Co. of America*, 148 F.2d 416 (2d Cir. 1945).

44 See *Timberlane Lumber Co. v. Bank of America*, 549 F.2d 597 (9th Cir. 1976).

45 509 U.S. 764 (Sup. Ct. 1993).

J. ruled that this situation created no conflict between U.S. and U.K. law, since the companies *could* have complied with the regulatory regimes in both countries. Does this "conflict test" amount to a recognition by the U.S. Supreme Court that international law does place a limitation on domestic jurisdiction?

Canadian Practice

In Canada, the provisions of the *Competition Act*[46] against combines and other market controlling and price fixing arrangements would presumably apply to conduct outside Canada designed to affect markets inside Canada and that would be an offence if committed in Canada,[47] although there have been cases of conduct outside Canada with effects on Canada that were considered beyond the scope of the Act.[48] It also contains a section directed against certain conduct of individuals abroad:

> 46(1) Any corporation, wherever incorporated, that carries on business in Canada and that implements, in whole or in part in Canada, a directive, instruction, intimation of policy or other communication to the corporation or any person from a person in a country other than Canada who is in a position to direct or influence the policies of the corporation, which communication is for the purpose of giving effect to a conspiracy, combination, agreement or arrangement entered into outside Canada that, if entered into in Canada, would have been in contravention of section 45, is, whether or not any director or officer of the corporation in Canada has knowledge of the conspiracy, combination, agreement or arrangement, guilty of an indictable offence and is liable on conviction to a fine in the discretion of the court.

The *Foreign Investment Review Act*,[49] now the *Investment Canada Act*,[50] has been applied to mergers of foreign corporations when the control over a Canadian business enterprise is thereby affected.[51]

---

46   R.S.C. 1985, c. C-34, as amended.

47   *R. v. Campbell* (1965), 46 D.L.R. (2d) 83 (Ont. C.A.), aff'd. (1966), 58 D.L.R. (2d) 673 (S.C.C.), where an overt act was done in Canada in furtherance of an agreement entered into in the United States.

48   See Canada, *Report of the Royal Commission on Farm Machinery: Special Report on Prices of Tractors and Combines in Canada and Other Countries* (1969) (price fixing of farm machinery in the U.K. that related to prices in Canada) and Restrictive Trade Practices Commission, *Report on Trade Practices in Phosphorous Products and Sodium Chlorate Industries* (1966); "The Japanese Drum Case," reported in R. Roberts, *Anti-combines and Anti-trust* (1980) at 328.

49   S.C. 1973-74, c. 46, as amended, repealed by S.C. 1985, c. 20.

50   R.S.C. 1985, c. 28 (1st Supp.), as amended.

51   *Dow Jones & Co. Inc. v. A.-G. of Canada* (1981), 122 D.L.R. (3d) 731 (F.C.A.) and *A.-G. of Canada v. Fallbridge Holdings Ltd.* (1986), 31 B.L.R. 57 (F.C.A.).

Clash of Foreign Policies: United States, Cuba, and the Helms-Burton Act

Extraterritorial assertions of jurisdiction are sometimes manifestations of a state's foreign policy, as a government attempts to use its regulatory powers to support specific goals on the international plane—and punish, directly or indirectly, those states that do not agree with its foreign policy objectives. One of the most controversial examples in recent years was the U.S. *Helms-Burton Act*,[52] which arose from that state's historical antipathy toward the Castro regime in Cuba. The notorious Title III of this statute awarded a right of action before U.S. courts to any U.S. national who claimed to have had property in Cuba confiscated by the Castro government, against anyone who "trafficked" in this property. The definition of "traffic" was fairly broad; as one commentator noted:

> [T]he Act contemplates that if an English company purchases sugar from a Cuban state enterprise and the English company also does business in the United States and accordingly is amenable to the judicial jurisdiction of a U.S. court, it would be liable to a U.S. national who could show that some of the English company's purchases consisted of sugar grown on the plantation that the plaintiff once owned.[53]

Reaction to the *Helms-Burton Act* was swift and fierce. Both the European Union[54] and Mexico[55] adopted blocking legislation regarding the Act. The Organization of American States issued a Resolution condemning this type of law, which, its Juridical Committee stated, violated both the property rights of foreign nationals and international law principles regarding the extension of extraterritorial jurisdiction.[56] Canada's response, an amendment to the *Foreign Extraterritorial Measures Act*, is discussed further below. Some commentators assert that the *Helms-Burton Act* is consistent with international law. What arguments would support this view?[57]

The clash of opposing views may be ameliorated by the fact that the *Helms-Burton Act* contains a provision that allows the President to suspend the application of Title III for renewable six-month periods.

---

52 The *Helms-Burton Act* is the common name for the *Cuban Liberty and Democratic Solidarity (Libertad) Act of 1996* (Pub. L. No. 104-114; 110 Stat. 785; (1996) 35 I.L.M. 357). See, generally, Fairley, *supra* note 38; A.F. Lowenfeld, "Congress and Cuba: The Helms-Burton Act" (1996) 90 A.J.I.L. 419; B.M. Clagett, "Title III of the Helms-Burton Act Is Consistent with International Law" (1996) 90 A.J.I.L. 434; and P. Glossop, "Canada's Foreign External Measures Act and U.S. Restrictions on Trade with Cuba" (1998) 37 Int. Law 93.

53 Lowenfeld, *supra* note 52 at 426.

54 European Council Regulation No. 2271/96, November 22, 1996, "Protecting Against the Effects of Extra-Territorial Application of Legislation Adopted by a Third County" (1997) 36 I.L.M. 125.

55 *Mexican Act To Protect Trade and Investment from Foreign Norms That Contravene International Law* (1997) 36 I.L.M. 133.

56 See "Freedom of Trade and Investment of the Hemisphere": Opinion of the Inter-American Juridical Committee in Response to Resolution AG/DOC.3375/96 of the General Assembly of the Organization of American States (1996) 35 I.L.M. 1329.

57 See Clagett, *supra* note 52 at 434.

Demands for Production of Documents Located Abroad[58]

Problems often arise when courts, or other authorities, seek to obtain evidence located abroad, in order to enforce their own laws of whatever kind. Such demands can cause particular difficulty when courts seek to enforce the forum state's procedural laws regarding evidence gathering against multinational corporations that might have branch offices located in numerous other states and are thus subject to those states' laws. It is not unusual, but highly controversial, for courts to enforce these procedural laws, even where to do so would cause the corporation to violate another state's laws.[59]

Without access to relevant business records located abroad, a major commercial crime case or an antitrust suit may be severely crippled. Naturally such cases have often led to diplomatic protests by the foreign countries involved. The Canadian government has appeared in some cases before the U.S. courts to protest this form of jurisdiction, though unsuccessfully.[60] For its part, the Supreme Court of Canada in *Gulf Oil Corp. v. Gulf Canada Ltd.*[61] refused to enforce a U.S. court order for the compulsion of documents held in Canada by Gulf Canada Ltd., because the order conflicted directly with regulations enacted by the Canadian government to deny exactly such an order as a matter of state policy and foreign relations.

Canadian Responses: Repulsion and Cooperation

Foreign Extraterritorial Measures Act
R.S.C. 1985, c. F-29, as amended

2.1 The Attorney General of Canada may, with the concurrence of the Minister of Foreign Affairs, by order, amend the schedule

(a) by adding the name of a foreign trade law or a reference to any provision of a foreign trade law if the Attorney General of Canada is of the opinion that the law or provision is contrary to international law or international comity; or

(b) by removing a name or reference to any provision set out in the schedule if the Attorney General of Canada is of the opinion that it is appropriate to do so. ...

3.(1) Where, in the opinion of the Attorney General of Canada, a foreign tribunal has exercised, is exercising or is proposing or likely to exercise jurisdiction or powers of a kind or in a manner that has adversely affected or is likely to adversely affect significant Canadian interests in relation to international trade or commerce involving a business carried on in whole or in part in Canada or that otherwise has infringed or is likely to infringe Canadian sovereignty, or jurisdiction or powers that is or are related to the enforcement of a foreign trade law or a provision of a foreign trade law set out in the schedule, the Attorney General of Canada may, by order, prohibit or restrict

---

58   See, generally, Castel, *supra* note 38 at 188.

59   See *e.g. U.S. v. First National City Bank*, 396 F.2d 897 (2d Cir. 1968).

60   See *United States v. Bank of Nova Scotia*, 740 F.2d 817 (11th Cir. 1984).

61   [1980] 2 S.C.R. 39.

(a) the production before or the disclosure or identification to, or for the purposes of, a foreign tribunal of records that, at any time while the order is in force, are in Canada or are in the possession or under the control of a Canadian citizen or a person resident in Canada;

(b) the doing of any act in Canada, in relation to records that at any time while the order is in force are in Canada or are in the possession or under the control of a Canadian citizen or a person resident in Canada, that will, or is likely to, result in the records, or information as to the contents of the records or from which the records might be identified, being produced before or disclosed or identified to, or for the purposes of, a foreign tribunal; and

(c) the giving by a person, at a time when he is a Canadian citizen or a resident of Canada, of information before, or for the purposes of, a foreign tribunal in relation to, or in relation to the contents or identification of, records that, at any time while the order is in force, are or were in Canada or under the control of a Canadian citizen or a person resident in Canada.

(2) Where production before or disclosure or identification to, or for the purposes of a foreign tribunal of a record and the giving by a person of information before, or for the purposes of, a foreign tribunal in relation to, or in relation to the contents or identification of, a record is prohibited or restricted by an order under subsection (1), a tribunal in Canada shall not, for the purposes of proceedings before the foreign tribunal,

(a) where the order is in the nature of a prohibition, receive the record or information; or

(b) where the order is in the nature of a restriction, receive the record or information if, as a result of so doing, the order may be contravened.

(3) An order under this section may

(a) be directed to a particular person or to a class of persons;

(b) relate to a particular foreign tribunal or to a class of foreign tribunals; and

(c) relate to a particular record or to a class of records.

Seizure of Records

4. Where, on an application by or on behalf of the Attorney General of Canada, a superior court is satisfied that an order under section 3 may not be complied with in relation to some or all of the records in Canada to which it relates, the court may issue a warrant authorizing a person named therein or a peace officer to seize those records and to deliver them to the court or a person designated by the court for safekeeping while the order under section 3 remains in force, on such terms as to access to the records or return of all or any of the records, as are fixed by the court having regard to the object to which the order under section 3 is directed.

Measures of a Foreign State or Foreign Tribunal

5.(1) Where, in the opinion of the Attorney General of Canada, a foreign state or foreign tribunal has taken or is proposing or is likely to take measures affecting international trade or commerce of a kind or in a manner that has adversely affected or is likely to adversely affect significant Canadian interests in relation to international trade or commerce involving business carried on in whole or in part in Canada or that otherwise has infringed or is likely to infringe Canadian sovereignty, the Attorney General of Canada may, with the concurrence of the Secretary of State for External Affairs, by order,

(a) require any person in Canada to give notice to him of such measures, or of any directives, instructions, intimations of policy or other communications relating to such measures from a person who is in a position to direct or influence the policies of the person in Canada; or

(b) prohibit any person in Canada from complying with such measures, or with any directives, instructions, intimations of policy or other communications relating to such measures from a person who is in a position to direct or influence the policies of the person in Canada.

(2) For the purposes of subsection (1), measures taken or to be taken by a foreign state or foreign tribunal include laws, judgments and rulings made or to be made by the foreign state or foreign tribunal and directives, instructions, intimations of policy and other communications issued by or to be issued by the foreign state or foreign tribunal.

(3) An order made under this section may be directed to a particular person or to a class of persons. ...

7.(1) Every person who contravenes an order made under section 3 or 5 that is directed to the person and that has been served on the person in accordance with section 6 is guilty of an offence and liable

(a) on conviction on indictment,

(i) in the case of a corporation, to a fine not exceeding $1,500,000, and

(ii) in the case of an individual, to a fine not exceeding $150,000 or to imprisonment for a term not exceeding five years, or to both; or

(b) on summary conviction,

(i) in the case of a corporation, to a fine not exceeding $150,000, and

(ii) in the case of an individual, to a fine not exceeding $15,000 or to imprisonment for a term not exceeding two years, or to both.

7.1 Any judgment given under the law of the United States entitled *Cuban Liberty and Democratic Solidarity (LIBERTAD) Act of 1996* shall not be recognized or enforceable in any manner in Canada. ...

Orders of the Attorney General

8.(1) Where a foreign tribunal has given a judgment in proceedings instituted under an antitrust law and, in the opinion of the Attorney General of Canada, the recognition or enforcement of the judgment in Canada has adversely affected or is likely to adversely affect significant Canadian interests in relation to international trade or commerce involving a business carried on in whole or in part in Canada or otherwise has infringed or is likely to infringe Canadian sovereignty, the Attorney General of Canada may

(a) in the case of any judgment, by order, declare that the judgment shall not be recognized or enforceable in any manner in Canada; or

(b) in the case of a judgment for a specified amount of money, by order, declare that, for the purposes of the recognition and enforcement of the judgment in

Canada, the amount of the judgment shall be deemed to be reduced to such amount as is specified in the order.

(1.1) Where a foreign tribunal has given a judgment in proceedings instituted under a foreign trade law or a provision of a foreign trade law set out in the schedule and, in the opinion of the Attorney General of Canada, the recognition or enforcement of the judgment in Canada has adversely affected or is likely to adversely affect significant interests in Canada, the Attorney General of Canada may

(a) in the case of any judgment, by order, declare that the judgment shall not be recognized or enforceable in any manner in Canada; or

(b) in the case of a judgment for a specified amount of money, by order, declare that, for the purposes of the recognition and enforcement of the judgment in Canada, the amount of the judgment shall be deemed to be reduced to such amount as is specified in the order.

(2) Every order made under subsection (1) or (1.1) shall be published in the *Canada Gazette* and each order comes into force on the later of the day it is published and a day specified in the order as the day on which it is to come into force.

(3) While an order made under subsection (1) or (1.1) is in force,

(a) in the case of an order made under paragraph (1)(a) or (1.1)(a), the judgment to which it relates shall not be recognized and is not enforceable in Canada; and

(b) in the case of an order made under paragraph (1)(b) or (1.1)(b), the judgment to which it relates may, if enforceable apart from this Act, be recognized and enforced in Canada as if the amount specified in the order were substituted for the amount of the judgment, and not otherwise.

(4) In any proceedings in Canada to recognize or enforce a judgment given by a foreign tribunal in proceedings instituted under an antitrust law, or a foreign trade law or a provision of a foreign trade law set out in the schedule, or to enforce a concurrent or subsequent judgment for contribution or indemnity related to that judgment, no inference shall be drawn from the fact that the Attorney General of Canada has not made an order under subsection (1) or (1.1) in respect of the judgment.

8.1 Where an order may not be made under section 8 in respect of a judgment because the judgment has been satisfied outside Canada, or where a judgment has been given under the law of the United States entitled *Cuban Liberty and Democratic Solidarity (LIBERTAD) Act of 1996*, the Attorney General of Canada may, on application by a party against whom the judgment was given who is a Canadian citizen, a resident of Canada, a corporation incorporated by or under a law of Canada or a province or a person carrying on business in Canada, by order, declare that that party may recover, under the provisions of section 9 that the Attorney General identifies, any or all amounts obtained from that party under the judgment, expenses incurred by that party, or loss or damage suffered by that party.

Recovery of Damages

9.(1) Where a judgment in respect of which an order has been made under section 8 has been given against a party who is a Canadian citizen, a resident of Canada, a corporation incorporated by or under a law of Canada or a province or a person carrying on business in Canada, or an order has been made under section 8.1 in favour of such a party in respect of a judgment, that party may, in Canada, sue for and recover from a person in whose favour the judgment is given

(a) in the case of an order made under paragraph 8(1)(a) or (1.1)(a),

(i) any amount obtained from that party by that person under the judgment,

(ii) all expenses incurred by that party in the course of defending the proceedings in which the judgment was awarded and in instituting proceedings under this Act, including all solicitor–client costs or judicial and extrajudicial costs, and

(iii) any loss or damages suffered by that party by reason of the enforcement of the judgment; and

(b) in the case of an order made under paragraph 8(1)(b) or (1.1)(b),

(i) any amount obtained from that party by that person under the judgment that is in excess of the amount to which the judgment is deemed to be reduced,

(ii) the amount that the Attorney General of Canada may specify in respect of the expenses incurred by that party in the course of defending the proceedings in which the judgment was awarded,

(iii) the expenses incurred by that party in instituting proceedings under this Act, including all solicitor–client costs or judicial and extrajudicial costs, and

(iv) such proportion of any loss or damages suffered by that party by reason of the enforcement of the judgment as the Attorney General may specify.

9.(1.1) Where proceedings are instituted under an antitrust law, or a foreign trade law or a provision of a foreign trade law set out in the schedule, and no final judgment has been given under those proceedings against a party who is a Canadian citizen, a resident of Canada, a corporation incorporated by or under a law of Canada or a province or a person carrying on business in Canada, that party may, in Canada, with the consent of the Attorney General of Canada, at any time during the proceedings sue the person who instituted the action and recover from that person all expenses incurred by the party in defending those proceedings and in instituting proceedings under this Act, including all solicitor–client costs or judicial and extrajudicial costs.

(2) A court that renders judgment in favour of a party pursuant to subsection (1) or (1.1) may, in addition to any other means of enforcing judgment available to the court, order the seizure and sale of any property in which the person against whom the judgment is rendered, or any person who controls or is a member of a group of persons that controls, in law or in fact, that person, has a direct or indirect beneficial interest. The property that may be seized and sold includes shares of any corporation incorporated by or under a law of Canada or a province, regardless of whether the share certificates are located inside or outside Canada.

NOTES

1) The *Foreign Extraterritorial Measures Act* was passed in reaction to increased extraterritorial assertions of jurisdiction affecting Canadians,[62] and was amended to

---

62   See W. Graham, "The Foreign Extraterritorial Measures Act" (1986) 11 Can. Bus. L.J. 410.

respond to the *Helms-Burton Act*. Notice how in sections 5, 8, and 9 the Attorney General can block the foreign court's orders and judgments and facilitate the "clawback" of any damages paid. On January 15, 1996 the federal government amended the *Foreign Extraterritorial Measures (United States) Order*, 1992, to provide for a general blocking order of this kind.[63]

2) H. Scott Fairley has commented: "The parry and riposte of blocking statutes to such extraterritorial lunges, even if properly executed, lead only to stalemate."[64] He also points out "that blocking statutes, in particular to the extent they create clawback rights of action in relation to the assets of foreign nationals [for example, section 9 of the *Foreign Extraterritorial Measures Act*], are themselves extraterritorial acts."[65]

3) Measures may only be taken under the *Foreign Extraterritorial Measures Act* when the foreign state order adversely affects significant Canadian interests in international trade or infringes Canadian sovereignty. These two criteria are quite different grounds for action. The infringement of sovereignty is a public matter touching high state policy and foreign relations, as in the *Gulf Oil* case. The test of adverse effects on Canadian trade also covers government policy, usually toward the economy, but it would additionally seem to permit action where an individual trader or corporation is likely to be injured.

4) A number of states have adopted legislation similar to the *Foreign Extraterritorial Measures Act. The Protection of Trading Interests Act* of the United Kingdom[66] clearly served as a model for the Canadian statute. Australia has enacted legislation to restrict the enforcement of foreign judgments,[67] and France has passed a law to the same effect, as well as to control the removal of records and information.[68]

Cooperation Agreements

Jurisdictional conflicts, particularly when brought about by the kind of aggressive "measure–countermeasure" approach described above, have a corrosive effect on interstate relations.[69] Accordingly, many states, including Canada, have sought to reach international accords in controversial areas. If the issue of unilateral exercise of extraterritorial jurisdiction cannot be resolved, perhaps conflicts can be reduced by

---

63 See SOR/96-84.

64 Fairley, *supra* note 38 at 180-81.

65 *Ibid.* at 180, footnote 80.

66 (U.K.) 1980, c. 11; see A.V. Lowe, "Blocking Extraterritorial Jurisdiction: The British Protection of Trading Interests Act, 1980" (1981) 75 A.J.I.L. 257; and T. Harris, "The Extraterritorial Application of U.S. Export Controls: A British Perspective" (1987) 19 Int. L. & Pol. 959 at 960-61.

67 See the *Foreign Antitrust Judgments (Restriction of Enforcement) Act* 1979, reprinted in (1979) 18 I.L.M. 869.

68 See the *Law Relating to the Communication of Economic, Commercial, Industrial, Financial or Technical Documents or Information to Foreign National or Legal Persons, Law No. 80-538*, J.O. (1980) No. 1799 and B. Herzog, "The 1980 French Law on Documents and Information" (1981) 75 A.J.I.L. 382.

69 See also, in this regard, the *Special Economic Measures Act*, S.C. 1992, c. 17, which allows for significant economic and other coercive measures to be taken against foreign states or their nationals where the government is of the opinion that there is a "serious international crisis" (s. 4(1)).

intergovernmental cooperation. Two areas in which cooperative action has been taken by Canada concern competition law enforcement and criminal proceedings.

One good example of an agreement on competition law enforcement is the *Canada–United States Agreement Regarding the Application of Their Competition and Deceptive Marketing Practices Laws*.[70] As the title indicates, this treaty is designed to harmonize and coordinate the respective states' enforcement activities with regard to their competition laws. While providing little in the way of binding obligations, the agreement does require each state to consult with and/or notify the other when investigating and prosecuting competition matters "that may affect important interests of the other Party" (art. II). It also contains several provisions allowing for the possibility of enforcement cooperation, particularly as against anti-competitive activities that have cross-border effects.[71] More generally, it requires each state to carefully consider the other's "important interests" that might be affected by enforcement activities and to seek to minimize these effects as much as it can.

In criminal matters, cooperation is becoming increasingly commonplace. Historically, states jealously guarded the exercise of criminal jurisdiction as being closely linked with the bedrock notions of sovereignty and independence, and they were highly averse to foreign states attempting to enforce their criminal laws or processes extraterritorially. This made it difficult for prosecution authorities to conduct cases where, for example, some of the evidence was located in another state. Requests for the foreign state to provide evidence had to be made through diplomatic channels (by way of a process called "letters rogatory"), which was cumbersome and often too time consuming to effectively aid in prosecution.

To overcome these difficulties and minimize conflict in this area, Canada has joined many states in concluding treaties that streamline the process of transferring evidence between jurisdictions.[72] The *Canada–United States Treaty on Mutual Legal Assistance in Criminal Matters*[73] is one such treaty. It sets up a scheme whereby prosecutors in the "requesting" state may apply to the government of the "requested" state for the latter to obtain and transmit evidence for use in a criminal case in the requesting state. Several grounds for refusal of these requests exist, but in practice these are conservatively applied so as to maintain smooth relations between treaty partners.

All of Canada's bilateral and multilateral mutual legal assistance arrangements are implemented by the *Mutual Legal Assistance in Criminal Matters Act*.[74] This statute provides the domestic authority required for Canadian authorities to, *inter alia*, execute search warrants, compel witnesses to testify, and enforce the production of documents, in order to send the evidence to the requesting state. The Crown must seek judicial authorization both

---

70   (1996) 36 I.L.M. 311.

71   See C. Goldman & J. Kissack, "Current Issues in Cross-Border Criminal Investigations: A Canadian Perspective" (1996) 16 Canadian Competition Record 81.

72   See generally R.J. Currie, "Peace and Public Order: International Mutual Legal Assistance 'The Canadian Way'" (1998) 7 Dal. J. Leg. Stud. 91; R. Goldstein & N. Dennison, "Mutual Legal Assistance in Canadian Criminal Courts" (2001) 45 Crim. L.Q. 126.

73   Can. T.S. 1990 No. 19; (1985) 24 I.L.M. 1092.

74   R.S. 1985, c.30 (4th Supp.), as amended.

for the gathering of the evidence and for its transmittal.[75] The Act also allows for other modes of cooperation contained in the treaties, such as the transfer of prisoners.

5. Scope of Universal Jurisdiction[76]

As the *Lotus* case above in Section A.1 shows, a state may exercise criminal jurisdiction, even extraterritorially, where doing so does not violate any other rule of international law. Conceptually, then, universal jurisdiction is a simple enough concept: any state may exercise criminal jurisdiction over individuals accused of those crimes that have attracted a sufficient level of international opprobrium to allow it. Applying universal jurisdiction does not require a link between the prosecuting state on the basis of, for example, territory or nationality, but stems from the nature of the crime and the collective interest of the international community in combating it. It is a powerful tool, for use against the most abhorrent of criminals.

The specific inquiry that must be made is this: which crimes attract universal jurisdiction? A classic example is piracy. At international law, pirates were viewed as such a scourge upon the community of states that the pirate was "no longer a national, but *hostis humani generis* and as such he is justiciable by any State anywhere."[77] Accordingly, any state could prosecute an individual committing piratical acts on the high seas. Similarly, it has been relatively clear since the *Eichmann* case[78] that any state could prosecute persons accused of crimes against humanity on a massive scale, on the basis of universal jurisdiction.

In contemporary practice, however, it is recognized that the exercise of universal jurisdiction can be a legally and politically contentious matter. Some states may be uncomfortable with prosecution by states that have no links to the matter, or they may characterize the prosecution as political interference in the affairs of another state.[79] These problems are compounded when prosecution of political figures is sought. Thus, the development of international criminal law has made the exercise of universal jurisdiction a much more complex matter than it was historically. Consider the extracts from the following high-profile cases.

---

75 For a review of some issues involved in the process, particularly the applicability of the Charter, see R.J. Currie, "Search Warrants Under the Mutual Legal Assistance in Criminal Matters Act" (2003), 12 C.R. (6th) 275.

76 See K.C. Randall, "Universal Jurisdiction Under International Law" (1988) 66 Texas L. Rev. 785; International Law Association, Committee on International Human Rights Law and Practice, *Final Report on the Exercise of Universal Jurisdiction in Respect of Gross Human Rights Offences* (2000); S. Macedo, ed., *Universal Jurisdiction: National Courts and the Prosecution of Serious Crimes Under International Law* (2004); B. Broomhall, "Towards the Development of an Effective System of Universal Jurisdiction for Crimes under International Law" (2001) New England L. Rev. 399; M.C. Bassiouni, "Universal Jurisdiction for International Crimes: Historical Perspectives and Contemporary Practice" (2001) Va. J. Int'l L. 81.

77 *Re Piracy Jure Gentium*, [1934] A.C. 586 (P.C.) at 589, per Lord Macmillan. The Latin phrase translates to "an enemy of humanity." See also A.P. Rubin, *The Law of Piracy*, 2d ed. (1998).

78 (1961), 36 I.L.R. 5 (Dist. Ct. Jerusalem), aff'd. (1961), 36 I.L.R. 277 (Israel S.C.).

79 See H.J. Steiner, "Three Cheers for Universal Jurisdiction—Or Is It Only Two?" (2004) 5 Theoretical Inquiries in Law 199.

R. v. Bow Street Magistrate, ex parte Pinochet (No. 3)
[2001] 1 A.C. 147 (H.L.)

[The state of Chile was ruled by the dictatorial military regime of Augusto Pinochet from 1973 to 1990. Massive and widespread human rights abuses took place, allegedly at the instigation of Pinochet himself. Pinochet visited the United Kingdom in October 1998 for medical treatment. A Spanish court had issued a warrant for Pinochet's arrest, having indicted him for crimes both against Spanish citizens and for genocide, torture, and hostage taking of Chileans, the latter on the basis of universal jurisdiction. It filed a petition in the United Kingdom requesting Pinochet's arrest and extradition, which Pinochet contested.

In a complex and wide-ranging judgment, the House of Lords considered various important issues of extradition and the law of state immunity. It ruled that Pinochet could be extradited for torture and conspiracy to torture, but the extradition was eventually waived on compassionate grounds due to the state of Pinochet's health. A portion of the lead judgment on the denial of immunity from arrest and extradition is reproduced in Chapter 11, Section D on "National Prosecution of International Crimes." The passage reproduced here is taken from the judgment of Lord Millett in which he considers the conditions under which universal jurisdiction can be exercised.]

LORD MILLET: … The landmark decision of the Supreme Court of Israel in *Attorney-General of Israel v. Eichmann* (1962) 36 I.L.R. 5 is also of great significance. … The court dealt separately with the questions of jurisdiction and Act of State. Israel was not a belligerent in the Second World War, which ended three years before the state was founded. Nor were the offences committed within its territory. The District Court found support for its jurisdiction in the historic link between the State of Israel and the Jewish people. The Supreme Court preferred to concentrate on the international and universal character of the crimes of which the accused had been convicted, not least because some of them were directed against non-Jewish groups (Poles, Slovenes, Czechs and gypsies).

As a matter of domestic Israeli law, the jurisdiction of the court was derived from an Act of 1950. Following the English doctrine of Parliamentary supremacy, the court held that it was bound to give effect to a law of the Knesset even if it conflicted with the principles of international law. But it went on to hold that the law did not conflict with any principle of international law. Following a detailed examination of the authorities, including the judgment of the Permanent Court of International Justice in the *Lotus* case, 7 September 1927, it concluded that there was no rule of international law which prohibited a state from trying a foreign national for an act committed outside its borders. There seems no reason to doubt this conclusion. The limiting factor that prevents the exercise of extra-territorial criminal jurisdiction from amounting to an unwarranted interference with the internal affairs of another state is that, for the trial to be fully effective, the accused must be present in the forum state.

Significantly, however, the court also held that the scale and international character of the atrocities of which the accused had been convicted fully justified the application of the doctrine of universal jurisdiction. It approved the general consensus of jurists that war crimes attracted universal jurisdiction: see, for example, Greenspan's *The Modern Law of Land Warfare* (1959) where he writes at p. 420 that:

> Since each sovereign power stands in the position of a guardian of international law, and is equally interested in upholding it, any state has the legal right to try war crimes, even though the crimes have been committed against the nationals of another power and in a conflict to which that state is not a party.

This seems to have been an independent source of jurisdiction derived from customary international law, which formed part of the unwritten law of Israel, and which did not depend on the statute. The court explained that the limitation often imposed on the exercise of universal jurisdiction, that the state which apprehended the offender must first offer to extradite him to the state in which the offence was committed, was not intended to prevent the violation of the latter's territorial sovereignty. Its basis was purely practical. The great majority of the witnesses and the greater part of the evidence would normally be concentrated in that state, and it was therefore the most convenient forum for the trial. ...

Article 5 of the Universal Declaration of Human Rights of 1948 and Article 7 of the International Covenant on Civil and Political Rights of 1966 both provided that no one shall be subjected to torture or to cruel, inhuman or degrading treatment or punishment. A resolution of the General Assembly in 1973 proclaimed the need for international co-operation in the detection, arrest, extradition and punishment of persons guilty of war crimes and crimes against humanity. A further resolution of the General Assembly in 1975 proclaimed the desire to make the struggle against torture more effective throughout the world. The fundamental human rights of individuals, deriving from the inherent dignity of the human person, had become a commonplace of international law. Article 55 of the Charter of the United Nations was taken to impose an obligation on all states to promote universal respect for and observance of human rights and fundamental freedoms.

The trend was clear. War crimes had been replaced by crimes against humanity. The way in which a state treated its own citizens within its own borders had become a matter of legitimate concern to the international community. The most serious crimes against humanity were genocide and torture. Large scale and systematic use of torture and murder by state authorities for political ends had come to be regarded as an attack upon the international order. Genocide was made an international crime by the Genocide Convention in 1948. By the time Senator Pinochet seized power, the international community had renounced the use of torture as an instrument of state policy. The Republic of Chile accepts that by 1973 the use of torture by state authorities was prohibited by international law, and that the prohibition had the character of *jus cogens* or *obligation erga omnes*. But it insists that this does not confer universal jurisdiction. ...

In my opinion, crimes prohibited by international law attract universal jurisdiction under customary international law if two criteria are satisfied. First, they must be contrary to a peremptory norm of international law so as to infringe a jus cogens. Secondly, they must be so serious and on such a scale that they can justly be regarded as an attack on the international legal order. Isolated offences, even if committed by public officials, would not satisfy these criteria. The first criterion is well attested in the authorities and text books: for a recent example, see the judgment of the international tribunal for the territory of the former Yugoslavia in *Prosecutor v. Anto Furundzija* (unreported) given on 10 December 1998, where the court stated:

> At the individual level, that is, of criminal liability, it would seem that one of the consequences of the jus cogens character bestowed by the international community upon the prohibition of torture is that every state is entitled to investigate, prosecute, and punish or extradite individuals accused of torture who are present in a territory under its jurisdiction.

The second requirement is implicit in the original restriction to war crimes and crimes against peace, the reasoning of the court in *Eichmann*, and the definitions used in the more recent Conventions establishing *ad hoc* international tribunals for the former Yugoslavia and Rwanda.

Every state has jurisdiction under customary international law to exercise extra-territorial jurisdiction in respect of international crimes which satisfy the relevant criteria. Whether its courts have extra-territorial jurisdiction under its internal domestic law depends, of course, on its constitutional arrangements and the relationship between customary international law and the jurisdiction of its criminal courts. The jurisdiction of the English criminal courts is usually statutory, but it is supplemented by the common law. Customary international law is part of the common law, and accordingly I consider that the English courts have and always have had extra-territorial criminal jurisdiction in respect of crimes of universal jurisdiction under customary international law.

In their handbook on the Convention against Torture (1984), Burgers and Danelius wrote at p. 1:

> Many people assume that the Convention's principal aim is to outlaw torture and other cruel, inhuman or degrading treatment or punishment. This assumption is not correct insofar as it would imply that the prohibition of these practices is established under international law by the Convention only and that the prohibition will be binding as a rule of international law only for those states which have become parties to the Convention. On the contrary, the Convention is based upon the recognition that the above-mentioned practices are already outlawed under international law. The principal aim of the Convention is to strengthen the existing prohibition of such practices by a number of supportive measures.

In my opinion, the systematic use of torture on a large scale and as an instrument of state policy had joined piracy, war crimes and crimes against peace as an international crime of universal jurisdiction well before 1984. I consider that it had done so by 1973. For my own part, therefore, I would hold that the courts of this country already possessed extra-territorial jurisdiction in respect of torture and conspiracy to torture on the scale of the charges in the present case and did not require the authority of statute to exercise it. ...

The Convention against Torture (1984) did not create a new international crime. But it redefined it. Whereas the international community had condemned the widespread and systematic use of torture as an instrument of state policy, the Convention extended the offence to cover isolated and individual instances of torture provided that they were committed by a public official. I do not consider that offences of this kind were previously regarded as international crimes attracting universal jurisdiction. The charges against Senator Pinochet, however, are plainly of the requisite character. The Convention thus affirmed and extended an existing international crime and imposed obligations on the parties to the Convention to take measures to prevent it and to punish those guilty of it. As Burgers and Danielus explained, its main purpose was to introduce an institutional mechanism to enable this to be achieved. Whereas previously states were entitled to take jurisdiction in respect of the offence wherever it was committed, they were now placed under an obligation to do so. Any state party in whose territory a person alleged to have committed the offence was found was bound to offer to extradite him or to initiate proceedings to prosecute him. The obligation imposed by the Convention resulted in the passing of section 134 of the Criminal Justice Act 1988.

I agree, therefore, that our courts have statutory extra-territorial jurisdiction in respect of the charges of torture and conspiracy to torture committed after the section had come into force and (for the reasons explained by my noble and learned friend, Lord Hope of Craighead) the charges of conspiracy to murder where the conspiracy took place in Spain.

NOTES

1) A majority of the Lords disagreed with Lord Millet that the United Kingdom could exercise universal jurisdiction over the crime of torture as of 1973. They found instead that Pinochet could only be extradited for torture that allegedly occurred after 1988, the year that the United Kingdom implemented the Torture Convention. This would have resulted in the extradition of Pinochet for a smaller number of charges than the Spanish government had requested. What effect would this have had? See the discussion of the extradition doctrine of "specialty" in Section B.2 below.

2) Lord Millet suggests that crimes that violate a *jus cogens* norm and occur on a large scale are automatically subject to universal jurisdiction. Is there a functional separation between the prohibition of torture as a *jus cogens* norm and the power of states to exercise jurisdiction on a universal basis? Professors Bantekas and Nash wrote this about Lord Millet's formula: "This statement, correct though it may be, lacks a most essential ingredient: the consent of States to subject an offence to universal jurisdiction through treaty or custom."[80] What do you think?

3) Even where customary international law allows states to exercise universal jurisdiction over a crime, note that this norm is essentially *permissive* in nature. States may prosecute, but have no obligation to do so. Did the implementation of the Torture Convention in the United Kingdom have a different effect? Refer to the discussion of *aut dedere, aut judicare* in subsection 6, below.

---

80   I. Bantekas & S. Nash, *International Criminal Law*, 2d ed. (2003) at 157.

4) In the *Eichmann* case,[81] referred to by Lord Millet, one of the issues considered by the Israeli courts was jurisdiction over the offence.[82] At the time of Eichmann's war crimes and crimes against humanity during World War II, the State of Israel did not exist; the crimes were committed in European states against citizens of European states, and Eichmann too was a foreigner. Thus, Israel could not exercise jurisdiction on the territorial or nationality bases of jurisdiction, or on a strict interpretation of the passive personality principle. However, the District Court based its jurisdiction on the universal principle, in that war criminals were enemies of humankind and Eichmann was in Israeli custody, and secondarily on the protective and passive personality principles. As discussed earlier in this section, the protective principle is used to protect a state's vital interests. There must be a linking point between the crime and the state. The "linking point" in this case was that the crimes were committed against Jewish people, although at the time no State of Israel was in existence. The Court concluded that the connection between the State of Israel and the Jewish people needed no explanation.

5) In *Demjanjuk v. Petrovsky*[83] John Demjanjuk was extradited by the United States to Israel to be prosecuted for crimes against humanity committed in Poland in World War II under the same 1951 statute as Eichmann. The jurisdictional basis upon which extradition was granted was the universal principle, even though Demjanjuk was in the custody of the United States. It was based on the nature of the crime being universally condemned. Was this a valid application of the universal principle?

Case Concerning the Arrest Warrant of April 11, 2000 (Yerodia Case)
Congo v. Belgium
I.C.J. 14 February 2002, reproduced in 41 I.L.M. 536

[On April 11, 2000 a Belgian court issued an arrest warrant for Abdulaye Yerodia Ndombasi (who was at that date the sitting foreign minister of the Democratic Republic of the Congo), charging him with war crimes and crimes against humanity. The Belgian statute under which Yerodia was charged allowed that state's courts to exercise universal jurisdiction over these crimes. Congo instituted proceedings in the ICJ to have the arrest warrant set aside because: (1) Belgium's exercise of universal jurisdiction was unlawful; and (2) as an incumbent foreign affairs minister, Yerodia was immune from Belgium's criminal jurisdiction. Since Congo chose to argue only the immunity issue in its final submissions, the Court declined to make substantial comments on universal jurisdiction. However, in a joint separate opinion, three of the judges addressed the issue:]

---

81   *Supra* note 78.

82   The other issues were jurisdiction over the person acquired by extra-legal means (considered below in Section B.1 on "Abduction From a Foreign State"), because Eichmann had been abducted from Argentina; the illegality of Eichmann's crimes against humanity and whether Israel's *Nazi and Nazi Collaborators (Punishment) Act, 1951* was *ex post facto* penal legislation; the argument that Eichmann's actions were acts of state and the defence of superior orders.

83   776 F.2d 571 (6th Cir. 1985).

JUDGES HIGGINS, KOOIJMANS, and BUERGENTHAL: ...

[The judges first reviewed state practice regarding the exercise of universal jurisdiction and then continued:]

[45] That there is no established practice in which States exercise universal jurisdiction, properly so called, is undeniable. As we have seen, virtually all national legislation envisages links of some sort to the forum State; and no case law exists in which pure universal jurisdiction has formed the basis of jurisdiction. This does not necessarily indicate, however, that such an exercise would be unlawful. In the first place, national legislation reflects the circumstances in which a State provides in its own law the ability to exercise jurisdiction. But a State is not required to legislate up to the full scope of the jurisdiction allowed by international law. The war crimes legislation of Australia and the United Kingdom afford examples of countries making more confined choices for the exercise of jurisdiction. Further, many countries have no national legislation for the exercise of well-recognized forms of extraterritorial jurisdiction, sometimes notwithstanding treaty obligations to enable themselves so to act. National legislation may be illuminating as to the issue of universal jurisdiction, but not conclusive as to its legality. Moreover, while none of the national case law to which we have referred happens to be based on the exercise of a universal jurisdiction properly so called, there is equally nothing in this case law which evidences an *opinio juris* on the illegality of such a jurisdiction. In short, national legislation and case law, that is, State practice, is neutral as to exercise of universal jurisdiction.

[46] There are, moreover, certain indications that a universal criminal jurisdiction for certain international crimes is clearly not regarded as unlawful. The duty to prosecute under those treaties which contain the *aut dedere aut prosequi* provisions opens the door to a jurisdiction based on the heinous nature of the crime rather than on links of territoriality or nationality (whether as perpetrator or victim). The 1949 Geneva Conventions lend support to this possibility, and are widely regarded as today reflecting customary international law. ...

[51] ...[T]he dictum [in *Lotus* regarding freedom to exercise jurisdiction in the absence of a prohibitive rule] represents the high-water mark of *laissez-faire* in international relations, and an era that has been significantly overtaken by other tendencies. The underlying idea of universal jurisdiction properly so called (as in the case of piracy, and possibly in the Geneva Conventions of 1949), as well as the *aut dedere aut prosequi* variation, is a common endeavour in the face of atrocities. The series of multilateral treaties with their special jurisdictional provisions reflect a determination by the international community that those engaged in war crimes, hijacking, hostage taking, torture should not go unpunished. Although crimes against humanity are not yet the object of a distinct convention, a comparable international indignation at such acts is not to be doubted. And those States and academic writers who claim the right to act unilaterally to assert a universal criminal jurisdiction over persons committing such acts, invoke the concept of acting as "agents for the international community." This vertical notion of the authority of action is significantly different from the horizontal system of international law envisaged in the "*Lotus*" case.

At the same time, the international consensus that the perpetrators of international crimes should not go unpunished is being advanced by a flexible strategy, in which newly established international criminal tribunals, treaty obligations and national courts all have their part to play. We reject the suggestion that the battle against impunity is "made over" to international treaties and tribunals, with national courts having no competence in such matters. Great care has been taken when formulating the relevant treaty provisions not to exclude other grounds of jurisdiction that may be exercised on a voluntary basis. (See Article 4(3) Hague Convention for the Suppression of Unlawful Seizure of Aircraft, 1970; Article 5(3) International Convention Against Taking of Hostages, 1979; Article 5(3) Convention Against Torture; Article 9, Statute of the International Criminal Tribunal for the Former Yugoslavia; and Article 19, Rome Statute of the International Criminal Court.)

[52] We may thus agree with the authors of the Oppenheim, 9th Edition, at page 998, that:

> While no general rule of positive international law can as yet be asserted which gives to states the right to punish foreign nationals for crimes against humanity in the same way as they are, for instance, entitled to punish acts of piracy, there are clear indications pointing to the gradual evolution of a significant principle of international law to that effect.

[53] This brings us once more to the particular point that divides the Parties in this case: is it a precondition of the assertion of universal jurisdiction that the accused be within the territory?

[54] Considerable confusion surrounds this topic, not helped by the fact that legislators, courts and writers alike frequently fail to specify the precise temporal moment at which any such requirement is said to be in play. Is the presence of the accused within the jurisdiction said to be required at the time the offence was committed? At the time the arrest warrant is issued? Or at the time of the trial itself? An examination of national legislation, cases and writings reveals a wide variety of temporal linkages to the assertion of jurisdiction. This incoherent practice cannot be said to evidence a precondition to any exercise of universal criminal jurisdiction. The fact that in the past the only clear example of an agreed exercise of universal jurisdiction was in respect of piracy, *outside of any territorial jurisdiction*, is not determinative. The only prohibitive rule (repeated by the Permanent Court in the "*Lotus*" case) is that criminal jurisdiction should not be exercised, without permission, within the territory of another State. The Belgian arrest warrant envisaged the arrest of Mr. Yerodia in Belgium, or the possibility of his arrest in third States at the discretion of the States concerned. This would in principle seem to violate no existing prohibiting rule of international law.

[55] In criminal law, in particular, it is said that evidence gathering requires territorial presence. But this point goes to *any* extraterritoriality, including those that are well established and not just to universal jurisdiction.

[56] Some jurisdictions provide for trial *in absentia*; others do not. If it is said that a person must be within the jurisdiction at the time of the trial itself, that may be a prudent guarantee for the right of fair trial but has little to do with bases of jurisdiction recognized under international law. ...

[58] If the underlying purpose of designating certain acts as international crimes is to authorize a wide jurisdiction to be asserted over persons committing them, there is no rule of international law (and certainly not the *aut dedere* principle) which makes illegal co-operative overt acts designed to secure their presence within a State wishing to exercise jurisdiction.

[59] If, as we believe to be the case, a State may choose to exercise a universal criminal jurisdiction *in absentia*, it must also ensure that certain safeguards are in place. They are absolutely essential to prevent abuse and to ensure that the rejection of impunity does not jeopardize stable relations between States. ... A State contemplating bringing criminal charges based on universal jurisdiction must first offer to the national State of the prospective accused person the opportunity itself to act upon the charges concerned. The Court makes reference to these elements in the context of this case at paragraph 16 of its Judgment.

Further, such charges may only be laid by a prosecutor or *juge d'instruction* who acts in full independence, without links to or control by the government of that State. Moreover, the desired equilibrium between the battle against impunity and the promotion of good inter-State relations will only be maintained if there are some special circumstances that do require the exercise of an international criminal jurisdiction and if this has been brought to the attention of the prosecutor or *juge d'instruction*. For example, persons related to the victims of the case will have requested the commencement of legal proceedings.

[60] It is equally necessary that universal criminal jurisdiction be exercised only over those crimes regarded as the most heinous by the international community.

[61] Piracy is the classical example. This jurisdiction was, of course, exercised on the high seas and not as an enforcement jurisdiction within the territory of a non-agreeing State. But this historical fact does not mean that universal jurisdiction only exists with regard to crimes committed on the high seas or in other places outside national territorial jurisdiction. Of decisive importance is that this jurisdiction was regarded as lawful because the international community regarded piracy as damaging to the interests of all. War crimes and crimes against humanity are no less harmful to the interests of all because they do not usually occur on the high seas. War crimes (already since 1949 perhaps a treaty-based provision for universal jurisdiction) may be added to the list. The specification of their content is largely based upon the 1949 Conventions and those parts of the 1977 Additional Protocols that reflect general international law. Recent years have also seen the phenomenon of an alignment of national jurisdictional legislation on war crimes, specifying those crimes under the statutes of the ICTY, ICTR and the intended ICC.

[62] The substantive content of the concept of crimes against humanity, and its status as crimes warranting the exercise of universal jurisdiction, is undergoing change. Article 6(c) of the Charter of the International Military Tribunal of 8 August, 1945, envisaged them as a category linked with those crimes over which the Tribunal had jurisdiction (war crimes, crimes against the peace). In 1950 the International Law Commission defined them as murder, extermination, enslavement, deportation or other inhuman acts perpetrated on the citizen population, or persecutions on political, racial or religious grounds if in exercise of, or connection with, any crime against peace or a

war crime (*YILC* 1950, Principle VI(c), pp. 374-377). Later definitions of crimes against humanity both widened the subject matter, to include such offences as torture and rape, and decoupled the link to other earlier established crimes. Crimes against humanity are now regarded as a distinct category ... .

[65] It would seem (without in any way pronouncing upon whether Mr. Yerodia did or did not perform the acts with which he is charged in the warrant) that the acts alleged do fall within the concept of "crimes against humanity" and would be within that small category in respect of which an exercise of universal jurisdiction is not precluded under international law.

NOTES

1) Does this opinion indicate that a *jus cogens* crime always attracts universal jurisdiction? If so, is this a desirable extension of the principle?

2) What was the importance for these judges of the fact that the arrest warrant was issued while Mr. Yerodia was not in Belgium? Note the sensitivity that these judges have to the implications that exercising universal jurisdiction *in absentia* may have for "the equilibrium between the battle against impunity and the promotion of good inter-State relations." Do the measures they propose strike the right balance?

3) In 1996 Professor Bassiouni argued that, conceptually, international crimes that attain *jus cogens* status constitute *erga omnes* obligations.[84] The specific obligations include universal jurisdiction and the duty to extradite or prosecute an alleged offender when apprehended. He admitted that current state practice did not reflect this level of obligatory force arising from *jus cogens* crimes. Based on the excerpts from the Pinochet case and *Congo v. Belgium*, above, do you think there has been any change?

4) As is apparent from these two cases, Belgium and Spain are two states that have been quite aggressive in attempting to enforce international criminal law through the assertion of universal jurisdiction. Under Spain's *Organic Law of the Judicial Power*, its courts may exercise universal jurisdiction over torture and have done so.[85] Belgian courts have exercised universal jurisdiction over a number of prominent world figures, including Israeli Prime Minister Ariel Sharon, though in the latter case the Court of Appeals ruled that this was not permitted *in absentia*.[86] Other states have been more reticent.

5) In Canada, section 8 of the *Crimes Against Humanity and War Crimes Act*[87] provides for universal jurisdiction over genocide, war crimes, and crimes against humanity, if "after the time the offence is alleged to have been committed, the person is present in Canada."

---

84   M.C. Bassiouni, "International Crimes: Jus Cogens and Obligatio Erga Omnes" (1996) 59 Law & Contemp. Probs. 63.

85   See the *Guatemala Genocide Case (Menchu Tum and Others)*, decision of Spanish Supreme Court, February 25, 2003, reprinted (2003) 42 I.L.M. 686.

86   *H.S.A. et al. v. S.A. et al. (Decision Related to the Indictment of Ariel Sharon, Amos Yaron, and Others)*, Belg. Cour. De Cass. (February 12, 2003), reprinted (with English translation) (2003) 42 I.L.M. 596.

87   *Supra* note 19.

6. Suppression of Transnational Crimes of International Concern

Beyond the core international crimes such as genocide, there are certain kinds of crimes that, while part of domestic criminal law, ordinarily have transnational aspects—that is, they affect in some way the citizens, resources, or interests of more than one state on a regular basis. Throughout the 20th century, in particular, there was recognition by states that joint activity in the suppression of these crimes would be beneficial in a number of ways. Cooperation was seen as a more efficient way for states to use their (sometimes scarce) resources to deal with transnational crime, and provided a means by which developing states could gain access to technical assistance that would otherwise be unavailable to them. Moreover, the larger the group of states that cooperated in combating a particular crime, the easier it was to exert pressure on those states seen as "havens" for criminals engaged in that activity.

The practical result of this cooperative outlook was what have been referred to as the "suppression conventions,"[88] multilateral treaties that obligate states to criminalize certain types of behaviour and to cooperate in prosecuting them. The suppression conventions deal with a multitude of topics, including slavery, counterfeiting, narcotics trafficking, terrorism, and organized crime.[89] The United Nations has often been the moving force behind these conventions, but not always. For example, the Organization for Economic Co-operation and Development (OECD) was the sponsor of the *Convention on Combating Bribery of Foreign Officials in International Business Transactions*.[90]

For present purposes, what is important about the suppression conventions is the means they provide for states to assert jurisdiction over individuals. This is accomplished in essentially two ways. First, each adhering state must criminalize a certain kind of behaviour—that is, provide for prescriptive jurisdiction over the offence. Second, when the state has custody of a person alleged to have engaged in the criminalized act, it must either extradite the individual to another party state that is willing to prosecute him, or prosecute the individual domestically. This latter modality is usually referred to as *aut dedere aut judicare*.[91]

One important point bears mention. The *aut dedere* obligation is a treaty mechanism whereby states that have custody of an alleged offender must, if they do not extradite him or her, submit the case to investigation with a view to prosecution. It effectively obligates the state to exercise extraterritorial criminal jurisdiction over the individual, potentially in a case where it has no other jurisdictional links, such as territoriality or nationality. This operates similarly to universal jurisdiction, and is sometimes referred to as such. However,

---

88 See N. Boister, " 'Transnational Criminal Law?' " (2003) 14 E.J.I.L. 953 at 955.

89 For a detailed and thorough list, see M.C. Bassiouni, ed., *International Criminal Law, vol. I: Crimes*, 2d ed. (1999) at 62-99.

90 Can. T. S. 1999 No. 23. Adopted November 21, 1997 and in force February 15, 1999. Canada signed the convention on December 17, 1997 and it is implemented by the *Corruption of Foreign Public Officials Act*, S.C. 1993, c. 34.

91 See generally M.C. Bassiouni & E. Wise, *Aut Dedere Aut Judicare: The Duty to Extradite or Prosecute in International Law* (1995).

the two concepts are different.[92] Universal jurisdiction is permissive in nature; it allows states to exercise extraterritorial jurisdiction over a small number of crimes and as against the rest of the world, but does not require them to do so. *Aut dedere*, by contrast, is obligatory as regards the particular crime in question, and operates only as between the parties to the treaty in which it is found.

Aside from terminological differences, however, interaction between the two regimes can create uncertainty. Consider the Convention Against Torture, reproduced in Chapter 11, Section A.3, which contains an extradite or prosecute obligation. Does the status of the prohibition on torture as a *jus cogens* norm automatically incorporate the *aut dedere* obligation, even for non-parties to the Convention? Or, does the *aut dedere* obligation regarding torture itself have customary law status? Recall that in the Pinochet case, a majority of the House of Lords answered this question negatively.

Suppression of Terrorism[93]

Terrorism is one of the most fully internationalized crimes. Acts of international terrorism are of concern to the entire international community. However, the manner in which that community has sought to deal with the problem has not been in the form of a single comprehensive treaty. Rather, a piecemeal approach has been used. Several multilateral "suppression" conventions have been adopted that deal with different types of terrorist acts such as hijacking and other attacks on civil aviation; attacks on diplomats and other internationally protected persons; the taking of hostages; offences against nuclear material; interference with maritime navigation and unlawful acts against fixed platforms located on the continental shelf; and on the suppression of terrorist bombings, terrorist financing, and nuclear terrorism. This convention-by-convention approach has been the only one possible because some states will not agree to one convention dealing with all aspects of terrorism together.[94] The overriding wish is to join as many states parties as possible against each kind of terrorist activity, and thus this piecemeal pattern of conventions has emerged.

In the following extract from one of those conventions, two features common to these treaties against terrorism will be apparent: first, the use of the different bases of

---

92   Per Judges Higgins, Kooijmans, and Buergenthal in the *Yerodia Case*, excerpted in Section A.5, above: "By the loose use of language [*aut dedere*] has come to be referred to as 'universal jurisdiction,' though this is really an obligatory territorial jurisdiction over persons, albeit in relation to acts committed elsewhere" (at para. 41).

93   See, generally, M.C. Bassiouni, ed., *International Terrorism and Political Crimes* (1975); C. Blakesley, *Terrorism, Drugs, International Law and the Protection of Human Liberty* (1992); A. Evans & J. Murphy, eds., *Legal Aspects of International Terrorism* (1978); R. Friedlander, *Terrorism* (1979-84), 4 vols.; and R. Higgins & M. Flory, eds., *Terrorism and International Law* (1997).

94   A comprehensive approach was taken in the 1937 *Convention on the Prevention and Punishment of Terrorism*, Hudson, *International Legislation* (2000) vol. 7 at 862. However, neither this Convention nor a draft Convention dealing with the setting up of an international criminal court ever came into force. Note the regional approach taken in the 1977 *European Convention on the Suppression of Terrorism*, 1977 Eur. T.S. No. 97.

jurisdiction over the offence; and, second, the concept of *aut dedere, aut judicare*—extradite or prosecute—both considered earlier in this chapter. It is incumbent on a ratifying state to establish in its territory jurisdiction over the crime. Then, if an alleged offender is detained and he or she is not extradited to another state, the case shall be submitted without exception to the local authorities for the purposes of prosecution.

International Convention for the Suppression of Terrorist Bombings
GA Res. 52/164, UN GAOR, 52d Sess., Supp. No. 49,
U.N. Doc. A/52/49 (1997) 389

Article 1

For the purposes of this Convention:

1. "State or government facility" includes any permanent or temporary facility or conveyance that is used or occupied by representatives of a State, members of Government, the legislature or the judiciary or by officials or employees of a State or any other public authority or entity or by employees or officials of an intergovernmental organization in connection with their official duties.

2. "Infrastructure facility" means any publicly or privately owned facility providing or distributing services for the benefit of the public, such as water, sewage, energy, fuel or communications.

3. "Explosive or other lethal device" means:

(a) An explosive or incendiary weapon or device that is designed, or has the capability, to cause death, serious bodily injury or substantial material damage; or

(b) A weapon or device that is designed, or has the capability, to cause death, serious bodily injury or substantial material damage through the release, dissemination or impact of toxic chemicals, biological agents or toxins or similar substances or radiation or radioactive material.

4. "Military forces of a State" means the armed forces of a State which are organized, trained and equipped under its internal law for the primary purpose of national defence or security and persons acting in support of those armed forces who are under their formal command, control and responsibility.

5. "Place of public use" means those parts of any building, land, street, waterway or other location that are accessible or open to members of the public, whether continuously, periodically or occasionally, and encompasses any commercial, business, cultural, historical, educational, religious, governmental, entertainment, recreational or similar place that is so accessible or open to the public.

6. "Public transportation system" means all facilities, conveyances and instrumentalities, whether publicly or privately owned, that are used in or for publicly available services for the transportation of persons or cargo.

Article 2

1. Any person commits an offence within the meaning of this Convention if that person unlawfully and intentionally delivers, places, discharges or detonates an

explosive or other lethal device in, into or against a place of public use, a State or government facility, a public transportation system or an infrastructure facility:

(a) With the intent to cause death or serious bodily injury; or

(b) With the intent to cause extensive destruction of such a place, facility or system, where such destruction results in or is likely to result in major economic loss.

2. Any person also commits an offence if that person attempts to commit an offence as set forth in paragraph 1 of the present article.

3. Any person also commits an offence if that person:

(a) Participates as an accomplice in an offence as set forth in paragraph 1 or 2 of the present article; or

(b) Organizes or directs others to commit an offence as set forth in paragraph 1 or 2 of the present article; or

(c) In any other way contributes to the commission of one or more offences as set forth in paragraph 1 or 2 of the present article by a group of persons acting with a common purpose: such contribution shall be intentional and either be made with the aim of furthering the general criminal activity or purpose of the group or be made in the knowledge of the intention of the group to commit the offence or offences concerned.

Article 3

This Convention shall not apply where the offence is committed within a single State, the alleged offender and the victims are nationals of that State, the alleged offender is found in the territory of that State and no other State has a basis under article 6, paragraph 1 or paragraph 2, of this Convention to exercise jurisdiction, except that the provisions of articles 10 to 15 shall, as appropriate, apply in those cases.

Article 4

Each State Party shall adopt such measures as may be necessary:

(a) To establish as criminal offences under its domestic law the offences set forth in article 2 of this Convention;

(b) To make those offences punishable by appropriate penalties which take into account the grave nature of those offences.

Article 5

Each State Party shall adopt such measures as may be necessary, including, where appropriate, domestic legislation, to ensure that criminal acts within the scope of this Convention, in particular where they are intended or calculated to provoke a state of terror in the general public or in a group of persons or particular persons, are under no circumstances justifiable by considerations of a political, philosophical, ideological, racial, ethnic, religious or other similar nature and are punished by penalties consistent with their grave nature.

Article 6

1. Each State Party shall take such measures as may be necessary to establish its jurisdiction over the offences set forth in article 2 when:

(a) The offence is committed in the territory of that State; or

(b) The offence is committed on board a vessel flying the flag of that State or an aircraft which is registered under the laws of that State at the time the offence is committed; or

(c) The offence is committed by a national of that State.

2. A State Party may also establish its jurisdiction over any such offence when:

(a) The offence is committed against a national of that State; or

(b) The offence is committed against a State or government facility of that State abroad, including an embassy or other diplomatic or consular premises of that State; or

(c) The offence is committed by a stateless person who has his or her habitual residence in the territory of that State; or

(d) The offence is committed in an attempt to compel that State to do or abstain from doing any act; or

(e) The offence is committed on board an aircraft which is operated by the Government of that State.

3. Upon ratifying, accepting, approving or acceding to this Convention, each State Party shall notify the Secretary-General of the United Nations of the jurisdiction it has established under its domestic law in accordance with paragraph 2 of the present article. Should any change take place, the State party concerned shall immediately notify the Secretary-General.

4. Each State Party shall likewise take such measures as may be necessary to establish its jurisdiction over the offences set forth in article 2 in cases where the alleged offender is present in its territory and it does not extradite that person to any of the States Parties which have established their jurisdiction in accordance with paragraph 1 or 2 of the present article.

5. This Convention does not exclude the exercise of any criminal jurisdiction established by a State Party in accordance with its domestic law.

Article 7

1. Upon receiving information that a person who has committed or who is alleged to have committed an offence as set forth in article 2 may be present in its territory, the State Party concerned shall take such measures as may be necessary under its domestic law to investigate the facts contained in the information.

2. Upon being satisfied that the circumstances so warrant, the State Party in whose territory the offender or alleged offender is present shall take the appropriate measures under its domestic law so as to ensure that person's presence for the purpose of prosecution or extradition.

3. Any person regarding whom the measures referred to in paragraph 2 of the present article are being taken shall be entitled to:

(a) Communicate without delay with the nearest appropriate representative of the State of which that person is a national or which is otherwise entitled to protect that person's rights or, if that person is a stateless person, the State in the territory of which that person habitually resides;

(b) Be visited by a representative of that State;

(c) Be informed of that person's rights under subparagraphs (a) and (b).

4. The rights referred to in paragraph 3 of the present article shall be exercised in conformity with the laws and regulations of the State in the territory of which the offender or alleged offender is present, subject to the provision that the said laws and regulations must enable full effect to be given to the purposes for which the rights accorded under paragraph 3 are intended.

5. The provisions of paragraphs 3 and 4 of the present article shall be without prejudice to the right of any State Party having a claim to jurisdiction in accordance with article 6, subparagraph 1(c) or 2(c), to invite the International Committee of the Red Cross to communicate with and visit the alleged offender.

6. When a State Party, pursuant to the present article, has taken a person into custody, it shall immediately notify, directly or through the Secretary-General of the United Nations, the States Parties which have established jurisdiction in accordance with article 6, paragraphs 1 and 2, and, if it considers it advisable, any other interested States Parties, of the fact that that person is in custody and of the circumstances which warrant that person's detention. The State which makes the investigation contemplated in paragraph 1 of the present article shall promptly inform the said States Parties of its findings and shall indicate whether it intends to exercise jurisdiction.

Article 8

1. The State Party in the territory of which the alleged offender is present shall, in cases to which article 6 applies, if it does not extradite that person, be obliged, without exception whatsoever and whether or not the offence was committed in its territory, to submit the case without undue delay to its competent authorities for the purpose of prosecution, through proceedings in accordance with the laws of that State. Those authorities shall take their decision in the same manner as in the case of any other offence of a grave nature under the law of that State.

2. Whenever a State Party is permitted under its domestic law to extradite or otherwise surrender one of its nationals only upon the condition that the person will be returned to that State to serve the sentence imposed as a result of the trial or proceeding for which the extradition or surrender of the person was sought, and this State and the State seeking the extradition of the person agree with this option and other terms they may deem appropriate, such a conditional extradition or surrender shall be sufficient to discharge the obligation set forth in paragraph 1 of the present article.

Article 9

1. The offences set forth in article 2 shall be deemed to be included as extraditable offences in any extradition treaty existing between any of the States Parties before the entry into force of this Convention. States Parties undertake to include such offences

as extraditable offences in every extradition treaty to be subsequently concluded between them.

2. When a State Party which makes extradition conditional on the existence of a treaty receives a request for extradition from another State Party with which it has no extradition treaty, the requested State Party may, at its option, consider this Convention as a legal basis for extradition in respect of the offences set forth in article 2. Extradition shall be subject to the other conditions provided by the law of the requested State.

3. States Parties which do not make extradition conditional on the existence of a treaty shall recognize the offences set forth in article 2 as extraditable offences between themselves, subject to the conditions provided by the law of the requested State.

4. If necessary, the offences set forth in article 2 shall be treated, for the purposes of extradition between States parties, as if they had been committed not only in the place in which they occurred but also in the territory of the States that have established jurisdiction in accordance with article 6, paragraphs 1 and 2.

5. The provisions of all extradition treaties and arrangements between States Parties with regard to offences set forth in article 2 shall be deemed to be modified as between State Parties to the extent that they are incompatible with this Convention.

Article 10

1. States Parties shall afford one another the greatest measure of assistance in connection with investigations or criminal or extradition proceedings brought in respect of the offences set forth in article 2, including assistance in obtaining evidence at their disposal necessary for the proceedings.

2. States Parties shall carry out their obligations under paragraph 1 of the present article in conformity with any treaties or other arrangements on mutual legal assistance that may exist between them. In the absence of such treaties or arrangements, States Parties shall afford one another assistance in accordance with their domestic law.

Article 11

None of the offences set forth in article 2 shall be regarded, for the purposes of extradition or mutual legal assistance, as a political offence or as an offence connected with a political offence or as an offence inspired by political motives. Accordingly, a request for extradition or for mutual legal assistance based on such an offence may not be refused on the sole ground that it concerns a political offence or an offence connected with a political offence or an offence inspired by political motives.

Article 12

Nothing in this Convention shall be interpreted as imposing an obligation to extradite or to afford mutual legal assistance, if the requested State Party has substantial grounds for believing that the request for extradition for offences set forth in article 2 or for mutual legal assistance with respect to such offences has been made for the purpose of prosecuting or punishing a person on account of that person's race, religion, nationality, ethnic origin or political opinion or that compliance with the request would cause prejudice to that person's position for any of these reasons. ...

Article 14

Any person who is taken into custody or regarding whom any other measures are taken or proceedings are carried out pursuant to this Convention shall be guaranteed fair treatment, including enjoyment of all rights and guarantees in conformity with the law of the State in the territory of which that person is present and applicable provisions of international law, including international law of human rights.

Article 15

States Parties shall cooperate in the prevention of the offences set forth in article 2, particularly:

(a) By taking all practicable measures, including, if necessary, adapting their domestic legislation, to prevent and counter preparations in their respective territories for the commission of those offences within or outside their territories, including measures to prohibit in their territories illegal activities of persons, groups and organizations that encourage, instigate, organize, knowingly finance or engage in the perpetration of offences as set forth in article 2;

(b) By exchanging accurate and verified information in accordance with their national law, and coordinating administrative and other measures taken as appropriate to prevent the commission of offences as set forth in article 2;

(c) Where appropriate, through research and development regarding methods of detection of explosives and other harmful substances that can cause death or bodily injury, consultations on the development of standards for marking explosives in order to identify their origin in post-blast investigations, exchange of information on preventive measures, cooperation and transfer of technology, equipment and related materials.

NOTES

1) Terrorist bombings unconnected with any other terrorist convention crimes illustrated the gaps in the piecemeal approach to dealing with international terrorism. No multilateral convention covered such crimes and thus no obligations to extradite or prosecute in that situation existed. The U.N. General Assembly remedied this deficiency by adopting the above convention.

2) The Terrorist Bombings Convention prescribes the bases of jurisdiction in article 6. Why are they divided into mandatory and optional bases? Does article 6(4) provide for a type of universal jurisdiction? What is the impact of article 6(5)?

3) By article 4(b) each state sets its own penalties for the offences prescribed in article 2. Why would the Convention not settle the penalties as well as the offences?

4) Notice how article 4(a) requires states parties to take legislative action to implement the Convention—that is, to proscribe the offences in article 2 within their own domestic legal systems. In Canada, see the *Criminal Code*, sections 7(3.72) and 431.2. Refer also to sections 3.75 and 83.01.

5) Article 8(1) deals with the mandatory obligation to extradite or to submit the case to a state's own authorities for the purpose of prosecution. Further, article 11 provides

that none of the offences set down in article 2 shall be regarded as political offences or offences inspired by political motives for the purposes of extradition or mutual legal assistance. This is a novel article. The earlier conventions did not address this ground for refusal. See section 46(1)(c) of the Canadian *Extradition Act*, and article 4(2) of the bilateral Canada–United States Treaty on Extradition, both reproduced later in Section B.2. However, note that article 12 provides that there is no obligation to extradite or afford mutual legal assistance where the person will be prosecuted or punished on account of his or her race, religion, nationality, ethnic origin, or political opinion.

6) Altogether there are over a dozen anti-terrorism conventions that prohibit interference with aircraft, ships, marine installations, and internationally protected persons and proscribe hostage taking, terrorist bombing, and terrorist financing. [95]

These Conventions and Protocols aim to ensure that alleged international terrorists will not go unprosecuted because of the obligation on states parties to extradite or to submit the case to their own authorities for the purposes of prosecution. As one writer has commented:

> The perceived problems are at least three fold: first, a lack of treaty obligations requiring extradition or prosecution in certain situations not covered by the existing scheme of conventions; second, third party frustration of the existing conventions; and third, the impact of the ideologically motivated offender seeking publicity for a cause.[96]

7) State-sponsored terrorism, discussed in Chapter 15, Section B.4 on "Collective Measures Pursuant to the U.N. Charter," is a violation of article 2(4) U.N. Charter, of the 1970 Declaration of Principles on International Law, reproduced in the Documentary Supplement, and an act of aggression under article 3(g) of the Definition of Aggression, reproduced in Chapter 15, Section A.

8) In 2001, Canada brought in the *Anti-Terrorism Act*[97] which, as the preamble states, was designed in part to "fully [implement] United Nations and other international instruments relating to terrorism." The Act contained numerous amendments to the *Criminal Code* to accomplish this purpose; see section 7 and Part II.1 of the Code. In terms of domestic application, the amendments went well beyond the international law

---

95   See the *Tokyo Convention on Offences and Certain Other Acts on Aircraft* (1963) 704 U.N.T.S. 219; Can. T.S. 1970 No. 5; *Hague Convention for the Suppression of Unlawful Seizure of Aircraft* (1970) 860 U.N.T.S. 105; Can. T.S. 1972 No. 23; *Montreal Convention for the Suppression of Unlawful Acts Against the Safety of Civil Aviation* (1971) 974 U.N.T.S. 177; Can. T.S. 1973 No. 6; *Montreal Protocol for the Suppression of Unlawful Acts of Violence at Airports Serving International Civil Aviation* (1988) 27 I.L.M. 627; *Convention on the Prevention and Punishment of Crimes Against Internationally Protected Persons Including Diplomatic Agents*, Can. T.S. 1977 No. 43; *Convention Against the Taking of Hostages* (1979) 18 I.L.M. 1456; *Convention for the Suppression of Unlawful Acts Against the Safety of Maritime Navigation* (1988) 27 I.L.M. 672 and *Protocol for the Suppression of Unlawful Acts Against the Safety of Fixed Platforms Located on the Continental Shelf* (1988) 27 I.L.M. 685; *Terrorist Bombing Convention*, reproduced in the text; *International Convention for the Suppression of the Financing of Terrorism* (December 9, 1999), U.N. Doc. A/RES/54/109; and *International Convention for the Suppression of Acts of Nuclear Terrorism*, U.N. Doc. A/59/766 (April 13, 2005).

96   S.A. Williams, "International Law and Terrorism: Age-Old Problems, Different Targets" (1988) 26 Can. Y.B. Int'l L. 87 at 88.

97   S.C. 2001, c. 41, in force January 17, 2002.

on the subject, criminalizing a great deal of behaviour by way of an expansive definition of "terrorist activity"; see s. 83.01(1)(b) of the *Criminal Code*.

B. JURISDICTION OVER THE PERSON

Beyond possessing prescriptive jurisdiction over the subject matter, a state also needs jurisdiction over the person in order to enforce its laws. Normally the state requires custody of the human or legal persons involved in order to execute its will. Occasionally states assert jurisdiction against the property of absent persons. *In rem* action against a ship is one example of a universal civil law process, which pressures the shipowner to come into the jurisdiction. Another example is seizure of enemy alien property in time of war, wherever the owner may be.

When the wrongdoer is within the country there is no difficulty in enforcing jurisdiction. The state has plenary territorial authority subject to international rules for the protection of human rights (considered in Chapter 12 on "Protection of Human Rights") and of the immunities of other states and their representatives (discussed in Chapter 5 on "Interstate Relations"). When a transnational element is introduced by the movement of the persons concerned between two or more states, the exercise of jurisdiction is more complicated. International law has developed piecemeal to deal with a variety of such situations in pragmatic ways. This section considers the following issues: abduction from a foreign state, extradition of fugitive offenders, and admission and expulsion of aliens. Jurisdiction over genocide, war crimes, crimes against humanity, and other offences against the peace and security of mankind will be considered in Chapter 11 on "International Criminal Law."

1. Abduction from a Foreign State

The exercise of jurisdiction that is prohibited or cannot be soundly based on any of the six principles previously considered may induce complaints from other states. The international responsibility that may befall a state that acts in excess of its jurisdiction is discussed in Chapter 10 on "State Responsibility." The question here is how an excess of jurisdiction internationally will affect the authority of the state internally.

If a fugitive from the criminal law of one state seeks refuge in another state, in order to be brought to trial, he or she must be returned to the state that seeks to prosecute him or her. His or her presence may be secured lawfully by extradition;[98] or unlawfully by kidnapping in the refuge state or by enticement to enter the state of prosecution by fraud. The questions that arise are: can an accused who has been obtained by extra-legal means contest the jurisdiction of the court over acts by law enforcement officers or other persons from the prosecuting state, and can such a challenge result in the court divesting itself of jurisdiction?[99] Or, is the kidnapping simply a violation of customary or conventional

---

98   Discussed in the next subsection.

99   See S.A. Williams, Comment (1975) 53 Can. Bar Rev. 404; S.A. Williams & J.-G. Castel, *supra* note 4 at c. 7; F.A. Mann, "Reflections on the Prosecution of Persons Abducted in Breach of International Law," in Yoram Dinstein, ed., *International Law at a Time of Perplexity: Essays in Honour of Shabtai Rosenne*

international law relating to the territorial sovereignty of the state of refuge that may be complained about by that state alone?

Although, in the past, states, including Canada and the United Kingdom, conducted kidnapping or luring, it is the contemporary position of the United States that is the focus of interest. The United States' practice has been that a fugitive should not succeed in escaping trial because he or she was illegally brought into the jurisdiction of the prosecuting state. The source of this practice can be found in the Roman law maxim *mala captus bene detentus*, which means that the court, once in possession of the accused, has jurisdiction and all that is required is a fair trial. As will be seen, this approach is controversial.

Conviction After Unlawful Arrest
by S.A. Williams (1975) 53 Can. Bar Rev. 404 (footnotes omitted)

One of the major problems raised by the present uncertain tendencies of the law concerning unlawful arrest is the question of policy. The interests of the individual offender are in juxtaposition with those of the state. Canadian as well as American courts have tended to promote the idea that illegality of some pre-trial events, although infringing the accused's rights, should not nullify his detention and excuse him from a crime he has committed. They have weighed the illegal arrest against the merits of the criminal charge. However, there is a conflicting theory as to the thought that criminals should be punished, and that is that a government should obey the law even where criminals are concerned. Jurisdiction gained through illegal acts tend to reward brutality and lawlessness. Thus, one must consider whether it is in the social interest to excuse a criminal because the police or government agents used illegal means to bring him before the court.

... Government officials should not have a separate set of rules as regards their conduct. Respect for the authority of a government will seriously be affected if it fails itself to observe the law faithfully, and individual citizens feel that their liberty is at stake. A government should set an example to its people and if it is known to be breaking the law in order to secure criminal convictions what hope is there for society in general. The right to be protected from abduction into the jurisdiction of a state is a basic human right in a free society. The misplaced sense of justice on the part of governments or individual agents not to comply with legal machinery to bring offenders into the jurisdiction of the court must be condemned. The official who acts in an unlawful way may be criminally liable for kidnapping. He may also be liable civilly to the victim for trespass to the person. The criminal penalties are seldom used as there is no tendency on the part of the states to prosecute their officers, and as regards the civil measures, there is little doubt that police officers are not affluent enough to warrant action against them personally unless their employers are made jointly liable.

(1989) 407-21; A.F. Lowenfeld, "U.S. Law Enforcement Abroad: The Constitution and International Law" (1989) 83 A.J.I.L. 880 and (1990) 84 A.J.I.L. 444; and "Kidnapping by Government Order: A Follow-up" (1990) 84 A.J.I.L. 712 and "Still More Kidnapping" (1990) 85 A.J.I.L. 655.

Thus, the most definite way by far of deterring the police from wilful lawlessness is to make it clear that criminals will not be tried who have been illegally secured.

United States v. Alvarez-Machain[100]
112 S.Ct. 2188 (1992) (footnotes omitted)

[On April 2, 1990, Dr. Alvarez-Machain, a Mexican resident in Mexico, was forcibly kidnapped from his medical office in Guadalajara, Mexico and flown by private plane to Texas, where he was arrested by U.S. Drug Enforcement Administration (DEA) officials. He was indicted for participating in the kidnap and murder of a DEA agent by keeping the agent alive so that others could torture and interrogate him. Mexico protested in a number of diplomatic notes to the United States and demanded Dr. Alvarez-Machain's return. At trial it was concluded that the DEA was responsible for Dr. Alvarez-Machain's abduction, although it was not personally involved in it. The District Court granted Dr. Alvarez-Machain's motion to dismiss the indictment based on the violation of the bilateral Extradition Treaty between Mexico and the United States.[101] The Court of Appeals for the Ninth Circuit upheld the decision to dismiss and to repatriate Dr. Alvarez-Machain,[102] on the basis that although the Extradition Treaty does not expressly prohibit abductions, the "purpose" of the Treaty was violated by such action. Also of importance to the Court was the formal protest by the offended state. The U.S. Government sought a review of this decision by the U.S. Supreme Court.]

THE CHIEF JUSTICE (for the majority): The issue in this case is whether a criminal defendant, abducted to the United States from a nation with which it has an extradition treaty, thereby acquires a defense to the jurisdiction of this country's courts. We hold that he does not, and that he may be tried in federal district court for violations of the criminal law of the United States.

... In construing a treaty, as in construing a statute, we first look to its terms to determine its meaning. *Air France v. Saks*, 470 U.S. 392, 397, 105 S.Ct. 1338, 1341, 84 L.Ed. 289 (1985); *Valentine v. United States ex. rel. Neidecker*, 299 U.S. 5, 11, 57 S.Ct. 100, 103, 81 L.Ed. 5 (1936). The Treaty says nothing about the obligations of the United States and Mexico to refrain from forcible abductions of people from the territory of the other nation, or the consequences under the Treaty if such an abduction

---

100 See A. Abramovsky, "Extraterritorial Abductions: America's 'Catch and Snatch' Policy Run Amok" (1991) 31 Va. J. Int'l L. 151; M. Glennon, "State-sponsored Abduction: A Comment on United States v. Alvarez-Machain" (1992) 86 A.J.I.L. 746; M. Halberstan, "In Defence of the Supreme Court Decision in Alvarez-Machain" (1992) 86 A.J.I.L. 739; and A. Wilder, "The Supreme Court Decision, Abduction from Mexico of Dr. Humberto Alvarez-Machain" (1992) 32 Va. J. Int'l L. 979.

101 (1979) 31 U.S.T. 5059; T.I.A.S. No. 9656.

102 The Court of Appeals relied on its decision in *U.S. v. Verdugo-Urquidez*, 939 F.2d 1341 (9th Cir. 1991). In that case the Court held that the Fourth Amendment to the U.S. Constitution is restricted to U.S. citizens outside the United States and U.S. citizens and aliens for occurrences in the United States. For a criticism of this decision, see A.F. Lowenfeld, "U.S. Law Enforcement Abroad: The Constitution and International Law, Continued" (1990) 84 A.J.I.L. 444 at 452-53, 492-93.

occurs. Respondent submits that Article 22(1) of the *Treaty* which states that it "shall apply to offenses specified in Article 2 [including murder] committed before and after this *Treaty* enters into force," 31 U.S.T., at 5073-5074, evidences an intent to make application of the Treaty mandatory for those offenses. However, the more natural conclusion is that Article 22 was included to ensure that the Treaty was applied to extraditions requested after the *Treaty* went into force, regardless of when the crime of extradition occurred.

More critical to respondent's argument is Article 9 of the *Treaty* which provides:

> 1. Neither Contracting Party shall be bound to deliver up its own nationals, but the executive authority of the requested Party shall, if not prevented by the laws of that Party, have the power to deliver them up if, in its discretion, it be deemed proper to do so.
>
> 2. If extradition is not granted pursuant to paragraph 1 of this Article, the requested Party shall submit the case to its competent authorities for the purpose of prosecution, provided that Party has jurisdiction over the offense. *Id.*, at 5065.

According to respondent, Article 9 embodies the terms of the bargain which the United States struck: if the United States wishes to prosecute a Mexican national, it may request that individual's extradition. Upon a request from the United States, Mexico may either extradite the individual, or submit the case to the proper authorities for prosecution in Mexico. In this way, respondent reasons, each nation preserved its right to choose whether its nationals would be tried in its own courts or by the courts of the other nation. This preservation of rights would be frustrated if either nation were free to abduct nationals of the other nation for the purposes of prosecution. More broadly, respondent reasons, as did the Court of Appeals, that all the processes and restrictions on the obligation to extradite established by the *Treaty* would make no sense if either nation were free to resort to forcible kidnapping to gain the presence of an individual for prosecution in a manner not contemplated by the *Treaty*. ...

We do not read the *Treaty* in such a fashion. Article 9 does not purport to specify the only way in which one country may gain custody of a national of the other country for the purposes of prosecution. In the absence of an extradition treaty, nations are under no obligation to surrender those in their country to foreign authorities for prosecution. *Rauscher*, 119 U.S., at 411-412, 7 S.Ct. at 236; *Factor v. Laubenheimer*, 290 U.S. 276, 287, 54 S.Ct, 191, 193, 78 L.Ed. 315 (1933); *cf. Valentine v. United States ex. rel. Neidecker*, *supra*, 299 U.S., at 8-9, 57 S.Ct., at 102 (United States may not extradite a citizen in the absence of a statute or treaty obligation). Extradition treaties exist so as to impose mutual obligations to surrender individuals in certain defined sets of circumstances, following established procedures. See 1 J. Moore, *A Treatise on Extradition and Interstate Rendition*, s. 72 (1891). The *Treaty* thus provides a mechanism which would not otherwise exist, requiring under certain circumstances, the United States and Mexico to extradite individuals to the other country, and establishing the procedures to be followed when the *Treaty* is invoked.

The history of negotiation and practice under the *Treaty* also fails to show that abductions outside of the *Treaty* constitute a violation of the *Treaty*. As the Solicitor General notes, the Mexican government was made aware, as early as 1906, of the *Ker* doctrine, and the United States' position that it applied to forcible abductions made outside of the terms of the United States-Mexico extradition treaty. Nonetheless, the current version of the *Treaty*, signed in 1978, does not attempt to establish a rule that would in any way curtail the effect of *Ker*. Moreover, although language which would grant individuals exactly the right sought by respondent had been considered and drafted as early as 1935 by a prominent group of legal scholars sponsored by the faculty of Harvard Law School, no such clause appears in the current treaty.

Thus, the language of the *Treaty*, in the context of its history, does not support the proposition that the *Treaty* prohibits abductions outside of its terms. The remaining question, therefore, is whether the Treaty should be interpreted so as to include an implied term prohibiting prosecution where the defendant's presence is obtained by means other than those established by the *Treaty*. See *Valentine*, 299 U.S., at 17, 57 S.Ct., at 106 ("Strictly the question is not whether there had been a uniform practical construction denying the power, but whether the power had been so clearly recognized that the grant should be implied").

Respondent contends that the *Treaty* must be interpreted against the backdrop of customary international law, and that international abductions are "so clearly prohibited in international law" that there was no reason to include such a clause in the *Treaty* itself. Brief for Respondent 11. The international censure of intentional abductions is further evidenced, according to respondent, by the *United Nations Charter* and the *Charter of the Organization of American States*. *Id.*, at 17, 57 S.Ct., at 106. Respondent does not argue that these sources of international law provide an independent basis for the right respondent asserts not to be tried in the United States, but rather they should inform the interpretation of the *Treaty* terms.

The Court of Appeals deemed it essential, in order for the individual defendant to assert a right under the *Treaty*, that the affected government had registered a protest. *Verdugo*, 939 F.2d, at 1357 ("in the kidnapping case there must be a formal protest from the offended government after the kidnapping"). Respondent agrees that the right exercised by the individual is derivative of the nation's right under the *Treaty*, since nations are authorized, notwithstanding the terms of an extradition treaty, to voluntarily render an individual to the other country on terms completely outside of those provided in the *Treaty*. The formal protest, therefore, ensures that the "offended" nation actually objects to the abduction and has not in some way voluntarily rendered the individual for prosecution. Thus the *Extradition Treaty* only prohibits gaining the defendant's presence by means other than those set forth in the *Treaty* when the nation from which the defendant was abducted objects.

This argument seems to us inconsistent with the remainder of respondent's argument. The *Extradition Treaty* has the force of law, and if, as respondent asserts, it is self-executing, it would appear that a court must enforce it on behalf of an individual regardless of the offensiveness of the practice of one nation to the other nation.

... More fundamentally, the difficulty with the support respondent garners from international law is that none of it relates to the practice of nations in relation to extradition treaties. ... In the instant case, respondent would imply terms in the extradition treaty from the practice of nations with regards to international law more generally. Respondent would have us find that the *Treaty* acts as a prohibition against a violation of the general principle of international law that one government may not "exercise its police power in the territory of another state." Brief for Respondent 16. There are many actions which could be taken by a nation that would violate this principle, including waging war, but it cannot seriously be contended an invasion of the United States by Mexico would violate the terms of the extradition treaty between the two nations.

In sum, to infer from this *Treaty* and its terms that it prohibits all means of gaining the presence of an individual outside of its terms goes beyond established precedent and practice. ... To imply from the terms of this *Treaty* that it prohibits obtaining the presence of an individual by means outside of the procedures the *Treaty* establishes requires a much larger inferential leap, with only the most general of international law principles to support it. The general principles cited by respondent simply fail to persuade us that we should imply in the *United States-Mexico Extradition Treaty* a term prohibiting international abductions.

Respondent and his amici may be correct that respondent's abduction was "shocking," Tr. of Oral Arg. 40, and that it may be in violation of general international law principles. Mexico has protested the abduction of respondent through diplomatic notes, App. 33-38, and the decision of whether respondent should be returned to Mexico, as a matter outside of the *Treaty*, is a matter for the Executive Branch. We conclude, however, that respondent's abduction was not in violation of the *Extradition Treaty between the United States and Mexico*, and therefore the rule of *Ker v. Illinois* is fully applicable to this case. The fact of respondent's forcible abduction does not therefore prohibit his trial in a court in the United States for violations of the criminal laws of the United States.

The judgment of the Court of Appeals is therefore reversed, and the case is remanded for further proceedings consistent with this opinion. So ordered.

STEVENS J. (Justices Blackmun and O'Connor concurring) dissenting: The Court correctly observes that this case raises a question of first impression. ... The case is unique for several reasons. It does not involve an ordinary abduction by a private kidnapper, or bounty hunter, as in *Ker v. Illinois*, 119 U.S. 436, 7 S.Ct. 225, 30 L.Ed. 421 (1886); nor does it involve the apprehension of an American fugitive who committed a crime in one State and sought asylum in another, as in *Frisbie v. Collins*, 342 U.S. 519, 72 S.Ct. 509, 96 L.Ed. 541 (1952). Rather, it involves this country's abduction of another country's citizen; it also involves a violation of the territorial integrity of that other country, with which this country has signed an extradition treaty.

The *Extradition Treaty* with Mexico is a comprehensive document containing 23 articles and an appendix listing the extraditable offenses covered by the agreement. The parties announces their purpose in the preamble: Two Governments desire "to cooperate more closely in the fight against crime and, to this end, to mutually render better assistance in matters of extradition." From the preamble, through the description of the parties' obligations with respect to offenses committed within as well as beyond the territory of a requesting party, the delineation of the procedures and evidentiary requirements for extradition, the special provisions for political offenses and capital punishment, and other details, the *Treaty* appears to have been designed to cover the entire subject of extradition. Thus, Article 22, entitled "Scope of Application" states that the "*Treaty* shall apply to offenses specified in Article 2 committed before and after this *Treaty* enters into force," and Article 2 directs that "[e]xtradition shall take place, subject to this *Treaty*, for wilful acts which fall within any of [the extraditable offences listed in] the clauses of the Appendix." Moreover, as noted by the Court, ... Article 9 expressly provides that neither Contracting Party is bound to deliver up its own nationals, although it may do so in its discretion, but if it does not do so, it "shall submit the case to its competent authorities for purposes of prosecution."

Petitioner's claim that the *Treaty* is not exclusive, but permits forcible governmental kidnapping, would transform these, and other, provisions into little more than verbiage. For example provisions requiring "sufficient" evidence to grant extradition (Art. 3), withholding extradition for political or military offenses (Art. 5), withholding extradition when the person sought has already been tried (Art. 6), withholding extradition when the statute of limitations for the crime has lapsed (Art. 7), and granting the requested State discretion to refuse to extradite an individual who would face the death penalty in the requesting country (Art. 8), would serve little purpose if the requesting country could simply kidnap the person. As the Court of Appeals for the Ninth Circuit recognized in a related case, "[e]ach of these provisions would be utterly frustrated if a kidnapping were held to be a permissible course of governmental conduct." *United States v. Verdugo-Urquidez*, 939 F.2d 1341, 1349 (1991). In addition, all of these provisions "only make sense if they are understood as requiring each treaty signatory to comply with those procedures whenever it wishes to obtain jurisdiction over an individual who is located in another treaty nation." *Id.*, at 1351.

It is true, as the Court notes, that there is no express promise by either party to refrain from forcible abductions in the territory of the other Nation. ... Relying on that omission, the Court, in effect, concludes that the *Treaty* merely creates an optional method of obtaining jurisdiction over alleged offenders, and that the parties silently reserved the right to resort to self help whenever they deem force more expeditious than legal process. If the United States, for example, thought it more expedient to torture or simply to execute a person rather than to attempt extradition, these options would be equally available because they, too, were not explicitly prohibited by the *Treaty*. That, however, is a highly improbable interpretation of a consensual agreement, which on its face appears to have been intended to set forth comprehensive and exclusive rules concerning the subject of extradition. In my opinion, "the manifest scope and object of the treaty itself," *Rauscher*, 119 U.S., at 422, 7 S.Ct., at 242, plainly imply a mutual undertaking to respect the territorial integrity of the other contracting party. That opinion is confirmed by a consideration of the "legal context" in which the *Treaty* was negotiated. *Cannon v. University of Chicago*, 441 U.S. 677, 699, 99 S.Ct. 1946, 1958, 60 L.Ed. 2d 560 (1979).

... As the Court observes at the outset of its opinion, there is reason to believe that respondent participated in an especially brutal murder of an American law enforcement agent. That fact, if true, may explain the Executive's intense interest in punishing respondent in our courts. Such an explanation, however, provides no justification for disregarding the Rule of Law that this Court has a duty to uphold. That the Executive may wish to reinterpret the *Treaty* to allow for an action that the *Treaty* in no way authorizes should not influence this Court's interpretation. Indeed, the desire for revenge exerts "a kind of hydraulic pressure ... before which even well settled principles of law will bend," *Northern Securities Co. v. United States*, 193 U.S. 197, 401, 24 S.Ct. 436, 468, 48 L.Ed. 679 (1904) (Holmes J., dissenting), but it is precisely at such moments that we should remember and be guided by our duty "to render judgment evenly and dispassionately according to law, as each is given understanding to ascertain and apply it." *United States v. Mine Workers*, 330 U.S. 258, 342, 67 S.Ct. 677, 720, 91 L.Ed. 884 (1947) (Rutledge J., dissenting). The way that we perform that duty in a case of this kind sets an example that other tribunals in other countries are sure to emulate.

The significance of this Court's precedents is illustrated by a decision of the Court of Appeal of the Republic of South Africa. Based largely on its understanding of the import of this Court's cases—including our decision in *Ker v. Illinois*—that court held that the prosecution of a defendant kidnapped by agents of South Africa in another country must be dismissed. *S. v. Ebrahim*, S. Afr. L. Rep. (Apr.-June 1991). The Court of Appeal of South Africa—indeed, I suspect most courts throughout the civilized world—will be deeply disturbed by the "monstrous" decision the Court announces today. For every Nation that has an interest in preserving the Rule of Law is affected, directly or indirectly, by a decision of this character. As Thomas Paine warned, an "avidity to punish is always dangerous to liberty" because it leads a Nation "to stretch, to misinterpret, and to misapply even the best of laws." To counter that tendency, he reminds us:

> He that would make his own liberty secure must guard even his enemy from oppression; for if he violates this duty he establishes a precedent that will reach to himself.

I respectfully dissent.

NOTES

1) In 1974, the Second Circuit Court of Appeals delivered a remarkable opinion in *United States v. Toscanino*.[103] The accused appealed his conviction on a narcotics charge, claiming that jurisdiction over him had been illegally acquired in that U.S. agents had kidnapped him in Uruguay, used illegal electronic surveillance, tortured him, and abducted him to the United States. The court distinguished the *Ker-Frisbie* line of authority discussed in *Alvarez*, finding that a court had to "divest itself of jurisdiction over the person of a defendant where it has been acquired as the result of the government's deliberate, unnecessary and unreasonable invasion of the accused's constitutional rights."[104] The *Alvarez* decision, however, was the nadir of a judicial climbdown from *Toscanino*, which subsequent appellate courts had either refused to apply or treated as a narrow "torture exception." In the light of the events of September 11, 2001, do you expect any changes in U.S. law or policy on this question?

2) Does the *Alvarez-Machain* case give a right to abduct abroad to U.S. law enforcement agents? Or was the matter framed much more narrowly? Refer to the jurisdictional issue

---

103   500 F.2d 267 (2d Cir. 1974).
104   *Ibid.* at 275.

outlined by the Chief Justice. Note that the Court stated the abduction may have been "shocking" but the Executive Branch must decide whether the respondent should be returned to Mexico, as the matter was outside of the Treaty. Canada presented an *amicus curiae* brief to the U.S. Supreme Court in which it condemned the U.S. conduct.[105]

3) The charges against Dr. Alvarez were dismissed for lack of evidence, and he was released. His civil action against his abductors and the U.S. government also made its way to the Supreme Court, where it was dismissed.[106]

4) Judge Stevens's dissent referred to the South African case of *State v. Ebrahim*.[107] In that case, Ebrahim, a South African citizen by birth and since 1962 a member of the military wing of the African National Congress (ANC), was forcibly abducted from his home in Swaziland and taken across the border into South Africa. In 1964 he had been convicted in South Africa of several acts of sabotage and had been sentenced to 15 years of imprisonment. Upon his release in 1979 he was restricted to Pinetown, Natal. In 1980 he fled to Swaziland. Upon his arrival in South Africa he was formally arrested and later charged and convicted of treason. He submitted in his application for release that his "abduction in Swaziland took place with the authority and knowledge of the South African Police or other agents of the South African state." It does not appear that the government of Swaziland protested at anytime. The Court, based on a combination of Roman-Dutch law and English common law and referring in particular to the *Toscanino* case considered above, held that the South African trial court had no jurisdiction to hear the case on account of the abduction and consequently his conviction and sentence were set aside.

5) *Ebrahim* is in fact illustrative of a line of international decisions that run counter to the *mala captus* doctrine that found favour in *Alvarez*. U.K. courts, for example, have on several occasions divested themselves of jurisdiction over fugitives who were detained through irregular or illegal conduct on the part of U.K. government officials, by applying the doctrine of "abuse of process."[108]

6) In *United States v. Yunis*,[109] the accused was lured from Lebanon to Cyprus by a friend who had been co-opted by the U.S. DEA and the CIA. He was arrested in international waters off the coast of Cyprus by an FBI agent who was posing as a drug dealer, with whom Yunis thought he would be working. Yunis was transferred to a U.S. Navy communications vessel, from there to the U.S. aircraft carrier "Saratoga," and finally by non-stop Navy jet aircraft to Andrews Air Force Base outside Washington D.C. Yunis's arrest had been authorized by a U.S. magistrate. He had, with others, hijacked a Royal Jordanian Airlines aircraft in Beirut, Lebanon. The aircraft was eventually blown up, but all the passengers, including three Americans, survived. Cyprus had at no time

---

105   Reproduced in (1992) 31 I.L.M. 919.

106   *Sosa v. Alvarez-Machain*, 542 U.S. 692 (2004).

107   (1991) 2 S.A. Rep. 553(a); translation into English from Afrikaans reprinted in (1992) 31 I.L.M. 888.

108   *R. v. Horseferry Road Magistrates' Court, ex parte Bennett*, [1993] 3 All E.R. 138 (H.L.); *R. v. Mullen*, [1999] 3 W.L.R. 777 (Crim. Ct. App.). See generally C. Warbrick, "Judicial Jurisdiction and Abuse of Process" (2000) 49 I.C.L.Q. 489. See also *R. v. Hartley*, [1978] 2 N.Z.L.R. 199 (New Zealand C.A.); *Levinge v. Director of Custodial Services et al.* (1987), 9 N.S.W.L.R. 546 (New South Wales S.C.).

109   681 F. Supp. 909 at 914-15 (D.D.C. 1988).

been informed about what was going on. The prosecution in the United States was founded on legislation contained, *inter alia*, in 18 U.S.C. § 02331 entitled "Terrorist Acts Against United States Nationals." Yunis was found guilty and sentenced to 30 years in prison. How is the *Yunis* case different from *Toscanino* or *Alvarez*? Does it make a difference that Yunis was arrested in international waters?

7) The Canadian cases of *R. v. Walton*[110] and *Re Hartnett and the Queen: Re Hudson and the Queen*[111] applied the *mala captus bene detentus* maxim with slight concern for the due process of law and the civil rights of the accused. Does the *Canadian Charter of Rights and Freedoms* alter this position? So far there have been no cases on point. The *amicus* brief filed by the government of Canada in *Alvarez* (see note 2, above) seems to indicate that there will be no official sanction of abductions.

8) Unlawful enforcement in another state also formed the basis of the *Jaffe* case.[112] Sidney Jaffe was kidnapped in Toronto by two "bounty hunters" employed by a U.S. bail bonding agency. Then they forcibly took him to Florida to answer outstanding criminal charges of fraud. Canada vigorously protested to the United States that the abduction was a violation of international law and Jaffe was eventually released. The "bounty hunters" were subsequently extradited from the United States to Canada and were convicted of the offence.

9) The question of the impact of abduction or irregular arrest on a court's jurisdiction is by no means stale; it has emerged in the recent caselaw of the Yugoslavia War Crimes Tribunal (ICTY). See *Prosecutor v. Slavko Dokmanovik, Decision on the Motion for Release by the Accused;*[113] *Prosecutor v. Dragan Nikolic, Decision on Interlocutory Appeal Concerning Legality of Arrest*, reproduced below. Do you agree or disagree with the Tribunal's approach in *Nikolic*? In particular, should there be impunity for international criminals out of respect for international borders or human rights?

Prosecutor v. Dragan Nikolic
ICTY Case No. IT-94-2-AR73, Appeals Chamber, June 3, 2003
(most footnotes omitted)

[The accused was indicted by the International Tribunal for crimes against humanity and war crimes on November 1, 1994. This appeal concerned the alleged illegal arrest and abduction of the accused from Serbia and Montenegro by unknown individuals and his transfer to Bosnia and Herzegovina, where he was arrested by SFOR on or about April 20, 2002 and subsequently taken to The Hague.]

THE APPEALS CHAMBER: ...

[3] The question presented in this appeal is whether the International Tribunal can exercise jurisdiction over the Appellant notwithstanding the alleged violations of

---

110 (1905), 10 C.C.C. 269 (O.C.A.).

111 (1973), 1 O.R. (2d) 206 (H.C.).

112 Discussed in Chapter 10, Section A.3 on "Attribution."

113 No. IT-95-13a-PT, Trial Chamber II, 22 October 1997.

Serbia and Montenegro's sovereignty and of the Accused's human rights committed by SFOR, and by extension OTP, acting in collusion with the unknown individuals who abducted the Accused from Serbia and Montenegro.

[The Appeals Chamber noted that there was no case law in the Tribunal directly on point and looked to national jurisprudence for guidance.]

[23] With regard to cases concerning the same kinds of crimes as those falling within the jurisdiction of the International Tribunal, reference may be made to *Eichmann* and *Barbie*. ... In *Barbie*, the French Court of Cassation (Criminal Chamber) asserted its jurisdiction over the accused, despite the claim that he was a victim of a disguised extradition, on the basis, *inter alia*, of the special nature of the crimes ascribed to the accused, namely, crimes against humanity.[114]

[24] Although it is difficult to identify a clear pattern in this case law, and caution is needed when generalizing, two principles seem to have support in State practice as evidenced by the practice of their courts. First, in cases of crimes such as genocide, crimes against humanity and war crimes which are universally recognised and condemned as such ... courts seem to find the special character of these offences and, arguably, in their seriousness, a good reason for not setting aside jurisdiction. Second, absent a complaint by the State whose sovereignty has been breached or in the event of a diplomatic resolution of the breach it is easier for courts to assert their jurisdiction. The initial *inuria* has in a way been cured and the risk of having to return the accused to the country of origin is no longer present. ...

[26] ... In the opinion of the Appeals Chamber, the damage caused to international justice by not apprehending fugitives accused of serious violations of international humanitarian law is comparatively higher than the injury, if any, caused to the sovereignty of a State by a limited intrusion in its territory, particularly when the intrusion occurs in default of the State's cooperation. Therefore, the Appeals Chamber does not consider that in cases of universally condemned offences, jurisdiction should be set aside on the ground that there was a violation of the sovereignty of a state, when the violation is brought about by the apprehension of fugitives from international justice, whatever the consequences for the international responsibility of the State or organization involved. This is all the more so in cases such as this one, in which the State whose sovereignty has allegedly been breached has not lodged any complaint and thus has acquiesced in the International Tribunal's exercise of jurisdiction.

[The Appeals Chamber then considered under what circumstances a human rights violation would require jurisdiction to be set aside.]

[30] ... Although the assessment of the seriousness of the human rights violations depends on the circumstances of each case and cannot be made *in abstracto*, certain human rights violations are of such a serious nature that they require that the exercise

---

114 *Fédération Nationale des Déportés et Internés Résistants et Patriotes* v. *Barbie* (1983), 78 I.L.R. 130-31.

of jurisdiction be declined. It would be inappropriate for a court of law to try the victims of these abuses. Apart from such exceptional cases, however, the remedy of setting aside jurisdiction will ... usually be disproportionate. The correct balance must, therefore, be maintained between the fundamental rights of the accused and the essential interests of the international community in the prosecution of persons charged with serious violations of international humanitarian law.

[31] In the circumstances, the evidence does not satisfy the Appeals Chamber that the rights of the Accused were egregiously violated in the process of his arrest. Therefore, the procedure adopted for his arrest did not disable the Trial Chamber from exercising its jurisdiction.

2. Extradition[115]

Introduction
from S.A. Williams and J.-G. Castel, *Canadian Criminal Law, International and Transnational Aspects* (1981) 337-40 (updated and some footnotes omitted)

Extradition can be defined as the giving up of a person by a state in whose territory he or she is present, at the request of another state in whose jurisdiction that person is accused of having committed or has been convicted of a crime. International law has developed this procedure as a means whereby fugitives from justice are extradited and tried or punished in the requesting state for the crimes they have committed against its laws.

In theory, extradition can be carried out on the basis of reciprocity or under a treaty. There is in fact no duty to extradite where there is no treaty,[116] ... although laws may be passed providing for extradition and provisions to that effect in the absence of a treaty are to be found in ... the Extradition Act.[117] ... Canada has extradition treaties with many states, including [Germany,[118] India,[119] Brazil], France, Greece, Hungary, Israel, Mexico, Nicaragua, Switzerland, Tonga, and the United States of America.

Most of Canada's extradition treaties were in fact concluded by Great Britain and pre-date 1925. Several of these are still in force together with any subsequent amendments made to them. One of the most famous was the Webster-Ashburton

---

115 G. Gilbert, *Transnational Fugitive Offenders in International Law* (1998); E. Krivel, et al., *A Practical Guide to Canadian Extradition* (2002); A.W. LaForest, *Extradition to and from Canada*, 3d ed. (1991); I. Shearer, *Extradition in International Law* (1971); S.A. Williams & J.-G. Castel, *supra* note 4 at c. 25; and M.C. Bassiouni, *International Extradition: United States, Law and Practice*, 4th ed. (2002).

116 See *Re Insull* (1933), 60 C.C.C. 254 at 257 (Ont. H.C.) where the court stated that: "Extradition is purely a creature of the treaty and the statute." See also *State of Utah v. Peters* (1936), 66 C.C.C. 75; [1936] 4 D.L.R. 509 (Alta. Dist. Ct.). Note, however, removal pursuant to the *Immigration and Refugee Protection Act*, S.C. 2001, c. 27, as amended, as a substitute for extradition.

117 S.C. 1999, c. 18, s. 10.

118 Can. T.S. 1979 No. 18.

119 Can. T.S. 1987 No. 14.

Treaty of 1842 concluded between the United States and Great Britain. It provided not only for the settlement of boundaries between British possessions in North America and the United States but also the suppression of the African slave trade, and the return of criminals in certain cases. This treaty continued in operation until recently, with amendments by supplementary Conventions.[120]

A new treaty came into force between Canada and the United States on March 22nd, 1976.[121] It will probably serve as a model for all future Canadian extradition treaties. It can be looked upon as heralding a second generation of Canadian extradition treaties. The old arrangements between the two states have been expressly terminated and replaced by the new treaty. ...

The reason behind the development of such arrangements is state sovereignty. States were, and even today are, unwilling to concede advantages to other states unless the concessions proceed on the basis of reciprocity. The treaties create mutual obligations to return accused or convicted persons.

I. DOMESTIC LEGISLATION

... The purpose behind the Canadian Extradition Act [reproduced hereafter] is to ensure that the domestic law conforms with Canada's external obligations. As extradition is a part of the criminal law, it falls within section 91(27) [of the *Constitution Act, 1867*] and a federal statute must give effect to the relevant treaties. The Act provides ... for the execution of the treaties ... .

As the matter of granting extradition is one of concern to the state to which a request is made, the regulation of the procedures is left to the domestic law of that state. Thus, there can often occur conflicts or divergences between the approaches taken by various states, notably concerning the extradition of nationals, the evidence required ... by the requested state, and the powers of the judiciary or executive in the matter.

II. REASONS BEHIND EXTRADITION

In addition to protecting the sovereignty of states, extradition is used to prevent a person escaping justice. It involves a common fight against crime. Certain considerations have helped to produce the present generally accepted rules concerning extradition.

First, a state in whose territory an accused person has sought refuge frequently cannot prosecute him, usually, because it lacks jurisdiction over the offense. Second, it is often more practicable for the state where the offense has been committed to try the offender not only for evidentiary reasons but also because that state is in fact most interested in the offense. Third, if extradition did not take place and states had no regard for one another's laws, crime would be encouraged. Criminals, especially in an era of fast and easy international transportation would flee to the nearest safe haven.

---

120 Can T.S. 1952 No. 12. See articles X and XI.

121 Can. T.S. 1976 No. 3, as amended by Protocol 1, Can. T.S. 1991 No. 37, and Protocol 2, online at: <http://www.treaty-accord.gc.ca/Treaties_CLF/TreatyResult.asp>, reproduced later in this subsection.

Extradition Act
S.C. 1999, c. 18 as am.

Part I
Interpretation

2. The definitions in this section apply in this Act. ...

"extradition agreement" means an agreement that is in force, to which Canada is a party and that contains a provision respecting the extradition of persons, other than a specific agreement.

"extradition partner" means a State or entity with which Canada is party to an extradition agreement, with which Canada has entered into a specific agreement or whose name appears in the schedule. ...

"Minister" means the Minister of Justice. ...

Part II
Extradition from Canada

Extraditable Conduct

3(1) A person may be extradited from Canada in accordance with this Act and a relevant extradition agreement on the request of an extradition partner for the purpose of prosecuting the person or imposing a sentence on—or enforcing a sentence imposed on—the person if

(a) subject to a relevant extradition agreement, the offence in respect of which the extradition is requested is punishable by the extradition partner, by imprisoning or otherwise depriving the person of their liberty for a maximum of two years or more, or by a more severe punishment; and

(b) the conduct of the person, had it occurred in Canada, would have constituted an offence that is punishable in Canada,

(i) in the case of a request based on a specific agreement, by imprisonment for a maximum term of five years or more, or by a more severe punishment, and

(ii) in any other case, by imprisonment for a maximum term of two years or more, or by a more severe punishment, subject to a relevant extradition agreement.

(2) For greater certainty, it is not relevant whether the conduct referred to in subsection (1) is named, defined or characterized by the extradition partner in the same way as it is in Canada. ...

Jurisdiction

5. A person may be extradited

(a) whether or not the conduct on which the extradition partner bases its request occurred in the territory over which it has jurisdiction; and

(b) whether or not Canada could exercise jurisdiction in similar circumstances.

Retrospectivity

6. Subject to a relevant extradition agreement, extradition may be granted under this Act whether the conduct or conviction in respect of which the extradition is requested occurred before or after this Act or the relevant extradition agreement or specific agreement came into force.

No Immunity

6.1 Despite any other Act or law, no person who is the subject of a request for surrender by the International Criminal Court or by any international criminal tribunal that is established by resolution of the Security Council of the United Nations and whose name appears in the schedule, may claim immunity under common law or by statute from arrest or extradition under this Act.

Functions of the Minister

7. The Minister is responsible for the implementation of extradition agreements, the administration of this Act and dealing with requests for extradition made under them. ...

Specific Agreements

10.(1) The Minister of Foreign Affairs may, with the agreement of the Minister, enter into a specific agreement with a State or entity for the purpose of giving effect to a request for extradition in a particular case.

(2) For greater certainty, if there is an inconsistency between this Act and a specific agreement, this Act prevails to the extent of the inconsistency. ...

Authority to Proceed

15.(1) The Minister may, after receiving a request for extradition and being satisfied that the conditions set out in paragraph 3(1)(a) and subsection 3(3) are met in respect of one or more offences mentioned in the request, issue an authority to proceed that authorizes the Attorney General to seek, on behalf of the extradition partner, an order of a court for the committal of the person under section 29.

(2) If requests from two or more extradition partners are received by the Minister for the extradition of a person, the Minister shall determine the order in which the requests will be authorized to proceed. ...

Arrest or Summons

16.(1) The Attorney General may, after the Minister issues an authority to proceed, apply ex parte to a judge in the province in which the Attorney General believes the person is or to which the person is on their way, or was last known to be, for the issuance of a summons to the person or a warrant for the arrest of the person. ...

Extradition Hearing

24.(1) The judge shall, on receipt of an authority to proceed from the Attorney General, hold an extradition hearing. ...

25. For the purposes of the *Constitution Act, 1982*, a judge has, with respect to the functions that the judge is required to perform in applying this Act, the same competence that that judge possesses by virtue of being a superior court judge. ...

Order of Committal

29.(1) A judge shall order the committal of the person into custody to await surrender if

(a) in the case of a person sought for prosecution, there is evidence admissible under this Act of conduct that, had it occurred in Canada, would justify committal for trial in Canada on the offence set out in the authority to proceed and the judge is satisfied that the person is the person sought by the extradition partner; and

(b) in the case of a person sought for the imposition or enforcement of a sentence the judge is satisfied that the conviction was in respect of conduct that corresponds to the offence set out in the authority to proceed and that the person is the person who was convicted. ...

Evidence

32.(1) ... The following shall also be admitted as evidence, even if it would not otherwise be admissible under Canadian law:

(a) the contents of the documents contained under subsection 33(3);

(b) the contents of the documents that are submitted in conformity with the terms of an extradition agreement; and

(c) evidence adduced by the person sought for extradition that is relevant to the tests set out in subsection 29(1) if the judge considers it reliable.

(2) Evidence gathered in Canada must satisfy the rules of evidence under Canadian law in order to be admitted.

Record of the Case

33.(1) The record of the case must include

(a) in the case of a person sought for the purpose of prosecution, a document summarizing the evidence available to the extradition partner for use in the prosecution; and

(b) in the case of a person sought for the imposition or enforcement of a sentence,

(i) a copy of the document that records the conviction of the person, and

(ii) a document describing the conduct for which the person was convicted. ...

(3) A record of the case may not be admitted unless

(a) in the case of a person sought for the purpose of prosecution, a judicial or prosecuting authority of the extradition partner certifies that the evidence summarized or contained in the record of the case is available for trial and

(i) is sufficient under the law of the extradition partner to justify prosecution, or

(ii) was gathered according to the law of the extradition partner; ...

34. A document is admissible whether or not it is solemnly affirmed or under oath. ...

Powers of the Minister

40.(1) The Minister may within a period of 90 days after the date of a person's committal to await surrender, personally order that the person be surrendered to the extradition partner. ...

(3) The Minister may seek assurances ... or may subject the surrender to any conditions ... including a condition that the person not be prosecuted, nor that a sentence be imposed on or enforced against the person, in respect of any offence or conduct other than that referred to in the order of surrender. ...

Reasons for Refusal

44.(1) The Minister shall refuse to make a surrender order if the Minister is satisfied that

(a) the surrender would be unjust or oppressive having regard to all the relevant circumstances; or

(b) the request for extradition is made for the purpose of prosecuting or punishing the person by reason of their race, religion, nationality, ethnic origin, language, colour, political opinion, sex, sexual orientation, age, mental or physical disability or status or that the person's position may be prejudiced for any of those reasons.

(2) The Minister may refuse to make a surrender order if the Minister is satisfied that the conduct ... is punishable by death under the laws that apply to the extradition partner. ...

46.(1) The Minister shall refuse to make a surrender order if the Minister is satisfied that

(a) the prosecution of a person is barred by prescription or limitations under the law that applies to the extradition partner;

(b) the conduct ... is a military offence that is not also an offence under criminal law; or

(c) the conduct in respect of which extradition is sought is a political offence or an offence of a political character.

(2) For the purpose of subparagraph (1)(c), conduct that constitutes an offence mentioned in a multilateral extradition agreement for which Canada, as a party, is obliged to extradite the person or submit the matter to its appropriate authority for prosecution does not constitute a political offence or an offence of a political character. The following conduct also does not constitute an offence of a political character:

(a) murder or manslaughter;

(b) inflicting serious bodily harm;

(c) sexual assault;

(d) kidnapping, abduction, hostage-taking or extortion;

(e) using explosives, incendiaries, devices or substances in circumstances in which human life is likely to be endangered or serious bodily harm or substantial property damage is likely to be caused; and

(f) an attempt or conspiracy to engage in, counselling, aiding or abetting another person to engage in, or being an accessory after the fact in relation to, the conduct referred to in any of paragraphs (a) to (e).

When Minister May Refuse to Make an Order

47. The Minister may refuse to make a surrender order if the Minister is satisfied that

(a) The person would be entitled, if that person were tried in Canada, to be discharged under the laws of Canada because of a previous acquittal or conviction;

(b) the person was convicted in their absence and could not, on surrender, have the case reviewed;

(c) the person was less than eighteen years old at the time of the offence and the law that applies to them in the territory over which the extradition partner has jurisdiction is not consistent with the fundamental principles governing the Young Offenders Act;

(d) the conduct is respect of which the request for extradition is made is the subject of criminal proceedings in Canada against the person; or

(e) none of the conduct in which the extradition partner bases its request occurred in the territory over which the extradition partner has jurisdiction.

47.1 The grounds for refusal set out in sections 44, 46 and 47 do not apply in the case of a person who is subject to a request for surrender by the International Criminal Court.

Discharge

48.(1) If the Minister decides not to make a surrender order, the Minister shall order the discharge of the person. ...

Appeal

49. A person may appeal against an order of committal—or the Attorney General, on behalf of the extradition partner, may appeal the discharge of the person or a stay of proceedings—to the court of appeal of the province in which the order of committal, the order discharging the person, or the order staying the proceedings was made. ...

Review of Order

57(1) Despite the Federal Courts Act, the court of appeal of the province in which the committal of the person was ordered has exclusive original jurisdiction to hear and determine applications for judicial review under this Act, made in respect of the decision of the Minister under section 40.

(2) An application for judicial review may be made by the person....

Delay for Surrender

62.(1) No person may be surrendered

(a) until a period of 30 days has expired after the date of the committal for surrender; or

(b) if an appeal or a judicial review in respect of a matter arising under this Act, or any appeal from an appeal or judicial review, is pending, until after the date of the final decision of the court on the appeal or judicial review.

Canada–United States Treaty on Extradition
Can. T.S. 1976 No. 3, Protocol 1 (1988)[122] and Protocol 2 (2001)[123]

Article 1

Each Contracting Party agrees to extradite to the other, in the circumstances and subject to the conditions described in this Treaty, persons found in its territory who have been charged with, or convicted of, any of the offenses covered by Article 2 of this Treaty committed within the territory of the other, or outside thereof under the conditions specified in Article 3(2) of this Treaty.

Article 2

(1) Extradition shall be granted for conduct which constitutes an offense punishable by the laws of both Contracting Parties by imprisonment or other form of detention for a term exceeding one year or any greater punishment.

(2) An offense is extraditable notwithstanding

(i) that conduct such as interstate transportation or use of the mails or of other facilities affecting interstate or foreign commerce, required for the purpose of establishing jurisdiction, forms part of the offense in the United States, or

(ii) that it relates to taxation or revenue or is one of a purely fiscal character.

Article 3

(1) For the purpose of this Treaty the territory of a Contracting Party shall include all territory under the jurisdiction of that Contracting Party, including air space and territorial waters and vessels and aircraft registered in that Contracting Party or aircraft leased without crew to a lessee who has his principal place of business, or, if the lessee has no such place of business, his permanent residence in, that Contracting Party if any such aircraft is in flight, or if any such vessel is on the high seas when the offense is committed. For the purposes of this Treaty an aircraft shall be considered in flight from the moment when power is applied for the purpose of the take-off until the moment when the landing run ends. ...

---

122 *Ibid.*

123 *Ibid.*

(2) When the offense for which extradition is requested was committed outside the territory of the requesting State, the executive or other appropriate authority of the requested State shall grant extradition if the laws of the requested State provide for jurisdiction over such an offense committed in similar circumstances. If the laws in the requested State do not so provide, the executive authority in the requested State may, in its discretion, grant extradition.

Article 4

(1) Extradition shall not be granted in any of the following circumstances:

(i) When the person whose surrender is sought is being proceeded against, or has been tried and discharged or punished in the territory of the requested State for the offense for which his extradition is requested.

(ii) When the prosecution for the offense has become barred by lapse of time according to the laws of the requesting State.

(iii) When the offense in respect of which extradition is requested is of a political character, or the person whose extradition is requested proves that the extradition request has been made for the purpose of trying or punishing him for an offense of the above-mentioned character. If any question arises as to whether a case comes within the provisions of this subparagraph, the authorities of the Government on which the requisition is made shall decide.

(2) For the purpose of this Treaty, the following offenses shall be deemed not to be offenses within subparagraph (iii) of paragraph 1 of this Article:

(i) An offense for which each Contracting Party has the obligation pursuant to a multilateral international agreement to extradite the person sought or to submit the case to its competent authorities for the purpose of prosecution;

(ii) Murder, manslaughter or other culpable homicide, malicious wounding or inflicting grievous bodily harm;

(iii) An offense involving kidnapping, abduction, or any form of unlawful detention, including taking a hostage;

(iv) An offense involving the placing or use of explosives, incendiaries or destructive devices or substances capable of endangering life or of causing grievous bodily harm or substantial property damage; and

(v) An attempt or conspiracy to commit, or counselling the commission of, any of the foregoing offenses, or aiding or abetting a person who commits or attempts to commit such offenses. …

Article 6

When the offense for which extradition is requested is punishable by death under the laws of the requesting State and the laws of the requested State do not permit such punishment for that offense, extradition may be refused unless the requesting State provides such assurances as the requested State considers sufficient that the death penalty shall not be imposed, or, if imposed, shall not be executed. …

Article 8

The determination that extradition should or should not be granted shall be made in accordance with the law of the requested State and the person whose extradition is sought shall have the right to use all remedies and recourses provided by such law.

Article 9

(1) The request for extradition shall be made through the diplomatic channel.

(2) The request shall be accompanied by a description of the person sought, a statement of the facts of the case, the text of the laws of the requesting State describing the offense and prescribing the punishment for the offense, and a statement of the law relating to the limitation of the legal proceedings.

(3) When the request relates to a person who has not yet been convicted, it must also be accompanied by a warrant of arrest issued by a judge or other judicial officer of the requesting State and by such evidence as, according to the laws of the requested State, would justify his arrest and committal for trial if the offense had been committed there, including evidence proving the person requested is the person to whom the warrant of arrest refers.

(4) When the request relates to a person already convicted, it must be accompanied by the judgement of conviction and sentence passed against him in the territory of the requesting State, by a statement showing how much of the sentence has not been served, and by evidence proving that the person requested is the person to whom the sentence refers.

Article 10

(1) Extradition shall be granted only if the evidence be found sufficient, according to the laws of the place where the person sought shall be found, either to justify his committal for trial if the offense of which he is accused had been committed in its territory or to prove that he is the identical person convicted by the courts of the requesting State.

(2) The documentary evidence in support of a request for extradition or copies of these documents shall be admitted in evidence in the examination of the request for extradition when:

(a) in the case of a request emanating from Canada, they are authenticated by an officer of the Department of Justice of Canada and are certified by the principal diplomatic or consular officer of the United States in Canada;

(b) in the case of a request emanating from the United States for a person who is sought for prosecution, they are certified by a judicial authority or prosecutor who attests that the evidence is available for trial and is sufficient to justify prosecution under the law of the prosecuting jurisdiction. In the case of a request emanating from the United States for a person who is sought in connection with a conviction, the documents must be certified by a judicial, prosecuting or correctional authority who attests to the fact that the documents are accurate; or

(c) they are certified or authenticated in any other manner accepted by the law of the requested State.

Article 11

(1) In case of urgency a Contracting Party may apply for the provisional arrest [for no longer than 60 days] of the person sought pending the presentation of the request for extradition through the diplomatic channel. ...

Article 12

(1) A person extradited under the present Treaty shall not be detained, tried or punished in the territory of the requesting State for an offense other than that for which extradition has been granted nor be extradited by that State to a third State unless:

(i) He has left the territory of the requesting State after his extradition and has voluntarily returned to it;

(ii) He has not left the territory of the requesting State within thirty days after being free to do so; or

(iii) The requested State has consented to his detention, trial, punishment for an offense other than that for which extradition was granted or to his extradition to a third State, provided such other offense is covered by Article 2.

(2) The foregoing shall not apply to offenses committed after the extradition.

Article 13

(1) A requested State upon receiving two or more requests for the extradition of the same person either for the same offense, or for different offenses, shall determine to which of the requesting States it will extradite the person sought.

(2) Among the matters which the requested State may take into consideration are the possibility of a later extradition between the requesting States, the seriousness of each offense, the place where the offense was committed, the dates upon which the requests were received and the provisions of any extradition agreements between the requested State and the other requesting State or States.

Article 14

(1) The requested State shall promptly communicate to the requesting State through the diplomatic channel the decision on the request for extradition.

(2) If a warrant or order for the extradition of a person sought has been issued by the competent authority and he is not removed from the territory of the requested State within such time as may be prescribed by the laws of that State, he may be set at liberty and the requested State may subsequently refuse to extradite that person for the same offense.

Article 17 bis

If both Contracting Parties have jurisdiction to prosecute the person for the offense for which extradition is sought, the executive authority of the requested State, after consulting with the executive authority of the requesting State, shall decide whether to extradite the person or to submit the case to its competent authorities for the purpose of prosecution. In making its decision, the requested State shall consider all relevant factors, including but not limited to:

(i) the place where the act was committed or intended to be committed or the injury occurred or was intended to occur;

(ii) the respective interests of the Contracting Parties;

(iii) the nationality of the victim or the intended victim; and

(iv) the availability and location of the evidence.

NOTES

1) Canada's current *Extradition Act*, in the making for many years, came into force on June 17, 1999. It repealed the old *Extradition Act*[124] and the *Fugitive Offenders Act*,[125] and merged extradition with rendition to Commonwealth countries into one comprehensive statute. It created a uniform procedure that will allow for the extradition of fugitives to states and to entities such as the *Ad Hoc* Criminal Tribunals for the former Yugoslavia and Rwanda, as well as to the new International Criminal Court (ICC).[126] Some of the highlights are that extradition from Canada is possible on the basis of bilateral or multilateral treaties or, in the absence of treaty, where a state or entity is designated under the schedule to the Act or where a special agreement is in place. The previous Act specified the crimes for which extradition might be granted in a cumbersome list. Extradition is now based on the criminality of the conduct in both states and a prescribed period of imprisonment or other deprivation of liberty for a maximum of two years or more, or by a more severe punishment subject to a relevant extradition agreement. The requirements for the forms of evidence that can be used to substantiate the *prima facie* case have also been modified. Do they satisfy the protections afforded an accused under the Canadian *Charter of Rights*?[127]

2) Note that the "record of the case" approach, as set out in sections 32 and 33 of the *Extradition Act* above, has already been incorporated into some of Canada's bilateral extradition treaties with civil law countries. For example, article 10(c) of the Extradition Treaty Between Canada and France[128] provides:

---

124 R.S.C. 1985, c. E-23, as amended S.C. 1992, c. 13.

125 R.S.C. 1985, c. F-32, as amended.

126 See the Act s. 2. The ICTY and the ICTR are already included in the Schedule.

127 See *United Mexican States v. Ortega*, 2005 BCCA 270; A.W. LaForest, "The Balance Between Liberty and Comity in the Evidentiary Requirements Applicable to Extradition Proceedings" (2002) 28 Queen's L.J. 95.

128 Can. T.S. 1989 No. 38.

[O]riginals or certified true copies of exhibits statements, depositions, minutes, reports, appendices or any other document, whether received, gathered or obtained in France or in some other place, shall be admitted in evidence as proof of the facts contained therein, if a "juge d'instruction" certifies that they were obtained in accordance with French law and they appear in the "dossier d'instruction" on the basis of which the arrest was issued.[129]

3) When a foreign state requests extradition from Canada, does it matter whether the offence was committed in that state or not? If a Canadian citizen assaulted and injured a Swiss citizen in France and returned to Canada, would an extradition request by Switzerland be within the scope of the Canadian Act? Should the request be granted? See sections 2, 5, and 47.[130]

4) The requirement of double criminality is of utmost importance for the accused individual. It is the principle that the acts committed must be a criminal offence in both the requesting and requested state.[131] It is usually included in extradition treaties. See the Canada–U.S. Treaty, article 2. Do sections 3(1), 3(2), and 29(1) of the *Extradition Act* satisfy this requirement?

5) Another important consideration in this context is the doctrine of "specialty" (or "speciality"), which provides that an extradited individual cannot be tried in the receiving state for any offences except those for which he or she was extradited. This principle, like double criminality, usually appears in extradition treaties;[132] see Article 12 of the Canada–U.S. Treaty. The right of specialty for individuals being extradited from Canada is provided for in section 80 of the Act.

6) Domestic extradition proceedings are often referred to as a "two-stage process," and the separate responsibilities of the extradition judge and the Minister of Justice are clearly identified in the Act. Notice that the accused has both a right of appeal from the extradition judge's order of committal[133] and a right of review of the Minister's decision. Does the Act achieve an appropriate balance among the protection of the accused, the authority of the extradition judge, and the discretion of the Minister?

In addition, under section 15, when the Justice Minister receives a request from an extradition partner, he or she must initially decide that the outlined conditions are met before issuing an "authority to proceed."

---

129 Regarding the constitutionality of the record of the case approach, see *United States of America v. Yang* (2001), 157 C.C.C. (3d) 225 (O.C.A.).

130 See under the old Act, *Re Federal Republic of Germany and Rauca* (1982), 38 O.R. (2d) 705; 141 D.L.R. (3d) 412 (H.C.), aff'd. 41 O.R. (2d) 225; 145 D.L.R. (3d) 638 (sub nom. *R. v. Rauca*). Compare *United States v. Lépine*, [1994] 1 S.C.R. 286.

131 S.A. Williams, "The Double Criminality Rule and Extradition" (1991) 15 Nova L. Rev. 581.

132 It has been opined that specialty is "a rule of general international law" (T. Stein, "Extradition," in R. Bernhardt, ed. 2 Encyc. Pub. Int. L. (1995) 327 at 330). See also *R. v. Parisien* (1988), 41 C.C.C. (3d) 223 (S.C.C.) at 227-228 per LaForest J.

133 The Supreme Court has spoken to the Charter-based procedural rights of the fugitive during the extradition hearing phase in, e.g., *United States v. Kwok*, [2001] 1 S.C.R. 532; *United States v. Cobb*, [2001] 1 S.C.R. 587; *United States v. Shulman*, [2001] 1 S.C.R. 616; *United States v. Tsioubris*, [2001] 1 S.C.R. 613.

7) There are a number of reasons why extradition may be refused apart from lack of fulfillment of the substantive grounds discussed above.[134] For example, some states refuse to extradite their own nationals.[135] Canada has taken the position that although to do so *prima facie* violates the right of a Canadian citizen to remain in Canada as provided in section 6(1) of the *Charter of Rights and Freedoms*,[136] extradition is a reasonable limitation of that right pursuant to section 1 of the Charter, even where there is a jurisdictional basis for prosecution in Canada.[137]

8) As to other grounds of refusal and how they have been dealt with in Canada, see *United States v. Schmidt*[138] where the Supreme Court of Canada held that double jeopardy was a defence to be raised at trial and not a matter for the requested state; and *Argentina v. Mellino*[139] and *United States v. Allard and Charette*[140] concerning unreasonable delay.

9) Extradition of individuals to face the death penalty abroad has been an especially controversial issue. In *Kindler v. Canada (Minister of Justice)*[141] and *Reference Re Ng Extradition (Canada)*,[142] the Supreme Court permitted extradition to a state that imposes the death penalty.[143] In 2001 the Court reversed this position, finding in the case of *United States v. Burns and Rafay* that extradition to face the death penalty would violate section 7 of the Charter except in exceptional circumstances.[144] The ruling meant that the government would be constitutionally required to seek assurances from the requested state, before extraditing, that the death penalty would not be applied. The Canada–U.S.

134　And see S.A. Williams, "Nationality, Double Jeopardy, Prescription and the Death Sentence as Bases for Refusing Extradition" (1991) 62 R.I.D.P. 259.

135　See J.-G. Castel & S.A. Williams, "The Extradition of Canadian Citizens and Sections 1 and 6(1) of the Canadian Charter of Rights and Freedoms" (1987) 25 Can. Y.B. Int'l L. 263.

136　As enacted by the *Canada Act 1982* (U.K.) 1982, c. 11.

137　See *Re Federal Republic of Germany v. Rauca*, *supra* note 130; *U.S. v. Cotroni*, [1989] 1 S.C.R. 1469 and *U.S. v. El Zein*, [1989] 1 S.C.R. 1469. Although the last two cases were heard separately in the Quebec courts, the Supreme Court of Canada consolidated them because they presented the same issue—namely, whether extradition was a reasonable limitation on Charter freedoms. The fugitives could have been prosecuted in Canada rather than extradited to the United States because elements of the offences occurred in both states. They sought to be distinguished from *Rauca*, since at that time prosecution in Canada for war crimes committed in World War II was not possible.

138　[1987] 1 S.C.R. 500. And see A.J. Spencer, "Fugitive Rights: The Role of the Charter in Extradition Cases" (1993) U.T. Fac. L.R. 53.

139　[1987] 1 S.C.R. 536. The Supreme Court held that the Charter right to a trial within a reasonable period of time in Canada is not infringed by delay in making the extradition request by the foreign state.

140　[1987] 1 S.C.R. 564.

141　[1991] 2 S.C.R. 779.

142　[1991] 2 S.C.R. 858.

143　See S.A. Williams, "Extradition and the Death Penalty Exception in Canada: Resolving the Ng and Kindler Cases" (1991) 13 Loyola of Los Angeles Int. & Comp. L.J. 799; and J.W. O'Reilly, "Case Comment: Ng and Kindler" (1992) 37 McGill L.J. 837. See also W.A. Schabas, *The Abolition of the Death Penalty in International Law*, 3d ed. (2002).

144　See R.J. Currie, "Charter Without Borders? The Supreme Court of Canada, Transnational Crime and Constitutional Rights and Freedoms" (2004) 27 Dal. L.J. 235.

Treaty makes specific provision for this potential; what about treaties that do not? Will the constraints of the Charter cause Canada to breach an interstate obligation to extradite?

10) The international law issues raised by the intersection of extradition and human rights are also profound.[145] If Canada extradites a fugitive to face human rights violations in the requesting state, would Canada itself be violating its obligations under international human rights instruments, such as the *International Covenant on Civil and Political Rights*? There is a line of international case law that suggests the answer is yes.[146] This was also the opinion of the U.N. Human Rights Committee, which ruled in 2003 that Canada had breached its obligations under the ICCPR when it extradited a fugitive to face the death penalty in Pennsylvania in 1998.[147] Similar issues may pertain to other modes of criminal cooperation, such as mutual legal assistance, described above in section A.4.[148]

11) Are there other human rights norms that should preclude extradition? If so, which ones?[149]

3. Admission and Exclusion of Aliens[150]

Admission of Immigrants and Refugees

States are free at customary international law to control the movement of foreigners, as opposed to nationals, across their frontiers.[151] Citizens have a right of entry to their national state: see the Universal Declaration of Human Rights article 13 and the International Covenant on Civil and Political Rights article 12, both reproduced in the Documentary Supplement and discussed in Chapter 12. However, states have ultimate control over the determination of who is a national: refer to Chapter 8, "Nationality," Section A on "Individuals." Control over the movement of aliens is a jealously protected

---

145 See J. Dugard & C. van den Wyngaert, "Reconciling Extradition With Human Rights" (1998) 92 A.J.I.L. 187.

146 Most notably the decision of the European Court of Human Rights in *Soering v. United Kingdom* (1989), Eur. Ct. H.R. (Ser. A) 161.

147 *Judge v. Canada* (No. 829/1998), U.N. Doc. CCPR/C/78/D/829/1998, decision date August 13, 2003. The Committee had made a similar finding with regard to Kenneth Ng; see *Ng v. Canada*, UN Doc. CCPR/C/49/D/469/1991.

148 See R.J. Currie, "Human Rights and International Mutual Legal Assistance: Resolving the Tension" (2000) 11 Crim. L.F. 143.

149 See *Canada (Minister of Justice) v. Pacificador* (2002), 60 O.R. (3d) 685 (C.A.), leave to appeal dismissed, S.C.C. Bulletin, 2003, p. 286.

150 A. Grahl-Madsen, *The Status of Refugees in International Law* (1966/1972) 2 vols.; G.S. Goodwin-Gill, *International Law and the Movement of Persons between States* (1978); E.M. Morgan, *International Law and the Canadian Courts* (1990) c. 3; R. Plender, *International Migration Law*, 2d ed. (1988); Sir R. Jennings & Sir A. Watts, eds., *Oppenheim's International Law*, 9th ed. (1992) 896-948; A.C. Evans, "The Political Status of Aliens in International Law, Municipal Law and European Law" (1981) 30 I.C.L.Q. 20; and L.C. Green, "Immigration, Extradition, and Asylum in Canadian Law and Practice," in R. St. J. Macdonald, D.M. Johnston, & G.L. Morris, eds., *Canadian Perspectives on International Law and Organization* (1974) at 244.

151 *Oppenheim's International Law*, *supra* note 150 at 897.

aspect of state sovereignty. Immigration is frequently a sensitive political matter. Mass displacement and migration are major problems in the world today. Thus the power to regulate immigration is very important. It was a major concern of the United States motivating introduction of the provision in the Charter of the League of Nations article 15, and now carried over as article 2(7) of the U.N. Charter, against intervention in matters essentially within the domestic jurisdiction of the state.[152] Management of the flow of immigrants is viewed as quintessentially a matter of domestic jurisdiction. As Hyndman has commented: "[s]tates the world over consistently have exhibited great reluctance to give up their sovereign right to decide which persons will, and which will not, be admitted to their territory, and given a right to settle there. They have refused to agree to international instruments which would impose on them duties to make grants of asylum."[153] A strong restatement of this right was made by the Privy Council in *Attorney General for Canada v. Cain*.[154]

The power to admit or exclude aliens is exercised at the border by the familiar techniques of passport inspections, visa requirements, and immigration controls. To discourage foreigners from even seeking entry, states may impose penalties on transportation companies, naval blockades, and discretionary immigration rules.

The sovereign right to exclude aliens is, however, subject to exceptions by agreement. Four classes of exceptional migrants are significant. First, international commerce demands the transnational movement of business people for the conduct of trade and investment. There is a long history of bilateral treaties of friendship and the more specific treaties of freedom, commerce, and navigation that grant reciprocal rights of entry and establishment to each other state's nationals for business purposes. The following articles of the United States–France Convention on Establishment exhibits provisions typical of these kinds of agreements:[155]

Article I

Each High Contracting Party shall accord equitable treatment to nationals and companies of the other High Contracting Party, both as to their persons and as to their property, enterprises and other interests, and shall assure them within its territories full legal and judicial protection.

Article II

1. Nationals of either High Contracting Party shall, subject to the laws relating to the entry and sojourn of aliens, be permitted to enter the territories of the other High Contracting Party, to travel therein freely, and to reside therein at places of their choice. They shall in

---

152 See D.H. Miller, *The Drafting of the Covenant* (1928) at 276. U.N. Charter article 2(7) is reproduced in the Documentary Supplement.

153 P. Hyndman, "Refugees Under International Law with a Reference to the Concept of Asylum" (1986) 60 Aus. L.J. 148 at 153.

154 [1906] A.C. 542 at 546. See also *Johnstone v. Pedlar*, [1921] 2 A.C. 262 (H.L.); *Gana v. Minister of Manpower and Immigration*, [1970] S.C.R. 699; and *Prata v. Minister of Manpower and Immigration*, [1976] 1 S.C.R. 376.

155 (1960) 11 U.S.T. 2398; T.I.A.S. No. 4625. See H. Walker Jr., "Modern Treaties of Friendship, Commerce and Navigation" (1958) 41 Minn. L.R. 805. See also NAFTA, c. 16 for the conditions of business travel between Canada, the United States, and Mexico, in (1993) 32 I.L.M. 296.

particular be permitted to enter the territories of the other High Contracting Party and to remain therein, for the purpose of:

(a) carrying on trade between the territories of the two High Contracting Parties and engaging in related commercial activities;

(b) developing and directing the operations of an enterprise in which they have invested, or in which they are actively in the process of investing, a substantial amount of capital.

2. Nationals of each High Contracting Party shall enjoy, within the territories of the other High Contracting Party, freedom of conscience, of worship, of information and of the press.

3. The provisions of the present Article shall be subject to the right of either High Contracting Party to take measures that are necessary for the maintenance of public order and for the protection of public health, morals, and safety. ...

Article V

1. Nationals and companies of either High Contracting Party shall be accorded national treatment with respect to engaging in all types of commercial, industrial, financial and other activities for gain within the territories of the other High Contracting Party, whether directly or through the intermediary of an agent or of any other natural or juridical person. Accordingly, such nationals and companies shall be permitted within such territories:

(a) to establish and to maintain branches, agencies, offices, factories and other establishments appropriate to the conduct of their business;

(b) to organize companies under the general company laws of such other High Contracting Party, and to acquire majority interests in companies of such other High Contracting Party;

(c) to control and manage the enterprises which they have established or acquired. Moreover, the enterprises which they control, whether in the form of an individual proprietorship, of a company or otherwise, shall, in all that relates to the conduct of the activities thereof, be accorded treatment no less favourable than that accorded like enterprises controlled by nationals and companies of such other High Contracting Party.

2. Each High Contracting Party reserves the right to determine the extent to which aliens may, within its territories, create, control, manage or acquire interests in, enterprises engaged in communications, air or water transport, banking involving depository or fiduciary functions, exploitation of the soil or other natural resources, and the production of electricity. ...

Article XIV

1. The term "national treatment" means treatment accorded to nationals and companies of either High Contracting Party within the territories of the other High Contracting Party upon terms no less favourable than the treatment therein accorded, in like situations, to the nationals and companies, as the case may be, of such other High Contracting Party.

A second class of welcome foreigners are diplomats. The conduct of interstate relations requires the exchange of diplomatic and other representatives. Indeed, to perform effectively these state agents are accorded, in addition to admission and accreditation to the host state, rights of immunity and inviolability. See the discussion of "Diplomatic Immunities" in Chapter 5, Section D.

Third, the European Union (EU) has created a unique level of transnational integration between member states for the transfer of goods, services, and people. The 1986 *Single*

European Act[156] established at the end of 1992 a single market that included, *inter alia*, the free movement without border restrictions of all people physically within the EU area. This level of unrestrained transnational activity goes far beyond the typical customs union that, though it reduces or eliminates border taxes and quotas, does not necessarily end frontier inspections and other controls. The North American Free Trade Agreement, for instance, is a kind of customs union enlarged by the inclusion of freer movement in services and investments, and some special supranational dispute resolution mechanisms. But it does not grant freedom of movement of people across the Canadian–American border, apart from the temporary entry for individuals on business.

The fourth significant group of admissible migrants are refugees.[157] Millions of people in all continents of the world are displaced and stateless. The international community first addressed the problems of these individuals in an organized multilateral way in the face of the flood of European refugees after World War II. The principal instrument then created and now still is the following convention.

Convention on the Status of Refugees

(1951) 189 U.N.T.S. 138; Can. T.S. 1969 No. 6, as amended by Protocol Relating to the Status of Refugees (1967) 606 U.N.T.S. 267; Can. T.S. 1969 No. 29

Article 1

A. For the purposes of the present Convention, the term "refugee" shall apply to any person who: ...

(2) ... owing to well-founded fear of being persecuted for reasons of race, religion, nationality, membership of a particular social group or political opinion, is outside the country of his nationality and is unable or, owing to such fear, is unwilling to avail himself of the protection of that country; or who, not having a nationality and being outside the country of his former habitual residence as a result of such events, is unable or, owing to such fear, is unwilling to return to it. ...

Article 32

1. The Contracting States shall not expel a refugee lawfully in their territory save on grounds of national security or public order.

2. The expulsion of such a refugee shall be only in pursuance of a decision reached in accordance with due process of law. Except where compelling reasons of national security otherwise require, the refugee shall be allowed to submit evidence to clear

---

156 [1997] O.J.L. 169, reprinted in (1986) 25 I.L.M.. 503. See also P. Weiss, *The Refugee Convention 1951: The Travaux Préparatoires Analysed* (1995); M. Zieck, *UNHCR and Voluntary Repatriation of Refugees* (1997); and P. Zambelli, *The Refugee Convention: A Compendium of Canadian and American Cases* (1999).

157 G.S. Goodwin-Gill, *The Refugee in International Law*, 2d ed. (1996); J.C. Hathaway, *The Law of Refugee Status* (1991); D.A. Martin, ed., *The New Asylum Seekers: Refugee Law in the 1980s* (1988); and A.E. Nash, *Human Rights and the Protection of Refugees under International Law* (1988).

himself, and to appeal to and be represented for the purpose before competent authority or a person or persons specially designated by the competent authority.

3. The Contracting States shall allow such a refugee a reasonable period within which to seek legal admission into another country. ...

Article 33

1. No Contracting States shall expel or return ("refouler") a refugee in any manner whatsoever to the frontiers of territories where his life or freedom would be threatened on account of his race, religion, nationality, membership of a particular social group or political opinion.

2. The benefit of the present provision may not, however, be claimed by a refugee whom there are reasonable grounds for regarding as a danger to the security of the country in which he is, or who, having been convicted by a final judgement of a particularly serious crime, constitutes a danger to the community of that country.

NOTES

1) The Refugee Convention does not confer upon refugees a right of entry to any state but, once admitted, they are guaranteed protection and other human rights intended to encourage their resettlement.

2) The definition of a "refugee" under the Convention is very restricted. First, only a person who "is outside the country of his nationality" qualifies. A displaced person within his or her own country is not protected by the Convention. Second, the applicant must have a fear of persecution that is well founded. Discrimination or prosecution in general is insufficient. These criteria exclude millions of people who seek refuge as a result of fleeing from natural disasters or civil war, and other millions of "economic migrants" who want to escape from poverty and starvation to a better life for themselves and their families. In addition, the fear of persecution must be based on race, religion, or nationality or membership of a particular group. The last category has provided, as intended, expanding grounds for applying the Convention.

3) In practice, the scope of refugee status has been expanded in several ways.[158] Organized international assistance to refugees is provided by the United Nations High Commissioner for Refugees (UNHCR). Although the original terms of reference of the High Commissioner described refugees in language similar to that in the Refugee Convention,[159] the General Assembly has authorized the Office to aid all kinds of involuntary migrants. "The essential criterion of refugee status under UNHCR auspices has come to be simply the existence of human suffering consequent to forced migration."[160] The work of the UNHCR, however, is to provide immediate material assistance and support in finding

---

158 See Hathaway, *supra* note 157 at 11. See also the enhancement by the Treaty of European Union (Maastricht Treaty), especially article K, O.J. C191 (1992) 31 I.L.M. 247.

159 *Statute of the Office of the United Nations High Commissioner for Refugees*, GA Res. 428 (V), UN GAOR, 5th Sess., Supp. No. 20, U.N. Doc. A/1775 (1950) 46.

160 Hathaway, *supra* note 157 at 13.

places of resettlement for refugees: it does not grant admission and asylum, for these are matters within the territorial authority of the receiving states. Yet states are free to apply their own expanded definition of refugees and on occasion many do so. This second way of extending the status of refugee frequently takes the selective form of a special program for a population group following a broadly based disturbance. The resettlement of the Vietnamese "boat people" in the 1970s is such an example.

4) The principal protection for a Convention refugee is the right of non-refoulement or not to be returned to the country of actual or potential persecution. See article 33.[161] The principal obligation of the receiving state is to help the refugee become resettled. It is not obliged to afford refugees opportunities to immigrate and become naturalized citizens, although the practice is common. The difference in status can be significant since the non-citizen refugee may, for instance, be allowed only limited political rights, be excluded from professional and other types of employment, and be restricted in acquiring property. In addition, a receiving state, stressed by the flow of refugees, may try to move them to a "safe" third state such as one of the countries of transit in their flight.

5) The most pressing need for millions of uprooted and migrant people is territorial asylum, but no general right to asylum is yet ensured by international law.[162] The Universal Declaration of Human Rights article 14, reproduced in the Documentary Supplement, states only that "[e]veryone has the right to seek and enjoy in other countries asylum from persecution." This provision does not oblige states to grant asylum, even if the Universal Declaration can be said to have achieved the status of customary international law. A U.N. conference on territorial asylum was held in 1977 but it failed to conclude a convention. The preoccupation of participating states appeared to be the safeguarding of their sovereign right to determine questions of asylum.

Territorial asylum is distinct from diplomatic asylum, which is the practice of affording a temporary place of retreat within one's foreign embassy to nationals of the host state, typically political figures. Technically the foreign state has no authority in the territorial state to provide refuge, but, since its diplomatic mission is inviolable by the host state, a kind of asylum is the practical result. However, there is no right for the fugitive to safe conduct out of the country.[163] See the *Asylum Case* discussed under customary sources of law in Chapter 3, Section C.2 on "Regional or Special Customary Law." Territorial asylum is incidentally a corollary of extradition in that a state, in refusing to surrender a fugitive to a requesting state on political or compassionate grounds, effectively grants refuge and protection.

6) Canada is a party to the Refugee Convention and in addition applies its own enhanced definition of refugees.[164] The Convention is implemented by the *Immigration*

---

161   And see G. Stenberg, *Non-Expulsion and Non-Refoulement* (1989).

162   See, generally, G.S. Goodwin-Gill, *supra* note 157 at c. 5; A. Grahl-Madsen, *Territorial Asylum* (1980) and J. Hucker, "Migration and Resettlement under International Law," in R. St. J. Macdonald, D.M. Johnston, & G.L. Morris, eds., *The International Law and Policy of Human Welfare* (1978) at 327.

163   *Haya de la Torre Case*, [1951] I.C.J. Rep. 71.

164   For an overview of Canadian law through 1987, see J.C. Hathaway, "Selective Concern: An Overview of Refugee Law in Canada" (1988) 33 McGill L.J. 676.

and Refugee Protection Act (IRPA).[165] Convention refugees have a right to remain in Canada, unless found to be serious criminals or security risks.[166] In the security-conscious years since 2001, there have been a number of high-profile cases of refugees whom the Canadian government has sought to return to their national states of origin because their association with terrorist organizations presented a security risk in Canada. The case of *Suresh* was especially notable because he successfully argued that the *Convention Against Torture*, which Canada has ratified, should constrain the government's authority to return a refugee who poses a security risk if to do so would likely deport him to torture. See the report of *Suresh v. Canada (Minister of Citizenship and Immigration)* reproduced in Chapter 4, Section D on "Jus Cogens in Canadian Law."

7) The Canadian legislation also links refugee status with immigration. Convention refugees have a right to be granted the standing of landed immigrants, which may mature into full Canadian citizenship.[167] Since *Singh*,[168] refugee claimants have also been afforded the protections of the *Canadian Charter of Rights and Freedoms*. They are entitled to the usual legal rights of individuals in Canada and cannot be deported or excluded without appropriate oral hearings according to Canadian standards of procedural fairness.

8) "The majority of persons admitted to Canada as refugees do not meet the Convention definition."[169] This is because the narrow definition is strictly applied by the courts, which have emphasized the need for persuasive evidence of individualized persecution. However, IRPA authorizes the Governor in Council to designate classes of people that may be granted admission, and thus asylum, "in accordance with Canada's humanitarian tradition with respect to the displaced and the persecuted."[170] This power to extend the scope of refugee status has been exercised from time to time for a variety of classes of migrants, such as Vietnamese "boat people" and self-exiled persons from former socialist states of Eastern Europe. The self-exiled persons class was particularly liberal since applicants needed only show that they were unwilling to return to their former country. No grounds of persecution or suffering were required; it was enough that the individual wanted to come to Canada. In the 1990s, refuge was offered to individuals from selected countries, whether they were outside the state or still within it, provided that they were seriously and personally affected by internal armed conflict or massive human rights abuses in their homeland. The countries named were Bosnia-Herzegovina, Cambodia, Colombia, Croatia, El Salvador, Guatemala, Liberia, and Sudan.[171] Although the availability of asylum for these extended classes of refugees to Canada may be praised for their generosity, they may also be criticized for being a partial and political selection of a few groups of displaced persons from many others equally deserving of attention.

---

165 S.C. 2001, c. 27, as amended.

166 *Ibid.*, ss. 101(1)(f) and 115(2).

167 *Ibid.*, s. 21(2).

168 *Re Singh and the Minister of Employment and Immigration*, [1985] 1 S.C.R. 177.

169 Hathaway, *supra* note 164 at 708.

170 Section 12(3).

171 SOR/97-183, as am. SOR/98-271.

Deportation of Aliens

As part of its territorial sovereignty, a state may arrest and deport illegal immigrants. The class includes not only individuals who have found their way into the country without passing through the immigration process but also those who attained admission by fraudulent application. States also reserve the right to expel legal immigrants, especially those who, before they become citizens, commit serious crimes or constitute national security risks. There are grounds to argue, however, that the state's discretion is not wholly unfettered, in that it must not be exercised in an arbitrary or discriminatory manner. See *Rankin v. Iran*, reproduced in Chapter 10, Section B.2(a) on "Protection of the Person: Admission and Expulsion."[172]

The power to deport unwanted aliens is limited in two respects. First, the expulsion must be undertaken in a manner that comports with international law. There have long been asserted some minimum standards for the treatment of aliens at customary international law. Refer to the discussion on the "Responsibility for Injuries to Aliens," in Chapter 10, Section B.1. More recently, there has grown up a large and much stronger body of international human rights that are equally applicable to nationals and foreigners within the territory of a state. See the Universal Declaration of Human Rights and the International Covenant on Civil and Political Rights, especially article 13, both reproduced in the Documentary Supplement and discussed in Chapter 12, Sections A.1 and B.2. In addition, national human rights legislation, such as the *Canadian Charter of Rights and Freedoms*, may afford further procedural protections in the way an alien is treated.

A second practical consideration in expelling aliens is that some other state must be willing to receive them. Since individuals have a right of entry to their national state, it is bound to receive its deported citizens. However, when the deportees have been stripped of their nationality or otherwise become stateless, it may be practically impossible to deport them.

Deportation as Disguised Extradition

In a case where Canada has custody of an alleged criminal but extradition is not possible, what are Canada's options? Based on the *Libman* case, discussed above in Section A.3 on "Scope of Territorial Jurisdiction," or if the offence is an international crime, Canada may itself have jurisdiction to prosecute. If that is not the situation, deportation may be an option, provided the person is not a Canadian citizen. The question then arises whether the person may be deported to the state that would like to prosecute.

---

172   And see *Oppenheim's International Law*, *supra* note 150 at 940; G.S. Goodwin-Gill, *supra* note 150 at 306-7.

Re Shepherd and Minister of Employment & Immigration
(1989), 70 O.R. (2d) 765 (C.A.)

[Shepherd, an American, had been charged with two rapes, two murders, and an aggravated assault on a police officer. He had escaped while awaiting trial in the United States and had come to Canada, where he avoided detection for 10 years. Upon eventually being identified he was ordered deported. Among other issues raised was the question of deportation being used as a disguised form of extradition. In dismissing the appeal, the Ontario Court of Appeal repeated the judgment of the lower court as follows:]

AUSTIN J.: ... The theme underlying many of the arguments raised on behalf of Shepherd was that this was really what the cases have referred to as a "disguised extradition." That is for reasons unknown to Shepherd, Canadian authorities decided to take the initiative and to bring deportation proceedings against Shepherd, not for the purpose of ridding the country of him, but for the purpose turning him over to American ... authorities. By taking the initiative, it is argued, Canada avoids having to consider art. 6 of the extradition treaty [the discretion to refuse extradition on account of the death penalty]. Looking at it from Shepherd's perspective, he is deprived of the possible benefit of art. 6.

... [From the case law] the following principles emerge:

1. If the purpose of the exercise is to deport the person because his presence is not conducive to the public good, that is a legitimate exercise of the power of deportation.

2. If the purpose is to surrender the person as a fugitive criminal to a state because it asked for him, that is not a legitimate exercise of the power of deportation.

3. It is open to the courts to inquire whether the purpose of the government was lawful or otherwise.

4. The onus is on the party alleging an unlawful exercise of power. It is a heavy onus.

5. To succeed, it would be necessary to hold that the Minister did not genuinely consider it in the public interest to expel the person in question.

6. The adoption of the Charter has not lessened the onus.

... [T]here is no evidence that this is an extradition in disguise ... . There is little ... to negative the proposition that the purpose of the exercise is to deport Shepherd because his presence here is not conducive to the public good. ... [There is nothing] to suggest that, from a Canadian point of view, the purpose of the proceedings was and is to surrender Shepherd as a fugitive criminal to a state because it asked for him. There is nothing to suggest that the Minister did not genuinely consider it in the public interest to expel Shepherd. There is, therefore, no basis upon which I can conclude that this is an extradition in disguise.[173]

---

173 See also *R. v. Broxton Prison (Governor), ex parte Soblen*, [1962] 3 All E.R. 641 (C.A.); and *Halm v. Canada (Minister of Employment & Immigration)* (1995), 104 F.T.R. 81 (F.C.T.D.).

CHAPTER TEN

State Responsibility

The rise of rules on international responsibility[1] is both a consequence of and a precondition for the emergence of an international legal system imposing positive obligations upon states. As such, state responsibility is one of the most fundamental principles of public international law, coextensive with the doctrine of the sovereign equality of states. Initially developed on the basis of compensation paid by states for injury to the person or property of aliens, the principle has now evolved to provide very broadly that every internationally wrongful act of a state entails its responsibility. Beyond this rather general principle, many questions are left open in the articulation of specific rules on state responsibility. This chapter presents the main elements of the general theory of state responsibility (Section A), and of the special regime of responsibility for injuries to aliens (Section B), before turning to the requirements for enforcing claims in that respect (Section C), and finally to the invocation of state responsibility (Section D).

A. GENERAL THEORY OF RESPONSIBILITY

The law of state responsibility concerns what happens when things go wrong and states behave in a manner that is inconsistent with their international obligations. To attempt to devise a general theory of state responsibility that will apply to all of international law is

---

1   In general, see C.F. Amerasinghe, *State Responsibility for Injuries to Aliens* (1967); F.G. Dawson & I.L. Head, *International Law, National Tribunals and the Rights of Aliens* (1971); F.V. Garcia-Amador, "State Responsibility—Some New Problems" (1958) 94 Hague Recueil 369; R.B. Lillich, *International Claims: Their Adjudication by National Commissions* (1962); R.B. Lillich & G.A. Christenson, *International Claims: Their Preparation and Presentation* (1962); R.B. Lillich, ed., *International Law of State Responsibility for Injuries to Aliens* (1983); R.B. Lillich, ed., *The Valuation of Nationalised Property in International Law* (1972-87) 4 vols.; C.H.P. Law, *The Local Remedies Rule in International Law* (1961); M.M. Whiteman, *Damages in International Law* (1937 and 1943) 3 vols.; *Restatement of the Law (Third), Foreign Relations Law of the United States* (1987), vol. 2, paras. 711-13; M. Spinedi & B. Simma, eds., *United Nations Codification of State Responsibility* (1987); I. Brownlie, *State Responsibility, Part I* (1983); S. Rosenne, ed., *The International Law Commission's Draft Articles on State Responsibility (Part 1, arts. 1-35)* (1991); Société française pour le droit international, *La responsabilité dans le système international* (1991); R. Lillich, D. Barstow McGraw, & D. Bederman, *The Iran-United States Tribunal: Its Contribution to the Law of State Responsibility* (1998); P. Klein, *La responsabilité des organisations internationales* (1998); R. Provost, *State Responsibility in International Law* (2002); J. Crawford, *The International Law Commission's Articles on State Responsibility—Introduction, Text and Commentaries* (2002).

to adhere to a dichotomy between primary and secondary rules. Primary rules include all substantive obligations under international law—for example, the duty to protect diplomatic personnel or the duty to refrain from the military use of outer space. Secondary rules in turn articulate the conditions under which a primary rule will be considered to have been breached and map out the consequences of such a breach. They will cover issues such as "defences" or circumstances precluding wrongfulness and the type of reparation that an injured state may demand. Although there are grounds to dispute the possibility of fully separating a substantive rule and the conditions and consequences of its breach, most writing on international responsibility has adopted that structure, following in this the lead of the International Law Commission (ILC).[2]

The law of state responsibility is one of the areas of international law where the urge to make analogies with municipal law is strongest. While there are clear parallels between the concept and rationale for responsibility under international law and municipal law, the particular dynamics of relations between international legal subjects has meant that principles borrowed from tort law or delictual responsibility cannot be easily transposed onto the international plane. Basic distinctions found in most national legal systems—for instance, the difference between civil and criminal responsibility or between responsibility in contracts and in torts—have no echo in international law. In a fundamental way, municipal law on responsibility is shaped by its jurisdictional nature—that is, the fact that disputes on issues giving rise to responsibility are often decided by tribunals. In international law, on the contrary, state responsibility is essentially non-jurisdictional, since parties to a dispute rarely turn to a jurisdictional mechanism to settle the matter. The fact that the law of state responsibility is applied most regularly in a non-jurisdictional setting, in the context of unstructured diplomatic relations, and the fact that there are relatively few cases that articulate the elements of state responsibility, have had a clear impact on its substance. This has slowly started to change over the last several years, with the creation of a number of bilateral and multilateral international institutions, such as the Iran–US Claims Tribunal and International Centre for Settlement of Investment Disputes (ICSID) panels, mandated to apply principles of international responsibility.

The following section sketches out the basic elements of the law of state responsibility, starting with its fundamental principles (Section A.1), then addressing the more pointed questions of the basis of responsibility (Section A.2), the need for an action to be imputable to a state (Section A.3), the occurrence of circumstances that preclude wrongfulness (Section A.4), the consequences of state responsibility (Section A.5), and, finally, the several elements of aggravated responsibility (Section A.6).

1. General Principles

The work of the ILC on the topic of state responsibility has become a necessary reference point for any analysis of that field of international law. State responsibility was one of the

---

2   See [1970] Y.B.I.L.C. vol. 2 (Part 2) at 306. See J. Combacau & D. Alland, " 'Primary' and 'Secondary' Rules in the Law of State Responsibility: Categorizing International Obligations," [1985] Nethl. Int'l L. Rev. 81-109.

initial topics that the U.N. General Assembly identified in 1949 as warranting the attention of the ILC in its work of codification and progressive development of international law. Initially centred on issues touching on the responsibility of states for injuries to aliens, the work of the ILC was enlarged in the early 1960s to cover all areas of the law of state responsibility, with priority being given to the elaboration of the general rules governing international responsibility of states. During the 50 years that the ILC has spent looking at this issue, five successive Special Rapporteurs drafted a total of 33 reports touching on most areas of the law of state responsibility and adopting a wide spectrum of different approaches. These reports and the recorded debates of their recommendations by the ILC represent a most significant body of thinking on the issue. Indeed, it can be said that the critical approaches embodied in some of the reports and debates has muddled rather than clarified or codified the law. Although many issues remained unresolved, the ILC in 1996 adopted on first reading a full set of Draft Articles. Three issues in particular were identified as key to any further consideration of the Draft Articles: international crimes, the regime of countermeasures, and the settlement of disputes. After several more years of difficult and at times acrimonious negotiations, the ILC finally and formally adopted in August 2001 its Draft Articles on the Responsibility of States for Internationally Wrongful Acts. The United Nations General Assembly took note of and annexed the Draft Articles in resolution 56/83 in 2001, with appropriate language emphasizing the importance of the subject. Further consideration of the possible conversion of the Draft Articles into a convention was purposely postponed until the 59th session of the Assembly in 2004, leaving their content to be taken up in the normal processes of the application and development of international law, and in particular endorsement by international tribunals.[3] While the Draft Articles have already exerted considerable influence on international practice and judicial decisions, some elements remain controversial or unsettled, such as the regime for countermeasures, the definition of injury, the invocation of responsibility by individuals, and state responsibility in relation to international organizations.

International Law Commission, Draft Articles on the Responsibility of States for Internationally Wrongful Acts
Report of the International Law Commission on the Work of Its Fifty-third Session,
UN GAOR, 56th Sess., Supp. No. 10, U.N. Doc. A/56/10 (2001) chp. IV.E.1

Article 1
Responsibility of a State for Its Internationally Wrongful Acts

Every internationally wrongful act of a State entails the international responsibility of that State.

---

3   The Draft Articles, the reports of the Special Rapporteurs, and the debates of the ILC can be found online at <http://www.un.org/law/ilc>.

Article 2
Elements of an Internationally Wrongful Act of a State

There is an internationally wrongful act of a State when conduct consisting of an action or omission:
> (a) Is attributable to the State under international law; and
> (b) Constitutes a breach of an international obligation of the State.

Article 3
Characterization of an Act of a State as Internationally Wrongful

The characterization of an act of a State as internationally wrongful is governed by international law. Such characterization is not affected by the characterization of the same act as lawful by internal law.

NOTES

1) Articles 1-3 can be taken as an expression of existing basic principles on state responsibility, from which the Articles as a whole proceed. They have generated little debate either within or outside the ILC. They reflect the idea that a new relationship arises automatically under international law from the wrongdoing of one or several other states, as a direct consequence of any internationally wrongful act.

2) Article 1 refers to an "internationally wrongful *act*." This should not be taken as an indication that only positive actions by a state may trigger its responsibility. Both actions and omissions are covered by the provision, as is more clearly evident from the French version of the same expression "*fait internationalement illicite*" (rather than "*acte*"), as well as from Article 2. Note that Article 1 does not contain any reference to damage as a condition of international responsibility. It is generally accepted that, unlike most municipal legal systems, damage is not a required element of the international responsibility of states. Some international obligations may be violated without any material or even identifiable moral damage to any other states. Such obligations include many flowing from human rights and environmental law standards. International responsibility is thus not to be seen as merely a means to allocate risks but, more generally, as a tool to enforce standards of conduct imposed on states and an attempt to maintain the rule of law within the international sphere.

3) The Articles deal only with the responsibility of the State for conduct that is internationally wrongful, meaning that it contravenes an international legal norm. There may be cases where international law will impose on States the obligation to compensate for the injurious consequences of conduct that is not prohibited by international law. This is the issue of strict liability that arises most often with respect to international environmental norms. This is not covered by the Articles but rather by a parallel project still ongoing at the ILC.

4) Article 3 is a reflection of the autonomous nature of the international and municipal legal systems. It mirrors article 27 of the Vienna Convention of the Law of Treaties (reproduced in the Documentary Supplement) in providing that a State cannot escape its international responsibility by invoking the fact that its conduct is permitted or required by municipal law.

2. Basis of Responsibility

The question of the basis of international responsibility—that is, whether responsibility is grounded in risk, damage, or fault—has generated much confusion. ILC Articles 1 and 2, in their statement of the basic elements of international responsibility, do not refer to the mental state of the actor involved in the commission of an internationally wrongful act. The Articles thus take a neutral stance, neither requiring nor excluding fault or negligence as an element of international responsibility. It has been suggested that the Articles therefore represent an "objective" regime of responsibility, existing in isolation of the notions of fault or risk. Yet, reference to an "objective" responsibility is somewhat misleading, because it suggests that the responsibility of a State can be engaged even where it has done nothing wrong. This certainly does not correspond to the thrust of the ILC Articles, which establish neither an objective nor a subjective regime. The Articles codify a *sui generis* regime of responsibility, common to no other legal system, rooted in the requirement that the State has behaved in a manner inconsistent with its international legal obligations (Article 12). The basis of State responsibility is neither fault nor risk but rather the breach of an international obligation. That being said, the nature of many substantive international obligations will invite an assessment of the mental state of the actor in order to determine whether the latter's behaviour was in conformity with a given obligation.

Corfu Channel Case (Merits)
United Kingdom v. Albania
[1949] I.C.J. Rep. 4 at 17-23

[In October 1946, a group of British warships passed through the straight between the island of Corfu and Albania. While in Albanian territorial waters, two of the warships hit mines, causing heavy damage to the ships and killing a number of sailors. The case was submitted to the ICJ by *compromis*, to decide the potential responsibility of Albania for the minelaying and of the United Kingdom for its subsequent unilateral clearing of the mines in Albanian waters. The United Kingdom was unable to prove either that Albania had itself laid the mines or that it had colluded with Yugoslavia to do so.]

THE COURT: …

Finally, the United Kingdom Government put forward the argument that, whoever the authors of the minelaying were, it could not have been done without the Albanian Government's knowledge.

It is clear that knowledge of the minelaying cannot be imputed to the Albanian Government by reason merely of the fact that a minefield discovered in Albanian territorial waters caused the explosions of which the British warships were the victims. It is true, as international practice shows, that a State on whose territory or in whose waters an act contrary to international law has occurred, may be called upon to give an explanation. It is also true that a State cannot evade such a request by limiting itself to a reply that it is ignorant of the circumstances of the act and of its authors. The State may, up to a certain point, be bound to supply particulars of the use made by it of the means of information and inquiry at its disposal. But it cannot be concluded from the mere fact of the control exercised by a State over its territory and waters that that State necessarily knew, or ought to have known, of any unlawful act perpetrated therein, nor yet that it necessarily knew, or should have known, the authors. This fact, by itself and apart from other circumstances, neither involves *prima facie* responsibility nor shifts the burden of proof.

On the other hand, the fact of this exclusive territorial control exercised by a State within its frontiers has a bearing upon the methods of proof available to establish the knowledge of that State as to such events. By reason of this exclusive control, the other State, the victim of a breach of international law, is often unable to furnish direct proof of facts giving rise to responsibility. Such a State should be allowed a more liberal recourse to inferences of fact and circumstantial evidence. This indirect evidence is admitted in all systems of law, and its use is recognized by international decisions. It must be regarded as of special weight when it is based on a series of facts linked together and leading logically to a single conclusion.

The Court must examine therefore whether it has been established by means of indirect evidence that Albania had knowledge of minelaying in her territorial waters independently of any connivance on her part in this operation. The proof may be drawn from inferences of fact, provided that they leave *no room* for reasonable doubt. The elements of fact on which these inferences can be based may differ from those which are relevant to the question of connivance … .

From all the facts and observations mentioned above, the Court draws the conclusion that the laying of the minefield which caused the explosions on October 22nd, 1946, could not have been accomplished without the knowledge of the Albanian Government.

The obligations resulting for Albania from this knowledge are not disputed between the Parties. Counsel for the Albanian Government expressly recognized that [*translation*] "if Albania had been informed of the operation before the incidents of October 22nd, and in time to warn the British vessels and shipping in general of the existence of mines in the Corfu Channel, her responsibility would be involved … ."

The obligations incumbent upon the Albanian authorities consisted in notifying, for the benefit of shipping in general, the existence of a minefield in Albanian territorial waters and in warning the approaching British warships of the imminent danger to which the minefield exposed them. Such obligations are based, not on the Hague Convention of 1907, No. VIII, which is applicable in time of war, but on certain general and well-recognized principles, namely: elementary considerations of humanity, even more exacting in peace than in war; the principle of the freedom of maritime communication; and every State's obligation not to allow [knowingly][4] its territory to be used for acts contrary to the rights of other States … .

4   The word "knowingly" is put here between square brackets because it does not appear in the official French version of the decision of the Court, which reads "*l'obligation, pour tout État, de ne pas laisser utiliser son territoire aux fins d'actes contraires aux droits d'autres États.*" Interestingly, this mistake in translation is rarely noted in literature based on the English translation, and has given rise to distinct theories of state responsibility in the Francophone and Anglophone legal communities.

In fact, nothing was attempted by the Albanian authorities to prevent the disaster. These grave omissions involve the international responsibility of Albania.

The Court therefore reaches the conclusion that Albania is responsible under international law for the explosions which occurred on October 22nd, 1946 in Albanian waters, and for the damage and loss of human life which resulted from them, and that there is a duty upon Albania to pay compensation to the United Kingdom.

NOTES

1) In this case, the Court found that the substantive obligations invoked by the United Kingdom could not derive from the 1907 Hague Convention No. VIII but, rather, the obligations stemmed from general international law. This conclusion does not affect the responsibility of the regime, since there is no distinction to make in international law on the basis of the source of the obligation, whether treaty, customary, or other (ILC Draft Articles on State Responsibility, article 12). Likewise, there is no distinction to make between obligations stemming from bilateral or multilateral sources. Finally, international responsibility may result from any breach irrespective of its seriousness, from the most minor infringement to massive and systematic violations of peremptory norms.

2) What is the basis of Albania's responsibility in the Court's reasoning—the simple knowledge and inaction of that state or the breach of an implied duty of due diligence? Compare the following passage from Judge Krylov's dissent in the same case, after he had concluded that Albanian knowledge of the laying of mines had not been proven:[5]

But is it perhaps the case that the Albanian authorities *ought* to have seen or heard the minelaying operation?

To answer that question in the affirmative would, in my opinion, be to found Albania's responsibility on the notion of *culpa*.

I employ this term, subject to a reservation. I consider that the terms of Roman law and of contemporary civil and criminal law may be used in international law, but with a certain flexibility and without making too subtle distinctions. There is no need to transfer the distinctions which we sometimes meet in certain systems of municipal law into the system of international law. Is it then possible to found the international responsibility of Albania on the notion of *culpa*? Can it be argued that Albania failed to exercise the diligence required by international law to prevent the laying of mines in the Corfu Channel? Can it be asserted that international law involves an obligation for a coastal State to prevent the laying of mines in its territorial waters? I do not think so. However perfectly the coastal watch of a coastal State may be organized, the clandestine laying of mines cannot be considered impossible, especially, one might add, in peace time when the coastal guards are not in a state of instant readiness. But the history of maritime war provides plenty of examples of clandestine minelaying.

Here I have an observation to make. The responsibility of a State in consequence of an international delinquency presupposes, at the very least, *culpa* on the part of that State. One cannot found the international responsibility of a State on the argument that the act of which

---

5   [1949] I.C.J. Rep. 4 at 71-72.

the State is accused took place in its territory—terrestrial, maritime, or aerial territory. One cannot transfer the theory of risk, which is developed in the municipal law of some States, into the domain of international law. In order to found the responsibility of the State recourse must be had to the notion of *culpa*. I refer to the famous English author, Oppenheim. In his work on international law, he writes that the conception of international delinquency presumes that the State acted "wilfully and maliciously," or in cases of acts of omission "with culpable negligence" (Vol. 1, para. 154). Mr. Lauterpacht, the editor of the 7th edition (1948), adds that one can discern among modern authors a definite tendency to reject the theory of absolute responsibility and to found the responsibility of States on the notion of *culpa* (p. 311).

As I have already stated, I cannot find in the organization and functioning of the Albanian coastal watch—having regard to the limited resources of that small country—such a lack of diligence as might involve the responsibility of Albania. I do not find any evidence of *culpable* negligence. ...

In view of the foregoing and owing to the inadequacy of the evidence produced by the British, I am unable to reach the conclusion that Albania was responsible for the explosions which took place on October 22nd, 1946 in Albanian waters. One cannot condemn a State on the basis of probabilities. To establish international responsibility, one must have clear and indisputable facts. In the present case these facts are absent.

3) One of the many relevant elements in assessing the place of fault in international responsibility is whether the internationally wrongful act is directly imputable to the state, or whether responsibility derives from the state's failure to react to private acts threatening the rights of other states.

4) Cases of intentional commission of a wrongful act by state agents on instruction of their government pose relatively few problems. One example is the *Rainbow Warrior Case*, in which a Greenpeace ship was destroyed by twin bomb blasts while moored at Auckland, New Zealand in July 1985, resulting in the death of a Dutch national. Two French agents were subsequently arrested and charged with conspiracy to commit arson, wilfully damaging the *Rainbow Warrior* by means of explosives, and murder. They were convicted on these counts and sentenced to a total of 10 years in prison. The French Government's initial reaction was to deny responsibility for the agents' actions. Though it recognized the identity and affiliation of the agents, it conceded only that the agents were dispatched on a mission of surveillance. In September of that year, however, it was acknowledged that the two agents had in fact been acting at the behest of the French Directorate-General of External Security. This admission notwithstanding, the French Government protested that the agents should be exempted from blame (and returned to France) because they were acting under orders. The response of the Government of New Zealand was to pursue its rights under international law. The matter was subsequently referred to the U.N. Secretary-General for arbitration, with the result being payment of compensation to New Zealand in the amount of $7 million and release of the two agents into French custody on condition that they be "isolated" at a French Polynesian military establishment for three years and not be allowed to leave without the consent of both governments.[6]

---

6   *Rainbow Warrior Case (New Zealand v. France)* (1987) 26 I.L.M. 1946. See also M. Pugh, "Legal Aspects of the Rainbow Warrior Affair" (1987) 36 I.C.L.Q. 655; and R.S. Clark, "State Terrorism: Some

5) When state agents are not under instruction to act illegally, but still act within their mandate, there is usually no requirement to show fault or negligence on the part of the agent in order to establish international responsibility. Thus in the *Jessie, Thomas F. Bayard, and Pescawha Claim*,[7] the American and British Claims Arbitration Tribunal noted that the good faith of state officials offered no defence against an international claim and concluded that "any government is responsible to other governments for errors in judgment of its officials purporting to act within the scope of their duties and vested with power to enforce their demands." This is also the position adopted by President Verzijl in the *Caire Claim* decided by the Franco–Mexican Claims Commission, where he wrote that he was "interpreting these principles [of state responsibility] in accordance with the doctrine of 'objective responsibility' of the state, that is responsibility for the commanded acts of officials or organs of a state, despite the absence of fault on its part."[8]

6) When the illegal acts are carried out by non-state actors and their action can in no way be imputed to the state, proof of some fault or negligence on the part of the state will usually be required in order to engage its responsibility. For example, the ICJ in the *U.S. Diplomatic and Consular Staff in Tehran Case* found that Iran had breached its international obligations in not reacting to protect the embassy and diplomatic personnel of the United States after an assault by private persons.[9] The holding in the *Corfu Channel Case* that a state must not let its territory be used for acts contrary to the rights of other states can also be seen as an articulation of this principle. Likewise, in the *Trail Smelter Arbitration* between the United States and Canada, reported in Chapter 14, Section B.2 on "Development of General Principles," the Tribunal said: "[N]o State has the right to use or permit the use of its territory in such a manner as to cause injury by fumes in or to the territory of another or the properties or persons therein, when the case is of serious consequence and the injury is established by clear and convincing evidence."[10] With respect to international peace and security, the Declaration on Friendly Relations (reproduced in the Documentary Supplement) holds that a state is under a general obligation to prevent the use of its territory by persons or groups planning to commit hostile acts against a foreign state. This obligation plays a central role in the international suppression of terrorism, because it prohibits states from harbouring on its territory terrorist groups planning to carry out attacks against states (see UN Security Council Resolution 1373 (2001)). This was the case in Afghanistan, where the Taliban regime refused to take action against Al-Qaida in the wake of the September 11, 2001 attacks against the United States. Note that the consequence of such a breach, the international responsibility of the state, is not necessarily coextensive with the legitimate use of force in self-defence. The issue of the legality of an armed response to terrorist

---

Lessons from the Sinking of the *Rainbow Warrior*" (1989) 20 Rutgers L.J. 393. Cf. A.F. Lowenfeld, "Agora: The Downing of Iran Air Flight 655" (1989) 83 A.J.I.L. 318.

7 (1926), 6 R.I.A.A. 57.

8 *The Caire Claim (France v. Mexico)* (1929), 5 R.I.A.A. 516 at 529-31 (translation).

9 *United States Diplomatic and Consular Staff in Teheran Case (United States v. Iran)*, [1980] I.C.J. Rep. 3 at paras. 57-70.

10 (1931-1941), 3 R.I.A.A. 1905 at 1965.

attacks is considered in Chapter 15. Do you think that state responsibility can be expected
to play a significant role in the suppression of terrorism? What does this say about the
function of state responsibility generally?

Yet another strand of analysis of the basis of responsibility in international law is the
absolute assumption of risk for certain types of activities. The classic reference mentioned
in support of this is the *Cosmos 954 Claim* presented by Canada against the U.S.S.R.

Cosmos 954 Claim (Canada v. U.S.S.R.)
(1979) 18 I.L.M. 899

[On September 18, 1977, the Soviet Union placed in orbit a satellite identified as
Cosmos 954, and, as required, officially informed the Secretary-General of the United
Nations of this fact. The satellite carried on board a nuclear reactor working on
uranium enriched with an isotope of uranium 235. On January 24, 1978, the satellite
entered the Earth's atmosphere, intruding into Canadian air space at about 11:53 a.m.
G.M.T. to the north of the Queen Charlotte Islands on the west coast of Canada. On
re-entry and disintegration, debris from the satellite was deposited on Canadian
territory, including portions of the Northwest Territories, Alberta, and Saskatchewan.
Immediately, the Canadian Armed Forces and the Atomic Energy Control Board of
Canada undertook operations directed at locating, recovering, removing, and testing
the debris and cleaning up the affected areas. The operations took place in two phases:
Phase I from January 24, 1978 to April 20, 1978 and Phase II from April 21, 1978 to
October 15, 1978. The total cost incurred by the various Canadian departments and
agencies involved in Phases I and II of the operations was around $14 million,
$6 million of which Canada claimed from the Soviet Union.

Canada's Statement of Claim was based jointly and separately on: (1) the relevant
international agreements and in particular the 1972 Convention on International
Liability for Damage Caused by Space Objects[11] to which both Canada and the Union
of Soviet Socialist Republics were parties, and (2) general principles of international
law. The statement of claim asserted:]

On behalf of CANADA: ...

(a) International Agreements

[15] Under Article II of the Convention on International Liability for Damage
caused by Space Objects, hereinafter also referred to as the Convention, "A launching
State shall be absolutely liable to pay compensation for damage caused by its space
object on the surface of the earth. ..." The Union of Soviet Socialist Republics, as the
launching State of the Cosmos 954 satellite, has an absolute liability to pay
compensation to Canada for the damage caused by this satellite. The deposit of
hazardous radioactive debris from the satellite throughout a large area of Canadian

---

11   Can. T.S. 1975 No. 7; 961 U.N.T.S. 187.

territory, and the presence of that debris in the environment rendering part of Canada's territory unfit for use, constituted "damage to property" within the meaning of the Convention.

[16] The intrusion into Canadian air space of a satellite carrying on board a nuclear reactor and the break-up of the satellite over Canadian territory created a clear and immediate apprehension of damage, including nuclear damage, to persons and property in Canada. The Government of the Union of Soviet Socialist Republics failed to give the Government of Canada prior notification of the imminent re-entry of the nuclear powered satellite and failed to provide timely and complete answers to the Canadian questions of January 24, 1978 concerning the satellite. It thus failed to minimize the deleterious results of the intrusion of the satellite into Canadian air space.

[17] Under general principles of international law, Canada had a duty to take the necessary measures to prevent and reduce the harmful consequences of the damage and thereby to mitigate damages. Thus, with respect to the debris, it was necessary for Canada to undertake without delay operations of search, recovery, removal, testing and clean-up. These operations were also carried out in order to comply with the requirements of the domestic law of Canada. Moreover, Article VI of the Convention imposes on the claimant State a duty to observe reasonable standards of care with respect to damage caused by a space object.

[18] The operations described in paragraph 8 ... [clean-up] would not have been necessary and would not have been undertaken had it not been for the damage caused by the hazardous radioactive debris from the Cosmos 954 satellite on Canadian territory and the reasonable apprehension of further damage in view of the nature of nuclear contamination. As a result of these operations, the areas affected have been restored, to the extent possible, to the condition which would have existed if the intrusion of the satellite and the deposit of the debris had not occurred. The Departments and Agencies of the Government of Canada involved in these operations incurred, as a result, considerable expense, particularly with regard to the procurement and use of services and equipment, the transportation of personnel and equipment and the establishment and operation of the necessary infrastructure. The costs included by Canada in this claim were incurred solely as a consequence of the intrusion of the satellite into Canadian air space and the deposit on Canadian territory of hazardous radioactive debris from the satellite.

[19] In respect of compensation for damage caused by space objects, the Convention provides for "... such reparation in respect of the damage as will restore ... [the claimant] to the condition which would have existed if the damage had not occurred" (Article XII). In accordance with its Preamble, the Convention seeks to ensure "... the prompt payment ... [under its terms] of a full and equitable measure of compensation to victims of such damage" (Fourth preambular paragraph). Canada's claim includes only those costs which were incurred in order to restore Canada to the condition which would have existed if the damage inflicted by the Cosmos 954 satellite had not occurred. The Convention also provides that "The compensation which the launching State shall be liable to pay for damage under this Convention shall be determined in accordance with international law and the principles of justice and equity ..." (Article XII). In calculating the compensation

claimed, Canada has applied the relevant criteria established by general principles of international law and has limited the costs included in its claim to those costs that are reasonable, proximately caused by the intrusion of the satellite and deposit of debris and capable of being calculated with a reasonable degree of certainty.

[20] The liability of the Union of Soviet Socialist Republics for damage caused by the satellite is also founded in Article VII of the Treaty on Principles Governing the Activities of States in the Exploration and Use of Outer Space, including the Moon and Other Celestial Bodies, done in 1967, and to which both Canada and the Union of Soviet Socialist Republics are parties. This liability places an obligation on the Union of Soviet Socialist Republics to compensate Canada in accordance with international law for the consequences of the intrusion of the satellite into Canadian air space and the deposit on Canadian territory of hazardous radioactive debris from the satellite.

(b) General Principles of International Law

[21] The intrusion of the Cosmos 954 satellite into Canada's air space and the deposit on Canadian territory of hazardous radioactive debris from the satellite constitutes a violation of Canada's sovereignty. This violation is established by the mere fact of the trespass of the satellite, the harmful consequences of this intrusion, being the damage caused to Canada by the presence of hazardous radioactive debris and the interference with the sovereign right of Canada to determine the acts that will be performed on its territory. International precedents recognize that a violation of sovereignty gives rise to an obligation to pay compensation.

[22] The standard of absolute liability for space activities, in particular activities involving the use of nuclear energy, is considered to have become a general principle of international law. A large number of states, including Canada and the Union of Soviet Socialist Republics, have adhered to this principle as contained in the 1972 Convention on International Liability for Damage caused by Space Objects. The principle of absolute liability applies to fields of activities having in common a high degree of risk. It is repeated in numerous international agreements and is one of "the general principles of law recognized by civilized nations" (Article 38 of the Statute of The International Court of Justice). Accordingly, this principle has been accepted as a general principle of international law.

[23] In calculating the compensation claimed, Canada has applied the relevant criteria established by general principles of international law according to which fair compensation is to be paid, by including in its claim only those costs that are reasonable, proximately caused by the intrusion of the satellite and deposit of debris and capable of being calculated with a reasonable degree of certainty.

NOTES

1) Negotiations toward a settlement did not begin for almost a year. Finally, after three sessions in February, June, and November 1980, a $3 million settlement that did not expressly acknowledge legal liability (*ex gratia* payment) was concluded in Moscow on

April 2, 1981. It took the form of a formal protocol signed by the Canadian Ambassador and the Soviet Deputy Minister of Foreign Affairs.[12]

2) The explosion of a Soviet nuclear reactor at Chernobyl in the spring of 1986 and the consequent pollution of several countries also raised the question of Soviet international responsibility. Do the principles in the previous cases provide any assistance on this question? Despite well-documented damage caused by nuclear fallout in a number of other countries, no claim was presented against the U.S.S.R. in the wake of the Chernobyl accident. On September 26, 1986, this nuclear accident led to the signature by 50 states, including Canada, of the Convention on Early Notification of a Nuclear Accident and the Convention on Assistance in the Case of Nuclear Accident or Radiological Emergency.[13]

3) The fact that payment in the *Cosmos 954* claim was made on an *ex gratia* basis, coupled with the absence of claims following the Chernobyl accident, sheds considerable doubt on whether a principle of absolute liabililty for ultra-hazardous activities has emerged in general international law.[14]

4) Since 1978, the ILC has been working on the subject of "International Liability for Injurious Consequences Arising out of Acts Not Prohibited by International Law." The topic covers primarily activities carried out in the territory or control of a state, the physical consequences of which cause or create a risk of causing significant transboundary harm. Such activities, which involve, *inter alia*, the storage, production, or carriage of dangerous substances, risks created by nuclear plants or oil refineries, or the introduction into the environment of dangerous genetically altered organisms and micro-organisms, would impose on the state of origin a duty to make reparation on the sole basis of the damage suffered by the injured State, and despite the absence of an internationally wrongful act. However, the rules to be developed must deal both with activities involving risks predominantly relevant to *prevention* and activities with harmful effects relevant to liability and *compensation*. Of course, the principles of prevention and reparation should be compatible with those applied where state responsibility is incurred for wrongful acts. This segment of the ILC's work has been segregated from its work on international responsibility because it involves not only the articulation of secondary rules, but also the elaboration of primary rules imposing new substantive obligations upon states.[15]

---

12 See P.G. Dembling, "Cosmos 954 and the Space Treaties" (1978) 6 J. Space L. 129; M. Mateesco-Matte, "Cosmos 954: pour une zone orbitale de securité" (1978) 3 Ann. Air & Space L. 483; S. Gorove, "Cosmos 954: Issues of Law and Policy" (1978) 6 J. Space L. 137; P.P.C. Haanappel, "Some Observations on the Crash of Cosmos 954" (1978) 6 J. Space L. 147; and B. Schwartz & M.L. Berlin, "After the Fall: An Analysis of Canadian Legal Claims for Damage Caused by Cosmos 954" (1982) 27 McGill L.J. 676.

13 (1986) 25 I.L.M. 1370 and 1377, respectively.

14 C. Jenks, "Liability for Ultra-Hazardous Activities in International Law" (1966-I) 117 R.C.A.D.I. 99.

15 A. Boyle, "State Responsibility and International Liability for Injurious Consequences of Acts Not Prohibited by International Law: A Necessary Distinction?" (1990) 39 I.C.L.Q. 1.

3. Attribution[16]

The issue of attribution, or whether an act may be imputed to a state, is a key element in international responsibility. The state will be held responsible if one of its organs has directly committed an internationally wrongful act (begging the question of what ought to be considered a state organ), or if it has endorsed the acts of non-state actors such as private persons, insurgent movements, and international organizations, or if it failed to react to private acts in a situation where international law required it to do so.

(a) Acts of the State

The state, being a political construct, cannot act without some form of human agency. To speak of acts of the state is to ask which persons ought to be considered as acting on behalf of the state. The general rule in international law is that the only conduct that may be attributed to the State is that of organs of government or of others who have acted under the direction, instigation, or control of those organs. As will be shown below, however, there are a limited number of instances in which the action of other non-state entities will be considered as attributable to the State.

International Law Commission, Draft Articles on the Responsibility of States for Internationally Wrongful Acts

Report of the International Law Commission on the Work of Its Fifty-third Session,
UN GAOR, 56th Sess., Supp. No. 10, U.N. Doc. A/56/10 (2001) chp. IV.E.1

Article 4
Conduct of Organs of a State

1. The conduct of any State organ shall be considered an act of that State under international law, whether the organ exercises legislative, executive, judicial or any other functions, whatever position it holds in the organization of the State, and whatever its character as an organ of the central government or of a territorial unit of the State.

2. An organ includes any person or entity which has that status in accordance with the internal law of the State.

Article 5
Conduct of Persons or Entities Exercising Elements of Governmental Authority

The conduct of a person or entity which is not an organ of the State under article 4 but which is empowered by the law of that State to exercise elements of the governmental

---

16   L. Condorelli, "L'imputation à l'État d'un fait internationallement illicite: solutions classiques et nouvelles tendances" (1984) 189 R.C.A.D.I. 9; H. Dipla, *La responsabilité de l'État pour violation des droits de l'homme: problèmes d'imputation* (1994); D. Caron, "The Basis of Responsibility: Attribution and Other Trans-Substantive Rules," in Lillich, Barstow & Bederman, *supra* note 1 at 109.

authority shall be considered an act of the State under international law, provided the person or entity is acting in that capacity in the particular instance.

Article 6
Conduct of Organs Placed at the Disposal of a State by Another State

The conduct of an organ placed at the disposal of a State by another State shall be considered an act of the former State under international law if the organ is acting in the exercise of elements of the governmental authority of the State at whose disposal it is placed.

Article 7
Excess of Authority or Contravention of Instructions

The conduct of an organ of a State or of a person or entity empowered to exercise elements of the governmental authority shall be considered an act of the State under international law if the organ, person or entity acts in that capacity, even if it exceeds its authority or contravenes instructions. ...

Article 9
Conduct Carried Out in the Absence or Default of the Official Authorities

The conduct of a person or group of persons shall be considered an act of a State under international law if the person or group of persons is in fact exercising elements of the governmental authority in the absence or default of the official authorities and in circumstances such as to call for the exercise of those elements of authority.

• • •

Article 11
Conduct Acknowledged and Adopted by a State as Its Own

Conduct which is not attributable to a State under the preceding articles shall nevertheless be considered an act of that State under international law if and to the extent that the State acknowledges and adopts the conduct in question as its own.

NOTES

1) Rules on state responsibility aim to cast as wide a net as possible on acts that may be linked to the state, either *de jure* or *de facto*. The internal structure of a state, including the constitutional division of powers among several levels of government or among various branches and the hierarchical arrangement of organs of the state, is immaterial when considering international responsibility. Thus any administrative, judicial, or legislative act of any level of government may trigger a violation of international law and engage the state's responsibility. In addition, acts of persons who are not organically connected to the state may nevertheless be considered acts of the state if in fact they amount to the exercise of some kind of sovereign authority.

2) Consider the case of Sydney Jaffe, a Canadian, who in September 1981 was forcibly abducted from Canada by two U.S. bail bondsmen allegedly acting under colour of authority of the state of Florida. Jaffe, accused of fraudulent land dealings in Florida, had "jumped" bail and returned to Canada. When the Florida state court issued a bench warrant for his arrest, the bail bondsmen kidnapped Jaffe from his home in Toronto and took him against his will back to Florida, where he was tried on 28 counts of fraud and for his failure to appear to answer the charges. Jaffe was convicted and sentenced to 35 years in jail and a fine of $152,250.

It was argued that the Florida state judge had provided the bail bonding agency with an incentive for the abduction because he had ordered the forfeiture of the $150,000 bond that the agency had put up for Jaffe. The Canadian Government protested to the U.S. Government about the abduction. The Canadian Embassy in Washington presented six diplomatic notes that objected to the breach of U.S. treaty obligations and the violation of Canadian sovereignty. Since at the time of Jaffe's abduction the rendition of fugitives from justice between the United States and Canada was governed by the Treaty on Extradition of December 3, 1971,[17] the action taken by the bail bondsmen at the instigation of Florida constituted a flagrant violation of that treaty, which was ignored. This internationally wrongful act entailed the responsibility of the United States toward Canada.

After many different initiatives, Jaffe succeeded in his appeal against the convictions for fraud and in November 1983 he was released from jail in Florida and allowed to return to Canada. In 1986 the two bail bondsmen were extradited to Canada and convicted for kidnapping Jaffe. On January 11, 1988 the Governments of Canada and the United States exchanged correspondence creating an understanding between them that they would cooperate to prevent transborder abduction.

In view of the Articles quoted above, do you believe that Jaffe's kidnapping should be attributed to the United States?

3) One of the problems associated with the attribution of an act to a state is that Article 4.2 contains a renvoi to municipal law with respect to the delineation of the state apparatus. Some concerns have been expressed that a state could successfully shield itself by legislating that a particular organ is not part of the state, which is problematic because a number of countries have increasingly tended to devolve to private actors functions that were traditionally performed by the state—for example, the operation of prison facilities or the interrogation of prisoners of war. In addition, international law does not contain a definition of "state functions," and it must be accepted that there are different cultural and political traditions about the proper role of the state. For instance, in many cultures some judicial decisions concerning family matters are rendered by religious bodies rather than by the state. The United Kingdom commented in this respect that "if [municipal] law itself designates the organ as an organ of the State, it may be appropriate for international law to adopt a similar position. If, however, the municipal law of a State does not treat an organ as part of the State, it does not necessarily follow that the organ's acts are not attributable to the State. The municipal law cannot have determinative effect in this context; attribution is a matter for international law."[18] This position is now reflected in ILC Article 4.

---

17   Can. T.S. 1976 No. 3; 27 U.S.T. 983.

18   U.N. Doc. A/CN.4/488 (1998) 37.

4) It has been suggested that whether an organ or entity should be considered a part of the state depends on the contents of its powers, the way in which these were conferred, their purpose, and the degree of accountability of the organ or entity to the government.[19] Does this approach really dispense with the need to rely on a specific vision of the state and its functions? Can international responsibility really accommodate a diversity of definitions of the state on the basis of diverse traditions?

T.H. Youmans Claim
United States v. Mexico
General Claims Commission (1926), 4 R.I.A.A. 110

THE COMMISSION (van Vollenhoven, Nielsen, MacGregor):

1. Claim for damages in the amount of $50,000.00 is made in this case by the United States of America against the United Mexican States in behalf of Thomas H. Youmans, the son of Henry Youmans, an American citizen, who, together with two other Americans, John A. Connelly and George Arnold, was killed at the hands of a mob on March 14, 1880, at Angangueo, State of Michoacán, Mexico. The occurrences giving rise to the claim as stated in the Memorial are substantially as follows:

2. At the time when the killing took place Connelly and Youmans were employed by Justin Arnold and Clinton Stephens, American citizens, who were engaged under a contract with a British corporation in driving a tunnel, known as the San Hilario Tunnel, in the town of Angangueo, a place having a population of approximately 7,000 people. The work was being done by Mexican laborers resident in the town under the supervision of the Americans. On the day when these men were killed Connelly, who was Managing Engineer in the construction of the tunnel at Angangueo, had a controversy with a laborer, Cayentano Medina by name, over a trifling sum of about twelve cents which the laborer insisted was due to him as wages. Connelly, considering the conduct of the laborer to be offensive, ejected the latter from the house in which Connelly lived and to which Medina had come to discuss the matter. Subsequently Medina, who was joined by several companions, began to throw stones at Connelly while the latter was sitting in front of his house and approached the American with a drawn machete. Connelly, with a view to frightening his assailant, fired shots into the air from a revolver. The American having withdrawn into the house, Medina attempted to enter, and his companions followed. Connelly thereupon fired at Medina with a shotgun and wounded him in the legs. Soon the house was surrounded by a threatening mob, which increased until it numbered about a thousand people. Connelly, Youmans, and Arnold, realizing the seriousness of their situation, prepared to defend themselves against the mob. Connelly's employer, Clinton Stephens, on hearing shots, went to the house and learned from Connelly what had happened. Upon Stephen's advice Connelly undertook to surrender himself to the local authorities, but was driven back into the house by the mob. The attack against Connelly when he endeavoured to surrender to police authorities was led by Pedro

---

19   J. Crawford, "First Report on State Responsibility," U.N. Doc. A/CN.4/490/Add.5 (1998) at para. 193.

Mondragón, a person styled the *Jefe de Manzana*, with whom Connelly had been on friendly terms. Stephens, followed by a part of the mob, proceeded to the *Casa Municipal* and requested the Mayor, Don Justo Lopez, to endeavour to protect the American in the house. The Mayor promptly went to the house, but was unable to quiet the mob. He then returned to his office and ordered José Maria Mora, *Jefe de la Tropa de la Seguridad Pública*, who held the rank of Lieutenant in the forces of the State of Michoacán, to proceed with troops to quell the riot and put an end to the attack upon the Americans. The troops, on arriving at the scene of the riot, instead of dispersing the mob, opened fire on the house, as a consequence of which Arnold was killed. The mob renewed the attack, and while the Americans defended themselves as best they could, several members of the mob approached the house from the rear, where there were no windows, and set fire to the roof. Connelly and Youmans were forced to leave, and as they did so they were killed by the troops and members of the mob. Their bodies were dragged through the streets and left under a pile of stones by the side of the road so mutilated as scarcely to be recognizable. At night they were buried by employees of the Mining Company in its cemetery at Trojes. ...

11. The claim made by the United States is predicated on the failure of the Mexican Government to exercise due diligence to protect the father of the claimant from the fury of the mob at whose hands he was killed. ... In connection with the contention with respect to the failure of the authorities to protect Youmans from the acts of the mob, particular emphasis is laid on the participation of soldiers which is asserted to be in itself a ground of liability. In behalf of the respondent Government it is contended that ... even if it were assumed that the soldiers were guilty of such participation, the Mexican Government should not be held responsible for the wrongful acts of ten soldiers and one officer of the State of Michoacán, who, after having been ordered by the highest official in the locality to protect American citizens, instead of carrying out orders given them acted in violation of them in consequence of which the Americans were killed. ...

13. With respect to the question of responsibility for the acts of soldiers there are citations in the Mexican Government's brief of extracts from a discussion of a subcommittee of the League of Nations Committee of Experts for the Progressive Codification of International Law. The passage quoted, which deals with the responsibility of a State for illegal acts of officials resulting in damages to foreigners, begins with a statement relative to the acts of an official accomplished "outside the scope of his competency, that is to say, if he has exceeded his powers." An illegal act of this kind, it is stated in the quotation, is one that can not be imputed to the State. Apart from the question whether the acts of officials referred to in this discussion have any relation to the rule of international law with regard to responsibility for acts of soldiers, it seems clear that the passage to which particular attention is called in the Mexican Government's brief is concerned solely with the question of the authority of an officer as defined by domestic law to act for his Government with reference to some particular subject. Clearly it is not intended by the rule asserted to say that no wrongful act of an official acting in the discharge of duties entrusted to him can impose responsibility on a Government under international law because any such wrongful act must be considered to be "outside the scope of his competency." If this were the meaning intended by the rule it would follow that no wrongful acts committed by an

official could be considered as acts for which his Government could be held liable. We do not consider that any of these passages from the discussion of the subcommittee quoted in the Mexican brief are at variance with the view which we take that the action of the troops in participating in the murder at Angangueo imposed a direct responsibility on the Government of Mexico.

14. Citation is also made in the Mexican brief to an opinion rendered by Umpire Lieber in which effect is evidently given to the well-recognized rule of international law that a Government is not responsible for malicious acts of soldiers committed in their private capacity. Awards have repeatedly been rendered for wrongful acts of soldiers acting under the command of an officer. ... Certain cases coming before the international tribunals may have revealed some uncertainty whether the acts of soldiers should properly be regarded as private acts for which there was no liability on the State, or acts for which the State should be held responsible. But we do not consider that the participation of the soldiers in the murder at Angangueo can be regarded as acts of soldiers committed in their private capacity when it is clear that at the time of the commission of these acts the men were on duty under the immediate supervision and in the presence of a commanding officer. Soldiers inflicting personal injuries or committing wanton destruction or looting always act in disobedience of some rules laid down by superior authority. There could be no liability whatever for such misdeeds if the view were taken that any acts committed by soldiers in contravention of instructions must always be considered as personal acts. ...

17. The Commission therefore decides that the Government of the United Mexican States must pay to the Government of the United States of America the sum of $20,000.00 (twenty thousand dollars) without interest on behalf of Thomas H. Youmans.

NOTES

1) The rule that a state may not invoke an abuse of authority by its agents to block a claim has long been accepted. As commented by the ILC:[20]

In the opinion of the Commission there is no need to reopen the discussion on the basic criterion which has been affirmed in diplomatic practice and in the decisions of international tribunals in this century, *i.e.* the criterion of the attribution to the State, as a subject of international law, of the acts and omissions of its organs which have acted in that capacity, even when they have contravened the provisions of municipal law concerning their activity. This criterion is based on the need for clarity and security in international relations which seems to be the dominant theme in modern international life. In international law, the State must recognize that it acts whenever persons or groups of persons whom it has instructed to act in its name in a given area of activity appear to be acting effectively in its name. Even when in so doing those persons or groups exceed the formal limits of their competence according to municipal law or contravene the provisions of that law or of administrative ordinances or internal instructions issued by their superiors, they are nevertheless acting, even though improperly, within the scope of the discharge of their functions. The State

---

20   See [1975] Y.B.I.L.C. vol. 2 at 67.

cannot take refuge behind the notion that, according to the provisions of its legal system, those actions or omissions ought not to have occurred or ought to have taken a different form. They have nevertheless occurred and the State is therefore obliged to assume responsibility for them and to bear the consequences provided for in international law.

2) Not all acts of state agents will trigger the international responsibility of the state. At a minimum, the actions must have been taken under cover of their official character; otherwise, it will be considered a private act. While this principle is clear and agreed upon, its application to concrete facts consistently raises difficulties. For example, in *Yeager v. Iran*, the Iran–U.S. Claims Tribunal found that bribes taken by a state airline employee were not imputable to the state, while theft carried out by revolutionary guards performing customs duties were so imputable.[21]

3) Taking into consideration the fact that, generally, the superior or subordinate position of an agent within the state apparatus does not affect the state's responsibility (Article 4.1), do you think that a broader scope of *ultra vires* acts of higher officials should trigger international responsibility? Are there distinctions to make according to the nature of the agent's functions—for example, between a soldier and a postal worker?

4) Is responsibility for *ultra vires* acts similar to liability for risk?

(b) Acts of Private Persons

In principle, the state is not responsible for the conduct of private persons or entities. Circumstances may arise, however, where such conduct is nevertheless attributable to the State because there exists a specific factual relationship of control of the State over the individuals. This control can take one of two forms: either a direct and positive control of the State over individuals, consisting of clear instructions and clear support to the conduct of the private persons—for example, recruiting, arming, and commanding mercenaries— or an indirect and more passive control of the state—for instance, a State purposely harbouring terrorist groups on its territory. In any circumstances, though, the control shall be effective enough to establish a real link between the person or group performing the act and the State machinery.

International Law Commission, Draft Articles on the Responsibility of States for Internationally Wrongful Acts
Report of the International Law Commission on the Work of Its Fifty-third Session,
UN GAOR, 56th Sess., Supp. No. 10, U.N. Doc. A/56/10 (2001) chp. IV.E.1

Article 8
Conduct Directed or Controlled by a State

The conduct of a person or group of persons shall be considered an act of a State under international law if the person or group of persons is in fact acting on the instructions of, or under the direction or control of, that State in carrying out the conduct.

---

21   (1987), 17 Iran–U.S. Cl. Tr. Rep. 92.

Military and Paramilitary Activities In and Against Nicaragua
Nicaragua v. United States (Merits)
[1986] I.C.J. Rep. 14 at 63-65

[Nicaragua presented a claim against the United States alleging that the latter had tried to destabilize the country by way of its control of the insurgent group known as the *contras*. One of the key issues was whether the acts of the *contras* could indeed be imputed to the United States or whether they should be considered acts of private persons for the purposes of the international responsibility of the United States.]

[113] The question of the degree of control of the *contras* by the United States Government is relevant to the claim of Nicaragua attributing responsibility to the United States for activities of the *contras* whereby the United States has, it is alleged, violated an obligation of international law not to kill, wound or kidnap citizens of Nicaragua. The activities in question are said to represent a tactic which includes "the spreading of terror and danger to non-combatants as an end in itself with no attempt to observe humanitarian standards and no reference to the concept of military necessity." In support of this, Nicaragua has catalogued numerous incidents, attributed to "CIA-trained mercenaries" or "mercenary forces," of kidnapping, assassination, torture, rape, killing of prisoners, and killing of civilians not dictated by military necessity … .

[114] In this respect, the Court notes that according to Nicaragua, the *contras* are no more than bands of mercenaries which have been recruited, organized, paid and commanded by the Government of the United States. This would mean that they have no real autonomy in relation to that Government. Consequently, any offences which they have committed would be imputable to the Government of the United States, like those of any other forces placed under the latter's command. In the view of Nicaragua, "*stricto sensu*, the military and paramilitary attacks launched by the United States against Nicaragua do not constitute a case of civil strife. They are essentially the acts of the United States." If such a finding of the imputability of the acts of the *contras* to the United States were to be made, no question would arise of mere complicity in those acts, or of incitement of the *contras* to commit them.

[115] The Court has taken the view … that United States participation, even if preponderant or decisive, in the financing, organizing, training, supplying and equipping of the *contras*, the selection of its military or paramilitary targets, and the planning of the whole of its operation, is still insufficient in itself, on the basis of the evidence in the possession of the Court, for the purpose of attributing to the United States the acts committed by the *contras* in the course of their military or paramilitary operations in Nicaragua. All the forms of United States participation mentioned above, and even the general control by the respondent State over a force with a high degree of dependency on it, would not in themselves mean, without further evidence, that the United States directed or enforced the perpetration of the acts contrary to human rights and humanitarian law alleged by the applicant State. Such acts could well be committed by members of the *contras* without the control of the United States. For this conduct to give rise to legal responsibility of the United States, it would in principle have to be proved that that State had effective control of the military or paramilitary operations in the course of which the alleged violations were committed.

NOTES

1) The *Nicaragua* case marks the outer limits of the state, indicating that the degree of control required in order for the act to be imputable to the state is that of effective control of the general operations of the group or persons. In that sense, the decision clearly inspired the formulation of Article 8. In the same case, Judge Ago noted in his dissent that it would "be inconsistent with the principles governing the question [of attribution] to regard members of the *contra* forces as persons or groups acting in the name and on behalf of the United States of America. Only in cases where certain members of those forces happened to have been specifically charged by United States authorities to commit a particular act, or carry out a particular task of some kind on behalf of the United States, would it be possible so to regard them."[22] The European Court of Human Rights (ECHR) in *Loizidou v. Turkey* adopted the wider criteria proposed by the Court in *Nicaragua* to conclude that the fact that Turkey "exercise[s] effective overall control" of the "Turkish Republic of Northern Cyprus" entailed its international responsibility for the latter's acts.[23]

2) The Appeals Chamber of the International Criminal Tribunal for the Former Yugoslavia (ICTY), in the *Prosecutor v. Tadic*, explicitly rejected the position adopted by the ICJ in *Nicaragua*. The ICTY found as follows: "The requirement of international law for the attribution to States of acts performed by private individuals is that the State exercise control over the individuals. The *degree of control* may, however, vary according to the factual circumstances of each case. The Appeals Chamber fails to see why in each and every circumstance international law should require a high threshold for the test of control." The ICTY concluded that the requisite degree of control by the Yugoslavian authorities over the armed forces was one of "*overall control* going beyond the mere financing and equipping of such forces and involving also participation in the planning and supervision of military operations."[24] That said, despite the explicit foray by the ICTY into the law of state responsibility, the issue it was directly concerned with was the application of international humanitarian law, more precisely the degree to which a foreign state must control an insurgent group in order for a civil war to become an international armed conflict. Which of the two approaches, *Nicaragua* or *Tadic*, do you think is best suited to the issue of international terrorism?

3) The *U.S. Diplomatic and Consular Staff in Tehran Case*[25] shows the different ways a state may be attributed with responsibility for the unlawful acts of private citizens. The ICJ held that responsibility for the seizure of the American embassy and hostages was not directly imputable to the state of Iran in the absence of evidence that the actions of the "militants" in occupying the premises were taken on the orders of government officials, this despite the earlier public encouragement of Ayatollah Khomeini for "dear pupils, students and theological students to expand with all their might their attacks against the United States." As to the seizure, therefore, Iran could only be responsible indirectly for

---

22   [1986] I.C.J. Rep. 14 at 188.

23   (1996), Eur. Ct. H.R. (Ser. A.) 2260 at para. 56.

24   Case IT-94-1 (1999) I.L.M., vol. 38, p. 1518, para.145.

25   [1980] I.C.J. Rep. 3, reported in Chapter 5, Section D on "Diplomatic Immunities." See paras. 56-62, 69-74, 79, 90-91, and 95.

failure to take appropriate steps to ensure the security of the embassy and its staff. However, when Ayatollah Khomeini and other members of the government, instead of taking measures to protect the embassy from further molestation, approved its continued occupation, the "militants" became, in legal effect, agents of Iran for whose persisting acts the state itself was directly responsible. This is codified in ILC Article 11, which attributes to the state private conduct that the latter acknowledges and adopts as its own.

(c) Acts of Insurgents

If the state assumes no responsibility for the acts of individuals not under its control then, *a fortiori*, it will in principle not incur international responsibility for the conduct of groups engaged in rebellion against the government. Exceptions to the principle centre on the state's due diligence obligation to protect the interests of other states on its territory and on the situations in which insurgents successfully overturn the government and assume power.

International Law Commission, Draft Articles on the Responsibility of States for Internationally Wrongful Acts
Report of the International Law Commission on the Work of Its Fifty-third Session,
UN GAOR, 56th Sess., Supp. No. 10, U.N. Doc. A/56/10 (2001) chp. IV.E.1

Article 10
Conduct of an Insurrectional or Other Movement

1. The conduct of an insurrectional movement which becomes the new government of a State shall be considered an act of that State under international law.

2. The conduct of a movement, insurrectional or other, which succeeds in establishing a new State in part of the territory of a pre-existing State or in a territory under its administration shall be considered an act of the new State under international law.

3. This article is without prejudice to the attribution to a State of any conduct, however related to that of the movement concerned, which is to be considered an act of that State by virtue of articles 4 to 9.

Asian Agricultural Products Ltd. v. Sri Lanka
International Centre for the Settlement of Investment Disputes Case No. Arb/87/3
(1990), 106 I.L.R. 416; (1991) 30 I.L.M. 577 at 611

President: Dr. Ahmed Sadek
Members of Tribunal: Prof. Berthold Goldman & Dr. Samuel K.B. Asante

[In 1987, the Sri Lankan army destroyed a plant owned by Asian Agricultural Products Ltd. (AAPL) on the basis of reports that it was being used by local rebels. After negotiations failed, AAPL presented a claim to the International Centre for Settlement of Investment Disputes (ICSID) for arbitration pursuant to the Sri Lanka–United

Kingdom Bilateral Investment Treaty, alleging that Sri Lanka had not exercised due diligence to prevent damages by the insurgent Tamil Tigers.]

THE TRIBUNAL: ...

72. It is a generally accepted rule of International Law, clearly stated in international arbitral awards and in the writings of the doctrinal authorities, that:

> (i) —A State on whose territory an insurrection occurs is not responsible for loss or damage sustained by foreign investors unless it can be shown that the Government of that state failed to provide the standard of protection required, either by treaty, or under general customary law, as the case may be; and
>
> (ii) —Failure to provide the standard of protection required entails the state's international responsibility for losses suffered, regardless of whether the damages occurred during an insurgents' offensive act or resulting from governmental counter-insurgency activities.

73. The long established arbitral case-law was adequately expressed by MAX HUBER, the *Rapporteur* in the *Spanish Zone of Morocco* claims (1923), in the following terms:

> The principle of non-responsibility in no way excludes the duty to exercise a certain degree of vigilance. If a state is not responsible for the revolutionary events themselves, it may nevertheless be responsible for what its authorities do or not do to ward the consequence, within the limits of possibility ... .

Furthermore, the famous arbitrator indicated that the "degree of vigilance" required in providing the necessary protection and security would differ according to the circumstances. ...

76. In the light of all the above-mentioned arbitral precedents, it would be appropriate to consider that adequate protection afforded by the host State authorities constitutes a primary obligation, the failure to comply with which creates international responsibility. Furthermore, "there is an extensive and consistent state practice supporting the duty to exercise due diligence" (BROWNLIE, *System of the Law of Nations*, *State Responsibility—Part I*, Oxford, 1986, p. 162).

As a doctrinal authority, relied upon by both Parties during the various stages of their respective pleadings in the present case, Professor Brownlie stated categorically that:

> There is general agreement among writers that the rule of non-responsibility cannot apply where the government concerned has failed to show due diligence (*Principles of Public International Law*, Third Edition, Oxford, 1979, p. 453).

After reviewing all categories of precedents, including more recent international judicial case-law, the learned Oxford University Professor arrived, not only to confirm that international responsibility arises from the mere "failure to exercise due diligence" in providing the required protection, but also to note "a sliding scale of liability related to the standard of due diligence" (*State Responsibility*, *op. cit.* p. 162 and p. 168).

77. A number of other contemporary international law authorities noticed the "sliding scale," from the old "subjective" criteria that takes into consideration the

relatively limited existing possibilities of local authorities in a given context, towards an "objective" standard of vigilance in assessing the required degree of protection and security with regard to what should be legitimately expected to be secured for foreign investors by a reasonably well organized modern State. ...

In the light of said uncontested evidence, the Tribunal is of the opinion that reasonably the Government should have at least tried to use such peaceful available high level channels of communication in order to get any suspect elements excluded from the farm's staff. This would have been essential to minimize the risks of killings and destruction when planning to undertake a vast military counter-insurgency operation in that area for regaining lost control.

85. ... The Tribunal notes in this respect that the failure to resort to such precautionary measures acquires more significance when taking into consideration that such measures fall within the normal exercise of governmental inherent powers—as a public authority—entitled to order undesirable persons out from security sensitive areas. The failure became particularity serious when the highest executive officer of the Company reconfirmed just ten days before his willingness to comply with any governmental requests in this respect.

Accordingly, the Tribunal considers that the Respondent through said inaction and omission violated its due diligence obligation which requires undertaking all possible measures that could be reasonably expected to prevent the eventual occurrence of killings and property destructions.

NOTES

1) As illustrated by this decision, the fact that an insurgent movement is active in a country does not automatically relieve the state of any international responsibility for insurgents' acts, even in those instances where the insurrection remains unsuccessful. The general duty of due diligence developed in the *Corfu Channel* case remains applicable, a point related not to attribution but to the scope of a state's primary obligations.

2) The label of "movement, insurrectional or other" can cover a wide spectrum of groups eventually leading a successful attempt to overthrow the government. The threshold for the application of the rule embodied in Article 10 is that the movement is advocating change outside the constitutional framework of the state.

3) An illustration of the attribution to the state of acts of revolutionary organizations is contained within a trilogy of cases dealing with the responsibility of Iran for the conduct of the Revolutionary Guards and others. In *Short v. Iran*[26] and *Rankin v. Iran*,[27] claims were brought against the Government of Iran for injury caused as a result of alleged anti-Americanism on the part of the revolutionary movement. In its decisions, the Tribunal emphasized that mere reference to actions of agents of the Iranian Government was insufficient to establish state responsibility. In the absence of an established policy directly attributable to the Islamic Government, state responsibility could not be engaged. The Tribunal did note in *Short*, however, that the determination would depend upon a

---

26   (1987), 16 Iran–U.S. Cl. Trib. Rep. 76.

27   (1987), 17 Iran–U.S. Cl. Trib. Rep. 135.

consideration of the facts in each case. This sensitivity to context is illustrated in *Yeager v. Iran*[28] in which, as noted earlier, the Tribunal found that the Revolutionary Guards (members of which had forced the claimant out of the country) were agents of the government for the purposes of engaging state responsibility.[29] In the case of a successful insurrection, does it seem coherent to hold the state responsible both for the actions of the rebels and those of the former government?

(d) Acts of International Organizations

International organizations are entities that can possess an international legal personality distinct from that of its member states, as was seen in the *Reparations* case, reproduced in Chapter 2, Section C.1 on "Other Legal Persons: International Organizations." As independent bodies, they do not fall under the sovereignty of any state. On the other hand, the legal personality of organizations is partly derivative of that of states, because the organization was created or recognized by states or because its members are states. Furthermore, because international organizations do not have a territorial basis, they most often operate on the territory of a given state. The principle remains that the fact that a state is a member of an international organization or that the organization is present on its territory will not entail the international responsibility of the state if a wrong is committed by the organization.

NOTES

1) In the *Reparations* case, the ICJ concluded that the United Nations could be endowed with international rights and duties.[30] While that case dealt with the possibility for the United Nations to bring a claim for injuries suffered by its agents, the principles exposed therein can be applied to the question of international responsibility. More recently, in the *Immunity of a Special Rapporteur* case, the ICJ noted that "the question of immunity from legal process is distinct from the issue of legal compensation for any damages incurred as a result of acts performed by the United Nations or by its agents acting in their official capacity. The United Nations may be required to bear responsibility for the damage arising from such acts."[31]

2) It is important to note that principles of state responsibility are not necessarily identical to those relating to the responsibility of international organizations, which led the ILC to exclude the latter altogether from consideration as part of its work on state responsibility (Article 57).[32] In 2000 the ILC decided to include the topic "Responsibility

---

28   (1987), 17 Iran–U.S. Cl. Trib. Rep. 92.

29   H. Atlam, "National Liberation Movements and International Responsibility," in Spinedi & Simma, *supra* note 1 at 35.

30   [1949] I.C.J. Rep. 174, reported in Chapter 2, Section C.1 on "International Organizations."

31   *Difference Relating to Immunity from Legal Process of a Special Rapporteur of the Commission on Human Rights*, [1999] I.C.J. Rep. 62 at 88-89, para. 66.

32   See [1975] Y.B.I.L.C. vol. 2 87 at paras. 8-9. See M. Hirsch, *The Responsibility of International Organizations Towards Third Parties* (1995); Klein, *supra* note 1.

of International Organizations" in its long-term program of work. A Special Rapporteur was appointed in 2002, and by 2004 the ILC had provisionally adopted Articles 1 (Scope of the present draft articles), 2 (Use of terms), 3 (General principles), 4 (General rule on attribution of conduct to an international organization), 5 (Conduct of organs or agents placed at the disposal of an international organization by a State or another international organization), 6 (Excess of authority or contravention of instructions), and 7 (Conduct acknowledged and adopted by an international organization as its own).[33]

3) The Secretary-General noted that "the applicability of international humanitarian law to United Nations forces when they are engaged as combatants in situations of armed conflict entails the international responsibility of the Organization and its liability in compensation for violations of international humanitarian law committed by members of United Nations forces." In 1993, Canadian armed forces were in Somalia as part of UNITAF, a "peace enforcement" mission under United States command authorized by the Security Council pursuant to Chapter VII of the U.N. Charter. One night, two Canadian soldiers caught an unarmed 16-year-old civilian, Shidane Arone, trying to break into their compound in Belet Huen. Arone was tortured and killed by his Canadian captors.[34] If an international claim were presented in this case, who should it be directed against?

4. Circumstances Precluding Wrongfulness

A certain number of defences or circumstances precluding wrongfulness can be invoked by a state as a shield against the invocation of international responsibility. Despite the expression, the effect of these defences is not to make lawful what would otherwise be unlawful, but rather to excuse non-performance of most obligations stemming from the rules on state responsibility while the circumstances persist.

International Law Commission, Draft Articles on the Responsibility of States for the Internationally Wrongful Acts
Report of the International Law Commission on the Work of Its Fifty-third Session, UN GAOR, 56th Sess., Supp. No. 10, U.N. Doc. A/56/10 (2001) chp. IV.E.1

Article 20
Consent

Valid consent by a State to the commission of a given act by another State precludes the wrongfulness of that act in relation to the former State to the extent that the act remains within the limits of that consent.

---

33 *Report of the International Law Commission on the Work of Its Fifty-sixth Session,* UN GAOR, 59th Sess., Supp. No. 10, U.N. Doc. A/59/10 (2004).

34 Several soldiers were prosecuted and convicted for this crime, and the entire Canadian Airborne Regiment was disbanded. See *Dishonoured Legacy: The Lessons of the Somalia Affair, Report of the Commission of Inquiry into the Deployment of Canadian Forces to Somalia* (1997) 5 vols. online: Department of National Defence and Canadian Forces <http://www.forces.gc.ca/site/Reports/somalia/index_e.asp>. See also G. Gaja, "Second Report on Responsibility of International Organizations," U.N. Doc. A/CN.4/541 (2004) 14-23.

Article 21
Self-Defence

The wrongfulness of an act of a State is precluded if the act constitutes a lawful measure of self-defence taken in conformity with the Charter of the United Nations.

Article 22
Countermeasures in Respect of an Internationally Wrongful Act

The wrongfulness of an act of a State not in conformity with an international obligation towards another State is precluded if and to the extent that the act constitutes a countermeasure taken against the latter State in accordance with Chapter II of Part Three.

Article 23
Force Majeure

1. The wrongfulness of an act of a State not in conformity with an international obligation of that State is precluded if the act is due to *force majeure*, that is the occurrence of an irresistible force or of an unforeseen event, beyond the control of the State, making it materially impossible in the circumstances to perform the obligation.

2. Paragraph 1 does not apply if:

    (a) The situation of *force majeure* is due, either alone or in combination with other factors, to the conduct of the State invoking it; or

    (b) The State has assumed the risk of that situation occurring.

Article 24
Distress

1. The wrongfulness of an act of a State not in conformity with an international obligation of that State is precluded if the author of the act in question has no other reasonable way, in a situation of distress, of saving the author's life or the lives of other persons entrusted to the author's care.

2. Paragraph 1 does not apply if:

    (a) The situation of distress is due, either alone or in combination with other factors, to the conduct of the State invoking it; or

    (b) The act in question is likely to create a comparable or greater peril.

Article 25
Necessity

1. Necessity may not be invoked by a State as a ground for precluding the wrongfulness of an act not in conformity with an international obligation of that State unless the act:

    (a) Is the only way for the State to safeguard an essential interest against a grave and imminent peril; and

    (b) Does not seriously impair an essential interest of the State or States towards which the obligation exists, or of the international community as a whole.

2. In any case, necessity may not be invoked by a State as a ground for precluding wrongfulness if:

(a) The international obligation in question excludes the possibility of invoking necessity; or

(b) The State has contributed to the situation of necessity.

Article 26
Compliance with Peremptory Norms

Nothing in this Chapter precludes the wrongfulness of any act of a State which is not in conformity with an obligation arising under a peremptory norm of general international law.

Article 27
Consequence of Invoking a Circumstance Precluding Wrongfulness

The invocation of a circumstance precluding wrongfulness in accordance with this Chapter is without prejudice to:

(a) Compliance with the obligation in question, if and to the extent that the circumstance precluding wrongfulness no longer exists;

(b) The question of compensation for any material loss caused by the act in question.

Case Concerning the Gabčíkovo-Nagymaros Project (Hungary/Slovakia)
[1997] I.C.J. Rep. 7 at 40-46

[In 1977, Hungary and Czechoslovakia concluded a treaty to build a series of dams in Slovakia and Hungary for the production of electricity, flood control, and improvement of navigation on the River Danube. Hungary in 1989 suspended and later abandoned the project, invoking grave risks to the environment and to the water supply of Budapest. Slovakia, as successor to Czechoslovakia, denied these allegations and insisted that Hungary carry out its treaty obligations. It planned and subsequently put into operation an alternative project only on Slovak territory, the operation of which affected Hungary's access to the waters of the Danube.]

THE COURT: ...

[51] The Court considers, first of all, that the state of necessity is a ground recognized by customary international law for precluding the wrongfulness of an act not in conformity with an international obligation. It observes moreover that such ground for precluding wrongfulness can only be accepted on an exceptional basis. ...

Thus, according to the [International Law] Commission, the state of necessity can only be invoked under certain strictly defined conditions which must be cumulatively satisfied; and the State concerned is not the sole judge of whether those conditions have been met.

[52] In the present case, the following basic conditions set forth in Draft Article 33 are relevant: it must have been occasioned by an "essential interest" of the State which is the author of the act conflicting with one of its international obligations; that interest must have been threatened by a "grave and imminent peril"; the act being challenged must have been the "only means" of safeguarding that interest; that act must not have "seriously impair[ed] an essential interest" of the State towards which the obligation existed; and the State which is the author of that act must not have "contributed to the occurrence of the state of necessity." Those conditions reflect customary international law ... .

[53] The Court has no difficulty in acknowledging that the concerns expressed by Hungary for its natural environment in the region affected by the Gabčíkovo-Nagymaros Project related to an "essential interest" of that State, within the meaning given to that expression in Article 33 of the Draft of the International Law Commission. ...

[54] ... The Court considers, however, that, serious though these uncertainties [as to the ecological impact of the dam] might have been, they could not, alone, establish the objective existence of a "peril" in the sense of a component element of a state of necessity. The word "peril" certainly evokes the idea of "risk"; that is precisely what distinguishes "peril" from material damage. But a state of necessity could not exist without a "peril" duly established at the relevant point in time; the mere apprehension of a possible "peril" could not suffice in that respect. It could moreover hardly be otherwise, when the "peril" constituting the state of necessity has at the same time to be "grave" and "imminent." "Imminence" is synonymous with "immediacy" or "proximity" and goes far beyond the concept of "possibility." As the International Law Commission emphasized in its commentary, the "extremely grave and imminent" peril must "have been a threat to the interest at the actual time."[35] That does not exclude, in the view of the Court, that a "peril" appearing in the long term might be held to be "imminent" as soon as it is established, at the relevant point in time, that the realization of that peril, however far off it might be, is not thereby any less certain and inevitable. ...

[55] ... The Court notes that the dangers ascribed to the upstream reservoir were mostly of a long-term nature and, above all, that they remained uncertain. ... It follows that, even if it could have been established—which, in the Court's appreciation of the evidence before it, was not the case—that the reservoir would ultimately have constituted a "grave peril" for the environment in the area, one would be bound to conclude that the peril was not "imminent" at the time at which Hungary suspended and then abandoned the works relating to the dam. ...

[56] ... The Court moreover considers that Hungary could, in this context also, have resorted to other means in order to respond to the dangers that it apprehended. In particular, within the framework of the original Project, Hungary seemed to be in a position to control at least partially the distribution of the water between the bypass canal, the old bed of the Danube and the side-arms. It should not be overlooked that the Dunakiliti dam was located in Hungarian territory and that Hungary could construct the works needed to regulate flows along the old bed of the Danube and the side-arms. ...

---

35   See [1980] Y.B.I.L.C. vol. 2 (Part 2) 49 at para. 33.

[57] The Court concludes from the foregoing that, with respect to both Nagymaros and Gabčíkovo, the perils invoked by Hungary, without prejudging their possible gravity, were not sufficiently established in 1989, nor were they "imminent"; and that Hungary had available to it at that time means of responding to these perceived perils other than the suspension and abandonment of works with which it had been entrusted. What is more, negotiations were under way which might have led to a review of the Project and the extension of some of its time-limits, without there being need to abandon it. The Court infers from this that the respect by Hungary, in 1989, of its obligations under the terms of the 1977 Treaty would not have resulted in a situation "characterized so aptly by the maxim *summum jus summa injuria*." ...[36]

In 1983, Hungary asked that the works under the Treaty should go forward more slowly, for reasons that were essentially economic but also, subsidiarily, related to ecological concerns. In 1989, when, according to Hungary itself, the state of scientific knowledge had undergone a significant development, it asked for the works to be speeded up, and then decided, three months later, to suspend them and subsequently to abandon them. The Court is not however unaware that profound changes were taking place in Hungary in 1989, and that, during that transitory phase, it might have been more than usually difficult to co-ordinate the different points of view prevailing from time to time.

The Court infers from all these elements that, in the present case, even if it had been established that there was, in 1989, a state of necessity linked to the performance of the 1977 Treaty, Hungary would not have been permitted to rely upon that state of necessity in order to justify its failure to comply with its treaty obligations, as it had helped, by act or omission, to bring it about.

NOTES

1) Hungary also invoked the possibility of taking countermeasures as a justification for its termination of the project, claiming that Slovakia's unilateral termination of the dam and interference with the waters of the Danube themselves amounted to an internationally wrongful act to which it could respond. The Court rejected this argument, concluding that both Hungary and Slovakia had breached international obligations.

2) The ICJ in its advisory opinion on *Legal Consequences of the Construction of a Wall in the Occupied Palestinian Territories* reaffirmed the customary character of the state-of-necessity exception.[37] In that case, the Court concluded that the exception could not be invoked successfully because it had not been shown that the construction of a wall along the route chosen by Israel was the only means available to protect itself against the threat of terrorist attacks.

3) If a state were to bomb an oil tanker that ran aground because of a storm, in order to set fire to its contents and thus prevent the massive pollution of its shores, such a situation would constitute a state of necessity precluding wrongfulness of the act. That

---

36   *Ibid.* at para. 31.

37   [2004] I.C.J. Rep. 1 at para. 140.

being said, should the coastal state still bear the risk and be considered liable for the destruction of the ship? Article 27(b) reserves, without deciding on the issue, the possibility that a state legitimately relying on a circumstance precluding wrongfulness might nevertheless be required to compensate for material losses caused by its actions.

4) On the conditions for lawful countermeasures, see below, Section D.2 on "Countermeasures."

5. Consequences of International Responsibility

The breach of an international obligation entails two types of legal consequences: first, it creates new obligations for the wrongdoer, principally, duties of cessation and non-repetition, and a duty to make full reparation; second, it creates new rights for the injured state.

International Law Commission, Draft Articles on the Responsibility of States for Internationally Wrongful Acts
Report of the International Law Commission on the Work of Its Fifty-third Session,
UN GAOR, 56th Sess., Supp. No. 10, U.N. Doc. A/56/10 (2001) chp. IV.E.1

Article 29
Continued Duty of Performance

The legal consequences of an internationally wrongful act under this Part do not affect the continued duty of the responsible State to perform the obligation breached.

Article 30
Cessation and Non-repetition

The State responsible for the internationally wrongful act is under an obligation:
(a) To cease that act, if it is continuing;
(b) To offer appropriate assurances and guarantees of non-repetition, if circumstances so require.

Article 31
Reparation

1. The responsible State is under an obligation to make full reparation for the injury caused by the internationally wrongful act.
2. Injury includes any damage, whether material or moral, caused by the internationally wrongful act of a State.

Article 32
Irrelevance of Internal Law

The responsible State may not rely on the provisions of its internal law as justification for failure to comply with its obligations under this Part.

Article 33
Scope of International Obligations Set Out in This Part

1. The obligations of the responsible State set out in this Part may be owed to another State, to several States, or to the international community as a whole, depending in particular on the character and content of the international obligation and on the circumstances of the breach.

2. This Part is without prejudice to any right, arising from the international responsibility of a State, which may accrue directly to any person or entity other than a State.

Article 34
Forms of Reparation

Full reparation for the injury caused by the internationally wrongful act shall take the form of restitution, compensation and satisfaction, either singly or in combination, in accordance with the provisions of this Chapter.

Article 35
Restitution

A State responsible for an internationally wrongful act is under an obligation to make restitution, that is, to re-establish the situation which existed before the wrongful act was committed, provided and to the extent that restitution:

(a) Is not materially impossible;

(b) Does not involve a burden out of all proportion to the benefit deriving from restitution instead of compensation.

Article 36
Compensation

1. The State responsible for an internationally wrongful act is under an obligation to compensate for the damage caused thereby, insofar as such damage is not made good by restitution.

2. The compensation shall cover any financially assessable damage including loss of profits insofar as it is established.

Article 37
Satisfaction

1. The State responsible for an internationally wrongful act is under an obligation to give satisfaction for the injury caused by that act insofar as it cannot be made good by restitution or compensation.

2. Satisfaction may consist in an acknowledgement of the breach, an expression of regret, a formal apology or another appropriate modality.

3. Satisfaction shall not be out of proportion to the injury and may not take a form humiliating to the responsible State.

NOTES

1) Article 29 expresses the principle that the issue of whether a primary obligation has been extinguished by its breach, on the one hand, and the application of rules on state responsibility, on the other hand, constitute two autonomous legal concepts. State responsibility is concerned with the legal consequences of the breach of an international obligation and not with the existence of such an obligation. Whether that obligation subsists despite the breach is a matter not of State responsibility but of the law of treaty.

2) Cessation is, together with reparation, the general and immediate consequence of an internationally wrongful act. In most international disputes, cessation will be the main focus of the controversy.

3) In the *LaGrand* case, the ICJ considered the legal consequences of the United States' failure to inform Karl and Walter LaGrand of their right to communicate with their consular representative, following their arrest for bank robbery and murder.[38] By the time the Court issued its decision on the merits, both brothers had been executed despite an order for provisional measures requiring a stay of the executions. Cessation in this specific case was no longer an issue. Compensation was requested, but clearly played a role secondary to a request for guarantees of non-repetition on the part of the United States. The Court found that the United States' repeated undertaking to enact a broad and detailed program to ensure compliance with the Vienna Convention on Consular Relations fulfilled its obligation in this respect. It noted, however, that any future breach would trigger not simply a duty to offer an apology, but also an obligation to provide an opportunity to reconsider any criminal conviction and sentence.

The obligation to make full reparation is the second general obligation of the responsible state. This general principle was first stated by the Permanent Court in the *Chorzow Factory Case*.

Chorzow Factory (Indemnity) Case
(1928), P.C.I.J. (Ser. A.) No. 17

[In its judgment No. 7 concerning *German Interests in Polish Upper Silesia, 1926*,[39] the PCIJ held that the attitude adopted by the Polish Government toward the Obserschlesische Stickstoffwerke A.-G. and the Bayerische Stickstoffwerke A.-G. in taking possession of the nitrate factory at Chorzow was incompatible with the provisions of the Geneva Convention 1922[40] between Germany and Poland, concerning Upper Silesia. The German Government now sought to recover an indemnity from Poland in respect of the damage suffered by these companies.

The Court, by nine votes to three, ruled that Poland owed reparation to Germany in respect of damage suffered by the two companies and reserved the amount of compensation due until after an expert inquiry had been held.]

---

38   *LaGrand (Germany v. United States of America)*, Merits, [2001] I.C.J. Rep. 466.

39   (1926), P.C.I.J. (Ser. A.) No. 7.

40   16 Martens, *Nouveau recueil général* (3d Ser.) 645.

THE COURT: ... It is a principle of international law that the reparation of a wrong may consist in an indemnity corresponding to the damage which the nationals of the injured State have suffered as a result of the act which is contrary to international law. This is even the most usual form of reparation. ... The reparation due by one State to another does not however change its character by reason of the fact that it takes the form of an indemnity for the calculation of which the damage suffered by a private person is taken as the measure. The rules of law governing the reparation are the rules of international law in force between the two States concerned, and not the law governing relations between the State which has committed a wrongful act and the individual who has suffered damage. Rights or interests of an individual, the violation of which rights causes damage, are always in a different plane to rights belonging to a State, which rights may also be infringed by the same act. The damage suffered by an individual is never therefore identical in kind with that which will be suffered by a State; it can only afford a convenient scale for the calculation of the reparation due to the State. ... The Court observes that it is a principle of international law, and even a general conception of law, that any breach of an engagement involves an obligation to make reparation. ... [I]n estimating the damage caused by an unlawful act, only the value of property, rights and interests which have been affected and the owner of which is the person on whose behalf compensation is claimed, or the damage done to whom is to serve as a means of gauging the reparation claimed, must be taken into account. This principle, which is accepted in the jurisprudence of arbitral tribunals, has the effect, on the one hand, of excluding from the damage to be estimated, injury resulting for third parties from the unlawful act and, on the other hand, of not excluding from the damage the amount of debts and other obligations for which the injured party is responsible. The damage suffered by the Oberschlesische in respect of the Chorzow undertaking is therefore equivalent to the total value—but to that total only—of the property, rights and interests of this Company in that undertaking, without deducting liabilities. ...

The action of Poland which the Court has judged to be contrary to the [1922] Geneva Convention [on Upper Silesia] is not an expropriation—to render which lawful only the payment of fair compensation would have been wanting; it is a seizure of property, rights and interests which could not be expropriated even against compensation, save under the exceptional conditions fixed by Article 7 of the said Convention. As the Court has expressly declared in Judgment No. 8, reparation is in this case the consequence not of the application of Articles 6 to 22 of the Geneva Convention, but of acts contrary to those Articles.

It follows that the compensation due to the German Government is not necessarily limited to the value of the undertaking at the moment of dispossession, plus interest to the day of payment. This limitation would only be admissible if the Polish Government had had the right to expropriate, and if its wrongful act consisted merely in not having paid to the two Companies the just price of what was expropriated; in the present case, such a limitation might result in placing Germany and the interests protected by the Geneva Convention, on behalf of which interests the German Government is acting, in a situation more unfavourable than that in which Germany and these interests would have been if Poland had respected the said Convention.

Such a consequence would not only be unjust, but also and above all incompatible with the aim of Article 6 and the following articles of the Convention—that is to say, the prohibition, in principle, of the liquidation of the property, rights and interests of German nationals and of companies controlled by German nationals in Upper Silesia—since it would be tantamount to rendering lawful liquidation and unlawful dispossession indistinguishable in so far as their financial results are concerned.

The essential principle contained in the actual notion of an illegal act—a principle which seems to be established by international practice and in particular by the decisions of arbitral tribunals—is that reparation must, as far as possible, wipe out all the consequences of the illegal act and reestablish the situation which would, in all probability, have existed if that act had not been committed. Restitution in kind, or, if this is not possible, payment of a sum corresponding to the value which a restitution in kind would bear; the award, if need be, of damages for loss sustained which would not be covered by restitution in kind or payment in place of it—such are the principles which should serve to determine the amount of compensation due for an act contrary to international law.

This conclusion particularly applies as regards the Geneva Convention, the object of which is to provide for the maintenance of economic life in Upper Silesia on the basis of respect for the *status quo*. The dispossession of an industrial undertaking— the expropriation of which is prohibited by the Geneva Convention—then involves the obligation to restore the undertaking and, if this be not possible, to pay its value at the time of the indemnification, which value is designed to take the place of restitution which has become impossible. To this obligation, in virtue of the general principles of international law, must be added that of compensating loss sustained as the result of the seizure. The impossibility, on which the Parties are agreed, of restoring the Chorzow factory could therefore have no other effect but that of substituting payment of the value of the undertaking for restitution; it would not be in conformity either with the principles of law or with the wish of the Parties to infer from that agreement that the question of compensation must henceforth be dealt with as though an expropriation properly so called was involved. ...

Faced with the task of determining what sum must be awarded to the German Government in order to enable it to place the dispossessed Companies as far as possible in the economic situation in which they would probably have been if the seizure had not taken place, the Court considers that it cannot be satisfied with the data for assessment supplied by the Parties. ...

And finally as regards the sum agreed on at one moment by the two Governments during the negotiations which followed Judgment No. 7—which sum, moreover, neither Party thought fit to rely on during the present proceedings—it may again be pointed out that the Court cannot take into account declarations, admissions or proposals which the Parties may have made during direct negotiations between themselves, when such negotiations have not led to a complete agreement. ... Possible but contingent and indeterminate damage ... in accordance with the jurisprudence of arbitral tribunals, cannot be taken into account. ...

It may be admitted, as the Court has said in Judgment No. 8, that jurisdiction as to the reparation due for the violation of an international convention involves jurisdiction as to the forms and methods of reparation. If the reparation consists in the payment of a sum of money, the Court may therefore determine the method of such payment. For this reason it may well determine to whom the payment shall be made, in what place and at what moment; in a lump sum or maybe by instalments; where payment shall be made; who shall bear the costs, etc. It is then a question of applying to a particular case the general rules regarding payment, and the Court's jurisdiction arises quite naturally out of its jurisdiction to award monetary compensations.

But this principle would be quite unjustifiably extended if it were taken as meaning that the Court might have cognizance of any question whatever of international law, even quite foreign to the convention under consideration, for the sole reason that the manner in which such question is decided may have an influence on the effectiveness of the reparation asked for. Such an argument seems hardly reconcilable with the fundamental principles of the Court's jurisdiction which is limited to cases specially provided for in treaties and conventions in force.

NOTES

1) The *Chorzow Factory Case* represents the classic exposition of the basic principles regarding the duty to provide reparation, which have been codified in Articles 34-37. The injured state may demand restitution in kind over other forms of reparation, if it is materially possible in the circumstances, since it is the form of reparation that is best suited to return the situation to the *status quo ante*. It can also combine this and other forms of reparation if restitution by itself cannot wipe out the consequences of the internationally wrongful act.

2) Even though the assessment of which types of reparation will be most appropriate will largely depend on the circumstances of each case, the Articles show a clear order of priority among the different means of reparation, with a preference for restitution.

3) In accordance with article 34, restitution is then the first of the forms of reparation. It is aimed at re-establishing, as far as possible, the *status quo ante*, and "may take the form of material restoration or return of territory, persons or property, or the reversal of some juridical act, or some combination of them."[41] See, for example, the *Temple of Preah Vihear Case*,[42] discussed in Chapter 7, Section B.1 on "Acquisition of Territory," in which Thailand was ordered to return certain religious artifacts taken from the temple prior to its return to Cambodia. Article 35 states the possibility of derogating from restitution whenever restitution is impossible, or when it would place a burden out of all proportion on the responsible state. That said, practice often centres on compensation for other reasons, and in particular because some cases involve breaches of contract, expropriation, or similar economic issues where compensation is the normal remedy.

4) Whenever full reparation cannot be achieved by restitution, or by restitution alone, the responsible State is under an obligation to compensate for damages caused by the internationally wrongful act. Compensation is intended only to indemnify quantifiable

---

41 *Report of the International Law Commission on the Work of Its Fifty-third Session*, UN GAOR, 56th Sess., Supp. No. 10, U.N. Doc. A/56/10 (2001) at 241.

42 Sub nom. *Cambodia v. Thailand*, [1962] I.C.J. Rep. 6 at 36-37.

losses suffered by the injured state, excluding exemplary or punitive damages that go beyond remedying the actual harm suffered as a result of the wrongful act.

5) Satisfaction, the third possible form of reparation, is a term primarily applied to compensation for the moral or non-material consequences of an act for which a state is internationally responsible. In principle, it is only in those cases where the injury cannot be made good by restitution or compensation that satisfaction may be required. Some of the common forms satisfaction may take include apologies or amends of a diplomatic character, a common feature of diplomatic practice. In some cases a sum is paid not as compensation for a material wrong, but as an additional reparation for the wrongful act committed. The *I'm Alone Case*[43] reported in Chapter 13, Section B.6 on "High Seas" is an example of satisfaction. The Commissioners recommended the payment by the United States of $25,000 as material amends in respect of the wrong committed by that country in sinking the Canadian vessel, an amount not linked to the value of the ship. They also recommended that the United States apologize to the Canadian Government. Likewise in the 1990 *Rainbow Warrior* arbitration, the Tribunal held that "an order for the payment of monetary compensation can be made in respect of the breach of international obligations involving ... serious moral and legal damage, even though there is no material damage."[44] However, the Tribunal declined to order monetary compensation on the grounds that New Zealand was seeking alternative remedies. Instead, it declared that condemnation of France for its breaches of treaty obligations owed to New Zealand, made public by the Tribunal's decision, was appropriate satisfaction for the legal and moral damage suffered by New Zealand.

6) Special remedial regimes may be established by states on a bilateral basis, such as the large number of mixed-claims commissions set up to adjudicate on specific classes of claims. The U.N. Compensation Fund for Claims Against Iraq provides a unique example of a dedicated multilateral remedial regime. In resolution 687 of April 3, 1991, the U.N. Security Council declared that Iraq was liable under international law for "any direct loss, damage, including environmental damage and depletion of natural resources, or injury to foreign Governments, nationals and corporations" as a result of its unlawful invasion and occupation of Kuwait. For this purpose, it established the U.N. Compensation Fund and the U.N. Commission and directed the Commission to administer the Fund, which is funded by Iraqi contributions based on a percentage of the value of that country's export of petroleum and petroleum products. The Commission has elaborated new techniques to deal with the more than 2.5 million claims it has received, and has awarded over US$18 billion to individuals, corporations, and states.[45]

---

43   (1935), 3 R.I.A.A. 1609; (1935) 29 A.J.I.L. 326.

44   (1990), 82 I.L.R. 499 at 575.

45   See Sokol Colloqium and R. Lillich, *The United Nations Compensation Commission: Thirteenth Sokol Colloquium* (1995); B. Graefrath, "Iraqi Reparations and the Security Council" (1995) 55 *Zeitschrift für ausländisches öffentliches Recht und Völkerrecht* 1; M. Frigessi di Rattalma, "Le régime de la responsabilité internationale institué par le Conseil d'administration de la Commission de compensation des Nations Unies" (1997) 101 Rev. gén. droit int. pub. 44; V. Heiskanen & R. O'Brien, "UN Compensation Commisssion Panel Sets Precedents on Government Claims" (1998) 92 A.J.I.L. 339; and H. Wassgren, "The UN Compensation Commission: Lessons of Legitimacy, State Responsibility, and War Reparations" (1998) 11 Leiden J. Int. L. 473. Decisions of the Compensation Commission are available at <www.unog.ch/uncc>.

6. Elements of Aggravated Responsibility

Traditionally, international law has not made any space for the criminality of state behaviour. As put by the International Military Tribunal in Nuremberg, "crimes against international law are committed by men, not by abstract entities, and only by punishing individuals who commit such crimes can the provisions of international law be enforced."[46] The Nuremberg Tribunal accordingly refrained from expressing any opinion as to the criminality of Germany or its allies. Yet it was perceived soon after World War II that the most serious breaches of international law by States—for example, genocide— which "shock the conscience of mankind,"[47] called for a treatment different than that for, say, a simple violation of a treaty of commerce. After two decades of acrimonious debates on the issue, both within the ILC and among states, in 1996, the ILC adopted Draft Article 19, which formally distinguished international crimes and international delicts. Paragraph 2 of Draft Article 19 read: "an internationally wrongful act which results from the breach by a State of an international obligation so essential for the protection of fundamental interests of the international community that its breach is recognized as a crime by that community as a whole constitutes an international crime." Many remained deeply opposed to this proposal, both because of doubts over the appropriateness of using the language of criminal law in relation to state behaviour and because the proposed consequences of an international crime did not seem markedly different from those of an ordinary international delict. Faced with an issue that could derail the entire project, Special Rapporteur James Crawford devised a compromise solution by folding the concerns contained in Draft Article 19 into other provisions detailing the consequences of breaches of *jus cogens* norms, thus eliminating the need for an article dealing specifically with crimes of states. As a result, while internationally wrongful acts of a State now form a single category and the criteria for such acts apply to all, with no distinction between delictual and criminal responsibility, some important elements of aggravated responsibility remain in place.

International Law Commission, Draft Articles on the Responsibility of States for Internationally Wrongful Acts

Report of the International Law Commission on the Work of Its Fifty-third Session,
UN GAOR, 56th Sess., Supp. No. 10, U.N. Doc. A/56/10 (2001) chp. IV.E.1

Article 40
Application of This Chapter

1. This Chapter applies to the international responsibility which is entailed by a serious breach by a State of an obligation arising under a peremptory norm of general international law.

---

46 International Military Tribunal for the Trial of the Major War Criminals, Judgment of 1 October 1946, reprinted in (1947) 41 A.J.I.L. 172 at 221.

47 *Reservations to the Convention on the Prevention and Punishment of the Crime of Genocide,* Advisory Opinion, [1951] I.C.J. Rep. 15 at 23.

2. A breach of such an obligation is serious if it involves a gross or systematic failure by the responsible State to fulfil the obligation.

Article 41
Particular Consequences of a Serious Breach of an Obligation under This Chapter

1. States shall cooperate to bring to an end through lawful means any serious breach within the meaning of article 40.

2. No State shall recognize as lawful a situation created by a serious breach within the meaning of article 40, nor render aid or assistance in maintaining that situation.

3. This article is without prejudice to the other consequences referred to in this Part and to such further consequences that a breach to which this Chapter applies may entail under international law.

NOTES

1) Article 40 sets out two criteria to distinguish "serious breaches of obligations under peremptory norms of general international law" from other types of breaches. One relates to the character of the obligation breached, the second to the intensity of the breach. First, the breach must concern an obligation arising under a peremptory norm of general international law or, in other words, a norm of *jus cogens*. The classical, and not exhaustive, examples of these are the prohibitions against aggression, torture, slavery, genocide, and apartheid. Second, article 40 limits the scope of the chapter to the most serious or systematic breaches of these norms. The commentaries suggest that to be regarded as serious or systematic, a violation would have to be carried out in an organized and deliberate way—that is, in a flagrant manner.

2) Two special legal obligations of States faced with the commission of "serious breaches" are set out in article 41. Paragraph 1 calls for a joint and coordinated effort by all States to counteract the effects of the most serious breaches of international law, without specifying the special modalities and forms of such cooperation. Since the gross violations of *jus cogens* norms interest the international community as a whole, it is felt that collective reactions will be better suited to answer them.

3) Paragraph 2 sets out a general duty of abstention, comprising both the obligation not to recognize as lawful the "serious breaches" and the obligation not to render aid or assistance in maintaining that situation. Thus, for example, the Security Council in Resolution 662 (1990) called on all states not to recognize the "eternal merger" of Kuwait and Iraq, proclaimed by the latter in the aftermath of its invasion.

4) The International Court of Justice (ICJ) in the *Barcelona Traction Case* recognized the existence of obligations *erga omnes*, in the violation of which every state can be said to have an interest. The incorporation of Article 19 in the 1996 Draft had been an attempt by the ILC to echo in some ways the significant difference between these and other obligations underlined by the ICJ. Does the regime now set up by Articles 40-41 seem to adequately express the concept articulated by the ICJ in *Barcelona Traction*?

B. RESPONSIBILITY FOR INJURY TO ALIENS[48]

With the expansion of colonial empires and the increase in international commercial trading in the 18th and 19th centuries, nationals of all states became more prone to being subjected to forms of treatment that they and their governments found objectionable. The espousal of claims by the state came as a peaceful alternative to the issuance of letters of reprisals, entitling the injured individuals to do themselves justice. The law of state responsibility for injury to aliens occupied a central place in the elaboration of the basic principles of international responsibility examined above, in Section A on "General Theory of Responsibility," for the reason that it is primarily in the context of mistreatment of foreign nationals, and subsequent claims by their state of nationality, that these rules were developed. The significance of this field has been lessened by the emergence of two normative regimes in public international law over the last century: first, the general principles of international responsibility studied earlier, detached from any reference to the treatment of aliens; and second, international human rights norms, which overlap to some degree with standards designed to protect aliens. Unlike the secondary rules studied in Section A, the norms surveyed in this section embody primary rules, setting out the parameters of lawful state behaviour in their treatment of aliens.

1. Standard of Treatment

The historical circumstances of the emergence of standards on the treatment of aliens help us to understand the controversy they triggered over whether there is a universal standard or merely a right of aliens to be treated on an equal footing with nationals. Broadly speaking, this controversy reflects conflicting economic and political interests. Colonial and now industrialized countries, on the one hand, have defended the international minimum standard in order to ensure protection of their nationals and their investments, irrespective of how the local state may treat its own nationals. Latin American and developing, decolonized countries, on the other hand, traditionally have argued in favour of the national treatment standard, invoking a state's right to control its own political and economic development.

Neer Claim
United States v. Mexico
General Claims Commission (1926), 4 R.I.A.A. 60 at 61-2

[The United States presented a claim against Mexico, following the murder of Neer, a U.S. citizen killed by unknown assailants while working in Mexico. The United States alleged that Mexico had not exercised due diligence in investigating the crime with a view to punishing its authors. The Commission unanimously rejected the claim.]

---

48   See Lillich, *International Claims: Their Adjudication by National Commissions, supra* note 1; R. Lillich, "Duties of States Regarding the Civil Rights of Aliens" (1978) 161 Hague Recueil 329; and A.-C. Evans, "The Political Status of Aliens in International Law, Municipal Law and European Community Law" (1981) 30 I.C.L.Q. 20.

VAN VOLLENHOVEN, Presiding Commissioner: Without attempting to announce a precise formula, it is in the opinion of the Commission possible ... to hold (first) that the propriety of governmental acts should be put to the test of international standards, and (second) that the treatment of an alien, in order to constitute an international delinquency, should amount to an outrage, to bad faith, to wilful neglect of duty, or to an insufficiency of governmental action so far short of international standards that every reasonable and impartial man would readily recognize its insufficiency. Whether the insufficiency proceeds from deficient execution of an intelligent law or from the fact that the laws of the country do not empower the authorities to measure up to international standards is immaterial.

NOTES

1) Hackworth put the issue as follows:[49]

The admission of aliens into a State immediately calls into existence certain correlative rights and duties. The alien has a right to the protection of the local law. He owes a duty to observe that law and assumes a relationship toward the State of his residence sometimes referred to as "temporary allegiance."

The State has the right to expect that the alien shall observe its laws and that his conduct shall not be incompatible with the good order of the State and of the community in which he resides or sojourns. It has the obligation to give him that degree of protection for his person and property which he and his State have the right to expect under local law, under international law, and under treaties and conventions between his State and the State of residence. Failure of the alien or of the State to observe these requirements may give rise to responsibility in varying degrees, the alien being amenable to the local law or subject to expulsion from the State, or both, and the State being responsible to the alien or to the State of which he is a national.

We are here concerned primarily with responsibility of the State. State responsibility may arise directly or indirectly. It does not arise merely because an alien has been injured or has suffered loss within the State's territory. If the alien has suffered an injury at the hands of a private person his remedy usually is against that person, and State responsibility does not arise in the absence of a dereliction of duty on the part of the State itself in connection with the injury, as for example by failure to afford a remedy, or to apply an existing remedy. When local remedies are available the alien is ordinarily not entitled to the interposition of his government until he has exhausted those remedies and has been denied justice. This presupposes the existence in the State of orderly judicial and administrative processes. In theory an unredressed injury to an alien constitutes an injury to his State, giving rise to international responsibility.

2) In cases like the *Neer Claim*, the local state maintained that no violation of international law had been committed as long as there was no discrimination against the

---

alien. It was thus a perfect defence to assert that nationals of the respondent state are treated in the same fashion as was the alien. However, international tribunals have generally taken the view that, although a state must, as a minimum, not discriminate against aliens, its conduct must ultimately be judged by international standards and that a state may not be heard in its defence to allege that its nationals are treated in exactly the same way as aliens. It may be said in defence of the position of the Latin American states that it may be justifiable to apply local standards to a natural or juristic person maintaining a permanent residence in a given state; the individual or corporation must be considered to have assumed the risks associated with residence in that state. Thus, if state A in time of war requisitions the property of a corporation of state B permanently established in state A, compensation should be limited to the same amount that nationals of state A are receiving, especially if property is being requisitioned by state B on the same basis as by state A. However, if means of transportation owned by an alien and temporarily within the jurisdiction of a state are requisitioned by that state in time of war in the exercise of its right of angary, full compensation according to international law ought to be paid for the property so taken.

When we turn from the protection of property to the protection of the person and of the fundamental rights and freedoms of individuals, it is difficult to maintain that an alien should have no protection under international law because all nationals of the state concerned are subjected to the same injustices. The treatment of aliens should no longer be viewed in terms of minimum standard of conduct or national treatment. It should be related to the binding rules of international law that, even in the absence of treaties, protect the most fundamental human rights. These rules that apply to both nationals and aliens alike have grown apace under the guidance of the United Nations. They have the effect of restricting the exercise of sovereignty by the territorial state toward all individuals, whether nationals or aliens. In 1957, the Special Rapporteur on State Responsibility of the International Law Commission suggested the following provision:[50]

> Draft Article 5.1 The State is under a duty to ensure to aliens the enjoyment of the same civil rights, and to make available to them the same individual guarantees as are enjoyed by its nationals. These rights and guarantees shall not, however, in any case be less than the "fundamental human rights" recognized and defined in contemporary international instruments.

This is complemented by international human rights standards on the prohibition of discrimination, which have been interpreted as prohibiting discrimination on the basis of nationality, including unjustified distinction between nationals and aliens.[51]

---

50   F.V. García Amador, "Second Report on the Law of State Responsibility for Injuries to Aliens," [1957] Y.B.I.L.C. vol. 2 104 at 112-13. See R. Lillich & S. Neff, "The Treatment of Aliens and International Human Rights Norms: Overlooked Developments at the U.N." (1978) 21 German Y.B. Int'l L. 97.

51   See U.N. Human Rights Committee, *Gueye v. France*, Comm. No. 196/1985 (3 April 1989); U.N. Human Rights Committee, "General Comment 15 (27) (The Position of Aliens under the Covenant)," U.N. Doc. CCPR/C/21/Add.5/Rev.1 (1986); *Proposed Amendment to the Naturalization Provisions of the Constitution of Costa Rica* (1984), Advisory Opinion OC-4/84, Inter_Am. Ct. H.R. (Ser. A) No. 4 at paras. 52-63.

Even if such a linking of human rights and standards on the treatment of aliens is accepted, aliens may be entitled to better remedies than nationals, since the home state may intervene diplomatically on behalf of their nationals or present a claim against the wrongdoing state to obtain redress. Also, in the case of taking of property belonging to aliens, they have, under general principles of international law, a right to be compensated, which may not be enjoyed by nationals of the expropriating or nationalizing state.

3) It must be pointed out that the national treatment standard or the international minimum standard only applies to certain areas of activity by aliens. In other areas, it is perfectly legitimate under customary international law for states to treat aliens as such in their discretion and to limit their activities—for instance, by preventing them from holding a public office. The mere fact that the law and procedure of the state in which the alien resides differ from those of the country of which he or she is a national does not of itself afford justification for complaint.

2. Protection of the Person

Before international human rights emerged into positive international law in the aftermath of World War II, a body of norms emerged that were related to the treatment of aliens, which provided protection somewhat comparable to human rights. These standards correspond to the problems most often faced by foreigners: admission and expulsion, detention and physical injury, and maladministration of justice. Primary rules on the law of state responsibility for injury to aliens had been the main focus of the initial work of the ILC on international responsibility in the 1950s. When the Commission decided to focus exclusively on general principles, the codification of standards on the treatment of aliens was abandoned. The project was resuscitated in the U.N. Sub-Commission on Prevention of Discrimination and Protection of Minorities, with the appointment of Special Rapporteur Baroness Elles. Her report eventually led to the adoption of the following Declaration by the General Assembly in 1985.[52]

Declaration on the Rights of Individuals Who Are Not Citizens of the Country in Which They Live
GA Res. 40/144, UN GAOR, 40th Sess., Supp. No. 53,
U.N. Doc. A/40/53 (1985) 252

Article 1

For the purposes of this Declaration, the term "alien" shall apply, with due regard to qualifications made in subsequent articles, to any individual who is not a national of the State in which he or she is present. ...

---

52   Sub-Commission on Prevention of Discrimination and Protection of Minorities, *International Provisions Protecting the Human Rights of Non-Citizens*, Study prepared by the Baroness Elles, U.N. Doc., E/CN.4/ Sub.2/392/Rev.1 (1980).

Article 5

1. Aliens shall enjoy, in accordance with domestic law and subject to the relevant international obligations of the State in which they are present, in particular the following rights:

(a) The right of life and security of person; no alien shall be subjected to arbitrary arrest or detention; no alien shall be deprived of his or her liberty except on such grounds and in accordance with such procedures as are established by law;

(b) The right to protection against arbitrary or unlawful interference with privacy, family, home or correspondence;

(c) The right to be equal before the courts, tribunals and all other organs and authorities administering justice and, when necessary, to free assistance of an interpreter in criminal proceedings and, when prescribed by law, other proceedings;

(d) The right to choose a spouse, to marry, to found a family;

(e) The right to freedom of thought, opinion, conscience and religion; the right to manifest their religion or beliefs, subject only to such limitations as are prescribed by law and are necessary to protect public safety, order, health or morals or the fundamental rights and freedoms of others;

(f) The right to retain their own language, culture and tradition;

(g) The right to transfer abroad earnings, savings or other personal monetary assets, subject to domestic currency regulations.

2. Subject to such restrictions as are prescribed by law and which are necessary in a democratic society to protect national security, public safety, public order, public health or morals or the rights and freedoms of others, and which are consistent with the other rights recognized in the relevant international instruments and those set forth in this Declaration, aliens shall enjoy the following rights:

(a) The right to leave the country;

(b) The right to freedom of expression;

(c) The right to peaceful assembly;

(d) The right to own property alone as well as in association with others, subject to domestic law.

3. Subject to the provisions referred to in paragraph 2, aliens lawfully in the territory of a State shall enjoy the right to liberty of movement and freedom to choose their residence within the borders of the State.

4. Subject to national legislation and due authorization, the spouse and minor or dependent children of an alien lawfully residing in the territory of a State shall be admitted to accompany, join and stay with the alien.

Article 6

No alien shall be subjected to torture or to cruel, inhuman or degrading treatment or punishment and, in particular, no alien shall be subjected without his or her free consent to medical or scientific experimentation.

Article 7

An alien lawfully in the territory of a State may be expelled therefrom only in pursuance of a decision reached in accordance with the law and shall, except where compelling reasons of national security otherwise require, be allowed to submit the reasons why he or she should not be expelled and to have the case reviewed by, and be represented for the purpose before, the competent authority or a person or persons specially designed by the competent authority. Individual or collective expulsion of such aliens on grounds of race, colour, religion, culture, descent or national or ethnic origin is prohibited.

Article 8

1. Aliens lawfully residing in the territory of a State shall also enjoy, in accordance with the national laws, the following rights, subject to their obligations under article 4:

(a) The right to safe and healthy working conditions, to fair wages and equal remuneration for work of equal value without distinction of any kind, in particular, women being guaranteed conditions of work not inferior to those enjoyed by men, with equal pay for equal work;

(b) The right to join trade unions and other organizations or associations of their choice and to participate in their activities. No restrictions may be placed on the exercise of this right other than those prescribed by law and which are necessary, in a democratic society, in the interests of national security or public order or for the protection of the rights and freedoms of others;

(c) The right to health protection, medical care, social security, social services, education, rest and leisure, provided that they fulfil the requirements under the relevant regulations for participation and that undue strain is not placed on the resources of the State.

2. With a view to protecting the rights of aliens carrying on lawful paid activities in the country in which they are present, such rights may be specified by the Governments concerned in multilateral or bilateral conventions.

Article 9

No alien shall be arbitrarily deprived of his or her lawfully acquired assets.

Article 10

Any alien shall be free at any time to communicate with the consulate or diplomatic mission of the State of which he or she is a national or, in the absence thereof, with the consulate or diplomatic mission of any other State entrusted with the protection of the interests of State of which he or she is a national in the State where he or she resides.

NOTES

1) The Declaration represents in part an attempt to codify customary standards on the treatment of aliens and in part an expansion of these standards. The rights contained in

article 8, for example, have not generally been found in practice related to the treatment of aliens. Given that economic, social, and cultural rights are now a part of customary law, what do you think of the expansion of standards related to aliens in that field?

2) The long-winded name of the Declaration results from the feeling among members of the Sub-Commission on Prevention of Discrimination and Protection of Minorities that the term "alien" was pejorative and should be avoided.

3) At present, there is no project to prepare a treaty on the basis of the above Declaration. Is this a serious shortcoming that should be corrected? Are there any advantages in not attempting to press further to obtain a binding instrument?

(a) Admission and Expulsion

Rankin v. Iran
(1987), 17 Iran-U.S. Cl. Trib. Rep. 135

[Rankin, who was employed by a U.S. company, requested and was granted permission to be evacuated out of Iran with other employees in the aftermath of the Islamic revolution in 1979. The Tribunal dismissed his claim for lost salary and abandoned property.]

THE TRIBUNAL: ... According to the practice of States, the writings of scholars, the decisions of international tribunals, and bilateral treaty provisions such as those contained in the Treaty of Amity, Economic Relations and Consular Rights of 1955 between Iran and the United States which entered into force on 16 June 1957, international law imposes certain restraints on the circumstances and the manner in which a State may expel aliens from its territory. A claimant alleging expulsion has the burden of proving the wrongfulness of the expelling State's action, in other words that it was arbitrary, discriminatory, or in breach of the expelling State's treaty obligations. These restraints have usually been considered in the context of specific measures directed against an individual emanating directly from the State or legally attributable to it. However, these general principles apply equally to a situation in which, while there is no law, regulation, or directive which forces the individual alien to leave, his or her continued presence in the host country is made impossible because of conditions generated by wrongful acts of the State or attributable to it.

NOTES

1) By way of example, the Tribunal in *Rankin v. Iran* noted that a state would violate customary international law "by expelling an alien who had a continued right to residence in Iran or by depriving an alien of a reasonable opportunity to protect his property interests prior to his expulsion."[53] For instance, in *Yeager v. Iran*, when "the Claimant was

---

53   (1987), 17 Iran–U.S. Cl. Trib. Rep. 135 at 147, note 20.

given only 30 minutes to pack a few personal belongings without advance notice" the Tribunal held his expulsion "was carried out with unnecessary haste and in violation of minimum procedural standards under customary international law."[54] What other limitations on a state's right to expel aliens exist? In particular, should international law require the existence of a "just cause" for expulsion? Consider the protection of an individual's human rights, discussed in Chapter 12 on "Protection of Human Rights."[55]

2) In *Re Janoczka*, it was stated:[56]

> The right of expulsion of a foreign citizen whose presence is found to be objectionable does not seem to be conditional on the acquiescence of the country of the foreign citizenship but apparently international comity requires that communication take place. Such communication takes the form of a passport application. At all events the practice to that effect does exist and must be recognized.

(b) Detention and Physical Injury

Quintanilla Claim
United States v. Mexico
General Claims Commission (1926), 4 R.I.A.A. 101 at 102-3

VAN VOLLENHOVEN, Presiding Commissioner:

[1] This claim is presented by the United Mexican States against the United States in behalf of F. Quintanilla and M.I. Perez de Quintanilla, Mexican nationals, father and mother of Alejo Quintanilla, a young man, who was killed on or about July 16, 1922, not far from Edinburg, Hidalgo County, Texas, U.S.A. On July 15, 1922, about 5 p.m., said Alejo Quintanilla in a lonely spot had lassoed a girl of fourteen years, Agnes Casey, who was on horseback, and thrown her from the horse; she screamed, and the young Mexican fled. She told the occurrence to her father, Tom Casey with whom Quintanilla had been employed some time before; the father the next morning went to lodge his complaint with the authorities, first to Edinburg (the County seat), where he did not find the sheriff, and then to Donna, where he found the deputy sheriff, one Sam A. Bernard. According to the record, this deputy sheriff with three other men, whose names are not mentioned, went to Quintanilla's house, took him from it, and the deputy sheriff with one Walter Weaver placed him in a motor car and drove with him, first to Casey's house, where they put on a new tire, and then in the direction of Edinburg to take him to the county jail. On July 18, 1922, about noon, Quintanilla's corpse was found near the side of this road, some three miles from

---

54   (1987), 17 Iran–U.S. Cl. Trib. Rep. 92 at 106-7.

55   See also G.S. Goodwin-Gill, *International Law and the Movement of Persons Between States* (1978); R. Plender, *International Migration Law*, 2d ed. (1988); R.L. Cave, "State Responsibility for Constructive Wrongful Expulsion of Foreign Nationals" (1987-88) 11 Fordham Int'l L.J. 802; and refer to Chapter 9, "State Jurisdiction Over Persons," Section B.3 on "Admission and Exclusion of Aliens."

56   [1933] 1 D.L.R. 123 at 128 (Man. C.A.).

Edinburg, traces showing that he had been taken there in a motor car. Bernard and Weaver were accused by the Mexican Consul at Hidalgo, Texas, and were accordingly arrested, but released on bail; Bernard's appointment as a deputy sheriff was cancelled by his sheriff on July 22, 1922. The public prosecutor made investigations and submitted the case to the Grand Jury, but the Grand Jury deferred it from 1922 to 1923, from 1923 to 1924, and never took action upon it. ...

[2] It appears from the record that Quintanilla was taken into custody on July 16, 1922, by a deputy sheriff of the State of Texas, to put him at the disposal of the judicial officers; it is left uncertain whether this official was provided with any authorization to take Quintanilla from his house and arrest him. The United States Government never reported what this deputy sheriff did with Quintanilla after he had taken him under custody. The young man apparently never reached the county jail. The deputy sheriff may have changed his mind and set him at liberty, and after that Quintanilla may have been murdered by an unknown person. An enemy of Quintanilla may have come up and taken him from the car. The companion of the deputy sheriff, who was not an official, may have killed Quintanilla; or the two custodians may have acted in self-defence. The United States Government has been silent on all of this. The only thing the record clearly shows is that Quintanilla was taken into custody by a State official, and that he never was delivered to any jail. The first question before this Commission, therefore, is whether under international law these circumstances present a case for which a Government must be held liable.

[3] The Commission does not hesitate to answer in the affirmative. The most notable parallel in international law relates to war prisoners, hostages, and interned members of a belligerent army and navy. ... The case before this Commission is analogous. A foreigner is taken into custody by a state official. It would go too far to hold that the Government is liable for everything which may befall him. But it has to account for him. The Government can be held liable if it is proven that it has treated him cruelly, harshly, unlawfully; so much the more it is liable if it can say only that it took him into custody—either in jail or in some other place and form—and that it ignores what happened to him.

[4] The question then arises whether this duty to account for a man in Governmental custody is modified by the fact that the custodian himself is accused of having killed his prisoner and, as an accused, cannot be made to testify against himself. The two things clearly are separate. If the Government is obligated to state what happened to the man in its custody, its officials are bound to inform their Governments. It might be that the custodians themselves perish in a calamity together with the men in their custody, and therefore can not furnish any information. But if they are alive, and are silent, the Government has to bear the consequences. The Commission holds, therefore, that under international law ... the respondent Government is liable for the damages originating in this act of a State official and resulting in injustice.[57]

---

57   See also *Noyes Claim (United States v. Panama)* (1933), 6 R.I.A.A. 308.

(c) Maladministration of Justice

B.E. Chattin Claim
United States v. Mexico
General Claims Commission (1927), 4 R.I.A.A. 282 at 283-99

VAN VOLLENHOVEN, Presiding Commissioner:

[1] This claim is made by the United States of America against the United Mexican States on behalf of B.E. Chattin, an American national. Chattin, who since 1908 was an employee (at first freight conductor, thereafter passenger conductor) of the Ferrocarril Sud-Pacífico de México (Southern Pacific Railroad Company of Mexico) and who in the Summer of 1910 performed his duties in the State of Sinaloa, was on July 9, 1910, arrested at Mazatlan, Sinaloa, on a charge of embezzlement; was tried there in January, 1911, convicted on February 6, 1911, and sentenced to two years' imprisonment; but was released from the jail at Mazatlán in May or June, 1911, as a consequence of disturbances caused by the Madero revolution. He then returned to the United States. It is alleged that the arrest, the trial and the sentence were illegal, that the treatment in jail was inhuman, and that Chattin was damaged to the extent of $50,000.00 which amount Mexico should pay. ...

[12] The next allegation on the American side is that Chattin's trial was held in an illegal manner. The contentions are: (a) that the Governor of the State, for political reasons, used his influence to have this accused and three of his fellow conductors convicted; (b) that the proceedings against the four conductors were consolidated without reason; (c) that the proceedings were unduly delayed; (d) that an exorbitant amount of bail was required; (e) that the accused was not duly informed of the accusations; (f) that the accused lacked the aid of counsel; (g) that the accused lacked the aid of an interpreter; (h) that there were no oaths required of the witnesses; (i) that there was no such a thing as a confrontation between the witnesses and the accused; and (j) that the hearings in open court which led to sentences of from two years' to two years and eight months' imprisonment lasted only some five minutes. ...

[15] For undue delay of the proceedings (allegation c), there is convincing evidence in more than one respect. The formal proceedings began on July 9, 1910. Chattin was not heard in court until more than one hundred days thereafter. The stubs and perhaps other pieces of evidence against Chattin were presented to the Court on August 3, 1910; Chattin however, was not allowed to testify regarding them until October 28, 1910. ...

[22] The whole of the proceedings discloses a most astonishing lack of seriousness on the part of the Court. ... It is not for the Commission to endeavour to reach from the record any conviction as to the innocence or guilt of Chattin and his colleagues; but even in case they were guilty, the Commission would render a bad service to the Government of Mexico if it failed to place the stamp of its disapproval and even indignation on a criminal procedure so far below international standards of civilization as the present one. If the wholesome rule of international law as to respect for the judiciary of another country ... shall stand, it would seem of the utmost necessity that

appellate tribunals when, in exceptional cases, discovering proceedings of this type should take against them the strongest measures possible under constitution and laws, in order to safeguard their country's reputation. ...

[29] Bringing the proceedings of Mexican authorities against Chattin to the test of international standards (paragraph 11), there can be no doubt of their being highly insufficient. Inquiring whether there is convincing evidence of these unjust proceedings (paragraph 11), the answer must be in the affirmative. Since this is a case of alleged responsibility of Mexico for injustice committed by its judiciary, it is necessary to inquire whether the treatment of Chattin amounts even to an outrage, to bad faith, to wilful neglect of duty, or to an insufficiency of governmental action recognizable by every unbiased man (paragraph 11); and the answer here again can only be in the affirmative.

[30] An illegal arrest of Chattin is not proven. Irregularity of court proceedings is proven with reference to absence of proper investigations, insufficiency of confrontations, withholding from the accused the opportunity to know all of the charges brought against him, undue delay of the proceedings, making the hearings in open court a mere formality, and a continued absence of seriousness on the part of the Court. Insufficiency of the evidence against Chattin is not convincingly proven; intentional severity of the punishment is proven, without its being shown that the explanation is to be found in unfairmindedness of the Judge. Mistreatment in prison is not proven. Taking into consideration, on the one hand, that this is a case of direct governmental responsibility, and, on the other hand, that Chattin, because of his escape, has stayed in jail for eleven months instead of for two years, it would seem proper to allow in behalf of this claimant damages in the sum of $5,000.00, without interest.

NOTES

1) Hackworth, in his *Digest of International Law*, described denial of justice thus:[58]

In a broad sense denial of justice may result from acts or omissions of authorities of any one or more of the three branches of government, *i.e.*, the executive, legislative, or judicial. There is a wide variance in the use of the term as is illustrated by the fact that some employ it to cover any delinquency on the part of an organ of the government resulting in injury to an alien, while others in employing the term restrict it to denial of access to judicial remedies. It is more frequently employed in connection with acts or omissions of the judicial branch, as distinguished from other branches of the government, since, generally speaking, exhaustion of available judicial remedies is a prerequisite to a valid complaint that the alien has been denied justice. Denial of justice may consist either of denial of access to the courts or of injustice at their hand. It may not be predicated solely on the fact that the decision of the court might have been different or that reasonable men might differ as to its correctness. Nations are considered to be equal, and with but few exceptions judgments of their courts of last resort are considered to be and are accepted as just and proper. There is, therefore, a strong presumption

---

58   Vol. 5 at 526-27. See also A.H. Feller, *The Mexican Claims Commissions 1923-1934: A Study in the Law and Procedure of International Tribunals* (1935).

in favor of their correctness, and a complainant who bases his grievance upon an alleged denial of justice by the courts assumes the obligation of establishing by clear evidence that the presumption does not apply to his case. As a general proposition if the decision appears to have been unjust and is shown to have been influenced by improper motives; if corruption of the court is shown to have existed; or if there was prejudice or discrimination against the alien because of his nationality or against aliens generally; or if there was unconscionable delay by the court or other grave irregularities resulting in serious injustice; the foundation is laid for diplomatic representation or for international adjudication.

2) The report of a Sub-Committee of the League of Nations Committee of Experts for the Progressive Codification of International Law provided the following description:

Denial of Justice consists in refusing to allow foreigners easy access to the courts to defend those rights which the national law accords them. A refusal of the competent judge to exercise jurisdiction also constitutes a denial of justice.[59]

3) In the *Neer Claim*, Commissioner Nielsen thought it "useful and proper to apply the term denial of justice in a broader sense than that of a designation solely of a wrongful act on the part of the judicial branch of the government. I consider that a denial of justice may, broadly speaking, be properly regarded as the general ground of diplomatic intervention."[60] A wider view is also expressed in the Harvard Draft Convention on the Responsibility of States for Damage Done in Their Territory to the Person or Property of Foreigners:[61]

Article 9

Denial of justice exists when there is a denial, unwarranted delay or obstruction of access to courts, gross deficiency in the administration of judicial or remedial process, failure to provide those guarantees which are generally considered indispensable to the proper administration of justice, or a manifestly unjust judgment. An error of a national court which does not produce manifest injustice is not a denial of justice.

3. Protection of Property[62]

One of the most hotly disputed fields within international law as it relates to the treatment of aliens is the extent to which a state may deprive aliens of their property. Property in this context is defined very broadly to include both tangible and intangible assets—from shipments of ore to concession contracts and artistic rights. The problem has been especially serious since the vast nationalizations following the Soviet revolution and the attempts by newly decolonized states to regain control over their natural resources.

---

59   (1926) 20 A.J.I.L. Sp. Supp. 177 at 202.

60   *U.S. v. Mexico* (1926), 4 R.I.A.A. 60 at 64.

61   (1929) 23 A.J.I.L. Sp. Supp. 131 at 134.

62   See, in addition to the sources mentioned *supra* note 1, Jiménez de Aréchaga, "State Responsibility for the Nationalization of Foreign Owned Property" (1978) 11 N.Y.U.J. Int. L. & Pol. 179; A. Mouri, *The International Law of Expropriation as Reflected in the Work of the Iran–U.S. Claims Tribunal* (1994); and International Centre for Settlement of Investment Disputes, *Investment Promotion and Protection Treaties* (1997).

Nationalizations of large enterprises or even entire sectors of the economy have thus replaced more limited takings of property in the context of a commercial dispute, which were the typical type of dispute in the previous century. Protection of aliens against expropriation is now directly linked to issues of state sovereignty, the right of peoples to self-determination, and the property rights of individuals and corporations.

In the 19th century, the responsibility of a state for expropriation (or nationalization, which is taken here as a species of expropriation) was regarded as a clear basis for an international claim. The greater control by states over the national economy and over almost every aspect of private enterprise and the nationalization measures adopted by many states, especially after World War II, make it difficult, if not impossible, to treat an expropriation of foreign property as contrary to international law, where it is based on grounds of public utility, security, or the national interest in accordance with a declared policy applied without discrimination to the citizens of the expropriating State and to aliens alike.

However, if the expropriation measure is in violation of a treaty or of a special arrangement between the government and aliens, or of a recognized principle of international law, the measure then becomes *per se* a wrongful act that involves state responsibility. The expropriation measure itself is the wrongful act, rather than the non-performance of obligations arising out of the expropriation, such as the failure to compensate.

Today, it appears that the right of a state to expropriate foreign property for a public purpose related to its internal needs is recognized by customary international law. However, expropriation measures that are arbitrary or discriminatory or that are motivated by considerations of a political nature unrelated to the internal well-being of the taking state are illegal and invalid and call for restitution or, if not possible, compensation.

What amounts to expropriation and what measure of compensation must be paid under international law are questions that have not yet been settled. Rules on these questions involve the delicate balancing of the need to provide some security in order to foster foreign investment and the need to control economic activities as an accessory to full national sovereignty.

(a) Basic Principles

North American Free Trade Agreement
(1993) 32 I.L.M. 296

Article 1110: Expropriation and Compensation

1. No Party shall directly or indirectly nationalize or expropriate an investment of an investor of another Party in its territory or take a measure tantamount to nationalization or expropriation of such an investment ("expropriation"), except:

(a) for a public purpose;

(b) on a non-discriminatory basis;

(c) in accordance with due process of law and the general principles of treatment provided in Article 1105; and

(d) upon payment of compensation in accordance with paragraphs 2 to 6.

2. Compensation shall be equivalent to the fair market value of the expropriated investment immediately before the expropriation took place ("date of expropriation"), and shall not reflect any change in value occurring because the intended expropriation had become known earlier. Valuation criteria shall include going concern value, asset value (including declared tax value of tangible property) and other criteria, as appropriate to determine fair market value.

3. Compensation shall be paid without delay and be fully realizable.

4. If payment is made in a G7 currency, compensation shall include interest at a commercially reasonable rate for that currency from the date of expropriation until the date of actual payment thereof.

5. If a Party elects to pay in a currency other than a G7 currency, the amount paid on the date of payment, if converted into a G7 currency at the market rate of exchange prevailing on that date, shall be no less than if the amount of compensation owed on the date of expropriation had been converted into that G7 currency at the market rate of exchange prevailing on that date, and interest had accrued at a commercially reasonable rate for that G7 currency from the date of expropriation until the date of payment.

6. Upon payment, compensation shall be freely transferable as provided in Article 1109.

7. This Article does not apply to the issuance of compulsory licenses granted in relation to intellectual property rights, or the revocation, limitation or creation of intellectual property rights to the extent that such issuance, revocation, limitation or creation is consistent with Chapter Seventeen (Intellectual Property).

8. For purposes of this Article and for greater clarity, a non-discriminatory measure of general application shall not be considered a measure tantamount to an expropriation of a debt security or loan covered by this Chapter solely on the ground that the measure imposes costs on the debtor that cause it to default on the debt.

Restatement of the Law (Third), Foreign Relations Law of the United States
American Law Institute (1987)

§712. Economic Injury to Nationals of Other States

A state is responsible under international law for injury resulting from:

1) a taking by the state of the property of a national of another state that is (a) not for a public purpose, or (b) discriminatory, or (c) not accompanied by provision for just compensation; for compensation to be just under this Subsection, it must, in the absence of exceptional circumstances, be in an amount equivalent to the value of the property taken, be paid at the time of taking, or within a reasonable time thereafter with interest from the date of taking, and be in a form economically usable by the foreign national;

2) a repudiation or breach by the state of a contract with a national of another state

(a) where the repudiation or breach is (i) discriminatory; or (ii) motivated by non-commercial considerations and compensatory damages are not paid; or

(b) where the foreign national is not given an adequate forum to determine his claim of breach or is not compensated for any breach determined to have occurred;

3) other arbitrary or discriminatory acts or omissions by the state that impair property or other economic interests of a national of another state.

Resolution on Permanent Sovereignty over Natural Resources
GA Res. 1803 (XVII), UN GAOR, 17th Sess., Supp. No. 17,
U.N. Doc. A/5217 (1962) 15

The General Assembly, ...
Declares that:

1. The right of peoples and nations to permanent sovereignty over their natural wealth and resources must be exercised in the interest of their national development and of the well-being of the people of the State concerned. ...

3. In cases where authorization is granted, the capital imported and the earnings on that capital shall be governed by the terms thereof, by the national legislation in force, and by international law. The profits derived must be shared in the proportions freely agreed upon, in each case, between the investors and the recipient State, due care being taken to ensure that there is no impairment, for any reason, of that State's sovereignty over its natural wealth and resources.

4. Nationalization, expropriation or requisitioning shall be based on grounds or reasons of public utility, security or the national interest which are recognized as overriding purely individual or private interests, both domestic and foreign. In such cases the owner shall be paid appropriate compensation, in accordance with the rules in force in the State taking such measures in the exercise of its sovereignty and in accordance with international law. In any case where the question of compensation gives rise to a controversy, the national jurisdiction of the State taking such measures shall be exhausted. However, upon agreement by sovereign States and other parties concerned, settlement of the dispute should be made through arbitration or international adjudication. ...

8. Foreign investment agreements freely entered into by or between sovereign States shall be observed in good faith; States and international organizations shall strictly and conscientiously respect the sovereignty of peoples and nations over their natural wealth and resources in accordance with the Charter and the principles set forth in the present resolution.

Charter of Economic Rights and Duties of States
GA Res. 3281 (XXIX), UN GAOR, 29th Sess., Supp. No. 31,
U.N. Doc. A/9631 (1974) 50

Article 2

1. Every State has and shall freely exercise full permanent sovereignty, including possession, use and disposal, over all its wealth, natural resources and economic activities.

2. Each State has the right:

(a) To regulate and exercise authority over foreign investment within its national jurisdiction in accordance with its laws and regulations and in conformity with its national objectives and priorities. No State shall be compelled to grant preferential treatment to foreign investment;

(b) To regulate and supervise the activities of transnational corporations within its national jurisdiction and take measures to ensure that such activities comply with its laws, rules and regulations and conform with its economic and social policies. Transnational corporations shall not intervene in the internal affairs of a host State. Every State should, with full regard for its sovereign rights, co-operate with other States in the exercise of the right set forth in this subparagraph;

(c) To nationalize, expropriate or transfer ownership of foreign property in which case appropriate compensation should be paid by the State adopting such measures, taking into account its relevant laws and regulations and all circumstances that the State considers pertinent. In any case where the question of compensation gives rise to a controversy, it shall be settled under the domestic law of the nationalizing State and by its tribunals, unless it is freely and mutually agreed by all States concerned that other peaceful means be sought on the basis of the sovereign equality of States and in accordance with the principle of free choice of means. ...

Article 16

1. It is the right and duty of all States, individually and collectively, to eliminate colonialism, *apartheid*, racial discrimination, neo-colonialism and all forms of foreign aggression, occupation and domination, and the economic and social consequences thereof, as a prerequisite for development. States which practise such coercive policies are economically responsible to the countries, territories and peoples affected for the restitution and full compensation for the exploitation and depletion of, and damages to, the natural and all other resources of those countries, territories and peoples. It is the duty of all States to extend assistance to them.

2. No State has the right to promote or encourage investments that may constitute an obstacle to the liberation of a territory occupied by force.

NOTES

1) Canada voted in favour of resolution 1803 (Permanent Sovereignty over Natural Resources) but abstained in the vote on resolution 3281 (Charter of Economic Rights and Duties of States), a pattern followed by many western states. The Canadian position on the Charter was explained in a statement made in the Second Committee of the 29th Session of the U.N. General Assembly by the Canadian Representative on December 6, 1974:[63]

My delegation does not deny the right of a state to nationalize foreign property but it does maintain that this right is conditional upon the payment of compensation. The question of what amount of compensation is just or equitable will naturally depend upon the particular

---

63   Press Release No. 43.

circumstances of each individual case, but my delegation is unable to accept a text which seeks to establish the principle that a state may nationalize or expropriate foreign property without compensation, in effect to confiscate such property. This, in the view of my delegation, is the effect of paragraph 2(c) of Article 2.

I wish to refer now, Mr. Chairman, to an issue which constitutes one of the most important obstacles to my Delegation's support of the Charter as a whole, namely the absence of any reference in Article 2 to the applicability of international law to the treatment of foreign investment. There is, of course, a very relevant distinction between the body of law to be applied in the event of a dispute and the tribunal which is to apply that law. It is clear that, in the absence of a relevant acceptance of the compulsory jurisdiction of the International Court of Justice (in the case of disputes between states) or some other agreement between the parties respecting disputes settlement, jurisdiction in respect of a dispute rests with the appropriate tribunal of the host state.

This does not, however, alter the fact that the host state's measures must be carried out in conformity with its international legal obligations. There is, of course, disagreement among states over whether such obligations arise only from treaties or from principles of customary international law as well.

2) The Charter was central to the push by developing states to adopt a New International Economic Order, with a watered-down obligation to provide compensation for expropriation as the lightning rod for the clash between industrialized and developing states. It suggests an alternative to the traditional "Hull doctrine," expressed by the American Secretary of State in 1938, and implied in resolution 1803 through the reference to the "appropriate compensation ... in accordance with international law." Instead of a "prompt, adequate and effective compensation," the Charter suggests "appropriate compensation ... taking into account its relevant laws and regulations and all circumstances that the State considers pertinent." Only domestic law and considerations, then, are linked to the issue of compensation. The Charter favours a historical perspective according to which, for example, the benefits obtained by western investors during colonization may be used to offset full compensation. Terminologically, the Charter states that compensation *should* be paid where resolution 1803 indicates that compensation *shall* be paid.

Texaco v. Libya
(1977), 53 I.L.R. 389; (1978) 17 I.L.M. 1

[By a series of decrees in 1973 and 1974, the Libyan government nationalized the rights and property of the two plaintiff oil companies, Texaco and California Asiatic, in Libya. The companies claimed that this action breached their Deeds of Concession from the Government and they sought arbitration, as was their right under those deeds. Libya opposed the appointment of an arbitrator, claiming that its acts of nationalization were not subject to arbitration because they were acts of sovereignty, and it took no further part in the case. One of the issues to be decided by the Arbitrator, Professor René Dupuy, was the legal status of resolution 1803 and of the Charter, reproduced above in this section.]

AWARD OF THE ARBITRATOR: ...

[83] The general question of the legal validity of the Resolutions of the United Nations has been widely discussed by the writers. This Tribunal will recall first that, under Article 10 of the U.N. Charter, the General Assembly only issues "recommendations," which have long appeared to be texts having no binding force and carrying no obligations for the Member States.

Refusal to recognize any legal validity of United Nations Resolutions must, however, be qualified according to the various texts enacted by the United Nations. These are very different and have varying legal value, but it is impossible to deny that the United Nations' activities have had a significant influence on the content of contemporary international law. In appraising the legal validity of the above-mentioned Resolutions, this Tribunal will take account of the criteria usually taken into consideration, i.e., the examination of voting conditions and the analysis of the provisions concerned.

[84(1)] With respect to the first point, Resolution 1803 (XVII) of 14 December 1962 [reproduced above in this section] was passed by the General Assembly by 87 votes to 2, with 12 abstentions. It is particularly important to note that the majority voted for this text, including many States of the Third World, but also several Western developed countries with market economies, including the most important one, the United States. The principles stated in this Resolution were therefore assented to by a great many States representing not only all geographical areas but also all economic systems.

From this point of view, this Tribunal notes that the affirmative vote of several developed countries with a market economy was made possible in particular by the inclusion in the Resolution of two references to international law, and one passage relating to the importance of international cooperation for economic development. ...

The reference to international law, in particular in the field of nationalization, was therefore an essential factor in the support given by several Western countries to Resolution 1803 (XVII).

[85] On the contrary, it appears to this Tribunal that the conditions under which Resolutions 3171 (XXVII), 3201 (S-VI) and 3281 (XXIX) (Charter of the Economic Rights and Duties of States) were notably different:

— Resolution 3171 (XXVII) was adopted by a recorded vote of 108 votes to 1, with 16 abstentions, but this Tribunal notes that a separate vote was requested with respect to the paragraph in the operative part mentioned in the Libyan Government's Memorandum whereby the General Assembly stated that the application of the principle according to which nationalizations effected by States as the expression of their sovereignty implied that it is within the right of each State to determine the amount of possible compensation and the means of their payment, and that any dispute which might arise should be settled in conformity with the national law of each State instituting measures of this kind. As a consequence of a roll-call, this paragraph was adopted by 86 votes to 11 (Federal Republic of Germany, Belgium, Spain, United States, France, Israel, Italy, Japan, The Netherlands, Portugal, United Kingdom), with 23 abstentions (South Africa, Australia, Austria, Barbados, Canada, Ivory Coast, Denmark, Finland, Ghana, Greece, Haiti, India, Indonesia, Ireland, Luxembourg,

Malawi, Malaysia, Nepal, Nicaragua, Norway, New Zealand, Philippines, Rwanda, Singapore, Sri Lanka, Sweden, Thailand, Turkey).

This specific paragraph concerning nationalizations, disregarding the role of international law, not only was not consented to by the most important Western countries, but caused a number of the developing countries to abstain.

— Resolution 3201 (S-VI) was adopted without a vote by the General Assembly, but the statements made by 38 delegates showed clearly and explicitly what was the position of each main group of countries. The Tribunal should therefore note that the most important Western countries were opposed to abandoning the compromise solution contained in Resolution 1803 (XVII).

— The conditions under which Resolution 3281 (XXIX), proclaiming the Charter of Economic Rights and Duties of States, was adopted also show unambiguously that there was no general consensus of the States with respect to the most important provisions and in particular those concerning nationalization. Having been the subject matter of a roll-call vote, the Charter was adopted by 118 votes to 6, with 10 abstentions.

The analysis of votes on specific sections of the Charter is most significant insofar as the present case is concerned. From this point of view, paragraph 2(c) of Article 2 of the Charter, which limits consideration of the characteristics of compensation to the State and does not refer to international law, was voted by 104 to 16, with 6 abstentions, all of the industrialized countries with market economies having abstained or having voted against it.

[86] ... while it is now possible to recognize that resolutions of the United Nations have a certain legal value, this legal value differs considerably, depending on the type of resolution and the conditions attached to its adoption and its provisions. Even under the assumption that they are resolutions of a declaratory nature, which is the case of the Charter of Economic Rights and Duties of States, the legal value is variable. Ambassador Castañeda, who was Chairman of the Working Group entrusted with the task of preparing this Charter, admitted that "it is extremely difficult to determine with certainty the legal force of declaratory resolutions," that it is "impossible to lay down a general rule in this respect," and that "the legal value of the declaratory resolutions therefore includes an immense gamut of nuances" ("La Valeur Juridique des Résolutions des Nations Unies," 129 R.C.A.D.I. 204 (1970), at 319-20).

As this Tribunal has already indicated, the legal value of the resolutions which are relevant to the present case can be determined on the basis of circumstances under which they were adopted and by analysis of the principles which they state:

— With respect to the first point, the absence of any binding force of the resolutions of the General Assembly of the United Nations implies that such resolutions must be accepted by the members of the United Nations in order to be legally binding. In this respect, the Tribunal notes that only Resolution 1803 (XVII) of 14 December 1962 was supported by a majority of Member States representing all of the various groups. By contrast, the other Resolutions mentioned above, and in particular those referred to in the Libyan Memorandum, were supported by a majority of States but not by any of the developed countries with market economies which carry on the largest part of international trade.

[87] ... (2) With respect to the second point, to wit the appraisal of the legal value on the basis of the principles stated, it appears essential to this Tribunal to distinguish between those provisions stating the existence of a right on which the generality of the States has expressed agreement and those provisions introducing new principles which were rejected by certain representative groups of States and having nothing more than a *de lege ferenda* value only in the eyes of the States which have adopted them: as far as the others are concerned, the rejection of these same principles implies that they consider them as being *contra legem*. With respect to the former, which proclaim rules recognized by the community of nations, they do not create a custom but confirm one by formulating it and specifying its scope, thereby making it possible to determine whether or not one is confronted with a legal rule. As has been noted by Ambassador Castañeda, "[such resolutions] do not create the law: they have a declaratory nature of noting what does exist" (129 R.C.A.D.I. 204 (1970), at 315).

On the basis of the circumstances of adoption mentioned above and by expressing an *opinio juris communis*, Resolution 1803 (XVII) seems to this Tribunal to reflect the state of customary law existing in this field. ...

[90] The argument of the Libyan Government, based on the relevant resolutions enacted by the General Assembly of the United Nations, that any dispute relating to nationalization or its consequences should be decided in conformity with the provisions of the municipal law of the nationalizing State and only in its courts, is also negated by a complete analysis of the whole text of the Charter of Economic Rights and Duties of States.

From this point of view, even though Article 2 of the Charter does not explicitly refer to international law, this Tribunal concludes that the provisions referred to in this Article do not escape all norms of international law. Article 33, paragraph 2, of this Resolution states as follows: "2. In their interpretation and application, the provisions of the present Charter are interrelated and each provision should be construed in the context of the other provisions." Now, among the fundamental elements of international economic relations quoted in the Charter, principle (j) is headed as follows: "Fulfillment in good faith of international obligations."

Analyzing the scope of these various provisions, Ambassador Castañeda, who chaired the Working Group charged with drawing up the Charter of Economic Rights and Duties of States, formally stated that the principle of performance in good faith of international obligations laid down in Chapter I(j) of the Charter applies to all matters governed by it, including, in particular, matters referred to in Article 2. Following his analysis, this particularly competent and eminent scholar concluded as follows:

> The Charter accepts that international law may operate as a factor limiting the freedom of the State should foreign interests be affected, even though Article 2 does not state this explicitly. This stems legally from the provisions included in other Articles of the Charter which should be interpreted and applied jointly with those of Article 2. ("La Charte des Droits et Devoirs Economiques des Etats. Note sur son Processus d'Elaboration." 20 A.F.D.I. 31 (1974) at 54.)

NOTES

1) As the *Texaco* award makes clear, the right of a state to expropriate property is uncontested and universally accepted as a direct corollary of the principle of permanent sovereignty over natural resources and economic development. The exercise of that right, however, is subject to a number of conditions.

2) What differences are there between resolution 1803 and the Charter? Note especially by what legal standards the matters of expropriation and of compensation are to be measured.

3) Note that both resolutions employ the term "appropriate compensation," but do they use them in the same sense? See the discussion below in Section B.3(c) on "Standard of Compensation and Method of Valuation."

4) In the Charter, what is meant by the phrase "compensation should be paid ... taking into account ... all circumstances that the state considers pertinent"? Does it mean that national treatment need not be offered to foreign investors? Should any of the following circumstances be taken into consideration to reduce or eliminate the compensation to be paid: the nature of the circumstances in which the foreign investment was made, the real enrichment of the expropriating state, excessive profits, unpaid taxes, questionable financial practices, environmental damage, and employee benefits?

5) What is the relevance of article 16 to the interpretation of article 2(2)(c) of the Charter?

6) What is the meaning of a "taking" of property? The concept could potentially be defined in such a broad manner to prevent any national regulation that negatively affects the enjoyment of property rights by an alien. The Iran–U.S. Claims Tribunal held in *Starett Housing Corp. v. Iran* that

> it is recognized in international law that measures taken by a State can interfere with property rights to such an extent that these rights are rendered so useless that they must be deemed to have been expropriated, even though the State does not purport to have expropriated them and the legal title to the property formally remains with the original owner.

Mere assumption of control, however, is not *per se* unlawful. As the Tribunal noted in *Tippetts, Abbett, McCarthy, Stratton v. TAMS-AFFA Consulting Engineers of Iran*,[64] expropriation will only be found in cases where it is clear that the owner was deprived of basic rights of ownership in a clearly non-ephemeral way. In determining whether there had been an expropriation, the Tribunal considered the intent of the government as being of less weight than the actual effect of the measures imposed on the owner.[65]

(b) Conditions

It is generally accepted that expropriation may be lawful only if it is in pursuance of a public purpose, if it is non-discriminatory, and if it gives rise to appropriate compensation.

---

64 (1983) 4 Iran–U.S. Cl. Trib. Rep. 122 at 154. Applying this formula, see also *Harza Engineering Co. v. Iran* (1982) 1 Iran–U.S. Cl. Trib. Rep. 499; *Otis Elevator Co. and the Islamic Republic of Iran* (1987), 14 Iran–U.S. Cl. Trib. Rep. 283; and *Payne v. Iran* (1986) 12 Iran–U.S. Cl. Trib. Rep. 3.

65 (1984), 6 Iran–U.S. Cl. Trib. Rep. 219.

The issue of "public purpose" was discussed by the Iran–U.S. Claims Tribunal in *Amoco International Finance Corp. v. Iran*:[66]

> [145] A precise definition of the "public purpose" for which an expropriation may be lawfully decided has neither been agreed upon in international law nor even suggested. It is clear that, as a result of the modern acceptance of the right to nationalize, this term is broadly interpreted, and that States, in practice, are granted extensive discretion. An expropriation, the only purpose of which would have been to avoid contractual obligations of the State or of an entity controlled by it, could not, nevertheless, be considered as lawful under international law. ... Such an expropriation, indeed, would be contrary to the principle of good faith and to accept it as lawful would run counter to the well-settled rule that a State has the right to commit itself by contract to foreign corporations. ... It is also generally accepted that a State has no right to expropriate a foreign concern only for financial purposes. It must, however, be observed that, in recent practice and mostly in the oil industry, States have admitted expressly, in a certain number of cases, that they were nationalizing foreign properties primarily in order to obtain a greater share, or even the totality, of the revenues drawn from the exploitation of a national natural resource, which, according to them, should accrue to the development of the country. Such a purpose has not generally been denounced as unlawful and illegitimate.
>
> [146] The Tribunal need not determine the delicate legal issues raised in the preceding paragraph. It cannot be doubted that the Single Article Act was adopted for a clear public purpose, namely to complete the nationalization of the oil industry in Iran initiated by the 1951 Nationalization of the Iranian Oil Industry Act, with a view to implementing one of the main economic and political objectives of the new Islamic Government. The decision of the Special Commission relative to Khemco was taken in apparent conformity with the Single Article Act. Even if financial considerations were considered in the adoption of such a decision—which would have been only natural, but which has not been evidenced—this fact would not be sufficient, in the opinion of the Tribunal, to prove that this decision was not taken for a public purpose.

While the requirement of public purpose or utility is generally uncontested, it has not proven to be a significant limitation to expropriation, as proof of the absence of a public purpose is extremely difficult. In *Libyan American Oil Co. v. Libya*[67] (Liamco Case) the arbitrator, Dr. Mahmassani, took the unusual position of rejecting this requirement to use instead the prohibition of discrimination, usually considered a distinct requirement:[68]

> As to the contention that the said measures were politically motivated and not in pursuance of a legitimate public purpose, it is the general opinion in international theory that the public utility principle is not a necessary requisite for the legality of a nationalization. This principle was mentioned by Grotius and other later publicists, but now there is no

---

66   (1987), 15 Iran–U.S. Cl. Trib. Rep. 189.

67   (1981) 20 I.L.M. 1. See also *B.P. v. Libya* (1973), 53 I.L.R. 297 and R.B. von Mehren & P.N. Kourides, "International Arbitrations Between States and Foreign Private Parties: The Libyan Nationalization Cases" (1981) 75 A.J.I.L. 476.

68   *Ibid.* at 58-60.

international authority, from a judicial or any other source, to support its application to nationalization. ...

However, political motivation may take the shape of discrimination as a result of political retaliation ... .

It is clear and undisputed that non-discrimination is a requisite for the validity of a lawful nationalization. This is a rule well established in international legal theory and practice ... . Therefore, a purely discriminatory nationalization is illegal and wrongful.

Libya's motive for nationalisation was its desire to preserve the ownership of its oil. ... The political motive [complained of] was not the predominant motive for nationalisation, and ... such motive *per se* does not constitute a sufficient proof of a purely discriminatory measure.

This position is inconsistent with resolution 1803, which requires a public purpose. Do you think that a prohibition of discrimination can achieve the same goals as the requirement of public utility? If expropriation must not discriminate against aliens, how can a government nationalize an industry wholly owned by foreign interests? Is the requirement better suited for discrete takings rather than nationalizations?

The principle of non-discrimination has not proven to be a significant limitation to the right of expropriation. It is indeed generally accepted that foreign investors can benefit from positive discrimination in cases of nationalization. Moreover, arbitrators have on many occasions acknowledged that major nationalizations often occur incrementally, in a manner which does not affect all foreign investors in a similar fashion.

(c) Standard of Compensation and Method of Valuation

The standard and method of compensation are still very controversial and remain central to the issue of the legality of expropriation of foreign property.

World Bank Guidelines on the Treatment of Foreign Direct Investment
(1992) 31 I.L.M. 1363 at 1382

IV. Expropriation and Unilateral Alterations or Termination of Contracts

1. A State may not expropriate or otherwise take in whole or in part a foreign private investment in its territory, or take measures which have similar effects, except where this is done in accordance with applicable legal procedures, in pursuance in good faith of a public purpose, without discrimination on the basis of nationality and against the payment of appropriate compensation.

2. Compensation for a specific investment taken by the State will, according to the details provided below, be deemed "appropriate" if it is adequate, effective and prompt.

3. Compensation will be deemed "adequate" if it is based on the fair market value of the taken asset as such value is determined immediately before the time at which the taking occurred or the decision to take the asset became publicly known.

4. Determination of the "fair market value" will be acceptable if conducted according to a method agreed by the State and the foreign investor (hereinafter referred to as the parties) or by a tribunal or another body designated by the parties.

5. In the absence of a determination agreed by, or based on the agreement of, the parties, the fair market value will be acceptable if determined by the State according to reasonable criteria related to the market value of the investment, i.e., in an amount that a willing buyer would normally pay to a willing seller after taking into account the nature of the investment, the circumstances in which it would operate in the future and its specific characteristics, including the period in which it has been in existence, the proportion of tangible assets in the total investment and other relevant factors pertinent to the specific circumstances of each case.

6. Without implying the exclusive validity of a single standard for the fairness by which compensation is to be determined and as an illustration of the reasonable determination by a State of the market value of the investment under Section 5 above, such determination will be deemed reasonable if conducted as follows:

(i) for a going concern with a proven record of profitability, on the basis of the discounted cash flow value;

(ii) for an enterprise which, not being a proven going concern, demonstrates lack of profitability, on the basis of the liquidation value;

(iii) for other assets, on the basis of (a) the replacement value or (b) the book value in case such value has been recently assessed or has been determined as of the date of the taking and can therefore be deemed to represent a reasonable replacement value.

For the purpose of this provision:

— a "*going concern*" means an enterprise consisting of income-producing assets which has been in operation for a sufficient period of time to generate the data required for the calculation of future income and which could have been expected with reasonable certainty, if the taking had not occurred, to continue producing legitimate income over the course of its economic life in the general circumstances following the taking by the State;

— "*discounted cash flow value*" means the cash receipts realistically expected from the enterprise in each future year of its economic life as reasonably projected minus that year's expected cash expenditure, after discounting this net cash flow for each year by a factor which reflects the time value of money, expected inflation, and the risk associated with such cash flow under realistic circumstances. Such discount rate may be measured by examining the rate of return available in the same market on alternative investments of comparable risk on the basis of their present value;

— "*liquidation value*" means the amounts at which individual assets comprising the enterprise or the entire assets of the enterprise could be sold under conditions of liquidation to a willing buyer less any liabilities which the enterprise has to meet;

— "*replacement value*" means the cash amount required to replace the individual assets of the enterprise in their actual state as of the date of the taking; and

— "*book value*" means the difference between the enterprise's assets and liabilities as recorded on its financial statements or the amount at which the taken tangible assets appear on the balance sheet of the enterprise, representing their cost after deducting accumulated depreciation in accordance with generally accepted accounting principles.

Shahin v. Iran

Iran–U.S. Claims Tribunal, Case No. 560-44/46/47-3 (October 12, 1994)[69]

[Shahin and other claimants were the shareholders of an Iranian construction company called Gostaresh Maskan Co. In 1979, following the Iranian revolution and the ensuing departure of the claimants, a new director was appointed by the Government to head the company. The claimants asserted that they had been deprived of their ownership rights, and claimed the equivalent to the full value of the company.]

AWARD:

[88] The Tribunal believes that, while international law undoubtedly sets forth an obligation to provide compensation for property taken, international law theory and practice do not support the conclusion that the "prompt, adequate and effective" standard represents the prevailing standard of compensation. ... Rather, customary international law favors an "appropriate" compensation standard. ... The gradual emergence of this rule aims at ensuring that the amount of compensation is determined in a flexible manner, that is, taking into account the specific circumstances of each case. The prevalence of the "appropriate" compensation standard does not imply, however, that the compensation quantum should be always "less than full" or always "partial." ...

[93] These three awards[70] show that the terms of the "appropriate compensation" standard or "fair compensation" standard must not be construed either to always require partial compensation or to always exclude full compensation. Regardless of the formulation of the standard, these awards reflect a consistent concern not to determine the amount of compensation rigidly, i.e., without taking into account the specific circumstances of each concrete case. ...

[94] Turning to the practice of the Tribunal, it appears that in past Awards the Tribunal has typically awarded compensation representing the full value of the expropriated property as determined by the Tribunal. ...

[95] Considering the scholarly opinions, arbitral practice and Tribunal precedents noted above, the Tribunal finds that once the full value of the property has been properly evaluated, the compensation to be awarded must be appropriate to reflect the pertinent facts and circumstances of each case.

[96] Despite the importance of the distinction, the Tribunal need not examine here the effect of the characterization of the taking as lawful or unlawful on the available compensation. The Claimants seek compensation for *damnum emergens* only (including compensation for tangible and intangible assets and future prospects). The Claimants do not seek additional compensation for *lucrum cessans* (that is, lost profits), which claim is typically conditioned on a prior characterization of the taking

---

69   Available on Westlaw, INT-IRAN database, accessed June 10, 1999.

70   The Tribunal refers to *Texaco Overseas Petroleum Company and California Asiatic Oil Company (TOPCO) v. Libyan Arab Republic* (1977), 53 I.L.R. 389; *Kuwait v. American Independent Oil Company (AMINOIL)* (1982), 66 I.L.R. 518; and *Libyan American Oil Company (LIAMCO) v. Libyan Arab Republic* (1977), 62 I.L.R. 140.

as unlawful. The appropriate amount to be awarded shall therefore be determined in such a manner as to include *damnum emergens* but not *lucrum cessans*.

SEPARATE OPINION OF STEPHEN ALLISON:

[3] I must respectfully, but profoundly, disagree with this interpretation of the law. The Award's advocacy of an ill-defined and essentially meaningless standard of "appropriate" compensation is unjustifiable and out of step with the times. In today's world where nations—great and small—have come increasingly to recognize their economic interdependence and the need to inspire confidence as the basis for their development and prosperity, a "flexible" rule that looks with indifference upon the deprivation of property for less than its fair value is counterproductive and backward-looking. Moreover, in this respect the Award misreads the state of customary international law as the twenty-first century approaches. ...

[38] Ever since the arrival of nation States upon the scene, international law has held that when a State takes the property of aliens, compensation representing the full equivalent of the property taken is required. Whatever label is attached to this principle ("just," "adequate," "equitable" or "appropriate" compensation), international tribunals have endeavored in practice to restore, if possible, the property taken or, failing that, to award damages corresponding to the loss sustained. Although the would-be architects of a new international economic order labored assiduously in the 1960's and 1970's to eviscerate this rule, these efforts failed. Their failure is evidenced by, *inter alia*, the many actions discussed above of the very same forces that sought to undermine the standard of prompt, adequate and effective compensation.

[39] To argue that this standard should be set aside in favor of "appropriate" compensation—meaning "flexible" or dependent upon the "circumstances"—is not to say that a time-honored rule of law should be calibrated or adjusted to modern conditions. To the contrary, it is to say that there is, in effect, no rule and to leave the result to caprice and subjective perception.

NOTES

1) The World Bank Guidelines and the *Shahin* case show how contemporary the dispute over the standard of compensation remains. The Guidelines clearly codify the "Hull doctrine" whereby "appropriate" compensation means adequate, prompt, and effective, whereas the Tribunal in *Shahin* prefers a gradual and flexible "appropriate compensation" standard.[71] Despite rejection in *Shahin* of the traditional "adequate, prompt, and effective" standard, how different are these two positions?

---

71   See UN GAOR C.2, 17th Sess., 846th Mtg., U.N. Doc. A/C.2SR.846 (1962) at para. 3, and UN GAOR C.2, 17th Sess., 850th Mtg., U.N. Doc. A/C.2/SR.850 (1962) at para. 16. See P. Smith, "Determining the Standard Compensation for the Expropriation of Nationalised Assets: Themes for the Future" (1997) 23 Monash U.L. Rev. 159; and T. Levy, "NAFTA's Provision for Compensation in the Event of Expropriation: A Reassessment of the 'Prompt, Adequate and Effective' Standard" (1995) 31 Stanford J. Int. L. 423.

2) Apart from the customary norm on compensation, a state may enter into a treaty that conventionally sets the compensation standard in case of expropriation. A large number of bilateral agreements on investment have been entered into that adopt the "adequate, prompt, and effective" standard. What is the possible impact on customary law of such an accumulation of bilateral treaties incorporating this disputed standard?

3) As noted in *Shahin*, a major issue related to the appropriateness of the compensation is whether the foreign investor's profits, both past and projected, should be protected, and whether the answer given should depend on the lawfulness of the taking. The Tribunal in *Amoco International Finance Corp. v. Iran* stated:[72]

> Obviously the value of an expropriated enterprise does not vary according to the lawfulness or the unlawfulness of the taking. This value cannot depend on the legal characterization of a fact totally foreign to the economic constituents of the undertaking, namely the conduct of the expropriating State. In the traditional language of international law it equates the *damnum emergens*, which must be compensated in any case. Such a conclusion was already accepted by this Tribunal in *Sedco Inc. v. National Iranian Oil Company*.[73] The difference is that if the taking is lawful the value of the undertaking at the time of the dispossession is the measure and the limit of the compensation, while if it is unlawful, this value is, or may be, only a part of the reparation to be paid. In any event, even in case of unlawful expropriation the damage actually sustained is the measure of the reparation, and there is no indication that "punitive damages" could be considered.

Should a higher standard of compensation generally be applied to an individual expropriation than to a program of nationalization?

4) The traditional legal basis for the claim that adequate, prompt, and effective compensation should be paid to foreign owners is the principle of respect for acquired rights in general and for private property rights in particular. But an alternative legal foundation for compensation could be the principle of unjust enrichment.[74] Some individuals—in this case aliens in a community—in consequence of no fault on their part, are being asked to make a sacrifice of their private property for the general welfare of the community, while other members of this community are not asked to make corresponding sacrifices. The compensation paid to the owners of the property taken represents precisely the corresponding contribution made by the rest of the community in order to equalize the financial incidence of the taking of individual property. The community has been enriched by the sacrifice of the individuals concerned and must compensate them for their deprivation, which was not shared by everyone. Thus what constitutes "fair," "just," or "adequate" compensation in any given case depends on one's assessment of the actual benefit that has accrued to the community at large from the property taken and the extent to which the rest of the community should share the

---

72   (1987), 15 Iran–U.S. Cl. Trib. Rep. 189 at 248.

73   Award No. ITL 59-129-3 (March 27, 1986) at pp. 11-12, reprinted in (1986) 25 I.L.M. 629.

74   See A.A. Fatouros, "Legal Security for International Investment" in W.G. Friedmann & R.C. Pugh, eds., *Legal Aspects of Foreign Investment* (1959) 699 at 723.

sacrifice thus made by the former owners. Of course, the compensation paid should not exceed the actual deprivation of the former owners.

In the *Lena Goldfields Arbitrations*,[75] compensation was given to prevent the unjust enrichment of the expropriating state. However, an examination of arbitral decisions seems to indicate that arbitrators of whatever theoretical viewpoint agree that full compensation must be paid in cases of unlawful expropriation, and that even in the case of lawful expropriation, full compensation is the starting point. Of course, much may depend on the method used to quantify the compensation.[76]

5) A second major issue with respect to compensation concerns the expropriating state's capacity to pay compensation. It seems reasonable to support the view that a foreign creditor should agree to accept payment of compensation in installments where it has a justified expectation of payments being adequate and effective. "Prompt" compensation does not necessarily mean payment in advance, but does imply payment within a reasonable period of time after the taking. In this connection the paying capacity as well as the enrichment of the debtor government should be taken into consideration. The amount of compensation should be reasonable and equitable, measured by the enrichment of the state, and effective in the sense that the compensation should be paid in a beneficial form that is of real economic value to the former owner. It is not the currency in which payment is effectuated that is decisive but rather its proper use. It is improper that compensation that has been promptly paid should be immediately frozen by foreign exchange laws precluding the removal of the compensation from the state granting it.

6) The standards of valuation to be used in order to establish the amount of compensation payable are numerous and at present there is no consensus about which is the most appropriate. Some of these standards are fair market value;[77] net book value;[78] discounted cash flow (DCF);[79] capitalization of expected benefits;[80] average profits made in a number of past years, loss of use of profits, equitable restitution;[81] and forced sale value. Less than full value has been accepted in lump-sum settlements with East European countries and in lowered book value settlements on an individual basis on behalf of the oil companies in the Middle East. The World Bank Guidelines represent but one attempt to systematize valuation practices in international law.

---

75   (1929-30), 5 Ann. Dig. 3.

76   See P.M. Norton, "A Law of the Future or a Law of the Past? Modern Tribunals and the International Law of Expropriation" (1991) 85 A.J.I.L. 474.

77   See, for instance, *Expropriation Act*, R.S.C. 1985, c. E-21, s. 25.

78   J.S. McCosker, "Book Values in Nationalization Settlements," in R.B. Lillich, *The Valuation of Nationalized Property in International Law* (1973) vol. 2 at 36.

79   See, for example, *Amoco International Finance Corp. v. Iran* (1987), 15 Iran–U.S. Cl. Trib. Rep. 189 at 253 *et seq.*

80   D.R. Weigel & B.H. Weston, "Valuation upon the Deprivation of Foreign Enterprise: A Policy-Oriented Approach to the Problem of Compensation under International Law" in Lillich, *The Valuation of Nationalised Property in International Law*, vol. 1, *supra* note 1 at 3.

81   D.A. Lapres, "Principles of Compensation for Nationalized Property" (1977) 26 I.C.L.Q. 97.

(d) Breach of Contract

Generally speaking, issues related to breach by the state of a contract with an alien raise many of the same problems as expropriation. Indeed, many writers simply assimilate the two. Breach of contract raises distinct questions, especially in the possibility that a state may contractually limit its sovereign right to take measures affecting an alien's contractual rights.

Texaco v. Libya
(1977), 53 I.L.R. 389; (1978) 17 I.L.M. 1

[A major task in this arbitration, introduced above in Section B.3(a) on "Basic Principles," was to determine the governing law. Clause 28 of the Deeds of Concession expressed a choice of applicable law:

> This concession shall be governed by and interpreted in accordance with the principles
> of the law of Libya common to the principles of international law and in the absence of
> such common principles then by and in accordance with the general principles of law,
> including those principles that may have been applied by international tribunals.

In the course of his interpretation and application of this clause, Professor René-Jean Dupuy, the sole arbitrator, had to consider the effects of nationalization in the face of a "stabilization legal clause."]

[59] ... [T]he right of a State to nationalize is unquestionable today. It results from international customary law, established as the result of general practices considered by the international community as being the law. The exercise of the national sovereignty to nationalize is regarded as the expression of the State's territorial sovereignty. Territorial sovereignty confers upon the State an exclusive competence to organize as it wishes the economic structures of its territory and to introduce therein any reforms which may seem to be desirable to it. It is an essential prerogative of sovereignty for the constitutionally authorized authorities of the State to choose and build freely an economic and social system. International law recognizes that a State has this prerogative just as it has the prerogative to determine freely its political regime and its constitutional institutions. The exclusive nature of such a right is in fact confirmed by the fact that in practice a decision to nationalize very often is made by the organ which is regarded as the supreme level in the internal hierarchy of State institutions. ...

[61] Even though, for a State, the decision of nationalizing is an expression of its sovereignty, which this Tribunal fully recognizes, does not the exercise of the right to nationalize know some limits in the international order? In particular, does the act of sovereignty which constitutes the nationalization authorize a State to disregard its international commitments assumed by it within the framework of its sovereignty?

It is clear from an international point of view that it is not possible to criticize a nationalization measure concerning nationals of the State concerned, or any measure affecting aliens in respect of whom the State concerned has made no particular commitment to guarantee and maintain their position. On the assumption that the nationalizing State has concluded with a foreign company a contract which stems from the municipal law of that State and is completely governed by that law the resolution of the new situation created by nationalization will be subject to the legal and administrative provisions then in force.

[62] But the case is totally different where the State has concluded with a foreign contracting party an internationalized agreement, either because the contract has been subjected to the municipal law of the host country, viewed as a mere law of reference, applicable as of the effective date of the contract, and "stabilized" on that same date by specific clauses, or because it has been placed directly under the aegis of international law. Under these two assumptions, the State has placed itself within the international legal order in order to guarantee vis-à-vis its foreign contracting party a certain legal and economic status over a certain period of time. ...

[70] It is therefore necessary to examine in the light of these principles whether the nationalization measures decreed by the Libyan Government with respect to the plaintiffs disregard any specific commitment undertaken by that Government, a commitment which should have been sufficient to protect the plaintiffs from such a decision.

The Deeds of Concession entered into by the parties do not include any provision by which the Libyan Government limited its recourse to nationalization. However, Clause 16 of the Deeds of Concession contains a stabilization clause with respect to the rights of the concession holder. As consideration for the economic risks to which the foreign contracting parties were subjected, the Libyan State granted them a concession of a minimum duration of 50 years and, more specifically, containing a non-aggravation clause, Clause 16, which provided:

> The Government of Libya will take all steps necessary to ensure that the company enjoys all the rights conferred by this concession. The contractual rights expressly created by this concession shall not be altered except by mutual consent of the parties.

Another paragraph was added to this provision under the Royal Decree of December 1961 and became an integral part of the contract on the basis of the Agreement of 1963. It provides:

> This Concession shall throughout the period of its validity be construed in accordance with the Petroleum Law and the Regulations in force on the date of execution of the agreement of amendment by which this paragraph (2) was incorporated into the concession agreement. Any amendment to or repeal of such Regulations shall not affect the contractual rights of the Company without its consent.

[71] Such a provision, the effect of which is to stabilize the position of the contracting party, does not, in principle, impair the sovereignty of the Libyan State. Not only has the Libyan State freely undertaken commitments but also the fact that this clause stabilizes the petroleum legislation and regulations as of the date of the execution of the agreement does not affect in principle the legislative and regulatory sovereignty of Libya. Libya reserves all its prerogatives to issue laws and regulations in the field of petroleum activities in respect of national or foreign persons with which it has not undertaken such a commitment. Clause 16 only makes such acts invalid as far as contracting parties are concerned—with respect to whom this commitment has

been undertaken—during the period of applicability of the Deeds of Concession. Any changes which may result from the adoption of new laws and regulations must, to affect the contracting parties, be agreed to by them. This is so not because the sovereignty of Libya would be reduced, but simply by reason of the fact that Libya has, through an exercise of its sovereignty, undertaken commitments under an international agreement, which, for its duration, is the law common to the parties.

Thus, the recognition by international law of the right to nationalize is not sufficient ground to empower a State to disregard its commitments, because the same law also recognizes the power of a State to commit itself internationally, especially by accepting the inclusion of stabilization clauses in a contract entered into with a foreign private party. ...

[73] Thus, in respect of the international law of contracts, a nationalization cannot prevail over an internationalized contract, containing stabilization clauses, entered into between a State and a foreign private company. ...

NOTES

1) The arbitrator pronounced the Deeds of Concession to be binding contracts that Libya had breached by its acts of nationalization. The award declared that Libya was "legally bound to perform these contracts." In fact, approximately eight months after the award on the merits was rendered, Libya and the companies reached a settlement of their disputes by means of an agreement for compensation.

2) Since most contracts with states are governed by local law, stabilization clauses are sought by foreign investors in an attempt to protect themselves from prejudicial statutory changes, including expropriation, by subsequent governments. In the *Texaco* case this contractual technique was successful: the arbitrator considered the stabilization clause legal under international law as a valid contractual expression of Libya's sovereign capacity to enter into agreements with foreign investors, rather than a limitation of its permanent sovereignty over natural resources and economic activities. But this position has been criticized by many writers and qualified in a number of awards. Thus in the *Aminoil Arbitration*, another instance of nationalization of a foreign oil company, this time by Kuwait, the majority opinion of the Tribunal stated:[82]

[93] It seems fair to say that what the Parties had in mind in drafting the stabilisation clauses in 1948 and 1961, was anything which, by reason of its confiscatory character, might cause serious financial prejudice to the interests of the Company. Thus, as mentioned earlier, Article 7(g) of 1961, instituting a new revised Article 11 of 1948, enumerated and strictly limited all the instances in which the Concession can terminate through a forfeiture

---

82   (1982) 21 I.L.M. 976 at 1023. Cf. Jiménez de Aréchaga, "State Responsibility for the Naturalization of Foreign Owned Property" (1978) 11 N.Y.U.J.I.L.P. 179; F.A. Mann, "The Aminoil Arbitration" (1983) 54 Brit. Y.B. Int'l L. 213; F.R. Tesón, "State Contracts and Oil Expropriations: The Aminoil–Kuwait Arbitration" (1983-84) 24 Va. J. Int'l L. 322 at 339; A. Redfern, "The Arbitration between the Government of Kuwait and Aminoil" (1984) 55 Brit. Y.B. Int'l L. 65; P. Kalm, "Contrats d'Etat et nationalisation" (1982) 109 J. Dr. Int. (Clunet) 844; and T. Wälde, "Stabilizing International Investment Commitments: International Law Versus Contract Interpretation" (1996) 31 Texas Int'l L.J. 215.

of the concessionaire's rights (for failure in its obligations), but is silent as to all acts that would lead to the ending of the Concession *without* having a confiscatory character. It can be held that the case of nationalisation is precisely one of those acts, since as a matter of international law it is subject *inter alia* to the payment of appropriate compensation.

[94] The case of nationalisation is certainly not expressly provided against by the stabilisation clauses of the Concession. But it is contended by Aminoil that notwithstanding this *lacuna*, the stabilisation clauses of the Concession ... are cast in such absolute and all-embracing terms as to suffice in themselves—unconditionally and in all circumstances—for prohibiting nationalisation. That is a possible interpretation on the purely formal plane; but, for the following reasons, it is not the one adopted by the Tribunal.

[95] No doubt contractual limitations on the State's right to nationalise are juridically possible, but what that would involve would be a particularly serious undertaking which would have to be expressly stipulated for, and be within the regulations governing the conclusion of State contracts; and it is to be expected that it should cover only a relatively limited period. In the present case however, the existence of such a stipulation would have to be presumed as being covered by the general language of the stabilisation clauses, and over the whole period of an especially long concession since it extended to 60 years. A limitation on the sovereign rights of the State is all the less to be presumed where the concessionaire is in any event in possession of important guarantees regarding its essential interests in the shape of a legal right to eventual compensation.

[96] Such is the case here—for if the Tribunal thus holds that it cannot interpret [the stabilization clause] as absolutely forbidding nationalisation, it is nevertheless the fact that these provisions are far from having lost all their value and efficacity on that account since, by impliedly requiring that nationalisation shall not have any confiscatory character, they reinforce the necessity for a proper indemnification as a condition of it.

What difficulties do you see in the position adopted by the *Texaco* award? Which approach to stabilization clauses seems preferable?

3) It is clear that agreements between two sovereign states with respect to economic matters are international agreements governed by public international law. Contracts between nationals and corporations of the host state and foreign private investors are private contracts governed by the law determined by the conflict of laws rules of either the host or foreign state. What is not clear is whether economic development contracts or concessions giving the right to exploit natural resources or to establish manufacturing industries between sovereign states and foreign private investors are international agreements or private contracts governed by public international law, the private law of the host or foreign state, or general principles of law recognized by civilized nations. Can a state contract away its sovereignty—that is, its power to take unilateral action in the future? Does a private investor have rights and duties under international law? It would seem that the basic question does not relate to sovereignty but to the nature of the obligation arising under the contract or concession. When a sovereign state contracts with an alien, it undertakes well-defined obligations, one of which is to respect the terms of the contract. Thus, if the contract is abrogated in the future by the host state, there is a breach of this obligation. Once it is determined that the contract has been broken according to the relevant applicable law, linking the breach with a violation of international law is easy.

4) The sanctity of the state's contractual obligation could be based on the concepts of acquired or vested rights (the property rights acquired or vested under the law of the host state cannot be destroyed without compensation and are entitled to international protection), unjust enrichment (the state unjustly enriched at the expense of the injured foreign investor is bound to make a just reparation), estoppel (the host state having enticed the foreign investor to act to his or her detriment cannot deny him or her recovery), abuse of rights (the host state cannot use its sovereign rights arbitrarily to the detriment of the foreign investor), or *pacta sunt servanda* (the host state is under a general obligation to observe and respect its contracts). These concepts are general principles of law recognized by civilized nations that are also sources of international law, as discussed in Chapter 3, Section D.

5) Economic development contracts or concessions may be legally abrogated or modified by virtue of the doctrine *rebus sic stantibus* (vital change of circumstances),[83] the passage of legislation for the protection of a *bona fide* public interest (health, safety, etc.), an express clause in the contract conferring that power on the host state in accordance with stipulated conditions, or as punishment for an offence against the criminal law of the host state (smuggling, tax evasion, or breach of currency laws), provided these offences are recognized by international law or the practice of states, and the punishment is reasonable according to civilized standards and proportional to the offence committed.

6) Another option stems from the Convention on the Settlement of Investment Disputes between States and Nationals of other States, to which Canada is not yet a party due to constitutional difficulties over its implementation.[84] The Convention provides facilities for submission to conciliation or arbitration of investment disputes between contracting states and nationals of other contracting states (articles 1-2). The facilities are provided by the ICSID, which has its seat at the principal offices of the World Bank. The Centre maintains a Panel of Conciliators and a Panel of Arbitrators from which the parties to a dispute may choose the members of the Conciliation Commission or the Arbitral Tribunal to which their dispute is to be submitted (articles 2-15, 28-31, and 36-40).

The jurisdiction of the Centre with regard to the settlement of disputes is founded on the *written consent* of the parties, which must be given for every case and extends to all "legal disputes arising out of an investment" between a contracting state or any constituent sub-division or agency of a contracting state and a national of another contracting state (whether a natural or juridical person) (article 25(1)). Thus, the mere fact that a state becomes a party to the Convention will not impose obligations on it as regards the settlement of

---

83 Explained in Chapter 3, Section B.4 on "Operation of Treaties."

84 (1965) 575 U.N.T.S. 159. And see S.J. Toope, *Mixed International Arbitration: Studies in Arbitration between States and Private Persons* (1990); C.F. Amerasinghe, "Dispute Settlement Machinery in Relations between States and Multinational Enterprises with Particular Reference to the ICSID" (1977) 11 Int. Lawyer 45; M.D. Rowat, "Multilateral Approaches to Improving the Investment Climate of Developing Countries: The Cases of ICSID and MIGA" (1992) 33 Harv. Int. L.J. 103; N. Nassar, "Internationalization of State Contracts—ICSID, The Last Citadel" (1997) 14 J. Int'l Arb. 185; and E. Gaillard, "Centre international pour le règlement des différends relatifs aux investissements (CIRDI)" (1998) 125 J.D.I. 241.

disputes, since it remains free to accept or reject the conciliation or arbitration organized by the Centre. Moreover, at any time, any contracting state "may ... notify the Centre of the Class or Classes of disputes which it would or would not consider submitting to the jurisdiction of the Centre" (article 25(4)). Both the Conciliation Commission (article 32(1)) and the Arbitral Tribunal (article 41(1)) are the judges of their own competence.

The Convention provides in article 42(1) that the Arbitral Tribunal shall decide a dispute in accordance with rules of law as may be agreed by the parties and that, in "the absence of such agreement, the Tribunal shall apply the law of the Contracting State party to the dispute (including its rules on the conflict of laws) and such rules of international law as may be applicable." The arbitral award must state the reasons on which it is based and is invalid if it fails to do so (article 52(1)(e)).

An award rendered under the Convention is binding on the parties and is not subject to any appeal or to any other remedy except those provided for in the Convention (article 53). The remedies provided for are revision (article 51) and annulment (article 52) of the award. In addition, either party may request the Arbitral Tribunal to interpret its award (article 53). Contracting states are bound to recognize and enforce an award as if it were a final judgment of a national court, subject only to a foreign state's customary rights to immunity from execution (articles 54-55).

The Convention also contains provisions on the status, immunities, and privileges of the Centre, conciliators, arbitrators, and certain other persons, including officials or employees of the Secretariat (articles 18-24). It also provides for the financing of the Centre by contracting states (article 17). Further, and this is important from the point of view of implementation by Canada, it is stipulated that each contracting state must take such legislative or other measures as may be necessary for making the provisions of the Convention effective in its territory (article 69).

C. DIPLOMATIC PROTECTION

As we have seen in Section B, international law imposes a number of duties upon states with respect to aliens present on their territory. These standards on the treatment of aliens complement in some ways international human rights standards, but operate according to a different framework. Whereas human rights endow individuals directly with rights under international law, standards on the treatment of aliens have traditionally been seen as vesting rights in the state. As a result, individuals may not independently bring an international claim against a wrongdoing state. Instead, a state may choose to endorse the claim of one of its nationals and take measures necessary so that international law is respected toward its citizens. The International Law Commission in 1996 initiated a project to codify the law of diplomatic protection, which it defines in Draft Article 1 as the "resort to diplomatic action or other means of peaceful settlement by a State adopting in its own right the cause of its national in respect of an injury to that national arising from an internationally wrongful act of another State."[85]

---

85   International Law Commission, *Draft Articles on Diplomatic Protection*, UN GAOR, 59th Sess., Supp.
     No. 10, U.N. Doc. A/59/10 (2004) 17.

1. Espousal and Nationality of Claims

International Law Commission, Draft Articles on Diplomatic Protection
Report of the International Law Commission on the Work of Its Fifty-sixth Session,
UN GAOR, 59th Sess., Supp. No. 10, U.N. Doc. A/59/10 (2004) 18

Article 3
Protection by the State of Nationality

1. The State entitled to exercise diplomatic protection is the State of nationality.

2. Notwithstanding paragraph 1, diplomatic protection may be exercised in respect of a non-national in accordance with draft article 8. ...

Article 5
Continuous Nationality

1. A State is entitled to exercise diplomatic protection in respect of a person who was its national at the time of the injury and is a national at the date of the official presentation of the claim

2. Notwithstanding paragraph 1, a State may exercise diplomatic protection in respect of a person who is its national at the date of the official presentation of the claim but was not a national at the time of injury, provided that the person has lost his or her former nationality and has acquired, for a reason unrelated to the bringing of the claim, the nationality of that State in a manner not inconsistent with international law.

3. Diplomatic protection shall not be exercised by the present State of nationality in respect of a person against a former State of nationality of that person for an injury incurred when that person was a national of the former State of Nationality and not of the present State of nationality. ...

Article 8
Stateless Persons and Refugees

1. A State may exercise diplomatic protection in respect of a stateless person who, at the time of the injury and at the date of the official presentation of the claim, is lawfully and habitually resident in that State.

2. A State may exercise diplomatic protection in respect of a person who is recognized as a refugee by that State when that person, at the time of the injury and at the date of the official presentation of the claim, is lawfully and habitually resident in that State.

3. Paragraph 2 does not apply in respect of an injury caused by an internationally wrongful act of the State of nationality of the refugee.

Mavrommatis Palestine Concessions Case
Greece v. U.K.
(1924), P.C.I.J. (Ser. A.) No. 2 at 12

[The Greek Government brought an action against the British Government for the alleged refusal of the Palestine authorities under British mandate to recognize the rights acquired by Mr. Mavrommatis, a Greek national, under contracts that he had entered into with the Ottoman Empire, the predecessor sovereign in Palestine.]

THE COURT: ... In the case of the Mavrommatis concessions it is true that the dispute was at first between a private person and a State—i.e. between M. Mavrommatis and Great Britain. Subsequently, the Greek Government took up the case. The dispute then entered upon a new phase; it entered the domain of international law, and became a dispute between two States.

... It is an elementary principle of international law that a State is entitled to protect its subjects, when injured by acts contrary to international law committed by another State, from whom they have been unable to obtain satisfaction through the ordinary channels. By taking up the case of one of its subjects and by resorting to diplomatic action or international judicial proceedings on his behalf, a State is in reality asserting its own rights—its right to ensure, in the person of its subjects, respect for the rules of international law.

The question, therefore, whether the present dispute originates in an injury to a private interest, which in point of fact is the case in many international disputes, is irrelevant from this standpoint. Once a State has taken up a case on behalf of one of its subjects before an international tribunal, in the eyes of the latter the State is sole claimant.

NOTES

1) In the *Reparations Case* the ICJ stated:

Competence to bring an international claim is, for those possessing it, the capacity to resort to the customary methods recognized by international law for the establishment, the presentation and the settlement of claims. Among these methods may be mentioned protest, request for an enquiry, negotiation, and request for submission to an arbitral tribunal or to the Court in so far as this may be authorized by the Statute.

This capacity certainly belongs to the State; a State can bring an international claim against another State. Such a claim takes the form of a claim between two political entities, equal in law, similar in form, and both the direct subjects of international law. It is dealt with by means of negotiation, and cannot, in the present state of the law as to international jurisdiction, be submitted to a tribunal, except with the consent of the States concerned.[86]

---

86   [1949] I.C.J. Rep. 174 at 177-78, reported in Chapter 2, Section C.1 on "International Organizations."

2) In the *Panevezys-Saldutiskis Railway Case*, the PCIJ stated:

In taking up the case of one of its nationals, by resorting to diplomatic action or international judicial proceedings on his behalf, a State is in reality asserting its own right, the right to ensure in the person of its nationals respect for the rules of international law. This right is necessarily limited to intervention on behalf of its own nationals because, in the absence of a special agreement, it is the bond of nationality between the State and the individual which alone confers upon the State the right of diplomatic protection, and it is as a part of the function of diplomatic protection that the right to take up a claim and to ensure respect for the rules of international law must be envisaged. Where the injury was done to the national of some other State, no claim to which such injury may give rise falls within the scope of the diplomatic protection which a State is entitled to afford nor can it give rise to a claim which that State is entitled to espouse.[87]

Draft Article 8 recognizes that the legal position of stateless persons and refugees under international law has evolved since that case, to exceptionally allow for some possibility of diplomatic protection by a state other than the state of nationality. Note, however, that state practice to that effect appears extremely limited.

3) International law requires that for a claim to be sustainable the claimant normally must be a national of the state that is presenting the claim, both at the time when the injury occurred and continuously thereafter up to the date of formal presentation of the claim. In practice, however, it is sufficient to prove nationality at the date of injury and of presentation of the claim.[88] Given the contemporary reality of a globalized work force in which individuals often settle in countries other than their own, does it make sense to hold on to a strict requirement of nationality?

4) Draft Article 6 codifies the accepted practice regarding individuals holding multiple nationality—that is, that diplomatic protection may be exercised individually or jointly by any of the states of nationality. Draft Article 7 states that a state of nationality may present a claim against another state of nationality only if the national link to the claimant state is predominant both at the time of injury and presentation of the claim.

5) As to whether an individual or a corporation is a national, an issue considered in Draft Articles 4 and 9, see Chapter 8 on "Nationality."

6) The right to exercise diplomatic protection is held by the state (Draft Article 2), which means that the decision whether to present a claim is a discretionary act. The South African Constitutional Court recently rejected an argument that a human right to diplomatic protection has emerged in international law, despite the inclusion of such a right in a number of national legal systems.[89] Likewise, a suggestion that there be a right

---

87   *Estonia v. Lithuania* (1939), P.C.I.J. (Ser. A/B) No. 76 at 16.

88   See "International Claims" (1957) 9 External Affairs 326; (1966) 18 External Affairs 11; E.B. Wang, "Nationality of Claims and Diplomatic Intervention" (1965) 43 Can. Bar Rev. 136; and E. Wyler, *La règle dite de la continuité de la nationalité dans le contentieux international* (1990).

89   *Kaunda v. South Africa*, Judgment of 4 August 2004, Case No. CCT 23/04 at para. 27.

to diplomatic protection in cases of violations of *jus cogens* norms benefiting individuals was rejected by the majority of the International Law Commission.[90]

2. Exhaustion of Local Remedies and Waiver of Claims[91]

International Law Commission, Draft Articles on Diplomatic Protection
Report of the International Law Commission on the Work of Its Fifty-sixth Session,
UN GAOR, 59th Sess., Supp. No. 10, U.N. Doc. A/59/10 (2004) 21

Article 14
Exhaustion of Local Remedies

1. A State may not bring an international claim in respect of an injury to a national or other person referred to in draft article 8 before the injured person has, subject to draft article 16, exhausted all local remedies.

2. "Local remedies" means legal remedies which are open to an injured person before the judicial or administrative courts or bodies, whether ordinary or special, of the State alleged to be responsible for the injury.

Article 15
Category of Claims

Local remedies shall be exhausted where an international claim, or request for a declaratory judgment related to the claim, is brought preponderantly on the basis of an injury to a national or other person referred to in draft article 8.

Article 16
Exceptions to the Local Remedies Rule

Local remedies do not need to be exhausted where:

   (a) The local remedies provide no reasonable possibility of effective redress;

   (b) There is undue delay in the remedial process which is attributable to the State alleged to be responsible;

   (c) There is no relevant connection between the injured person and the State alleged to be responsible or the circumstances of the case otherwise make the exhaustion of local remedies unreasonable;

   (d) The State alleged to be responsible has waived the requirement that local remedies be exhausted.

---

90   *Report of the International Law Commission on the Work of Its Fifty-second Session*, UN GAOR, 55th Sess., Supp. No. 10, U.N. Doc. A/55/10 (2000) 155.

91   See Law, *supra* note 1; A. Cançado Trindade, *The Application of the Rule of Exhaustion of Local Remedies in International Law* (1983); C. Amerasinghe, *Local Remedies in International Law*, 2nd ed. (2004); and John Dugard, "Third Report on Diplomatic Protection," U.N. Doc. A/CN.4/523 (2002).

Ambatielos Arbitration
Greece v. United Kingdom
(1956), 12 R.I.A.A. 83; 23 I.L.R. 306

[Greece espoused the claims of its national, Mr. Ambatielos, arising out of his contract with the U.K. government for the purchase of certain ships. In rejecting the claims, the Commission applied the international rule that requires prior exhaustion of local remedies.]

THE COMMISSION: ... The rule thus invoked by the United Kingdom Government is well established in international law. Nor is its existence contested by the Greek Government. It means that the State against which an international action is brought for injuries suffered by private individuals has the right to resist such an action if the persons alleged to have been injured have not first exhausted all the remedies available to them under the municipal law of that State. The defendant State has the right to demand that full advantage shall have been taken of all local remedies before the matters in dispute are taken on the international level by the State of which the persons alleged to have been injured are nationals.

In order to contend successfully that international proceedings are inadmissible, the defendant State must prove the existence, in its system of internal law, of remedies which have not been used. The views expressed by writers and in judicial precedents, however, coincide in that the existence of remedies which are obviously ineffective is held not to be sufficient to justify the application of the rule. Remedies which could not rectify the situation cannot be relied upon by the defendant State as precluding an international action.

The Greek Government contends that in the present case the remedies which English law offered to Mr. Ambatielos were ineffective and that, accordingly, the rule is not applicable.

The ineffectiveness of local remedies may result clearly from the municipal law itself. That is the case, for example, when a Court of Appeal is not competent to reconsider the judgment given by a Court of first instance on matters of fact, and when, failing such reconsideration, no redress can be obtained. ...

Furthermore, however, it is generally considered that the ineffectiveness of available remedies, without being legally certain, may also result from circumstances which do not permit any hope of redress to be placed in the use of those remedies. But in a case of that kind it is essential that such remedies, if they had been resorted to, would have proved to be *obviously futile*. ...

These "local remedies" include not only reference to the courts and tribunals, but also the use of the procedural facilities which municipal law makes available to litigants before such courts and tribunals. It is the whole system of legal protection, as provided by municipal law, which must have been put to the test before a State, as the protector of its nationals, can prosecute the claim on the international plane. ...

In the view of the Commission the non-utilization of certain means of procedure can be accepted as constituting a gap in the exhaustion of local remedies only if the use of these means of procedure were essential to establish the claimant's case before the municipal courts. ...

As regards Claim A [for compensation for breach of contract], the questions of the non-exhaustion of local remedies thus raised are:

(1) In the 1922 proceedings Mr. Ambatielos failed to call (as he could have done) the witnesses who, as he now says, were essential to establish his case. ...

Under English Law Mr. Ambatielos was not precluded from calling Major Laing as a witness.

In so far as concerns Claim A, the failure of Mr. Ambatielos to call Major Laing as a witness at the hearing before Mr. Justice Hill must therefore be held to amount to non-exhaustion of the local remedy available to him in the proceedings before Mr. Justice Hill.

It may be that the decision of Mr. Ambatielos not to call Major Laing as a witness, with the result that he did not exhaust local remedies, was dictated by reasons of expediency—quite understandable in themselves—in putting his case before Mr. Justice Hill. This, however, is not the question to be determined. The Commission is not concerned with the question as to whether he was right or wrong in acting as he did. He took his decision at his own risk.

(2) The second question as to non-exhaustion raised by the United Kingdom Government is the failure of Mr. Ambatielos to make use of or exhaust his appellate rights. ...

The Greek Government argues by way of explanation that to proceed with the general appeal once the decision of the Court of Appeal not to admit the Laing evidence had been given would have been futile because the Laing evidence was essential to enable the Court to arrive at a decision favourable to Mr. Ambatielos.

The reason why Mr. Ambatielos was not allowed to call Major Laing in the Court of Appeal was, in the words of Lord Justice Scrutton, that "One of the principal rules which this Court adopts is that it will not give leave to adduce further evidence which might have been adduced with reasonable care at the trial of the action."

Accordingly, the failure of Mr. Ambatielos to exhaust the local remedy before Hill J. by not calling Major Laing as a witness, is the reason why it was futile for him to prosecute his appeal.

It would be wrong to hold that a party who, by failing to exhaust his opportunities in the Court of first instance, has caused an appeal to become futile should be allowed to rely on this fact in order to rid himself of the rule of exhaustion of local remedies.

NOTES

1) The rule regarding exhaustion of local remedies gives diplomatic protection a subsidiary character. It is meant to afford a state an opportunity to redress its own internationally wrongful act by using its domestic legal system.[92]

2) The local remedies rule is inapplicable to a case of direct injury caused by one state to another—for example, the sinking of British warships in the *Corfu Channel Case*

---

92   See *Interhandel Case (Switzerland v. United States of America)*, Preliminary Objections, [1959] I.C.J. Rep. 6 at 27.

reported previously in Section A on "General Theory of Responsibility." What is the rationale for not requiring exhaustion of local remedies in cases of direct state injury?

3) Draft Article 14 makes clear that all judicial and administrative remedies, including all appeals, must be exhausted before a state may validly endorse a claim. That said, as the Commission in *Ambatielos* noted, failure to exhaust local remedies will not constitute a bar to a claim if it can be clearly established that in the circumstances of the case an appeal to a higher national tribunal would have been futile. Likewise, procedures of a purely discretionary nature, such as an appeal for clemency, need not be exhausted. Finally, as noted by the British Rules Regarding International Claims, "a claimant against another state [is not] required to exhaust justice in that state where there is no justice to exhaust."[93]

4) What is the nature of the requirement of exhaustion of local remedies? Is it a procedural block to the espousal of a claim by the state or is it an element of the injury? The answer given may have an impact on the timing of the occurrence of the injury, which may in some cases raise problems of jurisdiction *ratione temporis* or of application of the rule of continuity. The PCIJ in the *Phosphates in Morocco Case (Preliminary Objections)*[94] and the ICJ in the *ELSI Case*[95] favoured a procedural approach to this rule, although the proper answer will depend on the nature of the violated rule and the circumstances of the case.[96]

5) A state may expressly waive the requirement of exhaustion of local remedies, allowing claims against it to be brought by another state directly to an international tribunal. For example, article V of the Convention Establishing the Mexican–United States General Claims Commission provided that no claim should be "disallowed or rejected by the Commission by the application of the general principle of international law that the legal remedies must be exhausted as a condition precedent to the validity or allowance of any claim."[97]

Prior Waiver of Claim: The Calvo Clause

An alien who has been injured by a state in a manner wrongful under international law can always waive or settle his or her claim before diplomatic intervention by the state of which he or she is a national, provided that the waiver or settlement is not made under duress.

Some states, in an attempt to avoid foreign diplomatic intervention, have required aliens to waive such intervention in advance, and to submit all their disputes to the local law and courts exclusively. This is called the Calvo clause after its advocate, an Argentinian jurist named Carlos Calvo.

---

93   (1988) 37 I.C.L.Q. 1008.

94   (1938), P.C.I.J. (Ser. A/B) No. 74 at 27.

95   [1989] I.C.J. Rep. 15 at 46-48.

96   See J. Crawford, "Second Report on State Responsibility," U.N. Doc. A/CN.498 (1999) at paras. 136-148, and I. Brownlie, *Principles of Public International Law*, 6th ed. (2004) at 472-81.

97   (1923), 9 Bevans 935 at 938. See also the *Tattler Claim (U.S. v. Great Britain)* (1920), 6 R.I.A.A. 48.

North American Dredging Company Claim
(1926), 4 R.I.A.A. 26

[Article 18 of an agreement between the North American Dredging Company and the Government of Mexico provided that:

> The contractor and all persons who, as employees or in any other capacity, may be engaged in the execution of the work under this contract either directly or indirectly, shall be considered as Mexicans in all matters, within the Republic of Mexico, concerning the execution of such work and the fulfilment of this contract. They shall not claim, nor shall they have, with regard to the interests and the business connected with this contract, any other rights or means to enforce the same than those granted by the laws of the Republic to Mexicans, nor shall they enjoy any other rights than those established in favor of Mexicans. They are consequently deprived of any rights as aliens, and under no conditions shall the intervention of foreign diplomatic agents be permitted, in any matter related to this contract.

The United States on behalf of the company claimed damages for breach of the contract by the Government of Mexico. The Commission sustained the Mexican motion to dismiss the claim on the ground that a contract containing a Calvo clause precluded its consideration by an international commission.]

THE COMMISSION: ...

[14] Reading this article [article 18, quoted above] as a whole, it is evident that its purpose was to bind the claimant to be governed by the laws of Mexico and to use the remedies existing under such laws. ... But this provision did not, and could not, deprive the claimant of his American citizenship and all that that implies. It did not take from him his undoubted right to apply to his own Government for protection if his resort to the Mexican tribunals or other authorities available to him resulted in a denial or delay of justice as that term is used in international law. In such a case the claimant's complaint would be not that his contract was violated but that he had been denied justice. The basis of his appeal would be not a construction of his contract, save perchance in an incidental way, but rather an internationally illegal act.

[15] What, therefore, are the rights which claimant waived and those which he did not waive in subscribing to article 18 of the contract? (a) He waived his right to conduct himself as if no competent authorities existed in Mexico; as if he were engaged in fulfilling a contract in an inferior country subject to a system of capitulations; and as if the only real remedies available to him in the fulfilment, construction, and enforcement of this contract were international remedies. All these he waived and had a right to waive. (b) He did not waive any right which he possessed as an American citizen as to any matter not connected with the fulfilment, execution, or enforcement of this contract as such. (c) He did not waive his undoubted right as an American citizen to apply to his Government for protection against the violation of international law (internationally illegal acts) whether growing out of this contract or out of other situations. (d) He did not and could not affect the right of his Government to extend to him its protection in general or to extend to him its protection against breaches of

international law. But he did frankly and unreservedly agree that in consideration of the Government of Mexico awarding him this contract, he did not need and would not invoke or accept the assistance of his Government with respect to the fulfilment and interpretation of his contract and the execution of his work thereunder. ...

[18] If it were necessary to demonstrate how legitimate are the fears of certain nations with respect to abuses of the right of protection and how seriously the sovereignty of those nations within their own boundaries would be impaired if some extreme conceptions of this right were recognized and enforced, the present case would furnish an illuminating example. The claimant, after having solemnly promised in writing that it would not ignore the local laws, remedies, and authorities, behaved from the very beginning as if article 18 of its contract had no existence in fact. It used the article to procure the contract, but this was the extent of its use. It has never sought any redress by application to the local authorities and remedies which article 18 liberally granted it and which, according to Mexican law, are available to it, even against the Government, without restrictions, both in matter of civil and of public law. ...

[20] Under article 18 of the contract ... the present claimant is precluded from presenting to its Government any claim relative to the interpretation or fulfilment of this contract. If it had a claim for denial of justice, for delay of justice or gross injustice, or for any other violation of international law committed by Mexico to its damage, it might have presented such a claim to its Government, which in turn could have espoused it and presented it here. Although the claim as presented falls within the first clause of Article I of the Treaty, describing claims coming within this Commission's jurisdiction, it is not a claim that may be rightfully presented by the claimant to its Government for espousal and hence is not cognizable here.

NOTES

1) Whether Calvo clauses can effectively prevent a state from espousing a claim of one of its nationals has been yet another object of contention between industrialized and developing countries. The former have long argued that Calvo clauses cannot be given full effect because the right to present an international claim belongs to the state and not to the individual or corporation. Writers and tribunals have generally agreed with that position.[98]

2) In the above case, what is the practical impact of the Calvo clause? How does it relate to the requirement on exhaustion of local remedies?

---

98   See also Restatement, *supra* note 1 at s. 713, comment g and Reporter's Note 6; D. Shea, *The Calvo Clause: A Problem of Inter-American and International Law and Diplomacy* (1955); and D. Manning-Cabrol, "The Imminent Death of the Calvo Clause and the Rebirth of the Calvo Principle: Equality of Foreign and National Investors" (1995) 26 Law & Poly Int'l Bus. 1169.

3. Canadian Practice

Canadian Espousal of Claims
based on J.-G. Castel, *Legal Services Provided by the Department of External Affairs with Respect to International Judicial Co-operation and Other Matters*, Department of External Affairs (1987)

The Government of Canada may, in conformity with generally accepted principles of customary international law, only espouse claims in respect of loss of human life, property, rights, interests or debts of Canadians where the individuals concerned were Canadian citizens at the time of loss, confiscation, expropriation or nationalization. Further, the claim must have belonged to Canadian citizens at all times since they arose and the claimants must be Canadian citizens at the time these claims are presented.

The Government of Canada will normally not espouse a claim of a Canadian against a foreign state until all local legal remedies (i.e., the remedies available to him up to and including the court of final appeal in the foreign state) have been exhausted without satisfaction. However, if in exhausting these local legal remedies the claimant has met with prejudice or obstruction constituting a denial of justice, there may be grounds on which the Government of Canada could intervene on his behalf to secure redress.

In cases of special merit where the claimant does not fulfill the conditions set out above, the Government of Canada may consider using its "good offices" and direct an inquiry to foreign authorities but it will not formally espouse such a claim.

As regards claims by companies, the Government of Canada, pursuant to customary international law as interpreted in the *Barcelona Traction* case,[99] may espouse claims in respect of property nationalized or otherwise taken abroad only where the claims belong to a company incorporated under the laws of Canada or of any province of Canada and where the company was so incorporated on the date on which the claim arose.

There is a further requirement in Canadian practice, and that is that company claims will normally only be espoused by the Government of Canada where there is a "substantial" Canadian interest in the company. Whether such a "substantial" Canadian interest exists so as to justify Canadian diplomatic intervention will depend, *inter alia*, on factors such as where it carries on its business, whether it has active trading interests in Canada, and the extent to which the company is beneficially owned in Canada.

---

99   [1970] I.C.J. Rep. 3, reported in Chapter 8, Section B on "Corporations." But see *Case concerning Elettronica Sicula S.P.A. (ELSI)*, [1989] I.C.J. Rep. 15, also reproduced in Chapter 8, Section B, which involved proceedings by the United States against Italy in respect of a dispute arising out of the requisition by the government of Italy of the plant and related assets of an Italian company 100 percent owned by two U.S. corporations; and B. Stern, "La protection diplomatique des investissements internationaux. De Barcelona Traction à Electtronica Sicula ou les glissements progressifs de l'analyse" (1990) 117 J.D.I. 897.

Where Canadian citizens have an interest, as shareholders or otherwise, in a foreign company and where the state under the laws of which that company was incorporated and of which it is thus a national causes economic loss to the company, the Government of Canada may intervene to protect the interests of such citizens. Canadian citizens who are shareholders in a foreign company which suffered loss at the hands of a foreign government are thus eligible for espousal of their claims by the Government of Canada. Such claims, moreover, may be included in claims negotiations leading to lump-sum settlement agreements.

There are, nevertheless, questions of public policy in such cases and it is usually necessary, therefore, to consider each case on its merits. The Government of Canada may also intervene on behalf of a Canadian shareholder of a foreign company incorporated in a foreign state if that company is injured by the acts of a third state. In such a case, the intervention may be made in concert with the government of the state in which the company was incorporated.

Procedure

When a Canadian citizen brings to the attention of Foreign Affairs Canada a *prima facie* valid claim against a foreign state in respect of which he has exhausted all local legal remedies without success, the Department may decide to intervene formally through the exercise of good offices or espousal of the claim in accordance with established principles of international law. The decision as to which course of action is to be followed depends in large part on the facts of the individual case. When a state has undertaken a policy of general nationalization and, as a result, the property of a large number of Canadian citizens has been affected, it has been customary first to obtain an agreement in principle with the state concerned to negotiate a general settlement of Canadian claims. Such preliminary agreements are then publicized and interested persons are invited to file completed claims questionnaires with Foreign Affairs Canada. Following a period of assessment and preparation, those claims considered to be valid are made known to the other state and negotiations begin for a lump-sum settlement.

If such a settlement is reached, regulations respecting the distribution of the proceeds of the settlement are passed by Order-in-Council and the claims are subsequently formally referred to the Foreign Claims Commission (established in 1970) for a Report and Recommendation as to the amount to be awarded in respect of each claim of which it has notice. While the question of whether the claimant is eligible to participate in a claims settlement between Canada and a foreign state is subject to a report and recommendation of the Foreign Claims Commission, ministerial approval is required in order for an award to be made. Advancement of the claim during negotiations and its acceptance as being *prima facie* valid by the other side, create no rights to a share of the settlement for individual claimants. Such a right is created only by Ministerial approval of a Foreign Claims Commission Report and Recommendation on a particular claim.

While Canadian claims settlement agreements in the form of lump-sum settlements will reflect in a general way, the number and value of claims submitted by Canadian citizens to the Canadian Government, such settlements are not regarded as the total sum of a series of individually-accepted claims.

Foreign Affairs Canada has played a transactional role in processing Canadian claims to the United Nations Compensation Commission, established by Security Council Resolution 687 (1991) to provide reparation for injuries suffered as a result of the Iraqi invasion of Kuwait. The Compensation Commission paid any successful claims to the Canadian Government, which then distributed them to individual claimants (less a small processing fee).

Exercise of Good Offices

The Canadian Government, at its discretion, may in certain circumstances support and make diplomatic representations on behalf of a claim which is of uncertain validity, on the merits or on grounds of international law. For example, the Government may consider a request for assistance in respect to the claim of a new Canadian who was not a Canadian citizen at the time of the events giving rise to the claim. Under the rule of continuous nationality, the Government cannot formally espouse this claim (unless it rests on provisions of a specific treaty) but it may instruct the Canadian Embassy or Consulate in the foreign locality concerned to lend assistance short of espousal where such action is considered to be useful and appropriate.

Such informal assistance, where an effort is made to facilitate a settlement without the Government thereby becoming a party to the dispute, is often referred to as an exercise of "good offices." It may take many forms, including, for example, enquiries as to the present status of the dispute, as to the procedure which the claimant should follow to press his own claim under local laws, or it may be in the form of a request for reconsideration or review of a decision of an agency of the foreign government. An intervention as an exercise of good offices may, at the discretion of the Government, and depending upon the circumstances of the case, be made at a high level and may be accompanied by strong representations. As a practical matter, the distinction between formal espousal and an exercise of good offices may be somewhat blurred. It must be recognized, however, that in many cases the possibility of effective assistance by the Government of Canada in cases which do not meet the international requirements for espousal, will be severely circumscribed. Where, for example, a number of claims valid under international law are outstanding against, or under negotiation with the foreign government, support by Canada for other claims, without regard to traditional rules of eligibility, may prejudice efforts made to obtain satisfaction of the valid claims. In such a case, an informal exercise of good offices on behalf of a claimant may not only be futile but counter-productive. Accordingly, in the exercise of its sovereign discretion in presenting international claims, the Government of Canada will be closely guided by accepted principles of international law and practice.

D. INVOCATION OF STATE RESPONSIBILITY[100]

1. General Principles

The question who may claim the benefit of international responsibility is complex but essential to the theory that an internationally wrongful act creates a secondary obligation to provide reparation. Unlike most regimes in torts or civil liability in municipal legal systems, international responsibility is not necessarily defined in a direct relational manner between two parties. Traditionally, the consequences of a breach of an international obligation have been considered to relate only to those states that suffer injury as a result of the breach. Thus, responsibility was essentially a bilateral matter between the wrongdoing and injured states. Globalization and the proliferation of multilateral instruments, however, have rendered this traditional approach obsolete. The breach of a multilateral agreement may not directly harm any state but may nevertheless undermine the effectiveness of the legal regime as a whole. The multilateral context has therefore commanded a shift in the approach to state responsibility, emphasizing the restoration and maintenance of the rule of law rather than the simple adjustment of bilateral disputes.[101]

The ILC articles have incorporated that need to focus on re-establishing and upholding the international rule of law, in the interest of both the injured state and of the international community at large, by allowing invocation of State responsibility to both injured and, in certain circumstances, non-injured states.

(a) Invocation by the Injured State

Although virtually all states may, in certain instances, have a legal interest in invoking responsibility and ensuring compliance with an international obligation, the concept of the injured State remains central to the invocation of responsibility. As will be detailed below, States may be considered to have been injured either individually or collectively.

**International Law Commission, Draft Articles on Responsibility of States for
Internationally Wrongful Acts**
Report of the International Law Commission on the Work of Its Fifty-third Session,
UN GAOR, 56th Sess., Supp. No. 10, U.N. Doc. A/56/10 (2001) chp. IV.E.1

Article 42
Invocation of Responsibility by an Injured State

A State is entitled as an injured State to invoke the responsibility of another State if the obligation breached is owed to:

---

100 See C. Gray, *Judicial Remedies in International Law* (1987).

101 Dinah Shelton, "Righting the Wrongs: Reparations in the Articles on State Resonsibility" (2002) 96 A.J.I.L. 833.

    (a) That State individually; or

    (b) A group of States including that State, or the international community as a
whole, and the breach of the obligation:

        (i) Specially affects that State; or

        (ii) Is of such a character as radically to change the position of all the other
    States to which the obligation is owed with respect to the further performance
    of the obligation.

. . . .

<h2 style="text-align:center">Article 46</h2>
<h3 style="text-align:center">Plurality of Injured States</h3>

Where several States are injured by the same internationally wrongful act, each injured
State may separately invoke the responsibility of the State which has committed the
internationally wrongful act.

<h2 style="text-align:center">Article 47</h2>
<h3 style="text-align:center">Plurality of Responsible States</h3>

    1. Where several States are responsible for the same internationally wrongful act,
the responsibility of each State may be invoked in relation to that act.

    2. Paragraph 1:

    (a) Does not permit any injured State to recover, by way of compensation, more
than the damage it has suffered;

    (b) Is without prejudice to any right of recourse against the other responsible State.

<h3 style="text-align:center">NOTES</h3>

    1) The definition of "invocation" is not given in the ILC Articles. However, acccording
to the commentaries, "invocation should be understood as taking measures of a relatively
formal character—for example, the raising or presentation of a claim against another state
or the commencement of proceedings before an international court or tribunal. A state does
not invoke the responsibility of another state merely because it criticizes that state for the
breach and calls for observance of the obligation, or even reserves its rights or protests."[102]

    2) Article 42 codifies three hypothetical situations in which a state will be considered
entitled, as an injured state, to invoke the responsibility of another state. First, under
Article 42(a), a state will be considered injured when it has an individual right to the
performance of the obligation that has been breached. This will occur not only in the case
of breach of a bilateral treaty but also in other cases including unilateral commitments
made by one state to another, multilateral treaties where a particular obligation binds one
state party toward another, or general international law dealing with the relations between
states.[103] This will be the case, for example, if a foreign spy plane enters national airspace
without permission or if a state fails to protect the embassy of a foreign state.

---

102   Crawford, *supra* note 1 at 256.

103   Crawford, *supra* note 1 at art. 42, para. 6.

Second, according to article 42(b)(i), a state will be considered injured if it is the victim of a violation of a collective obligation owed to a group of states or the international community as a whole, and is "specially affected" by such a breach. This could include, for example, pollution of the high seas, in violation of the multilateral obligations set out in the United Nations Convention on the Law of the Sea, but that particularly affects the nearest coastal state.

Last, article 42(b)(ii) deals with those obligations whose breach will be considered as affecting in itself every other state to which they are owed. This paragraph covers "integral obligations" or "all or nothing" regimes characterized by the fact that "each state's continued performance of the obligation is in effect conditioned upon its performance by each other party" and that "a breach of such an obligation threatens the treaty structure as a whole."[104] Consequently, every state to which such obligations are owed will be considered injured by its breach. One example would be the breach of a treaty providing for nuclear non-proliferation.

3) Articles 46 and 47 deal with those cases where there are several injured States or several responsible States. It is stipulated that in those instances, any of the injured States is entitled to invoke the responsibility of any wrongdoer, as long as the required reparation does not exceed the actual harm that has been suffered by that State. These principles will be of particular interest when facing specific issues such as environmental protection, most often engaging a number of responsible as well as injured States.

(b) Invocation by Other States

The injury caused by an internationally wrongful act may be of a general nature, meaning that all states bound by a given norm will be considered injured by its violation. This corresponds to the category of obligations *erga omnes*, which do not create a series of parallel bilateral relationships, but only an omni-directional, non-bilateral relation with all other states bound by the norm. In the *Barcelona Traction Case*, the Court identified aggression, human rights, and the prohibition of genocide as three examples of norms *erga omnes*, the breach of which will injure every other state.[105] When a state tortures one of its own nationals, for instance, there is no specifically injured state, and the only basis on which international responsibility may be activated is the *erga omnes* dimension of the norm prohibiting torture. The significance of the emergence of this third type of international responsibility is illustrated by the hesitations of the ICJ in this respect, first seeming to accept the idea in the *South West Africa Cases* (Preliminary Objections) in 1962, then backtracking to refuse the idea of an *actio popularis*, whereby any state may take legal action to vindicate a public interest, in the Second Phase of the same case in

---

104 J. Crawford, J. Peel & S. Olleson, "The ILC's Articles on Responsibility of States for Internationally Wrongful Acts: Completion of the Second Reading" (2001) 12 EJIL 963 at 974.

105 *Barcelona Traction, Light and Power Co. Case*, *supra* note 99 at para. 33; see A. de Hoog, *Obligations Erga Omnes and International Crimes* (1996) and M. Ragazzi, *The Concept of International Obligations Erga Omnes* (1997).

1966,[106] before finally embracing the concept of obligations *erga omnes* in the *Barcelona Traction Case* in 1970.

International Law Commission, Draft Articles on the Responsibility of States for Internationally Wrongful Acts
Report of the International Law Commission on the Work of Its Fifty-third Session,
UN GAOR, 56th Sess., Supp. No. 10, U.N. Doc. A/56/10 (2001) chp. IV.E.1

Article 48
Invocation of Responsibility by a State Other Than an Injured State

1. Any State other than an injured State is entitled to invoke the responsibility of another State in accordance with paragraph 2 if:

(a) The obligation breached is owed to a group of States including that State, and is established for the protection of a collective interest of the group; or

(b) The obligation breached is owed to the international community as a whole.

2. Any State entitled to invoke responsibility under paragraph 1 may claim from the responsible State:

(a) Cessation of the internationally wrongful act, and assurances and guarantees of non-repetition in accordance with article 30; and

(b) Performance of the obligation of reparation in accordance with the preceding articles, in the interest of the injured State or of the beneficiaries of the obligation breached.

3. The requirements for the invocation of responsibility by an injured State under articles 43, 44 and 45 apply to an invocation of responsibility by a State entitled to do so under paragraph 1.

NOTES

1) Article 48 "recognizes that other States, by virtue of their participation in a multilateral regime or as a consequence of their membership of the international community, have a legal interest in the performance of certain multilateral obligations."[107] The notion of injury is in this context completely set aside, replaced by the broader concept of legal interest flowing from membership in a designated group to whom the obligation is owed, or to the international community as a whole. This corresponds to the spirit of the ILC articles, which is the maintenance of international legality at large and not simply the adjustment of bilateral disputes.

2) A distinction is drawn in article 48 between those obligations that are owed to the international community as a whole (obligations *erga omnes*) and those that only concern a limited group of States (obligation *erga omnes partes*). For a State other than those

---

106 *South West Africa Cases* (Preliminary Objections), [1962] I.C.J. Rep. 319; *South West Africa Cases* (Second Phase), [1966] I.C.J. Rep. 6 at 47.

107 Crawford, *supra* note 1 at 40.

injured to invoke responsibility in the latter case, an additional criterion is required. According to article 48 paragraph (1)(a), the obligation must have been established for the protection of a collective interest. It might concern, for example, the environment or security of a given region.

3) Invocation of State responsibility by the State other than those injured is of a more limited range than invocation by the injured State itself. As explained in the commentaries, "the position of the broader class of states interested in the breach of a collective or community obligation is ancillary or secondary. These states have the right to call for cessation of the internationally wrongful act and for assurances and guarantees of non-repetition. They may also insist on compliance by the responsible state."[108] They may not, however, claim compensation on their own account.

4) The distinction between injured and non-injured States has been criticized on the grounds that all States are in some sense legally injured when an obligation to which they subscribe has been breached.[109] Do you think the notion of "legal injury" could serve as a relevant basis of international responsibility?

2. Countermeasures[110]

Countermeasures are a typical feature of the decentralized system of implementation in international law. Due to the lack of compulsory jurisdiction on the international plane, it is only infrequently that international disputes relating to reparation for an internationally wrongful act are referred to adjudication. As a result, when a dispute does occur, there is often no international institution to which the injured state can turn for help in persuading the wrongdoing state to provide reparation. Countermeasures are a form of self help by which the injured state may lawfully apply pressure on the wrongdoing state to obtain the cessation of the wrongful act as well as reparation.

Countermeasures are acts that would normally be unlawful but are nevertheless considered licit by their character as a response to a prior internationally wrongful act of another state. They are to be distinguished from mere retortion measures, which are acts of an unfriendly nature but which breach no international obligation of the state such as, for example, the suspension of development assistance.

---

108 Crawford, *supra* note 1 at 45.

109 See B. Stern, "Et si l'on utilisait le concept de préjudice juridique? Retour sur une notion délaissée à l'occasion de la fin des travaux de la CDI sur la responsabilité des Etats," [2001] AFDI 3.

110 See E. Zoller, *Peacetime Unilateral Remedies: An Analysis of Countermeasures* (1984); O. Elagab, *The Legality of Non-Forcible Counter-Measures in International Law* (1988); L. Sicilianos, *Les réactions décentralisées à l'illicite* (1990); and D. Alland, *Justice privé et ordre juridique international—étude théorique des contre-mesures en droit international public* (1994).

International Law Commission, Draft Articles on the Responsibility of States for Internationally Wrongful Acts

Report of the International Law Commission on the Work of Its Fifty-third Session, UN GAOR, 56th Sess., Supp. No. 10, U.N. Doc. A/56/10 (2001), chp. IV.E.1

Article 49
Object and Limits of Countermeasures

1. An injured State may only take countermeasures against a State which is responsible for an internationally wrongful act in order to induce that State to comply with its obligations under Part Two.

2. Countermeasures are limited to the non-performance for the time being of international obligations of the State taking the measures towards the responsible State.

3. Countermeasures shall, as far as possible, be taken in such a way as to permit the resumption of performance of the obligation in question.

Article 50
Obligations Not Affected by Countermeasures

1. Countermeasures shall not affect:

(a) The obligation to refrain from the threat or use of force as embodied in the Charter of the United Nations;

(b) Obligations for the protection of fundamental human rights;

(c) Obligations of a humanitarian character prohibiting reprisals;

(d) Other obligations under peremptory norms of general international law.

2. A State taking countermeasures is not relieved from fulfilling its obligations:

(a) Under any dispute settlement procedure applicable between it and the responsible State;

(b) To respect the inviolability of diplomatic or consular agents, premises, archives and documents.

Article 51
Proportionality

Countermeasures must be commensurate with the injury suffered, taking into account the gravity of the internationally wrongful act and the rights in question.

Article 52
Conditions Relating to Resort to Countermeasures

1. Before taking countermeasures, an injured State shall:

(a) Call on the responsible State, in accordance with article 43, to fulfil its obligations under Part Two;

(b) Notify the responsible State of any decision to take countermeasures and offer to negotiate with that State.

2. Notwithstanding paragraph 1(b), the injured State may take such urgent countermeasures as are necessary to preserve its rights.

3. Countermeasures may not be taken, and if already taken must be suspended without undue delay if:

(a) The internationally wrongful act has ceased, and

(b) The dispute is pending before a court or tribunal which has the authority to make decisions binding on the parties.

4. Paragraph 3 does not apply if the responsible State fails to implement the dispute settlement procedures in good faith.

Article 53
Termination of Countermeasures

Countermeasures shall be terminated as soon as the responsible State has complied with its obligations under Part Two in relation to the internationally wrongful act.

NOTES

1) The expression "countermeasures" replaced the older term "reprisals" in the wake of the 1978 *Air Service Agreement Case*,[111] which affirmed the state's broad right to adopt countermeasures in reaction to a violation of its rights by another state.

2) A state may adopt countermeasures that need not mirror the initial violation to which they are a response. Thus, a state may react to the breach of a customary right of innocent passage of ships in the territorial sea by suspending a trade agreement. What is the link between this principle and the right of a state to suspend and terminate a treaty in case of breach by the other party (Vienna Convention on the Law of Treaties article 60, reproduced in the Documentary Supplement)? Can a state terminate a treaty by way of countermeasures?[112]

3) A set of both substantive and procedural limitations seeks to ensure that countermeasures remain within acceptable bounds and strictly correspond to the specific requirements of the situation. Among the several substantial safeguards, countermeasures shall be directed only at the responsible state(s) and not at third parties (article 49(1)); they are to be taken temporarily, for the duration of the internationally wrongful act (article 49(2)); they shall be as far as possible reversible in their effect and not affect the resumption of performance of the obligation at stake and the future legal relations between the states involved (article 49(3)). Lastly, countermeasures must be proportionate to the injury suffered (article 51) and shall never impair human rights, humanitarian norms, or peremptory norms (article 50(1)).

---

111 (1978), 18 R.I.A.A. 417.

112 See the *Case Concerning the Gabčíkovo-Nagymaros Project*, [1997] I.C.J. Rep. 7 at para. 106; P. Weckel, "Convergence du droit des traités et du droit de la responsabilité internationale: à la lumière de l'Arrêt du 25 septembre 1997 de la Cour internationale de Justice relatif au projet Gabcikovo-Nagymaros Hongrie/Slovaquie" (1998) 102 R.G.D.I.P. 647; J. Setear, "Responses to Breach of A Treaty and Rationalist International Relations Theory: the Rules of Release and Remediation in the Law of Treaties and the Law of State Responsibility" (1997) 83 Va. L. Rev. 1; and P. Weil, "Droit des traités et droit de la responsabilité" in M. Rama-Montaldo, ed., *El derecho internacional en un mundo en transformación* (1994) 523.

4) As to procedural limitations, the main and most controversial one is the constraint put on the adoption of countermeasures whenever there exists an international court or tribunal with authority to make decisions binding on the parties in relation to the dispute. Article 52 is "a rephrasing of the relevant holding from *Air Services Agreement* that once a dispute is submitted to a tribunal that has the 'means to achieve the objectives justifying the countermeasures,' the right to initiate countermeasures is vitiated and those already in force may be 'eliminated,' but only to the extent that the tribunal can provide equivalent 'interim measures of protection.' "[113] In its 2001 *LaGrand* judgment, the International Court of Justice found that provisional measures ordered by the Court were binding on parties, but the United States failed to comply with these measures.[114] Given the real possibility that a wrongdoing state may disregard court-imposed provisional measures, is it opportune to drastically restrict the recourse to countermeasures whenever a court or tribunal is asked to settle the dispute? Should restrictions to the taking of countermeasures be conditioned on the issuance of provisional measures by the tribunal and subsequent compliance by the alleged wrongdoer?

5) The Legal Bureau of the Department of External Affairs wrote in a memorandum dated November 24, 1989:[115]

> Some argue that the mere existence of a dispute settlement procedure in a treaty acts as an absolute bar to the parties to the treaty from taking counter-measures. This view is not entirely supported by State practice, nor by scholars commenting on the issue.
>
> The better view, in our opinion, is that the existence of an institutional framework for dispute settlement puts certain checks on the resort to counter-measures. For example, the exhaustion of the peaceful settlement procedure is a prerequisite to taking counter-measures. However, "it should be emphasized at the same time that the right to resort to counter-measures is merely held in abeyance. The implication, therefore, is that the right in question can be revived where the institutional framework proves to be ineffective.".... In other words, the existence of the dispute settlement mechanism is a *prima facie* ban to resorting to counter-measures. This ban can be overridden in certain circumstances, such as the inability of the tribunal to provide the protection sought.

---

113 David J. Bederman, "Counterintuiting Countermeasures" (2002) 96 A.J.I.L. 817 at 825.

114 *Supra* note 38 at paras. 92-109.

115 Reprinted in (1990) 28 Can. Y.B. Int'l L. 494.

CHAPTER ELEVEN

International Criminal Law

International criminal law[1] has evolved alongside international humanitarian law, also known as the law of armed conflict. They overlap to the extent that violations of international humanitarian law may be international crimes. However, international criminal law goes beyond armed conflicts of an international and internal nature and humanitarian protection encompassed therein. International criminal law reflects "the convergence of two disciplines: the penal aspects of international law and the international aspects of national criminal law."[2]

International crimes, *stricto sensu*, must be distinguished from crimes that are purely transnational in character. The latter are common domestic crimes with constituent elements in more than one state that require international cooperation to prosecute or punish. International crimes are different. They are offences that are prescribed at customary and/or conventional international law. The ambit of international criminal law is wide ranging.

During the 20th century there was a growing realization that individuals might be prosecuted and found liable for international criminal conduct, such as crimes against peace, war crimes, crimes against humanity, apartheid, genocide, torture, a variety of international terrorist acts, and the international traffic in narcotics and psychotropic substances.

In the absence of a permanent international criminal court, the operation of international criminal law has depended on two mechanisms: *ad hoc* tribunals and mixed national-international tribunals set up to deal with specific situations, and prosecution in domestic criminal courts. The International Military Tribunals (IMT) established after World War II at Nuremberg and Tokyo and, more recently, the *Ad Hoc* International Criminal Tribunals for the former Yugoslavia and Rwanda, the Special Panels in East Timor, and the Special Court for Sierre Leone exemplify the prosecution at the international level. They were

---

1   See generally M.C. Bassiouni, *Introduction to International Criminal Law* (2003); ed., *International Criminal Law*, 2d ed. (1998-1999) 3 vols.; I. Bantekas & S. Nash, *International Criminal Law*, 2d ed. (2003); A. Cassese, *International Criminal Law* (2003); K. Kittichaisaree, *International Criminal Law* (2001); G.-J. A. Knoops, *An Introduction to the Law of International Criminal Tribunals* (2003); P. Sands, *From Nuremberg to The Hague: The Future of International Criminal Justice* (2003); E. van Sliedregt, *The Criminal Responsibility in International Law for Serious Human Rights Violations* (2003). See also the ASIL Guide to Electronic Resources for International Law: International Criminal Law (by Gail Partin) at <www.asil.org/resource/crim1.htm>.

2   J. Paust *et al.*, *International Criminal Law*, 2d ed. (2000) at 3.

aimed at individuals alleged to have committed violations of customary and conventional law in the course of international or internal armed conflicts, crimes against humanity, and genocide. More generally, the international community has relied on the enforcement by domestic courts of acts proscribed by international criminal law. Some of these proscriptions impose on states an obligation *aut dedere, aut judicare*—that is, to extradite or to submit the accused to prosecution.[3] International cooperation in criminal matters is also supported by the use in good faith of bilateral treaties and multilateral conventions dealing specifically with extradition and other forms of mutual legal assistance.

The development of both the body of international crimes and the processes for their enforcement has proceeded at a great rate in recent years. Renewed political interest in a permanent international court and vigorous preparatory work first by the International Law Commission and subsequently by the Preparatory Committee established by the U.N. General Assembly have produced results. To meet the challenges to world order and international peace and security, and to secure adherence to the international rule of law by seeking to end impunity, the United Nations established a diplomatic conference in Rome in July 1998 at which the International Criminal Court (ICC) was established.

The following materials explore these developments from the Nuremberg Tribunal and the advancement of international humanitarian law after World War II, through the *Ad Hoc* Tribunals for the former Yugoslavia and Rwanda to the new ICC. They conclude with a discussion of the responsibilities of states for national criminal prosecution of international offences.

A. DEVELOPMENT OF INTERNATIONAL CRIMINAL LAW

1. Individual Responsibility After World War II

The London Agreement, 1945
Agreement by United Kingdom, United States of America, France, and
U.S.S.R. for the Prosecution and Punishment of the Major War
Criminals of the European Axis
82 U.N.T.S. 279.

[The Moscow Declaration of 1943 provided for the punishment by the Allies of Germans who might be found guilty of having committed war crimes. It stated:

> Those German officers and men and members of the Nazi party who have been responsible for, or have taken a consenting part in the above atrocities, massacres and executions, will be sent back to the countries in which their abominable deeds were done in order that they may be judged and punished according to the laws of these

---

3   See M.C. Bassiouni & E.M. Wise, *Aut Dedere Aut Judicare: The Duty to Extradite or Prosecute in International Law* (1995). Also note that the International Law Commission has begun work on the topic "The Obligation To Extradite or Prosecute (aut dedere aut judicare) in International Law": ILC, *Report of the Work of Its 56th Session*, GAOR 59th Sess., Supp. No. 10, U.N. Doc. A/59/10 (2004) at 305.

liberated countries and of the free governments which will be created therein ... without prejudice to the case of the major criminals, whose offenses have no particular geographical location and who will be punished by the joint decision of the Governments of the Allies.

On August 8, 1945, an agreement was concluded in London between the Governments of the United Kingdom, the United States, the U.S.S.R., and France, acting in the interests of all the United Nations, which provided for the establishment of an International Military Tribunal pursuant to the Moscow Declaration. Later, 19 governments of the United Nations adhered to the agreement.]

Article 1

There shall be established after consultation with the Control Council for Germany an International Military Tribunal for the trial of war criminals whose offences have no particular geographical location whether they be accused individually or in their capacity as members of organizations or groups or in both capacities.

Article 2

The constitution, jurisdiction and functions of the International Military Tribunal shall be those set out in the Charter annexed to this agreement, which Charter shall form an integral part of this Agreement. ...

Article 4

Nothing in this Agreement shall prejudice the provisions established by the Moscow Declaration concerning the return of war criminals to the countries where they committed their crimes. ...

Article 6

Nothing in this agreement shall prejudice the jurisdiction of the powers of any national or occupational court established or to be established in any allied territory or in Germany for the trial of war criminals.

The Nuremberg Charter, 1945
Charter of the International Military Tribunal
82 U.N.T.S. 279

II. JURISDICTION AND GENERAL PRINCIPLES

Article 6

The Tribunal established by the Agreement referred to in Article 1 hereof for the trial and punishment of the major war criminals of the European Axis countries shall have the power to try and punish persons who, acting in the interests of the European Axis countries, whether as individuals or as members of organizations, committed any of the following crimes.

The following acts, or any of them, are crimes coming within the jurisdiction of the Tribunal for which there shall be individual responsibility:

(a) Crimes against peace: namely, planning, preparation, initiation or waging of a war of aggression, or a war in violation of international treaties, agreements or assurances, or participation in a common plan or conspiracy for the accomplishment of any of the foregoing;

(b) War crimes: namely, violations of the laws or customs of war. Such violations shall include, but not be limited to, murder, ill-treatment or deportation to slave labour or for any other purpose of civilian population of or in occupied territory, murder or ill-treatment of prisoners of war or persons on the seas, killing of hostages, plunder of public or private property, wanton destruction of cities, towns or villages, or devastation not justified by military necessity;

(c) Crimes against humanity: namely, murder, extermination, enslavement, deportation, and other inhumane acts committed against any civilian population, before or during the war, or persecutions on political, racial or religious grounds in execution of or in connection with any crime within the jurisdiction of the Tribunal, whether or not in violation of the domestic law of the country where perpetrated.

Leaders, organizers, instigators and accomplices participating in the formulation or execution of a common plan or conspiracy to commit any of the foregoing crimes are responsible for all acts performed by any persons in execution of such plan.

Article 7

The official position of defendants, whether as Heads of State or responsible officials in Government Departments, shall not be considered as freeing them from responsibility or mitigating punishment.

Article 8

The fact that the Defendant acted pursuant to an order of his Government or of a superior shall not free him from responsibility, but may be considered in mitigation of punishment if the Tribunal determines that justice so requires.

Article 9

At the trial of any individual member of any group or organization the Tribunal may declare (in connection with any act of which the individual was convicted) that the group or organization of which the individual was a member was a criminal organization.

Nuremberg War Crimes Trials[4]
(1947), 1 Trial of the Major War Criminals 171

[Twenty-two defendants, the major war criminals whose crimes had no exact geographical location, were indicted before the IMT established at Nuremberg pursuant to an agreement between France, the United Kingdom, the United States, the U.S.S.R., and 19 other adherents. The defendants were charged with crimes against peace, war crimes, and crimes against humanity. They were also charged with participating in the formulation or execution of a common plan or conspiring to commit all these crimes.]

THE TRIBUNAL: ... The individual defendants are indicted under article 6 of the Charter ... .

Leaders, organizers, instigators and accomplices participating in the formulation or execution of a common plan or conspiracy to commit any of the foregoing crimes are responsible for all acts performed by any persons in execution of such plan. ...

The making of the Charter was the exercise of the sovereign legislative power by the countries to which the German Reich unconditionally surrendered; and the undoubted right of these countries to legislate for the occupied territories has been recognized by the civilized world. The Charter is not an arbitrary exercise of power on the part of the victorious nations, but in the view of the Tribunal, as will be shown, it is the expression of international law existing at the time of its creation; and to that extent is itself a contribution to international law. ...

It was submitted that international law is concerned with the actions of sovereign States, and provides no punishment for individuals; and further, that where the act in question is an act of State, those who carry it out are not personally responsible, but protected by the doctrine of the sovereignty of the State. In the opinion of the Tribunal, both these submissions must be rejected. That international law imposes duties and liabilities upon individuals as well as upon states has long been recognized. Crimes against international law are committed by men, not by abstract entities, and only by punishing individuals who commit such crimes can the provisions of international law be enforced. ...

The principle of international law, which under certain circumstances, protects the representatives of a State, cannot be applied to acts which are condemned as criminal by international law. The authors of these acts cannot shelter themselves behind their official position in order to be freed from punishment in appropriate proceedings. Article 7 of the Charter expressly declares: "The official position of defendants, whether as heads of State, or responsible officials in government departments, shall not be considered as freeing them from responsibility, or mitigating punishment."

---

4   See R. Woetzel, *The Nürnberg Trials in International Law*, rev. ed. (1962). The portion of the judgment concerning acts of aggression is reported in Chapter 15, Section B.1 on "The Right of Self-Defence." On war crimes, generally, see L.C. Green, *International Law: A Canadian Perspective*, 2d ed. (1988) at 340-357; and T. McCormack & G. Simpson, *Law of War Crimes, National and International Approaches* (1996).

On the other hand the very essence of the Charter is that individuals have international duties which transcend the national obligations of obedience imposed by the individual State. He who violates the laws of war cannot obtain immunity while acting in pursuance of the authority of the State if the State in authorizing action moves outside its competence under international law.

It was also submitted on behalf of these defendants that in doing what they did they were acting under the orders of Hitler, and therefore cannot be held responsible for the acts committed by them in carrying out these orders. The Charter specifically provides in Article 8: "The fact that the defendant acted pursuant to orders of his Government or of a superior shall not free him from responsibility, but may be considered in mitigation of punishment."

The provisions of this Article are in conformity with the law of all nations. That a soldier was ordered to kill or torture in violation of the international law of war has never been recognized as a defense to such acts of brutality, though, as the Charter here provides, the order may be urged in mitigation of the punishment. The true test, which is found in varying degrees in the criminal law of most nations, is not the existence of the order, but whether moral choice was in fact possible.

NOTES

1) The IMT held that "to initiate a war of aggression ... is the supreme international crime." In the course of its judgment, the Tribunal reviewed the aggressive acts pursued as a deliberate and essential part of Nazi foreign policy. It condemned the seizure of Austria, Belgium, Czechoslovakia, Denmark, Luxembourg, the Netherlands, Norway, and Poland and the aggressive acts against the former U.S.S.R., all in violation of customary and conventional international law. The IMT relied on the Kellogg-Briand Pact of 1928[5] renouncing war as an instrument of national policy as reinforced by other treaties in support of its judgment. The IMT emphasized here and with respect to the other crimes within its mandate that the maxims *nullum crimen sine lege, nulla poena sine lege* had been complied with, that the acts were criminal at international law at the time that they were committed. See the judgment of the IMT extracted in Chapter 15, Section B.1 on "The Right of Self-Defence."

2) Because of the grammatical construction of article 6(c) of the Charter, the Tribunal was constrained by the language to crimes against humanity committed during the war. It could entertain only crimes against humanity committed before the war that had been "undertaken" in execution of or in connection with crimes against peace or war crimes. Why do you think that the former U.S.S.R. insisted on this construction?

3) The IMT was composed of four judges and four alternates appointed by France, the United Kingdom, the United States, and the former U.S.S.R. At the conclusion of the trial of the 22 accused, 19 were held guilty and 3 were acquitted. Of the guilty, 12 were sentenced to death by hanging, 3 were sentenced to life imprisonment, and the remainder were sent to prison for lengthy terms. The major war criminals before the IMT included Hermann Goering, Rudolf Hess, Alfred Rosenberg, Hans Frank, and Albert Speer.

---

5   Can. T.S. 1929 No. 7; 94 L.N.T.S. 57.

4) In addition to the IMT, Allied Control Council Order No. 10, promulgated by the Allied Powers in 1945, authorized the Allied Commanders in the four zones of occupation in Germany to arrest suspected war criminals and establish tribunals to prosecute them. The United States established its military tribunal also at Nuremberg and pursued 12 indictments, naming 185 defendants.[6] Such prosecutions were not inhibited by the language of article 6(c) of the IMT Charter mentioned above. In *In Re Ohlendorf and Others*[7] the U.S. Military Tribunal held that Control Council Order No. 10 expressed a "codification and systemization of already existing legal principles, rules and customs, both with respect to war crimes and crimes against humanity."

5) After World War I, under articles 228 to 230 of the Versailles Treaty 1919, the German Government recognized the right of the Allied and Associated Powers to bring persons accused of committing acts in violation of the laws and customs of war to trial before military tribunals. A demand was submitted to Germany for the trial of 901 persons under the aforementioned articles. Germany refused and as a compromise the Allies accepted that Germany should prosecute a selected number of individuals. Of 45 names that were selected only 13 were actually tried.[8] Of these, 6 were acquitted. The heaviest sentence imposed was four years' imprisonment.

6) Many other trials have considered the applicability of international criminal law to individuals. Of special note are: the Tokyo War Trials and conviction by the IMT for the Far East of the 28 major war criminals of that arena;[9] *In Re Flick and Others*[10] where the United States Military Tribunal held that: "International law binds every citizen as does ordinary municipal law ... . The application of international law to individuals is no novelty"; and *In Re Ohlendorf and Others*[11] where the United States Military Tribunal held again that "[i]t is a fallacy of no small proportion that international obligations can apply only to the abstract entities called States."

7) The U.N. General Assembly affirmed the principles of international law recognized in the Nuremberg Charter and the judgment of the IMT on December 11, 1946.[12] The ILC at the behest of the General Assembly formulated the Nuremberg Principles.[13]

2. International Humanitarian Law

In the view of the International Military Tribunal, when the Nuremberg Charter, reproduced in Section A.1, defined the offences within its jurisdiction as crimes against peace, war crimes, and crimes against humanity, this was "not an arbitrary exercise of

---

6   See T. Taylor, *Final Report to the Secretary of the Army on the Nuremberg War Crimes Trials Under Control Council Order No. 10* (1949) 136-38, reproduced in Paust *et al.*, *supra* note 2 at 861.

7   (1948), I.L.R. 656.

8   See the *Dover Castle Case* and *The Llandovery Castle Case* (1923-24), 2 Ann. Dig. 429 and 436.

9   *International Military Tribunal, Tokyo* (1948) 15 Ann. Dig. 356.

10   (1947) 14 Ann. Dig. 266.

11   Also known as the Einsatzgruppen trial (1948), 15 I.L.R. 656.

12   GA Res. 95(I), UN GAOR, 1st Sess., U.N. Doc. A/64/Add.1, (1946) 188.

13   GA Res. 177(II), UN GAOR, 2d Sess., U.N. Doc. A/519 (1947) 111-112.

power on the part of the victorious nations, but ... the expression of international law existing at the time of its creation."[14] Even so, it could not be said that the body of international crimes was defined with precision. The process of refining and defining international criminal offences has proceeded since that time along several different and mostly complementary avenues.

The first significant development was the conclusion of the Geneva Conventions of 1949[15] sponsored by the International Committee of the Red Cross (ICRC). These rules of international humanitarian law, alias laws of armed conflict (also formerly known as the laws of war) both prescribe humanitarian protection and proscribe criminal conduct. They built on the First Geneva Convention of 1864 and The Hague Conventions of 1899 and 1907, which sought to protect wounded combatants and limit the means of combat. See the extract below on " 'Law of The Hague' and 'Law of Geneva' Distinguished." There are four Geneva Conventions, which address the protection of wounded soldiers (I), sick and shipwrecked sailors (II), prisoners of war (III), and civilians in occupied territory (IV). Their principal objective is to set standards for conduct in times of armed conflict for those who are not, or are no longer, combatants. To this extent these standards supplement the international protection of human rights, discussed in Chapter 12, in times of war. In addition, the Geneva Conventions establish "grave breaches" of these humanitarian standards as international crimes. Extracts are provided below of Geneva Convention IV to illustrate these principles.

Note that the Geneva Conventions operate only in the context of war, in particular international armed conflict. There is a single article, Article 3, common to all four Conventions, that specifies international standards of humanitarian conduct in situations of internal armed conflict. It is brief and general, and provides only basic humanitarian protections.

In recognition of these limitations and others, including the lack of protection of women from abuse, two additional protocols[16] to the Geneva Conventions were concluded in 1977. Protocol I extends the definition of international armed conflict to situations in which "peoples are fighting against colonial domination and alien occupation and against racist regimes in the exercise of their right of self-determination," so as to make provisions of the Conventions more widely applicable. Protocol I also enlarges the humanitarian standards and criminal offences in the Conventions in specific ways—see the portions reproduced below.

Protocol II applies to internal armed conflicts, defining them carefully so as to include all confrontations between government forces and organized armed groups, under

---

14   See the extract from the *Nuremberg War Crimes Trials* in Section A.1 and note 1 following it.

15   (1950) 75 U.N.T.S. 31, 85, 135, and 287. See F. Karlshoven, *The Law of Warfare* (1973); A. Cassese ed., *The New Humanitarian Law of Armed Conflict* (1979); J. Pictet, *Humanitarian Law and the Protection of War Victims* (1982); C. Swinarski, ed., *Studies and Essays on Humanitarian Law and Red Cross Principles* (1984); Delissen & Tanya, eds., *Humanitarian Law of Armed Conflict* (1991); McCombrey & White, *International Law and Armed Conflict* (1992); L.C. Green, *The Contemporary Law of Armed Conflict*, 2d ed. (2000) and *Essays on the Modern Law of War*, 2d ed. (1999); and M.C. Bassiouni, *International Criminal Law Conventions and Their Penal Provisions* (1997).

16   (1977) 1125 U.N.T.S. 3 and 609.

responsible command, which exercise control over part of state territory, but to exclude riots and other sporadic outbursts of violence. The Protocol then elaborates in considerable detail and length, in complement to the four Geneva Conventions, the standards and offences to be applied in internal conflicts.

The Geneva Conventions and Protocol I have been widely ratified and dissident regimes have been known to declare their adherence to them. Why would it be advantageous for rebel groups to adhere? Protocol II is also in force and effect but lacks the widespread support of the other Conventions. Why would states have less interest in ratifying it?

"Law of The Hague" and "Law of Geneva" Distinguished
from A. Eide, "The Laws of War and Human Rights—Differences and Convergences" in C. Swinarski ed., *Studies and Essays on International Humanitarian Law and Red Cross Principles in Honour of Jean Pictet* (1984) 675 at 677-78

The beginning of the law of war in its modern sense can be traced back to the 1860s, the two major events being the meetings in Geneva and in St. Petersburg. Admittedly, traditions of chivalry as well as canonical notions of immunity of noncombatants had existed in the medieval ages in Europe, and similar traditions were in existence also in other parts of the world. And yet, the modern law of warfare is the product of more recent experiences of war between nation-States, the inter-national wars.

The dynamic evolution started in Geneva, following the initiative taken by Henry Dunant after the battle of Solferino, with the convening of the Geneva International Conference in 1863 by which the Red Cross was founded, and the convening of the Geneva Diplomatic Conference of 1864 which adopted the *First Geneva Convention*, dealing with the amelioration of the condition of the wounded in armies in the field. The other major step was the convening in St. Petersburg in 1868 of an International Military Commission which adopted the *St. Petersburg Declaration*, by which the States represented renounced the use of certain explosive projectiles and formulated certain general principles concerning the laws of war.

The subsequent evolution does not need recounting here, but some points have to made for the purpose of the ensuing discussion.

The International Peace Conferences, convened in The Hague in 1899 and 1907 came up with the "laws of combat" which had already begun with the *St. Petersburg Declaration*. Sometimes this has also been called the "law of The Hague" because of the place of its origin.

There has, at times, been some disagreement whether or not to include "the law of The Hague" together with "the law of Geneva" into the wider concept of humanitarian law in armed conflict, or "the laws of war."

The "law of The Hague" was concerned with the conduct of warfare, in particular the limitations on means and methods. But it also dealt with the protection of prisoners of war, an area that was soon to be taken over by "the law of Geneva." The latter law was initially focussed on the protection of the victims of armed conflicts, but has gradually come to encompass additional areas. It has gone through many stages, from the narrow range of the *1864 Convention* to the broad range of concerns dealt with in the four *Geneva Conventions of 1949* and the two *Protocols of 1977*. The "law of The Hague" was the product of an episode, albeit an important one, in the history of international law, i.e. the Peace Conferences of 1899 and 1907. The "law of Geneva," on the other hand, came to obtain permanence and dynamism because of the existence, evolution and strength of the Red Cross.

The "law of Geneva" focussed initially on the prevention of suffering of the sick and wounded during armed conflict, but expanded substantially as a consequence of the broadening concern of the ICRC. The historical evolution has caused an ever increasing part of the laws of the war to be dealt with in Geneva. After the adoption of the two additional Protocols by the Diplomatic Conference in Geneva in 1977, it is artificial to distinguish between the laws of The Hague and the laws of Geneva. It may still be appropriate to distinguish between combat law and the other aspects of the laws of war, the humanitarian law in the most narrow sense.

Thus, the two initial tracks have merged into one. Humanitarian law has expanded in its concerns. Understandably, controversies and dilemmas have been faced when previous limitations had to be transcended.

One aspect of the evolution is that the laws of war increasingly have come to deal also with internal conflicts, thus transcending its initial limitation to international regulation.

Another aspect is that these laws came to deal also with problems not directly related to the armed confrontation between two opposing armed forces. The *Fourth Geneva Convention of 1949*, relative to the protection of civilian persons in time of war, applies also to situations of occupation, even when the occupation meets with little or no resistance.

Both of these aspects have caused the laws of war to come closer to the field regulated by the law of human rights. This was already in evidence with the adoption of the four Conventions in 1949, and further strengthened by the adoption of the two additional Protocols in 1977. *Protocol I* included under "international armed conflicts" also "wars of national liberation," and an elaboration was made of the rules of protection of persons in the power of a party to the conflict. *Protocol II*, dealing with non-international armed conflicts, contains provisions aimed at humane treatment of all persons. It provides some fundamental guarantees for all, goes on to establish safeguards for persons whose liberty has been restricted, and lays down important rule of law principles applying to penal prosecutions.

1949 Geneva Convention IV (Civilians)
(1950) 75 U.N.T.S. 287

Article 2

In addition to the provisions which shall be implemented in peacetime, the present Convention shall apply to all cases of declared war or of any other armed conflict which may arise between two or more of the High Contracting Parties, even if the state of war is not recognized by one of them.

The Convention shall also apply to all cases of partial or total occupation of the territory of a High Contracting Party, even if the said occupation meets with no armed resistance.

Although one of the Powers in conflict may not be a party to the present Convention, the Powers who are parties thereto shall remain bound by it in their mutual relations. They shall furthermore be bound by the Convention in relation to the said Power, if the latter accepts and applies the provisions thereof. ...

Article 4

Persons protected by the Convention are those who, at a given moment and in any manner whatsoever, find themselves, in case of a conflict or occupation, in the hands of a Party to the conflict or Occupying Power of which they are not nationals.

Nationals of a State which is not bound by the Convention are not protected by it. Nationals of a neutral State who find themselves in the territory of a belligerent State, and nationals of a co-belligerent State, shall not be regarded as protected persons while the State of which they are nationals has normal diplomatic representation in the State in whose hands they are. ...

Article 27

Protected persons are entitled, in all circumstances, to respect for their persons, their honour, their family rights, their religious convictions and practices, and their manners and customs. They shall at all times be humanely treated, and shall be protected especially against all acts of violence or threats thereof and against insults and public curiosity.

Women shall be especially protected against any attack on their honour, in particular against rape, enforced prostitution, or any form of indecent assault.

Without prejudice to the provisions relating to their state of health, age and sex, all protected persons shall be treated with the same consideration by the Party to the conflict in whose power they are, without any adverse distinction based, in particular, on race, religion or political opinion.

However, the Parties to the conflict may take such measures of control and security in regard to protected persons as may be necessary as a result of the war. ...

Article 32

The High Contracting Parties specifically agree that each of them is prohibited from taking any measure of such a character as to cause the physical suffering or extermination of protected persons in their hands. This prohibition applies not only to murder, torture, corporal punishment, mutilation and medical or scientific experiments not necessitated by the medical treatment of a protected person, but also to any other measures of brutality whether applied by civilian or military agents. ...

Article 146

The High Contracting Parties undertake to enact any legislation necessary to provide effective penal sanctions for persons committing, or ordering to be committed, any of the grave breaches of the present Convention defined in the following Article.

Each High Contracting Party shall be under the obligation to search for persons alleged to have committed, or to have ordered to be committed, such grave breaches, and shall bring such persons, regardless of their nationality, before its own courts. It may also, if it prefers, and in accordance with the provisions of its own legislation, hand such persons over for trial to another High Contracting Party concerned, provided such High Contracting Party has made out a *prima facie* case.

Each High Contracting Party shall take measures necessary for the suppression of all acts contrary to the provisions of the present Convention other than the grave breaches defined in the following Article.

In all circumstances, the accused persons shall benefit by safeguards of proper trial and defence, which shall not be less favourable than those provided by Article 105 and those following of the Geneva Convention relative to the Treatment of Prisoners of War of August 12, 1949.

Article 147

Grave breaches to which the preceding Article relates shall be those involving any of the following acts, if committed against persons or property protected by the present Convention: wilful killing, torture or inhuman treatment, including biological experiments, wilfully causing great suffering or serious injury to body or health, unlawful deportation or transfer or unlawful confinement of a protected person, compelling a protected person to serve in the forces of a hostile Power, or wilfully depriving a protected person of the rights of fair and regular trial prescribed in the present Convention, taking of hostages and extensive destruction and appropriation of property, not justified by military necessity and carried out unlawfully and wantonly.

Protocol I to the 1949 Geneva Conventions
(1977) 1125 U.N.T.S. 3

Article I
General Principles and Scope of Application

1. The High Contracting Parties undertake to respect and to ensure respect for this Protocol in all circumstances.

2. In cases not covered by this Protocol or by other international agreements, civilians and combatants remain under the protection and authority of the principles of international law derived from established custom, from the principles of humanity and from the dictates of public conscience.

3. This Protocol, which supplements the Geneva Conventions of 12 August 1949 for the protection of war victims, shall apply in the situations referred to in Article 2 common to those Conventions.

4. The situations referred to in the preceding paragraph include armed conflicts in which peoples are fighting against colonial domination and alien occupation and against racist regimes in the exercise of their right of self-determination, as enshrined in the Charter of the United Nations and the Declaration on Principles of International

Law concerning Friendly Relations and Co-operation among States in accordance with the Charter of the United Nations. ...

Article 75
Fundamental Guarantees

1. In so far as they are affected by a situation referred to in Article I of this Protocol, persons who are in the power of a Party to the conflict and who do not benefit from more favourable treatment under the Conventions or under this Protocol shall be treated humanely in all circumstances and shall enjoy, as a minimum, the protection provided by this Article without any adverse distinction based upon race, colour, sex, language, religion or belief, political or other opinion, national or social origin, wealth, birth or other status, or on any other similar criteria. Each Party shall respect the person, honour, convictions and religious practices of all such persons.

2. The following acts are and shall remain prohibited at any time and in any place whatsoever, whether committed by civilian or by military agents:

    (a) violence to the life, health, or physical or mental well-being of persons, in particular:

        (i) murder;

        (ii) torture of all kinds, whether physical or mental;

        (iii) corporal punishment; and

        (iv) mutilation;

    (b) outrages upon personal dignity, in particular humiliating and degrading treatment, enforced prostitution and any form of indecent assault;

    (c) the taking of hostages;

    (d) collective punishments; and

    (e) threats to commit any of the foregoing acts. ...

Article 76
Protection of Women

1. Women shall be the object of special respect and shall be protected in particular against rape, forced prostitution and any other form of indecent assault.

2. Pregnant women and mothers having dependent infants who are arrested, detained or interned for reasons related to the armed conflict, shall have their cases considered with the utmost priority. ...

Article 85
Repression of Breaches of This Protocol

1. The provisions of the Conventions relating to the repression of breaches and grave breaches, supplemented by this Section, shall apply to the repression of breaches and grave breaches of this Protocol.

2. Acts described as grave breaches in the Conventions are grave breaches of this Protocol if committed against persons in the power of an adverse Party protected by Articles 44, 45 and 73 of this Protocol, or against the wounded, sick and shipwrecked

of the adverse Party who are protected by this Protocol, or against those medical or religious personnel, medical units or medical transports which are under the control of the adverse Party and are protected by this Protocol.

3. In addition to the grave breaches defined in Article 11, the following acts shall be regarded as grave breaches of this Protocol, when committed wilfully, in violation of the relevant provisions of this Protocol, and causing death or serious injury to body or health:

(a) making the civilian population or individual civilians the object of attack;

(b) launching an indiscriminate attack affecting the civilian population or civilian objects in the knowledge that such attack will cause excessive loss of life, injury to civilians or damage to civilian objects, as defined in Article 57, paragraph 2(a)(iii);

(c) launching an attack against works or installations containing dangerous forces in the knowledge that such attack will cause excessive loss of life, injury to civilians or damage to civilian objects, as defined in Article 57, paragraph 2(a)(iii);

(d) making non-defended localities and demilitarized zones the object of attack;

(e) making a person the object of attack in the knowledge that he is *hors de combat*;

(f) the perfidious use, in violation of Article 37, of the distinctive emblem of the red cross, red crescent or red lion and sun or of other protective signs recognized by the Conventions or this Protocol.

4. In addition to the grave breaches defined in the preceding paragraphs and in the Conventions, the following shall be regarded as grave breaches of this Protocol, when committed wilfully and in violation of the Conventions or the Protocol:

(a) the transfer by the Occupying Power of parts of its own civilian population into the territory it occupies, or the deportation or transfer of all or parts of the population of the occupied territory within or outside this territory, in violation of Article 49 of the Fourth Convention;

(b) unjustifiable delay in the repatriation of prisoners of war or civilians;

(c) practices of *apartheid* and other inhuman and degrading practices involving outrages upon personal dignity, based on racial discrimination;

(d) making the clearly-recognized historic monuments, works of art or places of worship which constitute the cultural or spiritual heritage of peoples and to which special protection has been given by special arrangement, for example, within the framework of a competent international organization, the object of attack, causing as a result extensive destruction thereof, where there is no evidence of the violation by the adverse Party of Article 53, sub-paragraph (b), and when such historic monuments, works of art and places of worship are not located in the immediate proximity of military objectives;

(e) depriving a person protected by the Conventions or referred to in paragraph 2 of this Article of the rights of fair and regular trial.

5. Without prejudice to the application of the Conventions and of this Protocol, grave breaches of these instruments shall be regarded as war crimes.

1949 Geneva Conventions—Common Article 3
(1950) 75 U.N.T.S. 31, 85, 135, and 187

Article 3

In the case of armed conflict not of an international character occurring in the territory of one of the High Contracting Parties, each Party to the conflict shall be bound to apply, as a minimum, the following provisions:

1. Persons taking no active part in the hostilities, including members of armed forces who have laid down their arms and those placed *hors de combat* by sickness, wounds, detention, or any other cause, shall in all circumstances be treated humanely, without any adverse distinction founded on race, colour, religion or faith, sex, birth or wealth, or any other similar criteria.

To this end the following acts are and shall remain prohibited at any time and in any place whatsoever with respect to the above-mentioned persons:

    (a) violence to life and person, in particular murder of all kinds, mutilation, cruel treatment and torture;

    (b) taking of hostages;

    (c) outrages upon personal dignity, in particular humiliating and degrading treatment;

    (d) the passing of sentences and the carrying out of executions without previous judgment pronounced by a regularly constituted court, affording all the judicial guarantees which are recognized as indispensable by civilized peoples.

2. The wounded and sick shall be collected and cared for.

An impartial humanitarian body, such as the International Committee of the Red Cross, may offer its services to the Parties to the conflict.

The Parties to the conflict should further endeavour to bring into force, by means of special agreements, all or part of the other provisions of the present Convention.

The application of the preceding provisions shall not affect the legal status of the Parties to the conflict.

Protocol II to the 1949 Geneva Conventions
(1977) 1125 U.N.T.S. 609

Article I
Material Field of Application

1. This Protocol, which develops and supplements Article 3 common to the Geneva Conventions of 12 August 1949 without modifying its existing conditions of application, shall apply to all armed conflicts which are not covered by Article 1 of the Protocol Additional to the Geneva Conventions of 12 August 1949, and relating to the Protection of Victims of International Armed Conflicts (Protocol I) and which take place in the territory of a High Contracting Party between its armed forces and dissident armed forces or other organized armed groups which, under responsible command, exercise such control over a part of its territory as to enable them to carry out sustained and concerted military operations and to implement this Protocol. ...

3. This Protocol shall not apply to situations of internal disturbances and tensions, such as riots, isolated and sporadic acts of violence and other acts of a similar nature, as not being armed conflicts. ...

Article 4
Fundamental Guarantees

1. All persons who do not take a direct part or who have ceased to take part in hostilities, whether or not their liberty has been restricted, are entitled to respect for their person, honour and convictions and religious practices. They shall in all circumstances be treated humanely, without any adverse distinction. It is prohibited to order that there shall be no survivors.

2. Without prejudice to the generality of the foregoing, the following acts against the persons referred to in paragraph 1 are and shall remain prohibited at any time and in any place whatsoever:

   (a) violence to the life, health and physical or mental well-being of persons, in particular murder as well as cruel treatment such as torture, mutilations or any form of corporal punishment;

   (b) collective punishments;

   (c) taking of hostages;

   (d) acts of terrorism;

   (e) outrages upon personal dignity, in particular humiliating and degrading treatment, rape, enforced prostitution and any form of indecent assault;

   (f) slavery and the slave trade in all their forms;

   (g) pillage;

   (h) threats to commit any of the foregoing acts.

3. Multilateral Conventions Specifying International Crimes

Humanitarian law is only one source of international criminal responsibility. To the Geneva Conventions and Protocols must be added the specific treaties against genocide, torture, apartheid, and narcotics smuggling as well as the multilateral agreements against a variety of terrorist activities, discussed in Chapter 9, Section A.6 on "State Jurisdiction Over Persons: Suppression of Transnational Crime." Each of these treaties adds to the articulated body of international crimes. The first was the Convention on the Prevention and Punishment of the Crime of Genocide, done in 1948.[17] It is significant for proscribing genocide, defined as killing or causing serious harm "with intent to destroy ... a national, ethnical, racial or religious group," in times of peace or war. It is also important for its

---

17   (1951) 78 U.N.T.S. 277; Can. T.S. 1949 No. 27. See N. Robinson, *The Genocide Convention* (1960); L. Kuper, *Genocide* (1981); W. Schabas, *Genocide in International Law* (2000); and P. Akhavan, "Enforcement of the Genocide Convention: A Challenge to Civilization" (1995) 8 Harv. Hum. Rts. J. 229. See also *Reservations to the Convention on Genocide* (Advisory Opinion), [1951] I.C.J. Rep. 15; *Application of the Genocide Convention Case* (Bosnia and Herzegovina v. Yugoslavia (Serbia and Montenegro)), Provisional Measures [1993] I.C.J. Rep. 3 and 325, Preliminary Objections, [1996] I.C.J. Rep. 595.

standard-setting obligations on states parties "to prevent and to punish" genocide (article 1) without distinction between perpetrators, whether governors or governed (article 4). However, the means of enforcement (article 6) are weak, except in so far as they look forward perceptively to the recent development of international courts and tribunals. See the extract from the Genocide Convention below. Why did the United Nations not provide for universal jurisdiction? Does customary international law?

The Convention Against Torture and Other Cruel, Inhuman, or Degrading Treatment or Punishment,[18] done in 1984, is a more mature instrument against international crime. It defines torture in article 1 as

> [A]ny act by which severe pain or suffering, whether physical or mental, is intentionally inflicted on a person for such purposes as obtaining from him or a third person information or a confession, punishing him for an act he or a third person has committed or is suspected of having committed, or intimidating or coercing him or a third person, or for any reason based on discrimination of any kind, when such pain or suffering is inflicted by or at the instigation of or with the consent or acquiescence of a public official or other person acting in an official capacity. It does not include pain or suffering arising only from, inherent in or incidental to lawful sanctions.

Notice the limitation in this definition to torture inflicted by persons acting in an official capacity. Compare this definition to article 7(2)(e) of the Rome Statute on the International Criminal Court, reproduced in Section C. Is there a significant difference? The Convention Against Torture goes on to impose on states parties duties to "take effective legislative, administrative, judicial or other measures to prevent acts of torture in any territory under its jurisdiction" without exception whatsoever, "whether a state of war or a threat of war, internal political instability or any other public emergency, may be invoked as a justification." The Convention provides for universal jurisdiction and obliges states to extradite or prosecute offenders on the now well-established principle *aut dedere*, *aut judicare*, discussed under "Suppression of Transnational Crime" in Chapter 9, Section A.6.

Convention for the Prevention and Punishment of the Crime of Genocide
(1951) 78 U.N.T.S. 277; Can. T.S. 1949 No. 27

The Contracting Parties,

Having considered the declaration made by the General Assembly of the United Nations in its resolution 96 (I) dated 11 December 1946 that genocide is a crime under international law contrary to the spirit and aims of the United Nations and condemned by the civilized world,

Recognizing that at all periods of history genocide has inflicted great losses on humanity, and

---

18 (1984) 23 I.L.M. 1027 and (1985) 24 I.L.M. 535. See N. Rodley, *The Treatment of Prisoners Under International Law*, 2d ed. (1999); J. Burgers & H. Danelius, *The United Nations Convention Against Torture* (1988); R. St. J. MacDonald, "International Prohibitions Against Torture and Other Forms of Similar Treatment or Punishment," in Y. Dinstein, ed., *International Law at a Time of Perplexity* (1988) at 385.

Being convinced that in order to liberate mankind from such an odious scourge international co-operation is required,

Hereby agree as hereinafter provided:

Article 1

The Contracting Parties confirm that genocide whether committed in time of peace or in time of war, is a crime under international law which they undertake to prevent and to punish.

Article 2

In the present Convention genocide means any of the following acts committed with intent to destroy in whole or in part; a national, ethnical, racial or religious group, as such:

    (a) Killing members of the group;

    (b) Causing serious bodily or mental harm to members of the group;

    (c) Deliberately inflicting on the group conditions of life calculated to bring about its physical destruction in whole or in part;

    (d) Imposing measures intended to prevent births within the group;

    (e) Forcibly transferring children of the group to another group.

Article 3

The following acts shall be punishable:

    (a) Genocide;

    (b) Conspiracy to commit genocide;

    (c) Direct and public incitement to commit genocide;

    (d) Attempt to commit genocide;

    (e) Complicity in genocide.

Article 4

Persons committing genocide or any of the other acts enumerated in article 3 shall be punished, whether they are constitutionally responsible rulers, public officials or private individuals.

Article 5

The Contracting Parties undertake to enact in accordance with their respective Constitutions, the necessary legislation to give effect to the provisions of the present Convention and, in particular, to provide effective penalties for persons guilty of genocide or any of the other acts enumerated in article 3.

Article 6

Persons charged with genocide or any of the other acts enumerated in article 3 shall be tried by a competent tribunal of the State in the territory of which the act was committed or by such international penal tribunal as may have jurisdiction with respect to those Contracting Parties which shall have accepted its jurisdiction.

Article 7

Genocide and the other acts enumerated in article 3 shall not be considered as political crimes for the purpose of extradition.

The Contracting Parties pledge themselves in such cases to grant extradition in accordance with their laws and treaties in force.

Article 8

Any Contracting Party may call upon the competent organs of the United Nations to take such action under the Charter of the United Nations as they consider appropriate for the prevention and suppression of acts of genocide or any of the other acts enumerated in article 3.

Article 9

Disputes between the Contracting Parties relating to the interpretation, application or fulfilment of the present Convention, including those relating to the responsibility of a State for genocide or for any of the other acts enumerated in article 3, shall be submitted to the International Court of Justice at the request of any of the parties to the dispute.

Article 10

The present Convention of which the Chinese, English, French, Russian and Spanish texts are equally authentic, shall bear the date of 9 December 1948.

Convention Against Torture and Other Cruel, Inhuman, or Degrading Treatment or Punishment
(1984) 1465 U.N.T.S. 85; Can. T.S. 1987 No. 36

The States Parties to this Convention ...
Have agreed as follows:

PART I

Article 1

1. For the purposes of this Convention, torture means any act by which severe pain or suffering, whether physical or mental, is intentionally inflicted on a person for such purposes as obtaining from him or a third person information or a confession, punishing him for an act he or a third person has committed or is suspected of having

committed, or intimidating or coercing him or a third person, or for any reason based on discrimination of any kind, when such pain or suffering is inflicted by or at the instigation of or with the consent or acquiescence of a public official or other person acting in an official capacity. It does not include pain or suffering arising only from, inherent in or incidental to lawful sanctions.

2. This article is without prejudice to any international instrument or national legislation which does or may contain provisions of wider application.

Article 2

1. Each State Party shall take effective legislative, administrative, judicial or other measures to prevent acts of torture in any territory under its jurisdiction.

2. No exceptional circumstances whatsoever, whether a state of war or a threat of war, internal political instability or any other public emergency, may be invoked as a justification of torture.

3. An order from a superior officer or a public authority may not be invoked as a justification of torture.

Article 3

1. No State Party shall expel, return ("refouler") or extradite a person to another State where there are substantial grounds for believing that he would be in danger of being subjected to torture.

2. For the purpose of determining whether there are such grounds, the competent authorities shall take into account all relevant considerations including, where applicable, the existence in the State concerned of a consistent pattern of gross, flagrant or mass violations of human rights.

Article 4

1. Each State Party shall ensure that all acts of torture are offences under its criminal law. The same shall apply to an attempt to commit torture and to an act by any person which constitutes complicity or participation in torture.

2. Each State Party shall make these offences punishable by appropriate penalties which take into account their grave nature.

Article 5

1. Each State Party shall take such measures as may be necessary to establish its jurisdiction over the offences referred to in article 4 in the following cases:

(a) When the offences are committed in any territory under its jurisdiction or on board a ship or aircraft registered in that State;

(b) When the alleged offender is a national of that State;

(c) When the victim was a national of that State if that State considers it appropriate.

2. Each State Party shall likewise take such measures as may be necessary to establish its jurisdiction over such offences in cases where the alleged offender is present in any territory under its jurisdiction and it does not extradite him pursuant to article 8 to any of the States mentioned in Paragraph 1 of this article.

3. This Convention does not exclude any criminal jurisdiction exercised in accordance with internal law.

Article 6

1. Upon being satisfied, after an examination of information available to it, that the circumstances so warrant, any State Party in whose territory a person alleged to have committed any offence referred to in article 4 is present, shall take him into custody or take other legal measures to ensure his presence. The custody and other legal measures shall be as provided in the law of that State but may be continued only for such time as is necessary to enable any criminal or extradition proceedings to be instituted.

2. Such State shall immediately make a preliminary inquiry into the facts.

3. Any person in custody pursuant to paragraph 1 of this article shall be assisted in communicating immediately with the nearest appropriate representative of the State of which he is a national, or, if he is a stateless person, to the representative of the State where he usually resides.

4. When a State, pursuant to this article, has taken a person into custody, it shall immediately notify the States referred to in article 5, paragraph 1, of the fact that such person is in custody and of the circumstances which warrant his detention. The State which makes the preliminary inquiry contemplated in paragraph 2 of this article shall promptly report its findings to the said State and shall indicate whether it intends to exercise jurisdiction.

Article 7

1. The State Party in territory under whose jurisdiction a person alleged to have committed any offence referred to in article 4 is found, shall in the cases contemplated in article 5, if it does not extradite him, submit the case to its competent authorities for the purpose of prosecution.

2. These authorities shall take their decision in the same manner as in the case of any ordinary offence of a serious nature under the law of that State. ...

3. Any person regarding whom proceedings are brought in connection with any of the offences referred to in article 4 shall be guaranteed fair treatment at all stages of the proceedings.

Article 8

1. The offences referred to in article 4 shall be deemed to be included as extraditable offences in any extradition treaty existing between States Parties. States Parties undertake to include such offences as extraditable offences in every extradition treaty to be concluded between them.

NOTES

1) The above disparate treaties have together provided the reference points for the elaboration of the international crimes within the jurisdiction of the *Ad Hoc* International Tribunals, the mixed national–international courts and tribunals, and the International Criminal Court, discussed in the next two sections of this chapter. Meanwhile, the International Law Commission (ILC) undertook a separate project to develop a concerted code of international crimes.

2) The ILC was requested by the General Assembly in 1947[19] to formulate the Nuremberg Principles based on the Nuremberg Charter and Judgment considered earlier and to prepare a Draft Code of Offences (later termed Crimes) Against the Peace and Security of Mankind. The ILC submitted a draft code to the General Assembly in 1954, but consideration of it was postponed pending a Special Commission preparing a report on a draft definition of aggression. The General Assembly adopted such a definition in 1974, as can be seen in Chapter 15, "Limitation of the Use of Force," Section A on "Prohibition of the Use of Force," but no action was taken on the Draft Code until 1981 when the ILC was invited to resume its work on the subject.[20] Then, in 1991, the General Assembly mandated the ILC to deal with the question of an international criminal court as a matter of priority.[21] The ILC finally adopted the text of a Draft Code of Crimes Against the Peace and Security of Mankind in July 1996 and presented it to the U.N. later that year,[22] but the General Assembly has not pursued the topic.

3) Even so, the Draft Code is instructive for its description of the crime of aggression, which, as will be seen, is part of the mandate of the ICC but has yet to be defined in that context. The Draft Code only deals with individual and not state liability; however, the wording of article 16 on the crime of aggression links responsibility to the commission of aggression by a state. See the 1974 Definition of Aggression, reproduced in Chapter 15, Section A on "Prohibition of the Use of Force." Is this an appropriate, necessary, or fatal linkage? Consider what body determines whether a state has committed aggression.

---

19   *Supra* note 13 at 23.

20   GA Res. 36/106, UN GAOR, 36th Sess., Supp. No. 51, UN Doc. A/36/51 (1981) 239. For the historical background see "Report of the International Law Commission on the Work of its 35th Session," (UN Doc. A/38/10) in *Year Book of the International Law Commission 1983*, vol. 2, part 2 (1983) at 10-13 (UNDOC A/CN.4/SER.A/1983/Add.1).

21   GA Res. 46/54, UN GAOR, 46th Sess., Supp. No. 49, UN Doc. A/46/49 (1991) 286.

22   UN GAOR, 51st Sess. Supp. No. 10 (A/51/10) 9-120.

Draft Code of Crimes Against the Peace and Security of Mankind
GAOR, 51st Sess. Supp. No. 10, U.N. Doc. A/51/10 (1996)

Article 16
Crime of Aggression

An individual who, as leader or organiser, actively participates in or orders the planning, preparation, initiation or waging of aggression committed by a State shall be responsible for a crime of aggression.

B. PROSECUTION IN THE AD HOC INTERNATIONAL TRIBUNALS[23]

The atrocities committed in the territory of the former Yugoslavia and in Rwanda in the 1990s called for immediate action on an *ad hoc* basis. The extracts that follow demonstrate how the two Tribunals were established by the U.N. Security Council and give a sampling of some of the cases.

Charter of the United Nations
Articles 39, 41, and 42
Reproduced in the Documentary Supplement

1. The Ad Hoc International Criminal Tribunal for the Former Yugoslavia

In U.N. Security Council Resolution 808 of February 22, 1993,[24] it was decided that an international tribunal be established for the prosecution of those persons allegedly responsible for serious violations of international humanitarian law in the territory of the former Yugoslavia since 1991. The Secretary-General was requested to submit a report on all aspects of the matter, including specific proposals and options for the effective and

---

23 M.C. Bassiouni, *The Law of the International Criminal Tribunal for the Former Yugoslavia* (1996); V. Morris & M. Scharf, *An Insider's Guide to the International Criminal Tribunal for the Former Yugoslavia* (1995); J.R.W.D. Jones, *The Practice of the International Criminal Tribunals for the Former Yugoslavia and Rwanda*, 2d ed. (2000); M. Scharf, "The Tools for Enforcing International Criminal Justice in the New Millennium: Lessons from the Yugoslavia Tribunal" (2000) 49 DePaul L. Rev. 925; C. Blakesley, "Atrocity and Its Prosecution: The Ad Hoc Tribunals for the Former Yugoslavia and Rwanda" in T. McCormack & G. Simpson, *supra* note 4 at 189; D.P. Forsythe, "Politics and the International Tribunal for the Former Yugoslavia" (1994) 5 Crim.L.F. 401; H. von Hebel, "An International Tribunal for the Former Yugoslavia: An Act of Powerlessness or a New Challenge for the International Community?" (1993) 11 Nethl Q.H.R. 437; O. Gross, "The Grave Breaches System and the Armed Conflict in the Former Yugoslavia" (1995) 16 Mich. J. Int'l L. 783; and T. Meron, "War Crimes in Yugoslavia and Developments in International Law" (1994) 88 A.J.I.L. 78.

24 SC Res. 808 (1993) UN SCOR, 48th year, *Res. and Dec.*; U.N. Doc. S/INF/49 at 28. For details of the findings of the Commission of Experts established by the Secretary-General to provide him with conclusions on the evidence of grave breaches of the Geneva Conventions and other violations of international humanitarian law committed in the territory of the former Yugoslavia, see U.N. Doc. S/25274 (1993).

expeditious implementation of such a tribunal. His extensive report,[25] which took into consideration the suggestions put forward by U.N. member states, meetings of international experts, and non-governmental organizations, recommended that the tribunal be established by a decision of the Security Council on the basis of Chapter VII of the Charter, rather than by multilateral treaty because of the need to act expeditiously. Such Security Council action constituted a measure to maintain or restore international peace and security, following a determination of the existence of a threat to the peace, breach of the peace, or act of aggression and had effect immediately, binding member states to take whatever action was required.

On May 25, 1993 the Security Council, in Resolution 827, reproduced in part below, decided to set up the Tribunal and endorsed the 34-article Statute annexed to the Secretary-General's Report. The serious violations of international humanitarian law that are within the competence of the Tribunal as listed are (1) grave breaches of the 1949 Geneva Conventions, such as willful killing, torture, extensive destruction or appropriation of property not justified by military necessity and carried out unlawfully and wantonly, unlawful deportation or confinement of civilians, and hostage taking; (2) violations of the laws or customs of war; (3) genocide; and (4) crimes against humanity including murder, extermination, rape, deportation, persecution on political, racial, and religious grounds, and other inhumane acts. The seat of the Tribunal is at The Hague and its working languages are English and French.[26] There are 14 judges, who are elected by the General Assembly from a list submitted by the Security Council.[27] Since 2001, in order to expedite the number of trials, the Statute was amended to provide for an additional pool of 27 *ad litem* judges. A maximum of nine *ad litem* judges may be at the ICTY at one time.[28] The Tribunal consists of three Trial Chambers and an Appeals Chamber with seven judges.[29] There is an independent Prosecutor's Office, which for a time was occupied by Louise Arbour of Canada. The rights of an accused person are provided for in detail, including the right to be presumed innocent until proved guilty; the right to be informed promptly, in detail, and in a language that he or she understands, about the nature and cause of the charge; the right to counsel of choice; the right to be tried without undue delay; the right to examine the witnesses for the prosecution and to obtain defence witnesses; and the right not to be compelled to testify against himself or herself or to confess guilt.[30] Penalties are limited to imprisonment. However, in addition, property and proceeds of criminal conduct may be ordered returned to their rightful owners.[31]

---

25   U.N. Doc. S/25704 (1993).

26   Article 18(3) of the Statute of the International Tribunal provides that the accused has the right to necessary translation into and from a language that he or she understands.

27   Article 13. The judges may be re-elected but the judges *ad litem* may not be.

28   Canadian Sharon A. Williams sat as an *ad litem* judge from 2001-3.

29   Article 12(3). Note that two judges elected by the General Assembly for the ICTR sit in The Hague as members of the common Appeals Chamber for the two *Ad Hoc* Tribunals. Five judges sit on each appeal.

30   Article 21.

31   Article 24.

Security Council Resolution 827 (1993)
U.N. Doc. S/Res/827 (1993), as am. by U.N. Doc. S/Res/1166 (1998) and U.N.
Doc. S/Res/1329 (2000)

The Security Council ...

Convinced that in the particular circumstances of the former Yugoslavia the establishment as an *ad hoc* measure by the Council of an international tribunal and the prosecution of persons responsible for serious violations of international humanitarian law would enable this aim to be achieved and would contribute to the restoration and maintenance of peace; ...

Acting under Chapter VII of the Charter of the United Nations; ...

2. *Decides* hereby to establish an international tribunal for the sole purpose of prosecuting persons responsible for serious violations of international humanitarian law committed in the territory of the former Yugoslavia between 1 January 1991 and a date to be determined by the Security Council upon the restoration of peace and to this end to adopt the Statute of the International Tribunal annexed to the above-mentioned report;

3. *Requests* the Secretary-General to submit to the judges of the International Tribunal, upon their election, any suggestions received from States for the rules of procedure and evidence called for in Article 15 of the Statute of the International Tribunal;

4. *Decides* that all States shall cooperate fully with the International Tribunal and its organs in accordance with the present resolution and the Statute of the International Tribunal and that consequently all States shall take any measures necessary under their domestic law to implement the provisions of the present resolution and the Statute, including the obligation of States to comply with requests for assistance or orders issued by a Trial Chamber under Article 29 of the Statute;

5. *Urges* States and intergovernmental and non-governmental organizations to contribute funds, equipment and services to the International Tribunal, including the offer of expert personnel;

6. *Decides* that the determination of the seat of the International Tribunal is subject to the conclusion of appropriate arrangements between the United Nations and the Netherlands acceptable to the Council, and that the International Tribunal may sit elsewhere when it considers it necessary for the efficient exercise of its functions;

7. *Decides* also that the work of the International Tribunal shall be carried out without prejudice to the right of the victims to seek, through appropriate means, compensation for damages incurred as a result of violations of international humanitarian law;

8. *Requests* the Secretary-General to implement urgently the present resolution and in particular to make practical arrangements for the effective functioning of the International Tribunal at the earliest time and to report periodically to the Council;

9. *Decides* to remain actively seized of the matter.

ANNEX
Amended Statute of the International Criminal Tribunal for the Former Yugoslavia

Having been established by the Security Council acting under Chapter VII of the Charter of the United Nations, the International Tribunal for the Prosecution of Persons Responsible for Serious Violations of International Humanitarian Law Committed in the Territory of the Former Yugoslavia since 1991 (hereinafter referred to as "the International Tribunal") shall function in accordance with the provisions of the present Statute.

Article 1
Competence of the International Tribunal

The International Tribunal shall have the power to prosecute persons responsible for serious violations of international humanitarian law committed in the territory of the former Yugoslavia since 1991 in accordance with the provisions of the present Statute.

Article 2
Grave Breaches of the Geneva Conventions of 1949

The International Tribunal shall have the power to prosecute persons committing or ordering to be committed grave breaches of the Geneva Conventions of 12 August 1949, namely the following acts against persons or property protected under the provisions of the relevant Geneva Convention:

(a) wilful killing;

(b) torture or inhuman treatment, including biological experiments;

(c) wilfully causing great suffering or serious injury to body or health;

(d) extensive destruction and appropriation of property, not justified by military necessity and carried out unlawfully and wantonly;

(e) compelling a prisoner of war or a civilian to serve in the forces of a hostile power;

(f) wilfully depriving a prisoner of war or a civilian of the rights of fair and regular trial;

(g) unlawful deportation or transfer or unlawful confinement of a civilian;

(h) taking civilians as hostages.

Article 3
Violations of the Laws or Customs of War

The International Tribunal shall have the power to prosecute persons violating the laws or customs of war. Such violations shall include, but not be limited to:

(a) employment of poisonous weapons or other weapons calculated to cause unnecessary suffering;

(b) wanton destruction of cities, towns or villages, or devastation not justified by military necessity;

(c) attack, or bombardment, by whatever means, of undefended towns, villages, dwellings, or buildings;

(d) seizure of, destruction or wilful damage done to institutions dedicated to religion, charity and education, the arts and sciences, historic monuments and works of art and science;

(e) plunder of public or private property.

Article 4
Genocide

1. The International Tribunal shall have the power to prosecute persons committing genocide as defined in paragraph 2 of this article or of committing any of the other acts enumerated in paragraph 3 of this article.

2. Genocide means any of the following acts committed with intent to destroy, in whole or in part, a national, ethnical, racial or religious group, as such:

(a) killing members of the group;

(b) causing serious bodily or mental harm to members of the group;

(c) deliberately inflicting on the group conditions of life calculated to bring about its physical destruction in whole or in part;

(d) imposing measures intended to prevent births within the group;

(e) forcibly transferring children of the group to another group.

3. The following acts shall be punishable:

(a) genocide;

(b) conspiracy to commit genocide;

(c) direct and public incitement to commit genocide;

(d) attempt to commit genocide;

(e) complicity in genocide.

Article 5
Crimes Against Humanity

The International Tribunal shall have the power to prosecute persons responsible for the following crimes when committed in armed conflict, whether international or internal in character, and directed against any civilian population:

(a) murder;

(b) extermination;

(c) enslavement;

(d) deportation;

(e) imprisonment;

(f) torture;

(g) rape;

(h) persecutions on political, racial and religious grounds;

(i) other inhumane acts.

NOTES

1) Do you think that the establishment of such tribunals as the International Criminal Tribunal for the Former Yugoslavia (ICTY) and the International Criminal Tribunal for

Rwanda (ICTR) have helped to "usher in an era of peace and reconciliation"[32] by placing responsibility on individuals and leaders?

2) Both *Ad Hoc* Tribunals were set up by U.N. Security Council resolutions under Chapter VII of the U.N. Charter, as subsidiary organs of the Security Council. What do you think was the precondition for doing so under article 39 of the U.N. Charter? How was this met in the factual circumstances in both instances?

3) Look at articles 41 and 42 of the U.N. Charter, in the Documentary Supplement. In your opinion, do they allow for such tribunals as subsidiary organs of the Security Council?

4) The ICTY was faced at the outset with a challenge to its institutional legitimacy. In its first case, *Prosecutor v. Dusko Tadic*, reproduced below, it was held that the Security Council had the authority under Chapter VII of the Charter to establish the ICTY.

Prosecutor v. Dusko Tadic
Case No. IT-94-1, Trial Chamber decision on the Defence Motion on Jurisdiction, Aug. 10, 1995, rev'd. and aff'd. in part by the Appeals Chamber, October 2, 1995

[The first extract from the judgment of the Trial Chamber demonstrates that the ICTY was properly established and has subject-matter jurisdiction. It is followed by a second extract from the Appeals Chamber decision about "grave breaches" under the Geneva Conventions 1949.]

THE TRIAL CHAMBER: ...

2. It is said that, to be duly established by law, the International Tribunal should have been created either by treaty, the consensual act of nations, or by amendment of the Charter of the United Nations, not by resolution of the Security Council. Called in aid of this general proposition are a number of considerations: that before the creation of the International Tribunal in 1993 it was never envisaged that such an *ad hoc* criminal tribunal might be set up; that the General Assembly, whose participation would at least have guaranteed full representation of the international community, was not involved in its creation; that it was never intended by the Charter that the Security Council should, under Chapter VII, establish a judicial body, let alone a criminal tribunal; that the Security Council had been inconsistent in creating this tribunal while not taking a similar step in the case of other areas of conflict in which violations of international humanitarian law may have occurred; that the establishment of the International Tribunal had neither promoted, nor was capable of promoting, international peace, as the current situation in the former Yugoslavia demonstrates; that the Security Council could not, in any event, create criminal liability on the part of individuals and that this is what the creation of the International Tribunal did; that there existed and exists now no such international emergency as would justify the action of the Security Council; that no political organ such as the Security Council is

---

32   W. Andy Knight, "Legal Issues" in J. Tessitore & S. Woolfson, *A Global Agenda: Issues Before the 52nd General Assembly of the United Nations* (1998) 267, 268.

capable of establishing an independent and impartial tribunal; that there is an inherent defect in the creation, after the event of *ad hoc* tribunals to try particular types of offences and, finally, that to give the International Tribunal primacy over national courts is, in any event and in itself, inherently wrong. ...

8. For the Defence it is said that it is a basic human right of an accused to have a fair and public hearing by a competent, independent and impartial tribunal established by law. The Defence asserts that this right is protected by a panoply of principles of fundamental justice recognized by human rights law. There can be no doubt that the International Tribunal should seek to provide just such a trial; indeed, in enacting its Statute, care has been taken by the Security Council to ensure that this in fact occurs and the Judges of the International Tribunal, in framing its Rules, have also paid scrupulous regard to the requirements of a fair trial. For example, Article 21 of the Statute of the International Tribunal guarantees the accused the right to a fair trial and Article 20 obligates the Trial Chambers to ensure that trials are, in fact, fair. There are several other provisions to the same effect. However, it is one thing for the Security Council to have taken every care to ensure that a structure appropriate to the conduct of fair trials has been created; it is an entirely different thing in any way to infer from that careful structuring that it was intended that the International Tribunal be empowered to question the legality of the law which established it. The competence of the International Tribunal is precise and narrowly defined; as described in Article 1 of its Statute, it is to prosecute persons responsible for serious violations of international humanitarian law, subject to spatial and temporal limits, and to do so in accordance with the Statute. That is the full extent of the competence of the International Tribunal. ...

10. The Defence relies on, or at least refers to, what has been said by the International Court of Justice ("the Court") in three cases: Certain Expenses of the United Nations, 1962 I.C.J. 151, 168 (Advisory Opinion of 20 July) (the "Expenses Advisory Opinion"), Legal Consequences for States of the Continued Presence of South Africa in Namibia (South-West Africa) Notwithstanding Security Council Resolution 776, 1971 I.C.I. 16, 45 (Advisory Opinion of 21 June) (the "Namibia Advisory Opinion") and Questions of Interpretation and Application of the 1971 Montreal Convention Arising from the Aerial Incident at Lockerbie (*Libya v. U.S.*), 1992 I.C.J. 114, 176 (Provisional Measures Order of 14 April) (the "Lockerbie decision"). In the first of these, the Expenses Advisory Opinion, the Court specifically stated that, unlike the legal system of some States there exists no procedure for determining the validity of acts of organs of the United Nations. It referred to proposals at the time of drafting of the Charter that such a power should be given to the Court and to the rejection of those proposals.

11. In the second of these cases, the Namibia Advisory Opinion, the Court dealt very specifically with this matter, stating that: "Undoubtedly, the Court does not possess powers of judicial review or appeal in respect of the decisions taken by the United Nations organs concerned."

12. Finally, in the Lockerbie decision, Judge Weeramantry, in his dissenting opinion, but in this respect not in dissent from other members of the Court, said that "it is not for this Court to sit in review on a given resolution of the Security Council" and, that in relation to the exercise by the Security Council of its powers under Chapter VII:

[T]he determination under Article 39 of the existence of any threat to the peace ... is
one entirely within the discretion of the Council ... . The Council and no other is the
judge of the existence of the state of affairs which brings Chapter VII into operation ... .
Once [such a determination is] taken the door is opened to the various decisions the
Council may make under that Chapter.

13. These opinions of the Court clearly provide no basis for the International
Tribunal to review the actions of the Security Council, indeed, they are authorities to
the contrary.

14. In support of its submission that this Trial Chamber should review the actions
of the Security Council, the Defence contends that the decisions of the Security
Council are not sacrosanct. Certainly, commentators have suggested that there are
limits to the authority of the Security Council. It has been posited that such limits
may be based on Article 24(2), which provides that the Security Council: "shall act in
accordance with the Purposes and Principles of the United Nations. The specific
powers appointed to the Security Council for the discharge of these duties are laid
down in Chapters VI, VII, VIII, and XII." One commentator interprets this provision
to mean that the Security Council "cannot, in principle, act arbitrarily and unfettered
by any restraints." (D.W. Bowett, The Law of International Institutions 33, (1982).)
Another commentator has taken the position, that although the Security Council has
broad discretion in the field of international peace and security, it cannot "act
arbitrarily or use the existence of a threat to the peace as a basis for action which ... is
for collateral and independent purposes, such as the overthrow of a government or
the partition of a State." (Ian Brownlie, "The Decisions of Political Organs of the
United Nations and the Rule of Law," in *Essays in Honour of Wang Tieya 95* (1992).)

15. Support for the view that the Security Council cannot act arbitrarily or for an
ulterior purpose is found in the nature of the Charter as a treaty delegating certain
powers to the United Nations. In fact, such a limitation is almost a corollary of the
principle that the organs of the United Nations must act in accordance with the powers
delegated them. It is a matter of logic that if the Security Council acted arbitrarily or
for an ulterior purpose it would be acting outside the purview of the powers delegated
to it in the Charter.

16. Although it is not for this Trial Chamber to judge the reasonableness of the
acts of the Security Council, it is without doubt that, with respect to the former
Yugoslavia, the Security Council did not act arbitrarily. To the contrary, the Security
Council's establishment of the International Tribunal represents its informed judgment,
after great deliberation, that violations of international humanitarian law were occurring
in the former Yugoslavia and that such violations created a threat to the peace. ...

23. The making of a judgment as to whether there was such an emergency in the
former Yugoslavia as would justify the setting up of the International Tribunal under
Chapter VII is eminently one for the Security Council and only for it; it is certainly
not a justiciable issue but one involving considerations of high policy and of a political
nature. As to whether the particular measures of establishing the International Tribunal
is, in fact, likely to be conducive to the restoration of peace and security is, again,

pre-eminently a matter for the Security Council and for it alone and no judicial body, certainly not this Trial Chamber, can or should review that step. ...

27. That it was not originally envisaged that an *ad hoc* judicial tribunal might be created under Chapter VII, even if that be factually correct, is nothing to the point. Chapter VII confers very wide powers upon the Security Council and no good reason has been advanced why Article 41 should be read as excluding the step, very appropriate in the circumstances, of creating the International Tribunal to deal with the notorious situation existing in the former Yugoslavia. This is a situation clearly suited to adjudication by a tribunal and punishment of those found guilty of crimes that violate international humanitarian law. This is not, as the Defence puts it, a question of the Security Council doing anything it likes; it is a seemingly entirely appropriate reaction to a situation in which international peace is clearly endangered.

28. The Defence argues that the establishment of the International Tribunal is not a measure contemplated by Article 41 because the examples included in that Article focus on economic and political measures, not judicial measures. As the Defence concedes, however, the list in that Article is not exhaustive. Once again, the decision of the Security Council in this regard is fraught with fact-based, policy determinations that make this issue non-justiciable.

29. Further, the Defence contends that the International Tribunal is not an appropriate measure under Article 41 because it has failed to restore peace in the former Yugoslavia. However, the accused is but the first and, as yet, the only accused to be brought before the International Tribunal, and it is wholly premature at this initial stage of its functioning to attempt to assess the effectiveness of the International Tribunal as a measure to restore peace, even were it the function of the International Tribunal to do so. ...

32. Then it is said that international law requires that criminal courts be independent and impartial and that no court created by a political body such as the Security Council can have those characteristics. Of course, criminal courts world-wide are the creations of legislatures, eminently political bodies. The Court, in the Effect of Awards case, specifically held that a political organ of the United Nations—in that case, the General Assembly—could and had created "an independent and truly judicial body." (Effect of Awards of Compensation Made by the United Nations Administrative Tribunal, 1954 I.C.I. 47, 53 (Advisory Opinion of 13 July) ("Effect of Awards").) The question whether a court is independent and impartial depends not upon the body that creates it but upon its constitution, its judges and the way in which they function. The International Tribunal has, as its Statute and Rules attest, been constituted so as to ensure a fair trial to an accused and it is to be hoped that the way its Judges administer their jurisdiction will leave no room for complaints about lack of impartiality or want of independence.

33. The fact that the Security Council has established an *ad hoc* tribunal is also said to reveal invalidity because it is said to deny to the accused the right conferred by Article 14 of the International Convention on the Protection of Civil and Political Rights ("ICCPR") to be tried by a tribunal "established by law." However, on analysis this introduces no new concept; it is but another way of expressing the general

complaint that the creation of the International Tribunal was beyond the power of the Security Council.

34. It is noteworthy that, in the context of the International Covenant and its entitlement in Article 14 to trial by a "tribunal established by law," this phrase requires only that the tribunal be legally constituted. ...

51. The Report of the Secretary-General (U.N. Doc. S/25704 (3 May 1993)) (the "Report") makes it clear, in paragraph 34, that it was intended that the rules of international law that were to be applied should be "beyond any doubt part of customary law," so that problems of non-adherence of particular States to any international Convention should not arise. Hence, no doubt, the specific reference to the law of the Geneva Conventions in Article 2 since, as the Report states in paragraph 35, that law applicable in armed conflict has beyond doubt become part of customary law. But there is no ground for treating Article 2 as in effect importing into the Statute the whole of the terms of the Conventions, including the reference in common Article 2 of the Geneva Convention to international conflicts. As stated, Article 2 of the Statute is on its face, self-contained, save in relation to the definition of protected persons and things. It simply confers subject matter jurisdiction to prosecute what, if one were concerned with the Conventions, would indeed be grave breaches of those Conventions, but which are, in the present context, simple enactments of the Statute.

52. When what is in issue is what the Geneva Conventions contemplate in the case of grave breaches, namely their prosecution before a national court and not before an international tribunal, it is natural enough that there should be a requirement of internationality; a nation might well view with concern, as an unacceptable infringement of sovereignty, the action of a foreign court in trying an accused for grave breaches committed in a conflict internal to that nation. Such considerations do not apply to the International Tribunal, any more than do the references in the Conventions to High Contracting Parties and much else in the Conventions; all these are simply inapplicable to the International Tribunal. They do not apply because the International Tribunal is not in fact, applying conventional international law but, rather, customary international law, as the Secretary-General makes clear in his Report, and is doing so by virtue of the mandate conferred upon it by the Security Council. In the case of what are commonly referred to as "grave breaches," this conventional law has become customary law, though some of it may well have been conventional law before being written into the predecessors of the present Geneva Conventions.

53. It follows that the element of internationality forms no jurisdictional criterion of the offences created by Article 2 of the Statute of the International Tribunal. If it did, there are clear indications in the great volume of material before the Trial Chamber that the acts alleged in the indictment were in fact committed in the course of an international armed conflict. However, little of this material is such that judicial notice can be taken of it and none of it is in the form of, nor has it been tendered as, evidence. In these circumstances the Trial Chamber makes no finding regarding the nature of the armed conflict in question.

Prosecutor v. Dusko Tadic
Appeals Chamber Decision on the Defence Motion on Jurisdiction,
October 2, 1995

[The following extract discusses the applicability of the "grave breaches" provisions of the Geneva Conventions 1949.]

THE APPEALS CHAMBER: ...

79. Article 2 of the Statute of the International Tribunal provides:

> The International Tribunal shall have the power to prosecute persons committing or ordering to be committed grave breaches of the Geneva Conventions of 12 August 1949 ... .

By its explicit terms, and as confirmed in the Report of the Secretary-General, this Article of the Statute is based on the Geneva Conventions of 1949 and, more specifically, the provisions of those Conventions relating to "grave breaches" of the Conventions. Each of the four Geneva Conventions of 1949 contains a "grave breaches" provision, specifying particular breaches of the Convention for which the High Contracting Parties have a duty to prosecute those responsible. In other words, for these specific acts, the Conventions create universal mandatory criminal jurisdiction among contracting States. Although the language of the Conventions might appear to be ambiguous and the question is open to some debate (see, e.g. (*Amicus Curiae*) Submission of the Government of the United States of America Concerning Certain Arguments Made by Counsel for the Accused in the Case of *The Prosecutor of the Tribunal v. Dusko Tadic*, 17 July 1995, (Case No. IT-94-1-T), at 35-6 (hereinafter, U.S. *Amicus Curiae Brief*)), it is widely contended that the grave breaches provisions establish universal mandatory jurisdiction only with respect to those breaches of the Conventions committed in international armed conflicts. Appellant argues that, as the grave breaches enforcement system only applies to international armed conflicts, reference in Article 2 of the Statute to the grave breaches provisions of the Geneva Conventions limits the International Tribunal's jurisdiction under that Article to acts committed in the context of an international armed conflict.

The Trial Chamber has held that Article 2 [of the Statute of the Tribunal]:

> [H]as been so drafted as to be self-contained rather than referential, save for the identification of the victims of enumerated acts; that identification and that alone involves going to the Conventions themselves for the definition of "persons or property protected." ...
>
> [T]he requirement of international conflict does not appear on the face of Article 2. Certainly, nothing in the words of the Article expressly require its existence; once one of the specified acts is allegedly committed upon a protected person the power of the International Tribunal to prosecute arises if the spatial and temporal requirements of Article 1 are met. ...
>
> [T]here is no ground for treating Article 2 as in effect importing into the Statute the whole of the terms of the Conventions, including the reference in common Article 2 of the Geneva Convention to international conflicts. As stated, Article 2 of the Statute is

on its face, self-contained, save in relation to the definition of protected persons and things. (Decision at Trial, at paras. 49-51)

80. With all due respect, the Trial Chamber's reasoning is based on a misconception of the grave breaches provisions and the extent of their incorporation into the Statute of the International Tribunal. The grave breaches system of the Geneva Conventions establishes a twofold system: there is on the one hand an enumeration of offences that are regarded so serious as to constitute "grave breaches," closely bound up with this enumeration a mandatory enforcement mechanism is set up, based on the concept of a duty and a right of all Contracting States to search for and try or extradite persons allegedly responsible for "grave breaches." The international armed conflict element generally attributed to the grave breaches provisions of the Geneva Conventions is merely a function of the system of universal mandatory jurisdiction that those provisions create. The international armed conflict requirement was a necessary limitation on the grave breaches system in light of the intrusion on State sovereignty that such mandatory universal jurisdiction represents. States parties to the 1949 Geneva Conventions did not want to give other States jurisdiction over serious violations of international humanitarian law committed in their internal armed conflicts—at least not the mandatory universal jurisdiction involved in the grave breaches system.

81. The Trial Chamber is right in implying that the enforcement mechanism has of course not been imported into the Statute of the International Tribunal, for the obvious reason that the International Tribunal itself constitutes a mechanism for the prosecution and punishment of the perpetrators of "grave breaches." However, the Trial Chamber has misinterpreted the reference to the Geneva Conventions contained in the sentence of Article 2: "persons or property protected under the provisions of the relevant Geneva Conventions." (Statute of the Tribunal, art. 2.) For the reasons set out above, this reference is clearly intended to indicate that the offences listed under Article 2 can only be prosecuted when perpetrated against persons of property regarded as "protected" by the Geneva Conventions under the strict conditions set out by the Conventions themselves. Clearly, these provisions of the Geneva Conventions apply to persons or objects protected only to the extent that they are caught up in an international armed conflict. By contrast, those provisions do not include persons or property coming within the purview of common Article 3 of the four Geneva Conventions.

82. The above interpretation is borne out by what could be considered as part of the preparatory works of the Statute of the International Tribunal, namely the Report of the Secretary General. There, in introducing and explaining the meaning and purport of Article 2 and having regard to the "grave breaches" system of the Geneva Conventions, reference is made to "international armed conflicts" (Report of the Secretary-General at para. 37).

83. We find that our interpretation of Article 2 is the only one warranted by the text of the Statute and the relevant provisions of the Geneva Conventions, as well as by a logical construction of their interplay as dictated by Article 2. However, we are aware that this conclusion may appear not to be consonant with recent trends of both State practice and the whole doctrine of human rights which, as pointed out below (see paras. 97-127), tend to blur in many respects the traditional dichotomy between

international wars and civil strife. In this connection the Chamber notes with satisfaction the statement in the *amicus curiae* brief submitted by the Government of the United States, where it is contended that

> the "grave breaches" provisions of Article 2 of the International Tribunal Statute apply to armed conflicts of a non-international character as well as those of an international character. (U.S. Amicus Curiae Brief, at 35.)

This statement, unsupported by any authority, does not seem to be warranted as to the interpretation of Article 2 of the Statute. Nevertheless, seen from another viewpoint, there is no gainsaying its significance: that statement articulates the legal views of one of the permanent members of the Security Council on a delicate legal issue; on this score it provides the first indication of a possible change in *opinio juris* of States. Were other States and international bodies to come to share this view, a change in customary law concerning the scope of the "grave breaches" system might gradually materialize. Other elements pointing in the same direction can be found in the provision of the German Military Manual mentioned below (para. 131), whereby grave breaches of international humanitarian law include some violations of common Article 3. In addition, attention can be drawn to the Agreement of 1 October 1992 entered into by the conflicting parties in Bosnia-Herzegovina. Articles 3 and 4 of this Agreement implicitly provide for the prosecution and punishment of those responsible for grave breaches of the Geneva Conventions and Additional Protocol I. As the Agreement was clearly concluded within a framework of an internal armed conflict ... , it may be taken as an important indication of the present trend to extend the grave breaches provisions to such category of conflicts. One can also mention a recent judgement by a Danish court. On 25 November 1994 the Third Chamber of the Eastern Division of the Danish High Court delivered a judgement on a person accused of crimes committed together with a number of Croatian military police on 5 August 1993 in the Croatian prison camp of Dretelj in Bosnia (*The Prosecution v. Refik Saric*, unpublished (Den. H. Ct. 1994)). The Court explicitly acted on the basis of the "grave breaches" provisions of the Geneva Conventions, more specifically Articles 129 and 130 of Convention III and Articles 146 and 147 of Convention IV (*The Prosecution v. Refik Saric*, Transcript at 1 (25 Nov. 1994)), without however raising the preliminary question of whether the alleged offences had occurred within the framework of an international rather than an internal armed conflict (in the event the Court convicted the accused on the basis of those provisions and the relevant penal provisions of the Danish Penal Code (see *id*. at 7-8)). This judgement indicates that some national courts are also taking the view that the "grave breaches" system may operate regardless of whether the armed conflict is international or internal.

84. Notwithstanding the foregoing, the Appeals Chamber must conclude that, in the present state of development of the law, Article 2 of the Statute only applies to offences committed within the context of international armed conflicts.

85. Before the Trial Chamber, the Prosecutor asserted an alternative argument whereby the provisions on grave breaches of the Geneva Conventions could be applied to internal conflicts on the strength of some agreements entered into by the conflicting parties. For the reasons stated below, in Section IV C (para. 144) [defendant has not

been charged with a violation of such an agreement], we find it unnecessary to resolve this issue at this time … .

LI J. (concurring in part) …

7. Professor Meron states the customary international law of war crimes very correctly and clearly in the following terms:

> Whether the conflicts in Yugoslavia are characterized as internal or international is critically important. The fourth Hague Convention of 1907, which codified the principal laws of war and served as the normative core for the post-World War II war crimes prosecutions, applies to international wars only. The other principal prong of the penal laws of war, the grave breaches provisions of the Geneva Conventions and Protocol I is also directed to international wars. Violations of common Article 3 of the Geneva Conventions, which concerns internal wars, do not constitute grave breaches giving rise to universal criminal jurisdiction. Were any part of the conflict deemed internal rather than international, the perpetrators of even the worst atrocities might try to challenge prosecutions for war crimes or grave breaches, but not for genocide or crimes against humanity. (Meron, *War Crimes in Yugoslavia and the Development of International Law*, 88 AJIL 78, 80 (1994).)

8. The Final Report of 27 May 1994 of the Commission of Experts established pursuant to Security Council resolution 780 (1992) takes the same view as Professor Meron:

> If a conflict is classified as international, then the grave breaches of the Geneva Conventions, including Additional Protocol I, apply as well as violations of the laws and customs of war. The treaty and customary law applicable to international armed conflict is well-established. The treaty law designed for internal armed conflict is in common [A]rticle 3 of the Geneva Conventions, additional Protocol II of 1977, and [A]rticle 19 of the 1954 Hague Convention for the Protection of Cultural property in the Event of Armed Conflict. These legal sources do not use the terms "grave breaches" or "war crimes." Further, the content of customary law applicable to internal armed conflicts is debatable. As a result, in general, unless the parties to an internal armed conflict agree otherwise, the only offences committed in internal armed conflict for which universal jurisdiction exists are "crimes against humanity" and genocide, which apply irrespective of the conflicts' classification. (S/1994/674, p. 13, para. 42.)

NOTE

With the establishment of the ICTY and ICTR, systematic rape has been recognized as a war crime and a crime against humanity. The 1949 Geneva Conventions and their two Additional Protocols do not include rape as a grave breach subject to universal jurisdiction.[33] Neither did the Nuremberg Charter. With the advent of the two *Ad Hoc*

---

33   T. Meron, "Rape as a Crime Under International Humanitarian Law" (1993) 87 A.J.I.L. 425.

Tribunals and the new ICC, gender-related offences have been clearly proscribed as crimes subject to international condemnation and prosecution. Refer to the *"Celebici"* case below and the *Akayesu* case reproduced in the next subsection on the ICTR.

Prosecutor v. Delalic, Mucic, Delic & Landzo
IT-96-21 (Trial Chamber, ICTY) Summary of Judgment, (1999) 38 I.L.M. 57

[The actual judgment in this case was 500 pages. The Tribunal, therefore, read out a summary of its content, which is reproduced in part below. This case is referred to as the *"Celebici"* case, after the prison camp in Bosnia and Herzegovina where the alleged crimes occurred. The camp housed Bosnian Serbs arrested by the Bosnian forces.]

In Section I, the Judgement contains a description of the charges in the Indictment, which are various counts of violations of Article 2 of the Statute—grave breaches of the Geneva Conventions—and Article 3 of the Statute—violations of the laws or customs of war—alleged to have been committed within the Celebici prison-camp in the Konjic municipality in central Bosnia and Herzegovina over a period of months in 1992.

The fourth accused, Esad Landzo, is thus, pursuant to Article 7(1) of the Statute, charged with wilful killing and murder, torture and cruel treatment and wilfully causing great suffering of serious injury to body or health. The third accused, Hazim Delic, is similarly charged under Article 7(1) with wilful killing and murder, torture—including rape and cruel treatment, inhuman treatment, wilfully causing great suffering or serious injury to body or health, the unlawful confinement of civilians, and plunder of private property. Hazim Delic is also charged pursuant to Article 7(3) of the Statute with responsibility as a superior for the crimes which occurred in the Celebici prison-camp at this time.

The second accused, Zdravko Mucic, is also charged pursuant to Article 7(3) with responsibility as a superior for the crimes alleged in the indictment, due to his position as commander of the Celebici prison-camp at the relevant time. Mr. Mucic is further charged as a direct participant in the unlawful confinement of civilians, the plunder of private property and the wilful causing of great suffering or serious injury to body or health and cruel treatment for the inhumane conditions which existed in the Celebici prison-camp. The first accused, Zejni Delalic, is charged pursuant to Article 7(3) with responsibility as a superior for the crimes alleged in the Indictment, due to his overall command over the Celebici prison-camp at the relevant time. Mr. Delalic is also charged as a direct participant in the unlawful confinement of civilians. ...

Most importantly, it is found that, in the period relevant to the indictment, a situation of armed conflict existed in Bosnia and Herzegovina, which incorporated the municipality of Konjic. In Konjic, this armed conflict involved the forces of the Bosnian government—the territorial defence forces and the Ministry of Interior forces (MUP), for a time acting jointly with the Croatian defence Council (HVO)—engaging the Bosnian Serb forces—initially the JNA and then the Bosnian Serb army (VRS), joined by local volunteers and militia. It is, furthermore, found that there is a clear nexus between the acts of the accused alleged in the Indictment and this armed conflict. ...

The Trial Chamber finds that the conflict in Bosnia and Herzegovina must be regarded as an international armed conflict throughout 1992. There can be no question that forces external to Bosnia and Herzegovina, particularly the forces of the Yugoslav People's Army (JNA), participated in hostilities in that State. In mid-May 1992, there was an attempt by the authorities of the Federal Republic of Yugoslavia (Serbia and Montenegro) to create the appearance that they were no longer involved in Bosnia and Herzegovina, by the division of the JNA into the Bosnian Serb army (VRS) and the Yugoslav army (VJ). The Trial Chamber finds, however, that this was a deliberate attempt to mask the continued involvement of the FRY, whose government remained the controlling force behind the Bosnian Serbs.

The Trial Chamber also finds that, at all relevant times, the persons detained in the Celebici prison-camp, being the victims of the crimes alleged in the Indictment, were persons protected by the Fourth Geneva Convention concerning civilian populations. In particular, it is the firm belief of the Trial Chamber that civilians caught up in an international armed conflict resulting from the dissolution of a State cannot be denied the full protection of the Fourth Geneva Convention solely on the basis of their citizenship status under domestic law.

[The judgment contains a detailed discussion of the concept of command responsibility under customary international law and as incorporated in article 7(3). This is the first elucidation of the concept of command responsibility by an international judicial body since the cases decided in the wake of World War II. Most important, it is found that not only military commanders, but also civilians holding positions of authority, are encompassed by the doctrine. Furthermore, for the attribution of criminal responsibility, not only persons in *de jure* positions of superiority, but also those in such position *de facto*, may be held criminally responsible if they knew or had reason to know that offences had been or were about to be committed by their subordinates and failed to take the necessary and reasonable measures to prevent or punish such offences.]

With respect to Mr. Mucic, the Tribunal found that as the commander of the Celebici prison camp, he was clearly derelict in this duty and allowed those under his authority to commit the most heinous of offences, without taking any disciplinary action. Furthermore, as commander of the Celebici prison camp, he was the person with the primary responsibility for the conditions in which the prisoners were kept. As discussed in some depth in our written judgment, the trial Chamber is appalled by the inadequacy of the food and water supplies, and medical and sleeping facilities that were provided for the detainees, as well as the atmosphere of terror which reigned in the Celebici prison camp. ...

[Concerning Mr. Delic, the Trial Chamber stated that it was] ... appalled by the details of Mr. Delic's criminal actions, as recounted by many victims and witnesses. He displayed a singular brutality in causing the deaths of two men detained in the Celebici prison-camp and a calculated cruelty in the torture and mistreatment of many others. He raped two defenceless women on several occasions, seeking to exert his power over them and instill absolute fear in them. The Trial Chamber considers the rape of any person to be a despicable act which strikes at the very core of human dignity and physical integrity. As well as showing no mercy to his chosen victims, he has displayed no remorse before this Trial Chamber.

Throughout Mr. Delic's tenure as deputy commander in the Celebici prison-camp he was instrumental in creating an atmosphere of terror by his actions and his threats to and humiliation of the detainees. It appears that he took a sadistic pleasure in causing the detainees pain and suffering, most clearly illustrated by his frequent use of a device to inflict electrical shocks. Mr. Delic abused his position of authority and trust as deputy commander and, although he has been found not to have command responsibility for the offences of others within the prison-camp by his actions he encouraged others among the camp guards to engage in their own forms of mistreatment of the detainees.

Once again, the Trial Chamber would emphasize that the breakdown of society and the mechanisms which ordinarily sanction crimes during times of armed conflict must not be used in avoidance of the responsibility on all individuals to conduct themselves appropriately and exercise moral choice.

NOTES

1) In *Prosecutor v. Furundzija*,[34] the Trial Chamber held that torture is specifically prohibited by treaty law, particularly article 3 common to the Geneva Conventions 1949 and article 4 of Additional Protocol II. Further, in the *Nicaragua* case[35] the International Court of Justice confirmed that article 3 has the status of customary international law. The prohibition against torture imposes upon states an *erga omnes* obligation. Such prohibition is regarded as *jus cogens* with universal jurisdiction conferred on states.

2) *Furundzija* also considered a rape as a war crime, a crime against humanity, or an act of genocide and noted the formulation of the crime in the *Akayesu* case, reproduced below.

3) In June 1999, the U.N. Security Coucil adopted Resolution 1244[36] on the situation relating to Kosovo. It authorized a NATO-led force to establish a safe environment for all people in Kosovo and to facilitate the safe return to their homes of all displaced persons and refugees. It also authorized the Secretary-General to establish an international civil presence in Kosovo to provide an interim administration "while establishing and overseeing the development of provisional democratic self-governing institutions." In particular, in the context of this chapter, the Security Council recalled the jurisdiction and mandate of the ICTY and demanded full cooperation with it by all concerned, including the international security presence.

4) As of February 2005, 109 accused persons had appeared in proceedings before the ICTY. There were 51 accused in custody at the Detention Unit and 14 accused provisionally released. Seventeen arrest warrants had been issued against accused still at large including Radovan Karadzic, Ratko Mladic, and Ante Gotovina. Additional

---

34 Case No. IT-95-17/1-T (Trial Chamber, December 10, 1998), available online at: <www.un.org/icty/index.html>.

35 [1986] I.C.J. Rep. 14.

36 SC Res. 1244 (1999), UN SCOR, 54th year, *Res. and Dec.*; U.N. Doc. S/INF/55 at 32.

undisclosed indictments may have also been confirmed pursuant to Rule 53 of the Rules of Procedure and Evidence. Thirty-five accused were at the pre-trial stage of prosecution and 9 accused were being tried, including Slobodan Milosevic[37] and Momcilo Krajisnik.[38] Fifty-five persons had received Trial Chamber judgment and 14 persons were at the appeal stage. Thirty-three persons had received their final sentence and were awaiting transfer. Seventeen convicted persons had been transferred to serve their sentences in France, United Kingdom, Spain, Austria, Norway, Finland, Sweden, Italy, or Germany. Twelve convicted persons had served their sentences. Three persons had been found not guilty by the Appeals Chamber[39] and two accused had been acquitted by the Trial Chamber.[40] Ten cases had been terminated, five indictments having been withdrawn after transfer of the accused to the Tribunal, and five following the death of the accused.

5) The Detention Unit is located in The Hague and is managed by the Registry. The maximun sentence that can be imposed on an accused is life imprisonment. Sentences are served in a state that has signed an agreement with the United Nations to accept persons convicted by the ICTY. The expenses of the Tribunal were $271,854,600.00 in 2004-5 and are borne by the regular budget of the United Nations in accordance with article 17 of the United Nations Charter, as provided by article 32 of the ICTY Statute.

2. The Ad Hoc International Criminal Tribunal for Rwanda

In April 1994 the Presidents of Burundi and Rwanda were killed in an aircraft accident. Immediately, a campaign of widespread killing began in which approximately 800,000 people were massacred in just two months. Directed by leaders of the Hutu people, the massacres were aimed at annihilating the Tutsi population of Rwanda. The U.N. Security Council responded hesitantly, but, eventually, on becoming gravely concerned by the reports of genocide and other widespread and systematic violations of international humanitarian law, determined that the situation constituted a threat to international peace and security. Acting under Chapter VII of the Charter it again created an *Ad Hoc* Tribunal on November 8, 1994, in the following resolution.

Security Council Resolution 955 (1994)
U.N. Doc. S/Res/955 (1994)

The Security Council, ... [a]cting under Chapter VII of the Charter of the United Nations
    1. *Decides* hereby, having received the request of the Government of Rwanda (S/1994/1115), to establish an international tribunal for the sole purpose of prosecuting

---

37   Case No. IT-02-54, commenced 2 February 2002.

38   Case No. IT-00-39 & 40, commenced 3 February 2004.

39   Zoran Kupreskic, Mirjan Kupreskic, & Vlatko Kupreskic, Case No. IT-95-16 (Appeals Chamber, 23 October, 2001).

40   Zejnil Delalic, in the *"Celebici"* case, Case No. IT-96-21 (Appeals Chamber, 21 February 2001) and *Dragan Papic*, Case No. IT-95-16 (Appeals Chamber, 14 January 2000).

persons responsible for genocide and other serious violations of international humanitarian law committed in the territory of Rwanda and Rwandan citizens responsible for genocide and other such violations committed in the territory of neighbouring States, between 1 January 1994 and 31 December 1994 and to this end to adopt the Statute of the International Criminal Tribunal for Rwanda annexed hereto;

2. *Decides* that all States shall cooperate fully with the International Tribunal and its organs in accordance with the present resolution and the Statute of the International Tribunal and that consequently all States shall take any measures necessary under their domestic law to implement the provisions of the present resolution and the Statute, including the obligation of States to comply with requests for assistance or orders issued by a Trial Chamber under Article 28 of the Statute.

ANNEX
Statute of the International Criminal Tribunal for Rwanda

Article 1
Competence of the International Tribunal for Rwanda

The International Tribunal for Rwanda shall have the power to prosecute persons responsible for serious violations of international humanitarian law committed in the territory of Rwanda and Rwandan citizens responsible for such violations committed in the territory of neighbouring States between 1 January 1994 and 31 December 1994, in accordance with the provisions of the present Statute.

Article 2
Genocide

1. The International Tribunal for Rwanda shall have the power to prosecute persons committing genocide as defined in paragraph 2 of this Article or of committing any of the other acts enumerated in paragraph 3 of this Article.

2. Genocide means any of the following acts committed with intent to destroy, in whole or in part, a national, ethnical, racial or religious group, as such:

    (a) Killing members of the group;

    (b) Causing serious bodily or mental harm to members of the group;

    (c) Deliberately inflicting on the group conditions of life calculated to bring about its physical destruction in whole or in part;

    (d) Imposing measures intended to prevent births within the group;

    (e) Forcibly transferring children of the group to another group.

3. The following acts shall be punishable:

    (a) Genocide;

    (b) Conspiracy to commit genocide;

    (c) Direct and public incitement to commit genocide;

    (d) Attempt to commit genocide;

    (e) Complicity in genocide.

Article 3
Crimes Against Humanity

The International Tribunal for Rwanda shall have the power to prosecute persons responsible for the following crimes when committed as part of a widespread or systematic attack against any civilian population on national, political, ethnic, racial or religious grounds:

(a) Murder;

(b) Extermination;

(c) Enslavement;

(d) Deportation;

(e) Imprisonment;

(f) Torture;

(g) Rape;

(h) Persecutions on political, racial and religious grounds;

(i) Other inhumane acts.

Article 4
Violations of Article 3 Common to the Geneva Conventions and of Additional Protocol II

The International Tribunal for Rwanda shall have the power to prosecute persons committing or ordering to be committed serious violations of Article 3 common to the Geneva Conventions of 12 August 1949 for the Protection of War Victims, and of Additional Protocol II thereto of 8 June 1977. These violations shall include, but shall not be limited to:

(a) Violence to life, health and physical or mental well-being of persons, in particular murder as well as cruel treatment such as torture, mutilation or any form of corporal punishment;

(b) Collective punishments;

(c) Taking of hostages;

(d) Acts of terrorism;

(e) Outrages upon personal dignity, in particular humiliating and degrading treatment, rape, enforced prostitution and any form of indecent assault;

(f) Pillage;

(g) The passing of sentences and the carrying out of executions without previous judgement pronounced by a regularly constituted court, affording all the judicial guarantees which are recognized as indispensable by civilised peoples;

(h) Threats to commit any of the foregoing acts.

NOTES

1) Because the conflict in Rwanda was basically internal, the subject-matter jurisdiction of the ICTR differs from that of the ICTY. It is restricted to genocide, crimes against humanity, and violations of article 3 common to the Geneva Conventions 1949 and of article 4 of Additional Protocol II, reproduced above in Section A.2. In addition, while the

ICTY may only prosecute persons for crimes against humanity when committed in armed conflict, the ICTR may pursue them whenever committed as part of a widespread or systematic attack against any civilian population. The temporal jurisdiction of the ICTR is limited to the calendar year of 1994 and is not open ended as it is for the ICTY. Much of the rest of the Statute, however, parallels the ICTY. Originally both Tribunals shared the same Chief Prosecutor and Appeals Chamber, but subsequently a separate Prosecutor was established for the ICTR. The seat of the ICTR is in Arusha, Tanzania.

2) At the time the new Government of Rwanda was a non-permanent member of the Security Council and itself requested action to establish a criminal tribunal. In the event, however, Rwanda voted against Resolution 955 because it disagreed with aspects of the Statute, including the lack of the death penalty, which Rwanda retains domestically.

Prosecutor v. Akayesu
Case No. ICTR-96-4-T, Summary of Judgment, (1998) 37 I.L.M. 1399

[The actual judgment was almost 300 pages, so the Trial Chamber delivered a summary, which is extracted below. The accused was elected bourgmestre of Taba commune in 1993 and held that position until June 1994. He was indicted with 15 counts relating to genocide, crimes against humanity, and violations of article 3 common to the Geneva Conventions 1949 and Additional Protocol II. The Tribunal noted that the bourgmestre in Rwanda traditionally had extensive powers. The case is particularly significant because it was the first full trial of an accused for genocide.]

19. Based on the evidence submitted to the Chamber, it is clear that the massacres which occurred in Rwanda in 1994 had a specific objective, namely the extermination of the Tutsi, who were targeted especially because of their Tutsi origin and not because they were RPF fighters. In any case, the Tutsi children and pregnant women would, naturally, not have been among the fighters. The Chamber concludes that, alongside the conflict between the RAF and RPF, genocide was committed in Rwanda in 1994 against the Tutsi as a group. The execution of this genocide was probably facilitated by the conflict in the sense that the conflict with the RPF forces served as a pretext for the propaganda inciting genocide against the Tutsi by branding RPF fighters and Tutsi civilians together through the notion widely disseminated, particularly by Radio television Libre des Mille Collines (RTLM), to the effect that every Tutsi was allegedly an accomplice of the RPF soldiers or "Inkotanyi." However, the fact that the genocide occurred while the RAF were in conflict with the RPF, obviously, cannot serve as a mitigating circumstance for the genocide.

20. Consequently, the Chamber concludes from all the foregoing that it was, indeed, genocide that was committed in Rwanda in 1994, against the Tutsi as a group. The Chamber is of the opinion that the genocide appears to have been meticulously organized. ...

21. The Chamber holds that the genocide was organized and planned not only by members of the RAF, but also by the political forces who were behind the "Hutu-power," that it was executed essentially by civilians including the armed militia and

even ordinary citizens, and above all that the majority of the Tutsi victims were non-combatants, including thousands of women and children.

22. Having said that, the Chamber then recalled that the fact that genocide was, indeed, committed in Rwanda in 1994, and more particularly in Taba, cannot influence it in its findings in the present matter. It is the Chamber's responsibility alone to assess the individual criminal responsibility of the Accused, Jean-Paul Akayesu, for the crimes alleged against him, including genocide, for which the Prosecution has to show proof. Despite the indisputable atrociousness of the crimes and the emotions evoked in the international community, the judges have examined the facts adduced in a most dispassionate manner, bearing in mind that the accused is presumed innocent. ...

26. The Chamber finds that ... it has been established that throughout the period covered in the Indictment, Akayesu in his capacity as bourgmestre, was responsible for maintaining law and public order in the commune of Taba and that he had effective authority over the communal police. Moreover, as "leader" of Taba commune, of which he was one of the most prominent figures, the inhabitants respected him and followed his orders. Akayesu himself admitted before the Chamber that he had the power to assemble the population and that they obeyed his instructions. It has also been proven that a very large number of Tutsi were killed in Taba between 7 April and the end of June 1994 while Akayesu was bourgmestre of the Commune. Knowing of such killings, he opposed them and attempted to prevent them only until 18 April 1994, date after which he not only stopped trying to maintain law and order in his commune, but was also present during the acts of violence and killings and sometimes even gave orders himself for bodily or mental harm to be caused to certain Tutsi and endorsed and even ordered the killing of several Tutsi.

27. ... [T]he Prosecutor has shown beyond a reasonable doubt that between 7 April and the end of June 1994, numerous Tutsi who sought refuge at the Taba Bureau communal were frequently beaten by members of the Interahamwe on or near the premises of the Bureau communal. Some of them were killed. Numerous Tutsi women were forced to endure acts of sexual violence, mutilations and rape, often repeatedly, often publicly and often by more than one assailant. Tutsi women were systematically raped, as one female victim testified to by saying that "each time that you met assailants, they raped you." Numerous incidents of such rape and sexual violence against Tutsi women occurred inside or near the Bureau communal. It has been proven that some communal policemen armed with guns and the accused himself were present while some of these rapes and sexual violence were being committed. ...

29. As regards the facts alleged in paragraphs 14 and 15 of the Indictment, it is established that in the early hours of 19 April 1994, Akayesu joined a gathering in Gishyeshye and took this opportunity to address the public; he led the meeting and conducted the proceedings. He then called on the population to unite in order to eliminate what he referred to as the sole enemy, the accomplices of the Inkotanyi and the population understood that he was thus urging them to kill the Tutsi. ... The statements thus made by Akayesu at that gathering immediately led to widespread killings of Tutsi in Taba.

30. With respect to the allegations in paragraph 16 of the Indictment, it is also established that on 19 April 1994, Akayesu on two occasions threatened to kill victum U,

a Tutsi woman, while she was being interrogated. He detained her for several hours at the Bureau communal before allowing her to leave. In the evening of 20 April 1994, during a search conducted in the home of victim V, a Hutu man, Akayesu directly threatened to kill the latter. Victim V was thereafter beaten … in the presence of the accused. …

… [I]t is established that on or about 19 April 1994, Akayesu and a group of men under his control were looking for Ephrem Karangwa and destroyed his house and that of his mother. They then went to search the house of Ephrem Karangwa's brother-in-law in Musambira commune and found his three brothers there. When the three brothers, namely Simon Mutijima, Thaddee Uwanyiligira and Jean-Chrysostome Gakuba, tried to escape, Akayesu ordered that they be captured and ordered that they be killed and participated in their killing.

41. On the crime of genocide, the Chamber recalls that the definition given by Article 2 of the Statute is echoed exactly by the Convention for the Prevention and Repression of the Crime of Genocide. The Chamber notes that Rwanda acceded by legislative decree to the Convention on genocide on 12 February 1975. Thus, punishment of the crime of genocide did exist in Rwanda in 1994 at the time of the acts alleged in the Indictment, and the perpetrator was liable to be brought before the competent courts of Rwanda to answer for this crime.

42. Contrary to popular belief, the crime of genocide does not imply the actual extermination of a group in its entirety, but is understood as such once any one of the acts mentioned in Article 2 of the Statute is committed with the specific intent to destroy "in whole or in part" a national, ethnical, racial or religious group. Genocide is distinct from other crimes inasmuch as it embodies a special intent or *dolus specialis*. Special intent of a crime is the specific intention, required as a constitutive element of the crime, which requires that the perpetrator clearly seek to produce the act charged. The special intent in the crime of genocide lies in "the intent to destroy, in whole or in part, a national, ethnical, racial or religious group, as such."

43. Specifically, for any of the acts charged under Article 2(2) of the Statute to be a constitutive element of genocide, the act must have been committed against one or several individuals because such individual or individuals were members of a specific group and specifically because they belonged to this group. Thus, the victim is chosen not because of his individual identity, but rather on account of his being a member of a national, ethnical, racial or religious group. The victim of the act is therefore a member of a group, targeted as such; hence, the victim of the crime of genocide is the group itself and not the individual alone.

44. On the issue of determining the offender's specific intent, the Chamber considers that intent is a mental factor which is difficult, even impossible, to determine. This is the reason why, in the absence of a confession from the accused, his intent can be inferred from a certain number of presumptions of fact. The Chamber considers that it is possible to deduce the genocidal intent inherent in a particular act charged from the general context of the perpetration of other culpable acts systematically directed against that same group, whether these acts were committed by the same offender or by others. Other factors such as the scale of atrocities committed in a region or a country, their general nature, or, furthermore, the fact of deliberately and systematically targeting victims on account of their membership of a

particular group, while excluding the members of other groups, can enable the Chamber to infer the genocidal intent of a particular act.

45. Apart from the crime of genocide, Jean-Paul Akayesu is charged with complicity in genocide and direct and public incitement to commit genocide. ...

48. The second crime which comes within the jurisdiction of the Tribunal and of which Jean-Paul Akayesu is charged is that of crimes against humanity. On the law applicable to this crime, the Chamber reviewed the case law on this crime from the judgements rendered by the Nuremberg and Tokyo Tribunals to more recent cases, including the Touvier and Papon cases in France notably and the Eichmann trial in Israel. It indicated the circumstances under which the charge of crimes against humanity would be leveled, as provided for by Article 3 of the Statute, under which the act must be committed as part of a widespread or systematic attack directed against a civilian population on discriminatory grounds.

49. The third crime on which the Chamber rendered its conclusions is that for which it has competence pursuant to article 4 of the Statute, which provides that the Tribunal is empowered to prosecute persons committing or ordering to be committed serious violations of Article 3 common to the Geneva Conventions of 12 August 1949 for the protection of war Victims and of the Additional Protocol II thereto of June 8, 1977. The said Article 3 common to the Geneva Conventions extends a minimum threshold of humanitarian protection as well to all persons affected by a non-international conflict, a protection which was further developed and enhanced in the 1977 Additional Protocol II. The Chamber decided to analyse separately the respective conditions of applicability of Article 3 common to the Geneva Conventions and the Additional Protocol II thereto. It then analysed the conflict which took place in Rwanda in 1994 in the light of those conditions and concluded that each of the two legal instruments was applicable in this case. Furthermore, the Chamber is of the opinion that all the norms set forth under article 4 of its Statute constitute a part of Customary International Law. It finally recalled that the violation of the norms defined in article 4 of the Statute may, in principle, commit criminal responsibility of civilians and that the Accused belongs to the category of individuals who could be held responsible for serious infringement of international humanitarian law, particularly for serious violations of Article 3 common to the Geneva Conventions and the Additional Protocol II thereto. ...

In light of all the evidence before it, the Chamber is satisfied that the acts of rape and sexual violence described above were committed solely against Tutsi women, many of whom were subjected to the worst public humiliation, mutilated and raped several times, often in public in the Bureau Communal premises or in other public places, and often by more than one assailant. These rapes resulted in physical and psychological destruction of Tutsi women, their families and their communities. Sexual violence was an integral part of the process of destruction, specifically targeting Tutsi women and specifically contributing to their destruction and to the destruction of the Tutsi group as a whole. ...

53. On the basis of the substantial testimonies brought before it, the Chamber finds that in most cases, the rapes of Tutsi women in Taba were accompanied with the intent to kill those women. Many rapes were perpetrated near mass graves where the

women were taken to be killed. A victim testified that Tutsi women caught could be taken away by peasants and men with promises that they would be collected later to be executed. Following an act of gang rape, a witness heard Akayesu say "tomorrow they will be killed" and they were actually killed. In this respect, it appears clearly to the Chamber that the acts of rape and sexual violence, as other acts of serious bodily and mental harm committed against the Tutsi reflected the determination to make Tutsi women suffer and to mutilate them even before killing them, the intent being to destroy the Tutsi group while inflicting acute suffering on its members in the process.

54. The Chamber has already established that genocide was committed against the Tutsi group in Rwanda in 1994, throughout the period covering the events alleged in the Indictment. Owing to the very high number of atrocities committed against the Tutsi, their widespread nature not only in the commune of Taba, but also throughout Rwanda, and to the fact that the victims were systematically and deliberately selected because they belonged to the Tutsi group, with persons belonging to other groups being excluded, the Chamber is also able to infer, beyond reasonable doubt, the genocidal intent of the accused in the commission of the above-mentioned crimes; to the extent that the actions and words of Akayesu during the period of the facts alleged in the Indictment, the Chamber is convinced beyond reasonable doubt, on the basis of evidence adduced before it during the hearing, that he repeatedly made statements more or less explicitly calling for the commission of genocide. Yet, according to the Chamber, he who incites another to commit genocide must have the specific intent to commit genocide: that of destroying in whole, or in part, a national, ethnical, racial, or religious group, as such.

55. In conclusion, regarding Count One on genocide, the Chamber is satisfied beyond reasonable doubt that these various acts were committed by Akayesu with the specific intent to destroy the Tutsi group, as such. ... Furthermore, the Chamber is satisfied beyond reasonable doubt that in committing the various acts alleged, Akayesu had the specific intent of destroying the Tutsi group as such. ...

57. [Regarding] Count 3 of the Indictment on crimes against humanity, extermination, the Chamber concludes that the murder of the eight refugees described in paragraph 19 of the Indictment as well as the killing of Simon Mutijima, Thaddee Uwanyiligra and Jean Chrysostome Gakuba, Samuel, Tharcisse, Theogene, Phoebe Uwineze and her fiancé, facts described in paragraph 20 of the Indictment, constitute, beyond reasonable doubt, a crime of extermination perpetrated during a widespread and systematic attack against a civilian population on ethnic grounds and, as such, constitutes a crime against humanity for which Akayesu is individually criminally responsible.

58. Regarding Count Four, on the basis of the facts described in paragraphs 14 and 15 of the Indictment and which it believes are well founded, the Chamber is satisfied beyond reasonable doubt that by the speeches made in public, Akayesu had the intent to directly create a particular state of mind in his audience necessary to lead to the destruction of the Tutsi group as such. Accordingly, the Chamber finds that the said acts constitute the crime of direct and public incitement to commit genocide. In addition, the Chamber finds that the direct and public incitement to commit genocide engaged in by Akayesu, was indeed successful and did lead to the destruction of a great number of Tutsi in the commune of Taba. ...

64. With respect to Counts 6, 8, 10, 12 and 15, Akayesu is charged with violations of Common Article 3 of the Geneva Conventions of 1949 in counts 6, 8, 10 and 12 and with violations of Common Article 3 of the Geneva Conventions and of Additional Protocol II thereto of 1977 under count 15. The Chamber finds that it has been established beyond reasonable doubt that there was an armed conflict not of an international character between the Government of Rwanda and the RPF at the time of the facts alleged in the Indictment and that the said conflict was well within the provisions of Common Article 3 and of the Additional Protocol II. The Chamber however finds that the Prosecution has failed to show beyond reasonable doubt that Akayesu was a member of the armed forces and that he was duly mandated and expected in his capacity as a public official or agent or person otherwise vested with public authority of a *de facto* representative of the Government to support and carry out the war effort.

[The Chamber unanimously found the accused guilty of genocide, incitement to commit genocide, and crimes against humanity.]

NOTES

1) On July 9, 1997, Jean Kambanda, who was Prime Minister of the Interim Government of Rwanda from April 8, 1994 until July 17, 1994, was arrested in Kenya and transferred to the ICTR. In *Prosecutor v. Kambanda*,[41] the accused pleaded guilty to genocide, conspiracy to commit genocide, direct and public incitement to commit genocide, and crimes against humanity. The Trial Chamber verified that his guilty plea was voluntary, that he understood the charges, and that his plea was unequivocal. Mr. Kambanda also submitted to the Trial Chamber a document entitled "Plea Agreement" in which he made full admission of all relevant facts alleged in the indictment. He acknowledged that as Prime Minister he had exercised *de jure* authority and control over members of his government and the armed forces. He also admitted to having possessed *de jure* and *de facto* authority over senior civil servants and senior officers in the military. Mr. Kambanda was sentenced to life imprisonment.

2) One of the complexities of proving the commission of genocide is establishing the identity of the victims as a targeted group. Established in the wake of the Holocaust of World War II, the Genocide Convention's designation of "a national, ethnic, racial or religious group" may have seemed straightforward, but its application in Rwanda was troubling because there are not significant ethnic and racial differences between Tutsis and Hutu and they are all Rwandan nationals. Basically, they share the same language, culture, customs, religion, and most physical traits. Faced with this dilemma, the ICTR in

---

41   Case No. ICTR-97-23-S (Trial Chamber, 4 September 1998) 37 I.L.M. 1411. See also *Prosecutor v. Kayishema and Ruzindana*, Case No. ICTR-95-1 (Appeals Chamber, June 1, 2001); *Prosecutor v. Baglishema*, Case No. ICTR 95-1A-T (Trial Chamber, June 7, 2001); *Prosecutor v. Kunarac, Kovac and Vokovic*, Case No. IT-96-23 & IT-96-23/1 (Appeals Chamber, June 12, 2002); and *Prosecutor v. Niyitegika*, Case No. ICTR-96-14 (Trial Chamber, 16 May 2003). The cases are available online at: <www.ictr.org/default.htm>.

the *Akayesu* case devised a test that assessed whether the group had a stable and permanent membership, which was acquired, typically, by birth, as opposed to a group whose members might join by individual voluntary commitment, such as a political association. The Tutsis readily satisfied this test, but does it really reflect the nature of national or religious groups?

3) Noticeably, genocide does not include targeted political groups although attempts to destroy political opponents have long been known. Should such "politicide" be proscribed as a form of genocide?

4) Similar to the ICTY, judges *ad litem* have also been appointed to the ICTR.[42]

C. THE INTERNATIONAL CRIMINAL COURT

On July 17, 1998, in Rome, the United Nations Diplomatic Conference of Plenipotentiaries on the Establishment of an International Criminal Court adopted the Statute of the International Criminal Court (ICC).[43] The Rome Statute is the culmination of work that began in the International Law Commission,[44] continued in the *Ad Hoc* Committee set up by the General Assembly in 1994,[45] and in the Preparatory Committee (Prep. Com.), which met between 1996 and 1998 and prepared the draft text for the Diplomatic Conference.[46]

The five-week Rome Conference was the scene of intense negotiations "characterized by deep divides, a substantial volume of work and limited time."[47] The draft text had over 1,300 square brackets signifying matters that were unresolved and often contentious.

---

42 SC Res. 1431(2002) UN SCOR, *Res. and Dec.*; U.N. Doc. S/INF/58 at 205; and SC Res. 1512 (2003), UN SCOR, *Res. and Dec.*; U.N. Doc. S/INF/59 at 237, which increased the number who may serve at any one time from 4 to 9.

43 Much has now been written on the International Criminal Court. See for example, B. Ferencz, *An International Criminal Court: A Step Towards World Peace* (1980); M.C. Bassiouni, *The Statute of the International Criminal Court: A Documentary History* (1998); and "Explanatory Note on the ICC Statute" in *International Criminal Court: Ratification and National Implementing Legislation* (2000) 71 Rev. I.D.P. 1; H. von Hebel, J. Lammers, & J. Schukking, eds., *Reflections on the International Criminal Court* (1999); R.S. Lee, ed., *The International Criminal Court: The Making of the Rome Statute* (1999); and *The International Criminal Court: Elements of Crimes and Rules of Procedure and Evidence* (2001); S.A. Williams, "The Rome Statute on the International Criminal Court: From 1947-2000 and Beyond" (2000) 38 Osgoode Hall L.J. 297; O. Triffterer, ed., *Commentary on the Rome Statute of the International Criminal Court* (1999); W.A. Schabas, *An Introduction to the International Criminal Court*, 2d ed. (2004); A. Cassesse, P. Gaeta, & J. Jones, eds., *The Rome Statute of the International Criminal Court: A Commentary* (2002) 2 vols.; G-J.A. Knoops, *Surrendering to International Criminal Courts* (2002); and R. Dixon & K. Khan, eds., *Archbold International Criminal Courts: Practice, Procedure, and Evidence* (2003).

44 See the 1994 Draft Statute in *Report of the ILC on the Work of Its 46th Session*, UN GAOR, 49th Sess., Supp. No. 10, U.N. Doc. A/49/10.

45 GA Res. 49/53, UN GAOR, 49th Sess., Supp. No. 49, UN Doc. A/49/738 (1994) 293.

46 See M.C. Bassiouni, *The Statute of the International Criminal Court*, *supra* note 43; and D. Shelton, *International Crimes, Peace, and Human Rights: The Role of the International Criminal Court* (2000).

47 P. Kirsch, "Introduction," in von Hebel *et al.*, eds., *supra* note 43 at 2: P.Kirsch & J.T. Holmes, "The Rome Conference on the International Criminal Court: The Negotiating process" (1999) 93 A.J.I.L. 2.

Some of the issues that divided states were (1) which crimes would be included; (2) would the ICC have automatic jurisdiction over core crimes once a state had accepted the Court's jurisdiction or would an "opt-in" approach be taken case-by-case; (3) would certain states, and, if so, which ones, have to be parties to the Statute as a precondition to the ICC exercising jurisdiction; (4) would the Prosecutor be able to initiate prosecution; and (5) what role would the Security Council play? The Conference finally adopted a Statute that is a product of compromise, as the text reproduced below reflects.

1998 Rome Statute of the International Criminal Court
U.N. Doc. A/CONF. 183/9 (July 17, 1998) as corr. by U.N. Doc. PCNICC/1999/
INF/3, (1998) 37 I.L.M. 999

PREAMBLE
Conscious that all peoples are united by common bonds, their cultures pieced together in a shared heritage, and concerned that this delicate mosaic may be shattered at any time,

Mindful that during this century millions of children, women and men have been victims of unimaginable atrocities that deeply shock the conscience of humanity,

Recognizing that such grave crimes threaten the peace, security and well-being of the world,

Affirming that the most serious crimes of concern to the international community as a whole must not go unpunished and that their effective prosecution must be ensured by taking measures at the national level and by enhancing international cooperation,

Determined to put an end to impunity for the perpetrators of these crimes and thus to contribute to the prevention of such crimes,

Recalling that it is the duty of every State to exercise its criminal jurisdiction over those responsible for international crimes,

Reaffirming the Purposes and Principles of the Charter of the United Nations, and in particular that all States shall refrain from the threat or use of force against the territorial integrity or political independence of any State, or in any other manner inconsistent with the Purposes of the United Nations,

Emphasizing in this connection that nothing in this Statute shall be taken as authorizing any State Party to intervene in an armed conflict in the internal affairs of any State,

Determined to these ends and for the sake of present and future generations, to establish an independent permanent International Criminal Court in relationship with the United Nations system, with jurisdiction over the most serious crimes of concern to the international community as a whole,

Emphasizing that the International Criminal Court established under this Statute shall be complementary to national criminal jurisdictions,

Resolved to guarantee lasting respect for the enforcement of international justice,

Have agreed as follows:

PART 1: ESTABLISHMENT OF THE COURT

Article 1
The Court

An International Criminal Court ("the Court") is hereby established. It shall be a permanent institution and shall have the power to exercise its jurisdiction over persons for the most serious crimes of international concern as referred to in this Statute, and shall be complementary to national criminal jurisdictions. The jurisdiction and functioning of the Court shall be governed by the provisions of this Statute.

Article 2
Relationship of the Court with the United Nations

The Court shall be brought into relationship with the United Nations through an agreement to be approved by the Assembly of States Parties to this Statute and thereafter concluded by the President of the Court on its behalf.

Article 3
Seat of the Court

1. The seat of the Court shall be established at The Hague in the Netherlands ("the host State").

2. The Court shall enter into a headquarters agreement with the host State, to be approved by the Assembly of States Parties and thereafter concluded by the President of the Court on its behalf.

3. The Court may sit elsewhere, whenever it considers it desirable, as provided in this Statute.

Article 4
Legal Status and Powers of the Court

1. The Court shall have international legal personality. It shall also have such legal capacity as may be necessary for the exercise of its functions and the fulfilment of its purposes.

2. The Court may exercise its functions and powers, as provided in this Statute, on the territory of any State Party and, by special agreement, on the territory of any other State.

PART 2: JURISDICTION, ADMISSIBILITY, AND APPLICABLE LAW

Article 5
Crimes within the Jurisdiction of the Court

1. The jurisdiction of the Court shall be limited to the most serious crimes of concern to the international community as a whole. The Court has jurisdiction in accordance with this Statute with respect to the following crimes:

(a) The crime of genocide;

(b) Crimes against humanity;

(c) War crimes;

(d) The crime of aggression.

2. The Court shall exercise jurisdiction over the crime of aggression once a provision is adopted in accordance with articles 121 and 123 defining the crime and setting out the conditions under which the Court shall exercise jurisdiction with respect to this crime. Such a provision shall be consistent with the relevant provisions of the Charter of the United Nations.

Article 6
Genocide

For the purpose of this Statute, "genocide" means any of the following acts committed with intent to destroy, in whole or in part, a national, ethnical, racial or religious group, as such:

(a) Killing members of the group;

(b) Causing serious bodily or mental harm to members of the group;

(c) Deliberately inflicting on the group conditions of life calculated to bring about its physical destruction in whole or in part;

(d) Imposing measures intended to prevent births within the group;

(e) Forcibly transferring children of the group to another group.

Article 7
Crimes Against Humanity

1. For the purpose of this Statute, "crime against humanity" means any of the following acts when committed as part of a widespread or systematic attack directed against any civilian population, with knowledge of the attack:

(a) Murder;

(b) Extermination;

(c) Enslavement;

(d) Deportation or forcible transfer of population;

(e) Imprisonment or other severe deprivation of physical liberty in violation of fundamental rules of international law;

(f) Torture;

(g) Rape, sexual slavery, enforced prostitution, forced pregnancy, enforced sterilization, or any other form of sexual violence of comparable gravity;

(h) Persecution against any identifiable group or collectivity on political, racial, national, ethnic, cultural, religious, gender as defined in paragraph 3, or other grounds that are universally recognized as impermissible under international law, in connection with any act referred to in this paragraph or any crime within the jurisdiction of the Court;

(i) Enforced disappearance of persons;

(j) The crime of apartheid;

(k) Other inhumane acts of a similar character intentionally causing great suffering, or serious injury to body or to mental or physical health.

2. For the purpose of paragraph 1:

(a) "Attack directed against any civilian population" means a course of conduct involving the multiple commission of acts referred to in paragraph 1 against any civilian population, pursuant to or in furtherance of a State or organizational policy to commit such attack;

(b) "Extermination" includes the intentional infliction of conditions of life, inter alia the deprivation of access to food and medicine, calculated to bring about the destruction of part of a population;

(c) "Enslavement" means the exercise of any or all of the powers attaching to the right of ownership over a person and includes the exercise of such power in the course of trafficking in persons, in particular women and children;

(d) "Deportation or forcible transfer of population" means forced displacement of the persons concerned by expulsion or other coercive acts from the area in which they are lawfully present, without grounds permitted under international law;

(e) "Torture" means the intentional infliction of severe pain or suffering, whether physical or mental, upon a person in the custody or under the control of the accused; except that torture shall not include pain or suffering arising only from, inherent in or incidental to, lawful sanctions;

(f) "Forced pregnancy" means the unlawful confinement, of a woman forcibly made pregnant, with the intent of affecting the ethnic composition of any population or carrying out other grave violations of international law. This definition shall not in any way be interpreted as affecting national laws relating to pregnancy;

(g) "Persecution" means the intentional and severe deprivation of fundamental rights contrary to international law by reason of the identity of the group or collectivity;

(h) "The crime of apartheid" means inhumane acts of a character similar to those referred to in paragraph 1, committed in the context of an institutionalized regime of systematic oppression and domination by one racial group over any other racial group or groups and committed with the intention of maintaining that regime;

(i) "Enforced disappearance of persons" means the arrest, detention or abduction of persons by, or with the authorization, support or acquiescence of, a State or a political organization, followed by a refusal to acknowledge that deprivation of freedom or to give information on the fate or whereabouts of those persons, with the intention of removing them from the protection of the law for a prolonged period of time.

3. For the purpose of this Statute, it is understood that the term "gender" refers to the two sexes, male and female, within the context of society. The term "gender" does not indicate any meaning different from the above.

Article 8

War Crimes

1. The Court shall have jurisdiction in respect of war crimes in particular when committed as a part of a plan or policy or as part of a large-scale commission of such crimes.

2. For the purpose of this Statute, "war crimes" means:

(a) Grave breaches of the Geneva Conventions of 12 August 1949, namely, any of the following acts against persons or property protected under the provisions of the relevant Geneva Convention;

(i) Wilful killing;

(ii) Torture or inhuman treatment, including biological experiments;

(iii) Wilfully causing great suffering, or serious injury to body or health;

(iv) Extensive destruction and appropriation of property, not justified by military necessity and carried out unlawfully and wantonly;

(v) Compelling a prisoner of war or other protected person to serve in the forces of a hostile Power;

(vi) Wilfully depriving a prisoner of war or other protected person of the rights of fair and regular trial;

(vii) Unlawful deportation or transfer or unlawful confinement;

(viii) Taking of hostages.

(b) Other serious violations of the laws and customs applicable in international armed conflict, within the established framework of international law, namely, any of the following acts:

(i) Intentionally directing attacks against the civilian population as such or against individual civilians not taking direct part in hostilities;

(ii) Intentionally directing attacks against civilian objects, that is, objects which are not military objectives;

(iii) Intentionally directing attacks against personnel, installations, material, units or vehicles involved in a humanitarian assistance or peacekeeping mission in accordance with the Charter of the United Nations, as long as they are entitled to the protection given to civilians or civilian objects under the international law of armed conflict;

(iv) Intentionally launching an attack in the knowledge that such attack will cause incidental loss of life or injury to civilians or damage to civilian objects or widespread, long-term and severe damage to the natural environment which would be clearly excessive in relation to the concrete and direct overall military advantage anticipated;

(v) Attacking or bombarding, by whatever means, towns, villages, dwellings or buildings which are undefended and which are not military objectives;

(vi) Killing or wounding a combatant who, having laid down his arms or having no longer means of defence, has surrendered at discretion;

(vii) Making improper use of a flag of truce, of the flag or of the military insignia and uniform of the enemy or of the United Nations, as well as of the distinctive emblems of the Geneva Conventions, resulting in death or serious personal injury;

(viii) The transfer, directly or indirectly, by the Occupying Power of parts of its own civilian population into the territory it occupies, or the deportation or transfer of all of the population of the occupied territory within or outside this territory;

(ix) Intentionally directing attacks against buildings dedicated to religion, education, art, science or charitable purposes, historic monuments, hospitals and places where the sick and wounded are collected, provided they are not military objectives;

(x) Subjecting persons who are in the power of an adverse party to physical mutilation or to medical or scientific experiments of any kind which are neither justified by the medical, dental or hospital treatment of the person concerned nor carried out in his or her interest, and which cause death to or seriously endanger the health of such person or persons;

(xi) Killing or wounding treacherously individuals belonging to the hostile nation or army;

(xii) Declaring that no quarter will be given;

(xiii) Destroying or seizing the enemy's property unless such destruction or seizure be imperatively demanded by the necessities of war;

(xiv) Declaring abolished, suspended or inadmissible in a court of law the rights and actions of the nationals of the hostile party;

(xv) Compelling the nationals of the hostile party to take part in the operations of war directed against their own country, even if they were in the belligerent's service before the commencement of the war;

(xvi) Pillaging a town or place, even when taken by assault;

(xvii) Employing poison or poisoned weapons;

(xviii) Employing asphyxiating, poisonous or other gases, and all analogous liquids, materials or devices;

(xix) Employing bullets which expand or flatten easily in the human body, such as bullets with a hard envelope which does not entirely cover the core or is pierced with incisions;

(xx) Employing weapons, projectiles and material and methods of warfare which are of a nature to cause superfluous injury or unnecessary suffering or which are inherently indiscriminate in violation of the international law of armed conflict, provided that such weapons, projectiles and material and methods of warfare are the subject of a comprehensive prohibition and are included in an annex to this Statute, by an amendment in accordance with the relevant provisions set forth in articles 121 and 123;

(xxi) Committing outrages upon personal dignity, in particular humiliating and degrading treatment;

(xxii) Committing rape, sexual slavery, enforced prostitution, forced pregnancy, as defined in article 7, paragraph 2(f), enforced sterilization, or any other form of sexual violence also constituting a grave breach of the Geneva Conventions;

(xxiii) Utilizing the presence of a civilian or other protected person to render certain points, areas or military forces immune from military operations;

(xxiv) Intentionally directing attacks against buildings, material, medical units and transport, and personnel using the distinctive emblems of the Geneva

Conventions in conformity with international law;

(xxv) Intentionally using starvation of civilians as a method of warfare by depriving them of objects indispensable to their survival, including wilfully impeding relief supplies as provided for under the Geneva Conventions;

(xxvi) Conscripting or enlisting children under the age of fifteen years into the national armed forces or using them to participate actively in hostilities.

(c) In the case of an armed conflict not of an international character, serious violations of article 3 common to the four Geneva Conventions of 12 August 1949, namely, any of the following acts committed against persons taking no active part in the hostilities, including members of armed forces who have laid down their arms and those placed *hors de combat* by sickness, wounds, detention or any other cause:

(i) Violence to life and person, in particular murder of all kinds, mutilation, cruel treatment and torture;

(ii) Committing outrages upon personal dignity, in particular humiliating and degrading treatment;

(iii) Taking of hostages;

(iv) The passing of sentences and the carrying out of executions without previous judgement pronounced by a regularly constituted court, affording all judicial guarantees which are generally recognized as indispensable.

(d) Paragraph 2(c) applies to armed conflicts not of an international character and thus does not apply to situations of internal disturbances and tensions, such as riots, isolated and sporadic acts of violence or other acts of a similar nature.

(e) Other serious violations of the laws and customs applicable in armed conflicts not of an international character, within the established framework of international law, namely, any of the following acts:

(i) Intentionally directing attacks against the civilian population as such or against individual civilians not taking direct part in hostilities;

(ii) Intentionally directing attacks against buildings, material, medical units and transport, and personnel using the distinctive emblems of the Geneva Conventions in conformity with international law;

(iii) Intentionally directing attacks against personnel, installations, material, units or vehicles involved in a humanitarian assistance or peacekeeping mission in accordance with the Charter of the United Nations, as long as they are entitled to the protection given to civilians or civilian objects under the law of armed conflict;

(iv) Intentionally directing attacks against buildings dedicated to religion, education, art, science or charitable purposes, historic monuments, hospitals and places where the sick and wounded are collected, provided they are not military objectives;

(v) Pillaging a town or place, even when taken by assault;

(vi) Committing rape, sexual slavery, enforced prostitution, forced pregnancy, as defined in article 7, paragraph 2(f), enforced sterilization, and any other form of sexual violence also constituting a serious violation of article 3 common to the four Geneva Conventions;

(vii) Conscripting or enlisting children under the age of fifteen years into armed forces or groups or using them to participate actively in hostilities;

(viii) Ordering the displacement of the civilian population for reasons related to the conflict, unless the security of the civilians involved or imperative military reasons so demand;

(ix) Killing or wounding treacherously a combatant adversary;

(x) Declaring that no quarter will be given;

(xi) Subjecting persons who are in the power of another party to the conflict to physical mutilation or to medical or scientific experiments of any kind which are neither justified by the medical, dental or hospital treatment of the person concerned nor carried out in his or her interest, and which cause death to or seriously endanger the health of such person or persons;

(xii) Destroying or seizing the property of an adversary unless such destruction or seizure be imperatively demanded by the necessities of the conflict;

(f) Paragraph 2 (e) applies to armed conflicts not of an international character and thus does not apply to situations of internal disturbances and tensions, such as riots, isolated and sporadic acts of violence or other acts of a similar nature. It applies to armed conflicts that take place in the territory of a State when there is protracted armed conflict between governmental authorities and organized armed groups or between such groups.

3. Nothing in paragraphs 2(c) and (d) shall affect the responsibility of a Government to maintain or re-establish law and order in the State or to defend the unity and territorial integrity of the State, by all legitimate means.

Article 9
Elements of Crimes

1. Elements of Crimes shall assist the Court in the interpretation and application of articles 6, 7 and 8. They shall be adopted by a two-thirds majority of the members of the Assembly of States Parties.

2. Amendments to the Elements of Crimes may be proposed by:

(a) Any State Party;

(b) The judges acting by an absolute majority;

(c) The Prosecutor.

Such amendments shall be adopted by a two-thirds majority of the members of the Assembly of States Parties.

3. The Elements of Crimes and amendments thereto shall be consistent with this Statute.

Article 10

Nothing in this Part shall be interpreted as limiting or prejudicing in any way existing or developing rules of international law for purposes other than this Statute.

Article 11
Jurisdiction Ratione Temporis

1. The Court has jurisdiction only with respect to crimes committed after the entry into force of this Statute.

2. If a State becomes a Party to this Statute after its entry into force, the Court may exercise its jurisdiction only with respect to crimes committed after the entry into force of this Statute for that State, unless that State has made a declaration under article 12, paragraph 3.

Article 12
Preconditions to the Exercise of Jurisdiction

1. A State which becomes a Party to this Statute thereby accepts the jurisdiction of the Court with respect to the crimes referred to in article 5.

2. In the case of article 13, paragraph (a) or (c), the Court may exercise its jurisdiction if one or more of the following States are Parties to this Statute or have accepted the jurisdiction of the Court in accordance with paragraph 3:

(a) The State on the territory of which the conduct in question occurred or, if the crime was committed on board a vessel or aircraft, the State of registration of that vessel or aircraft;

(b) The State of which the person accused of the crime is a national.

3. If the acceptance of a State which is not a Party to this Statute is required under paragraph 2, that State may, by declaration lodged with the Registrar, accept the exercise of jurisdiction by the Court with respect to the crime in question. The accepting State shall cooperate with the Court without any delay or exception in accordance with Part 9.

Article 13
Exercise of Jurisdiction

The Court may exercise its jurisdiction with respect to a crime referred to in article 5 in accordance with the provisions of this Statute if:

(a) A situation in which one or more of such crimes appears to have been committed is referred to the Prosecutor by a State Party in accordance with article 14;

(b) A situation in which one or more of such crimes appears to have been committed is referred to the Prosecutor by the Security Council acting under Chapter VII of the Charter of the United Nations; or

(c) The Prosecutor has initiated an investigation in respect of such a crime in accordance with article 15.

Article 14
Referral of a Situation by a State Party

1. A State Party may refer to the Prosecutor a situation in which one or more crimes within the jurisdiction of the Court appear to have been committed requesting the Prosecutor to investigate the situation for the purpose of determining whether one or more specific persons should be charged with the commission of such crimes.

2. As far as possible, a referral shall specify the relevant circumstances and be accompanied by such supporting documentation as is available to the State referring the situation.

Article 15
Prosecutor

1. The Prosecutor may initiate investigations *proprio motu* on the basis of information on crimes within the jurisdiction of the Court.

2. The Prosecutor shall analyse the seriousness of the information received. For this purpose, he or she may seek additional information from States, organs of the United Nations, intergovernmental or non-governmental organizations, or other reliable sources that he or she deems appropriate, and may receive written or oral testimony at the seat of the Court.

3. If the Prosecutor concludes that there is a reasonable basis to proceed with an investigation, he or she shall submit to the Pre-Trial Chamber a request for authorization of an investigation, together with any supporting material collected. Victims may make representations to the Pre-Trial Chamber, in accordance with the Rules of Procedure and Evidence.

4. If the Pre-Trial Chamber, upon examination of the request and the supporting material, considers that there is a reasonable basis to proceed with an investigation, and that the case appears to fall within the jurisdiction of the Court, it shall authorize the commencement of the investigation, without prejudice to subsequent determinations by the Court with regard to the jurisdiction and admissibility of a case.

5. The refusal of the Pre-Trial Chamber to authorize the investigation shall not preclude the presentation of a subsequent request by the Prosecutor based on new facts or evidence regarding the same situation.

6. If, after the preliminary examination referred to in paragraphs 1 and 2, the Prosecutor concludes that the information provided does not constitute a reasonable basis for an investigation, he or she shall inform those who provided the information. This shall not preclude the Prosecutor from considering further information submitted to him or her regarding the same situation in the light of new facts or evidence.

Article 16
Deferral of Investigation or Prosecution

No investigation or prosecution may be commenced or proceeded with under this Statute for a period of 12 months after the Security Council, in a resolution adopted under Chapter VII of the Charter of the United Nations, has requested the Court to that effect; that request may be renewed by the Council under the same conditions.

Article 17
Issues of Admissibility

1. Having regard to paragraph 10 of the Preamble and article 1, the Court shall determine that a case is inadmissible where:

(a) The case is being investigated or prosecuted by a State which has jurisdiction over it, unless the State is unwilling or unable genuinely to carry out the investigation or prosecution;

(b) The case has been investigated by a State which has jurisdiction over it and the State has decided not to prosecute the person concerned, unless the decision resulted from the unwillingness or inability of the State genuinely to prosecute;

(c) The person concerned has already been tried for conduct which is the subject of the complaint, and a trial by the Court is not permitted under article 20, paragraph 3;

(d) The case is not of sufficient gravity to justify further action by the Court.

2. In order to determine unwillingness in a particular case, the Court shall consider, having regard to the principles of due process recognized by international law, whether one or more of the following exist, as applicable:

(a) The proceedings were or are being undertaken or the national decision was made for the purpose of shielding the person concerned from criminal responsibility for crimes within the jurisdiction of the Court referred to in article 5;

(b) There has been an unjustified delay in the proceedings which in the circumstances is inconsistent with an intent to bring the person concerned to justice;

(c) The proceedings were not or are not being conducted independently or impartially, and they were or are being conducted in a manner which, in the circumstances, is inconsistent with an intent to bring the person concerned to justice.

3. In order to determine inability in a particular case, the Court shall consider whether, due to a total or substantial collapse or unavailability of its national judicial system, the State is unable to obtain the accused or the necessary evidence and testimony or otherwise unable to carry out its proceedings.

Article 18
Preliminary Rulings Regarding Admissibility

1. When a situation has been referred to the Court pursuant to article 13(a) and the Prosecutor has determined that there would be a reasonable basis to commence an investigation, or the Prosecutor initiates an investigation pursuant to articles 13(c) and 15, the Prosecutor shall notify all States Parties and those States which, taking into account the information available, would normally exercise jurisdiction over the crimes concerned. The Prosecutor may notify such States on a confidential basis and, where the Prosecutor believes necessary to protect persons, prevent destruction of evidence or prevent the absconding of persons, may limit the scope of the information provided to States.

2. Within one month of receipt of that notice, a State may inform the Court that it is investigating or has investigated its nationals or others within its jurisdiction with respect to criminal acts which may constitute crimes referred to in article 5 and which relate to the information provided in the notification to States. At the request of that State, the Prosecutor shall defer to the State's investigation of those persons unless the Pre-Trial Chamber, on the application of the Prosecutor, decides to authorize the investigation.

3. The Prosecutor's deferral to a States investigation shall be open to review by the Prosecutor six months after the date of deferral or at any time when there has been a significant change of circumstances based on the State's unwillingness or inability genuinely to carry out the investigation.

4. The State concerned or the Prosecutor may appeal to the Appeals Chamber against a ruling of the Pre-Trial Chamber, in accordance with article 82, paragraph 2. The appeal may be heard on an expedited basis.

5. When the Prosecutor has deferred an investigation in accordance with paragraph 2, the Prosecutor may request that the State concerned periodically inform the Prosecutor of the progress of its investigations and any subsequent prosecutions. States Parties shall respond to such requests without undue delay.

6. Pending a ruling by the Pre-Trial Chamber, or at any time when the Prosecutor has deferred an investigation under this article, the Prosecutor may, on an exceptional basis, seek authority from the Pre-Trial Chamber to pursue necessary investigative steps for the purpose of preserving evidence where there is a unique opportunity to obtain important evidence or there is a significant risk that such evidence may not be subsequently available.

7. A State which has challenged a ruling of the Pre-Trial Chamber, under this article may challenge the admissibility of a case under article 19 on the grounds of additional significant facts or significant change of circumstances.

Article 19
Challenges to the Jurisdiction of the Court or the Admissibility of a Case

1. The Court shall satisfy itself that it has jurisdiction in any case brought before it. The Court may, on its own motion, determine the admissibility of a case in accordance with article 17.

2. Challenges to the admissibility of a case on the grounds referred to in article 17 or challenges to the jurisdiction of the Court may be made by:

(a) An accused or a person for whom a warrant of arrest or summons to appear has been issued under article 58;

(b) A State which has jurisdiction over a case, on the ground that it is investigating or prosecuting the case or has investigated or prosecuted; or

(c) A State from which acceptance of jurisdiction is required under article 12.

3. The Prosecutor may seek a ruling from the Court regarding a question of jurisdiction or admissibility. In proceedings with respect to jurisdiction or admissibility, those who have referred the situation under article 13 as well as victims, may also submit observations to the Court.

4. The admissibility of a case or the jurisdiction of the Court may be challenged only once by any person or State referred to in paragraph 2. The challenge shall take place prior to or at the commencement of the trial. In exceptional circumstances, the Court may grant leave for a challenge to be brought more than once or at a time later than the commencement of the trial.

Challenges to the admissibility of a case, at the commencement of a trial, or subsequently with the leave of the Court, may be based only on article 17, paragraph 1(c).

5. A State referred to in paragraph 2(b) and (c) shall make a challenge at the earliest opportunity.

6. Prior to the confirmation of the charges, challenges to the admissibility of a case or challenges to the jurisdiction of the Court shall be referred to the Pre-Trial

Chamber. After confirmation of the charges, they shall be referred to the Trial Chamber. Decisions with respect to jurisdiction or admissibility may be appealed to the Appeals Chamber in accordance with article 82.

7. If a challenge is made by a State referred to in paragraph 2(b) or (c), the Prosecutor shall suspend the investigation until such time as the Court makes a determination in accordance with article 17.

8. Pending a ruling by the Court, the Prosecutor may seek authority from the Court:

(a) To pursue necessary investigative steps of the kind referred to in article 18, paragraph 6;

(b) To take a statement or testimony from a witness or complete the collection and examination of evidence which had begun prior to the making of the challenge; and

(c) In cooperation with the relevant States, to prevent the absconding of persons in respect of whom the Prosecutor has already requested a warrant of arrest under article 58.

9. The making of a challenge shall not affect the validity of any act performed by the Prosecutor or any order or warrant issued by the Court prior to the making of the challenge.

10. If the Court has decided that a case is inadmissible under article 17, the Prosecutor may submit a request for a review of the decision when he or she is fully satisfied that new facts have arisen which negate the basis on which the case had previously been found inadmissible under article 17.

11. If the Prosecutor, having regard to the matters referred to in article 17, defers an investigation, the Prosecutor may request that the relevant State make available to the Prosecutor information on the proceedings. That information shall, at the request of the State concerned, be confidential. If the Prosecutor thereafter decides to proceed with an investigation, he or she shall notify the State in respect of the proceedings of which deferral has taken place.

Article 20
Ne Bis in Idem

1. Except as provided in this Statute, no person shall be tried before the Court with respect to conduct which formed the basis of crimes for which the person has been convicted or acquitted by the Court.

2. No person shall be tried before another court for a crime referred to in article 5 for which that person has already been convicted or acquitted by the Court.

3. No person who has been tried by another court for conduct also proscribed under articles 6, 7 or 8 shall be tried by the Court with respect to the same conduct unless the proceedings in the other court:

(a) Were for the purpose of shielding the person concerned from criminal responsibility for crimes within the jurisdiction of the Court; or

(b) otherwise were not conducted independently or impartially in. accordance with the norms of due process recognized by international law and were conducted in a manner which, in the circumstances, was inconsistent with an intent to bring the person concerned to justice.

Article 21
Applicable Law

1. The Court shall apply:

(a) In the first place, this Statute, Elements of Crimes and its Rules of Procedure and Evidence;

(b) In the second place, where appropriate, applicable treaties and the principles and rules of international law, including the established principles of the international law of armed conflict;

(c) Failing that, general principles of law derived by the Court from national laws of legal systems of the world including, as appropriate, the national laws of States that would normally exercise jurisdiction over the crime, provided that those principles are not inconsistent with this Statute and with international law and internationally recognized norms and standards.

2. The Court may apply principles and rules of law as interpreted in its previous decisions.

3. The application and interpretation of law pursuant to this article must be consistent with internationally recognized human rights, and be without any adverse distinction founded on grounds such as gender, as defined in article 7, paragraph 3, age, race, colour, language, religion or belief, political or other opinion, national, ethnic or social origin, wealth, birth or other status.

PART 3: GENERAL PRINCIPLES OF CRIMINAL LAW

Article 22
Nullum Crimen Sine Lege

1. A person shall not be criminally responsible under this Statute unless the conduct in question constitutes, at the time it takes place, a crime within the jurisdiction of the Court.

2. The definition of a crime shall be strictly construed and shall not be extended by analogy. In case of ambiguity, the definition shall be interpreted in favour of the person being investigated, prosecuted or convicted.

3. This article shall not affect the characterization of any conduct as criminal under international law independently of this Statute.

Article 23
Nulla Poena Sine Lege

A person convicted by the Court may be punished only in accordance with this Statute.

Article 24
Non-retroactivity Ratione Personae

1. No person shall be criminally responsible under this Statute for conduct prior to the entry into force of the Statute.

2. In the event of a change in the law applicable to a given case prior to a final judgement, the law more favourable to the person being investigated, prosecuted or convicted shall apply.

Article 25
Individual Criminal Responsibility

1. The Court shall have jurisdiction over natural persons pursuant to this Statute.

2. A person who commits a crime within the jurisdiction of the Court shall be individually responsible and liable for punishment in accordance with this Statute.

3. In accordance with this Statute, a person shall be criminally responsible and liable for punishment for a crime within the jurisdiction of the Court if that person:

(a) Commits such a crime, whether as an individual, jointly with another or through another person, regardless of whether that other person is criminally responsible;

(b) Orders, solicits or induces the commission of such a crime which in fact occurs or is attempted;

(c) For the purpose of facilitating the commission of such a crime, aids, abets or otherwise assists in its commission or its attempted commission including providing the means for its commission;

(d) In any other way contributes to the commission or attempted commission of such a crime by a group of persons acting with a common purpose. Such contribution shall be intentional and shall either:

(i) Be made with the aim of furthering the criminal activity or criminal purpose of the group, where such activity or purpose involves the commission of a crime within the jurisdiction of the Court; or

(ii) Be made in the knowledge of the intention of the group to commit the crime;

(e) In respect of the crime of genocide, directly and publicly incites others to commit genocide;

(f) Attempts to commit such a crime by taking action that commences its execution by means of a substantial step, but the crime does not occur because of circumstances independent of the person's intentions. However, a person who abandons the effort to commit the crime or otherwise prevents the completion of the crime shall not be liable for punishment under this Statute for the attempt to commit that crime if that person completely and voluntarily gave up the criminal purpose.

4. No provision in this Statute relating to individual criminal responsibility shall affect the responsibility of States under international law.

Article 26
Exclusion of Jurisdiction over Persons under Eighteen

The Court shall have no jurisdiction over any person who was under the age of 18 at the time of the alleged commission of a crime.

Article 27
Irrelevance of Official Capacity

1. This Statute shall apply equally to all persons without any distinction based on official capacity. In particular, official capacity as a Head of State or Government, a member of a Government or parliament, an elected representative or a government official shall in no case exempt a person from criminal responsibility under this Statute, nor shall it, in and of itself, constitute a ground for reduction of sentence.

2. Immunities or special procedural rules which may attach to the official capacity of a person, whether under national or international law, shall not bar the Court from exercising its jurisdiction over such a person.

Article 28
Responsibility of Commanders and Other Superiors

In addition to other grounds of criminal responsibility under this Statute for crimes within the jurisdiction of the Court:

1. A military commander or person effectively acting as a military commander shall be criminally responsible for crimes within the jurisdiction of the Court committed by forces under his or her effective command and control, or effective authority and control as the case may be, as a result of his or her failure to exercise control properly over such forces, where:

   (a) That military commander or person either knew or, owing to the circumstances at the time, should have known that the forces were committing or about to commit such crimes; and

   (b) That military commander or person failed to take all necessary and reasonable measures within his or her power to prevent or repress their commission or to submit the matter to the competent authorities for investigation and prosecution.

2. With respect to superior and subordinate relationships not described in paragraph 1, a superior shall be criminally responsible for crimes within the jurisdiction of the Court committed by subordinates under his or her effective authority and control, as a result of his or her failure to exercise control properly over such subordinates, where:

   (a) The superior either knew, or consciously disregarded information which clearly indicated, that the subordinates were committing or about to commit such, crimes;

   (b) The crimes concerned activities that were within the effective responsibility and control of the superior; and

   (c) The superior failed to take all necessary and reasonable measures within his or her power to prevent or repress their commission or to submit the matter to the competent authorities for investigation and prosecution.

Article 29
Non-applicability of Statute of Limitations

The crimes within the jurisdiction of the Court shall not be subject to any statute of limitations.

Article 30
Mental Element

1. Unless otherwise provided, a person shall be criminally responsible and liable for punishment for a crime within the jurisdiction of the Court only if the material elements are committed with intent and knowledge.

2. For the purposes of this article, a person has intent where:

(a) In relation to conduct, that person means to engage in the conduct;

(b) In relation to a consequence, that person means to cause that consequence or is aware that it will occur in the ordinary course of events.

3. For the purposes of this article, "knowledge" means awareness that a circumstance exists or a consequence will occur in the ordinary course of events. "Know" and "knowingly," shall be construed accordingly.

Article 31
Grounds for Excluding Criminal Responsibility

1. In addition to other grounds for excluding criminal responsibility provided for in this Statute, a person shall not be criminally responsible if, at the time of that person's conduct:

(a) The person suffers from a mental disease or defect that destroys that person's capacity to appreciate the unlawfulness or nature of his or her conduct, or capacity to control his or her conduct to conform to the requirements of law;

(b) The person is in a state of intoxication that destroys that person's capacity to appreciate the unlawfulness or nature of his or her conduct, or capacity to control his or her conduct to conform to the requirements of law, unless the person has become voluntarily intoxicated under such circumstances that the person knew, or disregarded the risk, that, as a result of the intoxication, he or she was likely to engage in conduct constituting a crime within the jurisdiction of the Court;

(c) The person acts reasonably to defend himself or herself or another person or, in the case of war crimes, property which is essential for the survival of the person or another person or property which is essential for accomplishing a military mission, against an imminent and unlawful use of force in a manner proportionate to the degree of danger to the person or the other person or property protected. The fact that the person was involved in a defensive operation conducted by forces shall not in itself constitute a ground for excluding criminal responsibility under this subparagraph;

(d) The conduct which is alleged to constitute a crime within the jurisdiction of the Court has been caused by duress resulting from a threat of imminent death or of continuing or imminent serious bodily harm against that person or another person, and the person acts necessarily and reasonably to avoid this threat, provided that the person does not intend to cause a greater harm than the one sought to be avoided. Such a threat may either be:

    (i) Made by other persons; or

    (ii) Constituted by other circumstances beyond that person's control.

2. The Court shall determine the applicability of the grounds for excluding criminal responsibility provided for in this Statute to the case before it.

3. At trial, the Court may consider a ground for excluding criminal responsibility other than those referred to in paragraph 1 where such a ground is derived from applicable law as set forth in article 21. The procedures relating to the consideration of such a ground shall be provided for in the Rules of Procedure and Evidence.

Article 32
Mistake of Fact or Mistake of Law

1. A mistake of fact shall be a ground for excluding criminal responsibility only if it negates the mental element required by the crime.

2. A mistake of law as to whether a particular type of conduct is a crime within the jurisdiction of the Court shall not be a ground for excluding criminal responsibility. A mistake of law may, however, be a ground for excluding criminal responsibility if it negates the mental element required by such a crime, or as provided for in article 33.

Article 33
Superior Orders and Prescription of Law

1. The fact that a crime within the jurisdiction of the Court has been committed by a person pursuant to an order of a Government or of a superior, whether military or civilian, shall not relieve that person of criminal responsibility unless:

    (a) The person was under a legal obligation to obey orders of the Government or the superior in question;

    (b) The person did not know that the order was unlawful; and

    (c) The order was not manifestly unlawful.

2. For the purposes of this article, orders to commit genocide or crimes against humanity are manifestly unlawful.

PART 4: COMPOSITION AND ADMINISTRATION OF THE COURT

Article 34
Organs of the Court

The Court shall be composed of the following organs:

    (a) The Presidency;

    (b) An Appeals Division, a Trial Division and a Pre-Trial Division;

    (c) The Office of the Prosecutor;

    (d) The Registry.

Article 35
Service of Judges

1. All judges shall be elected as full-time members of the Court and shall be available to serve on that basis from the commencement of their terms of office.

2. The judges composing the Presidency shall serve on a full-time basis as soon as they are elected.

3. The Presidency may, on the basis of the workload of the Court and in consultation with its members, decide from time to time to what extent the remaining judges shall be required to serve on a full-time basis. Any such arrangement shall be without prejudice to the provisions of article 40. ...

Article 48
Privileges and Immunities

1. The Court shall enjoy in the territory of each State Party such privileges and immunities as are necessary for the fulfilment of its purposes.

2. The judges, the Prosecutor, the Deputy Prosecutors and the Registrar shall, when engaged on or with respect to the business of the Court, enjoy the same privileges and immunities as are accorded to heads of diplomatic missions and shall, after the expiry of their terms of office, continue to be accorded immunity from legal process of every kind in respect of words spoken or written and acts performed by them in their official capacity.

3. The Deputy Registrar, the staff of the Office of the Prosecutor and the staff of the Registry shall enjoy the privileges and immunities and facilities necessary for the performance of their functions, in accordance with the agreement on the privileges and immunities of the Court.

4. Counsel, experts, witnesses or any other person required to be present at the seat of the Court shall be accorded such treatment as is necessary for the proper functioning of the Court, in accordance with the agreement on the privileges and immunities of the Court. ...

Article 51
Rules of Procedure and Evidence

1. The Rules of Procedure and Evidence shall enter into force upon adoption by a two-thirds majority of the members of the Assembly of States Parties.

2. Amendments to the Rules of Procedure and Evidence may be proposed by:
   (a) Any State Party;
   (b) The judges acting by an absolute majority; or
   (c) The Prosecutor.
Such amendments shall enter into force upon adoption by a two-thirds majority of the members of the Assembly of States Parties.

3. After the adoption of the Rules of Procedure and Evidence, in urgent cases where the Rules do not provide for a specific situation before the Court, the judges may, by a two-thirds majority, draw up provisional Rules to be applied until adopted, amended or rejected at the next ordinary or special session of the Assembly of States Parties. ...

5. In the event of conflict between the Statute and the Rules of Procedure and Evidence, the Statute shall prevail. ...

PART 5: INVESTIGATION AND PROSECUTION

Article 53
Initiation of an Investigation

1. The Prosecutor shall, having evaluated the information made available to him or her, initiate an investigation unless he or she determines that there is no reasonable basis to proceed under this Statute. In deciding whether to initiate an investigation, the Prosecutor shall consider whether:

(a) The information available to the Prosecutor provides a reasonable basis to believe that a crime within the jurisdiction of the Court has been or is being committed;

(b) The case is or would be admissible under article 17; and

(c) Taking into account the gravity of the crime and the interests of victims, there are nonetheless substantial reasons to believe that an investigation would not serve the interests of justice.

If the Prosecutor determines that there is no reasonable basis to proceed and his or her determination is based solely on subparagraph (c) above, he or she shall inform the Pre-Trial Chamber.

2. If, upon investigation, the Prosecutor concludes that there is not a sufficient basis for a prosecution because:

(a) There is not a sufficient legal or factual basis to seek a warrant or summons under article 58;

(b) The case is inadmissible under article 17; or

(c) A prosecution is not in the interests of justice, taking into account all the circumstances, including the gravity of the crime, the interests of victims and the age or infirmity of the alleged perpetrator, and his or her role in the alleged crime; the Prosecutor shall inform the Pre-Trial Chamber and the State making a referral under article 14 or the Security Council in a case under article 13, paragraph (b), of his or her conclusion and the reasons for the conclusion.

3.(a) At the request of the State making a referral under article 14 or the Security Council under article 13, paragraph (b), the Pre-Trial Chamber may review a decision of the Prosecutor under paragraph 1 or 2 not to proceed and may request the Prosecutor to reconsider that decision.

(b) In addition, the Pre-Trial Chamber may, on its own initiative, review a decision of the Prosecutor not to proceed if it is based solely on paragraph 1(c) or 2(c). In such a case, the decision of the Prosecutor shall be effective only if confirmed by the Pre-Trial Chamber.

4. The Prosecutor may, at any time, reconsider a decision whether to initiate an investigation or prosecution based on new facts or information. ...

PART 6: THE TRIAL

...

Article 66
Presumption of Innocence

1. Everyone shall be presumed innocent until proved guilty before the Court in accordance with the applicable law.

2. The onus is on the Prosecutor to prove the guilt of the accused.

3. In order to convict the accused, the Court must be convinced of the guilt of the accused beyond reasonable doubt.

Article 67
Rights of the Accused

1. In the determination of any charge, the accused shall be entitled to a public hearing, having regard to the provisions of this Statute, to a fair hearing conducted impartially, and to the following minimum guarantees, in full equality:

(a) To be informed promptly and in detail of the nature, cause and content of the charge, in a language which the accused fully understands and speaks;

(b) To have adequate time and facilities for the preparation of the defence and to communicate freely with counsel of the accused's choosing in confidence;

(c) To be tried without undue delay;

(d) Subject to article 63, paragraph 2 [concerning disruption of the trial by the accused], to be present at trial, to conduct the defence in person or through legal assistance of the accused's choosing ... .

(g) Not to be compelled to testify or to confess guilt and to remain silent, without such silence being a consideration in the determination of guilt or innocence; ...

Article 75
Reparation to Victims

1. The Court shall establish principles relating to reparations to, or in respect of, victims, including restitution, compensation and rehabilitation. ...

2. The Court may make an order directly against a convicted person specifying appropriate reparations ... . Where appropriate, the Court may order the award for reparations be made through the Trust Fund provided for in Article 79. ...

[The Trust Fund has been established by decision of the Assembly of States Parties. The Court is able to order money or other property collected through fines or forfeiture to be transferred to the Trust Fund.]

PART 9: INTERNATIONAL COOPERATION AND JUDICIAL ASSISTANCE

Article 86
General Obligation To Cooperate

States Parties shall, in accordance with the provisions of this Statute, cooperate fully with the Court in its investigation and prosecution of crimes within the jurisdiction of the Court.

Article 87
Requests for Cooperation: General Provisions

1.(a) The Court shall have the authority to make requests to States Parties for cooperation. The requests shall be transmitted through the diplomatic channel or any other appropriate channel as may be designated by each State Party upon ratification, acceptance, approval or accession. ...

7. Where a State Party fails to comply with a request to cooperate by the Court contrary to the provisions of this Statute, thereby preventing the Court from exercising its functions and powers under this Statute, the Court may make a finding to that effect and refer the matter to the Assembly of States Parties or, where the Security Council referred the matter to the Court, to the Security Council.

Article 88
Availability of Procedures under National Law

States Parties shall ensure that there are procedures available under their national law for all of the forms of cooperation which are specified under this Part.

Article 89
Surrender of Persons to the Court

1. The Court may transmit a request for the arrest and surrender of a person, together with the material supporting the request outlined in article 91, to any State on the territory of which that person may be found and shall request the cooperation of that State in the arrest and surrender of such a person. States Parties shall, in accordance with the provisions of this Part and the procedure under their national law, comply with requests for arrest and surrender. ...

Article 90
Competing Requests

1. A State Party which receives a request from the Court for the surrender of a person under article 89 shall, if it also receives a request from any other State for the extradition of the same person for the same conduct which forms the basis of the crime for which the Court seeks the person's surrender, notify the Court and the requesting State of that fact.

2. Where the requesting State is a State Party, the requested State shall give priority to the request from the Court if:

(a) The Court has, pursuant to article 18 or 19, made a determination that the case in respect of which surrender is sought is admissible and that determination takes into account the investigation or prosecution conducted by the requesting State in respect of its request for extradition; or

(b) The Court makes the determination described in subparagraph (a) pursuant to the requested State's notification under paragraph 1.

3. Where a determination under paragraph 2(a) has not been made, the requested State may, at its discretion, pending the determination of the Court under paragraph 2(b), proceed to deal with the request for extradition from the requesting State but shall not extradite the person until the Court has determined that the case is inadmissible. The Court's determination shall be made on an expedited basis.

4. If the requesting State is a State not Party to this Statute the requested State, if it is not under an international obligation to extradite the person to the requesting State, shall give priority to the request for surrender from the Court, if the Court has determined that the case is admissible. ...

Article 93
Other Forms of Cooperation

1. States Parties shall, in accordance with the provisions of this Part and under procedures of national law, comply with requests by the Court to provide the following assistance in relation to investigations or prosecutions:

(a) The identification and whereabouts of persons or the location of items;

(b) The taking of evidence, including testimony under oath, and the production of evidence, including expert opinions and reports necessary to the Court;

(c) The questioning of any person being investigated or prosecuted;

(d) The service of documents, including judicial documents;

(e) Facilitating the voluntary appearance of persons as witnesses or experts before the Court;

(f) The temporary transfer of persons as provided in paragraph 7;

(g) The examination of places or sites, including the exhumation and examination of grave sites;

(h) The execution of searches and seizures;

(i) The provision of records and documents, including official records and documents;

(j) The protection of victims and witnesses and the preservation of evidence;

(k) The identification, tracing and freezing or seizure of proceeds, property and assets and instrumentalities of crimes for the purpose of eventual forfeiture, without prejudice to the rights of bona fide third parties; and

(l) Any other type of assistance which is not prohibited by the law of the requested State, with a view to facilitating the investigation and prosecution of crimes within the jurisdiction of the Court. ...

Article 98
Cooperation with Respect to Waiver of Immunity and Consent To Surrender

1. The Court may not proceed with a request for surrender or assistance which would require the requested State to act inconsistently with its obligations under international law with respect to the State or diplomatic immunity of a person or property of a third State, unless the Court can first obtain the cooperation of that third State for the waiver of the immunity.

2. The Court may not proceed with a request for surrender which would require the requested State to act inconsistently with its obligations under international agreements pursuant to which the consent of a sending State is required to surrender a person of that State to the Court, unless the Court can first obtain the cooperation of the sending State for the giving of consent for the surrender. ...

Article 102
Use of Terms

For the purposes of this Statute:

(a) "surrender" means the delivering up of a person by a State to the Court, pursuant to this Statute.

(b) "extradition" means the delivering up of a person by one State to another as provided by treaty, convention or national legislation. ...

PART 11: ASSEMBLY OF STATES PARTIES

Article 112
Assembly of States Parties

1. An Assembly of States Parties to this Statute is hereby established. Each State Party shall have one representative in the Assembly who may be accompanied by alternates and advisers. Other States which have signed this Statute or the Final Act may be observers in the Assembly.

2. The Assembly shall:

(a) Consider and adopt, as appropriate, recommendations of the Preparatory Commission;

(b) Provide management oversight to the Presidency, the Prosecutor and the Registrar regarding the administration of the Court;

(c) Consider the reports and activities of the Bureau established under paragraph 3 and take appropriate action in regard thereto;

(d) Consider and decide the budget for the Court;

(e) Decide whether to alter, in accordance with article 36, the number of judges;

(f) Consider ... any question relating to non-cooperation;

(g) Perform any other function consistent with this Statute or the Rules of Procedure and Evidence. ...

5. The President of the Court, the Prosecutor and the Registrar or their representatives may participate, as appropriate, in meetings of the Assembly ... .

7. Each State Party shall have one vote. Every effort shall be made to reach decisions by consensus in the Assembly and in the Bureau. If consensus cannot be reached, except as otherwise provided in the Statute:

(a) Decisions on matters of substance must be approved by a two-thirds majority of those present and voting provided that an absolute majority of States Parties constitutes the quorum for voting;

(b) Decisions on matters of procedure shall be taken by a simple majority of States Parties present and voting.

NOTES

1) The Rome Statute was adopted with 120 states voting in favour, 7 voting against, and 21 abstentions. The United States called for an unrecorded vote in the final plenary on July 17, 1998. It is surmised that the 7 states voting against were the United States, China, Iraq, Israel, Libya, Qatar, and Yemen. The ICC came into operation on July 1, 2002, following the deposit of the 60th instrument of ratification. As of November 2005, 139 states had signed and 99 had ratified the Rome Statute, including Canada. In September 2002, the Assembly of States Parties adopted the Rules of Evidence and Procedure, the Elements of Crimes, and the Agreement on Privileges and Immunities of the Court. Pursuant to Article 2 of the Rome Statute, an agreement on the relationship between the Court and the United Nations has also been concluded between the President and the Secretary-General.

2) The 18 judges were elected by the Assembly of States Parties in February 2003.[48] Article 36(3) provides that the candidates for election shall have "established competence in criminal law and procedure, and the necessary relevant experience, whether as judge, prosecutor, advocate or in other similar capacity, in criminal proceedings" (List A candidates) or have "established competence in relevant areas of international law such as international humanitarian law and the law of human rights, and extensive experience in a professional legal capacity which is of relevance to the judicial work of the Court" (List B candidates). In the first election states parties were instructed to comply with the following voting requirements or their ballots would be declared invalid: under Article 36(7) no two judges may be of the same nationality; under Article 36(4) only nationals of states parties may be elected.

3) The Chief Prosecutor, Luis Moreno-Ocampo from Argentina, was elected by the same body in 2003.

4) There were many controversial issues—in fact, many make-or-break provisions—in the negotiating text. The following extract documents some of them.

---

48   Canadian Philippe Kirsch, who chaired the Committee of the Whole at the Rome Conference, was elected
      as a judge for a six-year term and subsequently was selected by the Judges as President for a two-year term.

Core Crimes in the Rome Statute

from Sharon A. Williams, "The Core Crimes in the Rome Statute on the
International Criminal Court" in The International Centre for Criminal Reform and
Criminal Justice Policy, *The Changing Face of International Criminal Law:
Selected Papers* (2001) at 63-72[49] (footnotes omitted with some additions)

There is broad consensus that an independent, just and effective international criminal court (ICC) is an imperative for the twenty first century. The ICC will have jurisdiction over some of the most serious international crimes, namely genocide, crimes against humanity, war crimes and aggression once a definition has been agreed upon. Its value is not only in prosecuting and punishing perpetrators of these crimes, but also in its deterrence capability. An impartial ICC with an independent Prosecutor's office will hopefully discourage those who seek to instigate and carry out barbarous atrocities in violation of international law. The major challenge for the international community is to make it truly effective, by global ratification, implementation domestically and fulfillment of obligations in good faith. ...

The philosophical and practical underpinnings of the court may be seen as deterrence, prosecution, justice for victims and promotion of peace and stability and reconciliation. The goal is to replace impunity with accountability and protect the fundamentals of human dignity. ...

Why has it taken so long for the international community to agree on the need to establish an ICC? Amongst the apparent obstacles was a reluctance to yield up any element of sovereignty to an international court, nationalistic pride in the superiority of domestic law, reticence to participate in establishing another international institution, problems on obtaining consensus on subject matter jurisdiction, applicable substantive and procedural rules and lastly the cost. ...

The negotiations on the crimes listed in article 5 were among some of the most delicate issues at the Rome Conference. One of the major guiding principles was that the crimes be reflective of customary international law and be limited to the most serious crimes of international concern to the international community as a whole. This latter provision appearing in the Preamble [article 1] and article 5 meant that the crimes had to be universally recognized. ...

[T]he crimes listed in article 5 ... are intimately connected with article 12 on preconditions to the exercise of jurisdiction by the court, article 13 on exercise of jurisdiction, and article 17 on complementarity. According to article 11 the ICC has jurisdiction only over crimes committed after the entry into force of the Statute. ... Even though the principle of legality, as contained in the *nullem crimen sine lege* rule [article 22], would be complied with when conduct is not retroactively being criminalized but it is simply an exercise of jurisdiction taken retrospectively, this temporal restriction was necessary to gain the wide support of states.

---

49   See also S.A. Williams, *supra* note 43; "Jurisdiction Ratione Temporis" in O. Triffterer, ed., *supra* note 43 at 323-28; "Article 12 Preconditions to the Exercise of Jurisdiction," in Triffterer *ibid.* at 329-42; "Article 13 Exercise of Jurisdiction" in Triffterer, *ibid.* at 343-52 and "Article 17 Issues of Admissibility" in Triffterer *ibid.* at 383-97.

The conference achieved the impossible in many ways, given the approximately 1,300 square brackets in the negotiating text indicating bones of contention, some of which were fundamental. The final text adopted in Rome is indicative of what was possible at the time. It is true that there are weaknesses but there are also many real successes. The Statute is a compromise that endeavours to satisfy many of the interests that were in operation in the Rome Conference and before and to make it acceptable to the majority of states.

Containing 128 articles, the Statute is an intricately woven package-deal. The core crimes cannot be looked at without note being taken of the vital importance to a credible and effective court of impartial investigations and an independent prosecutor who may initiate them *proprio motu* with certain inbuilt checks and balances [article 15]. Thus, the prosecutorial scheme does not depend solely on the initiation of investigations and consequent prosecutions by states parties [article 14] and the United Nations Security Council [article 13(b)]. As well, there are provisions for the due process of the accused [articles 66-67] and victims' rights [article 68]. There is no statute of limitations [article 29] and no reservations are allowed [article 120].

On the other hand, it would be naïve to suggest that there are not weaknesses in the Statute. ... Certain states and most NGOs pressed for the ICC to have universal jurisdiction or a variant thereof, over the listed crimes. In other words the ICC would have jurisdiction over a core crime as long as one or more of four directly involved states had consented by being a state party, that is the territorial state, the states of nationality of the perpetrator or the victim or the custodial state. However, at the end of the conference the result was restrictive preconditions in the final text of article 12. ... Until the final hours in Rome article 12 remained a make or break provision and still even today retains its notoriety. However, it must be understood that some states had pushed for tighter restrictions insisting on the necessity for the acceptance by the state of nationality of the accused or even the stricter requirement of acceptance conjunctively from a list of all involved states. Article 12 in its final form is the accommodation that was struck. There is also the transitional seven-year "opt out" provision for war crimes [article 124] and a renewable ability for the Security Council to block an investigation by the Prosecutor for twelve months, when it is acting under Chapter VII of the U.N. Charter [in article 16. See the example of such a resolution that follows this extract.] ...

Article 6 defines genocide. This turned out to be the least problematic crime and is defined in accordance with article II of the 1948 Convention on the Prevention and Punishment of Genocide [reproduced above in Section A.3]. ...

Article 7 on crimes against humanity ... clearly goes far beyond what is contained in the Nuremberg, Tokyo, ICTY and ICTR definitions ... . The final text of article 7, similar to genocide criminalizes the enumerated conduct in peacetime as well as in armed conflicts ... . The threshold set is that the conduct must be part of a "widespread or systematic attack directed against any civilian population." There must also be knowledge of the attack. Discriminatory intent is only required as an element of the crime of persecution contained in article 7(1)(h). Little consensus existed before Rome on these matters. The "widespread or systematic" requirement accords with customary international law and has been followed in the jurisprudence of the ICTY. It ensures that isolated or random acts are not encompassed. ...

Eleven offences are enumerated. These include not only those contained in the IMT Charters but also add the following: forcible transfer of population is added to deportation, imprisonment or other severe deprivation of physical liberty in violation of fundamental rules of international law, torture, rape, sexual slavery, enforced prostitution, forced pregnancy, enforced sterilization or any other form of sexual violence of comparable gravity, enforced disappearance of persons and apartheid. The express inclusion of crimes of sexual violence was a major accomplishment. It was understood that rape had been covered in the Nuremberg and Tokyo Charters by reference to "other inhumane acts." Following the lead in the ICTY and ICTR Statutes, the Rome Statute now explicitly provides for rape as well as the [other] gender based crimes. It was an important mission to have these crimes defined as criminal acts and not subsumed under classifications such as those dealing with violations of honour and dignity and humiliating and degrading treatment. Forced pregnancy was acutely controversial as some delegations had feared that the aim was to impose on states an obligation to provide access to abortion to forcibly impregnated women. The consensus that was reached was based on language added to the definitional paragraph and now contained in article 7(2)(f). Thus, for forced pregnancy there must be the unlawful confinement of a woman made pregnant forcibly. There must have been the intent of affecting the ethnic composition of any population or carrying out other grave violations of international law. In order to eliminate the concerns of Catholic and Arab states, a final sentence was added which states that "This definition shall not in any way be interpreted as affecting national laws relating to pregnancy." A similar provision is also found in article 8 on war crimes. ...

Article 8 on war crimes does not follow the simple Nuremberg model. It is a complex article containing fifty crimes. ... The Statute applies not only to international armed conflicts, but also to internal conflicts.

NOTES

1) Compare the definitions of the three core classes of crimes in articles 6-8 of the Rome Statute with their specifications in the Statutes of the ICTY and ICTR and the Genocide Convention, reproduced above in Sections B and A.2 respectively. How have these crimes become elaborated? Note that article 124 of the Rome Statute allows a state on becoming a party to defer application of article 8 on war crimes for seven years. In fact, very few signatories, notably France, have taken advantage of this option.

2) The crime of aggression, listed in article 5, is not yet defined; indeed, much difficulty is being encountered in doing so because of its link to state aggression and the inevitable political involvement of the Security Council that entails.[50]

---

50   See M. Politi & G. Nesi, eds., *The International Criminal Court and the Crime of Aggression* (2004); M Schuster, "The Rome Statute and the Crime of Aggression: A Gordian Knot in Search of a Sword" (2003) 14 Crim. L. Forum 17.

3) Concerning the initiation of proceedings by the Prosecutor under article 13, what are the checks and balances on his powers? Review articles 15-18 and 53. How are his powers affected if an accused claims the benefit of a state-granted amnesty? Consider article 53.

United States' Position Toward the Court

Article 12 of the Rome Statute, as discussed above, limits the ability of the ICC to take jurisdiction. When alleged core crimes have been committed on the territory of a non-party state, by nationals of that state or of another non-party state, the ICC has no jurisdiction unless there is a referral of the situation by the Security Council. The United States was never happy with these conditions. In Rome, at the proverbial 11th hour on July 17, 1998, the United States proposed an amendment to article 12 to permit the ICC to assert jurisdiction over nationals of a non-party state only when the state consented. Since the amendment was resoundingly defeated by a no-action motion, adopted by 113 in favour to 17 against with 25 abstentions, it seemed unlikely that the United States would sign the Statute. It considered the Statute fundamentally flawed. Yet, on December 31, 2000, the Clinton administration, in one of its final acts, did deposit the signature of the United States. However, with the new administration of President George W. Bush in place, on May 6, 2002, the United States government delivered a letter to Secretary-General Kofi Annan, in which formal notice was given that the United States had no intention of becoming a party. This act has been dubbed the "unsigning" of the Rome Statute. Consider article 18 of the 1969 Vienna Convention on the Law of Treaties. Does it sanction such a step?

Refer to article 17 of the Rome Statute on complementarity. Why do you think its inclusion has not assuaged the fears of the United States concerning a politically motivated prosecutor, court, and state party referrals? How would you interpret "unwilling" or "unable" genuinely to investigate and prosecute in article 17?

The United States has pursued two lines of action toward the new court. First, it has negotiated a growing series of bilateral treaties, numbering about 100 in June 2005, with both party and non-party states, that provide that United States personnel will not be surrendered to the ICC. These have been labelled article 98(2) agreements. Was article 98 included in the Statute for such a purpose? How do you think the ICC will interpret such a bilateral treaty entered into by a state party?

Second, the United States sought a resolution from the Security Council addressed to the ICC under the Statute article 16: see Security Council Resolution 1422, reproduced below. This unanimously adopted resolution was renewed by the Security Council on June 12, 2003 in Resolution 1487[51] by a vote of 12:0 with France, Germany, and Syria abstaining. In what way was the Security Council acting under Chapter VII of the Charter? What was the threat to international peace and security? Was its action consistent with article 16 of the Rome Statute?

The United States in pressing for the resolution had to overcome the potential veto by one or more of the other five permanent members of the Security Council, including France and the United Kingdom, which have ratified the Rome Statute. The United States

---

51   SC Res. 1487 (2003), UN SCOR, *Res. and Dec.*; U.N. Doc. S/INF/58 at 202.

let it be known that without passage of the resolutions it would veto the renewal of peacekeeping operations in Bosnia and Herzegovina and potentially all other peacekeeping operations. In 2004 the issue of renewal came up again in the Security Council. However, the United States withdrew the draft when the allegations of torture in Abu Ghraib prison in Iraq surfaced concerning United States military personnel.

Security Council Resolution 1422 (2002)
U.N. Doc. S/Res/1422, 12 July 2002

The Security Council,

Taking note of the entry into force on 1 July 2002, of the Statute of the International Criminal Court (ICC), done at Rome 17 July 1998 (The Rome Statute),

Emphasizing the importance to international peace and security of United Nations operations,

Noting that not all States are parties to the Rome Statute,

Noting that States Parties to the Rome Statute have chosen to accept its jurisdiction in accordance with the Statute and in particular the principle of complementarity,

Noting that States not Party to the Rome Statute will continue to fulfill their responsibilities in their national jurisdictions in relation to international crimes,

Determining that operations established or authorized by the United Nations Security Council are deployed to maintain or restore international peace and security,

Determining further that it is in the interests of international peace and security to facilitate Member States' ability to contribute to operations established or authorized by the United Nations Security Council,

Acting under Chapter VII of the Charter of the United Nations,

1. *Requests*, consistent with the provisions of article 16 of the Rome Statute, that the ICC, if a case arises involving current or former officials or personnel from a contributing State not a Party to the Rome Statute over acts or omissions relating to a United Nations established or authorized operation, shall for a twelve-month period starting 1 July 2002 not commence or proceed with investigation or prosecution of any such case, unless the Security Council decides otherwise;

2. *Expresses* the intention to renew the request in paragraph 1 under the same conditions each 1 July for further 12-month periods for as long as may be necessary;

3. *Decides* that Member States shall take no action inconsistent with paragraph 1 and with their international obligations;

4. *Decides* to remain seized of the matter.

Investigations by the Prosecutor

On June 21, 2004, the ICC Chief Prosecutor, Luis Moreno-Ocampo, officially opened the first investigation of the ICC concerning crimes allegedly committed on the territory of the Democratic Republic of the Congo following a referral by that state under articles 13(a) and 14 of the Statute. Similarly, on July 28, 2004, he opened an investigation into the situation concerning Northern Uganda. Both situations were referred by these states parties themselves. On the basis of article 17 dealing with complementarity, these two states could have investigated and prosecuted themselves and, unless unable or unwilling genuinely to do so, the ICC would not have taken jurisdiction. Although articles 13(a) and 14 simply say referral of a situation by a state party, it would seem that it was thought that it would be from a state party distinct from the locus of the alleged crimes. Nevertheless, the wording of these articles makes no such distinction.

The third investigation begun by the Prosecutor concerns violations of international law and human rights in the Darfur region of Sudan. The Security Council referred the situation in Darfur to the Chief Prosecutor in the following resolution.

Security Council Resolution 1593 (2005)
U.N. Doc. S/Res/1593, 31 March 2005

The Security Council,

Taking note of the report of the International Commission of Inquiry on violations of international humanitarian law and human rights law in Darfur (S/2005/60),

Recalling article 16 of the Rome Statute under which no investigation or prosecution may be commenced or proceeded with by the International Criminal Court for a period of 12 months after a Security Council request to that effect,

Also recalling articles 75 and 79 of the Rome statute and encouraging States to contribute to the ICC Trust Fund for Victims,

Taking note of the existence of agreements referred to in Article 98-2 of the Rome Statute,

Determining that the situation in Sudan continues to constitute a threat to international peace and security,

Acting under Chapter VII of the Charter of the United Nations,

1. *Decides* to refer the situation in Darfur since 1 July 2002 to the Prosecutor of the International Criminal Court;

2. *Decides* that the Government of Sudan and all other parties to the conflict in Darfur, shall cooperate fully with and provide any necessary assistance to the Court and the prosecutor pursuant to this resolution and, while recognizing that States not party to the Rome statute have no obligation under the Statute, urges all states and concerned regional and other international organizations to cooperate fully;

3. *Invites* the Court and the African Union to discuss practical arrangements that will facilitate the work of the Prosecutor and of the Court, including the possibility of conducting proceedings in the region, which would contribute to regional efforts in the fight against impunity;

4. *Also encourages* the Court, as appropriate and in accordance with the Rome Statute, to support international cooperation with domestic efforts to promote the rule of law, protect human rights and combat impunity in Darfur;

5. *Also emphasizes* the need to promote healing and reconciliation and encourages in this respect the creation of institutions, involving all sectors of Sudanese society, such as truth and/or reconciliation commissions, in order to complement judicial

processes and thereby reinforce the efforts to restore longlasting peace, with African Union and international support as necessary;

6. *Decides* that nationals, current or former officials or personnel from a contributing State outside Sudan which is not a party to the Rome Statute of the International Criminal Court shall be subject to the exclusive jurisdiction of that contributing State for all alleged acts or omissions arising out of or related to operations in Sudan established or authorized by the Council or the African Union, unless such exclusive jurisdiction has been expressly waived by that contributing State;

7. *Recognizes* that none of the expenses incurred in connection with the referral, including expenses related to investigations or prosecutions in connection with that referral, shall be borne by the United Nations and that such costs shall be borne by the parties to the Rome Statute and those States that wish to contribute voluntarily;

8. *Invites* the Prosecutor to address the Council within three months of the date of adoption of this resolution and every six months thereafter on actions taken pursuant to this resolution;

9. *Decides* to remain seized of the matter.

NOTES

1) As noted earlier, under article 13(b) of the Rome Statute, the Security Council is able to refer a "situation," not individual cases. In this first referral by the Security Council to the ICC, 11 states voted in favour and 4 abstained: Algeria, Brazil, China, and the United States.

2) Previously, the Security Council, by Resolution 1564 of September 18, 2004, created an independent International Commission of Inquiry "to investigate reports of violations of international humanitarian law and human rights law in Darfur by all parties and to identify the perpetrators of such violations with a view to ensuring that those responsible be held accountable." The Commission released its Report on January 25, 2005. It strongly recommended that the Security Council refer the situation to the ICC. Two months later, after much debate, it did so. Following the referral by the Security Council, the Secretary-General of the United Nations, Kofi Annan, submitted to the Office of the Prosecutor a list of 51 persons who are suspected of rape, slaughter, and pillage in Darfur. The sealed list was gathered by the Independent Commission. It is said to include government and military officials, leaders of the Janjaweed militia, and rebels. Nine boxes of documents, gathered by the Independent Commission, were received by the Chief Prosecutor on April 6, 2005.

3) Given the U.S. position that the Rome Statute is fundamentally flawed why do you think the United States agreed to abstain and not veto the referral? Does this signal a change in policy toward the ICC or was it a political decision given that the United States had already declared that, in its view, genocide was being committed? Consider the exemption contained in paragraph 6 of Resolution 1593 of nationals, current or former officials from States outside Sudan, that are not parties to the Rome Statute. Note also that Sudan itself is not a state party. Clearly, the referral to the ICC is a historic milestone for the Court, but does this exemption clause appear as a "double standard"?

4) What alternatives were there? Could the Security Council have established an *ad hoc* tribunal for Darfur or expanded the mandate of the ICTR? Why do you think that neither of these was done?

5) As indicated above, Algeria, Brazil, and China also abstained. Brazil abstained because of the exemption provision and Algeria and China preferred the option of referral to an African court or tribunal.

6) It remains to be seen whether Sudan will cooperate with the ICC. Refer back to article 17 on complementarity. This article applies to states parties and non-states parties. It creates no distinction.[52] However, note further article 18 on issues of admissibility, concerning notification by the Prosecutor to all states parties and those states that would normally exercise jurisdiction over the offences concerned and challenges to the admissibility of a case before the Court. Article 18 applies only when the Prosecutor is acting following a state party referral under article 13(a) or where the Prosecutor is acting *proprio motu* pursuant to articles 13(c) and 15. It does not apply where the Prosecutor is acting following a referral by the Security Council acting under Chapter VII of the U.N. Charter in accordance with article 13(b) of the Rome Statute.[53]

7) It should not be overlooked that there is a precedent for the Darfur Resolution. On August 1, 2003, in Security Council Resolution 1497, a multinational force was established for Liberia. Seemingly, this would have fallen under Resolution 1487 of 2003. However, paragraph 7 stated that the Security Council "[d]ecides that current or former officials or personnel from a contributing State that is not a party to the Rome Statute of the International Criminal Court shall be subject to the exclusive jurisdiction of that contributing State for all alleged acts or omissions arising out of or related to the Multinational Force or United Nations stabilization force in Liberia, unless such exclusive jurisdiction has been waived by that contributing State." This is the same type of immunity as included in the Darfur Resolution and is not the deferral expressed in Resolutions 1422 (2002) and 1497 (2003).

8) Note that Security Council Resolutions 1422 (2002), 1487 (2003), and 1497 (2003) speak of an exemption for "current or former officials or personnel" from a contributing state "that is not a party to the Rome Statute." The Darfur resolution is different in adding first "nationals." What is the significance of their inclusion?

D. NATIONAL PROSECUTION OF INTERNATIONAL CRIMES

The traditional way of enforcing international criminal law was, and still is, through national criminal justice systems. Each state has the jurisdictional power to enforce the laws, as discussed in Chapter 9, Section A.2, provided it is able to exercise authority over both the offence and the accused person. Under some international crime-creating treaties, like the Convention Against Torture, reproduced above in Section A.3, states have a duty to extradite or prosecute a suspect they are able to detain. Custody of the alleged

---

52   S.A.Williams, "Article 17: Issues of Admissibility" in Triffterer, *supra* note 43 at 383.

53   D.D. Ntanda Nsereko, "Article 18: Preliminary Rulings Regarding Admissibility" in Triffterer, *supra* note 43 at 395, 397-98.

perpetrator of an international crime committed abroad is also sufficient where the offence carries universal jurisdiction, such as grave breaches of the Geneva Conventions and genocide. This was the asserted basis of the Israeli Supreme Court's jurisdiction in the *Eichmann* case, extracted below.

With the establishment of the ICC, states have not lost the right to prosecute international criminals because the ICC has only complementary jurisdiction, but they have acquired considerable extra responsibilities under the Rome Statute, especially Part 9, to assist the ICC. As a party to the Rome Statute, Canada has responded with new legislation that both asserts Canadian jurisdiction over international criminal offences and authorizes Canadian courts and officials to fulfill any requests by the ICC for their assistance. See the *Crimes Against Humanity and War Crimes Act*, reproduced below. In addition, the 1999 *Extradition Act*, reproduced in Chapter 9, Section B.2, allows Canadian authorities to respond to requests from the ICC for the surrender of offenders.

Eichmann Case[54]
(1961), 36 I.L.R. 277 (Israel Sup. Ct.)

[The Israeli Supreme Court, sitting as a court of criminal appeal on May 29, 1962, dismissed an appeal by Adolf Eichmann from the judgment and sentence of the District Court. Eichmann had been abducted in 1960 from Argentina where he had lived since 1950 under an assumed name. He signed a paper purporting to consent to trial in Israel. He was charged with offences under the Nazi and Nazi Collaborators (Punishment) Law 1950, *inter alia*, for his part in the "Final Solution of the Jewish Problem with the intent to exterminate the Jewish people." The charges included crimes against the Jewish people, crimes against humanity, and war crimes.]

THE SUPREME COURT: ... It is impossible for a state to sanction an act that violates its severe prohibitions, and from this follows the idea ... that a person who was a party to such a crime must bear individual responsibility for it. ...

[I]t is the universal character of the crime in question which vests in every state the authority to try and punish those who participated in their commission.

NOTES

1) At the time of Eichmann's crimes the State of Israel did not exist; was the assertion of universal jurisdiction by the Israeli Supreme Court therefore legitimate?

2) Ordinarily, common law states mostly limit the exercise of criminal jurisdiction to their territory. For instance, the Canadian *Criminal Code*, section 6(2) states: "Subject to the Act or any other Act of parliament, no person shall be convicted ... of an offence committed outside Canada." Assertions of universal jurisdiction over international

---

54   See H.Arendt, *Eichmann in Jerusalem* (1964); P. Papadatos, *The Eichmann Trial*; and L.C. Green, "The Eichmann Case" (1962) 38 Brit. Y.B. Int'l L. 181.

criminal offences have been infrequent and exceptional, but are growing more common. Here is the principal Canadian statute.

Crimes Against Humanity and War Crimes Act[55]
S.C. 2000, c. 24, as amended S.C. 2001, c. 32 ss. 59-61

INTERPRETATION

2.(1) The definitions in this subsection apply in this Act.

"conventional international law" means any convention, treaty or other international agreement

> *(a)* that is in force and to which Canada is a party; or
>
> *(b)* that is in force and the provisions of which Canada has agreed to accept and apply in an armed conflict in which it is involved.

"International Criminal Court" means the International Criminal Court established by the Rome Statute … .

(2) Unless otherwise provided, words and expressions used in this Act have the same meaning as in the *Criminal Code*. …

OFFENCES WITHIN CANDA

[Sections 4-5 proscribe genocide, crimes against humanity, and war crimes committed in Canada.]

OFFENCES OUTSIDE CANADA

6.(1) Every person who, either before or after the coming into force of this section, commits outside Canada

> *(a)* genocide
>
> *(b)* a crime against humanity, or
>
> *(c)* a war crime,

is guilty of an indictable offence and may be prosecuted for that offence in accordance with section 8.

(1.1) Every person who conspires or attempts to commit, is an accessory after the fact in relation to, or counsels in relation to, an offence referred to in subsection (1) is guilty of an indictable offence.

(2) Every person who commits an offence under subsection (1) or (1.1)

> *(a)* shall be sentenced to imprisonment for life, if an intentional killing forms the basis of the offence; and
>
> *(b)* is liable to imprisonment for life, in any other case.

(3) The definitions in this subsection apply in this section.

---

55   See Madeleine J. Schwarz, "Prosecuting Crimes against Humanity in Canada: What Must Be Proved" (2002) 46 Crim. L.Q. 40.

"crime against humanity" means murder, extermination, enslavement, deportation, imprisonment, torture, sexual violence, persecution or any other inhumane act or omission that is committed against any civilian population or any identifiable group and that, at the time and in the place of its commission, constitutes a crime against humanity according to customary international law or conventional international law or by virtue of its being criminal according to the general principles of law recognized by the community of nations, whether or not it constitutes a contravention of the law in force at the time and in the place of its commission.

"genocide" means an act or omission committed with intent to destroy, in whole or in part, an identifiable group of persons, as such, that at the time and in the place of its commission, constitutes genocide according to customary international law or conventional international law or by virtue of its being criminal according to the general principles of law recognized by the community of nations, whether or not it constitutes a contravention of the law in force at the time and in the place of its commission.

"war crime" means an act or omission committed during an armed conflict that, at the time and in the place of its commission, constitutes a war crime according to customary international law or conventional international law applicable to armed conflicts, whether or not it constitutes a contravention of the law in force at the time and in the place of its commission.

(4) For greater certainty, crimes described in articles 6 and 7 and paragraph 2 of article 8 of the Rome Statute are, as of July 17, 1998, crimes according to customary international law, and may be crimes according to customary international law before that date. This does not limit or prejudice in any way the application of existing or developing rules of international law.

(5) For greater certainty, the offence of crime against humanity was part of customary international law or was criminal according to the general principles of law recognized by the community of nations before the coming into force of either of the following:

(a) the Agreement for the prosecution and punishment of the major war criminals of the European Axis, signed at London on August 8, 1945; and

(b) the proclamation by the Supreme Commander for the Allied Powers, dated January 19, 1946.

7.(1) A military commander commits an indictable offence if

(a) the military commander, outside Canada,

(i) fails to exercise control properly over a person under their effective command and control or effective authority and control, and as a result the person commits an offence under section 4, or

(ii) fails, before or after the coming into force of this section, to exercise control properly over a person under their effective command and control or effective authority and control, and as a result the person commits an offence under section 6;

(b) the military commander knows, or is criminally negligent in failing to know, that the person is about to commit or is committing such an offence; and *(c)* the military commander subsequently

(i) fails to take, as soon as practicable, all necessary and reasonable measures within their power to prevent or repress the commission of the offence, or the further commission of offences under section 4 or 6, or

(ii) fails to take, as soon as practicable, all necessary and reasonable measures within their power to submit the matter to the competent authorities for investigation and prosecution.

(2) A superior commits an indictable offence if

(a) the superior, outside Canada,

(i) fails to exercise control properly over a person under their effective authority and control, and as a result the person commits an offence under section 4, or

(ii) fails, before or after the coming into force of this section, to exercise control properly over a person under their effective authority and control, and as a result the person commits an offence under section 6;

(b) the superior knows that the person is about to commit or is committing such an offence, or consciously disregards information that clearly indicates that such an offence is about to be committed or is being committed by the person;

(c) the offence relates to activities for which the superior has effective authority and control; and

(d) the superior subsequently

(i) fails to take, as soon as practicable, all necessary and reasonable measures within their power to prevent or repress the commission of the offence, or the further commission of offences under section 4 or 6, or

(ii) fails to take, as soon as practicable, all necessary and reasonable measures within their power to submit the matter to the competent authorities for investigation and prosecution.

(2.1) Every person who conspires or attempts to commit, is an accessory after the fact in relation to, or counsels in relation to, an offence referred to in subsection (1) or (2) is guilty of an indictable offence.

(3) A person who is alleged to have committed an offence under subsection (1), (2) or (2.1) may be prosecuted for that offence in accordance with section 8.

(4) Every person who commits an offence under subsection (1), (2) or (2.1) is liable to imprisonment for life.

(5) Where an act or omission constituting an offence under this section occurred before the coming into force of this section, subparagraphs (1)*(a)*(ii) and 2*(a)*(ii) apply to the extent that, at the time and in the place of the act or omission, the act or omission constituted a contravention of customary international law or conventional international law or was criminal according to the general principles of law recognized by the community of nations, whether or not it constituted a contravention of the law in force at the time and in the place of its commission.

(6) The definitions in this subsection apply in this section.

"military commander" includes a person effectively acting as a military commander and a person who commands police with a degree of authority and control comparable to a military commander.

"superior" means a person in authority, other than a military commander.

8. A person who is alleged to have committed an offence under section 6 or 7 may be prosecuted for that offence if

(a) at the time the offence is alleged to have been committed,

(i) the person was a Canadian citizen or employed by Canada in a civilian or military capacity,

(ii) the person was a citizen of a state that was engaged in an armed conflict against Canada, or was employed in a civilian or military capacity by such a state,

(iii) the victim of the alleged offence was a Canadian citizen, or

(iv) the victim of the alleged offence was a citizen of a state that was allied with Canada in an armed conflict; or

(b) after the time the offence is alleged to have been committed, the person is present in Canada.

PROCEDURE AND DEFENCES

9.(1) Proceedings for an offence under this Act alleged to have been committed outside Canada for which a person may be prosecuted under this Act may, whether or not the person is in Canada, be commenced in any territorial division in Canada and the person may be tried and punished in respect of that offence in the same manner as if the offence had been committed in that territorial division.

(2) For greater certainty, in a proceeding commenced in any territorial division under subsection (1), the provisions of the *Criminal Code* relating to requirements that the accused appear at and be present during proceedings and any exceptions to those requirements apply.

(3) No proceedings for an offence under any of sections 4 to 7 of this Act ... may be commenced without the personal consent in writing of the Attorney General or Deputy Attorney General of Canada, and those proceedings may be conducted only by the Attorney General of Canada or counsel acting on their behalf.

(4) No proceedings for an offence under section 18 [re bribery of judges and officials of the International Criminal Court] may be commenced without the consent of the Attorney General of Canada.

10. Proceedings for an offence alleged to have been committed before the coming into force of this section shall be conducted in accordance with the laws of evidence and procedure in force at the time of the proceedings.

11. In proceedings for an offence under any of sections 4 to 7, the accused may, subject to sections 12 to 14 and to subsection 607(6) of the *Criminal Code*, rely on any justification, excuse or defence available under the laws of Canada or under international law at the time of the alleged offence or at the time of the proceedings.

12.(1) If a person is alleged to have committed an act or omission that is an offence under this Act, and the person has been tried and dealt with outside Canada in respect of the offence in such a manner that, had they been tried and dealt with in Canada, they would be able to plead *autrefois acquit*, *autrefois convict* or pardon, the person is deemed to have been so tried and dealt with in Canada.

(2) Despite subsection (1), a person may not plead *autrefois acquit, autrefois convict* or pardon in respect of an offence under any of sections 4 to 7 if the person was tried in a court of a foreign state or territory and the proceedings in that court

    (a) were for the purpose of shielding the person from criminal responsibility; or

    (b) were not otherwise conducted independently or impartially in accordance with the norms of due process recognized by international law, and were conducted in a manner that, in the circumstances, was inconsistent with an intent to bring the person to justice.

13. Despite section 15 of the *Criminal Code*, it is not a justification, excuse or defence with respect to an offence under any of sections 4 to 7 that the offence was committed in obedience to or in conformity with the law in force at the time and in the place of its commission.

14.(1) In proceedings for an offence under any of sections 4 to 7, it is not a defence that the accused was ordered by a government or superior—whether military or civilian—to perform the act or omission that forms the subject-matter of the offence, unless

    (a) the accused was under a legal obligation to obey orders of the government or superior;

    (b) the accused did not know that the order was unlawful; and

    (c) the order was not manifestly unlawful.

(2) For the purpose of paragraph (1)*(c)*, orders to commit genocide or crimes against humanity are manifestly unlawful.

(3) An accused cannot base their defence under subsection (1) on a belief that an order was lawful if the belief was based on information about a civilian population or an identifiable group of persons that encouraged, was likely to encourage or attempted to justify the commission of inhumane acts or omissions against the population or group.

NOTES

1) Section 15 of the Act provides for parole eligibility; sections 16-26 deal with offences against the administration of justice of the International Criminal Court; and sections 30-32 concern the establishment and other matters related to the Crimes Against Humanity Fund. The Schedule to the Act, pursuant to section 2(1), extracts articles 6, 7, and 8(2) of the Rome Statute defining genocide, crimes against humanity, and war crimes, reproduced above in Section C.

2) Does the *Crimes Against Humanity Act* comply with the *Canadian Charter of Rights and Freedoms*, in particular section 11(g), which states:

    11. Any person charged with an offence has the right …

    (g) not to be found guilty on account of any act or omission unless, at the time of the act or omission, it constituted an offence under Canadian or international law or was criminal according to the general principles of law recognized by the community of nations.

3) Are the definitions of genocide, crimes against humanity, and war crimes in section 6(2) the same as those in the Rome Statute? As a party to the Rome Statute, Canada is

bound to implement its provisions in Canadian law, but does it have authority to legislate differently from them?

4) The Rome Statute operates only in respect of crimes committed after it came into force on July 1, 2002: see article 11. Under the Canadian Act, may Canadian courts try persons accused of committing genocide, crimes against humanity, or war crimes in Rwanda in 1994, or in Europe during World War II?

5) The core offences in the Act are often not directly committed by senior military officers and political leaders. In what circumstances may they be held accountable?

6) What bases of jurisdiction does Canada assert in the Act? Do the crimes defined in section 6 justify their assertion?

7) Compare the issue of superior orders in section 14 with the Nuremberg Charter, article 8, reproduced in Section A.1 and the statutes of the *Ad Hoc* Tribunals and the International Criminal Court, reproduced in Sections B.1, B.2, and C above. How significant are their differences?

8) The first indictment under the *Crimes Against Humanity and War Crimes Act* and the first ever charge of genocide to be laid by Canada was announced in October 2005 against Désiré Munyaneza. He was arrested in Toronto and charged with seven counts of genocide, crimes against humanity, and war crimes allegedly committed in leading attacks on Tutsis seeking refuge at Butare, Rwanda during the conflict there in 1994. In one other case, *Andeel v. Canada (Minister for Citizenship and Immigration)*,[56] an immigration officer denied an application for permanent residence on the grounds that the applicant had been complicit in offences under the Act. However, the Federal Court quashed the decision for insufficiency of evidence.

Immunity from Arrest and Prosecution?

It is clear that no individual, even a head of state, is immune from arrest and prosecution for alleged criminal acts by international law before an international court or tribunal. See the judgment of the Nuremberg Tribunal in Section A.1 above and article 27 of the Rome Statute of the ICC in Section C above. But the situation is different when the accused is a high official of one state and is sought for trial in another state. While the ICC is a supra-national court, a national court ordinarily has no jurisdiction over a foreign state or its organs and agencies because it is a sovereign equal. The scope of the customary international law of state immunity in civil actions is regulated in Canada by the *State Immunity Act*, which is discussed in Chapter 5, Section C. But that Act, by section 18, expressly does not apply to criminal proceedings, which therefore continue to be governed by customary international law. What, then, is the customary international law about individuals who claim immunity from national arrest and prosecution because they are or were state officials at the time of their alleged commission of an international crime? The question was first considered by the House of Lords in the ground-breaking case of *Pinochet* but shortly afterward it was also addressed by the ICJ in the *Yerodia* case, reproduced after *Pinochet*.

---

56 (2003), 240 F.T.R. 1.

R. v. Bow Street Magistrate, ex parte Pinochet (No. 3)[57]
[2000] 1 A.C. 147 (H.L.)

[Spain requested the United Kingdom to extradite Senator Pinochet, the former President of Chile, to face charges involving hostage taking, torture, and murder of numerous individuals, including Spanish citizens in Chile and elsewhere while he was head of state. Pinochet claimed immunity from arrest and prosecution. This was the third time the House of Lords rendered judgment in the case. The first judgment of the Law Lords was set aside by the second because one of them had failed to disclose his connection to an intervenor in the case. The third hearing involved seven Law Lords, who each rendered a decision. The lead speech for the majority of 6:1 was given by Lord Browne-Wilkinson.]

LORD BROWNE-WILKINSON: My Lords,

As is well known, this case concerns an attempt by the Government of Spain to extradite Senator Pinochet from this country to stand trial in Spain for crimes committed (primarily in Chile) during the period when Senator Pinochet was head of state in Chile. The interaction between the various legal issues which arise is complex. I will therefore seek, first, to give a short account of the legal principles which are in play in order that my exposition of the facts will be more intelligible.

Outline of the Law

In general, a state only exercises criminal jurisdiction over offences which occur within its geographical boundaries. If a person who is alleged to have committed a crime in Spain is found in the United Kingdom, Spain can apply to the United Kingdom to extradite him to Spain. The power to extradite from the United Kingdom for an "extradition crime" is now contained in the *Extradition Act 1989*. That Act defines what constitutes an "extradition crime." For the purposes of the present case, the most important requirement is that the conduct complained of must constitute a crime under the law both of Spain and of the United Kingdom. This is known as the double criminality rule.

Since the Nazi atrocities and the Nuremberg trials, international law has recognised a number of offences as being international crimes. Individual states have taken jurisdiction to try some international crimes even in cases where such crimes were not committed within the geographical boundaries of such states. The most important of such international crimes for present purposes is torture which is regulated by the International Convention Against Torture and other Cruel, Inhuman or Degrading

---

57   See Bradley & Goldsmith, "Pinochet and International Human Rights Litigation" (1999) 97 Mich. L. Rev. 2129; Wilson, "Prosecuting Pinochet: International Crimes in Spanish Domestic Law" (1999) 21 Hum. Rts. Q. 927; R. Wedgwood, "Augusto Pinochet and International Law" (2000) 46 McGill L.J. 241; V.N. Opara, "Sovereign and Diplomatic Immunity as Customary International Law: Beyond R. v. Bow Street Metropolitan Stipendiary Magistrate and Others, Ex Parte Pinochet Ugarte" (2003) 21 Wis. Int'l L.J. 255. See also the reports collected around the Pinochet proceedings in (1999) 93 A.J.I.L. 690 and the judicial comments in *Jones v. Ministry of the Interior of the Kingdom of Saudi Arabia*, [2004] EWCA Civ. 1394.

Treatment or Punishment, 1984 (1990) (cm. 1775). The obligations placed on the United Kingdom by that Convention (and on the other 110 or more signatory states who have adopted the Convention) were incorporated into the law of the United Kingdom by section 134 of the *Criminal Justice Act 1988*. That Act came into force on 29 September 1988. Section 134 created a new crime under United Kingdom law, the crime of torture. As required by the Torture Convention "all" torture wherever committed world-wide was made criminal under United Kingdom law and triable in the United Kingdom. No one has suggested that before section 134 came into effect torture committed outside the United Kingdom was a crime under United Kingdom law. Nor is it suggested that section 134 was retrospective so as to make torture committed outside the United Kingdom before 29 September 1988 a United Kingdom crime. Since torture outside the United Kingdom was not a crime under U.K. law until 29 September 1988, the principle of double criminality which requires an Act to be a crime under both the law of Spain and of the United Kingdom cannot be satisfied in relation to conduct before that date if the principle of double criminality requires the conduct to be criminal under United Kingdom law *at the date it was committed*. If, on the other hand, the double criminality rule only requires the conduct to be criminal under U.K. law *at the date of extradition* the rule was satisfied in relation to all torture alleged against Senator Pinochet whether it took place before or after 1988. The Spanish courts have held that they have jurisdiction over all the crimes alleged.

In these circumstances, the first question that has to be answered is whether or not the definition of an "extradition crime" in the Act of 1989 requires the conduct to be criminal under U.K. law at the date of commission or only at the date of extradition.

This question, although raised, was not decided in the Divisional Court. At the first hearing in this House [2000] 1 A.C. 61 it was apparently conceded that all the matters charged against Senator Pinochet were extradition crimes. It was only during the hearing before your Lordships that the importance of the point became fully apparent. As will appear, in my view only a limited number of the charges relied upon to extradite Senator Pinochet constitute extradition crimes since most of the conduct relied upon occurred long before 1988. In particular, I do not consider that torture committed outside the United Kingdom before 29 September 1988 was a crime under U.K. law. It follows that the main question discussed at the earlier stages of this case—is a former head of state entitled to sovereign immunity from arrest or prosecution in the U.K. for acts of torture—applies to far fewer charges. But the question of state immunity remains a point of crucial importance since, in my view, there is certain conduct of Senator Pinochet (albeit a small amount) which does constitute an extradition crime and would enable the Home Secretary (if he thought fit) to extradite Senator Pinochet to Spain unless he is entitled to state immunity. Accordingly, having identified which of the crimes alleged is an extradition crime, I will then go on to consider whether Senator Pinochet is entitled to immunity in respect of those crimes. But first I must state shortly the relevant facts.

The Facts

On 11 September 1973 a right-wing coup evicted the left-wing regime of President Allende. The coup was led by a military junta, of whom Senator (then General) Pinochet was the leader. At some stage he became head of state. The Pinochet regime remained in power until 11 March 1990 when Senator Pinochet resigned.

There is no real dispute that during the period of the Senator Pinochet regime appalling acts of barbarism were committed in Chile and elsewhere in the world: torture, murder and the unexplained disappearance of individuals, all on a large scale. Although it is not alleged that Senator Pinochet himself committed any of those acts, it is alleged that they were done in pursuance of a conspiracy to which he was a party, at his instigation and with his knowledge. He denies these allegations. None of the conduct alleged was committed by or against citizens of the United Kingdom or in the United Kingdom.

In 1998 Senator Pinochet came to the United Kingdom for medical treatment. The judicial authorities in Spain sought to extradite him in order to stand trial in Spain on a large number of charges. Some of those charges had links with Spain. But most of the charges had no connection with Spain. The background to the case is that to those of left-wing political convictions Senator Pinochet is seen as an arch-devil: to those of right-wing persuasions he is seen as the saviour of Chile. It may well be thought that the trial of Senator Pinochet in Spain for offences all of which related to the state of Chile and most of which occurred in Chile is not calculated to achieve the best justice. But I cannot emphasise too strongly that that is no concern of your Lordships. Although others perceive our task as being to choose between the two sides on the grounds of personal preference or political inclination, that is an entire misconception. Our job is to decide two questions of law: are there any extradition crimes and, if so, is Senator Pinochet immune from trial for committing those crimes. If, as a matter of law, there are no extradition crimes or he is entitled to immunity in relation to whichever crimes there are, then there is no legal right to extradite Senator Pinochet to Spain or, indeed, to stand in the way of his return to Chile. If, on the other hand, there are extradition crimes in relation to which Senator Pinochet is not entitled to state immunity then it will be open to the Home Secretary to extradite him. The task of this House is only to decide those points of law.

[Lord Browne-Wilkinson then explained how Spain had issued several warrants for Senator Pinochet's arrest that together contained 32 charges against him. However, his Lordship determined that, by the operation of the double criminality rule of extradition, only two categories of offences survived as extraditable crimes. They involved a limited number of charges of torture and conspiracy to torture and to murder.]

Torture

Apart from the law of piracy, the concept of personal liability under international law for international crimes is of comparatively modern growth. The traditional subjects of international law are states not human beings. But consequent upon the war crime trials after the 1939-45 World War, the international community came to recognise that there could be criminal liability under international law for a class of crimes such as war crimes and crimes against humanity. Although there may be legitimate doubts as to the legality of the *Nuremberg Charter: Charter of the International Military Tribunal*, adopted by the Big Four Powers (1945), in my judgment those doubts were stilled by the Affirmation of the Principles of International Law recognised by the Charter of Nuremberg Tribunal adopted by the United Nations General Assembly on 11 December 1946 (G.A. Res. 95, 1st Sess., 1144; U.N. Doc. A/236 (1946). That Affirmation affirmed the principles of international law recognised by the Charter of the Nuremberg Tribunal and the judgment of the Tribunal and directed the committee on the codification of international law to treat as a matter of primary importance plans for the formulation of the principles recognised in the Charter of the Nuremberg Tribunal. At least from that date onwards the concept of personal liability for a crime in international law must have been part of international law. In the early years state torture was one of the elements of a war crime. In consequence torture, and various other crimes against humanity, were linked to war or at least to hostilities of some kind. But in the course of time this linkage with war fell away and torture, divorced from war or hostilities, became an international crime on its own: see *Oppenheim's International Law*, vol. I, 9th ed. (1992) (ed. Sir Robert Jennings Q.C. and Sir Arthur Watts Q.C.), p. 996; note 6 to article 18 of the International Law Commission Draft Code of Crimes Against the Peace and Security of Mankind; *Prosecutor v. Furundzija* (unreported) 10 December 1998, International Criminal Tribunal for the Former Yugoslavia case, No. IT-95-17/7-T10. Ever since 1945, torture on a large scale has featured as one of the crimes against humanity: see, for example, U.N. General Assembly Resolutions 3059, 3452 and 3453 passed in 1973 and 1975; Statutes of the International Criminal Tribunals for former Yugoslavia (article 5) and Rwanda (article 3).

Moreover, the Republic of Chile accepted before your Lordships that the international law prohibiting torture has the character of *jus cogens* or a peremptory norm, i.e. one of those rules of international law which have a particular status. In *Furundzija*, paragraphs 153 and 154, the Tribunal said:

> Because of the importance of the values it protects, [the prohibition of torture] has evolved into a peremptory norm or *jus cogens*, that is, a norm that enjoys a higher rank in the international hierarchy than treaty law and even "ordinary" customary rules. The most conspicuous consequence of this higher rank is that the principle at issue cannot be derogated from by states through international treaties or local or special customs or even general customary rules not endowed with the same normative force ... . Clearly, the *jus cogens* nature of the prohibition against torture articulates the notion that the prohibition has now become one of the most fundamental standards of the international community. Furthermore, this prohibition is designed to produce a deterrent effect, in that it signals to all members of the international community and the individuals over whom they wield authority that the prohibition of torture is an absolute value from which nobody must deviate.

See also the cases cited in Note 170 to the *Furundzija* case.

The *jus cogens* nature of the international crime of torture justifies states in taking universal jurisdiction over torture wherever committed. International law provides that offences *jus cogens* may be punished by any state because the offenders are "common enemies of all mankind and all nations have an equal interest in their apprehension and prosecution": *Demjanjuk v. Petrovsky* (1985) 603 F. Supp. 1468; 776 F. 2d. 571.

It was suggested by Miss Montgomery, for Senator Pinochet, that although torture was contrary to international law it was not strictly an international crime in the highest sense. In the light of the authorities to which I have referred (and there are many others) I have no doubt that long before the Torture Convention of 1984 state torture was an international crime in the highest sense.

But there was no tribunal or court to punish international crimes of torture. Local courts could take jurisdiction: see the *Demjanjuk* case; *Attorney-General of Israel v. Eichmann* (1962) 36 I.L.R. 277. But the objective was to ensure a general jurisdiction so that the torturer was not safe wherever he went. For example, in this case it is alleged that during the Pinochet regime torture was an official, although unacknowledged, weapon of government and that, when the regime was about to end, it passed legislation designed to afford an amnesty to those who had engaged in institutionalised torture. If these allegations are true, the fact that the local court had jurisdiction to deal with the international crime of torture was nothing to the point so long as the totalitarian regime remained in power: a totalitarian regime will not permit adjudication by its own courts on its own shortcomings. Hence the demand for some international machinery to repress state torture which is not dependent upon the local courts where the torture was committed. In the event, over 110 states (including Chile, Spain and the United Kingdom) became state parties to the Torture Convention. But it is far from clear that none of them practised state torture. What was needed therefore was an international system which could punish those who were guilty of torture and which did not permit the evasion of punishment by the torturer moving from one state to another. The Torture Convention was agreed not in order to create an international crime which had not previously existed but to provide an international system under which the international criminal—the torturer—could find no safe haven. Burgers and Danelius (respectively the chairman of the United Nations Working Group on the 1984 Torture Convention and the draftsmen of its first draft) say, in their *Handbook on the Convention Against Torture and Other Cruel, Inhuman, or Degrading Treatment or Punishment* (1988), p. 131, that it was "an essential purpose [of the Convention] to ensure that a torturer does not escape the consequences of his act by going to another country."

The Torture Convention
[reproduced above in Section A.3]

Article 1 of the Convention defines torture as the intentional infliction of severe pain and of suffering with a view to achieving a wide range of purposes "when such pain or suffering is inflicted by or at the instigation of or with the consent or acquiesence of a public official or other person acting in an official capacity." Article 2(1) requires each state party to prohibit torture on territory within its own jurisdiction and article 4 requires each state party to ensure that "all" acts of torture are offences under its criminal law. Article 2(3) outlaws any defence of superior orders. Under article 5(1) each state party has to establish its jurisdiction over torture (a) when committed within territory under its jurisdiction, (b) when the alleged offender is a national of that state, and (c) in certain circumstances, when the victim is a national of that state. Under article 5(2) a state party has to take jurisdiction over any alleged offender who is found within its territory. Article 6 contains provisions for a state in whose territory an alleged torturer is found to detain him, inquire into the position and notify the states referred to in article 5(1) and to indicate whether it intends to exercise jurisdiction. Under article 7 the state in whose territory the alleged torturer is found shall, if he is not extradited to any of the states mentioned in article 5(1), submit him to its authorities for the purpose of prosecution. Under article 8(1) torture is to be treated as an extraditable offence and under article 8(4) torture shall, for the purposes of extradition, be treated as having been committed not only in the place where it occurred but also in the state mentioned in article 5(1).

Who Is an "Official" for the Purposes of the Torture Convention?

The first question on the Convention is to decide whether acts done by a head of state are done by "a public official or a person acting in an official capacity" within the meaning of article 1. The same question arises under section 134 of the *Criminal Justice Act 1988*. The answer to both questions must be the same. In his judgment at the first hearing, Lord Slynn, at pp. 1476-1477, held that a head of state was neither a public official nor a person acting in an official capacity within the meaning of article 1: he pointed out that there are a number of international conventions (for example the Statute of the International Criminal Tribunal for the Former Yugoslavia (1993) and the Statute of the International Criminal Tribunal for Rwanda (1994)) which refer specifically to heads of state when they intend to render them liable. Lord Lloyd apparently did not agree with Lord Slynn on this point since he thought that a head of state who was a torturer could be prosecuted in his own country, a view which could not be correct unless such head of state had conducted himself as a public official or in an official capacity.

It became clear during the argument that both the Republic of Chile and Senator Pinochet accepted that the acts alleged against Senator Pinochet, if proved, were acts done by a public official or person acting in an official capacity within the meaning of article 1. In my judgment these concessions were correctly made. Unless a head of state authorising or promoting torture is an official or acting in an official capacity within article 1, then he would not be guilty of the international crime of torture even within his own state. That plainly cannot have been the intention. In my judgment it would run completely contrary to the intention of the Convention if there was anybody who could be exempt from guilt. The crucial question is not whether Senator Pinochet falls within the definition in article 1: he plainly does. The question is whether, even so, he is procedurally immune from process. To my mind the fact that a head of state can be guilty of the crime casts little, if any, light on the question whether he is immune from prosecution for that crime in a foreign state.

Universal Jurisdiction

There was considerable argument before your Lordships concerning the extent of the jurisdiction to prosecute torturers conferred on states other than those mentioned in article 5(1). I do not find it necessary to seek an answer to all the points raised. It is enough that it is clear that in all circumstances, if the article 5(1) states do not choose to seek extradition or to prosecute the offender, other states must do so. The purpose of the Convention was to introduce the principle aut dedere aut punire—either you extradite or you punish: *Burgers and Danelius Handbook* p. 131. Throughout the negotiation of the Convention certain countries wished to make the exercise of jurisdiction under article 5(2) dependent upon the state assuming jurisdiction having refused extradition to an article 5(1) state. However, at a session in 1984 all objections to the principle of aut dedere aut punire were withdrawn. "The inclusion of universal jurisdiction in the draft Convention was no longer opposed by any delegation": Working Group on the Draft Convention U.N. Doc. E/CN. 4/1984/72, para. 26. If there is no prosecution by, or extradition to, an article 5(1) state, the state where the alleged offender is found (which will have already taken him into custody under article 6) must exercise the jurisdiction under article 5(2) by prosecuting him under article 7(1).

I gather the following important points from the Torture Convention: 1) Torture within the meaning of the Convention can only be committed by "a public official or other person acting in an official capacity," but these words include a head of state. A single act of official torture is "torture" within the Convention; 2) Superior orders provide no defence; 3) If the states with the most obvious jurisdiction (the article 5(1) states) do not seek to extradite, the state where the alleged torturer is found must prosecute or, apparently, extradite to another country, i.e. there is universal jurisdiction. 4) There is no express provision dealing with state immunity of heads of state, ambassadors or other officials. 5) Since Chile, Spain and the United Kingdom are all parties to the Convention, they are bound under treaty by its provisions whether or not such provisions would apply in the absence of treaty obligation. Chile ratified the Convention with effect from 30 October 1988 and the United Kingdom with effect from 8 December 1988.

State Immunity

This is the point around which most of the argument turned. It is of considerable general importance internationally since, if Senator Pinochet is not entitled to immunity in relation to the acts of torture alleged to have occurred after 29 September 1988, it will be the first time so far as counsel have discovered when a local domestic court has refused to afford immunity to a head of state or former head of state on the grounds that there can be no immunity against prosecution for certain international crimes.

Given the importance of the point, it is surprising how narrow is the area of dispute. There is general agreement between the parties as to the rules of statutory immunity and the rationale which underlies them. The issue is whether international law grants state immunity in relation to the international crime of torture and, if so, whether the Republic of Chile is entitled to claim such immunity even though Chile, Spain and the United Kingdom are all parties to the Torture Convention and therefore "contractually" bound to give effect to its provisions from 8 December 1988 at the latest.

It is a basic principle of international law that one sovereign state (the forum state) does not adjudicate on the conduct of a foreign state. The foreign state is entitled to procedural immunity from the processes of the forum state. This immunity extends to both criminal and civil liability. State immunity probably grew from the historical immunity of the person of the monarch. In any event, such personal immunity of the head of state persists to the present day: the head of state is entitled to the same immunity as the state itself. The diplomatic representative of the foreign state in the forum state is also afforded the same immunity in recognition of the dignity of the state which he represents. This immunity enjoyed by a head of state in power and an ambassador in post is a complete immunity attaching to the person of the head of state or ambassador and rendering him immune from all actions or prosecutions whether or not they relate to matters done for the benefit of the state. Such immunity is said to be granted *ratione personae*.

What then when the ambassador leaves his post or the head of state is deposed? The position of the ambassador is covered by the Vienna Convention on Diplomatic Relations (1961). After providing for immunity from arrest (article 29) and from criminal and civil jurisdiction (article 31), article 39(1) provides that the ambassador's privileges shall be enjoyed from the moment he takes up post; and subsection (2) provides:

> When the functions of a person enjoying privileges and immunities have come to an end, such privileges and immunities shall normally cease at the moment when he leaves the country, or on expiry of a reasonable period in which to do so, but shall subsist until that time, even in case of armed conflict. However, with respect to acts performed by such a person in the exercise of his functions as a member of the mission, immunity shall continue to subsist.

The continuing partial immunity of the ambassador after leaving post is of a different kind from that enjoyed *ratione personae* while he was in post. Since he is no longer the representative of the foreign state he merits no particular privileges or immunities as a person. However in order to preserve the integrity of the activities of the foreign state during the period when he was ambassador, it is necessary to provide that immunity is afforded to his *official* acts during his tenure in post. If this were not done the sovereign immunity of the state could be evaded by calling in question acts done during the previous ambassador's time. Accordingly under article 39(2) the ambassador, like any other official of the state, enjoys immunity in relation to his official acts done while he was an official. This limited immunity, *ratione materiae*, is to be contrasted with the former immunity *ratione personae* which gave complete immunity to all activities whether public or private.

In my judgment at common law a former head of state enjoys similar immunities, *ratione materiae*, once he ceases to be head of state. He too loses immunity *ratione personae* on ceasing to be head of state: see Sir Arthur Watts Q.C., Hague Lectures, "The Legal Position in International Law of Heads of States, Heads of Government and Foreign Ministers" 1994-III 247 Recueil des cours, p. 88 and the cases there cited. He can be sued on his private obligations: *Ex-King Farouk of Egypt v. Christian Dior* (1957) 24 I.L.R. 228; *Jimenez v. Aristeguieta* (1962) 311 F. 2d 547. As ex head of state he cannot be sued in respect of acts performed whilst head of state in his public capacity:

Hatch v. Baez (1876) 7 Hun. 596. Thus, at common law, the position of the former ambassador and the former head of state appears to be much the same: both enjoy immunity for acts done in performance of their respective functions whilst in office. ...

The question then which has to be answered is whether the alleged organisation of state torture by Senator Pinochet (if proved) would constitute an act committed by Senator Pinochet as part of his official functions as head of state. It is not enough to say that it cannot be part of the functions of the head of state to commit a crime. Actions which are criminal under the local law can still have been done officially and therefore give rise to immunity *ratione materiae*. The case needs to be analysed more closely.

Can it be said that the commission of a crime which is an international crime against humanity and *jus cogens* is an act done in an official capacity on behalf of the state? I believe there to be strong ground for saying that the implementation of torture as defined by the Torture Convention cannot be a state function. This is the view taken by Sir Arthur Watts Q.C. in his Hague Lecture, who said, at p. 82:

> While generally international law ... does not directly involve obligations on individuals personally, that is not always appropriate, particularly for acts of such seriousness that they constitute not merely international wrongs (in the broad sense of a civil wrong) but rather international crimes which offend against the public order of the international community. States are artificial legal persons: they can only act through the institutions and agencies of the state, which means, ultimately through its officials and other individuals acting on behalf of the state. For international conduct which is so serious as to be tainted with criminality to be regarded as attributable only to the impersonal state and not to the individuals who ordered or perpetrated it is both unrealistic and offensive to common notions of justice. The idea that individuals who commit international crimes are *internationally* accountable for them has now become an accepted part of international law. Problems in this area—such as the non-existence of any standing international tribunal to have jurisdiction over such crimes, and the lack of agreement as to what acts are internationally criminal for this purpose—have not affected the general acceptance of the principle of individual responsibility for international criminal conduct.

Later, at p. 84, he said: "It can no longer be doubted that as a matter of general customary international law a head of state will personally be liable to be called to account if there is sufficient evidence that he authorised or perpetrated such serious international crimes."

It can be objected that Sir Arthur was looking at those cases where the international community has established an international tribunal in relation to which the regulating document *expressly* makes the head of state subject to the tribunal's jurisdiction: see, for example, the Nuremberg Charter article 7; the Statute of the International Criminal Tribunal for former Yugoslavia; the Statute of the International Criminal Tribunal for Rwanda and the Statute of the International Criminal Court. It is true that in these cases it is expressly said that the head of state or former head of state is subject to the court's jurisdiction. But those are cases in which a new court with no existing jurisdiction is being established. The jurisdiction being established by the Torture Convention and the Hostages Convention is one where existing domestic courts of all the countries are being authorised and required to take jurisdiction internationally. The question is whether, in this new type of jurisdiction, the only possible view is that those made subject to the jurisdiction of each of the state courts of the world in relation to torture are not entitled to claim immunity.

I have doubts whether, before the coming into force of the Torture Convention, the existence of the international crime of torture as *jus cogens* was enough to justify the conclusion that the organisation of state torture could not rank for immunity purposes as performance of an official function. At that stage there was no international tribunal to punish torture and no general jurisdiction to permit or require its punishment in domestic courts. Not until there was some form of universal jurisdiction for the punishment of the crime of torture could it really be talked about as a fully constituted international crime. But in my judgment the Torture Convention did provide what was missing: a worldwide universal jurisdiction. Further, it required all member states to ban and outlaw torture: article 2. How can it be for international law purposes an official function to do something which international law itself prohibits and criminalises? Thirdly, an essential feature of the international crime of torture is that it must be committed "by or with the acquiesence of a public official or other person acting in an official capacity." As a result all defendants in torture cases will be state officials. Yet, if the former head of state has immunity, the man most responsible will escape liability while his inferiors (the chiefs of police, junior army officers) who carried out his orders will be liable. I find it impossible to accept that this was the intention.

Finally, and to my mind decisively, if the implementation of a torture regime is a public function giving rise to immunity *ratione materiae*, this produces bizarre results. Immunity *ratione materiae* applies not only to ex-heads of state and ex-ambassadors but to all state officials who have been involved in carrying out the functions of the state. Such immunity is necessary in order to prevent state immunity being circumvented by prosecuting or suing the official who, for example, actually carried out the torture when a claim against the head of state would be precluded by the doctrine of immunity. If that applied to the present case, and if the implementation of the torture regime is to be treated as official business sufficient to found an immunity for the former head of state, it must also be official business sufficient to justify immunity for his inferiors who actually did the torturing. Under the Convention the international crime of torture can only be committed by an official or someone in an official capacity. They would all be entitled to immunity. It would follow that there can be no case outside Chile in which a successful prosecution for torture can be brought unless the State of Chile is prepared to waive its right to its officials' immunity. Therefore the whole elaborate structure of universal jurisdiction over torture committed by officials is rendered abortive and one of the main objectives of the Torture Convention—to provide a system under which there is no safe haven for torturers—will have been frustrated. In my judgment all these factors together demonstrate that the notion of continued immunity for ex-heads of state is inconsistent with the provisions of the Torture Convention.

For these reasons in my judgment if, as alleged, Senator Pinochet organised and authorised torture after 8 December 1988, he was not acting in any capacity which gives rise to immunity *ratione materiae* because such actions were contrary to international law, Chile had agreed to outlaw such conduct and Chile had agreed with the other parties to the Torture Convention that all signatory states should have jurisdiction to try official torture (as defined in the Convention) even if such torture were committed in Chile.

As to the charges of murder and conspiracy to murder, no one has advanced any reason why the ordinary rules of immunity should not apply and Senator Pinochet is entitled to such immunity.

For these reasons, I would allow the appeal so as to permit the extradition proceedings to proceed on the allegation that torture in pursuance of a conspiracy to commit torture, including the single act of torture which is alleged in charge 30, was being committed by Senator Pinochet after 8 December 1988 when he lost his immunity.

In issuing to the magistrate an authority to proceed under section 7 of the *Extradition Act 1989*, the Secretary of State proceeded on the basis that the whole range of torture charges and murder charges against Senator Pinochet would be the subject matter of the extradition proceedings. Your Lordships' decision excluding from consideration a very large number of those charges constitutes a substantial change in the circumstances. This will obviously require the Secretary of State to reconsider his decision under section 7 in the light of the changed circumstances.

Case Concerning the Arrest Warrant of 11 April 2000 (Yerodia Case)[58]
Congo v. Belgium
I.C.J. 14 February 2002, 41 I.L.M. 536

[An international arrest warrant was issued by an investigating judge in Brussels, Belgium against Abdoulaye Yerodia Ndombasi, who was at the time the Minister of Foreign Affairs of the Congo. In the warrant, which was issued *in absentia* and circulated internationally, Yerodia was accused of inciting racial hatred by speeches he had made in the Congo in 1998 and was charged, under a Belgian statute, with war crimes and with crimes against humanity. Congo instituted proceedings in the ICJ to have the arrest warrant set aside because: (1) Belgium's exercise of universal jurisdiction was invalid, and (2) Yerodia was immune from Belgium's criminal jurisdiction. Since Congo chose to argue only the immunity issue in its final submissions, the Court's judgment addressed only this issue, but some judges gave separate opinions on the issue of universal jurisdiction, which are reproduced in Chapter 9, Section A.5.]

---

58   See A. Cassese, "When May Senior Officials Be Tried for International Crimes? Some Comments on the Belgium v. Congo Case" (2002) 13 E.J.I.L. 853; S. Wirth, "Immunity for Core Crimes: The ICJ's Judgements in the Congo v. Belgium Case" (2002) 13 E.J.I.L. 877. Compare *Prosecutor v. Charles Taylor*, Case No. SCSL-2003-01-1, Sierra Leone Special Court, Appeals Chamber decision on Immunity from Jurisdiction, May 31, 2004, summary online at: <www.sc-sl.org/Summary-SCSL-03-01-I-059.html>.

THE COURT: ...

[47] The Congo maintains that, during his or her term of office, a Minister for Foreign Affairs of a sovereign State is entitled to inviolability and to immunity from criminal process being "absolute or complete," that is to say, they are subject to no exception. Accordingly, the Congo contends that no criminal prosecution may be brought against a Minister for Foreign Affairs in a foreign court as long as he or she remains in office, and that any finding of criminal responsibility by a domestic court in a foreign country, or any act of investigation undertaken with a view to bringing him or her to court, would contravene the principle of immunity from jurisdiction. According to the Congo, the basis of such criminal immunity is purely functional, and immunity is accorded under customary international law simply in order to enable the foreign State representative enjoying such immunity to perform his or her functions freely and without let or hindrance. The Congo adds that the immunity thus accorded to Ministers for Foreign Affairs when in office covers all their acts, including any committed before they took office, and that it is irrelevant whether the acts done whilst in office may be characterized or not as "official acts."

[48] The Congo states further that it does not deny the existence of a principle of international criminal law, deriving from the decisions of the Nuremberg and Tokyo international military tribunals, that the accused's official capacity at the time of the acts cannot, before any court, whether domestic or international, constitute a "ground of exemption from his criminal responsibility or a ground for mitigation of sentence." The Congo then stresses that the fact that an immunity might bar prosecution before a specific court or over a specific period does not mean that the same prosecution cannot be brought, if appropriate, before another court which is not bound by that immunity, or at another time when the immunity need no longer be taken into account. It concludes that immunity does not mean impunity.

[49] Belgium maintains for its part that, while Ministers for Foreign Affairs in office generally enjoy an immunity from jurisdiction before the courts of a foreign State, such immunity applies only to acts carried out in the course of their official functions, and cannot protect such persons in respect of private acts or when they are acting otherwise than in the performance of their official functions.

[50] Belgium further states that, in the circumstances of the present case, Mr. Yerodia enjoyed no immunity at the time when he is alleged to have committed the acts of which he is accused, and that there is no evidence that he was then acting in any official capacity. It observes that the arrest warrant was issued against Mr. Yerodia personally. ...

[51] The Court would observe at the outset that in international law it is firmly established that, as also diplomatic and consular agents, certain holders of high-ranking office in a State, such as the Head of State, Head of Government and Minister for Foreign Affairs, enjoy immunities from jurisdiction in other States, both civil and criminal. For the purposes of the present case, it is only the immunity from criminal jurisdiction and the inviolability of an incumbent Minister for Foreign Affairs that fall for the Court to consider.

[52] A certain number of treaty instruments were cited by the Parties in this regard. These included, first, the Vienna Convention on Diplomatic Relations of 18 April 1961, which states in its preamble that the purpose of diplomatic privileges and

immunities is "to ensure the efficient performance of the functions of diplomatic missions as representing States." It provides in Article 32 that only the sending State may waive such immunity. On these points, the Vienna Convention on Diplomatic Relations, to which both the Congo and Belgium are parties, reflects customary international law. The same applies to the corresponding provisions of the Vienna Convention on Consular Relations of 24 April 1963, to which the Congo and Belgium are also parties. The Congo and Belgium further cite the New York Convention on Special Missions of 8 December 1969, to which they are not, however, parties. They recall that under Article 21, paragraph 2, of that Convention:

> The Head of the Government, the Minister for Foreign Affairs and other persons of high rank, when they take part in a special mission of the sending State, shall enjoy in the receiving State or in a third State, in addition to what is granted by the present Convention, the facilities, privileges and immunities accorded by international law.

These conventions provide useful guidance on certain aspects of the question of immunities. They do not, however, contain any provision specifically defining the immunities enjoyed by Ministers for Foreign Affairs. It is consequently on the basis of customary international law that the Court must decide the questions relating to the immunities of such Ministers raised in the present case.

[53] In customary international law, the immunities accorded to Ministers for Foreign Affairs are not granted for their personal benefit, but to ensure the effective performance of their functions on behalf of their respective States. In order to determine the extent of these immunities, the Court must therefore first consider the nature of the functions exercised by a Minister for Foreign Affairs. He or she is in charge of his or her Government's diplomatic activities and generally acts as its representative in international negotiations and intergovernmental meetings. Ambassadors and other diplomatic agents carry out their duties under his or her authority. His or her acts may bind the State represented, and there is a presumption that a Minister for Foreign Affairs, simply by virtue of that office, has full powers to act on behalf of the State (see, e.g., Art. 7, para. 2 (a), of the 1969 Vienna Convention on the Law of Treaties). In the performance of these functions, he or she is frequently required to travel internationally, and thus must be in a position freely to do so whenever the need should arise. He or she must also be in constant communication with the Government, and with its diplomatic missions around the world, and be capable at any time of communicating with representatives of other States. The Court further observes that a Minister for Foreign Affairs, responsible for the conduct of his or her State's relations with all other States, occupies a position such that, like the Head of State or the Head of Government, he or she is recognized under international law as representative of the State solely by virtue of his or her office. He or she does not have to present letters of credence: to the contrary, it is generally the Minister who determines the authority to be conferred upon diplomatic agents and countersigns their letters of credence. Finally, it is to the Minister for Foreign Affairs that chargés d'affaires are accredited.

[54] The Court accordingly concludes that the functions of a Minister for Foreign Affairs are such that, throughout the duration of his or her office, he or she when abroad

enjoys full immunity from criminal jurisdiction and inviolability. That immunity and that inviolability protect the individual concerned against any act of authority of another State which would hinder him or her in the performance of his or her duties.

[55] In this respect, no distinction can be drawn between acts performed by a Minister for Foreign Affairs in an "official" capacity, and those claimed to have been performed in a "private capacity," or, for that matter, between acts performed before the person concerned assumed office as Minister for Foreign Affairs and acts committed during the period of office. Thus, if a Minister for Foreign Affairs is arrested in another State on a criminal charge, he or she is clearly thereby prevented from exercising the functions of his or her office. The consequences of such impediment to the exercise of those official functions are equally serious, regardless of whether the Minister for Foreign Affairs was, at the time of arrest, present in the territory of the arresting State on an "official" visit or a "private" visit, regardless of whether the arrest relates to acts allegedly performed before the person became the Minister for Foreign Affairs or to acts performed while in office, and regardless of whether the arrest relates to alleged acts performed in an "official" capacity or a "private" capacity. Furthermore, even the mere risk that, by travelling to or transiting another State a Minister for Foreign Affairs might be exposing himself or herself to legal proceedings could deter the Minister from travelling internationally when required to do so for the purposes of the performance of his or her official functions. ...

[56] The Court will now address Belgium's argument that immunities accorded to incumbent Ministers for Foreign Affairs can in no case protect them where they are suspected of having committed war crimes or crimes against humanity. In support of this position, Belgium refers in its Counter-Memorial to various legal instruments creating international criminal tribunals, to examples from national legislation, and to the jurisprudence of national and international courts. Belgium begins by pointing out that certain provisions of the instruments creating international criminal tribunals state expressly that the official capacity of a person shall not be a bar to the exercise by such tribunals of their jurisdiction. Belgium also places emphasis on certain decisions of national courts, and in particular on the judgments rendered on 24 March 1999 by the House of Lords in the United Kingdom and on 13 March 2001 by the Court of Cassation in France in the Pinochet and Qaddafi cases respectively, in which it contends that an exception to the immunity rule was accepted in the case of serious crimes under international law. Thus, according to Belgium, the Pinochet decision recognizes an exception to the immunity rule when Lord Millett stated that "[i]nternational law cannot be supposed to have established a crime having the character of a *jus cogens* and at the same time to have provided an immunity which is co-extensive with the obligation it seeks to impose," or when Lord Phillips of Worth Matravers said that "no established rule of international law requires state immunity rationae materiae to be accorded in respect of prosecution for an international crime." As to the French Court of Cassation, Belgium contends that, in holding that, "under international law as it currently stands, the crime alleged [acts of terrorism], irrespective of its gravity, does not come within the exceptions to the principle of immunity from jurisdiction for incumbent foreign Heads of State," the Court explicitly recognized the existence of such exceptions.

[57] The Congo, for its part, states that, under international law as it currently stands, there is no basis for asserting that there is any exception to the principle of absolute immunity from criminal process of an incumbent Minister for Foreign Affairs where he or she is accused of having committed crimes under international law. In support of this contention, the Congo refers to State practice, giving particular consideration in this regard to the Pinochet and Qaddafi cases, and concluding that such practice does not correspond to that which Belgium claims but, on the contrary, confirms the absolute nature of the immunity from criminal process of Heads of State and Ministers for Foreign Affairs. Thus, in the Pinochet case, the Congo cites Lord Browne-Wilkinson's statement that "[t]his immunity enjoyed by a head of state in power and an ambassador in post is a complete immunity attached to the person of the head of state or ambassador and rendering him immune from all actions or prosecutions ... ." According to the Congo, the French Court of Cassation adopted the same position in its Qaddafi judgment, in affirming that "international custom bars the prosecution of incumbent Heads of State, in the absence of any contrary international provision binding on the parties concerned, before the criminal courts of a foreign State." As regards the instruments creating international criminal tribunals and the latter's jurisprudence, these, in the Congo's view, concern only those tribunals, and no inference can be drawn from them in regard to criminal proceedings before national courts against persons enjoying immunity under international law. ...

[58] The Court has carefully examined State practice, including national legislation and those few decisions of national higher courts, such as the House of Lords or the French Court of Cassation. It has been unable to deduce from this practice that there exists under customary international law any form of exception to the rule according immunity from criminal jurisdiction and inviolability to incumbent Ministers for Foreign Affairs, where they are suspected of having committed war crimes or crimes against humanity. The Court has also examined the rules concerning the immunity or criminal responsibility of persons having an official capacity contained in the legal instruments creating international criminal tribunals, and which are specifically applicable to the latter (see Charter of the International Military Tribunal of Nuremberg, Art. 7; Charter of the International Military Tribunal of Tokyo, Art. 6; Statute of the International Criminal Tribunal for the former Yugoslavia, Art. 7, para. 2; Statute of the International Criminal Tribunal for Rwanda, Art. 6, para. 2; Statute of the International Criminal Court, Art. 27). It finds that these rules likewise do not enable it to conclude that any such an exception exists in customary international law in regard to national courts. Finally, none of the decisions of the Nuremberg and Tokyo international military tribunals, or of the International Criminal Tribunal for the former Yugoslavia, cited by Belgium deal with the question of the immunities of incumbent Ministers for Foreign Affairs before national courts where they are accused of having committed war crimes or crimes against humanity. The Court accordingly notes that those decisions are in no way at variance with the findings it has reached above. In view of the foregoing, the Court accordingly cannot accept Belgium's argument in this regard.

[59] It should further be noted that the rules governing the jurisdiction of national courts must be carefully distinguished from those governing jurisdictional immunities:

jurisdiction does not imply absence of immunity, while absence of immunity does not imply jurisdiction. Thus, although various international conventions on the prevention and punishment of certain serious crimes impose on States obligations of prosecution or extradition, thereby requiring them to extend their criminal jurisdiction, such extension of jurisdiction in no way affects immunities under customary international law, including those of Ministers for Foreign Affairs. These remain opposable before the courts of a foreign State, even where those courts exercise such a jurisdiction under these conventions.

[60] The Court emphasizes, however, that the immunity from jurisdiction enjoyed by incumbent Ministers for Foreign Affairs does not mean that they enjoy impunity in respect of any crimes they might have committed, irrespective of their gravity. Immunity from criminal jurisdiction and individual criminal responsibility are quite separate concepts. While jurisdictional immunity is procedural in nature, criminal responsibility is a question of substantive law. Jurisdictional immunity may well bar prosecution for a certain period or for certain offences; it cannot exonerate the person to whom it applies from all criminal responsibility.

[61] Accordingly, the immunities enjoyed under international law by an incumbent or former Minister for Foreign Affairs do not represent a bar to criminal prosecution in certain circumstances. First, such persons enjoy no criminal immunity under international law in their own countries, and may thus be tried by those countries' courts in accordance with the relevant rules of domestic law. Secondly, they will cease to enjoy immunity from foreign jurisdiction if the State which they represent or have represented decides to waive that immunity. Thirdly, after a person ceases to hold the office of Minister for Foreign Affairs, he or she will no longer enjoy all of the immunities accorded by international law in other States. Provided that it has jurisdiction under international law, a court of one State may try a former Minister for Foreign Affairs of another State in respect of acts committed prior or subsequent to his or her period of office, as well as in respect of acts committed during that period of office in a private capacity. Fourthly, an incumbent or former Minister for Foreign Affairs may be subject to criminal proceedings before certain international criminal courts, where they have jurisdiction. Examples include the International Criminal Tribunal for the former Yugoslavia, and the International Criminal Tribunal for Rwanda, established pursuant to Security Council resolutions under Chapter VII of the United Nations Charter, and the future International Criminal Court created by the 1998 Rome Convention. The latter's Statute expressly provides, in Article 27, paragraph 2, that

> [i]mmunities or special procedural rules which may attach to the official capacity of a person, whether under national or international law, shall not bar the Court from exercising its jurisdiction over such a person.

. . .

[62] Given the conclusions it has reached above concerning the nature and scope of the rules governing the immunity from criminal jurisdiction enjoyed by incumbent Ministers for Foreign Affairs, the Court must now consider whether in the present

case the issue of the arrest warrant of 11 April 2000 and its international circulation violated those rules. ...

[70] The Court notes that the issuance, as such, of the disputed arrest warrant represents an act by the Belgian judicial authorities intended to enable the arrest on Belgian territory of an incumbent Minister for Foreign Affairs on charges of war crimes and crimes against humanity. The fact that the warrant is enforceable is clearly apparent from the order given to "all bailiffs and agents of public authority ... to execute this arrest warrant" ... and from the assertion in the warrant that "the position of Minister for Foreign Affairs currently held by the accused does not entail immunity from jurisdiction and enforcement." The Court notes that the warrant did admittedly make an exception for the case of an official visit by Mr. Yerodia to Belgium, and that Mr. Yerodia never suffered arrest in Belgium. The Court is bound, however, to find that, given the nature and purpose of the warrant, its mere issue violated the immunity which Mr. Yerodia enjoyed as the Congo's incumbent Minister for Foreign Affairs. The Court accordingly concludes that the issue of the warrant constituted a violation of an obligation of Belgium towards the Congo, in that it failed to respect the immunity of that Minister and, more particularly, infringed the immunity from criminal jurisdiction and the inviolability then enjoyed by him under international law.

[71] The Court also notes that Belgium admits that the purpose of the international circulation of the disputed arrest warrant was "to establish a legal basis for the arrest of Mr. Yerodia ... abroad and his subsequent extradition to Belgium." The Respondent maintains, however, that the enforcement of the warrant in third States was "dependent on some further preliminary steps having been taken" and that, given the "inchoate" quality of the warrant as regards third States, there was no "infringe[ment of] the sovereignty of the [Congo]." It further points out that no Interpol Red Notice was requested until 12 September 2001, when Mr. Yerodia no longer held ministerial office. The Court cannot subscribe to this view. As in the case of the warrant's issue, its international circulation from June 2000 by the Belgian authorities, given its nature and purpose, effectively infringed Mr. Yerodia's immunity as the Congo's incumbent Minister for Foreign Affairs and was furthermore liable to affect the Congo's conduct of its international relations. Since Mr. Yerodia was called upon in that capacity to undertake travel in the performance of his duties, the mere international circulation of the warrant, even in the absence of "further steps" by Belgium, could have resulted, in particular, in his arrest while abroad. The Court observes in this respect that Belgium itself cites information to the effect that Mr. Yerodia, "on applying for a visa to go to two countries, [apparently] learned that he ran the risk of being arrested as a result of the arrest warrant issued against him by Belgium," adding that "[t]his, moreover, is what the [Congo] ... hints when it writes that the arrest warrant 'sometimes forced Minister Yerodia to travel by roundabout routes.' " Accordingly, the Court concludes that the circulation of the warrant, whether or not it significantly interfered with Mr. Yerodia's diplomatic activity, constituted a violation of an obligation of Belgium towards the Congo, in that it failed to respect the immunity of the incumbent Minister for Foreign Affairs of the Congo and, more particularly, infringed the immunity from criminal jurisdiction and the inviolability then enjoyed by him under international law. ...

[78] For these reasons,

THE COURT: ...

(2) By thirteen votes to three,

Finds that the issue against Mr. Abdulaye Yerodia Ndombasi of the arrest warrant of 11 April 2000, and its international circulation, constituted violations of a legal obligation of the Kingdom of Belgium towards the Democratic Republic of the Congo, in that they failed to respect the immunity from criminal jurisdiction and the inviolability which the incumbent Minister for Foreign Affairs of the Democratic Republic of the Congo enjoyed under international law; ...

(3) By ten votes to six,

Finds that the Kingdom of Belgium must, by means of its own choosing, cancel the arrest warrant of 11 April 2000 and so inform the authorities to whom that warrant was circulated.

NOTES

1) *Pinochet*'s case revolved around torture as defined in the Convention Against Torture. In Canadian law, torture is proscribed in the *Criminal Code* section 269.1 in terms that reflect the Convention, and also in the *Crimes Against Humanity and War Crimes Act*, reproduced above, by its implementation of article 7 of the Rome Statute of the ICC. The two definitions are not identical, so of what precedential value is the *Pinochet* case in Canada?

2) May the principle of *Pinochet*'s case be extended beyond torture to other international crimes? To crimes that have attained the status of *jus cogens*? To all crimes of universal jurisdiction or that require a state to prosecute or extradite?

3) What is the effect of the ICJ's determination of the customary international law of immunity from criminal process in *Yerodia* on the principles expounded in *Pinochet*?

4) How is the distinction made in *Yerodia* between public and private wrongdoings to be drawn in practice? Are all international crimes committed in a private capacity, even when perpetrated by a person in public office and as part of government policy?

5) The cases of *Pinochet* and *Yerodia* dealt only with the highest officials of state. In what circumstances might there be immunity from criminal process for lower state officials?

CHAPTER TWELVE

Protection of Human Rights

Over the last 50 years, human rights have emerged as one of the most significant agents of change in the creation of international legal norms. In this short period of time, human rights have permeated nearly all areas of international law, from recognition of states and international trade to protection of the environment and international peace and security. Although its actual impact on international relations and the conduct of states remains highly variable, human rights law constitutes a powerful legal and rhetorical tool in the hands of lawyers, activists, governments, and organizations. It is not an easy tool to wield, however, because its disjointed evolution resulted in a "system" that is shapeless and at times inconsistent. This chapter presents (1) a brief description of the evolution and particular features of human rights norms (Section A); (2) the varied content of human rights and the challenges they present (Section B); and (3) the mechanisms in treaty and general international law available to ensure compliance and enforcement (Section C).

A. INTRODUCTION

1. Development[1]

The place of human rights in the international legal system before World War II was limited at best. While the idea that individuals are endowed with fundamental or natural rights can be traced back to Greek and Roman philosophy, with significant echoes in

---

1   H. Lauterpacht, *International Law and Human Rights* (1973); M. McDougal, H. Lasswell & L. Chen, *Human Rights and World Public Order* (1980); K. Vasak & P. Alston, eds., *The International Dimensions of Human Rights* (1982) 2 vols.; T. Meron, ed., *Human Rights in International Law; Legal and Policy Issues* (1984/1985); J. Donnelly, *Universal Human Rights in Theory and Practice*, 2d ed. (2003); I. Brecher, ed., *Human Rights Development and Foreign Policy: Canadian Perspectives* (1989); H. Hannum, ed., *Guide to International Rights Practice*, 4th ed. (2004); I. Cotler & F.P. Eliadis, *International Human Rights Law, Theory and Practice* (1992); P. Alston, ed., *The United Nations and Human Right: A Critical Appraisal* (1992); R. Lillich & F. Newman, eds., *International Human Rights; Problems of Law and Policy*, 2d ed. (1996); A. Robertson & J. Merrils, *Human Rights in the World; An Introduction to the Study of the International Protection of Human Rights*, 4th ed. (1996); W. Schabas, *Précis du droit international des droits de la personne, avec une attention particulière au droit du Canada et du Québec* (1997); S. Watson, *Efficacy and Validity in the International Protection of Human Rights* (1999); H. Steiner & P. Alston, *International Human Rights in Context: Law, Politics, Morals*, 2d ed. (2000); R. Provost, *International Human Rights and Humanitarian Law* (2002); M. Nowak, *Introduction to the International Human Rights Regime* (2003); and R. Smith, *International Human Rights* (2003).

medieval natural law doctrines, such rights were not recognized as creating binding limitations on the sovereign's absolute power over his or her subjects. On the contrary, state sovereignty became the central pillar of the law of nations, a concept largely incompatible with the adoption of international human rights standards. The slow emergence of human rights in positive international law has involved a constant struggle to roll back the concept of state sovereignty from its absolutist beginnings.

Some norms that we would now regard as human rights were adopted in the wake of World War I. The peace treaties signed by the various belligerents included, in an attempt to stabilize various parts of Eastern Europe, specific protections for minority groups. Members of minorities were guaranteed the right to life and liberty without discrimination, equality before the law, free exercise of religion, and control over education. The League of Nations Covenant did not refer to human rights, and proposals to include a prohibition of racial discrimination and universal protection of minorities were voted down, but a system of mandates was created for former colonies whereby inhabitants were recognized as holding certain basic rights. Finally, the International Labour Organisation (ILO) was created in 1919 to address the conditions of workers. It adopted a number of important international conventions touching on forced labour, working conditions, minimum age of employment, and the like. To this could be added, from the late 18th century, international customary standards on the treatment of aliens, which guaranteed a minimum level of equality under the law, due process, and protection against expropriation without compensation. Any violation of these standards gave the victim's state of nationality a discretionary right to exercise diplomatic protection and seek compensation from the violating state (see Chapter 10, Section B). These norms followed the expansion of European colonial empires and the need to protect nationals travelling on the outer edges of these empires. Standards on the protection of aliens were the object of a protracted debate between developed and developing countries, with the former arguing for an international minimal standard applicable to all aliens, the content of which mirrored parts of contemporary human rights. Developing countries rejected such a universal standard that, in effect, created rights in favour of aliens that citizens often did not enjoy under municipal laws. The debate became largely moot after the emergence of universal human rights norms, except for rules relating to expropriation.[2]

The Holocaust and other atrocities committed during World War II acted as a catalyst for the rise of a movement seeking to integrate binding human rights standards in international law. Experience revealed that international standards protecting aliens and other special classes of individuals such as diplomats were insufficient, and that international law should include fundamental rights applying equally to everyone everywhere, including citizens residing in their own states. Public pressure likely encouraged the United States, which formulated the working draft of the U.N. Charter (the so-called Dumbarton Oaks proposals), to incorporate a vague reference to human

---

2   Discussed in Chapter 10, Section B.1 on "State Responsibility." The last salvo in the debate was the adoption by the U.N. General Assembly of the *Declaration on the Human Rights of Individuals Who Are Not Citizens of the Country in Which They Live*, GA Res. 40/144, UN GAOR, 40th Sess., Supp. No. 53, U.N. Doc. A/40/53 (1985) 252, reproduced in Chapter 10, Section B.2.

rights. However, those proposals attempted to preserve the status and control over international affairs of the states that became the Permanent Members of the U.N. Security Council (UNSC). The document reflected their absorption with military security; it did not represent the views of some other countries or of private interests. The relatively strong human rights provisions ultimately inscribed in the Charter were largely the result of determined lobbying by a group of non-governmental organizations and individuals invited to the San Francisco Conference, aided by delegations from smaller nations.[3]

The U.N. Charter not only contains numerous and somewhat cryptic references to human rights, but also entrenches them as one of the purposes of the U.N. Organization (see Art. 1(3) of the U.N. Charter reproduced in the Documentary Supplement). That fact commenced the slow process of elevating human rights from a subsidiary role to a primary one both for the United Nations and in international law in general. Their further development was taken up by the General Assembly and the Economic and Social Council. The Council established the Human Rights Commission and entrusted to that body the task of drafting an international bill of rights. The Commission began its work in 1946, but the divergence of views among member states forced it to plan to create not one but three documents: (1) a declaration defining the human rights in the Charter, (2) a treaty that states could ratify to make those rights legally binding, and (3) a procedural mechanism to ensure that states would implement them.

In 1948, two years after it had begun its work, the Commission on Human Rights completed a draft declaration for presentation to the General Assembly as a resolution. This choice of forum for the declaration answered the concerns of most states, because General Assembly resolutions are not automatically legally binding. It also helped the Commission, which, armed with such a resolution, possessed a more authoritative mandate to prepare a binding human rights treaty and implementation process. The draft was first scrutinized by the General Assembly's Committee on Social, Cultural and Humanitarian Questions (the Third Committee), which had to meet for 81 sessions before its members were ready to report out a draft of the Universal Declaration. In the Third Committee, Canada surprised observers by joining six Soviet bloc states in abstaining on the vote to accept the Declaration. Professor Humphrey records that a Canadian delegate unconvincingly claimed Canada had declined to support the proposal because the federal government feared encroaching on provincial constitutional powers. More likely, the legal and business communities in Canada pressured the Government to resist the proclamation of a document seen as too "revolutionary" or Marxist. Humphrey has suggested that the Canadian delegation later altered its position and voted in favour of the resolution in the General Assembly because "the government did not relish the company in which it found itself."[4]

---

3   J.T.P. Humphrey, *Human Rights and the United Nations: A Great Adventure* (1984) at 12-13.

4   See *ibid.* at 72 and 79; A.J. Hobbins, "Eleanor Roosevelt, John Humphrey and Canadian Opposition to the Universal Declaration of Human Rights; Looking Back on the 50th Anniversary of the UNDHR" (1998) 53 Int. J. 325; and W. Schabas, "Canada and the Adoption of the Universal Declaration of Human Rights" (1998) 43 McGill L. J. 403. Other reasons behind Canada's position appear in a telegram sent to Lester Pearson, then the Foreign Affairs Minister: "Quite apart from the question of provincial jurisdiction, the Cabinet holds strongly to the view that the language is sometime so lacking in precision

On December 10, 1948, the General Assembly quickly adopted the resolution contained in the Committee's report. Of the 56 U.N. member states at the time, 48 voted in favour of the resolution, 0 voted against it, and 8 (Byelorussia, Czechoslovakia, Poland, Soviet Union, Ukraine, Yugoslavia, South Africa, and Saudi Arabia) abstained. The eight delegations that abstained in the General Assembly vote did not hide their objections, some of which bear repeating because they foreshadow a number of major, contemporary problems in international human rights law. The Eastern bloc states, for example, complained that the Declaration's foundation in Western ideology, the economic system of free enterprise, and the political philosophy of liberalism, placed too great an emphasis on a narrow band of civil and political rights and failed to grant adequate recognition either to economic, social, and cultural rights or to collective rights and duties. A delegate from the Soviet Union also complained that it failed to mention national sovereignty. Additionally, South Africa, already suffering from attacks in the United Nations for its domestic policy of apartheid, had the prescience to object that the resolution could well lead to the Universal Declaration becoming the definitive statement of the human rights contained in the U.N. Charter, and thus being elevated to a binding norm of international law. Saudi Arabia based its objection on another ground: the inclusion of the right of persons to change their religion or belief contradicted the rule of the Koran.[5]

Charter of the United Nations
Preamble and Articles 1, 8, 13, 55, 56, 62, 73, 74, and 76
Reproduced in the Documentary Supplement

Universal Declaration of Human Rights
Reproduced in the Documentary Supplement

NOTES

1) If the U.N. Charter heralded a major step in the development of international human rights law, the Universal Declaration commenced a second stage in the process. The growing fear by states that international human rights norms might well become binding international legal obligations was apparent during the Commission and

---

as to make some articles incapable of application. For example, unless Article 28 is given a very broad interpretation and application, Article No. 19, conferring the right to public employment irrespective of political creed, must be read as requiring the employment of Communists in the government service, while Article 16 would permit the unrestricted activities of sects such as Jehovah's Witnesses," reprinted in, H. MacKenzie, ed., *Documents on Canadian External Relations* (1994) vol. 14 at 359.

John Humphrey, a McGill law professor serving as the first Director of the U.N. Division on Human Rights, had a major influence on human rights as the author of the initial draft of the *Universal Declaration*. A printed version of John Humphrey's first long-hand manuscript may be read in (1995) 33 Can. Y.B. Int'l L. 333.

5   Humphrey, *supra* note 3 at 73. On the *Universal Declaration*, see A. Eide, ed., *The Universal Declaration of Human Rights; A Commentary* (1992); and A. Verdoodt, *Naissance et signification de la Déclaration universelle des droits de l'homme* (1964).

Committee debates on the Declaration, and intensified as the United Nations pressed further to draft a human rights treaty. The drafting process also became embroiled in ideological battles between various groups of states holding different opinions as to which rights ought to be included. As a result, the process slowed even more, and in 1952 the Commission was forced to split the draft into two separate treaties: one for civil and political rights, and another for social, economic, and cultural rights. Moreover, states could not agree on a common enforcement mechanism for both treaties because of fundamental differences in the rights contained in each. After 18 years of debate, states finally accepted three instruments that elaborated on the rights in the Universal Declaration: the International Covenant on Civil and Political Rights (ICCPR),[6] the International Covenant on Economic, Social and Cultural Rights (ICESCR),[7] and an Optional Protocol to the Covenant on Civil and Political Rights.[8] The last treaty grants individuals a right of petition to the U.N. Human Rights Committee if they believe that a state that has ratified the Protocol has violated their rights under the ICCPR. Owing to the continued resistance of states to incur duties in what was previously their reserved domain, it took another decade before getting the 35 ratifications needed for the Covenants to enter into force.

2) The adoption and entry into force of the two Covenants signalled the acceleration of human rights law's penetration of international law. There are now 191 states parties to the U.N. Charter, compared with 149 parties to the ICCPR; 104 parties to the (First) Optional Protocol; 146 parties to the ICESCR; 165 parties to the Convention on the Elimination of All Forms of Racial Discrimination; 170 parties to the Convention on the Elimination of All Forms of Discrimination Against Women; and 191 parties to the Convention on the Rights of the Child, to mention only these very important treaties.[9] Human rights are now well-entrenched within the international legal system to the point where no government challenges the existence of such rights or their applicability to state behaviour taking place wholly within national territory. The debate has shifted to the content of human rights, the need to adapt them to varied contexts, and specific applications to concrete situations.

2. Special Nature of Human Rights

Human rights are in some respects distinct from most international law, particularly in that they seek to govern the relations of a state and individuals under its control rather than interstate relations. The decision of the U.N. Human Rights Committee (UNHRC) in the case of *Toonen v. Australia* illustrates some of these features in this subsection, as well as other issues in the rest of this chapter.

---

6   (1966) 999 U.N.T.S. 171; Can. T.S. 1976 No. 47, reproduced in the Documentary Supplement.

7   (1966) 993 U.N.T.S. 3; Can.T.S. 1976 No. 46, reproduced in the Documentary Supplement.

8   (1966) 999 U.N.T.S. 302; Can. T.S. 1976 No. 47, reproduced below in Section C on "Compliance and Enforcement." The General Assembly on December 15, 1989 adopted a Second Optional Protocol to the *International Covenant on Civil and Political Rights: Aiming at the Abolition of the Death Penalty*, GA Res. 44/128, UN GAOR, 44th Sess., Supp. No. 49, U.N. Doc. A/44/49 (1989) 206.

9   Status of ratification of various treaties deposited with the U.N. Secretary General as of May 11, 1999, available online: <http://untreaty.un.org>.

Toonen v. Australia
U.N. HRC Communication No. 488/1992; (1994) 1-3 Int. Hum. Rts. Rep. 97

[Nicholas Toonen is an Australian national and gay rights activist living in the state of Tasmania. He petitioned the Human Rights Committee seeking a declaration that two provisions of the Tasmanian *Criminal Code* prohibiting "unnatural sexual intercourse" (s. 122) and "indecent practice between male persons" (s. 123) contravened articles 2(1), 17, and 26 of the ICCPR (reproduced in the Documentary Supplement). He alleged that he and other homosexuals and lesbians in Tasmania had been the victims of a campaign of official and unofficial hatred. The Australian government, as the state party, forwarded the arguments of the Tasmanian state government while disputing the validity of many of them. The Human Rights Committee deemed the communication admissible and proceeded to examine the merits of the petition.]

8.1 The Committee is called upon to determine whether Mr. Toonen has been the victim of an unlawful or arbitrary interference with his privacy, contrary to article 17, paragraph 1, and whether he has been discriminated against in his right to equal protection of the law, contrary to article 26.

8.2 Inasmuch as article 17 is concerned, it is undisputed that adult consensual sexual activity in private is covered by the concept of "privacy," and that Mr. Toonen is actually and currently affected by the continued existence of the Tasmanian laws. The Committee considers that Sections 122(a), (c) and 123 of the Tasmanian Criminal Code "interfere" with the author's privacy, even if these provisions have not been enforced for a decade. In this context, it notes that the policy of the Department of Public Prosecutions not to initiate criminal proceedings in respect of private homosexual conduct does not amount to a guarantee that no actions will be brought against homosexuals in the future, particularly in the light of undisputed statements of the Director of Public Prosecutions of Tasmania in 1988 and those of members of the Tasmanian Parliament. The continued existence of the challenged provisions therefore continuously and directly "interferes" with the author's privacy.

8.3 The prohibition against private homosexual behaviour is provided for by law, namely, Sections 122 and 123 of the Tasmanian Criminal Code. As to whether it may be deemed arbitrary, the Committee recalls that pursuant to its General Comment 16(32) on article 17, the "introduction of the concept of arbitrariness is intended to guarantee that even interference provided for by the law should be in accordance with the provisions, aims and objectives of the Covenant and should be, in any event, reasonable in the circumstances."[10] The Committee interprets the requirement of reasonableness to imply that any interference with privacy must be proportional to the end sought and be necessary in the circumstances of any given case.

---

10   General Comment 16(32) (article 17) in "General Comments Adopted by the Committee under Article 40, paragraph 4 of the International Covenant on Civil and Political Rights—General Comments 1(13) to 17(35)" (U.N. Doc. CCPR/C/21/Rev.1) in *Official Records of the Human Rights Committee 1988/89*, vol. 2, 291 at 301.

8.4 While the State party acknowledges that the impugned provisions constitute an arbitrary interference with Mr. Toonen's privacy, the Tasmanian authorities submit that the challenged laws are justified on public health and moral grounds, as they are intended in part to prevent the spread of HIV/AIDS in Tasmania, and because, in the absence of specific limitation clauses in article 17, moral issues must be deemed a matter for domestic decision.

8.5 As far as the public health argument of the Tasmanian authorities is concerned, the Committee notes that the criminalization of homosexual practices cannot be considered a reasonable means or proportionate measure to achieve the aim of preventing the spread of AIDS/HIV. The Australian Government observes that statutes criminalizing homosexual activity tend to impede public health programmes "by driving underground many of the people at the risk of infection." Criminalization of homosexual activity thus would appear to run counter to the implementation of effective education programmes in respect of the HIV/AIDS prevention. Secondly, the Committee notes that no link has been shown between the continued criminalization of homosexual activity and the effective control of the spread of the HIV/AIDS virus.

8.6 The Committee cannot accept either that for the purposes of article 17 of the Covenant, moral issues are exclusively a matter of domestic concern, as this would open the door to withdrawing from the Committee's scrutiny a potentially large number of statutes interfering with privacy. It further notes that with the exception of Tasmania, all laws criminalizing homosexuality have been repealed throughout Australia and that, even in Tasmania, it is apparent that there is no consensus as to whether Sections 122 and 123 should not also be repealed. Considering further that these provisions are not currently enforced, which implies that they are not deemed essential to the protection of morals in Tasmania, the Committee concludes that the provisions do not meet the "reasonableness" test in the circumstances of the case, and that they arbitrarily interfere with Mr. Toonen's right under article 17, paragraph 1.

8.7 The State party has sought the Committee's guidance as to whether sexual orientation may be considered an "other status" for the purposes of article 26. The same issue could arise under article 2, paragraph 1, of the Covenant. The Committee confines itself to noting, however, that in its view the reference to "sex" in articles 2, paragraph 1, and 26 is to be taken as including sexual orientation.

9. The Human Rights Committee, acting under article 5, paragraph 4, of the Optional Protocol to the International Covenant on Civil and Political Rights, is of the view that the facts before it reveal a violation of articles 17, paragraph 1, juncto 2, paragraph 1, of the Covenant.

10. Under article 2(3)(a) of the Covenant, the author, victim of a violation of articles 17, paragraph 1, juncto 2, paragraph 1, of the Covenant, is entitled to a remedy. In the opinion of the Committee, an effective remedy would be the repeal of Sections 122(a), (c) and 123 of the Tasmanian Criminal Code.

11. Since the Committee has found a violation of Mr. Toonen's rights under articles 17(1) and 2(1) of the Covenant requiring the repeal of the offending law, the Committee does not consider it necessary to consider whether there has also been a violation of article 26 of the Covenant.

12. The Committee would wish to receive, within 90 days of the date of the transmittal of its Views, information from the State party on the measures taken to give effect to the Views.

NOTES

1) In the *Toonen* case, the petitioner's communication related primarily to statutory provisions and statements by Tasmanian officials. There is no "international" element to this complaint, in the sense that all facts took place within Australian territory and involved only the Australian state and its nationals. The traditional position of states under international law was that such questions were part of their domestic jurisdiction, implying that it was governed by no international norm and that no other state could legitimately interfere to question the state's conduct. Although the principle of non-intervention in the internal affairs of other states is reaffirmed in article 2(7) of the U.N. Charter, human rights have now carved a very significant exception to that rule, placing issues of respect for fundamental rights such as those raised in *Toonen* squarely within the confines of international concern.

2) The ICJ in the *Case Concerning Reservations to the Convention on Genocide* put forward the idea that, in human rights treaties, "the contracting States do not have any interest of their own; they merely have, one and all, a common interest, namely, the accomplishment of those high purposes which are the *raison d'être* of the convention."[11] The link between this common interest and the interplay of rights and obligations was further articulated by the Inter-American Court of Human Rights in its *Advisory Opinion on the Effect of Reservations on the Entry into Force of the American Convention on Human Rights*:[12]

> The Court must emphasize, however, that modern human rights treaties in general, and the American Convention in particular, are not multilateral treaties of the traditional type concluded to accomplish the reciprocal exchange of rights for the mutual benefit of the contracting States. Their object and purpose is the protection of the basic rights of individual human beings irrespective of their nationality, both against the State of their nationality and all other contracting States. In concluding these human rights treaties, the States can be deemed to submit themselves to a legal order within which they, for the common good, assume various obligations, not in relation to other States, but towards all individuals within their jurisdiction.
>
> Human rights impose on states obligations *erga omnes*, i.e. towards all, meaning they do not involve the creation of multiple bilateral relations between all state parties, similar to, for example, trade conventions. Because the international community as a whole has an interest in the state's non-reciprocal undertaking to respect human rights, all states bound by the same norm as well as institutions like the Human Rights Committee can be said to have a legal interest. This fundamental feature of human rights will have a profound impact on, among other things, the effect of reservations, treaty relations, and enforcement measures.[13]

---

11   *Case Concerning Reservation to the Convention on Genocide*, Advisory Opinion, [1951] I.C.J. Rep. 15 at 23.

12   *The Effect of Reservations on the Entry into Force of the American Convention on Human Rights (Arts. 74 and 75)* (1982), Advisory Opinion OC-2/82, Inter-Am. Ct. H.R. (Ser. A), No. 2 at para. 29.

13   See R. Provost, "Reciprocity in Human Rights and Humanitarian Law" [1994] 65 Brit. Y.B. Int'l L. 383.

3) In *Toonen*, the author of the petition alleged that he and others were the object of discrimination originating not only in the Tasmanian state, to be assimilated to Australia in this respect, but also in the behaviour of private persons. This raises the question of the applicability of human rights to violations coming from non-state actors as well as the possible international responsibility of the Australian state for such behaviour. The first issue is often described as the *Drittwirkung* (literally "effect on third parties") of human rights norms—that is, their applicability to inter-individual relations. Although the preamble of the ICCPR refers to individual duties to other individuals, and instruments like the Universal Declaration on Human Rights are not explicitly directed only at government action, international human rights norms were framed essentially as a bulwark protecting individuals against abuses originating in the state. Given the experiences of World War II, which acted as a background to the drafting of many of these instruments, such a position is understandable. It does, however, place outside of human rights law's scope many egregious violations that can be just as serious as those committed by state agents. Feminist critiques of human rights have denounced such a construction of human rights as flawed, because it closes the door to invoking human rights norms against such widespread evil as domestic abuse, much more likely to affect women's enjoyment of basic rights than state violations. They also argue that this position reinforces the artificial public/private dichotomy:

> Long-term domination of all bodies wielding political power nationally and internationally means that issues traditionally of concern to men become seen as general human concerns, while "women's concerns" are relegated to a special, limited category. Because men generally are not the victims of sex discrimination, domestic violence, and sexual degradation and violence, for example, these matters can be consigned to a separate sphere and tend to be ignored. The orthodox face of international law and politics would change dramatically if their institutions were truly human in composition: their horizons would widen to include issues previously regarded as domestic.[14]

One obstacle standing in the way of expanding the reach of human rights to cover violations by non-state actors, not only in the private sphere but also in the public sphere by insurgent or terrorist groups, is the fact that state responsibility stands as the central pillar of human rights law. All norms are articulated in terms of the possible responsibility of a state for not complying with its obligations, with an extremely limited role for individual criminal responsibility.[15]

Velásquez Rodríguez Case
(1988), Inter-Am. Ct. H.R. (Ser. C.) No. 4; 9 Hum. Rts. L.J. 212

[In this landmark decision of the Inter-American Court of Human Rights, the petitioners presented a claim against Honduras following the disappearance of a number of students after their abduction by seven armed men dressed in civilian

---

14   K. Askin & D. Koenig, *Women and International Human Rights* (1999) 3 vols. (Transnational 1999-2001); H. Charlesworth & C. Chinkin, *The Boundaries of International Law: A Feminist Analysis* (2000).

15   But see Chapter 11, "International Criminal Law."

clothing and using an unlicensed car. Although the petitioners could not categorically prove the involvement of State agents, the Court nevertheless found Honduras responsible on the basis of the State's duty not only to "respect" but also to "ensure" rights, found in article 1(1) of the American Convention on Human Rights.]

166. The second obligation of the States Parties is to "ensure" the free and full exercise of the rights recognized by the Convention to every person subject to its jurisdiction. This obligation implies the duty of the States Parties to organize the governmental apparatus and, in general, all the structures through which public power is exercised, so that they are capable of juridically ensuring the free and full enjoyment of human rights. As a consequence of this obligation, the States must prevent, investigate and punish any violation of the rights recognized by the Convention and, moreover, if possible attempt to restore the right violated and provide compensation as warranted for damages resulting from the violation.

167. The obligation to ensure the free and full exercise of human rights is not fulfilled by the existence of a legal system designed to make it possible to comply with this obligation—it also requires the government to conduct itself so as to effectively ensure the free and full exercise of human rights. ...

172. ... An illegal act which violates human rights and which is initially not directly imputable to a State (for example, because it is the act of a private person or because the person responsible has not been identified) can lead to international responsibility of the State, not because of the act itself, but because of the lack of due diligence to prevent the violation or to respond to it as required by the Convention.

174. The State has a legal duty to take reasonable steps to prevent human rights violations and to use the means at its disposal to carry out a serious investigation of violations committed within its jurisdiction, to identify those responsible, to impose the appropriate punishment and to ensure the victim adequate compensation.

175. This duty to prevent includes all those means of a legal, political, administrative and cultural nature that promote the protection of human rights and ensure that any violations are considered and treated as illegal acts, which, as such, may lead to the punishment of those responsible and the obligation to indemnify the victims for damages. ...

176. The State is obligated to investigate every situation involving a violation of the rights protected by the Convention. If the State apparatus acts in such a way that the violation goes unpunished and the victim's full enjoyment of such rights is not restored as soon as possible, the State has failed to comply with its duty to ensure the free and full exercise of those rights to the persons within its jurisdiction. The same is true when the State allows private persons or groups to act freely and with impunity to the detriment of the rights recognized by the Convention.

177. In certain circumstances, it may be difficult to investigate acts that violate an individual's rights. The duty to investigate, like the duty to prevent, is not breached merely because the investigation does not produce a satisfactory result. Nevertheless, it must be undertaken in a serious manner and not as a mere formality preordained to be ineffective. An investigation must have an objective and be assumed by the State as its own legal duty, not as a step taken by private interests that depends upon the

initiative of the victim or his family or upon their offer of proof, without an effective search for the truth by the government. This is true regardless of what agent is eventually found responsible for the violation. Where the acts of private parties that violate the Convention are not seriously investigated, those parties are aided in a sense by the government, thereby making the State responsible on the international plane.

178. In the instant case, the evidence shows a complete inability of the procedures of the State of Honduras, which were theoretically adequate, to carry out an investigation into the disappearance of Manfredo Velásquez, and of the fulfillment of its duties to pay compensation and punish those responsible, as set out in Article 1(1) of the Convention.

NOTES

1) A duty to "ensure rights" similar to article 1(1) of the ACHR is also found in the ICCPR (article 2(1)) as well as in most human rights treaties.[16] Should this be seen as an exception to the rule, discussed in Chapter 10, Section A.3(b) on "Acts of Private Persons," that there is no State responsibility for private behaviour unless it is imputable to the State?

2) In *Toonen* the Human Rights Committee did not need to examine Australia's duty to ensure the protection of human rights because it found direct State action in breach of the Covenant. Absent any direct State action, what steps ought to have been taken by Australia to "ensure" that Toonen was not the object of discrimination on the basis of sexual orientation?

3) Australia, in the wake of the Committee's decision in *Toonen*, adopted a federal statute aimed at overriding Tasmania's *Criminal Code* provisions found to be contrary to the ICCPR. After much constitutional wrangling, Tasmania itself eventually repealed the impugned provisions.

The Tasmanian state government argued in *Toonen* that whether or not homosexual activities should be given protection was essentially a moral issue and hence a matter of purely domestic concern. This argument, rejected by the Human Rights Committee, raises questions about the foundations of human rights law and whether they ought to be related to certain identified moral codes. Charles Taylor has argued that:

> What should be emphasized is that the system of positive rights rests on a set of deep-rooted moral beliefs concerning the human person and the dignity and liberty that we must accord that person. Every moral system has a conception of what one might call human dignity, that is to say, of the quality which, in man, compels us to treat him with respect or, in other words, a conception which defines what it is to have respect for human beings.
>
> Underlying the systems of personal rights is a whole set of conceptions which make liberty, power of initiative, the right to lodge claims and to determine society's actions,

---

16   See *Herrera Rubio v. Colombia*, Comm. No. 161/1983, Human Rights Committee, UN GAOR, 31st Sess., Supp. No. 40, U.N. Doc. A/43/40 (1987) 190 at 198; Human Rights Committee, *Compilation of General Comments and General Recommendations Adopted by Human Rights Treaty Bodies*, UN ESCOR, 1992, U.N. Doc. HRI/GEN/1/Rev.1 (General Recommendation No. 19, "Violence Against Women") at 84; and *Commission nationale des droits de l'homme v. Chad*, Comm. No. 74/92, October 11 1995 (1997) 18 Hum. Rts. L. J. 34, paras. 19-22 (African Commission on Human and Peoples' Rights).

integral parts of human dignity. If they were to disappear from our civilization, the systems of personal rights would not survive for long. Such systems derive from this conception of human dignity and they would not outlive it. ...

It is none the less true that enumerations of rights, even when they are relative or circumstantial, are based on the conceptions of human dignity referred to above. Clearly, a list of positive rights is drawn up on the basis of a specific context, but always in the light of our basic convictions. We decide, for instance, that certain rights should take precedence over others: that the child's right to education should have primacy over the parents' right when there is a conflict between the two; we do the same in the case of the right to life, when the parents refuse their children medical attention for religious reasons, for instance. Similarly, we may decide that the collective rights of a community to safeguard its language warrant restricting the right of individuals to use the language of their choice when dealing with the public authorities.

This kind of decision, which is inevitable in drawing up a list of positive rights, is taken in the light of our basic conceptions, due consideration being given to what we believe to be the circumstances. It is our conception of the human person that makes us consider certain requirements to be more fundamental than others. It is because we attach so much importance in our post-Romantic era to the full development of the capacities of the individual that we regard education as such a basic right that we suspend parents' rights when they come into conflict with it. It is because we believe that the preservation of language is essential for human fulfilment that we are prepared to give it priority over the choice of a working language by business enterprises, for example.

Our enumeration will therefore depend on our conception of the human person. But it will also be drawn up in the light of conditions in a specific context. For instance, whatever the importance of the language, there can be no justification for restricting freedom of choice if the language is not actually threatened by such freedom under the prevailing conditions. If the life of the child is not in danger, and if the refusal of medical attention will only prolong the period of convalescence, there are fewer grounds for overruling the parents' decision. This is why the two levels must be distinguished.

Does this mean that any attempt to draw up a list of universal rights is futile? No, it does not, because there are still rights which are so fundamental that we can more or less commit ourselves in advance to upholding them in all possible contexts.[17]

Looking back at the decision of the Human Rights Committee, how clearly do you perceive moral choices in the drafting of the ICCPR? Do you think that states would likely have voted in favour of a prohibition of discrimination on the basis of sexual orientation in 1966? in 1992, the year *Toonen* was decided? This question is related to issues of cultural pluralism and the need to adapt rights to different contexts, which we will examine in the following section.

---

17   C. Taylor, "Human Rights: The Legal Culture" in A. Diemer *et al.*, eds., *Philosophical Foundations of Human Rights*, with introduction by P. Ricoeur (1986) 49 at 53-55.

B. HUMAN RIGHTS STANDARDS

The human rights "system" appears in many ways so fluid and disorganized that it is often difficult to grasp its key features. There have been attempts to superimpose classifications of various kinds to present human rights more systematically, but the variety of rights and regimes in treaty and customary law broadly resists generalizations. The difficulty is heightened by the challenge of cultural difference, which forces a questioning of the universal character of human rights, as well as by the incorporation into the human rights system of collective rights.

1. Classifying Rights

One classification of the various substantive rights protected by international law, the "generation approach," has been presented as helpful to understand differences in the nature of protected interests and in difficulties of implementation. Another classification is hierarchical, seeking to establish priorities among the various rights.

Generations of Rights

Karel Vasak first proposed a classification of human rights on the basis of three "generations" of rights, inspired by the motto of the French revolution, liberté (first generation—civil and political rights), égalité (second generation—economic, social, and cultural rights), fraternité (third generation—collective rights), as a way of understanding the different dynamic of each category of rights.[18] The first generation comprises civil and political rights, which protect the individual against interferences from the state. These are said to be framed in negative terms ("right against" or "freedom from") and impose on the state a duty to refrain from acting in an injurious manner. First-generation rights include those listed in articles 2 to 21 of the Universal Declaration of Human Rights, such as the right to life, the right to be free from torture, and the right not to be the object of discrimination. These rights, most directly inspired by Western philosophy, were presented as fundamental by Western states during the drafting of the Universal Declaration and the two Covenants. They are grounded in the idea of individual liberty— human rights acting as a shield against abusive intrusions by the state. The second generation of human rights comprises economic, social, and cultural rights, which represent claims by individuals for an equitable share of economic and social resources. They are said to be framed in positive terms ("right to"), imposing active duties on states. They include rights listed in articles 22 to 27 of the Universal Declaration of Human Rights, such as the right to social security, the right to work, and the right to education. They were promoted mainly by East Bloc and developing countries, as elements needed to stem the excesses of free-market economies and capitalism and to ensure equality of all participants. Finally, third-generation human rights are collective human rights relying on universal solidarity (hence the reference to fraternité). They represent collective claims to the sharing of global power and wealth, put forward most forcefully by developing

---

18   Karel Vasak, ed., *The International Dimensions of Human Rights* (1982).

states. The Universal Declaration of Human Rights alludes to such a right when it entrenches a right to a social and international legal order in which other rights can be realized (article 28). The right to self-determination, the right to development, the right to peace, and the right to a healthy environment are examples of third-generation human rights.

The very ordering of these three generations is a matter of considerable debate, since it seems to imply a priority of first-generation human rights over second- and third-generation rights, a claim hotly disputed by many states:

> This is not to imply that each of these three generations of rights is equally acceptable to all or that they or their separate elements are greeted with equal urgency. First-generation proponents, for example, are inclined to exclude second- and third-generation rights from their definition of human rights altogether (or, at best, to label them as "derivative"). In part this is due to the complexities that inform the process of putting these rights into action. The suggestion of greater feasibility that attends first-generation rights because they stress the absence rather than the presence of government is somehow transformed into a prerequisite of a comprehensive definition of human rights, such that aspirational and vaguely asserted claims to entitlement are deemed not to be rights at all. The most forceful explanation, however, is more ideologically or politically motivated. Persuaded that egalitarian claims against the rich, particularly where collectively espoused, are unworkable without a severe decline in liberty and quality (in part because they involve state intervention for the redistribution of privately held resources), first-generation proponents, inspired by the natural law and laissez-faire traditions, are partial to the view that human rights are inherently independent of civil society and are individualistic.
>
> Conversely, second- and third-generation defenders often look upon first-generation rights, at least as commonly practised, as insufficiently attentive to material human needs, and, indeed, as legitimating instruments in service to unjust domestic, transnational and international social orders—hence constituting a "bourgeois illusion." Accordingly, while not placing first-generation rights outside their definition of human rights, they tend to assign such rights a low status and therefore to treat them as long-term goals that will come to pass only with fundamental economic and social transformations to be realized progressively and fully consummated only sometime in the future.
>
> In sum, different conceptions of rights, particularly emerging conceptions, contain the potential for challenging the legitimacy and supremacy not only of one another but, more importantly, of the political-social systems with which they are most intimately associated. As a consequence there is sharp disagreement about the legitimate scope of human rights and about the priorities that are claimed among them.[19]

First-generation rights are presented as negative, cost-free, immediate, apolitical, and justiciable, whereas second- and third-generation rights would be positive, resource-driven, progressive, political, and non-justiciable. Do you agree that such distinctions can

---

19   B. Weston, "Human Rights" in *The New Encyclopaedia Britannica*, 15th ed. (1992) vol. 20 at 656 and 659. See also C. Flinterman, "Three Generations of Human Rights" in Jan Berting *et al.*, eds., *Human Rights in a Pluralist World: Individuals and Collectivities* (1990) at 75; and C. Scott, "The Interdependence and Permeability of Human Rights Norms: Towards a Partial Fusion of the International Covenants on Human Rights" (1989) 27 Osgood Hall L.J. 769.

be made between the rights of the various generations, since it could be argued that a rigid compartmentalization of human rights obscures the interdependence and permeability of human rights norms? Interdependence relates to the fact that often the realization of a right is necessarily linked to rights of other generations. For example, the right to food (second generation) can hardly become a reality without freedom of movement (first generation), allowing farmers to sell their products, and the right to a healthy environment (third generation). Permeability underscores the idea that most rights overlap the boundaries of the generation with which they are associated. For instance, the right to education (second generation) necessarily implies freedom of expression (first generation) and the right of collectivities to control education (third generation). This is supported by the Vienna Declaration and Programme of Action, adopted by the World Conference on Human Rights in 1993, which holds that "all human rights are universal, indivisible, interdependent and interrelated."[20] In *Toonen* the arguments were framed in terms of civil and political rights, because a petition to the Human Rights Committee must allege a violation of the ICCPR in order to be admissible. Do you think that the facts of that case raise issues related to rights of other generations?

Hierarchies of Rights

"A system builder by vocation, the jurist cannot dispense with a minimum of conceptual scaffolding."[21] Perhaps because of the ineluctable influence of municipal law, international lawyers tend to replicate in the international legal system the hierarchical structure of norms found in municipal law. The increasing constitutionalization of basic rights no doubt fans the idea that some human rights ought to be considered as superior to others, which is at odds with the general structure of international law where, as a rule, no set priority exists among norms. Human rights instruments do not contain clear indications that some categories of rights ought to be considered as superior to others. The question is important because human rights are framed in such a general way that conflicts among rights are a constant occurrence. The ICJ in the *Barcelona Traction Case* referred to "*basic* rights of the human person" as generating *erga omnes* obligations.[22] Likewise, the International Law Commission in its Draft Articles on the Responsibility of States for Internationally Wrongful Acts refers to "*fundamental* human rights" as a limit to countermeasures (article 50(1)(b)).[23] Absent any indication of rank in human rights instruments, it has not been possible to find a consensus on a list of "superior" human rights. As seen in the discussion of generations of rights, great differences of opinion exist over which rights are more fundamental. Some have suggested that the small number of rights that may not be suspended during a state of emergency (a phenomenon

(> rights are owed to all.

20 World Conference on Human Rights, *Vienna Declaration and Program of Action* U.N. Doc. A/CONF/ 157/23 (1993) para. 5.

21 P. Weil, "Towards Relative Normativity in International Law" (1983) 77 A.J.I.L. 413 at 440.

22 [1970] I.C.J. Rep. 4 at para. 33.

23 International Law Commission, *Report on the Work of Its 53rd Session*, UN GAOR 56th Sess., Supp. No. 10, U.N. Doc. A/56/10 (2001) chp. IV.E.1.

discussed below) are thereby labelled as superior. There are wide variations in the lists of non-derogable rights in different treaties, however, and some rights that would otherwise be seen as basic, such as due process, are not included in the list of some treaties, including the ICCPR. The *travaux préparatoires* of human rights treaties do not reveal that any priority was to be given to non-derogable rights. The one explicit ranking of norms in international law, embodied in the concept of *jus cogens*, is at first sight an attractive vehicle for setting apart some human rights as more basic than others. Although the very concept has attracted considerable support in the wake of its incorporation into article 53 of the Vienna Convention on the Law of Treaties (reproduced in the Documentary Supplement), there is, once again, no discernible consensus as to which norms ought to be considered *jus cogens*.[24] The characterization of the right to self-determination as a *jus cogens* norm, for example, could entail that it ought to override other rights such as individual freedom of expression. As concluded by Meron, "rather than grapple with the harder questions of rationalizing human rights law making and distinguishing between rights and claims, some commentators are resorting increasingly to superior rights in the hope that no state will dare—politically, morally and perhaps even legally—to ignore them. In these ways, hierarchical terms contribute to the unnecessary mystification of human rights, rather than to their greater clarity."[25]

2. Treaty Human Rights

Human rights entrenched in treaties present the significant advantage that their very existence cannot be disputed, an issue often presenting great challenges when referring to customary law. The flip side of this benefit is that treaty norms are binding solely on states who have ratified the treaty, with only diffused and disputed effects on non-party states. Treaties on human rights also usually provide for the creation of some form of compliance mechanism, although these vary widely in nature and effectiveness. Key features of universal and regional treaty regimes are discussed below.

(a) Universal Norms

International Covenant on Civil and Political Rights
Reproduced in the Documentary Supplement

International Covenant on Economic, Social, and Cultural Rights
Reproduced in the Documentary Supplement

---

24   The most commonly proposed human rights norms are self-determination, the prohibition of genocide, and the prohibitions of racial discrimination, slave trade, and piracy: I. Brownlie, *Principles of Public International Law*, 6th ed. (2003) at 488-89.

25   T. Meron, "On a Hierarchy of International Human Rights" (1986) 80 A.J.I.L. 1 at 22 (footnote omitted).

NOTES

1) The two pillars of universal treaty human rights are the ICCPR and the ICESCR, the development of which was outlined above in Section A.1 on "Development." The Covenants represent concrete and binding translations of the non-binding principles found in the Universal Declaration of Human Rights. As always, some things were lost in translation, most notably the right to obtain asylum in another country in case of persecution (article 14) and the right to own property (article 17). Conversely, the Covenants include rights not mentioned in the Declaration, first and foremost the right to self-determination, but also the right of minorities, protection against expulsion, the right of a child to a nationality, and many economic, social, and cultural rights. Some of the variations are a direct consequence of the growth and diversification of the community of states between 1948 and 1966, due to decolonization. In 1966, for example, the right to property was objectionable to many developed states because it could be used to deny the right to compensation for expropriated property. Rights expressed as general principles in the Declaration are expanded and made more specific in the Covenants (compare, for example, freedom of expression in article 19 of the Declaration and in articles 19-20 of the ICCPR).[26] These differences are due partly to the legal character of the documents. The Universal Declaration is a declaration of principles while the Covenants create legally binding treaty obligations, which inevitably have to be expressed precisely and with appropriate qualifications.

2) The ICCPR provides for the creation of an 18-member Human Rights Committee composed of nationals of the states parties to the treaty who must serve "in their personal capacity" (article 28). The Committee members are elected by the states parties, by secret ballot, from a list of nominees composed of no more than two nationals per state submitted by each state (article 29). The Committee can hear petitions from individuals or states alleging a breach of the Covenant by any state that has accepted such a competence. Every party to the ICCPR must present periodic reports on their progress in implementing the rights recognized therein, which are reviewed by the Human Rights Committee (see below, Section C.1 on "Compliance and Enforcement: Treaty Mechanisms"). Finally, the Committee may from time to time adopt general comments on the content or meaning of rights entrenched in the Covenant. The helpfulness of these general comments has varied greatly, a result of the need for consensus among the Committee members, but more recent general comments have been instructive and forward-looking—for example, General Comment 24 on reservations, discussed below in Section 2(c) on "Reservations, Limitations, and Derogations."

---

26 On the Covenants, see M. Nowak, *U.N. Covenant on Civil and Political Rights: ICCPR Commentary* (1993); M. Bossuyt, *Guide to the "travaux préparatoires" of the International Covenant on Civil and Political Rights* (1987); S. Carlson & G. Gisvold, *Practical Guide to the International Covenant on Civil and Political Rights* (2003); A. Eide, C. Krause, & A. Rosas, *Economic, Social and Cultural Rights* (2001); M. Craven, *The International Covenant on Economic, Social and Cultural Rights: A Perspective on Its Development* (1995); and L. Lamarche, *Perspectives occidentales du droit international des droits économiques de la personne* (1995/1996).

Committee on Economic, Social and Cultural Rights, General Comment 3,
The Nature of States Parties Obligations (article 2, para. 1 of the Covenant)
U.N. Doc. HRI/GEN/1/Rev. 1, 5th Sess., 1990 (1994) at 45

1. Article 2 [of the ICESCR] is of particular importance to a full understanding of the Covenant and must be seen as having a dynamic relationship with all of the other provisions of the Covenant. It describes the nature of the general legal obligations undertaken by States parties to the Covenant. Those obligations include both what may be termed (following the work of the International Law Commission) obligations of conduct and obligations of result. While great emphasis has sometimes been placed on the difference between the formulations used in this provision and that contained in the equivalent article 2 of the International Covenant on Civil and Political Rights, it is not always recognized that there are also significant similarities. In particular, while the Covenant provides for progressive realization and acknowledges the constraints due to the limits of available resources, it also imposes various obligations which are of immediate effect. Of these, two are of particular importance in understanding the precise nature of States parties obligations. One of these, which is dealt with in a separate General Comment, and which is to be considered by the Committee at its sixth session, is the "undertaking to guarantee" that relevant rights "will be exercised without discrimination ... ."

2. The other is the undertaking in article 2(1) "to take steps," which in itself is not qualified or limited by other considerations. The full meaning of the phrase can also be gauged by noting some of the different language versions. In English the undertaking is "to take steps," in French it is "to act" ("s'engage ... agir") and in Spanish it is "to adopt measures" ("a adoptar medidas"). Thus while the full realization of the relevant rights may be achieved progressively, steps towards that goal must be taken within a reasonably short time after the Covenant's entry into force for the States concerned. Such steps should be deliberate, concrete and targeted as clearly as possible towards meeting the obligations recognized in the Covenant.

3. The means which should be used in order to satisfy the obligation to take steps are stated in article 2(1) to be "all appropriate means, including particularly the adoption of legislative measures." The Committee recognizes that in many instances legislation is highly desirable and in some cases may even be indispensable. For example, it may be difficult to combat discrimination effectively in the absence of a sound legislative foundation for the necessary measures. In fields such as health, the protection of children and mothers, and education, as well as in respect of the matters dealt with in articles 6 to 9, legislation may also be an indispensable element for many purposes.

4. The Committee ... wishes to emphasize, however, that the adoption of legislative measures, as specifically foreseen by the Covenant, is by no means exhaustive of the obligations of States parties. Rather, the phrase "by all appropriate means" must be given its full and natural meaning. While each State party must decide for itself which means are the most appropriate under the circumstances with respect to each of the rights, the "appropriateness" of the means chosen will not always be self-evident. It is therefore desirable that States parties' reports should indicate not

only the measures that have been taken but also the basis on which they are considered to be the most "appropriate" under the circumstances. However, the ultimate determination as to whether all appropriate measures have been taken remains one for the Committee to make.

5. Among the measures which might be considered appropriate, in addition to legislation, is the provision of judicial remedies with respect to rights which may, in accordance with the national legal system, be considered justiciable. The Committee notes, for example, that the enjoyment of the rights recognized, without discrimination, will often be appropriately promoted, in part, through the provision of judicial or other effective remedies. Indeed, those States parties which are also parties to the International Covenant on Civil and Political Rights are already obligated (by virtue of arts. 2 (paras. 1 and 3), 3 and 26) of that Covenant to ensure that any person whose rights or freedoms (including the right to equality and non-discrimination) recognized in that Covenant are violated, "shall have an effective remedy" (art. 2(3)(a)). In addition, there are a number of other provisions in the International Covenant on Economic, Social and Cultural Rights, including articles 3, 7(a)(i), 8, 10(3), 13(2)(a), (3) and (4) and 15(3) which would seem to be capable of immediate application by judicial and other organs in many national legal systems. Any suggestion that the provisions indicated are inherently non-self-executing would seem to be difficult to sustain. ...

9. The principal obligation of result reflected in article 2(1) is to take steps "with a view to achieving progressively the full realization of the rights recognized" in the Covenant. The term "progressive realization" is often used to describe the intent of this phrase. The concept of progressive realization constitutes a recognition of the fact that full realization of all economic, social and cultural rights will generally not be able to be achieved in a short period of time. In this sense the obligation differs significantly from that contained in article 2 of the International Covenant on Civil and Political Rights which embodies an immediate obligation to respect and ensure all of the relevant rights. Nevertheless, the fact that realization over time, or in other words progressively, is foreseen under the Covenant should not be misinterpreted as depriving the obligation of all meaningful content. It is on the one hand a necessary flexibility device, reflecting the realities of the real world and the difficulties involved for any country in ensuring full realization of economic, social and cultural rights. On the other hand, the phrase must be read in the light of the overall objective, indeed the raison d'être, of the Covenant which is to establish clear obligations for States parties in respect of the full realization of the rights in question. It thus imposes an obligation to move as expeditiously and effectively as possible towards that goal. Moreover, any deliberately retrogressive measures in that regard would require the most careful consideration and would need to be fully justified by reference to the totality of the rights provided for in the Covenant and in the context of the full use of the maximum available resources ...

13. A final element of article 2(1), to which attention must be drawn, is that the undertaking given by all States parties is "to take steps, individually and through international assistance and cooperation, especially economic and technical ... ." The Committee notes that the phrase "to the maximum of its available resources" was

intended by the drafters of the Covenant to refer to both the resources existing within a State and those available from the international community through international cooperation and assistance.

NOTES

1) The substantive rights of the ICESCR deal with work, trade unions, social security, the family, standards of living, health, education, culture, and the benefits of scientific progress. This Covenant shares some similarities with the ICCPR in that it contains general provisions making its specific rights applicable "without discrimination of any kind such as race, colour, language, religion, political or other opinion, national or social origin, property, birth or other status" (article 2(1)). In addition, article 3 of both Covenants dictates that states ensure "the equal right of men and women to the enjoyment of all" the rights set out in them, respectively.

2) Unlike the ICCPR, the ICESCR in article 2(1) requires states to take steps to realize the economic and social rights "to the maximum of its available resources." When considering the amount of resources available for the purpose, does the state have complete discretion in the allocation of its gross national product? Might this matter be part of the scrutiny of a state's report under the ICESCR?

3) Implementation provisions are much weaker in the ICESCR than in the ICCPR. In particular, the ICESCR does not provide for the creation of a committee similar to the Human Rights Committee. Nevertheless, the Economic and Social Council in 1985 created a Committee on Economic, Social and Cultural Rights with a structure very similar to that of the Human Rights Committee to monitor state compliance with its obligations under the ICESCR. The Treaty requires states to submit reports "on the measures which they have adopted and the progress made in achieving the observance of" those rights (article 16(1)). The reports are examined by the Committee on Economic Social and Cultural Rights, which then issues comments on the state's progress. There is no right to petition the Committee on Economic, Social and Cultural Rights at present.[27] In general, this type of right does not benefit from an implementation machinery comparable to civil and political rights.

The two Covenants are completed by a large number of other universal human rights treaties dealing with particular rights or categories of persons in need of protection. Some of the most important among these other treaties include:

— The 1948 Convention on the Prevention and Punishment of Genocide, which was the first human rights treaty adopted after World War II.[28] It seeks to prohibit any

---

27 The Economic Committee has proposed a draft Protocol to the ICESCR that would create a right of individual petition alleging a breach of the Covenant: *Draft Optional Protocol to the International Covenant on Economic, Social and Cultural Rights*, UN ESCOR, 53d Sess., U.N. Doc. E/CN.4/1997/105. The proposal is still pending before an open-ended working group of the Human Rights Commission: *Report of the Secretary-General in Response to Commission Resolution 2003/18*, U.N. Doc. E/CN.4/2004/WG.23/2.

28 (1948) 78 U.N.T.S.; Can. T. S. 1949 No. 27. See N. Robinson, *The Genocide Convention: A Commentary* (1960); L. Kuper, *Genocide* (1981/1982); W. Schabas, *Genocide in International Law* (2000); and P. Akhavan, "Enforcement of the Genocide Convention: A Challenge to Civilization" (1995) 8 Harv. Hum. Rts. J. 229.

action intended to bring about the partial or total destruction of a national, ethnical, racial, or religious group. Under the Genocide Convention, states have an obligation to enact municipal criminal legislation and to prosecute or extradite anyone suspected of having participated in the crime of genocide.

— The 1966 International Convention on the Elimination of All Forms of Racial Discrimination was adopted in the context of a reaction against the apartheid regime in South Africa and of the civil rights movement in the United States.[29] The Convention prohibits any distinction, exclusion, or preference based on race, colour, descent, or national or ethnic origins that has an impact on the equal recognition, enjoyment, or exercise of human rights. A Committee on the Elimination of Racial Discrimination is created to review the states parties' periodic reports and to hear inter-state and individual petitions.

— The 1979 Convention on the Elimination of All Forms of Discrimination Against Women (CEDAW) was adopted in order to supplement the broad statements of the equality of sexes found in the Preamble of the U.N. Charter, in the Universal Declaration of Human Rights (article 2) and in the two Covenants (article 3).[30] The Convention identifies a number of areas in which discrimination against women persists, and establishes goals and measures to be taken by states parties. A Committee on the Elimination of Discrimination Against Women was established to review periodic state reports. In 1999, the U.N. General Assembly adopted a Protocol to CEDAW that gives individuals and groups the right to petition the Committee, in addition to giving the Committee the power to initiate inquiries into situations of grave or systematic violations of women's rights.[31]

— The 1984 Convention Against Torture and Other Cruel, Inhuman or Degrading Treatment or Punishment is meant to giving binding effect to the prohibition proclaimed earlier by way of a General Assembly Resolution.[32] The Convention prohibits the state-sanctioned infliction of pain and suffering aimed at obtaining information, punishing, or intimidating a person, but it does not cover pain or suffering connected to lawful sanctions. A Committee Against Torture was created

---

29 (1966) 660 U.N.T.S. 195; Can. T.S. 1970 No. 28. See N. Lerner, *The U.N. Convention on the Elimination of All Forms of Racial Discrimination*, 2d ed. (1980); and T. Meron, "The Meaning and Reach of the International Convention on the Elimination of All Forms of Racial Discrimination" (1985) 79 A.J.I.L. 283. More information on the work of this and other U.N. treaty bodies is available online: <http://www.unhchr.ch> accessed May 6, 1999.

30 (1979) 1249 U.N.T.S. 13; Can. T.S. 1982 No. 31. See L. Rehof, ed., *Guide to the Travaux Préparatoires to the Convention on the Elimination of All Forms of Discrimination Against Women* (1993); and Askin & Koenig, *supra* note 14.

31 GA Res. 54/4, UN GAOR, 54th Sess., Supp. No. 49, U.N. Doc. A/54/49 (1999). The Protocol entered into force in 2000.

32 (1984) 1465 U.N.T.S. 85; Can. T.S. 1987 No. 36. See J. Burger & H. Danelius, eds., *The United Nations Convention against Torture: A Handbook on the Convention Against Torture and Other Cruel, Inhuman, or Degrading Treatment or Punishment* (1988).

to review periodic state reports, hear inter-state and individual petitions, and to undertake confidential enquiries into situations of systematic resort to torture.

— The 1989 Convention on the Rights of the Child is one of the most recent but also the most widely ratified human rights instrument.[33] It provides for the protection of a wide array of civil, political, economic, social, and cultural rights for children, including a number of rights specific to children—for example, the right to participate in decision making affecting them. The Committee on the Rights of the Child is given power to review periodic state reports. Two protocols were adopted in 1998 to address the problem of child pornography and prostitution, and to regulate the involvement of children in armed conflicts.[34]

(b) Regional Norms

Regional Norms in Europe[35]

Having experienced the horrors of the two world wars and the atrocities associated with them, a strong demand existed in the Western European states for a supranational human rights regime. Many linked the rise of state human rights violations with conditions that could lead once more to the war and brutality of the previous 30 years, and hoped that international human rights obligations monitored by an international organization would prevent, or at least warn about, their development in time for the international community to intervene. It had been clear that one of the first purposes of the creation of a regional political organization, the Council of Europe, would be to adopt common human rights standards. Difficulties encountered in the United Nations in the drafting of the Universal Declaration prompted Western European states to go ahead and formulate the first binding human rights treaty. The European Convention for the Protection of Human Rights and Fundamental Freedoms (ECHR)[36] entered into force more than 12 years before the United Nations had agreed on the texts of the treaties comprising its international bill of rights. Since that time, the Council of Europe has created a number of other human rights

---

33   GA Res. 44/25, UN GAOR, 44th Sess., Supp. No. 49, U.N. Doc. A/44/49 (1989) 166; Can. T.S. 1992 No. 3. See S. Detric *et al.*, eds., *The United Nations Convention on the Rights of the Child: A Guide to the "Travaux préparatoires"* (1992); and E. Verhellen, ed., *Monitoring Children's Rights* (1996).

34   Although a protocol aiming to give the Committee on the Rights of the Child power to receive individual petitions had been mooted at the same time, no such instrument had been adopted as of January 2005.

35   See F. Jacobs & R. White, *The European Convention on Human Rights*, 3d ed. (2001); J. Merrills and A. Robertson, *Human Rights in Europe*, 4th ed. (2001); A.R. Mowbray, *Cases and Materials on the European Convention on Human Rights* (2001); M. Janis, R. Kay, & A. Bradley, eds., *European Human Rights Law: Text and Materials*, 2d ed. (2000). E. Decaux, P.-H. Imbert, & L. Pettit, eds., *La Convention européenne des droits de l'homme* (1995); D. Harris & M. O'Boyle, eds., *Law of the European Convention on Human Rights*, 3d ed. (1998); R. MacDonald, F. Matscher, & H. Petzold, eds., *The European System for the Protection of Human Rights* (1993); P. Van Dijk & F. Van Hoof, *Theory and Practice of the European Convention on Human Rights*, 3d ed. (1998).

36   Eur. T.S. 1950 No. 5, reproduced below, in force since 1953. There are now 45 parties to the ECHR. Canada, although it cannot become a party to the ECHR, became a permanent observer at the Council of Europe in May 1996.

instruments, including 14 Protocols to the ECHR, the European Social Charter, which sets out economic, social, and cultural rights, and other specialized treaties such as the European Convention for the Prevention of Torture and Inhuman or Degrading Treatment or Punishment, the European Convention on Recognition and Enforcement of Decisions Concerning Custody of Children and on Restoration of Custody of Children, and the Framework Convention for the Protection of National Minorities.[37]

European Convention for the Protection of Human Rights and Fundamental Freedoms
213 U.N.T.S. 222; Eur. T.S. 1950 No. 5

Article 2

1. Everyone's right to life shall be protected by law. No one shall be deprived of his life intentionally save in the execution of a sentence of a court following his conviction of a crime for which this penalty is provided by law.

2. Deprivation of life shall not be regarded as inflicted in contravention of this article when it results from the use of force which is no more than absolutely necessary:

(a) in defence of any person from unlawful violence;

(b) in order to effect a lawful arrest or to prevent the escape of a person lawfully detained;

(c) in action lawfully taken for the purpose of quelling a riot or insurrection.

Article 3

No one shall be subjected to torture or to inhuman or degrading treatment or punishment.

Article 4

1. No one shall be held in slavery or servitude.

2. No one shall be required to perform forced or compulsory labour.

3. For the purpose of this Article the term—forced or compulsory labour—shall not include:

(a) any work required to be done in the ordinary course of detention imposed according to the provisions of Article 5 of this Convention or during conditional release from such detention;

(b) any service of a military character or, in case of conscientious objectors in countries where they are recognised, service exacted instead of compulsory military service;

(c) any service exacted in case of an emergency or calamity threatening the life or well-being of the community;

(d) any work or service which forms part of normal civil obligations.

---

37 The text and status of ratification of these conventions is available from the Directorate of Human Rights of the Council of Europe at <http://www.humanrights.coe.int/Intro/eng/General/welc2dir.htm>.

Article 5

1. Everyone has the right to liberty and security of person. No one shall be deprived of his liberty save in the following cases and in accordance with a procedure prescribed by law:

(a) the lawful detention of a person after conviction by a competent court;

(b) the lawful arrest or detention of a person for non-compliance with the lawful order of a court or in order to secure the fulfilment of any obligation prescribed by law;

(c) the lawful arrest or detention of a person effected for the purpose of bringing him before the competent legal authority on reasonable suspicion of having committed an offence or when it is reasonably considered necessary to prevent his committing an offence or fleeing after having done so;

(d) the detention of a minor by lawful order for the purpose of educational supervision or his lawful detention for the purpose of bringing him before the competent legal authority;

(e) the lawful detention of persons for the prevention of the spreading of infectious diseases, of persons of unsound mind, alcoholics or drug addicts or vagrants;

(f) the lawful arrest or detention of a person to prevent his effecting an unauthorised entry into the country or of a person against whom action is being taken with a view to deportation or extradition.

2. Everyone who is arrested shall be informed promptly, in a language which he understands, of the reasons for his arrest and of any charge against him.

3. Everyone arrested or detained in accordance with the provisions of paragraph 1(c) of this article shall be brought promptly before a judge or other officer authorised by law to exercise judicial power and shall be entitled to trial within a reasonable time or to release pending trial. Release may be conditioned by guarantees to appear for trial.

4. Everyone who is deprived of his liberty by arrest or detention shall be entitled to take proceedings by which the lawfulness of his detention shall be decided speedily by a court and his release ordered if the detention is not lawful.

5. Everyone who has been the victim of arrest or detention in contravention of the provisions of this article shall have an enforceable right to compensation.

Article 6

1. In the determination of his civil rights and obligations or of any criminal charge against him, everyone is entitled to a fair and public hearing within a reasonable time by an independent and impartial tribunal established by law. Judgment shall be pronounced publicly but the press and public may be excluded from all or part of the trial in the interests of morals, public order or national security in a democratic society, where the interests of juveniles or the protection of the private life of the parties so require, or to the extent strictly necessary in the opinion of the court in special circumstances where publicity would prejudice the interests of justice.

2. Everyone charged with a criminal offence shall be presumed innocent until proved guilty according to law.

3. Everyone charged with a criminal offence has the following minimum rights:

(a) to be informed promptly, in a language which he understands and in detail, of the nature and cause of the accusation against him;

(b) to have adequate time and facilities for the preparation of his defence;

(c) to defend himself in person or through legal assistance of his own choosing or, if he has not sufficient means to pay for legal assistance, to be given it free when the interests of justice so require;

(d) to examine or have examined witnesses against him and to obtain the attendance and examination of witnesses on his behalf under the same conditions as witnesses against him;

(e) to have the free assistance of an interpreter if he cannot understand or speak the language used in court.

Article 7

1. No one shall be held guilty of any criminal offence on account of any act or omission which did not constitute a criminal offence under national or international law at the time when it was committed. Nor shall a heavier penalty be imposed than the one that was applicable at the time the criminal offence was committed.

2. This article shall not prejudice the trial and punishment of any person for any act or omission which, at the time when it was committed, was criminal according to the general principles of law recognized by civilised nations.

Article 8

1. Everyone has the right to respect for his private and family life, his home and his correspondence.

2. There shall be no interference by a public authority with the exercise of this right except such as is in accordance with the law and is necessary in a democratic society in the interests of national security, public safety or the economic well-being of the country, for the prevention of disorder or crime, for the protection of health or morals, or for the protection of the rights and freedoms of others.

Article 9

1. Everyone has the right to freedom of thought, conscience and religion; this right includes freedom to change his religion or belief and freedom, either alone or in community with others and in public or private, to manifest his religion or belief, in worship, teaching, practice and observance.

2. Freedom to manifest one's religion or beliefs shall be subject only to such limitations as are prescribed by law and are necessary in a democratic society in the interests of public safety, for the protection of public order, health or morals, or for the protection of the rights and freedoms of others.

Article 10

1. Everyone has the right to freedom of expression. This right shall include freedom to hold opinions and to receive and impart information and ideas without interference by public authority and regardless of frontiers. This Article shall not prevent States from requiring the licensing of broadcasting, television or cinema enterprises.

2. The exercise of these freedoms, since it carries with it duties and responsibilities, may be subject to such formalities, conditions, restrictions or penalties as are prescribed by law and are necessary in a democratic society, in the interests of national security, territorial integrity or public safety, for the prevention of disorder or crime, for the protection of health or morals, for the protection of the reputation or rights of others, for preventing the disclosure of information received in confidence, or of maintaining the authority and impartiality of the judiciary.

Article 11

1. Everyone has the right to freedom of peaceful assembly and to freedom of association with others, including the right to form and to join trade unions for the protection of his interests.

2. No restrictions shall be placed on the exercise of these rights other than such as are prescribed by law and are necessary in a democratic society in the interests of national security or public safety, for the prevention of disorder or crime, for the protection of health or morals or for the protection of the rights and freedoms of others. This article shall not prevent the imposition of lawful restrictions on the exercise of these rights by members of the armed forces, of the police or of the administration of the State.

Article 12

Men and women of marriageable age have the right to marry and to found a family, according to the national laws governing the exercise of this right.

Article 13

Everyone whose rights and freedoms as set forth in this Convention are violated shall have an effective remedy before a national authority notwithstanding that the violation has been committed by persons acting in an official capacity.

Article 14

The enjoyment of the rights and freedoms set forth in this Convention shall be secured without discrimination on any ground such as sex, race, colour, language, religion, political or other opinion, national or social origin, association with a national minority, property, birth or other status.

NOTES

1) Four of the 14 Protocols add to or elaborate on the rights in the ECHR and the mechanisms for their implementation. Protocol 1 protects the right to peaceful enjoyment of possessions (article 1) and to education in conformity with parents' "religious and philosophical convictions" (article 2), and obligates member states "to hold free elections at reasonable intervals by secret ballot, under conditions which will ensure the freedom of expression of the opinion of the people in the choice of the legislature." Protocol 4 prohibits imprisonment for the inability to fulfill contractual obligations (article 1), restrictions on liberty of movement out of or within the State and on choice of residency within the state (article 2), the expulsion or refusal to permit re-entry of nationals (article 3), and the collective expulsion of aliens (article 4). Protocol 6 abolishes the death penalty (article 1) except in times of war or imminent threat of war (article 2). Protocol 7 prohibits the expulsion of aliens lawfully resident in the state (article 1) and guarantees the right of appeal upon conviction of a criminal offence (article 2), protects individuals against multiple criminal proceedings or repeated punishment for the same offence (article 4), ensures compensation for victims of the miscarriage of justice (article 3), and provides for the rights and responsibilities of spouses before, during, and after marriage (article 5). Protocol 12 establishes a general prohibition of discrimination on any ground (article 1). Protocol 13 abolishes the death penalty unconditionally (article 1), with no right to make derogations (article 2) or reservations (article 3).

2) The rights entrenched in the ECHR all fall within the broad category of civil and political rights, and generally are similar to those found in the ICCPR. Some notable variations, however, include the lack of any reference to the right of self-determination (article 1), the right to recognition as a person before the law (article 16), the rights of the child (article 24), and protection of minorities (article 27). Why do you think that the ECHR omits any mention of the right to self-determination, which is found in both Covenants? Compare ICCPR articles 2(1), 17, and 26, invoked by the petitioner in *Toonen*, to ECHR articles 8 and 14. Are there any significant differences in the form and substance of these rights? Do you think that the case would have been decided differently if it had been presented to the ECHR?

3) In recent years, reasons for joining the Council of Europe and ratifying ECHR have moved from the ideological plane to an economic one. The European Union (EU) now expects states who intend to apply for membership to demonstrate an acceptable human rights stance by first joining the Council of Europe and then ratifying the ECHR. This has been a major reason why, in the past few years, a small rush of "democratic" Eastern European states have lined up to ratify the treaty. The latest round of new parties to the ECHR include Romania and Slovenia in 1993; Lithuania in 1995; Albania and Estonia in 1996; Croatia, Latvia, Macedonia, Moldova, and Ukraine in 1997; Russia in 1998; Georgia in 1999; Armenia, Azerbaijan, and Bosnia-Herzegovina in 2002; and Serbia and Montenegro in 2004.[38] Additionally, the EU itself has pledged to respect

---

38   See 63 Human Rights Information Bulletin (July to November 2004), online: <http://www.coe.int/T/E/Human_rights/hribe.asp#TopOfPage>.

fundamental human rights as guaranteed in the ECHR, as provided in article F2 of the 1992 Treaty of Maastricht creating the European Union. Such commitment to human rights was confirmed by the solemn proclamation in 2000, in Nice, of a Charter of Fundamental Rights of the European Union. If the Charter's legal status remains unclear, it has the merit, however, to offer, for the first time in the history of the EU, a catalogue of civil, political, economic, and social rights of European citizens. The proposed constitution for the EU provides for eventual ratification of the ECHR by the EU, a prospect made possible by a 2004 amendment to the ECHR.[39] One of the political bases of the ECHR, as inscribed in its Preamble, was that "European countries ... are like-minded and have a common heritage of political tradition, ideals, freedoms, and the rule of law"; is that still true of a 45-party ECHR extending to Eastern Europe and Asia? Should the European Court apply a "sliding scale" of human rights norms to accommodate different levels of capabilities of states? Is that different from universal human rights standards such as those entrenched in the ICCPR?

4) The ECHR initially created a three-pronged, powerful and sophisticated machinery to oversee the implementation of the rights guaranteed therein: the Commission, which acted as fact-finding, conciliation, and reporting organ; the Court, which adjudicated on whether a breach had occurred; and the Committee of Ministers, a political body with power to decide whether there had been a breach of the Convention for cases not proceeding from the Commission to the Court, and the organ entrusted with ensuring the execution of judgments for cases that did proceed to the Court. However, the ECHR mechanism was unable to respond to the exponential growth in petitions, from around 2,000 in 1980 to more than 12,000 in 1997, resulting from the eastward expansion of the Council of Europe. In 1993, states parties decided to reform the structure of the ECHR machinery to eliminate the Commission and create a unified Court, which took over in 1998. Further enlargement of the Council of Europe, composed by 2005 of over 800 million individuals, has meant a continued vertiginous rise in applications to the Court. In 2003, some 39,000 applications were lodged, resulting in a backlog of 65,000 applications pending a decision on admissibility and 16,500 cases pending before chambers by the beginning of 2004. In reaction to the mounting threat to the viability of the European Court, the Council of Europe adopted Protocol 14 in June 2004, amending the ECHR to give the Court more power to effectively and rapidly deal with applications, more than 90 percent of which are eventually declared inadmissible.[40]

5) The new European Court, which has a number of full-time judges equivalent to the number of states parties (at present 45), may be directly petitioned by individuals or states. The Court is divided into four sections that are broadly representative of the various

---

39   See P. Alston, ed., *L'Union européenne et les droits de l'homme* (2001); T. Hervey & J. Kenner, eds., *Economic and Social Rights under the EU Charter of Fundamental Rights* (2003); Lord Goldsmith, "A Charter of Rights, Freedoms, and Principles" in M. Andenas & J.A. Usher, eds., *The Treaty of Nice and Beyond* (2003) 387 and S.D. Scott, "The EU Charter of Rights: A Poor Attempt to Strengthen Democracy and Citizenship?" (*ibid.* at 399).

40   See Council of Europe, "Protocol No. 14 to the Convention for the Protection of Human Rights and Fundamental Freedoms, Amending the Control System of the Convention" (2004) 62 Human Rights Information Bulletin 63 and, "Explanatory Report" (*ibid.* at 66).

legal systems and present a geographical and gender equilibrium. Each section designates a Rapporteur and establishes a Committee of three judges, both of which may play a role in the decision on the initial admissibility of an individual application. With the entry into force of the 2004 Protocol 14, a single judge may declare an application inadmissible. Individual applications not deemed inadmissible may be decided on the merits, in certain cases, by a three-judge committee. In other cases, including all inter-state applications, a decision on the merits is made by a chamber composed of five or seven judges. Following a final decision, a party to the case may seek leave to have the case referred to a Grand Chamber. If leave is granted by a 5-judge panel of the Grand Chamber, then the full Grand Chamber, composed of 17 judges, sits to make a final decision.[41]

6) The ECHR focuses exclusively on civil and political rights, which led the Council of Europe to adopt the European Social Charter in 1961 to entrench economic and social rights.[42] The Charter protects 19 fundamental rights related to employment, social security, social services, equality, health, and the protection of disabled persons and migrant workers. Interestingly, the Charter adopts an *à la carte* approach, whereby states are given a choice of which rights they will guarantee. A 1996 Revised European Social Charter, which entered into force on July 1, 1999, modernized and expanded the protections granted by the Charter. Under the Revised Charter, states parties must file periodic reports on their efforts to implement the rights guaranteed by the Charter. These reports are examined by a Committee of Independent Experts and may lead to recommendations by the Governmental Committee and the Committee of Ministers. In addition, a 1995 Protocol, which entered into force in 1998, provides that trade unions, NGOs, and other groups may petition the Committee of Independent Experts.[43]

7) In 1975, virtually all European states as well as Canada and the United States participated in the Conference on Security and Co-operation in Europe (CSCE) in Helsinki, where they signed a document pledging allegiance to the peaceful settlement of disputes and to respect human rights.[44] Following the changes in Eastern Europe, the human rights portfolio of the CSCE has expanded. Most CSCE signatory states have gathered at a series of meetings dealing specifically with the "Human Dimension of the CSCE" to examine the changing character of Eastern Europe. For example, a meeting in 1990 produced the Document of the Copenhagen Meeting of the Conference on the

---

41   In May 1999, the Committee of Ministers of the Council of Europe created the position of Commissioner for Human Rights, to be elected by the Parliamentary Assembly and entrusted with the task of making recommendations and issuing reports on respect for human rights within the member states of the Council of Europe: Council of Europe, Committee of Ministers, 104th Sess., *Resolution (99)50 on the Council of Europe Commissioner for Human Rights* (1999) 46 Human Rights Bulletin 56. The first Commissioner is Alvaro Gil-Robes, of Spain.

42   (1961) 529 U.N.T.S. 89. See L. Samuel, *Fundamental Social Rights: Case Law of the European Social Charter*, 2d ed. (2002); D. Harris & J. Darcy, *The European Social Charter*, 2d ed. (2001); and A. Jaspers & L. Betten, eds., *25 Years; European Social Charter* (1988).

43   More information on the *European Social Charter* is available online: <http://www.humanrights.coe.int/Intro/eng/General/welc2dir.htm>.

44   (1975) 14 I.L.M. 1292. As its contents make clear, this document was not intended to have binding legal effect. This and other OSCE documents are available online: <http://www.osce.org>.

Human Dimension of the CSCE. It sets out basic civil and political rights and specifically links them to the ICCPR, the ICESCR, and the ECHR. Considering the atrocities committed by the Serbs, Croatians, and Bosnians in their territorial disputes, the instrument's Preamble is noteworthy: the signatory States "recognize that pluralistic democracy and the rule of law are essential for ensuring respect for all human rights and fundamental freedoms, the development of human contacts and the resolution of other issues of a related humanitarian character."[45]

The CSCE met again and signed the Charter of Paris for a New Europe in November 1990, which formally recognized the end of the Cold War, pledged friendly relations among states and reinforced the belief that respect for civil and political rights issues leads to economic liberty and social justice.[46] Considering the ethnic tensions, especially in Eastern Europe, one of the Charter's paragraphs is particularly significant: "We affirm that the ethnic, cultural, linguistic and religious identity of national minorities will be protected and that persons belonging to national minorities have the right freely to express, preserve and develop that identity without discrimination and in full equality before the law."[47] The 1990 meeting signalled the start of a greater institutionalization of the CSCE, which became the Organization for Security and Co-operation in Europe (OSCE) in 1994. Of particular interest to human rights are the Office for Democratic Institutions and Human Rights, active in monitoring elections and human rights, the Representative on Freedom for the Media, and the High Commissioner on National Minorities. One example of the unique contribution of an organization such as the OSCE is the role given to it by the 1995 General Framework Agreement for Peace in Bosnia and Herzegovina (the "Dayton Peace Agreement"): it has responsibility to promote democratization, monitor human rights and media freedom, and supervise free and fair elections—all tasks that bodies like the European Court or the Human Rights Committee cannot perform.

Regional Norms in the Americas[48]

Seven months before the United Nations adopted the Universal Declaration on Human Rights, the Organization of American States (OAS) adopted its own American Declaration

---

45   Council Eur. Doc. H/INF (91)1 at 115. The quotation comes from the text of the document in Appendix 63 at 266, reproduced in (1990) I.L.M. 1305 at 1307.

46   See Council Eur. Doc. H/INF (91) 2, 94 and Appendix 43 at 183 for a partial text. The full text is reproduced in (1991) 30 I.L.M. 190. After pledging that the protection and promotion of human rights and fundamental freedoms "is the first responsibility of government" and that "[r]espect for them is an essential safeguard against an over-mighty State," the *Charter of Paris for a New Europe* provides that, "[t]he free will of the individual, exercised in democracy and protected by the rule of law, forms the necessary basis for successful economic and social development. We will promote economic activity which respects and upholds human dignity." See I.L.M. *ibid.*

47   Doc. H/INF *Ibid.* Appendix 43, 183 at 183-84.

48   See J. Pasqualucci, *The Practice and Procedure of the Inter-American Court of Human Rights* (2003); H. Tigroudja & I. Panoussis, *La Cour interaméricaine des droits de l'homme* (2003); D. Harris & S. Livingstone, *The Inter-American System of Human Rights* (1998); S. Davidson, *The Inter-American*

on the Rights and Duties of Man.[49] The document is in many ways similar to the Universal Declaration; it was not meant to create binding obligations for OAS member states, and it contains both civil and political rights and economic, social, and cultural rights. A significant difference, however, is the chapter on duties (articles XXIX-XXXVIII), which includes individual duties to educate one's children (article XXX), to acquire an elementary education (article XXXI), to pay taxes (article XXXVI), and to work according to one's capacity (article XXXVII). The OAS created the Inter-American Commission on Human Rights in 1959, initially to promote awareness and respect for human rights and make recommendations to states, a task expanded to the consideration of individual communications alleging violations of human rights by OAS member states after 1965. The American Convention on Human Rights (ACHR) was adopted by the OAS General Assembly in 1969, entering into force in 1978. There are two protocols to the ACHR: one from 1988 on economic, social, and cultural rights; the other from 1990 on the abolition of the death penalty.[50] In addition, the OAS has sponsored the 1985 Inter-American Convention to Prevent and Punish Torture, the 1994 Convention on Forced Disappearances, the 1994 Inter-American Convention on the Prevention, Punishment and Eradication of Violence Against Women ("Convention of Belem do Para"), and the 1999 Convention on the Elimination of All Forms of Discrimination Against Persons with Disabilities.[51] Canada has ratified none of these Inter-American human rights instruments.

American Convention on Human Rights
1144 U.N.T.S. 123; OAS T.S. 1969 No. 36

Article 4: Right to Life

1. Every person has the right to have his life respected. This right shall be protected by law and, in general, from the moment of conception. No one shall be arbitrarily deprived of his life.

2. In countries that have not abolished the death penalty, it may be imposed only for the most serious crimes and pursuant to a final judgment rendered by a competent court and in accordance with a law establishing such punishment, enacted prior to the commission of the crime. The application of such punishment shall not be extended to crimes to which it does not presently apply.

Human Rights System (1997); T. Buergenthal & D. Shelton, *Protecting Human Rights in the Americas; Cases and Materials*, 4th ed. (1995); and B. Santoscoy, *La Commission interaméricaine des droits de l'homme et de le développement de sa compétence par le système des pétitions individuelles* (1995). Documents and information on human rights in the Americas are available online: <http://www.oas.org>.

49 OAS, 9th International Conference of American States, Res. XXX (1948), reprinted in *Basic Documents Pertaining to Human Rights in the Inter-American System*, OEA/Ser.L.V/II.82, Doc. 6 Rev. 1 (1992) at 17. Updated to July 2003 online at <http://www.corteidh.or.cr/public/Basingl0.pdf> at 19.

50 OAS Tr. Ser. 1988 No.69; OAS Tr. Ser. 1990 No. 73.

51 These instruments may be found at <http://www.oas.org>.

3. The death penalty shall not be reestablished in states that have abolished it. ...

4. In no case shall capital punishment be inflicted for political offenses or related common crimes.

5. Capital punishment shall not be imposed upon persons who, at the time the crime was committed, were under 18 years of age or over 70 years of age; nor shall it be applied to pregnant women.

6. Every person condemned to death shall have the right to apply for amnesty, pardon, or commutation of sentence, which may be granted in all cases. Capital punishment shall not be imposed while such a petition is pending decision by the competent authority. ...

Article 9:   Freedom from Ex Post Facto Laws

No one shall be convicted of any act or omission that did not constitute a criminal offense, under the applicable law, at the time it was committed. A heavier penalty shall not be imposed than the one that was applicable at the time the criminal offense was committed. If subsequent to the commission of the offense the law provides for the imposition of a lighter punishment, the guilty person shall benefit therefrom. ...

Article 11:   Right to Privacy

1. Everyone has the right to have his honor respected and his dignity recognized.

2. No one may be the object of arbitrary or abusive interference with his private life, his family, his home, or his correspondence, or of unlawful attacks on his honor or reputation.

3. Everyone has the right to the protection of the law against such interference or attacks. ...

Article 14:   Right of Reply

1. Anyone injured by inaccurate or offensive statements or ideas disseminated to the public in general by a legally regulated medium of communication has the right to reply or to make a correction using the same communications outlet, under such conditions as the law may establish.

2. The correction or reply shall not in any case remit other legal liabilities that may have been incurred.

3. For the effective protection of honor and reputation, every publisher, and every newspaper, motion picture, radio, and television company, shall have a person responsible who is not protected by immunities or special privileges. ...

Article 18:   Right to a Name

Every person has the right to a given name and to the surnames of his parents or that of one of them. The law shall regulate the manner in which this right shall be ensured for all, by the use of assumed names if necessary.

Article 19: Rights of the Child

Every minor child has the right to the measures of protection required by his condition as a minor on the part of his family, society, and the state.

Article 20: Right to Nationality

1. Every person has the right to a nationality.

2. Every person has the right to the nationality of the state in whose territory he was born if he does not have the right to any other nationality.

3. No one shall be arbitrarily deprived of his nationality or of the right to change it.

Article 21: Right to Property

1. Everyone has the right to the use and enjoyment of his property. The law may subordinate such use and enjoyment to the interest of society.

2. No one shall be deprived of his property except upon payment of just compensation, for reasons of public utility or social interest, and in the cases and according to the forms established by law.

3. Usury and any other form of exploitation of man by man shall be prohibited by law. ...

Article 24: Right to Equal Protection

All persons are equal before the law. Consequently, they are entitled, without discrimination, to equal protection of the law.

NOTES

1) In addition to the provisions quoted above, the ACHR guarantees the right to recognition as a person (article 3), the right to humane treatment (article 5), freedom from slavery (article 6), the right to personal liberty (article 7), the right to a fair trial (article 8), the right to compensation (article 10), freedom of conscience and religion (article 12), freedom of thought and expression (article 13), the right of assembly (article 15), freedom of association (article 16), freedom of movement and residence (article 22), the right to participate in government (article 23), and the right to judicial protection (article 25). There is only a general reference to economic, social, and cultural rights in article 26, with the more substantive rights of that nature entrenched in a 1988 protocol to the ACHR. The long list of duties found in the American declaration has been pared down in the ACHR to a single provision (article 32) stressing individual responsibilities to one's family, community, and humankind. Generally, the ACHR follows the rights entrenched in the ICCPR quite closely, with a few significant exceptions, including the right to property (article 21), the right to reply to libellous statements using the same medium (article 14), and the right to obtain asylum in case of political persecution (article 22(7)). Compare the right to life as guaranteed in article 4 of the ACHR to equivalent provisions in the ICCPR (article 6) and ECHR (article 2).

2) The Inter-American Commission on Human Rights, composed of seven independent experts elected for four-year terms, is based in Washington, D.C., and exercises
functions under the ACHR in addition to those under the OAS Charter described earlier.
It can hear petitions presented by individuals, organizations, and states, in addition to
possessing broad fact-finding capacities. The Inter-American Court of Human Rights,
based in San José, Costa Rica, is composed of seven independent judges elected for six
years by states parties. It hears cases submitted to it by the Commission or by states
parties. It also has power to issue advisory opinions. The powers of the Inter-American
Commission and Court of Human Rights are further discussed below in Section C on
"Compliance and Enforcement."

3) Canada ratified the OAS Charter in 1990, thus becoming a member of that
organization, and announced that ratification of the ACHR would be forthcoming in
1991.[52] More than a decade later, however, ratification has still to occur.[53] Some of the
provisions found in the ACHR present difficulties for Canada, including the apparent
incompatibility of legalized abortion with a right to life "from the moment of conception"
(article 4(1)), as well as the obligation to allow a right of reply in the media in case of
libellous statements (article 14), perhaps not fully compatible with freedom of expression
under the *Canadian Charter of Rights and Freedoms*. Because many of the rights guaranteed
by the ACHR touch on issues of provincial jurisdiction, Canada's ratification is conditioned
upon a prior agreement with the provinces to ensure that a ratified treaty will be implemented at both levels.[54] Do you think that it is preferable for Canada to abstain from
ratifying the ACHR than for it to ratify with a large number of reservations? Non-ratification
does hinder Canada's ability to effectively speak on human rights in the Americas. For
example, Canada's intervention to persuade Peru not to withdraw its acceptance of the
jurisdiction of the Inter-American Court of Human Rights in 1999 was met with a rebuke
that, as a non-party to the ACHR, Canada was in no position to tell anyone what to do.

52   See Standing Senate Committee on Human Rights, *Enhancing Canada's Role in the OAS: Canadian
     Adherence to the American Convention on Human Rights* (2003); I. Almeida & M. Porret, *Renewing
     Canada's Commitment to Human Rights; Strategic Actions for At Home and Abroad* (2004); N. Farrell,
     "The American Convention on Human Rights: Canada's Present Law and the Effect of Ratification" (1992)
     30 Can Y.B. Int'l L. 233; C. Hilling, "La participation canadienne au système interaméricain de protection
     des droits et libertés: les obligation immédiates et les perspectives d'avenir" in CCIL, *Canada and the
     Americas* (1991) CCIL Proc. 223; and W. Schabas, "Substantive and Procedural Hurdles to Canada's
     Ratification of the American Convention on Human Rights" (1991) 12 Hum. Rts. L.J. 405.

53   Canada proposed Mme. Justice Bertha Wilson as a candidate for election to the Inter-American Court of
     Human Rights in 1991, as an indication of its willingness not only to ratify the ACHR but also to accept the
     competence of the court. In one of the darker moments of the OAS, Canada's candidate was defeated by the
     former justice minister of Nicaraguan dictator Anathasio Somosa, an event that, according to Schabas,
     cooled Canada's enthusiasm for the ACHR. See Schabas, *supra* note 1 at 127; and D. Cassel, "Somoza's
     Revenge: A New Judge for the Inter-American Court of Human Rights" (1992) 13 Hum. Rts. L.J. 137.

54   See Senate Report, *supra* note 52 at 39-50 for a full analysis of the compatibility of Canadian law with
     the ACHR. Negotiations are pursued within the Permanent Federal-Provincial-Territorial Committee of
     Officials on Human Rights. See D. Turp, "Le Comite permanent fédéral-provincial-territorial des
     fonctionnaires charges des droits de la personne et sa participation a la mise en oeuvre des traités" (1984-
     85) 2 Can. Y.B. Hum. Rts. 77.

4) Although Canada is not a party to the ACHR, it has ratified the OAS Charter and, by the same token, undertaken to comply with the rights guaranteed in the American Declaration of the Rights and Duties of Man. Under article 20 of its Statute, the Inter-American Commission on Human Rights has jurisdiction to examine petitions alleging violations of human rights by states who are parties to the OAS Charter but not the ACHR.[55] Indeed, there have been petitions alleging that Canada was not in compliance with the rights entrenched in the American Declaration. In addition, the Inter-American Court of Human Rights concluded in its *Advisory Opinion on the Interpretation of the American Declaration of the Rights and Duties of Man Within the Framework of Article 64 of the American Convention on Human Rights* that it had the power to render opinions interpreting the American Declaration insofar as that was necessary for the construction of the ACHR or other human rights treaties.[56] The net result is that the Court may flesh out rights in the Declaration that are binding on Canada, despite the fact that Canada has not accepted the Court's jurisdiction.

Regional Norms in Africa[57]

Africa is the most recent region to adopt its own human rights treaty, which it did under the auspices of the Organisation for African Unity (OAU). This constituted a new direction for the organization, founded in 1963, which had up to then been concerned primarily with decolonization and regional stability. In answer to repeated calls from the United Nations to create an African human rights instrument, the OAU adopted the African Charter on Human and Peoples' Rights (ACHPR) in Nairobi in 1981. The guidelines given to the drafters are instructive of the nature of the ACHPR: it had to be grounded in African traditions and values; embody an equilibrium between individual and collective rights, between civil and political rights and economic, social, and cultural rights, and between rights and duties; specify the content of the rights of peoples; and create a commission to protect the rights entrenched in the Charter while still remaining under the control of the OAU Assembly of Heads of States and Governments.[58] The resulting document is both distinctive and controversial. Two protocols to the ACHPR were adopted respectively in 1998 and 2003 on the creation of an African Court on Human and Peoples' Rights and on the rights of women in Africa. In addition, a separate Charter on the Rights and Welfare of the Child was adopted by the OAU in 1990.

---

55   OAS, General Assembly, 9th Sess., *Statute of the Inter-American Commission on Human Rights*, OR OEA/Ser.P/IX.0.2/80, vol. 1 at 98. reproduced in *Basic Documents, supra* note 49 at 93. Updated to July 2003 online <http://www.corteidh.or.cr/public/Basingl0.pdf> at 137.

56   (1989), Advisory Opinion OC-10/90, Inter-Am. Ct. H.R. (Ser. A) No. 10 at para. 44.

57   See R. Murray, *Human Rights in Africa* (2004); F. Ouguergouz, *The African Charter on Human and Peoples' Rights* (2003); M. Evans & R. Murray, *The African Charter on Human and Peoples' Rights* (2002); E. Ankumah, *The African Commission on Human and Peoples' Rights* (1996); V. Yemet, *La Charte africaine des droits de l'homme et des peuples* (1996); and K. M'baye, *Les Droits de l'homme en Afrique* (1992).

58   M'baye, *supra* note 57 at 151.

African Charter on Human and Peoples' Rights
OAU Doc. CAB/LEG/67/3 Rev. 5; (1982) 21 I.L.M. 58

Article 1

The Member States of the Organization of African Unity parties to the present Charter shall recognize the rights, duties and freedoms enshrined in this Chapter and shall undertake to adopt legislative or other measures to give effect to them.

Article 2

Every individual shall be entitled to the enjoyment of the rights and freedoms recognized and guaranteed in the present Charter without distinction of any kind such as race, ethnic group, color, sex, language, religion, political or any other opinion, national and social origin, fortune, birth or other status.

Article 3

1. Every individual shall be equal before the law.
2. Every individual shall be entitled to equal protection of the law.

Article 4

Human beings are inviolable. Every human being shall be entitled to respect for his life and the integrity of his person. No one may be arbitrarily deprived of this right.

Article 5

Every individual shall have the right to the respect of the dignity inherent in a human being and to the recognition of his legal status. All forms of exploitation and degradation of man particularly slavery, slave trade, torture, cruel, inhuman or degrading punishment and treatment shall be prohibited. ...

Article 15

Every individual shall have the right to work under equitable and satisfactory conditions, and shall receive equal pay for equal work.

Article 16

1. Every individual shall have the right to enjoy the best attainable state of physical and mental health.
2. States parties to the present Charter shall take the necessary measures to protect the health of their people and to ensure that they receive medical attention when they are sick.

Article 17

1. Every individual shall have the right to education.
2. Every individual may freely take part in the cultural life of his community.
3. The promotion and protection of morals and traditional values recognized by the community shall be the duty of the State. ...

Article 18

1. The family shall be the natural unit and basis of society. It shall be protected by the State which shall take care of its physical health and morals.
2. The State shall have the duty to assist the family which is the custodian of morals and traditional values recognized by the community.
3. The State shall ensure the elimination of every discrimination against women and also ensure the protection of the rights of the woman and the child as stipulated in international declarations and conventions.
4. The aged and the disabled shall also have the right to special measures of protection in keeping with their physical or moral needs.

Article 19

All peoples shall be equal; they shall enjoy the same respect and shall have the same rights. Nothing shall justify the domination of a people by another.

Article 20

1. All peoples shall have the right to existence. They shall have the unquestionable and inalienable right to self-determination. They shall freely determine their political status and shall pursue their economic and social development according to the policy they have freely chosen.
2. Colonized or oppressed peoples shall have the right to free themselves from the bonds of domination by resorting to any means recognized by the international community.
3. All peoples shall have the right to the assistance of the States parties to the present Charter in their liberation struggle against foreign domination, be it political, economic or cultural.

Article 21

1. All peoples shall freely dispose of their wealth and natural resources. This right shall be exercised in the exclusive interest of the people. In no case shall a people be deprived of it.
2. In case of spoliation the dispossessed people shall have the right to the lawful recovery of its property as well as to an adequate compensation.
3. The free disposal of wealth and natural resources shall be exercised without prejudice to the obligation of promoting international economic cooperation based on mutual respect, equitable exchange and the principles of international law.

4. States parties to the present Charter shall individually and collectively exercise the right to free disposal of their wealth and natural resources with a view to strengthening African unity and solidarity.

5. States parties to the present Charter shall undertake to eliminate all forms of foreign economic exploitation particularly that practiced by international monopolies so as to enable their peoples to fully benefit from the advantages derived from their national resources.

Article 22

1. All peoples shall have the right to their economic, social and cultural development with due regard to their freedom and identity and in the equal enjoyment of the common heritage of mankind.

2. States shall have the duty, individually or collectively, to ensure the exercise of the right to development.

Article 23

1. All peoples shall have the right to national and international peace and security. The principles of solidarity and friendly relations implicitly affirmed by the Charter of the United Nations and reaffirmed by that of the Organization of African Unity shall govern relations between States.

2. For the purpose of strengthening peace, solidarity and friendly relations, States parties to the present Charter shall ensure that:

(a) any individual enjoying the right of asylum under Article 12 of the present Charter shall not engage in subversive activities against his country of origin or any other State party to the present Charter;

(b) their territories shall not be used as bases for subversive or terrorist activities against the people of any other State party to the present Charter.

Article 24

All peoples shall have the right to a general satisfactory environment favourable to their development.

Article 25

States parties to the present Charter shall have the duty to promote and ensure through teaching, education and publication, the respect of the rights and freedoms contained in the present Charter and to see to it that these freedoms and rights as well as corresponding obligations and duties are understood.

Article 26

States parties to the present Charter shall have the duty to guarantee the independence of the Courts and shall allow the establishment and improvement of appropriate national institutions entrusted with the promotion and protection of the rights and freedoms guaranteed by the present Charter.

Article 27

1. Every individual shall have duties towards his family and society, the State and other legally recognized communities and the international community.

2. The rights and freedoms of each individual shall be exercised with due regard to the rights of others, collective security, morality and common interest.

Article 28

Every individual shall have the duty to respect and consider his fellow beings without discrimination, and to maintain relations aimed at promoting, safeguarding and reinforcing mutual respect and tolerance.

Article 29

The individual shall also have the duty:

1. To preserve the harmonious development of the family and to work for the cohesion and respect of the family; to respect his parents at all times, to maintain them in case of need;

2. To serve his national community by placing his physical and intellectual abilities at its service;

3. Not to compromise the security of the State whose national or resident he is;

4. To preserve and strengthen social and national solidarity, particularly when the latter is threatened;

5. To preserve and strengthen the national independence and the territorial integrity of his country and to contribute to its defence in accordance with the law;

6. To work to the best of his abilities and competence, and to pay taxes imposed by law in the interest of the society;

7. To preserve and strengthen positive African cultural values in his relations with other members of the society, in the spirit of tolerance, dialogue and consultation and, in general, to contribute to the promotion of the moral well being of society;

8. To contribute to the best of his abilities, at all times and at all levels, to the promotion and achievement of African unity.

NOTES

1) In addition to the rights quoted above, the ACHPR guarantees the right to liberty and security of the person (article 6), due process rights (article 7), freedom of conscience (article 8), freedom of expression (article 9), freedom of association (articles 10-11), freedom of movement (article 12), the right to participate in government (article 13), and the right to property (article 14). The rights found in the ACHPR are generally inspired by earlier universal and regional instruments, but at times with a particular African slant. For example, the ACHPR introduces ethnicity as an explicit prohibited ground of discrimination in article 2, a reflection of the inter-ethnic tensions in many African countries. Likewise, references to slavery and the slave trade and freedom from foreign domination are reflections of the region's history. The OAU's concern for political

stability and territorial integrity are echoed in a state's duty to prevent its territory from being used for terrorist acts (article 23(2)(b)) and an individual duty to preserve national territorial integrity (article 29(5)). Like the ACHR and unlike the ICCPR, it guarantees the right to property (article 14), although the idea of compensation in case of expropriation included in the ACHR is not replicated in the ACHPR. Compare the formulation of article 1 of the ACHPR to the duty to "respect and ensure" rights found in the ICCPR (article 2(1)) and ACHR (article 1(1)) as interpreted by the Inter-American Court of Human Rights in the *Velásquez Rodríguez Case*, reproduced above in Section A.2.

2) Unlike the ICCPR and ECHR, the ACHPR covers not only civil and political rights but also economic, social, and cultural rights. Compare the formulation of the state's obligations under ACHPR articles 15-17 to those imposed by ICESCR article 2(1), discussed earlier.

3) The most creative and controversial portions of the ACHPR concern peoples' rights and individual duties. They reflect what is presented as the African vision of the individual, not viewed in an atomistic fashion as in the West, but rather as necessarily and dialectically connected to several overlapping communities, starting with the family and growing wider through community, ethnic groups, and so on. As such, although the ACHPR neither overlooks individual rights nor formally subordinates them to group rights, it does seem to give a measure of priority to collective rights. With respect to duties, the ACHPR departs from all other human rights instruments to create duties that are more than limitations or the other side of rights. Indeed, the ACHPR lacks a provision on limitation of individual rights found in the Universal Declaration on Human Rights (article 30), ICCPR (article 5), the ECHR (article 17), and the ACHR (article 29). It is interesting to note that the ACHPR does not create a broad individual duty to respect the fundamental rights of others, but simply one not to discriminate. Most duties are owed to the community and the state. These duties have been criticized as out of place because they do not fit within the protection of individuals and peoples. Some also fear that individual duties might be used by governments as an excuse to disregard individual rights.[59]

4) The institutional content of the ACHPR is less innovative than its normative content. It provides for the creation of an African Commission on Human and Peoples' Rights, made of 11 independent experts elected by the OAU Assembly of Heads of States and Governments for a period of six years. The Commission's mandate is close to that of the Inter-American Commission. It is charged with the promotion, interpretation, and protection of the rights entrenched in the ACHPR. There is a built-in political control of the African Commission's power to examine communications from individuals and groups, with the ultimate decision to make an in-depth study of any case left to the OAU Assembly of Heads of States and Governments. The African Commission has few powers, very little means, and so far has had difficulty establishing its credibility among African governments and activists.

5) The idea of establishing an African Court of Human Rights predated the founding of the OAU. As early as 1961, during the African Conference on the Rule of Law in

---

59   See M. wa Mutua, "The Banjul Charter and the African Cultural Fingerprint: An Evaluation of the Language of Duties" (1995) 35 Va. J. Int. L. 339; U. Umozurike, "The African Charter on Human and Peoples' Rights" (1983) 77 A.J.I.L. 902; and S.C. Agbakwa, "A Path Least Taken: Economic and Social Rights and the Prospects of Conflict Prevention and Peacebuilding in Africa" (2003) 47 J. Afr. L. 38.

Lagos, a recommendation was made to create such an institution. During the negotiation of the ACHPR, however, it was felt that a pragmatic compromise had to be found in order to attract broad support. It appeared that the establishment of a court was premature at the time and that the only feasible solution was to adopt weak enforcement machinery, the subsequent establishment of a court depending on how the initial organ would function. As the idea progressed among African states that the protection of human and peoples' rights was no longer a purely domestic matter, so did the idea of an African Court aimed at complementing and reinforcing the mission of the Commission. A protocol to the ACHPR was finally adopted at the Summit of the OAU in Ouagadougou, in June 1998, establishing the African Court on Human and Peoples' Rights.[60] The Court has jurisdiction over "all cases and disputes submitted to it concerning the interpretation and application of the Charter, [the] protocol and any other relevant Human Rights instrument ratified by the States concerned" (article 3(1)). Unlike other regional institutions, the jurisdiction of the Court is not limited to the implementation of the ACHPR, but extends to any treaty dealing with human rights applicable in Africa. Individuals and NGOs may petition the Court only if the state party against which they want to proceed has previously accepted the jurisdiction of the Court to entertain such complaints (article 34(6)). As of 2005, 19 of 53 States had ratified the Protocol creating the Court, which entered into force on January 25, 2004. Among them, only Burkina Faso has made a declaration under article 34(6).

6) The OAU was replaced in 2001 by the African Union (AU).[61] The Constitutive Act of the AU, adopted on July 11, 2000 in Lomé, grants a much greater place to respect for human rights, democratic principles, and the rule of law than the Charter of the OAU. According to article 3, the AU is set up in order to "promote and protect human and peoples' rights in accordance with the *African Charter on Human and Peoples' Rights* and other relevant human rights instruments." Remarkably, and quite originally, article 4(h) recognizes a genuine right of humanitarian intervention in certain instances by laying down "the right of the Union to intervene in a Member State pursuant to a decision of the Assembly in respect of grave circumstances, namely war crimes, genocide and crimes against humanity."[62]

(c) Reservations, Limitations, and Derogations

Human rights embodied in treaties are the result of long and usually difficult negotiations and, as such, represent a compromise of divergent views. Once the formulation of a human right has been agreed upon and entrenched into a binding instrument, however, it is subject to further assaults on the part of states seeking to minimize its legal impact.

---

60   M. wa Mutua, "The African Human Rights Court: A Two Legged Stool?" (1999) 21 H.R. Quart. 342. M. Mutoy, "La Cour africaine des droits de l'homme et des peuples: mimétisme institutionnel ou avancée judiciaires?" (1998) 102 R.G.D.I.P. 765-80.

61   On the African Union see T. Maluwa, "Reimagining African Unity: Some Preliminary Reflections on the Constitutive Act of the African Union" (2001) 9 African Y.B. Int'l L. 3; and S. Bula-Bula, "Les fondements de l'Union Africaine" (2001) 9 African Y.B. Int'l L. 39.

62   See the discussion on reservations in Chapter 3, "Creation and Ascertainment of International Law," Section B.2 on "Treaty Making."

Reservation, limitation clauses, and derogation during times of emergency are three tools that allow states to both ratify human rights treaties and restrict their scope of application.

Reservations and Limitations to Human Rights Conventions

States often will hesitate before making reservations to a treaty because, as a rule, they will produce a reciprocal effect, meaning that other states will be able to invoke the reservation in their relation with the reserving state. In the field of human rights, however, reservations pose a special problem because treaties create obligations *erga omnes* with very little role for reciprocity. As a result, reservations have an essentially unilateral effect and cannot be invoked by other states. States have used reservations rather liberally when ratifying human rights treaties. There are, for instance, more than 150 reservations to the ICCPR. The problem in this area has been to determine what reservations are acceptable, who should make that determination, and what is the effect of an invalid reservation.[63]

The acceptability of reservations to treaties is usually not an issue addressed directly by most treaties, which remain silent in that respect. In the field of human rights, a few treaties like the Convention against Torture mention that reservations must be compatible with the object and purpose of the convention. This limitation indeed has grown to be accepted as representing a customary limitation to the making of reservations, so that any reservation incompatible with the object and purpose of the treaty is, *ipso facto*, invalid (Vienna Convention on the Law of Treaties article 19(c)). This in turns begs the question how to define the object and purpose of a human rights treaty, a point on which treaties are usually silent as well. The Inter-American Court of Human Rights in its advisory opinion on *Restrictions to the Death Penalty* (American Convention on Human Rights articles 4(2) and 4(4)) addressed this issue:

> 61. Consequently, the first question which arises when interpreting a reservation is whether it is compatible with the object and purpose of the treaty. Article 27 of the Convention allows the States Parties to suspend, in time of war, public danger, or other emergency that threatens their independence or security, the obligations they assumed by ratifying the Convention, provided that in doing so they do not suspend or derogate from certain basic or essential rights, among them the right to life guaranteed by Article 4. It would follow therefrom that a reservation which was designed to enable a State to suspend any of the non-derogable fundamental rights must be deemed to be incompatible with the object and purpose of the Convention and, consequently, not permitted by it.
>
> The situation would be different if the reservation sought merely to restrict certain aspects of a nonderogable right without depriving the right as a whole of its basic purpose.

---

63   Since 1995, the International Law Commission has been considering the topic of reservations to treaties, on the basis of a series of reports by Special Rapporteur Alain Pellet. The results of the ILC's work as well as the Special Rapporteur's reports are available at www.un.org/law/ilc. See also C. Chinkin & J. Gardner, *Human Rights as General Norms and a State's Right To Opt Out: Reservations and Objections to Human Rights Conventions* (1997); L. Lijnzaad, *Reservations to UN Human Rights Treaties: Ratify and Ruin?* (1995); W. Schabas, "Reservations to Human Rights Treaties: Time for Innovation and Reform" (1994) 32 Can. Y.B. Int'l L. 39; and refer to Chapter 3, "Creation and Ascertainment of International Law," Section B.2 on "Treaty Making."

Since the reservation referred to by the Commission in its submission does not appear to be of a type that is designed to deny the right to life as such, the Court concludes that to that extent it can be considered, in principle, as not being incompatible with the object and purpose of the Convention.[64]

The UNHRC has also found a link between non-derogable rights and reservations, holding that "[w]hile there is no automatic correlation between reservations to non-derogable provisions, and reservations which offend against the object and purpose of the Covenant, a State has a heavy onus to justify such a reservation."[65] The Human Rights Committee also proposed a general rule whereby treaty provisions codifying norms that are already part of customary law cannot be the object of reservations, a position that has been the object of some criticism. It must be noted that both non-derogable rights and human rights also contained in customary law have been the object of many reservations. Some states make very general reservations—for instance, the Maldives' reservation to the Convention on the Elimination of All Forms of Discrimination Against Women:

> The Government of the Republic of Maldives will comply with the provisions of the Convention, except those which the Government may consider contradictory to the principles of the Islamic Sharia upon which the laws and traditions of the Maldives is founded. Furthermore, the Republic of Maldives does not see itself bound by any provisions of the Convention which obliges it to change its Constitution and laws in any manner.[66]

The latter sentence, which attempts to subject the Convention to national laws, is in substance similar to the U.S. reservation to article 7 of the ICCPR.[67] The Committee has challenged the validity of such general reservations, which have been objected to by many other states parties to the same treaties.

Bodies established by human rights treaties, including the Human Rights Committee and the Committee on the Elimination of All Forms of Discrimination Against Women, have taken an aggressive stance in asserting their power to judge the compatibility of a reservation with the object and purpose of a convention. The Human Rights Committee, for example, clearly stated in its comments on the United States' initial report that it considered the U.S. reservation to article 7 to be invalid.[68] Some states have noted that the treaties do not expressly accord such a power to those bodies, and have challenged the

---

64 *Restriction to the Death Penalty* (1983), Advisory Opinion OC-3/83, Inter-Am. Ct. H.R. (Ser. A.) No. 3.

65 Human Rights Committee, *General Comment Adopted by the Human Rights Committee Under Article 40, Paragraph 4 of the International Covenant on Civil and Political Rights*, UN ESCOR, 1994, U.N. Doc. CCPR/C/21/Rev. 1/Add. 6 (General Comment 24(52), "General Comment on Issues Relating to Reservations Made Upon Ratification or Accession to the Covenant of the Optional Protocols Thereto, or in Relation to Declarations Under Article 41 of the Covenant").

66 *Multilateral Treaties Deposited with the Secretary General*, U.N. Doc. ST/LEG/Ser.E.

67 "The United States considers itself bound by article 7 to the extent that 'cruel, inhuman or degrading treatment or punishment' means the cruel and unusual treatment or punishment prohibited by the Fifth, Eighth, and/or Fourteenth Amendments to the Constitution of the United States," *ibid.*

68 Human Rights Committee, *Consideration of Reports Submitted by States Parties Under Article 40 of the Covenant: International Covenant on Civil and Political Rights: Comments of the Human Rights Committee: United States of America*, UN ESCOR, 1995, U.N. Doc. CCPR/C/79/Add.50 (1995) para. 14.

latter's right to pronounce on the compatibility of a reservation with the object and purpose of a treaty. The alternative is to rely on objections to reservations by other states parties, although the effect of such objections is not clear under article 21 of the Vienna Convention on the Law of Treaties (reproduced in the Documentary Supplement).

Another difficult question is the effect of invalid reservations. Is the state still to be considered a party to the treaty, minus the reservation, or does a finding of incompatibility mean that, for instance, the United States is not to be considered a party to the ICCPR? One argument provides that the treaty body ought to decide whether the reservation is severable from the state's consent to the treaty, so that an invalid reservation would still leave the state as a party to the treaty. A number of states, including the United States, strenuously object to such a position, and insist that reservations are an integral part of consent to a treaty.

It is important to note that many of the rights entrenched in human rights conventions can be limited, under normal circumstances, for public policy reasons. The presence of limitation or "clawback" clauses in the treaty definition of some rights allows states to trench on rights in a manner that would otherwise constitute a violation of that right. For example, the ICCPR guarantees freedom of religion but permits the right to manifest one's religion to be subject to "such limitations as are prescribed by law and are necessary to protect public safety, order, health, or morals or the fundamental rights and freedoms of others" (ICCPR article 18(3)). There, specific restrictions are an alternative to general limitation clauses that apply to all rights in a given instrument, such as article 29(2) of the Universal Declaration of Human Rights (or article 1 of the *Canadian Charter of Rights and Freedoms*). The formulation of limitation clauses varies greatly from right to right and from instrument to instrument. Despite the fact that some limitation clauses are framed in a very general manner, treaty bodies have devised principles that provide guidance on what limitations are permissible under a given instrument. Thus, in *Toonen*, the author of the communication relied on the right to be protected against "arbitrary or unlawful interference with his privacy" (ICCPR article 17).[69] The state of Tasmania argued that the *Criminal Code* provisions criminalizing homosexual relations were neither arbitrary nor unlawful, but that they could indeed be justified on public health and moral grounds. Despite the vagueness of the limitation clause, the Human Rights Committee considered the limitation to be arbitrary, using a test based on the legitimacy of the aims and proportionality of measures adopted. Similar tests have been used with respect to other human rights instruments, sometimes encapsulated in the notion of a "margin of appreciation," and have provided the inspiration for the test adopted by the Supreme Court of Canada in the *Oakes* case.[70]

---

69   Compare that provision to the limitation of the right to privacy under ECHR article 8(2).

70   *R. v. Oakes*, [1986] 1 R.C.S. 103. See Schabas, *supra* note 1 at 279-86 and H. Yourow, *The Margin of Appreciation Doctrine in the Dynamics of European Human Rights Jurisprudence* (1996).

Derogations from Human Rights in Times of Emergency

Most human rights treaties contain a clause permitting the suspension of many fundamental human rights during a time of emergency.[71] The rationale for these clauses is said to be that there can be no protection of fundamental rights without a minimally stable society in which the state can enforce the rule of law. The ICCPR allows for derogation in article 4 (reproduced in the Documentary Supplement), while the ECHR does so in article 15:

Article 15

1. In time of war or other public emergency threatening the life of the nation any High Contracting Part may take measures derogating from its obligations under this Convention to the extent strictly required by the exigencies of the situation, provided that such measures are not inconsistent with its other obligations under international law.

2. No derogation from Article 2, except in respect of deaths resulting from lawful acts of war, or from Articles 3, 4 (para. 1) and 7 shall be made under this provision.

3. Any High Contracting Party availing itself of this right of derogation shall keep the Secretary-General of the Council of Europe fully informed of the measures which it has taken and the reasons therefor. It shall also inform the Secretary-General of the Council of Europe when such measures have ceased to operate and the provisions of the convention are again fully executed.

Some significant variations in the formulation of the circumstances justify derogation, with the ICCPR avoiding any reference to "war" in article 4 and the ACHR allowing for derogation in "time of war, public danger, or other emergency that threatens the independence or security of a State Party" (ACHR article 27).

Brannigan & McBride v. United Kingdom
ECHR, Ser. A., No. 258-B; (1993), 17 Eur. Hum. Rts. Rep. 539

[The two applicants challenged the legality of their detention by British forces in Northern Ireland, alleging that their right to be "brought promptly before a judge" (ECHR article 5(3)) had been breached. The United Kingdom had given notice of a state of emergency in Northern Ireland and argued that any breach of article 5 would be covered by the derogation under article 15.]

[41] The applicants argued that it would be inconsistent with Article 15(2) if, in derogating from safeguards recognised as essential for the protection of non-derogable rights such as Articles 2 and 3, the national authorities were to be afforded a wide margin of appreciation. This was especially so where the emergency was of a quasi-

---

71   See J. Oráa, *Human Rights in States of Emergency in International Law* (1992); J. Fitzpatrick, *Human Rights in Crisis: The International System for Protecting Human Rights During States of Emergency* (1994); and R. Ergec, *Les droits de l'homme a l'épreuve des circonstances exceptionnelles. Études sur l'Article 15 de la Convention européennes des droits de l'homme* (1987).

permanent nature such as that existing in Northern Ireland. To do so would also be inconsistent with the *Brogan and others*[72] judgment where the Court had regarded judicial control as one of the fundamental principles of a democratic society and had already—they claimed—extended to the Government a margin of appreciation by taking into account in paragraph 58 the context of terrorism in Northern Ireland.

[42] In their written submissions, Amnesty International maintained that strict scrutiny was required by the Court when examining derogation from fundamental procedural guarantees which were essential for the protection of detainees at all times, but particularly in times of emergency. Liberty, Interights and the Committee on the Administration of Justice ("Liberty and Others") submitted for their part that, if States are to be allowed a margin of appreciation at all, it should be narrower the more permanent the emergency becomes.

[43] The Court recalls that it falls to each Contracting State, with its responsibility for "the life of [its] nations," to determine whether that life is threatened by a "public emergency" and, if so, how far it is necessary to go in attempting to overcome the emergency. By reason of their direct and continuous contact with the pressing needs of the moment, the national authorities are in principle in a better position than the international judge to decide both on the presence of such an emergency and on the nature and scope of derogations necessary to avert it. Accordingly, in this matter a wide margin of appreciation should be left to the national authorities.[73]

Nevertheless, Contracting Parties do not enjoy an unlimited power of appreciation. It is for the Court to rule on whether inter alia the States have gone beyond the "extent strictly required by the exigencies" of the crisis. The domestic margin of appreciation is thus accompanied by a European supervision. At the same time, in exercising its supervision the Court must give appropriate weight to such relevant factors as the nature of the rights affected by the derogation, the circumstances leading to, and the duration of, the emergency situation.

2. *Existence of a Public Emergency Threatening the Life of the Nation*

[44] Although the applicants did not dispute that there existed a public emergency "threatening the life of the nation," they submitted that the burden rested on the Government to satisfy the Court that such an emergency really existed.

[45] It was, however, suggested by Liberty and Others in their written submissions that at the relevant time there was no longer any evidence of an exceptional situation of crisis. They maintained that reconsideration of the position could only properly have led to a further derogation if there was a demonstrable deterioration in the situation since August 1984 when the Government withdrew its previous derogation. For the Standing Advisory Commission on Human Rights, on the other hand, there was a public emergency in Northern Ireland at the relevant time of a sufficient magnitude to entitle the Government to derogate.

---

72   *Brogan and others v. United Kingdom* (1988), 145B Eur. Ct. H.R. (Ser. A.) 16, 11 Eur. Hum. Rts. Rep. 117.

73   *Ireland v. United Kingdom* (1978), 25 Eur. Ct. H. R. (Ser. A.) 4, 2 Eur. Hum. Rts. Rep. 25 at para. 207.

[46] Both the Government and the Commission, referring to the existence of public disturbance in Northern Ireland, maintained that there was such an emergency.

[47] Recalling its case law in *Lawless v. Ireland*[74] and *Ireland v United Kingdom* and making its own assessment, in the light of all the material before it as to the extent and impact of terrorist violence in Northern Ireland and elsewhere in the United Kingdom, the Court considers there can be no doubt that such a public emergency existed at the relevant time. ...

[The Court then went on to examine whether the measures were strictly required by the exigencies of the situation, asking in turn: was the derogation a genuine response to an emergency situation? Was the derogation premature? Was the absence of judicial control of extended detention justified? Are there sufficient safeguards against abuses? The Court found that the British Government was within its margin of appreciation with respect to each of these points.]

4. Other Obligations under International Law

[67] The Court recalls that under Article 15(1) measures taken by the State derogating from Convention obligations must not be "inconsistent with its other obligations under international law."

[68] In this respect, before the Court the applicants contended for the first time that it was an essential requirement for a valid derogation under Article 4 of the 1966 United Nations International Covenant on Civil and Political Rights ("the Covenant"), to which the United Kingdom is a Party, that a public emergency must have been "officially proclaimed." Since such proclamation had never taken place the derogation was inconsistent with the United Kingdom's other obligations under international law. In their view this requirement involved a formal proclamation and not a mere statement in Parliament.

[69] For the Government, it was open to question whether an official proclamation was necessary for purposes of Article 4 of the Covenant, since the emergency existed prior to the ratification of the Covenant by the United Kingdom and has continued to the present day. In any event, the existence of the emergency and the fact of derogation were publicly and formally announced by the Secretary of State for the Home Department to the House of Commons on 22 December 1988. Moreover, there had been no suggestion by the United Nations Human Rights Committee that the derogation did not satisfy the formal requirements of Article 4.

[70] The Delegate of the Commission considered the Government's argument to be tenable.

[71] The relevant part of Article 4 of the Covenant states: "In time of public emergency which threatens the life of the nation and the existence of which is officially proclaimed ..."

[72] The Court observes that it is not its role to seek to define authoritatively the meaning of the terms "officially proclaimed" in Article 4 of the Covenant.

---

74 *Lawless v. Ireland* (1961), 3 Eur. Ct. H.R. (Ser. A.) 4, 1 Eur. Hum. Rts. Rep. 15 at para. 28.

Nevertheless it must examine whether there is any plausible basis for the applicant's argument in this respect.

[73] In his statement of 22 December 1988 to the House of Commons the Secretary of State for the Home Department explained in detail the reasons underlying the Government's decision to derogate and announced that steps were being taken to give notice of derogation under both Article 15 of the European Convention and Article 4 of the Covenant. He added that there was "a public emergency within the meaning of these provisions in respect of terrorism connected with the affairs of Northern Ireland in the United Kingdom. ..."

In the Court's view, the above statement, which was formal in character and made public the Government's intentions as regards derogation, was well in keeping with the notion of an official proclamation. It therefore considers that there is no basis for the applicants' arguments in this regard.

5. Summary

[74] In the light of the above examination, the Court concludes that the derogation lodged by the United Kingdom satisfies the requirements of Article 15 and that therefore the applicants cannot validly complain of a violation of Article 5(3). It follows that there was no obligation under Article 5(5) to provide the applicants with an enforceable right to compensation.

NOTES

1) Some rights are shielded from the possibility of derogation in times of emergency and must be complied with at all times by the state. The lists of non-derogable rights vary significantly from one instrument to the next, with the shortest core of rights to be found in ICCPR article 4(1) and the longest in ACHR article 27(1). The *Brannigan & McBride* case highlights the link between these lists, as ECHR article 15 could not validate emergency measures inconsistent with "other obligations under international law," including other human rights treaties like the ICCPR. This means that states parties to several human rights instruments are bound to comply with the highest common denominator of non-derogable rights. The obligations under international law referred to in derogation provisions should also be understood to include, in particular, relevant international humanitarian law standards.[75]

2) As noted by the Court in *Brannigan & McBride*, states are given a margin of appreciation in the assessment of both the existence of an emergency and whether the measures are strictly required by the exigencies of the situation. Some challenge the

---

75   The first instance in which a human rights body directly applied humanitarian law is provided by decision of the Inter-American Commission on Human Rights in *Abella v. Argentina (La Tablada Case)* (1997), Inter-Am. Comm. H.R. Rep. No. 55/97, Case No. 11, 137, OEA/Ser.L/V/II.97, Doc. 38, a decision that must be read in the light of the position of the Inter-American Court of Human Rights in *Las Palmeras* (2000) (Judgment on Preliminary Objections) Inter-Am. Ct. H.R. (Ser. C) No. 67. Both are available online: <http://www.cidh.oas.org>.

soundness of this doctrine, which has yet to be explicitly adopted by the UNHRC or the Inter-American organs. Do you agree with the explanation given by the Court in paragraph 43? Is a margin of appreciation equally justified for assessing the existence of an emergency and for judging whether measures are strictly required?

3) Despite the margin of appreciation that States enjoy as to the qualification of emergency, international law poses conditions as to the nature and extent of the derogatory measures that can be adopted. In particular, and as recalled by the International Court of Justice in its advisory opinion concerning the *Legal Consequences of the Construction of a Wall in the Occupied Palestinian Territory*,[76] "it is not sufficient that such restrictions be directed to the ends authorized; they must also be necessary for the attainment of those ends. As the Human Rights Committee put it, they 'must conform to the principle of proportionality' and 'must be the least intrusive instrument amongst those which might achieve the desired result.'" In that case, the Court concluded that the information available did not support a finding that the measures adopted by Israel were strictly required by the exigencies of the situation.

4) The control of derogation by treaty bodies is variable. The Inter-American Commission on Human Rights indicates that derogation may be one of the factors triggering a country report, while the Human Rights Committee has adopted the practice of requesting supplementary periodic reports whenever states give notice of derogation. The ECHR, on the other hand, does not act independently and will review derogations only in the context of a case brought before it.

5) As an eminently indeterminate notion, the state of emergency lends itself easily to abuse by states anxious to provide a facade of legality to the perpetration of human rights abuses. Particularly in the Latin American context, it has served perhaps more as a tool to breach human rights than as an instrument to protect democracy and political stability. Do you agree that derogation clauses are a necessary and useful part of human rights treaties? In his dissent in *Brannigan & McBride*, Judge Makarczyk noted:

> A derogation made by any State affects not only the position of that State, but also the integrity of the Convention system of protection as a whole. It is relevant for other Member States—old and new—and even for States aspiring to become Parties which are in the process of adapting their legal systems to the standards of the Convention. For the new Contracting Parties, the fact of being admitted, often after long periods of preparation and negotiation, means not only the acceptance of Convention obligations, but also recognition by the community of European States of their equal standing as regards the democratic system and the rule of law. In other words, what is considered by the old democracies as a natural state of affairs, is seen as a privilege by the newcomers which is not to be disposed of lightly. A derogation made by a new Contracting Party from Eastern and Central Europe would call into question this new legitimacy and is, in my opinion, quite improbable. Any decision of the Court concerning Article 15 should encourage and confirm this philosophy. In any event it should not reinforce the views of those in the new Member States for whom European standards clash with interests which they have inherited from the past. I am not convinced that the reasoning adopted by the majority fulfils these requirements. This is

---

76   [2004] I.C.J. Rep. 136 at para. 136.

especially so as the derogation concerns a provision of the Convention which, for some, should not be the subject of any derogation at all.

6) Some human rights treaties do not include derogation provisions. The ILO has stated that despite the fact that treaties adopted under its aegis are silent in this respect, there is nevertheless an implied right to suspend some rights in times of emergency. The African Commission on Human and Peoples' Rights, on the contrary, refused an argument presented by Chad that there is an implied derogation clause in the ACHPR to conclude that no derogation was permissible under that treaty.[77] What is the significance of the silence of the ICESCR in this respect?

3. Customary Human Rights

Many states around the world, with governments of all political persuasion, are reluctant to ratify some or most human rights conventions for reasons ranging from ideological opposition to the content of a given treaty to concern over national sovereignty. For situations that relate to states not party to the relevant human rights treaty, the question of whether or not the international norms have acquired customary status is of critical importance.

Restatement of the Law (Third), Foreign Relations Law of the United States
American Law Institute (1987)

[The Restatement is an unofficial compendium of existing law prepared by academics in the United States. It is generally considered highly persuasive both within and outside the United States.]

§702   Customary International Law of Human Rights

A state violates international law if, as a matter of state policy, it practices, encourages, or condones

- (a) genocide,
- (b) slavery or slave trade,
- (c) the murder or causing the disappearance of individuals,
- (d) torture or other cruel, inhuman, or degrading treatment or punishment,
- (e) prolonged arbitrary detention,
- (f) systematic racial discrimination, or
- (g) a consistent pattern of gross violations of internationally recognized human rights.

Comment

a. *Scope of customary law of human rights.* This section includes as customary law only those human rights whose status as customary law is generally accepted (as of 1987) and whose scope and content are generally agreed. The list is not necessarily

---

77   See *Commission nationale des droits de l'homme et des libertés v. Chad, supra* note 16.

complete, and is not closed: human rights not listed in this section may have achieved the status of customary law, and some rights might achieve that status in the future. ...

Reporters Notes

1. *Customary law of human rights.* This section adopts the view that customary international law prohibits the particular human rights violations indicated, if the violations are state policy. This view is accepted by virtually all states; ... no state claims the right to commit the practices set forth in this section as state policy, and few, if any, would deny that they are violations of international law. Other rights may already have become customary law and international law may develop to include additional rights. It has been argued that customary international law is already more comprehensive than here indicated and forbids violation of any of the rights set forth in the Universal Declaration.

NOTES

1) The list of human rights given in the Restatement can be taken as a conservative minimum of rights accepted as customary law. The Restatement has been criticized as overly restrictive in refusing to acknowledge that other rights have already become customary—for example, the right to be free from discrimination on the basis of sex. As noted by some, the rights considered as customary by the Restatement are those, and only those, that are either entrenched in the U.S. Bill of Rights or accepted by the U.S. Government.[78] Compare the Restatement list to that given by the Human Rights Committee in its General Comment on Reservations:

[P]rovisions in the Covenant that represent customary international law (and a fortiori when they have the character of peremptory norms) may not be the subject of reservations. Accordingly, a State may not reserve the right to engage in slavery, to torture, to subject persons to cruel, inhuman or degrading treatment or punishment, to arbitrarily deprive persons of their lives, to arbitrarily arrest and detain persons, to deny freedom of thought, conscience and religion, to presume a person guilty unless he proves his innocence, to execute pregnant women or children, to permit the advocacy of national, racial or religious hatred, to deny to persons of marriageable age the right to marry, or to deny to minorities the right to enjoy their own culture, profess their own religion, or use their own language. And while reservations to particular clauses of Article 14 [of the ICCPR] may be acceptable, a general reservation to the right to a fair trial would not be.[79]

2) The customary status of the Universal Declaration of Human Rights has been much debated.[80] Initially adopted as a non-binding resolution of the U.N. General

---

78   See B. Simma & P. Alston, "The Sources of Human Rights Law: Custom, Jus Cogens, and General Principles: (1992) Austrl. Y.B. Int'l L. 82 at 95.

79   Human Rights Committee, *supra* note 65 at para. 8.

80   See H. Hannum, "The Status of the Universal Declaration of Human Rights in National and International Law" (1995-96) 25 Georgia J. Int'l & Comp. L. 287.

Assembly, some argue that the innumerable references to the Declaration in international instruments as well as statements by a great number of states to the effect that they adhere to its principles mean that the Declaration has now ripened into custom. Many of the rights found in the Universal Declaration are listed above as customary. Referring to the role of "soft law"[81] in the creation of international norms, review the provisions of the Declaration that do not appear in the list given by the Human Rights Committee, and see whether they can be considered to represent customary standards.

3) Apart from the fact that customary norms bind all states, what are the consequences of concluding that a human right has become part of custom? On reservations? On municipal law? On the interpretation of human rights treaties?

4. Universality of Human Rights and Cultural Diversity

Cultural relativism has come to replace arguments based on state sovereignty as the greatest challenge to human rights law. From the outset, the Preamble of the Universal Declaration of Human Rights grounded human rights in the "recognition of the inherent dignity and of the equal and inalienable rights of all members of the human family." The criticism by Western governments and NGOs of the human rights record of many non-Western governments vis-à-vis civil and political rights triggered challenges by these governments of the West's compliance with economic, social, and cultural rights, putting human rights issues squarely in the political field. Those who espouse cultural relativism posit that international human rights norms are a Western construct imposed on the rest of the world. Cultural relativism thus grew partly as a defence against what was perceived as a form of neo-colonialism. It is also fed by post-modern rejections of essentialism and claims to objective rationality and universality.

"Human Rights: A Precious Tree and the Soil To Grow It In"
Voice of Vietnam Radio (1995)[82]

The ways in which the human rights offensive of the Western countries has been intensified have caused many people to worry that this issue could be the greatest source of ideological and cultural conflict in decades to come. People have come to realize more and more clearly that human rights is not only a temporary goal but also a long-term national policy and that apart from being part of an overall strategy, human rights is by itself a strategy devised by individuals who assume the role of world leader. ...

Here, it is necessary to point out a regrettable mistake, or to be more precise, the authoritarian imposition of the Western countries. They consider the common Western cultural values as a whole; as soon as somebody does something that goes against their belief, they immediately bring in a judgmental verdict of human rights violations.

---

81   Discussed in Chapter 3, "Creation and Ascertainment of International Law," after the Notes in Section A on "Sources of Law."

82   Excerpts from an article in the army newspaper "Quan Doi Nhan Dan," broadcast on the Voice of Vietnam Radio, Hanoi, in Vietnamese 1430 gmt June 5, 1995 (c) BBC Monitoring Summary of World Broadcasts.

It seems that they either do not know or try to ignore the fact that human rights cannot be separated from historical, geographical and cultural conditions and the development level of different countries and peoples. A faithful follower of Jesus Christ cherishes different spiritual values from those of a disciple of Allah. A Somalian citizen living in his blistering desert would not be able to dream about the material conditions of an American. ...

We can affirm that the Western countries are trying to make human rights a new form of conflict in terms of culture and ideology. It is beginning to appear as a serious confrontation between the West and the East, bearing the typical characteristic of a new cold peace after the Cold War. We do not deny that Western cultures have many material and spiritual values that deserve respect. Some of these values have been inherited worldwide since they are accepted universal values. However, it is impossible to demand that all Western cultural values be imposed on the East or on the world in general. A plant, however precious it is, should be grown in suitable soil, otherwise the fruit it gives will be poisonous.

NOTES

1) Abdullah An-Na'im has suggested that one of the main factors leading to human rights violations was the lack of cultural legitimacy within a given community. If international human rights standards are perceived as alien or even contrary to religious or cultural tenets, there is very little incentive for self-compliance by the authorities. He suggests as a solution to this impasse that two simultaneous dialogues be encouraged: one between the various cultures, so that international human rights are not perceived to lead to the necessary imposition by one (Western) culture of its values on other cultures; the other, within each culture, between various groups in order to redefine some of its elements and hopefully adapt them to some international human rights standards.[83] Both dialogues present significant challenges: the first, because the Western side of this dialogue is perceived as being already embodied in international instruments like the Universal Declaration of Human Rights; the second, because some cultures do not accept the possibility of an internal challenge to accepted doctrine or fail to make room for all participants in an internal dialogue. The issue of female genital mutilation is one example of these challenges: it is attacked on the one hand as a violation of the right to bodily integrity of young girls, a breach of the right to health, and discrimination on the basis of sex; it is defended on the other as beyond debate because it is required by Shari'a or as necessary to fully bring young women within the fold of their community.[84]

2) Relativist arguments rarely challenge the very existence of human rights law. Even the commentary from the Voice of Vietnam Radio, quoted above, acknowledges that

---

83   See A. An-Na-im, "Human Rights in the Muslim World: Socio-Political Conditions and Scriptural Imperatives" (1990) 3 Harv. Hum. Rts. J. 13. See generally, A. An-Na'im, ed., *Human Rights in Cross-Cultural Perspectives; A Quest for Consensus* (1992); and W. Schmale, ed., *Human Rights and Cultural Diversity* (1993).

84   See for example, K. Savell, "Wrestling with Contradiction: Human Rights and Traditional Practices Affecting Women" (1996) 41 McGill L.J. 781.

human rights are a "precious tree." The debate usually centres on the specific meaning of a given right or its application to a particular situation. In *Toonen*, for example, the Human Rights Committee found that adult consensual sexual activity in private is covered by the concept of privacy entrenched in ICCPR article 17 and that the reference to "sex" as a prohibited ground of discrimination in ICCPR articles 2(1) and 26 is to be understood as including sexual orientation. The Committee followed an earlier decision of the ECHR in *Dudgeon v. United Kingdom*, which had also found that the criminalization of homosexual relations violated the right to privacy (ECHR article 8).[85] Does this mean that the criminalization of such relations in, for example, the Sudan necessarily violates international human rights law? What is the impact of the African Charter's omission of a right to privacy? The World Conference on Human Rights in 1993 adopted the Vienna Declaration and Programme of Action, which reads in part:

> 1. The World Conference on Human Rights reaffirms the solemn commitment of all States to fulfil their obligations to promote universal respect for, and observance and protection of, all human rights and fundamental freedoms for all in accordance with the Charter of the United Nations, other instruments relating to human rights, and international law. The universal nature of these rights and freedoms is beyond question. ...
>
> 5. All human rights are universal, indivisible and interdependent and interrelated. The international community must treat human rights globally in a fair and equal manner, on the same footing, and with the same emphasis. While the significance of national and regional particularities and various historical, cultural and religious backgrounds must be borne in mind, it is the duty of States, regardless of their political, economic and cultural systems, to promote and protect all human rights and fundamental freedoms.[86]

Do you believe that this statement, adopted by consensus with the participation of all states, provides an answer to the general question of cultural relativism? To the specific question of whether the Sudan's position violates international human rights law?

5. Collective Rights and Self-Determination

Collective rights raise additional problems, particularly from a First World perspective. Their potential to clash with individual rights—for example, affirmative action to protect one group may interfere with individual rights to equality—and the possibility of their expansion to include a myriad of issues—for example, the right to development; the rights of people to a clean environment—make them hard to define with any precision and difficult to reconcile with other rights. As a result, many states have been reluctant to accept the concept of collective rights in the same way they have accepted individual human rights. States that choose to adhere to collective rights face accusations of being biased in their selection and definition of whom and what they choose to protect. Similarly, the critics of collective rights preach against them because they fear that governments can

---

85   (1981), 4 Eur. Hum. Rts. Rep. 149.

86   *Vienna Declaration, supra* note 20. See also the reaffirmation of human rights and states' responsibilities to respect them made by the world leaders at the 2005 World Summit in 2005 *World Summit Outcome*, U.N. Doc. A/60/L.1 (2005) at paras. 121 & 122.

rely on them to deprive persons of their individual human rights. They also maintain that collective rights, while legitimate international legal and political issues, are not "human rights" concerns and that to treat them as such confuses the focus of the human rights movement and thereby threatens the support for it in international and domestic forums. On the other hand, the promotion of collective rights, or certain of them, are viewed as the most important goal by indigenous peoples, who often see themselves as colonized within a nation state, and by other groups who seek self-determination.

Mi'kmaq Case
U.N. HRC Communication No. 205/1986 (1990 and 1992)[87]

Decision on Admissibility

1. The authors of the communication (initial letter of 30 January 1986 and subsequent correspondence) are Grand Chief Donald Marshall, Grand Captain Alexander Denny and Adviser Simon Marshall, the officers of the Grand council of the Mi'kmaq tribal society in Canada. They allege violations by the Government of Canada of article 1 of the International Covenant on Civil and Political Rights. They submit the communication both as individually affected alleged victims and as trustees for the welfare and the rights of the Mi'kmaq people as a whole. They are represented by counsel.

2.1 It is stated that the Mi'kmaq are a people who have lived in their traditional territories in North America since time immemorial and that they, as a free and independent nation, concluded treaties with the France and British colonial authorities, which guaranteed their separate national identity and rights of hunting, fishing and trading throughout Nova Scotia. The authors give a historical survey of events affecting the sovereignty of the Mi'kmaq people over their traditional territories, Mikmakik.

2.2 They state that for more than 100 years, Mi'kmaq territories and political rights have been in dispute with the Government of Canada, which had claimed absolute sovereignty over Mikmakik by virtue of its independence, since 1867, from the United Kingdom. The authors further state that, although it was argued by the State party in its rule 91 submissions of 21 July 1981 and 10 June 1982 in the case of *A.D. v. Canada*, No. 478/1988, that the United Kingdom of Great Britain and Northern Ireland gave Canada plenary legislative authority over the case of "Indians" in North America, it is their view that Mikmakik was never part of Europe's American colonies, but enjoyed, by treaty, the status of a separate and distinct commonwealth under the British Crown and could not have lost its right of self-determination as a result of dealings between Canada and the Crown. They state that the Mi'kmaqs' right of self-determination has never been surrendered and that their land, Mikmakik, must be considered as a Non-Self-Governing Territory within the meaning of the Charter of the United Nations. In substantiation of the right of the Mi'kmaqs of self-determination, the authors argue that article 1, paragraph 2 of the Charter, article 1, paragraph 1 of the International

---

87   U.N. Doc. CCPR/C/34/D/205/1986, reproduced in *Selected Decisions of the Human Rights Committee under the Optional Protocol*, vol. 4 at 40 (U.N. Doc. CCPR/C/OP/4).

Covenant on Civil and Political Rights and (amongst others) General Assembly resolutions 1514 (XV) of 14 December 1960 and 2625 (XIV) of 24 October 1970, guarantee all peoples' right to self-determination, *i.e.*, their right to "freely determine their political status and freely pursue their economic, social and cultural development." As a minimum, the authors submit this includes the choice of independence, some degree of association or federation with an existing state or integration with an existing state, cf. General Assembly resolution 1514 (XV) of 14 December 1960.

2.3 Allegedly, in recognition of past injustices, by Constitution Act, 1982; Canada "recognized and affirmed" the "existing aboriginal and treaty rights of the aboriginal peoples of Canada" (art. 35). The authors submitted in accordance with article 37 of the *Constitution Act, 1982*, the specification of these "existing" rights must be negotiated with indigenous representatives "Invited" for this purpose by the Prime Minister of Canada. Such meetings, the authors state, were held in 1984, 1985 and 1987. Their request to participate was allegedly denied, "on the extraordinary ground that direct discussions with Mi'kmaqs are not 'practical' and other 'Indians' can negotiate our future political status for us." This allegedly racist position, viz, "that any members of the 'Indian' race can exercise Mi'kmaq peoples' rights to self-determination," is the basis of the communication. ...

4.1 In its submission dated 9 February 1987, the State party objects to the admissibility of the communication on the following grounds.

4.2 Firstly, with regard to the authors' claim that the Mi'kmaq tribal society has a right of self-determination, the State party contends that this right cannot be invoked in circumstances that would prejudice the national unity and territorial integrity of a sovereign State, such as Canada, and that the author's communication should therefore be declared inadmissible pursuant to article 3 of the Optional Protocol to the International Covenant on Civil and Political Rights, as incompatible *rationes materiae* with the provisions of the Covenant.

4.3 Secondly, the State party argues that the Mi'kmaq tribal society does not constitute a "people" within the meaning of article 1 of the Covenant. The term "people" cannot apply to a thinly scattered minority dispersed among the majority. Only 14,072 Mi'kmaqs are registered under the *Indian Act*, and they are scattered throughout the provinces of Nova Scotia, New Brunswick, Prince Edward Island and Quebec, an area where more than 2,000,000 Canadian residents intermingle with the Mi'kmaqs. The communication would therefore be declared inadmissible as incompatible *rationae personae* with article 1 of the Covenant.

4.4 Thirdly, the State party maintains that the right of self-determination is a collective right and cannot, therefore, be available in and of itself to providing the necessary contextual background for the exercise of individual human rights. This interpretation is said to be justified by the fact that the rights enshrined in article 1 are set apart from all the other rights in both the International Covenant on Civil and Political Rights and the International Covenant on Economic, Social and Cultural Rights; furthermore, the inclusion of the same rights at the beginning of the International Covenant on Economic, Social and Cultural Rights, which does not contain an individual complaint mechanism, can also support the claim that article 1 of each Covenant is exclusively structural in nature and not, by itself amenable to allegations of a breach by individuals. Since the Committee's jurisdiction, as defined by the Optional Protocol, cannot be invoked when the alleged violations concern a collective right, the State party submits that the communication of the Mi'kmaq tribal society should be dismissed.

4.5 Fourthly, the State party rejects the authors' assertion that a 1752 treaty entered into between British colonial authorities and the Mi'kmaqs (the "Halifax Treaty") confirms the existence of the latter as a separate national entity. It affirms that international law and Canadian domestic law do not recognize Indian treaties as international documents confirming the existence of tribal societies to independent and sovereign States.

4.6 With regard to the author's allegation that the denial of their right to participate in the so-called constitutional conference between the Government of Canada and selected indigenous organizations on the status of "aboriginal peoples" in Canada infringed their right of self-determination protected by article 1 of the Covenant, the State party observes, "The Government of Canada contends that, even if the authors could bring a communication on the basis of article 1, they have wrongly characterized the constitutional conferences as relating to the right of self-determination. Participation in such discussions has no direct connection with the right of self-determination which the Mi'kmaq tribal society seeks to enjoy. The communication is therefore incompatible *rationes materiae* with the provisions of the Covenant and should be declared inadmissible, pursuant to article 3 of the Optional Protocol." ...

5.1 Commenting on the State party's submission, the author's own submissions, dated 10 March 1987, contend that their allegations with respect to a violation of article 1 are well founded; they further ascertain that the State party has violated article 25 of the Covenant and request in their [petition] measures in accordance with Rule 86 of the Human Rights Committee's provisions rules of procedures.

5.2 In the context of an alleged violation of article 1 of the Covenant, the authors assert that the Mi'kmaq tribal society is merely proposing an alternative form of federalism and asserting its right of self-determination in a manner consistent with the national unity of Canada; to this extent, no conflict can be said to exist with the Covenant on Civil and Political Rights.

5.3 With regard to the State party's claim that the Mi'kmaq Tribal Society does not constitute a "people" within the meaning of article 1 of the Covenant on Civil and Political Rights, the authors assert that this response is in direct contradiction to the State party's own explicit statement, to the 1986 Sessional Working Group on Economic, Social and Cultural Rights of ECOSOC, that "native people were not considered as a cultural minority but as a distinct people with a unique role in Canada." They point out that the Government of Canada cannot refer to the Indian tribes as a "people" for the purposes of one International Covenant but not the other. The authors further contend that the Mi'kmaq do not live "thinly scattered" throughout the Canadian national population but in geographically-distinct communities, most of them designed by the Government of Canada itself as "Indian reserves," from which non-Mi'kmaq persons are explicitly excluded from residence by the *Indian Act*.

5.4 As regards the State party's objection to the standing of the authors before the Committee, the authors observe that if an earlier communication to the Committee concerning the rights of the Mi'kmaq (No. 78/1980, *A.D. v. Canada*) was held inadmissible on the grounds that the author had not proven his authority to represent the Grand Council or the Mi'kmaq community as a whole, this could only be construed as implying that the Committee considered it possible for individuals to invoke article 1—with the proviso that they could show they were themselves directly affected and genuinely representative of the others. The authors further reiterate their view that the right of self-determination has an individual dimension, that is an individual right *exercised through collective means.* In their view, the submission of 9 February 1987 by the Government of Canada misconstrues the Human Rights Committee's General Comment on article 1 (CCPR/C21Add.3) to the effect that self-determination is an "essential condition for the effective guarantee and observance of individual human rights": this ought to be interpreted in the sense that self-determination *is* a human right and does not provide a mere "contextual background" for the enjoyment of Human Rights.

5.5 With regard to the State party's claim that the "Halifax Treaty" of 1752 between British colonial authorities and the Mi'kmaqs does not confirm the existence of the latter as a separate national entity, the authors allege that this goes counter to international practice and that the reasons adduced by the Canadian Government in this respect, namely that the Mi'kmaqs are "Indians" and the Grand Council consists of "native chiefs," constitute a discrimination on the basis of race, colour and national origin, and as such are incompatible with article 2, paragraph 1 of the Covenant.

5.6 The authors also reject the Canadian Government's assertion that the constitutional conference and the proposed constitutional accord with Canada's "aboriginal peoples" do not affect the Mi'kmaq tribal society's rights under article 1 of the Covenant. They maintain that the right of self-determination *does* include a peoples' right to choose their political status and their own political institutions and that, if the proposed constitutional accord places limits on their right to govern themselves or to determine the nature of their relationship with the Covenant of Canada, this will necessarily involve self-determination within the meaning of article 1 of the Covenant. At this point in time, the authors expressed their view that, independent of a violation of article 1 of the Covenant, the Canadian constitutional accord process, as was constituted at the time in question, also violated article 25 of the Covenant, in so far as it was non-representative and deprived a particular racial, ethnic or national class of persons of the right to participate meaningfully in decisions directly affecting them. ...

14.1 Before considering any claims contained in a communication, the Human Rights Committee shall, in accordance with Rule 87 of its rules of procedure, decide whether or not it is admissible under the Optional Protocol to the Covenant.

14.2 With regard to the State party's contention that the authors' communication as pertaining to the right of self-determination should be declared inadmissible because "the Committee's jurisdiction, as defined by the Optional Protocol, cannot be invoked by an individual when the alleged violation concerns a collective right," the Committee observes as follows: While article 1 of the Covenant recognizes and protects in the most resolute terms a people's right of self-determination and its right to dispose of its natural resources, as an essential condition for the effective guarantee and observance of individual human rights and for the promotion and strengthening of those rights, this provision can neither be invoked by individuals, nor by peoples under the Optional Protocol. Firstly, as observed by the Committee in earlier cases ... individuals cannot claim under Optional Protocol to be victims of a violation of the right of self-determination, which is a right conferred upon peoples, as such. Finally, as the Committee has also observed in its views on communication No. 167/1984, the Optional Protocol does not constitute a machinery through which peoples can advance their rights. It provides a procedure under which individuals can claim that their individual rights, as set out in Part III of the Covenant (articles 6 to 27, inclusive) have been violated. The question whether the Mi'kmaq tribal society constitutes a "people," as asserted by the authors but contested by the State party, is not relevant in this respect. ...

14.4 Notwithstanding the observation in paragraph 14.2 above, the Optional Protocol does not preclude a group of individuals, who claim to be similarly affected, from together submitting a communication about alleged breaches of their rights as set out in Part III of the Covenant. Although initially drafted in terms of an alleged breach of the right of self-determination, the authors, subsequently, and after receiving the State party's objections to the admissibility of the communication as it then stood, asserted that the fact that the Mi'kmaqs were excluded from participating in the constitutional conferences also reveals a breach of article 25 of the Covenant. ...

14.6 The Committee believes that there are certain questions of law and facts relating to article 25(a) of the Covenant that can only be determined on the merits. The Committee will have to address the issue whether or not the constitutional conferences constituted a "conduct of public affairs" and whether the right under article 25(a) is available only to individual citizens, or to groups or representatives of groups also. In this context, the committee would wish to know, in particular, the precise legal nature and scope of competence given to the constitutional conferences, as well as the criteria for participation therein.

15. In the light of the above, the Human Rights Committee decides:

(a) That the communication is inadmissible in respect of article 1; ...

(c) That the communication is admissible in so far as it may raise issues under article 25(a) of the Covenant; ... .

Decision on the Merits

The Complaint

3.1 The authors sought, unsuccessfully, to be invited to attend the constitutional conferences as representatives of the Mi'kmaq people. The refusal of the State party to permit specific representation for the Mi'kmaqs at the constitutional conference is the basis of the complaint.

3.2 Initially, the authors claimed that the refusal to grant a seat at the constitutional conferences to representatives of the Mi'kmaq tribal society denied them the right of self-determination, in violation of article 1 of the International Covenant on Civil and Political Rights. They subsequently revised that claim and argued that the refusal also infringed their right to take part in the conduct of public affairs, in violation of article 25(a) of the Covenant.

The State Party's Observations and Authors' Comments

4.1 The State party argues that the restrictions on participation in the constitutional conferences were not unreasonable, and that the conferences were not conducted in a way that was contrary to the right to participate in "the conduct of public affairs." In particular, the State party argues that "the rights of citizens to participate in 'the conduct of public affairs' does not ... require direct input into the duties and responsibilities of a government properly elected. Rather, this right is fulfilled ... when 'freely chosen representatives' conduct and make decisions on the affairs with which they are entrusted by the constitution." The State party submits that the circumstances of the instant case "do not fall within the scope of activities which individuals are entitled to undertake by virtue of article 25 of the Covenant. This article could not possibly require that all citizens of a country be invited to a constitutional conference."

4.2 The authors contend, *inter alia*, that the restrictions were unreasonable and that their interests were not properly represented at the constitutional conferences. First, they stress that they could not choose which of the "national associations" would represent them, and, furthermore, that they did not confer on the Assembly of First Nations (AFN) any right to represent them. Secondly, when the Mi'kmaqs were not allowed direct representation, they attempted, without success, to influence the AFN. In particular, they refer to a 1987 hearing conducted jointly by the AFN and several Canadian Government departments, at which Mi'kmaq leaders submitted a package of constitutional proposals and protested "in the strongest terms any discussion of Mi'kmaq treaties at the constitutional conferences in the absence of direct Mi'kmaq representation." The AFN, however, did not submit any of the Mi'kmaq position papers to the constitutional conferences nor incorporated them in its own positions.

Issues and Proceedings before the Committee

5.1 The communication was declared admissible on 25 July 1990, in so far as it may raise issues under article 25(a) of the Covenant. ...

5.2 Article 25 of the Covenant stipulates that:

> every citizen shall have the right and the opportunity, without any of the distinctions mentioned in article 2 and without unreasonable restrictions:
>
>> (a) to take part in the conduct of public affairs, directly or through freely chosen representatives;
>>
>> (b) to vote and to be elected in genuine periodic elections ... ;
>>
>> (c) to have access, on general terms of equality, to public service. ...

At issue in the present case is whether the constitutional conferences constituted a "conduct of public affairs" and if so, whether the authors, or any other representatives chosen for that purpose by the Mi'kmaq tribal society, had the right, by virtue of article 25(a), to attend the conferences.

5.3 The State party has informed the Committee that, as a general rule, constitutional conferences in Canada are attended only by the elected leaders of the federal and 10 provincial governments. In the light of the composition, nature and scope of activities of constitutional conferences in Canada, as explained by the State party, the Committee cannot but conclude that they do indeed constitute a conduct of public affairs. The fact that an exception was made, by inviting representatives of aboriginal peoples in addition to elected representatives to take part in the deliberations of the constitutional conferences on aboriginal matters, cannot change this conclusion.

5.4 It remains to be determined what is the scope of the right of every citizen, without unreasonable restrictions, to take part in the conduct of public affairs, directly or through freely chosen representatives. Surely, it cannot be the meaning of article 25(a) of the Covenant that every citizen may determine either to take part directly in the conduct of public affairs or to leave it to freely chosen representatives. It is for the legal and constitutional system of the State party to provide for the modalities of such participation.

5.5 It must be beyond dispute that the conduct of public affairs in a democratic State is the task of representatives of the people, elected for that purpose, and public officials appointed in accordance with the law. Invariably, the conduct of public affairs affects the interest of large segments of the population or even the population as a whole, while in other instances it affects more directly the interest of more specific groups of society. Although prior consultations, such as public hearings or consultations with the most interested groups may often be envisaged by law or have evolved as public policy in the conduct of public affairs, article 25(a) of the Covenant cannot be understood as meaning that any directly affected group, large or small, has the unconditional right to choose the modalities of participation in the conduct of public affairs. That, in fact, would be an extrapolation of the right to direct participation by the citizens, far beyond the scope of article 25(a).

6. Notwithstanding the right of every citizen to take part in the conduct of public affairs without discrimination and without unreasonable restrictions, the Committee concludes that, in the specific circumstances of the present case, the failure of the State party to invite representatives of the Mi'kmaq tribal society to the constitutional conferences on aboriginal matters, which constituted conduct of public affairs, did not infringe that right of the authors or other members of the Mi'kmaq tribal society. Moreover, in the view of the Committee, the participation and representation at these conferences have not been subjected to unreasonable restrictions. Accordingly, the Committee is of the view that the communication does not disclose a violation of article 25 or any other provisions of the Covenant.

NOTES

1) The existence of a right to self-determination is now well established. It has been enshrined in a number of international treaties, including the U.N. Charter and the ICCPR and ICESCR (all reproduced in the Documentary Supplement), and proclaimed by a large number of resolutions, most significantly the 1960 Declaration on the Granting of Independence to Colonial Territories and Peoples[88] and the 1970 Declarations on Principles of International Law Concerning Friendly Relations and Co-operation Among

---

88   GA. Res. 1514(XV), UN GAOR, 15th Sess., Supp. No. 16 U.N. Doc. A/L.323/Add.1-6 (1960) 66.

States (reproduced in the Documentary Supplement). See the discussion of the right in Chapter 2, Section C.4(b) on "Peoples Seeking Self-Determination."

2) The ICJ recognized in the *East Timor Case* that the right to self-determination was "one of the essential principles of contemporary international law," generating obligations *erga omnes* for all states.[89] The reference to obligations *erga omnes* is significant, in that it would require all states to work toward the full realization of the right to self-determination not only of peoples under their control, but also under the control of other states. In the context of East Timor, this would have led to the conclusion that states like Australia should have refrained from giving effect to Indonesia's occupation of the island inasmuch as the East Timorese were prevented from freely determining their political status, an issue that the Court in that case could not address because of lack of jurisdiction.[90] In its advisory opinion on *Legal Consequences of the Construction of a Wall in the Occupied Palestinian Territory*,[91] the Court furthered that reasoning in finding that "the obligations violated by Israel include certain obligations *erga omnes*. [S]uch obligations are by their very nature 'the concern of all States' and, 'in view of the importance of the rights involved, all States can be held to have a legal interest in their protection.' ... The obligations *erga omnes* violated by Israel are the obligation to respect the right of the Palestinian people to self-determination, and certain of its obligations under international humanitarian law." The Court therefore concluded that "given the character and the importance of the rights and obligations involved, the Court is of the view that all States are under an obligation not to recognize the illegal situation resulting from the construction of the wall. ... They are also under an obligation not to render aid or assistance in maintaining the situation created by such construction. It is also for all States ... to see to it that any impediment, resulting from the construction of the wall, to the exercise by the Palestinian people of its right to self-determination is brought to an end." What do you think may constitute "assistance or aid in maintaining the situation"? May a state be held responsible for publicly defending the necessity of the wall on the basis of Israel's right to self-defence?

3) In the *Mi'kmaq* case, Canada denied that the Mi'kmaq were a people within the meaning of ICCPR article 1. Because it decided that the claim was inadmissible, the Human Rights Committee did not provide its views on the point. Likewise, in the *Reference re Secession of Québec*, the Supreme Court of Canada skirted the issue of whether there was a Québec people within the meaning of international law:

> International law grants the right to self-determination to "peoples." Accordingly, access to the right requires the threshold step of characterizing as a people the group seeking self-determination. However, as the right to self-determination has developed by virtue of a combination of international agreements and conventions, coupled with state practice, with little formal elaboration of the definition of "peoples," the result has been that the precise meaning of the term "people" remains somewhat uncertain.

---

89   [1995] I.C.J. Rep. 90 at para. 29.

90   See *Report of the Human Rights Committee*, UN GAOR, 39th Sess., Supp. No. 40, U.N. Doc. A/39/40 (1984) General Comment 12 at 142.

91   *Supra* note 76 at paras. 155 & 159.

It is clear that "a people" may include only a portion of the population of an existing state. The right to self-determination has developed largely as a human right, and is generally used in documents that simultaneously contain references to "nation" and "state." The juxtaposition of these terms is indicative that the reference to "people" does not necessarily mean the entirety of a state's population. To restrict the definition of the term to the population of existing states would render the granting of a right to self-determination largely duplicative, given the parallel emphasis within the majority of the source documents on the need to protect the territorial integrity of existing states, and would frustrate its remedial purpose.[92]

There is also no set definition of the concept of "people" in the draft Declaration on the Rights of Indigenous Peoples (see below) being studied at the United Nations.[93] A number of lists of defining traits have been proposed to define the concept of peoples. The suggested criteria include some or all of the following: a common historical tradition, racial or ethnic identity, cultural homogeneity, linguistic unity, religious or ideological affinity, territorial connection, common economic life, self-identification, etc.[94] Do you believe that such a definition leads to the conclusion that the Mi'kmaq are a "people"? That there is a Quebec "people"? Can peoples be overlapping, so that an individual could belong to several at the same time? In its *Opinion No. 2*, the Arbitration Committee of the International Conference on Yugoslavia (or "Badinter Committee," established by the European Union) found that "the principle of the right to self-determination serves to safeguard human rights. By virtue of that right every individual may choose to belong to whatever ethnic, religious or language community he or she wishes."[95] Does a full right of exit seem consistent with the concept of peoplehood?

4) Compare the definition of peoples to that of minorities, which have been defined as "a group of citizens of a state, constituting a numerical minority and in a non-dominant position in that state, endowed with ethnic, religious or linguistic characteristics which differ from those of the majority of the population, having a sense of solidarity with one another, motivated, if only implicitly, by a collective will to survive and whose aim is to achieve equality with the majority in fact and in law."[96] Article 27 of the ICCPR provides that "minorities shall not be denied the right, in community with the other members of their group, to enjoy their own culture, to profess and practise their own religion, or to use their own language." The Human Rights Committee noted that the right of minorities

---

92   *Reference Re Secession of Quebec*, [1998] 2 S.C.R. 217 at paras. 123-24, reproduced in Chapter 2, Section C.4.

93   Commission on Human Rights, Sub-Commission on Prevention of Discrimination and Protection of Minorities, *Technical Review of the United Nations Draft Declaration on the Rights of Indigenous Peoples*, UN ESCOR, 1994, U.N. Doc. E/CN.4/SUB.2/1994/2/Add.1 (1994). See Commission on Human Rights, *Report of the Working Group Established in Accordance with Commission on Human Rights Resolution 1995/32*, UN ESCOR U.N. Doc. E/CN.4/1998/106/CORR.1.

94   See UNESCO, *Final Report and Recommendations of an International Meeting of Experts on the Further Study of the Concept of the Rights of People*, SHS-89/CONF.602/7 (1990).

95   (1990) 3 Eur. J. Int'l L. 184.

96   J. Deschênes, *Proposal Concerning a Definition of the Term "Minority,"* U.N. Doc. E/CN.4/Sub.2/1985/31 at para. 181.

to enjoy their own culture is particularly broad and may consist of a way of life closely associated with a specific territory including traditional hunting and fishing activities.[97] How does the protection given to communities compare to the bundle of rights associated with the right of peoples to self-determination? How far can the protection of minorities go toward meeting the traditional demands of aboriginal peoples in Canada?

5) The Supreme Court of Canada was non-committal vis-à-vis a right to external self-determination in a context other than colonial or alien occupation. In view of the wording of the Declaration on Friendly Relations (reproduced in the Documentary Supplement) and the references to self-determination in the context of, for example, the former Yugoslavia, does this caution seem warranted? Consider the discussion in Chapter 2, Section C.4(b) on "Peoples Seeking Self-Determination."

6) In contrast to a set of result-oriented rules providing a solution to an abnormal situation, some have suggested that the principle of self-determination is more process-oriented:

Self-determination law, as applied during the inter-war era, allows a "softer" approach to international conflict. It allows procedural and material guidelines to be devised that seek to regulate conflict in a pragmatic, ad hoc fashion and look towards the re-creation of communal identities which once again can form the basis of a statal organisation. Thus it allows, for example, the balancing of individual rights and collective political goals; the use of recognition policies as a means to bring about attenuation or settlement; the creation of ad hoc procedures in order to determine the fate of particular communities living in disputed territories; collective diplomatic and at some point also military intervention to safeguard human rights and to enable the cessation of fighting, and so on.[98]

7) How does the situation of aboriginal peoples like the Mi'kmaq fit in the interpretation of the right to self-determination given in the *Quebec Secession Reference*?

U.N. Draft Declaration on the Rights of Indigenous Peoples[99]
U.N. Doc. E/CN.4/Sub.2/1994/2/Add.1 (1994)

[The United Nations has been working on the elaboration of a Declaration on the Rights of Indigenous Peoples since 1982, when a Working Group on Indigenous

---

97   Human Rights Committee, *Compilation of General Comments and General Recommendations Adopted by Human Rights Treaty Bodies*, UN ESCOR, 1994, U.N. Doc. HRI/GEN/1/Rev.1 (General Comment 23(50), The Rights of Minorities (article 27)) at 38. See *Bernard Ominayak, Chief of the Lubicon Lake Band v. Canada*, Comm. No. 167/1984 (1990) 11 Hum. Rts. L.J. 305.

98   M. Kosenniemi, "National Self-Determination Today: Problems of Legal Theory and Practice" (1994) 43 I.C.L.Q. 241 at 266. See also B. Kingsbury, " 'Indigenous Peoples' in International Law: A Construcctivist Approach to the Asian Controversy" (1998) 92 A.J.I.L. 414.

99   The Economic and Social Council in 2000 created the Permanent Forum on Indigenous Issues, a body of 16 independent experts meeting annually to study and report on issues affecting indigenous peoples <http://www.un.org/esa/socdev/unpfii/>. See J. Anaya, *Indigenous Peoples in International Law*, 2d ed. (2004); J. Anaya, ed., *International Law and Indigenous Peoples* (2003); P. Thornberry, *Indigenous Peoples and Human Rights* (2002); and M.C. Lam, *At the Edge of State: Indigenous Peoples and Self-Determination* (1998/2000).

Peoples of the Sub-Commission on the Prevention of Discrimination and Protection of Minorities was created. It took the independent experts of the Working Group more than a decade to agree on a text, with significant participation, in the later years, by aboriginal NGOs. The Draft Declaration was adopted in 1994 by the Sub-Commission and submitted to the UNCHR for consideration. The Commission reacted by referring the matter to an open-ended inter-sessional working group, entrusted with the task of drafting a declaration. The nature of the Commission (and its working group) as a political body made of state representatives has translated into great difficulties in obtaining consensus on the draft declaration. Some had hoped that the Declaration could be adopted to mark the end of the International Decade of the World's Indigenous People (1994–2004), but consideration of the draft by the working group was far from completed by that time.]

Article 1

Indigenous peoples have the right to the full and effective enjoyment of all human rights and fundamental freedoms recognized in the Charter of the United Nations, the Universal Declaration of Human Rights and international human rights law.

Article 2

Indigenous individuals and peoples are free and equal to all other individuals and peoples in dignity and rights, and have the right to be free from any kind of adverse discrimination, in particular that based on their indigenous origin or identity.

Article 3

Indigenous peoples have the right of self-determination. By virtue of that right they freely determine their political status and freely pursue their economic, social and cultural development.

Article 4

Indigenous peoples have the right to maintain and strengthen their distinct political, economic, social and cultural characteristics, as well as their legal systems, while retaining their rights to participate fully, if they so choose, in the political, economic, social and cultural life of the State.

Article 5

Every indigenous individual has the right to a nationality.

PART II

Article 6

Indigenous peoples have the collective right to live in freedom, peace and security as distinct peoples and to full guarantees against genocide or any other act of violence, including the removal of indigenous children from their families and communities under any pretext. In addition, they have the individual rights to life, physical and mental integrity, liberty and security of person.

Article 7

Indigenous peoples have the collective and individual right not to be subjected to ethnocide and cultural genocide, including prevention of and redress for:

(a) any action which has the aim or effect of depriving them of their integrity as distinct peoples, or of their cultural values or ethnic identities;

(b) any action which has the aim or effect of dispossessing them of their lands, territories or resources;

(c) any form of population transfer which has the aim or effect of violating or undermining any of their rights;

(d) any form of assimilation or integration by other cultures or ways of life imposed on them by legislative, administrative or other measures;

(e) any form of propaganda directed against them.

Article 8

Indigenous peoples have the collective and individual right to maintain and develop their distinct identities and characteristics, including the right to identify themselves as indigenous and to be recognized as such.

Article 9

Indigenous peoples and individuals have the right to belong to an indigenous community or nation, in accordance with the traditions and customs of the community or nation concerned. No disadvantage of any kind may arise from the exercise of such a right.

Article 10

Indigenous peoples shall not be forcibly removed from their lands or territories. No relocation shall take place without the free and informed consent of the indigenous peoples concerned and after agreement on just and fair compensation and, where possible, with the option of return.

Article 11

Indigenous peoples have the right to special protection and security in periods of armed conflict. States shall observe international standards, in particular the Fourth Geneva Convention of 1949, for the protection of civilian populations in circumstances of emergency and armed conflict, and shall not:

(a) recruit indigenous individuals against their will into the armed forces and, in particular, for use against other indigenous peoples;

(b) recruit indigenous children into the armed forces under any circumstances;

(c) force indigenous individuals to abandon their lands, territories or means of subsistence, or relocate them in special centres for military purposes;

(d) force indigenous individuals to work for military purposes under any discriminatory conditions.

PART III

Article 12

Indigenous peoples have the right to practice and revitalize their cultural traditions and customs. This includes the right to maintain, protect and develop the past, present and future manifestations of their cultures, such as archaeological and historical sites, artefacts, designs, ceremonies, technologies and visual and performing arts and literature, as well as the right to the restitution of cultural, intellectual, religious and spiritual property taken without their free and informed consent or in violation of their laws, traditions and customs. ...

PART V

Article 19

Indigenous peoples have the right to participate fully, if they so choose, at all levels of decision-making in matters which may affect their rights, lives and destinies through representatives chosen by themselves in accordance with their own procedures, as well as to maintain and develop their own indigenous decision-making institutions.

Article 20

Indigenous peoples have the right to participate fully, if they so choose, through procedures determined by them, in devising legislative or administrative measures that may affect them.

States shall obtain the free and informed consent of the peoples concerned before adopting and implementing such measures.

Article 21

Indigenous peoples have the right to maintain and develop their political, economic and social systems, to be secure in the enjoyment of their own means of subsistence and development, and to engage freely in all their traditional and other economic activities. Indigenous peoples who have been deprived of their means of subsistence and development are entitled to just and fair compensation. ...

PART VI

Article 25

Indigenous peoples have the right to maintain and strengthen their distinctive spiritual and material relationship with the lands, territories, waters and coastal seas and other resources which they have traditionally owned or otherwise occupied or used, and to uphold their responsibilities to future generations in this regard.

Article 26

Indigenous peoples have the right to own, develop, control and use the lands and territories, including the total environment of the lands, air, waters, coastal seas, sea-ice, flora and fauna and other resources which they have traditionally owned or otherwise occupied or used. This includes the right to the full recognition of their laws, traditions, and customs, land-tenure systems and institutions for the development and management of resources, and the right to effective measures by States to prevent any interference with, alienation of or encroachment upon these rights.

Article 27

Indigenous peoples have the right to the restitution of the lands, territories and resources which they have traditionally owned or otherwise occupied or used, and which have been confiscated, occupied, used or damaged without their free and informed consent. Where this is not possible, they have the right to just and fair compensation. Unless otherwise freely agreed upon by the peoples concerned, compensation shall take the form of lands, territories and resources equal in quality, size and legal status.

Article 28

Indigenous peoples have the right to the conservation, restoration, and protection of the total environment and the productive capacity of their lands, territories and resources, as well as to assistance for this purpose from States and through international cooperation. Military activities shall not take place in the lands and territories of indigenous peoples, unless otherwise freely agreed upon by the peoples concerned. States shall take effective measures to ensure that no storage or disposal of hazardous materials shall take place in the lands and territories of indigenous peoples. States shall also take effective measures to ensure, as needed, that programmes for monitoring, maintaining and restoring the health of indigenous peoples, as developed and implemented by the peoples affected by such materials, are duly implemented.

Article 29

Indigenous peoples are entitled to the recognition of the full ownership, control and protection of their cultural and intellectual property. They have the right to special measures to control, develop and protect their sciences, technologies and cultural manifestations, including human and other genetic resources, seeds, medicines, knowledge of the properties of fauna and flora, oral traditions, literatures, designs and visual and performing arts.

Article 30

Indigenous peoples have the right to determine and develop priorities and strategies for the development or use of their lands, territories and other resources, including the right to require that States obtain their free and informed consent prior to the approval of any project affecting their lands, territories and other resources, particularly in connection with the development, utilization or exploitation of mineral, water or other resources. Pursuant to agreement with the indigenous peoples concerned, just and fair compensation shall be provided for any such activities and measures taken to mitigate adverse environmental, economic, social, cultural or spiritual impact.

PART VII

Article 31

Indigenous peoples, as a specific form of exercising their right to self-determination, have the right to autonomy or self-government in matters relating to their internal and local affairs, including culture, religion, education, information, media, health, housing, employment, social welfare, economic activities, land and resources management, environment and entry by non-members, as well as ways and means for financing these autonomous functions.

Article 32

Indigenous peoples have the collective right to determine their own citizenship in accordance with their customs and traditions. Indigenous citizenship does not impair the right of indigenous individuals to obtain citizenship of the States in which they live. Indigenous peoples have the right to determine the structures and to select the membership of their institutions in accordance with their own procedures.

Article 33

Indigenous peoples have the right to promote, develop and maintain their institutional structures and their distinctive juridical customs, traditions, procedures and practices, in accordance with internationally recognized human rights standards.

Article 34

Indigenous peoples have the collective right to determine the responsibilities of individuals to their communities.

Article 35

Indigenous peoples, in particular those divided by international borders, have the right to maintain and develop contacts, relations and cooperation, including activities for spiritual, cultural, political, economic and social purposes, with other peoples across borders. States shall take effective measures to ensure the exercise and implementation of this right.

Article 36

Indigenous peoples have the right to the recognition, observance and enforcement of treaties, agreements and other constructive arrangements concluded with States or their successors, according to their original spirit and intent, and to have States honour and respect such treaties, agreements and other constructive arrangements. Conflicts and disputes which cannot otherwise be settled should be submitted to competent international bodies agreed to by all parties concerned.

NOTES

1) The Draft Declaration may be seen as an articulation of the right to internal self-determination, which may explain the significant opposition it has generated from many states. It can also be seen as an elaboration of the protection of the rights of minorities. Looking at the content of the proposed Draft Declaration, to which of these norms does the Draft seem to relate most closely?

2) Does the interpretation given by the Supreme Court of Canada in the *Quebec Secession Reference*, reproduced in Chapter 2, Section C.4(b) on "Peoples Seeking Self-Determination," imply that aboriginal peoples who cannot exercise their internal self-determination then have a right to external self-determination, including secession? Can that be supported by the Draft Declaration?

3) Imagine that the Declaration had been unanimously adopted by the U.N. General Assembly by the time the Human Rights Committee considered the merits of the *Mi'kmaq Case*. How would it have affected its outcome?

4) Notice that the Draft Declaration studiously avoids defining "Indigenous Peoples." The International Labour Organization has not shirked this politically laden task. It concluded Convention No. 169 on Indigenous and Tribal Peoples in Independent Countries 1989 to protect the social, cultural, religious, and spiritual values and practices of "tribal peoples in independent countries" and others who are "indigenous on account of their descent." Even so, the convention provides that the use of the term "peoples" "shall not be construed as having any implications as regards the rights which may attach to the term under international law."

5) The right of peoples to self-determination and the rights of minorities are two instances of collective rights that have gained a large measure of currency in the international community. A certain number of other collective rights have been suggested and even entrenched into binding and non-binding instruments, but have not attained a status comparable to the two others. The African Charter on Human and Peoples' Rights provides an interesting list of rights of peoples, including the rights of peoples to equality, to existence, to dispose of their wealth and resources, to development, to international peace and security, and to a satisfactory environment (articles 19-24 reproduced above in Section B.2(b) under "Regional Norms in Africa"). Do you think that it is legitimate and useful to use the discourse of human rights to frame these collective claims? In what ways are the dynamics of collective rights distinct from those of individual rights? Can a state argue that it is the legitimate representative of a people and claim the rights listed above?

C. COMPLIANCE AND ENFORCEMENT

International human rights sometimes have been criticized as utopian ideals that have little bearing on the way states actually behave. While an outright dismissal of human rights law as mere idealism seems unwarranted, they do acutely suffer from many of the same compliance problems affecting public international law as a whole. States have been reluctant to impose upon themselves binding human rights obligations, and even more so to agree to create institutions with power to oversee compliance with such obligations. The various international institutions that do exist to promote compliance with human rights form a shapeless quilt with little unifying theme. Some categories of rights are systematically underprotected around the world—for example, economic, social, and cultural rights—while other rights are protected in some countries by several competing international mechanisms—for example, civil and political rights in Europe. Even within the U.N. system, there was until recently little coordination between the various bodies entrusted with the task of ensuring compliance with human rights. The creation of the office of U.N. High Commissioner for Human Rights by the General Assembly in December 1993 sought to remedy this situation and provide some needed coherence.[100] The High Commissioner's responsibilities include the promotion and protection of all human rights in terms not limited to human rights entrenched in U.N.-sponsored treaties. As such, the High Commissioner may be seen, in some sense, as a universal human rights ombudsman overseeing compliance with all human rights around the world.

Human rights treaties usually provide for the creation of some type of compliance mechanism, opening more avenues unavailable to enforce compliance than are available for customary human rights. Treaty and non-treaty mechanisms are examined in turn.

1. Treaty Mechanisms

Four types of mechanisms have been created by human rights treaties to promote compliance: (1) petitions to a treaty body, (2) periodic reports, (3) enquiries, and (4) advisory opinions. Most treaties do not create all these mechanisms but only some of them, with significant variations from treaty to treaty.

Petitions[101]

A number of human rights treaties provide for the possibility of an individual, an organization, a state, or a combination thereof, presenting a communication alleging that a state

---

100 *High Commissioner for the Promotion and Protection of all Human Rights*, G A Res. 48/141, UN GAOR, 48th Sess., (1993). The first High Commissioner for Human Rights was Jose Ayala-Lasso of Ecuador from 1994 to 1997. The current High Commissioner is Louise Arbour of Canada.

101 For an extended overview of petition mechanisms and their treatment of cases involving Canada, see Schabas, *supra* note 1 at 133-99. See generally P. Alston & J. Crawford, eds., *The Future of UN Human Rights Treaty Monitoring* (2000); and D. McGoldrick, *The Human Rights Committee* (1994); Petitions and views of treaty bodies are frequently published in the *Human Rights Law Journal*, as well as being available online on the websites of the U.N. High Commissioner for Human Rights at <http://

party is failing to comply with treaty obligations. Treaties creating petition mechanisms include the ICCPR, ECHR, ACHR, ACHPR, the Convention Against Torture, and the Convention on the Elimination of Racial Discrimination. The jurisdiction of a treaty body to entertain such petitions is sometimes optional—that is, a state may ratify a treaty but refuse to accept the treaty body's competence to receive communications concerning its compliance with the human rights entrenched in the treaty. Such is the case of the ICCPR, where the Human Rights Committee's competence to receive petitions both from states and from individuals is purely optional for states parties. Other treaties, for instance, the ECHR and the ACHR, require that all parties submit to the competence of the treaty body.

Optional Protocol to the ICCPR
999 U.N.T.S. 302; Can. T.S. 1976 No. 47

Article 2

Subject to the provisions of article 1, individuals who claim that any of their rights enumerated in the Covenant have been violated and who have exhausted all available domestic remedies may submit a written communication to the Committee for consideration.

Article 3

The Committee shall consider inadmissible any communication under the present Protocol which is anonymous, or which it considers to be an abuse of the right of submission of such communications or to be incompatible with the provisions of the Covenant.

Article 4

1. Subject to the provisions of article 3, the Committee shall bring any communications submitted to it under the present Protocol to the attention of the State Party to the present Protocol alleged to be violating any provision of the covenant.

2. Within six months, the receiving State shall submit to the Committee written explanations or statements clarifying the matter and the remedy, if any, that may have been taken by that State.

Article 5

1. The Committee shall consider communications received under the present Protocol in the light of all written information made available to it by the individual and by the State Party concerned.

2. The Committee shall not consider any communication from an individual unless it has ascertained that:

---

www.unhchr.ch/>, the Council of Europe at <http://www.humanrights.coe.int/Intro/eng/General/ welc2dir.htm> and the Organization of American States at <http://www.oas.org>.

(a) The same matter is not being examined under another procedure of international investigation or settlement;

(b) The individual has exhausted all available domestic remedies. This shall not be the rule where the application of the remedies is unreasonably prolonged.

3. The Committee shall hold closed meetings when examining communications under the present Protocol.

4. The Committee shall forward its views to the State Party concerned and to the individual. ...

Article 7

Pending the achievement of the objectives of resolution 1514 (XV) adopted by the General Assembly of the United Nations on 14 December 1960 concerning the Declaration on the Granting of Independence to Colonial Countries and Peoples, the provisions of the present Protocol shall in no way limit the right of petition granted to these peoples by the Charter of the United Nations and other international conventions and instruments under the United Nations and its specialized agencies.

Article 8

1. The present Protocol is open for signature by any State which has signed the Covenant.

2. The present Protocol is subject to ratification by any State which has ratified or acceded to the Covenant. Instruments of ratification shall be deposited with the Secretary-General of the United Nations.

3. The present Protocol shall be open to accession by any State which has ratified or acceded to the Covenant.

4. Accession shall be effected by the deposit of an instrument of accession with the Secretary-General of the United Nations.

5. The Secretary-General of the United Nations shall inform all States which have signed the present Protocol or acceded to it of the deposit of each instrument of ratification or accession. ...

Article 10

The provisions of the present Protocol shall extend to all parts of federal States without any limitations or exceptions.

NOTES

1) As of 2005, 104 states had ratified the Optional Protocol, out of 152 parties to the ICCPR. Some states have not ratified the Protocol because they firmly believe that individuals should have no standing at international law or because they consider that such a competence is anathema to national sovereignty. On the other hand, a significant number of states have accepted the competence of several treaty bodies with overlapping jurisdiction. This explains the rule found in article 5(2)(a) of the Optional Protocol to the

ICCPR whereby the Human Rights Committee cannot consider a communication relating to a matter already under examination by another international body.

2) The position of the individual before a treaty body is highly variable, from simple information provider—for example, before the Human Rights Committee—to full party— for example, before the ECHR. It is a reflection of the nature of the bodies themselves, which should not necessarily be all assimilated to international tribunals:

> The [Human Rights] Committee is neither a court nor a body with a quasi-judicial mandate, like the organs created under another international human rights instrument, the European Convention on Human Rights. ... Still, the Committee applies the provisions of the Covenant and of the Optional Protocol in a judicial spirit and performs functions similar to those of the European Commission of Human Rights, in as much as the consideration of applications from individuals is concerned. Its decisions on the merits are, in principle, comparable to the reports of the European Commission, non-binding recommendations. The two systems differ, however, in that the Optional Protocol does not provide explicitly for friendly settlement between the parties and, more importantly, in that the Committee has no power to hand down binding decisions as does the European Court of Human Rights. States parties to the Optional Protocol endeavour to observe the Committee's views, but in case of non-compliance the Optional Protocol does not provide for an enforcement mechanism or for sanctions.[102]

As noted by the Committee, its "views" are not binding on states. The record of state compliance with decisions of the Human Rights Committee has been variable, with a small number of states systematically ignoring the conclusions of the Committee, and the majority making good-faith efforts to implement the Committee's conclusions. The eventual repeal by Tasmania of the *Criminal Code* provisions found to be inconsistent with the ICCPR in the *Toonen* case is but one example of the impact that non-binding views may have. By contrast, decisions of the ECHR and Inter-American Court of Human Rights are binding on states.

3) The petition systems instituted by the various human rights treaties are used more and more frequently. The workload of the various bodies varies widely, from 3 cases per year for the Committee against Torture to 170 cases per year for the Human Rights Committee. The Human Rights Committee now issues approximately 120 views on individual cases every year.[103]

4) Despite their high ideals, the work performed by human rights bodies in the context of petitions has not always been beyond reproach. The Committee on International Human Rights of the Association of the Bar of the City of New York thus criticized the Inter-American Commission on Human Rights in the following terms:

> The problems that confront the Inter-American Commission in cases of individual complaints alleging human rights violations, moreover, are especially difficult. Just investigating such a case can be daunting, according to accounts from Commission staff and

---

102 Human Rights Committee, *Selected Decisions of the Human Rights Committee Under the Optional Protocol: Seventeenth to Thirty-Second Sessions* (1990) at 1-2.

103 *Effective Functioning of Human Rights Mechanisms Treaty Bodies*, UN ESCOR, 2004, U.N. Doc. E/CN.4/2004/98.

consultants, because of threats to the lives of witnesses, as well as the difficulties of travel and communication over large distances. Further, the Commission's power under the American Convention, much less its residual jurisdiction under the OAS Charter, do not give it enough authority to obtain redress from a recalcitrant government without strong support from the OAS itself. ...

Nor is the difficulty of the cases or the obstruction of governments alone sufficient to explain why the Commission's decisions are often not persuasive or well-reasoned, nor why they are so long delayed. According to the Commission, it "opened" 181 individual cases in 1991, reporting to the OAS in 19, leaving a backlog of 978 cases pending. The Commission does not report how many complaints it receives each year, nor the current status of them. ...

Critics described the problems with the Commission's treatment of individual petitions in several ways. It was said that the Commission does not follow its own regulations, that it is confused about its functions, and, most bluntly, that its decisions are politicized. The [New York Bar Association] Committee has concluded that all of these are aspects of one problem: the Commission does not function well as a neutral, quasi-judicial adjudicative body for individual cases. ...

The budgetary situation of the Inter-American Commission on Human Rights is, in a word, a scandal. The budget is much too small, viewed either as a percentage of the OAS budget, or from the point of view of the work to be done by the Commission. In addition, the Commission has too little control over the allocation and expenditure of its budget. Although human rights have been designated a priority for the OAS, the funds for the Commission are an extremely small percentage of the OAS budget ... . All sources agreed that while the members of the OAS give lip-service to human rights, many of them who are in fact offended by the attentions of the Commission, work to keep it starved for funds so that it will not be able to function as effectively as it could.[104]

While such sweeping criticism should not be extended to all human rights bodies, or even to all the work of the Inter-American Commission on Human Rights, it does highlight some reasons why states may be reluctant to agree to accept the competence of such bodies. In particular, increases in the volume of cases have not always translated into increased resources, so that some bodies like the Human Rights Committee now have a large backlog of cases and unanswered correspondence. This is a serious situation since many of the cases dealt with by the Human Rights Committee or the Inter-American Commission on Human Rights require urgent action in order to be meaningful. The lengthy delays before the Inter-American Commission, in some cases extending to many years between the issuance of provisional measures and a decision on the merits, have been cited as one reason explaining Canada's reluctance to ratify the ACHR.

Periodic Reporting

A significant number of human rights treaties require that all states parties submit periodic reports relating their progress in implementing the rights entrenched in the

---

104 Committee on International Human Rights of the Association of the Bar of the City of New York, "The Inter-American Commission: A Promise Unfulfilled" (1993) 48 The Record 589.

treaty. Treaty-reporting obligations are required, *inter alia*, by the ICCPR, ICESCR, CEDAW, ACHPR, the Convention on the Rights of the Child, and the Convention Against Torture (but not the ECHR or the ACHR). The presentation of these reports to supervisory bodies such as the Human Rights Committee provides an opportunity for a dialogue on human rights issues between the independent experts and senior state representatives.[105]

Treaty bodies have set up guidelines for the reports that demand sufficient particulars about a state's legal and governmental systems to permit detailed examinations and discussion of its actions in carrying out treaty obligations. For example, reports under the ICCPR are required to be in two parts. The first is a description of the general legal framework within which civil and political rights are protected in the reporting state. This part should contain a statement about what rights are protected, when derogations can occur, how the provisions of the ICCPR can be invoked before, and directly enforced by, domestic tribunals, what authorities have jurisdiction respecting human rights, what remedies individuals might have, and what measures have been taken to ensure the domestic implementation of the provisions of the ICCPR. The second part is more detailed and requires that states outline, in relation to the provisions of each substantive article in the ICCPR, all legislative and other measures in force in regard to each right, any restrictions or limitations of a *de jure*, *de facto*, or temporary nature affecting the enjoyment of such rights, and any other factors or difficulties affecting the enjoyment of them.[106]

The reporting standards established by the Committee have made that mechanism a useful tool for the implementation of rights since they generate a large body of information and opinion that appears to be helpful in the interpretation of the substantive provisions of the Covenant in a way that should make them both universal and functional. However, the submitted reports reflect a great divergency of both ideology and competence, and even willing participation, that divide states on human rights issues. Additionally, their variety underlines the difficulty that the Committee members face in understanding and coping with the vast array of legal and political systems represented by the states parties to the Covenant.[107]

The preparation of periodic reports that conform to the treaty body guidelines is a lengthy and expensive process. In Canada, it requires the preparation of preliminary reports by provincial and federal governments before a national report can be compiled. Efforts to involve civil society in the process are a laudable but further time-consuming practice for Canada. If developed countries are at times reluctant to expand the necessary resources to meet their reporting obligations, developing nations often find themselves completely devoid of the resources necessary to prepare such reports. The problem is compounded by the accumulation of reporting obligations under up to half-a-dozen treaties. In addition, some states neglect to prepare and file periodic reports for political

105 See Alston & Crawford, *supra* note 101. For a survey of reports by Canada before the various treaty bodies, see Schabas, *supra* note 1 at 219-47.

106 United Nations, *Manual on Human Rights Reporting Under Six Major International Human Rights Instruments* (1997).

107 The reports under the various U.N. treaties as well as the Concluding Observations of the treaty bodies are available online: <http://www.unhchr.ch>.

reasons, thus avoiding a potentially damaging public assessment of their human rights record. There is no sanction for states failing to live up to their reporting obligations, save the limited opprobrium of being named in the treaty body's annual report as a delinquent state. Some states have accumulated a great number of overdue reports—for example, Guyana as of 2005 owed 22 reports to various U.N. treaty bodies, including the initial report under the Convention for the Elimination of Racial Discrimination due in 1978.[108] In reaction to this problem, a partial amalgamation of reports has occurred, in the form of a core state report to which a treaty-specific portion is added for each submission. In addition, nearly all treaty bodies have started examining the situation of human rights in countries where reports are long overdue, even when no report has been submitted, although the basis of such a power has been questioned by some.[109]

The Human Rights Committee and other treaty bodies have adopted the practice of issuing written comments in response to each state's report. Such comments, after identifying positive aspects and factors and difficulties affecting the implementation of treaty human rights, then go on to survey "subjects of concern" and make recommendations. For example, the review by the Committee on Economic, Social and Cultural Rights of the last report from Canada under the ICESCR included the following concerns:

15. The Committee is deeply concerned at the information that provincial courts in Canada have routinely opted for an interpretation of the Charter which excludes protection of the right to an adequate standard of living and other Covenant rights. The Committee notes with concern that the courts have taken this position despite the fact that the Supreme Court of Canada has stated, as has the Government of Canada before this Committee, that the Charter can be interpreted so as to protect these rights.

16. The Committee is also concerned about the inadequate legal protection in Canada of women's rights which are guaranteed under the Covenant, such as the absence of laws requiring employers to pay equal remuneration for work of equal value in some provinces and territories, restricted access to civil legal aid, inadequate protection from gender discrimination afforded by human rights laws and the inadequate enforcement of those laws.

17. The Committee is greatly concerned at the gross disparity between Aboriginal people and the majority of Canadians with respect to the enjoyment of Covenant rights. There has been little or no progress in the alleviation of social and economic deprivation among Aboriginal people. In particular, the Committee is deeply concerned at the shortage of adequate housing, the endemic mass unemployment and the high rate of suicide, especially among youth, in the Aboriginal communities. Another concern is the failure to provide safe and adequate drinking water to Aboriginal communities on reserves. The delegation of the State Party conceded that almost a quarter of Aboriginal household dwellings required major repairs and lacked basic amenities ... .

---

108 As of 2004, there were a total of 845 reports overdue under the various U.N. human rights treaties imposing reporting duties: *Effective Functioning, supra* note 103.

109 *Effective Implementation of International Instruments on Human Rights Including Reporting Obligations Under International Instruments on Human Rights*, UN GAOR, 53d Sess., Annex, Agenda Item 113(a) of the Preliminary List, U.N. Doc. A/53/125 (1998) paras. 25-28.

20. The Committee is concerned that newly-introduced successive restrictions on unemployment insurance benefits have resulted in a dramatic drop in the proportion of unemployed workers receiving benefits to approximately half of previous coverage, in the lowering of benefit rates, in reductions in the length of time for which benefits are paid and in increasingly restricted access to benefits for part-time workers. While the new programme is said to provide better benefits for low-income families with children, the fact is that fewer low-income families are eligible to receive any benefits at all. Part-time, young, marginal, temporary and seasonal workers face more restrictions and are frequently denied benefits, although they contribute significantly to the fund ... .

24. The Committee is gravely concerned that such a wealthy country as Canada has allowed the problem of homelessness and inadequate housing to grow to such proportions that the mayors of Canada's 10 largest cities have now declared homelessness a national disaster ... .

28. The Committee is concerned that the significant reductions in provincial social assistance programmes, the unavailability of affordable and appropriate housing and widespread discrimination with respect to housing create obstacles to women escaping domestic violence. Many women are forced, as a result of those obstacles, to choose between returning to or staying in a violent situation, on the one hand, or homelessness and inadequate food and clothing for themselves and their children, on the other ... .

31. The Committee notes that Bill 22, entitled "An act to prevent unionization," was adopted by the Ontario Legislative Assembly on 24 November 1998. The Act denies to workfare participants the rights to join a trade union, to bargain collectively and to strike. In response to a request from the Committee, the Government provided no information in relation to the compatibility of the Act with the Covenant. The Committee considers the Act to be a clear violation of article 8 of the Covenant and calls upon the State Party to take measures to repeal the offending provisions ... .

39. The Committee is concerned that loan programmes for post-secondary education are available only to Canadian citizens and permanent residents and that recognized refugees who do not have permanent residence status, as well as asylum seekers, are ineligible for these loan programmes. The Committee views also with concern the fact that tuition fees for university education in Canada have dramatically increased in the past few years, making it very difficult for those in need to attend university in the absence of a loan or grant. A further subject of concern is the significant increase in the average student debt on graduation.[110]

Often, the treaty body will have obtained information regarding these areas of concerns not from the state's own report but rather from parallel reports prepared by local and international NGOs and communicated informally to the independent experts. This was the case in the discussion of Canada's report, for which numerous Canadian NGOs were

---

110 *Consideration of Reports Submitted by States Parties Under Articles 16 and 17 of the Covenant: Concluding Observations of the Committee on Economic, Social and Cultural Rights: Canada*, UN ESCOR, 1998, U.N. Doc. E/C.12/1/Add. 31. Many of the same issues were noted by the Human Rights Committee in its review of Canada's report under the ICCPR, *Consideration of Reports Submitted by States Parties Under Article 40 of the Covenant: International Covenant on Civil and Political Rights: Concluding Observations of the Human Rights Committee: Canada*, UN ESCOR, 1999, U.N. Doc. CCPR/C/79/Add.105. Canada's periodic reports are available online: <www.pch.gc.ca/ddp-hrd>.

in Geneva.[111] Conversely, the comments issued by the treaty bodies on concluding their review are often seized upon by local NGOs and the press to legitimate their critique of the government's human rights record. Thus, in the aftermath of Canada's review in Geneva, the Grand Council of the Crees used the report to criticize the Federal Government's funding of aboriginal peoples.[112]

Enquiries

The possibility of a treaty body initiating, of its own authority, an enquiry into the situation of human rights in a given country represents a potentially powerful tool for ensuring compliance with fundamental rights. The Inter-American Commission on Human Rights is unique in being given sweeping powers to prepare in-depth reports on any OAS member state it selects. Such powers derive both from the Commission's status under the OAS Charter as well as under the ACHR. Since 1961, the Commission has made 87 visits to 23 different countries, issuing a total of 56 country reports, some of them several hundred pages. Recent country reports include Haiti, El Salvador, Colombia, and Guatemala. The Commission also includes in its annual report briefer assessments of the human rights situations of countries that had been the focus of the Commission's work in the past. It identified the following criteria to determine which countries ought to be the object of special attention:

> First: States ruled by governments that did not reach power by means of popular elections using secret, honest, regular and free vote, in accordance with internationally accepted rules of law; second: States where the free exercise of the rights embodied in the American Convention or in the American Declaration have been suspended in full or in part, by means of imposition of exceptional measures such as state of emergency, state of siege or other; third: States against which there is proof that they have committed widespread and grave violations of rights secured in the American Convention, in the American Declaration, or in other applicable instruments, that have suspended rights whose effect may not be interrupted, and have committed summary executions, tortures and forced disappearances of persons; and fourth: States that are in a process of transition with respect to any of the three aforementioned situations.[113]

Country reports allow the Inter-American Commission on Human Rights to investigate and comment on respect for human rights in countries where the government is non-cooperative or even hostile to international supervision. It further allows the Commission

---

111 These included the Charter Committee on Poverty Issues, Low Income Families Together, and the National Anti-Poverty Organization: see. P. Foster, "No Apologies on Human Rights," *National Post* (December 2, 1998) C7.

112 See, "Crees Condemns Federal Government's Reaction to Human Rights Criticism by U.N. Committee on Economic, Social and Cultural Rights," *Canada Newswire* (December 7, 1998).

113 *Annual Report of the Inter-American Commission on Human Rights: 1997*, OEA/Ser.L/V/II.98 doc.6. In the *Annual Report of the Inter-American Commission on Human Rights: 2000*, OEA/Ser./L/V/II.111 doc. 20, the Commission added a fifth criterion touching on temporary or structural situations that seriously affect the enjoyment of rights guaranteed by the ACHR.

to cast its net very broadly to assess the general state of human rights in a given country, or to focus on particular issues—for example, the treatment of Miskito Indians in Nicaragua, the situation of asylum seekers in Canada, or the impact on human rights of efforts to combat terrorism.[114] A somewhat similar right to perform in-country visits to investigate allegations of torture is given to the Committee Against Torture under the 2002 Protocol to the Convention Against Torture.

Advisory Opinions

The ACHR and the ECHR both endow the courts that they create with power to issue advisory opinions. Likewise, the African Court on Human and Peoples' Rights is given an advisory jurisdiction by the Protocol to the ACHPR (article 4). On the other hand, no similar power is given to the Inter-American commission, or to any U.N. treaty bodies. The power to request an advisory opinion is granted more or less liberally depending on the instrument. The ECHR is very restrictive, giving that right only to the Committee of Ministers (article 44). The ACHR, on the other hand, allows any member state of the OAS, even if not a party to the ACHR, to request an opinion from the Court (article 64). The Inter-American Commission and other OAS organs may also present such requests.[115] The advisory jurisdiction of the Inter-American Court is extremely broad, extending not only to the interpretation of the ACHR but also to "other treaties concerning the protection of human rights in the American states" (article 64), terms that the Court has construed very liberally. The ECHR, for its part, prohibits advisory opinions relating to the content or scope of any of the fundamental rights entrenched in the treaty. As a result of these variations, the Inter-American Court has developed a rich body of jurisprudence under its advisory powers, initially much more significant than under its contentious powers. The 18 advisory opinions issued so far by the Inter-American Court of Human Rights have covered derogations in times of emergency, the death penalty, rights of journalists, citizenship and discrimination, sexual equality, and the interpretation of human rights instruments.[116] The European Court, for its part, declined to answer what would have been its first advisory opinion in June 2004. Such opinions, as their name implies, are merely advisory and create no obligation for states, although they generally carry significant persuasive power.

---

114   Inter-American Commission on Human Rights, *Report on the Situation of Human Rights of a Segment of the Nicaraguan Population of Misquito Origin: 1983*, OEA/Ser.L/V/II.62, Doc. 10, Rev. 3; Inter-American Commission on Human Rights, *Report on the Situation of Human Rights of Asylum Seekers Within the Canadian Refugee Determination System: 2000*, OEA/Ser.L/V/II.106, Doc. 40, Rev.; Inter-American Commission on Human Rights, *Report on Terrorism and Human Rights: 2002*, OEA/Ser.L/V/II.116, Doc. 5, Rev. 1.

115   The ACHPR Protocol is even broader in this respect, giving any African organization recognized by the AU power to request an advisory opinion from the African Court on Human and Peoples' Rights (article 4).

116   The opinions are available online: <www1.umn.edu/humanrts/iachr/seriesa.html>.

2. Non-Treaty Mechanisms[117]

A number of mechanisms exist outside the structures created by human rights treaties to stimulate compliance with customary human rights. Such non-treaty mechanisms include the structures established by international organs like the U.N., as well as actions undertaken by other actors such as states and NGOs. The significant advantage they possess over their treaty counterparts is that they are not subject to optional acceptance by states. On the other hand, they tend to be more diffuse and, generally, more politicized than treaty mechanisms.

The most structured and influential non-treaty mechanisms are the various institutions created by the U.N. Commission on Human Rights.[118] The Commission (distinct from the Human Rights Committee, discussed previously) is a subsidiary body of the Economic and Social Council, formed of 53 state representatives. It has a Sub-Commission on the Promotion and Protection of Human Rights composed of 26 experts of varying degrees of independence from their governments. After 20 years of total inaction regarding compliance with human rights, a new political balance within the Economic and Social Council permitted in 1967 the adoption of resolution 1235, allowing the Commission and Sub-Commission to examine information relevant to gross violations of human rights and to "make a thorough study of situations which reveal a consistent pattern of violations of human rights" by appointing a Special Rapporteur. This public procedure was complemented in 1971 by ECOSOC resolution 1503, creating a confidential alternative to study consistent patterns of gross violations of human rights.

The multi-stage and rather complex "1503 Procedure" considers individual communications to see whether they reveal evidence of massive and systematic abuses. As such, it does not offer individual relief to the author of the communication, but rather uses the communication as a source of information. If indeed there emerges such pattern of violations, the Commission may decide to appoint a Special Rapporteur or *ad hoc* committee to investigate further and report back to the Commission. The effectiveness of these procedures is significantly hampered by the fact that the Commission and Sub-Commission are not insulated from political influence. As such certain states—for example, Uganda and Uruguay during the 1970s or China in the 1990s—were able to manipulate these bodies and avoid scrutiny at times when there were certainly ample grounds to justify a thorough study. Worse still, the fact that the 1503 Procedure is confidential has been used by some governments to argue against consideration in other forums of situations already the object of a 1503 Procedure.

The Commission has considered hundreds of thousands of communications since 1972 and has examined the situations of more than three dozen different states.[119]

The Commission on Human Rights' machinery was substantially improved in the 1980s with the creation of thematic rapporteurs appointed to research a specific problem

---

117 See N. Rodley, "United Nations Non-treaty Procedures for Dealing with Human Rights Violations," in Hannum, *supra* note 1 at 60.

118 See H. Tolley, *The U.N. Commission on Human Rights* (1987).

119 See P. Alston, "The Commission on Human Rights," in Alston, *supra* note 1 at 126.

without geographic restrictions. Thematic rapporteurs, usually highly reputable independent experts, have been named by the Commission to study, for instance, the effects of illicit movement of toxic waste on the enjoyment of human rights, religious intolerance, and violence against women.[120]

Other non-treaty mechanisms working toward greater compliance with human rights standards include the various reports written by international and local NGOs like Amnesty International, Human Rights Watch, and the Lawyers Committee for Human Rights. NGOs play an essential role in collecting and disseminating information on violations of human rights and generating public pressure on governments and international organizations to react to such situations. Without their work toward the "marshalling of shame" over the last 50 years, it is clear that the human rights system would not be what it is today. At the same time NGOs are answerable to no one, and a blanket designation of a myriad of organizations as NGOs hides great disparities in the quality of their contribution to the advancement of human rights. In some contexts, NGOs may also act as *de facto* filters for access to treaty mechanisms by granting or denying legal assistance to potential petitioners. Hard questions must be asked about the independence and impartiality of any given NGO.[121]

States themselves may rely on general institutions of international law such as counter-measures to unilaterally adopt sanctions against other states disregarding fundamental rights, although they rarely do so. For example, in December 1983, the Netherlands suspended a development cooperation agreement in reaction to massive violations of human rights associated with a coup in Surinam. Some states like the United States have legislation that links aid and human rights, warranting that aid should not be extended to governments that engage in systematic violations of human rights.[122] States are generally quite reluctant to identify human rights as a centrepiece of their foreign policy in a manner that will prevent giving priority to other concerns should political expediency demand it. Canada, for example, like many other states, has no equivalent to the U.S. statute mentioned earlier, despite the fact that human rights have become more and more important in all aspects of its foreign policy, including the granting of development assistance.[123]

---

120 The reports are available online: <http://www.unhchr.ch>.

121 See M. Posner & C. Whittome, "The Status of Human Rights NGOs" (1994) 25 Colum. Hum. Rts. L. Rev. 269; and N. Rodley, "The work of Non-Governmental Organizations in the World-Wide Promotion and Protection of Human Rights" (1991) 90/1 U.N. Bulletin of Human Rights 84.

122 *Alien Tort Statute*, 28 U.S.C. § 1350 (1948); s. 502B, *Foreign Assistance Act of 1961*, as amended 22 U.S.C. §2304 (1961).

123 See "Notes for an Address by the Honourable Lloyd Axworthy, Minister of Foreign Affairs, at the Faculty of Law of McGill University, 1Human Rights and Canadian Foreign Policy: Principled Pragmatism'" Montreal, October 16, 1997, online: <http://webapps.dfait-maeci.gc.ca/minpub/Publication.asp?publication_id=376362>.

Civil Suits in National Courts

Filartiga v. Peña-Irala
630 F.2d 876 (2d Cir. 1980); (1980) 19 I.L.M. 966

[Filartiga was a Paraguayan national whose 17-year-old son had been kidnapped and tortured by Peña-Irala, who was Inspector General of Police in Asuncion, Paraguay, under the dictatorship of President Stroessner. Both Filartiga and Peña-Irala eventually became residents of the United States, where Filartiga filed a lawsuit claiming US$10 million in compensatory and punitive damages for his son's death.]

KAUFMAN CIR. J.: ... Appellants rest their principal argument in support of federal jurisdiction upon the Alien Tort Statute which provides: "The district courts shall have original jurisdiction of any civil action by an alien for a tort only, committed in violation of the law of nations or a treaty of the United States." Since appellants do not contend that their action arises directly under a treaty of the United States, a threshold question on the jurisdictional issue is whether the conduct alleged violates the law of nations. In light of the universal condemnation of torture in numerous international agreements, and the renunciation of torture as an instrument of official policy by virtually all of the nations of the world (in principle if not in practice), we find that an act of torture committed by a state official against one held in detention violates established norms of the international law of human rights, and hence the law of nations. ...

Having examined the sources from which customary international law is derived— the usage of nations, judicial opinions and the works of jurists—we conclude that official torture is now prohibited by the law of nations. The prohibition is clear and unambiguous, and admits of no distinction between treatment of aliens and citizens ... . While the ultimate scope of those rights will be a subject for continuing refinement and elaboration, we hold that the right to be free from torture is now among them. We therefore turn to the question whether the other requirements for jurisdiction are met. ...

Appellee submits that even if the tort alleged is a violation of modern international law, federal jurisdiction may not be exercised consistent with the dictates of Article III of the Constitution. The claim is without merit. Common law courts of general jurisdiction regularly adjudicate transitory tort claims between individuals over whom they exercise personal jurisdiction, wherever the tort occurred. Moreover, as part of an articulated scheme of federal control over external affairs, Congress provided, in the First Judiciary Act, Sec. 9(b), 1 Stat. 73, 77 (1789), for federal jurisdiction over suits by aliens where principles of international law are in issue. The constitutional basis for the Alien Tort Statute is the Law of Nations, which has always been part of the federal common law.

It is not extraordinary for a court to adjudicate a tort claim arising outside of its territorial jurisdiction. A state or nation has a legitimate interest in the orderly resolution of disputes among those within its borders, and where the *lex loci delicti commissi* is applied, it is an expression of comity to give effect to the laws of the state where the wrong occurred. ...

The law of nations forms an integral part of the common law, and a review of the history surrounding the adoption of the Constitution demonstrates that it became a part of the common law of the United States upon the adoption of the Constitution. Therefore, the enactment of the Alien Tort Statute was authorized by Article III. ... During the eighteenth century, it was taken for granted on both sides of the Atlantic that the law of nations forms a part of the common law. ...

Although the Alien Tort Statue has rarely been the basis for jurisdiction during its long history, in light of the foregoing discussion, there can be little doubt that this action is properly brought in federal court.

NOTES

1) The case was remanded to trial, where Filartiga won a judgment by default and was awarded over US$10 million against Peña-Irala, an amount that he was never able to collect. *Filartiga* was the first successful case using the *Alien Tort Statute* to claim damages for human rights violations. It has been followed by a number of other cases that have broadly accepted its holding.[124]

2) In 2004, the United States Supreme Court had its first opportunity to pronounce on this line of cases in *Sosa v. Alvarez-Machain*.[125] Alvarez-Machain, relying on the *Alien Tort Statute*, sued Sosa and various U.S. government agencies and individuals for illegally abducting him in Mexico and forcibly transferring him to the United States. In its decision, the Supreme Court acknowledged that the *Alien Tort Statute* did afford a plaintiff a cause of action, most clearly with respect to violations of the law of nations as it stood in 1789 such as infringements of the rights of ambassadors, violations of safe-conduct, and actions arising out of prize captures and piracy. The majority of the Court found that federal courts have some discretion to create new causes of action that would reflect developments of customary international law over the last two centuries, but only in cases where these norms enjoy "definite content and acceptance" similar to the 1789 standards. The dissenters denied that federal courts possessed any discretion to create new causes of action beyond those known in 1789. The Supreme Court's decision in *Sosa* thus neither rejects the *Filartiga* approach nor embraces a broad construction of the jurisdiction of American Courts to entertain tortious claims based on violations of international human rights standards. Within the confines of the strict limits defined by the majority in *Sosa*, it seems that claims based on violations amounting to international crimes could still be pursued under the *Alien Tort Statute*.

3) What seem to be the advantages of enforcing international human rights by way of private civil suits before national courts? Who would be the typical defendants in such suits?

---

124 See R. Steinhardt, "Fulfilling the Promise of Filartiga: Litigating Human Rights Claims Against the Estate of Ferdinand Marcos" (1995) 20 Yale J. Int. L. 65; and "Symposium: Human Rights on the Eve of the Next Century: U.N. Human Rights Standards and U.S. Law" (1997) 66 Fordham L. Rev. *passim*.

125 124 S. Ct. 2739.

4) Would it be possible to file the same type of civil suits before Canadian courts without a statute similar to the *Alien Tort Statute*? To paraphrase *Filartiga*, can international customary law be said to form part of Canadian common law?[126]

5) Some of these issues were raised in a decision of the Ontario Court of Appeal, *Bouzari v. Iran*, in which the plaintiff filed a civil suit against Iran for abduction and torture some years before he came to Canada as a landed immigrant. The Court found that both the doctrine of *forum non conveniens* under private international law and the Canadian *State Immunity Act (SIA)* barred such an action before Canadian courts. In particular, the Court rejected an argument based on the *jus cogens* character of the prohibition of torture whereby all states would be under an obligation to permit a civil suit against a foreign state for torture committed abroad:

> Both under customary international law and international treaty there is today a balance struck between the condemnation of torture as an international crime against humanity and the principle that states must treat each other as equals not to be subjected to each other's jurisdiction. It would be inconsistent with this balance to provide a civil remedy against a foreign state for torture committed abroad. In the future, perhaps as the international human rights movement gathers greater force, this balance may change, either through the domestic legislation of states or by international treaty. However, this is not a change to be effected by a domestic court adding an exception to the *SIA* that is not there, or seeing a widespread state practice that does not exist today.[127]

---

126 See Chapter 4, Section A.1 on "Customary Law in Canada." See also C. Scott, ed., *Torture as Tort* (2001).

127 (2004) 243 D.L.R. (4th) 406 para. 95 (Ont. C.A.) (leave to appeal to the Supreme Court of Canada denied, 27 Jan. 2005), reproduced in part in Chapter 5, Section C.4.

CHAPTER THIRTEEN

Law of the Sea

A. INTRODUCTION[1]

The law of the sea is one of the most ancient and complex branches of international law. It dates back to the Roman period when the doctrine of the open seas was first formulated. The Romans believed that the open seas were *communis omnium naturali jure*, common to all by the operation of natural law. For a short time during the 17th century, the Spanish and the Portuguese attempted to challenge this notion by reaching an agreement to divide the Atlantic ocean between them. However, at the same time, Grotius reintroduced the notion of freedom of the high seas, whereby the open seas would remain free of all claims, and this view eventually won the day. Nevertheless, although the doctrine of the freedom of the high seas became a cornerstone principle of international law, states were still permitted to make certain territorial claims in the seas immediately adjacent to their coastline.[2] Indeed, for the most part, the evolution of the law of the sea has focused on solving questions of territorial claims and their delineation.

Despite its antiquity, the law of the sea is also one of the most dynamic and changing areas of law. Few areas of public international law have been of greater interest and significance to Canada. Canada has the world's longest coastline and vast oceanic resources; not surprisingly the law of the sea has been a major concern of successive Canadian governments.

---

1   See I. Brownlie, *Principles of Public International Law*, 6th ed. (2003) at 173-245; R.R. Churchill & A.V. Lowe, *The Law of the Sea*, 3d ed. (1999); C.J. Colombos, *The International Law of the Sea*, 6th ed. (1967); R.-J. Dupuy & D. Vignes, eds., *Traité du Nouveau Droit de la Mer* (1985); J.B. Morell, *The Law of the Sea, An Historical Analysis of the 1982 Treaty and Its Rejection by the United States* (1992); D.P. O'Connell, *The International Law of the Sea* (1982-84) 2 vols.; C. Rousseau, *Droit International Public* (1980) vol. 4, (1987) at 269-601; and E.D. Brown, *The International Law of the Sea* (1994) 2 vols. See also B. Johnson & M.W. Zacher, eds., *Canadian Foreign Policy and the Law of the Sea* (1977); D.M. Johnston, *Canada and the New International Law of the Sea* (1985); D. McRae & G. Munro, eds., *Canadian Oceans Policy: National Strategies and the New Law of the Sea* (1989); and D. VanderZwaag, ed., *Canadian Ocean Law and Policy* (1992). Extensive documentation is available in *New Directions in the Law of the Sea* (1973-81) 11 vols., kept up to date by a New Series, 2 vols., looseleaf; S. Oda, *The International Law of the Ocean Development*, looseleaf (1977) 2 vols.; K.R. Simmonds, ed., *New Directions in the Law of the Sea* (1994) 5 vols.; and E.D. Brown, *Sea-Bed Energy and Mineral Resources and the Law of the Sea* (1986) 3 vols. The United Nations, Office of Legal Affairs, Division for Ocean Affairs and the Law of the Sea (DOALOS), maintains an excellent website: <www.un.org/Depts/los/index.htm>, hereinafter DOALOS website.

2   Churchill & Lowe, *supra* note 1 at c. 4.

The international community has a considerable stake in ensuring stability and certainty in the law of the sea, but new uses of the oceans and new technologies, in this century as in the past, have put pressure on old rules and have forced change. What is most remarkable about the law of the sea is that, given the high degree of common use, a clear rule of some sort has always emerged within a relatively short period of time.

Customary law has long been and continues to be a central element of the law of the sea. Virtually all modern rules of the law of the sea are grounded in custom. However, major efforts were made to codify the law during the course of the 20th century. The first efforts related to the status of certain international straits; they were followed by drafts proposed by the League of Nations in 1930.[3] After lengthy preparatory work by the International Law Commission (ILC), the First U.N. Conference on the Law of the Sea, convened at Geneva in 1958, adopted four comprehensive conventions: the Convention on the Territorial Sea and the Contiguous Zone; the Convention on the High Seas; the Convention on Fishing and Conservation of the Living Resources of the High Seas; and the Convention on the Continental Shelf.[4] All four Conventions entered into force and were ratified by a considerable number of states. Many that did not ratify considered that the conventions on the territorial sea, high seas, and continental shelf codified important areas of the law, and thus in practice followed them relatively closely. Canada was in this position, although it eventually ratified the Convention on the Continental Shelf.

The four Geneva Conventions represented a considerable achievement but they fell short of universal acceptance and, as the *North Sea Continental Shelf Cases*[5] showed, not all the provisions of these law-making conventions codified or achieved the status of customary international law. The Convention on Fishing on the High Seas met the greatest resistance as it appeared to many coastal states to restrict their jurisdiction to the advantage of distant water states. In practice, for Canada, fisheries were governed by bilateral arrangements with the United States (such as the Halibut Treaty[6] and the Fraser River Salmon Fisheries Treaty[7]), general reciprocal fisheries treaties,[8] or regional arrangements such as the International Convention for the Northwest Atlantic Fisheries.[9]

Within a decade of the adoption of the 1958 Geneva Conventions it became clear that the process of change was continuing. Some old law was crumbling, as in the area of fisheries, and complex new problems were emerging with respect to the exploitation of polymetallic nodules to be found in large areas of the deep ocean floor. In December 1967 the spectre of the extension of continental shelf claims out into the middle of the

---

3   See Rousseau, *supra* note 1 at 405-22 and 364-66.

4   516 U.N.T.S. 205; 450 U.N.T.S. 82; 559 U.N.T.S. 285; 499 U.N.T.S. 311; Can. T.S. 1970 No. 4, respectively.

5   [1969] I.C.J. Rep. 3, reported in Chapter 3, Section C.1 on "General Customary Law."

6   Can. T.S. 1931 No. 2.

7   Can. T.S. 1937 No. 10; since replaced by the 1985 Pacific Salmon Treaty, Can. T.S. 1985 No. 7; see below, "West Coast Fisheries" in Section E.1 on "Fisheries."

8   Can. T.S.1970 No. 11; Can. T.S. 1972 No. 13; Can. T.S. 1973 Nos. 16 and 23; Can. T.S. 1974 No. 14; Can. T.S.1976 No. 32; and Can. T.S.1977 No. 23.

9   Can. T.S. 1950 No. 10; Can. T.S.1967 No. 17; Can. T.S. 1969 No. 34, since replaced by the *Convention for Future Multilateral Cooperation in the Northwest Atlantic Fisheries*, Can. T.S. 1979 No. 11.

ocean was raised at the United Nations. As a result, an *ad hoc* committee was established to explore the issues. One year later the "Seabed Committee" was established with 36 members and was given a mandate to identify the issues and prepare the agenda of a new conference on the law of the sea.

The Third U.N. Conference on the Law of the Sea held its first session in December 1973 and its final 11th session in December 1982. The U.N. Convention on the Law of the Sea,[10] which emerged from that conference, is the most ambitious effort at codification and progressive development of international law ever attempted by the United Nations. It comprises 17 parts, 320 articles, and 9 annexes. The Convention covers all the traditional law of the sea (with the partial exception of military uses) including territorial sea, high seas, rights of navigation, international straits, and the continental shelf. It also contains extensive additions to the law on new topics (the common heritage of mankind beyond national jurisdiction, archipelagic states, the exclusive economic zone, protection of the marine environment and marine scientific research) or new law on traditional topics (innocent passage, transit passage through straits, fisheries, and delimitation of the continental shelf). There are also extensive provisions on compulsory dispute settlement.

The U.N. Convention on the Law of the Sea entered into force in accordance with article 308 on November 16, 1994, 12 months following the date of deposit of the 60th instrument of ratification. By October 2005, 149 states had ratified the 1982 Convention.[11] The relatively long interim period before the Convention entered into force is due largely to the reservations of the developed countries, led by the United States, concerning the Convention's rules governing the exploitation of the resources of the International Seabed Area. Informal consultations, commenced in July 1990, culminated in the adoption on July 28, 1994 of the Agreement relating to the implementation of Part XI of the U.N. Convention on the Law of the Sea of December 10, 1982,[12] which entered into force on July 28, 1996. This Agreement consists of 10 articles dealing principally with procedural aspects such as signature, entry into force, and provisional application. The main purpose of the Agreement was to amend Part XI of the Convention, even before it came into force, with regard to deep seabed mining. These provisions are found in an annex, divided into nine sections, which deal with such issues as costs to states parties, institutional arrangements, and decision-making mechanisms for the International Seabed Authority.

State practice and the other *indicia* of customary international law continue to be an important source of law. Throughout the interim period before the entry into force of the 1982 Convention, states increasingly acted as though the Convention reflected the new customary international law. This is particularly the case with respect to the new forms of jurisdiction within the Exclusive Economic Zone that many states have been exercising, at least partially, since 1977.

---

10   *Third U.N. Conference on the Law of the Sea,* Official Records (1973-1984) vols. 1-18. The Convention (U.N. Doc. A/CONF.62/122) appears in Vol. 17 at 151-221, and is reprinted in (1982) 21 I.L.M. 1261.

11   DOALOS website, *supra* note 1. Canada ratified the Convention in November 2003. At present, only the United States, among industrialized states, remains a non-party.

12   The full text of the Agreement is available online: DOALOS website, *supra* note 1.

Although Canada signed the Convention in 1982, it was not until November 2003 that Canada ratified it. What legal, political, economic, and social arguments militated for and against Canadian ratification? Consider this issue in the light of the discussion of the substance of the Convention throughout this chapter.[13]

A further important source of the law of the sea is the host of more specialized conventions (many drawn up under the aegis of the International Maritime Organization, the U.N. Conference on Trade and Development, the U.N. Environment Program, and other U.N. agencies), dealing with such topics as navigation, ship registration, environmental protection, passage through straits, continental shelf, and economic zone delimitation. Judicial and arbitral decisions have also played an important part in developing the law of the sea in the past five decades.

B. MARINE ZONES

1. Territorial Sea[14]

(a) Definition and Delimitation

United Nations Convention on the Law of the Sea
Articles 2-14
Reproduced in the Documentary Supplement

NOTES

1) The concept of the territorial sea has not changed from 1958 to 1982. However, archipelagic states (discussed below) are now permitted to claim areas of territorial sea within archipelagic water.

2) The 1982 Convention has finally resolved the vexed question of the outer limit of the territorial sea. Subject to acceptance of the new regime of passage through straits (discussed below), this limit is fixed at 12 nautical miles. Some 140 states claim territorial seas of 12 nautical miles or less.[15]

3) The articles of the 1982 Convention otherwise closely follow the 1958 Geneva Convention on the Territorial Sea and the Contiguous Zone. This includes articles 5-14, which deal with the drawing of baselines from which the territorial sea is to be measured.

---

13   And see T.L. McDorman, "Will Canada Ratify the Law of the Sea Convention?" (1988) 25 San Diego L.R. 535 and "Canada Ratifies the 1982 United Nations Convention on the Law of the Sea: At Last" (2004) 35 Ocean Dev. & Int'l L. 103.

14   See P.C. Jessup, *The Law of Territorial Waters and Maritime Jurisdiction* (1927); D.P. O'Connell, *supra* note 1 at cc. 3-10, 17, 23, and 24; J.-Y. Morin, "Les eaux territoriales du Canada au regard du droit international" (1963) 1 Can. Y.B. Int'l L. 82; and Churchill & Lowe, *supra* note 1 at 31-101.

15   *Law of the Sea (Report of the Secretary-General)* (March 4, 2004) A/59/62, online: <http://daccessdds.un.org/doc/UNDOC/GEN/N04/261/40/PDF/N04/261/40.pdf?OpenElement>. A table of claims to maritime jurisdiction by states is maintained on the DOALOS website at <www.un.org/Depts/los/LEGISLATIONANDTREATIES/claims.htm>.

While the "normal" baselines are stated in article 5 to be the "low-water line along the coast," there are a number of exceptions to this rule, including the provision respecting deltas in article 7(2), which was added at the behest of Bangladesh for reasons of local geography. The provisions dealing with straight baselines, which may be drawn to join a number of points along a coast, are grounded in customary law as evidenced by state practice and the decision of the World Court in the *Anglo-Norwegian Fisheries Case*.[16] In the 2001 *Qatar v. Bahrain Maritime Delimitation and Territorial Questions* case,[17] the ICJ had to evaluate apparent straight baselines constructed by Bahrain.

THE COURT: ...

210. Bahrain has contended that, as a multiple-island State, its coast consists of the lines connecting its outermost islands and such low-tide elevations as lie within their territorial waters. Without explicitly referring to Article 4 of the 1958 Convention on the Territorial Sea and the Contiguous Zone or Article 7 of the 1982 Convention on the Law of the Sea, Bahrain in its reasoning and in the maps provided to the Court applied the method of straight baselines. ...

211. Bahrain maintains that as a multiple-island State characterized by a cluster of islands off the coast of its main islands, it is entitled to draw a line connecting the outermost islands and low-tide elevations. According to Bahrain, in such cases the external fringe should serve as the baseline for the territorial sea.

212. The Court observes that the method of straight baselines, which is an exception to the normal rules for the determination of baselines, may only be applied if a number of conditions are met. This method must be applied restrictively. Such conditions are primarily that either the coastline is deeply indented and cut into, or that there is a fringe of islands along the coast in its immediate vicinity.

213. The fact that a State considers itself a multiple-island State or a *de facto* archipelagic State does not allow it to deviate from the normal rules for the determination of baselines unless the relevant conditions are met. The coasts of Bahrain's main islands do not form a deeply indented coast, nor does Bahrain claim this. It contends, however, that the maritime features off the coast of the main islands may be assimilated to a fringe of islands which constitute a whole with the mainland.

214. The Court does not deny that the maritime features east of Bahrain's main islands are part of the overall geographical configuration; it would be going too far, however, to qualify them as a fringe of islands along the coast. The islands concerned are relatively small in number. Moreover, in the present case it is only possible to speak of a "cluster of islands" or an "island system" if Bahrain's main islands are included in that concept. In such a situation, the method of straight baselines is applicable only if the State has declared itself to be an archipelagic State under Part IV of the 1982 Convention on the Law of the Sea, which is not true of Bahrain in this case.

215. The Court, therefore, concludes that Bahrain is not entitled to apply the method of straight baselines.

---

16   [1951] I.C.J. Rep. 116.

17   [2001] I.C.J. Rep. 40.

Diagram of the Construction of Baselines

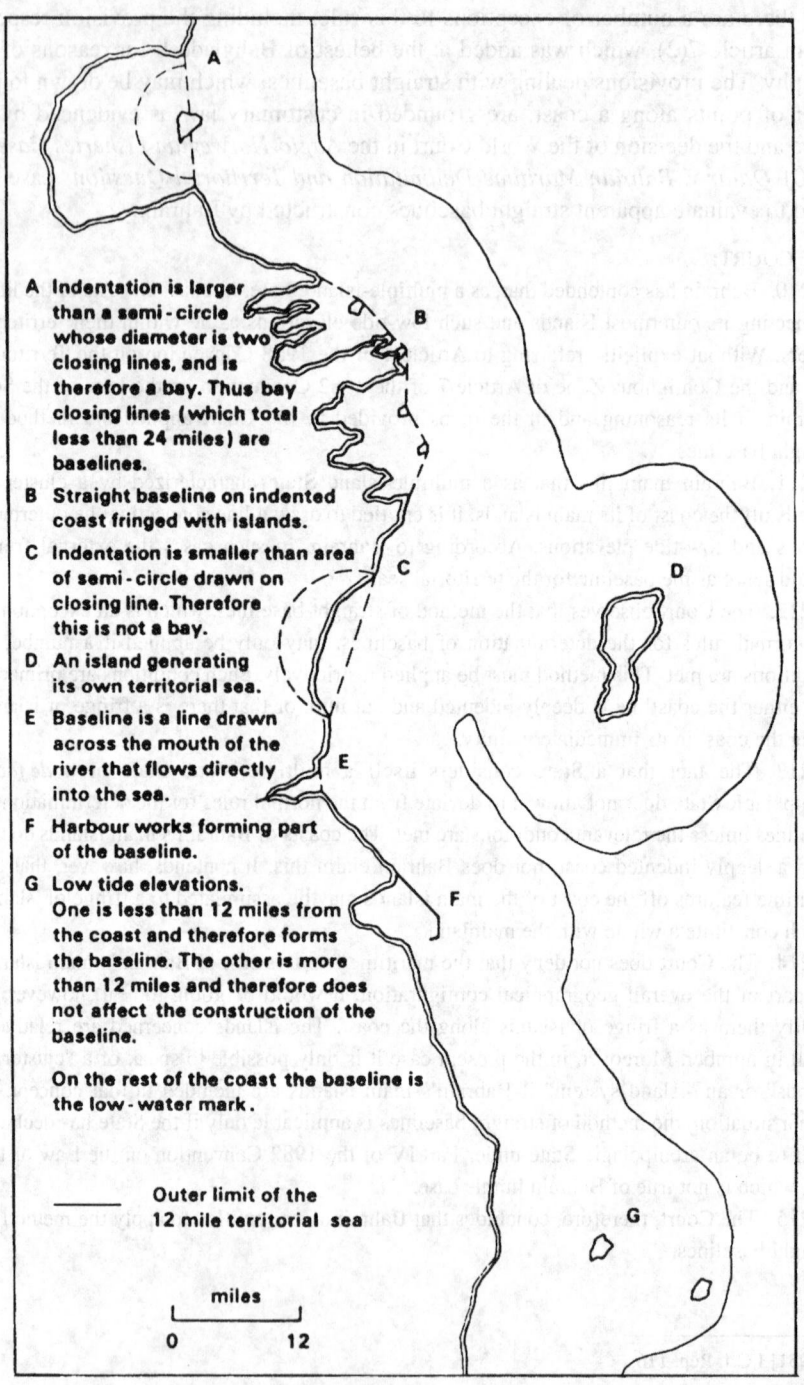

A Indentation is larger
   than a semi - circle
   whose diameter is two
   closing lines, and is
   therefore a bay. Thus bay
   closing lines (which total
   less than 24 miles) are
   baselines.

B Straight baseline on indented
   coast fringed with islands.

C Indentation is smaller than area
   of semi - circle drawn on
   closing line. Therefore
   this is not a bay.

D An island generating
   its own territorial sea.

E Baseline is a line drawn
   across the mouth of the
   river that flows directly
   into the sea.

F Harbour works forming part
   of the baseline.

G Low tide elevations.
   One is less than 12 miles from
   the coast and therefore forms
   the baseline. The other is more
   than 12 miles and therefore does
   not affect the construction of the
   baseline.

   On the rest of the coast the baseline is
   the low - water mark.

   _____ Outer limit of the
           12 mile territorial sea

           miles
   └─────────┘
   0   12

4) A number of countries, including Canada, have constructed straight baselines that are longer than 50 miles. How long may a baseline be in order to respect article 7 of the 1982 Convention and customary international law?

5) Article 10(6) is of particular interest to Canada and to those other states having historic claims over more extensive zones of the sea adjacent to their coasts than a literal application of these articles would allow. Attempts were made during the Third U.N. Conference on the Law of the Sea to reinforce recognition of such claims. However, the general sentiment in the conference was against such a move. For this reason, the article reproduces the same language as article 7(6) of the 1958 Geneva Convention on the Territorial Sea. Does this imply confirmation or discouragement of the right to maintain historic claims in the light of the new jurisdiction granted to states over the Exclusive Economic Zone? Or does it simply imply that historic claims continue to be judged upon their own merits?

Oceans Act
S.C. 1996, c. 31

4. *Territorial sea of Canada*—The territorial sea of Canada consists of a belt of sea that has as its inner limit the baselines described in section 5 and as its outer limit

    (a) subject to paragraph (b), the line every point of which is at a distance of 12 nautical miles from the nearest point of the baselines; or

    (b) in respect of the portions of the territorial sea of Canada for which geographical coordinates of points have been prescribed pursuant to subparagraph 25(a)(ii), lines determined from the geographical coordinates of points so prescribed.

5.(1) *Determination of the baselines*—Subject to subsections (2) and (3), the baseline is the low-water line along the coast or on a low-tide elevation that is situated wholly or partly at a distance not exceeding the breadth of the territorial sea of Canada from the mainland or an island.

(2) *Geographical coordinates of points*—In respect of any area for which geographical coordinates of points have been prescribed pursuant to subparagraph 25(a)(i) and subject to any exceptions in the regulations for

    (a) the use of the low-water line along the coast between given points, and

    (b) the use of the low-water lines of low-tide elevations that are situated wholly or partly at a distance not exceeding the breadth of the territorial sea of Canada from the mainland or an island,

the baselines are straight lines interpreted as geodesics joining the consecutive geographical coordinates of points so prescribed.

(3) *Baselines where historic title*—In respect of any area not referred to in subsection (2), the baselines are the outer limits of any area, other than the territorial sea of Canada, over which Canada has a historic or other title of sovereignty.

(4) *Low-tide elevations*—For the purposes of this section, a low-tide elevation is a naturally formed area of land that is surrounded by and above water at low tide but submerged at high tide.

6. *Internal waters of Canada*—The internal waters of Canada consist of the waters on the landward side of the baselines of the territorial sea of Canada.

7. *Part of Canada*—For greater certainty, the internal waters of Canada and the territorial sea of Canada form part of Canada.

NOTES

1) Canada has exercised jurisdiction over the territorial sea on its east and west coasts out to 12 nautical miles since 1970, first under the *Territorial Sea and Fishing Zones Act* and now under its replacement, the *Oceans Act*. Canada has proclaimed several sets of straight baselines: in 1967 along the coasts of Newfoundland and Labrador; in 1969 along the coast of Nova Scotia and the western coasts of the Queen Charlotte Islands and Vancouver Island; and in 1985 along the outer coasts of the Arctic archipelago. There are gaps in the straight baselines on the east and west coasts—the mouths of the Queen Charlotte Sound, Bay of Fundy, and Gulf of St. Lawrence. In these areas Canada has used "fishery closing lines." Despite section 4(3) of the *Oceans Act*, no territorial sea has in fact been constructed seaward of the fishery closing lines.[18] The straight baselines and fishery closing lines are illustrated on the following maps.[19] To what degree is the *Oceans Act* consistent with the provisions of the Law of the Sea Convention? With customary international law as evidenced in the *Qatar v. Bahrain Case*?

2) As sections 3, 6, and 7 of the Act state, all the areas of the sea to landward of the baselines are internal waters of Canada and thus are as fully part of its sovereign territory as the land mass. For certain regulatory purposes connected to shipping and customs, Canada makes a further subdivision of its internal waters with respect to the Great Lakes and their means of access from the oceans via the St. Lawrence River. Thus within the regime of internal waters the *Canada Shipping Act*[20] distinguishes the "inland waters of Canada," meaning:

all the rivers, lakes and other navigable fresh waters within Canada, and includes the St. Lawrence River as far seaward as a straight line drawn
   (a) from Cap des Rosiers to West Point Anticosti Island, and
   (b) from Anticosti Island to the north shore of the St. Lawrence River along the meridian of longitude sixty-three degrees west.

---

18   See T.L. McDorman, "Canada's Ocean Limits and Boundaries: An Overview" in L.K. Kriwoken *et al.*, eds., *Oceans Law and Policy in the Post-UNCED Era: Australian and Canadian Perspectives* (1996) 113 at 114-19. See also L.L. Herman, "Proof of Offshore Territorial Claims in Canada" (1982) 7 Dal. L.J. 3.

19   Based on C.R.C., cc. 1547 and 1550. Canadian jurisdiction over Arctic waters, including a map of baselines, is considered in Chapter 7, Section C.1 on "The Arctic."

20   R.S.C. 1985, c. S-9, s. 2. A similar definition is contained in the *Customs Act*, R.S.C. 1985 (2nd Supp.) c. 1, s. 2(1).

Map of Canadian Baselines, East Coast
Derived from (1982-83), 7 Dal. L.J. 32, 33, and 35

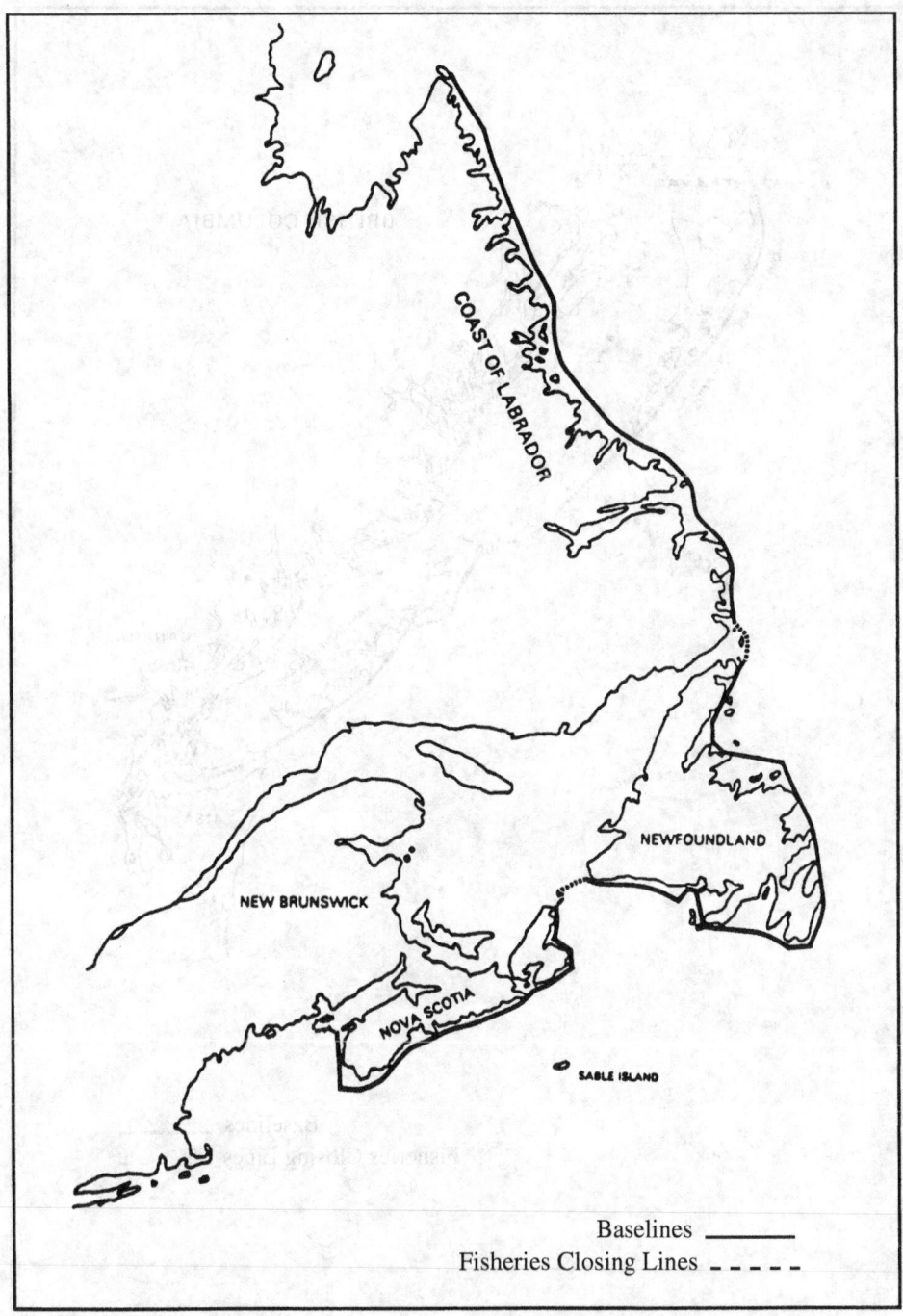

COAST OF LABRADOR

NEWFOUNDLAND

NEW BRUNSWICK

NOVA SCOTIA

SABLE ISLAND

Baselines _____
Fisheries Closing Lines _ _ _ _ _

Map of Canadian Baselines, West Coast
Derived from (1982-83), 7 Dal. L.J. 34 and 35

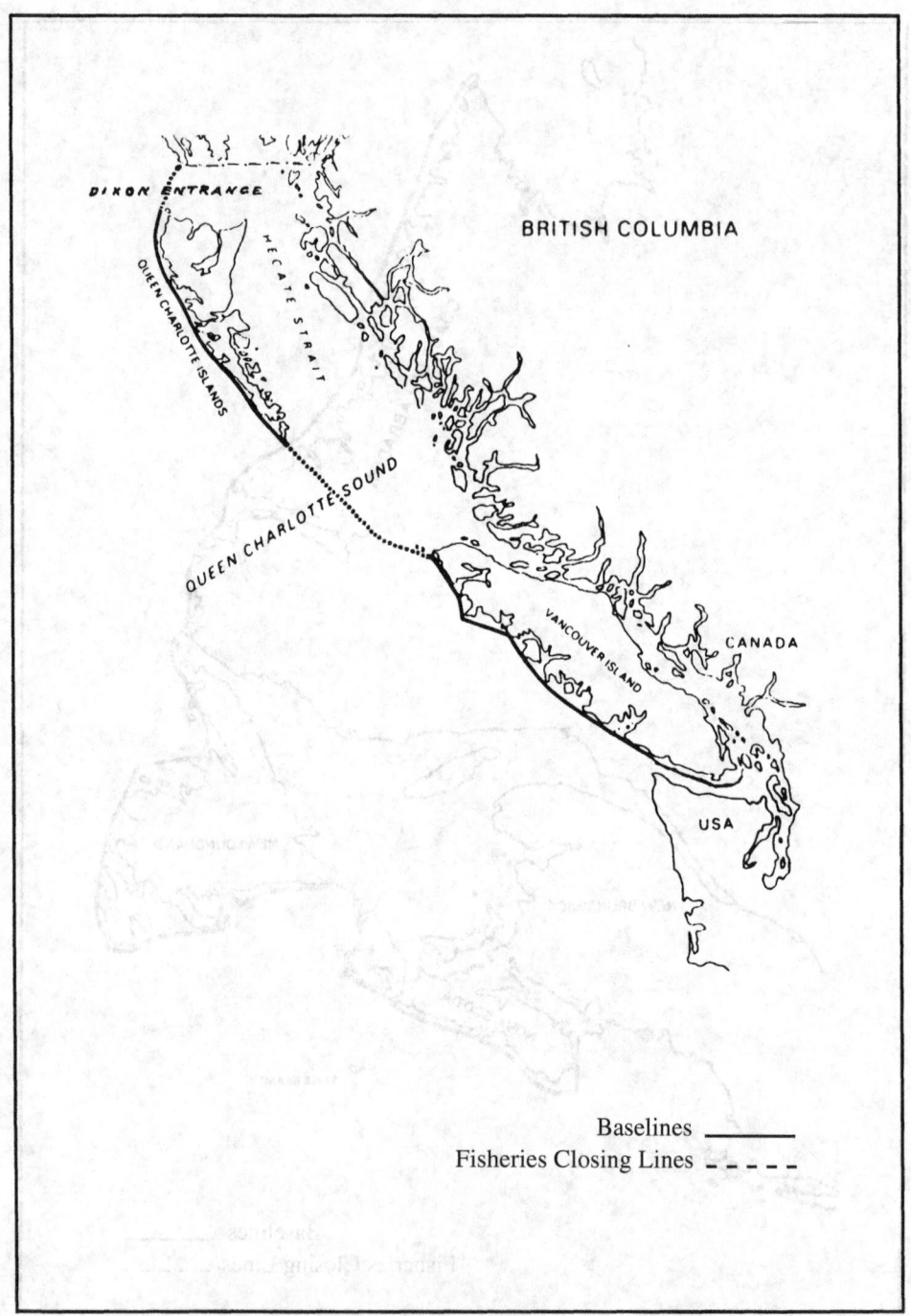

(b) Islands and Archipelagos[21]

United Nations Convention on the Law of the Sea
Articles 46-49, 121
Reproduced in the Documentary Supplement

NOTES

1) The rule on islands repeats article 10(1) of the 1958 Geneva Convention on the Territorial Sea and the Contiguous Zone. Article 121(3) is an innovation designed to restrict abusive claims to exclusive economic zones on the basis of claims to reefs and low tide elevations.

2) Is Canada justified in claiming an exclusive fishing zone and continental shelf 200 miles beyond Sable Island—a small sand bar situated at some 125 miles from Nova Scotia and inhabited only by birds, wild ponies, and a few government biologists?

3) The sovereignty over archipelagic waters recognized in article 49 is subject to the right of innocent passage (article 52). By article 53, the archipelagic state may designate sea lanes and air routes through its waters, but in doing so it must include all the passage routes normally used for international navigation and overflight.

4) Does Canada have any interest in claiming the status of an archipelagic state? Does it have any right to? Is it relevant that Canada's Arctic archipelago ratio of water to land is 1:0.9—that is, some 5 times more favourable than the water to land ratio of Indonesia, which promulgated archipelagic baselines as long ago as 1957?

5) In the *Qatar v. Bahrain* case, the ICJ did not consider the baselines constructed by Bahrain to be archipelagic baselines because Bahrain had not "declared itself to be an archipelagic State under Part IV of the 1982 Convention on the Law of the Sea."[22] Presumably, this declaratory requirement arises from article 47(8) and (9) of the 1982 Convention. What is the legal status of archipelagic baselines constructed before the entry into force of the 1982 Convention? Can Ecuador construct archipelagic straight baselines for the Galapagos Islands?

(c) Innocent Passage Through the Territorial Sea

United Nations Convention on the Law of the Sea
Articles 17-26
Reproduced in the Documentary Supplement

---

21   See D.P. O'Connell, *supra* note 1 at 236; P.E.J. Rodgers, *Midocean Archipelagos and International Law* (1981); L.L. Herman, "The Modern Concept of the Off-Lying Archipelago in International Law" (1985) 23 Can. Y.B. Int'l L. 172; B. McKinnon, "Arctic Baselines: A Litore Usque Ad Litus" (1987) 66 Can. Bar Rev. 790; and Churchill & Lowe, *supra* note 1 at 118-31.

22   See excerpt from *Qatar v. Bahrain*, above at para. 214.

NOTES

1) The right of foreign vessels, including military vessels, to pass through the territorial sea is fundamental to international commerce and navigation. Many major shipping routes pass close to the shoreline or through narrow international straits. Customary international law[23] and the 1958 Geneva Convention defined innocent passage very much as it is found in articles 17, 18, and 19(1). A general balance was struck between sovereignty and the right of navigation. With the extension of claims beyond 3 miles and the proliferation of laws on pollution from ships after 1969, the maritime powers became alarmed at the possible erosion of the right of innocent passage and so, at the Third U.N. Conference, they insisted upon a much more precise definition of the right.

2) Article 21 gives the coastal state authority to make certain regulations respecting innocent passage, but what power does it have to enforce them? What measures may be taken under the permission in article 25 to take "necessary steps … to prevent passage which is not innocent"? Can the coastal state ever prevent innocent passage?

3) There is no mention of innocent passage rights in the *Oceans Act* or any other Canadian legislation. Should the international right be made explicit in national legislation? Does it matter?

4) The passage by vessels carrying nuclear materials (fuel for reprocessing or the reprocessed fuel) has raised questions as to whether these vessels are inherently non-innocent and thus not entitled to the right of innocent passage. Some states have enacted laws to prevent the passage of such vessels through their territorial waters. Moreover, the right of a coastal state to receive prior notification of the intended passage of these vessels is a matter of some debate. Is innocent passage as set out in the 1982 Convention subject to evolution?

(d) Jurisdiction in Internal Waters

Since the sea on the landward side of a state's baselines is internal to that state, it has sovereignty over those waters as completely as over its land territory. Thus, within internal waters, such as a port, the coastal state has absolute jurisdiction over the visiting vessels and crew, and the vessel and crew are subject to and must comply with the laws and regulations of the coastal state. But a state does not have to exercise its authority and frequently does not choose to do so with respect to visiting merchant vessels, at least when its interests and population are not affected. A typical incident would be a disturbance among the crew aboard a foreign ship while in port. The port state might take no action on the assumption that the flag state also has jurisdiction, as discussed in Chapter 8, Section C on "Ships," and has a greater interest to act.

Examples of the balance between port and coastal state and flag state jurisdiction are provided by the *Criminal Code* section 477.1, dealing with offences in marine areas under Canadian jurisdiction,[24] discussed below in Section B.1(e) on "Exercise of Jurisdiction by Canada."

---

23   See the *Corfu Channel Case*, [1949] I.C.J. Rep. 4, reported below, in Section B.3 on "International Straits."

24   R.S.C. 1985, c. C-46, s. 477.1, as am. by S.C. 1990, cc. 44 & 315; S.C. 1996, c. 31, s. 68; and S.C. 2001, c. 27, s. 247.

One area where the ability of a coastal state (port state) to exert its laws over visiting vessels that is becoming increasingly important is vessel standards for safety and reduction of pollution. A network of Port State Control Memoranda of Understanding directs port states to undertake inspections of visiting vessels to ensure those vessels comply with national and international standards regarding vessel safety and pollution prevention.[25] Canada participates in two of these MOUs[26] and, as a consequence, undertakes to apply national laws (for example, the *Canada Shipping Act*) to visiting vessels. Can a port state apply its national laws to foreign vessels and arrest or detain the vessel for activities (for example, illegal fishing or pollution discharges) that took place outside of the port state? Would this extraterritorial application of law be inconsistent with international law?

One consequence of the absolute authority of the coastal or port state over internal waters is that, absent an explicit treaty requirement, states are under no obligation to provide port access to foreign vessels. Canada, for example, has denied entry to its ports of fishing vessels from certain states in retaliation for alleged abusive fishing activities by those states. Moreover, Canada has denied entry to its ports of stricken vessels that may pose unacceptable environmental risks, although this raises questions about where such vessels are to go and whether "passing the buck" is an appropriate response.[27]

A well-recognized exception to the jurisdiction of the port state is the immunity granted to a ship that enters one of its harbours in distress. The plea of entry in distress is often raised by those who stand accused of smuggling, previously for rum running and nowadays for drug trading. In these circumstances the courts have admitted the right to immunity but have applied it strictly. The right of distress was expressed in *Cashin v. The King*[28] to be a rule of customary international law to the effect that:

> a ship, compelled through stress of weather, duress or other unavoidable cause to put into a foreign port, is ... exempt from liability to the penalties and forfeitures which, had she entered the port voluntarily, she would have incurred.

The right of distress is not solely a matter of sheltering from harsh weather but may arise from the urgent need to make repairs or to cope with a mutiny, or any other cause of

---

25 See generally Z.O. Ozcayir, *Port State Control* (2001) and T. Keselj, "Port State Jurisdiction in Respect of Pollution of Ships: The 1982 United Nations Convention on the Law of the Sea and the Memorandum of Understanding" (1999) 30 Ocean Dev. & Int'l L. 127.

26 The *Paris Port State Control MOU*, reproduced in (1982) 21 I.L.M. 1, and the *Tokyo Port State Control MOU*, reproduced in R.S. Lee & M. Hayashi, eds., *New Directions in the Law of the Sea: Regional and National Developments*, Release 97-1 (1997). Both these MOUs have websites; see: <www.parismou.org> and <www.tokyo-mou.org>.

27 See *Case Concerning Military and Paramilitary Activities in and against Nicaragua (Nicaragua v. United States)*, [1986] I.C.J. Rep. 14. See also L. de La Fayette, "Access to Ports in International Law" (1996) 11 Int'l J. of Marine and Coastal L. 1 and A. Chircop & O. Linden, eds., *Places of Refuge for Ships: Emerging Environmental Concerns of a Maritime Custom* (2005).

28 [1935] 4 D.L.R. 547 at 551-52 (Ex. Ct.). However, the Court excluded exemption from Canadian revenue laws in apparent contradiction with the principle it had just stated.

genuine necessity. But there must be a real and irresistible distress; a little bad weather or self-induced difficulties will not suffice to support a plea for immunity from jurisdiction.[29]

The right of distress used to be recognized in Canada in the *Customs Act* but was omitted from the revised Act adopted in 1988.[30] What are the legal consequences of this omission?

(e) Exercise of Jurisdiction by Canada

A number of specific laws protect the internal waters and territorial sea of Canada or govern conduct on board ships that are fishing, surveying, or exercising the right of innocent passage.[31] But, until the adoption of the *Canadian Laws Offshore Application Act* in 1990, the general body of Canadian law, apart from the *Criminal Code*, did not apply to these coastal areas or activities. "The basic rule of public law governing the application of Canadian law to the offshore is that no law, whether statute or common law, extends beyond the low water-mark unless specifically extended by Parliament or a Provincial Legislature."[32] Furthermore, a province, generally speaking, has no authority to apply its laws extraterritorially.

The principle of territorial restriction of Canadian law is still the basic rule of the *Criminal Code*, by virtue of section 6(2). However the *Criminal Code* has long applied to the territorial sea, and in 1990, section 477.1 was adopted to ensure its application to all activities off the coast of Canada in marine areas subject to Canadian sovereignty and jurisdiction.[33] This change was effected by the *Canadian Laws Offshore Application Act*, which also made a plenary extension of federal and provincial laws into the offshore areas. The *Oceans Act* has now replaced the *Canadian Laws Offshore Application Act* and has made a further amendment to the *Criminal Code*, as follows.

---

29   *The Queen City v. The King*, [1931] S.C.R. 387; *R. v. Flahaut*, [1935] 2 D.L.R. 685 (N.B. C.A.); and *R. v. Salvador* (1981), 45 N.S.R. (2d) 192 (S.C. A.D.).

30   See *Customs Act*, R.S.C. 1970, c. C-40, s. 173 and R.S.C. 1985 (2d Supp.) c. 1, respectively.

31   The principal Canadian statutes are the *Canada Shipping Act*, R.S.C. 1985, c. S-9; the *Coastal Fisheries Protection Act*, R.S.C. 1985, c. C-33; the *Customs Act*, R.S.C. 1985 (2d Supp.) c. 1; the *Fisheries Act*, R.S.C. 1985, c. F-14; and the *Oceans Act*, S.C. 1996, c. 31. See also the *Customs and Excise Offshore Application Act*, R.S.C. 1985, c. C-53; and R. Hornby, "The Canadian Laws Offshore Application Act: The Legislative Incorporation of Rights over the Continental Shelf" (1991) 29 Can. Y.B. Int'l L. 355; and see A. Chircop & H. Kindred, *et al.*, "Legislating for Integrated Marine Management: Canada's Proposed Oceans Act of 1996" (1995) 34 Can. Y.B. Int'l L. 305

32   A.L.C. de Mestral, "The Law Applicable to the Canadian East-Coast Offshore" (1983) 21 Alta. L.R. 63 at 64.

33   Note that s. 477.1 replaced the former section 433 and must be read in conjunction with ss. 6, 7, 477, 477.3, and 477.4.

Criminal Code

R.S.C. 1985, c. C-46, ss. 477.1 and 477.3, as amended by S.C. 1990, c. 44, s. 15;
S.C. 1996, c. 31, ss. 68 and 70; S.C. 2001, c. 27, s. 247

s. 477.1(1) Every person who commits an act or omission that, if it occurred in Canada, would be an offence under a federal law, within the meaning of section 2 of the *Oceans Act*, is deemed to have committed that act or omission in Canada if it is an act or omission

(a) in the exclusive economic zone of Canada, that

(i) is committed by a person who is in the exclusive economic zone of Canada in connection with exploring or exploiting, conserving or managing the natural resources, whether living or non-living, of the exclusive economic zone of Canada, and

(ii) is committed by or in relation to a person who is a Canadian citizen or a permanent resident within the meaning of subsection 2(1) of the *Immigration and Refugee Protection Act*,

(b) that is committed in a place in or above the continental shelf of Canada and that is an offence in that place by virtue of section 20 of the *Oceans Act*,

(c) that is committed outside Canada on board or by means of a ship registered or licensed, or for which an identification number has been issued, pursuant to any Act of Parliament;

(d) that is committed outside Canada, in the course of hot pursuit; or

(e) that is committed outside the territory of any state by a Canadian citizen. ...

s. 477.3(1) Every power of arrest, entry, search or seizure or other power that could be exercised in Canada in respect of an act or omission referred to in section 477.1 may be exercised, in the circumstances referred to in that section,

(a) at the place or on board the ship or marine installation or structure, within the meaning of section 2 of the *Oceans Act*, where the act or omission occurred; or

(b) where hot pursuit has been commenced, at any place on the seas, other than a place that is part of the territorial sea of any other state.

(2) A justice or judge in any territorial division in Canada has jurisdiction to authorize an arrest, entry search or seizure or an investigation or other ancillary matter related to an offence

(a) committed in or on the territorial sea of Canada or any area of the sea that forms part of the internal waters of Canada, or

(b) referred to in section 477.1.

Oceans Act

S.C. 1996, c. 31

8.(1) *Rights of Her Majesty*—For greater certainty, in any area of the sea not within a province, the seabed and subsoil below the internal waters of Canada and the territorial sea of Canada are vested in Her Majesty in right of Canada.

(2) *Saving*—Nothing in this section abrogates or derogates from any legal right or interest held before February 4, 1991.

9.(1) *Application of provincial law*—Subject to this section and to any other Act of Parliament, the laws of a province apply in any area of the sea

    (a) that forms part of the internal waters of Canada or the territorial sea of Canada;

    (b) that is not within any province; and

    (c) that is prescribed by the regulations.

(2) *Limitation*—Subject to any regulations made pursuant to paragraph 26(1)(d), subsection (1) does not apply in respect to any provision of a law of a province that

    (a) imposes a tax or royalty; or

    (b) relates to mineral or other non-living natural resources.

(3) *Interpretation*—For the purposes of this section, the laws of a province shall be applied as if the area of the sea in which those laws apply under this section were within the territory of that province.

(4) *Sums due to province*—Any sum due under a law of province that applies in an area of the sea under this section belongs to Her Majesty in right of the province.

(5) *Limitation*—For greater certainty, this section shall not be interpreted as providing a basis for any claim, by or on behalf of a province, in respect of any interest in or legislative jurisdiction over any area of the sea in which a law of a province applies under this section or the living or non-living resources of that area, or as limiting the application of any federal laws.

10. *Contiguous zone of Canada*—The contiguous zone of Canada consists of an area of the sea that has as its inner limit the outer limit of the territorial sea of Canada and as its outer limit the line every point of which is at a distance of 24 nautical miles from the nearest point of the baselines of the territorial sea of Canada, but does not include an area of the sea that forms part of the territorial sea of another state or in which another state has sovereign rights.

11. *Prevention in contiguous zone of infringement of federal laws*—A person who is responsible for the enforcement of a federal law that is a customs, fiscal, immigration or sanitary law and who has reasonable grounds to believe that a person in the contiguous zone of Canada would, if that person were to enter Canada, commit an offence under that law may, subject to Canada's international obligations, prevent entry of that person into Canada or the commission of the offence and, for greater certainty, section 25 of the Criminal Code applies in respect of the exercise by a person of any powers under this section.

12.(1) *Enforcement of contiguous zone of federal laws*—Where there are reasonable grounds to believe that a person has committed an offence in Canada in respect of a federal law that is a customs, fiscal, immigration or sanitary law, every power of arrest, entry, search or seizure or other power that could be exercised in Canada in respect of that offence may also be exercised in the contiguous zone of Canada.

(2) *Limitation*—A power of arrest referred to in subsection (1) shall not be exercised in the contiguous zone of Canada on board any ship registered outside Canada without the consent of the Attorney General of Canada.

NOTES

1) Section 477.1 of the *Criminal Code*, adopted after several years of study, is designed to resolve the many jurisdictional uncertainties in the offshore areas, such as the authority of the police or the law applicable to oil rigs and other installations on the continental shelf beyond the territorial sea. While these provisions produce clarity in Canadian law, what is the authority internationally to assert such jurisdiction? Consider the "Bases of Criminal Jurisdiction" of a state described in Chapter 9, Section A.2.

2) Why is it necessary to apply provincial laws in offshore areas? Why is federal authority over navigation and fisheries not sufficient? Consider, for instance, the assertion of Canadian laws in the contiguous zone.

3) Section 10 of the *Oceans Act* declares Canada's contiguous zone. In the 1930s, the French writer A. Gidel[34] developed the notion of a contiguous zone that would represent an extension of a coastal state's jurisdiction into the area of the high seas contiguous to its territorial sea. The extension of jurisdiction constituted a further infringement of the principle of the freedom of the high seas, but this was considered acceptable as long as it occurred for defined purposes—for example, for the application of immigration or sanitary laws. Today, more than 70 states have claimed jurisdiction over a contiguous zone.[35] Article 33(2) of the 1982 Convention provides that the contiguous zone may not extend beyond 24 nautical miles from the coastal state's baselines, so it is a belt of coastal seas up to 12 nautical miles wide beyond the 12-mile limit of the territorial sea.

4) The limited purpose of the contiguous zone is to allow a state to protect its coastal waters from the effects of certain activities beyond its territorial sea, such as infringement of customs, fiscal, immigration, or sanitary laws. Smuggling fits as an example and the *Hovering Acts* were early assertions of this jurisdiction.[36] Security is not specifically mentioned as being relevant within the contiguous zone. Should it be?

2. Historic Waters of Canada

Like many countries, Canada claims that certain bodies of water that might otherwise be classified as part of the high seas or an exclusive economic zone are more properly regarded as internal waters. These historic claims have usually developed over long periods of time and are grounded in special reasons of geography, security, or economic necessity. They all imply a closer relationship between waters and the surrounding land than is generally the case, thus justifying the argument that the waters form an integral part of the land and must be subject to the complete sovereignty of the coastal state. The possible existence of historic waters is acknowledged in the U.N. Law of the Sea

---

34 A. Gidel, "La Mer territoriale et la zone contigue" (1934) 48 Hague Recueil 133 at 241.

35 *Law of the Sea Report, supra* note 15.

36 For example, see *Croft v. Dunphy*, [1933] A.C. 156 (P.C.); *Cashin v. The King*, [1935] Ex. C.R. 103; 4 D.L.R. 547; and J. Brierly, "The Doctrine of the Contiguous Zone and the Dicta in Croft v. Dunphy" (1933) 14 Brit. Y.B. Int'l L. 155. With the adoption of the *Customs Act*, R.S.C. 1985 (2d Supp.) c. 1 in 1986, the offence of "hovering" in "Canadian customs waters" was repealed because it was no longer deemed necessary in the light of Canada's 12-mile territorial sea.

Convention article 10(6), reported in the preceding subsection on the "Territorial Sea." However, the criteria for the proof of a claim of historic waters are not defined there but rest on customary international law. The strength of Canada's claims varies from one area to another; they raise problems of regional attachment and, with respect to the Arctic, form part of the Canadian mystique of Canada as a northern power. It would be unwise to underestimate Canadian attachment to these claims or the seriousness of the international problems that they raise for other states, in particular the United States.[37]

The following commentary does not purport to give an exhaustive picture of Canadian claims but simply highlights some important ones. Many of these claims have been asserted by members of the Canadian Government in the course of parliamentary debates. Thus, concerning Hudson Bay, in 1957 the Minister of Northern Affairs and Natural Resources asserted:

> The waters of Hudson Bay are Canadian waters by historic title in accordance with the universally accepted international law doctrine applying to historic bays. Canada regards as inland water all the water west of a line drawn across the entrance to Hudson Strait from Button Island to Hatton Headland on Resolution Island.[38]

As to the Bay of Fundy, in 1962 Prime Minister Diefenbaker said:

> The Bay of Fundy has always been considered, since the earliest days, first by Great Britain and thereafter by successive Canadian governments, as Canadian territorial waters. As far back as 1763 it was described in official documents as being comprised within the boundaries of what is now Canada. There are strong geographic and economic considerations for this.[39]

Regarding the Gulf of St. Lawrence, Prime Minister St.-Laurent in 1949 stated:

> We intend to contend and hope to be able to get acquiescence in the contention that the waters west of Newfoundland constituting the Gulf of St. Lawrence shall become an inland sea. We hope that, with Newfoundland as a part of Canadian territory, the Gulf of St. Lawrence west of Newfoundland will all become territorial waters of Canada, whereas before there would be only the usual off-shore portion that would thus become part of the territorial waters. Of course that is a matter which is not governed by statutes; it is governed by the comity of nations. It is our intention to assert that position and it is our hope that it will be recognized as a valid contention.[40]

---

37   For an early review of the issues, see "Historic Bays," memorandum of the Secretariat of the United Nations (U.N. Doc. A/CONF.13/1), *First U.N. Conference on the Law of the Sea*, Official Records, vol. 1 (1958) 1. See also L. Bouchez, *The Regime of Bays in International Law* (1964) at 199-302; O'Connell, *supra* note 1 at 417-38; M.P. Strohl, *The International Law of Bays* (1963) at 231-367; T.L. McDorman, *supra* note 18 at 114-17; and D. Pharand, *Canada's Arctic Waters in International Law* (1988) at 91-105.

38   *House of Commons Debates*, 2 (1957-58) at 1169 (Hon. Alvin Hamilton). See V.K. Johnston, "Canada's Title to Hudson Bay and Hudson Strait" (1934) 15 Brit. Y.B. Int'l L. 1.

39   *House of Commons Debates*, 2 (1962-63) at 1650 (Hon. John Diefenbaker). See G.V. LaForest, "Canadian Inland Waters of the Atlantic Provinces and the Bay of Fundy Incident" (1963) 1 Can. Y.B. Int'l L. 149.

40   *House of Commons Debates*, 1 (1949) at 368 (Hon. Louis St. Laurent). See F. Rigaldies, "Le statut du golfe du Saint-Laurent en droit international public" (1985) 23 Can. Y.B. Int'l L. 80.

On March 6, 1974, recalling the statement of Prime Minister St.-Laurent, the Department of External Affairs issued a communiqué stating that the Gulf of St. Lawrence was composed of Canadian internal waters by virtue of historic title.

The Bureau of Legal Affairs of the Department of External Affairs has also written[41] that Canada has similar historic claims to the waters of Dixon Entrance, Hecate Strait, and Queen Charlotte Sound on the British Columbia coast. These bodies of water together with the Bay of Fundy and the Gulf of St. Lawrence have since been declared exclusive Canadian fishing zones under the former *Territorial Sea and Fishing Zones Act* and now, under the *Oceans Act*. The extent of Canada's sovereignty in Arctic waters and their recent enclosure is discussed in Chapter 7, Section C.1 on "The Arctic." It should be recalled that the preamble to the Order in Council drawing the baselines in the Arctic states that these baselines are declaratory of pre-existing historic baselines.

The courts have also had occasion to consider some of Canada's claims to historic waters, typically in the context of determining the extent of territorial jurisdiction offshore. In *Direct U.S. Cable Co. v. Anglo-American Telegraph Co.*,[42] a dispute arose between competing telegraphic companies about the laying of transatlantic cables through Conception Bay. The Privy Council decided that Newfoundland legislation governed the rights of the companies inasmuch as the waters of Conception Bay formed part of Newfoundland. In *Mowat v. McFee*[43] a fisherman objected to the seizure of his boat and nets by a fisheries officer for salmon fishing in the Bay of Chaleur in violation of the *Fisheries Act*. The Supreme Court, in rejecting his writ for trespass, held the *Fisheries Act* applied to the full extent of the Bay of Chaleur since the whole of its waters were within the Dominion of Canada.

The decisions of the courts have not often discussed the concept of historic waters at international law. Their judgments have frequently been based on the English common law principle that the limit of territorial authority was the low-water mark along the coast, even though international law would respect a greater assertion of sovereignty. In the application of this principle the courts have admitted a number of modifications. They have recognized that the territorial limit could be extended seawards, so far as permitted in international law, by the express declaration of a competent legislature. The two previous cases exemplify this process. The courts have also accepted as part of sovereign territory any area of the sea that is *inter fauces terrae* (literally, within the jaws of the land). Thus bays and estuaries between jutting headlands might be treated as part of the country or province into which they project. On occasion, owing to their geographical interrelation to the surrounding land, these portions of the sea have alternatively been called inland waters.

The *Reference Re Ownership of the Bed of the Strait of Georgia*[44] was a case involving inland waters in this sense. The Supreme Court was asked to determine whether the

---

41 Letter (December 17, 1973) reprinted in (1974) 12 Can. Y.B. Int'l L. 279. And see C. Bourne & D. McRae, "Maritime Jurisdiction in the Dixon Entrance: The Alaska Boundary Re-examined" (1976) 14 Can. Y.B. Int'l L. 175.

42 (1877), 2 App. Cas. 394.

43 (1880), 5 S.C.R. 66.

44 [1984] 1 S.C.R. 388. See G. Marston, "The Strait of Georgia Reference" (1985) 23 Can. Y.B. Int'l L. 34.

seabed covered by the waters between mainland British Columbia and Vancouver Island was the property of Canada or of British Columbia. The Court held in favour of the Province on the basis of the territorial description of the colonies of Vancouver Island and British Columbia when they were united and the wording of the British Statute forming the new colony. It made its interpretation of those documents in part by assimilating the sea in the Georgia Strait to waters *inter fauces terrae*.

For an important decision of the U.S. Supreme Court concerning the alleged historic waters of the State of Alaska, see *U.S. v. Alaska*, where the Court took a conservative view of Alaska's claim in applying a test of "continuous and exclusive assertions of dominion."[45]

3. International Straits[46]

United Nations Convention on the Law of the Sea
Articles 37-45
Reproduced in the Documentary Supplement

NOTES

1) Before 1982, the law governing navigation through international straits rested upon customary international law and a number of bilateral or regional conventions dealing with particular straits, such as the Montreux Convention 1936 on Passage Through the Dardanelles,[47] as well as the 1958 Geneva Convention on the Territorial Sea and Contiguous Zone article 16(4), which prohibited the suspension of innocent passage of foreign ships "through straits which are used for international navigation." The extension of the territorial sea from 3 to 12 miles has had the effect of enclosing many major straits. As part of the negotiations at the Third U.N. Conference on the Law of the Sea the maritime powers called for the establishment of a new right of "transit passage" through straits. This right is a guarantee of transit, not simply of innocent passage. It applies to civil and military vessels and constitutes a considerable strengthening of the right of navigation.

2) May the right of transit be controlled or prevented? Compare articles 42 and 44 with articles 21, 24, and 25 on innocent passage through the territorial sea. What is the effect of article 45?

3) Is the right of transit passage binding upon coastal states that encompass straits? If so, on what basis? What straits are subject to the right of transit passage? Does the Northwest

---

45   422 U.S. 184 (1975).

46   See E. Brüel, *International Straits: a Treatise on International Law* (1947) 2 vols.; R. Lapidoth, *Les détroits en droit international* (1972); D.P. O'Connell, *supra* note 1 at 299-337; Churchill & Lowe, *supra* note 1 at 102-17; D. Pharand, *The Northwest Passage Arctic Straits* (1984); B.B. Jia, *The Regime of Straits in International Law* (1998); S. Nandan & D. Anderson, "Straits used for International Navigation: A Commentary on Part III of the United Nations Convention on the Law of the Sea 1982" (1989) 60 Brit. Y.B. Int'l L. 159; W.L. Schachte Jr., "International Straits and Navigational Freedoms" (1993) 24 Ocean Dev. & Int'l L. 179; and A. Mayama, "The Influence of the Straits Transit Regime of the Law of Neutrality at Sea" (1995) 26 Ocean Dev. and Int'l L. 1.

47   173 L.N.T.S. 213.

Passage meet the definition of a "strait used for international navigation"? The Government of Canada has always maintained the contrary. See article 234, discussed later in Section E.2 on "Protection of the Marine Environment" under the heading "Pollution Prevention in Arctic Waters," and Chapter 7, Section C.1 on "The Arctic." Consider the following case.

Corfu Channel Case (Merits)
United Kingdom v. Albania
[1949] I.C.J. Rep. 4

[Two out of a squadron of four British warships were heavily damaged by mines during transit of the Corfu Channel while within the territorial sea of Albania. Subsequently, other British warships mineswept the Channel. By agreement, the parties submitted three questions to the Court.

The first question, which asked whether Albania was responsible under international law for the mines and the damage they caused to the British Ships, was answered affirmatively. (It is discussed in Chapter 10, Section A.2 on "Basis of Responsibility.") The second and third questions asked whether the United Kingdom under international law had violated the sovereignty of the Albanian People's Republic by reason of the acts of the Royal Navy in Albanian waters on October 22 and on November 12 and 13, 1946 and whether there was any duty to give satisfaction.]

THE COURT: ... will first consider whether the sovereignty of Albania was violated by reason of the acts of the British Navy in Albanian waters on October 22nd, 1946.

On May 15th, 1946, the British cruisers Orion and Superb, while passing southward through the North Corfu Channel, were fired at by an Albanian battery in the vicinity of Saranda. ...

The United Kingdom Government at once protested to the Albanian Government, stating that innocent passage through straits is a right recognized by international law. There ensued a diplomatic correspondence in which the Albanian Government asserted that foreign warships and merchant vessels had no right to pass through Albanian territorial waters without prior notification to, and the permission of the Albanian authorities. This view was put into effect by a communication of the Albanian Chief of Staff, dated May 17th, 1946, which purported to subject the passage of foreign warships and merchant vessels in Albanian territorial waters to previous notification to and authorization by the Albanian Government. The diplomatic correspondence continued, and culminated in a United Kingdom note of August 2nd, 1946, in which the United Kingdom Government maintained its view with regard to the right of innocent passage through straits forming routes for international maritime traffic between two parts of the high seas. The note ended with the warning that if Albanian coastal batteries in the future opened fire on any British warship passing through the Corfu Channel, the fire would be returned. ...

The Court will now consider the Albanian contention that the United Kingdom Government violated Albanian sovereignty by sending the warships through this Strait without the previous authorization of the Albanian Government [on October 22].

It is, in the opinion of the Court, generally recognized and in accordance with international custom that States in time of peace have a right to send their warships through straits used for international navigation between two parts of the high seas without the previous authorization of a coastal State, provided that the passage is innocent. Unless otherwise prescribed in an international convention, there is no right for a coastal State to prohibit such passage through straits in time of peace.

The Albanian Government does not dispute that the North Corfu Channel is a strait in the geographical sense; but it denies that this Channel belongs to the class of international highways through which a right of passage exists, on the grounds that it is only of secondary importance and not even a necessary route between two parts of the high seas, and that it is used almost exclusively for local traffic to and from the ports of Corfu and Saranda.

It may be asked whether the test is to be found in the volume of traffic passing through the Strait or in its greater or lesser importance for international navigation. But in the opinion of the Court the decisive criterion is rather its geographical situation as connecting two parts of the high seas and the fact of its being used for international navigation. Nor can it be decisive that this Strait is not a necessary route between two parts of the high seas, but only an alternative passage between the Aegean and the Adriatic Seas. It has nevertheless been a useful route for international maritime traffic. ...

The Court is further informed that the British Navy has regularly used this Channel for eighty years or more, and that it has also been used by the navies of other States.

One fact of particular importance is that the North Corfu Channel constitutes a frontier between Albania and Greece, that a part of it is wholly within the territorial waters of these States, and that the Strait is of special importance to Greece by reason of the traffic to and from the port of Corfu.

Having regard to these various considerations, the Court has arrived at the conclusion that the North Corfu Channel should be considered as belonging to the class of international highways through which passage cannot be prohibited by a coastal State in time of peace.

On the other hand, it is a fact that the two coastal States did not maintain normal relations, that Greece had made territorial claims precisely with regard to a part of Albanian territory bordering on the Channel, that Greece had declared that she considered herself technically in a state of war with Albania, and that Albania, invoking the danger of Greek incursions, had considered it necessary to take certain measures of vigilance in this region. The Court is of opinion that Albania, in view of these exceptional circumstances, would have been justified in issuing regulations in respect of the passage of warships through the Strait, but not in prohibiting such passage or in subjecting it to the requirement of special authorization.

For these reasons the Court is unable to accept the Albanian contention that the Government of the United Kingdom has violated Albanian sovereignty by sending the warships through the Strait without having obtained the previous authorization of the Albanian Government.

In these circumstances, it is unnecessary to consider the more general question, much debated by the Parties, whether States under international law have a right to send warships in time of peace through territorial waters not included in a strait.

The Albanian Government has further contended that the sovereignty of Albania was violated because the passage of the British warships on October 22nd, 1946, was not an innocent passage. ...

It is shown by the Admiralty telegram of September 21st, ... and admitted by the United Kingdom Agent, that the object of sending the warships through the Strait was not only to carry out a passage for purposes of navigation, but also to test Albania's attitude. As mentioned above, the Albanian Government, on May 15th, 1946, tried to impose by means of gunfire its view with regard to the passage. As the exchange of diplomatic notes did not lead to any clarification, the Government of the United Kingdom wanted to ascertain by other means whether the Albanian Government would maintain its illegal attitude and again impose its view by firing at passing ships. The legality of this measure taken by the Government of the United Kingdom cannot be disputed, provided that it was carried out in a manner consistent with the requirements of international law. The "mission" was designed to affirm a right which had been unjustly denied. The Government of the United Kingdom was not bound to abstain from exercising its right of passage, which the Albanian Government had illegally denied.

It remains, therefore, to consider whether the manner in which the passage was carried out was consistent with the principle of innocent passage and to examine the various contentions of the Albanian Government in so far as they appear to be relevant. ...

[Albania had contended that the British ships manoeuvred in combat formation with soldiers on board and guns at the ready, but the Court found that they did not. Albania had also asserted that the crews were at action stations, that the ships were in such force as to evince an intention to intimidate, and that they had observed and reported upon the coastal defences. The Court observed:]

[T]he Commander-in-Chief reported that the passage "was made with ships at action stations in order that they might be able to retaliate quickly if fired upon again." In view of the firing from the Albanian battery on May 15th, this measure of precaution cannot, in itself, be regarded as unreasonable. But four warships—two cruisers and two destroyers—passed in this manner, with crews at action stations, ready to retaliate quickly if fired upon. They passed one after another through this narrow channel, close to the Albanian coast, at a time of political tension in this region. The intention must have been, not only to test Albania's attitude, but at the same time to demonstrate such force that she would abstain from firing again on passing ships. Having regard, however, to all the circumstances of the case, as described above, the Court is unable to characterize these measures taken by the United Kingdom authorities as a violation of Albania's sovereignty.

With regard to the observations of coastal defences made after the explosions, these were justified by the fact that two ships had just been blown up and that, in this critical situation, their commanders might fear that they would be fired on from the coast, as on May 15th.

Having thus examined the various contentions of the Albanian Government in so far as they appear to be relevant, the Court has arrived at the conclusion that the

United Kingdom did not violate the sovereignty of Albania by reason of the acts of the British Navy in Albanian waters on October 22nd, 1946.

In addition to the passage of the United Kingdom warships on October 22nd, 1946, the second question in the Special Agreement relates to the acts of the Royal Navy in Albanian waters on November 12th and 13th, 1946. This is the minesweeping operation called "Operation Retail" by the Parties during the proceedings. …

The United Kingdom Government does not dispute that "Operation Retail" was carried out against the clearly expressed wish of the Albanian Government. It recognizes that the operation had not the consent of the international mine clearance organizations, that it could not be justified as the exercise of a right of innocent passage, and lastly that, in principle, international law does not allow a State to assemble a large number of warships in the territorial waters of another State and to carry out minesweeping in those waters. The United Kingdom Government states that the operation was one of extreme urgency, and that it considered itself entitled to carry it out without anybody's consent.

[T]he explosions of October 22nd, 1946, in a channel declared safe for navigation, and one which the United Kingdom Government, more than any other government, had reason to consider safe, raised quite a different problem from that of a routine sweep carried out under the orders of the mine clearance organizations. These explosions were suspicious; they raised a question of responsibility.

Accordingly, this was the ground on which the United Kingdom Government chose to establish its main line of defence. According to that Government, the *corpora delicti* must be secured as quickly as possible, for fear they should be taken away, without leaving traces, by the authors of the minelaying or by the Albanian authorities. This justification took two distinct forms in the United Kingdom Government's arguments. It was presented first as a new and special application of the theory of intervention, by means of which the State intervening would secure possession of evidence in the territory of another State, in order to submit it to an international tribunal and thus facilitate its task.

The Court cannot accept such a line of defence. The Court can only regard the alleged right of intervention as the manifestation of a policy of force, such as has, in the past, given rise to most serious abuses and such as cannot, whatever be the present defects in international organization, find a place in international law. Intervention is perhaps still less admissible in the particular form it would take here; for, from the nature of things, it would be reserved for the powerful States, and might easily lead to perverting the administration of international justice itself.

The United Kingdom Agent, in his speech in reply, has further classified "Operation Retail" among methods of self-protection or self-help. The Court cannot accept this defence either. Between independent States, respect for territorial sovereignty is an essential foundation of international relations. The Court recognizes that the Albanian Government's complete failure to carry out its duties after the explosions, and the dilatory nature of its diplomatic notes, are extenuating circumstances for the action of the United Kingdom Government. But to ensure respect for international law, of which it is the organ, the Court must declare that the action of the British Navy constituted a violation of Albanian sovereignty.

This declaration is in accordance with the request made by Albania through her Counsel, and is in itself appropriate satisfaction.

4. Exclusive Economic Zone[48]

United Nations Convention on the Law of the Sea
Articles 55-60
Reproduced in the Documentary Supplement

Oceans Act
S.C. 1996, c. 31

13.(1) *Exclusive economic zone of Canada*—The exclusive economic zone of Canada consists of an area of the sea beyond and adjacent to the territorial sea of Canada that has as its inner limit the outer limit of the territorial sea of Canada and as its outer limit

(a) subject to paragraph (b), the line every point of which is at a distance of 200 nautical miles from the nearest point of the baselines of the territorial sea of Canada; or

(b) in respect of a portion of the exclusive economic zone of Canada for which geographical coordinates of points have been prescribed pursuant to subparagraph 25(a)(iii), lines determined from the geographical coordinates of points so prescribed.

(2) *Determination of the outer limit of the exclusive economic zone of Canada*— For greater certainty, paragraph (1)(a) applies regardless of whether regulations are made pursuant to subparagraph 25(a)(iv) prescribing geographical coordinates of points from which the outer limit of the exclusive economic zone of Canada may be determined.

14. *Sovereign rights and jurisdiction of Canada*—Canada has

(a) sovereign rights in the exclusive economic zone of Canada for the purpose of exploring and exploiting, conserving and managing the natural resources, whether living or non-living, of the waters superjacent to the seabed and of the seabed and its subsoil, and with regard to other activities for the economic exploitation and exploration of the exclusive economic zone of Canada, such as the production of energy from the water, currents and winds;

---

48 See W.C. Extavour, *The Exclusive Economic Zone* (1979); D. Attard, *The Exclusive Economic Zone in International Law* (1987); B. Kwiatkowski, *The 200 Mile Exclusive Economic Zone in the Law of the Sea* (1989); F. Orrego Vicuna, *The Exclusive Economic Zone: Régime and Legal Nature Under International Law* (1989); D. Pharand & U. Leanza, eds., *The Continental Shelf and the Exclusive Economic Zone: Delimitation and Legal Regime* (1993); T. Akintoba, *African States and Contemporary International Law: A Case Study of the 1982 Law of the Sea Convention and the EEZ* (1996); and Churchill & Lowe, *supra* note 1 at 160-80.

(b) jurisdiction in the exclusive economic zone of Canada with regard to

    (i) the establishment and use of artificial islands, installations and structures,

    (ii) marine scientific research, and

    (iii) the protection and preservation of the marine environment; and

(c) other rights and duties in the exclusive economic zone of Canada provided for under international law.

15.(1) *Rights of Her Majesty*—For greater certainty, any rights of Canada in the seabed and subsoil of the exclusive economic zone of Canada and their resources are vested in Her Majesty in right of Canada.

(2) *Saving*—Nothing in this section abrogates or derogates from any legal right or interest held before February 4, 1991.

16. *Fishing zones of Canada*—The fishing zones of Canada consist of areas of the sea adjacent to the coast of Canada that are prescribed in the regulations.

NOTES

1) The scope of a state's rights under article 56(1)(a) with respect to fishing are elaborated by articles 61-67, which are discussed later in Section E.1 on "Fisheries." Together with Part XI dealing with the seabed beyond national jurisdiction, the provisions on the exclusive economic zone constitute the principal innovations of the 1982 Convention. These articles are remarkable in many respects, not least in respect of the speed with which they appear to have become rules of international law by virtue of state practice. Almost as soon as agreement was expected to be reached at the Third U.N. Conference on the Law of the Sea in 1975, 200-mile fishing zones were proclaimed by such influential states as the United States, Canada, the European Community members, the former U.S.S.R., and Japan. At the same time, a number of states proclaimed full-fledged exclusive economic zones; Mexico and France were among the first. Approximately 110 states, including Canada, the United States, Russia, and the United Kingdom have proclaimed exclusive economic zones.[49]

2) One of the principal problems in negotiating the exclusive economic zone was the definition of the nature of the zone. This was not simply a matter of abstract theory since a decision to retain the status of high seas would have left many aspects of high seas freedoms unchanged. On the other hand, a decision to equate the zone with the territorial sea would have raised the spectre of restrictions on freedom of navigation. The ultimate resolution clearly creates a regime of law that is *sui generis*, while article 58(2) expressly preserves all high seas freedoms that are not incompatible with the rights enjoyed by coastal states in the zone. But how should a conflict of uses of the zone be resolved—in favour of the coastal state's sovereign rights or the other states' high seas freedoms? Does the coastal state have authority to police the zone? Consider articles 59 and 73, in the Documentary Supplement.

---

49   *Law of the Sea Report, supra* note 15.

3) Although coastal states clearly may claim an exclusive economic zone, they must assert the jurisdiction expressly since the rights do not arise by mere operation of the law, as with the continental shelf. Note too that by article 57 the zone may extend 200 nautical miles from a state's baselines, not from the outer frontier of its territorial sea.

4) What is the distinction between "sovereign rights" and "jurisdiction"? Are non-parties and non-signatories to the 1982 Convention required to respect exclusive economic zone claims by coastal states?

5) The exclusive economic zone encompasses all the waters over which Canada has historic claims to full sovereignty. At the U.N. Conference, Canada argued successfully for a new, more functional law of the sea, which lays less stress on sovereignty: should Canada now abandon its historic claims? How good are Canada's claims, set out above in Section B.2 on "Historic Waters in Canada" in the face of the U.N. Convention?

6) Canada waited until the 1990s to exercise its legislative authority to establish an exclusive economic zone. Canada had a patchwork of fishing zones, pollution laws that applied in the fishing zones, an Arctic waters pollution prevention zone of 100 miles, and oil and gas legislation applicable to the full extent of the continental margin. The 1996 *Oceans Act* attempted to consolidate many aspects of these various enactments, with the exception of the *Arctic Waters Pollution Prevention Act*.[50] The Act entrenches the assertion of Canada's maritime jurisdiction alongside a clear framework for ocean management.[51] What factors may have driven Canada in the mid-1990s to take the initiative to consolidate its legislation and organize the management of Canada's oceans, culminating in the passage of the *Oceans Act*?

5. Continental Shelf[52]

The Truman Proclamation
(September 28, 1945) 10 Fed. Reg. 12303

Whereas the Government of the United States of America, aware of the long range world-wide need for new sources of petroleum and other minerals, holds the view that efforts to discover and make available new supplies of these resources should be encouraged; and ...

Whereas recognized jurisdiction over these resources is required in the interest of their conservation and prudent utilization when and as development is undertaken; and

---

50   R.S.C. 1985, c. A-12.

51   See A. Chircop & H. Kindred, *et al.*, *supra* note 31.

52   See R.D. Eckert, *The Enclosure of Ocean Resources* (1979); M.L. Jewett, "The Evolution of the Legal Regime of the Continental Shelf" (1984) 22 Can. Y.B. Int'l L. 153 and (1985) 23 Can. Y.B. Int'l L. 201; T. McDorman, "The Entry into Force of the 1982 LOS Convention and the Article 76 Outer-Continental Shelf Regime" (1995) 10 Int. J. Mar. of Coast. L. 165; R. Hornby, "The Canadian Offshore Application Act: the Legislative Incorporation of Rights over the Continental Shelf" (1991) 29 Can. Y.B. Int'l L. 355; and Churchill & Lowe, *supra* note 1 at 141-58.

Whereas it is the view of the Government of the United States that the exercise of jurisdiction over the natural resources of the subsoil and sea bed of the continental shelf by the contiguous nation is reasonable and just, since the effectiveness of measures to utilize or conserve these resources would be contingent upon cooperation and protection from the shore, since the continental shelf may be regarded as an extension of the land mass of the coastal nation and thus naturally appurtenant to it, since these resources frequently form a seaward extension of a pool or deposit lying within the territory, and since self-protection compels the coastal nation to keep close watch over activities off its shores which are of the nature necessary for utilization of these resources:

Now therefore, I, Harry S. Truman, President of the United States of America, do hereby proclaim the following policy of the United States of America with respect to the natural resources of the subsoil and sea bed of the continental shelf.

Having concern for the urgency of conserving and prudently utilizing is natural resources, the Government of the United States regards the natural resources of the subsoil and sea bed of the continental shelf beneath the high seas but contiguous to the coasts of the United States as appertaining to the United States, subject to its jurisdiction and control. In cases where the continental shelf extends to the shores of another state, or is shared with an adjacent state, the boundary shall be determined by the United States and the state concerned in accordance with equitable principles. The character as high seas of the waters above the continental shelf and the right to their free and unimpeded navigation are in no way thus affected.

Geneva Convention on the Continental Shelf
(1958) 499 U.N.T.S. 311

Article 1

For the purpose of these articles, the term "continental shelf" is used as referring (a) to the seabed and subsoil of the submarine areas adjacent to the coast but outside the areas of the territorial sea, to a depth of 200 metres or, beyond that limit, to where the depth of the superjacent waters admits of the exploitation of the natural resources of the said areas; (b) to the seabed and subsoil of similar submarine areas adjacent to the coasts of islands.

United Nations Convention on the Law of the Sea
Articles 76-82
Reproduced in the Documentary Supplement

Oceans Act
S.C. 1996, c. 31

17.(1) *Continental Shelf of Canada*—The continental shelf of Canada is the seabed and subsoil of the submarine areas, including those of the exclusive economic zone of Canada, that extend beyond the territorial sea of Canada throughout the natural prolongation of the land territory of Canada

(a) subject to paragraphs (b) and (c), to the outer edge of the continental margin, determined in the manner under international law that results in the maximum extent of the continental shelf of Canada, the outer edge of the continental margin being the submerged prolongation of the land mass of Canada consisting of the seabed and subsoil of the shelf, the slope and the rise, but not including the deep ocean floor with its oceanic ridges or its subsoil;

(b) to a distance of 200 nautical miles from the baselines of the territorial sea of Canada where the outer edge of the continental margin does not extend up to that distance; or

(c) in respect of a portion of the continental shelf of Canada for which geographical coordinates of points have been prescribed pursuant to subparagraph 25(a)(iii), to lines determined from the geographical coordinates of points so prescribed.

(2) For greater certainty, paragraphs (1)(a) and (b) apply regardless of whether regulations are made pursuant to subparagraph 25(a)(iv) prescribing geographical coordinates of points from which the outer edge of the continental margin or other outer limit of the continental shelf of Canada may be determined.

18. *Sovereign rights of Canada*—Canada has sovereign rights over the continental shelf of Canada for the purpose of exploring it and exploiting the mineral and other non-living natural resources of the seabed and subsoil of the continental shelf of Canada, together with living organisms belonging to sedentary species, that is to say, organisms that, at the harvestable stage, either are immobile on or under the seabed of the continental shelf of Canada or are unable to move except in constant physical contact with the seabed or the subsoil of the continental shelf of Canada.

19.(1) *Rights of Her Majesty*—For greater certainty, any rights of Canada in the continental shelf of Canada are vested in Her Majesty in right of Canada.

(2) *Saving*—Nothing in this section abrogates or derogates from any legal right or interest held before February 4, 1991.

20.(1) *Application of federal laws—continental shelf installations*—Subject to any regulations made pursuant to paragraph 26(1)(j) or (k), federal laws apply

(a) on or under any marine installation or structure from the time it is attached or anchored to the continental shelf of Canada in connection with the exploration of that shelf or the exploitation of its mineral or other non-living resources until the marine installation or structure is removed from the waters above the continental shelf of Canada;

(b) on or under any artificial island constructed, erected or placed on the continental shelf of Canada; and

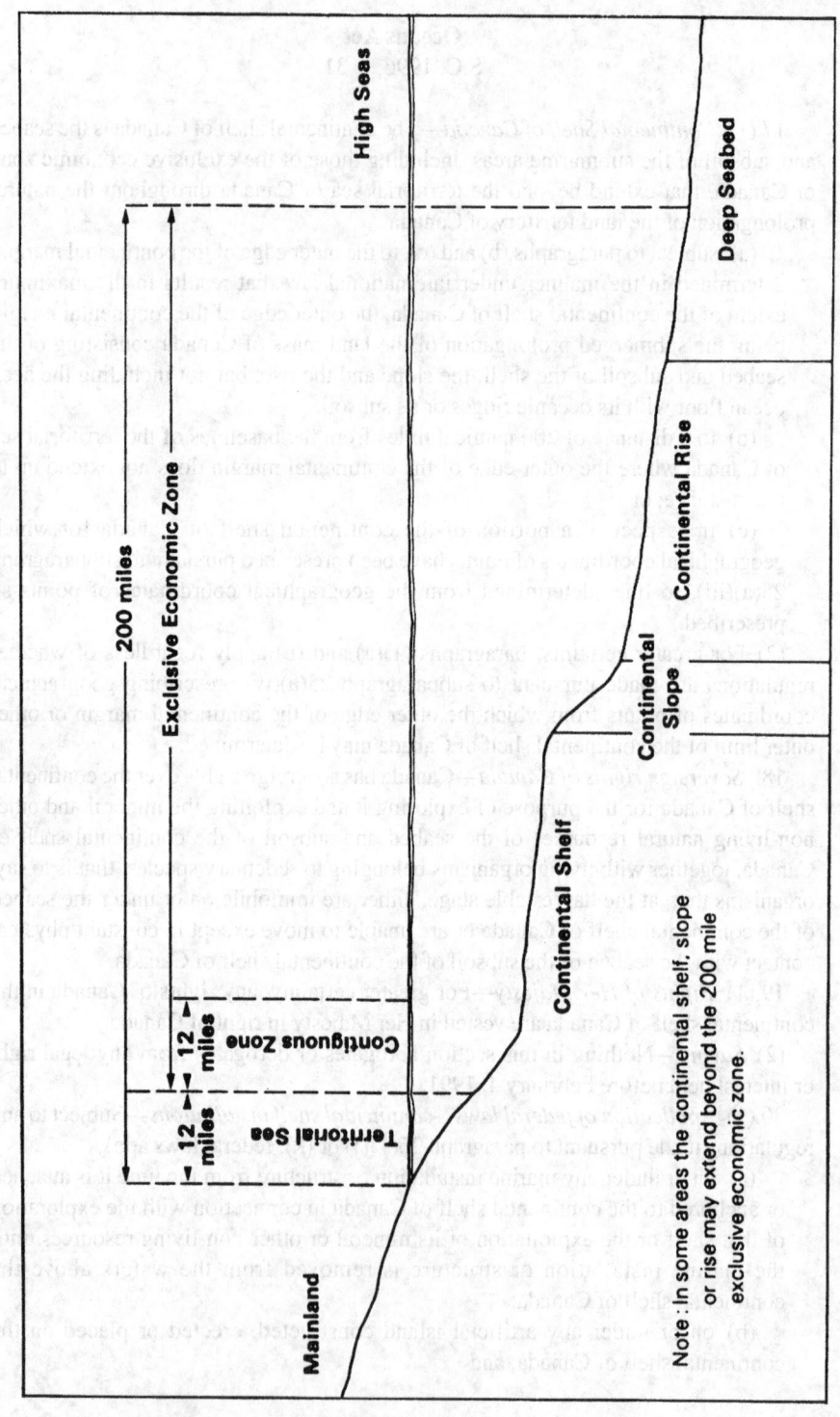

Divisions of the Continental Margin

Note : In some areas the continental shelf, slope or rise may extend beyond the 200 mile exclusive economic zone.

(c) within such safety zone surrounding any marine installation or structure or artificial island referred to in paragraph (a) or (b) as is determined by or pursuant to the regulations.

(2) *Interpretation*—For the purposes of subsection (1), federal laws shall be applied

(a) as if the places referred to in that subsection formed part of the territory of Canada;

(b) notwithstanding that by their terms their application is limited to Canada; and

(c) in a manner that is consistent with the rights and freedoms of other states under international law and, in particular, with the rights and freedoms of other states in relation to navigation and overflight.

21.(1) *Application of provincial law*—Subject to this section and to any other Act of Parliament, the laws of a province apply to the same extent as federal laws apply pursuant to section 20 in any area of the sea

(a) that forms part of the exclusive economic zone of Canada or is above the continental shelf of Canada;

(b) that is not within any province; and

(c) that is prescribed by the regulations.

(2) *Limitation*—Subject to any regulations made pursuant to paragraph 26(1)(d), subsection (1) does not apply in respect of any provision of a law of a province that

(a) imposes a tax or royalty; or

(b) relates to mineral or other non-living natural resources. ...

23.(1) *Certificate—Minister of Foreign Affairs*—In any legal or other proceedings, a certificate issued by or under the authority of the Minister of Foreign Affairs containing a statement that any geographic location specified in the certificate was, at any time material to the proceedings,

(a) in the internal waters of Canada,

(b) in the territorial sea of Canada,

(c) in the contiguous zone of Canada,

(d) in the exclusive economic zone of Canada, or

(e) in or above the continental shelf of Canada

is conclusive proof of the truth of the statement without proof of the signature or official character of the person appearing to have issued the certificate. ...

26.(1) The Governor in Council may, on the recommendation of the Minister of Justice, make regulations

(a) prescribing a work or a class of works for the purpose of the definition "marine installation or structure" in section 2;

(b) making any law of a province applicable in respect of any part of the area of the sea in which laws of the province apply under section 9 or 21, even though the law, by its own terms, is applicable only in respect of a particular area within the province; ...

(k) making federal laws or laws of a province or any of their provisions applicable, in such circumstances as are specified in the regulations,

(i) in the exclusive economic zone of Canada or in a portion of that zone,

(ii) in or above the continental shelf of Canada or a portion of that shelf, or

(iii) in any area beyond the continental shelf of Canada, where that application is made pursuant to an international agreement or arrangement entered into by Canada.

NOTES

1) Every coastal state possesses sovereign rights over the continental shelf appertaining to its coast. These rights are enjoyed by operation of the law alone, without the necessity of an explicit claim, and are exclusive to that state. In this respect the 1982 Convention has simply maintained the rules of customary law and of the 1958 Geneva Convention on the Continental Shelf. The principal defect of the 1958 Convention was the absence of fixed outer limits to the continental shelf. After laborious negotiation, the Third U.N. Conference was able to reach an agreement on a complex new definition that grants all states jurisdiction over the seabed out to 200 nautical miles, regardless of the actual extent of the *physical* continental shelf, and further defines the juridical continental shelf to be the continental margin, which allows so-called wide margin states jurisdiction over the seabed well beyond 200 nautical miles (subject to restrictions discussed below). Part of the *quid pro quo* of this entitlement is the duty of revenue sharing respecting resources beyond 200 nautical miles, as stated in article 82.

2) The *Oceans Act* is fully consistent with the rights accorded to states over the continental shelf, as set out in article 76 of the 1982 Convention. The upshot of this provision for Canada is that on the Pacific coast, Canada may control the seabed to a distance of 200 nautical miles in spite of the fact that there is only a narrow continental shelf and, on the Atlantic coast, Canadian jurisdiction extends over the continental margin far beyond 200 nautical miles.[53] In a Report prepared on Canada and article 76 of the 1982 Convention,[54] it was estimated that the aggregate additions of jurisdiction beyond the 200 nautical miles limit in the Atlantic and the Arctic would represent an area almost equal to the three Prairie provinces combined.

3) In March 1997, the states parties to the 1982 Convention established the Commission on the Limits of the Continental Shelf, which is provided for under Article 76 and Annex II of the Convention. Under Article 76(8), coastal states that claim jurisdiction over the continental shelf beyond 200 nautical miles must provide information on the outer limits of these claims to the Commission, which will make recommendations respecting the outer limits to the coastal state. The Commission was another part of the *quid pro quo* for coastal state rights extending beyond 200 miles regarding the continental shelf. A unique type of body composed of scientific and technical experts (and no lawyers), the Commission is to assist coastal states in ascertaining the outer limits of their continental shelf. The ultimate determination/location of a state's outer limit of the

---

53   A. Chircop & H. Kindred, *et al.*, *supra* note 31 at 312.

54   Geological Survey of Canada, *Canada and Article 76 of the Law of the Sea, Defining the Limits of Canadian Resource Jurisdiction Beyond 200 Nautical Miles in the Atlantic and Arctic Oceans*, R. McNab, ed. (Open File 3209, May 1994).

continental shelf is left to the state, although Article 76(8) does state that limits established on the basis of the Commission's recommendations "shall be final and binding."[55] Article 4 of Annex II requires a state that intends to establish outer limits of a continental shelf claim beyond 200 nautical miles to submit data and information regarding its proposed limits to the Commission within 10 years of the Convention entering into force for that party (although subsequent meetings of the states parties have purported to extend this time limit). What would be the legal consequences of not submitting a claim to the Commission within the limitation period?

4) Although Canada has not established the outer limits of its continental shelf in accordance with Article 76 or submitted information to the Commission, oil and gas permits have been issued for shelf areas beyond 200 nautical miles and fishers have been prosecuted for illegally harvesting sedentary species on the outer shelf. In *R. v. Perry*,[56] the accused fisher unsuccessfully raised the defence that there was a lack of certainty as to the extent of the Canadian continental shelf, as defined in section 17 of the *Oceans Act*. Reviewing section 17, how valid was the defence? The federal government chose not to use section 23(1) of the *Oceans Act*. Why might the prosecutors have decided against this course of action?

5) A coastal state has sovereign rights regarding the resources of the continental shelf including the sedentary species (for example, snow crabs) on the shelf. Article 78 indicates that while a state may claim jurisdiction over the resources of the shelf, this does not affect rights to the waters above the shelf. However, the argument can be raised that a state's rights regarding sedentary species also includes conservation and management measures. To what extent would those measures (for example, a prohibition on trawling for non-sedentary species that had an impact on sedentary species) be consistent with article 78?

6) The question of federal versus provincial jurisdiction over the mineral resources in the offshore area has been before the Supreme Court of Canada three times. In the landmark 1967 case *Reference Re: Ownership of Offshore Mineral Rights (British Columbia)*,[57] the Court decided in favour of the federal government. The essence of the case was that when British Columbia entered Confederation it did not include the adjacent offshore area; thus the area was not "in the Province" and must fall within the authority of the federal government. This case dealt only with the offshore area seaward of Vancouver Island and the Queen Charlotte Islands. Reference has been made above to the 1984 *Reference Re Ownership of the Bed of the Strait of Georgia and Related Areas*,[58] where the Supreme Court included the Strait of Juan de Fuca, the Strait of Georgia, Johnstone Strait, and the Queen Charlotte Strait as having been part of British Columbia in 1871.

How confident should one be that the reasoning of the Court in the *B.C. Offshore Reference* would extend to the determination of federal–provincial jurisdiction in offshore areas of the other provinces and territories that entered Confederation? What about other

---

55   See T.L. McDorman, "The Role of the Commission on the Limits of the Continental Shelf: A Technical Body in a Political World" (2002) 17 Int'l J. of Marine and Coastal L. 301.

56   (2003), 222 Nfld. & P.E.I.R. 313.

57   [1967] S.C.R. 792.

58   [1984] 1 S.C.R. 388.

areas on the west coast, including Hecate Strait between the mainland and the Queen Charlotte Islands and Queen Charlotte Sound between Vancouver Island and the Queen Charlotte Islands?

7) Also in 1984, the Supreme Court addressed the continental shelf adjacent to Newfoundland. The Newfoundland government argued that when it joined Canada in 1949, the province included the adjacent continental shelf. The argument was based on the assertion that a coastal state's right to sovereign rights over the continental shelf had become part of customary international law by 1949 and Newfoundland was an independent state, however briefly, prior to its entry into Canada. The Supreme Court concluded:

(1) Continental shelf rights are, in pith and substance, an extra-territorial manifestation of external sovereignty.

(2) Canada has the right to explore and exploit in the continental shelf off Newfoundland because:

   (a) any continental shelf rights available in international law in 1949 would have been acquired by the Crown in right of the United Kingdom, not the Crown in right of Newfoundland;

   (b) even if Newfoundland could have held continental shelf rights prior to Union, they would have passed to Canada by virtue of the Terms of Union;

   (c) in any event, international law did not recognize continental shelf rights by 1949; such rights were not indisputably recognized before the Geneva Convention of 1958.

(3) Canada has legislative jurisdiction in relation to the right to explore and exploit in the continental shelf off Newfoundland by virtue of the peace, order, and good government power in its residual capacity.[59]

Irrespective of the outcome in the above case, the federal government and Newfoundland reached agreement regarding a "sharing" of the management and revenues from offshore Newfoundland hydrocarbon development.[60]

8) In the light of federal–provincial arrangements that exist for offshore oil and gas on the east coast, as between the federal and provincial governments, who would be obligated to contribute the funds necessary to meet the revenue-sharing obligation in Article 82?

9) It is noteworthy that the application of provincial laws in the exclusive economic zone under section 21 of the *Oceans Act* is limited by section 20, which specifies the application of federal laws on continental shelf installations. It seems, therefore, that the application of provincial laws relating to the EEZ may only extend to activities associated

59   [1984] 1 S.C.R. 86 at 128-29. See also *Re Mineral and Other Natural Resources of the Continental Shelf* (1983), 145 D.L.R. (3d) 9 (Nfld. C.A.).

60   *Canada-Newfoundland Atlantic Accord Implementation Act*, S.C. 1987, c. 3 and its complementary Newfoundland & Labrador legislation, S.N. 1986, c. 37, now R.S.N. (1990) c. C-2. Nova Scotia has a similar arrangement; see *Canada-Nova Scotia Offshore Petroleum Resources Accord Implementation Act*, S.C. 1988, c. 28 and the complementary Nova Scotia Act, S.N.S. 1987, c. 3, as amended.

with the continental shelf where they take place within the waters of the province. Does the ministerial power under section 26 resolve this issue?

10) Does the *Oceans Act* properly resolve the problems posed by the need to apply provincial laws in the offshore areas? Are all the constitutional problems resolved? For instance, is it appropriate to incorporate, as federal law, provincial laws that are only adopted in English? How would you go about enforcing a security interest in equipment on board an oil rig on the Canadian continental shelf that is registered in a foreign country?

6. High Seas[61]

United Nations Convention on the Law of the Sea
Articles 86-111
Reproduced in the Documentary Supplement

NOTES

1) The relevant articles of the 1982 Convention on the Law of the Sea are a codification of customary international law and are virtually identical to those of the 1958 Geneva Convention on the High Seas. They represent the central core of the international law of the sea, including such fundamental concepts as freedom of navigation, flag-state jurisdiction, and the prohibition of piracy. One change to be noted is that allowing hot pursuit to begin in the exclusive economic zone.

2) As these articles spell out, the authority of the flag state over its ships on the high seas involves both rights and duties of states. By virtue of the Convention and customary international law, the flag state exercises nearly exclusive jurisdiction over persons and cargo as well as the design, crewing, maintenance, and navigation of the vessel. The nationality and flag of a vessel are governed by articles 90 to 94.[62] In principle, the nationality of a ship depends on the flag it flies. However, article 91 of the 1982 Convention stipulates that a "genuine link" must exist between the state and the ship flying its flag. It is not clear, however, what precisely constitutes a "genuine link." Despite the existence of the "genuine link" criterion, attempts to restrict or regulate the vessel registration practices of states have not been successful.[63] This was confirmed in the 1999 *M/V Saiga (No. 2) Case (Saint Vincent and the Grenadines v. Guinea)*[64] before the International Tribunal for the Law of the Sea (ITLOS):

---

61   See I. Brownlie, *supra* note 1 at c. 11; D.P. O'Connell, *supra* note 1 at c. 21; and Churchill & Lowe, *supra* note 1 at 203-22.

62   See Churchill & Lowe, *supra* note 1 at 208-20. And see the discussion of the nationality of ships in Chapter 8, Section C on "Ships."

63   The 1986 *United Nations Convention on Conditions for Registration of Ships* (1986) 7 United Nations Law of the Sea Bulletin 87, has not entered into force.

64   (1999) 38 I.L.M. 1323. The International Tribunal for the Law of the Sea (ITLOS) has a website on which its decisions are located: <www.itlos.org>. ITLOS is discussed below in Section F on "Dispute Settlement in the Law of the Sea."

63. Article 91 leaves to each State exclusive jurisdiction over the granting of its nationality to ships. In this respect, article 91 codifies a well-established rule of general international law. Under this article, it is for Saint Vincent and the Grenadines to fix the conditions for the grant of its nationality to ships, for the registration of ships in its territory and for the right to fly its flag. These matters are regulated by a State in its domestic law. Pursuant to article 91, paragraph 2, Saint Vincent and the Grenadines is under an obligation to issue to ships to which it has granted the right to fly its flag documents to that effect. The issue of such documents is regulated by domestic law.

64. International law recognizes several modalities for the grant of nationality to different types of ships. In the case of merchant ships, the normal procedure used by States to grant nationality is registration in accordance with domestic legislation adopted for that purpose. This procedure is adopted by Saint Vincent and the Grenadines in the *Merchant Shipping Act*.

65. Determination of the criteria and establishment of the procedures for granting and withdrawing nationality to ships are matters within the exclusive jurisdiction of the flag State. ...

66. The Tribunal considers that the nationality of a ship is a question of fact to be determined, like other facts in dispute before it, on the basis of evidence adduced by the parties.

67. Saint Vincent and the Grenadines has produced evidence before the Tribunal to support its assertion that the *Saiga* was a ship entitled to fly its flag at the time of the incident giving rise to the dispute. In addition to making references to the relevant provisions of the *Merchant Shipping Act*, Saint Vincent and the Grenadines has drawn attention to several indications of Vincentian nationality on the ship or carried on board. These include the inscription of "Kingstown" as the port of registry on the stern of the vessel, the documents on board and the ship's seal which contained the words "SAIGA Kingstown" and the then current charter-party which recorded the flag of the vessel as "Saint Vincent and the Grenadines."

68. The evidence adduced by Saint Vincent and the Grenadines has been reinforced by its conduct. Saint Vincent and the Grenadines has at all times material to the dispute operated on the basis that the *Saiga* was a ship of its nationality. It has acted as the flag State of the ship during all phases of the proceedings. It was in that capacity that it invoked the jurisdiction of the Tribunal in its Application for the prompt release of the *Saiga* and its crew under article 292 of the Convention and in its Request for the prescription of provisional measures under article 290 of the Convention.

In the 2001 *Grand Prince Case (Belize v. France)*,[65] again before ITLOS, the Tribunal took the view that the evidence put forward by Belize failed to establish that Belize was the flag state. Interestingly, there had not been significant argument in the case about the validity of the flag and the Tribunal appears to have acted largely on its own. Is there such a thing as a vessel without a flag (a stateless vessel) and, if so, what international law rules might apply to such a vessel?

3) It is the notion of the "flag of convenience" vessel that has made the genuine link requirement of interest. In loose terms, a flag of convenience vessel is a vessel that is flying a flag to which the vessel has little direct relationship—that is, the ownership may be elsewhere; the crew may be from elsewhere; and the registering state, other than

---

65   Available on the ITLOS website, *supra* note 64.

collecting fees, has little relationship with the vessel. In the shipping world, flags of convenience are used to minimize taxes and crewing costs and to avoid unionization and equipment requirements. For many, flags of convenience are seen as a subterfuge used by vessel owners to avoid labour and equipment standards. The impression, generally false, is that flag-of-convenience vessels are substandard vessels and environmental disasters waiting to occur. Flags of convenience do, however, allow shipowners to avoid certain obligations, because in most cases treaties are only binding on states that become parties. The vessel owner can reflag a vessel in a state that is not a party to a particular treaty and thus avoid the application of the treaty. This scenario has become a particular problem regarding fishing vessels, and the flag-of-convenience phenomenon is seen as minimizing the effective enforcement of national laws, allowing vessel owners and states to avoid responsibility, particularly with respect to high seas fisheries.

4) The exclusivity of flag-state jurisdiction on the high seas is restricted with respect to ships engaged in piracy and slavery. Moreover, the exclusivity is restricted by the law of armed conflict, and may be further restricted by U.N. Security Council Resolutions. Finally, whether by agreement[66] or in response to a specific request, a flag state may consent to restrict its exclusivity. The Canadian Navy's interdiction operations (boarding and inspecting vessels) in the Arabian Gulf in the 1990s and 2000s were justified as being pursuant to a U.N. Security Council Resolution. The exclusivity of flag-state jurisdiction on the high seas, and in many situations within the EEZ,[67] has become a prominent issue in recent years in the light of terrorism concerns. In December 2002, Spanish naval forces boarded a Cambodian flag vessel (it was reportedly a North Korean vessel but it was later determined to be registered in Cambodia) approximately 600 miles off the coast of Oman. The vessel was carrying Scud missiles from North Korea to Yemen. It was released and allowed to take its cargo to Yemen. Was the boarding legal? Does international law prohibit the trade or carrying on board vessels of Scud missiles, and, if so, would this matter? While in this case the captain of the vessel did not consent to the boarding, would the consent of the captain be sufficient to make the boarding legal? If the Cambodian vessel were traversing Canada's EEZ, would the Canadian Navy have any international legal justification to board the vessel? If the Cambodian vessel were a fishing vessel, and still carrying Scud missiles, could Canada board and inspect the vessel?

5) The exclusivity of flag-state jurisdiction as regards fishing vessels on the high seas was directly at issue when Canada seized and arrested the Spanish vessel the *Estai* in March 1995 outside Canada's 200 nautical mile zone. This incident is dealt with below in Section E.1 on "East Coast Fisheries and the Estai."

6) What are the potential conflicts between the flag state's right of freedom of navigation and the coastal state's rights in its exclusive economic zone?

---

66 Read carefully the 1988 U.N. *Convention Against Illicit Traffic in Narcotic Drugs and Psychotropic Substances*, Can. T.S. 1990 No. 42 and the 2000 *Protocol Against the Smuggling of Migrants by Land, Sea, and Air, Supplementing the UN Convention Against Transnational Organized Crime*, GA Res. 55/25, annex III, UN GAOR, 55th Sess., Supp. No. 49 U.N. Doc. A/55/49 (2000) at 65, not yet in force.

67 Recall that the EEZ is a *sui generis* zone within which both high seas rights and coastal state rights coexist.

7) Although pirates were driven from the shores of North America and Europe long ago, they are still a commonplace hazard to shipping around the coasts of West Africa, Indonesia, and some other parts of Asia. Piracy[68] is the classic example of an offence of universal jurisdiction—that is, every state may arrest and prosecute pirates apprehended on the high seas, regardless of their nationality. Piracy *jure gentium* is strictly defined in the Convention but individual states, who are of necessity the enforcers of the law against pirates, are not inhibited by this definition from prescribing the crime and its penalties in different terms in their national legislation. In Canada, for instance, section 75 of the *Criminal Code* makes it an offence, punishable by imprisonment for life, to do "any act that, by the law of nations, is piracy." Section 76 adds an offence, carrying 14 years' incarceration, relating to "piratical acts," which include stealing a Canadian ship or its cargo, causing a mutiny, or counselling others to mutiny. However, to the extent that national proscriptions of piracy exceed international law, jurisdiction to enforce them cannot be based on the universality principle. More recently, international jurisdiction has been extended by agreement in an effort to suppress terrorist attacks on ships that do not qualify as acts of piracy.[69]

8) The right of hot pursuit[70] of fugitive ships is respected yet precisely regulated in the Convention. When paragraphs 1, 2, and 4 of article 111 are read together, it is clear that hot pursuit may only begin if the escaping ship has failed to stop after it has been given a visual or auditory signal, which it could reasonably have received, while it was in a marine zone of the coastal state. A strict reading of article 111 indicates that a radio signal is not sufficient to found the right of pursuit, even though nowadays the offending vessel is likely to carry radar equipment by which it may identify its pursuers and head for the high seas long before they can come within sight or hailing distance. It is also clear that a foreign ship may only be pursued for a violation of the laws applicable in the particular marine zone in which it was signalled to stop. These rules, though detailed, are still not a complete code but are supplemented by customary international law, as the following case demonstrates.

---

68   See B.H. Dubner, *The Law of International Sea Piracy* (1980); B.H. Dubner, "Human Rights and Environmental Disaster—Two Problems That Defy the Norms of the International Law of Sea Piracy" (1997) 23 Syr. J. Int'l L. & Com. 1; J. Noyes, "An Introduction to the International Law of Piracy" (Essays on Piracy: Symposium on Piracy in Contemporary National and International Law) (1990) 21 Cal. W. Int'l L.J. 105; and S. Pyeatt Menefee, "The New Jamaica Discipline: Problems with Piracy, Maritime Terrorism and the 1982 Convention on the Law of the Sea" (1990) 6 Conn. J. Int'l L. 127.

69   See the *Convention for the Suppression of Unlawful Acts Against the Safety of Maritime Navigation*, Can. T.S. 1993 No. 9; (1988) 27 I.L.M. 672 and *Protocol for the Suppression of Unlawful Acts Against the Safety of Fixed Platforms Located on the Continental Shelf*, Can. T.S. 1993 No. 10; (1988) 27 I.L.M. 685. See also the discussion under "Suppression of Terrorism" in Chapter 9, Section A.2.

70   See generally, N.M. Poulantzas, *The Right of Hot Pursuit in International Law* (2002) and R.C. Reuland, "The Customary Right of Hot Pursuit onto the High Seas: Annotations to Art. 111 of the Law of the Sea Convention" (1993) 33 Virg. J. Int. L. 557. The first case of the new International Tribunal for the Law of the Sea involved hot pursuit and the interpretation of art. 111: see the *M/V Saiga* available on the ITLOS website, *supra* note 64.

The I'm Alone[71]
Canada v. United States
(1935) 29 A.J.I.L. 327

[On March 22, 1929, the *I'm Alone*, a rum-runner of Canadian registry, was sunk on the high seas some 200 miles from the coast by the U.S. Revenue cutter, the *Dexter*, after a lengthy pursuit. According to the U.S. government, pursuit began $10\frac{1}{2}$ miles from the coast, within the 12-mile customs zone. The Canadian government contended that it began $14\frac{1}{2}$ miles from the coast. In any event, the pursuit began outside the 3-mile territorial sea. The *I'm Alone* was originally sighted and followed by the *Wolcott*, also a U.S. revenue vessel.

On these facts the Arbitral Commissioners held that there was a right of hot pursuit and that pursuit had been continuous. However, the Commissioners also held that the intentional sinking of a foreign registered vessel violated both the treaty in force between the United States and Canada (U.K.) and customary international law.]

THE COMMISSIONERS (Willis van Devanter and Lyman P. Duff): ... Only questions numbered One and Three and the answers given thereto are now material. These are stated in the interim report as follows:

The question numbered one is in the following terms:

The first question is whether the Commissioners may inquire into the beneficial or ultimate ownership of the *I'm Alone* or of the shares of the corporation that owned the ship. If the Commissioners are authorized to make this inquiry, a further question arises as to the effect of indirect ownership and control by citizens of the United States upon the Claim; viz., whether it would be an answer to the Claim under the Convention, or whether it would go to mitigation of damages, or whether it would merely be a circumstance that should actuate the claimant Government in refraining from pressing the claim, in whole or in part.

The answer given to this question is as follows:

The Commissioners think they may inquire into the beneficial or ultimate ownership of the *I'm Alone* and of the shares of the corporation owning the ship; as well as into the management and control of the ship and the venture in which it was engaged; and that this may be done as a basis for considering the recommendations which they shall make. But the Commissioners reserve for further consideration the extent to which, if at all, the facts of such ownership, management and control may affect particular branches or phases of the claim presented.

---

71 See W.C. Dennis, "The Sinking of the I'm Alone" (1929) 23 A.J.I.L. 351; G.G. Fitzmaurice, "The Case of the I'm Alone" (1936) 17 Brit. Y.B. Int'l L. 82; and N.A.M. MacKenzie, "Comment" (1929)7 Can. Bar Rev. 407.

The question numbered three is in the following terms:

The third question is based upon the assumption that the United States Government had the right of hot pursuit in the circumstances and was entitled to exercise the rights under Article 2 of the Convention at the time when the *Dexter* joined the *Wolcott* in the pursuit of the *I'm Alone*. It is also based upon the assumption that the averments set forth in paragraph eight of the Answer are true. The question is whether in the circumstances, the Government of the United States was legally justified in sinking the *I'm Alone*.

The answer given to this question is as follows:

On the assumptions stated in the question, the United States might, consistently with the Convention, use necessary and reasonable force for the purpose of affecting the objects of boarding, searching, seizing and bringing into port the suspected vessel; and if sinking should occur incidentally, as a result of the exercise of necessary and reasonable force for such purpose, the pursuing vessel might be entirely blameless. But the Commissioners think that, … the admittedly intentional sinking of the suspected vessel was not justified by anything in the Convention.

The preliminary questions having been answered, the Commissioners made the following recommendations as to the future conduct of the case:

First: that the agents be instructed by their respective Governments to prepare and submit to the Commissioners separate statements setting forth in detail the contentions of their respective Governments as to the ultimate beneficial interests in the vessel and in the cargo, together with specifications of the documents and witnesses relied upon to substantiate their respective contentions:

Second: that the agents be similarly instructed to submit to the Commissioners either a joint statement or separate statements (in either case specifically itemized) of the sums which should be payable by the United States in case the Commissioners finally determine that compensation is payable by that Government.

Statements were submitted to the Commissioners pursuant to these recommendations; and, on December 28, 1934, the Commissioners convened for the purpose of hearing further evidence and oral argument touching the matters in dispute; and the hearing was concluded on January 3, 1935. The Commissioners now present their joint final report.

It will be recalled that the *I'm Alone* was sunk on the 22nd day of March, 1929, on the high seas, in the Gulf of Mexico, by the United States revenue cutter *Dexter*. By their interim report the Commissioners found that the sinking of the vessel was not justified by anything in the Convention. The Commissioners now add that it could not be justified by any principle of international law.

The vessel was a British ship of Canadian registry; after her construction she was employed for several years in rum running, the cargo being destined for illegal introduction into, and sale in the United States. In December, 1928, and during the early months of 1929, down to the sinking of the vessel on the 22nd day of March, of that year, she was engaged in carrying liquor from Belize, in British Honduras, to an agreed point or points in the Gulf of Mexico, in convenient proximity to the coast of

Louisiana, where the liquor was taken from her in smaller craft, smuggled into the United States, and sold there.

We find as a fact that, from September, 1928, down to the date when she was sunk, the *I'm Alone*, although a British ship of Canadian registry, was *de facto* owned, controlled, and at the critical times, managed, and her movements directed and her cargo dealt with and disposed of, by a group of persons acting in concert who were entirely, or nearly so, citizens of the United States, and who employed her for the purposes mentioned. The possibility that one of the group may not have been of United States nationality we regard as of no importance in the circumstances of this case.

The Commissioners consider that, in view of the facts, no compensation ought to be paid in respect of the loss of the ship or the cargo.

The act of sinking the ship, however, by officers of the United States Coast Guard, was, as we have already indicated, an unlawful act; and the Commissioners consider that the United States ought formally to acknowledge its illegality, and to apologize to His Majesty's Canadian Government therefor; and, further, that as a material amend in respect of the wrong the United States should pay the sum of $25,000 to His Majesty's Canadian Government; and they recommend accordingly.

The Commissioners have had under consideration the compensation which ought to be paid by the United States to His Majesty's Canadian Government for the benefit of the captain and members of the crew, none of whom was a party to the illegal conspiracy to smuggle liquor into the United States and sell the same there. The Commissioners recommend that compensation be paid as follows:

For the captain, John Thomas Randell, the sum of $7,906.00

For John Williams, deceased, to be paid to his proper representatives, $1,250.50

For Jens Jansen, $1,098.00

For James Barrett, $1,032.00

For William Wordsworth, deceased, to be paid to his proper representatives, $907.00

For Eddie Young, $999.50

For Chesley Hobbs, $1,323.50

For Edward Fouchard, $965.00

For Amanda Mainguy, as compensation in respect of the death of Leon Mainguy, for the benefit of herself and the children of Leon Mainguy (Henriette Mainguy, Jeanne Mainguy and John Mainguy), the sum of $10,185.00.

NOTES

1) What principles of customary international law are applied in this early case that are not reflected in the rules on hot pursuit contained in the 1982 U.N. Convention? Do they still operate?

2) Notice the discrete awards of compensation payable by the United States for its illegal act. Why did the Government of Canada recover $25,000? Although individually evaluated awards were made to Canada for each of the crew members, why was no award made for the loss of the Canadian flag ship?

3) Since no statute implements the rules on hot pursuit in Canada,[72] Canadian courts have applied the right as a matter of customary international law. In doing so they have allowed a liberal right of pursuit, which at times is difficult to regard as compatible with international law. For instance, in the case of *R. v. Sunila and Soleyman*,[73] the arrested foreign ship had been followed continuously by a Canadian destroyer after its rendezvous with a shore boat inside the territorial sea (to transfer an illicit cargo of drugs). The vessel was, however, many miles onto the high seas before it was ever ordered to heave to. Though the Court was well aware of the rules in the 1958 Geneva Convention, which in this respect are repeated verbatim in the 1982 U.N. Convention, and even regarded them, rightly, as a codification of customary laws, it held that to expect the pursuing destroyer to have signalled the fleeing ship before coming within range to prevent its escape would have been unreasonable and that the arrest was properly conducted.[74] The court also made a generous interpretation of the combination of vessels used by the drug smugglers when it declared, without discussion, that the foreign ship was a mother ship of the Canadian shore boat, even though they and their crews had different nationalities and shared no personal connections.[75]

C. DEEP SEABED[76]

Until recent decades the status of the seabed beyond national jurisdiction was only a problem of theoretical interest. One could maintain that it constituted *res nullius* or *res communis*,[77] and there appeared to be little doubt that the freedoms of the high seas included the freedom to take living and non-living resources from the seabed, insofar as this was a practical possibility. By the late 1960s, interest was focused upon the extraction of magnesium, lead, zinc, nickel, and copper from the polymetallic nodules to be found on many parts of the ocean floor. Experiments began and feasibility studies were done on possible industrial exploitation. Several large international consortia were formed to

---

72   However, arrest in order to enforce a federal law by exercising the right of hot pursuit is recognized by the recently amended provisions of the *Criminal Code*, s. 477.3(1) (b), adopted in S.C. 1990, c. 44, s. 15, as am. S.C. 1996, c. 31, s. 70.

73   (1986), 71 N.S.R. (2d) 300 (S.C. A.D.), purportedly applying *The Ship North v. The King* (1906), 37 S.C.R. 385. See also *Fudge v. The King*, [1940] Ex. C.R. 187.

74   Cf. *Gillam v. U.S.*, 27 F.2d 296 (4th Cir. 1928).

75   See *The Henry L. Marshall*, 286 F. 260 (S.D. N.Y. 1922). Cf. *The Tenyu Maru*, 4 Alaska R. 136 (1910) and *The Marjorie E. Bachman*, 4 F.2d 405 (D. Mass. 1925).

76   See M. Nordquist & J. Norton Moore, eds., *Entry into Force of the Law of the Sea Convention* (1995); T. Treves, "Deep Sea-Bed Mining: The Practice of Pioneer Investors," in R. Wolfrum, ed., *Law of the Sea at the Crossroads: The Continuing Search for a Universally Applicable Regime* (1991) at 331-49 ; Y. Li, *Transfer of Technology for Deep Sea-Bed Mining: The 1982 Law of the Sea Convention and Beyond* (1994); D. Anderson, "Efforts to Ensure Universal Participation in the United Nations Convention on the Law of the Sea" (1993) 42 I.C.L.Q. 654; and D. Anderson, "Further Efforts to Ensure Universal Participation in the United Nations Convention on the Law of the Sea" (1994) 43 I.C.L.Q. 886; see also the website of the International Seabed Authority, available online: <www.isa.org.jm/>.

77   See Section A, "Introduction," in Chapter 7 for an explanation of these terms.

investigate the prospects. To date, technical and economic factors have inhibited exploitation, and commercial development does not seem likely in the foreseeable future.

However, as a result of fears of extended national continental shelf claims and suggestions that revenue could be generated from these resources to assist the Third World, intense interest was focused on the Third U.N. Conference on the Law of the Sea, which began in December 1973. By then, U.N. resolutions had already been adopted declaring these resources to be the common heritage of mankind. In addition, in 1969, U.N. General Assembly resolution 2574(XXIV) called for a moratorium on activities in the deep seabed until an international regime could be established to govern those activities.

Moratorium Resolution
G.A. Res. 2574 (XXIV), U.N. GAOR, 24th Sess., Supp. No. 30 at 11 (1969)

The General Assembly ...
Declares that, pending the establishment of the aforementioned international regime:

(a) States and persons, physical or juridical, are bound to refrain from all activities of exploitation of the resources of the area of the sea-bed and ocean floor, and the subsoil thereof, beyond the limits of national jurisdiction;

(b) No claim to any part of that area or its resources shall be recognized.

Seabed Declaration
Declaration of principles governing the sea-bed and the ocean floor, and subsoil thereof, beyond the limits of national jurisdiction
G.A. Res. 2749 (XXV), U.N. GAOR, 25th Sess., Supp. No. 28 at 4;
U.N. Doc. A/8028 (1970)

The General Assembly solemnly declares that: ...

1. The seabed and ocean floor, and the subsoil thereof, beyond the limits of national jurisdictions (hereinafter referred to as the area), as well as the resources of the area, are the common heritage of mankind.

2. The area shall not be subject to appropriation by any means by States or persons, natural or juridical, and no State shall claim or exercise sovereignty or sovereign rights over any part thereof.

3. No State or person, natural or juridical, shall claim, exercise or acquire rights with respect to the area or its resources incompatible with the international regime to be established and the principles of this Declaration.

4. All activities regarding the exploration and exploitation of the resources of the area and other related activities shall be governed by the international regime to be established ...

7. The exploration of the area and the exploitation of its resources shall be carried out for the benefit of mankind as a whole. ...

14. Every State shall have the responsibility to ensure that activities in the area, including those relating to its resources, whether undertaken by governmental

agencies, or non-governmental entities or persons under its jurisdiction, or acting on its behalf, shall be carried out in conformity with the international regime to be established. The same responsibility applies to international organizations and their members for activities undertaken by such organizations or on their behalf. Damage caused by such activities shall entail liability.

NOTES

1) The 1970 Seabed Declaration was adopted without a dissenting vote. The resolution calling for a moratorium was adopted in 1969 with a large measure of support (62 votes), but a number of states interested in seabed mining voted against (28) or abstained (28).

2) There has been wide acceptance of the idea that the resources of the seabed are "the common heritage of mankind" in the sense that they are not subject to the sovereignty or sovereign rights of any state or person. From this perspective, the problem for the U.N. Law of the Sea Conference was to negotiate an agreement for the exploitation of seabed minerals that was consistent with this idea and satisfied all countries.[78] Developed and developing countries were deeply divided on this issue.

Eventually the international regime referred to in article 3 of the Seabed Declaration was created on paper by Part XI of the U.N. Convention on the Law of the Sea. Unfortunately, the United States objected to a number of provisions, refused to sign the Convention, and furthermore succeeded in establishing an alternative regime of mutual recognition of claims with some of the potential producers among developed States.

3) What does it mean to say the seabed and its resources are "the common heritage of mankind"? Compare the principles of the Seabed Declaration with the use of a similar phrase in the Moon Treaty, reproduced in Chapter 7, Section D.2 on "Outer Space." How are the benefits of the common heritage to be acquired and distributed?

4) In 1980, the U.S. Congress passed the *Deep Seabed Hard Mineral Resources Act*.[79] This legislation was designed to provide suitable domestic authorization and international protection for U.S. corporations wishing to engage in deepsea mining. At the time, Congress stated that exploration and commercial exploitation of the mineral resources of the deep seabed are freedoms of the high seas, which are restrained only to the extent of reasonable regard for the exercise by other states of these or other freedoms recognized at international law. Therefore, Congress established an interim legal regime for deepsea mining "until such time as a Law of the Sea Treaty enters into force with respect to the United States." In creating this interim regime, the United States limited the exercise of its authority to persons and vessels engaged in deepsea mining who are subject to its jurisdiction, and did not assert sovereignty or exclusive rights to the seabed or its resources as such.

---

78   See R.C. Ogley, *Internationalizing the Seabed* (1984) at 194.

79   30 U.S.C., §§1401-3, §§1411-28, §§1441-44, and §§1461-71 (1980), reprinted in (1980) 19 I.L.M. 1003.

United Nations Convention on the Law of the Sea
Articles 1, 136-141, 150-153
Reproduced in the Documentary Supplement

NOTES

1) Articles 156-191 of the 1982 Convention establish the body known as the International Seabed Authority to administer Part XI of the Convention. The Authority came into existence on November 16, 1994, upon entry into force of the 1982 Convention. The Authority became fully operational as an autonomous international organization in June 1996, when it established its headquarters in Kingston, Jamaica. The function of the Authority is to control all resource-related conduct in the international seabed area by states and other entities, including international consortia and private national companies.

2) All states parties to the 1982 Convention are automatically equal members of the Authority. The governing bodies of the Authority consist of the Assembly, which is made up of all members of the Authority, and the Council, consisting of 36 members elected for a term of 4 years. The members of the Council are chosen in a carefully structured process so as to fairly reflect the diversity of states' interests. Group A of the Council is composed of four states from among the largest consumers of net importers of minerals to be derived from seabed mining, Group B of four states from those with the largest investment in seabed mining, Group C of four states that are major land-based net exporters of minerals found on the deep seabed, Group D of six developing states representing special interests, and Group E of 18 states reflecting geographical distribution and balance between developed and developing states.

The subsidiary organs of the Authority include the Legal and Technical Commission, composed of 22 members elected by the Assembly for a period of 5 years, and the Finance Committee, composed of 15 members, also elected by the same means and for the same term.[80] The Assembly is the general policy organ and decides matters of substance by two-thirds majority vote. The Enterprise functions as the operative arm of the Authority for the exploration and exploitation of the resources of the Area. Finally, the Authority as a whole is an international legal person with responsibilities, privileges, and immunities for itself, its staff and the representatives of its member states comparable to any other intergovernmental organization.

3) As was noted above, the problem for the U.N. Law of the Sea Conference was to negotiate an agreement for the exploitation of seabed minerals that was consistent with the principle of the common heritage of mankind and satisfied all countries. Generally speaking, developing countries wanted to see the area wholly controlled by the Seabed Authority and its resources extracted by the Enterprise. Developed states desired a system of national or private corporate undertakings that, at most, would be licensed and regulated by the international Authority. The compromise that was finally arranged in 1982 is substantially set out in articles 150, 152, and 153, although further negotiations regarding their implementation took place until 1994 (discussed later). The text of Part XI provides that distribution of rights of access to the seabed will be made by the Authority

---

80   See online: International Seabed Authority <http://www.isa.org.jm/en/default.htm>.

according to the principles and policies contained in articles 150 and 152. What guiding economic and social policies do they express? Do they provide a consistent set of principles that will support the rational management of seabed resources?

4) During the Conference on the Law of the Sea, a special regime was established for pioneer investors, mostly from developed states, in certain areas of the international seabed. The regime included three categories of pioneer investors: (1) the four states that would have invested at least $30 million toward the preparation for deep seabed mining by January 1, 1983, 10 percent of which was earmarked already for the development of a certain mining site; (2) four private consortia, two of which include Canadian mining companies; and (3) developing countries that had registered by January 1, 1985.[81]

Canada concurred because the arrangements appeared to be the best means of protecting the interests of the Canadian members of the international mining consortia. While these negotiations took place, the pioneer investors, including Canada, signed the Agreement on the Resolution of Practical Problems with respect to Deep Sea Mining Areas in 1987[82] to ensure in the meantime that there existed no overlapping of deep seabed mining claims among them.

The Preparatory Commission Negotiations 1983–1994

The principal hindrance to the adoption of the 1982 Convention remained the objections of the United States and other developed states that the regime, as it stood, was based on economic organizational principles that would have interfered with market forces and would have impinged upon private investment.[83] Moreover, a requirement existed that commercial enterprises transfer their particular mining technology to the Enterprise, the operative arm of the Authority, or to developing countries to enable the latter to engage in the same activities as the developed states. In addition, the United States objected strongly to the proposed limitations of production by the Enterprise so that land-based producers would be protected from a reduction in the price on world markets of minerals produced from the seabed. Finally, the United States had reservations in terms of the proposed institutional organization of the Authority because it appeared clear that the large number of participants from developing countries would mean that developing states would dominate the Authority and that the United States might be bound without its consent by amendments to the Convention unless it could be guaranteed a seat on the Council of the Authority.[84]

Negotiations to ensure that these obstacles posed by Part XI of the 1982 Convention could be overcome began in earnest in 1990, upon the personal commitment of the U.N. Secretary-General to reach agreement between the developing and the developed states.

---

81   See *U.N. Law of the Sea Bulletin, Special Issue III: Registration of Pioneer Investors* (September 1991). See also M. Hayashi, "Registration of the First Group of Pioneer Investors by the Preparatory Commission for the International Sea-Bed Authority and for the International Tribunal for the Law of the Sea" (1989) 20 Ocean Dev. & Int'l L. 1.

82   (1987) 26 I.L.M. 1505.

83   W.S. Scholz, "Observations on the Draft Agreement Reforming Deep Seabed Mining," in Nordquist & Moore, *supra* note 76 at 69-71.

84   *Ibid.*

The process of negotiation gained even greater momentum after the election of the Clinton administration in the United States, when the industrialized countries were more able to demonstrate their readiness to negotiate seriously.[85]

The most significant compromise reached in the negotiations, which lasted until 1994, involved the nature of the Enterprise. On the one hand, developed states aimed ideally at an Enterprise that would work by way of joint ventures with private sector consortia but not before mining the deep seabed had become an economic and practical reality. On the other hand, developing states attached great importance to the creation of an effective Enterprise that would be directly involved in the realization of the notion of the deep seabed as the common heritage of mankind. According to the compromise, the Secretariat of the Authority is to perform the functions of the Enterprise until the Council has decided upon the details of how the Enterprise may function independently. Further, the system of joint ventures was recognized and emphasis on this system is evidenced in the Annexes to the Agreement.[86]

Overall, it appears that states were able to reach a consensus and to conclude more fruitful negotiations than in the period 1983-1990 by virtue of a change in political and economic views that occurred during that decade, such as a growing reliance on market principles and market-oriented approaches to economic alliances.[87]

Article 7 of the Agreement relating to the Implementation of Part XI of the U.N. Convention on the Law of the Sea of 10 December 1982 (the Agreement)[88] provides for provisional application by states that gave their consent to its adoption by the U.N. General Assembly if the Agreement had entered into force by November 16, 1994. In fact, the Agreement did not enter into force until July 28, 1996. The Agreement provides for the continuation of provisional membership in the International Seabed Authority for those States that applied it provisionally before July 28, 1996 but have not yet ratified the 1982 Convention. If a state could demonstrate to the Council of the Authority that it had made good-faith efforts to comply with the 1982 Convention, the period of provisional membership could be extended until November 1998. Canada, among other states, participated in the Authority as a provisional member from the adoption of the Agreement until November 1998.[89] At the same time in 2003 that Canada ratified the Law of the Sea Convention, it also ratified the Implementation of Part XI Agreement.

With respect to the private sector consortia, which had previously claimed certain rights to mine the deep seabed, Annex 1, section 1 of the Agreement sets out grandfather provisions for the Japanese, French, Russian, Chinese, and Indian pioneer investors who had already registered their seabed mining claims with the Preparatory Commission before the entry into force of the Convention in 1994. Nonetheless, other consortia licensed in states to which the grandfather provisions do not apply are to explore the

---

85   Anderson, "Further Efforts" *supra* note 76.

86   *Ibid.* at 890-91.

87   *Ibid.* at 893.

88   GA Res. 48/263, UN GAOR, 48th Sess., Supp. No. 49/A, U.N. Doc. A/48/49/Add. 1 reprinted in (1994) 33 I.L.M.1309.

89   See online: <http:/www.un.org/Depts/los/los94.st.tm>.

seabed on the basis of rights and obligations "similar to and not less favourable" than the best granted to those that already enjoy exploration rights, by virtue of the principle of non-discrimination entrenched in both in 1982 Convention and the Agreement.[90]

In August 1997 the plans for exploration by seven registered pioneer investors were submitted to the Council and considered to be approved in accordance with the provisions of the Agreement, and in 2001-2 the seven entities signed 15-year deep-seabed exploration contracts with the Authority.[91] The areas allocated under these contracts are in the Central Pacific and the Indian Ocean,[92] the goal being to locate exploitable deposits of polymetallic nodules that are rich in manganese, nickel, cobalt, and copper.

In July 2000, the Assembly of the Seabed Authority approved the Regulations on Prospecting and Exploration for Polymetallic Nodules in the Area,[93] consisting of 40 regulations that set out the framework for the exploration regime, and annexes that include a model contract and standard clauses (that provided the basis for the initial contracts referred to above). The terms in the regulations are based mainly on provisions in the two basic instruments governing the Authority's work, the 1982 Convention, and the 1994 Implementation Agreement. Of note are a number of provisions respecting protection and preservation of the marine environment, both in general (Regulation 31), and via a specific requirement that demands applicants for an exploration contract complete an assessment of the potential impact of their exploration activities on the environment and to present a proposal on measures to avoid environmental hazards in the course of operations (Regulation 18 (b), (c), and (d)).

D. BOUNDARY DELIMITATION PROBLEMS [94]

The problem of bilateral delimitation of the continental shelf is as old as the concept of continental shelf jurisdiction. With the emergence of the exclusive economic zone, maritime boundary delimitation became a major diplomatic and legal problem. The

---

90   See Agreement, *supra* note 88, Annex 1, Section 1, article 6(iii) at 10 and W.S. Scholz, *supra* note 83 at 78.

91   The seven entities are (1) The Government of India; (2) French Institute of Research for the Exploitation of the Sea (IFREMER)/French Association of Studies and Research of Nodules (AFERNOD) of France; (3) Deep Ocean Resources Development (DORD) of Japan; (4) YUZHMORGEOLOGIYA of Russia; (5) China Ocean Mineral Resources Research and Development Association (COMRA) of the People's Republic of China; (6) The Interoceanmetal Joint Organization (IOM) of Bulgaria, Cuba, the Czech Republic, Poland, Russia, and the Slovak Republic; and (7) The Government of the Republic of Korea. See: online: International Seabed Authority <http://www.isa.org.jm/en/seabedarea/pioneers.investors.stm>; *Press Release SEA/1565: Council Of Seabed Authority Notes Approval Of Work Plans By Seven Pioneer Investors* (Aug. 29, 1997), online: United Nations <http://www.un.org/News/Press/docs/1997/19970829.SEA1565.html>.

92   See online: International Seabed Authority <http://www.isa.org.jm/en/seabedarea/contractorareas.stm>.

93   ISBA/6/A/18 (Oct. 4, 2000), online: International Seabed Authority <http://www.isa.org.jm/en/documents/OFFICIAL_DOCUMENTS/DOC_2000/ISBA_6_A_18_E.pdf>.

94   See M.D. Evans, *Relevant Circumstances and Maritime Delimitation* (1989); S.P. Jagota, *Maritime Boundary* (1985); D.M. Johnston & P.M. Saunders, *Ocean Boundary Making: Regional Issues and Development* (1988); D.M. Johnston, *The Theory and History of Ocean Boundary-Making* (1988); P. Weil, *Perspectives du Droit de la Délimitation Maritime* (1988), translated by M. MacGlashan as

Truman Proclamation of 1945 speaks of delimitation of a boundary between neighbours "in accordance with equitable principles." The ILC developed a proposal that laid considerable stress upon equidistance. It was enshrined in article 6 of the 1958 Geneva Convention on the Continental Shelf but it met with almost equal favour and disfavour according to the geographic situations of states. As the decision in the *North Sea Continental Shelf* cases indicated, the contents of article 6 did not become a rule of customary international law binding upon non-parties to the Convention.[95] This judgment did much to reinforce the importance of equity as the basis of delimitation, but subsequent decisions, insofar as they are capable of a principled interpretation, tend to show that equidistance and equity are not as far apart as might be thought and that in any case a host of factors (social, economic, geographic, geologic, geomorphologic, historical, proportionality, or general direction of the coast) are applicable to the determination of each boundary.

When the opportunity came to set down principles for delimiting maritime boundaries at the Third U.N. Conference on the Law of the Sea, the states opposed to the equidistance rule were able to demonstrate convincingly that it could not be the basis of consensus, even though an equally large number of states, including Canada, supported retention of the contents of article 6 in the new Convention. The results of a protracted and often bitter negotiation were the two parallel articles 74 and 83 on delimitation of the EEZ and the continental shelf, respectively.

With the emergence of the right to a 200-mile EEZ it became largely theoretical to envisage delimitation of the continental shelf alone or separate sea water and seabed boundaries. The first major delimitation dispute subsequent to the conclusion of the U.N. Convention in 1982 was the Gulf of Maine case between Canada and the United States.[96] In that case, the parties asked the tribunal to settle a "single maritime boundary" rather than separate shelf and fishing zone frontiers. Subsequently, Canada and France similarly sought a single boundary in their dispute over fishing zones and continental shelf rights off the coasts of St. Pierre and Miquelon and Newfoundland.[97]

States have made frequent use of international adjudication to resolve or assist in resolving overlapping maritime claims. As noted above, Canada has twice accepted international adjudication as a means to resolve maritime boundary disputes. The following is a list of the most significant maritime boundary international adjudications.

P. Weil, *Law on Maritime Delimitation: Reflections* (1989); and Nuno Marques Atunes, *Towards the Conceptualisation of Maritime Delimitation* (2003). Reference should also be made to the *International Maritime Boundaries* series (currently at four volumes), a continuing project of the American Society of International Law, published by Martinus Nijhoff. This series provides detailed commentary on negotiated maritime boundary agreements. In addition, Volume 1 (1993) and Volume 5 (expected in 2005) contain articles reviewing almost all aspects on maritime boundary delimitation. Volumes 1 and 2, edited by J.I. Charney & L.M. Alexander, were published in 1993 with Volume 3 published in 1998. Volume 4, under the editorship of Charney & R.W. Smith came out in 2002. Volume 5 is expected in 2005 with editors D. Colson & R.W. Smith.

95 [1969] I.C.J. Rep. 3, reported in Chapter 3, Section C.1 on "General Customary Law."

96 [1984] I.C.J. Rep. 246.

97 (1992) 31 I.L.M. 1145.

- 1909 Grisbadarna Arbitration (Sweden/Norway), 11 UN R.I.A.A. 147;

- 1969 North Sea Continental Shelf Cases, [1969] I.C.J. Rep. 3;

- 1977 Anglo-French Continental Shelf Arbitration (1979) 18 I.L.M. 397;

- 1981 Dubai/Sharjah Border Arbitration (1993) 91 I.L.R. 543;

- 1982 Tunisia/Libya Continental Shelf Case, [1982] I.C.J. Rep. 18;

- 1984 Canada/United States Gulf of Maine Case, [1984] I.C.J. Rep. 246;

- 1985 Guinea/Guinea Bissau Maritime Boundary Arbitration (1985) 25 I.L.M. 251;

- 1985 Libya/Malta Continental Shelf Case, [1985] I.C.J. Rep. 13;

- 1992 Canada–France Maritime Boundary Arbitration (1992) 31 I.L.M. 1145;

- 1992 Land, Island, and Maritime Frontier Case (El Salvador/Honduras), [1992] I.C.J. Rep. 351;

- 1993 Greenland/Jan Mayen Maritime Delimitation (Denmark v. Norway), [1993] I.C.J. Rep. 38;

- 1999 Eritrea–Yemen Maritime Delimitation Arbitration (2001) 40 I.L.M. 983;

- 2001 Maritime Delimitation and Territorial Questions between Qatar and Bahrain, [2001] I.C.J. Rep. 40; and

- 2002 Case Concerning the Land and Maritime Boundary between Cameroon and Nigeria (Equatorial Guinea intervening), [2002] I.C.J. Rep. 303.

In October 2005 there were five pending cases that involve maritime boundary delimitation, two before the International Court (*Nicaragua v. Columbia* and *Nicaragua v. Honduras*) and three before arbitral bodies (*Malaysia v. Singapore*; *Guyana v. Suriname*; and *Barbados v. Trinidad and Tobago*). Finally, note should be made of the 2001/2002 arbitration between Newfoundland and Labrador and Nova Scotia.[98] While this was an internal Canadian matter regarding the maritime boundary between the offshore areas of the two provinces, the relevant legislation directed that the tribunal apply the existing international law on maritime boundary delimitation, a choice of law that necessitated treating the two provinces as if they were states for purposes of the arbitration.

Through the above international cases, an analytic framework has developed that tribunals tend to apply in maritime boundary cases. The goal of the framework is to assist

---

98   Arbitration between Newfoundland and Labrador and Nova Scotia Concerning Portions of the Limits of their Offshore Areas as Defined in the *Canada–Nova Scotia Offshore Petroleum Resources Accord Implementation Act* and the *Canada–Newfoundland Atlantic Accord Implementation Act*, Award of the Tribunal in the First Phase, May 2001 and in the Second Phase, 26 March 2002: <www.nr.gov.nl.ca/mines&en/publications/offshore/dispute/decision.pdf>. See V. Hughes, "The Nova Scotia–Newfoundland Dispute over the Limits of Their Respective Offshore Areas" (2000) 38 Can. Y.B. Int'l L. 189 and V. Hughes, "Nova Scotia–Newfoundland Dispute over Offshore Areas: The Delimitation Phase" (2002) 40 Can. Y.B. Int'l L. 373.

a tribunal in balancing all the relevant criteria and factors in order for the tribunal to construct a maritime boundary that is an "equitable result." The International Court in the *Cameroon v. Nigeria* case described the analytic framework as follows:

288. The Court has on various occasions made it clear what the applicable criteria, principles and rules of delimitation are when a line covering several zones of coincident jurisdictions is to be determined. They are expressed in the so-called equitable principles/ relevant circumstances method. This method, which is very similar to the equidistance/ special circumstances method applicable in delimitation of the territorial sea, involves first drawing an equidistance line, then considering whether there are factors calling for the adjustment or shifting of that line in order to achieve an "equitable result."

289. Thus, in the case concerning *Maritime Delimitation in the Area between Greenland and Jan Mayen (Denmark v. Norway)*, the Court, which had been asked to draw a single maritime boundary, took the view, with regard to delimitation of the continental shelf, that

"even if it were appropriate to apply ... customary law concerning the continental shelf as developed in the decided cases, it is in accord with precedents to begin with the median line as a provisional line and then to ask whether 'special circumstances' require any adjustment or shifting of that line" (*I.C.J. Reports 1993, Judgment*, p. 61, para. 51).

In seeking to ascertain whether there were in that case factors which should cause it to adjust or shift the median line in order to achieve an "equitable result," the Court stated:

"[i]t is thus apparent that special circumstances are those circumstances which might modify the result produced by an unqualified application of the equidistance principle. General international law, as it has developed through the case-law of the Court and arbitral jurisprudence, and through the work of the Third United Nations Conference on the Law of the Sea, has employed the concept of 'relevant circumstances.' This concept can be described as a fact necessary to be taken into account in the delimitation process." (*Ibid.*, p. 62, para. 55.)

In the case concerning *Maritime Delimitation and Territorial Questions between Qatar and Bahrain (Qatar v. Bahrain)* the Court further stated that

"[f]or the delimitation of the maritime zones beyond the 12-mile zone it [would] first provisionally draw an equidistance line and then consider whether there [were] circumstances which must lead to an adjustment of that line" (*I.C.J. Reports 2001*, para. 230).

290. The Court will apply the same method in the present case.

The result was that an equidistance line was left unadjusted and was decreed by the Court as the maritime boundary between the states. Note that the emphasis by the Court on an equidistance line being the provisional line has not been adopted as frequently in other cases as the Court suggests. Nevertheless, the analytic framework of a provisional line to be adjusted to reach an equitable result has become the standard formulation of international maritime boundary delimitation law. Left out of the equation is how to determine the provisional line (equidistance clearly gets the nod); what factors/ circumstances are to be taken into account in adjusting a provisional line; and how the result is to be judged as attaining an equitable result. It is important to note that of all the possible criteria and considerations that may play a role in maritime boundary delimitation, it is coastal geography and geographic characteristics such as islands (rather than politics, environment, fisheries, oil reserves, etc.) that have come to dominate.

Most bilateral maritime boundaries are resolved through negotiation. In negotiations, while the factors, circumstances, and criteria that arise in international adjudication are frequently used to support a state's position, ultimately the states agree on a boundary that is acceptable to them (an "equitable result").

Geneva Convention on the Continental Shelf
(1958) 499 U.N.T.S. 311

Article 6

1. Where the same continental shelf is adjacent to the territories of two or more States whose coasts are opposite each other, the boundary of the continental shelf appertaining to such States shall be determined by agreement between them. In the absence of agreement, and unless another boundary line is justified by special circumstances, the boundary is the median line, every point of which is equidistant from the nearest points of the baselines from which the breadth of the territorial sea of each State is measured.

2. Where the same continental shelf is adjacent to the territories of two adjacent States, the boundary of the continental shelf shall be determined by agreement between them. In the absence of agreement, and unless another boundary line is justified by special circumstances, the boundary shall be determined by application of the principle of equidistance from the nearest points of the baselines from which the breadth of the territorial sea of each State is measured.

3. In delimiting the boundaries of the continental shelf, any lines which are drawn in accordance with the principles set out in paragraphs 1 and 2 of this article should be defined with reference to charts and geographical features as they exist at a particular date, and reference should be made to fixed permanent identifiable points on the land.

United Nations Convention on the Law of the Sea
Articles 74 and 83
Reproduced in the Documentary Supplement

Maritime Boundaries of Canada[99]

Canada has six ocean areas where bilateral maritime boundary problems have arisen: the Gulf of Maine region; the waters around the French islands of St. Pierre and Miquelon; the eastern Arctic and sub-Arctic region fronting and adjacent to Greenland (Denmark); the western Arctic in the Beaufort Sea; the Juan de Fuca Strait region in the southwest corner of British Columbia; and the Dixon Entrance region between British Columbia and Alaska.

When the extension of offshore jurisdiction first created potential bilateral problems in the 1970s, Canada was actively involved in negotiations with its three neighbours (France, Greenland (Denmark), and the United States). During this period, Canada's only successfully negotiated ocean boundaries were the continental shelf delimitation agreement reached with Denmark in 1973[100] and a territorial sea agreement reached with France in 1972.[101] A maritime boundary agreement that predates both these by well over a century is the 1846 United Kingdom–United States Oregon Treaty[102] that ultimately, with the help of the Emperor of Germany in 1871, created the maritime boundary between British Columbia and the state of Washington in the Georgia Strait and Strait of Juan de Fuca.[103]

Regarding Canada and Greenland (Denmark) in the eastern Arctic and sub-Arctic, a substantial area has been delimited, although a very small gap in the delimitation exists because of the sovereignty dispute over Hans Island. The southern extent of the boundary may need to be re-examined in the light of possible continental shelf claims. More interesting is the fact that the 1973 boundary does not extend into the Lincoln Sea, north of Greenland and Canada's Arctic islands. The location of this boundary, which can be expected to extend beyond 200 nautical miles to deal with the continental shelf, may determine whether it is Greenland/Denmark or Canada that can lay claim to the North Pole.

The only area where the territorial sea and exclusive economic-zone boundaries have been fully resolved is between Canada and France in the St. Pierre and Miquelon region. As noted above, in 1972 Canada and France agreed to a territorial sea boundary in the ocean area between Newfoundland and the French islands. In the 1980s unsuccessful boundary negotiations created a fisheries crisis that led the two countries to arbitral adjudication.[104] In 1992, a five-member Arbitration panel determined the maritime

---

99 Excellent surveys of Canada's bilateral ocean boundary issues are provided by D. Russell, "International Ocean Boundary Issues and Management Arrangements" in VanderZwaag, *supra* note 1 at 463-507; D. McRae, "Delimitation Problems of Canada (First Part)" in D. Pharand & U. Leanza, eds., *The Continental Shelf and Exclusive Economic Zone: Delimitation and Legal Regime* (1993) at 159-69; D. Pharand, "Delimitation Problems of Canada (Second Part)" in Pharand & Leanza, at 171-79; and D.H. Gray, "Canada's Unresolved Maritime Boundaries" (1994) 48 Geomatica 131-44.

100 Can. T.S. 1974 No. 9.

101 Can. T.S. 1979 No. 37.

102 *Treaty Establishing the Boundary in the Territory on the Northwest Coast of America Lying Westward of the Rocky Mountains*, done at Washington, 15 June 1846, came into force 5 August 1846, reprinted in C. Parry, ed., *The Consolidated Treaty Series*, vol. 100 (1969) at 39-42.

103 See McDorman, *supra* note 18 at 131-32, nn. 50 and 51.

104 See T.L. McDorman, "The Search for Resolution of the Canada–France Ocean Dispute adjacent to St. Pierre and Miquelon" (1994) 15 Dal. L.J. 35.

boundary between the two states. The most prominent feature of the maritime boundary is a 10.5 nautical-mile-wide corridor that extends 200 nautical miles from St. Pierre and Miquelon with the entire French zone being within Canada's 200 nautical mile zone.

In 1977-78 Canada and the United States engaged in negotiations with the goal of simultaneously resolving its maritime boundary problems in the Gulf of Maine, Beaufort Sea, Dixon Entrance, and seaward of the Strait of Juan de Fuca regions. These negotiations ultimately foundered. The emphasis of the negotiations then shifted to the Gulf of Maine region where bilateral fishery problems demanded attention.

In 1979 Canada and the United States completed an integrated fisheries management agreement for the Gulf of Maine region. This complicated and imaginative cross-boundary fisheries agreement was ultimately unacceptable to U.S. interests and never came into force. However, the companion agreement to litigate the ocean boundary dispute went forward and in 1984 a chamber of the International Court of Justice delimited a maritime boundary between Canada and the United States in the Gulf of Maine region.

With regard to the maritime boundaries between Canada and the United States, the Department of External Affairs has written:

> While the judgment, in October 1984, of a Chamber of the International Court of Justice (ICJ) fixed a single maritime boundary between Canada and the United States in a large portion of the Gulf of Maine area, several maritime boundaries remain unsettled between the two countries.[105]

Gulf of Maine—Landward and Seaward Extensions
Under the terms of the agreement submitting the Gulf of Maine maritime boundary dispute to a Chamber of the ICJ, the Chamber was to fix the single maritime boundary seaward from a point 39 nautical miles from the terminus of the land boundary. The reason for not having the Chamber rule on the maritime boundary landward from this point related largely to the dispute over Machias Seal Island, which is claimed by both countries. The eventual seaward extension of the continental shelf dividing line will also have to be agreed in due course.

Strait of Juan de Fuca
The international boundary inside the Strait was fixed in the last century and is not the subject of dispute.

There is no agreement between Canada and the United States regarding the extension of the maritime boundary seaward of the Strait. The United States' position has been to espouse equidistance, using a line drawn by reference to coastal sinuosities.

Dixon Entrance
Inside the Entrance, the Canadian position is that the "A-B Line," established by the 1903 Alaska Boundary Tribunal, is the international boundary with respect to both land and sea. The Americans, who earlier claimed a three-mile territorial sea and a nine-mile contiguous fishing zone in the area, now maintain that the maritime boundary should follow a median line, more or less equally dividing the waters inside the Entrance between Canada and the United States.

---

105 From a memorandum of the Bureau of Legal Affairs on *Current Issues of International Law of Particular Importance to Canada* (October 1986) 16.

There is no agreement between Canada and the United States regarding the extension of the maritime boundary seaward of the Dixon Entrance. The United States' position has been to espouse equidistance. [Alaska has been pressing the U.S. federal government to take a more aggressive stance on this matter since 1990.]

Beaufort Sea
The USA claims a maritime boundary based on equidistance from the termination of the land boundary on the 141st meridian. The Canadian position, based on our interpretation of the language of Article III of the 1825 Russian-British Convention of St. Petersburg, is that the maritime boundary should follow the 141st meridian—in effect, a direct seaward extension of the land boundary.

No formal negotiations with the United States to resolve any of these boundary issues have taken place since the Gulf of Maine case.

E. RESOURCE MANAGEMENT AND ENVIRONMENTAL PROTECTION

1. Fisheries[106]

Few areas of the law of the sea reveal better the processes of development of international law than the law of fisheries during the last five decades. Originally the rule was simply one of freedom to fish beyond three miles. This rule was altered somewhat by the 1958 Geneva Convention on Fishing on the High Seas, which recognized the "special interest" of the coastal state and allowed it to impose temporary conservation measures beyond the territorial sea subject to reaching an agreement with interested states within 12 months. This regime did not protect the interests of coastal states. Iceland was the first to react. An extended exclusive fisheries jurisdiction was proclaimed, thus beginning a series of "cod wars."[107] Norway and Canada also found the regime unworkable.

Canada worked closely with the other signatories of the International Convention for the Northwest Atlantic Fisheries (ICNAF) first negotiated in 1949.[108] This organization recognized Canada's interest but only as one more member state and did not necessarily give priority to Canada as a coastal state. In 1970, Canada extended its territorial sea from 3 to 12 nautical miles and closed the Bay of Fundy, the Gulf of St. Lawrence, and Queen Charlotte Sound to foreign fishing.[109] The exclusion of foreign fishers was

---

106 See W.T. Burke, *The New International Law of Fisheries* (1994); S. M. Kaye, *International Fisheries Management* (2001); E. Hey, ed., *Developments in International Fisheries Law* (1999); and Churchill & Lowe, *supra* note 1 at c. 14.

107 See, for example, the *Fisheries Jurisdiction Case (United Kingdom v. Iceland) Interim Measures*, [1972] I.C.J. Rep. 12 and *Merits*, [1974] I.C.J. Rep. 3.

108 157 U.N.T.S. 157; Can. T.S.1950 No. 10, as amended.

109 See the discussion and maps relating to the *Oceans Act*, above in Section B.1(a) on "Definition and Delimitation of the Territorial Sea," as well as the materials herein. See also A.E. Gotlieb, "The Canadian Contribution to the Concept of a Fishing Zone in International Law" (1964) 2 Can. Y.B. Int'l L. 55 and J.-Y. Morin, "Les zones de peche de Terre-Neuve et du Labrador à la lumière de l'evolution du droit international" (1968) 6 Can. Y.B. Int'l L. 91.

rendered uncontroversial by the prior negotiation of phase-out agreements with those states that had traditionally fished these waters.[110] These agreements proved to be only temporary way stations to a larger objective. During the mid-1970s Canada sought and achieved recognition of its priority interests in ICNAF.

At the same time, Canada was promoting the concept of exclusive fisheries jurisdiction within a 200 mile exclusive economic zone at the Third U.N. Law of the Sea Conference. Agreement on the broad outlines of exclusive fisheries jurisdiction was reached during the course of 1974-75. Mexico was the first major state to adopt a 200-mile exclusive economic zone in 1975. The United States followed for fisheries in 1976; the European Community (EC) and the former U.S.S.R. adopted exclusive economic zones soon after, and on January 1, 1977, Canada extended its fisheries jurisdiction to 200 miles on the east and west coasts, with fisheries jurisdiction extended to 200 miles in the Arctic on March 1, 1977.

The multilateral groundwork had been laid. The regional groundwork was assured by denunciation of the ICNAF and signature of a new regional arrangement, governing scientific research and fisheries beyond 200 miles, the Convention on Future Multilateral Cooperation in the Northwest Atlantic Fisheries (NAFO).[111] Bilateral problems were avoided by signing a second series of phasing-out agreements based on the fisheries articles of the emerging draft text of the U.N. Convention. The first and most significant was the Canada–Norway Agreement[112] on their mutual fisheries relations, which proved to be the general model for a series of subsequent agreements with other countries,[113] including the first of a series of abortive reciprocal arrangements with the United States.[114] The essence of these agreements was to permit foreign fishing subject to Canadian law, and subject to there being fish surplus to Canadian harvesting capacity. These agreements, together with denunciation of ICNAF, reversed any direct threat of challenge and reinforced Canada's assertion that a 200-mile fishing zone was justified by customary international law as evidenced by the negotiating texts at the Law of the Sea Conference.[115]

Unfortunately, adoption of the 200-mile exclusive fishing zone has not proven to be the panacea predicted by Canadian negotiators at the Third U.N. Conference on the Law of the Sea. Within the 200-mile Canadian zone, fish stocks available to Canadian fishers increased with the withdrawal of foreign fishing in the late 1970s only to go into a steep decline at the end of the 1980s, due to a mixture of greed, regulatory mismanagement,

---

110 For example, U.S.A., Can. T.S. 1970 No. 11, as amended; Norway, Can. T.S. 1971 No. 27; and U.S.S.R., Can. T.S. 1971 No. 9.

111 Can. T.S. 1979 No. 11.

112 Can. T.S. 1976 No. 4.

113 Poland, Can. T.S. 1976 No. 5; U.S.S.R., Can. T.S. 1976 No. 6; Spain, Can. T.S.1976 No. 7; Portugal, Can. T.S. 1977 No. 2; Cuba, Can. T.S. 1977 No. 17; Bulgaria, Can. T.S. 1977 No. 28; German Democratic Republic, Can. T.S. 1977 No. 30; Romania, Can. T.S. 1978 No. 2; Japan, Can. T.S. 1978 No. 8; EEC, Can. T.S. 1979 No. 33 and Can. T.S. 1981 No. 30; and Poland, Can. T.S.1982 No 8.

114 Can. T.S. 1973 No. 23.

115 See A.L.C. de Mestral, "Accord entre le Canada et la Norvège sur leur relations en matière de pêche" (1976) 14 Can. Y.B. Int'l L. 270.

and possibly environmental factors. In 1992, the Canadian Minister of Fisheries had to close the northern cod fishery. Exacerbating this situation was the problem of overfishing by foreign and Canadian boats on two areas of the Canadian continental margin lying beyond 200 miles (known locally as the nose and tail of the Grand Banks), outside Canada's exclusive fisheries jurisdiction. Spanish and Portuguese boats in particular were accused of overfishing by Canada, while the EC in general refused even to abide by the NAFO Commission's recommended quotas until 1992. Only the crisis in the cod fishery in 1992 convinced the EC to restrict its fishing efforts in these areas. At the U.N. Conference on Environment and Development held at Rio de Janeiro, Brazil, in June 1992, Canada sought to gather support for new rules governing fishing for such stocks. Although not immediately successful, Canada did obtain a commitment from the international community to convene a conference on these issues in 1993, which led to a new multilateral convention in 1995 (see below).

United Nations Convention on the Law of the Sea
Articles 55-67
Reproduced in the Documentary Supplement

Canadian Fishing Zones

Pursuant to the powers in the former *Territorial Sea and Fishing Zones Act*,[116] the Canadian Government declared exclusive Canadian fishing zones by stages. In 1970, it established three zones by promulgating fisheries closing lines for the Gulf of St. Lawrence, the Bay of Fundy, and Queen Charlotte Sound. Then in 1977 it created three more zones, one each in the Atlantic, the Arctic, and the Pacific, extending 200 nautical miles beyond the previous closing lines and the straight baselines around the coast. See the following maps.[117] Upon creation of the offshore zones, the existing *Fisheries Act* and *Coastal Fisheries Protection Act*[118] applied automatically throughout their full extent and provided the basis for the making of elaborate new regulations.[119]

NOTES

1) Does Canada have an internationally enforceable obligation to share the fish of its 200-mile zone that are surplus to Canadian harvesting capacity? Can a foreign state, such as Norway, declare that Canada has a surplus?

---

116 R.S.C. 1985, c. T-8, s. 4, since replaced by the *Oceans Act*, S.C. 1996, c. 31.

117 Prepared by the Canadian Hydrographic Service and based on C.R.C. 1978, cc. 1547 and 1548, as amended SOR/79-107 and SOR/85-229. See also the Arctic fishing zone declared by C.R.C. 1978, c. 1549 and illustrated on a map of "The Canadian Arctic" in Chapter 7, Section C.1 on "The Arctic."

118 Respectively, *Fisheries Act*, R.S.C. 1985, c. F-14 and *Coastal Fisheries Protection Act*, R.S.C. 1985, c. C-33.

119 *Inter alia*, the *Coastal Fisheries Protection Regulations*, C.R.C. 1978, c. 413, as amended.

Map of Fishing Zones 1, 2, and 4

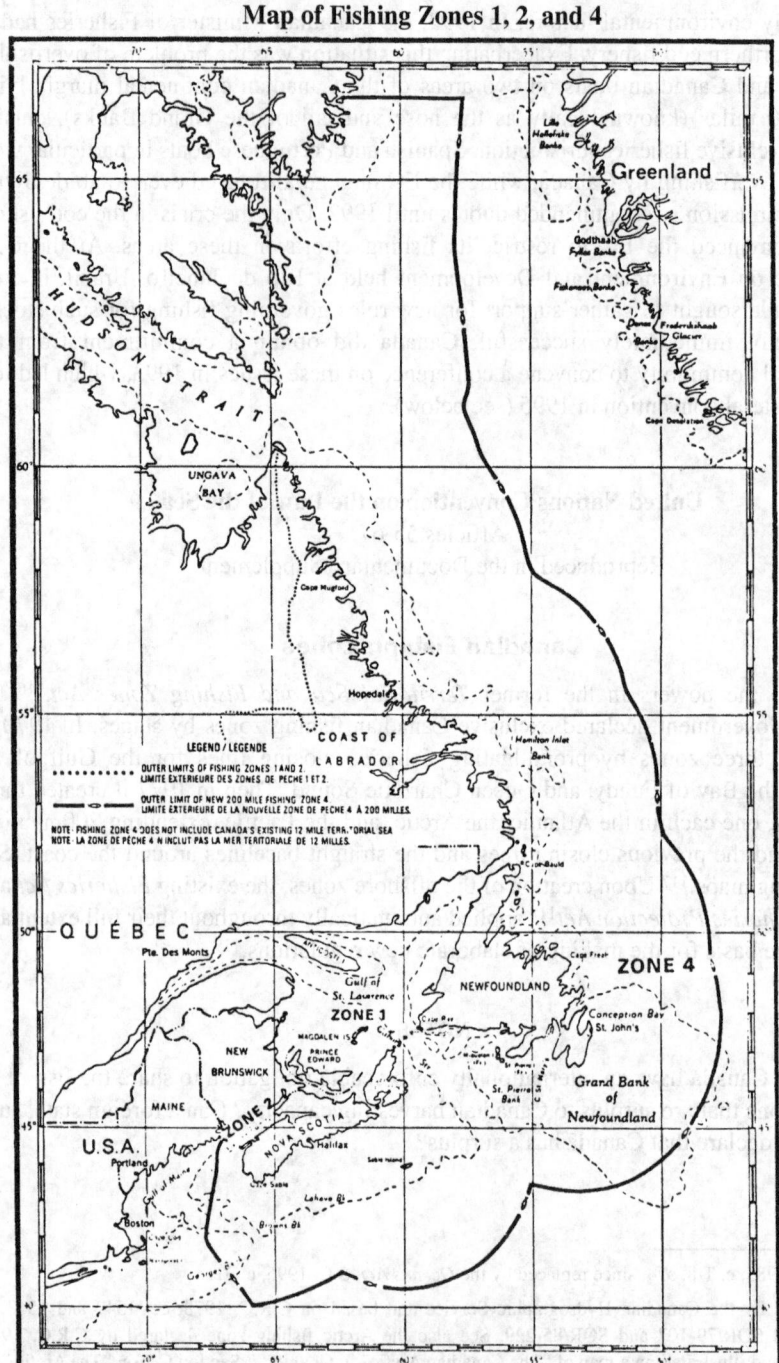

LIMITS OF CANADIAN FISHING ZONE/LIMIT DES ZONES DE PECHE CANADIENS
(EAST COAST)   (CÔTE EST)

Map of Fishing Zones 3 and 5

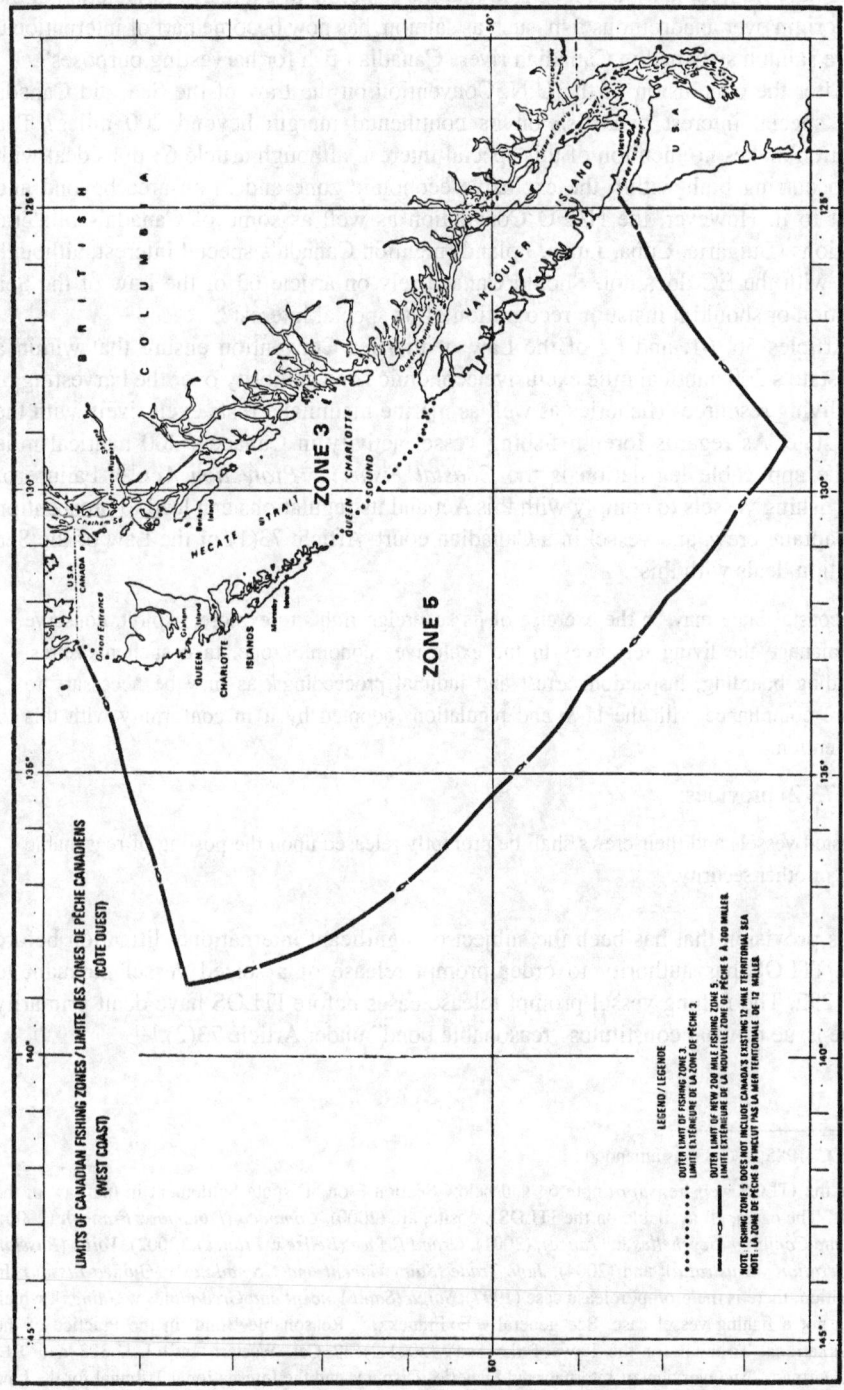

2) In the light of Article 66 of the Law of the Sea Convention (reproduced in the Documentary Supplement), can it be said that the principle of exclusive jurisdiction of the state of origin over anadromous fish, such as salmon, has now become part of international law? Are salmon spawned in Canadian rivers Canadian fish for harvesting purposes?

3) After the conclusion of the U.N. Convention on the Law of the Sea, did Canada lose its special interest over fish on its continental margin beyond 200 miles? The Convention makes no mention of this special interest, although article 63 does deal with stocks occurring both within the exclusive economic zone and in an area beyond and adjacent to it. However, the NAFO Convention as well as some of Canada's bilateral conventions (Bulgaria, Cuba, Japan, Poland) mention Canada's special interest, although the one with the EC does not. Should Canada rely on article 63 of the Law of the Sea Convention or should it insist on recognition of its special interest?

4) Articles 56, 61, and 62 of the Law of the Sea Convention ensure that within a coastal state's 200 nautical mile exclusive economic zone authority over the harvesting of marine living resources (fisheries as well as marine mammals) rests exclusively with the coastal state. As regards foreign fishing vessel activity in Canada's 200 nautical mile zone, the applicable legislation is the *Coastal Fisheries Protection Act*.[120] Failure of foreign fishing vessels to comply with this Act and its regulations can lead to prosecution of the captain, crew, and vessel in a Canadian court. Article 73(1) of the Law of the Sea Convention deals with this:

> The coastal State may, in the exercise of its sovereign rights to explore, exploit, conserve and manage the living resources in the exclusive economic zone, take such measures, including boarding, inspection, arrest and judicial proceedings, as may be necessary to ensure compliance with the laws and regulations adopted by it in conformity with this Convention.

Article 73(2) provides:

> Arrested vessels and their crews shall be promptly released upon the posting of reasonable bond or other security.

It is this provision that has been the subject of significant international litigation before ITLOS. ITLOS has authority to order prompt release of a seized vessel pursuant to Article 292. The fishing vessel prompt release cases before ITLOS have dealt primarily with the issue of what constitutes "reasonable bond" under Article 73(2).[121]

---

120 R.S.C. 1985, c. C-33, as amended.

121 See the ITLOS website, *supra* note 64 and below Section F on "Dispute Settlement in the Law of the Sea." The cases, all available on the ITLOS website, are (2000), *Comouco (Panama v. France)*; (2000), *Monte Confurco (Seychelles v. France)*; (2001), *Grand Prince (Belize v. France)*; (2002), *Volga (Russian Federation v. Australia)*; and (2004), *Juno Trade (Saint Vincent and Grenadines v. Guinea-Bissau)*. In addition, there is the prompt release case (1997), *Saiga (Saint Vincent and Grenadines v. Guinea)*, which was not a fishing vessel case. See generally E. Franckx, " 'Reasonable Bond' in the Practice of the International Tribunal for the Law of the Sea" (2001-2) 32 Cal. Western Int'l L.J. 303 and T.L. McDorman, "An Overview of International Fisheries Disputes and the International Tribunal for the Law of the Sea" (2002) 40 Can. Y.B. Int'l L. 119.

5) Canada's fishing relations with France have been most difficult to manage because of French claims arising from the presence of the islands of Saint-Pierre and Miquelon close to the Canadian coastline. The history of bilateral relations has been marked by a special treaty and an arbitration over its application, as the following materials explain.

Canada–France Agreement on Mutual Fishing Relations
Can. T.S. 1979 No. 37

Article 1

The Government of France renounces the privileges established to its advantage in fishery matters by the Convention signed at London, on April 8, 1904, between the United Kingdom and France. The present agreement supersedes all previous treaty provisions relating to fishing by French nationals off the Atlantic coast of Canada.

Article 2

In return, the Canadian Government undertakes in the event of a modification to the juridical regime relating to the waters situated beyond the present limits of the territorial sea and fishing zones of Canada on the Atlantic coast, to recognize the right of French nationals to fish in these waters subject to possible measures for the conservation of resources, including the establishment of quotas. The French Government undertakes for its part to grant reciprocity to Canadian nationals off the coast of Saint-Pierre and Miquelon.

Article 3

Fishing vessels registered in metropolitan France may continue to fish from January 15 to May 15 each year, up to May 15, 1986, on an equal footing with Canadian vessels, in the Canadian fishing zone within the Gulf of St. Lawrence, east of the meridian of longitude 61 degrees 30 min west, subject to the provisions of Articles 5 and 6.

Article 4

In view of the special situation of Saint-Pierre and Miquelon and as an arrangement between neighbours:

(a) French coastal fishing boats registered in Saint-Pierre and Miquelon may continue to fish in the areas where they have traditionally fished along the coasts of Newfoundland, and Newfoundland coastal fishing boats shall enjoy the same right along the coasts of Saint-Pierre and Miquelon;

(b) A maximum of ten French trawlers registered in Saint-Pierre and Miquelon, of a maximum length of 50 metres, may continue to fish along the coasts of Newfoundland, of Nova Scotia (with the exception of the Bay of Fundy), and in the Canadian fishing zone within the Gulf of St. Lawrence, on an equal footing with Canadian trawlers; Canadian trawlers registered in the ports on the Atlantic coast of Canada may continue to fish along the coasts of Saint-Pierre and Miquelon on an equal footing with French trawlers.

Article 5

French fishing vessels covered by the provision of Article 3 must not direct their fishing effort to the taking of species other than those which they have traditionally exploited in the five-year period immediately preceding this agreement, nor shall they substantially increase the level of such effort.

Article 6

1. Canadian fishery regulations shall be applied without discrimination in fact or in law to the French fishing vessels covered by Articles 3 and 4, including regulations concerning the dimensions of vessels authorized to fish less than 12 miles from the Atlantic coast of Canada.

2. French fishery regulations shall be applied under the same conditions to the Canadian fishing vessels covered by Article 4.

3. Before promulgating new regulations applicable to these vessels, the authorities of each of the parties shall give three months prior notice to the authorities of the other party.

Article 7

The French patrol vessel which usually accompanies the French fishing fleet may continue to exercise its functions of assistance in the Gulf of St. Lawrence.

Article 8

The line defined in the annex to the present agreement determines, in the area between Newfoundland and the islands of Saint-Pierre and Miquelon, the limit of the territorial waters of Canada and of the zones submitted to the fishery jurisdiction of France.

Article 9

No provision of the present agreement shall be interpreted as prejudicing the views and future claims of either party concerning internal waters, territorial waters or jurisdiction with respect to fisheries or the resources of the continental shelf, or the bilateral or multilateral agreements to which either government is a party.

Article 10

1. The contracting parties shall establish a Commission to consider all disputes concerning the application of this agreement.

2. The Commission shall consist of one national expert nominated by each of the parties for ten years. In addition, the two Governments shall designate by mutual agreement a third expert who shall not be a national of either party.

3. If, in connection with any dispute referred to the Commission by either of the contracting parties, the Commission has not within one month reached a decision acceptable to the contracting parties, reference shall be made to the third expert. The Commission shall then sit as an arbitral tribunal under the chairmanship of the third expert.

4. Decisions of the Commission sitting as an arbitral tribunal shall be taken by a majority, and shall be binding on the contracting parties.

La Bretagne Arbitration

The treaty with France was the last of the first series of "phasing-out" agreements signed by Canada between 1970 and 1972. It is different from the others because of the location of the French islands of Saint-Pierre and Miquelon within what is now the 200-mile fishing zone of Canada. Thus article 2 recognizes the right of French nationals to fish in Canadian waters along the Atlantic coast. Article 3 has excluded fishing vessels from metropolitan France from fishing in the Gulf of St. Lawrence since May 15, 1986 but articles 4 and 6 allow 10 boats registered in Saint-Pierre and Miquelon to fish there as well as along the Atlantic coast, subject to Canadian fishery regulations.

The scope of these provisions became the subject of arbitration between Canada and France in 1986[122] as a result of Canadian fears about French overfishing. When Canada proclaimed its 200-mile fishing zone, France also claimed a similar zone in a large area offshore from Saint-Pierre and Miquelon. Since the two countries had overlapping jurisdictional claims, neither were able to restrict the activities of the other in the disputed areas. As the 1986 deadline for the exclusion of metropolitan French vessels from the Gulf of St. Lawrence approached, France increased its fishing activities in the disputed area and for the first time added factory freezer trawlers, of maximum size for entry into the Gulf, to the registry of Saint-Pierre and Miquelon. Matters came to a head when applications were made to Canadian authorities in 1985 for licences for three vessels out of Saint-Pierre, La Bretagne, and two other similar 50-metre factory trawlers with fish filleting capacity, to operate both within and without the Gulf of St. Lawrence. The amended licence eventually granted by Canada carried a limitation:

> In accordance with the current Canadian prohibition against the filleting of traditional groundfish species at sea by Canadian vessels, the La Bretagne is permitted to process groundfish species in the Gulf of St. Lawrence to the headed, gutted form only.

The French government objected to this proviso as a limitation of their nationals' rights in violation of the treaty. The two states failed to settle their differences by negotiation but did agree to arbitration over the application of the treaty, particularly articles 4 and 6, in this situation. Canada contended that the treaty "sanctions the right for trawlers registered in Saint-Pierre and Miquelon to fish in the Canadian fishing zone within the Gulf of St. Lawrence, on an equal footing with Canadian vessels in compliance, without discrimination in fact or in law, with Canadian fishery regulations which prohibit filleting in the Gulf." France asserted with respect to article 4(b) "that its sole object is the right to fish exercised by the French trawlers registered in Saint-Pierre and Miquelon and that, as filleting the fish taken is not to fish, Canada may not use the regulatory power which derives from article 6 … for purposes other than the protection of the fishery resources of its exclusive fishing zone."[123]

---

122 *Dispute Concerning Filleting within the Gulf of St. Lawrence* (1986) 90 R.G.D.I.P. 713.

123 *Ibid.*, para. 24.

The majority of the Tribunal, P. de Visscher (Belg., Chairman) and J.-P. Queneudec (Fr.), D. Pharand (Can.) dissenting, in effect preferred the French interpretation of the treaty. There was no disagreement that Canada, consistent with the U.N. Law of the Sea Convention articles 56, 61, and 62, could exercise sovereign rights in respect of its exclusive fisheries zone subject only to its special agreement with France. However, the majority considered that the French trawlers' rights in article 4(b) to enjoy fishing "on an equal footing" with Canadian vessels grants them a right of access to exploit the resource on the same basis as Canadian trawlers but does not subject them in all respects to the national treatment given to Canadians. In particular, the "Canadian Regulations" referred to in article 6, whatever they may mean for Canadians, do not extend in the context of the Canada–France treaty as of 1972, or the parties' subsequent practice, or the U.N. Convention, beyond those laws that fix the conditions solely for fish-catching activities. Since Canada cannot prohibit fish-processing aboard French vessels, the majority had only to hold that a freezer trawler is a kind of trawler within article 4(b) to enjoin the Canadian prevention of their operation in the Gulf of St. Lawrence.

As a result of this award, Canada is unable to regulate the manner of handling the fish caught by Saint-Pierre boats in the Gulf of St. Lawrence but it retains a measure of control over the volume of fish taken by reason of the allocation of quotas to France. By virtue of article 2, French nationals have a right to fish in Canadian waters, but Canada equally has a right to conserve the fish stocks by quotas. These quotas were set by agreement between Canada and France up to 1992, in anticipation of the decision delimiting the maritime boundary between Canada and the French territories. Following that arbitral decision in June 1992, noted in the last section on "Boundary Delimitation Problems," the two states negotiated a long-term fisheries agreement.[124]

NOTE

How is it that France has been so successful in maintaining its historic fishing rights off Canadian coasts when other countries with equally long-standing claims have given them up?

East Coast Fisheries and the Estai

In 1992, depletion of the fish stocks forced the Canadian government to reduce its annual northern cod quota to one-half of mid-1980s levels. In the same year the Department of Fisheries and Oceans imposed a moratorium on northern cod fishing, which has been extended beyond the two years initially envisaged by the Canadian Government. In 1994, Canada asked NAFO to disallow fishing for northern cod within the NAFO Regulatory Area. In May of that same year, Canada went one step further by amending the *Coastal Fisheries Protection Act.* This amendment raised a number of eyebrows in the international community, in particular section 7, which states that a protection officer may board and inspect a fishing vessel within either Canadian fisheries waters or the NAFO Regulatory Area and section 9, which permits a protection officer on reasonable

---

124 *Proces-Verbal Applying the March 27, 1972 Agreement between Canada and France on their Mutual Fishing Relations*, done December 2, 1994.

grounds to seize a fishing vessel and any goods aboard that fishing vessel. At the same time, Canada submitted a reservation with the ICJ in order to exclude from the compulsory jurisdiction of the ICJ any dispute with another State regarding the fishery conservation and management measures taken and the enforcement of such measures.[125] In addition, soon after the amendments were made to the *Coastal Fisheries Protection Act*, Canada adopted regulations to ban fishing by vessels flying the flag of certain nationalities within the NAFO Regulatory Area.[126] The Canadian Director-General for Fisheries at that time stated that the new regulations were justified because "some 34 vessels from States that are not NAFO members continue to fish outside the 200-mile limit."[127]

In fall 1994, on the advice of its Scientific Council, the 15 members of NAFO decided for the first time to regulate catches of turbot (Greenland halibut) in the NAFO Regulatory Area. A Total Allowable Catch (TAC) of 27,000 tonnes was set for that stock in 1995. On February 1, 1995, Canada forced a vote in NAFO to divide the catch. (Normally all decisions are arrived at by consensus.) Canada received 60 percent (16,300 tonnes) and the Europeans received 12 percent (3,400 tonnes). (In the previous three years, Spanish vessels had been catching about 50,000 tonnes of turbot.)

The Europeans had asked for 75 percent of the TAC, and refused to accept the division. Because of the forced vote, the EU was able to invoke the objection procedure contained in the NAFO Convention, which allowed the EU to disregard the NAFO Commission's decision on the turbot quota and, as a consequence, the EU set its own catch limits. On February 22, 1995, the EU set for itself a quota of 18,630 tonnes, almost 70 percent of the TAC and more than five times the amount allocated to it by the decision of the NAFO Commission. As an internal EU matter, it was determined that only Spain and Portugal would share the revised quota.

Citing the imminent prospect of Spanish and Portuguese vessels irreparably depleting the Greenland halibut stock, on March 3, 1995, Canada added these two states to the Coastal Fisheries Protection Regulations in a separate list of flag states whose vessels could be arrested in the NAFO Regulatory Area pursuant to the *Coastal Fisheries Protection Act* and Regulations. Special conservation and management measures were also added to the regulations to apply only to the vessels of states appearing on the new list. Canada accompanied these amendments with a call to the EU for a 60-day moratorium on Greenland halibut catches in the interests of conservation. On March 6, 1995, the European Council of Ministers formally rejected the proposed moratorium.

On March 9, 1995, Canadian patrol vessels intercepted, fired at, stopped, boarded, and arrested a Spanish fishing trawler, the *Estai*, found fishing on the Nose of the Grand Banks, 245 nautical miles from the Canadian shore. The *Estai* was subsequently diverted to St. John's, Newfoundland, where the master of the vessel was detained and charged

---

125 Canada's declaration recognizing the compulsory jurisdiction of the ICJ is reproduced in Chapter 6, Section D.2 on "Jurisdiction of the Court." And see J.A. de Yturriaga, *The International Regime of Fisheries: From UNCLOS 1982 to the Presential Sea* (1997) at 239.

126 See Press Release of the Department of Fisheries and Oceans, Doc. NR-HQ-95-27 E, March 3, 1995 available online at <http://www.dfo-mpo.gc.ca/media/newsrel/1995/hq-ac27_e.htm>. And see SOR/94-362.

127 R. Appelbaum, "The UN Conference on Straddling Stocks and Highly Migratory Fish Stocks: The Current Canadian Perspective" in Nordquist & Moore, *supra* note 76 at 301.

with a violation of the *Coastal Protection Fisheries Act*. As expected, the EC protested vehemently against the action of the Canadian authorities and Canada immediately entered into bilateral negotiations with the Community. On April 16, 1995, the two parties reached an agreement on strengthening enforcement of international conservation measures in the NAFO Regulatory Area, which was later jointly submitted to NAFO and adopted on September 15, 1995. They also agreed upon the distribution of quotas and Canada made a commitment to the EC to repeal the provisions of its regulation of March 3, 1995 prohibiting vessels from Spain and Portugal from fishing for Greenland halibut.

Nevertheless, on March 28, 1995, Spain instituted proceedings against Canada at the ICJ, alleging the violation of various principles and norms of international law—in particular, the very principle of the freedom of the high seas and a serious infringement of the sovereign rights of Spain. On the basis of the reservation submitted by Canada subsequent to the amendment of the *Coastal Protection Fisheries Act*, on April 21, 1995, Canada declared to the Court that it lacked jurisdiction. The Court subsequently agreed that it had no jurisdiction to adjudicate the dispute: this decision is reproduced in part in Chapter 6, Section D.2 on "Jurisdiction of the Court."[128]

Coastal Fisheries Protection Act
R.S.C. 1985, c. C-33, as amended by S.C. 1994, c. 14,
reproduced in (1994) 33 I.L.M. 1383

5.1 Parliament recognizing
(a) that straddling stocks on the Grand Banks of Newfoundland are a major renewable world food source ...
(c) that there is an urgent need for all fishing vessels to comply in both Canadian fisheries waters and the NAFO Regulatory Area with sound conservation and management measures for those stocks ...
(d) that some foreign fishing vessels continue to fish for those stocks in the NAFO Regulatory Area in a manner that undermines the effectiveness of sound conservation and management measures,
declares that the purpose of section 5.2 is to enable Canada to take urgent action necessary to prevent further destruction of those stocks and to permit their rebuilding, while continuing to seek effective international solutions to the situation ...
5.2 No person being aboard a foreign fishing vessel of a prescribed class, shall, in the NAFO Regulatory Area, fish or prepare to fish for a straddling stock in contravention of any of the prescribed conservation and management measures.

---

128   See *Fisheries Jurisdiction Case (Spain v. Canada)*, [1998] I.C.J. Rep. 432.

Inspection, Arrest, Seizure and Forfeiture

7. A protection officer may

(a) for the purpose of ensuring compliance with this Act and the regulations, board and inspect any fishing vessel found within Canadian fisheries waters or the NAFO Regulatory Area; and

(b) with a warrant issued under section 7.1, search any fishing vessel found within Canadian fisheries waters or the NAFO Regulatory Area and its cargo.

7.1(1) A justice of the peace who on ex parte application is satisfied by information on oath that there are reasonable grounds to believe that there is in any place, including any premises, vessel or vehicle, any fish or other thing that was obtained by or used in or that will afford evidence in respect of, a contravention of this Act or the regulations, may issue a warrant authorizing the protection officer named in the warrant to enter and search the place for the fish or other thing subject to any conditions that may be specified in the warrant.

(2) A protection officer may exercise the powers referred to in paragraph 7(b) without a warrant if the conditions for obtaining a warrant exist but, by reason of exigent circumstances, it would not be practical to obtain a warrant.

8. A protection officer may arrest without warrant any person who the officer suspects on reasonable grounds has committed an offence under this Act.

8.1 A protection officer may, in the manner and to the extent prescribed by the regulations, use force that is intended or is likely to disable a foreign fishing vessel, if the protection officer

(a) is proceeding lawfully to arrest the master or other person in command of the vessel; and

(b) believes on reasonable grounds that the force is necessary for the purpose of arresting that master or other person.

9. Where a protection officer suspects on reasonable ground that an offence under this Act has been committed, the officer may seize

(a) any fishing vessel by means of or in relation to which the officer believes on reasonable grounds the offence was committed;

(b) any goods aboard a fishing vessel described in paragraph (a), including fish, tackle, rigging, apparel, furniture, stores and cargo.

NOTES

1) For the purposes of section 5.2, the "prescribed class" of vessels included foreign vessels without nationality and fishing vessels flying the flag of Belize, Cayman Islands, Honduras, Panama, Saint-Vincent and the Grenadines, Sierra Leone and, until Canada reached agreement with the EU for their removal from this list, Spain and Portugal.[129]

2) Canada was not called upon to provide a legal justification for its interference on the high seas with the Spanish vessel that was *prima facie* inconsistent with the NAFO Convention, the Law of the Sea Convention (to which at that time Canada was not a

---

129 See SOR/94-362.

party), and the customary law of the sea.[130] The two justifications usually suggested as being arguable were reprisal and necessity. The reprisal argument might have followed these lines: the seizure of the *Estai* was in response to the vessel's illegality (fishing in breach of NAFO regulations or an abuse of right) and, therefore, the Canadian action, otherwise illegal, was permitted. How strong is this argument? See the discussion of countermeasures in Chapter 10, Section D.2 on "Countermeasures."

The environmental necessity argument found more favour among many. The example most often given of necessity against an ecological disaster is the British action in 1967 of bombing the stricken Liberian flag vessel the *Torrey Canyon* on the high seas because of the pollution danger posed by the grounded vessel. Article 25 of the ILC Draft Articles on Responsibility of States for Internationally Wrongful Acts (reproduced in Chapter 10, Section A.4 on "Circumstances Precluding Wrongfulness") provides some support for the argument of the existence of environmental necessity. The questions that may be raised are: was the interest of Canada in "grave and imminent peril," and to what extent had Canada contributed to the peril it was saving itself from? How strong is the argument that Canada might have made regarding environmental necessity?

3) In her recent book entitled *Non-Flag State Enforcement in High Seas Fisheries*, R.G. Rayfuse concluded as follows:

> The examination of practice ... has revealed that although the primacy of flag state jurisdiction remains the bedrock of international fisheries law the principle *has* been modified. ... [W]ithin the confines of RFOs [Regional Fisheries Organizations such as NAFO] non-flag jurisdiction is a real and growing phenomenon. The practice does not go so far as to admit of a right of universal jurisdiction to unilaterally enforce conservation and management measures adopted by RFOs. Neither does it go so far as to admit of a right of non-flag sanction in respect of measures adopted, as asserted in the Canadian action with respect to the *Estai*. Neither does it admit of a right to enforce unilaterally adopted conservation and management measures which purport to apply to high seas fisheries ... . Rather, consistent with other developments in the law of the sea, consent of the flag state to non-flag action is still required.[131]

Straddling Fish Stocks

Straddling stocks of fish represent species that remain within the jurisdiction of a coastal state's EEZ for a large part of their existence but then later migrate from the jurisdictional zone to the high seas where they are susceptible to being harvested by fleets from distant water fishing nations. The turbot at the centre of the *Estai* incident is a straddling stock. While the straddling stocks occupy the zone of the coastal state, they are considered economic resources by the state that usually sets quotas for its own fisheries purposes and simultaneously may take measures to manage and conserve the fishery. As an increasing number of coastal states claim a 200-mile jurisdiction along their coasts, a larger number

---

130   See above Section B.6, Notes, number 4.

131   R.G. Rayfuse, *Non-Flag State Enforcement in High Seas Fisheries* (2004) at 357.

of straddling stocks are subject to the monopoly of one coastal state for long periods of time. In order to resolve the competition for straddling stocks, a commitment must be made for their effective management, which requires cooperation between coastal and non-coastal states alike. The challenge for the international community is to establish a system of incentives that are strong enough to counterbalance the strong desire of both coastal and distant water fishing states to exploit straddling stocks to the fullest extent.[132]

Article 116 of the 1982 Law of the Sea Convention states that

[a]ll States have the right for their nationals to engage in fishing on the high seas subject to
    (a) their treaty obligations;
    (b) the rights and duties as well as the interests of coastal states provided in Article 63.

Article 63(2), the only provision in the Law of the Sea Convention that deals explicitly with straddling stocks, directs:

Where the same stock ... occur both within the exclusive economic zone and in an area beyond and adjacent to the zone, the coastal State and the States fishing for such stocks in the adjacent area shall seek, either directly or through appropriate subregional or regional organizations, to agree upon the measures necessary for the conservation of these stocks in the adjacent area.

Short of agreement, is it possible for a coastal state to extend its material legal claim to manage straddling stocks when the stocks are located beyond the coastal state's EEZ, especially in the light of article 89 of the 1982 Convention, which provides that "no State may validly purport to subject any part of the high seas to its sovereignty"?

Canada has played an instrumental role in the effort to provide an international solution to the dilemma posed by the gradual depletion of straddling stock resources. In 1990, Canada embarked upon a "legal initiative" in order to address its frustration with the UNCLOS framework.[133] In May 1991, experts from Canada, Chile, and New Zealand agreed on a text featuring recommendations on the coordination of conservation measures between coastal and non-coastal states and protection from the negative impact caused by high seas fishing activities in the EEZ.[134] This text was presented by Canada along with 12 other coastal states and was considered during the U.N. Conference on Environment and Development, known as "The Earth Summit" in Rio de Janeiro on June 1992. At that Conference, Canada was able to obtain the agreement of 40 states to organize the Conference on Straddling Fish Stocks and Highly Migratory Fish Stocks.[135]

---

132 J.E. Colburn, "Turbot Wars: Straddling Stocks, Regime Theory, and A New U.N. Agreement" (1997) 6 J. Transnat. L. & Pol. at 326-28.

133 P. Fauteux, "L'initiative juridique canadienne sur la peche en haute mer" (1993) 31 Can. Y. B. Int'l L. 33 at 56.

134 Ibid. at 55. See also M. Keiver, "The Turbot War: Gunboat Diplomacy or Refinement of the Law of the Sea" (1996) 37 Cahiers de Droit 543 at 574-80.

135 The Conference was officially convened by the U.N. General Assembly by resolution 47/192, December 22, 1992, GA Res. 47/192, UN GAOR, 47th Sess., Supp. No. 49, U.N. Doc. A/47/49 at 145.

The Conference took place over five substantive sessions from April 1993 to August 1995. Throughout most of the negotiations, the Canadian Fisheries Minister, Brian Tobin, sought to achieve five broad objectives: (1) a legally binding U.N. Convention; (2) the implementation of a precautionary approach; (3) compatibility between conservation measures inside and outside 200 miles; (4) compulsory and binding dispute settlement resolution measures; and (5) high seas enforcement.[136] The Agreement on Straddling Fish Stocks and Highly Migratory Fish Stocks was concluded August 4, 1995 upon the three essential pillars of conservation measures, effective enforcement, and dispute settlement, whether or not the parties to the Agreement are also parties to the 1982 Convention.[137] Canada ratified the Fish Stocks Agreement on August 3, 1999. The Agreement entered into force on December 11, 2001. The EC and its member states became a party to the Agreement on 19 January 2004.[138] Pursuant to Article 36, within four years of entry into force of the Agreement, the U.N. Secretary-General "shall convene a conference with a view to assessing the effectiveness of this Agreement."

U.N. Fish Stocks Agreement
Agreement for the Implementation of the Provisions of the United Nations Convention on the Law of the Sea of 10 December 1982 Relating to the Conservation and Management of Straddling Fish Stocks and Highly Migratory Fish Stocks 1995 (1995) 34 I.L.M. 1542[139]

Article 2
Objective

The objective of this Agreement is to ensure the long-term conservation and sustainable use of straddling fish stocks and highly migratory fish stocks through effective implementation of the relevant provisions of the Convention.

Article 3
Application

(1) Unless otherwise provided, this Agreement applies to the conservation and management of straddling fish stocks and highly migratory fish stocks beyond areas under national jurisdiction, except that articles 6 and 7 apply also to the conservation and management of such stocks within areas under national jurisdiction, subject to

---

136   Keiver, *supra* note 134 at 579.

137   (1995) 34 I.L.M. 1542.

138   Ratification information is available online at DOALOS website, *supra* note 1.

139   See F. Orrego Vicuna, *The Changing International Law of High Seas Fisheries* (1999); M. Hayashi, "The Straddling and Highly Migratory Fish Stocks Agreement" in Hey, *supra* note 106 at 55-83; and P. Orebech, K. Sigurjonsson, & T.L. McDorman, "The 1995 United Nations Straddling and Highly Migratory Fish Stocks Agreement: Management, Enforcement, and Dispute Settlement" (1998) 12 Int. J. Mar. and Coastal L. 119.

the different legal regimes that apply within areas under national jurisdiction and in areas beyond national jurisdiction as provided for in the Convention. ...

Article 4
Relationship Between This Agreement and the 1982 Convention

Nothing in this Agreement shall prejudice the rights, jurisdiction and duties of States under the Convention. This Agreement shall be interpreted and applied in the context of and in a manner consistent with the Convention. ...

Article 5
General Principles

In order to conserve and manage straddling fish stocks and highly migratory fish stocks, coastal States and States fishing on the high seas shall, in giving effect to their duty to cooperate in accordance with the Convention:

(a) adopt measures to ensure long-term sustainability of straddling fish stocks and highly migratory fish stocks and promote the objective of their optimum utilization;

(b) ensure that such measures are based on the best scientific evidence available and are designed to maintain or restore stocks at levels capable of producing maximum sustainable yield, as qualified by relevant environmental and economic factors, including the special requirements of developing States, and taking into account fishing patterns, the interdependence of stocks and any generally recommended international minimum standards, whether subregional, regional or global;

(c) apply the precautionary approach in accordance with article 6;

(d) assess the impacts of fishing, other human activities and environmental factors on target stocks and species belonging to the same ecosystem or associated with or dependent upon the target stocks;

(e) adopt, where necessary, conservation and management measures for species belonging to the same ecosystem or associated with or dependent upon the species above levels at which their reproduction may become seriously threatened;

(f) minimize pollution, waste, discards, catch by lost or abandoned gear, catch of non-target species, both fish and non-fish species (hereinafter referred to as non-target species) and impacts on associated or dependent species, in particular endangered species, through measures including, to the extent practicable, the development and use of selective, environmentally safe and cost-effective fishing gear and techniques;

(g) protect biodiversity in the marine environment;

(h) take measures to prevent or eliminate overfishing and excess fishing capacity and to ensure that levels of fishing effort do not exceed those commensurate with the sustainable use of fishery resources;

(i) take into account the interest of artisanal and subsistence fishers;

(j) collect and share, in a timely manner, complete and accurate data concerning fishing activities on, *inter alia*, vessel position, catch of target and non-target species and fishing effort, as set out in Annex I, as well as information from national and international research programmes;

(k) promote and conduct scientific research and develop appropriate technologies in support of fishery conservation and management; and

(l) implement and enforce conservation and management measures through effective monitoring, control and surveillance.

Article 6
Application of the Precautionary Approach

(1) States shall apply the precautionary approach widely to conservation, management and exploitation of straddling fish stocks and highly migratory fish stocks in order to protect the living marine resources and preserve the marine environment. ...

Article 8
Cooperation for Conservation and Management

(1) Coastal States and States fishing on the high seas shall, in accordance with the Convention, pursue cooperation in relation to straddling fish stocks and highly migratory fish stocks either directly or through appropriate subregional or regional fisheries management organizations or arrangements, taking into account the specific characteristics of the subregion or region, to ensure effective conservation and management of such stocks.

(2) States shall enter into consultations in good faith and without delay, particularly where there is evidence that the straddling fish stocks and highly migratory fish stocks concerned may be under threat of over-exploitation or where a new fishery is being developed for such stocks. ...

(3) Where a subregional or regional fisheries management organization or arrangement has the competence to establish conservation and management measures for particular straddling fish stocks or highly migratory fish stocks, States fishing for the stocks on the high seas and relevant coastal States shall give effect to their duty to cooperate by becoming members of such organization or participants in such arrangement, or by agreeing to apply the conservation and management measures established by such organization or arrangement.

(4) Only those States which are members of such an organization or participants in such an arrangement, or which agree to apply the conservation and management measures established by such organization or arrangement, shall have access to the fishery resources to which those measures apply. ...

Article 17
Non-members of Organizations and Non-participants in Arrangements

(1) A State which is not a member of a subregional or regional fisheries management organization or is not a participant in a subregional or regional fisheries management arrangement, and which does not otherwise agree to apply the conservation and management measures established by such organization or arrangement, is not discharged from the obligation to cooperate, in accordance with the Convention and this Agreement, in the conservation and management of the relevant straddling fish stocks and highly migratory fish stocks.

(2) Such State shall not authorize vessels flying its flag to engage in fishing operations for the straddling fish stocks or highly migratory fish stocks which are subject to the conservation and management measures established by such organization or arrangement. ...

Article 18
Duties of the Flag State

(1) A State whose vessels fish on the high seas shall take such measures as may be necessary to ensure that vessels flying its flag comply with subregional and regional conservation and management measures and that such vessels do not engage in any activity which undermines the effectiveness of such measures.

(2) A State shall authorize the use of vessels flying its flag for fishing on the high seas only where it is able to exercise effectively its responsibilities in respect of such vessels under the Convention and this Agreement. ...

Article 19
Compliance and Enforcement by the Flag State

(1) A State shall ensure compliance by vessels flying its flag with subregional and regional conservation and management measures for straddling fish stocks and highly migratory fish stocks. To this end, that State shall:

(a) enforce such measures irrespective of where violations occur;

(b) investigate immediately and fully any alleged violation of subregional or regional conservation and management measures, which may include the physical inspection of the vessels concerned, and report promptly to the State alleging the violation and the relevant subregional or regional organization or arrangement on the progress and outcome of the investigation;

(c) require any vessel flying its flag to give information to the investigating authority regarding vessel position, catches, fishing gear, fishing operations and related activities in the area of an alleged violation;

(d) if satisfied that sufficient evidence is available in respect of an alleged violation, refer the case to its authorities with a view to instituting proceedings, without delay, in accordance with its laws and, where appropriate, detain the vessel concerned; and

(e) ensure that, where it has been established, in accordance with its laws, a vessel has been involved in the commission of a serious violation of such measures, the vessel does not engage in fishing operations on the high seas until such time as all outstanding sanctions imposed by the flag State in respect of the violation have been complied with. ...

Article 21
Subregional and Regional Cooperation in Enforcement

(1) In any high seas area covered by a subregional or regional fisheries management organization or arrangement, a State Party which is a member of such organization or a participant in such arrangement may, through its duly authorized inspectors,

board and inspect, in accordance with paragraph 2, fishing vessels flying the flag of another State Party to this Agreement, whether or not such State Party is also a member of the organization or a participant in the arrangement, for the purpose of ensuring compliance with conservation and management measures for straddling fish stocks and highly migratory fish stocks established by that organization or arrangement.

(2) States shall establish, through subregional or regional fisheries management organization or arrangements, procedures for boarding and inspection pursuant to paragraph 1, as well as procedures to implement other provisions of this article. Such procedures shall be consistent with this article and the basic procedures set out in article 22 and shall not discriminate against non-members of the organization or non-participants in the arrangement. Boarding and inspection as well as any subsequent enforcement action shall be conducted in accordance with such procedures. States shall give due publicity to procedures established pursuant to this paragraph. ...

(4) Prior to taking action under this article, inspecting States shall, either directly or through the relevant subregional or regional fisheries management organization or arrangement, inform all States whose vessels fish on the high seas in the subregion or region of the form of identification issued to their duly authorized inspectors. The vessels used for boarding and inspection shall be clearly marked and identifiable as being on government service. At the time of becoming a Party to this Agreement, a State shall designate an appropriate authority to receive notifications pursuant to this article and shall give due publicity of such designation through the relevant subregional or regional fisheries management organization or arrangement.

(5) Where, following boarding and inspection, there are clear grounds for believing that a vessel has engaged in any activity contrary to the conservation and management measures referred to in paragraph 1, the inspecting State shall, where appropriate, secure evidence and shall promptly notify the flag State of the alleged violation.

(6) The flag State shall respond to the notification referred to in paragraph 5 within three working days of its receipt, or such other period as may be prescribed in procedures established in accordance with paragraph 2, and shall either:

(a) fulfil, without delay, its obligations under article 19 to investigate and, if evidence so warrants, take enforcement action with respect to the vessel, in which case it shall promptly inform the inspecting State of the results of the investigation and of any enforcement action taken; or

(b) authorize the inspecting State to investigate.

(7) Where the flag State authorizes the inspection State to investigate an alleged violation, the inspecting State shall, without delay, communicate the results of that investigation to the flag State. The flag State shall, if evidence so warrants, fulfil its obligations to take enforcement action with respect to the vessel. Alternatively, the flag State may authorize the inspecting State to take such enforcement action as the flag State may specify with respect to the vessel, consistent with the rights and obligations of the flag State under this Agreement.

(8) Where, following boarding and inspection, there are clear grounds for believing that a vessel has committed a serious violation, and the flag State has either failed to respond or failed to take action as required under paragraphs 6 or 7, the inspectors may remain on board and secure evidence and may require the master to assist in further

investigation including, where appropriate, by bringing the vessel without delay to the nearest appropriate port, or to such other port as may be specified in procedures established in accordance with paragraph 2. The inspecting State shall immediately inform the flag State of the name of the port to which the vessel is to proceed. The inspecting State and the flag State and, as appropriate, the port State shall take all necessary steps to ensure the well-being of the crew regardless of their nationality. ...

(11) For the purpose of this article, a serious violation means:

(a) fishing without a valid licence, authorization or permit issued by the flag State in accordance with article 18, paragraph 3(a);

(b) failing to maintain accurate records of catch and catch-related data, as required by the relevant subregional or regional fisheries management organization or arrangement, or serious misreporting of catch, contrary to the catch reporting requirements of such organization or arrangement;

(c) fishing in a closed area, fishing during a closed season or fishing without, or after attainment of, a quota established by the relevant subregional or regional fisheries management organization or arrangement;

(d) directed fishing for a stock which is subject to a moratorium or for which fishing is prohibited;

(e) using prohibited fishing gear;

(f) falsifying or concealing the markings, identity or registration of a fishing vessel;

(g) concealing, tampering with or disposing of evidence relating to an investigation;

(h) multiple violations which together constitute a serious disregard of conservation and management measures; or

(i) such other violations as may be specified in procedures established by the relevant subregional or regional fisheries management organization or arrangement.

NOTES

1) What does the precautionary approach as set out in article 6 really mean?[140]

2) Do the new compliance and enforcement mechanisms provide a satisfactory means to implement the management of fisheries on the High Seas and to prevent disputes of the kind that arose between Canada and Spain?

3) Articles 21 and 22 provide for a boarding and inspection regime for straddling stocks that are "covered" by a regional fisheries management organization such as NAFO. NAFO has its own boarding and inspection regime. For those states members of NAFO and party to the 1995 Agreement, such as Canada and the EC, what is the relationship between the NAFO boarding and inspection regime and articles 21 and 22 of the 1995 Agreement? Does the NAFO boarding and inspection regime trump articles 21 and 22 of the 1995 Agreement or does the 1995 Agreement trump the NAFO regime? Assuming the application of articles 21 and 22, what rights would Canada have regarding an EC fishing vessel to (a) board; (b) inspect; (c) direct a fishing vessel to port; and (d) prosecute the vessel?

---

140 See Jaye Ellis, "The Straddling Stocks Agreement and the Precautionary Principle as Interpretive Device and Rule of Law" (2001) 32 Ocean Dev. & Int'l L. 289.

4) In what way and to what extent is the obligation on states in articles 8(3) and (4) stronger than that in article 63(2) of the Law of the Sea Convention?

5) The United States is a party to the 1995 Agreement (ratified August 21, 1996, three years before Canada) but not the Law of the Sea Convention. Canada ratified the 1995 Agreement four years before becoming a party to the Law of the Sea Convention. Yet, the 1995 Agreement is directly tied to the Law of the Sea Convention (see the title of the 1995 Agreement). How can this be explained?

6) Serious concerns exist in Canada regarding foreign overfishing beyond the east coast 200 nautical mile zone. These concerns and recommendations for action were detailed by the House of Commons Standing Committee on Fisheries and Oceans in its report of June 2002 entitled "Foreign Overfishing: Its Impacts and Solutions—Conservation on the Nose and Tail of the Grand Banks and the Flemish Cap" and reiterated in its March 2003 report entitled "Custodial Management Outside Canada's 200 Mile Limit." What options does Canada have in international law for dealing with alleged foreign overfishing beyond the 200 nautical mile zone?

7) In addition to NAFO, there are an increasing number of regional fisheries management agreements that deal with straddling fish stocks and regional agreements that deal with highly migratory fish stocks (for example, tuna).[141] One issued faced by these international fisheries organizations is rooted in international law, in that the regulations adopted by the organizations are only binding on their member states. In some situations, fishing vessel owners from a state that is a member of a regional fisheries organization will reflag their vessels in a state that is not a member with the intent of avoiding the regulations of the organization. The 1993 Agreement to Promote Compliance with International Conservation and Management Measures by Fishing Vessels on the High Seas (the FAO Compliance Agreement)[142] is an attempt to discourage states from agreeing to reflag fishing vessels.

8) In 2001 the Council of the Food and Agriculture Organization of the UN (FAO) adopted the International Plan of Action to Prevent, Deter, and Eliminate Illegal, Unreported, and Unregulated Fishing (IPOA-IUU).[143] While not a legally binding document, this Plan of Action is designed to provide guidance to states. Paragraph 1 of the Plan of Action outlines its rationale:

> [T]he issue of illegal, unreported and unregulated (IUU) fishing in world fisheries is of serious and increasing concern. IUU fishing undermines efforts to conserve and manage fish stocks in all capture fisheries. When confronted with IUU fishing, national and regional

---

141 See A.K. Sydnes, "Regional Fishery Organizations: How and Why Organizational Diversity Matters" (2001) 32 Ocean Dev. and Int'l L. 349. See also R. Rayfuse, "Canada and Regional Fisheries Organizations: Implementing the UN Fish Stocks Agreement" (2003) 34 Ocean Dev. & Int'l L. 209.

142 (1994) 33 I.L.M. 968. The *Compliance Agreement* entered into force on 24 April 2003; Canada ratified on 20 May 1994. See D.A. Bolton, "The Compliance Agreement" in Hey, *supra* note 106 at 31-53.

143 FAO, *International Plan of Action to Prevent, Deter, and Eliminate Illegal, Unreported and Unregulated Fishing* (2001). See W. Edeson, "The International Plan of Action on Illegal, Unreported, and Unregulated Fishing: The Legal Context of a Non-Legally Binding Instrument" (2001) 16 Int. J. of Marine and Coastal L. 603.

fisheries management organizations can fail to achieve management goals. This situation leads to the loss of both short- and long-term social and economic opportunities and to negative effects on food security and environmental protection. ... Existing international instruments addressing IUU fishing have not been effective due to a lack of political will, priority, capacity and resources to ratify or accede to and implement them.

What other reasons might be suggested for the ineffectiveness of international instruments in dealing with overfishing and IUU fishing?

West Coast Fisheries

Arguably the most vital natural resource in the Pacific Northwest region of North America is anadromous fish, the most important of which is salmon. Anadromous fish are born in fresh waters, migrate to the salt waters of the ocean for a number of years and then, when fully matured, return to fresh waters to spawn. The traditional principle of the freedom of the high seas for navigation and fishing has given way to a different view with respect to fishing for anadromous stocks. All states-of-origin for salmon agree that there is no longer a right to fish for salmon on the high seas.[144] Beyond this understanding, disagreement and, at times, bitter dispute has prevailed over the regulation of the salmon fisheries for nearly a century.

On February 11, 1992, the United States, Canada, Japan, and the Russian Federation signed the Convention for the Conservation of Anadromous Stocks in the North Pacific Ocean (1992 North Pacific Salmon Treaty). The operative provision of the 1992 Treaty is article 1, which asserts a complete ban on high seas salmon fishing extending across the North Pacific Ocean and adjacent seas north of 33 degrees latitude contiguous to the 200-nautical-mile EEZs of each of the signatories.[145] In addition, article V sets out enforcement measures: signatories who find vessels fishing illegally on the high seas may bring those boats into their ports and bring the violators before the prosecuting authorities in that country. Most illegal fishing in the North Pacific takes on two forms: (1) the reflagging of vessels from signatory States to flags of non-signatory States and; (2) the use of driftnets.[146] In addition, the Treaty established a new international body, the North Pacific Anadromous Fish Commission (NPAFC) in order to supervise oceanic research and cooperation between States. This body also plays an important role in the coordination of enforcement efforts among the signatories of the 1992 North Pacific Salmon Treaty.

The 1992 Treaty is consistent with the relevant provision of the 1982 Convention on the Law of the Sea. Article 66(1) of the 1982 Convention grants states-of-origin "primary interest in and responsibility for" anadromous stocks. Hence, the state-of-origin principle has been fully entrenched in the 1982 Convention and thus, arguably, in customary

---

144 K.B. Bryan, "Swimming Upstream: Trying To Enforce the 1992 North Pacific Salmon Treaty" (1995) 28 Cornell Int'l L.J. 241 at 247.

145 *Convention for the Conservation of Anadromous Stocks in the North Pacific Ocean*, February 11, 1992, T.I.A.S. No. 11465, signed in Moscow on February 11, 1992, available online: <www.npafc.org>.

146 See Bryan, *supra* note 144 at 252-56.

international law. Moreover, article 66(3) asserts that fishing for anadromous stocks may occur only within the 200-mile EEZ of a coastal state and that any high seas fishing outside the EEZ must be preceded by negotiation with the state-of-origin.

The more difficult issue has been between Canada and the United States. Attempts at joint management of the resource go back to the early 1900s. In 1908, the first attempt to establish cooperative management of Fraser River salmon was unsuccessful. In 1930, the Convention for the Protection, Preservation, and Extension of Sockeye Salmon Fisheries in the Fraser River was concluded.[147] Despite these efforts, however, the resource continued to be a source of friction and controversy, with periodic "fish wars" erupting during which each side attempted to intensify interceptions.

The growth in population of the North American continent has placed pressure upon the salmon fisheries in both Canada and the United States. Toward the end of the 1960s, salmon stocks along the Pacific shoreline of North America began to decline at an unprecedented rate. The decline in stocks, the fear of foreign overfishing from third country fleets, and the desire to benefit from aggressive hatchery enhancement programs brought the two nations to the negotiating table and, on April 24, 1970, the United States and Canada agreed to a bilateral fishing agreement, which called for expanded negotiations on issues of mutual concern.[148] The most persistently difficult matter that plagued the negotiations well into the mid-1970s concerned interception of the migrating fish. Pacific salmon usually travel northward once they reach the ocean and therefore they must return southward when they make their way back to the rivers of origin to spawn. Consequently, American-origin salmon from the rivers of Washington and Oregon may be intercepted by Canadian fishers off the B.C. coast, whereas Canadian origin salmon may be intercepted by Alaskan fishers as the fish return to B.C. rivers to spawn. The failure to reach agreement on the interception issue turned the bilateral negotiations into a stalemate.

In the early 1980s, a crisis provided the incentive for the two countries to renew serious negotiations; during this period the numbers of chinook salmon returning to their rivers of origin fell to a distressing level. The main hindrance to reaching agreement between the United States and Canada lay in the conflicts that existed between domestic actors, particularly on the U.S. side, where fishers and politicians from Washington and Oregon on the one hand differed with Alaska fishers, on the other.[149] For instance, Alaska relied on interceptions and held the view that it should not reduce this activity, whereas Washington and Oregon were preoccupied with the recovery of their endangered stocks and aimed to restrain Canadian interception.[150] By January 1984, both parties retreated from the negotiations only to return upon the direct initiative of the Reagan Administration.

---

147 8 U.S.T. 1058.

148 *Agreement on Reciprocal Fishing Privileges in Certain Areas Off Their Coasts*, Can. T.S. 1970 No. 11. See R.J. Schmidt Jr., "International Negotiations Paralyzed by Domestic Politics: Two-Level Game Theory and the Problem of the Pacific Salmon Commission" (1996) 26 Envtl. Law 95 at 102.

149 See, generally, R.J. Schmidt Jr., *supra* note 148 at 104-20.

150 See T.L. McDorman, "The West Coast Salmon Dispute: A Canadian View of the Breakdown of the 1985 Treaty and the Transit License Measure" (1995) 17 Loy. L.A. Int'l & Comp. L.J. 477 at 493.

The later, more focused negotiations culminated in the Pacific Salmon Treaty between Canada and the United States,[151] which entered into force on March 18, 1985.

The 1985 Treaty expresses two cornerstone principles: the two states must (1) refrain from overfishing while providing for optimum production and (2) ensure equitable benefits based upon the production of salmon originating in the waters of either nation.[152] The 1985 Pacific Salmon Treaty established the Pacific Salmon Commission, which was entrusted with the task of implementing the provisions of the Treaty. Canada and the United States each have equal representation on the Commission and its three advisory panels, and all decisions are reached by consensus. At the time, these treaty arrangements raised "an expectation that the United States and Canada would present an example to the world of cooperative resource management and the mutual benefits which can flow therefrom."[153] Unfortunately, both parties found it virtually impossible to apply the equitable principle entrenched in the Treaty and, consequently, the Pacific Salmon Commission became a largely ineffectual bilateral institution.

By 1992, Canada and the United States still could not agree on a joint management plan for Pacific salmon. Moreover, the number of interceptions of Canadian origin salmon by U.S. fishers increased dramatically. Between 1985 and 1992 U.S. interceptions increased from six million to nine million salmon, while Canadian interceptions decreased from five million to three and a half million during the same period.[154]

Canadian negotiators began to lose their patience with the continued failure of the Americans to present a united position. As a measure designed to place pressure on the Americans, Canada announced in June 1994 that U.S. fishing vessels crossing certain inside water passages along the coast of British Columbia would be obliged to obtain a transit licence at a cost of C$1,500. Arguably, the Canadian measure was successful insofar as it resulted in the personal intervention of U.S. Vice-President Gore, who assured Canada that the United States would reverse the trend of increased interception of Canadian salmon and that the United States would begin to regulate for the protection of sensitive stocks.[155] However, government-to-government negotiations continued unsuccessfully.

---

151 Can. T.S. 1985 No. 23. See also T. Healy, "Where Artificial Constraints Kill: The Dispute between Canada and the United States over Pacific Salmon" (1995) 12 Ariz. J. Int'l & Comp. L. 303; T.C. Jensen, "The United States–Canada Pacific Salmon Interception Treaty: An Historical and Legal Overview" (1986) 16 Envtl. L. 363; B.R.H. Johnston, "Swimming Against a Legal Current: A Critical Analysis of the Pacific Salmon Treaty" (1998) 7 Dal. J. Leg. Studies 125; G. Munro, T. McDorman, & R. McKelvey, *Transboundary Fishery Resources and the Canada–United States Pacific Salmon Treaty* (1998) 33 Canadian–American Public Policy 1; and R.J. Schmidt, Jr., *supra* note 148.

152 R.J. Schmidt Jr., *supra* note 148 at 106-7. See also T.L. McDorman, "A Canadian View of the Canada–United States Pacific Salmon Treaty: The International Legal Context" (1998) 6 Willamette J. Int'l L. & Disp. Resol. 79.

153 Munro, McDorman, & McKelvey, *supra* note 151 at 1-2.

154 Figures from 1992 Pacific Salmon Commission data. See T.L. McDorman, *supra* note 150 at 106-7.

155 See T.L. McDorman, *supra* note 150 at 496.

In June 1999, the U.S. and Canadian negotiators reached an agreement on the elements of a 10-year accord to conserve and manage Pacific salmon.[156] It is designed to ensure the sustainability of the five Pacific salmon species (sockeye, pink, chinook, coho, and chum) through a combination of scientific cooperation, new funds to improve fisheries management and aid recovery of weakened salmon stocks, and necessary limits on salmon catches.

NOTES

1) What are the factors that made the Pacific salmon dispute so intractable?[157] Negotiations involving all the stakeholders seemed like a good process at the time. In what ways might the process have been made more productive?

2) In response to the imposition of a transit licence by Canadian authorities in June 1994, the U.S. Senate passed a Bill[158] that asserted that vessels using Inside Passage waters are exercising an international right of innocent passage and that the Inside Passage waters are therefore part of Canada's territorial sea. Canada, however, contended that the waterways for which a transit licence was required were part of Canada's internal waters. What type of considerations are necessary in order to arrive at a convincing conclusion as to whether the Inside Passage is part of Canada's territorial sea or internal waters? Refer to the discussion above in Section B.2 on "Historic Waters of Canada."

Whaling[159]

The International Convention for the Regulation of Whaling (ICRW),[160] signed on December 2, 1946, established the International Whaling Commission (IWC).[161] The goal of the IWC is to conserve stocks and to structure the development of the global whaling industry by re-evaluating annually measures set out in the Schedule to the Convention. The IWC formulates its regulations for the control of whaling on the basis of information provided by the Commission's Scientific Committee. In 1982, the IWC decided on a worldwide moratorium on commercial whaling to take effect as of 1987.

---

156 *Exchange of Notes Constituting an Agreement Relating to the Treaty Concerning Pacific Salmon of January 28, 1985, with Attachments (A to E)*, Can. T.S. 1999 No. 58. See T.L. McDorman, "A Canadian View of the 1999 Canada–United States Pacific Salmon Agreement: A Positive Turning Point?" (1998) 6 Willamette J. of Int'l L. and Disp. Resol. 94 and T.L. McDorman, "The 1999 Canada–United States Pacific Salmon Agreement: Resolved and Unresolved Issues" (2000) 15 J. of Envtl. L. and Litig. 1.

157 See the analysis based on game theory in Munro, McDorman, & McKelvey, *supra* note 151.

158 The Senate Bill was subsequently merged with a House of Representatives Bill and became the *Fisheries Act* of 1995, the relevant provision of which is section 401; 109 U.S. Stat. 366.

159 See P.J. Stoett, *The International Politics of Whaling* (1997); R.L. Friedheim, ed., *Towards a Sustainable Whaling Regime* (2001); W.C.G. Burns & A. Gillespie, eds., *The Future of Cetaceans in a Changing World* (2003). See also Burke, *supra* note 106 at 255-302.

160 161 U.N.T.S. 72.

161 See website of the International Whaling Commission <www.iwcoffice.org>.

Canada is one of the original signatories of the 1946 ICRW; however, Canada withdrew its membership from the Convention in 1982 amid controversy over its decision not to support a moratorium on the hunting of sperm whales. Nonetheless, Canada still makes a contribution to the IWC to the extent that Canadian scientists collaborate with the Commission's Scientific Committee, and each year Canada sends a delegation to the IWC annual meeting as observers.[162]

With the exception of article 65, the 1982 Convention on the Law of the Sea is silent with respect to whaling. According to article 65, states have a duty of cooperation in order to conserve marine mammals and, particularly, with respect to whales, states are expected to "work through the appropriate international organizations" to this end. Although the IWC is presently the main international organization working toward the goal of whale conservation and management, does observance of article 65 by a State necessarily entail membership in the IWC? Viewed another way, now that Canada is a party to the 1982 Convention, is Canada required to comply with the regulations of the IWC?[163]

The moratorium imposed on commercial whaling by the IWC did not apply to subsistence whaling, which is carried out by some aboriginal peoples. Traditionally, Canada's Inuit hunted whales and relied on whale byproducts for food, social, and other needs. The IWC annually sets quotas on the limited number of whales that may be harvested by aboriginals.[164] In 1996, Canada permitted the harvesting of two bowhead whales by the Inuit. This action was met with disapproval by the IWC. The United States also condemned the Canadian measure and in fact threatened to respond with trade sanctions against Canada. Pursuant to the U.S. Pelly Amendment,[165] the U.S. President may choose to impose trade sanctions against a state that the United States considers to have acted contrary to the international conservation program of the IWC. However, in this case, no trade sanctions were ever imposed on Canada. To what extent, if at all, may the United States compel a member and a non-member of the ICRW alike to adhere to the regulations of the IWC?

2. Protection of the Marine Environment[166]

United Nations Convention on the Law of the Sea
Articles 192-194, 197-201, 204-222, 226, 228, 234, 235
Reproduced in the Documentary Supplement

---

162 See T. McDorman, "Canada and Whaling: An Analysis of Article 65 of the Law of the Sea Convention" (1998) 29 Ocean Devel. & Int'l L. 179 at 180.

163 See the discussion *ibid.* at 181-87.

164 See N. Doubleday, "Aboriginal Subsistence Whaling: The Right of Inuit to Hunt Whales and Implications for International Environmental Law" (1989) 17 Denver J. Int'l L. & Pol. 373.

165 22 U.S.C. § 1978 (1996).

166 J.W. Kindt, *Marine Pollution and the Law of the Sea* (1986) 4 vols.; D. VanderZwaag, *Canada and Marine Environmental Protection: Charting A Legal Course Toward Sustainable Development* (1995); D. Brubaker, *Marine Pollution and International Law* (1993); M. Gavouneli, *Pollution from Offshore*

NOTES

1) Part XII of the Convention, consisting of articles 192 to 237, establishes a general framework for global and regional cooperation in the prevention of pollution of the sea. It expects states to monitor the marine environment, and to assess and publish the potential impacts of marine activities under their jurisdiction. It requires states to adopt laws against pollution from land-based and seabed activities, by dumping and through the atmosphere, as well as from ships. It obliges states to enforce these laws and applicable international standards, subject to certain safeguards regarding, for instance, investigation of foreign ships and rights of passage, and subject to the immunity of warships. It holds states responsible for the fulfillment of these obligations both by their own acts and by others within their jurisdiction.

In addition to setting out the general scope of the duties on all states to protect the marine environment, the Convention also sets a balance for their execution by coastal and flag states, who do not share the same interests in prescribing and enforcing pollution standards. To some extent, it moderates national jurisdiction to prescribe pollution laws by reference to "generally accepted international rules." As to enforcement power, it is shared three ways among flag, coastal, and port states, whose authority is consequently to be found not only in Part XII but also in the articles on particular marine zones elsewhere in the Convention. See, for example, the previous materials on rights in the "Territorial Sea" and in the "Exclusive Economic Zone" in Sections B.1 and B.4, respectively. Part XII grants primacy to flag-state enforcement in areas beyond the territorial sea where valid but overlapping jurisdiction may arise. In particular, article 228 obliges the coastal state to suspend proceedings against a foreign ship if the flag state also prosecutes it. However, this limit on the coastal state's jurisdiction is itself suspended when there has been major damage to the coastal state or the flag state has repeatedly disregarded its enforcement duties.

2) This part of the 1982 Convention is almost entirely new law when compared with the four 1958 Geneva Conventions. However, since 1958, a host of specialized conventions on ship safety, ship construction, pollution from ships, and pollution of the seas from land-based sources have been adopted under the aegis of the International Maritime Organization (IMO), the U.N. Environment Programme, the United Nations itself, and on a regional and bilateral basis. See the commentary on "Regional and Specialized Agreements on Prevention of Marine Pollution" next in this section. It can thus be argued that there is a solid groundwork of principles and treaty law that are in part codified by the 1982 Convention. Indeed, the Convention itself refers to this body of international law in several articles where it calls on states to comply with "generally accepted international rules and standards." See, for example, article 211(2). However, this approach is not free of controversy and it is certainly open to states to argue that Part XII cannot be invoked against them until they ratify the Convention.

3) Of particular interest to Canada is article 234, which gives coastal states extensive discretionary powers, which normally would be denied to them by the Convention, in ice-

---

Installations (1995); L.S. Johnson, *Coastal State Regulation of International Shipping* (2004); and E.J. Molenaar, *Coastal State Jurisdiction over Vessel-Source Pollution* (1998).

covered areas. Canada was one of the prime movers of this article and the Canadian delegation worked hard to obtain the consent of the United States and the former U.S.S.R., in particular, as well as broad support within the conference. What is the legal status of article 234?

4) The body of international law on the protection of the marine environment is influenced by the precautionary principle or approach. According to this principle/ approach, it is better to prevent pollution than to depend on control strategies or clean-ups after an accident, both of which are rather costly for States.[167] This preventative approach to marine pollution, which is consistent with the precautionary principle, can be seen in principle 7 of the Stockholm Declaration on the Human Environment in 1972:[168]

> States shall take all possible steps to prevent pollution of the seas by substances that are liable to create hazards to human health, to harm living resources and marine life, to damage amenities or to interfere with other legitimate uses of the sea.

5) In 2003 the Privy Council Office of the Government of Canada released a document entitled "A Framework for the Application of Precaution in Science-based Decision Making about Risk." At page 5, it states: "The Government does not yet consider the precautionary principle/approach to be a rule of customary international law."

6) In the *MOX Plant Case (Ireland v. United Kingdom)*, the request for provisional measures by Ireland, before ITLOS, Ireland argued that the precautionary principle "places the burden on the United Kingdom to demonstrate that no harm would arise" from the operation of the MOX plant and that this "might usefully inform the assessment by the Tribunal of the urgency of the [provisional] measures."[169] The case involved the international movement of radioactive materials and the protection of the Irish Sea from potential increased radioactive contamination. Despite the uncertain science, the risk of harm, and the involvement of nuclear materials, the decision of ITLOS on provisional measures, except for comment in three separate opinions, was silent on the question of precaution.[170]

Regional and Specialized Agreements on Prevention of Marine Pollution

At the same time that the international community was defining a comprehensive legal framework for the protection of the marine environment at the U.N. Conference on the Law of the Sea, states were actively pursuing specific goals by way of specialized legal instruments. The decades of the 1970s and 1980s witnessed the emergence of an impressive body of international treaty law dealing with different aspects of marine

---

167 D. VanderZwaag, *Canada and Marine Environmental Protection, supra* note 166 at 12.

168 U.N. Doc. A/CONF. 48/14/Rev. 1 reproduced in (1972) 11 I.L.M. 1416.

169 (2001), *MOX Plant Case (Ireland v. United Kingdom)*, para. 71, available on the ITLOS website, *supra* note 64, and (2002) 41 I.L.M. 405.

170 Ireland and the United Kingdom proceeded to arbitration on the merits of the dispute. However, in June 2003 the chair of the tribunal suspended the proceedings when it became clear that a case before the European Court of Justice was going to proceed that raised internal EC questions about the Ireland–United Kingdom dispute.

environmental protection. The Stockholm Conference on the Human Environment gave a tremendous impetus to this effort in 1972.

The first area of activity to be the subject of a massive effort at international law making was that of ship-source pollution. A number of new conventions dealing with the design and construction of ships were negotiated, the most important being the International Convention for the Prevention of Pollution from Ships (MARPOL) of 1973.[171] This Convention, and its many annexes and subsequent protocols, is an extensive code dealing with discharges from all types of "ships," including hydrofoils, submersibles, and fixed and floating platforms. This treaty is complemented by three other major conventions: the 1969 International Convention on Civil Liability for Oil Pollution Damage,[172] the 1971 International Convention on the Establishment of an International Fund for Compensation for Oil Pollution Damage,[173] and the 1976 London Convention on Civil Liability for Oil Pollution Damage Resulting From Exploration for and Exploitation of Seabed Mineral Resources.[174] The dumping of wastes at sea has been the object of major international concern in the form of the 1972 London Convention on the Prevention of Marine Pollution by Dumping of Wastes and Other Matter.[175] This Convention and its annexes have been modified throughout the succeeding years by the parties.[176] Another Convention developed under the aegis of the IMO, a U.N. specialized agency located in London,[177] deals with the transportation of, and pollution from, hazardous chemicals.[178] The most recent IMO marine pollution convention is the International Convention for the Control and Management of Ships' Ballast Water and Sediments, 2004. Finally, intervention against maritime casualties to prevent further environmental

---

171   (1973) 12 I.L.M. 1319 and (1979) 17 I.L.M. 546. See also the 1954 *International Convention for the Prevention of Pollution of the Sea by Oil* (OILPOL), Can. T.S. 1958 No. 31, as amended Can. T.S. 1967 No. 29. The latest agreement is directed to the readiness of crew and equipment aboard ship to deal with an emergency: see the 1990 *International Convention on Oil Pollution Preparedness, Response and Cooperation* (1991) 30 I.L.M. 735.

172   (1970) 9 I.L.M. 45. And see the 1976 *Civil Liability Protocol* (1977) 16 I.L.M. 617; Can. T.S. 1989 No. 46. Both agreements are in force for Canada. See also *1984 Protocol*, Misc. No. 8 (1986), Cmnd. 9927, and *1992 Protocol*, IMO Doc. LEG/CONF. 9/15 (1992).

173   (1972) 11 I.L.M. 284; Can. T.S. 1989 No. 47. See also *1976 Protocol* (1977) 16 I.L.M. 621, to which Canada acceded in 1989, *1984 Protocol* (1984) 23 I.L.M. 195, and *1992 Protocol*, IMO Doc. LEG/CONF. 9/16 (1992). Compensation may also be available in Canada from the Ship-source Oil Pollution Fund established under the *Marine Liability Act*, S.C. 2001, c. 6, s. 77; see the annual reports of the Fund published by the Administrator.

174   (1977) 16 I.L.M. 1450.

175   (1972) 11 I.L.M. 1291; Can. T.S. 1979 No. 36.

176   See in particular the 1996 *Protocol to the Convention on the Prevention of Marine Pollution by Dumping of Wastes and Other Matter* (1997) 36 I.L.M. 1, not yet in force.

177   For an excellent but overlooked examination of the work of the IMO, see P. Boisson, *Safety at Sea: Policies, Regulations, and International Law* (1999).

178   The *International Convention on Liability and Compensation for Damage in connection with the Carriage of Hazardous and Noxious Substances by Sea* (HNS Convention) (1996) 35 I.L.M. 1415 (not yet in force).

damage in the event of catastrophic situations is the subject of the 1969 International Convention relating to Intervention on the High Seas in Cases of Oil Pollution Casualties.[179]

The countries of Western Europe showed the utility of regional agreements to deal with the marine environment by adopting conventions covering the Baltic in 1974[180] and the North Sea as early as 1969. The regional approach became the cornerstone of the course taken under the aegis of the U.N. Environment Programme (UNEP) to deal with seabed, land-based, and atmospheric pollution of the marine environment. The "regional seas" program of UNEP has been the impetus for the negotiation of an extraordinary network of conventions and protocols binding the states of different regions of the world. These conventions and protocols include the 1976 Barcelona Convention for the Mediterranean,[181] the 1978 Kuwait Convention for the Gulf,[182] the 1981 Abidjan Convention for West Africa,[183] the 1983 Cartagena Convention for the Caribbean,[184] and the 1986 Noumea Convention for the South-Pacific.[185] These conventions and protocols deal with the differing problems faced in each region.

None of these conventions is perfect. Many were only developed after catastrophes such as the shipwreck and resulting oil spill of the *Amoco Cadiz*. They all suffer from problems resulting from tardy or incomplete implementation and enforcement by national authorities. Despite the important work of the IMO and UNEP, they also suffer collectively from the absence of a world body capable of effective enforcement against delinquent states. Nevertheless, they reflect a considerable achievement in international law making, and they go much of the way toward completing the network of conventions on the different sources of marine pollution envisaged in Part XII of the Law of the Sea Convention.[186]

The Rio Conference on Environment and Development of 1992 laid less emphasis on the development of new law to protect the marine environment, but did stress the need for states to implement the existing law, with a view to protecting the oceans of the world from further degradation. Agenda 21 contributed to setting priority actions that States are

---

179 (1970) 9 I.L.M. 25. See also the *Protocol Relating to Intervention on the High Seas in Cases of Pollution by Substances Other than Oil* (1974) 13 I.L.M. 605.

180 *Helsinki Convention on the Protection of the Marine Environment of the Baltic Sea Area* (1974) 13 I.L.M. 546.

181 *Barcelona Convention for the Protection of the Mediterranean Sea Against Pollution, and its 1976 and 1980 Protocols* (1976)15 I.L.M. 290, 300, and 306 and (1980) 19 I.L.M. 869.

182 *Kuwait Regional Convention for Cooperation on the Protection of the Marine Environment from Pollution, and its Protocol* (1978) 17 I.L.M. 511 and 526.

183 *Abidjan Convention for Cooperation in the Protection and Development of the Marine and Coastal Environment of the West and Central African Region, and its Protocol* (1981) 20 I.L.M. 746 and 756.

184 *Cartagena Convention for the Protection and Development of the Marine Environment of the Wider Caribbean Region, and its Protocols* (1983) 22 I.L.M. 227 and 240. See also 1990 *Protocol Concerning Specially Protected Areas and Wildlife* (1990) 1 Y.B. Int'l Env. Law 450.

185 *Convention for the Protection of the National Resources and Environment of the South Pacific Region, and its Protocols* (1987) 26 I.L.M. 38 and 58. See also *Protocol Concerning Co-operation in Combating Pollution Emergencies in the South Pacific Region* (1987) 26 I.L.M. 59.

186 See the references in note 166.

to consider for controlling land-based marine pollution.[187] The longest chapter of Agenda 21 is chapter 17 on the protection of oceans and coastal areas from sea-based human activities. A conservative estimate is that 80 per cent of marine pollution comes from land-based sources. Following from the Rio Conference, in 1995 the Global Programme of Action for the Protection of the Marine Environment from Land-Based Activities was established and the Washington Declaration on Protection of the Marine Environment from Land-Based Activities adopted.[188] Although it is not a legally binding document, the Washington Declaration contains commitments made by governments to address the problem of land-based marine pollution. The Europeans have gone the furthest in a treaty context in dealing with land-based marine pollution through the 1992 Convention for the Protection of the Marine Environment of the North-East Atlantic (the OSPAR Convention).[189]

Pollution Prevention in Arctic Waters

In 1970, Canada enacted the *Arctic Waters Pollution Prevention Act*,[190] which gave the federal government wide powers to regulate shipping within 100 nautical miles of land in the Arctic. The provisions of the Act apply to "arctic waters," which are described as frozen or liquid waters "adjacent to the mainland and islands of the Canadian Arctic within the area enclosed by the 60th parallel of north latitude, the 141st meridian of longitude and a line measured seaward from the nearest Canadian land a distance of 100 nautical miles."[191] The Act prescribes offences and penalties for pollution of arctic waters by the deposit of waste, which is comprehensively defined to cover any substance that would degrade the waters to an extent detrimental to their use by man or by wildlife and plants that are useful to man. Offending conduct may also result in civil responsibility for pollution damage on an absolute liability basis.

The Act provides regulatory powers regarding (1) the financial responsibility of anyone engaging in activities in the arctic waters or the seabed under them, (2) the creation of shipping safety control zones, (3) the prescription of minimum standards for ships, including hull and fuel tank construction, navigational aids, safety equipment, pilotage

---

187 VanderZwaag, *supra* note 166 at 132-33.

188 See the GPA website at <www.gpa.unep.org> for documents and current activities.

189 (1993) 32 I.L.M. 1069. The OSPAR Convention replaced the *Convention on the Prevention of Marine Pollution from Land-Based Sources* (the Paris Convention) (1974) 13 I.L.M. 352, the first treaty to establish detailed rules on land-based marine pollution, and the 1972 *Convention for the Prevention of Marine Pollution by Dumping from Ships and Aircraft* (the Oslo Convention), 932 U.N.T.S. 4.

190 R.S.C. 1985, c. A-12, and C.R.C. 1978, cc. 353-56, as amended. See J.A. Beesley, "The Canadian Approach to International Environmental Law" (1973) 11 Can. Y.B. Int'l L. 3; R.B. Bilder, "The Canadian Arctic Waters Pollution Prevention Act: New Stresses on the Law of the Sea" (1970-71) 69 Mich. L.R. 1; L. Henkin, "Arctic Anti-Pollution: Does Canada Make or Break International Laws?" (1971) 65 A.J.I.L. 131; and R. St. J. Macdonald, G.L. Morris, & D.M. Johnston, "The Canadian Initiative to Establish a Maritime Zone for Environmental Protection: Its Significance for Mulitlateral Development of International Law" (1971) 21 U.T.L.J. 247. See also Chapter 7, Section C.1 on "The Arctic."

191 *Ibid.* at s. 3(1). An exception is made where the coasts of Canada and Greenland are opposed at less than 100 miles, when a line of equidistance is used instead.

and icebreaker escorts, and (4) the destruction or removal of ships in distress that are causing pollution by depositing waste. The provisions of the Act and the regulations are enforced by Pollution Prevention Officers who have wide powers, including authority to seize a ship anywhere in the Arctic waters or the territorial sea of Canada on reasonable suspicion of having committed an offence.

When the *Arctic Act* was passed, Canada received strong international protests, especially from the United States. Is the Act legitimated by article 234 of the U.N. Convention? Is Canada now prohibited from enforcing pollution standards that are more severe than those prescribed by "generally accepted international rules and standards" against foreign ships in other areas of the sea? Consider article 211. What conclusions can be drawn from the adoption of the 1988 Agreement on Cooperation in the Arctic,[192] by which both Canada and the United States agreed to ask permission of the other before sending icebreaking vessels into Arctic areas under their respective jurisdiction?

Canada, along with seven other polar nations, has since 1996 been working through the Arctic Council[193] to address issues regarding marine environmental protection in the Arctic. Within this framework, it is the Protection of the Arctic Marine Environment (PAME) expert working group that

> addresses policy and non-emergency pollution prevention and control measures related to the protection of the Arctic marine environment from land and sea-based activities, including marine shipping, offshore oil and gas development, land-based activities and ocean disposal.[194]

Other expert groups also deal with matters that touch upon Arctic marine issues.

---

192 Can. T.S. 1988 No. 29.

193 The Arctic Council came into being pursuant to the 1996 *Declaration on the Establishment of the Arctic Council*. See the Arctic Council website at <www.arctic-council.org>. The Arctic Council is not a treaty-based international government organization. Paragraph 2 of the 1996 Declaration provides:

> Members of the Arctic Council are: Canada, Denmark, Finland, Iceland, Norway, the Russian Federation, Sweden and the United States of America (the Arctic States).
> The Inuit Circumpolar Conference, the Saami Council and the Association of Indigenous Minorities in the Far North, Siberia, the Far East of the Russian Federation are Permanent Participants in the Arctic Council. Permanent participation is equally open to other Arctic organizations of indigenous peoples with majority Arctic indigenous constituency, representing:
> (a) a single indigenous people resident in more than one arctic State; or
> (b) more than one Arctic indigenous people resident in a single Arctic State.
> The determination that such an organization has met this criterion is to be made by decision of the Council. The number of Permanent Participants should at any time be less than the number of members.
> The category of Permanent Participation is created to provide for active participation and full consultation with the Arctic indigenous representatives within the Arctic Council.

> In addition to the three organizations of indigenous peoples noted above in the 1996 Declaration, three other groups are now recognized as Permanent Participants in the Arctic Council: the Aleut International Association, the Arctic Athabaskan Council, and the Gwich'in Council International.

194 Cited from <www.arctic-council.org/en/main/infopage/1/>. PAME has its own web pages accessible through the Arctic Council website, *supra* note 193.

Canada's Oceans Management Strategy

In addition to its environment protection measures in Arctic waters, Canada has more recently pioneered an integrated management strategy for its marine areas as a whole. Part II of the *Oceans Act, 1996* provides for the development of integrated management plans for Canadian estuarine, coastal, and marine waters. The federal government in collaboration with the provinces and territories is empowered to create advisory bodies and environmental quality guidelines. The Act permits the establishment of "marine protected areas" (MPAs) for the protection of marine species and their habitat and provides for enforcement of MPA regulations. Pursuant to the *Oceans Act*, in 2002 the federal government released "Canada's Ocean Strategy: Our Oceans, Our Future" and the companion "Policy and Operational Framework for Integrated Ocean Management of Estuarine, Coastal and Marine Environments in Canada."[195] Two marine protected areas have been established pursuant to the *Oceans Act*: in 2004, the Gully Marine Protected Area located on the edge of the Scotian Shelf near Sable Island;[196] and in 2003, the Endeavour Hydrothermal Vents Marine Protected Area that covers 100 square kilometres on the west coast.[197] There are 11 other areas being considering as possible future marine protected areas.

F. DISPUTE SETTLEMENT IN THE LAW OF THE SEA

United Nations Convention on the Law of the Sea
Part XV, Articles 279-299
Reproduced in the Documentary Supplement

Choice of Dispute Settlement Bodies

The entry into force of the Law of the Sea Convention in 1994 was particularly significant in terms of the settlement of law of the sea disputes. Part XV of the 1982 Convention stipulates that in case of a dispute between two States, the parties are to proceed "expeditiously to an exchange of views regarding its settlement by negotiation or other peaceful means." As a consequence, a state that has acceded to the 1982 Convention and that finds itself involved in a dispute under the Convention must submit the conflict to compulsory dispute settlement.

Alas, several exceptions to this last statement must be noted. These are found in articles 297 and 298. The most important exclusion arises under article 297(3)(a) whereby disputes regarding the exercise by a coastal state of its sovereign rights respecting marine living resources within its 200 nautical mile exclusive economic zone is not subject to compulsory adjudication. Pursuant to article 298 states may elect to exclude from compulsory

---

195 The Canada's Oceans Strategy website is <www.cos-soc.gc.ca>.

196 *Gully Marine Protected Area Regulations*, SOR/2004-112, May 7, 2004.

197 *Endeavour Hydrothermal Vents Marine Protected Area Regulations*, SOR/2003-87, March 4, 2003.

adjudication disputes concerning bilateral maritime boundaries, historic bays or titles, and military activities. Unlike many states, at the time of ratification of the Law of the Sea Convention, Canada elected to use the opportunity provided in article 298 to exclude compulsory adjudication for any disputes arising concerning the above noted matters.[198]

A difficult issue during the negotiation of the Law of the Sea Convention dispute settlement regime concerned the choice of adjudicative body to which disputes should be sent. Some states favoured the flexibility of *ad hoc* arbitral tribunals; others preferred the ICJ. Still others favoured the creation of a new and specialized oceans tribunal. In the end all the interests were satisfied. First, ITLOS was established.[199] Second, two forms of arbitration are provided for under the Convention: arbitral tribunals under Annex VII, which can deal with a full range of disputes (see below); and specialized tribunals under Annex VIII, which are restricted to matters related to fisheries, protection, and preservation of the marine environment; marine scientific research; and navigation. Third, article 287(1) provides that a state may select the body (ICJ, ITLOS, Annex VII Arbitration; Annex VIII Arbitration) that it wishes to hear a dispute arising from under the Convention. Annex VII Arbitration is the default dispute settlement body where: (1) a state has made no selection (article 287(3)); and (2) states involved in a dispute have not accepted the same bodies. At the time of ratification of the Law of the Sea Convention, Canada made the following declaration pursuant to Article 287(1):

> With regard to article 287 of the Convention on the Law of the Sea, the Government of Canada hereby chooses the following means for the settlement of disputes concerning the interpretation or application of the Convention without specifying that one has precedence over the other:
>
> (a) the International Tribunal for the Law of the Sea established in accordance with Annex VI of the Convention; and
>
> (b) an arbitral tribunal constituted in accordance with Annex VII of the Convention.

While it appears that ITLOS is only one of four possible choices of procedure for dispute settlement under the Law of the Sea Convention, this is but part of the ITLOS story. As has already been noted in the fisheries context, ITLOS has heard and decided on a number of cases regarding prompt release of seized vessels on the payment of reasonable bond.[200] Article 292 provides that ITLOS has jurisdiction over a prompt release request where it is alleged that a state has not complied with its obligations under the Law of the Sea Convention to release a vessel on the payment of reasonable bond (for example, Article 73(2)) and the involved states have not agreed on another tribunal or court to hear the request for prompt release. Also, pursuant to Article 290, ITLOS is the default

---

198 See "Declaration of Canada at time of Ratification" available on the DOALOS website, *supra* note 1.

199 See *Annex VI of the Law of the Sea Convention*, "The Statute of the International Tribunal for the Law of the Sea." See also the ITLOS website, *supra* note 64. See generally G. Eiriksson, *The International Tribunal for the Law of the Sea* (2000); P. Chandrasekhara Rao & R. Khan, eds., *The International Tribunal for the Law of the Sea: Law and Practice* (2001); and M.H. Nordquist & J.N. Moore, eds., *Current Marine Environmental Issues and the International Tribunal for the Law of the Sea* (2001).

200 See above in Section E.1 on "Fisheries" and *supra* note 121.

tribunal where a state, having initiated dispute settlement against another state, seeks an order for provisional measures and a tribunal or court has yet to be established or agreed on to hear the case. ITLOS has dealt with four requests for provisional measures: (1999), "*M/V Saiga*" (*Saint Vincent and the Grenadines v. Guinea*); (1999), *Southern Bluefin Tuna* (*New Zealand v. Japan; Australia v. Japan*); the previously mentioned (2001), *MOX Plant* case (*Ireland v. United Kingdom*); and (2003), *Case Concerning Land Reclamation* (*Malaysia v. Singapore*).[201]

Of these four cases where the dispute settlement regime of the Law of the Convention was invoked and provisional measures sought, thus far only one has led to a decision on the merits of the dispute. Saint Vincent and the Grenadines and Guinea agreed to have the merits of their dispute regarding the seizure by Guinea of a tanker ("*M/V Saiga*") under the flag of Saint Vincent and the Grenadines dealt with by ITLOS. ITLOS sided with the flag state, indicating that the customs law sought to be applied by Guinea had no application and that the force used by Guinea in boarding the tanker was excessive.[202] In the *Southern Bluefin Tuna* case, the arbitration tribunal established pursuant to the Law of the Sea Convention decided that it was without jurisdiction to proceed to the merits.[203] In the *MOX Plant* case, the arbitration tribunal established pursuant to the Law of the Sea Convention suspended consideration of the case pending a decision from within the European Community on the relationship between the Community and its member states regarding matters before the tribunal.[204] The *Case Concerning Land Reclamation* (*Malaysia v. Singapore*) is proceeding but, as of 2005, at a slow pace.

The dispute settlement regime of the Law of the Sea Convention was activated twice in 2004 for maritime boundary disputes between Barbados and Trinidad and Tobago and between Guyana and Suriname.[205] Decisions can be expected in late 2005 or 2006.

The dispute settlement regime of the Law of the Sea Convention is intimately tied to the dispute settlement regime adopted under the 1995 U.N. Fish Stocks Agreement.[206] Article 30(1) of the Fish Stocks Agreement provides that disputes concerning the Agreement are to be resolved using the Law of the Sea Convention regime. Furthermore, a state's choice of adjudicative procedure for the Law of the Sea Convention will, unless otherwise indicated, apply for disputes arising under the Fish Stocks Agreement.[207]

---

201   All these cases are available on the ITLOS website, *supra* note 64.

202   (1999), *M/V Saiga (Saint Vincent and the Grenadines v. Guinea)*, Judgment, on the ITLOS website, *supra* note 64.

203   (2000) 39 I.L.M. 1359. See B. Oxman, "Complementary Agreements and Compulsory Jurisdiction" (2001) 95 A.J.I.L. 277.

204   Information on the MOX Plant arbitration is available on the website of the Permanent Court of Arbitration at <www.pca-cpa.org>.

205   See the website of the Permanent Court of Arbitration, *ibid.*

206   See T.L. McDorman, "The Dispute Settlement Regime of the Straddling and Highly Migratory Fish Stocks Convention" (1997) 35 Can. Y.B. Int'l L. 57.

207   United Nations Conference on Straddling Fish Stocks and Highly Migratory Fish Stocks, *Agreement for the Implementation of the Provisions of the United Nations Convention of the Law of the Sea of 10 December 1982, Relating to the Conservation and Management of Straddling Fish Stocks and Highly Migratory Fish Stocks*, Article 30(3). Reprinted in (1995) 34 I.L.M. 1542 and above in Section E.1 on "Fisheries."

Canada, having ratified the 1995 Agreement prior to ratification of the Law of the Sea Convention, acted under article 30(4) of the Agreement[208] to select Annex VII arbitration as its dispute settlement procedure for matters arising under the Agreement.

An evaluation of the first 10 years of the dispute settlement regime of the Law of the Sea Convention and, in particular, the work of ITLOS, is a subjective task, as reflected in the following comment.

> Examining the importance and effectiveness of international adjudication and formal third-party dispute settlement solely by direct usage and results does not provide a full picture. In the international ocean sector, the existence within the 1982 LOS Convention and the 1995 High Seas Fishing Agreement of third-party dispute resolution processes helps to establish the *expectation* that disputes will be resolved peacefully, equitably and, where necessary, by third-party adjudication. Moreover, when disputes arise the 1982 LOS Convention and the 1995 High Seas Fishing Agreement provide a *structured process* for the disputing states to follow which, on its own, can assist the countries in reaching their own resolution. Of critical importance is the reality that the existence and acceptance of institutionalized international third-party dispute resolution can influence the *manner, style and immediacy of negotiations* to resolve a dispute.[209]

Note that the ICJ has continued to play a vital role in international maritime boundary delimitation and it appears that this function will continue, given its relative success in this area. Arbitration has been used by many governments during and subsequent to the period leading up to the adoption of the U.N. Convention on the Law of the Sea. Arbitration will doubtless continue to be the preferred option for some countries or in certain circumstances. Canada has had recourse to arbitration as well as to the ICJ. Decisions in this area seem to be taken on a pragmatic basis by most governments, when and as they have recourse to compulsory dispute settlement.

Conciliation continues to be an option under the U.N. Charter and general principles of public international law. However, there is little evidence that conciliation is a preferred option for many governments at the present time.

---

208 This provision was applicable to those states that were a party to the 1995 Agreement but not the Law of the Sea Convention and provided the same choices available to states under article 287 of the Law of the Sea Convention.

209 T.L. McDorman, "Global Ocean Governance and International Adjudicative Dispute Resolution" (2000) 43 Ocean & Coastal Management 255 at 270-71. Along similar lines regarding the work of ITLOS, see McDorman, *supra* note 121 at 144-48.

CHAPTER FOURTEEN

Protection of the Environment

A. INTRODUCTION[1]

International protection of the environment as a discrete area of concern is an important development in the public international law system. Paralleling the growth of domestic legal regulation of the environment, international law has developed to respond to the rapidly increasing harm inflicted on the environment and the threat of future degradation.

The world environment contains diverse elements including terrestrial areas, fresh and marine water spaces, and the airspace and atmosphere surrounding the planet. The Earth is inhabited by various forms of life—human, flora, and fauna. The environment and its inhabitants have been damaged and face the prospect of future deterioration, mainly due to the activities of the human race. As both the industrialization process and world population have exploded over the past century, the consequential dangers to the environment have become apparent. Marine and freshwater pollution, transboundary air pollution, depletion of the ozone layer, global warming, the elimination of species of flora and fauna, threats to wildlife habitat, and deforestation are some of the most serious occurrences.

In opposition to the fundamental ordering of public international law, based on the nation-state and the jurisdictional fences demarcating them, pollution and other assaults on the environment cannot always be confined within state boundaries. Transboundary pollution affects states other than the source nation. Deterioration of the ozone layer and global warming stem from activities in many states and affect all nations. Ecosystems cross national boundaries and are multidimensional. The ranges of many migratory species of animals encompass the territories of two or more nations. Clearly, effective legal protection of the environment requires international legal regulation. Furthermore, a number of international environmental concerns require global regulation for effective control.

Although international regulation of environmental matters has existed in specific areas since the 19th century,[2] states only began to focus on international protection of the

---

1   See generally P.W. Birnie & A.E. Boyle, *International Law and the Environment*, 2d ed. (2002); E. Brown Weiss, *et al.*, *International Environmental Law: Basic Instruments and References* (1992) and *International Environmental Law: Basic Instruments and References 1992-1999* (1999); E. Brown Weiss *et al.*, *International Environmental Law and Policy* (1998); H. Hohmann, *Basic Documents of International Environmental Law* (1992) 3 vols.; A. Kiss & D. Shelton, *International Environmental Law*, 3d ed. (2004); V.P. Nanda & G. Pring, *International Environmental Law and Policy for the 21st Century* (2003); and P. Sands, *Principles of International Environmental Law*, 2d ed. (2003).

2   See Sands, *supra* note 1 at xxv, 25.

environment as a matter of pressing concern in the 1960s. The past five decades have seen the considerable growth of international law in this area and the development of a distinct discipline. However, the product has been mainly in the form of treaty law, on a bilateral, regional, and multilateral basis, and sometimes employing the framework convention-protocol combination. The development of norms of customary international law on international protection of the environment has been slower. Traditional areas of international law such as sovereignty, jurisdiction, and state responsibility continue to provide foundational support, and some concepts and principles of international environmental law have been borrowed and adapted from extant sectors of public international law. However, new ideas have been developed because the traditional principles of international law alone are inadequate to meet the challenge of international environmental protection.

The following sections address the basic principles of international environmental law and the relevant players in the international system. In addition, some contemporary developments and evolving principles of international environmental law are examined. The developing international legal protection of the air, atmosphere, freshwater resources, biodiversity, and terrestrial environment are also surveyed.

B. DEVELOPMENT OF INTERNATIONAL ENVIRONMENTAL LAW

1. Introduction

Emergence of International Environmental Law
from P. Sands, *Principles of International Environmental Law*, 2d ed. (2003)
(footnotes omitted)

Modern international environmental law can be traced directly to international legal developments which took place in the second half of the nineteenth century. Thus, although the current form and structure of the subject has become recognisable only since the mid-1980s, a proper understanding of modern principles and rules requires a historic sense of earlier scientific, political and legal developments. International environmental law has evolved over at least four distinct periods, reflecting developments in scientific knowledge, the application of new technologies and an understanding of their impacts, changes in political consciousness and the changing structure of the international legal order and institutions.

The first period began with bilateral fisheries treaties in the nineteenth century, and concluded with the creation of the new international organisations in 1945. During this period, peoples and nations began to understand that the process of industrialisation and development required limitations on the exploitation of certain natural resources (flora and fauna) and the adoption of appropriate legal instruments. The second period commenced with the creation of the UN and culminated with the UN Conference on the Human Environment, held in Stockholm in June 1972. Over this period, a range of international organisations with competence in environmental matters was created, and legal instruments were adopted, at both the regional and global level, which addressed particular sources of pollution and the conservation of general and particular environmental resources, such as oil pollution, nuclear testing, wetlands, the marine environment and its living resources, the quality of freshwaters, and the dumping of waste at sea. The third period ran from the 1972 Stockholm Conference and concluded with the UN Conference on Environment and Development (UNCED) in June 1992. During this period, the UN tried to put in place a system for co-ordinating responses to international environmental issues, regional and global conventions were adopted, and for the first time the production, consumption and international trade in certain products was banned at the global level. The fourth period was set in motion by UNCED, and may be characterised as the period of integration: when environmental concerns should, as a matter of international law and policy, be integrated into all activities. This has also been the period in which increased attention has been paid to compliance with international environmental obligations, with the result that there has been a marked increase in international jurisprudence.

In tracing the development of the subject, general tendencies and themes may be discerned. First, the development of principles and rules of international environmental law—through treaties, other international acts and custom—has tended to react to events or incidents or the availability of scientific evidence, rather than anticipate general or particular environmental threats and put in place an anticipatory legal framework. Secondly, developments in science and technology have played a significant catalytic role: without the availability of scientific evidence, new rules of law are unlikely to be put in place. Thirdly, ... the principles and rules of international law have developed as a result of a complex interplay between governments, non-state actors and international organisations. The extent to which a particular area is subject to legal rules will depend upon pressure being imposed by non-state actors, the existence of appropriate institutional fora in which rules can be developed, and sufficient will on the part of states to transform scientific evidence and political pressures into legal obligations. And, fourthly, it is only very recently—within the past decade—that issues of international environmental law have become a regular subject of international adjudication, and that international courts have begun to contribute to the definition and application of the subject.

Issues of State Responsibility
from J. Brunnée, "Of Sense and Sensibility: Reflections on International Liability Regimes as Tools for Environmental Protection" (2004) 53 I.C.L.Q. 351 at 353-54 (footnotes omitted)

In principle, it is accepted that a State that violates international environmental law incurs State responsibility. But there is strikingly little State practice and most transnational environmental concerns are resolved through negotiation or adoption of an agreement that regulates the issue at hand. Only in a handful of cases have environmental concerns actually given rise to formal dispute settlement. The resulting decisions provide some clues regarding the primary rules of international environmental law, but they actually offer little insight into State responsibility for environmental harm. Many crucial details remain unsettled. For example, it is unclear whether and to what extent States are entitled to invoke the responsibility of another State when it violates obligations that are owed *erga omnes* or to a group of States. There is also little guidance on the extent to which purely ecological harm would be compensable. In any event, it is unlikely that a State responsibility approach could play a role in addressing global environmental problems. Apart from the fact that it is not conducive to promoting the necessary cooperative steps, the multiplicity of polluters and victims would likely pose insurmountable evidentiary difficulties.

Since State responsibility is contingent upon a violation of a rule of international law, the limitations of relevant international environmental norms also impact on the role that State responsibility can play in the environmental context. Important aspects even of central international environmental norms remain opaque. To begin with, the legal status and content of several key norms, such as the precautionary principle, sustainable development, common concern, or common but differentiated responsibilities, remain contested. While this fact does not impede these norms' ability to influence international environmental policy and shape environmental agreements, it does impact on their usefulness in a litigation context.

Further constraints flow from the standard of liability in international environmental law. Fault liability, encapsulated in the requirement of due diligence, is the background rule under customary law. For example, the foundational obligation to avoid significant transboundary harm requires only that reasonable (regulatory) efforts are made to prevent harm. The difficulties that a claimant would face in establishing a lack of diligence on the part of another State compound other evidentiary challenges, such as those related to causation. Only in relation to specific high-risk activities might there be a strict liability standard. However, it is debatable whether that is so as a matter of customary law, or only pursuant to specific treaty regimes.

In short, there is a vicious circle of sorts at play here. The various uncertainties in primary norms make it difficult to deploy them for State responsibility purposes. In turn, it seems that States are not anxious to resolve the ambiguities, as they serve as a convenient buffer against State responsibility.

NOTES

1) The extent to which the classical rules of international law can provide a viable framework for addressing international environmental problems in the inter-state context may be examined in the context of three aspects: (1) the existence of legal obligations to protect the environment; (2) the conditions upon which responsibility may be incurred by a state; and (3) the liability that ensues from breach of an obligation for which the state can be held responsible.[3]

---

3   Note, "Developments in the Law—International Environmental Law" (1991) 104 Harv. L. Rev. 1484. See generally Birnie & Boyle, *supra* note 1 at 181-200; X. Hanqin, *Transboundary Damage in International Law* (2003); M. Bowman & A. Boyle, eds., *Environmental Damage in International and Comparative Law* (2002).

2) Alleged breaches of international environmental law obligations involve issues of state responsibility. For an analysis of the factors necessary for a claim by one state against another, see Chapter 10, "State Responsibility," in particular the International Law Commission's (ILC) Draft Articles on Responsibility of States for Internationally Wrongful Acts.

3) State responsibility principles require that the conduct of private entities must be attributable to a state before state responsibility can arise: see the discussion in Chapter 10, Section A.3 on "State Responsibility: Attribution." Since international environmental damage stems predominantly from the actions of private persons, a particular problem in the field of state responsibility is the attribution of their conduct to a state. State responsibility for the acts of private persons is a function of state control over those activities and the obligation is imposed on a state to use "due diligence" to prevent conduct that would be in breach of its international obligations if carried out by that state.[4] When transboundary pollution occurs, does state responsibility arise when no action is taken to prosecute the perpetrators or access to the courts by the victims is denied or obstructed?

4) In 2001 the ILC also completed Draft Articles on Prevention of Transboundary Harm from Hazardous Activities.[5] Harm caused to the environment is included. The ILC is currently examining the topic of international liability in cases of loss from transboundary harm arising out of hazardous activities.

5) Based on model uniform legislation, some Canadian provinces and U.S. states have established legislation that gives out of jurisdiction victims standing to sue in the courts of the jurisdiction in which the polluter is situated.[6]

6) Another development is the establishment of some treaties containing civil liability regimes in which persons who engage in activities or operate facilities that may be hazardous to the environment are held liable for ensuing losses. Most of these treaties are in discrete areas, primarily covering nuclear power use, marine oil pollution, freshwater pollution, and the transboundary movement of hazardous waste.[7] Are civil liability treaties a positive and feasible response to the weaknesses of state responsibility in the environmental field?

---

4   "Developments in the Law—International Environmental Law," *supra* note 3 at 1495; Birnie & Boyle, *supra* note 1 at 112-13; and, generally, G. Handl, "State Liability for Accidental Transnational Environmental Damage by Private Persons" (1980) 74 A.J.I.L. 525.

5   *Report of the International Law Commission on the Work of Its Fifty-third Session*, UN GAOR, 56th Sess., Supp. No. 10, U.N. Doc. A/56/10 (2001) chp. IV. E.1.

6   For example, *Transboundary Pollution Reciprocal Access Act*, R.S.O. 1990, c. T.18; *The Transboundary Pollution Reciprocal Access Act*, C.C.S.M, c. T145; *Environment Act*, S.N.S. 1994-95, ch. 1, as am., Part XVI.; and *Transboundary Pollution (Reciprocal Access) Act*, R.S.P.E.I. 1988, c. T-5. See also Birnie & Boyle, *supra* note 1 at 271-72.

7   On nuclear power see *infra* note 104; on marine oil pollution see Chapter 13, Section E.2; on 2003 U.N. *ECE Protocol on Civil Liability and Compensation for Damage Caused by the Transboundary Effects of Industrial Accidents on Transboundary Waters*, see *infra* note 183; *1999 Basel Convention Protocol on Liability and Compensation for Damage Resulting from Transboundary Movements of Hazardous Wastes and Their Disposal*, *infra* note 254. The Council of Europe's *1993 Lugano Convention on Civil Liability for Damage Resulting from Activities Dangerous to the Environment* (1993) 32 I.L.M. 1230, not in force as of July 1, 2004, is the only treaty with general coverage. See also Council of Europe *Convention on the Protection of the Environment Through Criminal Law* (1999) 38 I.L.M. 259, not in force as of July 1,

7) Is it possible to apply the traditional principles of state responsibility to allocate blame with respect to the depletion of the stratospheric ozone layer and climate change?

8) States' duties to prevent or minimize environmental injury are also important, since harm to the environment may be irreversible. The preventive approach imposes procedural norms on states before the occurrence of harm to the environment.[8] In this regard, obligations to monitor the environment, exchange information and data, warn of transboundary risks to the environment, notify and consult before engaging in hazardous activities affecting bordering states, and cooperate with other states are developing norms of international environmental law. For example, procedural obligations are evident in the *Lake Lanoux Arbitration* and in principles 18 and 19 of the Rio Declaration on Environment and Development, reprinted below in Section B.2 on "Development of General Principles." Requirements for environmental impact assessments and the precautionary approach or principle are further examples of proactive measures to combat potential environmental harm. These concepts will be discussed further in Sections B.3(e) on "The Precautionary Principle" and B.3(f) on "Environmental Impact Assessments."

9) In the *Case Concerning the Gabcíkovo-Nagymaros Project*, the International Court of Justice (ICJ) considered Hungary's argument against Slovakia that it was entitled to abandon work on a project to construct a dam and system of locks in both states, and terminate the foundational 1977 bilateral treaty, without incurring state responsibility on the ground of a "state of ecological necessity."[9] The Court found that a state of necessity is recognized by customary international law as an exceptional ground for precluding the wrongfulness of an act that is contrary to international law and noted that grave danger to the environment could lead to a state of necessity, but decided that the case before them did not meet other criteria for such a finding.[10] The Court found that developments in international environmental law were insufficiently connected to the aims of the treaty to alter the obligations therein, but that the treaty itself permitted the parties to include newly developed environmental norms in the implementation of the agreement.

2004. See principle 13 of the *Rio Declaration on Environment and Development*, below in Section B.2 on "Development of General Principles"; J. Brunnée, "Of Sense and Sensibility: Reflections on International Liability Regimes as Tools for Environmental Protection" (2004) 53 I.C.L.Q. 351 at 358-67; L. de la Fayette, "The Concept of Environmental Damage in International Liability Regimes" in M. Bowman & A. Boyle, eds., *Environmental Damage in International and Comparative Law* (2002) at 149.

8   Sands, *supra* note 1 at 246-49; N. de Sadeleer, *Environmental Principles: From Political Slogans to Legal Rules* (2002) at 61-90.

9   (*Hungary/Slovakia*) [1997] I.C.J. Rep. 7; (1998) 37 I.L.M. 168 paras. 49-59. See, generally, P.R. Williams, "International Environmental Dispute Resolution: The Dispute Between Slovakia and Hungary Concerning Construction of the Gabcíkovo and Nagymaros Dams" (1994) 19 Columbia J. Env. L. 1; Sands, *supra* note 1 at 469-77.

10   *Hungary/Slovakia, supra* note 9 at paras. 49-59; Birnie & Boyle, *supra* note 1 at 108.

2. Development of General Principles

Territorial Sovereignty v. Territorial Integrity
from J. Brunnée, *Acid Rain and Ozone Layer Depletion: International Law and Regulation* (1988) at 85-87 (footnotes and subtitles omitted)

Until the time of the Stockholm Conference the international legal approach to transboundary pollution had largely been confined to adapting traditional principles to environmental scenarios. The rules governing transfrontier air pollution had to be derived from other, at times not even environmental, contexts. The emphasis of the traditional approach was on one state's action causing specific damage in another state's territory. The starting points in the search for a legal solution to the new problems were the two conflicting notions of territorial sovereignty and territorial integrity. According to the principle of territorial sovereignty, a state has the right to use its territory in whatever way it deems suitable, even if such utilization could cause environmental harm beyond its territory (Harmon doctrine). According to the principle of territorial integrity, however, a state is entitled to be free of infringements upon its territory. Consequently, no other state may engage in or tolerate activities on its territory which produce deleterious impacts on the environment of the neighbouring state.

These two principles indicate one of the tensions that international law must continuously overcome and not in the environmental context only. Clearly, neither principle, in its absolute form, can solve transboundary pollution problems. While, in the interests of peaceful coexistence, no state should use its territory without consideration of possible harm inflicted upon neighbors, it is also clear that certain activities in one state's territory inevitably have impact upon another state's territory. Both considerations are rooted in the same fact: a state's air neither originates nor stays within its boundaries, but moves uncontrollably from country to country.

The arising *transboundary* environmental problems are a result of man's arbitrarily having drawn boundaries and thus having created separate units of what truly is an entity. Just as these territorial divisions do not correspond to the environmental reality (interrelatedness), the rules of international law created to justify and consolidate them were unfit to solve the problems due to an artificially divided environment. Rules aiming at a solution to transfrontier pollution problems had therefore to be based on a balance between the two rival notions of territoriality. This corresponds to the prevalent view in international law which holds that the rights emanating from territorial sovereignty imply a duty to consider another state's territorial integrity. Thus, there is neither a rule of international law which absolutely prohibits pollution of transboundary impact, nor one which allows it without condition. Yet, while there accordingly is a limit to a state's activities on its territories, it is all the more difficult to determine where the line is to be drawn and where transfrontier pollution becomes unlawful. ...

The principle of "good neighborliness" resulting in "the reciprocal consideration or the mutual limitation of ..." territorial sovereignty and territorial integrity, is an expression of the search for balance between conflicting interests. According to this principle, no state is entitled to use its territory or permit it to be used in a way that would infringe upon the rights of another state. ...

The principle can be traced back to the Roman law maxim of *sic utere tuo ut alienum non laedas* (one must use his own so as not to injure another) subsequently adopted by both civil and common law, and also frequently referred to in modern international law. As far as adoption by civil and common law goes, it can be stated that the principle has precedents in legal concepts common to numerous nations. ...

The international case law relating to the principle of good neighborliness in an environmentally relevant context is scarce, but some significant decisions have confirmed and specified the rather broad notion.

Trail Smelter Arbitration
United States v. Canada
(1931-1941), 3 R.I.A.A. 1905

[In 1896, a smelter was started near Trail, British Columbia. In 1906, the Consolidated Mining and Smelting Company of Canada, Limited acquired and operated the smelter. From 1925, at least, to 1937, damage occurred in the State of Washington, resulting from the sulphur dioxide emitted from the smelter. In 1935, Canada and the United States agreed to arbitrate the following issues:

1) Has damage caused by the Trail Smelter in the State of Washington occurred since the first day of January 1932, and, if so, what indemnity should be paid therefor?

2) In the event of the answer to the first part of the preceding question being in the affirmative, should the Trail Smelter be required to refrain from causing damage in the State of Washington in the future and, if so, to what extent?

3) In the light of the answer to the preceding question, what measures or regime, if any, should be adopted or maintained by the Trail Smelter?

4) What indemnity or compensation, if any, should be paid on account of any decision or decisions rendered by the Tribunal pursuant to the two preceding questions?

In answering these questions, the Tribunal was instructed to "apply the law and practice followed in dealing with cognate questions in the United States of America as well as international law and practice ... ."

By an Interim Decision, delivered on April 16, 1938, the Tribunal reported its "final decision" on Question 1. Concerning Question 1, the Government of the United States claimed damages of $1,849,156.16 with interest of $250,855.01, divided into seven categories, in respect of (1) cleared land and improvements; (2) uncleared land and improvements; (3) livestock; (4) property; (5) wrong done to the United States in violation of sovereignty; (6) interest on $350,000 accepted in satisfaction of the damage done to January 1, 1932, but not paid on that date; and (7) business enterprises.

The Tribunal disallowed the claims of the United States with reference to items (3), (4), (5), (6), and (7) but allowed them, in part, with respect to the remaining items (1) and (2). It found that damage caused by the Trail Smelter in the United States had occurred since January 1, 1932 through October 1, 1937, for which compensation in the amount of $78,000 plus interest at 6 percent per year should be paid by Canada. Reparation for damage occurring after October 1, 1937 was left to be determined in the final decision.

Answering Questions 2 and 3, the Tribunal decided that the Trail Smelter should be subject to a temporary régime for a trial period in order to enable the Tribunal to establish a permanent régime in its final decision based on a "more adequate and intensive study." Its Final Decision was reported on March 11, 1941.]

THE TRIBUNAL: ... The second question ... is as follows:

> In the event of the answer to the first part of the preceding question being in the affirmative, whether the Trail Smelter should be required to refrain from causing damage in the State of Washington in the future and, if so, to what extent?

Damage has occurred since January 1, 1932, as fully set forth in the previous decision. To that extent, the first part of the preceding question has thus been answered in the affirmative.

As has been said above, the report of the International Joint Commission ... contained a definition of the word "damage" excluding "occasional damage that may be caused by SO_2 fumes being carried across the international boundary in air pockets or by reason of unusual atmospheric conditions," as far, at least, as the duty of the Smelter to reduce the presence of that gas in the air was concerned. ...

The first problem which arises is whether the question should be answered on the basis of the law followed in the United States or on the basis of international law. The Tribunal, however, finds that this problem need not be solved here as the law followed in the United States in dealing with the quasi-sovereign rights of the States of the Union, in the matter of air pollution, whilst more definite, is in conformity with the general rules of international law.

Particularly in reaching its conclusions as regards this question as well as the next, the Tribunal has given consideration to the desire of the high contracting parties "to reach a solution just to all parties concerned."

As Professor Eagleton puts it in *Responsibility of States in International Law*, 1928, at 80: "A State owes at all times a duty to protect other States against injurious acts by individuals from within its jurisdiction." A great number of such general pronouncements by leading authorities concerning the duty of a State to respect other States and their territory have been presented to the Tribunal. These and many others have been carefully examined. International decisions, in various matters, from the *Alabama* case onward, and also earlier ones, are based on the same general principle, and, indeed, this principle, as such, has not been questioned by Canada. But the real difficulty often arises rather when it comes to determine what, *pro subjecta materie*, is deemed to constitute an injurious act. ...

No case of air pollution dealt with by an international tribunal has been brought to the attention of the Tribunal nor does the Tribunal know of any such case. The nearest analogy is that of water pollution. But, here also, no decision of an international tribunal has been cited or has been found.

There are, however, as regards both air pollution and water pollution, certain decisions of the Supreme Court of the United States which may legitimately be taken as a guide in this field of international law, for it is reasonable to follow by analogy, in international cases, precedents established by that Court in dealing with controversies between States of the Union or with other controversies concerning the quasi-sovereign rights of such States, where no contrary rule prevails in international law and no reason for rejecting such precedents can be adduced from the limitations of sovereignty inherent in the Constitution of the United States. ...

Great progress in the control of fumes has been made by science in the last few years and this progress should be taken into account.

The Tribunal, therefore, finds that the above decisions, taken as a whole, constitute an adequate basis for its conclusions, namely, that, under the principles of international law, as well as of the laws of the United States, no State has the right to use or permit the use of its territory in such a manner as to cause injury by fumes in or to the territory of another or the properties or persons therein, when the case is of serious consequence and the injury is established by clear and convincing evidence.

The decisions of the Supreme Court of the United States which are the basis of these conclusions are decisions in equity and a solution inspired by them, together with the régime hereinafter prescribed, will, in the opinion of the Tribunal, be "just to all parties concerned," as long, at least, as the present conditions in the Columbia River Valley continue to prevail.

Considering the circumstances of the case, the Tribunal holds that the Dominion of Canada is responsible in international law for the conduct of the Trail Smelter. Apart from the undertakings in the Convention, it is, therefore, the duty of the Government of the Dominion of Canada to see to it that this conduct should be in conformity with the obligation of the Dominion under international law as herein determined.

The Tribunal, therefore, answers Question No. 2 as follows: (2) So long as the present conditions in the Columbia River Valley prevail, the Trail Smelter shall be required to refrain from causing any damage through fumes in the State of Washington; the damage herein referred to and its extent being such as would be recoverable under the decisions of the courts of the United States in suits between private individuals. The indemnity for such damage should be fixed in such manner as the Governments, acting under Article XI of the Convention, should agree upon.[11]

---

11   Further to the case, a supplementary agreement to the Convention established a tribunal to decide questions of indemnity and the future regime arising from the operation of the smelter; see Exchange of Notes, November 17, 1949 and January 24, 1950, 151 U.N.T.S. 171; 3 U.S.T. 539.

Corfu Channel Case (Merits)
United Kingdom v. Albania
[1949] I.C.J. Rep. 4, reported in Chapter 10, Section A.2

Lake Lanoux Arbitration
France v. Spain
(1957), 12 R.I.A.A. 281; 24 I.L.R. 101

[France proposed to use Lake Lanoux for hydroelectric purposes but Spain objected that the scheme would interfere with the flow of boundary waters contrary to a treaty of 1866 between the two states. The Tribunal first found in favour of France that its development scheme would not breach the treaty, and in so doing it made an important statement of principle about possible liability for pollution. The Tribunal went on to consider what conduct was expected of France toward Spain in the realization of its scheme. In particular, Spain argued that the proposed scheme required the prior agreement of both states.]

THE TRIBUNAL: ... To admit that jurisdiction in a certain field can no longer be exercised except on the condition of, or by way of, an agreement between two States, is to place an essential restriction on the sovereignty of a State, and such restriction could only be admitted if there were clear and convincing evidence. Without doubt, international practice does reveal some special cases in which this hypothesis has become reality; thus, sometimes two States exercise conjointly jurisdiction over certain territories (joint ownership, *co-imperium*, or *condominium*); likewise, in certain international arrangements, the representatives of States exercise conjointly a certain jurisdiction in the name of those States or in the name of organizations. But these cases are exceptional, and international judicial decisions are slow to recognize their existence, especially when they impair the territorial sovereignty of a State, as would be the case in the present matter. ...

That is why international practice prefers to resort to less extreme solutions by confining itself to obliging the States to seek, by preliminary negotiations, terms for an agreement, without subordinating the exercise of their competences to the conclusion of such an agreement. Thus, one speaks, although often inaccurately, of the "obligation of negotiating an agreement." In reality, the engagements thus undertaken by States take very diverse forms and have a scope which varies according to the manner in which they are defined and according to the procedures intended for their execution; but the reality of the obligations thus undertaken is incontestable and sanctions can be applied in the event, for example, of an unjustified breaking off of the discussions, abnormal delays, disregard of the agreed procedures, systematic refusals to take into consideration adverse proposals of interests, and, more generally, in cases of violation of the rules of good faith.

... States are today perfectly conscious of the importance of the conflicting interests brought into play by the industrial use of international rivers, and of the necessity to reconcile them by mutual concessions. The only way to arrive at such compromises of interests is to conclude agreements on an increasingly comprehensive basis. International practice reflects the conviction that States ought to strive to conclude such agreements: there would thus appear to be an obligation to accept in good faith all communications and contracts which could, by a broad comparison of interests and by reciprocal good will, provide States with the best conditions for concluding agreements. ...

But international practice does not so far permit more than the following conclusion: the rule that States may utilize the hydraulic power of international watercourses only on condition of a *prior* agreement between the interested States cannot be established as a custom, even less as a general principle of law. ...

The ... question is to determine the method by which these interests can be safeguarded. If that method necessarily involves communications, it cannot be confined to purely formal requirements, such as taking note of complaints, protests or representations made by the downstream State. The Tribunal is of the opinion that, according to the rules of good faith, the upstream State is under the obligation to take into consideration the various interests involved, to seek to give them every satisfaction compatible with the pursuit of its own interests, and to show that in this regard it is genuinely concerned to reconcile the interests of the other riparian State with its own. ...

As a matter of form, the upstream State has, procedurally, a right of initiative; it is not obliged to associate the downstream State in the elaboration of its schemes. If, in the course of discussions, the downstream State submits schemes to it, the upstream State must examine them, but it has the right to give preference to the solution contained in its own scheme provided that it takes into consideration in a reasonable manner the interests of the downstream State. ...

When one examines the question of whether France, either in the course of the dealings or in her proposals, has taken Spanish interests into sufficient consideration, it must be stressed how closely linked together are the obligation to take into consideration, in the course of negotiations, adverse interests and the obligation to give a reasonable place to these interests in the solution finally adopted. A State which has conducted negotiations with understanding and good faith ... is not relieved from giving a reasonable place to adverse interests in the solution it adopts simply because the conversations have been interrupted, even though owing to the intransigence of its partner. ...

[The Tribunal held that, although the parties had failed to reach agreement, France had sufficiently involved Spain in the preparation of its development scheme.]

Stockholm Declaration on the Human Environment
U.N. Doc. A/CONF.48/14/Rev. 1 (1973); (1972) 11 I.L.M. 1416

Principle 1

Man has the fundamental right to freedom, equality and adequate conditions of life, in an environment of a quality that permits a life of dignity and well-being, and he bears a solemn responsibility to protect and improve the environment for present and future generations. ...

Principle 21

States have, in accordance with the Charter of the United Nations and the principles of international law, the sovereign right to exploit their own resources pursuant to their own environmental policies, and the responsibility to ensure that activities within their jurisdiction or control do not cause damage to the environment of other States or of areas beyond the limits of national jurisdiction.

Rio Declaration on Environment and Development
U.N. Doc. A/CONF.151/5/Rev. 1; (1992) 31 I.L.M. 874

Preamble

The United Nations Conference on Environment and Development, Having met at Rio de Janeiro from 3 to 14 June 1992,

Reaffirming the Declaration of the United Nations Conference on the Human Environment, adopted at Stockholm on 16 June 1972, and seeking to build upon it,

With the goal of establishing a new and equitable global partnership through the creation of new levels of cooperation among States, key sectors of societies and people,

Working towards international agreements which respect the interests of all and protect the integrity of the global environmental and developmental system,

Recognizing the integral and interdependent nature of the Earth, our home,

Proclaims that:

Principle 1

Human beings are at the centre of concerns for sustainable development. They are entitled to a healthy and productive life in harmony with nature.

Principle 2

States have, in accordance with the Charter of the United Nations and the principles of international law, the sovereign right to exploit their own resources pursuant to their own environmental and developmental policies, and the responsibility to ensure that activities within their jurisdiction or control do not cause damage to the environment of other States or of areas beyond the limits of national jurisdiction.

Principle 3

The right to development must be fulfilled so as to equitably meet developmental and environmental needs of present and future generations.

Principle 4

In order to achieve sustainable development, environmental protection shall constitute an integral part of the development process and cannot be considered in isolation from it.

Principle 5

All States and all people shall cooperate in the essential task of eradicating poverty as an indispensable requirement for sustainable development, in order to decrease the disparities in standards of living and better meet the needs of the majority of the people of the world.

Principle 6

The special situation and needs of developing countries, particularly the least developed and those most environmentally vulnerable, shall be given special priority. International actions in the field of environment and development should also address the interests and needs of all countries.

Principle 7

States shall cooperate in a spirit of global partnership to conserve, protect and restore the health and integrity of the Earth's ecosystem. In view of the different contributions to global environmental degradation, States have common but differentiated responsibilities. The developed countries acknowledge the responsibility that they bear in the international pursuit of sustainable development in view of the pressures their societies place on the global environment and of the technologies and financial resources they command.

Principle 8

To achieve sustainable development and a higher quality of life for all people, States should reduce and eliminate unsustainable patterns of production and consumption and promote appropriate demographic policies.

Principle 9

States should cooperate to strengthen endogenous capacity-building for sustainable development by improving scientific understanding through exchanges of scientific and technological knowledge, and by enhancing the development, adaptation, diffusion and transfer of technologies, including new and innovative technologies.

Principle 10

Environmental issues are best handled with the participation of all concerned citizens, at the relevant level. At the national level, each individual shall have appropriate access to information concerning the environment that is held by public authorities, including information on hazardous materials and activities in their communities, and the opportunity to participate in decision-making processes. States shall facilitate and encourage public awareness and participation by making information widely available. Effective access to judicial and administrative proceedings, including redress and remedy, shall be provided.

Principle 11

States shall enact effective environmental legislation. Environmental standards, management objectives and priorities should reflect the environmental and developmental context to which they apply. Standards applied by some countries may be inappropriate and of unwarranted economic and social cost to other countries, in particular developing countries.

Principle 12

States should cooperate to promote a supportive and open international economic system that would lead to economic growth and sustainable development in all countries, to better address the problems of environmental degradation. Trade policy measures for environmental purposes should not constitute a means of arbitrary or unjustifiable discrimination or a disguised restriction on international trade. Unilateral actions to deal with environmental challenges outside the jurisdiction of the importing country should be avoided. Environmental measures addressing transboundary or global environmental problems should, as far as possible, be based on an international consensus.

Principle 13

States shall develop national law regarding liability and compensation for the victims of pollution and other environmental damage. States shall also cooperate in an expeditious and more determined manner to develop further international law regarding liability and compensation for adverse effects of environmental damage caused by activities within their jurisdiction or control to areas beyond their jurisdiction.

Principle 14

States should effectively cooperate to discourage or prevent the relocation and transfer to other States of any activities and substances that cause severe environmental degradation or are found to be harmful to human health.

Principle 15

In order to protect the environment, the precautionary approach shall be widely applied by States according to their capabilities. Where there are threats of serious or irreversible damage, lack of full scientific certainty shall not be used as a reason for postponing cost-effective measures to prevent environmental degradation.

Principle 16

National authorities should endeavour to promote the internalization of environmental costs and the use of economic instruments, taking into account the approach that the polluter should, in principle, bear the cost of pollution, with due regard to the public interest and without distorting international trade and investment.

Principle 17

Environmental impact assessment, as a national instrument, shall be undertaken for proposed activities that are likely to have a significant adverse impact on the environment and are subject to a decision of a competent national authority.

Principle 18

States shall immediately notify other States of any natural disasters or other emergencies that are likely to produce sudden harmful effects on the environment of those States. Every effort shall be made by the international community to help States so afflicted.

Principle 19

States shall provide prior and timely notification and relevant information to potentially affected States on activities that may have a significant adverse transboundary environmental effect and shall consult with those States at an early stage and in good faith. ...

Principle 22

Indigenous people and their communities, and other local communities, have a vital role in environmental management and development because of their knowledge and traditional practices. States should recognize and duly support their identity, culture and interests and enable their effective participation in the achievement of sustainable development. ...

Principle 24

Warfare is inherently destructive of sustainable development. States shall therefore respect international law providing protection for the environment in times of armed conflict and cooperate in its further development, as necessary.

NOTES

1) Can the general principle of law *sic utere tuo ut alienum non laedas*, sometimes treated as the equivalent to the "good neighbourliness" principle, be discerned in the previous material? See also article 74 of the U.N. Charter (reproduced in the Documentary Supplement).

2) The *Trail Smelter Arbitration* holding is considered to be a principle of customary international law and it forms the foundation for later developments in international environmental law.[12] Professor Williams has noted that

---

12   For example, see Sands, *supra* note 1 at 242; Birnie & Boyle, *supra* note 1 at 109, 504-6. See, generally, A.K. Kuhn, "The Trail Smelter Arbitration" (1941) 35 A.J.I.L. 665; J.E. Read, "The Trail Smelter Dispute" (1963) 1 Can. Y.B. Int'l L. 213.

what the Tribunal said as to liability can be considered as *obiter dicta*, on account of the fact that Canada had admitted liability for damage suffered in the United States resulting from sulphur dioxide emissions from the Cominco smelter at Trail, British Columbia. The Tribunal's function was only to assess the nature and extent of the compensation to be paid by Canada. Also, the principle of international law stated by the Tribunal can be questioned as it would be difficult to say that in 1931-41 there was sufficient state practice and *opinio juris*. The Tribunal referred also to the law of the United States.[13] Reference to domestic legal systems and decisions by national tribunals is valid as a subsidiary source of international law. Nevertheless, the bold principle it was propounding should have found support in more than a few United States municipal air pollution cases, as well as to analogies with water pollution. These criticisms aside, it is clear the holding of the Tribunal has today become an integral part of international environmental law and can be said to have widespread acceptance by states.[14]

The holding in the *Trail Smelter* case has been criticized for establishing a high and ambiguous prerequisite of "serious damage" for state liability to ensue and for not covering shared resources or the global commons.[15]

3) Although the *Corfu Channel Case* did not involve the environment, some of the statements of the ICJ, in particular its pronouncement that every state has an "obligation not to allow knowingly its territory to be used for acts contrary to the rights of other States" can be interpreted as an affirmation of a state's responsibility to take precautions against the exportation of pollution that might reasonably be prevented and to pay compensation for the damage caused when it does occur. What does a close reading of this part of the judgment suggest are the scope and limits of a state's environmental responsibilities?[16]

4) The Stockholm Declaration was adopted by acclamation at the 1972 U.N. Conference on the Human Environment. Containing 26 principles, the Declaration represents a basic charter laying down the foundation for the future development of international environmental law. Many scholars have expressed the view that principle 21 of the Declaration reflects an existing rule of customary international law.[17] It is reflected in article 30 of the Charter of the Economic Rights and Duties of States,[18] the 1982 U.N.

---

13   It was directed to apply U.S. law by the *compromis*.

14   S.A. Williams, "Public International Law Governing Transboundary Pollution," [1984] Int'l Bus. Lawyer 243 at 246. See also K. Mickelson, "Rereading Trail Smelter" (1993) 31 Can. Y.B. Int'l L. 219.

15   J. Brunnée, "The Responsibility of States for Environmental Harm in a Multinational Context—Problems and Trends" (1993) 34 C. de D. 827 at 831.

16   See the discussion of this case in Chapter 10, Section A.2 on "Basis of Responsibility."

17   For example, Sands, *supra* note 1 at 235-36, 246; Kiss & Shelton, *supra* note 1 at 46; Birnie & Boyle, *supra* note 1 at 109-11; and M. Akehurst, "International Liability for Injurious Consequences Arising Out of Acts Not Prohibited by International Law" (1985) Nethl. Y.B. Int'l L. 3 at 5. See J. Brunnée, "The Stockholm Declaration and the Structure and Processes of International Environmental Law" in M.H. Nordquist, J.N. Moore, & S. Mahmoudi, eds., *The Stockholm Declaration and Law of the Marine Environment* (2003) 67 at 68; J. Brunnée, *Acid Rain and Ozone Layer Depletion: International Law and Regulation* (1988) at 92 on the conceptual limitations of principle 21.

18   U.N. GA Res. 3281/(XXIX), UN GAOR, 29th Sess., Supp. No. 31 at 50, U.N. Doc. A/9631 (1974); (1975) 14 I.L.M. 251.

Law of the Sea Convention,[19] and a number of multilateral agreements and instruments including article 3 of the Convention on Biological Diversity.[20] Australia and New Zealand argued in the *Nuclear Tests Cases*[21] that the Stockholm Declaration reflects the attitude of the international community.

5) The 1992 Rio Declaration on Environment and Development, discussed further in note 9 below, reaffirms the Stockholm Declaration and seeks to build upon it. In particular, compare principle 2 of the Rio Declaration with principle 21 of the Stockholm Declaration. Principle 2 of the Rio Declaration has been replicated in a number of treaties and, in its 1996 Advisory Opinion on the *Legality of the Threat or Use of Nuclear Weapons*, the ICJ responded to the argument that any use of nuclear weapons would be unlawful by reference to international law on the environment, including principle 21 of the Stockholm Declaration and principle 2 of the Rio Declaration, by stating:

> The Court recognizes that the environment is under daily threat and that the use of nuclear weapons could constitute a catastrophe for the environment. The Court also recognizes that the environment is not an abstraction but represents the living space, the quality of life and the very health of human beings, including generations unborn. The existence of the general obligation of States to ensure that activities within their jurisdiction and control respect the environment of other States or of areas beyond national control is now part of the corpus of international law relating to the environment.[22]

6) Do the obligations in principle 21 of the Stockholm Declaration and principle 2 of the Rio Declaration cover activities occurring outside a state's territory to the extent that the state was exercising control over the injurious conduct? If so, could private activities in space, on the high seas or on the deep seabed, fall within the scope of the principles?[23] What are some of the limitations in the application of principle 21 and principle 2 in the light of contemporary environmental concerns?

---

19   See articles 192-194, reproduced in the Documentary Supplement.

20   These include both regional and global instruments—for example, OECD *Principles Concerning Transfrontier Pollution*, Council Rec. C(74) 224, (1975) 14 I.L.M. 242; *ECE Convention on Long-Range Transboundary Air Pollution*, Preamble, *infra* note 81; *Vienna Convention for the Protection of the Ozone Layer*, Preamble, *infra* note 106; *1991 Canada-U.S. Agreement on Air Quality*, Preamble, below in Section C.1 on "Transboundary Air Pollution and Acid Deposition"; *United Nations Framework Convention on Climate Change*, Preamble, below in section E on "Global Warming and Climate Change"; *Convention on Biological Diversity*, article 3, below in Section H.3 on "Conservation of Biological Diversity"; and *Statement of Principles for a Global Consensus on the Management, Conservation and Sustainable Development of All Types of Forests*, principle 1(a), below in Section H.1 on "Protection of Land Spaces" in Note 5.

21   [1974] I.C.J. Rep. 253 and 457.

22   [1996] I.C.J. Rep. 226; (1996) 35 I.L.M. 814 at para. 29. Principle 2 of the Rio Declaration is replicated in *e.g.*: *U.N. Framework Convention on Climate Change*, Preamble, below in Section E on "Global Warming and Climate Change"; *U.N. Convention to Combat Desertification*, Preamble, below in Section H.1 on "Protection of Land Spaces" in Note 4; and *Stockholm Convention on Persistent Organic Pollutants*, Preamble, *infra* note 86.

23   See Handl, "State Liability for Accidental Transnational Environmental Damage by Private Persons," *supra* note 4 at 528-29.

7) The Stockholm Declaration was accompanied by 109 recommendations. In December 1972, the U.N. General Assembly endorsed the recommendations and created a new subsidiary organ, the U.N. Environment Programme (UNEP) to carry them out.[24] Headquartered in Nairobi, Kenya, UNEP was designed, *inter alia*, to "promote international co-operation in the field of the environment and to recommend, as appropriate, policies to this end; [t]o provide general policy guidance for the direction and co-ordination of environmental programmes within the United Nations system ... [and] ... to keep under review the world environmental situation in order to ensure that emerging environmental problems of wide international significance receive appropriate and adequate consideration by Governments."[25] UNEP acts as a management body and a catalyst on environmental matters within the U.N. system. It places particular emphasis on the needs of developing states. UNEP's mandate has evolved; it includes policy advice and assisting states in the development of international environmental law. Under its auspices, a substantial number of multilateral treaties have been negotiated and adopted and a variety of environmental law standards, guidelines, and principles have been drafted. UNEP-sponsored treaties include the regional seas conventions, the Vienna Convention for the Protection of the Ozone Layer, the Montreal Protocol on Substances that Deplete the Ozone Layer, and the Basel Convention on the Control of Transboundary Movements of Hazardous Wastes and Their Disposal.[26] UNEP was involved in the drafting of the U.N. Framework Convention on Climate Change, together with other international organizations and bodies, and in the development of the Convention on Biological Diversity.[27] It also acts as the secretariat for a number of environmental treaties. UNEP has been criticized as follows: it is not an independent international organization; it can only advise and persuade states to adhere to instruments and programs; and it has suffered from a shortage of funds and personnel.[28] What reforms, if any, should be pursued to increase the effectiveness of UNEP? Is an international organization for the environment needed?

---

24 *Institutional and Financial Arrangements for International Environmental Co-operation*, GA Res. 2997/
27, UN GAOR, 27th Sess., Supp. No. 30, U.N. Doc. No. A/8730 (1972) at 43. See, generally,
A. Timoshenko, "UNEP Initiatives to Promote Compliance with Multilateral Environmental Agreements"
in A. Kiss, D. Shelton, & K. Ishibashi, eds., *Economic Globalization and Compliance with International
Environmental Agreements* (2003) at 125; S. Charnowitz, "A World Environmental Organization" (2002)
27 Colum. J. Envtl. L. 323; J. Hierlmeier, "UNEP: Retrospect and Prospect—Options for Reforming the
Global Environmental Governance Regime" (2002) 14 Geo. Int'l Envtl. L. Rev. 767; P. Sands, *supra* note
1 at 83-85; and C.A. Petsonk, "The Role of the United Nations Environment Programme (UNEP) in the
Development of International Environmental Law" (1990) 5 Am. U. J. Int'l L. & Pol'y 351.

25 GA Res. 2997/27, *supra* note 24, pt. I, at paras. 2(a), (b), and (d).

26 See below in Sections D on "Protection of the Ozone Layer," F on "Protection of the Marine
Environment," and I on "The Environment and International Trade."

27 "Preparation of an International Legal Instrument on the Biological Diversity of the Planet," UNEP
Governing Council Decision 15/34 (May 25, 1989); Petsonk, *supra* note 24 at 386-88. See below in
Sections E on "Global Warming and Climate Change" and H.3 on "Conservation of Biological Diversity"
on the Conventions.

28 Hierlmeier, *supra* note 24 at 782-87.

8) The U.N. General Assembly also adopted a resolution in 1982, containing the World Charter for Nature.[29] Professor Williams has commented:

This Charter reinforces the concept of conservation of all areas of the earth and special protection to unique areas and samples of the different ecosystems and habitats of rare and endangered species. It stresses that discharge of pollutants into natural systems should be avoided, but where this is not possible, such pollutants shall be treated at source. This would appear in the context of transboundary pollution to posit the view that states must ensure that activities located within their jurisdictions do not damage natural systems within their own territory, within other states or in areas beyond national jurisdiction.[30]

9) The U.N. Conference on Environment and Development (UNCED) was held from June 3 to 14, 1992 in Rio de Janeiro.[31] The Conference objectives included the recommendation of measures to be taken at the international and national levels to protect the environment, the creation of policies for sustainable and environmentally sound development, and the further development of international environmental law. Various legal instruments were adopted or signed during UNCED. Two treaties were signed: the United Nations Framework Convention on Climate Change and the Convention on Biological Diversity.[32] A non-binding statement of principles on the management, conservation, and sustainable development of all types of forests was adopted.[33] Also, a detailed plan of action for governments, called Agenda 21, was drafted.[34] In addition, the Rio Declaration on Environment and Development was adopted during the Conference. Note the manner in which the Rio Declaration addresses a wide variety of contemporary developments and evolving norms concerning environmental protection. Although the Rio Declaration is not a legally binding instrument, its provisions can be used as evidence to support the development of customary international law in the areas covered.[35] What is your opinion on the reconciliation of environmental protection and development achieved in the Declaration?

10) The General Assembly established the Commission on Sustainable Development (CSD) in December 1992 to oversee the implementation of Agenda 21, the Rio Declaration, and the Forest Principles, and to work toward sustainable development

---

29   GA Res. 37/7, UN GAOR, 37th Sess., Supp. No. 51 at 17, U.N. Doc. A/37/51 (1982); (1983) 22 I.L.M. 455.

30   Williams, *supra* note 14 at 248.

31   See L. Campiglio *et al.*, eds., *The Environment After Rio: International Law and Economics* (1994) and M. Pallemaerts, "La Conférence de Rio: Grandeur ou Décadence du Droit International de l'Environnement" (1995) 28 Rev. B.D.I. 175.

32   See below in Sections E on "Global Warming and Climate Change" and H.3 on "Conservation of Biological Diversity."

33   See below in Section H.1 on "Protection of Land Spaces."

34   The comprehensive Agenda 21 is divided into four sections: (1) Social and Economic Dimensions, (2) Conservation and Management of Resources for Development, (3) Strengthening the Role of Major Groups, and (4) Means of Implementation. See also N.A. Robinson, ed., *Agenda 21 and the UNCED Proceedings* (1992) 2 vols. and N.A. Robinson, ed., *Agenda 21: Earth's Action Plan* (1993).

35   J.D. Kovar, "A Short Guide to the Rio Declaration" (1993) 4 Colo. J. Int'l Envtl. L. & Pol'y 119. See *supra* note 22 on principle 2 of the Rio Declaration.

generally. The CSD, which is a functional commission of the Economic and Social Council of the United Nations (ECOSOC), is composed of 53 state representatives elected from U.N. members and meets in annual sessions. The CSD Secretariat is located in New York.

11) The idea that some environmental matters may constitute a "common concern of humankind" took hold with the inclusion of the notion in the Preambles of the Rio Earth Summit treaties: the U.N. Framework Convention on Climate Change and the Convention on Biological Diversity.[36] Professor Brunnée has stated that:

> Unlike Principle 21, the concept of common concern does not spell out a specific rule for the conduct of states. Nonetheless, it signals that states' freedom of action may be subject to limits even where other states' sovereign rights are not affected in the transboundary sense envisaged by Principle 21. Such limits flow from the fact that the concept identifies certain issues as of concern to all members of the international community. It entitles, and perhaps even requires, all states to participate in international efforts to address the concern.[37]

3. Selected Contemporary Developments

The field of environmental law has produced some of the more important and cross-cutting new concepts in international law, and has elicited some innovative approaches to concrete problems. The legal force of these concepts is an important question for discussion.

(a) The Roles of Non-State Actors

Non-state actors include intergovernmental organizations, non-governmental organizations, corporations, and communities of scientists and academics.

An increasing number of intergovernmental organizations (IGOs) have become involved in developing measures for the protection of the environment. Various U.N. bodies, such as UNEP and the CSD, and specialized agencies, such as the International Maritime Organization (IMO), the Food and Agricultural Organization (FAO), and the World Meteorological Organization (WMO) are playing important roles. Also, regional international organizations, such as the Organisation for Economic Co-operation and Development (OECD) and the supranational European Union (EU) have addressed environmental protection within their mandates.

An increasing number of multilateral environmental agreements establish institutional structures, such as a Conference of the Parties (COP) or Meeting of the Parties (MOP), which are given extensive functions and powers, such as the powers to adopt protocols, amendments, and adjustments to the treaty, make regulations, and monitor state party compliance with the treaty.[38] Churchill and Ulfstein argue that these autonomous

---

36 See below in Sections E on "Global Warming and Climate Change" and H.3 on "Conservation of Biological Diversity." See Birnie & Boyle, *supra* note 1 at 97-100; Brunnée, "The Stockholm Declaration and the Structure and Processes of International Environmental Law," *supra* note 17 at 69, 76.

37 Brunnée, "The Stockholm Declaration," *supra* note 17 at 69.

38 See *e.g. Vienna Convention for the Protection of the Ozone Layer and its Montreal Protocol*, below in Section D on "Protection of the Ozone Layer," and the *U.N. Framework Convention on Climate Change* and its *Kyoto Protocol*, below in Section E on "Global Warming and Climate Change." See R.R. Churchill

institutional arrangements may be classified as less formal forms of IGOs.[39] What is your view on this position?

In addition, non-governmental organizations (NGOs) engage in various activities that influence the direction of international environmental law such as disseminating information, advising, lobbying for changes in the law, participating in international conferences to develop international instruments, and monitoring the conservation of the environment.[40] For example, the World Wildlife Fund has fulfilled these functions to protect endangered species and wildlife generally. In some treaties, NGO participation as observers at COPs or as advisers is expressly included.[41] The Canadian Government has even included NGOs in the government delegation at treaty conferences on the environment.

In Chapter 2, "International Legal Persons," Section C.2, the international legal status of NGOs was examined. In the international environmental law context, it has been suggested that, contrary to existing international law principles, NGOs should be given formal legal status in the international system, the concept of environmental rights should be established on this plane, and NGOs should be granted formal standing to enforce these rights before international tribunals and institutions.[42] What is your view on these proposals and their viability considering extant international norms?

Scientists influence international environmental law making through the provision of scientific knowledge to governments, IGOs, and NGOs. This information may lead to the negotiation of international instruments or the strengthening of provisions in existing agreements. For example, the work of the Intergovernmental Panel on Climate Change (IPCC) contributed to the initiation of international negotiations of a treaty on climate change and its subsequent evolution. Scientists can also be included on regulatory committees in environmental treaty regimes.

& G. Ulfstein, "Autonomous Institutional Arrangements in Multilateral Environmental Agreements: A Little-Noticed Phenomenon in International Law" (2002) 94 A.J.I.L. 623; J. Brunnée, "Between Sovereignty, Efficiency, and Legitimacy: Lawmaking under Multilateral Environmental Agreements" in O.C. Okafor & O. Aginam, eds., *Humanizing Our Global Order: Essays in Honour of Ivan Head* (2003) at 62. On compliance, see, generally, E. Brown Weiss & H.K. Jacobson, eds., *Engaging Countries: Strengthening Compliance with International Environmental Accords* (1998); M. Ehrmann, "Procedures of Compliance Control in International Environmental Treaties" (2002) 13 Colo. J. Int'l Envtl. L. & Pol'y 377; E. Brown Weiss, "Understanding Compliance with International Environmental Agreements: The Baker's Dozen Myths" (1998-99) 32 U. Rich. L. Rev. 1555; and G. Handl, "Compliance Control Mechanisms and International Environmental Obligations" (1997) 5 Tul. J. Int'l & Comp. L. 29.

39   Churchill & Ulfstein, *supra* note 38 at 658.

40   See Sands, *supra* note 1 at 112-15; J. Cameron, "Future Directions in International Environmental Law: Precaution, Integration and Non-state Actors" (1996) 19 Dal. L.J. 122; and D.A. Wirth, "Reexamining Decision-Making Processes in International Environmental Law" (1994) 79 Iowa L. Rev. 769.

41   See *e.g. World Heritage Convention*, article 13(7), below in Section H.1 on "Protection of Land Spaces"; CITES, article 11(6)-(7), below in Section H.2 on "Protection of Wildlife"; *Convention on Biological Diversity*, article 23(5), below in Section H.3 on "Conservation of Biological Diversity"; *Climate Change Convention*, article 7(6), below in Section E on "Global Warming and Climate Change."

42   P.J. Sands, "The Environmental Community and International Law" (1989) 30 Harv. Int'l L.J. 393 at 394.

(b) Sustainable Development

The World Commission on Environment and Development was established by the United Nations as an independent body to re-examine the concerns arising out of the interrelated issues of development, economy, and environment. Chaired by Dr. Gro Harlem Brundtland, the Commission issued its now famous report *Our Common Future*[43] (the Brundtland Report) in 1987, defining sustainable development as "development that meets the needs of the present without compromising the ability of future generations to meet their own needs."[44] It recognized that contemporary environmental problems result both from underdevelopment and untrammelled industrialization. The Commission supported economic growth, but only that which is environmentally and socially sustainable. The Commission not only called for multilateral solutions, it also emphasized that action to achieve sustainable development must occur at all levels. Recommendations for institutional and legal reform were made throughout the Report. In particular, legal principles were proposed to attain sustainable development.[45] Sustainable development is expressly mentioned in numerous principles of the Rio Declaration on Environment and Development and is a guiding theme of the entire Declaration, reproduced above in Section B.2 on "Development of General Principles." The Commission on Sustainable Development, discussed above, also promotes the concept. The concept of sustainable development is included in numerous international agreements and instruments, and is being incorporated in domestic law and policy.[46] In the *Case Concerning the Gabčíkovo-*

---

43 *Our Common Future* (1987). See also Experts Group on Environmental Law of the World Commission on Environment and Development, *Environmental Protection and Sustainable Development: Legal Principles and Recommendations* (1987) (hereinafter "WCED Experts"); Sands, *supra* note 1 at 252-56; M.-C. Cordonier-Segger & A. Khalfan, *Sustainable Development Law: Principles, Practices, and Prospects* (2004); A. Boyle & D. Freestone. eds. *International Law and Sustainable Development* (1999); W. Lang, ed., *Sustainable Development and International Law* (1995); K. Ginther *et al.*, eds., *Sustainable Development and Good Governance* (1995); M.-C. Cordonier-Segger, *infra* note 247; A.B.M. Marong, "From Rio to Johannesburg: Reflections on the Role of International Legal Norms in Sustainable Development" (2003) 16 Geo. Int'l Envtl. L. Rev. 21; O. Aginam, "Saving the Tortoise, the Turtle, and the Terrapin: The Hegemony of Global Environmentalism and the Marginalization of Third-World Approaches to Sustainable Development" in *Humanizing Our Global Order: Essays in Honour of Ivan Head*, *supra* note 38 at 12; and A. Rochette, "Stop the Rape of the World: An Ecofeminist Critique of Sustainable Development" (2002) 51 U.N.B.L.J. 145.

44 *Our Common Future* (1987) at 43.

45 WCED Experts, *supra* note 43 at 7. See Summary in *Our Common Future*, *supra* note 43, Annex 1.

46 For example, *U.N. Framework Convention on Climate Change*, articles 2, 3(4), and its *Kyoto Protocol, article 2(1)*, below in Section E on "Global Warming and Climate Change"; *U.N. Convention to Combat Desertification*, Preamble, article 9(1), below in Section H.1 on "Protection of Land Spaces"; *Convention on Biological Diversity*, Preamble, articles 1 and 10, and its *Cartagena Protocol on Biosafety*, Preamble, below in Section H.3 on "Conservation of Biological Diversity"; *North American Free Trade Agreement*, Preamble, *infra* note 247; *Agreement Establishing The World Trade Organization*, Preamble, *infra* note 246; WTO *Turtle-Shrimp* Appellate Body Report, paras. 129, 153-155, *infra* note 249; *Rotterdam Convention on the Prior Informed Consent Procedure for Certain Hazardous Chemicals and Pesticides in International Trade*, Preamble, *infra* note 255; *Consolidated Treaty Establishing the European Community*, articles 2, 6, O.J. C 325 (December 24, 2002); *Charter of Fundamental Rights of the European Union*, article 37, O.J. C 364 (December 7, 2000); *UNCED Forest Principles*, Preamble, *infra* note 215; and

Nagymaros Project, while the Court only briefly mentioned the concept of sustainable development, the Separate Opinion of Vice-President Weeramantry contains an extensive survey of the development of sustainable development in international law and concludes:

> The principle of sustainable development is ... a part of modern international law by reason not only of its inescapable logical necessity, but also by reason of its wide and general acceptance by the global community.[47]

According to Philippe Sands, the concept of sustainable development contains four components: (1) preservation of natural resources for the benefit of future generations (intergenerational equity), (2) exploitation of natural resources only in a manner that is "sustainable" (sustainable use), (3) "equitable" use of natural resources (equitable use or intragenerational equity), and (4) resource management in which environmental considerations are integrated into development plans and projects and development needs are considered in the application of environmental objectives (integration).[48] Publicists differ on the issue whether the concept of sustainable development has become a principle of customary international law.[49]

Can sustainable development be given a precise meaning? Does sustainable development have different meanings for countries of the South and industrialized states?

(c) Intergenerational Equity

The notion of intergenerational equity has been advanced by some jurists.[50] It views the environment in terms of our relationship to past, present, and future generations of humanity and contains intergenerational rights and obligations. Professor Brown Weiss considers that there are three core principles to intergenerational equity:

> First, each generation should be required to conserve the diversity of the natural and cultural resource base, so that it does not unduly restrict the options available to future generations

---

Agenda 21, especially c. 7, *supra* note 34. See also International Law Association, *New Delhi Declaration of Principles of International Law Relating to Sustainable Development*, Conf. Res. 3/2002 (2002). In Canada, see *e.g. Oceans Act*, S.C. 1996, c. 31, as am., Preamble, s. 30(a); *Canadian Environmental Protection Act 1999* (CEPA), S.C. 1999, c. 33, as am., Preamble, s. 3; *Canadian Environmental Assessment Act* (CEAA), S.C. 1992, c. 37, as am., Preamble, ss. 2(1), 4(1)(b); and Government of Canada, the Commissioner of the Environment and Sustainable Development, Office of the Auditor General.

47   *Supra* note 9 at 95. The Court stated, "[t]his need to reconcile economic development with protection of the environment is aptly expressed in the concept of sustainable development," *supra* note 9 at para. 40.

48   Sands, *supra* note 1 at 253.

49   See *e.g.* Sands, *supra* note 1 at 254; as opposed to Birnie & Boyle, *supra* note 1 at 13, 85; Marong, *supra* note 43 at 21, 43-52. See discussion of publicists in Brunnée, "The Stockholm Declaration and the Structure and Processes of International Environmental Law," *supra* note 17 at 77.

50   See E. Brown Weiss, *In Fairness to Future Generations: International Law, Common Patrimony, and Intergenerational Equity* (1989); E. Agius & S. Busuttil, eds., *Future Generations and International Law* (1997); E. Brown Weiss, "Our Rights and Obligations to Future Generations for the Environment" (1990) 84 A.J.I.L. 198; and L. Gündling, "Our Responsibility to Future Generations" (1990) 84 A.J.I.L. 207. See also Sands, *supra* note 1 at 256-57; Birnie & Boyle, *supra* note 1 at 89-91.

in solving their problems and satisfying their own values, and should also be entitled to diversity comparable to that enjoyed by previous generations. This principle is called "conservation of options." Second, each generation should be required to maintain the quality of the planet so that it is passed on in no worse condition than that in which it was received, and should also be entitled to planetary quality comparable to that enjoyed by previous generations. This is the principle of "conservation of quality." Third, each generation should provide its members with equitable rights of access to the legacy of past generations and should conserve this access for future generations. This is the principle of "conservation of access."[51]

The concept of intergenerational equity is evident in principle 1 of the Stockholm Declaration, principle 3 of the Rio Declaration, the Preamble of the World Charter for Nature, article 4 of the World Heritage Convention, article 3(1) of the Convention on Climate Change, and in various other treaties on the environment.[52] In the *Minors Oposa* case, the Philippine Supreme Court had to decide whether the plaintiffs, various minors, had a cause of action in seeking an order to halt timber licensing to prevent deforestation in the Philippines.[53] The Supreme Court held that the plaintiffs did have standing to file a class action suit

> for themselves, for others of their generation and for the succeeding generations. ... Their personality to sue in behalf of the succeeding generations can only be based on the concept of intergenerational responsibility insofar as the right to a balanced and healthy ecology is concerned. Such a right, as hereinafter expounded, considers the "rhythm and harmony of nature." Nature means the created world in its entirety. Such rhythm and harmony indispensably include, *inter alia*, the judicious disposition, utilization, management, renewal and conservation of the country's forest, mineral, land, waters, fisheries, wildlife, off-shore areas and other natural resources to the end that their exploration, development and utilization be equitably accessible to the present as well as future generations. Needless to say, every generation has a responsibility to the next to preserve that rhythm and harmony for the full enjoyment of a balanced and healthy ecology. Put a little differently, the minors' assertion of their right to a sound environment constitutes, at the same time, the performance of their obligation to ensure the protection of that right for generations to come.[54]

---

51 Brown Weiss, "Our Rights and Obligations to Future Generations," *supra* note 50 at 201-2.

52 *Stockholm Declaration*, above in Section B.2 on "Development of General Principles"; *World Charter for Nature, supra* note 29; *Convention for the Protection of the World Cultural and National Heritage*, below in Section H.1 on "Protection of Land Spaces"; *U.N. Framework Convention on Climate Change*, below in Section E on "Global Warming and Climate Change." For other treaties see *e.g. CITES*, Preamble, below in Section H.2 on "Protection of Wildlife"; U.N. *ECE Convention on the Protection and Use of Transboundary Watercourses and International Lakes*, article 2(5)(c), below in Section G.1 on "General Principles"; and *Convention on Biological Diversity*, Preamble, below in Section H.3 on "Conservation of Biological Diversity."

53 *Minors Oposa v. Secretary of the Department of Environment and Natural Resources* (1994) 33 I.L.M. 173. See D.B. Gatmaytan, "The Illusion of Intergenerational Equity: Oposa v. Factoran as Pyrrhic Victory" (2003) 15 Geo. Int'l Envtl. L. Rev. 457; and M.A.S.Z. Manguiat & V.P.B. Yu III, "Maximizing the Value of Oposa v. Factoran" (2003) 15 Geo. Int'l Envtl. L. Rev. 487.

54 *Minors Oposa, supra* note 53 at 185 (footnotes omitted).

In the 1995 *Nuclear Tests Case Order*, Judge Weeramantry rendered a dissenting opinion that included an examination of the concept of intergenerational equity, describing it as "an important and rapidly developing principle of contemporary environmental law."[55]

What is the connection between the idea of intergenerational equity and the concept of sustainable development? Could the notion of intergenerational equity, with its emphasis on both rights and obligations, develop into a principle of international law?

(d) The Environment, Human Rights, and Humanitarian Law

Human rights breaches that involve environmental protection aspects have been addressed through existing human rights laws and remedial mechanisms—typically based on rights to life, privacy, property, health, or minority rights, although there are some developments supporting an independent right to a healthy or satisfactory environment.[56] The African Charter on Human and Peoples' Rights and the Protocol of San Salvador to the American Convention on Human Rights in the Area of Economic, Social and Cultural Rights are regional human rights treaties that include a right to a healthy or satisfactory environment.[57] Would such a human right be classified as a collective or individual right? Is it possible to formulate a right to a "pure" or "clean" environment?

Apart from the question of substantive human rights and the environment, the evolution of procedural rights of individuals to information on the environment, participation in decision making on the environment, and access to domestic remedies in environmental matters is another important development on the international level. These procedural rights are increasingly being included in treaties and other international instruments.[58]

---

55   [1995] I.C.J. Rep. 288. See B. Kwiatkowska, "New Zealand v. France Nuclear Tests: The Dismissed Case of Lasting Significance" (1996) 37 Va. J. Int'l L. 107.

56   See A.E. Boyle & M.R. Anderson, eds., *Human Rights Approaches to Environmental Protection* (1996); D. Shelton, "The Environmental Jurisprudence of International Human Rights Tribunals" in R. Picolotti & J.D. Taillant, eds., *Linking Human Rights and the Environment* (2003) at 1; M. Grandbois & M.-H. Bérard, "La Reconnaissance internationale des droits environnementaux: le droit de l'environnement en quête d'effectivité" (2003) 44 C. de D. 427; S.J. Anaya & C. Grossman, "The Case of Awas Tingni v. Nicaragua: A New Step in the International Law of Indigenous Peoples" (2002) 19 Ariz. J. Int'l & Comp. L. 1; and R. Desgagné, "Integrating Environmental Values into the European Convention on Human Rights" (1995) 89 A.J.I.L. 263. But see *Rodolfo Ullonoa v. Southern Peru Copper Corp.* (2d. Cir. 2003), 343 F. 3d 140. See also S. Attapattu, "The Right to a Healthy Life or the Right to Die Polluted?: The Emergence of a Human Right to a Healthy Environment Under International Law" (2002-3) 16 Tul. Envtl. L.J. 65; J. Lee, "The Underlying Legal Theory to Support a Well-Defined Human Right to a Healthy Environment as a Principle of Customary International Law" (2000) 25 Colum. J. Envtl. L. 283; and D. Shelton, "Human Rights, Environmental Rights, and the Right to Environment" (1991) 28 Stan. J. Int'l L. 103.

57   African Charter on Human and Peoples' Rights, article 24 (1982) 21 I.L.M. 58 (in force October 21, 1986): "All peoples shall have the right to a general satisfactory environment favourable to their development"; Additional Protocol to the American Convention on Human Rights in the Area of Economic, Social and Cultural Rights (Protocol of San Salvador), article 11 (1989) 28 I.L.M. 156 (in force November 16, 1999): "1. Everyone shall have the right to live in a healthy environment and to have access to basic public services. 2. The States Parties shall promote the protection, preservation, and improvement of the environment." (As of October 2005 Canada was not a party to the Protocol.)

International humanitarian law has also developed provisions for the protection of the environment during armed conflict.[59]

(e) The Precautionary Principle

The precautionary principle or approach entails that anticipatory action be taken to prevent or reduce the occurrence of adverse environmental consequences arising out of activities or the use of substances where the risk of such harm occurring is scientifically uncertain or has not been excluded from possibility.[60] Article 7 of the 1990 Bergen ECE Ministerial Declaration on Sustainable Development—the first international definition of general application—states:

> In order to achieve sustainable development, policies must be based on the precautionary principle. Environmental measures must anticipate, prevent and attack the causes of

---

58   See *e.g. 1998 Aarhus Convention on Access to Information, Public Participation in Decision-Making and Access to Justice in Environmental Matters* (1999) 38 I.L.M. 517 (in force October 30, 2001). See, generally, A. Kiss, "Environmental Information and Public Participation in Decision-Making" in *Economic Globalization and Compliance With International Environmental Agreements, supra* note 24 at 193; L.C. Reif, "International Environmental and Human Rights Law: The Role of Soft Law in the Evolution of Procedural Rights to Information, Participation in Decisionmaking, and Access to Domestic Remedies in Environmental Matters," in M.K. Young & Y. Iwasawa, eds., *Trilateral Perspectives on International Legal Issues: Relevance of Domestic Law and Policy* (1996) at 73.

59   See 1977 Protocol I to the 1949 Geneva Conventions, Can. T.S. 1991 No. 2, articles 35, 55; *Convention on the Prohibition of Military or Any Other Hostile Use of Environmental Modification Techniques*, Can. T.S. 1981 No. 40; *Advisory Opinion on the Legality of the Threat or Use of Nuclear Weapons, supra* note 22; and *Rio Declaration*, principle 24, above in Section B.2 on "Development of General Principles." See also S.C. Res. 687 (1991), Section E, para. 16 (reproduced in Chapter 15) (Iraq liable under international law for environmental damage); and S.C. Res. 692, U.N. Doc. S/RES/692, (1991) 30 I.L.M. 864 (U.N. Compensation Commission for claims under S.C. Res. 687). See, generally, L.B. de Chazournes & P. Sands, eds., *International Law, the International Court of Justice and Nuclear Weapons* (1999); H.B. Schiefer, ed., *Verifying Obligations Respecting Arms Control and the Environment: A Post Gulf War Assessment* (1992); G. Plant, *Environmental Protection and the Law of War* (1992); M.C. Power, "La protection de l'environnement en droit international humanitaire: Le cas du Kosovo" (2001-2) 33 Ottawa L. Rev. 225; R.J. Parsons, "The Fight To Save the Planet: U.S. Armed Forces, 'Greenkeeping,' and Enforcement of the Law Pertaining to Environmental Protection During Armed Conflict" (1998) 10 Geo. Int'l Envtl. L. Rev. 441; and M.N. Schmitt, "Green War: An Assessment of the Environmental Law of International Armed Conflict" (1997) 22 Yale Int'l L.J. 1.

60   See *e.g.* Cameron, *supra* note 40; Sands, *supra* note 1 at 266-79; Birnie & Boyle, *supra* note 1 at 115-21; de Sadeleer, *supra* note 8 at 91-226; A. Trouwborst, *Evolution and Status of the Precautionary Principle in International Law* (2002); P. Harremoës et al., eds., *The Precautionary Principle in the 20th Century: Late Lessons From Early Warnings* (2002); T. O'Riordan et al., eds., *Reinterpreting the Precautionary Principle* (2001); D. Freestone & E. Hey, eds., *The Precautionary Principle and International Law: The Challenge of Implementation* (1996); H. Hohmann, *Precautionary Legal Duties and Principles of Modern International Environmental Law* (1994); J.S. Applegate, "The Taming of the Precautionary Principle" (2002) 27 Wm. & Mary Envtl. L. & Pol'y Rev. 13; S. Boutillon, "The Precautionary Principle: Development of an International Standard" (2001-2) 23 Mich. J. Int'l L. 429; and O. McIntyre & T. Mosedale, "The Precautionary Principle as a Norm of Customary International Law" (1997) 9 J. Envtl. L. 221. See also discussion in Brunnée, "The Stockholm Declaration and the Structure and Processes of International Environmental Law," *supra* note 17 at 77-80.

environmental degradation. Where there are threats of serious or irreversible damage, lack
of full scientific certainty should not be used as a reason for postponing measures to prevent
environmental degradation.[61]

The precautionary principle or approach has been inserted in some treaties in the past
two decades and is found in some domestic legal systems, including Canada's.[62] For
example, article 3(3) of the U.N. Framework Convention on Climate Change, reproduced
below in Section E on "Global Warming and Climate Change," states that the parties
"should take precautionary measures" but links this to situations "where there are threats
of serious or irreversible damage." Principle 15 of the 1992 Rio Declaration on Environment
and Development, reproduced above in Section B.2 on "Development of General Principles,"
requires that states apply the precautionary approach according to their capabilities.

In their dissenting opinions in the 1995 *Nuclear Tests Case Order*, Judge *Ad Hoc* Sir
Geoffrey Palmer concluded that "the norm involved in the precautionary principle has
developed rapidly and may now be a principle of customary international law relating to the
environment" and Judge Weeramantry stated that the precautionary principle is "a principle
which is gaining increasing support as part of the international law of the environment."[63]

In the WTO *Beef Hormones* case, the Appellate Body said with respect to the
precautionary principle:

> The status of the precautionary principle in international law continues to be the subject of
> debate among academics, law practitioners, regulators and judges. The precautionary
> principle is regarded by some as having crystallized into a general principle of customary
> international environmental law. Whether it has been widely accepted by [WTO] Members
> as a principle of general or customary international law appears less than clear.[64]

---

61   Rep. in Hohmann, ed., *supra* note 1, vol. 1 at 558-59; Sands, *supra* note 1 at 269.

62   See *e.g. Consolidated Treaty Establishing the European Community*, article 174(2), *supra* note 46, and
      other European regional treaties including U.N. *ECE Convention on the Protection and Use of
      Transboundary Watercourses and International Lakes*, article 2(5)(a), below in Section G.1 on "General
      Principles"; *Convention on Biological Diversity*, Preamble, and its *2000 Cartagena Biosafety Protocol*,
      Preamble, articles 1, 10(6), and 11(8), below in Section H.3 on "Conservation of Biological Diversity";
      Stockholm Convention on Persistent Organic Pollutants, Preamble, article 1, *infra* note 86; and 1991
      *Bamako Convention on the Ban of Import into Africa and the Control of Transboundary Movement and
      Management of Hazardous Wastes Within Africa*, article 4(3)(f). For Canada see *e.g. Oceans Act*, Preamble,
      s. 30(c), *supra* note 46; CEAA, *supra* note 46, s. 4(1)(a); *Species at Risk Act*, Preamble, s. 38, *infra* note 233;
      CEPA, Preamble, ss. 2(1)(a), 6(1.1), *supra* note 46; and *114957 Canada Ltée (Spraytech, Societé
      d'arrosage) v. Hudson (Town)*, [2001] 2 S.C.R. 241 at paras. 30-32. See H. Trudeau, "Du Droit International
      au Droit Interne: L'Emergence du Principe de Precaution en Droit de L'Environnement" (2003) 28 Queen's
      L.J. 455; D. Vanderzwaag, S.D. Fuller, & R.A, Myers, "Canada and the Precautionary Principle/Approach in
      Ocean and Coastal Management: Wading and Wandering in Tricky Currents" (2002) 34 Ottawa L. Rev. 117.

63   *Supra* note 55, Judge *Ad Hoc* Palmer at 412 and Judge Weeramantry at 342. However, in 2003 the Privy
      Council Office of the Government of Canada released a document entitled *A Framework for the Application
      of Precaution in Science-based Decision Making about Risk*, which states at page 5: "The Government
      does not yet consider the precautionary principle/approach to be a rule of customary international law."

64   European Communities: *Measures Concerning Meat and Meat Products (Hormones)*, WT/DS26/AB/R,
      WT/DS48/AB/R (January 16, 1998) at para. 123 (Appellate Body Report). The Appellate Body declined
      to take a position on the status of the principle, *ibid.*

Some publicists consider that the precautionary principle has become a principle of customary international law, while others are more circumspect.[65]

Depending on the circumstances, implementation of the precautionary approach may be achieved through environmental quality objectives, environmental impact assessments, emission controls, or the prohibition of polluting substances. In your view, has the precautionary principle become a principle of customary international law?

(f) Environmental Impact Assessments

Environmental impact assessment (EIA) is a procedure used to determine whether proposed activities and projects will have a negative impact on the surrounding environment in the state in which the activity is to proceed and, if relevant, in neighbouring states. The EIA is increasingly required in both the national and international spheres: it is a decision-making tool that includes public participation and forces the decision maker to consider the environmental effects of the project.[66] Thus, the EIA is a procedural mechanism that takes a preventive approach to environmental protection.

Some treaty law developments have required EIAs when a proposed activity might have had a negative transboundary effect on the environment.[67] In addition, the U.N. Convention on Environmental Impact Assessment in a Transboundary Context (Espoo Convention) was signed on February 25, 1991 and entered into force on September 10, 1997.[68] The Treaty provides for an EIA procedure that must be undertaken for any proposed activity listed in Appendix I that is likely to cause significant adverse transboundary impact. Notification of and consultation with affected parties are required. Participation in the assessment process by the affected parties and the public in those states is also required. Post-assessment consultation must take place between the state of origin and affected parties on the potential transboundary impact of the proposed activity

---

65 See *e.g.* Trouwborst, *supra* note 60 at 244-45, 276, 284; Sands, *supra* note 1 at 279 (customary status in EU area); Hohmann, *supra* note 60 at 335-45; McIntyre & Mosedale, *supra* note 60. In contrast, see *e.g.* Birnie & Boyle, *supra* note 1 at 118-20; Boutillon, *supra* note 60 (an international law standard); Applegate, *supra* note 60.

66 See Sands, *supra* note 1 at 799-800; Birnie & Boyle, *supra* note 1 at 130-35; J.H. Knox, "The Myth and Reality of Transboundary Environmental Impact Assessment" (2002) 96 A.J.I.L. 291; and J. Woodliffe, "Environmental Damage and Environmental Impact Assessment" in *Environmental Damage in International and Comparative Law, supra* note 3 at 133.

67 For example, *U.N. Convention on the Law of the Sea*, article 206, reproduced in the Documentary Supplement; *Canada–United States Agreement on Air Quality*, articles 3(2)(b) and 5, below in Section C.1 on "Transboundary Air Pollution and Acid Deposition"; *Noumea Convention for the Protection of the Natural Resources and Environment of the South Pacific Region*, article 16, (1987) 26 I.L.M. 38; *Protocol to the Antarctic Treaty on Environmental Protection*, article 8 (1991) 30 I.L.M. 1461; and *Biodiversity Convention*, article 14, below in Section H.3 on "Conservation of Biological Diversity." For Canada, see CEAA, *supra* note 46.

68 (1991) 30 I.L.M. 802, with 2001 Amendment (not in force as of October 2005). Negotiated under the auspices of the U.N. Economic Commission for Europe (ECE). As of October 2005, 40 member states (including Canada, but not the United States) were Convention parties. See also its 2003 Protocol on Strategic Environmental Assessment (not in force as of October 2005): <http://www.unece.org>; and U.N. ECE Convention on the Transboundary Effects of Industrial Accidents (1992) 31 I.L.M. 1330.

and methods of reducing or eliminating its impact. The parties must ensure that, in the final decision, due account is taken of the assessment outcome, public comment, and consultations. Appendix I activities include crude oil refineries, nuclear facilities, large-diameter oil and gas pipelines, installations for the disposal of toxic and dangerous wastes, large dams and reservoirs, pulp and paper plants, major mining operations, and deforestation of large areas.

See also principle 17 of the Rio Declaration, reproduced, above, in Section B.2 on "Development of General Principles." In the *Nuclear Tests Case Order*, Judge *Ad Hoc* Palmer stated in his dissenting opinion that "[a]s the law now stands it is a matter of legal duty to first establish before undertaking an activity that the activity does not involve any unacceptable risk to the environment. An EIA is simply a means of establishing a process to comply with that international legal duty," but concluded only that "customary international law may have developed a norm of requiring environmental impact assessment where activities may have a significant effect on the environment."[69]

In the *Case Concerning the Gabcíkovo-Nagymaros Project*, Judge Weeramantry in his separate opinion stated:

> Environmental law in its current state of development would read into treaties which may reasonably be considered to have a significant impact upon the environment, a duty of environmental impact assessment and this means also, whether the treaty expressly so provides or not, a duty of monitoring the environmental impacts of any substantial project during the operation of the scheme.[70]

Do you think that a principle of customary international law requiring EIAs has formed? Would such a principle cover all activities with negative environmental impacts, including transboundary effects? Could a requirement to conduct an EIA be implied from other obligations, such as principle 21 of the Stockholm Declaration or the duty of a state to notify other states of a proposed activity that may cause transboundary damage, considered in the *Lake Lanoux Arbitration*, both reproduced above in Section B.2 on "Development of General Principles"?

(g) Common But Differentiated Responsibilities

The notion of common but differentiated responsibilities attempts to recognize the common responsibilities of all states in dealing with environmental matters, and to account for both the historically larger role of industrialized nations in activities contributing to environmental degradation and the relatively greater difficulties of developing countries in responding to international legal regulation in environmental matters. As Philippe Sands states:

---

69   *Supra* note 55 at 411-12. In his Dissenting Opinion in the same case, Judge Weeramantry stated that "this principle is gathering strength and international acceptance, and has reached the level of general recognition at which this Court should take notice of it" (at 344).

70   *Supra* note 9 at 112.

The principle of common but differentiated responsibility includes two elements. The first concerns the common responsibility of states for the protection of the environment, or parts of it, at the national, regional, and global levels. The second concerns the need to take account of differing circumstances, particularly in relation to each state's *contribution* to the creation of a particular environmental problem and its *ability* to prevent, reduce and control the threat. In practical terms, the application of the principle of common but differentiated responsibility has at least two consequences. First, it entitles, or may require, all concerned states to participate in international response measures aimed at addressing environmental problems. Secondly, it leads to environmental standards which impose differing obligations on states.[71]

Principle 7 of the Rio Declaration, reproduced above in Section B.2 on "Development of General Principles," declares that "States have common but differentiated responsibilities" and some environmental treaties include this formulation of states' responsibilities.[72] The application of the concept has resulted in various mechanisms being inserted in treaties on the environment. First, there may be a grace period given to developing country treaty parties before their legal obligations are activated.[73] Second, the legal obligations of industrialized states parties may be set at more stringent levels than those for developing states parties, or developing states parties may not have to shoulder specific commitments at all.[74] Third, there may be clauses that provide for the transfer of financial and technological assistance from industrialized to developing states parties and other creative mechanisms.[75] Do you think that the concept of common but differentiated responsibilities has developed into a principle of customary international law?

(h) Polluter-Pays Concept

The polluter-pays concept states that the entity that has caused pollution or other environmental harm should be responsible for the consequential costs and measures called for by the authorities of the state in order to remedy the situation.[76] The application

---

71   Sands, *supra* note 1 at 286. See also Birnie & Boyle, *supra* note 1 at 100-4; P. Cullet, *Differential Treatment in International Environmental Law* (2003); C.D. Stone, "Common but Differentiated Responsibilities in International Law" (2004) 98 A.J.I.L. 276; and D. French, "Developing States and International Environmental Law: The Importance of Differentiated Obligations" (2000) 49 I.C.L.Q. 34.

72   For example, *U.N. Framework Convention on Climate Change*, article 3(1), below in Section E on "Global Warming and Climate Change" and its *Kyoto Protocol*, article 10, *ibid.*; *Stockholm Convention on Persistent Organic Pollutants*, Preamble, *infra* note 86.

73   For example, *1987 Montreal Protocol on Substances That Deplete the Ozone Layer*, article 5, *infra* note 107.

74   For example, *U.N. Framework Convention on Climate Change*, article 4, below in Section E on "Global Warming and Climate Change," and its *Kyoto Protocol*, articles 2-7, *ibid.*

75   For example, *Convention on Biological Diversity*, articles 16, 20-21 (access to and transfer of technology, financial assistance), below in Section H.3 on "Conservation of Biological Diversity"; *Kyoto Protocol*, article 12 (clean development mechanism), below in Section E on "Global Warming and Climate Change"; and *Stockholm Convention on Persistent Organic Pollutants*, articles 11-13 (research, technical, and financial assistance), *infra* note 86.

76   Birnie & Boyle, *supra* note 1 at 92-95 and Sands, *supra* note 1 at 279-85; de Sadeleer, *supra* note 8 at 21-60.

of the polluter-pays concept allocates the economic costs of environmentally harmful activity to the polluter and to the goods or services it produces. The international instruments that incorporate the polluter-pays idea primarily involve the European region and industrialized countries.[77] Principle 16 of the Rio Declaration, reproduced above in Section B.2 on "Development of General Principles," contains a weak polluter-pays concept. As a result, commentators do not consider that the concept has gained sufficiently widespread state practice to constitute a principle of customary international law binding on all states.[78] Could the polluter-pays concept be considered a principle of regional customary international law?

C. REGULATION OF TRANSBOUNDARY AIR POLLUTION

1. Transboundary Air Pollution and Acid Deposition[79]

One consequence of the modern industrial era is the emission of pollutants into the air from activities occurring in a state. These pollutants are carried over extended distances, often crossing state boundaries, causing environmental damage to the air, waters, and terrestrial resources of one or more other states. Acid deposition, popularly called "acid rain," has caused major damage to the ground and surface water, terrestrial environment, and buildings in Europe, eastern Canada, and the northeastern United States. Acid deposition is caused by the emission into the air of sulphur dioxide and nitrogen oxides from the burning of fossil fuels by power generators, industrial plants, and motor vehicles. These pollutants are transformed into the secondary pollutant of acid deposition when they chemically react with water vapour, forming sulphuric or nitric acid contained in dry or wet precipitation.[80] In addition, nitrogen oxides combine with volatile organic compounds (VOCs) and produce ground-level ozone, which, in turn, is a major component of smog. Further, persistent organic pollutants (POPs) and heavy metals are also found in transboundary air pollution.

Long-range transboundary air pollution resulted in the classic *Trail Smelter* arbitral decision. Protection of the air and atmosphere has become an important priority in recent years. The European forum was the site of the first regional conventions, using the format

---

77   For example, various OECD and EC instruments discussed in Sands, *supra* note 1 at 281-84; *Consolidated Treaty Establishing the European Community*, article 174(2), *supra* note 46; U.N. *ECE Convention on the Protection and Use of Transboundary Watercourses and International Lakes*, article 12(5)(b), below in Section G.1 on "International Rivers and Lakes"; and *Lugano Convention on Civil Liability for Damage Resulting From Activities Dangerous to the Environment*, *supra* note 7. But see *Stockholm Convention on Persistent Organic Pollutants*, Preamble, *infra* note 86.

78   Birnie & Boyle, *supra* note 1 at 92-93 and Sands, *supra* note 1 at 280.

79   See, generally, P.N. Okowa, *State Responsibility for Transboundary Air Pollution in International Law* (2000); Brunnée, *Acid Rain and Ozone Layer Depletion: International Law and Regulation*, *supra* note 17; and C. Flinterman, B. Kwiatkowska, & J. Lammers, eds., *Transboundary Air Pollution* (1986).

80   See Brunnée, *Acid Rain and Ozone Layer Depletion: International Law and Regulation*, *supra* note 17 at 8-14.

of a framework convention with detailed protocols (the "protocol system") that has become the common approach in the more recent initiatives to protect the atmosphere.

On a regional basis, many international developments have centred on Europe. The Council of Europe, the OECD, the Nordic Council, and the European Union have all addressed the issue of transboundary air pollution in a variety of measures. The U.N. Economic Commission for Europe (ECE) began to examine environmental concerns at the end of the 1960s. Due to the geographic configuration of Europe, many states found they were both the victims and the source of long-range transboundary air pollution. In 1979, the ECE produced the Convention on Long-Range Transboundary Air Pollution (LRTAP Convention).[81] Both Canada and the United States are contracting parties. The LRTAP Convention expresses general principles with few substantive obligations and no specific limitations on emissions of pollutants. The contracting parties agreed that they "shall endeavour to limit and, as far as possible, gradually reduce and prevent air pollution including long-range transboundary air pollution."[82] The parties also agreed to develop policies and strategies to combat air pollution, exchange information, cooperate in the conduct of research, enter into consultations on proposed or ongoing activities with a significant risk of transboundary air pollution, and implement a cooperative program for the monitoring and evaluation of long-range air pollution in Europe. The LRTAP Convention acts as a framework that has been reinforced by Protocols that address financing and specific air pollutants. There are Protocols that impose concrete obligations on the contracting parties to reduce emissions of sulphur dioxide, nitrogen oxides, volatile organic compounds (VOCs), POPs, heavy metals, and ammonia.[83]

POPs are toxic persistent substances, typically pesticides, industrial chemicals, and byproduct contaminants—for example, DDT and PCBs—that can be carried by wind and water currents and bioaccumulate in living organisms, including humans. Indigenous peoples and wildlife in colder climates, such as the Canadian Arctic, are especially

---

81   1983 U.K.T.S. 57, Cmnd. 9034; (1979) 18 I.L.M. 1442. See Birnie & Boyle, *supra* note 1 at 508-13.

82   LRTAP Convention, *supra* note 81, article 2.

83   *1985 Protocol to the LRTAP Convention on the Reduction of Sulphur Emissions or Their Transboundary Fluxes by at Least 30 Percent (Helsinki Protocol)*, Can. T.S. 1987 No. 34; (1988) 27 I.L.M. 707; *1988 Protocol to the LRTAP Convention Concerning the Control of Emissions of Nitrogen Oxides or Their Transboundary Fluxes (Sophia Protocol)* (1989) 28 I.L.M. 214; *1991 Protocol to the LRTAP Convention Concerning the Control of Emissions of Volatile Organic Compounds or Their Transboundary Fluxes* (1992) 31 I.L.M. 573; *Protocol to the LRTAP Convention on the Further Reduction of Sulphur Emissions (Oslo Protocol)* (1994) 33 I.L.M. 1540; 1998 *Protocol to the LRTAP Convention on Persistent Organic Pollutants (Aarhus Protocol)* (1998) 37 I.L.M. 505; 1998 *Protocol to the LRTAP Convention on Heavy Metals (Aarhus Protocol)*: <http://www.unece.org/env/lrtap/> (covers lead, cadmium, mercury); *1999 Protocol to the LRTAP Convention To Abate Acidification, Eutrophication and Ground-Level Ozone (Gothenburg Protocol)*: <http://www.unece.org/env/lrtap/> (covers sulphur dioxide, nitrogen oxides, VOCs, ammonia). See W.J. Shapiro, "Air and Atmosphere: Protocol To Abate Acidification, Eutrophication and Ground-Level Ozone" (1999) Colo. J. Int'l Envtl. L. Pol'y 208. See also *Protocol on Long-Term Financing of the Co-operative Programme for Monitoring and Evaluation of the Long-Range Transmission of Air Pollutants in Europe (EMEP)*, Can. T.S. 1988 No. 39; (1988) 27 I.L.M. 701. As of October 2005, all the Protocols are in force internationally and Canada is a contracting party to the *Helsinki, Sophia, Oslo, Aarhus* (heavy metals) and *Aarhus* (POPs) Protocols, but it has only signed, but not ratified the *VOC* and *Gothenburg* Protocols.

impacted by POPs, which accumulate to a much higher degree in cold temperatures.[84] In 1998, under the auspices of UNEP, governments from around the world began negotiating a multilateral treaty to control POPs, avoiding the framework convention-protocol format and opting instead for immediate controls over a limited number of POPs.[85] The Stockholm Convention on Persistent Organic Pollutants was adopted on May 22, 2001 and entered into force on May 17, 2004.[86] Canada is a contracting party. The Stockholm Convention on POPs obligates parties to eliminate or strictly limit the production, use, import, and export of 12 POPs (including dioxins, furans, PCBs, and some pesticides).[87] The Annexes to the Convention and a Register provide for general or specific exemptions to the controls, for example, the production and use of DDT to kill malaria-carrying mosquitoes, in states parties according to WHO guidelines when there are no other locally safe, effective, and affordable alternatives.[88] Parties are required to take measures to eliminate or reduce releases of the regulated POPs from stockpiles, unintentional production (byproducts), wastes, and waste disposal.[89] Additional chemicals can be incorporated into the control regime.[90]

In the Canada–United States context,[91] Canada has been damaged by acid deposition, much of which originates in the United States, whereas only a small amount of the acid deposition falling in that country is caused by Canadian pollutants. Bilateral consultations on the issue commenced in the late 1970s and, in 1980, the two states signed a Memorandum of Intent Concerning Transboundary Air Pollution.[92] It did not contain any concrete obligations on reduction or limitation of polluting emissions but instead recorded the intention of the two states to work toward the negotiation of a bilateral agreement on transboundary air pollution. The two states also agreed to develop domestic policies and strategies, to exchange information on research, and to expand their historical practice of advance notification and consultation on proposed actions involving a significant actual

---

84   P.L. Lallas, "The Stockholm Convention on Persistent Organic Pollutants" (2001) 95 A.J.I.L. 692 at 694. See *infra* note 232.

85   See Lallas, *ibid.*; J.A. Mintz, "Two Cheers for Global POPs: A Summary and Assessment of the Stockholm Convention on Persistent Organic Pollutants" (2001) 14 Geo. Int'l Envtl. L. Rev. 319; P.L. Lallas, "The Role of Process and Participation in the Development of Effective International Environmental Agreements: A Study of the Global Treaty on Persistent Organic Pollutants (POPs)" (2000-1) 19 UCLA J. Envtl. L. & Pol'y 83.

86   *Stockholm Convention on Persistent Organic Pollutants* (2001) 40 I.L.M. 532. As of October 1, 2005, there were 110 parties. See also *Rotterdam Convention on the Prior Informed Consent Procedure for Certain Hazardous Chemicals and Pesticides in International Trade*, *infra* note 255.

87   *Stockholm Convention*, articles 3-6, Annexes A-C, *supra* note 86.

88   *Stockholm Convention*, article 4, Annexes A, B, part II(2), *supra* note 86; Lallas, *supra* note 84 at 699-701.

89   *Stockholm Convention*, articles 5-6, Annex C, *supra* note 86.

90   *Stockholm Convention*, article 8, *supra* note 86.

91   M. Grandbois, "Le contrôle juridique des précipitations acides" (1985) 26 C. de D. 591 and O. Corter & A. Schaus, "La responsabilité internationale des États-Unis pour la dommages causés par les précipitations acides sur le territoire Canadien" (1989) 27 Can. Y.B. Int'l L. 227. See also the earlier *Trail Smelter Arbitration*, above in Section B.2 on "Development of General Principles."

92   (1981) 20 I.L.M. 690. See Brunnée, *Acid Rain and Ozone Layer Depletion: International Law and Regulation*, *supra* note 17 at 198-202.

or potential risk of transboundary air pollution. The political environment stalled progress until March 1991 when a bilateral treaty on air quality was signed into force. Although the Agreement initially focused on reduction of acid rain precursors, it was amended in 2000, with the addition of Annex 3 to regulate VOCs and nitrogen oxides and reduce ground-level ozone.[93]

Canada–United States Agreement on Air Quality
Can. T.S. 1991 No. 3; 30 I.L.M. 676; as amended by 2000 Protocol,
Can. T.S. 2000 No. 26

Convinced that transboundary air pollution can cause significant harm to natural resources of vital environmental, cultural and economic importance, and to human health in both countries;

Desiring that emissions of air pollutants from sources within their countries not result in significant transboundary air pollution;

Convinced that transboundary air pollution can effectively be reduced through cooperative or coordinated action providing for controlling emissions of air pollutants in both countries, ...

Reaffirming Principle 21 of the Stockholm Declaration ... ;

Convinced that a healthy environment is essential to assure the well-being of present and future generations in Canada and the United States, as well as of the global community;

Have agreed as follows:

Article I
Definitions

For the purposes of this Agreement:

1. *"Air pollution"* means the introduction by man, directly or indirectly, of substances into the air resulting in deleterious effects of such a nature as to endanger human health, harm living resources and ecosystems and material property and impair or interfere with amenities and other legitimate uses of the environment, and "air pollutants" shall be construed accordingly;

2. *"Transboundary air pollution"* means air pollution whose physical origin is situated wholly or in part within the area under the jurisdiction of one Party and which has adverse effects, other than effects of a global nature, in the area under the jurisdiction of the other Party; ...

4. *"International Joint Commission"* means the International Joint Commission established by the Boundary Waters Treaty.

---

93   *Protocol Between Canada and the U.S.A. Amending the Air Quality Agreement*, Can. T.S. 2000 No. 26
(in force December 7, 2000); <http://www.ec.gc.ca/air/can_usa_e.html>. See Environment Canada, U.S.
Environmental Protection Agency, *Cleaner Air Through Cooperation Canada–United States: Progress Under the Air Quality Agreement* (2003); International Joint Commission, *Summary of Critical Air Quality Issues in the Transboundary Region* (January 2004).

Article II
Purpose

The purpose of the Parties is to establish, by this Agreement, a practical and effective instrument to address shared concerns regarding transboundary air pollution.

Article III
General Air Quality Objective

1. The general objective of the Parties is to control transboundary air pollution between the two countries.

2. To this end, the Parties shall:

(a) in accordance with Article IV, establish specific objectives for emissions limitations or reductions of air pollutants and adopt the necessary programs and other measures to implement such specific objectives;

(b) in accordance with Article V, undertake environmental impact assessment, prior notification, and, as appropriate, mitigation measures;

(c) carry out coordinated or cooperative scientific and technical activities, and economic research, in accordance with Article VI, and exchange information, in accordance with Article VII;

(d) establish institutional arrangements, in accordance with Articles VIII and IX; and

(e) review and assess progress, consult, address issues of concern, and settle disputes, in accordance with Articles X, XI, XII and XIII.

Article IV
Specific Air Quality Objectives

1. Each Party shall establish specific objectives, which it undertakes to achieve, for emissions limitations or reductions of such air pollutants as the Parties agree to address. Such specific objectives will be set forth in annexes to this Agreement.

2. Each Party's specific objectives for emissions limitations or reductions are set forth in annexes to this Agreement as follows:

(a) Specific objectives for sulphur dioxide and nitrogen oxides, which will reduce transboundary flows of these acidic deposition precursors, are set forth in Annex 1.

(b) Specific objectives for volatile organic compounds and nitrogen oxides, which will reduce transboundary flows of tropospheric ozone and these precursors, thereby helping both countries attain their respective air quality goals over time, are set forth in Annex 3. ...[94]

---

94   Annex 1 required of the United States: (1) reduction of annual sulphur dioxide emissions by approximately 10 million tons from 1980 levels by 2000; (2) a permanent national emission cap of 8.95 million tons of sulphur dioxide per year for electric utilities by 2010; (3) national cap for sulphur dioxide emissions from industrial sources at 5.6 million tons starting in 1995; and (4) reduction of total annual nitrogen oxides emissions by approximately 2 million tons from 1980 levels by 2000 and the implementation of nitrogen oxides control programs for mobile sources and boilers.

3. Each Party shall adopt the programs and other measures necessary to implement its specific objectives set forth in any annexes.

4. If either Party has concerns about the programs or other measures of the other Party referred to in paragraph 3, it may request consultations in accordance with Article XI.

Article V
Assessment, Notification and Mitigation

1. Each Party shall, as appropriate and as required by its laws, regulations and policies, assess those proposed actions, activities and projects within the area under its jurisdiction that, if carried out, would be likely to cause significant transboundary air pollution, including consideration of appropriate mitigation measures.

2. Each Party shall notify the other Party concerning a proposed action, activity or project subject to assessment under paragraph 1 as early as practicable in advance of a decision concerning such action, activity or project and shall consult with the other Party at its request in accordance with Article XI.

3. In addition, each Party shall, at the request of the other Party, consult in accordance with Article XI concerning any continuing actions, activities or projects that may be causing significant transboundary air pollution, as well as concerning changes to its laws, regulations or policies that, if carried out, would be likely to affect significantly transboundary air pollution.

4. Consultations pursuant to paragraphs 2 and 3 concerning actions, activities or projects that would be likely to cause or may be causing significant transboundary air pollution shall include consideration of appropriate mitigation measures.

5. Each Party shall, as appropriate, take measures to avoid or mitigate the potential risk posed by actions, activities or projects that would be likely to cause or may be causing significant transboundary air pollution.

6. If either Party becomes aware of an air pollution problem that is of joint concern and requires an immediate response, it shall notify and consult the other Party forthwith. ...

For Canada, Annex 1 demanded: (1) reduction of sulphur dioxide emissions in the seven easternmost provinces to 2.3 million tonnes per year by 1994 and the achievement of a cap on sulphur dioxide emissions in the seven easternmost provinces at 2.3 million tonnes per year from 1995 through December 31, 1999; (2) achievement of a permanent national emissions cap of 3.2 million tonnes per year by 2000; (3) reduction of nitrogen oxides from stationary sources by specified amounts by 2000 and, by January 1, 1995, the development of further annual national emission reduction requirements to be achieved by 2000 and/or 2005; and (4) the implementation of a more stringent nitrogen oxides program for mobile sources.

Annex 3 covers south-central Ontario and southern Quebec, 18 Northeastern and Midwestern U.S. states, and the District of Columbia. The U.S. commitments involve a nitrogen oxides emission reduction program to reduce summertime emissions in the U.S. region, and VOC and nitrogen oxides reductions via U.S. vehicle, fuel quality, and consumer/commercial product rules and standards. Canadian commitments involve new regulatory standards for vehicles and fuels as part of a Clean Air agenda, the implementation of Canada-wide standards for ground-level ozone, plus the imposition of maximum caps on nitrogen oxides emissions from fossil-fuel power plants in southern Ontario and southern Quebec aligned with U.S. standards by 2007.

Article VIII
The Air Quality Committee

1. The Parties agree to establish and maintain a bilateral Air Quality Committee to assist in the implementation of this Agreement. The Committee shall be composed of an equal number of members representing each Party. It may be supported by subcommittees, as appropriate. ...

Article IX
Responsibilities of the International Joint Commission

1. The International Joint Commission is hereby given, by a Reference pursuant to Article IX of the Boundary Waters Treaty, the following responsibilities for the sole purpose of assisting the Parties in the implementation of this Agreement:

(a) to invite comments, including through public hearings as appropriate, on each progress report prepared by the Air Quality Committee pursuant to Article VIII;

(b) to submit to the Parties a synthesis of the views presented pursuant to sub-paragraph (a), as well as the record of such views if either Party so requests; and

(c) to release the synthesis of views to the public after its submission to the Parties.

2. In addition, the Parties shall consider such other joint references to the International Joint Commission as may be appropriate for the effective implementation of this Agreement. ...

Article XIII
Settlement of Disputes

1. If, after consultations in accordance with Article XI, a dispute remains between the Parties over the interpretation or the implementation of this Agreement, they shall seek to resolve such dispute by negotiations between them. Such negotiations shall commence as soon as practicable, but in any event not later than ninety days from the date of receipt of the request for negotiation, unless otherwise agreed by the Parties.

2. If a dispute is not resolved through negotiation, the Parties shall consider whether to submit that dispute to the International Joint Commission in accordance with either Article IX or Article X of the Boundary Waters Treaty. If, after such consideration, the Parties do not elect either of those options, they shall, at the request of either Party, submit the dispute to another agreed form of dispute resolution.

NOTES

1) The International Joint Commission (IJC) was created by the 1909 Boundary Waters Treaty[95] between the United States and Great Britain, on behalf of Canada, for the

---

95   U.K.T.S. 1910 23; U.S. T.S. No. 548; 12 Bevans 319. See M. Cohen, *The Regime of Boundary Waters— The Canadian–United States Experience* (1977); R. Spencer, *et al.*, eds., *The International Joint Commission Seventy Years On* (1981); S.J. Toope & J. Brunnée, "Freshwater Regimes: The Mandate of the International Joint Commission" (1998) 15 Ariz. J. Int'l & Comp. L. 273; and <http://www.ijc.org/>.

purpose of aiding in the settlement and prevention of disputes over the uses of the boundary waters. The 1909 Treaty also declared that the boundary waters "shall not be polluted on either side to the injury of health or property on the other,"[96] although it did not give the IJC an express mandate regarding pollution. The IJC was given a number of powers, variously of an administrative, investigative, and adjudicative character. Under article IX, upon the request of one of the two governments, the IJC must examine, report, and make recommendations on a difference between the two states or their inhabitants along the common border. References under article IX have been used frequently. Article X confers arbitral powers on the IJC upon the request of both states. However, this function has not been used to date. Although mainly concerned with boundary water issues, the IJC has played a role in air pollution problems.[97] The 1991 Canada–United States Air Quality Agreement adds to the duties of the IJC in this field through assistance in the implementation of the treaty and the resolution of bilateral air pollution disputes.[98]

2) Transboundary notifications under article V of the Air Quality Agreement cover a range of common air pollutants when they are a new source of air pollution of specified amounts and within a specified range of the border. There are also ongoing informal consultations and regular reporting under the Agreement.

3) The 2000 Protocol also stipulates that in 2004 Canada and the United States would assess progress in implementing Annex 3 on ground-level ozone precursors with a view to negotiating further reductions. The two governments are also examining "particulate matter" (PM) to decide whether a PM Annex should be added to the Air Quality Agreement.[99] PM is composed of both solid and liquid matter in air from anthropogenic and natural sources, is harmful to human respiratory health, and is a major component of regional haze.[100]

4) How might the Agreement affect, or be affected by, other obligations between the parties—for example, customary international law regarding the environment?

2. Transboundary Nuclear Pollution

Apart from the spectre of nuclear warfare, transboundary nuclear pollution is a threat arising out of the contemporary use of nuclear technology as an energy source. The 1986 Chernobyl nuclear power plant incident served as a stark reminder of the effects of radioactivity on human life and the environment. It also demonstrated that nuclear accidents can have rapid and profound transboundary effects, and raised the question of

---

96   *Boundary Waters Treaty, supra* note 95 at article IV. See discussion below in Section G.2 on "Canada–United States Great Lakes Water Regimes."

97   See Brunnée, *Acid Rain and Ozone Layer Depletion: International Law and Regulation, supra* note 17 at 194-98.

98   See *Summary of Critical Air Quality Issues in the Transboundary Region, supra* note 93; J.L. Roelofs, "United States–Canada Air Quality Agreement: A Framework for Addressing Transboundary Air Pollution Problems" (1993) 26 Cornell Int'l L.J. 421.

99   *Cleaner Air Through Cooperation, supra* note 93 at 9.

100 *Ibid.* at 3.

the role that international law can play in preventing and responding to such accidents.[101] The 1986 Convention on Early Notification of a Nuclear Accident[102] and the 1986 Convention on Assistance in the Case of a Nuclear Accident or Radiological Emergency[103] were drafted under the auspices of the International Atomic Energy Agency (IAEA) shortly thereafter. There are also treaties on nuclear safety and civil liability.[104]

D. PROTECTION OF THE OZONE LAYER

The depletion of the stratospheric ozone layer[105] is a phenomenon that has been observed since the early 1970s. The ozone layer screens the Earth from harmful amounts of ultraviolet radiation. It is depleted by chemicals released into the atmosphere from industrial and human activities, including chlorofluorocarbons (CFCs), halons, carbon tetrachloride, methyl bromide, and hydrofluorocarbons (HCFCs). The 1985 Vienna Convention for the Protection of the Ozone Layer[106] was the first multilateral agreement on protection of the ozone layer. However, like the ECE LRTAP Convention, it contains few substantive obligations, serving instead as a framework treaty that depends upon the creation of a Protocol to establish specific obligations with respect to individual ozone depleting chemicals (ODCs). Article 2(1) of the Vienna Convention states that the "Parties shall take appropriate measures in accordance with the provisions of this Convention and of those protocols in force to which they are party to protect human health and the

---

101 See, generally, P.J. Sands, ed., *Chernobyl: Law and Communication* (1988); G. Handl, "Transboundary Nuclear Accidents: The Post-Chernobyl Multilateral Legislative Agenda" (1988) 15 Ecology L.Q. 203; M. Heller, "Chernobyl Fallout: Recent IAEA Conventions Expand Transboundary Nuclear Pollution Law" (1987) 23 Stan. J. Int'l L. 651; and G. Handl, "Après Tchernobyl: Quelques réflexions sur le programme législatif multilateral a l'ordre du jour" (1988) 92 R.G.D.I.P. 5.

102 Can. T.S. 1990 No. 21. In force October 27, 1986. In force for Canada February 18, 1990.

103 (1986) 25 I.L.M. 1377. In force February 26, 1987. In force for Canada September 12, 2002.

104 For example, 1979 IAEA *Convention on the Physical Protection of Nuclear Material* (1979) 18 I.L.M. 1419 (in force in 1987); 1994 IAEA *Convention on Nuclear Safety* (1994) 33 I.L.M. 1518 (in force in 1996); and 1997 IAEA *Joint Convention on the Safety of Spent Fuel Management and on the Safety of Radioactive Waste Management* (1997) 36 I.L.M. 1435 (in force in 2001). Canada is a contracting party to these IAEA Conventions. See also 1963 *Vienna Convention on Civil Liability for Nuclear Damage* (1963) 2 I.L.M. 727 and 1997 *Protocol to Amend the Vienna Convention and 1997 Convention on Supplementary Compensation for Nuclear Damage* (1997) 36 I.L.M. 1461.

105 See, generally, Brunnée, *Acid Rain and Ozone Layer Depletion: International Law and Regulation*, supra note 17; R.E. Benedick, *Ozone Diplomacy: New Directions in Safeguarding the Planet* (1991); L. Thoms, "A Comparative Analysis of International Regimes on Ozone and Climate Change with Implications for Regime Design" (2002-3) 41 Colum. J. Transnat'l L. 795; E. DeSombre, "The Experience of the Montreal Protocol: Particularly Remarkable and Remarkably Particular" (2000-1) 19 J. Envtl. L. 49; L.A. Duval, "The Future of the Montreal Protocol: Money and Methyl Bromide" (1999) 18 Va. Envtl. L.J. 609; O. Yoshida, "Soft Enforcement of Treaties: The Montreal Protocol's Noncompliance Procedure and the Functions of Internal International Institutions" (1999) 10 Colo. J. Int'l Envtl. L. & Pol'y 95; S. Oberthür, "Montreal Protocol: 10 Years After" (1997) 27 Envtl. Pol'y & L. 432; and E. Barratt-Brown, "Building a Monitoring and Compliance Regime Under the Montreal Protocol" (1991) 16 Yale J. Int'l L. 519.

106 Can. T.S. 1988 No. 23; (1987) 26 I.L.M. 1516: <http://www.unep.org/ozone/index.asp>. In force September 22, 1988.

environment against adverse effects resulting or likely to result from human activities which modify or are likely to modify the ozone layer." The Vienna Convention also contains provisions on, *inter alia*, the conduct of research and scientific assessments, and cooperation in the legal, scientific, and technical fields, including the exchange of information among the contracting parties.

The 1987 Montreal Protocol to the Vienna Convention[107] was designed to phase out production and consumption of covered ODCs, followed. In its original form, it covered five types of CFCs and three halons (Annex A). However, further ODCs and control measures were added to the regime by Amendments and more informal Adjustments, which accelerated phase-out schedules and tightened controls: London Amendments and Adjustments (1990), Copenhagen Amendments and Adjustments (1992), Vienna Adjustments (1995), Montreal Amendments and Adjustments (1997), and Beijing Amendments and Adjustments (1999). Canada and the United States have ratified or accepted all of the Amendments. Adjustments are automatically binding on all Protocol parties. The Ozone Secretariat is located at UNEP in Nairobi, Kenya. The Montreal Protocol as adjusted and amended is an example of a framework treaty-protocol regime that has been successful in introducing extensive control measures and the relatively speedy phase-out of ODCs. Almost 100 chemicals are covered. However, some of the Amendments have not been ratified by all of the Montreal Protocol parties.

NOTES

1) The Montreal Protocol in its unamended form froze production and consumption of the covered CFCs at 1986 levels beginning July 1, 1989, to be reduced by 20 percent on July 1, 1993 and 50 percent on July 1, 1998. Covered halons were frozen at 1986 levels, beginning in 1992. Article 4 of the Protocol uses trade restrictions against non-party states to support the control mechanism. In addition, the Protocol provides for information exchange, periodic assessment, and review of control measures, regular meetings of the parties, and promotes research and technical assistance to facilitate participation in the Protocol, particularly with respect to the developing states. Article 5 of the Protocol provides incentives for developing states to become contracting parties to the Protocol by giving them, under controlled circumstances, a 10-year grace period before compliance with the control measures is required.

2) Difficulties were initially experienced in persuading developing states to accede to the Protocol in the light of both the financial burden involved and the fact that, historically, industrialized states have produced most ODCs. However, most developing states have subsequently become contracting parties to the Protocol, including the populous nations of India, China, and Brazil.

3) At the second meeting of the Montreal Protocol parties (MOP), the London Adjustments and Amendments to the Montreal Protocol were adopted on June 29, 1990.[108] The London Adjustments to the Protocol cover the CFCs and halons listed in Annex A. Production and consumption of Annex A CFCs were to be totally phased out

---

107   Can. T.S. 1989 No. 42; (1987) 26 I.L.M. 1541: <http://www.unep.org/ozone/index.asp>. As of October 1, 2005, there were 189 contracting parties to the Montreal Protocol, including Canada and the United States.

by the year 2000, a target to be reached through a 50 percent reduction of 1986 levels starting in 1995 and an 85 percent cut in 1997.[109] A reduction schedule for Annex A halons was inserted, with a freeze on consumption and production at 1986 levels occurring between 1992 and 1995, with a 50 percent reduction starting in 1995, and a complete phase-out of non-essential uses starting in the year 2000. Halon production limits could be exceeded by 10 percent from 1992 to 1999 and by 15 percent starting in 2000 to satisfy the basic domestic needs of the article 5 parties; a production or consumption level in excess of the control level was permitted, starting in 1995, if "necessary to satisfy essential uses for which no adequate alternatives are available."[110] The London Amendments to the Protocol were extensive. The range of controlled substances in article 2 was expanded to include other fully halogenated CFCs, carbon tetrachloride, and methyl chloroform as listed in Annex B, and reduction schedules for these substances were specified.[111] Articles 4 and 5 were amended, including more extensive controls on trade with non-parties.[112] An important achievement was the establishment of a financial mechanism, including a Multilateral Fund, to assist the lesser developed article 5 parties to meet their Protocol obligations.[113] The mechanism provides technical and financial cooperation and the transfer of technologies. The Fund aids developing parties by financing capacity building and projects to phase out ODCs.

The 1990 MOP did not impose binding controls on HCFCs, which have less severe ozone-depleting effects and are used as a CFC replacement. In the Amendments, HCFCs were defined as a "transitional substance" and placed in Annex C, with only reporting requirements imposed.

4) The fourth MOP of the Montreal Protocol, held in Copenhagen from November 23 to 25, 1992, resulted in the adoption of further Adjustments and Amendments to the Protocol and a number of Decisions concerning its application.[114] The Copenhagen Adjustments to the Protocol accelerated the schedule for the phase-out of substances already regulated by the Protocol so that their production and consumption was to be

---

108 (1991) 30 I.L.M. 539, online: <http://www.unep.org/ozone/index.asp>. The Adjustments to the Protocol became effective on March 7, 1991 and the London Amendments entered into force on August 10, 1992. As of October 1, 2005, there were 179 parties to the London Amendments.

109 *London Amendments*, Annex I, article 2A, *ibid.*

110 *London Amendments*, Annex I, article 2B, *ibid.*

111 *London Amendments*, Annex II, articles 2C, 2D, and 2E, *ibid.* Fully halogenated CFCs were reduced by 20 percent from 1989 levels starting in 1993, reduced by 85 percent in 1997, and phased out starting in the year 2000. Carbon tetrachloride was reduced by 85 percent of 1989 levels in 1995 and phased out by 2000. Methyl chloroform was frozen at 1989 levels starting in 1993, reduced by 30 percent starting in 1995, by 70 percent in 2000, and phased out by 2005. Production limits could be exceeded as specified to satisfy the basic domestic needs of article 5 parties.

112 *London Amendments*, Annex II, articles 4 and 5, *ibid.*

113 *London Amendments*, Annex II, article 10, *ibid.*; Decision IV/18 of the Meetings of the Parties. The Multilateral Fund secretariat is located in Montreal. Financial contributions come from non-article 5 parties. See also the GEF *infra* note 127.

114 See UNEP/OzL.Pro.4/2/Rev.2 (November 24, 1992) and UNEP/OzL.Pro.4/L.1/Rev.2 (November 24, 1992). The Copenhagen Amendments entered into force on June 14, 1994. As of October 1, 2005, there were 168 contracting parties to these Amendments.

eliminated by the following dates: CFCs by January 1, 1996; halons by January 1, 1994; and other fully halogenated CFCs, carbon tetrachloride, and methyl chloroform by January 1, 1996. Limited exemptions were permitted with respect to production levels to satisfy the basic domestic needs of the article 5 parties and with respect to production and consumption levels as deemed necessary by the Parties for essential uses.

The Copenhagen Amendments to the Montreal Protocol, *inter alia*, add the following as controlled substances: HCFCs (Annex C), with a phase-out of consumption occurring by the year 2030; hydrobromofluorocarbons (HBFCs) (Annex C), with the elimination of production and consumption by January 1, 1996, and with exceptions as determined by the Parties to be necessary to satisfy essential uses; and methyl bromide (Annex E), with production and consumption limited to 1991 levels starting January 1, 1995, but permitting production limits to be exceeded by up to 10 percent in order to satisfy the basic domestic needs of article 5 parties. Methyl bromide is used as a soil and crop fumigant.

5) The seventh MOP, held in Vienna in 1995, addressed the control of HCFCs and methyl bromide. A phase-out schedule for methyl bromide for industrialized states parties was agreed on, with a 25 percent reduction to occur in 2001, a 50 percent reduction in 2005, and a total phase-out in 2010. The Parties also agreed to stabilize the production and consumption of methyl bromide in developing states parties by 2002.[115] For HCFCs, the baselines for reductions in industrialized parties was set at 1989 levels, plus 2.8 percent. The Parties also agreed that consumption of HCFCs in developing states parties was to be phased out by 2040.[116]

6) The ninth MOP of the Montreal Protocol, held in Montreal from September 15 to 17, 1997, resulted in further Adjustments and Amendments.[117] The phase-out schedule for methyl bromide for industrialized states parties was accelerated, with a 25 percent reduction to occur in 1999, a 50 percent reduction in 2001, a 70 percent drop in 2003, and full elimination in 2005. The Parties also agreed to phase out methyl bromide in developing states parties with a 20 percent reduction in 2005 and a total phase-out in 2015. Exceptions are permitted for critical uses. An Amendment to the Montreal Protocol was adopted, addressing the black market trade in ODCs, which requires all parties to implement an import and export licensing system to help the parties control such trade.[118]

7) The Beijing Amendments and Adjustments were adopted at the 11th MOP, held in Beijing November 29 to December 3, 1999.[119] The Amendments established control measures for the production of HCFCs (Annex C) and introduced restrictions on trade of HCFCs with non-parties.[120] The earlier Copenhagen Amendments had addressed controls

---

115 Oberthür, *supra* note 105 at 432.

116 *Ibid.* at 434.

117 *Ibid.* The *Montreal Amendments* entered into force on November 10, 1999. As of October 1, 2005, there were 135 parties to the Montreal Amendments.

118 Decision IX/8, UNEP/OzL.Pro.9/12 (September 25, 1997).

119 See <http://www.unep.org/ozone/index.asp>. The *Beijing Amendments* entered into force on February 25, 2002. As of October 1, 2005, there were 98 parties to the *Beijing Amendments*.

120 *Ibid.* A freeze on production was required in 2004 using 1989 baselines for non-article 5 parties. Article 5 parties must freeze HCFC production starting 2016 using 2015 baselines.

on consumption of HCFCs. The Beijing Amendments also imposed an immediate phase-out on the production and consumption of bromo-chloromethane (BCM) (Annex C) and prohibited trade with non-parties.[121] The Beijing Adjustments amended the allowances for meeting the basic domestic needs of article 5 states parties.[122]

8) In March 2004 an Extraordinary MOP was held, resulting in 11 developed states parties (including Canada, the United States, and some EU states) obtaining exemptions from their methyl bromide obligations for critical uses, allowing the use of specific amounts of methyl bromide for 2005.[123]

9) For those states parties that have ratified all the Amendments up to 2004, the following final phase-out dates must be implemented: for developed states—halons (1994); CFCs, carbon tetrachloride, methyl chloroform, and HBFCs (1996); BCM (2002); methyl bromide (2005); consumption of HCFCs (2030); and stabilization of HCFC production (2004).[124] Article 5 states must adhere to the following final phase-out dates: HBFCs (1996); BCM (2002); CFCs, halons, and carbon tetrachloride (2010); methyl chloroform and methyl bromide (2015); consumption of HCFCs (2040); and stabilization of HCFC production (2016).[125] After phase-out dates, no party can produce the controlled ODCs, except for critical or essential uses.[126]

10) The Global Environment Facility (GEF) is a financial mechanism under the management of the World Bank, UNEP, and the U.N. Development Programme (UNDP) that issues grants and mobilizes co-financing from other sources for environmental projects in developing states and countries with economies in transition.[127] Although it was created on a trial basis in 1991, it became a permanent mechanism in 1994. The GEF financing is directed at projects in the areas of depletion of the ozone layer, climate change, biological diversity, international waters, land degradation, and persistent organic pollutants.

11) Article 8 of the Montreal Protocol stated that at the first meeting of the Parties "procedures and institutional mechanisms for determining non-compliance with the provisions of this Protocol and for treatment of Parties found to be in non-compliance" shall be considered and approved. An Implementation Committee was established in 1990 at the second MOP, on an interim basis, and formally in 1992 at the fourth MOP.[128] The Implementation Committee reviews and monitors compliance of the provisions of the Protocol by individual contracting parties. The compliance procedure can be activated

---

121 *Ibid.* Effective 2002, BCM is a new ODC introduced commercially in 1998.

122 *Ibid.*

123 "Summary of Extraordinary Meeting of the Parties to the Montreal Protocol" (March 29, 2004), vol. 19 no. 37 *Earth Negotiations Bulletin.*

124 Ozone Secretariat UNEP, *Handbook for the International Treaties for the Protection of the Ozone Layer,* 6th ed. (2003) at 61-69. For Canada see regulations to CEPA, *supra* note 46.

125 *Handbook, supra* note 124.

126 *Ibid.* at 70.

127 *Instrument Establishing the Global Environment Facility* (1994) 33 I.L.M. 1273. See also <http://www.gefweb.org>.

128 See *e.g. Handbook, supra* note 124 at 295-97; and Yoshida, *supra* note 105.

by one or more contracting parties who are concerned about their own implementation progress or another party's implementation of its Protocol obligations. Also, if the Protocol Secretariat, UNEP, becomes aware of potential non-compliance by a contracting party who does not subsequently respond to a request for information, the Secretariat can inform the Implementation Committee. The Implementation Committee receives information from parties, undertakes its own information gathering, tries to reach an amicable solution of a particular matter based on respect for the terms of the Protocol, and reports to the meeting of the Parties, including recommendations that it thinks appropriate. In response, the Parties may call for steps to obtain full compliance with the Protocol and can decide on measures that may assist with achieving compliance.[129] Examples of measures that may be taken by the meeting of the Parties are assistance in forms such as technical and financial aid, the issue of a caution, or suspension of rights and privileges of a contracting party under the Protocol. The Montreal Protocol mechanism has been influential in the creation of similar compliance procedures in other treaties.[130]

E. GLOBAL WARMING AND CLIMATE CHANGE

Global warming and climate change[131] are no longer discounted in the international legal system, although the delay in activating a multilateral emissions reduction regime is indicative of the divergent economic and political views concerning the consequences of such a regime. The atmosphere is composed of a variety of gases, including some "greenhouse gases" such as carbon dioxide, methane, and nitrous oxide, which reflect heat back toward the Earth. Global warming is a phenomenon whereby the accumulation of certain gases emitted into the atmosphere aggravates the normal "greenhouse effect," trapping heat that would usually escape and leading to climatic change and sea level rise.[132] Greenhouse gases are emitted from the burning of fossil fuels and other industrial

---

129   See *Handbook, supra* note 124 and Yoshida, *supra* note 105.

130   See Handl, "Compliance Control Mechanisms and International Environmental Obligations," *supra* note 38 at 33.

131   See, generally, P.D. Cameron & D. Zillman, eds., *Kyoto: From Principles to Practice* (2001); S. Oberthür & H.E. Ott, *The Kyoto Protocol: International Climate Policy for the 21st Century* (1999); M. Grubb, with C. Vrolijk & D. Brack, *The Kyoto Protocol: A Guide and Assessment* (1999); M. Doelle, "From Kyoto to Marrakech; A Long Walk Through the Desert: Mirage or Oasis?" (2002) 25 Dal. L.J. 113; V.P. Nanda, "The Kyoto Protocol on Climate Change and the Challenges to its Implementation: A Commentary" (1999) 10 Colo. J. Int'l Envtl. L. & Pol'y 319; C. Georgetti, "From Rio to Kyoto: A Study of the Involvement of Non-Governmental Organizations in the Negotiations on Climate Change" (1999) 7 N.Y.U. Envtl. L.J. 201; A.G. Hanafi, "Joint Implementation: Legal and Institutional Issues for an Effective International Program to Combat Climate Change" (1998) 22 Harv. Envtl. L. Rev. 441; P.G.G. Davies, "Global Warming and the Kyoto Protocol" (1998) 47 I.C.L.Q. 446; E. McCoy, "Climate Change: Tax Changes, Emission Credits, and Joint Rules Key in Aftermath of Kyoto" (1998) 28 Envtl. Pol'y & L. 651; D. Bodansky, "The United Nations Framework Convention on Climate Change: A Commentary" (1993) 18 Yale J. Int'l. L. 451; and D. Zaelke & J. Cameron, "Global Warming and Climate Change—An Overview of the International Legal Process" (1990) 5 Am. U. J. Int'l L. & Pol'y 513.

132   Zaelke & Cameron, *supra* note 131 at 253-55.

and agricultural activities. Furthermore, massive deforestation, by eliminating a source of carbon dioxide absorption, intensifies the process. Activities in industrialized countries account for the majority of greenhouse gas emissions.[133] However, it is expected that greenhouse gases from developing countries will start to catch up in the 21st century.

The U.N. General Assembly raised the issue of climate change in its 1988 First Resolution on Protection of Global Climate for Present and Future Generations of Mankind, wherein the General Assembly recognized that "climate change is a common concern of mankind," stated that action should be taken to deal with climate change within a global framework that could possibly include a treaty on climate change, and endorsed the establishment of the Intergovernmental Panel on Climate Change (IPCC) by UNEP and the World Meteorological Organization (WMO) to provide scientific assessment of the nature and impact of climate change.[134] In 1989, in the Second Resolution on Protection of Global Climate for Present and Future Generations of Mankind, the General Assembly supported the initiative of UNEP and the WMO to begin negotiations on a framework convention on climate and associated protocols containing concrete commitments.[135] A number of non-binding declarations on climate change were made by governments at the end of the 1980s and in the early 1990s, calling for the development of international law and the reduction of greenhouse gases.[136]

On the basis of the scientific studies performed by the IPCC, UNEP and the WMO started work on the drafting of a treaty on climate change. In late 1990, the U.N. General Assembly consolidated negotiations in a single Intergovernmental Negotiating Committee (INC), supported by UNEP and the WMO, to complete the Framework Convention on Climate Change for signature at the 1992 U.N. Conference on Environment and Development (UNCED).[137] On December 11, 1997, at the third Conference of the Parties (COP), the parties reached agreement on the Kyoto Protocol to the Framework Convention (in force February 16, 2005—see note 6 following Kyoto Protocol to the U.N. Framework Convention on Climate Change, reproduced below), which contains greenhouse gas emission reduction obligations for the industrialized states and transition economy parties.

---

133 Bodansky, *supra* note 131 at 457.

134 GA Res. 43/53, paras. 1, 2, 5 and 10, UN GAOR, 43rd Sess., Supp. No. 49, U.N. Doc. A/RES/43/53 at 133; (1988) 28 I.L.M. 1326. Adopted without a vote, December 6, 1988.

135 GA Res. 44/207, paras. 10 and 12, UN GAOR, 44th Sess., Supp. No. 49, U.N. Doc. A/RES/44/207 (1989) at 130. Adopted without a vote, December 22, 1989.

136 See *e.g.* the 1989 *Declaration of The Hague* (1989) 28 I.L.M. 1308; the 1989 *Malé Declaration on Global Warming and Sea Level Rise* and the 1989 *Noordwijk Declaration on Atmospheric Pollution and Climate Change*, both in M. Molitor, *International Environmental Law: Primary Materials* (1990) at 100, 109; and the 1990 *Ministerial Declaration of the World Climate Conference* (1990) 1 Y.B. Int'l. Env. L. 473.

137 UNEP *Governing Council Decision 15/36 on Global Climate Change* (1989) 28 I.L.M. 330.

United Nations Framework Convention on Climate Change
U.N. Doc. A/AC.237/18 (Part II)/Add.1 and Corr. 1;
(1992) 31 I.L.M. 851 (footnotes omitted)

The Parties to this Convention,
Acknowledging that change in the Earth's climate and its adverse effects are a common concern of humankind, ...

Recalling also that States have, in accordance with the Charter of the United Nations and the principles of international law, the sovereign right to exploit their own resources pursuant to their own environmental and developmental policies, and the responsibility to ensure that activities within their jurisdiction or control do not cause damage to the environment of other States or of areas beyond the limits of national jurisdiction, ...

Determined to protect the climate system for present and future generations,
Have agreed as follows:

Article 1
Definitions

For the purposes of this Convention:

1. "Adverse effects of climate change" means changes in the physical environment or biota resulting from climate change which have significant deleterious effects on the composition, resilience or productivity of natural and managed ecosystems or on the operation of socio-economic systems or on human health and welfare.

2. "Climate change" means a change of climate which is attributed directly or indirectly to human activity that alters the composition of the global atmosphere and which is in addition to natural climate variability observed over comparable time periods.

3. "Climate system" means the totality of the atmosphere, hydrosphere, biosphere and geosphere and their interactions.

4. "Emissions" means the release of greenhouse gases and/or their precursors into the atmosphere over a specified area and period of time.

5. "Greenhouse gases" means those gaseous constituents of the atmosphere, both natural and anthropogenic, that absorb and re-emit infrared radiation. ...

7. "Reservoir" means a component or components of the climate system where a greenhouse gas or a precursor of a greenhouse gas is stored.

8. "Sink" means any process, activity or mechanism which removes a greenhouse gas, an aerosol or a precursor of a greenhouse gas from the atmosphere.

9. "Source" means any process or activity which releases a greenhouse gas, an aerosol or a precursor of a greenhouse gas into the atmosphere.

Article 2
Objective

The ultimate objective of this Convention and any related legal instruments that the Conference of the Parties may adopt is to achieve, in accordance with the relevant provisions of the Convention, stabilization of greenhouse gas concentrations in the atmosphere at a level that would prevent dangerous anthropogenic interference with the climate system. Such a level should be achieved within a time-frame sufficient to allow ecosystems to adapt naturally to climate change, to ensure that food production is not threatened and to enable economic development to proceed in a sustainable manner.

Article 3
Principles

In their actions to achieve the objective of the Convention and to implement its provisions, the Parties shall be guided, *inter alia*, by the following:

1. The Parties should protect the climate system for the benefit of present and future generations of humankind, on the basis of equity and in accordance with their common but differentiated responsibilities and respective capabilities. Accordingly, the developed country Parties should take the lead in combating climate change and the adverse effects thereof.

2. The specific needs and special circumstances of developing country Parties, especially those that are particularly vulnerable to the adverse effects of climate change, and of those Parties, especially developing country Parties, that would have to bear a disproportionate or abnormal burden under the Convention, should be given full consideration.

3. The Parties should take precautionary measures to anticipate, prevent or minimize the causes of climate change and mitigate its adverse effects. Where there are threats of serious or irreversible damage, lack of full scientific certainty should not be used as a reason for postponing such measures, taking into account that policies and measures to deal with climate change should be cost-effective so as to ensure global benefits at the lowest possible cost. To achieve this, such policies and measures should take into account different socio-economic contexts, be comprehensive, cover all relevant sources, sinks and reservoirs of greenhouse gases and adaptation, and comprise all economic sectors. Efforts to address climate change may be carried out cooperatively by interested Parties.

4. The Parties have a right to, and should, promote sustainable development. Policies and measures to protect the climate system against human-induced change should be appropriate for the specific conditions of each Party and should be integrated with national development programmes, taking into account that economic development is essential for adopting measures to address climate change.

5. The Parties should cooperate to promote a supportive and open international economic system that would lead to sustainable economic growth and development in all Parties, particularly developing country Parties, thus enabling them better to address the problems of climate change. Measures taken to combat climate change, including unilateral ones, should not constitute a means of arbitrary or unjustifiable discrimination or a disguised restriction on international trade.

Article 4

Commitments

1. All Parties, taking into account their common but differentiated responsibilities and their specific national and regional development priorities, objectives and circumstances, shall:

(a) Develop, periodically update, publish and make available to the Conference of the Parties, in accordance with Article 12, national inventories of anthropogenic emissions by sources and removals by sinks of all greenhouse gases not controlled by the Montreal Protocol, using comparable methodologies to be agreed upon by the Conference of the Parties;

(b) Formulate, implement, publish and regularly update national and, where appropriate, regional programmes containing measures to mitigate climate change by addressing anthropogenic emissions by sources and removals by sinks of all greenhouse gases not controlled by the Montreal Protocol, and measures to facilitate adequate adaptation to climate change;

(c) Promote and cooperate in the development, application and diffusion, including transfer, of technologies, practices and processes that control, reduce or prevent anthropogenic emissions of greenhouse gases not controlled by the Montreal Protocol in all relevant sectors, including the energy, transport, industry, agriculture, forestry and waste management sectors;

(d) Promote sustainable management, and promote and cooperate in the conservation and enhancement, as appropriate, of sinks and reservoirs of all greenhouse gases not controlled by the Montreal Protocol, including biomass, forests and oceans as well as other terrestrial, coastal and marine ecosystems;...

2. The developed country Parties and other Parties included in annex I[138] commit themselves specifically as provided for in the following:

(a) Each of these Parties shall adopt national policies and take corresponding measures on the mitigation of climate change, by limiting its anthropogenic emissions of greenhouse gases and protecting and enhancing its greenhouse gas sinks and reservoirs. These policies and measures will demonstrate that developed countries are taking the lead in modifying longer-term trends in anthropogenic emissions consistent with the objective of the Convention, recognizing that the return by the end of the present decade to earlier levels of anthropogenic emissions of carbon dioxide and other greenhouse gases not controlled by the Montreal Protocol would contribute to such modification, and taking into account the differences in these Parties' starting points and approaches, economic structures and resource bases, the need to maintain strong and sustainable economic growth, available technologies and other individual circumstances, as well as the need for equitable and appropriate contributions by each of these Parties to the global effort regarding that objective. These Parties may implement such policies and measures jointly

---

138 The EC, industrialized states (*e.g.* Canada, the United States, western European states, Japan, Australia, New Zealand) and countries whose economies are in transition in Central and Eastern Europe.

with other Parties and may assist other Parties in contributing to the achievement of the objective of the Convention and, in particular, that of this subparagraph;

(b) In order to promote progress to this end, each of these Parties shall communicate, within six months of the entry into force of the Convention for it and periodically thereafter, and in accordance with Article 12, detailed information on its policies and measures referred to in subparagraph (a) above, as well as on its resulting projected anthropogenic emissions by sources and removals by sinks of greenhouse gases not controlled by the Montreal Protocol for the period referred to in subparagraph (a), with the aim of returning individually or jointly to their 1990 levels these anthropogenic emissions of carbon dioxide and other greenhouse gases not controlled by the Montreal Protocol. This information will be reviewed by the Conference of the Parties, at its first session and periodically thereafter, ...

**Kyoto Protocol to the United Nations Framework
Convention on Climate Change**
(1998) 37 I.L.M. 32

The Parties to this Protocol,

Being Parties to the United Nations Framework Convention on Climate Change, hereinafter referred to as "the Convention,"

In pursuit of the ultimate objective of the Convention as stated in its Article 2,

Recalling the provisions of the Convention,

Being guided by Article 3 of the Convention,...

Have agreed as follows:

Article 1

For the purposes of this Protocol, the definitions contained in Article 1 of the Convention shall apply. In addition:

1. "Conference of the Parties" means the Conference of the Parties to the Convention.

2. "Convention" means the United Nations Framework Convention on Climate Change, adopted in New York on 9 May, 1992.

3. "Intergovernmental Panel on Climate Change" means the Intergovernmental Panel on Climate Change established in 1988 jointly by the World Meteorological Organization and the United Nations Environment Programme.

4. "Montreal Protocol" means the Montreal Protocol on Substances that Deplete the Ozone Layer, adopted in Montreal on 16 September 1987 and as subsequently adjusted and amended. ...

6. "Party" means, unless the context otherwise indicates, a Party to this Protocol.

7. "Party included in Annex I" means a Party included in Annex I to the Convention, as may be amended, or a Party which has made a notification under Article 4, paragraph 2(g), of the Convention.

Article 2

1. Each Party included in Annex I in achieving its quantified emission limitation and reduction commitments under Article 3, in order to promote sustainable development, shall:

(a) Implement and/or further elaborate policies and measures in accordance with its national circumstances, such as:

(i) Enhancement of energy efficiency in relevant sectors of the national economy;

(ii) Protection and enhancement of sinks and reservoirs of greenhouse gases not controlled by the Montreal Protocol, taking into account its commitments under relevant international environmental agreements; promotion of sustainable forest management practices, afforestation and reforestation;

(iii) Promotion of sustainable forms of agriculture in light of climate change considerations;

(iv) Research on, and promotion, development and increased use of, new and renewable forms of energy, of carbon dioxide sequestration technologies and of advanced and innovative environmentally sound technologies;

(v) Progressive reduction or phasing out of market imperfections, fiscal incentives, tax and duty exemptions and subsidies in all greenhouse gas emitting sectors that run counter to the objective of the Convention and application of market instruments;

(vi) Encouragement of appropriate reforms in relevant sectors aimed at promoting policies and measures which limit or reduce emissions of greenhouse gases not controlled by the Montreal Protocol;

(vii) Measures to limit and/or reduce emissions of greenhouse gases not controlled by the Montreal Protocol in the transport sector;

(viii) Limitation and/or reduction of methane through recovery and use in waste management, as well as in the production, transport and distribution of energy; ...

Article 3

1. The Parties included in Annex I shall, individually or jointly, ensure that their aggregate anthropogenic carbon dioxide equivalent emissions of the greenhouse gases listed in Annex A[139] do not exceed their assigned amounts, calculated pursuant to their quantified emission limitation and reduction commitments inscribed in Annex B[140] and in accordance with the provisions of this Article, with a view to reducing their overall emissions of such gases by at least 5 per cent below 1990 levels in the commitment period 2008 to 2012.

2. Each Party included in Annex I shall, by 2005, have made demonstrable progress in achieving its commitments under this Protocol.

---

139 Annex A lists carbon dioxide, methane, nitrous oxide, hydrofluorocarbons, perfluorocarbons, and sulphur hexafluoride.

140 The EC, industrialized states (including Canada), and states with economies in transition in Central and Eastern Europe.

3. The net changes in greenhouse gas emissions by sources and removals by sinks resulting from direct human-induced land-use change and forestry activities, limited to afforestation, reforestation, and deforestation since 1990, measured as verifiable changes in carbon stocks in each commitment period shall be used to meet the commitments under this Article of each Party included in Annex I. The greenhouse gas emissions by sources and removals by sinks associated with those activities shall be reported in a transparent and verifiable manner and reviewed in accordance with Articles 7 and 8. ...

9. Commitments for subsequent periods for Parties included in Annex I shall be established in amendments to Annex B to this Protocol ... . The Conference of the Parties serving as the meeting of the Parties to this Protocol shall initiate the consideration of such commitments at least seven years before the end of the first commitment period referred to in paragraph 1 above.

10. Any emission reduction units, or any part of an assigned amount, which a Party acquires from another Party in accordance with the provisions of Article 6 or of Article 17 shall be added to the assigned amount for the acquiring Party.

11. Any emission reduction units, or any part of an assigned amount, which a Party transfers to another Party in accordance with the provisions of Article 6 and of Article 16 *bis* shall be subtracted from the assigned amount for the transferring Party.

12. Any certified emission reductions which a Party acquires from another Party in accordance with the provisions of Article 12 shall be added to the assigned amount for the acquiring Party.

13. If the emissions of a Party included in Annex I during a commitment period are less than its assigned amount under this Article, this difference shall, on request of that Party, be added to the assigned amount for that Party for subsequent commitment periods.

14. Each Party included in Annex I shall strive to implement the commitments mentioned in paragraph 1 above in such a way as to minimize adverse social, environmental and economic impacts on developing country Parties. ...

Article 4

1. Any Parties included in Annex I that have reached an agreement to fulfil their commitments under Article 3 jointly, shall be deemed to have met those commitments provided that their total combined aggregate anthropogenic carbon dioxide equivalent emissions of the greenhouse gases listed in Annex A do not exceed their assigned amounts calculated pursuant to their quantified emission limitation and reduction commitments inscribed in Annex B and in accordance with the provisions of Article 3. The respective emission level allocated to each of the Parties to the agreement shall be set out in that agreement. ...

Article 6

1. For the purpose of meeting its commitments under Article 3, any Party included in Annex I may transfer to, or acquire from, any other such Party emission reduction units resulting from projects aimed at reducing anthropogenic emissions by sources

or enhancing anthropogenic removals by sinks of greenhouse gases in any sector of the economy, provided that:

(a) Any such project has the approval of the Parties involved;

(b) Any such project provides a reduction in emissions by sources, or an enhancement of removals by sinks, that is additional to any that would otherwise occur;

(c) It does not acquire any emission reduction units if it is not in compliance with its obligations under Articles 5 and 7; and

(d) The acquisition of emission reduction units shall be supplemental to domestic actions for the purposes of meeting commitments under Article 3. ...

Article 10

All Parties, taking into account their common but differentiated responsibilities and their specific national and regional development priorities, objectives and circumstances, without introducing any new commitments for Parties not included in Annex I, but reaffirming existing commitments in Article 4, paragraph 1, of the Convention, and continuing to advance the implementation of these commitments in order to achieve sustainable development, taking into account Article 4, paragraphs 3, 5 and 7 of the Convention, shall:

(a) Formulate, where relevant and to the extent possible, cost-effective national and, where appropriate, regional programmes to improve the quality of local emission factors, activity data and/or models which reflect the socio-economic conditions of each Party for the preparation and periodic updating of national inventories of anthropogenic emissions by sources and removals by sinks of all greenhouse gases not controlled by the Montreal Protocol. ...

(b) Formulate, implement, publish and regularly update national and, where appropriate, regional programmes containing measures to mitigate climate change and measures to facilitate adequate adaptation to climate change. ...

(c) Cooperate in the promotion of effective modalities for the development, application and diffusion of, and take all practicable steps to promote, facilitate and finance, as appropriate, the transfer of, or access to, environmentally sound technologies, know-how, practices and processes pertinent to climate change, in particular to developing countries, including the formulation of policies and programmes for the effective transfer of environmentally sound technologies that are publicly owned or in the public domain and the creation of an enabling environment for the private sector, to promote and enhance the transfer of, and access to, environmentally sound technologies. ...

Article 12

1. A clean development mechanism is hereby defined.

2. The purpose of the clean development mechanism shall be to assist Parties not included in Annex I in achieving sustainable development and in contributing to the ultimate objective of the Convention, and to assist Parties included in Annex I in achieving compliance with their quantified emission limitation and reduction commitments under Article 3.

3. Under the clean development mechanism:

(a) Parties not included in Annex I will benefit from project activities resulting in certified emission reductions; and

(b) Parties included in Annex I may use the certified emission reductions accruing from such project activities to contribute to compliance with part of their quantified emission limitation and reduction commitments under Article 3, as determined by the Conference of the Parties serving as the meeting of the Parties to this Protocol. ...

Article 17

The Conference of the Parties shall define the relevant principles, modalities, rules and guidelines, in particular for verification, reporting and accountability for emissions trading. The Parties included in Annex B may participate in emissions trading for the purposes of fulfilling their commitments under Article 3. Any such trading shall be supplemental to domestic actions for the purpose of meeting quantified emission limitation and reduction commitments under that Article.

NOTES

1) The U.N. Framework Convention on Climate Change (UNFCCC) was opened for signature on June 5, 1992 at UNCED and entered into force on March 21, 1994. Canada is a contracting party.[141] The UNFCCC does not impose binding reductions in greenhouse gas emissions, although in article 4(2)(a) and (b) the developed and transition economy states parties listed in Annex I commit themselves to adopt national policies and measures to limit, *inter alia*, greenhouse gases not covered by the Montreal Protocol, with the aim of returning to their 1990 emission levels.[142] Furthermore, article 4(2)(d) required the Conference of the Parties (COP) to review the adequacy of subparagraphs (a) and (b) at its first session, making amendments thereto if appropriate, and to undertake a second review prior to the end of 1998. In article 4, the UNFCCC created a procedure for the observation and review of greenhouse gas emissions through the establishment and reporting of national inventories of sources and sinks, and other state action taken to mitigate climate change. Such information is communicated to the COP. The UNFCCC contains provisions for the support of research, observation, education, training, and public awareness programs on climate change and its effects. Are there other alternatives to the format used in the UNFCCC that could have been more effective?

2) Article 7 of the UNFCCC established the COP as the supreme body of the treaty with a mandate to keep the implementation of the Convention and any future related legal

---

141 As of October 1, 2005, 189 states and the EC had ratified the FCCC, online: <http://unfccc.int>. Canada signed the Convention on June 12, 1992 and ratified it on December 4, 1992. See, generally, Bodansky, *supra* note 131.

142 See above in Section D on "Protection of the Ozone Layer" for the Montreal Protocol and note 138 for Annex I states.

instruments under review and to make the decisions necessary to promote effective implementation.

3) Article 11 of the UNFCCC established a mechanism for the provision of financial resources, including technology transfer, on grant or concessional terms. The Global Environment Facility (GEF) serves as the UNFCCC and Kyoto Protocol financial mechanism.[143]

4) The first COP (COP-1) was held in Berlin, Germany March 28 to April 7, 1995.[144] COP-1 resulted in an agreement known as the "Berlin Mandate." It stated that the objectives of the developed parties to reduce greenhouse gas emissions to 1990 levels by 2000 pursuant to article 4(2)(a) and (b) of the UNFCCC were inadequate.[145] It also mandated a process to negotiate a protocol or other legal instrument that would include new emission reduction commitments for developed country parties and parties in transition to a market economy (as listed in Annex I of the UNFCCC), with the aim of concluding and adopting an agreement at COP-3.[146] The decision to locate the UNFCCC Secretariat in Bonn, Germany was also made at COP-1.[147]

5) COP-2 was held in Geneva, Switzerland on July 8 to 19, 1996.[148] The Geneva Ministerial Declaration, issued at the end of the meeting, stated that the second assessment report of the IPCC provided a scientific basis for urgently strengthening action, particularly on the part of Annex I states to reduce greenhouse gas emissions and called on all UNFCCC parties to support the development of a protocol or other legal instrument in accordance with the Berlin Mandate.[149] The Declaration clarified that any resulting legal instrument, including emission reduction targets and schedules, would be legally binding and completed at COP-3.[150]

6) COP-3 was held in Kyoto, Japan on December 1 to 11, 1997. On December 11, 1997 the Kyoto Protocol to the UNFCCC was adopted.[151] Canada signed the Kyoto Protocol on April 29, 1998 and ratified it on December 17, 2002. Pursuant to article 25 of the Protocol, it was to enter into force when at least 55 parties representing Annex I parties, accounting for at least 55 percent of 1990 global carbon dioxide emissions, ratified the Convention.[152] As of November 18, 2004, 126 states had ratified the Protocol,

---

143 See *supra* note 127. At the COP-7 in Marrakesh in 2001, three new funds were created, to be managed by the GEF: The Special Climate Change Fund, the Least Developed Countries Fund (both under the UNFCCC), and the Adaptation Fund (under the Kyoto Protocol).

144 S. Oberthür, "The First Conference of the Parties" (1995) 25 Envtl. Pol'y & L. 144.

145 *United Nations Framework Convention on Climate Change First Conference of the Parties: Decisions Adopted by the Conference of the Parties*, Decision 1/CP.1 (1995) 34 I.L.M. 1676.

146 *Ibid.*

147 Decision 16/CP.1 (1995) 34 I.L.M. 1676 at 1710.

148 S. Oberthür, "The Second Conference of the Parties" (1996) 26 Envtl. Pol'y & L. 195.

149 FCCC/CP/1996/15/ADD.1, (1996) 7 Y.B. Int'l. Env. L. 535.

150 *Supra*, note 148 at 199.

151 (1998) 37 I.L.M. 32.

152 *Ibid.*, article 25.

representing 44.2 percent of required emissions.[153] The United States, the largest producer of greenhouse gases at 36.1 percent, signed the Protocol in 1998, but announced in March 2001 that it would not ratify.[154] However, on November 18, 2004, Russia deposited its ratification, thus increasing the participation level to 61.6 percent and bringing the Protocol into force on February 16, 2005.[155]

7) The Kyoto Protocol regulates the six major greenhouse gases: carbon dioxide, methane, nitrous oxide, hydrofluorocarbons, perfluorocarbons, and sulphur hexafluoride, as set out in Annex A. In article 3(1) of the Kyoto Protocol, the industrialized and transition economy contracting parties in Annex I of the UNFCCC have agreed that their emissions of the Annex A greenhouse gases will not exceed their assigned amounts listed in Annex B "with a view to reducing their overall emissions" in the initial 2008 to 2012 commitment period, to obtain a minimum 5 percent reduction below 1990 emission levels.[156] Each Annex I state has committed to an individual emission reduction percentage as codified in Annex B. For example, the EU and most of its member states have agreed to reduce their emissions to 92 percent of 1990 base year emissions—that is, an 8 percent cut. The United States originally agreed to a 7 percent reduction; Canada and Japan have each agreed to cut their emissions by 6 percent; and New Zealand, Russia, and the Ukraine have each promised to maintain their emissions at 1990 levels. In contrast, some states have been granted increases: Norway (1 percent), Australia (8 percent), and Iceland (10 percent). The developing country parties do not have any greenhouse gas emission reduction obligations in the Kyoto Protocol.[157] Given that Canadian greenhouse gas emissions have increased since 1990, what implications do the Canadian commitments in the Kyoto Protocol have on domestic implementation now that the Kyoto Protocol has come into force?[158]

8) The Kyoto Protocol allows for a "net" method of reducing greenhouse gases in article 3(3) by accounting for both emission reductions from various sources and credits gained from the action of "sinks" in absorbing these gases through actions such as reforestation and afforestation.[159] Joint fulfillment of emission reduction commitments between developed states parties is permitted in article 4, benefiting, for example, the EU. The mechanism of "joint implementation" is created in article 6, allowing Annex I

---

153 See <http://unfccc.int>. Many industrialized UNFCCC states (*e.g.* Canada, EU states, Japan, New Zealand) had ratified by this date, although Australia and the United States had not.

154 See Birnie & Boyle, *supra* note 1 at 533; Sands, *supra* note 1 at 370. The U.S. administration gave the following reasons: Protocol obligations could harm their economy and developing countries do not have any emission reduction obligations.

155 See <http://unfccc.int>.

156 Pursuant to article 3(8), Annex B states can use 1990 or 1995 as the base year for emission reductions of hydrofluorocarbons, perfluorocarbons, and sulphur hexafluoride. Pursuant to article 3(5) and (6), Annex I states that are economies in transition can use different base years for emission reduction calculation.

157 D.E. Cooper, "The Kyoto Protocol and China: Global Warming's Sleeping Giant" (1999) 11 Geo. Int'l Envtl. L. Rev. 401.

158 See *Climate Change Plan for Canada*, started in November 2002, online: <www.climatechange.gc.ca>.

159 A. Gillespie, "Sinks and the Climate Change Regime: The State of Play" (2003) 13 Duke Env. L. & Pol'y F. 279.

states to transfer among themselves "emission reduction units," which result from projects that reduce greenhouse gas sources or increase their removal through sinks.[160] Article 17 permits international trading of emission reduction units between the Annex B industrialized and economies in transition states parties to fulfill their commitments under Article 3. This will allow Annex B states to sell excess emission credits or purchase needed credits in order to meet their national targets.[161]

9) For developing countries, although they do not have emission reduction commitments in the Kyoto Protocol, article 12 does establish a "clean development mechanism" (CDM), which permits Annex I states to finance emission-reduction projects in developing state countries. Article 12(2) states that the purpose of the CDM is to aid developing states parties "in achieving sustainable development and in contributing to the ultimate objective of the Convention." Further, the Annex I parties will be able to use emission reduction credits resulting from these projects to assist in meeting their own national reduction targets under article 3. Article 10 refers to the "common but differentiated responsibilities" of all parties and requires all parties to create national programs on climate change and cooperate in matters of technology transfer, research, and education. Do you think that the Kyoto Protocol contains an appropriate level of commitment with respect to developing country parties?

10) Pursuant to Kyoto Protocol articles 13 and 14, the COP of the UNFCCC will act as the COP for the Kyoto Protocol and the UNFCCC secretariat will also serve as the Protocol secretariat. Two subsidiary bodies created by articles 9 and 10 of the UNFCCC—the Subsidiary Body for Scientific and Technological Advice and the Subsidiary Body for Implementation—are given the same roles in article 15 of the Protocol—that is, assisting the COP in promoting compliance with the terms of the UNFCCC and the Kyoto Protocol.

11) The Kyoto Protocol contains reporting and other compliance provisions. Under article 18, non-compliance procedures were to be clarified by the COP. Article 5 requires that every Annex I Party shall establish a national system for estimating greenhouse gas emissions by sources and their removals by sinks. Article 7 requires that Annex I parties include supplemental information necessary to ensure compliance with article 3 in their annual inventories of greenhouse gas emission by sources and removals by sinks. Pursuant to article 8, the information submitted under article 7 will be reviewed by expert review teams. Article 8(3) states that "[t]he review process shall provide a thorough and comprehensive technical assessment of all aspects of the implementation by a Party of this Protocol." Pursuant to article 8(6), the COP will receive this information and has the mandate to make decisions on all matters concerning the implementation of the Kyoto Protocol.

At COP-7 in 2001, a compliance mechanism was approved in a draft decision.[162] A Compliance Committee composed of facilitative and enforcement branches is to be

---

160 Hanafi, *supra* note 131.

161 S. Jinnah, "Emissions Trading Under the Kyoto Protocol: NAFTA and WTO Concerns" (2003) 15 Geo. Int'l Envtl. L. Rev. 709. The EU has created a multinational emissions trading scheme for its 25 member states, in effect in 2005, "European Parliament Adopts Emissions Trading Scheme" (July 10, 2003), vol. 7, no. 25 Bridges Weekly Trade News Digest.

162 See M. Montini, "Improving Compliance with Multilateral Environmental Agreements Through Positive Measures: The Case of the Kyoto Protocol on Climate Change" in *Economic Globalization and*

established.[163] The facilitative branch will provide advice to states parties concerning implementation of the Protocol, facilitate financial and technical assistance, and make recommendations.[164] The enforcement branch will address non-compliance of Annex I parties with their emission reduction and reporting obligations and will determine eligibility for use of the Protocol "flexibility" mechanisms (joint implementation, emissions trading, CDM).[165] The enforcement branch has a variety of powers to induce a party to comply, including declarations of non-compliance, orders to develop a compliance action plan, and suspension of eligibility to use the flexibility mechanisms.[166]

12) COP-4 was held in Buenos Aires, Argentina in November 1998. It resulted in a "Buenos Aires Adoption Plan," which established the year 2000 as the deadline for implementing the various mechanisms in the Kyoto Protocol. While the first COP-6, held in The Hague in November 2000, failed to reach agreement on these issues, COP-6, Part II, held in Bonn in July 2001, reached political agreements on implementation details.[167] At COP-7, held in Marrakesh later in 2001, most of the Bonn Agreements were converted into draft decisions known as the "Marrakesh Accords" (including, for example, joint implementation, emissions trading, CDM projects, and the compliance mechanism).[168] Accords on land use, land use change, and forestry (LULUCF) activities, aspects of articles 5, 7, and 8, and the creation of new funds were also adopted.[169] It was also agreed in the Marrakesh Accords that the use of the flexibility mechanisms is to be supplemental to domestic action and that Annex I parties must ensure that domestic action on their part comprises a significant component of their emission reduction activities pursuant to article 3.[170] At COP-8, in New Delhi in late 2002, the COP adopted, *inter alia*, the New Delhi Declaration on Climate Change, which reiterated the common but differentiated responsibilities of states parties and their national development situations in implementing their UNFCCC obligations.[171] COP-9 was held in Milan in December 2003 and COP-10

Compliance With International Environmental Agreements, supra note 24, 157 at 176-79; J. Brunnée, "The Kyoto Protocol: Testing Ground for Compliance Theories?" (2003) 63 Heidelberg J. Int'l L. 255; J. Brunnée, "A Fine Balance: Facilitation and Enforcement in the Design of a Compliance Regime for the Kyoto Protocol" (1999-2000) 13 Tul. Envtl. L.J. 223.

163   Montini, *supra* note 162 at 176; Brunnée, "The Kyoto Protocol: Testing Ground for Compliance Theories?," *supra* note 162 at 273. NGOs and IGOs can submit information to both branches, Brunnée, *supra* note 162 at 275.

164   Montini, *supra* note 162; Brunnée, *supra* note 162.

165   Montini, *supra* note 162 at 176-77; Brunnée, *supra* note 162 at 273-74.

166   Montini, *supra* note 162; Brunnée, *supra* note 162 at 274. The Committee makes final determinations on substantive matters and only due process issues can be appealed to the MOP: see Brunnée, *supra* note 162 at 276.

167   See Sands, *supra* note 1 at 370; P.D. Cameron, "The Kyoto Process: Past, Present and Future" in *Kyoto: From Principles to Practice, supra* note 131 at 15.

168   Sands, *supra* note 1 at 370, 377.

169   Gillespie, *supra* note 159 at 288-91, 296-300; Sands, *supra* note 1 at 377. See also comments *supra* note 143 and <http://www.gefweb.org>.

170   Sands, *supra* note 1 at 373.

171   See Stone, *supra* note 71 at 280.

was held in Buenos Aires in December 2004. The coming into force of the Protocol should enable draft decisions to be formally adopted.

13) Is the approach taken in the Kyoto Protocol the most realistic to achieve continued and more substantive international agreement to combat the problem?[172] What effect does the principle of sustainable development, discussed previously in Section B.3(b) on "Sustainable Development," have on the problem?

F. PROTECTION OF THE MARINE ENVIRONMENT

With regard to the oceans, great concern about their degradation has now found expression in Part XII of the U.N. Convention on the Law of the Sea, which deals with protection and preservation of the marine environment. In addition, there is a substantial record of other multilateral agreements on specific aspects or areas of pollution of the sea. See the discussion of this topic in Chapter 13, Section E.2 on "Protection of the Marine Environment."

G. INTERNATIONAL RIVERS AND LAKES[173]

1. General Principles

The fact that many major rivers and lakes or, more generally, freshwater drainage basins, in all parts of the world traverse national frontiers is a complicating reality with which riparian states have to live. The waters of an international drainage basin are a shared resource, so conditions for the shared use of the waters are essential. The process for the apportionment of access is complicated by the variety of uses, sometimes conflicting, which co-basin states may claim. Thus, navigation, hydroelectric power, human consumption, irrigation, and other uses may all have to be accommodated in an international regime.

By the end of the 19th century, greater demands made on international rivers spurred the development of legal theories over rights of access. To begin, states made assertions of exclusive rights to the waters of international rivers. An upstream state might claim unlimited territorial sovereignty over the river (the Harmon Doctrine), while a downstream

---

172 Cf. B. Pardy, "The Kyoto Protocol: Bad News for the Global Environment" (2004) 14 J. Envtl. L. & Pol'y 27 and M. Doelle, "The Kyoto Protocol: Reflections on Its Significance on Its Entry Into Force" (2004) 27 Dal. L.J. 555.

173 See, generally, S.C. McCaffrey, *The Law of International Watercourses: Non-Navigational Uses* (2001); International Bureau of the Permanent Court of Arbitration, ed., *Resolution of International Water Disputes* (2003); I. Kaya, *Equitable Utilization: The Law of the Non-Navigational Uses of International Watercourses* (2003); A. Tanzi & M. Arcari, *The United Nations Convention on the Law of International Watercourses* (2001): P. Wouters, ed., *International Water Law: Selected Writings of Professor Charles B. Bourne* (1997); M. Woodhouse, "Is Public Participation a Rule of the Law of International Watercourses?" (2003) 43 Nat. Res. J. 137; J. Brunnée & S.J. Toope, "The Changing Nile Basin Regime: Does Law Matter?" (2002) 43 Harv. Int'l L.J. 105; R. Paisley, "Adversaries into Partners: International Water Law and the Equitable Sharing of Downstream Benefits" (2002) 3 Melbourne J. Int'l L. 280; S.C. McCaffrey, "An Overview of the U.N. Convention on the Law of the Non-Navigational Uses of International Watercourses" (2000) J. Land Resources & Envtl. L. 57; and J. Brunnée & S.J. Toope, "Environmental Security and Freshwater Resources: Ecosystem Regime Building" (1997) 91 A.J.I.L. 26.

state might assert a riparian right to the unfettered natural flow, or prior use, and thus appropriation, of the waters.[174] But these approaches did not respond to the needs of other co-basin states and consequently they did not survive.

The principle of shared use ("equitable utilization" or "limited territorial sovereignty") has now met with general approval and has been supported by the work of the International Law Association (ILA). The 1966 Helsinki Rules on the Uses of Waters of International Rivers and the 1982 Montreal Rules on Water Pollution in an International Drainage Basin have been regularly referred to, even though they emanate from an unofficial source, and have now been revised by the ILA's 2004 Berlin Rules on Water Resources.[175] Consider also the *Lake Lanoux Arbitration*, discussed above in Section B.2 on "Development of General Principles" and the *Gabcíkovo-Nagymaros Project* case, discussed above in Section B.1 "Introduction."

Under the auspices of the U.N. Economic Commission for Europe (ECE), a regional framework Convention on the Protection and Use of Transboundary Watercourses and International Lakes was concluded on March 17, 1992 and entered into force on October 6, 1996. The ILC has also directed its energies toward the development of the law in this area and its work was relied on to draft the U.N. Convention on the Law of the Non-Navigational Uses of International Watercourses, which was adopted by the General Assembly and opened for signature on May 21, 1997. As of October 2005, the U.N. Convention had not entered into force. Like the ECE Convention, the U.N. Convention will act as a framework, envisaging the creation of regional or bilateral agreements between U.N. Convention riparian states applying the Convention rules to specific international watercourses.

ECE Convention on the Protection and Use of Transboundary Watercourses and International Lakes
(1992) 31 I.L.M. 1312

PREAMBLE

The Parties to this Convention, ...

Concerned over the existence and threats of adverse effects, in the short or long term, of changes in the conditions of transboundary watercourses and international lakes on the environment, economies and well-being of the member countries of the Economic Commission for Europe (ECE). ...

---

174 See McCaffrey, *The Law of International Watercourses: Non-Navigational Uses, supra* note 173 at 114-37; and S.C. McCaffrey, "The Harmon Doctrine One Hundred Years Later: Buried, Not Praised" (1996) 36 Nat. Res. J. 549.

175 See *Helsinki Rules on the Uses of Waters of International Rivers*, International Law Association (ILA), 52nd Conference, August 1966; *Montreal Rules on Water Pollution in an International Drainage Basin*, ILA, 60th Conference, August 1982. Berlin Rules on Water Resources, ILA, 71st Conference, August 2004. See also McCaffrey, *The Law of International Watercourses: Non-Navigational Uses, supra* note 173 at 137-49.

Emphasizing that cooperation between member countries in regard to the protection and use of transboundary waters shall be implemented primarily through the elaboration of agreements between countries bordering the same waters, especially where no such agreements have yet been reached.

Have agreed as follows:

Article 1
Definitions

For the purposes of this Convention,

1. "Transboundary waters" means any surface or ground waters which mark, cross or are located on boundaries between two or more States; wherever transboundary waters flow directly into the sea, these transboundary waters end at a straight line across their respective mouths between points on the low-water line of their banks;

2. "Transboundary impact" means any significant adverse effect on the environment resulting from a change in the conditions of transboundary waters caused by a human activity, the physical origin of which is situated wholly or in part within an area under the jurisdiction of a Party, within an area under the jurisdiction of another Party. Such effects on the environment include effects on human health and safety, flora, fauna, soil, air, water, climate, landscape and historical monuments or other physical structures or the interaction among these factors; they also include effects on the cultural heritage or socio-economic conditions resulting from alterations to those factors;

3. "Party" means, unless the text otherwise indicates, a Contracting Party to this Convention;

4. "Riparian Parties" means the Parties bordering the same transboundary waters;

5. "Joint body" means any bilateral or multilateral commission or other appropriate institutional arrangements for cooperation between the Riparian Parties;

6. "Hazardous substances" means substances which are toxic, carcinogenic, mutagenic, teratogenic or bio-accumulative, especially when they are persistent;

7. "Best available technology" (the definition is contained in annex I to this Convention).

PART I
PROVISIONS RELATING TO ALL PARTIES

Article 2
General Provisions

1. The Parties shall take all appropriate measures to prevent, control and reduce any transboundary impact.

2. The Parties shall, in particular, take all appropriate measures:

(a) To prevent, control and reduce pollution of waters causing or likely to cause transboundary impact;

(b) To ensure that transboundary waters are used with the aim of ecologically sound and rational water management, conservation of water resources and environmental protection;

(c) To ensure that transboundary waters are used in a reasonable and equitable way, taking into particular account their transboundary character, in the case of activities which cause or are likely to cause transboundary impact;

(d) To ensure conservation and, where necessary, restoration of ecosystems.

3. Measures for the prevention, control and reduction of water pollution shall be taken, where possible, at source.

4. These measures shall not directly or indirectly result in a transfer of pollution to other parts of the environment.

5. In taking the measures referred to in paragraphs 1 and 2 of this article, the Parties shall be guided by the following principles:

(a) The precautionary principle, by virtue of which action to avoid the potential transboundary impact of the release of hazardous substances shall not be postponed on the ground that scientific research has not fully proved a causal link between those substances, on the one hand, and the potential transboundary impact, on the other hand;

(b) The polluter-pays principle, by virtue of which costs of pollution prevention, control and reduction measures shall be borne by the polluter;

(c) Water resources shall be managed so that the needs of the present generation are met without compromising the ability of future generations to meet their own needs. ...

Article 3
Prevention, Control, and Reduction

1. To prevent, control and reduce transboundary impact, the Parties shall develop, adopt, implement and, as far as possible, render compatible relevant legal, administrative, economic, financial and technical measures, in order to ensure, *inter alia*, that:

(a) The emission of pollutants is prevented, controlled and reduced at source through the application of, *inter alia*, low- and non-waste technology;

(b) Transboundary waters are protected against pollution from point sources through the prior licensing of waste-water discharges by the competent national authorities, and that the authorized discharges are monitored and controlled; ...

(h) Environmental impact assessment and other means of assessment are applied;

(i) Sustainable water-resources management, including the application of the ecosystems approach, is promoted;

(j) Contingency planning is developed;

(k) Additional specific measures are taken to prevent the pollution of groundwaters;

(l) The risk of accidental pollution is minimized. ...

Article 9
Bilateral and Multilateral Cooperation

1. The Riparian Parties shall on the basis of equality and reciprocity enter into bilateral or multilateral agreements or other arrangements, where these do not yet

exist, or adapt existing ones, where necessary to eliminate the contradictions with the basic principles of this Convention, in order to define their mutual relations and conduct regarding the prevention, control and reduction of transboundary impact. The Riparian Parties shall specify the catchment area, or part(s) thereof, subject to cooperation. These agreements or arrangements shall embrace relevant issues covered by this Convention, as well as any other issues on which the Riparian Parties may deem it necessary to cooperate.

United Nations Convention on the Law of the Non-Navigational Uses of International Watercourses
U.N. Doc. A/51/869; (1997) 36 I.L.M. 703 (not in force)

PART I
INTRODUCTION

Article 1[176]
Scope of the Present Convention

1. The present Convention applies to uses of international watercourses and of their waters for purposes other than navigation and to measures of protection, preservation and management related to the uses of those watercourses and their waters.

2. The uses of international watercourses for navigation is not within the scope of the present Convention except insofar as other uses affect navigation or are affected by navigation.

Article 2
Use of Terms

For the purposes of the present Convention:

(a) "Watercourse" means a system of surface waters and ground waters constituting by virtue of their physical relationship a unitary whole and normally flowing into a common terminus;

(b) "International watercourse" means a watercourse, parts of which are situated in different States;

(c) "Watercourse State" means a State Party to the present Convention in whose territory part of an international watercourse is situated, or a Party that is a regional economic integration organization, in the territory of one or more of whose Member States part of an international watercourse is situated; ...

---

176 During the drafting of the agreement, the following statement of understanding was noted with respect to article 1: "(a) The concept of 'preservation' referred to in this article and the Convention includes also the concept of 'conservation'; (b) the present Convention does not apply to the use of living resources that occur in international watercourses, except to the extent provided for in part IV and except insofar as other uses affect such resources" (1997) 36 I.L.M. 703 at 719.

Article 3[177]
Watercourse Agreements

1. In the absence of an agreement to the contrary, nothing in the present Convention shall affect the rights or obligations of a watercourse State arising from agreements in force for it on the date on which it became a party to the present Convention.

2. Notwithstanding the provisions of paragraph 1, parties to agreements referred to in paragraph 1 may, where necessary, consider harmonizing such agreements with the basic principles of the present Convention.

3. Watercourse States may enter into one or more agreements, hereinafter referred to as "watercourse agreements," which apply and adjust the provisions of the present Convention to the characteristics and uses of a particular international watercourse or part thereof.

4. Where a watercourse agreement is concluded between two or more watercourse States, it shall define the waters to which it applies. Such an agreement may be entered into with respect to an entire international watercourse or any part thereof or a particular project, programme or use except insofar as the agreement adversely affects, to a significant extent, the use by one or more other watercourse States of the waters of the watercourse, without their express consent. ...

PART II
GENERAL PRINCIPLES

Article 5
Equitable and Reasonable Utilization and Participation

1. Watercourse States shall in their respective territories utilize an international watercourse in an equitable and reasonable manner. In particular, an international watercourse shall be used and developed by watercourse States with a view to attaining optimal and sustainable utilization thereof and benefits therefrom, taking into account the interests of the watercourse States concerned, consistent with adequate protection of the watercourse.

2. Watercourse States shall participate in the use, development and protection of an international watercourse in an equitable and reasonable manner. Such participation includes both the right to utilize the watercourse and the duty to cooperate in the protection and development thereof, as provided in the present Convention.

---

177   The following statement of understanding was noted for article 3: "(a) The present Convention will serve as a guideline for future watercourse agreements and, once such agreements are concluded, it will not alter the rights and obligations provided therein, unless such agreements provide otherwise; (b) The term 'significant' is not used in this article or elsewhere in the present Convention in the sense of 'substantial.' What is to be avoided are localized agreements, or agreements concerning a particular project, programme or use, which have a significant adverse effect upon third watercourse States. While such an effect must be capable of being established by objective evidence and not be trivial in nature, it need not rise to the level of being substantial." *Ibid.*

Article 6[178]
Factors Relevant to Equitable and Reasonable Utilization

1. Utilization of an international watercourse in an equitable and reasonable manner within the meaning of article 5 requires taking into account all relevant factors and circumstances, including:

(a) Geographic, hydrographic, hydrological, climatic, ecological and other factors of a natural character;

(b) The social and economic needs of the watercourse States concerned;

(c) The population dependent on the watercourse in each watercourse State;

(d) The effects of the use or uses of the watercourses in one watercourse State on other watercourse States;

(e) Existing and potential uses of the watercourse;

(f) Conservation, protection, development and economy of use of the water resources of the watercourse and the costs of measures taken to that effect;

(g) The availability of alternatives, of comparable value, to a particular planned or existing use.

2. In the application of article 5 or paragraph 1 of this article, watercourse States concerned shall, when the need arises, enter into consultations in a spirit of cooperation.

3. The weight to be given to each factor is to be determined by its importance in comparison with that of other relevant factors. In determining what is a reasonable and equitable use, all relevant factors are to be considered together and a conclusion reached on the basis of the whole.

Article 7[179]
Obligation Not To Cause Significant Harm

1. Watercourse States shall, in utilizing an international watercourse in their territories, take all appropriate measures to prevent the causing of significant harm to other watercourse States.

2. Where significant harm nevertheless is caused to another watercourse State, the States whose use causes such harm shall, in the absence of agreement to such use, take all appropriate measures, having due regard for the provisions of articles 5 and 6, in consultation with the affected State, to eliminate or mitigate such harm and, where appropriate, to discuss the question of compensation.

---

178 The following statement of understanding was noted for article 6(1)(e): "In order to determine whether a particular use is equitable and reasonable, the benefits as well as the negative consequences of a particular use should be taken into account." *Ibid.*

179 The following statement of understanding was noted for article 7(2): "In the event such steps as are required by article 7(2) do not eliminate the harm, such steps as are required by article 7(2) shall then be taken to mitigate the harm." *Ibid.*

Article 8
General Obligation To Cooperate

1. Watercourse States shall cooperate on the basis of sovereign equality, territorial integrity, mutual benefit and good faith in order to attain optimal utilization and adequate protection of an international watercourse. ...

Article 10[180]
Relationship Between Different Kinds of Uses

1. In the absence of agreement or custom to the contrary, no use of an international watercourse enjoys inherent priority over other uses.
2. In the event of a conflict between uses of an international watercourse, it shall be resolved with reference to articles 5 to 7, with special regard being given to the requirements of vital human needs. ...

PART IV
PROTECTION, PRESERVATION AND MANAGEMENT

Article 20
Protection and Preservation of Ecosystems

Watercourse States shall, individually and, where appropriate, jointly, protect and preserve the ecosystems of international watercourses.

Article 21[181]
Prevention, Reduction, and Control of Pollution

1. For the purposes of this article, "pollution of an international watercourse" means any detrimental alteration in the composition or quality of the waters of an international watercourse which results directly or indirectly from human conduct.
2. Watercourse States shall, individually and, where appropriate, jointly, prevent, reduce and control the pollution of an international watercourse that may cause significant harm to other watercourse States or to their environment, including harm to human health or safety, to the use of the waters for any beneficial purpose or to the living resources of the watercourse. Watercourse States shall take steps to harmonize their policies in this connection.

---

180 The following statement of understanding was noted for article 10: "In determining 'vital human needs,' special attention is to be paid to providing sufficient water to sustain human life, including both drinking water and water required for production of food in order to prevent starvation." *Ibid.*

181 The following statement of understanding was noted for articles 21-23: "As reflected in the commentary of the International Law Commission, these articles impose a due diligence standard on watercourse States." *Ibid.*

Berlin Rules on Water Resources
International Law Association, 71st Conference, August 2004

CHAPTER I
SCOPE

Article 1
Scope

1. These Rules express international law applicable to the management of the waters of international drainage basins and applicable to all waters, as appropriate.

2. Nothing in these Rules affects rights or obligations created by treaty or special custom. ...

Article 3
Definitions

For the purposes of these Articles, these terms have the following meanings: ...

3. A "basin State" is a State the territory of which includes any portion of an international drainage basin. ...

7. "Environment" includes the waters, land, air, flora, and fauna that exist in a particular region at a particular time.

8. "Environmental harm" includes:

   a. injury to the environment and any other loss or damage caused by such harm; and

   b. the costs of reasonable measures to restore the environment actually undertaken or to be undertaken. ...

13. An "international drainage basin" is a drainage basin extending over two or more States.

14. "Management of waters" and "to manage waters" includes the development, use, protection, allocation, regulation, and control of waters. ...

16. "Pollution" means any detrimental change in the composition or quality of waters that results directly or indirectly from human conduct. ...

20. "Vital human needs" means waters used for immediate human survival, including drinking, cooking, and sanitary needs, as well as water needed for the immediate sustenance of a household.

21. "Waters" means all surface water and groundwater other than marine waters. ...

CHAPTER III
INTERNATIONALLY SHARED WATERS

Article 10
Participation by Basin States

1. Basin States have the right to participate in the management of waters of an international drainage basin in an equitable, reasonable, and sustainable manner.

2. Basin States shall define the waters to which an international agreement regarding the management of waters of an international drainage basin applies; such an international agreement may apply to all or part of the waters of an international drainage basin or to a particular project or use, except that a use by one or more basin States shall not cause a significant adverse effect on the rights of or uses in another basin State without the latter State's express consent.

Article 11
Cooperation

Basin States shall cooperate in good faith in the management of waters of an international drainage basin for the mutual benefit of the participating States.

Article 12
Equitable Utilization

1. Basin States shall in their respective territories manage the waters of an international drainage basin in an equitable and reasonable manner having due regard for the obligation not to cause significant harm to other basin States.

2. In particular, basin States shall develop and use the waters of the basin in order to attain the optimal and sustainable use thereof and benefits therefrom, taking into account the interests of other basin States, consistent with adequate protection of the waters.

Article 13
Determining an Equitable and Reasonable Use

1. Equitable and reasonable use within the meaning of Article 12 is to be determined through consideration of all relevant factors in each particular case.

2. Relevant factors to be considered include, but are not limited to:

    a. Geographic, hydrographic, hydrological, hydrogeological, climatic, ecological, and other natural features;

    b. The social and economic needs of the basin States concerned;

    c. The population dependent on the waters of the international drainage basin in each basin State;

    d. The effects of the use or uses of the waters of the international drainage basin in one basin State upon other basin States;

    e. Existing and potential uses of the waters of the international drainage basin;

    f. Conservation, protection, development, and economy of use of the water resources of the international drainage basin and the costs of measures taken to achieve these purposes;

    g. The availability of alternatives, of comparable value, to the particular planned or existing use;

    h. The sustainability of proposed or existing uses; and

    i. The minimization of environmental harm.

3. The weight of each factor is to be determined by its importance in comparison with other relevant factors. In determining what is a reasonable and equitable use, all

relevant factors are to be considered together and a conclusion reached on the basis of the whole.

Article 14
Preferences among Uses

1. In determining an equitable and reasonable use, States shall first allocate waters to satisfy vital human needs.

2. No other use or category of uses shall have an inherent preference over any other use or category of uses. ...

Article 16
Avoidance of Transboundary Harm

Basin States, in managing the waters of an international drainage basin, shall refrain from and prevent acts or omissions within their territory that cause significant harm to another basin State having due regard for the right of each basin State to make equitable and reasonable use of the waters. ...

CHAPTER V
PROTECTION OF THE AQUATIC ENVIRONMENTS

Article 22
Ecological Integrity

States shall take all appropriate measures to protect the ecological integrity necessary to sustain ecosystems dependent on particular waters.

Article 23
The Precautionary Approach

1. In implementing obligations under this Chapter, States shall apply the precautionary approach.

2. States shall take all appropriate measures to prevent, eliminate, reduce, or control harm to the aquatic environment when there is a serious risk of significant adverse effect on or to the sustainable use of waters even without conclusive proof of a causal relation between an act or omission and its expected effects. ...

Article 27
Pollution

1. States shall prevent, eliminate, reduce, or control pollution in order to minimize environmental harm.

NOTES

1) The principle of "reasonable and equitable utilization," found in article 2(2)(c) of the U.N. ECE Convention on Transboundary Watercourses and International Lakes, article 5 of the U.N. Convention on the Law of the Non-Navigational Uses of International Watercourses, and article 12 of the Berlin Rules is a legal expression of the common interest in a shared resource of basin states.[182] In looking at the relationship between different types of uses, what role does the concept of "vital human needs" play in the 1997 U.N. Convention and the Berlin Rules?

2) The U.N. ECE Convention on the Protection and Use of Transboundary Watercourses and International Lakes is the first multilateral treaty to regulate the use of international watercourses over an entire region, and is now being supplemented by two protocols on civil liability and on water health.[183] It was signed by European states and the EC, but neither Canada nor the United States is a signatory. A number of sub-regional agreements have been created founded on the ECE Convention.[184]

3) The 1997 U.N. Convention on the Law of the Non-Navigational Uses of International Watercourses is primarily the product of the work of the ILC.[185] The ILC first adopted a full set of articles on the Law of the Non-Navigational Uses of International Watercourses in 1991.[186] In 1994, it submitted a final set of Draft Articles to the General Assembly with a recommendation that a treaty be formulated from them.[187] Following the ILC articles closely, the treaty was structured as a framework that states can modify in agreement with other states to meet the requirements of the particular watercourse and

---

182   See McCaffrey, *The Law of International Watercourses: Non-Navigational Uses*, *supra* note 173 at 324-45; and X. Fuentes, "The Criteria for the Equitable Utilization of International Rivers" (1996) 67 Brit. Y.B. Int'l L. 337.

183   As of October 1, 2005, the Convention had 35 parties, online: <http://www.unece.org/env>. See also U.N. *ECE Protocol on Civil Liability and Compensation for Damage Caused by the Transboundary Effects of Industrial Accidents on Transboundary Waters*, May 21, 2003, not in force as of October 1, 2005, and Canada not a signatory at that date; U.N. ECE Protocol on Water and Health, June 17, 1999, in force as of August 4, 2005, but Canada was not a signatory at that date. In 2003, the ECE Convention was amended to allow states outside the ECE region to accede to it, especially relevant for states bordering the ECE area: see U.N. ECE, *The 1992 UNECE Convention on the Protection and Use of Transboundary Watercourses and International Lakes: What Is It, Why It Matters?* (2004) at 5.

184   See *e.g.* 1994 *Danube River Convention*; 1998 *Rhine Convention*; *The 1992 UNECE Convention on the Protection and Use of Transboundary Watercourses and International Lakes: What Is It, Why It Matters?*, *supra* note 183 at 5.

185   See McCaffrey, *The Law of International Watercourses: Non-Navigational Uses*, *supra* note 173 at 301-22; S.C. McCaffrey & M. Sinjela, "The 1997 United Nations Convention on International Watercourses" (1998) 92 A.J.I.L. 97; Fuentes, *supra* note 182; C.B. Bourne, "The Primacy of the Principle of Equitable Utilization in the 1997 Watercourses Convention" (1997) 35 Can. Y.B. Int'l L. 215; and A.E. Utton, "Which Rule Should Prevail in International Water Disputes: That of Reasonableness or that of No Harm?" (1996) 36 Nat. Res. J. 635.

186   See S. McCaffrey, "The Law of International Watercourses—The ILC Completes Its Draft Articles" (1992) 22 Envtl. Pol'y & L. 66 and (1992) 3 Col. J. Int'l Envtl. L. & Pol'y 1.

187   S.C. McCaffrey, "The International Law Commission Adopts Draft Articles on International Watercourses" (1995) 89 A.J.I.L. 395 at 395.

the states concerned.[188] Articles 5 to 7 of the Convention contain the central legal obligations of contracting parties, attempting to implement both the "equitable utilization" and "no significant harm" principles in the use of an international watercourse.[189] Other articles cover exchange of information, notification of and consultations with respect to planned measures, joint management of the watercourse, installations, regulation of international watercourses, harmful conditions and emergency situations, international watercourses and installations in times of armed conflict, and dispute settlement. What differences of approach and substantive content can you see in comparing the ECE Convention and the U.N. Convention? Is the "equitable utilization" principle given greater weight than that of "no significant harm" in the U.N. Convention, or vice versa?

4) Stephen McCaffrey has argued that the U.N. Convention has "significant value" whether or not it enters into force because: (1) it is based on an ILC draft and "the most important elements of the Convention—equitable utilization, prevention of harm, prior notification, protection of ecosystems—are, in large measure, codifications of norms that either exist or, in the case of ecosystem protection, are at least emerging";[190] (2) it was negotiated in a fully open multilateral forum and "reflects the views of the international community on the subject";[191] and (3) the Convention can be used to interpret other watercourse agreements whether or not the U.N. Convention is binding on the states party to these other agreements.[192] Do you agree with these views?

5) In the *Gabcíkovo-Nagymaros Project* case, the ICJ noted the adoption of the 1997 U.N. Convention and stated:

> The Court considers that Czechoslovakia, by unilaterally assuming control of a shared resource, and thereby depriving Hungary of its right to an equitable and reasonable share of the natural resources of the Danube—with the continuing effects of the diversion of these waters on the ecology of the riparian area ...—failed to respect the proportionality which is required by international law.[193]

6) The ILA considers that its 2004 Berlin Rules on Water Resources are a comprehensive list of the predominantly customary international law norms on water resources, covering both international drainage basins and fresh water within a state to the extent that international law covers the latter. In addition to the articles listed above, the Berlin Rules contain provisions on conjunctive and integrated management of waters, sustainability, minimization of environmental harm, right of access to water, public participation and access to information, protection of indigenous and other particular communities, the right to compensation, alien species, hazardous substances, establishing water quality standards, impact assessments, extreme situations, groundwater, navigation,

---

188 See McCaffrey & Sinjela, *supra* note 185 at 98 and 106.

189 *Ibid.* at 101. But see Bourne, *supra* note 185 at 218-25.

190 McCaffrey, *The Law of International Watercourses: Non-Navigational Uses*, *supra* note 173 at 316.

191 *Ibid.*

192 *Ibid.*

193 *Case Concerning the Gabcíkovo-Nagymaros Project, supra* note 9, para. 85.

protection of waters and water installations during war or armed conflict, international cooperation and administration, state responsibility, legal remedies, and settlement of international disputes. Comparing the 1997 U.N. Convention and the ILA Berlin Rules, do you see any discrepancies in approach and content?

2. Canada–United States Great Lakes Water Regimes

By 1970 the Great Lakes system had become seriously polluted. The pollution had many sources, including industrial processes, urban usages, and shipping wastes. The poor condition of the lake waters was revealed convincingly in a study and report by the International Joint Commission (IJC).[194] Pursuant to the 1909 Boundary Waters Treaty, in the course of 90 years the IJC has helped to resolve a variety of transboundary difficulties, most frequently concerning navigation and water diversion projects, along many parts of the common frontier. But none of its efforts has had such an impact as its report on the polluted condition of Lake Erie, Lake Ontario, and the international section of the St. Lawrence River, which led swiftly to the first Canada–United States Great Lakes Water Quality Agreement in 1972.[195] The original arrangements, which were directed only to the boundary waters within the Great Lakes System, have now been superseded by the 1978 Agreement, amended most recently in 1987.[196] The Agreement attempts to restore and maintain the environmental integrity of the Great Lakes Basin Ecosystem and to eliminate or reduce the discharge of pollutants into the Great Lakes System.[197] The IJC is given the responsibility of assisting in the implementation of the Agreement through information collection and dissemination, assistance in the coordination of joint activities and research, the tendering of advice and recommendations to the parties and the provincial and state governments, and the conduct of investigations referred to it by the parties.[198] In recent years the parties to the Great Lakes Water Quality

---

194 The *Boundary Waters Treaty* and the IJC have been discussed previously in Section C.1 on "Transboundary Air Pollution and Acid Deposition" under the Canada–United States Air Quality Agreement, and in Chapter 6, Section E. See also Toope & Brunnée, "Freshwater Regimes: The Mandate of the International Joint Commission," *supra* note 95; and L.B. Dworsky, A.E. Utton, & D.J. Allee, "The Great Lakes: Transboundary Issues for the Mid-90s" (1995) 26 U. Tol. L. Rev. 347.

195 Can. T.S. 1972 No. 12.

196 Can. T.S. 1978 No. 20; 30 U.S.T. 1383. Amended by Can. T.S. 1983 No. 22 and Can. T.S. 1987 No. 32.

197 Article II. Article I defines (g) "Great Lakes Basin Ecosystem" as "the interacting components of air, land, water and living organisms, including humans, within the drainage basin of the St. Lawrence River at or upstream from the point at which this river becomes the international boundary between Canada and the United States" and (h) "Great Lakes System" as "all of the streams, rivers, lakes and other bodies of water that are within the drainage basin on the St. Lawrence River at or upstream from the point at which this river becomes the international boundary." See G. Francis, "Binational Cooperation for Great Lakes Water Quality: A Framework for the Groundwater Connection" (1989) 65 Chicago-Kent L. Rev. 359 and E. Brown Weiss, "New Directions for the Great Lakes Water Quality Agreement: A Commentary" (1989) 65 Chicago-Kent L. Rev. 375.

198 See Toope & Brunnée, "Freshwater Regimes: The Mandate of the International Joint Commission," *supra* note 95.

Agreement have focused on implementation of its terms and, in this respect, a Canada–Ontario Agreement Respecting the Great Lakes Basin Ecosystem is in place.[199]

The U.S. Great Lakes states, Ontario, and Québec signed the Great Lakes Charter in 1985[200] to provide for consultation and long-term cooperative management of the Great Lakes ecosystem. Does this agreement have the force of a treaty?

The consumption and potential diversion or large-scale export of the waters of the Great Lakes is as much a transboundary management problem as is the protection of their quality.[201] The Great Lakes Charter did address diversions and consumptive use, indicating an intent not to permit diversions that would have any significant adverse impacts, but provided only for consultations to seek consent.[202] In 2001, an Annex was added to the Charter in which the Great Lakes provinces and states agreed to draft, within three years, a binding agreement on water management and conservation, including regulation of proposals to withdraw water from the basin.[203] Considerable progress had been made and revised draft implementing agreements were issued on June 30, 2005 for public review.[204] The Canadian government also moved to amend the *International Boundary Waters Treaty Act* and regulations in December 2002, prohibiting the bulk removal of boundary waters from all Canadian basins for any purpose, including export.[205]

H. PROTECTION OF WILDLIFE AND TERRESTRIAL RESOURCES

Treaties for the protection of wildlife were among the earliest agreements concerning international environmental protection. However, they affected a limited range of species. Concern for the broader protection of biological diversity and wildlife habitat, and the movement to preserve terrestrial spaces for their own value, have developed more recently.

---

199 Dating back to 1994, the current Agreement was reached in 2002; see <http://www.ene.gov.on.ca/water.htm>.

200 <http://www.cglg.org/pub/charter>; Great Lakes Governors Task Force on Water Diversion and Great Lakes Institutions, *Final Report and Recommendations—A Report to the Governors and Premiers of the Great Lakes States and Provinces* (1985).

201 See the *Boundary Waters Treaty*, *supra* note 95; M. Valiente, "The Great Lakes Charter Annex 2001: Legal Dimensions of Provincial Participation" (2003) 13 J. Envtl. L. & Practice 47; and S. Frerichs & K. Easter, "Regulation of Interbasin Transfers and Consumptive Uses From the Great Lakes" (1990) 30 Nat. Res. J. 561.

202 *Great Lakes Charter*, *supra* note 200, Principles III-IV; Valiente, *supra* note 201 at 52-53.

203 Council of Great Lakes Governors, *The Great Lakes Charter Annex: A Supplementary Agreement to the Great Lakes Charter* (June 18, 2001), online: <http://www.cglg.org/projects/water/docs/GreatLakesCharterAnnex.pdf>; Valiente, *supra* note 201 at 48-50, 56-57.

204 See <http://www.cglg.org>; A. Mitchell, "Great Lakes proposal 'seriously flawed'" (September 20, 2004) *The Globe and Mail* at A8.

205 *International Boundary Waters Treaty Act*, R.S.C. 1985, c. I-17, as am. by S.C. 2001, c. 40, *International Boundary Waters Regulations*, SOR/2002-445 (in force December 10, 2002); *Boundary Waters Treaty*, *supra* note 95. Also, licences will be required for water-related projects in Canada that affect the level of flow of waters in boundary waters. See also IJC, *Protection of the Waters of the Great Lakes. Final Report to the Governments of Canada and the United States* (2000), recommending prohibition of removal of water from the basin unless listed criteria are satisfied.

The following are the major multilateral treaties that attempt to conserve wildlife, biological diversity, habitat, and land spaces. Collectively they indicate that the international community is responding to the need to preserve species and terrestrial spaces. Other multilateral, regional, and bilateral treaties are also in place to protect specific forms of wildlife such as marine mammals and birds, and regional treaties have been negotiated to protect wildlife and habitat.

1. Protection of Land Spaces

Convention for the Protection of the World Cultural and Natural Heritage
Can. T.S. 1976 No. 45; (1972) 11 I.L.M. 1358

I. DEFINITIONS OF THE CULTURAL AND THE NATURAL HERITAGE

Article 2

For the purposes of this Convention, the following shall be considered as "natural heritage":

— natural features consisting of physical and biological formations or groups of such formations, which are of outstanding universal value from the aesthetic or scientific point of view;
— geological and physiographical formations and precisely delineated areas which constitute the habitat of threatened species of animals and plants of outstanding universal value from the point of view of science or conservation;
— natural sites or precisely delineated natural areas of outstanding universal value from the point of view of science, conservation or natural beauty.

Article 3

It is for each State Party to this Convention to identify and delineate the different properties situated on its territory mentioned in Articles 1 and 2 above.

II. NATIONAL PROTECTION AND INTERNATIONAL PROTECTION OF THE CULTURAL AND NATURAL HERITAGE

Article 4

Each State Party to this Convention recognizes that the duty of ensuring the identification, protection, conservation, presentation and transmission to future generations of the cultural and natural heritage referred to in Articles 1 and 2 and situated on its territory, belongs primarily to that State. It will do all it can to this end, to the utmost of its own resources and, where appropriate, with any international assistance and co-operation, in particular, financial, artistic, scientific and technical, which it may be able to obtain.

Article 5

To ensure that effective and active measures are taken for the protection, conservation and presentation of the cultural and natural heritage situated on its territory, each State Party to this Convention shall endeavour, in so far as possible, and as appropriate for each country:

(a) to adopt a general policy which aims to give the cultural and natural heritage a function in the life of the community and to integrate the protection of that heritage into comprehensive planning programmes;

(b) to set up within its territories, where such services do not exist, one or more services for the protection, conservation and presentation of the cultural and natural heritage with an appropriate staff and possessing the means to discharge their functions;

(c) to develop scientific and technical studies and research and to work out such operating methods as will make the State capable of counteracting the dangers that threaten its cultural or natural heritage;

(d) to take the appropriate legal, scientific, technical, administrative and financial measures necessary for the identification, protection, conservation, presentation and rehabilitation of this heritage; and

(e) to foster the establishment or development of national or regional centres for training in the protection, conservation and presentation of the cultural and natural heritage and to encourage scientific research in this field.

Article 6

1. Whilst fully respecting the sovereignty of the States on whose territory the cultural and natural heritage mentioned in Articles 1 and 2 is situated, and without prejudice to property rights provided by national legislation, the States Parties to this Convention recognize that such heritage constitutes a world heritage for whose protection it is the duty of the international community as a whole to co-operate. ...

3. Each State Party to this Convention undertakes not to take any deliberate measures which might damage directly or indirectly the cultural and natural heritage referred to in Articles 1 and 2 situated on the territory of other State Parties to this Convention.

Convention on Wetlands of International Importance Especially as Waterfowl Habitat
Can. T.S. 1981 No. 9; (1972) 11 I.L.M. 969

Article 1

1. For the purpose of this Convention wetlands are areas of marsh, fen, peatland or water, whether natural or artificial, permanent or temporary, with water that is static or flowing, fresh, brackish or salt, including areas of marine water the depth of which at low tide does not exceed six metres.

2. For the purpose of this Convention waterfowl are birds ecologically dependent on wetlands.

Article 2

1. Each Contracting Party shall designate suitable wetlands within its territory for inclusion in a List of Wetlands of International Importance, hereinafter referred to as "the List." ...

2. Wetlands should be selected for the List on account of their international significance in terms of ecology, botany, zoology, limnology or hydrology. In the first instance wetlands of international importance to waterfowl at any season should be included.

3. The inclusion of a wetland in the List does not prejudice the exclusive sovereign rights of the Contracting Party in whose territory the wetland is situated.

4. Each Contracting Party shall designate at least one wetland to be included in the List when signing this Convention or when depositing its instrument of ratification or accession. ...

5. Any Contracting Party shall have the right to add to the List further wetlands situated within its territory, to extend the boundaries of those wetlands already included by it in the List, or, because of its urgent national interests, to delete or restrict the boundaries of wetlands already included by it in the List. ...

6. Each Contracting Party shall consider its international responsibilities for the conservation, management and wise use of migratory stocks of waterfowl, both when designating entries for the List and when exercising its right to change entries in the List relating to wetlands within its territory.

Article 3

1. The Contracting Parties shall formulate and implement their planning so as to promote the conservation of the wetlands included in the List, and as far as possible the wise use of wetlands in their territory. ...

Article 4

1. Each Contracting Party shall promote the conservation of wetlands and waterfowl by establishing nature reserves on wetlands, whether they are included in the List or not, and provide adequately for their wardening.

2. Where a Contracting Party in its urgent national interest, deletes or restricts the boundaries of a wetland included in the List, it should as far as possible compensate for any loss of wetland resources, and in particular it should create additional natural reserves for waterfowl and for the protection, either in the same area or elsewhere, of an adequate portion of the original habitat.

NOTES

1) The Convention for the Protection of the World Cultural and Natural Heritage (UNESCO or World Heritage Convention) entered into force on December 17, 1975. Canada acceded to the Convention with effect from October 23, 1976.[206] Canadian natural sites on the World Heritage List include the Rocky Mountain National Parks, Wood Buffalo National Park, and Nahanni National Park. Article 8 of the Convention establishes a World Heritage Committee. Pursuant to article 11, states parties submit inventories of properties for potential inclusion in a protected World Heritage List. The Committee determines which properties are placed in the List given the definitions in articles 1 and 2 of the Convention. Article 11(3) states that the inclusion of a property in the List requires the consent of the state concerned. The Committee also maintains a List of World Heritage in Danger. The Committee is assisted in its decisions by the World Conservation Union (ICUN) and the International Council on Monuments and Sites. The Convention also establishes a World Heritage Fund, provided through state party and other contributions, to be used for the protection of the world heritage as directed by the Committee upon the application of contracting parties.

2) The extent of the legal obligations imposed on contracting parties to the World Heritage Convention was explored in *Commonwealth of Australia v. State of Tasmania*.[207] The Government of Australia was a contracting party to the Convention. The State of Tasmania planned to build a dam on a river in territory that had been included on the World Heritage List. The federal government attempted to protect the area through legislation. The Tasmanian Government attacked the constitutional validity of the laws. In the course of its decision on Australian constitutional powers, a majority of the High Court found that articles 4 and 5 of the Convention imposed a legal obligation on Australia to protect the site. To what extent does the World Heritage Convention protect wildlife habitat?

3) The Convention on Wetlands of International Importance (Ramsar Convention) entered into force on December 21, 1975, with Canada acceding to the Convention with effect from May 15, 1981.[208] Wetlands as defined will include marshes, water meadows, coastal beaches, and tidal flats. Wetlands have been endangered by drainage and land reclamation, damming of rivers, and pollution. Wetlands need protection because they

---

206 As of October 1, 2005, 178 states had signed the Convention; see <http://whc.unesco.org/>; J.C. Kunich, "World Heritage in Danger in the Hotspots" (2003) 78 Indiana L.J. 619.

207 (1983), 46 A.L.R. 625 (H.C.). See also *e.g. State of Queensland v. Commonwealth of Australia* (1989), 86 A.L.R. 519; *Richardson v. Forestry Commission* (1988), 164 C.L.R. 261; and *Friends of Hinchinbrook Society Inc. v. Minister for Environment* (1997), 147 A.L.R. 608 (F.C.); *Booth v. Bosworth*, [2001] F.C.A. 1453.

208 A Protocol to the *Ramsar Convention* was adopted in 1982 concerning amendment of the Convention and equal validity of language texts. See Can. T.S. 1986 No. 46, online: <http://www.ramsar.org>. See, generally, D. Farrier & L. Tucker, "Wise Use of Wetlands Under the Ramsar Convention: A Challenge for Meaningful Implementation of International Law" (2000) 12 J. Envtl. L. 21; and M.J. Bowman, "The Ramsar Convention Comes of Age" (1995) 42 Nethl. Int'l L. Rev. 1. By October 1, 2005, there were 146 contracting parties to the Ramsar Convention and 1,462 sites were on the List of Wetlands of International Importance, with Canada having designated 37 sites including Point Pelee, Queen Maud Gulf, and Whooping Crane Summer Range; see <http://www.wetlands.org>.

fulfill a variety of functions: serving as habitat for waterfowl and other species; storing water; controlling floods; protecting land areas from erosion; and diluting wastes. The Ramsar Convention assists in the conservation of species, specifically waterfowl, and other forms of wildlife that depend on wetlands for their habitat. From a reading of the Convention, how strong are the legal obligations imposed on contracting parties? Compare the operational provisions of the World Heritage Convention.

4) The issue of desertification is important for a growing number of countries, especially African states.[209] The Convention to Combat Desertification entered into force on December 26, 1996; Canada is a party.[210] The focus of the Convention is innovative—it attempts to combat desertification and mitigate the effects of drought by using an integrated approach that includes all levels of governance, moving from the local community to the international level, and addresses the socio-economic factors as well as the biological and physical aspects that contribute to desertification. Article 4 of the Convention contains the general obligations of contracting parties, and article 4(2) states that the parties shall:

(a) adopt an integrated approach addressing the physical, biological and socio-economic aspects of the processes of desertification and drought;

(b) give due attention, within the relevant international and regional bodies, to the situation of affected developing country Parties with regard to international trade, marketing arrangements and debt with a view to establishing an enabling international economic environment conducive to the promotion of sustainable development;

(c) integrate strategies for poverty eradication into efforts to combat desertification and mitigate the effects of drought;

(d) promote cooperation among affected country Parties in the fields of environmental protection and the conservation of land and water resources, as they relate to desertification and drought;

(e) strengthen subregional, regional and international cooperation;

(f) cooperate within relevant intergovernmental organizations; ...

Article 5 of the Convention contains the obligations of affected country parties. These include addressing the underlying causes of desertification, paying special attention to contributory socio-economic factors, and facilitating the participation of local populations, particularly women and youth, with the support of NGOs.[211] Article 6 lists the obligations

---

209   W.C. Burns, "The International Convention to Combat Desertification: Drawing a Line in the Sand?" (1995) 16 Mich. J. Int'l. L. 831 at 833.

210   U.N. *Convention to Combat Desertification in Those Countries Experiencing Serious Drought and/or Desertification, Particularly in Africa* (1994) 33 I.L.M. 1328, online: <http://www.unccd.int>. The Convention was opened for signature on October 14, 1994 and Canada ratified on December 1, 1995. By October 1, 2005, 191 states had ratified. The Convention Secretariat is located in Bonn, Germany and the GEF serves as the Convention's financial mechanism. See L.C. Clark, "Comment: A Call to Restructure Existing International Environmental Law in Light of Africa's Renaissance: The United Nations Convention to Combat Desertification and the New Partnership for Africa's Development (NEPAD)" (2003) 27 Seattle U. L. Rev. 525; A. Iles, "The Desertification Convention: A Deeper Focus on Social Aspects of Environmental Degradation?" (1995) 36 Harv. Int'l L.J. 207; and Burns, *supra* note 209.

211   *Convention to Combat Desertification*, article 5(c) and (d), *ibid.*

of developed country parties. Article 7 states that, in implementing the Convention, parties shall give priority to affected African states parties while not neglecting affected developing states parties in other regions. A central part of the Convention is the development of action plans by governments at the national, subregional, and regional levels.

5) Deforestation and the conservation of forests have also gained the attention of the international community.[212] Forests serve many purposes. For example, they are important sites of biological diversity, act as carbon sinks, are homes for indigenous peoples, and are a source of economic and medicinal wealth. An existing agreement on tropical forests that touches on the issue is the 1994 International Tropical Timber Agreement (ITTA 1994): it is a commodity agreement that supports the International Tropical Timber Organization.[213] The Agreement includes some sustainable development objectives and provides for projects on reforestation and forest management.[214] Negotiations to draft a successor agreement to ITTA 1994 are under way. The protection of all types of forests was discussed at the 1992 U.N. Conference on Environment and Development. The negotiation of a treaty on forestry protection was rejected in the period leading up to UNCED, but the 1992 Conference produced a non-binding Statement of Principles for a Global Consensus on the Management, Conservation and Sustainable Development of All Types of Forests.[215] The Statement is a product of compromise, and includes as "Principles/Elements," the following:

1(a) States have, in accordance with the Charter of the United Nations and the principles of international law, the sovereign right to exploit their own resources pursuant to their own environmental policies and have the responsibility to ensure that activities within their jurisdiction or control do not cause damage to the environment of other States or of areas beyond the limits of national jurisdiction.

(b) The agreed full incremental cost of achieving benefits associated with forest conservation and sustainable development requires increased international cooperation and should be equitably shared by the international community.

2(a) States have the sovereign and inalienable right to utilize, manage and develop their forests in accordance with their development needs and level of socio-economic development and on the basis of national policies consistent with sustainable development and legislation, including the conversion of such areas for other uses within the overall socio-economic development plan and based on rational land-use policies.

---

212 See, generally, Canadian Council on International Law, ed., *Global Forests and International Environmental Law* (1996); T. Hock, "The Role of Eco-Labels in International Trade: Can Timber Certification be Implemented as a Means to Slowing Deforestation?" (2001) 12 Colo. J. Int'l. Envtl. L. & Pol'y 347; N. Chalifour, "Global Trade Rules and the World's Forests: Taking Stock of the World Trade Organization's Implications for Forests" (2000) 12 Geo. Int'l Envtl. L. Rev. 575; and H.M. Schally, "Forests: Toward an International Legal Regime?" (1993) 4 Y.B. Int'l. Envtl. L. 30.

213 The 1994 *International Tropical Timber Agreement* entered into force on January 1, 1997 (1994) 33 I.L.M. 1016. The ITTO has 59 member states.

214 See 1994 *International Tropical Timber Agreement*, article 1, *ibid.*

215 U.N. Doc. A/CONF. 151/6/Rev.1; (1992) 31 I.L.M. 881. See M. Steiner, "Reassessing the 1992 Forest Principles Statement: The Journey from Rio to Johannesburg: Ten Years of Forest Negotiations, Ten Years of Successes and Failures" (2002) 32 Golden Gate U.L. Rev. 629.

(b) Forest resources and forest lands should be sustainably managed to meet the social, economic, ecological, cultural and spiritual human needs of present and future generations. These needs are for forest products and services, such as wood and wood products, water, food, fodder, medicine, fuel, shelter, employment, recreation, habitats for wildlife, landscape diversity, carbon sinks and reservoirs, and for other forest products. Appropriate measures should be taken to protect forests against harmful effects of pollution, including air-borne pollution, fires, pests and diseases in order to maintain their full multiple value.

The Convention on Biological Diversity, discussed below, in Section H.3 on "Conservation of Biological Diversity," and the World Heritage Convention, discussed above, in Section H.1 on "Protection of Land Spaces," can also assist in the preservation of forests. The Climate Change Convention and its Kyoto Protocol, discussed above, in Section E on "Global Warming and Climate Change," can also provide some forest protection because forests act as carbon sinks.

6) In the years since the Earth Summit, governments have been meeting to further international cooperation on forest protection. In 1995, the Commission on Sustainable Development (CSD) created the Intergovernmental Panel on Forests (IPF). The mandate of the IPF was to develop proposals for the conservation and sustainable development of forests. The IPF submitted its final report to the CSD in April 1997; it contained many recommendations for action, but the IPF did not agree on some important points, including trade-related issues and whether a treaty on forests should be negotiated.[216] At the 1997 special session of the General Assembly, international discussions on forests were continued through the establishment of the Intergovernmental Forum on Forests (IFF), created under the CSD.[217] The IFF was mandated to facilitate the implementation of the IPF's proposals, consider international mechanisms, including the possibility of a treaty, and report to the CSD in 2000. In late 2000, it was replaced by the United Nations Forum on Forests (UNFF), which was created as an ECOSOC subsidiary body.[218] The aim of the UNFF is to promote the management, conservation, and sustainable development of all types of forests.[219] Given the conflicting uses and interests in different types of forests around the world, is the negotiation of a multilateral treaty on the protection of all types of forests a realistic objective?

---

216 See L. Reif, "Environment Policy: The Rio Summit Five Years Later," in F.O. Hampson & M.A. Molot, eds., *Canada Among Nations 1998: Leadership and Dialogue* (1998) 267 at 278.

217 The IFF was established by ECOSOC Res. 1997/65 (July 25, 1997).

218 Established by ECOSOC Res. E/2000/35 (October 18, 2000).

219 "Summary of the Fourth Session of the United Nations Forum on Forests" (May 17, 2004), vol. 13 no. 116 Earth Negotiations Bulletin.

2. Protection of Wildlife[220]

Convention on International Trade in Endangered Species of Wild Fauna and Flora
(1973) 993 U.N.T.S. 243; Can. T.S. 1975 No. 32

Article I
Definitions

For the purpose of the present Convention, unless the context otherwise requires:

(a) "Species" means any species, subspecies, or geographically separate population thereof;

(b) "Specimen" means:

(i) any animal or plant, whether alive or dead;

(ii) in the case of an animal: for species included in Appendices I and II, any readily recognizable part or derivative thereof; and for species included in Appendix III, any readily recognizable part or derivative thereof specified in Appendix III in relation to the species; and

(iii) in the case of a plant: for species included in Appendix I, any readily recognizable part or derivative thereof; and for species included in Appendices II and III, any readily recognizable part or derivative thereof specified in Appendices II and III in relation to the species;

(c) "Trade" means export, re-export, import and introduction from the sea;

(d) "Re-export" means export of any specimen that has previously been imported;

(e) "Introduction from the sea" means transportation into a State of specimens of any species which were taken in the marine environment not under the jurisdiction of any State; ...

Article II
Fundamental Principles

1. Appendix I shall include all species threatened with extinction which are or may be affected by trade. Trade in specimens of these species must be subject to particularly strict regulation in order not to endanger further their survival and must only be authorized in exceptional circumstances.

---

220 See, generally, R. Reeve, *Policing International Trade in Endangered Species: The CITES Treaty and Compliance* (2002); P. van Heijnsbergen, *International Legal Protection of Wild Fauna and Flora* (1997); D. Favre, *International Trade in Endangered Species: A Guide to CITES* (1989); S. Lyster, *International Wildlife Law* (1985); and M. Gray Davidson, "Protecting Coral Reefs: The Principal National and International Legal Instruments" (2002) 26 Harv. Envtl. L. Rev. 499.

2. Appendix II shall include:

(a) all species which although not necessarily now threatened with extinction may become so unless trade in specimens of such species is subject to strict regulation in order to avoid utilization incompatible with their survival; and

(b) other species which must be subject to regulation in order that trade in specimens of certain species referred to in sub-paragraph (a) of this paragraph may be brought under effective control.

3. Appendix III shall include all species which any Party identifies as being subject to regulation within its jurisdiction for the purpose of preventing or restricting exploitation, and as needing the cooperation of other parties in the control of trade.

4. The Parties shall not allow trade in specimens of species included in Appendices I, II and III except in accordance with the provisions of the present Convention.

Article III
Regulation of Trade in Specimens of Species Included in Appendix I

1. All trade in specimens of species included in Appendix I shall be in accordance with the provisions of this Article.

2. The export of any specimen of a species included in Appendix I shall require the prior grant and presentation of an export permit. An export permit shall only be granted when the following conditions have been met:

(a) a Scientific Authority of the State of export has advised that such export will not be detrimental to the survival of that species;

(b) a Management Authority of the State of export is satisfied that the specimen was not obtained in contravention of the laws of that State for the protection of fauna and flora;

(c) a Management Authority of the State of export is satisfied that any living specimen will be so prepared and shipped as to minimize the risk of injury, damage to health or cruel treatment; and

(d) a Management Authority of the State of export is satisfied that an import permit has been granted for the specimen.

3. The import of any specimen of a species included in Appendix I shall require the prior grant and presentation of an import permit and either an export permit or a re-export certificate. An import permit shall only be granted when the following conditions have been met:

(a) a Scientific Authority of the State of import has advised that the import will be for purposes which are not detrimental to the survival of the species involved;

(b) a Scientific Authority of the State of import is satisfied that the proposed recipient of a living specimen is suitably equipped to house and care for it; and

(c) a Management Authority of the State of import is satisfied that the specimen is not to be used for primarily commercial purposes. ...

Article IV
Regulation of Trade in Specimens of Species Included in Appendix II

1. All trade in specimens of species included in Appendix II shall be in accordance with the provisions of this Article.

2. The export of any specimen of a species included in Appendix II shall require the prior grant and presentation of an export permit. An export permit shall only be granted when the following conditions have been met:

(a) a Scientific Authority of the State of export has advised that such export will not be detrimental to the survival of that species;

(b) a Management Authority of the State of export is satisfied that the specimen was not obtained in contravention of the laws of that State for the protection of fauna and flora; and

(c) a Management Authority of the State of export is satisfied that any living specimen will be so prepared and shipped as to minimize the risk of injury, damage to health or cruel treatment.

3. A Scientific Authority in each Party shall monitor both the export permits granted by that State for specimens of species included in Appendix II and the actual exports of such specimens. Whenever a Scientific Authority determines that the export of specimens of any such species should be limited in order to maintain that species throughout its range at a level consistent with its role in the ecosystems in which it occurs and well above the level at which that species might become eligible for inclusion in Appendix I, the Scientific Authority shall advise the appropriate Management Authority of suitable measures to be taken to limit the grant of export permits for specimens of that species.

4. The import of any specimen of a species included in Appendix II shall require the prior presentation of either an export permit or a re-export certificate. ...

Article V
Regulation of Trade in Specimens of Species Included in Appendix III

1. All trade in specimens of species included in Appendix III shall be in accordance with the provisions of this Article.

2. The export of any specimen of a species included in Appendix III from any State which has included that species in Appendix III shall require the prior grant and presentation of an export permit. An export permit shall only be granted when the following conditions have been met:

(a) a Management Authority of the State of export is satisfied that the specimen was not obtained in contravention of the laws of that State for the protection of fauna and flora; and

(b) a Management Authority of the State of export is satisfied that any living specimen will be so prepared and shipped as to minimize the risk of injury, damage to health or cruel treatment.

3. The import of any specimen of a species included in Appendix III shall require, except in circumstances to which paragraph 4 of this Article applies [re-export and granting of a re-export certificate by the State of re-export], the prior presentation of a certificate of origin and, where the import is from a State which has included that species in Appendix III, an export permit.

NOTES

1) Canada is a party to the Convention on International Trade in Endangered Species of Wild Fauna and Flora (CITES).[221] CITES controls international trade in endangered species through an import and export permit regime detailed in articles II to V. Depending on the degree of endangerment, species are listed in three Appendices, with Appendix I containing those species that are threatened with extinction. By August 2004, about 5,000 species of animals and 28,000 species of plants were listed in the Appendices.[222] Article VII of CITES provides for a variety of exemptions from the permit system. For example, article VII(2) excludes specimens acquired before the provisions of CITES applied to them ("pre-Convention" specimens). Article VII(3) excludes specimens that are "personal or household effects" with specified exceptions to prevent abuse. Provision is also made to exempt the following from permit requirements: specimens bred in captivity or artificially propagated for commercial purposes, those in customs control trans-shipment, specimens on scientific loan, on exchange or donated, and specimens forming part of a travelling exhibition. Article VIII requires that contracting parties take appropriate measures to enforce CITES and to prohibit trade in specimens contrary to the treaty, including measures to penalize trade in and/or possession of such specimens and provision for their confiscation or return to the state of export.

2) CITES issued the Fort Lauderdale Criteria at the ninth Conference of the Parties (COP-9) in 1994 (revised in 2002), which adopted scientific criteria for listing species in the Appendices; permitted "split listing"—that is, listing some populations of a species in Appendix I and others in Appendix II; and adopted the precautionary principle for use when CITES is considering proposals to amend Appendices I or II.[223]

3) One issue, highlighting the weaknesses in CITES and the friction between "sustainable use" proponents and preservationists, was the 1989 uplisting of the African elephant from Appendix II to Appendix I in an attempt to halt the ivory trade that was resulting in the massive killing of these animals. The action illustrated two weaknesses in CITES—the ability of contracting parties to make specific reservations to CITES with

---

221 In force for Canada July 9, 1975. Implemented by *Wild Animal and Plant Protection and Regulation of International and Interprovincial Trade Act*, S.C. 1992, c. 52, as am., and regulations. By October 1, 2005, CITES had 169 parties. See <http://www.cites.org>. See also Reeve, *supra* note 220; Favre, *supra* note 220; S. Young, "Contemporary Issues of the Convention on International Trade in Endangered Species of Wild Fauna and Flora (CITES) and the Debate Over Sustainable Use" (2003) 14 Colo. J. Int'l Envtl. L. & Pol'y 167; M.E. Zimmerman, "The Black Market for Wildlife: Combating Transnational Organized Crime in the Illegal Wildlife Trade" (2003) 36 Vand. J. Transnat'l L. 1657; and L.P. Marshall, "Canada's Implementation of the Convention on International Trade in Endangered Species of Wild Fauna and Flora (Cites): The Effect of the Biodiversity Focus of International Environmental Law" (1999) 9 J. Envtl. L. & Practice 31.

222 See <http://www.cites.org/eng/disc/species.shtml>. All primates, elephants, cats, bears, rhinoceroses, and cetaceans are in Appendices I or II, *supra* note 221.

223 CITES, Res. Conf. 9.24 (Rev.CoP12). See Young, *supra* note 221 at 177-78; Note "The CITES Fort Lauderdale Criteria: The Uses and Limits of Science in International Conservation Decisionmaking" (2001) 114 Harv. L. Rev. 1769.

respect to listed species, which was taken advantage of by a number of ivory-producing and consuming states upon the uplisting, and the interpretation of the definition of a pre-Convention specimen in article VII(2), the exemption section that was cited by some states parties to justify trade in their stockpiles of ivory acquired before joining CITES.[224] More recently, split listing is being implemented. Elephant populations in southern Africa are healthier than those in Eastern Africa. As a result, in 1997 at COP-10, elephant populations in Botswana, Namibia, and Zimbabwe were downlisted to Appendix II and the same occurred with South Africa's elephants in 2000 at COP-11.[225]

4) CITES is limited in its protection of endangered species. It does not cover endangered species that are either not traded at all or not traded within the CITES definition. CITES does not protect endangered species against other threats, the prime example being the destruction of habitat.

5) There is also a Convention on the Conservation of Migratory Species of Wild Animals (the Bonn Convention).[226] Canada is not a contracting party to this treaty. The Bonn Convention attempts to protect migratory species of wild animals whose ranges cross state boundaries by imposing legal obligations on range state contracting parties for species listed in Appendix I, defined as those migratory species in danger of extinction throughout all or a significant portion of their range. For example, article III(5) requires that the range states shall prohibit the taking of Appendix I animals, with limited exceptions that include taking for scientific purposes and to accommodate the needs of traditional subsistence users of a particular species. Article III(4) is less stringent, stating that Appendix I range states "shall endeavour" to, *inter alia*, conserve and, where feasible and appropriate, restore those habitats that are important in removing the species from danger of extinction and to prevent, remove, minimize, or compensate for the adverse effects of activities or obstacles that seriously impede or prevent the migration of the species. The Bonn Convention also encourages range states parties to conclude agreements covering the conservation and management of migratory species listed in Appendix II, being those migratory species that have an unfavourable conservation status or a conservation status that would benefit significantly from the international cooperation arising out of the agreement. Also, as discussed above, the Ramsar Convention assists in the protection of migratory species that depend on wetlands for their habitat.

6) Canada has formal bilateral treaty relationships with the United States to protect migratory species. The vintage of the 1916 Convention Between the United Kingdom

---

224 See Young, *supra* note 221 at 175-76, 183-86; M.J. Glennon, "Has International Law Failed the Elephant?" (1990) 84 A.J.I.L. 1; and IUCN Environmental Law Programme, "The African Elephant Case" (1998) 28 Envtl. Pol'y & L. 21.

225 See CITES, Res. Conf. 10.10 (Rev. CoP12), "Trade in elephant specimens," containing provisions on control of internal ivory trade, monitoring of illegal hunting of and trade in elephant specimens under CITES supervision, capacity-building assistance for range states, and annual export quotas for raw ivory.

226 (1980) 19 I.L.M. 15. In force November 1, 1983. See C. Shine, "Selected Agreements Concluded Pursuant to the Convention on the Conservation of Migratory Species of Wild Animals" in D. Shelton, ed., *Commitment and Compliance: The Role of Non-Binding Norms in the International Legal System* (2000) at 196.

and the United States for the Protection of Migratory Birds[227] is evident in its perspective. For example, it sets hunting and closed seasons for the birds covered, generally prohibits the taking of nests or eggs of those birds covered, and allows the issue of permits to kill those birds covered that, under extraordinary conditions, may become seriously injurious to the agricultural or other interests in any particular community. There is no real provision for bird habitat protection. In 1987, the Agreement on the Conservation of the Porcupine Caribou Herd was concluded.[228] The taking of appropriate action to conserve the herd and its habitat, and the establishment of an advisory board are among its provisions.

7) A variety of other bilateral and multilateral treaties protect wildlife such as marine mammals, including whales[229] and Antarctic marine living resources.[230] There are also regional agreements and initiatives, such as in the Americas.[231] Further, international cooperation on Arctic issues, including environmental protection, is increasing.[232]

---

227 12 Bevans 375; Can. T.S. No. 628, implemented in the *Migratory Birds Convention Act, 1994*, S.C. 1994, c. 22, as am. See A. Thompson & N. Morgan, "Migratory Birds," in Canadian Bar Association, *Sustainable Development in Canada: Options for Law Reform* (1990) at 242. The Act of 1994 was amended in 2005 by *An Act to amend the Migratory Birds Convention Act, 1994 and the Canadian Environmental Protection Act, 1999*, S.C. 2005, c. 23. It clarifies the application of the Act to Canada's Exclusive Economic Zone (s. 2) and creates a number of offences related to pollution from ships (s. 4). As of February 2005, this Bill had not proceeded beyond first reading.

228 Can. T.S. 1987 No. 31. In force July 17, 1987. See B. Docherty, "Challenging Boundaries: The Arctic National Wildlife Refuge and International Environmental Law Protection" (2001-2002) 10 N.Y.U. Envtl. L.J. 70.

229 *Convention for the Regulation of Whaling* (1931), Can. T.S. 1935 No. 23 and *International Convention for the Regulation of Whaling* (1946) 161 U.N.T.S. 72, with 1956 Protocol, 338 U.N.T.S. 366. In 1982, the International Whaling Commission (IWC) adopted a moratorium on commercial whaling, effective in 1986. See R.B. Ackerman, "Japanese Whaling in the Pacific Ocean: Defiance of International Whaling Norms in the Name of 'Scientific Research,' Culture, and Tradition" (2002) 25 B.C. Int'l. & Comp. L. Rev. 323; T.L. McDorman, "Canada and Whaling: An Analysis of Article 65 of the Law of the Sea Convention" (1998) 29 Ocean Devel. & Int'l L. 179; and A. D'Amato & S. Chopra, "Whales: Their Emerging Right to Life" (1991) 85 A.J.I.L. 21. Whales are also protected under CITES, see *supra* note 222. See also *e.g.* 1973 *Agreement on the Conservation of Polar Bears*, Can. T.S. 1976 No. 24; and 1957 *Interim Convention on the Conservation of North Pacific Fur Seals*, 314 U.N.T.S. 105; and 1972 *Convention for the Conservation of Antarctic Seals*, Can. T.S. 1990 No. 40.

230 *Convention on the Conservation of Antarctic Marine Living Resources* (CCAMLR), Can. T.S. 1988 No. 37; (1980) 19 I.L.M. 841. The *Protocol on Environmental Protection to the Antarctic Treaty* (1991) 30 I.L.M. 1461, which entered into force on January 14, 1998, *inter alia*, protects Antarctic flora and fauna. Canada ratified the Protocol on November 13, 2003 and implemented it in the *Antarctic Environmental Protection Act*, S.C. 2003, c. 20.

231 For example, *Convention on Nature Protection and Wild Life Preservation in the Western Hemisphere*, 161 U.N.T.S. 193, entered into force April 30, 1942; initiatives arising out of the Summits of the Americas Declarations. See K. Rogers & J.A. Moore, "Revitalizing the Convention on Nature Protection and Wild Life Preservation in the Western Hemisphere: Might Awakening a Visionary but 'Sleeping' Treaty Be the Key to Preserving Biodiversity and Threatened Natural Areas in the Americas?" (1995) 36 Harv. Int'l L.J. 465; and D.L. Van Cott, "Regional Environmental Law in the Americas: Assessing the Contractual Environment" (1995) 26 U. Miami Inter-Am. L. Rev. 489.

232 For example, establishment of the Arctic Council in 1996 and the 1991 *Arctic Environmental Protection Strategy* (1996) 35 I.L.M. 1386 and (1991) 30 I.L.M. 1624. See also S.R. Hamilton, "Toxic Contamination and the Arctic: Thinking Globally and Acting Locally To Protect Arctic Ecosystems and

8) The Canadian Government's attempts to pass federal endangered species legislation did not meet with success until the *Species at Risk Act* was passed in 2002 and fully entered into force in 2004.[233] Given that the habitat of wild species falls mainly under provincial jurisdiction, some Canadian provinces have passed endangered species legislation.[234]

3. Conservation of Biological Diversity[235]

Convention on Biological Diversity
U.N. Doc. UNEP/Bio.Div./N7INC.5/4; (1992) 31 I.L.M. 822

The Contracting Parties,

Conscious of the intrinsic value of biological diversity and of the ecological, genetic, social, economic, scientific, educational, cultural, recreational and aesthetic values of biological diversity and its components,

Conscious also of the importance of biological diversity for evolution and for maintaining life sustaining systems of the biosphere,

Affirming that the conservation of biological diversity is a common concern of humankind,

Reaffirming that States have sovereign rights over their own biological resources,

Reaffirming also that States are responsible for conserving their biological diversity and for using their biological resources in a sustainable manner, ...

Noting also that where there is a threat of significant reduction or loss of biological diversity, lack of full scientific certainty should not be used as a reason for postponing measures to avoid or minimize such a threat,

---

People" (2004) 15 Colo. J. Int'l Envtl. L. & Pol'y 71; M.A. Verhaag, "It Is Not Too Late: The Need for a Comprehensive International Treaty To Protect the Arctic Environment" (2003) 15 Geo. Int'l Envtl. L. Rev. 555; D. VanderZwaag, R. Huebert, & S. Ferrara, "The Arctic Environmental Protection Strategy, Arctic Council, and Multilateral Environmental Initiatives: Tinkering While the Arctic Marine Environment Totters" (2002) 30 Den. J. Int'l L. & Pol'y 131; and D. Rothwell, "International Law and the Protection of the Arctic Environment" (1995) 44 I.C.L.Q. 280. Treaty law on POPs, discussed above in Section C.1 on "Transboundary Air Pollution and Acid Deposition," will also benefit the Arctic area.

233 *Species at Risk Act*, S.C. 2002, c. 29. See also *Canada Wildlife Act*, R.S.C. 1985, c. W-9, as am.

234 For example, Ontario, Quebec, Manitoba, Nova Scotia, and New Brunswick. Some other provinces and territories have statutes that address endangered species incidentally in wildlife legislation.

235 See *e.g.* Secretariat of the Convention on Biological Diversity, *Handbook of the Convention on Biological Diversity* (2001); W. Lesser, *Sustainable Use of Genetic Resources Under the Convention on Biological Diversity* (1998); F. McConnell, *The Biodiversity Convention: A Negotiating History* (1996); M. Bowman & C. Redgwell, eds., *International Law and the Conservation of Biological Diversity* (1996); J. Amiott, "Investigating the Convention on Biological Diversity's Protections for Traditional Knowledge" (2003) 11 Mo. Envtl. L. & Pol'y Rev. 3; L.A. Firestone, "You Say Yes, I Say No: Defining Community Prior Informed Consent Under the Convention on Biological Diversity" (2003) 16 Geo. Int'l Envtl. L. Rev. 171; L. Glowka, "Bioprospecting, Alien Invasive Species, and Hydrothermal Vents: Three Emerging Legal Issues in the Conservation and Sustainable Use of Biodiversity" (2000) 13 Tul. Envtl. L.J. 329; and Symposium: "Biodiversity: Opportunities and Issues" (1995) 28 Vand. J. Transnat'l. L. 613.

Noting further that the fundamental requirement for the conservation of biological diversity is the *in-situ* conservation of ecosystems and natural habitats and the maintenance and recovery of viable populations of species in their natural surroundings,

Noting further that *ex-situ* measures, preferably in the country of origin, also have an important role to play, ...

Determined to conserve and sustainably use biological diversity for the benefit of present and future generations,

Have agreed as follows:

Article 1
Objectives

The objectives of this Convention, to be pursued in accordance with its relevant provisions, are the conservation of biological diversity, the sustainable use of its components and the fair and equitable sharing of the benefits arising out of the utilization of genetic resources, including by appropriate access to genetic resources and by appropriate transfer of relevant technologies, taking into account all rights over those resources and to technologies, and by appropriate funding.

Article 2
Use of Terms

For the purposes of this Convention:

"Biological diversity" means the variability among living organisms from all sources including, *inter alia*, terrestrial, marine and other aquatic ecosystems and the ecological complexes of which they are part; this includes diversity within species, between species and of ecosystems.

"Biological resources" includes genetic resources, organisms or parts thereof, populations, or any other biotic component of ecosystems with actual or potential use or value for humanity.

"Biotechnology" means any technological application that uses biological systems, living organisms, or derivatives thereof, to make or modify products or processes for specific use. ...

"Domesticated or cultivated species" means species in which the evolutionary process has been influenced by humans to meet their needs.

"Ecosystem" means a dynamic complex of plant, animal and micro-organism communities and their non-living environment interacting as a functional unit.

"Ex-situ conservation" means the conservation of components of biological diversity outside their natural habitats.

"Genetic material" means any material of plant, animal, microbial or other origin containing functional units of heredity.

"Genetic resources" means genetic material of actual or potential value.

"Habitat" means the place or type of site where an organism or population naturally occurs. ...

"In-situ conservation" means the conservation of ecosystems and natural habitats and the maintenance and recovery of viable populations of species in their natural surroundings and, in the case of domesticated or cultivated species, in the surroundings where they have developed their distinctive properties.

"Protected area" means a geographically defined area which is designated or regulated and managed to achieve specific conservation objectives. ...

"Sustainable use" means the use of components of biological diversity in a way and at a rate that does not lead to the long-term decline of biological diversity, thereby maintaining its potential to meet the needs and aspirations of present and future generations.

"Technology" includes biotechnology.

Article 3
Principle

States have, in accordance with the Charter of the United Nations and the principles of international law, the sovereign right to exploit their own resources pursuant to their own environmental policies, and the responsibility to ensure that activities within their jurisdiction or control do not cause damage to the environment of other States or of areas beyond the limits of national jurisdiction.

Article 4
Jurisdictional Scope

Subject to the rights of other States, and except as otherwise expressly provided in this Convention, the provisions of this Convention apply, in relation to each Contracting Party:

(a) In the case of components of biological diversity, in areas within the limits of its national jurisdiction; and

(b) In the case of processes and activities, regardless of where their effects occur, carried out under its jurisdiction or control, within the area of its national jurisdiction or beyond the limits of national jurisdiction.

Article 5
Cooperation

Each Contracting Party shall, as far as possible and as appropriate, cooperate with other Contracting Parties, directly or, where appropriate, through competent international organizations, in respect of areas beyond national jurisdiction and on other matters of mutual interest, for the conservation and sustainable use of biological diversity.

Article 6
General Measures for Conservation and Sustainable Use

Each Contracting Party shall, in accordance with its particular conditions and capabilities:

(a) Develop national strategies, plans or programmes for the conservation and sustainable use of biological diversity or adapt for this purpose existing strategies, plans or programmes which shall reflect, *inter alia*, the measures set out in this Convention relevant to the Contracting Party concerned; and

(b) Integrate, as far as possible and as appropriate, the conservation and sustainable use of biological diversity into relevant sectoral or cross-sectoral plans, programmes and policies.

Article 7
Identification and Monitoring

Each Contracting Party shall, as far as possible and as appropriate, in particular for the purposes of Articles 8 to 10:

(a) Identify components of biological diversity important for its conservation and sustainable use having regard to the indicative list of categories set down in Annex I;

(b) Monitor, through sampling and other techniques, the components of biological diversity identified pursuant to subparagraph (a) above, paying particular attention to those requiring urgent conservation measures and those which offer the greatest potential for sustainable use;

(c) Identify processes and categories of activities which have or are likely to have significant adverse impacts on the conservation and sustainable use of biological diversity, and monitor their effects through sampling and other techniques; and

(d) Maintain and organize, by any mechanism data, derived from identification and monitoring activities pursuant to subparagraphs (a), (b) and (c) above.

Article 8
In-situ Conservation

Each Contracting Party shall, as far as possible and as appropriate:

(a) Establish a system of protected areas or areas where special measures need to be taken to conserve biological diversity;

(b) Develop, where necessary, guidelines for the selection, establishment and management of protected areas or areas where special measures need to be taken to conserve biological diversity;

(c) Regulate or manage biological resources important for the conservation of biological diversity whether within or outside protected areas, with a view to ensuring their conservation and sustainable use;

(d) Promote the protection of ecosystems, natural habitats and the maintenance of viable populations of species in natural surroundings;

(e) Promote environmentally sound and sustainable development in areas adjacent to protected areas with a view to furthering protection of these areas;

(f) Rehabilitate and restore degraded ecosystems and promote the recovery of threatened species, *inter alia*, through the development and implementation of plans or other management strategies;

(g) Establish or maintain means to regulate, manage or control the risks associated with the use and release of living modified organisms resulting from biotechnology which are likely to have adverse environmental impacts that could affect the conservation and sustainable use of biological diversity, taking also into account the risks to human health;

(h) Prevent the introduction of, control or eradicate those alien species which threaten ecosystems, habitats or species;

(i) Endeavour to provide the conditions needed for compatibility between present uses and the conservation of biological diversity and the sustainable use of its components;

(j) Subject to its national legislation, respect, preserve and maintain knowledge, innovations and practices of indigenous and local communities embodying traditional lifestyles relevant for the conservation and sustainable use of biological diversity and promote their wider application with the approval and involvement of the holders of such knowledge, innovations and practices and encourage the equitable sharing of the benefits arising from the utilization of such knowledge, innovations and practices;

(k) Develop or maintain necessary legislation and/or other regulatory provisions for the protection of threatened species and populations;

(l) Where a significant adverse effect on biological diversity has been determined pursuant to Article 7, regulate or manage the relevant processes and categories of activities; and

(m) Cooperate in providing financial and other support for *in-situ* conservation outlined in subparagraphs (a) to (l) above, particularly to developing countries. ...

Annex I
Identification and Monitoring

1. Ecosystems and habitats: containing high diversity, large numbers of endemic or threatened species, or wilderness; required by migratory species; of social, economic, cultural or scientific importance; or, which are representative, unique or associated with key evolutionary or other biological processes;

2. Species and communities which are: threatened; wild relatives of domesticated or cultivated species; of medicinal, agricultural or other economic value; or social, scientific or cultural importance; or importance for research into the conservation and sustainable use of biological diversity, such as indicator species; and

3. Described genomes and genes of social, scientific or economic importance.

NOTES

1) The Convention on Biological Diversity entered into force on December 29, 1993, and Canada is a contracting party.[236]

2) The approach of the Biodiversity Convention is one of "sustainable use," which attempts to balance the conservation and economic aspects of biological diversity. It is

---

236 Canada ratified the Convention on December 4, 1992. By October 1, 2005, the Convention had 188 contracting parties. The U.S. had signed the Convention but had not ratified it. See <http://www.biodiv.org>. See also Canada's *Species at Risk Act, supra* note 233, Preamble.

hoped that the economic benefits obtained from the equitable sharing of the uses of genetic resources will flow to lesser developed contracting parties, which in turn will promote increased protection of biodiversity. The Convention also lists *ex situ* conservation measures to be taken by parties pursuant to article 9. Article 10 addresses the actions to be taken by parties to promote the sustainable use of the components of biological diversity. Article 15(1) addresses access to genetic resources and, in recognition of the "sovereign rights of states over their natural resources," states that the authority to determine access rests with national governments. However, article 15(2) provides that the parties "shall endeavour to create conditions to facilitate access to genetic resources for environmentally sound uses by other Contracting Parties and not to impose restrictions that run counter to the objectives of this Convention."[237] Article 15 provides further that access shall be subject to the prior informed consent of the party providing the resources, and that each party shall take measures in accordance with the Convention with the objective of sharing equitably with the contracting party providing the resources the results of research and development and benefits arising from the use of the genetic resources. Access to and transfer of technology is regulated under article 16, focusing on "technologies that are relevant to the conservation and sustainable use of biological diversity or make use of genetic resources and do not cause significant damage to the environment."[238] Also, access and transfer shall take place on fair and most favourable terms, recognizing and consistent with intellectual property rights attached to the technology. Article 19 provides for the participation of parties who provided the genetic resources in biotechnological research activities and distribution of the benefits.

3) Article 20 of the Biodiversity Convention states, *inter alia*, that developed country parties shall provide financial resources to enable developing states parties to meet the incremental costs of implementing their Convention obligations. A financial mechanism is created in article 21 to facilitate the flow of financial resources to developing country parties; it will function under the authority of the Conference of the Parties (COP). The Global Environment Facility (GEF) includes biological diversity as one of its covered areas and the GEF serves as the Biodiversity Convention's financial mechanism.[239]

4) The COP oversees and reviews the implementation of the Convention, including the adoption of amendments and protocols. The COP chose Montreal as the headquarters of the Biodiversity Secretariat. At COP-7 in 2004, drafting of a regime to regulate the fair and equitable sharing of benefits arising from the use of genetic resources continued.[240]

5) The Cartagena Protocol on Biosafety, which covers the safe transboundary movement, transit, handling, and use of living modified organisms (LMOs) resulting from biotechnology that may have adverse effects on the conservation and sustainable use of biological diversity, including human health, was adopted on January 29, 2000 and

---

237 *Convention on Biological Diversity*, article 15(2).

238 *Ibid.* article 16(1).

239 See *supra* note 127.

240 "Summary of the Seventh Conference of the Parties to the Convention on Biological Diversity" (February 23, 2004) vol. 9 no. 284 *Earth Negotiations Bulletin*.

entered into force on September 11, 2003.[241] The Biosafety Protocol regulates transboundary movement of LMOs through the use of an advance informed agreement (AIA) procedure before an LMO is imported into a contracting party.[242] The Protocol adopts the precautionary approach.[243] A Biosafety Clearing House is created for the exchange of information and to assist parties in implementing the Protocol, particularly developing states and states that are centres of origin and centres of genetic diversity.[244] Implementation of and compliance with the Protocol are also supported with provisions on capacity building, compliance procedures and mechanisms, and a financial mechanism (the Biological Diversity Convention's mechanism).[245]

6) The obligations of the contracting parties to the Biodiversity Convention are framed in relatively weak language. Do you think that the broad coverage and soft language of the Convention impede implementation of and compliance with its provisions?

I. THE ENVIRONMENT AND INTERNATIONAL TRADE

There are increasing intersections between the areas of environmental protection and international trade and investment. These interactions can be placed in a number of perspectives. The international trade treaties, such as those of the World Trade Organization (WTO) Agreement (which contains the General Agreement on Tariffs and Trade (GATT)),[246] the North American Free Trade Agreement (NAFTA), the Canada–Chile Free Trade Agreement, and other free trade agreements entered into by Canada,[247] are based on the philosophy that government barriers to free trade in goods must be minimized or eliminated.

---

241 (2000) 39 I.L.M. 1027, articles 1, 4-6, online: <http://www.biodiv.org/biosafety/>. As of October 1, 2005, the Biosafety Protocol had 125 parties. Canada signed on April 19, 2001, but had not ratified by October 2005. See C. Bail, R. Faulkner, & H. Marquard, eds., *The Cartagena Protocol on Biosafety: Reconciling Trade in Biotechnology with Environment & Development* (2002); O. Rivera-Torres, "The Biosafety Protocol and the WTO" (2003) 26 B.C. Int'l. & Comp. L. Rev. 263; G. Nakseu Nguefang, "Le principe de précaution dans le contexte du Protocol international sur la prévention des risques biotechnologiques" (2002) 43 C. de D. 39; T.P. Stewart & D.S. Johanson, "A Nexus of Trade and the Environment: The Relationship between the Cartagena Protocol on Biosafety and the SPS Agreement of the World Trade Organization" (2003) 14 Colo. J. Int'l. Envtl. L. & Pol'y 1; and S. Safrin, "Treaties in Collision? The Biosafety Protocol and the World Trade Organization Agreements" (2002) 96 A.J.I.L. 606.

242 *Biosafety Protocol, supra* note 241 at articles 7-10, 12. Article 13 provides a simplified procedure as an alternative to the AIA as long as adequate measures are applied to the LMO transboundary movement in accordance with the Protocol's objectives.

243 *Biosafety Protocol, supra* note 241 at Preamble, articles 1, 10(6), 11(8).

244 *Biosafety Protocol, supra* note 241 at article 20.

245 *Biosafety Protocol, supra* note 241 at articles 22, 28, 34. The Protocol uses the Biodiversity Convention's institutional mechanisms.

246 Reproduced in P. Raworth & L.C. Reif, *The Law of the WTO: Final Text of the GATT Uruguay Round Agreements* (1995).

247 NAFTA signed December 17, 1992, in force January 1, 1994 (1993) 32 I.L.M. 296 and 612; Canada–Chile FTA signed December 5, 1996, in force July 5, 1997 (1997) 36 I.L.M. 1079. See also Canada's FTAs with Israel and Costa Rica. Negotiations for other FTAs are also under way. See M.-C. Cordonier Segger, "Sustainable Development in the Negotiation of the FTAA" (2004) 27 Fordham Int'l. L.J. 1118.

On this basis, government border or internal measures to protect the environment or conserve resources must comply with international trade law or risk being classified as an unlawful trade restriction.[248] For example, Article XX of the GATT, and various provisions of the NAFTA, the Canada–Chile FTA, and the Canada–Costa Rica FTA address government measures aimed at environmental protection and conservation.[249]

The North American Agreement on Environmental Cooperation (NAAEC), a NAFTA side agreement, attempts to improve the environment and the substance and enforcement of the environmental laws in the NAFTA states parties.[250] The general obligations of the states parties include ensuring that domestic laws provide for high levels of environmental protection, effectively enforcing environmental laws and providing appropriate access to procedurally fair judicial or administrative remedies for the enforcement of those laws. Also, a citizens' submission procedure was established in articles 14 and 15 of the NAAEC, whereby persons and NGOs can complain to the Secretariat of the Commission on Environmental Cooperation (CEC) that a party is failing to effectively enforce its environmental law, with the result that a factual record may be prepared by the Secretariat if it considers that the submission warrants one and the Council (the government minister

---

248 See *e.g.* F. Francioni, ed., *Environment, Human Rights, and International Trade* (2001); D. McRae, "Trade and the Environment: Competition, Cooperation, or Confusion?" (2003) 41 Alb. L. Rev. 745; K. Bartenstein & S. Lavallée, "L'écolabel est-il un outil du protectionisme "vert"?" (2003) 44 C. de D. 361; V. Ramangkura, "Thai Shrimp, Sea Turtles, Mangrove Forests, and the WTO: Innovative Environmental Protection Under the International Trade Regime" (2003) 15 Geo. Int'l Envtl. L. Rev. 677; S. Charnowitz, "The Law of Environmental 'PPMs' in the WTO: Debunking the Myth of Illegality" (2002) 27 Yale J. Int'l. L. 59; G.C. Shaffer, "The World Trade Organization Under Challenge: Democracy and the Law and Politics of the WTO's Treatment of Trade and Environment Matters" (2001) 25 Harv. Env. L. Rev. 1; M. Grandbois, "Le droit de l'environnement et le commerce international: quelques enjeux déterminants" (1999) 40 C. de D. 545; and T.J. Schoenbaum, "International Trade and Protection of the Environment: The Continuing Search for Reconciliation" (1997) 91 A.J.I.L. 268.

249 See *supra* note 247. In the GATT, articles XX(b) and (g) are used to uphold measures to protect the environment, through interpretation by GATT/WTO panel reports. See *e.g.* WTO panel and appellate body reports in United States: *Import Prohibition of Certain Shrimp and Shrimp Products (Turtle-Shrimp)* (1998) 37 I.L.M. 832 (Panel Report) and (1999) 38 I.L.M. 118 (Appellate Body Report). In the NAFTA see *e.g.* article 104 (paramountcy of trade-restrictive provisions in listed environment treaties), article 904 (right to take standards-related measures, including to protect the environment), article 1114 (environmental measures affecting investment), article 2101 (incorporation of GATT article XX, with environmental measures expressly included), article 2005(3) (certain environment-related complaints must be decided under the NAFTA and not the WTO if the respondent requests), and article 2015 (scientific review board reports may be used for factual issues in panel processes). See similar provisions in the Canada–Chile FTA—for example, articles A-04, G-14, N-05, and O-01. See also Canada–Costa Rica FTA, articles I.4, XIV.1, online: <http://www.dfait-maeci.gc.ca/tna-nac/Costa_Rica_toc_en.asp>. On the NAFTA, see *e.g.* T. Waelde & A. Kolo, "Environmental Regulation, Investment Protection and 'Regulatory Taking' in International Law" (2001) 50 I.C.L.Q. 811; J.A. Soloway, "Environmental Regulation as Expropriation: The Case of NAFTA's Chapter 11" (2000) 33 Can. Bus. L.J. 92; R. Housman, "The North American Free Trade Agreement's Lessons for Reconciling Trade and the Environment" (1994) 30 Stan. J. Int'l L. 379.

250 (1993) 32 I.L.M. 1480.

representatives) instructs it to do so.[251] By October 2005, 10 factual records had been issued out of a total of 52 submissions received.[252] Both the Canada–Chile and Canada–Costa Rica FTAs are accompanied by side agreements on environmental protection.[253]

Treaties can be created to protect an endangered resource by controlling its international trade. As discussed above, CITES is an example of this mechanism. Alternatively, treaties have been used to restrict trade in substances that are harmful to the environment. The Basel Convention on the Control of Transboundary Movements of Hazardous Wastes and Their Disposal[254] is one example of this type of agreement. Other examples are the Cartagena Protocol on Biosafety, discussed above in Section H.3 on "Conservation of Biological Diversity," and the Stockholm Convention on Persistent Organic Pollutants, discussed earlier in Section C.1 on "Transboundary Air Pollution and Acid Deposition." The Montreal Protocol on Substances That Deplete the Ozone Layer, discussed above, imposes export and import restrictions on trade with non-parties. The Rotterdam Convention on the Prior Informed Consent Procedure for Certain Hazardous Chemicals and Pesticides in International Trade was opened for signature in September 1998 and entered into force on February 24, 2004.[255] It provides for exchange of

---

251 See *e.g.* M. Fitzmaurice, "Public Participation in the North American Agreement on Environmental Cooperation" (2003) 52 I.C.L.Q. 333; and N. Gal-Or, "Multilateral Trade and Supranational Environmental Protection: The Grace Period of the CEC, or a Well-Defined Role?" (1996) 9 Geo. Int'l Envtl. L. Rev. 53.

252 <http://www.cec.org/citizen/>.

253 Canada–Chile *Agreement on Environmental Cooperation* (1997) 36 I.L.M. 1193 (in force July 5, 1997); Canada–Costa Rica *Agreement on Environmental Cooperation*, online: <http://www.ec.gc.ca/international/costarica/index_e.htm>.

254 (1989) 28 I.L.M. 657. In force for Canada November 26, 1992. See also *Basel Convention Protocol on Liability and Compensation for Damage Resulting from Transboundary Movements of Hazardous Wastes and Their Disposal*, adopted in 1999, online: <http://www.basel.int>, not in force and Canada had not signed as of October 1, 2005; the 1991 OAU *Bamako Convention on the Ban of the Import into Africa and the Control of Transboundary Movement and Management of Hazardous Wastes Within Africa* (1991) 30 I.L.M. 775 and Canada–U.S. *Agreement Concerning the Transboundary Movement of Hazardous Waste*, Can. T.S. 1986 No. 39, in force November 8, 1986. See, generally, Birnie & Boyle, *supra* note 1 at 428-39; K. Kummer, *International Management of Hazardous Wastes* (1995); B. Kwiatkowska & A.H.A. Soons, eds., *Transboundary Movements and Disposal of Hazardous Wastes in International Law: Basic Documents* (1993); and G.F.S. Soares & E.V. Vargas, "The Basel Liability Protocol on Liability and Compensation for Damage Resulting from Transboundary Movements of Hazardous Wastes and Their Disposal" (2001) 12 Y.B. Int'l Envtl. L. 69.

255 (1999) 38 I.L.M. 1. As of October 1, 2005, 100 states (including Canada) and the EC were parties to the Convention. See <http://www.pic.int>; C. Redgwell, "Regulating Trade in Dangerous Substances: Prior Informed Consent under the 1998 Rotterdam Convention" in *Economic Globalization and Compliance with International Environmental Agreements*, *supra* note 24 at 75; M.A. Mekouar, "Pesticides and Chemicals: The Requirement of Prior Informed Consent" in *Commitment and Compliance: The Role of Non-Binding Norms in the International Legal System*, *supra* note 226 at 146; and J. Ross, "Legally Binding Prior Informed Consent" (1999) 10 Colo. J. Int'l Envtl. L. & Pol'y 499.

information and lists banned or severely restricted industrial chemicals and pesticides in Annex III. These industrial chemicals and pesticides cannot be exported to another state unless the importing state gives its prior informed consent (PIC). The Rotterdam Convention originally covered 22 pesticides and 5 industrial chemicals, including DDT, PCBs, chlordane, lindane, and mercury compounds. The first Conference of the Parties to the Rotterdam Convention, held in September 2004, resulted in the addition of 14 new substances to Annex III.[256]

---

256 In force February 1, 2005. "Asbestos Sparks Controversy at Rotterdam Convention Meeting" (September 22, 2004) vol. 8 no. 31 Bridges Weekly Trade News Digest. Chrysotile asbestos was not included in the list because producer states, including Canada, blocked the move.

CHAPTER FIFTEEN

Limitation of the Use of Force

The dual concepts of sovereignty and equality[1] remain cornerstones of public international law. Being sovereign and equal, states have certain rights and correlative duties. The central element of these rights and obligations is the rules of international law pertaining to the use of force.[2]

Until as recently as the beginning of the 20th century, international law did not impose limits on states' rights to resort to war. Indeed, use of armed force was seen as a lawful means for states to promote their interests or resolve disputes. The two world wars of the 20th century each prompted efforts to place legal limits on interstate use of force. The post World War I efforts to proscribe war were undertaken by the League of Nations and through the Kellogg-Briand Pact. Following World War II, a sweeping prohibition on the use of force was enshrined in the U.N. Charter. States were not to use force unilaterally, except in self-defence. Responses to threats to international peace and security, including military steps, were to be within the exclusive authority of the U.N. Security Council.[3] However, due to the tensions of the Cold War, the U.N.'s collective security system failed to operate as envisioned by the drafters of the Charter. In particular, Security Council action was often blocked through a veto exercised by one of its permanent members.

---

1   See discussion on statehood in Chapter 2, Section B on "States and Statehood." See article 2 of the U.N. Charter reproduced in the Documentary Supplement and article 6 of the Charter of the Organization of American States, 1948, 119 U.N.T.S. 48; U.S.T. 2394; and Protocol of Amendment, 1967, 21 U.S.T. 607; (1967) 6 I.L.M. 310; Can. T.S. 1990 No. 23.

2   See, generally, B. Asrat, *Prohibition of the Use of Force Under the U.N. Charter* (1991); D. Bowett, *Self-Defence in International Law* (1958); I. Brownlie, *International Law and the Use of Force by States* (1963); W.E. Butler, *The Non-Use of Force in International Law* (1989); A. Cassese, ed., *The Current Legal Regulations of the Use of Force* (1986); L. Fisler Damrosch and D.J. Scheffer, *Law and Force in the New International Order* (1991); Y. Dinstein, *War, Aggression and Self-Defence* (1994); T.M. Franck, *Recourse to Force: State Action Against Threats and Armed Attacks* (2002); C. Gray, *International Law and the Use of Force* (2000); L. Henkin, *et al.*, *Right v. Might*, 2d ed. (1991); M. McDougal and F. Feliciano, *Law and Minimum World Public Order* (1961); J.N. Moore, ed., *Law and Civil War in the Modern World* (1974); J.F. Murphy, *The United Nations and the Control of International Violence* (1982); R. Falk, *Legal Order in a Violent World* (1968); and J. Stone, *Aggression and World Order* (1958).

3   For a historical overview, see *e.g.* M.N. Shaw, *International Law*, 5th ed. (2003) c. 20. On the drafting history of the U.N. Charter provisions on the use of force, see also Franck, *Recourse to Force*, *supra* note 2, c. 1.

After the end of the Cold War in 1989, the Security Council entered a period of activity that was seen by many as heralding a new world order, and as illustrating the U.N.'s ability both to respond to acts of aggression and to play a major role in safeguarding international peace.[4] Yet, this period of optimism and activity quickly gave way to new challenges to the collective security system. The Security Council's failure to act decisively in the face of the Rwandan genocide, the NATO intervention in Kosovo, and the events following the attacks on the United States on September 11, 2001, all prompted renewed questioning of the U.N.'s effectiveness, or even its relevance.[5]

This chapter provides an overview of the evolution of the law on the use of force in the 20th century, and of its key features and challenges at the beginning of the 21st century. It examines the U.N. Charter's prohibition of the use of force, as well the exceptions to that prohibition. The chapter reviews the circumstances under which individual states can lawfully resort to military force. Particular emphasis is placed in this context on the scope of states' right to self-defence. Attention is also paid to the renewed debate on whether international law permits "humanitarian intervention" in another state and on whether such interventions would require authorization by the Security Council. Against this backdrop, the chapter considers the role of the U.N. Security Council in ensuring international peace and security, and the evolution of that role. Finally, the chapter examines the evolution of the U.N.'s peacekeeping role, and the role that regional organizations have played in interventions in sovereign states.

A. PROHIBITION OF THE USE OF FORCE

The League of Nations was created in 1919. Its object was to promote international co-operation, peace, and security through disarmament, the peaceful resolution of disputes, a guarantee of the sovereignty and independence of member states, and sanctions.[6] However, the Covenant left it up to each member state to decide whether or not a breach had taken place and to take sanctions. With comparatively minor scale crises this system worked, but it was totally inadequate when the major powers were involved. For example, there was little response of any practical nature with respect to the German, Italian, and Japanese acts of aggression in Czechoslovakia, Abyssinia, and Manchukuo, respectively in the 1930s.[7] The League failed to avert World War II and was formally ended in 1946.

---

4   See *e.g.* B. Urquhart, "The UN and International Security after the Cold War," in A. Roberts and B. Kingsbury, eds., *United Nations, Divided World: The UN's Role in International Relations* (1996) at 81.

5   See *e.g.* M. Glennon, "Why the Security Council Failed" (May/June 2003) 82(3) Foreign Aff. 36. But see also E.C. Luck, "The End of an Illusion" and A.-M. Slaughter, "Misreading the Record" in E.C. Luck, A.-M. Slaughter, and I. Hurd, "Stayin' Alive: The Rumors of the UN's Death Have Been Exaggerated" (July/August 2003) 82(4) Foreign Aff. 201.

6   See the *Covenant of the League of Nations*, 12 Martens Nouveau Receuil (3d ed.) 323 and U.K.T.S. 1919 No. 4, articles 8, 10-17.

7   Shaw, *supra* note 3 at 1166.

General Treaty for the Renunciation of War, 1928[8]
Can. T.S. 1929 No. 7; 94 L.N.T.S. 57

[This Treaty is otherwise known as the Pact of Paris or the Kellogg-Briand Pact after the United States' Secretary of State and the French Foreign Minister. It was signed by 15 states and had the object of filling the gap left in the Covenant of the League, which did not prohibit war or the use of force *per se*, but sought only to restrict it to reasonable levels.[9] It is still in force, but may be said to have been superseded by article 2(4) of the U.N. Charter,[10] discussed below.]

The Signatory States ...

Persuaded that the time has come when a frank renunciation of war as an instrument of national policy should be made to the end that the peaceful and friendly relations now existing between their peoples may be perpetuated;

Convinced that all changes in their relations with one another should be sought only by pacific means and be the result of the peaceful and orderly process and that any Signatory Power which shall hereafter seek to promote its national interest by resort to war should be denied the benefits furnished by this Treaty ...

Article I

The High Contracting Parties solemnly declare in the names of their respective peoples that they condemn recourse to war for the solution of international controversies, and renounce it as an instrument of national policy in their relations with one another.

Article II

The High Contracting Parties agree that the Settlement or solution of all disputes or conflicts of whatever nature or of whatever origin they may be, which might arise among them, shall never be sought except by pacific means.

NOTES

1) Did the 1928 Treaty condemn aggressive acts short of war? Brownlie[11] takes the view that the subsequent state practice "leaves little room for doubt that it was understood to prohibit any substantial use of force." For a contrary view see Bowett.[12] Did the Treaty have any enforcement mechanisms?

---

8   See C. Colombos, "The Paris Pact, Otherwise Called the Kellogg Pact" (1928) 14 Grotius 87; Q. Wright, "The Meaning of the Pact of Paris" (1933) 27 A.J.I.L. 51; and Asrat, *supra* note 2 at 31-37.

9   Shaw, *supra* note 3 at 1017; and Stone, "Aggression," *supra* note 2 at 15.

10   Reproduced in the Documentary Supplement.

11   Brownlie, *Use of Force, supra* note 2 at 87.

12   Bowett, *Self-Defence, supra* note 2 at 136.

2) In the context of responsibility for crimes against peace,[13] see article 227 of the Versailles Treaty,[14] which provided for the arraignment of Kaiser Wilhelm II, the former German Emperor for "a supreme offence against international morality and the sanctity of treaties."[15]

3) In the period since the inception of the United Nations, the use of force against a state in any manner inconsistent with the purposes and principles of the U.N. Charter is prohibited.

The Prohibition of the Use of Force and the Principle of Non-Intervention

United Nations Charter
Article 2(3), (4), and (7)

and

Declaration on Principles of International Law Concerning Friendly Relations and Co-operation among States in Accordance with the Charter of the United Nations
Both reproduced in the Documentary Supplement

Charter of the Organization of American States
(1948) 119 U.N.T.S. 48, as amended (1967) 6 I.L.M. 310; Can. T.S. 1990 No. 23

Article 18

No State or group of States has the right to intervene, directly or indirectly, for any reason whatever in the internal or external affairs of any other state. The foregoing principle prohibits not only armed force but also any other form of interference or attempted threat against the personality of the State or against its political, economic and cultural elements.

Article 19

No State may use or encourage the use of coercive measures of an economic or political character in order to force the sovereign will of another State and obtain from it advantages of any kind.

---

13 See M.R. Garcia-Mora, "Crimes Against Peace in International Law: From Nürnberg to the Present" (1964) 53 Ky. L.J. 35 and "Crimes Against Peace" (1965) 34 Fordham L. Rev. 1; see also Chapter 11 on "International Criminal Law."

14 2 Bevans 43.

15 The Dutch Government refused to surrender the Kaiser on the ground that it had no duty "to associate itself with this high act of policy of the powers," and the trial was not proceeded with. See J.W. Garner, *International Law and the World War* (1920) vol. 2 at 488-95.

Article 20

The territory of a State is inviolable; it may not be the object, even temporarily, of military occupation or of other measures of force taken by another State, directly or indirectly, on any grounds whatever. No territorial acquisitions or special advantages obtained either by force or by means of coercion shall be recognized.

Article 21

The American States bind themselves in their international relations not to have recourse to the use of force, except in the case of self-defense in accordance with existing treaties or in fulfilment thereof.

Military and Paramilitary Activities In and Against Nicaragua (Nicaragua v. United States of America), Merits, Judgment
[1986] I.C.J. Reports 14

[In the Merits phase of this case, Nicaragua claimed, *inter alia*, that the United States had acted in violation of article 2(4) of the U.N. Charter and of the customary international law obligation to refrain from the threat or use of force, and that its conduct amounted to intervention in the internal affairs of Nicaragua. The United States did not file any pleadings on the merits of the case and was not represented at the hearings before the International Court of Justice (ICJ). However, in its counter-memorial on the earlier adjudicated questions of jurisdiction and admissibility,[16] the United States had claimed that by providing, upon request, proportionate and appropriate assistance to third states not before the Court it was acting in reliance on the inherent right to collective self-defence in article 51 of the Charter.]

[172] The Court has now to turn its attention to the question of the law applicable to the present dispute. In formulating its view on the significance of the United States multilateral treaty reservation, the Court has reached the conclusion that it must refrain from applying the multilateral treaties invoked by Nicaragua in support of its claims, without prejudice either to other treaties or to the other sources of law enumerated in Article 38 of the Statute. ...

[175] The Court does not consider that, in the areas of law relevant to the present dispute, it can be claimed that all the customary rules which may be invoked have a content exactly identical to that of the rules contained in the treaties which cannot be applied by virtue of the United States reservation. On a number of points, the areas governed by the two sources of law do not exactly overlap, and the substantive rules in which they are framed are not identical in content. But in addition, even if a treaty norm and a customary norm relevant to the present dispute were to have exactly the same content, this would not be a reason for the Court to take the view that the operation of

---

16   [1984] I.C.J. Rep. 392.

the treaty process must necessarily deprive the customary norm of its separate applicability. Nor can the multilateral treaty reservation be interpreted as meaning that, once applicable to a given dispute, it would exclude the application of any rule of customary international law the content of which was the same as, or analogous to, that of the treaty-law rule which had caused the reservation to become effective.

[176] As regards the suggestion that the areas covered by the two sources of law are identical, the Court observes that the United Nations Charter, the convention to which most of the United States argument is directed, by no means covers the whole area of the regulation of the use of force in international relations. On one essential point, this treaty itself refers to pre-existing customary international law; this reference to customary law is contained in the actual text of Article 51, which mentions the "inherent right" ... of individual or collective self-defence, which "nothing in the present Charter shall impair" and which applies in the event of an armed attack. The Court therefore finds that Article 51 of the Charter is only meaningful on the basis that there is a "natural" or "inherent" right of self-defence, and it is hard to see how this can be other than of a customary nature, even if its present content has been confirmed and influenced by the Charter. Moreover the Charter, having itself recognized the existence of this right, does not go on to regulate directly all aspects of its content. For example, it does not contain any specific rule whereby self-defence would warrant only measures which are proportional to the armed attack and necessary to respond to it, a rule well established in customary international law. Moreover, a definition of the "armed attack," which, if found to exist, authorizes the exercise of the "inherent right" of self-defence, is not provided in the Charter, and is not part of treaty law. It cannot therefore be held that Article 51 is a provision which "subsumes and supervenes" customary international law. It rather demonstrates that in the field in question, the importance of which for the present dispute need hardly be stressed, customary international law continues to exist alongside treaty law. The areas governed by the two sources of law thus do not overlap exactly, and the rules do not have the same content. This could also be demonstrated for other subjects, in particular for the principle of non-intervention. ...

[187] The Court must therefore determine, first, the substance of the customary rules relating to the use of force in international relations, applicable to the dispute submitted to it. ...

[188] [B]oth Parties take the view that the principles as to the use of force incorporated in the United Nations Charter correspond, in essentials, to those found in customary international law. The Parties thus both take the view that the fundamental principle in this area is expressed in the terms employed in Article 2, paragraph 4, of the United Nations Charter. They therefore accept a treaty-law obligation to refrain in their international relations from the threat or use of force against the territorial integrity or political independence of any State, or in any other manner inconsistent with the purposes of the United Nations. The Court has however to be satisfied that there exists in customary international law an *opinio juris* as to the binding character of such abstention. This *opinio juris* may, though with all due caution, be deduced from, *inter alia*, the attitude of the Parties and the attitude of States towards certain General Assembly resolutions, and particularly resolution 2625(XXV) entitled "Declaration on Principles of International Law concerning

Friendly Relations and Cooperation among States in accordance with the Charter of the United Nations." The effect of consent to the text of such resolutions cannot be understood as merely that of a "reiteration or elucidation" of the treaty commitment undertaken in the Charter. On the contrary, it may be understood as an acceptance of the validity of the rule or set of rules declared by the resolution by themselves. The principle of non-use of force, for example, may thus be regarded as a principle of customary international law, not as such conditioned by provisions relating to collective security, or to the facilities or armed contingents to be provided under Article 43 of the Charter. It would therefore seem apparent that the attitude referred to expresses an *opinio juris* respecting such rule (or set of rules), to be thenceforth treated separately from the provisions, especially those of an institutional kind, to which it is subject on the treaty-law plane of the Charter. ...

[191] ... [I]t will be necessary to distinguish the most grave forms of the use of force (those constituting an armed attack) from other less grave forms. In determining the legal rule which applies to these latter forms, the Court can again draw on the formulations contained in the Declaration on Principles of International Law concerning Friendly Relations and Cooperation among States in accordance with the Charter of the United Nations ... . Alongside certain descriptions which may refer to aggression, this text includes others which refer only to less grave forms of the use of force. ...

[193] The general rule prohibiting force allows for certain exceptions. In view of the arguments advanced by the United States to justify the acts of which it is accused by Nicaragua, the Court must express a view on the content of the right of self-defence, and more particularly the right of collective self-defence. First, with regard to the existence of this right, it notes that in the language of Article 51 of the United Nations Charter, the inherent right (or "*droit naturel*") which any State possesses in the event of an armed attack, covers both collective and individual self-defence. Thus, the Charter itself testifies to the existence of the right of collective self-defence in customary international law. Moreover, just as the wording of certain General Assembly declarations adopted by States demonstrates their recognition of the principle of the prohibition of force as definitely a matter of customary international law, some of the wording in those declarations operates similarly in respect of the right of self-defence (both collective and individual). Thus, in the declaration quoted above on the Principles of International Law concerning Friendly Relations and Co-operation among States in accordance with the Charter of the United Nations, the reference to the prohibition of force is followed by a paragraph stating that

nothing in the foregoing paragraphs shall be construed as enlarging or diminishing in any way the scope of the provisions of the Charter concerning cases in which the use of force is lawful.

This resolution demonstrates that the States represented in the General Assembly regard the exception to the prohibition of force constituted by the right of individual or collective self-defence as already a matter of customary international law.

[194] With regard to the characteristics governing the right of self-defence, since the Parties consider the existence of this right to be established as a matter of customary international law, they have concentrated on the conditions governing its

use. In view of the circumstances in which the dispute has arisen, reliance is placed by the Parties only on the right of self-defence in the case of an armed attack which has already occurred, and the issue of the lawfulness of a response to the imminent threat of armed attack has not been raised. Accordingly the Court expresses no view on that issue. The Parties also agree in holding that whether the response to the attack is lawful depends on observance of the criteria of the necessity and the proportionality of the measures taken in self-defence. Since the existence of the right of collective self-defence is established in customary international law, the Court must define the specific conditions which may have to be met for its exercise, in addition to the conditions of necessity and proportionality to which the Parties have referred.

[195] In the case of individual self-defence, the exercise of this right is subject to the State concerned having been the victim of an armed attack. Reliance on collective self-defence of course does not remove the need for this. There appears now to be general agreement on the nature of the acts which can be treated as constituting armed attacks. In particular, it may be considered to be agreed that an armed attack must be understood as including not merely action by regular armed forces across an international border, but also "the sending by or on behalf of a State of armed bands, groups, irregulars or mercenaries, which carry out acts of armed force against another State of such gravity as to amount to" (*inter alia*) an actual armed attack conducted by regular forces, "or its substantial involvement therein." This description, contained in Article 3, paragraph (g), of the Definition of Aggression annexed to General Assembly resolution 3314(XXIX), may be taken to reflect customary international law. The Court sees no reason to deny that, in customary law, the prohibition of armed attacks may apply to the sending by a State of armed bands to the territory of another State, if such an operation, because of its scale and effects, would have been classified as an armed attack rather than as a mere frontier incident had it been carried out by regular armed forces. But the Court does not believe that the concept of "armed attack" includes … also assistance to rebels in the form of the provision of weapons or logistical or other support. Such assistance may be regarded as a threat or use of force, or amount to intervention in the internal or external affairs of other States. It is also clear that it is the State which is the victim of an armed attack which must form and declare the view that it has been so attacked. There is no rule in customary international law permitting another State to exercise the right of collective self-defence on the basis of its own assessment of the situation. Where collective self-defence is invoked, it is to be expected that the State for whose benefit this right is used will have declared itself to be the victim of an armed attack. …

[199] At all events, the Court finds that in customary international law … there is no rule permitting the exercise of collective self-defence in the absence of a request by the State which regards itself as the victim of an armed attack. The Court concludes that the requirement of a request by the State which is the victim of the alleged attack is additional to the requirement that such a State should have declared itself to have been attacked. …

[202] The principle of non-intervention involves the right of every sovereign State to conduct its affairs without outside interference; though examples of trespass against this principle are not infrequent, the Court considers that it is part and parcel of customary international law. [It is] a corollary of the principle of the sovereign equality

of States. A particular instance of this is General Assembly resolution 2625(XXV), the Declaration on Principles of International Law concerning Friendly Relations and Co-operation among States. ...

[205] ... [T]he principle [of non-intervention] forbids all States or groups of States to intervene directly or indirectly in internal or external affairs of other States. A prohibited intervention must accordingly be one bearing on matters in which each State is permitted, by the principle of State sovereignty, to decide freely. One of these is the choice of a political, economic, social and cultural system, and the formulation of foreign policy. Intervention is wrongful when it uses methods of coercion in regard to such choices, which must remain free ones. The element of coercion, which defines, and indeed forms the very essence of, prohibited intervention, is particularly obvious in the case of an intervention which uses force, either in the direct form of military action, or in the indirect form of support for subversive or terrorist armed activities within another State. ...

[209] The Court therefore finds that no ... general right of intervention, in support of an opposition within another State, exists in contemporary international law. The Court concludes that acts constituting a breach of the customary principle of non-intervention will also, if they directly or indirectly involve the use of force, constitute a breach of the principle of non-use of force in international relations. ...

[210] When dealing with the rule of the prohibition of the use of force, the Court considered the exception to it constituted by the exercise of the right of collective self-defence in the event of armed attack. Similarly, it must now consider the following question: if one State acts towards another State in breach of the principle of non-intervention, may a third State lawfully take such action by way of counter-measures against the first State as would otherwise constitute an intervention in its internal affairs? A right to act in this way in the case of intervention would be analogous to the right of collective self-defence in the case of an armed attack, but both the act which gives rise to the reaction, and that reaction itself, would in principle be less grave. ...

[211] The Court has recalled above (paragraphs 193 to 195) that for one State to use force against another, on the ground that that State has committed a wrongful act of force against a third State, is regarded as lawful, by way of exception, only when the wrongful act provoking the response was an armed attack. Thus the lawfulness of the use of force by a State in response to a wrongful act of which it has not itself been the victim is not admitted when this wrongful act is not an armed attack. In the view of the Court, under international law in force today—whether customary international law or that of the United Nations system—States do not have a right of "collective" armed response to acts which do not constitute an "armed attack." ...

[226] The Court ... has now to appraise the facts in relation to the legal rules applicable. ...

[227] ... For the most part, the complaints by Nicaragua are of the actual use of force against it by the United States. Of the acts which the Court has found imputable to the Government of the United States, the following are relevant in this respect:

— the laying of mines in Nicaraguan internal or territorial waters in early 1984 ... ;

— certain attacks on Nicaraguan ports, oil installations and a naval base. ...

These activities constitute infringements of the principle of the prohibition of the use of force, defined earlier, unless they are justified by circumstances which exclude their unlawfulness, a question now to be examined. The Court has also found ... the existence of military manoeuvres held by the United States near the Nicaraguan borders; and Nicaragua has made some suggestion that this constituted a "threat of force," which is equally forbidden by the principle of non-use of force. The Court is however not satisfied that the manoeuvres complained of, in the circumstances in which they were held, constituted on the part of the United States a breach, as against Nicaragua, of the principle forbidding recourse to the threat or use of force.

[228] Nicaragua has also claimed that the United States has violated Article 2, paragraph 4, of the Charter, and has used force against Nicaragua in breach of its obligation under customary international law in as much as it has engaged in

> recruiting, training, arming, equipping, financing, supplying and otherwise encouraging, supporting, aiding, and directing military and paramilitary actions in and against Nicaragua. ...

[T]he Court finds that, subject to the question whether the action of the United States might be justified as an exercise of the right of self-defence, the United States has committed a *prima facie* violation of that principle by its assistance to the *contras* in Nicaragua, by "organizing or encouraging the organization of irregular forces or armed bands ... for incursion into the territory of another State," and "participating in acts of civil strife ... in another State," in the terms of General Assembly resolution 2625 (XXV). According to that resolution, participation of this kind is contrary to the principle of the prohibition of the use of force when the acts of civil strife referred to "involve a threat or use of force." In the view of the Court, while the arming and training of the *contras* can certainly be said to involve the threat or use of force against Nicaragua, this is not necessarily so in respect of all the assistance given by the United States Government. In particular, the Court considers that the mere supply of funds to the *contras*, while undoubtedly an act of intervention in the internal affairs of Nicaragua, as will be explained below, does not in itself amount to a use of force.

[229] The Court must thus consider whether, as the Respondent claims, the acts in question of the United States are justified by the exercise of its right of collective self-defence against an armed attack. ...

[230] As regards El Salvador, the Court has found ... that it is satisfied that between July 1979 and the early months of 1981, an intermittent flow of arms was routed via the territory of Nicaragua to the armed opposition in that country. The Court was not however satisfied that assistance has reached the Salvadorian armed opposition, on a scale of any significance, since the early months of 1981, or that the Government of Nicaragua was responsible for any flow of arms at either period. Even assuming that the supply of arms to the opposition in El Salvador could be treated as imputable to the Government of Nicaragua, to justify invocation of the right of collective self-defence in customary international law, it would have to be equated with an armed attack by Nicaragua on El Salvador. As stated above, the Court is unable to consider that, in customary international law, the provision of arms to the opposition in another State constitutes an armed attack on that State. Even at a time

when the arms flow was at its peak, and again assuming the participation of the Nicaraguan Government, that would not constitute such armed attack. ...

[232] ... [T]he Court is entitled to take account, in judging the asserted justification of the exercise of collective self-defence by the United States, of the actual conduct of El Salvador, Honduras and Costa Rica at the relevant time, as indicative of a belief by the State in question that it was the victim of an armed attack by Nicaragua...

[233] The Court has seen no evidence that the conduct of those States was consistent with such a situation, either at the time when the United States first embarked on the activities which were allegedly justified by self-defence, or indeed for a long period subsequently. [W]hile El Salvador did in fact officially declare itself the victim of an armed attack, and did ask for the United States to exercise its right of collective self-defence, this occurred only on a date much later than the commencement of the United States activities which were allegedly justified by this request. ... It was only in its Declaration of Intervention filed on 15 August 1984 that El Salvador referred to requests addressed at various dates to the United States for the latter to exercise its right of collective self-defence. ...

[234] As to Honduras and Costa Rica, they also were prompted by the institution of proceedings in this case to address communications to the Court; in neither of these is there mention of armed attack or collective self-defence. ...

[235] There is also an aspect of the conduct of the United States which the Court is entitled to take into account as indicative of the view of that State on the question of the existence of an armed attack. At no time, up to the present, has the United States Government addressed to the Security Council, in connection with the matters the subject of the present case, the report which is required by Article 51 of the United Nations Charter in respect of measures which a State believes itself bound to take when it exercises the right of individual or collective self-defence. The Court, whose decision has to be made on the basis of customary law, ... is [nonetheless] justified in observing that this conduct of the United States hardly conforms with the latter's avowed conviction that it was acting in the context of collective self-defence as consecrated by Article 51 of the Charter. ...

[236] Similarly, while no strict legal conclusion may be drawn from the date of El Salvador's announcement that it was the victim of an armed attack, and the date of its official request addressed to the United States concerning the exercise of collective self-defence, those dates have a significance as evidence of El Salvador's view of the situation. The declaration and the request of El Salvador, made publicly for the first time in August 1984, do not support the contention that in 1981 there was an armed attack capable of serving as a legal foundation for United States activities which began in the second half of that year. The States concerned did not behave as though there were an armed attack at the time when the activities attributed by the United States to Nicaragua, without actually constituting such an attack, were nevertheless the most accentuated. ...

[239] The Court comes now to the application ... of the principle of non-intervention in the internal affairs of States. ...

[240] Nicaragua has laid much emphasis on the intentions it attributes to the Government of the United States in giving aid and support to the *contras*. It contends

that the purpose of the policy of the United States and its actions against Nicaragua in pursuance of this policy was, from the beginning, to overthrow the Government of Nicaragua. ...

[241] The Court however does not consider it necessary to seek to establish whether the intention of the United States to secure a change of governmental policies in Nicaragua went so far as to be equated with an endeavour to overthrow the Nicaraguan Government. It appears to the Court to be clearly established first, that the United States intended, by its support of the *contras*, to coerce the Government of Nicaragua in respect of matters in which each State is permitted, by the principle of State sovereignty, to decide freely (see paragraph 205 above); and secondly that the intention of the *contras* themselves was to overthrow the present Government of Nicaragua. ... The Court considers that in international law, if one State, with a view to the coercion of another State, supports and assists armed bands in that State whose purpose is to overthrow the government of that State, that amounts to an intervention by the one State in the internal affairs of the other, whether or not the political objective of the State giving such support and assistance is equally far-reaching. ...

[242] The Court therefore finds that the support given by the United States, up to the end of September 1984, to the military and paramilitary activities of the *contras* in Nicaragua, by financial support, training, supply of weapons, intelligence and logistic support, constitutes a clear breach of the principle of non-intervention. ...

[244] As already noted, Nicaragua has also asserted that the United States is responsible for an "indirect" form of intervention in its internal affairs inasmuch as it has taken, to Nicaragua's disadvantage, certain action of an economic nature. The Court's attention has been drawn in particular to the cessation of economic aid in April 1981; the 90 per cent reduction in the sugar quota for United States imports from Nicaragua in April 1981, and the trade embargo adopted on 1 May 1985. While admitting in principle that some of these actions were not unlawful in themselves, counsel for Nicaragua argued that these measures of economic constraint add up to a systematic violation of the principle of non-intervention.

[245] ... [T]he Court has merely to say that it is unable to regard such action on the economic plane as is here complained of as a breach of the customary-law principle of non-intervention.

[246] Having concluded that the activities of the United States in relation to the activities of the *contras* in Nicaragua constitute *prima facie* acts of intervention, the Court must next consider whether they may nevertheless be justified on some legal ground. As the Court has stated, the principle of non-intervention derives from customary international law. It would certainly lose its effectiveness as a principle of law if intervention were to be justified by a mere request for assistance made by an opposition group in another State. ... Indeed, it is difficult to see what would remain of the principle of non-intervention in international law if intervention, which is already allowable at the request of the government of a State, were also to be allowed at the request of the opposition. This would permit any State to intervene at any moment in the internal affairs of another State, whether at the request of the government or at the request of its opposition. Such a situation does not in the Court's view correspond to the present state of international law.

[247] [As the] Court has already indicated ... the conduct of the United States towards Nicaragua cannot be justified by the right of collective self-defence in response to an alleged armed attack on one or other of Nicaragua's neighbours. So far as regards the allegations of supply of arms by Nicaragua to the armed opposition in El Salvador, the Court has indicated that ... the supply of arms and other support to such bands cannot be equated with armed attack. Nevertheless, such activities may well constitute a breach of the principle of the non-use of force and an intervention in the internal affairs of a State, that is, a form of conduct which is certainly wrongful, but is of lesser gravity than an armed attack. The Court must therefore enquire now whether the activities of the United States towards Nicaragua might be justified as a response to an intervention by that State in the internal affairs of another State in Central America. ...

[249] On the legal level the Court cannot regard response to an intervention by Nicaragua as such a justification. While an armed attack would give rise to an entitlement to collective self-defence, a use of force of a lesser degree of gravity cannot, as the Court has already observed (paragraph 211 above), produce any entitlement to take collective counter-measures involving the use of force. The acts of which Nicaragua is accused, even assuming them to have been established and imputable to that State, could only have justified proportionate counter-measures on the part of the State which had been the victim of these acts, namely El Salvador, Honduras or Costa Rica. They could not justify counter-measures taken by a third State, the United States, and particularly could not justify intervention involving the use of force. ...

[257] The Court has noted ... the attitude of the United States, as expressed in the finding of the Congress of 29 July 1985, linking United States support to the *contras* with alleged breaches by the Government of Nicaragua of its "solemn commitments to the Nicaraguan people, the United States, and the Organization of American States." Those breaches were stated to involve questions such as the composition of the government, its political ideology and alignment, totalitarianism, human rights, militarization and aggression. ...

[263] ... However the regime in Nicaragua be defined, adherence by a State to any particular doctrine does not constitute a violation of customary international law; to hold otherwise would make nonsense of the fundamental principle of State sovereignty, on which the whole of international law rests, and the freedom of choice of the political, social, economic and cultural system of a State. Consequently, Nicaragua's domestic policy options, even assuming that they correspond to the description given of them by the Congress's finding, cannot justify on the legal plane the various actions of the Respondent complained of. The Court cannot contemplate the creation of a new rule opening up a right of intervention by one State against another on the ground that the latter has opted for some particular ideology or political system. ...

[265] Similar considerations apply to the criticisms expressed by the United States of the external policies and alliances of Nicaragua. ... [From the standpoint of international law,] it is sufficient to say that State sovereignty evidently extends to the area of its foreign policy, and that there is no rule of customary international law to prevent a State from choosing and conducting a foreign policy in co-ordination with that of another State.

[266] The Court also notes that these justifications, advanced solely in the political context ... , were not advanced as legal arguments. The respondent State has always confined itself to the classic argument of self-defence, and has not attempted to introduce a legal argument derived from a supposed rule of "ideological intervention," which would have been a striking innovation. ...

[268] ... [W]hile the United States might form its own appraisal of the situation as to respect for human rights in Nicaragua, the use of force could not be the appropriate method to monitor or ensure such respect. With regard to the steps actually taken, the protection of human rights, a strictly humanitarian objective, cannot be compatible with the mining of ports, the destruction of oil installations, or again with the training, arming and equipping of the *contras*. The Court concludes that the argument derived from the preservation of human rights in Nicaragua cannot afford a legal justification for the conduct of the United States, and cannot in any event be reconciled with the legal strategy of the respondent State, which is based on the right of collective self-defence.

[269] The Court now turns to another factor. ... This is the militarization of Nicaragua, which the United States deems excessive and such as to prove its aggressive intent. ... It is irrelevant and inappropriate, in the Court's opinion, to pass upon this allegation by the United States, since in international law there are no rules, other than such rules as may be accepted by the State concerned, by treaty or otherwise, whereby the level of armaments of a sovereign State can be limited, and this principle is valid for all States without exception.

NOTES

1) Article 2(4) is regarded as codifying a rule of customary international law binding on all states.[17]

2) Article 2(4) does not refer to "war" but to "force."[18] What does "the threat or use of force" in article 2(4) mean? Does it prohibit economic measures or political pressure? Goodrich, Hambro, and Simons[19] argue that it is directed against armed force alone. Do you agree? Does the 1970 Declaration clarify article 2(4) of the Charter concerning whether economic or political measures short of armed force are prohibited? Article 51 of the Charter discussed below in Section B.1 on "The Right of Self-Defence," talks specifically of "armed force" as does the Preamble to the Charter. Is this further evidence for a broad interpretation of article 2(4)?

3) Note that the 1970 Declaration on Principles of International Law Concerning Friendly Relations (Declaration on Friendly Relations) was adopted by consensus. It

---

17   See *Military Activities In and Against Nicaragua*, [1986] I.C.J. Rep. 14 at paras. 175-176, 188; and R. St. J. Macdonald, "Nicaragua Case: New Answers to Old Questions?" (1986) 24 Can. Y.B. Int'l L. 127.

18   See E. Lauterpacht, "The Legal Irrelevance of the State of War" (1968) 62 A.S.I.L. Proc. 58 at 62; and M.C. Bassiouni and B. Ferencz, "The Crime Against Peace," in M.C. Bassiouni, ed., *International Criminal Law* (1986) vol. I 167 at 176-78.

19   L.M. Goodrich, *et al.*, *Charter of the United Nations*, 3d ed. (1969) 49. See also R. Higgins, *The Development of International Law through the Political Organs of the United Nations* (1963) 167-239.

elaborates on some of the provisions of the U.N. Charter. It is, nevertheless, still only a U.N. General Assembly resolution. What status does it have? Is it a reflection of customary international law? Is it a guide to interpretation of Charter articles?[20]

4) Although the Charter of the United Nations contains no provision that deals explicitly with the principle of non-intervention by states, this principle must be regarded as implicit in it. The principle is embodied in article 2(1), which proclaims the sovereign equality of states and thus prohibits one state from interfering in the affairs of another state and protects the second state against such interference. In customary law, sovereign equality was the foundation of the duty of non-intervention, and sovereign equality would be meaningless if states were entitled to intervene in the domestic affairs of other states. Thus, the legal concept of non-intervention as between member states of the United Nations could be regarded as springing from the concepts of respect for the personality and political independence of the state, concepts that constituted elements of sovereign equality, as well as from the principle of juridical equality.

In addition, since article 2(7) of the U.N. Charter prohibits intervention by the organization in the domestic affairs of member states, that prohibition should extend *a fortiori* to member states in their relations with each other. The principle of non-intervention could then be considered as a corollary of the principle of respect for the territorial integrity and political independence of states protected by article 2(4) of the Charter, which postulates implicitly the free and unhampered development of states as an aspect of their national independence.

In 1965, the General Assembly adopted an eight-point Declaration on the Inadmissibility of Intervention in the Domestic Affairs of States and the Protection of Their Independence and Sovereignty.[21] In 1966, in examining the status of the implementation of the Declaration, the Assembly expressed deep concern at the evidence of unceasing armed intervention and other forms of interference by certain states in the domestic affairs of others in different parts of the world, resulting in increased international tension. It reaffirmed all the principles and rules embodied in the Declaration, it urged the immediate cessation of intervention, in any form whatever, and it called upon all states to carry out faithfully their obligations under the Charter and the provisions of the Declaration.

The duties to avoid the use of force and refrain from intervention in another state are reiterated again in the first and third principles of the 1970 Declaration on Friendly Relations, reproduced in the Documentary Supplement.

5) In the *Nicaragua* case, reproduced above, the ICJ confirmed that the principle of non-intervention, despite examples of not infrequent violation, is part of customary international law. The Court found numerous examples of expressions of *opinio juris* to support this view. This *opinio juris* on the part of states is backed up by established

---

20 G. Arangio-Ruiz, *The U.N. Declaration on Friendly Relations and the System of the Sources of International Law* (1979) and R. Rosenstock, "The Declaration of Principles of International Law Concerning Friendly Relations: A Survey" (1971) 65 A.J.I.L. 713. And see the discussion of the Declaration in Chapter 2, Section B on "States and Statehood."

21 GA Res. 2131(XX) UN GAOR, 20th Sess., U.N. Doc. A/6014 (1966), reprinted in (1966) 60 A.J.I.L. 662. Adopted by 109 votes in favour, 0 against, and 1 abstention.

practice. This is so, notwithstanding the lack of specific reference to the principle of non-intervention in the U.N. Charter. The Court was of the opinion that "it was never intended that the Charter should embody written confirmation of every essential principle of international law in force."

6) The Organization of American States (OAS) was created in 1948 and binds together over 30 states in North, Central, and South America, including Canada and the United States. The OAS Charter spells out much more affirmatively than the U.N. Charter the principle of non-intervention by member states. Even so, how do its provisions differ specifically from the universal principles of the U.N. Charter as interpreted by the General Assembly's resolutions?

7) A not dissimilar organization to the OAS has taken shape in Europe under the auspices of the Conference on Security and Co-Operation in Europe (CSCE), later the Organization of Security and Co-operation in Europe (OSCE). The first summit-level meeting of the CSCE occurred at Helsinki in 1975 and was significant for achieving agreement on a set of 10 principles concerning peace, security, and human rights across an ideologically divided Europe. However, further progress was not possible while the Cold War persisted. Thereafter, activity picked up rapidly and meetings of the Organization were held regularly, culminating on November 21, 1990 with the Charter of Paris.[22] Adopted by 34 participating states, this Charter declared a new era of democracy, peace, and unity in Europe and, for its promotion, established guidelines for the future about human rights and the rule of law, military forces and security, economic co-operation, environmental protection, and culture. Most important, the Charter laid the foundation for a full-scale organization to fulfill its purposes and principles. A set of institutional arrangements were adopted.

The tone of the Charter of Paris is one of affirmative co-operation to find new ways to advance peace and security in order to address the needs and aspirations of the peoples of Europe. Thus, on the topic of security, the Charter eschews the negative language of non-intervention, preferring the statement that the parties "are determined to co-operate in defending democratic institutions against activities that violate the independence, sovereign equality or territorial integrity of the participating states. These include illegal activities involving outside pressure, coercion and subversion." Is this likely to be a better or worse legal approach to controlling intervention in one state by another?

8) On October 6, 1992 the U.N. Security Council took the unprecedented step of unanimously adopting a resolution establishing a commission to investigate the atrocities committed in the former Yugoslavia, mainly in Bosnia-Herzegovina. A Canadian, Commander W.J. Fenrick, was appointed to this Commission. Further, in February 1993, by resolution 808, the Security Council acting under Chapter VII of the U.N. Charter, called for the setting up of an International Criminal Tribunal (ICT) for the former Yugoslavia (ICTFY), for the prosecution of serious violations of international humanitarian law, including murder, torture, and the so-called ethnic cleansing. In November 1994, again acting under Chapter VII, the Security Council created the

---

22   (1991) 30 I.L.M. 190. The original Helsinki Accords of the CSCE are discussed in Chapter 3 in the text at note 21.

International Criminal Tribunal for Rwanda (ICTR) to prosecute individuals responsible for the genocide during the Rwandan civil conflict between January 1 and December 31, 1994. These *Ad Hoc* Tribunals are considered in Chapter 11, Section B on "International Criminal Law: Prosecution in the Ad Hoc International Tribunals." Do these steps violate the non-intervention principle?

9) On April 29, 1999, the Federal Republic of Yugoslavia (FRY) instituted proceedings before the ICJ against the United States of America, the United Kingdom, France, Germany, Italy, the Netherlands, Belgium, Canada, Portugal, and Spain. It has accused them, together with other member states of NATO of, *inter alia*, bombing Yugoslav territory in violation of their U.N. obligations not to use force against another state, intervening in the domestic affairs of Yugoslavia, violating its sovereignty, using prohibited weapons, and deliberately inflicting conditions of life calculated to cause the physical destruction of a national group. In each case Yugoslavia also filed a request for provisional measures. The ICJ, in oral pleadings on May 10–12, 1999, was asked to order the respondent states to "cease immediately acts of use of force" and to "refrain from any act or threat or use of force against the Federal Republic of Yugoslavia."[23] The ICJ handed down its decision on provisional measures in the *Case Concerning Legality of Use of Force*[24] on June 2, 1999. The Court rejected the request by FRY by a vote of 12 to 4. The Court in so doing first accepted the submission that had been put forward by Canada that the Court lacked *prima facie* jurisdiction in that the FRY had only deposited its declaration of acceptance of jurisdiction under the Optional Clause contained in article 36(2) of the ICJ statute on April 25, 1999. The NATO bombings had been initiated on March 24, 1999. Second, the Court agreed with Canada's submission that the Genocide Convention, to which both Canada and Yugoslavia are parties did not provide *prima facie* jurisdiction for the measures sought. Applying its decision in the *Application of the Convention on the Prevention and Punishment of the Crime of Genocide, Provisional Measures, Order of 13 September 1993*,[25] the ICJ stated "that the essential characteristic of genocide (as defined in the Genocide Convention article II) is the intended destruction of 'a national, ethnical, racial or religious group.'" It concluded that the threat of use of force "cannot constitute an act of genocide within the meaning" of article 2 and further that at that stage of the proceedings the NATO bombings did not "entail the element of intent, towards" such a group.[26] However, it was made clear by the ICJ that its findings on the FRY's application for provisional measures "in no way prejudge the jurisdiction of the Court to deal with the merits of the case or any questions relating to the admissibility of the application or relating to the merits themselves."[27] The Court did not at the provisional-measures stage opine on the legality of the NATO aerial action or on the

---

23   ICJ Press Communiqué 99/17.

24   *Yugoslavia v. Canada* (June 2, 1999) General List No. 106, online: <http://www.icj-cij.org/icjwww/idocket/iyca/iycaframe.htm>.

25   [1993] I.C.J. Rep. 325 at para. 42.

26   *Yugoslavia v. Canada, supra* note 24 at para. 39, quoting from the *Legality of the Threat or Use of Nuclear Weapons*, Advisory Opinion, [1996] I.C.J. Rep. 226 at para. 26.

27   *Ibid.* at para. 42.

alleged violations of international law committed by FRY in Kosovo. Indeed, the decision shows the deep concern of the Court with "the human tragedy, the loss of life, and the enormous suffering in Kosovo ... and with the continuing loss of life and human suffering in all parts of Yugoslavia";[28] with the use of force in Yugoslavia that raises "serious issues of international law";[29] with the purposes and principles of the U.N. Charter and its own responsibilities in the maintenance of peace and security;[30] and with obligations of all parties to the dispute to act in conformity with the Charter and other rules of international law, including humanitarian law. It is of interest to note that the ICJ concluded by stating that there is a fundamental distinction to be made between the issue of acceptance of the jurisdiction of the Court by a state and the compatibility of particular acts with international law. Further, the Court stressed that whether or not there is such acceptance, states remain responsible for acts in violation of international law that are attributable to them and that the parties in this dispute should take care not to "aggravate or extend the dispute."[31]

Having ruled on the provisional measures issue, the ICJ remained seized of the case. However, in July 2000, Canada submitted preliminary objections relating to the Court's jurisdiction to hear the case on the merits. In December 2004, the Court ruled to dismiss the case. Accepting Canada's argument, the Court concluded that it lacked jurisdiction because the Applicant was not a Member of the United Nations when the proceedings were instituted, and thus was not a state party to the Statute of the ICJ. That conclusion meant that the Applicant did not have access to the ICJ under Article 35(1) of the Court's Statute. The Court allowed that, while Article 35(1) gives access to the states parties to the Statute, Article 35(2) is intended to provide access to certain states that are not parties to the Statute. However, the Court held that paragraph 2 presupposes that such states access the Court on the basis of a treaty already in force at the time that the ICJ Statute entered into force. Therefore, the Applicant could not succeed with its argument that the Court had jurisdiction over the case on the basis of the Genocide Convention, which only entered into force on January 12, 1951, after the entry into force of the Statute.[32]

If the ICJ had granted provisional measures, would Canada and the other respondent states have complied? Do orders for provisional or interim measures have the force of law or are they purely advisory? See the discussion of provisional measures in the Notes in Chapter 6, Section D.3 on "Decisions of the Court." Do you think that the NATO bombings were intended as the use of force "against the territorial integrity" of the FRY and constitute a violation of article 2(4) of the U.N. Charter? Can it be argued that NATO's use of force was serving the goals of the United Nations as listed in article 1 of the Charter in that it was to further the causes of peace, security, self-determination of

---

28   *Ibid.* at para. 15.

29   *Ibid.* at para. 16.

30   *Ibid.* at para. 17.

31   *Ibid.* at paras. 43-45.

32   *Case concerning Legality of Use of Force (Serbia and Montenegro v. Canada)*, Preliminary Objections (December 15, 2004) paras. 44-90, 91-114, online: <http://www.icj-cij.org/icjwww/idocket/iyca/iycaframe.htm>. Note that, with effect from February 4, 2003, the applicant Federal Republic of Yugoslavia was renamed "Serbia and Montenegro."

peoples, and the protection of human rights? Does article 2(7) prohibit or not prohibit intervention where genocide or ethnic cleansing is taking place, as it was in Kosovo? As discussed in Chapter 11 on "International Criminal Law," genocide and crimes against humanity are considered two of the most serious crimes against the international community, are violations of *erga omnes* obligations, and are subject to universal jurisdiction. See also Section B.3 in this chapter on "Humanitarian Intervention" as a justification for the use of force and a potentially emerging limitation to the principle of non-intervention.

Use of Force, Aggression and Armed Attack

Definition of Aggression[33]
U.N. GA Res. 3314(XXIX), UN GAOR, 29th Sess., Supp. No. 31,
U.N. Doc. A/9631 (1974) at 142; reprinted in (1974) 13 I.L.M. 710

The General Assembly

Basing itself on the fact that one of the fundamental purposes of the United Nations is to maintain international peace and security and to take effective collective measures for the prevention and removal of threats to the peace, and for the suppression of acts of aggression or other breaches of the peace,

Recalling that the Security Council, in accordance with article 39 of the Charter of the United Nations, shall determine the existence of any threat to the peace, breach of the peace or act of aggression and shall make recommendations, or decide what measures shall be taken in accordance with articles 41 and 42, to maintain or restore international peace and security,

Recalling also the duty of States under the Charter to settle their international disputes by peaceful means in order not to endanger international peace, security and justice,

Bearing in mind that nothing in this definition shall be interpreted as in any way affecting the scope of the provisions of the Charter with respect to the functions and powers of the organs of the United Nations,

Considering also that, since aggression is the most serious and dangerous form of the illegal use of force, being fraught, in the conditions created by the existence of all types of weapons of mass destruction, with the possible threat of a world conflict and all its catastrophic consequences, aggression should be defined at the present stage,

Reaffirming the duty of States not to use armed force to deprive peoples of their right to self-determination, freedom and independence, or to disrupt territorial integrity,

Reaffirming also that the territory of a State shall not be violated by being the object, even temporarily, of military occupation or of other measures of force taken by another State in contravention of the Charter, and that it shall not be the object of acquisition by another State resulting from such measures or the threat thereof,

---

33   See B. Ferencz, *Defining Aggression* (1975) 2 vols.; N. Nyiri, *The United Nations' Search for a Definition of Aggression* (1989); and J. Stone, *Conflict Through Consensus: U.N. Approaches to Aggression* (1977).

Reaffirming also the provisions of the Declaration on Principles of International Law concerning Friendly Relations and Co-operation among States in accordance with the Charter of the United Nations,

Convinced that the adoption of a definition of aggression ought to have the effect of deterring a potential aggressor, would simplify the determination of acts of aggression and the implementation of measures to suppress them and would also facilitate the protection of the rights and lawful interests of, and the rendering of assistance to, the victim,

Believing that, although the question whether an act of aggression has been committed must be considered in light of all the circumstances of each particular case, it is nevertheless desirable to formulate basic principles as guidance for such determination,

Adopts the following Definition:

Article 1

Aggression is the use of armed force by a State against the sovereignty, territorial integrity or political independence of another State, or in any other manner inconsistent with the Charter of the United Nations, as set out in this Definition.

Explanatory note: In this Definition the term "State"

(a) Is used without prejudice to questions of recognition or to whether a State is a Member of the United Nations, and

(b) Includes the concept of a "group of States" where appropriate.

Article 2

The first use of armed force by a State in contravention of the Charter shall constitute *prima facie* evidence of an act of aggression although the Security Council may in conformity with the Charter, conclude that a determination that an act of aggression has been committed would not be justified in the light of other relevant circumstances including the fact that the acts concerned or their consequences are not of sufficient gravity.

Article 3

Any of the following acts, regardless of a declaration of war, shall, subject to and in accordance with the provisions of article 2, qualify as an act of aggression:

(a) The invasion or attack by armed forces of a State of the territory of another State, or any military occupation, however temporary, resulting from such invasion or attack, or any annexation by the use of force of the territory of another State or part thereof;

(b) Bombardment by the armed forces of a State against the territory of another State or the use of any weapons by a State against the territory of another State;

(c) The blockade of the ports or coasts of a State by the armed forces of another State;

(d) An attack by the armed forces of a State on the land, sea or air forces, or marine and air fleets of another State;

(e) The use of armed forces of one State which are within the territory of another State with the agreement of the receiving State, in contravention of the conditions provided for in the agreement or any extension of their presence in such territory beyond the termination of the agreement;

(f) The action of a State in allowing its territory, which it has placed at the disposal of another State, to be used by that other State for perpetrating an act of aggression against a third State;

(g) The sending by or on behalf of a State of armed bands, irregulars or mercenaries, which carry out acts of armed force against another State of such gravity as to amount to the acts listed above, or its substantial involvement therein.

Article 4

The acts enumerated above are not exhaustive and the Security Council may determine that other acts constitute aggression under the provision of the Charter.

Article 5

No consideration of whatever nature, whether political, economic, military or otherwise, may serve as a justification for aggression.

A war of aggression is a crime against international peace. Aggression gives rise to international responsibility.

No territorial acquisition or special advantage resulting from aggression are or shall be recognized as lawful.

Article 6

Nothing in this Definition shall be construed as in any way enlarging or diminishing the scope of the Charter including its provisions concerning cases in which the use of force is lawful.

Article 7

Nothing in this Definition, and in particular article 3, could in any way prejudice the right to self-determination, freedom and independence, as derived from the Charter, of peoples forcibly deprived of that right and referred to in the Declaration on Principles of International Law concerning Friendly Relations and Co-operation among States in accordance with the Charter of the United Nations particularly peoples under colonial and racist regimes or other forms of alien domination: nor the right of these peoples to struggle to that end and to seek and receive support in accordance with the principles of the Charter and in conformity with the above-mentioned Declaration.

Article 8

In their interpretation and application the above provisions are interrelated and each provision should be construed in the context of the other provisions.

Comments by Canadian Delegation
October 10, 1974, Press Release No. 14

Article 1

The Canadian Government is satisfied with the basic definition of aggression as contained in Article 1. Although cases of indirect aggression are not specifically referred to in the article, this aspect of the problem is adequately dealt with elsewhere in the declaration.

The explanatory note to Article 1 makes it clear that the concept of statehood, however defined, is not an essential element of the definition of aggression, thereby recognizing one of the realities of international life and, at the same time, avoiding a restriction on the scope of the definition so as not to unduly hamper its applicability.

Article 2

The wording of Article 2 represents a carefully worked out compromise following considerable difficulties regarding the inclusion of the concept of aggressive intent. This compromise is a workable one. It retains the notion of the use of armed force as the essential element to be considered by the Security Council in its determination as to the fact of aggression. At the same time, by constituting armed force as *prima facie* evidence of aggression it leaves the field of inquiry open to the other aspects of each particular case. This is further emphasized by the use of the term "other relevant circumstances." This approach reflects the realities of international conflict. In a great number of cases the simple act of armed force cannot be the only criterion to be identified. Aggressive intent is one of the other criteria which should be taken into consideration. The Canadian Government attaches considerable importance to intent as one of the necessary elements which, in combination, constitute the wrongful act. This is the *mens rea* of the criminal law. Admittedly, it is difficult to establish and prove this element, more so in the area of international conflict. Nonetheless, it is of central importance and in many cases could be one of the most important factors to be considered by the Security Council.

As understood by Canada, the use of armed force raises a rebuttable presumption that an act of aggression has been committed. It is an important, but not an exclusive determinant. The existence of an aggressive intent may be significant as one of the other "relevant factors" that can either rebut or support this presumption.

Article 3

The list of acts of aggression on paras. (a) to (h) of Article 3 is intended to be illustrative rather than exhaustive. It would be unnecessary, impractical and perhaps impossible to have it otherwise.

Moreover, it is clear that Article 3 is made subject to the previous article. It is important to read the two articles in conjunction for it then becomes obvious that this is a two-stage process, governed by Article 2 and supplemented by Article 3.

The Council will of course weigh all the circumstances of a particular act or use of armed force as it sees fit. The process of determination would be as follows: first, with the aid of this non-exhaustive list as a guideline, the Council would examine the particular act in question. If the act fell within one of the five categories the Council's deliberations would be substantially simplified. Whether it did or not, however, by virtue of Article 2, the act would still constitute only *prima facie* evidence of aggression. The Council would then broaden the scope of its inquiry into the other relevant circumstances in order to arrive at a final determination. The conclusion to be drawn then is that this list is intended to be an aid, albeit an important one. It is not necessary that one of the five categories be automatically applied to any situation which arises without further inquiry. It may well be, of course, that the Council could decide upon a course other than a determination of an act of aggression, for example, with a view to encouraging the parties to seek a peaceful settlement of their differences.

The wording of Article 3(d) might possibly be interpreted sufficiently widely to include enforcement measures taken by a coastal state, perhaps even within its territorial sea, but certainly within an economic or fishing zone, even if these measures related to fisheries or pollution control. The Canadian Delegation placed on record its understanding that nothing in this definition, and in particular Article 3(d) shall be construed as in any way prejudicing or diminishing the authority of a coastal state to exercise its rights in maritime zones within the limits of its national jurisdiction.

Paragraphs (f) and (g) describe situations which have long been a source of international tension and conflict yet which fall short of what has traditionally been thought of as acts of aggression, at least when we equate this concept with acts of war.

Paragraph (f) addresses itself to the situation wherein one state allows its territory to be used to further the aggressive purposes of another state against a third. This is an important aspect of the problem of aggression and one which should be recognized.

Nevertheless, this criterion should be applied with caution. It should be remembered that the knowledge or control which states may have regarding the improper use of their territory may vary considerably. Such a state may be more offended against than offending, a variable which will have to be carefully examined in every case.

Paragraph (g) provides further elaboration on the idea of indirect aggression. The inclusion of this paragraph is an indication of the acceptance of the thesis that the distinction between direct and indirect aggression is artificial. The determining factor should be the degree of force used and the degree of responsibility which can be attributed to the state rather than the means or modalities by which that force is used. This paragraph represents a recognition of the fact that aggression which is perpetrated under the guise of a third or intermediary agent is just as much an act of aggression as an outright attack by one state on another. It attempts to outlaw one aspect of the serious problem of terrorism which starkly confronts the international community. It is true that terroristic acts may be of a relatively limited nature. It is equally true that they may be of such magnitude as to leave no doubt of their intent and purpose and thereby constitute an act of aggression as harmful and offensive as any other.

The acquiescence in or indeed encouragement by one state of attacks of armed bands against a second state is rejected by the world community in this paragraph. State complicity in acts of international terrorism is a problem with which the world community has yet to come to grips. This paragraph is an encouraging sign of movement in the right direction. ...

Article 5

While the first paragraph of this article is perhaps a truism, the second is of value in that it makes reference to international law and in particular affirms the continuing validity of the principles of the Nuremberg Charter and the Declaration of Friendly Relations.

The last paragraph is a necessary corollary to the fact of the illegality of aggression in that it stipulates the fruits of aggression will not be recognized. While this paragraph singles out territorial acquisition as a harmful effect of aggression, there are many others including loss of life and destruction of property and institutions which are equally opprobrious. ...

Article 7

The seventh article was the subject of considerable controversy in the Special Committee. As it provides that the right of self-determination, freedom and independence will not be prejudiced by the definition, equal emphasis must be given to the proposition that Article 7 be interpreted subject to the Charter of the U.N.

Canada supports people engaged in the struggle for self-determination and human dignity. However, the settlement of such political conflicts need not be accomplished by violent means. The reference to struggle must mean struggle by peaceful means and not one which condones the use of force contrary to the provisions of the Charter. Furthermore, the article must not be interpreted as endorsing assault on the territorial integrity of any state or condoning the dismemberment of any state by violent means. ·

Recent events may serve to make us hopeful that this article will be of limited application in the future. However, it represents a recognition that the definition cannot be applied in a manner which would detract from the rights of peoples under colonial domination to self-determination in accordance with the Charter.

NOTES

1) The search for a generally acceptable definition of aggression was begun by the United Nations over 50 years ago, and was continued intermittently since then by the International Law Commission (ILC) and four U.N. Special Committees. The ILC first presented to the U.N. General Assembly a Draft Code of Offences (now called "Crimes") in 1954.[34] It was primarily concerned with aggression and intervention but failed to be adopted because of lack of agreement at the time on a definition of aggression and problems closely related to it.[35] The current Draft Code was presented to the U.N. General

---

34   In U.N. GA Res. 177(II) UN GAOR, 2d Sess., Supp. No. 1, U.N. Doc. A/519 (1947) at III, the U.N. General Assembly directed the newly formed ILC to (1) formulate the principles of international law recognized in the Charter of the Nuremberg Tribunal and in the Judgment of the Tribunal and (2) prepare a draft code of offences against the peace and security of mankind. The Draft Code may be found in UN GAOR 9th Sess., Supp. No. 9, U.N. Doc. A/2693 (1954) at 11.

35   The General Assembly, in resolution 897(IX) of December 4, 1954, because of these problems and the fact that a Special Committee had been entrusted with defining aggression, decided to postpone consideration of the Draft Code until the Special Committee had submitted its report. Even though that

Assembly for consideration in 1996. It is reproduced and discussed in Chapter 11 on "International Criminal Law," Section A.3. The definition of aggression provided in what became General Assembly resolution 3314 was drafted by the 35-member U.N. Special Committee on the Question of Defining Aggression that was established in 1967 with a membership chosen to reflect the principal legal system and geographical areas of the world.

2) Because the final result is a product of compromise, of necessity it contains elements that some U.N. members would have preferred to see omitted and does not go as far in other areas as some members had hoped; nevertheless, it received approval by consensus without a formal vote. (A decision is reached by consensus when no state objects to it formally. There is still a consensus when negative views are put on the record before or after the decision is taken but without a formal objection being raised.)

3) As Canada had insisted upon at the outset, the definition as drafted does not purport in any way to limit the primary responsibility of the Security Council for the maintenance of international peace and security pursuant to article 24 of the U.N. Charter, nor does it purport to fetter the ultimate discretion of the Security Council in determining under article 39 of the Charter whether an act of aggression has been committed in a particular instance. However, the definition serves as a useful guide to the Security Council, when it has to decide under article 39 of the Charter whether the direct or indirect use of armed force by a state has been such as to constitute an illegal use of force in contravention of the Charter. For consideration of the crime of aggression by an individual as included in the ILC's Draft Code of Crimes Against the Peace and Security of Mankind and its inclusion in article 5 of the 1998 Rome Statute on the ICC, see Chapter 11, "International Criminal Law," Sections A.3 and C.

4) Acts of intervention and aggression are illegal *per se*. States have not sought to justify their actions by stating that there is no rule or rules to prohibit their conduct; rather, they have tried to bring what has occurred within the legitimate exceptions that are recognized.

5) According to the ICJ in the *Nicaragua* case, reproduced above in this section, the term "armed attack" in article 51 is considerably more narrow than the concept of "use of force" in article 2(4). The Court's approach to the distinction, which remains controversial, has important implications. In particular, the ICJ concluded that the right to use armed force in self-defence was triggered only by uses of force that, due to their gravity, amounted to "armed attacks," and not by "less grave forms of the use of force."[36] The Court confirmed this view in its decision in the *Case Concerning Oil Platforms (Islamic Republic of Iran v. United States of America)*.[37] Do you agree that states should not be entitled to take defensive military countermeasures against such smaller-scale uses of force? Compare Articles 49–54 of the ILC's Draft Articles on the Law of State Responsibility, reproduced in Chapter 10, Section D.2 on "Countermeasures." Compare

---

report resulted in the 1974 *Definition of Aggression*, it took until December 19, 1981 for the General Assembly, by resolution 36/106, to invite the Commission to resume its work. See S.A. Williams, "The Draft Code of Offences Against the Peace and Security of Mankind," in M.C. Bassiouni, ed., *International Criminal Law* (1986) vol. I 109; also B. Ferencz, *An International Criminal Court—A Step Towards World Peace* (1980) 2 vols. and M.C. Bassiouni, *Draft Statute*, Ass. Int. Dr. Pénal, N. 9 (1992).

36 *Nicaragua* case, *supra* note 17 at paras. 191, 195.

37 Judgement of 6 November 2003, online: <www.icj-cij.org> at paras. 51, 64.

also the Dissenting Opinion of Judge Sir Robert Jennings in the *Nicaragua* case, and the Separate Opinion of Judge Simma in the *Case Concerning Oil Platforms*.[38]

6) In the *Nicaragua* case the ICJ thus highlights the need to define the scope of the interrelated norms prohibiting intervention, use of force, and armed attacks. One particularly important set of questions in this context is the following: when do various forms of state assistance to and involvement in armed activities undertaken by irregular forces amount to violation of the non-intervention principle and when do they violate the prohibition on the threat or use of force? And at what point do such forms of support amount to an "armed attack," entitling a victim state to resort to force in self-defence? What answers does the ICJ provide to these questions? Do you agree with the Court's approach? See further in Section B.1, below.

Arms Control

While this chapter is concerned with states' right to resort to military force (*jus ad bellum*), it should be noted that international law also places restrictions on the means by which war is conducted (*jus in bello*). *Jus in bello* encompasses international humanitarian law, discussed in Chapter 11. Further limitations flow from treaty-based efforts to promote disarmament and restrict the use of certain types of weapons.

From the beginning of the United Nations, disarmament, particularly nuclear disarmament, has been the major and a continuing preoccupation of the world organization. The very first resolution adopted by the General Assembly on January 24, 1946 called for the "elimination from national armaments of atomic weapons and of all other major weapons adaptable to mass destruction." That resolution, as well as many that followed, failed to prevent what eventually came to be known as the nuclear arms race. Owing to Great Power disagreements, more than 40 years since the first use of an atomic weapon at Hiroshima there has been virtually no progress toward nuclear disarmament. However, during that period some 20 multilateral and bilateral arms regulation agreements have been concluded, including the 1963 Limited Nuclear Test Ban Treaty, the 1967 Treaty of Tlatelolco (creating a nuclear-free zone in Latin America), the Outer Space Treaty of 1967, the 1968 Treaty on the Non-Proliferation of Nuclear Weapons, and the 1972 U.S.-U.S.S.R. bilateral treaty limiting the acquisition of anti-ballistic missile systems (the ABM Treaty).[39]

The dramatic easing of tension between the Soviet Union and the United States led in 1987 to the conclusion of the Treaty on the Elimination of Their Intermediate-Range and Shorter-Range Missiles (INF Treaty).[40] The subsequent demise of Communism in the U.S.S.R. and Eastern Europe produced additional important disarmament agreements in

---

38   *Nicaragua* case, *supra* note 17 at 543-44, Jennings J., dissenting.; *ibid.* at paras. 12-13, Simma J., separate opinion. See also Section B.1 on "The Right of Self-Defence."

39   480 U.N.T.S. 281; Can. T.S. 1964 No. 1; (1963) 2 I.L.M. 889; 634 U.N.T.S. 281; (1967) 6 I.L.M. 521; 610 U.N.T.S. 205; Can. T.S. 1967 No. 19; 729 U.N.T.S. 161, Can. T.S. 1970 No. 7; (1968) 7 I.L.M. 811; and 23 U.S.T. 3435; T.I.A.S. No. 7503; (1972) 11 I.L.M. 784, respectively.

40   (1998) 27 I.L.M. 84.

quick succession: the Treaty on Conventional Forces in Europe in 1990, the Strategic Arms Reduction Treaty (START I) in 1991, the Open Skies Treaty in 1992, and the START II Treaty and the Chemical Weapons Convention in 1993.[41] The pace of agreement of new disarmament treaties slowed in the second half of the 1990s, which were marked most notably by the conclusion and ratification, in quick succession, of the Landmines Convention and the achievement of the Comprehensive Nuclear Test Ban Treaty,[42] even though it has yet to come into force.

Post-war disarmament negotiations have been held in various forums, with varying numbers of participating states. Some of the most important arms limitation agreements have been concluded through bilateral—for example, the ABM Treaty—and trilateral negotiations—for example, the Limited Test Ban Treaty—while the United Nations continues to provide the principal forum for multilateral debates. Currently, the main worldwide negotiating body for arms control is the Conference on Disarmament (CD), created in 1978. The CD is composed of eight nuclear-weapon states and 56 other states representing all regions of the world. Although formally not a U.N. body, the CD reports annually to the U.N. General Assembly and is guided in its work by relevant General Assembly resolutions. Since its establishment, the CD has dealt with issues such as a ban on chemical and radiological weapons, arms control in outer space, and nuclear arms control. The progress of its work has been slow, but it has seen the birth of the Chemical Weapons Convention and the Comprehensive Nuclear Test Ban Treaty.

With respect to the question of the legality of nuclear weapons it should be noted that it has two aspects—one concerning their possession and the other concerning their use. On the question of first use of nuclear weapons, a fairly widespread view seems to be that the state initiating a nuclear exchange would act in violation of international law. First use (some would say any use, even in retaliation) would clearly violate the well-established principles of the laws of war. In their rhetoric, at least, all nuclear weapons states have repeatedly expressed abhorrence of these weapons and declared the total elimination of nuclear arsenals as a high-priority national goal. However, whereas two nuclear weapon states (the Russian Federation and China) have publicly and unconditionally renounced the first use of nuclear weapons, the United States and its NATO allies do not exclude first use in the event of aggression in Europe. The legality of possessing nuclear weapons, in the absence of any explicit prohibition by treaty, presents a more difficult question. Probably the predominant view among lawyers is that nuclear weapons are legal. That view is supported by legal and practical arguments, including the assumption that a state is free to do whatever it is not explicitly forbidden to do; the belief that nuclear weapons provide the most effective defence against aggression and have been largely responsible for preventing the outbreak of a major war; and the fact of a wide acceptance of nuclear weapons so that they are usually discussed in the context of disarmament rather than of illegality.

---

41   (1991) 30 I.L.M. 6; online: <www.state.gov/t/ac/trt/18535.htm>; Can. T.S. 2002 No. 3; online: <www.ceip.org/files/projects/npp/resources/start2text.htm>; and 1974 U.N.T.S. 45, 317, Can. T.S. 1997 No. 44; (1993) 32 I.L.M. 800, respectively.

42   2056 U.N.T.S. 211; Can. T.S. 1999 No. 4; (1997) 36 I.L.M. 1507; and (1996) 35 I.L.M. 1439, respectively.

On the second question—concerning the use of nuclear weapons—the ICJ has been asked for an advisory opinion on two occasions. The World Health Organization (WHO) presented the first request, but the Court in *Legality of the Use by a State of Nuclear Weapons in Armed Conflict*[43] determined that WHO lacked the constitutional authority to ask the question posed. The case is discussed in Chapter 6, Section D.3 on "Decisions of the Court" under "Advisory Opinions." Shortly afterward, the U.N. General Assembly made a similar request. It asked for an advisory opinion on the question: Is the threat or use of nuclear weapons in any circumstance permitted under international law? See *Legality of the Threat or Use of Nuclear Weapons Case*, reproduced in Chapter 6, Section D.3.[44]

B. JUSTIFICATIONS FOR THE USE OF FORCE

Excuses for Intervention
from S.A. Williams and A.L.C. de Mestral, *An Introduction to International Law* 2d ed. (1987) 48-50 (footnotes omitted)

There are several exceptional cases in which there may be legitimate intervention. First is the case of collective intervention by enforcement action under the authority of the Security Council of the United Nations pursuant to Chapter VII of the Charter, or possibly sanctioned by the General Assembly under the Uniting for Peace Resolution of November 3, 1950. Otherwise, the United Nations is prohibited under article 2(7) from intervening. It has been argued, however, that mere discussion and placing an item on the agenda of a United Nations organ does not constitute intervention.

Second, but more controversial and debatable is where a state seeks to protect the rights and personal safety of its nationals who are in the state in which it proposes to intervene. An example of this would be the Israeli intervention at Entebbe Airport in Uganda in 1976 to rescue the Israeli hostages held there by terrorists with the alleged complicity of the Ugandan Government. The essential features are the necessity of intervention on account of the imminent danger; no other recourse open for protection and proportionality in the action taken. It is necessarily very much a subjective decision by the intervening state and is open to abuse.

A third exception is the case of individual or collective self-defence, where intervention is found to be necessary to repel the danger of armed attack: Article 51 of the U.N. Charter recognizes the right of self-defence "if an armed attack occurs ... until the Security Council has taken measures necessary to maintain international peace and security." Disagreement has been voiced over the wording. ...

Fourth is the case of one state acting in the affairs of a protectorate state which it is obligated to assist usually under a treaty.

---

43   [1996] I.C.J. Rep. 66.

44   For commentary on the case, see the references in Chapter 6, note 151.

Fifth, an exception lies where the state intervened in has committed a gross breach of international law against the intervening state. This principle has been extended by some to cover situations of so-called humanitarian intervention, where a state treats its people in a substandard way, such that they are denied their fundamental human rights. It is argued that if such states do not reform their ways after international protests, by ameliorating human conditions within their territory, then humanitarian considerations out-weigh the reasons against intervention. One interpretation of this is that where there is no personal and selfish motive on the part of the intervening states, there can be justification. This is acutely controversial and it could easily be used as an excuse for meddling in the affairs of another state.

Sixth is the case where the lawful government of the state intervened in has invited the intervention, although the invitation must be genuine and real. It may be necessary in such a situation to divine the motives of the intervenors. In the case of internal strife, an invitation by the government cannot justify intervention, as when the outcome of the domestic war is doubtful, the government cannot hold itself out to speak for the state. On the other hand, if a civil war or civil strife has been aided by subversive help from another outside state, the government does have a legitimate right to ask for help.

1. The Right of Self-Defence[45]

United Nations Charter
Article 51
Reproduced in the Documentary Supplement

In the *Nicaragua* case, reproduced above in Section A, the ICJ affirmed that a customary international law right to self-defence exists alongside article 51. But note that the text of article 51 is more limited in its scope than the right granted under customary law, which raises a number of significant questions. Which differences are highlighted in the *Nicaragua* case? Must article 51 be interpreted literally and the right of self-defence restricted to cases of "armed attack"? Must such an armed attack emanate from another state to trigger the right to self-defence? Must article 51 be read to mean if and only if an armed attack occurs? What has happened to the customary law rule of pre-emptive self-defence? Has it survived the Charter? Has an even broader right to self-defence emerged in the aftermath of the terrorist attacks of September 11, 2001? These and other questions are explored in this section.

---

45   See, generally, Bowett, *Self-Defence*, *supra* note 2; Dinstein, *supra* note 2; O. Schachter, "Self-Defence and the Rule of Law" (1989) 83 A.J.I.L. 259; and Macdonald, *supra* note 17 at 143.

The Legality of Anticipatory Self-Defence and Preventive Strikes

The Caroline
United Kingdom v. United States
(1837), 2 Moore 409

[The 1837 Canadian Rebellion found active support from volunteers in the United States. These volunteers joined with the rebels and encamped on Navy Island and the Chippewa Channel in Canadian waters. From there this force raided the Canadian riverside and British ships. The U.S. authorities knew of these activities but did not stop them. The ship *Caroline* was involved in supplying men and materials to Navy Island. On December 29-30, 1837, the British seized the *Caroline*, which was docked at Fort Schlosser on the U.S. side. They set her alight and sent her over Niagara Falls. Two U.S. citizens were killed. This action was discussed in correspondence between the British and United States Governments, when the British sought to obtain the release of one McLeod, a British subject who had been arrested on charges of murder and arson.]

MR. WEBSTER to Mr. Fox (April 24, 1841): ... It will be for ... [Her Majesty's] Government to show a necessity of self-defence, instant, over-whelming, leaving no choice of means, and no moment for deliberation. It will be for it to show, also, that the local authorities of Canada, even supposing the necessity of the moment authorized them to enter the territories of the United States at all, did nothing unreasonable or excessive; since the act, justified by the necessity of self-defence, must be limited by that necessity, and kept clearly within it. It must be shown that admonition or remonstrance to the persons on board the Caroline was impracticable, or would have been unavailing; it must be shown that day-light could not be waited for; that there could be no attempt at discrimination between the innocent and the guilty; that it would not have been enough to seize and detain the vessel; but that there was a necessity, present and inevitable, for attacking her in the darkness of the night, while moored to the shore, and while unarmed men were asleep on board, killing some and wounding others, and then drawing her into the current, above the cataract, setting her on fire, and, careless to know whether there might not be in her the innocent with the guilty, or the living with the dead, committing her to a fate which fills the imagination with horror. A necessity for all this, the Government of the United States cannot believe to have existed.

LORD ASHBURTON to Mr. Webster (July 28, 1842): ... It is so far satisfactory to perceive that we are perfectly agreed as to the general principles of international law applicable to this unfortunate case. Respect for the inviolable character of the territory of independent nations is the most essential foundation of civilization.

NOTES

1) Clearly, the U.S. Government accepted the justification of self-defence. The British argued that what had been done was out of the necessity of self-preservation. There was, it was stated, a danger of future threats. However, on the facts as it saw them, the United States rejected the plea. This incident was the first apparent recognition internationally of pre-emptive (or "anticipatory") self-defence. To be legitimate, self-defence must not only be born out of necessity, it must also be proportionate to the harm to be countered. Note in this context that the ICJ held in its Advisory Opinion on the *Legality of the Threat or Use of Nuclear Weapons* case[46] that the dual condition of necessity and proportionality, well-established in customary international law, applies equally to article 51 of the U.N. Charter, whatever the means of force employed.

2) Judge Schwebel, the U.S. judge on the ICJ, stated in his dissenting opinion in the *Nicaragua* case[47] that he did not agree with construing article 51 of the U.N. Charter as if it were worded: "Nothing in the present Charter shall impair the inherent right of individual or collective self-defence, if and only if, an armed attack occurs." He was of the view that the wording and intent of article 51 do not eliminate the right of self-defence under customary international law or confine its overall scope to the expression of article 51. The Court itself stated that its judgment did not address the question of anticipatory self-defence.[48] There continues to be debate on whether or not a customary international law right to anticipatory self-defence has survived the advent of the Charter and its article 51.[49] See also paras. 188 and 192 in the report of the U.N. High-level Panel on Threats, Challenges, and Change, reproduced below in this section. What is the legal impact, if any, of these statements?

3) Although article 2 of the Definition of Aggression, reproduced above in Section A, states that: "The first use of armed force by a state in contravention of the Charter shall constitute *prima facie* evidence of an act of aggression," it qualifies this presumption in the face of "other relevant circumstances."[50]

---

46   *Supra* note 43.

47   *Nicaragua* case, *supra* note 17 at 347, Schwebel J. dissenting.

48   *Ibid.* at para 194.

49   See *e.g.* Jutta Brunnée and Stephen J. Toope, "The Use of Force: International Law After Iraq" (October 2004) 53 I.C.L.Q. 785 at 792; M. Byers, "Preemptive Self-defense: Hegemony, Equality, and Strategies of Legal Change" (2003) vol. 11 no. 2 J. of Pol. Phil. 171 at 180.

50   See also the Comments by the Canadian Delegation on article 2 in the previous subsection.

Nuremberg War Crimes Trials
(1947), 1 Trial of the Major War Criminals 171 at 206-9

[The following extract is taken from the Final Judgment of the International Military Tribunal (IMT) at Nuremberg. The 22 defendants, the major war criminals whose crimes had no exact geographical location, were indicted with crimes against peace, war crimes, and crimes against humanity. They were also charged with participating in the formulation or execution of a common plan or conspiring to commit all these crimes. The Tribunal held that to initiate a war of aggression is the supreme international crime. It further held that under article 6 of the Charter of the IMT that there was individual responsibility for such offences.][51]

THE TRIBUNAL: On the 1st March, Hitler issued a directive regarding the Weser Exercise which contained the words:

> The development of the situation in Scandinavia requires the making of all preparations for the occupation of Denmark and Norway by a part of the German Armed Forces. This operation should prevent British encroachment on Scandinavia and the Baltic; further, it should guarantee our own base in Sweden and give our Navy and Air Force a wider start line against Britain. ... The crossing of the Danish border and the landings in Norway must take place simultaneously. ... It is most important that the Scandinavian States as well as the Western opponents should be taken by surprise by our measures.

On the 24th March the naval operation orders for the Weser Exercise were issued, and on the 30th March the defendant Doenitz as Commander in Chief of U-boats issued his operational order for the occupation of Denmark and Norway. On the 9th April 1940, the German forces invaded Norway and Denmark.

... [I]t is clear that as early as October 1939 the question of invading Norway was under consideration. The defense that has been made here is that Germany was compelled to attack Norway to forestall an Allied invasion, and her action was therefore preventive.

It must be remembered that preventive action in foreign territory is justified only in case of "an instant and overwhelming necessity for self-defense, leaving no choice of means and no moment of deliberation." ("The Caroline Case," *Moore's Digest of International Law*, Vol. II, at 412). How widely the view was held in influential German circles that the Allies intended to occupy Norway cannot be determined with exactitude. Quisling asserted that the Allies would intervene in Norway with the tacit consent of the Norwegian Government. The German Legation at Oslo disagreed with this view, although the Naval Attaché at that Legation shared it.

... [I]t is clear that when the plans for an attack on Norway were being made, they were not made for the purpose of forestalling an imminent Allied landing, but, at the most, that they might prevent an Allied occupation at some future date.

---

51   See Chapter 11, Section A.1 on "Individual Responsibility after World War II" for this portion of the case.

When the final orders for the German invasion of Norway were given, the diary of the Naval Operations Staff for 23 March, 1940 records:

A mass encroachment by the English into Norwegian territorial waters ... is not to be expected at the present time.

And Admiral Assmann's entry 26 March says:

British landing in Norway not considered serious.

It was further argued that Germany alone could decide, in accordance with the reservations made by many of the Signatory Powers at the time of the conclusion of the Kellogg-Briand Pact, whether preventive action was a necessity, and that in making her decision her judgment was conclusive. But whether action taken under the claim of self-defense was in fact aggressive or defensive must ultimately be subject to investigation and adjudication if international law is ever to be enforced.

In the light of all the available evidence it is impossible to accept the contention that the invasions of Denmark and Norway were defensive, and in the opinion of the Tribunal they were acts of aggressive war.

Israeli Attack on Iraqi Nuclear Research Centre

Security Council Debate
June 12, 1981, U.N. Doc., S/PV 2280, reprinted in (1981) 20 I.L.M. 965

[On Sunday, June 7, 1981, at 6:37 p.m. local time in Iraq, Israeli military aircraft flew over Iraq and bombed the nuclear installation situated near Baghdad. Iraq asserted this was an act of aggression, while Israel claimed that it was an act of self-preservation. Here is an excerpt from the Security Council's debate[52] followed by other materials from its reports:]

MR. HAMMADI (Iraq): Mr. President, allow me first to express to you, and through you to the members of the Security Council, my gratitude for convening this meeting and for giving me the opportunity to address the Council on the question of the flagrant act of aggression committed by Israel against Iraq.

On Sunday, 7 June 1981, at 1837 hours Baghdad local time, Israeli war-planes raided the nuclear installations situated near Baghdad, causing many civilian casualties and much material damage. The Zionist aggressors announced on the following day their responsibility for the attack, brazenly claiming the total destruction of the installations. ...

MR. BLUM (Israel): ... On Sunday, 7 June 1981, the Israeli Air Force carried out an operation against the Iraqi reactor called "Osiraq." That reactor was in its final stages

---

52   Also note R.A. Friedlander, "Might Can Also Be Right: The Israeli Nuclear Reactor Bombing and International Law" (1980) 28 Chitty's L.J. 352.

of construction near Baghdad. The pilots' mission was to destroy it. They executed their mission successfully.

In destroying Osiraq, Israel performed an elementary act of self-preservation, both morally and legally. In so doing, Israel was exercising its inherent right of self-defence as understood in general international law and as preserved in Article 51 of the United Nations Charter.

A threat of nuclear obliteration was being developed against Israel by Iraq, one of Israel's most implacable enemies. Israel tried to have that threat halted by diplomatic means. Our efforts bore no fruit. Ultimately we were left with no choice. We were obliged to remove that mortal danger. We did it cleanly and effectively. The Middle East has become a safer place. We trust that the international community has also been given pause to make the world a safer place. ...

[Meanwhile, the International Atomic Energy Agency (IAEA) passed a resolution[53] in which it condemned Israel for "this premeditated and unjustified attack" on the Iraqi nuclear research centre and recommended the suspension of technical assistance to Israel by the Agency. It also recommended that the U.N. General Assembly consider Israel's membership to the United Nations and it reminded states of the U.N. resolution calling for an end to the transfer of nuclear materials and technology to Israel. This IAEA resolution was communicated to the Security Council, which noted it in the preamble to the following resolution of its own.]

Security Council Resolution 487 (1981)[54]
U.N. Doc. S/RES/487, June 19, 1981

The Security Council ...

Fully aware of the fact that Iraq has been a party to the Treaty on the Non-Proliferation of Nuclear Weapons since it came into force in 1970, that in accordance with that Treaty Iraq has accepted Agency safeguards on all its nuclear activities, and that the Agency has testified that these safeguards have been satisfactorily applied to date,

Noting furthermore that Israel has not adhered to the non-proliferation Treaty on Non-Proliferation of Nuclear Weapons,

Deeply concerned about the danger to international peace and security created by the premeditated Israeli air attack on Iraqi nuclear installations on 7 June 1981, which could at any time explode the situation in the area, with grave consequences for the vital interests of all States,

---

53   UN SCOR, 36th year, Supp. (January-March, 1981) 64; U.N. Doc. S/14532 of June 15, 1981. The Board of Governors adopted the resolution by a vote of 29 in favour to 2 against (Canada, United States) with 3 abstentions (Australia, Sweden, and Switzerland).

54   Adopted unanimously, June 19, 1981.

Considering that, under the terms of Article 2, paragraph 4, of the Charter of the United Nations: "All Members shall refrain in their international relations from the threat or use of force against the international integrity or political independence of any State, or in any other manner inconsistent with the purposes of the United Nations,"

1. *Strongly condemns* the military attack by Israel in clear violation of the Charter of the United Nations and the norms of international conduct;

2. *Calls upon* Israel to refrain in the future from any such acts or threats thereof;

3. *Further considers* that the said attack constitutes a serious threat to the entire safeguards regime of the International Atomic Energy Agency, which is the foundation of the Treaty on the Non-Proliferation of Nuclear Weapons;

4. *Fully recognizes* the inalienable sovereign right of Iraq, and all other States, especially the developing countries, to establish programmes of technological and nuclear development to develop their economy and industry for peaceful purposes in accordance with their present and future needs and consistent with the internationally accepted objectives of preventing nuclear-weapons proliferation;

5. *Calls upon* Israel urgently to place its nuclear facilities under the safeguards of the International Atomic Energy Agency;

6. *Considers* that Iraq is entitled to appropriate redress for the destruction it has suffered, responsibility for which has been acknowledged by Israel;

7. *Requests* the Secretary-General to keep the Security Council regularly informed of the implementation of the present resolution.

NOTES

1) What was the relevance to this incident of the fact that Iraq, according to Mr. Blum, had been in a state of war with Israel since 1948?

2) In the Security Council debate,[55] Mr. Blum argued that the Israeli Government had the right to protect the lives of Israeli citizens. In doing so it was exercising its inherent right under article 51 of the Charter. Note the following details provided by Mr. Blum: the strike was on a Sunday, late in the day, and the loss of life was minimal. What is their relevance?

3) Why do you think the Security Council voted unanimously against Israel? Note that Iraq was a party to the Non-Proliferation Treaty[56] and had accepted IAEA safeguards. Israel had not. The United States, through its ambassador, Ms. Kirkpatrick, stated after the vote that the United States was of the view that the Israelis only violated the U.N. Charter because Israel had not exhausted peaceful means for the resolution of the dispute.[57] Note that the United States and Canada had voted against the IAEA Resolution.

4) The Canadian view on the legality of the "first strike" was presented in a memorandum of November 27, 1981 from the Legal Bureau of the Department of External Affairs.[58] It stated:

---

55   U.N. Doc. S/PV 2280, June 12, 1981 at 37-60.

56   729 U.N.T.S. 16; Can. T.S. 1970 No. 7; (1968) 7 I.L.M. 811.

57   See U.N. Doc. S/PV, 2288. June 19, 1981 at 58-73.

58   (1982) 20 Can. Y.B. Int'l L. 303.

The basic rules pertaining to the use of force by States are laid down in Art. 2(4) and Art. 51 of the United Nations Charter. The first one prohibits the use of force, including the threat of such use, against any State, whereas the second rule, as an exception to the first one, declares that every State has an "inherent right" to use force "if an armed attack occurs against it." The use of armed force would thus appear confined to situations where it is necessary to repel actual aggression as defined by examples in Art. 3 of the U.N.G.A. resolution No. 2625 XXV of December 14, 1974. In all other circumstances States would have an obligation to resort to pacific means of settlement of international disputes according to Art. 2(3) and Chapter VI of the U.N. Charter, unless the U.N. Security Council decides otherwise.

It is, however, well known that modern weapons in possession of some States, much more powerful than others, as well as the exercise of the veto power within the U.N. Security Council, have both significantly modified the conditions in which resort could be made to the right of self-defence based on Art. 51 of the Charter. In practical terms, no help would be expected by some States from the United Nations, while the use of rapid and all-destructive weapons leaves no room for awaiting of an attack, if the concept of self-defence is to serve its original purpose.

Some States and some writers are therefore favourable to that traditional concept (which fell from respect) that anticipatory self-defence is permissible under international law, although this view is vigorously disputed by others. In the opinion of the former, Art. 51 of the Charter cannot be interpreted so as to prevent a State from acting in its own defence. It would therefore be permitted to engage in anticipatory "attack in self-defence" if:

— an armed aggression is imminent according to clear evidence based on the facts;

— this armed aggression, if allowed to happen, might put in jeopardy the existence of the victim-State (as opposed to inflicting even serious damages).

The proof of the necessity of such self-preservation falls on the State that accomplishes the "first-strike" action. Such an occurrence would only be conceivable in the case of the small State, from the point of view of which no effective self-defence is possible after the moment of a massive armed attack by a more powerful neighbour or an over-whelming coalition of other States. This conclusion appears at least indirectly supported by the terms of Art. 2 of the aforementioned U.N.G.A. resolution on Definition on Aggression: "The first use of armed force by a State in contravention of the Charter shall constitute *prima facie* evidence of an act of aggression although the Security Council may, in conformity with the Charter, conclude that a determination that an act of aggression has been committed would not be justified in the light of other relevant circumstances."

5) The assertion of self-defence to justify the Cuban Quarantine[59] raises a number of interesting issues. On October 22, 1962, an announcement was made by President Kennedy that the United States intended to carry out a strictly imposed quarantine on all

---

59   As to the Cuban Quarantine, see L.C. Meeker, "Defensive Quarantine and the Law" (1963) 57 A.J.I.L. 515 and Q. Wright, "The Cuban Quarantine" (1963) A.J.I.L. 546. And see generally A. Chayes, *The Cuban Missile Crisis* (1974).

offensive military weapons and materials being shipped to Cuba. The U.N. Security Council took no action. The Council of the OAS adopted a resolution[60] that recommended that its member states in accordance with articles 6 and 8 of the Rio Treaty[61] should take all individual and collective measures, including the armed force deemed necessary, to prevent Cuba from continuing to receive military material from the Sino-Soviet powers. The resolution states that such supplies would threaten the peace and security of the continent. By such a quarantine, the Cuban missiles were prevented from becoming an active threat.

Was this quarantine and the resulting interceptions of two ships (one a U.S.S.R. tanker and one a foreign ship under charter to the U.S.S.R.) on the high seas justifiable, or were they acts of aggression? Was the quarantine in breach of article 2(4) of the U.N. Charter? Was it justifiable under Chapter VIII of the U.N. Charter concerning Regional Arrangements?[62] See also below, Section D on "The United Nations and Regional Arrangements."

6) Retortion is a form of self-help open to a state in reply to an injury done to it by another state. This injury may be caused by lawful or unlawful acts. Retortion is a legal but unfriendly act. The classic examples are the severing of diplomatic relations and the cutting off of economic aid.

Reprisals or countermeasures differ from acts of retortion in that they are illegal acts, done in retaliation and not self-defence.[63] Since the inception of the United Nations the customary international law right to reprisal has been curtailed by articles 2(4) and 51 of the Charter. However, it has been argued that countermeasures short of force may still be taken legitimately.[64] Refer to Chapter 10, Section D.2 on "Countermeasures."

7) In 1981 the United States sent U.S. Navy jet fighters across the line proclaimed by Libya as marking the baseline from which the territorial waters of Libya would be measured. Waters behind the line would be internal. The United States stated that they were asserting internationally accepted rights as the line drawn across the Gulf of Sidra some 130 miles from the Libyan coast was in violation of international law. See Chapter 13, Section B.1 on "Territorial Sea." The U.S. fighters shot down two Libyan planes after one attacked them. Was this a case of self-defence by the United States? Was it provocation? Again in March 1986 the United States crossed the "line of death" as proclaimed by Muammar Gaddafi. It sent part of the U.S. 6th Fleet and responded to a missile attack by Libya by sinking at least three Libyan boats, and hitting a shore battery. Was the United States acting in an acceptable way? Further, was the subsequent U.S. action in bombing certain "strategic targets" in Libya justifiable on account of Libya's alleged part in encouraging international terrorism and thus complicity in an international

---

60   (1962) 47 U.S. Dept. of State Bull. 734.

61   The Inter-American Treaty of Reciprocal Assistance (1947) 21 U.N.T.S. 93.

62   See D. Acheson, "Comments" (1963) 57 A.S.I.L. Proc. 13.

63   See the *Naulilaa Case* (*Portugal v. Germany*) (1928), 2 R.I.A.A. 1011.

64   See Shaw, *supra* note 3 at 1023. See also on this matter D. Bowett, "Economic Coercion and Reprisals by States" (1972) 13 Va. J. Int. L. 1 and R. Lillich, ed., *Economic Coercion and the New International Economic Order* (1976) 73.

crime? Were these actions of the United States taken in self-defence, pre-emptive self-defence, or as a countermeasure?[65]

National Security Strategy of the United States of America
US Policy Document (September 2002) at 13, 15-16.

[N]ew deadly challenges have emerged from rogue states and terrorists. ... [T]he nature and motivations of these new adversaries, their determination to obtain destructive powers hitherto available only to the world's strongest states, and the greater likelihood that they will use weapons of mass destruction against us, make today's security environment more complex and dangerous. ...

It has taken almost a decade for us to comprehend the true nature of this new threat. Given the goals of rogue states and terrorists, the United States can no longer solely rely on a reactive posture as we have in the past. The inability to deter a potential attacker, the immediacy of today's threats, and the magnitude of potential harm that could be caused by our adversaries' choice of weapons, do not permit that option. We cannot let our enemies strike first. ...

For centuries, international law recognized that nations need not suffer an attack before they can lawfully take action to defend themselves against forces that present an imminent danger of attack. Legal scholars and international jurists often conditioned the legitimacy of preemption on the existence of an imminent threat—most often a visible mobilization of armies, navies, and air forces preparing to attack.

We must adapt the concept of imminent threat to the capabilities and objectives of today's adversaries. Rogue states and terrorists do not seek to attack us using conventional means. They know such attacks would fail. Instead, they rely on acts of terror and, potentially, the use of weapons of mass destruction—weapons that can be easily concealed, delivered covertly, and used without warning.

The targets of these attacks are our military forces and our civilian population, in direct violation of one of the principal norms of the law of warfare. As was demonstrated by the losses on September 11, 2001, mass civilian casualties is the specific objective of terrorists and these losses would be exponentially more severe if terrorists acquired and used weapons of mass destruction.

The United States has long maintained the option of preemptive actions to counter a sufficient threat to our national security. The greater the threat, the greater is the risk of inaction—and the more compelling the case for taking anticipatory action to defend ourselves, even if uncertainty remains as to the time and place of the enemy's attack. To forestall or prevent such hostile acts by our adversaries, the United States will, if necessary, act preemptively.

---

65   See G.F. Intoccia, "American Bombing of Libya: An International Legal Analysis" (1987) 19 Case W. Res. J. Int'l L. 177 and G.B. Roberts, "Self-Help Combatting State Sponsored Terrorism: Self-Defence and Peacetime Reprisals" (1987) 19 Case W. Res. J. Int'l L. 243. Compare also the ICJ's decision in the *Oil Platforms* case, referred to in Note 37, following the *Nicaragua* case excerpts in Section A above (follows Canadian comments).

The United States will not use force in all cases to preempt emerging threats, nor should nations use preemption as a pretext for aggression. Yet in an age where the enemies of civilization openly and actively seek the world's most destructive technologies, the United States cannot remain idle while dangers gather. We will always proceed deliberately, weighing the consequences of our actions. To support preemptive options, we will:

- build better, more integrated intelligence capabilities to provide timely, accurate information on threats, wherever they may emerge;
- coordinate closely with allies to form a common assessment of the most dangerous threats; and
- continue to transform our military forces to ensure our ability to conduct rapid and precise operations to achieve decisive results.

The purpose of our actions will always be to eliminate a specific threat to the United States or our allies and friends. The reasons for our actions will be clear, the force measured, and the cause just.

A More Secure World: Our Shared Responsibility
Report of the High-level Panel on Threats, Challenges, and Change,
U.N. Doc. A/59/565 (29 November 2004) at 54-55

[188] The language of [Article 51 of the U.N. Charter] is restrictive. ... However, a threatened State, according to long established international law, can take military action as long as the threatened attack is *imminent*, no other means would deflect it and the action is proportionate. The problem arises where the threat is not imminent but still claimed to be real: for example the acquisition, with allegedly hostile intent, of nuclear weapons-making capability.

[189] Can a State, without going to the Security Council, claim in these circumstances the right to act, in anticipatory self-defence, not just pre-emptively (against an imminent or proximate threat) but preventively (against a non-imminent or non-proximate one)? Those who say "yes" argue that the potential harm from some threats (e.g., terrorists armed with a nuclear weapon) is so great that one simply cannot risk waiting until they become imminent, and that less harm may be done (e.g. avoiding a nuclear exchange or radioactive fallout from reactor destruction) by acting earlier.

[190] The short answer is that if there are good arguments for preventive military action, with good evidence to support them, they should be put to the Security Council, which can authorize such action if it chooses to. If it does not so choose, there will be, by definition, time to pursue other strategies, including persuasion, negotiation, deterrence and containment—and to visit again the military option.

[191] For those impatient with such a response, the answer must be that, in a world full of perceived potential threats, the risk to global order and the norm of non-intervention on which it continues to be based is simply too great for the legality of unilateral preventive action, as distinct for collectively endorsed action, to be accepted. Allowing one to act is to allow all.

[192] We do not favour the rewriting or reinterpretation of Article 51.... .

[194] We emphasize that the concerns we expressed about the legality of the preventive use of military force in the case of self-defence under Article 51 are not applicable in the case of collective action authorized under Chapter VII. In the world of the twenty-first century, the international community does have to be concerned about nightmare scenarios combining terrorists, weapons of mass destruction and irresponsible States, ... which may conceivably justify the use of force, not just reactively but preventively and before a latent threat becomes imminent. The question is not whether such action can be taken: it can, by the Security Council as the international community's collective security voice, at any time it deems that there is a threat to international peace and security.

NOTES

1) While "anticipatory" or "pre-emptive" self-defence would presuppose an imminent threat, "preventive" self-defence would entitle a state to take military measures against potential or merely emerging threats. The legality of preventive war was forcefully rejected by the IMT in the *Nuremberg War Crimes Trials* (see earlier this section). Similarly, the responses to the Israeli bombing of the Osiraq reactor suggest that states considered preventive strikes to be beyond the scope of self-defence (see excerpts earlier in this section). However, in the aftermath of the terrorist attacks on the United States on September 11, 2001, the debate on whether purely preventive measures may be taken in self-defence has been reignited.

2) Is the U.S. National Security Strategy's goal to "preempt emerging threats" compatible with states' existing right to self-defence; is the Security Strategy proposing that international law be adjusted to meet new threats; or, is the United States asserting that it possesses special rights to defend itself?[66]

3) The U.S. National Security Strategy suggests *inter alia* that the concept of "imminent threat" must be adapted in the light of contemporary threats. How might one approach such adaptation? Consider the following proposal.

[T]here may be some advantage to [a] new concept of "catastrophic threat," or more properly, the "threat of catastrophic attack." Faced with an attack of this kind, it would ... be appropriate to begin to think beyond imminence to reasonable foreseeability, ie, away from temporal notions of threat and towards action required to neutralise the risk of catastrophic harm.[67]

Would the proposed formula be more appropriate than the current narrow concept of imminence? Thomas Franck has argued, by contrast, that the preventive strike doctrine is "not system transformation but system abrogation."[68] Do you agree?

---

66 For a range of perspectives, see contributions to the symposium on "Future Implications of the Iraq Conflict" (2003) 97 A.J.I.L. 543-642. And see Detlev Vagts, "Hegemonic International Law" (2001) 95 A.J.I.L. 843.

67 See written evidence of D. Bethlehem, cited in U.K. House of Commons Foreign Affairs Committee, *Foreign Policy Aspects of the War Against Terrorism, vol. I* (29 July 2004) at 139.

68 T.M. Franck, "What Happens Now? The United Nations After Iraq" (2003) 97 A.J.I.L. 607 at 620.

4) Was the military intervention in Iraq in March 2003 an application of the newly asserted doctrine of preventive self-defence? What justifications did the U.S. government offer for the intervention? What about the United Kingdom and Australia? On the American position, see the "U.S. Letter to the President of the U.N. Security Council" of March 20, 2003, reproduced in Section 4 below. Compare also the "U.S. Letter to the President of the U.N. Security Council" of October 7, 2001 (reproduced below in this Section) sent upon initiation of military actions in Afghanistan. Has the right to self-defence evolved as a result of the developments surrounding the Iraq intervention?

Attacks by Non-State Actors and Self-Defence

In the *Nicaragua* case, reproduced in Section A, above, the ICJ held that there is now "general agreement on the nature of the acts that can be treated as constituting armed attacks." These acts encompass not only action by regular armed forces across international borders, but also the sending of armed bands, groups, irregulars, or mercenaries, whose conduct is so grave as to amount to an actual armed attack conducted by regular forces. The court viewed the description of such acts contained in article 3(g) of the Definition of Aggression to reflect customary international law. However, the court also insisted that mere assistance to or support of irregulars did not amount to an armed attack and thus would not give rise to a right to use of force in self-defence.[69]

After World War II, subversion has been among the most common and most dangerous forms of intervention, whether it consists of hostile propaganda or of incitement to revolt or violently overthrow the established order. Such forms of subversion, which are themselves ancient, have come to characterize the ideological struggles that divide the world. During the Cold War, the goal was often not just to overthrow a rival or hostile government, but to change completely the political, economic, and social structure of another state in the name of supposedly superior ideological principles. Has the end of the Cold War changed this? What has been the impact of the terrorist attacks of September 11, 2001 on these questions? Do attacks by non-state actors amount to armed attacks in the meaning of article 51 of the U.N. Charter? Under what circumstances can terrorist attacks be attributed to a state? Do the narrow criteria for armed attacks outlined in the *Nicaragua* case still hold? Consider the following materials.

On September 11, 2001, four commercial airliners were hijacked after take-off from Boston, Newark, and Dulles airports in the United States. Shortly thereafter, two planes slammed into the World Trade Center towers in New York City, one crashed into the Pentagon in Washington, D.C., and another into a field in Pennsylvania. It was determined relatively quickly that the hijackers were part of the Al-Qaida terrorist network, which appeared to be led by Saudi-born Osama bin Laden. The U.N. Security Council had previously determined that the Taliban regime in Afghanistan had allowed terrorist organizations, including Al-Qaida, to operate training camps in Afghanistan, and was providing safe haven to Osama bin Laden. In several resolutions, the Security Council demanded that the Taliban stop sheltering terrorists and turn over Osama bin Laden. It

---

69   *Nicaragua* case, *supra* note 17 at para. 195.

also imposed sanctions on the Taliban regime to pressure it into compliance.[70] Immediately after the September 11, 2001 attacks, the Security Council adopted resolution 1368, recognizing states' right to individual and collective self-defence. In resolution 1373, acting under Chapter VII of the U.N. Charter, the Council required that states take a broad range of actions to suppress terrorism. On October 7, 2001, the United States sent a letter to the Security Council President, reporting that it had initiated military actions in Afghanistan in the exercise of its right of individual and collective self-defence.

Security Council Resolution 1368 (2001)[71]
U.N. Doc. S/RES/1368, 12 September 2001

The Security Council,

Reaffirming the principles and purposes of the Charter of the United Nations,

Determined to combat by all means threats to international peace and security caused by terrorist acts,

Recognizing the inherent right of individual or collective self-defence in accordance with the Charter,

1. *Unequivocally condemns* in the strongest terms the horrifying terrorist attacks which took place on 11 September 2001 in New York, Washington (D.C.) and Pennsylvania and *regards* such acts, like any act of international terrorism, as a threat to international peace and security;

2. *Expresses* its deepest sympathy and condolences to the victims and their families and to the People and Government of the United States of America;

3. *Calls* on all States to work together urgently to bring to justice the perpetrators, organizers and sponsors of these terrorist attacks and *stresses* that those responsible for aiding, supporting or harbouring the perpetrators, organizers and sponsors of these acts will be held accountable;

4. *Calls also* on the international community to redouble their efforts to prevent and suppress terrorist acts including by increased cooperation and full implementation of the relevant international anti-terrorist conventions and Security Council resolutions, in particular resolution 1269 of 19 October 1999;

5. *Expresses* its readiness to take all necessary steps to respond to the terrorist attacks of 11 September 2001, and to combat all forms of terrorism, in accordance with its responsibilities under the Charter of the United Nations

6. *Decides* to remain seized of the matter.

---

70   See SC Res. 1214 (1998), UN SCOR, 53rd year, *Res. and Dec.*; U.N. Doc. S/INF/54 at 82 (adopted by unanimous vote); SC Res. 1267 (1999), UN SCOR, 54th year, *Res. and Dec.*; U.N. Doc. S/INF/55 at 148 (adopted by unanimous vote); SC Res. 1333 (2000), UN SCOR, 55th year, *Res. and Dec.*; U.N. Doc. S/INF/56 at 32 (adopted by a vote of 13 in favour to 2 against (China and Malaysia)).

71   Adopted by unanimous vote.

Security Council Resolution 1373 (2001)[72]
U.N. Doc. S/RES/1373, 28 September 2001

The Security Council,

Reaffirming its resolutions 1269 (1999) of 19 October 1999 and 1368 (2001) of 12 September 2001,

Reaffirming also its unequivocal condemnation of the terrorist attacks which took place in New York, Washington, D.C., and Pennsylvania on 11 September 2001, and expressing its determination to prevent all such acts,

Reaffirming further that such acts, like any act of international terrorism, constitute a threat to international peace and security,

Reaffirming the inherent right of individual or collective self-defence as recognized by the Charter of the United Nations as reiterated in resolution 1368 (2001),

Reaffirming the need to combat by all means, in accordance with the Charter of the United Nations, threats to international peace and security caused by terrorist acts,

Deeply concerned by the increase, in various regions of the world, of acts of terrorism motivated by intolerance or extremism,

Calling on States to work together urgently to prevent and suppress terrorist acts, including through increased cooperation and full implementation of the relevant international conventions relating to terrorism,

Recognizing the need for States to complement international cooperation by taking additional measures to prevent and suppress, in their territories through all lawful means, the financing and preparation of any acts of terrorism,

Reaffirming the principle established by the General Assembly in its declaration of October 1970 (resolution 2625 (XXV)) and reiterated by the Security Council in its resolution 1189 (1998) of 13 August 1998, namely that every State has the duty to refrain from organizing, instigating, assisting or participating in terrorist acts in another State or acquiescing in organized activities within its territory directed towards the commission of such acts,

Acting under Chapter VII of the Charter of the United Nations,

1. *Decides* that all States shall:

(a) Prevent and suppress the financing of terrorist acts;

(b) Criminalize the wilful provision or collection, by any means, directly or indirectly, of funds by their nationals or in their territories with the intention that the funds should be used, or in the knowledge that they are to be used, in order to carry out terrorist acts;

(c) Freeze without delay funds and other financial assets or economic resources of persons who commit, or attempt to commit, terrorist acts or participate in or facilitate the commission of terrorist acts; of entities owned or controlled directly or indirectly by such persons; and of persons and entities acting on behalf of, or at the direction of such persons and entities, including funds derived or generated

---

72   Adopted by unanimous vote.

from property owned or controlled directly or indirectly by such persons and associated persons and entities;

(d) Prohibit their nationals or any persons and entities within their territories from making any funds, financial assets or economic resources or financial or other related services available, directly or indirectly, for the benefit of persons who commit or attempt to commit or facilitate or participate in the commission of terrorist acts, of entities owned or controlled, directly or indirectly, by such persons and of persons and entities acting on behalf of or at the direction of such persons;

2. *Decides also* that all States shall:

(a) Refrain from providing any form of support, active or passive, to entities or persons involved in terrorist acts, including by suppressing recruitment of members of terrorist groups and eliminating the supply of weapons to terrorists;

(b) Take the necessary steps to prevent the commission of terrorist acts, including by provision of early warning to other States by exchange of information;

(c) Deny safe haven to those who finance, plan, support, or commit terrorist acts, or provide safe havens;

(d) Prevent those who finance, plan, facilitate or commit terrorist acts from using their respective territories for those purposes against other States or their citizens;

(e) Ensure that any person who participates in the financing, planning, preparation or perpetration of terrorist acts or in supporting terrorist acts is brought to justice and ensure that, in addition to any other measures against them, such terrorist acts are established as serious criminal offences in domestic laws and regulations and that the punishment duly reflects the seriousness of such terrorist acts;

(f) Afford one another the greatest measure of assistance in connection with criminal investigations or criminal proceedings relating to the financing or support of terrorist acts, including assistance in obtaining evidence in their possession necessary for the proceedings;

(g) Prevent the movement of terrorists or terrorist groups by effective border controls and controls on issuance of identity papers and travel documents, and through measures for preventing counterfeiting, forgery or fraudulent use of identity papers and travel documents;

3. *Calls* upon all States to:

(a) Find ways of intensifying and accelerating the exchange of operational information, especially regarding actions or movements of terrorist persons or networks; forged or falsified travel documents; traffic in arms, explosives or sensitive materials; use of communications technologies by terrorist groups; and the threat posed by the possession of weapons of mass destruction by terrorist groups;

(b) Exchange information in accordance with international and domestic law and cooperate on administrative and judicial matters to prevent the commission of terrorist acts;

(c) Cooperate, particularly through bilateral and multilateral arrangements and agreements, to prevent and suppress terrorist attacks and take action against perpetrators of such acts;

(d) Become parties as soon as possible to the relevant international conventions and protocols relating to terrorism, including the International Convention for the Suppression of the Financing of Terrorism of 9 December 1999;

(e) Increase cooperation and fully implement the relevant international conventions and protocols relating to terrorism and Security Council resolutions 1269 (1999) and 1368 (2001);

(f) Take appropriate measures in conformity with the relevant provisions of national and international law, including international standards of human rights, before granting refugee status, for the purpose of ensuring that the asylum seeker has not planned, facilitated or participated in the commission of terrorist acts;

(g) Ensure, in conformity with international law, that refugee status is not abused by the perpetrators, organizers or facilitators of terrorist acts, and that claims of political motivation are not recognized as grounds for refusing requests for the extradition of alleged terrorists;

4. *Notes* with concern the close connection between international terrorism and transnational organized crime, illicit drugs, money-laundering, illegal arms-trafficking, and illegal movement of nuclear, chemical, biological and other potentially deadly materials, and in this regard emphasizes the need to enhance coordination of efforts on national, subregional, regional and international levels in order to strengthen a global response to this serious challenge and threat to international security;

5. *Declares* that acts, methods, and practices of terrorism are contrary to the purposes and principles of the United Nations and that knowingly financing, planning and inciting terrorist acts are also contrary to the purposes and principles of the United Nations;

6. *Decides* to establish, in accordance with rule 28 of its provisional rules of procedure, a Committee of the Security Council, consisting of all the members of the Council, to monitor implementation of this resolution, with the assistance of appropriate expertise, and calls upon all States to report to the Committee, no later than 90 days from the date of adoption of this resolution and thereafter according to a timetable to be proposed by the Committee, on the steps they have taken to implement this resolution;

7. *Directs* the Committee to delineate its tasks, submit a work programme within 30 days of the adoption of this resolution, and to consider the support it requires, in consultation with the Secretary-General;

8. *Expresses* its determination to take all necessary steps in order to ensure the full implementation of this resolution, in accordance with its responsibilities under the Charter;

9. *Decides* to remain seized of this matter.

U.S. Letter to the President of the U.N. Security Council, 7 October 2001
U.N. Doc. S/2001/946, 7 October 2001

In accordance with Article 51 of the Charter of the United Nations, I wish, on behalf of my Government, to report that the United States of America, together with other States, has initiated actions in the exercise of its inherent right of individual and collective self-defence following the armed attacks that were carried out against the United States on 11 September 2001.

On 11 September 2001, the United States was the victim of massive and brutal attacks in the states of New York, Pennsylvania and Virginia. These attacks were specifically designed to maximize the loss of life; they resulted in the death of more than 5,000 persons, including nationals of 81 countries, as well as the destruction of four civilian aircraft, the World Trade Center towers and a section of the Pentagon. Since 11 September, my Government has obtained clear and compelling information that the Al-Qaeda organization, which is supported by the Taliban regime in Afghanistan, had a central role in the attacks. There is still much we do not know. Our inquiry is in its early stages. We may find that our self-defence requires further actions with respect to other organizations and other States.

The attacks on 11 September 2001 and the ongoing threat to the United States and its nationals posed by the Al-Qaeda organization have been made possible by the decision of the Taliban regime to allow the parts of Afghanistan that it controls to be used by this organization as a base of operation. Despite every effort by the United States and the international community, the Taliban regime has refused to change its policy. From the territory of Afghanistan, the Al-Qaeda organization continues to train and support agents of terror who attack innocent people throughout the world and target United States nationals and interests in the United States and abroad.

In response to these attacks, and in accordance with the inherent right of individual and collective self-defence, United States armed forces have initiated actions designed to prevent and deter further attacks on the United States. These actions include measures against Al-Qaeda terrorist training camps and military installations of the Taliban regime in Afghanistan. In carrying out these actions, the United States is committed to minimizing civilian casualties and damage to civilian property. In addition, the United States will continue its humanitarian efforts to alleviate the suffering of the people of Afghanistan. We are providing them with food, medicine and supplies.

I ask that you circulate the text of the present letter as a document of the Security Council.

(Signed) John D. Negroponte

NOTES AND QUESTIONS

1) Assuming that the terrorist attack on the United States on September 11, 2001 was an "armed attack," could the air strikes against Afghanistan that began almost a month later on October 7, 2001 still be justified as self-defence?

2) Was the terrorist attack on the United States on September 11, 2001 an "armed attack" within the meaning of Article 51 of the U.N. Charter and relevant customary international law?[73] Must an "armed attack" emanate from another state to give rise to a right to self-defence? In its Advisory Opinion on the *Legal Consequences of the Construction of a Wall in the Occupied Palestinian Territory*, the ICJ considered, *inter alia*, the argument that the security barrier could be justified as a self-defence measure. The Court concluded:

[138] Annex I to the report of the Secretary-General states that, according to Israel: "the construction of the Barrier is consistent with Article 51 of the Charter of the United Nations,

---

73   See S.D. Murphy, "Terrorism and the Concept of 'Armed Attack' in Article 51 of the U.N. Charter" (2002) 43 Harv. Int'l L. J. 41.

its inherent right to self-defence and Security Council resolutions 1368 (2001) and 1373 (2001)." More specifically, Israel's Permanent Representative to the United Nations asserted in the General Assembly on 20 October 2003 that "the fence is a measure wholly consistent with the right of States to self-defence enshrined in Article 51 of the Charter"; the Security Council resolutions referred to, he continued, "have clearly recognized the right of States to use force in self-defence against terrorist attacks," and therefore surely recognize the right to use non-forcible measures to that end (A/ES-10/PV.21, p. 6).

[139] ... Article 51 of the Charter ... recognizes the existence of an inherent right of self-defence in the case of armed attack by one State against another State. However, Israel does not claim that the attacks against it are imputable to a foreign State.[74]

But consider also the following excerpt from the Declaration of Judge Buergenthal on this point:

[6] [T]he United Nations Charter, in affirming the inherent right of self-defence, does not make its exercise dependent upon an armed attack by another State, leaving aside for the moment the question whether Palestine, for the purposes of this case, should not be and is not in fact being assimilated by the Court to a State. ... Moreover, in the resolutions cited by the Court, the Security Council has made clear that "international terrorism constitutes a threat to international peace and security" while "*reaffirming* the inherent right of individual or collective self-defence as recognized by the Charter of the United Nations as reiterated in resolution 1368 (2001)." ... In its resolution 1368 (2001), adopted only one day after the September 11, 2001 attacks on the United States, the Security Council invokes the right of self-defence in calling on the international community to combat terrorism. In neither of these resolutions did the Security Council limit their application to terrorist attacks by State actors only, nor was an assumption to that effect implicit in these resolutions. In fact, the contrary appears to have been the case.[75]

3) Did the intervention in Afghanistan fit within the parameters outlined by the ICJ in the *Nicaragua* case for attribution of attacks by non-state actors to states?[76]

4) Have the Afghanistan intervention and attendant legal justifications prompted a shift in the nature of the required link between the target state of a self-defence action and perpetrators of attacks, including terrorists? Should the criteria of the law of state responsibility for imputing acts of non-state actors to states apply in the context of self-defence? Compare Articles 8, 9, and 11 of the ILC's Draft Articles on Responsibility of States for Internationally Wrongful Acts, reproduced in Chapter 10, Section A.3. Compare also the decision of the ICJ in the *Corfu Channel* case, reproduced in Chapter 10, Section A.2. Is the Court's conclusion that every state has an obligation "not to allow [knowingly] its territory to be used for acts contrary to the rights of other States" relevant in this

---

74   *Legal Consequences of the Construction of a Wall in the Occupied Palestinian Territory*, Adv. Op., 9 July 2004, paras. 138-139.

75   *Ibid.*, Declaration of Judge Buergenthal, para. 6. See also the Separate Opinion of Judge Higgins, [2004] I.C.J. Rep. 136 at para. 33; and the Separate Opinion of Judge Kooijmans, [2004] I.C.J. Rep. 136 at para. 35.

76   *Nicaragua* case, *supra* note 17 at paras. 195, 228.

context? Is mere "harbouring" of terrorists enough to make a state a legitimate target of military action taken in self-defence? What amounts to "harbouring" of terrorists?[77]

5) What is the relevance of the criteria of "necessity" and "proportionality" in the context of self-defence actions against or in another state in response to actual or threatened terrorist attacks?[78]

6) Do the following statements bear on the question whether, and under what circumstances, attacks by non-state actors amount to armed attacks in the meaning of article 51 of the U.N. Charter?

Statement by the North Atlantic Council
Press Release (2001) 124, September 12, 2001

The Council agreed that if it is determined that this attack was directed from abroad against the United States, it shall be regarded as an action covered by Article 5 of the Washington Treaty, which states that an armed attack against one or more of the Allies in Europe or North America shall be considered an attack against them all.

The commitment to collective self-defence embodied in the Washington Treaty was first entered into in circumstances very different from those that exist now, but it remains no less valid and no less essential today, in a world subject to the scourge of international terrorism. ...

Article 5 of the 1949 Treaty of Washington, which established the North Atlantic Treaty Organization (NATO), provides:

> The Parties agree that an armed attack against one or more of them in Europe or North America shall be considered an attack against them all and consequently they agree that, if such an armed attack occurs, each of them, in exercise of the right of individual or collective self-defence recognised by Article 51 of the Charter of the United Nations, will assist the Party or Parties so attacked by taking forthwith, individually and in concert with the other Parties, such action as it deems necessary, including the use of armed force, to restore and maintain the security of the North Atlantic area.
>
> Any such armed attack and all measures taken as a result thereof shall immediately be reported to the Security Council. Such measures shall be terminated when the Security Council has taken the measures necessary to restore and maintain international peace and security.

---

77   See S.R. Ratner, "Jus ad Bellum and Jus in Bello After September 11" (2002) 96 A.J.I.L. 905 at 908-10; G. Travalio and J. Altenburg, "State Responsibility for Sponsorship of Terrorist and Insurgent Groups: Terrorism, State Responsibility, and the Use of Military Force" (2003) 4 Chicago J. Int'l. L. 97; Brunnée and Toope, *supra* note 49 at 794-96.

78   See Travalio and Altenburg, *supra* note 77.

Statement by NATO Secretary General, Lord Robertson
October 2, 2001

This morning, the United States briefed the North Atlantic Council on the results of the investigation into who was responsible for the horrific terrorist attacks which took place on 11 September. ...

Today's was [a] classified briefing and so I cannot give you all the details. ...

The facts are clear and compelling. The information presented points conclusively to an Al-Qaida role in the 11 September attacks.

We know that the individuals who carried out these attacks were part of the world-wide terrorist network of Al-Qaida, headed by Osama bin Laden and his key lieutenants and protected by the Taleban.

On the basis of this briefing, it has now been determined that the attack against the United States on 11 September was directed from abroad and shall therefore be regarded as an action covered by Article 5 of the Washington Treaty, which states that an armed attack on one or more of the Allies in Europe or North America shall be considered an attack against them all.

NOTE

Collective self-defence is a concept introduced by the U.N. Charter without defining it. Consequently, considerable controversy has ensued over its scope. Must the state exercising the right show that the use of armed force against the victim state was also an attack against itself? What degree of proximity, whether geographical, economic, political, or cultural, must the collectively acting states bear to the victim of the attack? NATO and the Warsaw Pact were constructed as mutual defence arrangements by which an attack on any one member would be regarded as an attack on all, justifying a collective response.[79] The *Nicaragua* case did not limit collective self-defence in this way; instead, it introduced two novel prerequisites to the legitimate exercise of the right. First, the victim state must make a formal and public statement that it has been attacked. Second, assisting states must receive a formal and public request for and from the victim.[80] It is understandable that the Court wanted to limit the unrestricted participation of states willing to assist, but its approach may be criticized for overlooking the fact that collective self-defence is essentially the right of the assisting state, not the victim.

2. Self-Defence of Nationals

As with anticipatory self-defence, this justification for intervention raises questions about the interpretation of article 51 of the U.N. Charter. Is a state justified in taking self-help measures to protect its nationals if they are in imminent danger? Must all peaceful avenues first have been exhausted?

---

79   See also below, Section D on "The United Nations and Regional Arrangements."

80   *Nicaragua* case, *supra* note 17 at paras. 193-199. And see Macdonald, *supra* note 17 at 149.

In the 19th century, this type of intervention was accepted as lawful.[81] It was based on the doctrines of self-preservation, self-defence, and necessity. The mainstay of the argument was that nationals of a state are an extension of the state and their protection is crucial.[82] The question is once again whether this pre-Charter protection has survived.[83] Consider the following United Nations' debate.

The Entebbe Raid[84]

[On June 28, 1976, after a stop-over in Athens, an Air France airplane, with over 250 passengers and 12 crew en route from Israel to France was hijacked by terrorists. The airplane was forced to land at Benghazi, Libya and then finally at Entebbe Airport, Uganda. The hijackers, acting on behalf of the Popular Front for the Liberation of Palestine, demanded the release of about 153 terrorists imprisoned in France, Israel, Kenya, Switzerland, and West Germany. On June 30, 1976, they set free 47 passengers who were not Israeli citizens. The next day they freed an additional 100. The other 104 passengers and crew remained at Entebbe until rescued by an Israeli military commando unit on July 3, 1976, which then flew them to Israel. The reports following the rescue indicated that 3 hostages, 1 Israeli soldier, 7 of the hijackers, and a number of Ugandan soldiers were killed. Opinions conflicted at the time about whether the Ugandan Government had tried to protect the hostages and negotiate their release or whether it had been collaborating with the hijackers.

The Security Council debated the incident without reaching any definite conclusion. The following excerpts from the Security Council's debate expose the contending characterizations of the Israeli action.]

MR. HERZOG (Israel):[85] ... Uganda violated a basic tenet of international law in failing to protect foreign nationals on its territory. Furthermore, it behaved in a manner which constituted a gross violation of the 1970 Hague Convention on the Suppression of Unlawful Seizure of Aircraft. This Convention had been ratified by both Israel and Uganda.[86]

... The right of a State to take military action to protect its nationals in mortal danger is recognized by all legal authorities in international law. In Self-Defence in International Law, Professor Bowett states, on page 87, that "The right of the State to intervene by the use or threat of force for the protection of its nationals suffering

---

81   See Brownlie, *Use of Force, supra* note 2 at 289.

82   *Ibid.* See also E. de Vattel, *Le Droit des gens*, Book II, c. vi at 71 and Borchard, *Diplomatic Protection of Citizens Abroad* (1915) 31.

83   Brownlie, *Use of Force, supra* note 2 at 289-301, considers this doubtful.

84   See L.C. Green, "Rescue at Entebbe—Legal Aspects" (1976) 6 Israel Y.B.H.R. 312 and L.M. Salter, "Commando Coup at Entebbe: Humanitarian Intervention or Barbaric Aggression?" (1977) 11 Int. Law 331.

85   U.N. Doc. S/PV 1939, July 9, 1976 at 51-59, reprinted in (1976) 15 I.L.M. at 1228.

86   860 U.N.T.S. 105; Can. T.S. 1972 No. 23.

injuries within the territory of another State is generally admitted, both in the writings of jurists and in the practice of States." In the arbitration between Great Britain and Spain in 1925, one of the series known as the Spanish Moroccan claims, Judge Huber, as Rapporteur of the Commission, stated:

> However, it cannot be denied that at a certain point the interest of a State in exercising protection over its nationals and their property can take precedence over territorial sovereignty, despite the absence of any conventional provisions. This right of intervention has been claimed by all States. Only its limits are disputed. We now envisage action by the protecting State which involves a *prima facie* violation of the independence and territorial inviolability of the territorial State. In so far as this action takes effect in derogation of the sovereignty of the territorial States, it must necessarily be exceptional in character and limited to those cases in which no other means of protection are available. It presupposes the inadequacy of any other means of protection against some injury, actual or imminent, to the person or property of nations and, moreover, an injury which results either from the acts of the territorial State and its authorities or from the acts of individuals or groups of individuals which the territorial State is unable, or unwilling, to prevent.

In the *Law of Nations*, Sixth Edition, page 627, Brierly states as follows:

> Whether the landing of detachments of troops to save the lives of nationals under imminent threat of death or serious injury owing to the breakdown of law and order may be justifiable is a delicate question. Cases of this form of intervention have been not infrequent in the past and, when not attended by suspicion of being a pretext for political pressure, have generally been regarded as justified by the sheer necessity of instant action to save the lives of innocent nationals whom the local government is unable or unwilling to protect.

He goes on to observe that:

> Every effort must be made to get the United Nations to act. But, if the United Nations is not in a position to move in time and the need for instant action is manifest it would be difficult to deny the legitimacy of action in defence of nationals which every responsible Government would feel bound to take if it had the means to do so. This is, of course, on the basis that the action was strictly limited to securing the safe removal of the threatened national.
>
> In support of this contention, O'Connell states in *International Law*, Second Edition, at 303:

> ... Article 2(4) of the United Nations Charter should be interpreted as prohibiting acts of force against the territorial integrity and political independence of nations, and not to prohibit a use of force which is limited in intention and effect to the protection of a State's own integrity and its nationals' vital interests, when the machinery envisaged by the United Nations Charter is ineffective in the situation.

The act of hijacking can well be regarded as one of piracy. Pirates have been *hostis humani generis*—enemies of the human race—since the early days of international law in the Middle Ages. During the war against the slave trade and piracy, certain norms were established in international law which permitted intervention of ships engaged in slave trade between Africa and America and against the centres of piracy in North Africa. The principle of national sovereignty was overruled by the higher principles of man's liberty.

... The right of self-defence is enshrined in international law and in the Charter of the United Nations and can be applied on the basis of the classic formulation, as was done in the well-known Caroline case. ... That was exactly the situation which faced the Government of Israel.

... What mattered to the Government of Israel in this instance was the lives of the hostages, in danger of their very lives. No consideration other than this humanitarian consideration motivated the Government of Israel. Israel's rescue operation was not directed against Uganda. Israeli forces were not attacking Uganda—and they were certainly not attacking Africa. They were rescuing their nationals from a band of terrorists and kidnappers who were being aided and abetted by the Ugandan authorities. The means used were the minimum necessary to fulfil that purpose, as is laid down in international law.

Some parallels could be drawn with the right of an individual to use appropriate means to defend himself if he kills someone who is trying to kill him. He is not liable to be found guilty of murder. Judgment takes into account the context and purpose of the act. The same applies to the use of force in international affairs.

MR. OYONO (United Republic of Cameroon):[87] ... Israel took the initiative of attacking the territory of Uganda—a sovereign State separated from Israel by more than 3,000 kilometres—with commandos from its regular army, airlifted by three military planes. In so doing, Israel deliberately initiated hostilities against Uganda and for that reason is the aggressor in this affair, as defined by international law.

The Security Council, which is responsible for international peace and security, must vigorously condemn this barbaric act which constitutes a flagrant violation of the norms of international law and flouts the spirit and letter of the United Nations Charter, Article 2, paragraph 4. ...

In the spirit of the Charter, that prohibition means that Member States have an obligation to settle their international disputes by peaceful means in order to maintain international peace and security. I need hardly remind you that our Organization is not dedicated to anarchy or to the notion that might makes right, but is an organized community whose mutually accepted principles and rules must be scrupulously respected, and their violation adequately punished.

It is the corner-stone of our Organization that there can be no justification for the use of force against the sovereignty, independence or territorial integrity of a State, unless we wish to imperil international co-operation in its present form and indeed the very existence of States that do not yet possess modern, sophisticated systems of detection and deterrence.

---

87   *Supra* note 85 at 92.

MR. SCRANTON (United States):[88] ... Israel's action in rescuing the hostages necessarily involved a temporary breach of the territorial integrity of Uganda. Normally, such a breach would be impermissible under the Charter of the United Nations. However, there is a well established right to use limited force for the protection of one's own nationals from an imminent threat of injury or death in a situation where the State in whose territory they are located is either unwilling or unable to protect them. The right, flowing from the right of self-defence, is limited to such use of force as is necessary and appropriate to protect threatened nationals from injury.

The requirements of this right to protect nationals were clearly met in the Entebbe case. Israel had good reason to believe that at the time it acted Israeli nationals were in imminent danger of execution by the hijackers. Moreover, the actions necessary to release the Israel nationals or to prevent substantial loss of Israeli lives had not been taken by the Government of Uganda, nor was there a reasonable expectation such actions would be taken. In fact, there is substantial evidence that the Government of Uganda co-operated with and aided the hijackers. A number of the released hostages have publicly related how the Ugandan authorities allowed several additional terrorists to reinforce the original group after the plane landed, permitted them to receive additional arms and additional explosives, participated in guarding the hostages and, according to some accounts, even took over sole custody of some or all of the passengers to allow the hijackers to rest. The ease and success of the Israeli effort to free the hostages further suggests that the Ugandan authorities could have overpowered the hijackers and released the hostages if they had really had the desire to do so.

The apparent support given to the hijackers by the Ugandan authorities causes us to question whether Uganda lived up to its international legal obligations under the Hague Convention. The rights of a State carry with them important responsibilities which were not met by Uganda in this case. The Israeli military action was limited to the sole objective of extricating the passengers and crew and terminated when that objective was accomplished. The force employed was limited to what was necessary for the rescue of the passengers and crew.

That Israel might have secured the release of its nationals by complying with the terrorists' demands does not alter these conclusions. No State is required to yield control over persons in lawful custody in its territory under criminal charges. Moreover, it would be a self-defeating and dangerous policy to release prisoners, convicted in some cases of earlier acts of terrorism, in order to accede to the demands of terrorists.

It should be emphasized that this assessment of the legality of Israeli actions depends heavily on the unusual circumstances of this specific case. In particular, the evidence is strong that, given the attitude of the Ugandan authorities, co-operation with or reliance on them in rescuing the passengers and crew was impracticable. It is to be hoped that these unique circumstances will not arise in the future.

---

88   U.N. Doc. S/PV 1941, July 12, 1976, reprinted in (1976) 15 I.L.M. 1232.

NOTES

1) This justification for intervention is open to abuse unless safeguarded by certain prerequisite conditions. What should they be? Is there any basis for this excuse in the U.N. Charter? What arguments could be made to support the view that such action is not contrary to article 2(4) of the Charter? Could a state exercise the justification to protect its nationals' property abroad, rather than their lives?[89]

2) The *U.S. Diplomatic and Consular Staff in Tehran* case[90] concerned Iran's responsibility to the United States for certain American hostages. In addition to the case, the United States also made an unsuccessful attempt to rescue the hostages. The World Court did not rule on this action. Could the United States claim that its intervention was a legitimate act of self-defence of its nationals?

3) In the United States' intervention in Grenada in 1983[91] and in Panama in 1989, the justification of self-defence of its nationals was also announced.

In Grenada, following the collapse of governmental institutions that occurred in the wake of a coup d'état, in which the Prime Minister Maurice Bishop was murdered, some 1,000 U.S. citizens, mainly students, elderly retirees, and missionaries were allegedly in danger. According to Deputy Secretary of State Kenneth Dam the concern "was heightened by the murder of Bishop, members of his cabinet and union leaders, the curfew and the difficulty of getting accurate information. And in the absence of a functioning government, credible assurances of their well-being and future prospects were impossible to obtain."[92] In response, a multinational force of Commonwealth Caribbean troops and the U.S. military invaded Grenada and quickly overwhelmed the interim government. Within two months, the U.S. military withdrew, leaving the internal security of Grenada in the hands of the participating Caribbean forces.

The principal objectives of the U.S. invasion of Panama were to capture General Noriega, who was wanted on massive drug smuggling charges in Florida, and to remove his unconstitutional and tyrannical regime. President Bush, shortly after the U.S. forces had been sent into Panama, stated that General Noriega had declared "a state of war with the United States" and that he had "publicly threatened the lives of Americans in Panama."[93] The intervention was successful from the United States' point of view and Americans in Panama were protected, but not without loss of life and property among the

---

89   See Brownlie, *Use of Force*, *supra* note 2 at 301, who answers in the negative. His view is that if it were otherwise the host state of foreign investment or a state permitting ownership of property by foreigners would be severely limited in the exercise of its sovereignty.

90   [1979] I.C.J. Rep. 23.

91   See W.C. Gilmore, *The Grenada Intervention* (1984) and S. Davidson, *Grenada* (1987).

92   See U.S. Digest, c. 4, §1; reprinted in (1984) 78 A.J.I.L. 200-4. For opposing views on the lawfulness of the intervention, see C. Joyner, "The United States Action in Grenada, Reflections on the Lawfulness of Invasion" (1984) 78 A.J.I.L. 131; and J. Norton Moore, "Grenada and the International Double Standard" (1984) 78 A.J.I.L. 145.

93   See Statement of the President of December 20, 1989, Office of the Press Secretary, the White House, quoted in V. Nanda, "The Validity of United States Intervention in Panama under International Law" (1990) 84 A.J.I.L. 494.

local population.[94] Did the actions of the United States in these instances meet the tests for self-defence outlined in the *Caroline* case?[95]

4) The United States discovered that there had been an Iraqi plan to kill President George Bush in April 1993. It had not been implemented. The U.S. response was to send missiles into Iraq from U.S. aircraft carriers to bomb the Iraqi intelligence headquarters in Baghdad. Some missiles went astray and about six civilians were killed. The U.S. claimed that its conduct had been "proportionate and was linked directly to the operation against President Bush. It was designed to damage the terrorist infrastructure of the Iraqi regime, reduce its ability to promote terrorism and deter further acts of aggression against the United States."[96] Was this action of the United States anticipatory self-defence or a reprisal?

3. Humanitarian Intervention

In the 19th century it seems that the majority of international law publicists admitted that a right of humanitarian intervention existed, on the basis that a state that had abused its sovereign powers by inflicting excessively inhumane treatment on persons within its borders, whether nationals or aliens, made itself liable to intervention by any state prepared to do so to ameliorate conditions there.[97] Examples of state practice given in support included the 1827 intervention by Austria, Great Britain, France, Prussia, and Russia in aid of Greek insurgents,[98] and the French action and occupation of parts of Syria in 1860-61 to prevent the massacre of Maronite Christians.[99]

In creating the U.N. Charter, the world community evidenced a distrust for unilateral action on the part of states. The prohibition in article 2(7) of intervention in the domestic affairs of states is one of the fundamental principles of the modern international system. Although article 51 allows for self-defence in certain defined circumstances, including arguably the defence of a state's own nationals, as discussed in the previous section, a general right to intervene forcibly for humanitarian reasons remains acutely controversial. A primary concern is that if the claim to self-defence of nationals is open to abuse, general humanitarian intervention would be even more susceptible to aspersions being

---

94   See T. Farer, "Panama: Beyond the Charter Paradigm" (1990) 84 A.J.I.L. 503 and A. D'Amato, "The Invasion of Panama Was a Lawful Response to Tyranny" (1990) 84 A.J.I.L. 516.

95   (1837) 2 Moore 409, reproduced above in Section B.1 on "The Right of Self-Defence."

96   U.N. Doc. S/PV 3245 at 6.

97   See I. Brownlie, *Use of Force*, *supra* note 2 at 338.

98   *Ibid.* at 339 referring to Stowell, *Intervention in International Law* (1921) 126, 489. Brownlie, however, argues that the intervening states did not actually refer to such a justification and had other grounds as well. See also I. Brownlie, "Thoughts on Kind-Hearted Gunmen," in R. Lillich, ed., *Humanitarian Intervention and the United Nations* (1973); "Humanitarian Intervention," in J.N. Moore, ed., *Law and Civil War in the Modern World* (1974) 217; M. Akehurst, "Humanitarian Intervention," in H. Bull, ed., *Intervention in World Politics* (1984); and T.J. Farer, "An Inquiry into the Legitimacy of Humanitarian Intervention," in L. Fisler Damrosch and D.J. Scheffer, *supra* note 2 at 185.

99   See Brownlie, *Use of Force*, *supra* note 2 at 339. See also S. Kloepfer, "The Syrian Crisis, 1860-61: A Case Study in Classic Humanitarian Intervention" (1985) 23 Can. Y.B. Int'l L. 246.

cast on its altruistic and genuine nature.[100] Most notably, the concern is that some governments could use the claim of right to intervene as an excuse for meddling in the affairs of a less powerful state.

This legitimate fear of abuse of humanitarian intervention engendered the restraint placed on it by the United Nations unless taken pursuant to a decision of the Security Council under its special powers contained in Chapter VII of the Charter, discussed later in this chapter in Section B.4 on "Collective Measures Pursuant to the U.N. Charter" under the heading "Responses to State-Sponsored Terrorism." Such was the case of the Security Council authorizing assistance to the Kurds in Iraq in resolution 688 of April 5, 1991.[101] It should be noted that most members of the Council were of the view that the Kurdish situation was itself a threat to international peace and security. The measures taken by the United Nations in matters ostensibly within the domestic purview of Iraq are indicative of the potential future role and expanded mandate that that organization may have in situations where there are serious questions of human rights violations, a need for humanitarian assistance, and a lack of democracy. The Iraq–Kuwait crisis brought about far-reaching and ground-breaking consequences for international peace and security, which redefined the peacekeeping role of the United Nations.[102] Notwithstanding the cautious wording of resolution 688, a precedent was set for future situations involving serious humanitarian concerns.

Security Council Resolution 688 (1991)[103]
U.N. SCOR, 46th Year, 2982d Mtg; U.N. Doc. S.RES/688 (1991);
reprinted in (1991) 30 I.L.M. 858

The Security Council
    Mindful of its duties and its responsibilities under the Charter of the United Nations for the maintenance of international peace and security,
    Recalling the provisions of Article 2, paragraph 7 of the Charter of the United Nations,
    Gravely concerned by the repression of the Iraqi civilian population in many parts of Iraq, including most recently in Kurdish populated areas which led to a massive

---

100 See Brownlie, "Humanitarian Intervention," *supra* note 98 at 217-28. For recent, comprehensive treatments of humanitarian intervention and the arguments for and against it, see *e.g.* S. Chesterman, *Just War or Just Peace? Humanitarian Intervention and International Law* (2001); J.L. Holzgrefe and R.O. Keohane, eds., *Humanitarian Intervention: Ethical, Legal, and Political Dilemmas* (2003); N. Wheeler, *Saving Strangers: Humanitarian Intervention in International Society* (2000).

101 Reproduced below. Adopted by 10 votes in favour to 3 against (Cuba, Yemen, and Zimbabwe) with 2 abstentions (China and India).

102 J. Tessitore and S. Woolfson, *A Global Agenda: Issues Before the 46th General Assembly of the United Nations* (1991) xi. See V. Nanda, "Tragedies in Northern Iraq, Liberia, Yugoslavia, and Haiti—Revisiting the Validity of Humanitarian Intervention under International Law—Part I" (1992) 20 Denv. J. Int'l L. & Pol'y 305 and C. Bourloyannis, "The Security Council of the United Nations and the Implementation of International Humanitarian Law" (1992) 20 Denv. J. Int'l L. & Pol'y 335.

103 Adopted by 10 votes in favour, 3 against (Cuba, Yemen, and Zimbabwe), and 2 abstentions (China and India).

flow of refugees towards and across international frontiers and to cross border incursions, which threaten international peace and security in the region,

Deeply disturbed by the magnitude of the suffering involved, ...

Reaffirming the commitment of all Member States to the sovereignty, territorial integrity and political independence of Iraq and all other States in the area, ...

1. *Condemns* the repression of the Iraqi civilian population in many parts of Iraq, including most recently in Kurdish populated areas, the consequences of which threaten international peace and security in the region;

2. *Demands* that Iraq, as a contribution to removing the threat to international peace and security in the region, immediately end this repression ... ;

3. *Insists* that Iraq allow immediate access by international humanitarian organizations to all those in need of assistance in all parts of Iraq and to make available all necessary facilities for their operations;

4. *Requests* the Secretary-General to pursue his humanitarian efforts in Iraq and to report forthwith, if appropriate on the basis of a further mission to the region, on the plight of the Iraqi civilian population, and in particular the Kurdish population, suffering from the repression in all its forms inflicted by the Iraqi authorities;

5. *Also requests* the Secretary-General to use all the resources at his disposal, including those of the relevant United Nations agencies, to address urgently the critical needs of the refugees and displaced Iraqi population;

6. *Appeals* to all Member States and to all humanitarian organizations to contribute to these humanitarian relief efforts;

7. *Demands* that Iraq cooperate with the Secretary-General to these ends;

8. *Decides* to remain seized of the matter.

Security Council Resolution 794 (1992)[104]
S/RES/794 of 3 December 1992

The Security Council,

... *Recognizing* the unique character of the present situation in Somalia and *mindful* of its deteriorating, complex and extraordinary nature, requiring an immediate and exceptional response,

Determining that the magnitude of the human tragedy caused by the conflict in Somalia, further exacerbated by the obstacles being created to the distribution of humanitarian assistance, constitutes a threat to international peace and security,

Gravely alarmed by the deterioration of the humanitarian situation in Somalia and underlining the urgent need for the quick delivery of humanitarian assistance in the whole country,

... *Commending* the ongoing efforts of the United Nations, its specialized agencies and humanitarian organizations and of non-governmental organizations and of States to ensure delivery of humanitarian assistance in Somalia,

---

104 Adopted by unanimous vote.

Responding to the urgent calls from Somalia for the international community to take measures to ensure the delivery of humanitarian assistance in Somalia,

Expressing grave alarm at continuing reports of widespread violations of international humanitarian law occurring in Somalia, ...

Sharing the Secretary-General's assessment that the situation in Somalia is intolerable and that it has become necessary to review the basic premises and principles of the United Nations effort in Somalia, and that UNOSOM's existing course would not in present circumstances be an adequate response to the tragedy in Somalia,

... *Noting* the offer by Member States aimed at establishing a secure environment for humanitarian relief operations in Somalia as soon as possible,

Determined further to restore peace, stability and law and order with a view to facilitating the process of a political settlement under the auspices of the United Nations, aimed at national reconciliation in Somalia, and *encouraging* the Secretary-General and his Special Representative to continue and intensify their work at the national and regional levels to promote these objectives,

Recognizing that the people of Somalia bear ultimate responsibility for national reconciliation and the reconstruction of their own country,

1. *Reaffirms* its demand that all parties, movements and factions in Somalia immediately cease hostilities, maintain a cease-fire throughout the country, and cooperate with the Special Representative of the Secretary-General as well as with the military forces to be established pursuant to the authorization given in paragraph 10 below in order to promote the process of relief distribution, reconciliation and political settlement in Somalia;

2. *Demands* that all parties, movements and factions in Somalia take all measures necessary to facilitate the efforts of the United Nations, its specialized agencies and humanitarian organizations to provide urgent humanitarian assistance to the affected population in Somalia;

3. *Also demands* that all parties, movements and factions in Somalia take all measures necessary to ensure the safety of United Nations and all other personnel engaged in the delivery of humanitarian assistance, including the military forces to be established pursuant to the authorization given in paragraph 10 below; ...

6. *Decides* that the operations and the further deployment of the 3,500 personnel of the United Nations Operation in Somalia (UNOSOM) authorized by paragraph 3 of resolution 775 (1992) should proceed at the discretion of the Secretary-General in the light of his assessment of conditions on the ground; and *requests* him to keep the Council informed and to make such recommendations as may be appropriate for the fulfilment of its mandate where conditions permit; ...

10. *Acting* under Chapter VII of the Charter of the United Nations, *authorizes* the Secretary-General and Member States cooperating to implement the offer referred to in paragraph 8 above to use all necessary means to establish as soon as possible a secure environment for humanitarian relief operations in Somalia;

11. *Calls* on all Member States which are in a position to do so to provide military forces and to make additional contributions, in cash or in kind, in accordance with paragraph 10 above and *requests* the Secretary-General to establish a fund through

which the contributions, where appropriate, could be channelled to the States or operations concerned;

12. *Authorizes* the Secretary-General and the Member States concerned to make the necessary arrangements for the unified command and control of the forces involved, which will reflect the offer referred to in paragraph 8 above;

13. *Requests* the Secretary-General and the Member States acting under paragraph 10 above to establish appropriate mechanisms for coordination between the United Nations and their military forces; ...

21. *Decides* to remain actively seized of the matter.

NOTES

1) Concerning the plight of the Kurds in the north of Iraq and the Shi'ite muslims in the south of Iraq, it can be argued that humanitarian assistance was slow in coming. Leading up to the Security Council resolution 688 it was estimated that between 400 and 1,000 Kurdish refugees were dying every day at the Turkish border. Resolution 688 could not be avoided. Why did this collective action take so long? Was it in the minds of the coalition governments that *realpolitik* demanded that the balance of power in the region not collapse by the institution of a separate state for the Kurds? Would the Kurdish minorities in Syria, Turkey, and Iran have made similar demands?[105]

2) Did the Security Council, in resolution 688, authorize a humanitarian intervention to protect the Kurds in Iraq?

3) How does resolution 794, adopted in 1992 to address a humanitarian crisis in Somalia and to enable relief efforts, differ from resolution 688? Was the case of Somalia, as the resolution's preamble proclaims, "unique"? Was it within the Security Council's powers to determine that the humanitarian crises in Iraq and Somalia, respectively, constituted "threats to international peace and security"?

4) What accounts for the Security Council's failure to act decisively in the face of the Rwandan genocide in 1994? In this context, consider the materials on the "Peacekeeping Role of the United Nations," below in Section C.[106]

5) Is intervention to restore democracy part of humanitarian intervention? It seems that this was one of the grounds used by the United States in its intervention in Panama.[107] Is there a difficulty in defining democracy? Is this reason simply not acceptable in the light of the provisions of the U.N. Charter already discussed? But consider also the provisions of article 21 of the Universal Declaration of Human Rights, reproduced in the Documentary Supplement and discussed in Chapter 12, Section A.1.

---

105 See S.A. Williams, "Commentary on Panel on The Gulf War: Collective Security, War Powers, and Laws of War" (1991) 85 A.S.I.L. Proc. 16 at 17.

106 For a detailed account, see M. Barnett, *Eyewitness to a Genocide: The United Nations and Rwanda* (2002).

107 See *Keesing's Record of World Events* (1989) 37112; Nanda, *supra* note 93 at 498; and A. D'Amato, *supra* note 94 at 517-19.

6) In September 1991, the elected President of Haiti, Jean-Bertrand Aristide, was swept out of the country by a military coup. Subsequently, the U.N. General Assembly passed a resolution unanimously demanding respect for the Haitian Constitution, the return of Father Aristide to the Presidency and observance of human rights in Haiti.[108] Was this a legitimate exercise of authority by the General Assembly? How much further action to restore democracy might it have taken under the Charter?[109]

7) Is it acceptable as humanitarian intervention or under a separate justification to give assistance to peoples struggling for self-determination? Refer to the 1970 Declaration of Principles of International Law in the Documentary Supplement and articles 7 and 8 of the 1974 Definition of Aggression reported earlier in this chapter, Section A on the "Prohibition of the Use of Force."[110] It should be noted that article 1(4) of Protocol I,[111] Additional to the Geneva Conventions of 1949, Relating to the Protection of Victims of International Armed Conflicts[112] provides that international armed conflicts with all the concomitant rights and obligations under the Geneva Conventions and Protocol I, including combatant and prisoner of war status, methods and means of waging war, and protection of the civilian population apply to "armed conflicts in which peoples are fighting against colonial domination and alien occupation and against racist regimes in the exercise of their rights of self-determination, as enshrined in the Charter of the United Nations and the Declaration on Principles of International Law concerning Friendly Relations and Co-operation among States in accordance with the Charter of the United Nations."

8) Giving aid to rebel or terrorist movements is prohibited. See the 1970 Declaration of Principles on International Law, reproduced in the Documentary Supplement and article 3(g) of the 1974 Definition of Aggression, reproduced above in Section A on the "Prohibition of the Use of Force."

9) Are there any circumstances in which states can lawfully undertake a humanitarian intervention without Security Council authorization? Can the NATO bombings in 1999 of the Federal Republic of Yugoslavia (FRY), which had not been authorized by the U.N. Security Council, be justified as humanitarian intervention to end the "ethnic cleansing" of the Kosovar population? Kosovo is part of FRY, since renamed Serbia and Montenegro. However, 90 percent of Kosovo is populated by ethnic Albanians. Does humanitarian intervention interface here with the right of the Albanian Kosovars to self-determination? Did the incapacity of the U.N. Security Council to act in this case because of the potential use of the veto by China and the Russian Federation play a part?[113]

---

108 U.N. Doc. A/46/L.8/Rev. 1 (1991).

109 See T.M. Franck, "The Emerging Right to Democratic Governance" (1992) 86 A.J.I.L. 46.

110 See also the discussion on self-determination of peoples in Chapter 2, Section C.4(b).

111 (1977) 1125 U.N.T.S. 3, reproduced in Chapter 11, Section A.2.

112 Can. T.S. 1991 No. 2. On the Conventions and Protocols, see F. Kalshoven, *Constraints on the Laws of War* (1987) and the references in Chapter 11, note 15.

113 For a range of scholarly views on the legality of the Kosovo intervention, see "Editorial Comments: NATO's Kosovo Intervention" (1999) 93 A.J.I.L. 824-62. See also B. Simma, "NATO, the UN and the Use of Force: Legal Aspects" (1999) 10 E.J.I.L. 1.

10) Is it legally significant that a Russian draft resolution, condemning NATO's "unilateral use of force" as a "flagrant violation of the United Nations Charter," and demanding immediate cessation of NATO aggression, was defeated by a vote of 12:3?[114]

11) Could a subsequent approval by the Security Council have provided valid Chapter VII authorization of the NATO intervention? Does silence or failure to condemn constitute approval?[115] See also the discussion of Gulf War II in 2003, to be found below in Section B.4, and Section D on "The United Nations and Regional Arrangements."

12) Consider the following public statement by then NATO Secretary-General Javier Solana. Did it provide a legal justification for the bombing campaign? What accounts for the statement's approach to justification?

I have just directed ... General Clark to initiate air operations in the Federal Republic of Yugoslavia. ...

All efforts to achieve a negotiated, political solution to the Kosovo crisis having failed, no alternative is open but to take military action. ...

Let me be clear: NATO is not waging war against Yugoslavia.

We have no quarrel with the people of Yugoslavia who for too long have been isolated in Europe because of the policies of their government.

Our objective is to prevent more human suffering and more repression and violence against the civilian population of Kosovo.

We must also act to prevent instability spreading in the region. ...

We must halt the violence and bring an end to the humanitarian catastrophe now unfolding in Kosovo.

We know the risks of action but we have all agreed that inaction brings even greater dangers. ...

We must stop an authoritarian regime from repressing its people in Europe at the end of the 20th century.

We have a moral duty to do so.[116]

13) Consider also the following statement by U.N. Secretary-General Kofi Annan. Did it endorse the intervention?

I speak to you at a grave moment for the international community.

Throughout the last year, I have appealed on many occasions to the Yugoslav authorities and the Kosovo Albanians to seek peace over war, compromise over conflict. I deeply regret that, in spite of all the efforts made by the international community, the Yugoslav authorities have persisted in their rejection of a political settlement, which would have halted the bloodshed in Kosovo and secured an equitable peace for the population there. It is indeed

---

114 For the text of the draft resolution, see U.N. Doc. S/1999/328, 26 March 1999. The three states voting for the resolution were China, Namibia, and Russia. Argentina, Bahrain, Brazil, Canada, France, Gabon, Gambia, Malaysia, the Netherlands, Slovenia, the United Kingdom, and the United States voted against.

115 See J. Lobel and M. Ratner, "Bypassing the Security Council: Ambiguous Authorizations To Use Force, Ceasefires, and the Iraqi Inspection Regime" (1999) 93 A.J.I.L. 124.

116 NATO Press Release (1999) 040, 23 March 1999.

tragic that diplomacy has failed, but there are times when the use of force may be legitimate in the pursuit of peace.

In helping maintain international peace and security, Chapter VIII of the United Nations Charter assigns an important role to regional organizations. But as Secretary-General I have many times pointed out, not just in relation to Kosovo, that under the Charter the Security Council has primary responsibility for maintaining international peace and security—and this is explicitly acknowledged in the North Atlantic Treaty. Therefore the Council should be involved in any decision to resort to the use of force.[117]

The Responsibility To Protect

Report of the International Commission on Intervention and State Sovereignty (ICISS), *The Responsibility To Protect* (December 2001) at vii-ix, xi-xii.

FOREWORD

This report is about the so-called "right of humanitarian intervention": the question of when, if ever, it is appropriate for states to take coercive—and in particular military—action, against another state for the purpose of protecting people at risk in that other state. At least until the horrifying events of 11 September 2001 brought to center stage the international response to terrorism, the issue of intervention for human protection purposes has been seen as one of the most controversial and difficult of all international relations questions. With the end of the Cold War, it became a live issue as never before. Many calls for intervention have been made over the last decade— some of them answered and some of them ignored. But there continues to be disagreement as to whether, if there is a right of intervention, how and when it should be exercised, and under whose authority.

The Policy Challenge

External military intervention for human protection purposes has been controversial both when it has happened—as in Somalia, Bosnia and Kosovo—and when it has failed to happen, as in Rwanda. For some the new activism has been a long overdue internationalization of the human conscience; for others it has been an alarming breach of an international state order dependent on the sovereignty of states and the inviolability of their territory. For some, again, the only real issue is ensuring that coercive interventions are effective; for others, questions about legality, process and the possible misuse of precedent loom much larger.

NATO's intervention in Kosovo in 1999 brought the controversy to its most intense head. Security Council members were divided; the legal justification for military action without new Security Council authority was asserted but largely unargued; the moral or humanitarian justification for the action, which on the face of it was much

---

117 Secretary-General's Statement on NATO Military Action Against Yugoslavia, UN Press Release SG/SM/6938, March 24, 1999. See also below, Section D. on "The United Nations and Regional Arrangements."

stronger, was clouded by allegations that the intervention generated more carnage than it averted; and there were many criticisms of the way in which the NATO allies conducted the operation.

At the United Nations General Assembly in 1999, and again in 2000, Secretary-General Kofi Annan made compelling pleas to the international community to try to find, once and for all, a new consensus on how to approach these issues, to "forge unity" around the basic questions of principle and process involved. He posed the central question starkly and directly:

> [I]f humanitarian intervention is, indeed, an unacceptable assault on sovereignty, how should we respond to a Rwanda, to a Srebrenica—to gross and systematic violations of human rights that affect every precept of our common humanity?

It was in response to this challenge that the Government of Canada, together with a group of major foundations, announced at the General Assembly in September 2000 the establishment of the International Commission on Intervention and State Sovereignty (ICISS). Our Commission was asked to wrestle with the whole range of questions— legal, moral, operational and political—rolled up in this debate, to consult with the widest possible range of opinion around the world, and to bring back a report that would help the Secretary-General and everyone else find some new common ground.

The Commission's Report

The report which we now present has been unanimously agreed by the twelve Commissioners. Its central theme, reflected in the title, is "The Responsibility to Protect," the idea that sovereign states have a responsibility to protect their own citizens from avoidable catastrophe—from mass murder and rape, from starvation— but that when they are unwilling or unable to do so, that responsibility must be borne by the broader community of states. The nature and dimensions of that responsibility are argued out, as are all the questions that must be answered about who should exercise it, under whose authority, and when, where and how. We hope very much that the report will break new ground in a way that helps generate a new international consensus on these issues. It is desperately needed. ...

The Report and the Events of 11 September 2001

The Commission's report was largely completed before the appalling attacks of 11 September 2001 on New York and Washington DC, and was not conceived as addressing the kind of challenge posed by such attacks. Our report has aimed at providing precise guidance for states faced with human protection claims in other states; it has not been framed to guide the policy of states when faced with attack on their own nationals, or the nationals of other states residing within their borders.

The two situations in our judgement are fundamentally different. The framework the Commission, after consultations around the world, has developed to address the first case (coping with human protection claims in other states) must not be confused with the framework necessary to deal with the second (responding to terrorist attacks in one's own state). Not the least of the differences is that in the latter case the U.N.

Charter provides much more explicit authority for a military response than in the case of intervention for human protection purposes: Article 51 acknowledges "the inherent right of individual or collective self-defence if an armed attack occurs against a Member of the United Nations," though requiring that the measures taken be immediately reported to the Security Council. In Resolutions 1368 and 1373, passed unanimously in the aftermath of the September attacks, the Security Council left no doubt as to the scope of measures that states could and should take in response.

While for the reasons stated we have not—except in passing—addressed in the body of our report the issues raised by the 11 September attacks, there are aspects of our report which do have some relevance to the issues with which the international community has been grappling in the aftermath of those attacks. In particular, precautionary principles outlined in our report do seem to be relevant to military operations, both multilateral and unilateral, against the scourge of terrorism. We have no difficulty in principle with focused military action being taken against international terrorists and those who harbour them. But military power should always be exercised in a principled way, and the principles of right intention, last resort, proportional means and reasonable prospects outlined in our report are, on the face of it, all applicable to such action. ...

THE RESPONSIBILITY TO PROTECT

Core Principles

(1) Basic Principles

A. State sovereignty implies responsibility, and the primary responsibility for the protection of its people lies with the state itself.

B. Where a population is suffering serious harm, as a result of internal war, insurgency, repression or state failure, and the state in question is unwilling or unable to halt or avert it, the principle of non-intervention yields to the international responsibility to protect.

(2) Foundations

The foundations of the responsibility to protect, as a guiding principle for the international community of states, lie in:

A. obligations inherent in the concept of sovereignty;

B. the responsibility of the Security Council, under Article 24 of the U.N. Charter, for the maintenance of international peace and security;

C. specific legal obligations under human rights and human protection declarations, covenants and treaties, international humanitarian law and national law;

D. the developing practice of states, regional organizations and the Security Council itself.

(3) Elements

The responsibility to protect embraces three specific responsibilities:

A. The responsibility to prevent: to address both the root causes and direct causes of internal conflict and other man-made crises putting populations at risk.

B. The responsibility to react: to respond to situations of compelling human need with appropriate measures, which may include coercive measures like sanctions and international prosecution, and in extreme cases military intervention.

C. The responsibility to rebuild: to provide, particularly after a military intervention, full assistance with recovery, reconstruction and reconciliation, addressing the causes of the harm the intervention was designed to halt or avert.

(4) Priorities

A. Prevention is the single most important dimension of the responsibility to protect: prevention options should always be exhausted before intervention is contemplated, and more commitment and resources must be devoted to it.

B. The exercise of the responsibility to both prevent and react should always involve less intrusive and coercive measures being considered before more coercive and intrusive ones are applied.

Principles for Military Intervention

(1) The Just Cause Threshold

Military intervention for human protection purposes is an exceptional and extraordinary measure. To be warranted, there must be serious and irreparable harm occurring to human beings, or imminently likely to occur, of the following kind:

A. large scale loss of life, actual or apprehended, with genocidal intent or not, which is the product either of deliberate state action, or state neglect or inability to act, or a failed state situation; or

B. large scale "ethnic cleansing," actual or apprehended, whether carried out by killing, forced expulsion, acts of terror or rape.

(2) The Precautionary Principles

A. Right intention: The primary purpose of the intervention, whatever other motives intervening states may have, must be to halt or avert human suffering. Right intention is better assured with multilateral operations, clearly supported by regional opinion and the victims concerned.

B. Last resort: Military intervention can only be justified when every non-military option for the prevention or peaceful resolution of the crisis has been explored, with reasonable grounds for believing lesser measures would not have succeeded.

C. Proportional means: The scale, duration and intensity of the planned military intervention should be the minimum necessary to secure the defined human protection objective.

D. Reasonable prospects: There must be a reasonable chance of success in halting or averting the suffering which has justified the intervention, with the consequences of action not likely to be worse than the consequences of inaction.

(3) Right Authority

A. There is no better or more appropriate body than the United Nations Security Council to authorize military intervention for human protection purposes. The task is not to find alternatives to the Security Council as a source of authority, but to make the Security Council work better than it has.

B. Security Council authorization should in all cases be sought prior to any military intervention action being carried out. Those calling for an intervention should formally request such authorization, or have the Council raise the matter on its own initiative, or have the Secretary-General raise it under Article 99 of the U.N. Charter.

C. The Security Council should deal promptly with any request for authority to intervene where there are allegations of large scale loss of human life or ethnic cleansing. It should in this context seek adequate verification of facts or conditions on the ground that might support a military intervention.

D. The Permanent Five members of the Security Council should agree not to apply their veto power, in matters where their vital state interests are not involved, to obstruct the passage of resolutions authorizing military intervention for human protection purposes for which there is otherwise majority support.

E. If the Security Council rejects a proposal or fails to deal with it in a reasonable time, alternative options are:

I. consideration of the matter by the General Assembly in Emergency Special Session under the "Uniting for Peace" procedure; and

II. action within the area of jurisdiction by regional or sub-regional organizations under Chapter VIII of the Charter, subject to their seeking subsequent authorization from the Security Council.

F. The Security Council should take into account in all its deliberations that, if it fails to discharge its responsibility to protect in conscience-shocking situations crying out for action, concerned states may not rule out other means to meet the gravity and urgency of that situation—and that the stature and credibility of the United Nations may suffer thereby.

(4) Operational Principles

A. Clear objectives; clear and unambiguous mandate at all times; and resources to match.

B. Common military approach among involved partners; unity of command; clear and unequivocal communications and chain of command.

C. Acceptance of limitations, incrementalism and gradualism in the application of force, the objective being protection of a population, not defeat of a state.

D. Rules of engagement which fit the operational concept; are precise; reflect the principle of proportionality; and involve total adherence to international humanitarian law.

E. Acceptance that force protection cannot become the principal objective.

F. Maximum possible coordination with humanitarian organizations.

A More Secure World: Our Shared Responsibility
Report of the High-level Panel on Threats, Challenges, and Change,
U.N. Doc. A/59/565 (29 November 2004) at 57-58.

203. We endorse the emerging norm that there is a collective international responsibility to protect, exercisable by the Security Council authorizing military intervention as a last resort, in the event of genocide and other large-scale killing, ethnic cleansing or serious violations of humanitarian law which sovereign Governments have proved powerless or unwilling to prevent. ...

205. If the Security Council is to win the respect it must have as the primary body in the collective security system, it is critical that its most important and influential decisions, those with large-scale life-and-death impact, be better made, better substantiated and better communicated. ...

206. The guidelines we propose will not produce agreed conclusions with push-button predictability. The point of adopting them is ... to maximize the possibility of achieving Security Council consensus around when it is appropriate or not to use coercive action, including armed force; to maximize international support for whatever the Council decides; and to minimize the possibility of individual Member States bypassing the Security Council.

207. In considering whether to authorize ... the use of military force, the Security Council should always address ... at least the following five basic criteria of legitimacy:

(a) *Seriousness of the threat.* Is the threatened harm to State or human security of a kind, and sufficiently clear and serious, to justify prima facie the use of military force? In the case of internal threats, does it involve genocide and other large-scale killing, ethnic cleansing or serious violations of humanitarian law, actual or imminently apprehended?

(b) *Proper purpose.* Is it clear that the primary purpose of the proposed military action is to halt or avert the threat in question, whatever other purposes or motives may be involved?

(c) *Last resort.* Has every non-military option for meeting the threat in question been explored, with reasonable grounds for believing that other measures will not succeed?

(d) *Proportional measures.* Are the scale, duration and intensity of the proposed military action the minimum necessary to meet the threat in question?

(e) *Balance of consequences.* Is there a reasonable chance of the military action being successful in meeting the threat in question, with the consequences of action not likely to be worse than the consequences of inaction?

208. The above guidelines for authorizing the use of force should be embodied in declaratory resolutions of the Security Council and General Assembly.

NOTES

1) The debate on whether, in what circumstances, and by whom there should be outside intervention in a sovereign state to avert or halt humanitarian disasters has been marked by a gradual shift away from discussions of a *right* to humanitarian intervention and toward a *responsibility* to protect particularly threatened populations. The ICISS report is among the most comprehensive articulations of this framework. Do you agree with the Commission's assertion that the notion of a "responsibility to protect" provides a more appropriate conceptual framework than that of delimitation of a right to humanitarian intervention? Do you agree with the proposition that states have a legal responsibility to protect populations of other states in the case of extreme human rights abuses?

2) The report of the Independent International Commission on Kosovo, chaired by the eminent South African jurist Richard Goldstone, concluded that the 1999 NATO military intervention was "illegal but legitimate. It was illegal because it did not receive prior approval from the United Nations Security Council. However, ... the intervention was justified because all diplomatic avenues had been exhausted and because the intervention had the effect of liberating the majority population of Kosovo from a long period of oppression under Serbian rule."[118] Some commentators have suggested that humanitarian intervention (without Security Council authorization) should remain illegal, while potentially legitimate in a narrow range of cases. Do you agree?

3) The ICISS report is one of several efforts aimed at formulating "guidelines" that could assist decision makers in future cases of extreme crisis. The development of such guidelines, along with the "emerging norm" of a responsibility to protect, was endorsed by the High-level Panel on Threats, Challenges, and Change, which the U.N. Secretary-General had convened in 2003 to examine global threats and challenges to international peace and security and to identify the contribution that collective action can make in addressing these challenges. Guidelines have also been advocated by some governments, such as the British and Dutch governments. Other states, especially in the developing world, remain suspicious of any effort to establish a legal basis for humanitarian or "protective" interventions. The United States too has shown little enthusiasm for relevant initiatives. What considerations animate these positions? Do you think that "guidelines" would improve on the existing situation? Compare the role played by the General Assembly's "Definition of Aggression," discussed above in Section A. Note that the High-level Panel report envisages the application of the suggested guiding principles not just in the context of the responsibility to protect but for all collective decisions on the use of force. Subsequently, the U.N. Secretary-General accepted the High-level Panel's report and embraced the responsibility to protect in his own report to the General Assembly in March 2005, titled *In Larger Freedom: Towards Development, Security, and Human Rights for All*. Later still, the World Summit of heads of states and governments in September 2005 endorsed the responsibility to protect populations from genocide, war crimes, ethnic cleansing, and crimes against humanity as a responsibility for each individual state and for the international community through the United Nations.[119]

---

118 Independent International Commission on Kosovo, *The Kosovo Report: Conflict, International Response, Lessons Learned*, Executive Summary—Main Findings (2000).

4) Consider the following concerns, sketched by U.N. Secretary-General Kofi Annan in his 1999 address to the U.N. General Assembly:

> To those for whom the greatest threat to the future of international order is the use of force in the absence of a Security Council mandate, one might ask—not in the context of Kosovo—but in the context of Rwanda: If, in those dark days and hours leading up to the genocide, a coalition of States had been prepared to act in defence of the Tutsi population, but did not receive prompt Council authorization, should such a coalition have stood aside and allowed the horror to unfold?
>
> To those for whom the Kosovo action heralded a new era when States and groups of States can take military action outside the established mechanisms for enforcing international law, one might ask: Is there not a danger of such interventions undermining the imperfect, yet resilient, security system created after the Second World War, and of setting dangerous precedents for future interventions without a clear criterion to decide who might invoke these precedents, and in what circumstances?[120]

What constitutes "right authority" for interventions to protect threatened populations? Should authority rest exclusively with the Security Council? Consider the approach sketched out in the ICISS report's "Core Principles." Would the "Uniting for Peace" process, discussed below in Section 4, provide a viable alternative if the Security Council failed to act? Should individual states be entitled to launch a protective intervention? What about regional organizations, such as NATO? See also below, Section D on "The United Nations and Regional Arrangements."

Invitation

When an invitation is issued by one government to another to participate in its domestic or external affairs, such involvement would not be classed as intervention or aggression. However, the requesting government must be in control of the country and must be the lawful government. Naturally, the invitation must be genuine and voluntary and no untoward pressure must have been put on it that would vitiate the agreement. The invitation must have emanated from a person with the authority to make it. This issue was raised in the context of the Grenada intervention[121] when Sir Paul Scoon, the Governor-General of Grenada, exercised purported constitutional power to invite the United States and the Organization of Eastern Caribbean States to assist.[122] Such a request may be seen

---

119 See Report of the Secretary-General, U.N. Doc. A/59/2005 at para. 135, and *2005 World Summit Outcome*, U.N. Doc. A/60/L.1 at paras. 138 and 139. For a discussion, see N.J. Wheeler, "Legitimating Humanitarian Intervention: Principles and Procedures" (2001) 2 Melbourne J. Int'l L. 301.

120 Secretary-General Presents His Annual Report to General Assembly, Press Release SG/SM/7136 GA/9596 (20 September 1999).

121 Discussed above in the text accompanying note 92.

122 See C. Joyner, *supra* note 92 and Moore, "Grenada," *supra* note 92. Note also J.L. Hargrove, "Intervention by Invitation and the Politics of the New World Order," in L. Fisler Damrosch and D.J. Scheffer, *supra* note 2 at 113.

as a legitimate response to acts of aggression by a third state in contravention of article 2(4) of the Charter. Thus, there is nothing wrong in State A giving help to State B, which is being threatened or attacked by State C. Such action could fall within the "inherent right of ... collective self-defence" contained in article 51 of the Charter and at customary international law, provided the relevant conditions are satisfied.[123] For instance, after the invasion of Kuwait by Iraq on August 2, 1990 the Kuwaiti government in exile appealed for help to the international community. The assistance given by the coalition states was authorized under the various U.N. Security Council resolutions to be discussed in the next section. However, even without such cohesive action at the United Nations an argument for collective self-defence based on invitation could have been made.[124]

A different question is whether a state may respond to an invitation to assist another state in quelling a revolution or other serious unrest. It seems that to give such assistance is legitimate, as long as the government that has issued the invitation is not suppressing a self-determination movement.[125] In the case of a legitimate request, it may strengthen the move to intervene if the insurgents are already receiving outside support. Would it make a difference if they have not yet established effective control over any sizeable part of the country?

4. Collective Measures Pursuant to the U.N. Charter

United Nations Charter
Articles 2(7), 24, 25, and 39-51
Reproduced in the Documentary Supplement

NOTES

The U.N. Security Council is the organ that is given primary responsibility for international peace and security under article 24 of the Charter. By article 25 its decisions, as opposed to its hortatory resolutions, are binding on member states: see the interpretation by the ICJ in the *Namibia Case* reproduced in Chapter 2, Section C on "Other Legal Persons." Pursuant to Chapter VII of the Charter, decisions relating to threats to the peace, breaches of the peace, or acts of aggression are so binding. In order for the Security Council to exercise the powers in Chapter VII it has first to determine the existence of a threat to or breach of the peace. It managed to do so only in three situations prior to the Iraq–Kuwait crisis of 1990.

The first occasion was in 1950 following the invasion of South Korea by North Korea. The Security Council adopted a resolution determining the breach, called for the cessation

---

123 *Nicaragua* case, *supra* note 17 at paras. 193-199, and the discussion Notes in subsection B.1 on "The Right of Self-Defence."

124 See generally Shaw, *supra* note 3 at 1036. Note that in resolution 661 of August 6, 1990, reproduced in the next Section, the Security Council affirmed the collective right of self-defence in the Preamble.

125 See the 1970 Declaration of Principles of International Law, reproduced in the Documentary Supplement and the 1977 Protocol I Additional to the 4 Geneva Conventions, *supra* note 111.

of hostilities and the withdrawal of the North Korean forces, and called on member states to assist the United Nations in Korea.[126] When the North Koreans neither ceased hostilities nor withdrew their forces to the 38th parallel as called for, the Security Council recommended in a second resolution that member states furnish such assistance to the Republic of Korea as was necessary to repel the armed attack and restore international peace and security in the area.[127] The third resolution on Korea welcomed the support already given to assist the Republic of Korea in defending itself against armed attack and recommended that all member states providing armed forces and other assistance pursuant to the earlier resolutions make such forces and assistance available to a unified command under the United States. The United States was requested to designate the commander of such forces.[128] The major question concerning the Korean resolutions is whether the action by the Security Council in adopting them was constitutional in the absence of the U.S.S.R. Refer to the powers of the Security Council contained in U.N. Charter articles 24-28, reproduced in the Documentary Supplement. Was the U.S.S.R. itself in violation of article 28 by being absent? Can article 27 be read to mean the permanent members present and voting? What if all of the permanent members were absent at the same time?

The second occasion when the Security Council acted under Chapter VII was following the Argentine invasion of the Falklands/Malvinas Islands. On April 3, 1982 the Security Council adopted a resolution in which it determined that a breach of the peace existed and demanded the immediate cessation of hostilities, followed by the immediate withdrawal of the Argentine forces.[129]

The third occasion was in the Iran–Iraq Gulf War 1980-1988, when the Security Council adopted a resolution in which it determined that there was a breach of the peace in that conflict, acting specifically under articles 39 and 40 of the Charter.[130]

Until the post–Cold War cohesiveness in the Security Council, which in 1999 was sorely tested over Kosovo, as it was also after 1997 over continued sanctions against Iraq and then the 2003 invasion of Iraq, the exercise of the veto by one of the permanent members too often created an impasse in that body. Recognizing this inherent weakness in the system, the General Assembly sought to complete the authorization of collective measures by way of the Uniting for Peace Resolution. The documents that follow relate

---

126 See S.C. Res. 82 (1950), U.N. SCOR, 5th year, *Res. and Dec.* 5; U.N. Doc. S/INF/5/Rev. 1, adopted by 9 votes in favour to 0 against with 1 abstention (Yugoslavia). The U.S.S.R. was not present.

127 See S.C. Res. 83 (1950), U.N. SCOR, 5th year, *Res. and Dec.* 5; U.N. Doc. S/INF/5/Rev. 1 at 3, adopted by 7 votes in favour to 1 against (Yugoslavia) with 2 abstentions. The U.S.S.R. was not present.

128 See S.C. Res. 84 (1950), U.N. SCOR, 5th year, *Res. and Dec.* 5; U.N. Doc. S/INF/5/Rev. 1, adopted by 7 votes in favour to 0 against with three abstentions. The U.S.S.R. was not present.

129 U.N. Doc. S/RES/502 (1982); reprinted in (1982) 21 I.L.M. 679, adopted by a vote of 10 in favour to 1 against (Panama) with 4 abstentions (China, Poland, Spain, and the U.S.S.R.). See R. Perl, *The Falkland Islands Dispute in International Law and Politics* (1983).

130 U.N. Doc. S/RES/598 (1987) 26 I.L.M. 1479. Adopted unanimously. See M. Weller, "Comments: The Use of Force and Collective Security," in I. Dekker and H. Post, eds., *The Gulf War of 1980-1988* (1992) 71; S. Dallal, "International Law and the United Nations' Role in the Gulf Crisis" (1992) 18 Syracuse J. Int'l L. & Com. 111; and J. Quigley, "The New World Order and the Rule of Law" (1992) 18 Syracuse J. Int'l L. & Com. 75.

briefly to this action by the General Assembly and in more detail to the role of the Security Council under Chapter VII. Reference should also be made to the discussion of U.N. principles, organs, and processes in Chapter 2, Section C.1 on "International Organizations."

Uniting for Peace Resolution[131]
GA Res. 377A(V), UN GAOR, 5th Sess., Supp. No. 20,
U.N. Doc. A/1775 (1951) at 10

The General Assembly, ...

Finding that international tension exists on a dangerous scale, ...

Reaffirming the importance of the exercise by the Security Council of its primary responsibility for the maintenance of international peace and security, and the duty of the permanent members to seek unanimity and to exercise restraint in the use of veto.

Reaffirming that the initiative in negotiating the agreements for armed forces provided for in Article 43 of the Charter belongs to the Security Council, and desiring to ensure that, pending the conclusion of such agreements, the United Nations has at its disposal means for maintaining international peace and security.

Conscious that failure of the Security Council to discharge its responsibilities on behalf of all the Member States, particularly those responsibilities referred to in the two preceding paragraphs, does not relieve Member States of their obligations or the United Nations of its responsibility under the Charter to maintain international peace and security.

Recognizing in particular that such failure does not deprive the General Assembly of its rights or relieve it of its responsibilities under the Charter in regard to the maintenance of international peace and security.

Recognizing that discharge by the General Assembly of its responsibility in these respects calls for possibilities of observation which would ascertain the facts and expose aggressors; for the existence of armed forces which could be used collectively; and for the possibility of timely recommendation by the General Assembly to Members of the United Nations for collective action which, to be effective, should be prompt.

A.1. *Resolves* that if the Security Council, because of lack of unanimity of the permanent members, fails to exercise its primary responsibility for the maintenance of international peace and security in any case where there appears to be a threat to the peace, breach of the peace or act of aggression, the General Assembly shall consider the matter immediately with a view to making appropriate recommendations to Members for collective measures, including in the case of a breach of the peace or act of aggression the use of armed force when necessary, to maintain or restore international peace and security. If not in session at the time, the General Assembly may meet in an emergency special session within twenty-four hours of the request therefor. Such

---

131   See J. Andrassy, "Uniting for Peace" (1956) 50 A.J.I.L. 563; H. Reicher, "The Uniting for Peace Resolution on the Thirtieth Anniversary of Its Passage" (1981) 20 Colum. J. Transnat'l L. 1; and L.H. Woolsey, "The 'Uniting for Peace' Resolution of the United Nations" (1951) 45 A.J.I.L. 129.

emergency special session shall be called if requested by the Security Council on the vote of any seven members, or by a majority of the Members of the United Nations; ...

C.7. *Invites* each Member of the United Nations to survey its resources in order to determine the nature and scope of the assistance it may be in a position to render in support of any recommendations of the Security Council or of the General Assembly for the restoration of international peace and security;

8. *Recommends* to the Members of the United Nations that each Member maintain within its national armed forces elements so trained, organized and equipped that they could promptly be made available, in accordance with its constitutional processes, for service as a United Nations unit or units, upon recommendation by the Security Council or General Assembly, without prejudice to the use of such elements in exercise of the right of individual or collective self-defence recognized in Article 51 of the Charter.

NOTES

1) The Uniting for Peace Resolution was adopted by 52 votes for and 5 against with 2 abstentions. The General Assembly adopted this then controversial resolution at the time of the Security Council's impasse over the Korean crisis in 1950. It has been used a number of times since Korea, including for Suez in 1956, Hungary in 1956, Jordan and Lebanon in 1958, the Congo in 1960, Afghanistan in 1980, and Namibia in 1981.

2) What is the effect of the General Assembly "making appropriate recommendations to Members for collective measures"? Are member states bound to undertake the measures if they disagree with them? What authority does the General Assembly have with regard to collective measures? Consider the U.N. Charter articles 10-17, reproduced in the Documentary Supplement. Does this resolution enlarge the Assembly's powers? Can it? When several members of the U.N., including the U.S.S.R. and France, objected to paying for peacekeeping expenses assessed as part of their financial contributions to the U.N. by the General Assembly under its budgetary power in article 17(2), the GA asked the ICJ for an advisory opinion. The objectors claimed that the peacekeeping forces raised under the Uniting for Peace Resolution for Suez in 1956 (UNEF) and for the Congo in 1960 (ONUC) were unconstitutional. In *Certain Expenses of the United Nations Case*[132] the ICJ, noting that the Security Council's responsibility under article 24 is primary and not exclusive, advised that by articles 14 and 18 the GA may take decisions (subject to article 12) recommending measures in respect of international peace and security that would constitute "expenses of the Organization" within article 17(2). The Court also opined that the U.N. Charter, through article 11(2), draws a distinction between enforcement action, which only the SC may authorize under Chapter VII, and other measures to preserve peace and security. The Court declared that the peacekeeping operations of the UNEF and ONUC, which essentially were ceasefire monitoring missions, were not enforcement actions, but were legitimately recommended and expensed by the GA.

3) Under article 51 of the U.N. Charter, a state's right of self-defence, discussed previously in Section B.1 on "The Right of Self-Defence," subsists until the Security

---

132 [1962] I.C.J. Rep. 151.

Council has acted to maintain international peace and security. However, because of the veto power contained in article 27(3) it may be impossible for the Security Council to do so. In that case the right of self-defence under article 51 will continue.

4) Note that article 39 of the U.N. Charter speaks of "any threat to the peace, breach of the peace, or act of aggression." What can constitute "any threat to the peace"? Does this mean "international peace"? Does a threat to the peace also constitute a violation of article 2(4) of the Charter?

5) The first occasion when the Security Council exercised something approaching its full powers under Chapter VII of the U.N. Charter was the Iraq–Kuwait crisis, which arose in 1990. The following documentation provides the opportunity to assess the operational strengths and weaknesses of the Chapter VII provisions.

The 1990-91 Iraq–Kuwait Crisis: Gulf War I

On August 2, 1990 Iraq under the leadership of President Saddam Hussein invaded another state, Kuwait, with, it was estimated, over 100,000 troops. These troops had been amassed along the border between the two states the week before. Within 48 hours Iraq had control of Kuwait. On August 8, 1990 President Hussein announced "the comprehensive and eternal merger" of the two countries. Kuwait was to be "Province No. 19" of Iraq. It has been surmised in retrospect that President Hussein thought that the major powers on the Security Council would simply view this step as regional *realpolitik*, and not become involved in a distant and expensive conflict.[133]

This was a serious miscalculation. It failed to envisage the universal condemnation of one of the most blatant acts of armed aggression since World War II. Also, it did not allow for the changes in international outlook in the then Soviet Union and the fact that that state would join the consensus and not use the veto. The invasion of Kuwait by Iraq on August 2, 1990 and the Gulf War of January and February 1991 put the Security Council on the forefront of the international stage. It had not played such a dynamic role since the Korean crisis in 1950. The crisis illustrated the "sheer necessity of the United Nations as a forum for international conflict resolution."[134] Twelve resolutions swiftly condemning the invasion were adopted between August and the end of November 1990. Three others were adopted in April 1991 after the cessation of hostilities. They are reproduced in part below, following a brief chronology of the crisis.

---

133 Tessitore and Woolfson, *supra* note 102. And see *Agora: The Gulf Crisis in International and Foreign Relations Law* (1991) 85 A.J.I.L. 63 and 506.

134 *Supra* note 102 at 4.

Diary of the Iraq–Kuwait Crisis

1990

Aug. 1/2 — Iraqi troops entered Kuwait "at the invitation of a new provisional government to restore order"—per Iraqi representative to U.N.

Aug. 2 — Security Council condemned Iraq's invasion and demanded unconditional withdrawal. See Resolution 660.

Aug. 6 — Security Council decided upon comprehensive economic sanctions. See Resolution 661.

Aug. 8 — U.S. forces entered Saudi Arabia by agreement and took up positions along the Saudi–Kuwait border.

Aug. 8 — Iraq announced the annexation of Kuwait.

Aug. 9 — Security Council declared the annexation of Kuwait to be illegal, null and void. See Resolution 662.

Aug. 10 — Iraq began to detain foreigners and to abduct diplomats.

Aug. 12 — U.S. began to blockade Iraqi oil exports by sea with ships and aircraft.

Aug. 18 — Security Council demanded Iraq release abducted diplomats and respect their immunity. See Resolution 664.

Aug. 23 — Secretary General Perez de Cuellar first met with Iraqi authorities.

Aug. 25 — Security Council authorized measures to enforce economic sanctions. See Resolution 665.

Sept. 13 — Security Council established machinery to determine whether the civilian populations of Kuwait and Iraq were suffering as a result of the economic sanctions and, if so, to deliver humanitarian assistance in the form of foodstuffs and medical supplies through the Red Cross and other agencies.

Sept. 16 — Security Council ordered Iraq to release all foreigners and to stop interfering with diplomatic personnel.

Sept. 24 — After several states, including Jordan, sought assistance to overcome the economic side effects of the sanctions against Iraq, Security Council invited the Committee of Security Council members, established under Resolution 661 (Aug. 6, above) to recommend appropriate action.

Sept. 25 — Security Council strengthened the enforcement of sanctions by measures against aircraft and ships and affirmed that Iraq and Iraqis who mistreated Kuwaitis were liable for grave breaches of the Fourth Geneva Convention on humanitarian standards toward persons in occupied territory. See Resolution 670.

Oct. 29 — One month later, as the crisis deepened the Security-Council reiterated its demands of Iraq to stop molesting the Kuwaiti population and dismantling Kuwait, and requested the Secretary-General to use his good offices to reach a peaceful solution to the crisis. See Resolution 674.

Nov. 28 — After Iraq began to destroy civilian records in Kuwait, the Security Council mandated the Secretary-General to take custody of the population register.

Nov. 29 — Security Council authorized the use of "all necessary means" to implement Resolution 660 (August 2, above) if Iraq had not complied by January 15, 1991. See Resolution 678.

1991

Jan. 17 — Operation Desert Storm began.

Jan. 21 — General Assembly called for the convening by Security Council of an International Peace Conference on the Middle East.

Feb. 28 — End of hostilities. Kuwait was liberated and Iraq's forces were crushed, but President Hussein survived.

Mar. 3 — Secretary-General announced a mission to Iraq and Kuwait "to assess the humanitarian needs arising in the immediate post crisis environment."

Apr. 3 — Security Council Resolution 687 established detailed terms of submission by Iraq, including return of all Kuwaitis and Kuwaiti property, respect for the international border with Kuwait, destruction of all chemical, biological, and nuclear weapons and capabilities under international supervision, payment of compensation for damage caused by the invasion of Kuwait out of a fund constituted from Iraq's oil exports, renunciation of terrorism, and acceptance of a U.N. Observation Mission to monitor a demilitarized frontier zone.

April — Throughout the month conditions akin to civil war ensued in Iraq when Kurds in the north and Shi'ite Muslims in the south rebelled against Baghdad and were brutally suppressed by President Hussein's remaining armed forces.

Apr. 5 — Security Council condemned Iraq's repression of its civilian population, especially the Kurdish people, and demanded its end. See Resolution 688 (1991) reproduced in the previous subsection on "Humanitarian Intervention."

Apr. 17 — General Assembly appropriated US$61 million for the operation of the Observation Mission for the first six months.

Apr. 18 — Secretary-General reached agreement with Iraq for establishment of U.N. Humanitarian Centre in Iraq to alleviate the suffering of the population.

Security Council Resolution 660 (1990)[135]
U.N. Doc. S/RES/660, August 2, 1990

The Security Council,

Alarmed by the invasion of Kuwait on 2 August 1990 by the military forces of Iraq,

Determining that there exists a breach of international peace and security as regards the Iraqi invasion of Kuwait,

Acting under Articles 39 and 40 of the Charter of the United Nations,

1. *Condemns* the Iraqi invasion of Kuwait;

2. *Demands* that Iraq withdraw immediately and unconditionally all its forces to the positions in which they were located on 1 August 1990;

3. *Calls upon* Iraq and Kuwait to begin immediately intensive negotiations for the resolution of their differences and supports all efforts in this regard, and especially those of the League of Arab States;

4. *Decides* to meet again as necessary to consider further steps to ensure compliance with the present resolution.

Security Council Resolution 661 (1990)[136]
U.N. Doc. S/RES/661, August 6, 1990

The Security Council, ...

Deeply concerned that ... [resolution 660 (1990)] has not been implemented and that the invasion by Iraq of Kuwait continues with further loss of human life and material destruction,

Determined to bring the invasion and occupation of Kuwait by Iraq to an end and to restore the sovereignty, independence and territorial integrity of Kuwait,

Noting that the legitimate Government of Kuwait has expressed its readiness to comply with resolution 660 (1990),

Mindful of its responsibilities under the Charter of the United Nations for the maintenance of international peace and security,

Affirming the inherent right of individual or collective self-defence, in response to the armed attack by Iraq against Kuwait, in accordance with Article 51 of the Charter,

Acting under Chapter VII of the Charter of the United Nations,

1. *Determines* that Iraq so far has failed to comply with paragraph 2 of resolution 660 (1990) and has usurped the authority of the legitimate Government of Kuwait;

2. *Decides*, as a consequence, to take the following measures to secure compliance of Iraq with paragraph 2 of resolution 660 (1990) and to restore the authority of the legitimate Government of Kuwait;

---

135 Adopted by a vote of 14 in favour and 0 against. One member, Yemen, did not participate in the vote. Note that the resolutions from August-November 1991 are contained in Can. T.S. 1990 No. 44.

136 Adopted by a vote of 13 in favour to 2 against and 2 abstentions (Cuba and Yemen).

3. *Decides* that all States shall prevent:

(a) The import into their territories of all commodities and products originating in Iraq or Kuwait exported therefrom after the date of the present resolution;

(b) Any activities by their nationals or in their territories which would promote or are calculated to promote the export or trans-shipment of any commodities or products from Iraq or Kuwait; and any dealings by their nationals or their flag vessels or in their territories in any commodities or products originating in Iraq or Kuwait and exported therefrom after the date of the present resolution, including in particular any transfer of funds to Iraq or Kuwait for the purposes of such activities or dealings;

(c) The sale or supply by their nationals or from their territories or using their flag vessels of any commodities or products, including weapons or any other military equipment, whether or not originating in their territories but not including supplies intended strictly for medical purposes, and, in humanitarian circumstances, foodstuffs, to any person or body in Iraq or Kuwait or to any person or body for the purposes of any business carried on in or operated from Iraq or Kuwait, and any activities by their nationals or in their territories which promote or are calculated to promote such sale or supply of such commodities or products;

4. *Decides* that all States shall not make available to the Government of Iraq or to any commercial, industrial or public utility undertaking in Iraq or Kuwait, any funds or any other financial or economic resources and shall prevent their nationals and any persons within their territories from removing from their territories or otherwise making available to that Government or to any such undertaking any such funds or resources and from remitting any other funds to persons or bodies within Iraq or Kuwait, except payments exclusively for strictly medical or humanitarian purposes and, in humanitarian circumstances, foodstuffs;

5. *Calls upon* all States, including States non-members of the United Nations, to act strictly in accordance with the provisions of the present resolution notwithstanding any contract entered into or licence granted before the date of the present resolution; ...

9. *Decides* that, ... nothing in the present resolution shall prohibit assistance to the Government of Kuwait, and calls upon all States:

(a) To take appropriate measures to protect assets of the legitimate Government of Kuwait and its agencies;

(b) Not to recognize any regime set up by the occupying Power.

Security Council Resolution 662 (1990)[137]
U.N. Doc. S/RES/662, August 9, 1990

The Security Council, ...

Gravely alarmed by the declaration by Iraq of a "comprehensive and eternal merger" with Kuwait,

Demanding once again that Iraq withdraw immediately and unconditionally all its forces to the positions in which they were located on 1 August 1990,

Determined to bring the occupation of Kuwait by Iraq to an end and to restore the sovereignty, independence and territorial integrity of Kuwait,

Determined also to restore the authority of the legitimate Government of Kuwait,

1. *Decides* that annexation of Kuwait by Iraq under any form and whatever pretext has no legal validity, and is considered null and void;

2. *Calls upon* all States, international organizations and specialized agencies not to recognize that annexation, and to refrain from any action or dealing that might be interpreted as an indirect recognition of the annexation;

3. *Demands* that Iraq rescind its actions purporting to annex Kuwait;

4. *Decides* to keep this item on its agenda and to continue its efforts to put an early end to the occupation.

Security Council Resolution 664 (1990)[138]
U.N. Doc. S/RES/664, August 18, 1990

The Security Council,

Recalling the Iraqi invasion and purported annexation of Kuwait and resolutions 660, 661 and 662,

Deeply concerned for the safety and well being of third state nationals in Iraq and Kuwait,

Recalling the obligations of Iraq in this regard under international law,

Welcoming the efforts of the Secretary-General to pursue urgent consultations with the Government of Iraq following the concern and anxiety expressed by the members of the Council on 17 August 1990,

Acting under Chapter VII of the United Nations Charter,

1. *Demands* that Iraq permit and facilitate the immediate departure from Kuwait and Iraq of the nationals of third countries and grant immediate and continuing access of consular officials to such nationals;

2. *Also demands* that Iraq take no action to jeopardize the safety, security or health of such nationals;

3. *Reaffirms* its decision in resolution 662 (1990) that annexation of Kuwait by Iraq is null and void, and therefore demands that the government of Iraq rescind its

---

137 Adopted by unanimous vote.

138 Adopted by unanimous vote.

orders for the closure of diplomatic and consular missions in Kuwait and the withdrawal of the immunity of their personnel, and refrain from any such actions in the future.

Security Council Resolution 665 (1990)[139]
U.N. Doc. S/RES/665, August 25, 1990

The Security Council, ...

Having decided in resolution 661 (1990) to impose economic sanctions under Chapter VII of the Charter of the United Nations,

Determined to bring an end to the occupation of Kuwait by Iraq which imperils the existence of a Member State and to restore the legitimate authority, and the sovereignty, independence and territorial integrity of Kuwait which requires the speedy implementation of the above resolutions,

Deploring the loss of innocent life stemming from the Iraqi invasion of Kuwait and determined to prevent further such losses,

Gravely alarmed that Iraq continues to refuse to comply with resolutions 660 (1990), 661 (1990), 662 (1990) and 664 (1990) and in particular at the conduct of the Government of Iraq in using Iraqi flag vessels to export oil,

1. *Calls upon* those Member States cooperating with the Government of Kuwait which are deploying maritime forces to the area to use such measures commensurate to the specific circumstances as may be necessary under the authority of the Security Council to halt all inward and outward maritime shipping in order to inspect and verify their cargoes and destinations and to ensure strict implementation of the provisions related to such shipping laid down in resolution 661 (1990);

2. *Invites* Member States accordingly to cooperate as may be necessary to ensure compliance with the provisions of resolution 661 (1990) with maximum use of political and diplomatic measures, in accordance with paragraph 1 above;

3. *Requests* all States to provide in accordance with the Charter such assistance as may be required by the States referred to in paragraph 1 of this resolution;

4. *Also requests* the States concerned to coordinate their actions in pursuit of the above paragraphs of this resolution using as appropriate mechanisms of the Military Staff Committee and after consultation with the Secretary-General to submit reports to the Security Council and its Committee established under resolution 661 (1990) to facilitate the monitoring of the implementation of this resolution.

---

139   Adopted by a vote of 13 in favour to 0 against with 2 abstentions (Cuba and Yemen).

Security Council Resolution 670 (1990)[140]
U.N. Doc. S/RES/670, September 25, 1990

The Security Council, ...

Acting under Chapter VII of the Charter of the United Nations,

1. *Calls upon* all States to carry out their obligations to ensure strict and complete compliance with resolution 661 (1990) and in particular paragraphs 3, 4 and 5 thereof;

2. *Confirms* that resolution 661 (1990) applies to all means of transport, including aircraft;

3. *Decides* that all States, notwithstanding the existence of any rights or obligations conferred or imposed by any international agreement or any contract entered into or any licence or permit granted before the date of the present resolution, shall deny permission to any aircraft to take off from their territory if the aircraft would carry any cargo to or from Iraq or Kuwait other than food in humanitarian circumstances, subject to authorization by the Council or the Committee established by resolution 661 (1990) and in accordance with resolution 666 (1990), or supplies intended strictly for medical purposes or solely for UNIIMOG [United Nations Iran–Iraq Military Observer Group];

4. *Decides also* that all States shall deny permission to any aircraft destined to land in Iraq or Kuwait, whatever its State of registration, to overfly its territory unless:

(a) the aircraft lands at an airfield designated by that State outside Iraq or Kuwait in order to permit its inspection to ensure that there is no cargo on board in violation of resolution 661 (1990) or the present resolution, and for this purpose the aircraft may be detained for as long as necessary; or

(b) the particular flight has been approved by the Committee established by resolution 661 (1990); or

(c) the flight is certified by the United Nations as solely for the purposes of the Military Observer Group;

5. *Decides further* that each State shall take all necessary measures to ensure that any aircraft registered in its territory or operated by an operator who has his principle place of business or residence in its territory complies with the provisions of resolution 661 (1990) and the present resolution; ...

8. *Also calls upon* all States to detain any ships of Iraqi registry which enter their ports and which are being or have been used in violation of resolution 661 (1990), or to deny such ships entrance to their ports except in circumstances recognized under international law as necessary to safeguard human life;

9. *Reminds* all States of their obligation under resolution 661 (1990) with regard to the freezing of Iraqi assets, and the protection of the assets of the legitimate Government of Kuwait and its agencies, located within their territory and to report to the Committee established under resolution 661 (1990) regarding those assets.

---

140 Adopted by a vote of 14 in favour and 1 against (Cuba).

Security Council Resolution 674 (1990)[141]
U.N. Doc. S/RES/674, October 29, 1990

The Security Council, ...
   Acting under Chapter VII of the Charter of the United Nation, ...

A.

   1. *Demands* that the Iraqi authorities and occupying forces immediately cease and desist from taking third-State nationals hostage, mistreating and oppressing Kuwaiti and third-State nationals and any other actions, such as those reported to the Security Council ... that violate the decisions of this Council, the Charter of the United Nations, the Fourth Geneva Convention, the Vienna Conventions on Diplomatic and Consular Relations and international law; ...

   10. *Requires* that Iraq comply with the provisions of the present resolution and its previous resolutions, failing which the Security Council will need to take further measures under the Charter;

   11. *Decides* to remain actively and permanently seized of the matter until Kuwait has regained its independence and peace has been restored in conformity with the relevant resolutions of the Security Council.

B.

   12. *Reposes its trust* in the Secretary-General to make available his good offices and, as he considers appropriate, to pursue them and to undertake diplomatic efforts in order to reach a peaceful solution to the crisis caused by the Iraqi invasion and occupation of Kuwait on the basis of Security Council resolutions 660 (1990), 662 (1990) and 664 (1990), and calls upon all States, both those in the region and others, to pursue on this basis their efforts to this end, in conformity with the Charter, in order to improve the situation and restore peace, security and stability;

   13. Requests the Secretary-General to report to the Security Council on the results of his good offices and diplomatic efforts.

Security Council Resolution 678 (1990)[142]
U.N. Doc. S/RES/678, November 29, 1990

The Security Council, ...
   Noting that, despite all efforts by the United Nations, Iraq refuses to comply with its obligation to implement resolution 660 (1990) and the above-mentioned subsequent relevant resolutions, in flagrant contempt of the Security Council,

---

141   Adopted by a vote of 13 in favour to 0 against with 2 abstentions (Cuba and Yemen).

142   Adopted by a vote of 12 in favour to 2 against (Cuba and Yemen) and 1 abstention (China).

Mindful of its duties and responsibilities under the Charter of the United Nations for the maintenance and preservation of international peace and security,

Determined to secure full compliance with its decisions,

Acting under Chapter VII of the Charter,

1. *Demands* that Iraq comply fully with resolution 660 (1990) and all subsequent relevant resolutions, and decides, while maintaining all its decisions, to allow Iraq one final opportunity, as a pause of goodwill, to do so;

2. *Authorizes* Member States co-operating with the Government of Kuwait, unless Iraq on or before 15 January 1991 fully implements, as set forth in paragraph 1 above, the foregoing resolutions, to use all necessary means to uphold and implement resolution 660 (1990) and all subsequent relevant resolutions and to restore international peace and security in the area;

3. *Requests* all States to provide appropriate support for the actions undertaken in pursuance of paragraph 2 of the present resolution;

4. *Requests* the States concerned to keep the Security Council regularly informed on the progress of actions undertaken pursuant to paragraphs 2 and 3 of the present resolution;

5. *Decides* to remain seized of the matter.

Security Council Resolution 687 (1991)[143]
U.N. Doc. S/RES/687, April 3, 1991

The Security Council, ...

Welcoming the restoration to Kuwait of its sovereignty, independence and territorial integrity and the return of its legitimate Government,

Affirming the commitment of all Member States to the sovereignty, territorial integrity and political independence of Kuwait and Iraq, and noting the intention expressed by the Member States cooperating with Kuwait under paragraph 2 of resolution 678 (1990) to bring their military presence in Iraq to an end as soon as possible consistent with paragraph 8 of resolution 686 (1991), ...

Bearing in mind its objective of restoring international peace and security in the area as set out in recent resolutions of the Security Council,

Conscious of the need to take the following measures acting under Chapter VII of the Charter,

1. *Affirms* all thirteen resolutions noted above, except as expressly changed below to achieve the goals of this resolution, including a formal cease-fire;

A.

2. *Demands* that Iraq and Kuwait respect the inviolability of the international boundary and the allocation of islands set out in the "Agreed Minutes Between the State of Kuwait and the Republic of Iraq Regarding the Restoration of Friendly

---

143 Adopted by a vote of 12 in favour to 1 against (Cuba) with 2 abstentions (Ecuador and Yemen).

Relations, Recognition and Related Matters," signed by them in the exercise of their sovereignty at Baghdad on 4 October 1963 and registered with the United Nations and published by the United Nations in document 7063, United Nations, *Treaty Series*, 1964;

3. *Calls upon* the Secretary-General to lend his assistance to make arrangements with Iraq and Kuwait to demarcate the boundary between Iraq and Kuwait, drawing on appropriate material, including the map transmitted by Security Council document S/22412 and to report back to the Security Council within one month;

4. *Decides* to guarantee the inviolability of the above-mentioned international boundary and to take as appropriate all necessary measures to that end in accordance with the Charter of the United Nations;

B.

5. *Requests* the Secretary-General, after consulting with Iraq and Kuwait, to submit within three days to the Security Council for its approval a plan for the immediate deployment of a United Nations observer unit to monitor the Khor Abdullah and a demilitarized zone, which is hereby established, extending ten kilometres into Iraq and five kilometres into Kuwait from the boundary referred to in the "Agreed Minutes Between the State of Kuwait and the Republic of Iraq Regarding the Restoration of Friendly Relations, Recognition, and Related Matters" of 4 October 1963; to deter violations of the boundary through its presence in and surveillance of the demilitarized zone; to observe any hostile or potentially hostile action mounted from the territory of one State to the other; and for the Secretary-General to report regularly to the Security Council on the operations of the unit, and immediately if there are serious violations of the zone or potential threats to peace; ...

C.

7. *Invites* Iraq to reaffirm unconditionally its obligations under the Geneva Protocol for the Prohibition of the Use in War of Asphyxiating, Poisonous or Other Gases, and of Bacteriological Methods of Warfare, signed at Geneva on 17 June 1925, and to ratify the Convention on the Prohibition of the Development, Production and Stockpiling of Bacteriological (Biological) and Toxin Weapons and on Their Destruction, of 10 April 1972;

8. *Decides* that Iraq shall unconditionally accept the destruction, removal, or rendering harmless, under international supervision, of:

(*a*) All chemical and biological weapons and all stocks of agents and all related subsystems and components and all research, development, support and manufacturing facilities;

(*b*) All ballistic missiles with a range greater than 150 kilometres and related major parts, and repair and production facilities;

9. *Decides also*, for the implementation of paragraph 8 above, the following

(*a*) Iraq shall submit to the Secretary-General, within fifteen days of the adoption of the present resolution, a declaration of the locations, amounts and types of all items specified in paragraph 8 and agree to urgent, on-site inspection as specified below;

(*b*) The Secretary-General, in consultation with the appropriate Governments and, where appropriate, with the Director-General of the World Health Organization, within forty-five days of the passage of the present resolution, shall develop, and submit to the Council for approval, a plan calling for the completion of the following acts within forty-five days of such approval:

(*i*) The forming of a Special Commission, which shall carry out immediate on-site inspection of Iraq's biological, chemical and missile capabilities, based on Iraq's declarations and the designation of any additional locations by the Special Commission itself;

(*ii*) The yielding by Iraq of possession to the Special Commission for destruction, removal or rendering harmless, taking into account the requirements of public safety, of all items specified under paragraph 8(a) above, including items at the additional locations designated by the Special Commission under paragraph 9(b)(i) above and the destruction by Iraq, under the supervision of the Special Commission, of all its missile capabilities, including launchers, as specified under paragraph 8(b) above;

(*iii*) The provision by the Special Commission of the assistance and cooperation to the Director-General of the International Atomic Energy Agency required in paragraphs 12 and 13 below;

10. *Decides further* that Iraq shall unconditionally undertake not to use, develop, construct or acquire any of the items specified in paragraphs 8 and 9 above and requests the Secretary-General, in consultation with the Special Commission, to develop a plan for the future ongoing monitoring and verification of Iraq's compliance with this paragraph, to be submitted to the Security Council for approval within one hundred and twenty days of the passage of this resolution;

11. *Invites* Iraq to reaffirm unconditionally its obligations under the Treaty on the Non-Proliferation of Nuclear Weapons of 1 July 1968;

12. *Decides* that Iraq shall unconditionally agree not to acquire or develop nuclear weapons or nuclear-weapons-usable material or any subsystems or components or any research, development, support or manufacturing facilities related to the above; to submit to the Secretary-General and the Director-General of the International Atomic Energy Agency within fifteen days of the adoption of the present resolution a declaration of the locations, amounts, and types of all items specified above; to place all of its nuclear-weapons-usable materials under the exclusive control, for custody and removal, of the International Atomic Energy Agency, with the assistance and cooperation of the Special Commission as provided for in the plan of the Secretary-General discussed in paragraph 9 (b) above; to accept ... urgent on-site inspection and the destruction, removal or rendering harmless as appropriate of all items specified above; and to accept ... the future ongoing monitoring and verification of its compliance with these undertakings; ...

D.

15. *Requests* the Secretary-General to report to the Security Council on the steps taken to facilitate the return of all Kuwaiti property seized by Iraq, including a list of any property that Kuwait claims has not been returned or which has not been returned intact;

E.

16. *Reaffirms* that Iraq, without prejudice to the debts and obligations of Iraq arising prior to 2 August 1990, which will be addressed through the normal mechanisms, is liable under international law for any direct loss, damage, including environmental damage and the depletion of natural resources, or injury to foreign Governments, nationals and corporations, as a result of Iraq's unlawful invasion and occupation of Kuwait;

17. *Decides* that all Iraqi statements made since 2 August 1990 repudiating its foreign debt are null and void, and demands that Iraq adhere scrupulously to all of its obligations concerning servicing and repayment of its foreign debt;

18. *Decides also* to create a fund to pay compensation for claims that fall within paragraph 16 above and to establish a Commission that will administer the fund;

19. *Directs* the Secretary-General to develop and present to the Security Council for decision, no later than thirty days following the adoption of the present resolution, recommendations for the fund to meet the requirement for the payment of claims established in accordance with paragraph 18 above and for a programme to implement the decisions in paragraphs 16, 17 and 18 above, including: administration of the fund; mechanisms for determining the appropriate level of Iraq's contribution to the fund based on a percentage of the value of the exports of petroleum and petroleum products from Iraq not to exceed a figure to be suggested to the Council by the Secretary-General, taking into account the requirements of the people of Iraq, Iraq's payment capacity as assessed in conjunction with the international financial institutions taking into consideration external debt service, and the needs of the Iraqi economy; arrangements for ensuring that payments are made to the fund; the process by which funds will be allocated and claims paid; appropriate procedures for evaluating losses, listing claims and verifying their validity and resolving disputed claims in respect of Iraq's liability as specified in paragraph 16 above; and the composition of the Commission designated above;

F.

20. *Decides*, effective immediately, that the prohibitions against the sale or supply to Iraq of commodities or products, other than medicine and health supplies, and prohibitions against financial transactions related thereto contained in resolution 661 (1990) shall not apply to foodstuffs notified to the Security Council Committee established by resolution 661 (1990) concerning the situation between Iraq and Kuwait or, with the approval of that Committee, under the simplified and accelerated "no-objection" procedure, to materials and supplies for essential civilian needs as identified in the report of the Secretary-General dated 20 March 1991, and in further findings of humanitarian need by the Committee;

21. *Decides* that the Security Council shall review the provisions of paragraph 20 above every sixty days in the light of the policies and practices of the Government of Iraq, including the implementation of all relevant resolutions of the Security Council, for the purpose of determining whether to reduce or lift the prohibitions referred to therein;

22. *Decides also* that upon the approval by the Security Council of the programme called for in paragraph 19 above and upon Council agreement that Iraq has completed

all actions contemplated in paragraphs 8, 9, 10, 11, 12, and 13 above, the prohibitions against the import of commodities and products originating in Iraq and the prohibitions against financial transactions related thereto contained in resolution 661 (1990) shall have no further force or effect;

23. *Decides further* that, pending action by the Security Council under paragraph 22 above, the Security Council Committee established by resolution 661 (1990) shall be empowered to approve, when required to assure adequate financial resources on the part of Iraq to carry out the activities under paragraph 20 above, exceptions to the prohibition against the import of commodities and products originating in Iraq;

24. *Decides* that, in accordance with resolution 661 (1990) and subsequent related resolutions and until a further decision is taken by the Security Council, all States shall continue to prevent the sale or supply, or the promotion or facilitation of such sale or supply, to Iraq by their nationals, or from their territories or using their flag vessels or aircraft, of:

(*a*) Arms and related *matériel* of all types, specifically including the sale or transfer through other means of all forms of conventional military equipment, including for paramilitary forces, and spare parts and components and their means of production, for such equipment;

(*b*) Items specified and defined in paragraphs 8 and 12 above not otherwise covered above;

(*c*) Technology under licensing or other transfer arrangements used in the production, utilization or stockpiling of items specified in subparagraphs (*a*) and (*b*) above;

(*d*) Personnel or materials for training or technical support services relating to the design, development, manufacture, use, maintenance or support of items specified in subparagraphs (*a*) and (*b*) above;

25. *Calls upon* all States and international organizations to act strictly in accordance with paragraph 24 above, notwithstanding the existence of any contracts, agreements, licences or any other arrangements; ...

G.

30. *Decides* that, in furtherance of its commitment to facilitate the repatriation of all Kuwaiti and third country nationals, Iraq shall extend all necessary cooperation to the International Committee of the Red Cross, providing lists of such persons, facilitating the access of the International Committee of the Red Cross to all such persons wherever located or detained and facilitating the search by the International Committee of the Red Cross for those Kuwaiti and third country nationals still unaccounted for; ...

H.

32. *Requires* Iraq to inform the Security Council that it will not commit or support any act of international terrorism or allow any organization directed towards commission of such acts to operate within its territory and to condemn unequivocally and renounce all acts, methods and practices of terrorism;

I.

33. *Declares* that, upon official notification by Iraq to the Secretary-General and to the Security Council of its acceptance of the provisions above, a formal cease-fire is effective between Iraq and Kuwait and the Member States cooperating with Kuwait in accordance with resolution 678 (1990);

34. *Decides* to remain seized of the matter and to take such further steps as may be required for the implementation of the present resolution and to secure peace and security in the area.

NOTES AND QUESTIONS

1) At the time of the adoption of these resolutions the Security Council was composed of the five permanent members: China, France, United Kingdom, United States, and U.S.S.R., and the non-permanent members: Canada, Colombia, Côte d'Ivoire, Ethiopia, Finland, Malaysia, Romania, Yemen, and Zaire. The experience of the United Nations in trying to resolve the Iraq–Kuwait crisis raises a large number of instructive questions.

2) What was the legal force of Security Council resolution 660 (August 2)? Refer to the U.N. Charter article 25, reproduced in the Documentary Supplement, and to the *Namibia* case, reproduced in Chapter 2, Section C on "Other Legal Persons."

3) Where was the legal authority for the Security Council to order sanctions in resolution 661 (August 6)? See articles 31, 32, and 39-41.

4) How did the entry of U.S. forces into Saudi Arabia differ legally from the entry of Iraqi troops into Kuwait? See articles 2(4) and 51, the commentary in Section B.3 on "Humanitarian Intervention" under the heading "Invitation" and the definition of aggression, reproduced above in Section A on "Prohibition of the Use of Force."

5) The United States asserted a right of collective self-defence with Kuwait and Saudi Arabia. Note how in resolution 661 (August 6), the Security Council recognized for the first time that collective self-defence applied in a given case, even where the assisting state has not itself been attacked and has no special treaty arrangement to give assistance. Are there limits to participation in collective acts of self-defence or may any friendly state join in?[144]

6) Once the Security Council was seized with the Iraq crisis, was the right of individual or collective self-defence under article 51 suspended?[145]

7) By what authority did the U.N. Secretary-General meet with Iraqi officials on August 23? See articles 97-101. Compare resolution 674 (October 9).

8) What was the legal basis for the U.S. naval blockade when it began on August 12? Consider resolution 665 (August 25). Was it lawful for Jordan to continue exports and imports with Iraq by truck and plane? Consider resolution 661 (August 6).

---

144 See *Nicaragua* case, *supra* note 17; Macdonald, *supra* note 17 at 143; and O. Schachter, "United Nations Law in the Gulf Conflict" (1991) 85 A.J.I.L. 452 at 457. Refer to the discussion of collective self-defence in the notes above in Section B.1 on "The Right of Self-Defence."

145 See E. Rostow, "Until What? Enforcement Action or Collective Self-Defence?" (1991) 85 A.J.I.L. 506 at 510-14.

9) Where was the legal authority for the Security Council on September 24 to deal with the economic effects of sanctions on co-operating member states? See article 50.

10) Where was the legal authority for the Security Council to authorize "measures" to enforce sanctions in resolution 665 (August 25)? What more could it do short of the use of force? See article 42.

11) What was the significance of the reference in resolution 665 (August 25) to the "Military Staff Committee"? See article 47.

12) What were the legal obligations of U.N. member states with respect to Security Council resolutions 661 (August 6) and 665 (August 25)? See articles 25, 48, and 49.

13) The economic sanctions imposed by these resolutions are the most extensive ever declared by the Security Council. Was it necessary that economic sanctions or other measures be taken and proved inadequate before the Security Council was able to authorize the use of armed force?

14) Operation Desert Storm was undertaken pursuant to resolution 678 (November 29). What were the limits on U.N. member states on the kind and amount of force used and the territorial range of their operations? Review resolutions 660 (August 2) and 678 (August 29).

15) There were no further Security Council resolutions after number 678 on November 29, 1990 and before Operation Desert Storm commenced on January 17, 1991. Were any necessary? Were any to be expected? What more might the Security Council have done?

16) Was Operation Desert Storm a U.N. force or even a U.N. action? Why was it not coordinated or commanded by the Security Council or the Military Staff Committee? See articles 46-49.

17) In its resolutions the Security Council generally concluded by deciding "to remain seized of the matter." What is the significance of this decision? See article 12.

18) Where was the legal authority for the General Assembly to become involved in the Iraq–Kuwait crisis by its resolution of April 17, 1991? See articles 10-17.

19) In April 1991 while the Security Council condemned Iraq for repression of the Kurds and the Secretary-General sought to establish humanitarian centres, some members of the Coalition forces organized safe havens and provided basic services to the population in several places inside Iraq. What was their legal authority for doing so? Are there lawful grounds for this kind of humanitarian intervention? See articles 2(1) and (7) and resolution 688 (April 5, 1991), reproduced in Section B.3 on "Humanitarian Intervention."

20) While the Security Council responded vigorously to the humanitarian plight of the Kuwaitis, it was slow to act in the face of the repression of Iraq's own population. What marks the legal difference between the two situations? Are there lawful grounds for humanitarian intervention by the United Nations under Chapter VII of the Charter in one situation but not the other? Consider the fact that subsequently the U.N. intervened in 1992 in Somalia and in 1994 in Rwanda in situations that were almost entirely internal conflicts.

21) Later in 1991, in the face of the perceived intransigence of President Hussein, some Coalition partners declared no-fly zones for Iraqi aircraft within Iraq and enforced them with their own military airplanes. These restrictions, which continued throughout the 1990s, were marked by Iraqi resistance and some conflict. Where is the legal authority for these actions by Coalition forces? Review resolution 687 (April 3, 1991).

22) The illegal occupation of Kuwait also raised many other issues of international law discussed elsewhere in this book. Consider, for example, the question whether

Saddam Hussein should be prosecuted for international crimes, treated in Chapter 11 on "International Criminal Law"; the taking of hostages, treated in Chapter 9, Section A.2 on "Bases of Criminal Jurisdiction"; the violation of diplomatic immunities, taken up in Chapter 5, Section D on "Diplomatic Immunities"; and state responsibility for injuries to aliens and their property, dealt with in Chapter 10, Section B on "Responsibility for Injury to Aliens."

23) In 1995, the U.N. Security Council authorized an "oil for food" deal with Iraq.[146] This agreement, which was concluded in May 1996, allowed Iraq for the first time to sell its oil since the sanctions were imposed at the end of the Gulf War. This initiative was aimed at alleviating the hardship of sanctions on ordinary Iraqi citizens by allowing Iraq to sell US$2 billion worth of oil every six months. The income provided Iraq with US$1.3 billion worth of food, medical supplies, and other essential commodities. The remaining US$700 million went for compensation of Kuwaiti nationals and others injured by the Iraqi aggression and also toward U.N. expenses in Iraq.[147] This deal was tied to the earlier 1991 resolution 687, reproduced above, concerning the dismantling of the nuclear weapons program in Iraq and the destruction of stockpiles of chemical and biological weapons.

The oil for food program was terminated on November 21, 2003, when operations and responsibilities were handed over to the Coalition Provisional Authority for Iraq established after Gulf War II. In April 2004, the U.N. Secretary-General appointed an Independent Inquiry Committee to investigate the administration and management of the program, addressing allegations of corruption and bribery in connection with the oil sales. Five reports were issued in the course of 2005 by the Inquiry Committee. While the Inquiry exonerated the Secretary-General of any personal wrongdoing, it criticized him for lack of diligence or effectiveness in pursuing an investigation after he learned of his son's involvement. More broadly, although the Inquiry noted that the oil for food program succeeded in maintaining minimal standards of nutrition in Iraq, it condemned the weak administrative practices and inadequate control and auditing that allowed for widespread corruption of the program. These findings reflected negatively on the whole system of decision making, accountability, and management throughout the United Nations, much of which was rooted in unclear separation of the roles and responsibilities of the Secretary-General and the Security Council. The Inquiry called for wide-scale reforms within the United Nations. Meanwhile at least two senior U.N. staff members associated with the program were indicted for corruption.

The 2003 Invasion of Iraq: Gulf War II

By resolution 687 (1991), the Security Council had established the terms and conditions for a formal ceasefire between Iraq and the Coalition of Member States co-operating with Kuwait. Section C of the resolution addressed the elimination, under international supervision, of Iraq's weapons of mass destruction and ballistic missiles with a range greater than 150 kilometres, together with related items and production facilities. It also

146 U.N. S.C. Res. 986 (1995).

147 G.A.P. Fitzpatrick, "The Middle East and the Persian Gulf," in Tessitore and Woolfson, *supra* note 102 at 62.

called for measures to ensure that the acquisition and production of prohibited items are not resumed. In May 1991, the United Nations Special Commission (UNSCOM) was established to implement the non-nuclear provisions of the resolution and to assist the International Atomic Energy Agency (IAEA) in the nuclear areas. While Iraq initially allowed UNSCOM to monitor military installations, it later denied access to sites designated by UNSCOM, expelled U.S. national members of UNSCOM, and, by so doing, flagrantly violated previous resolutions. These actions were condemned by the Security Council.[148] But it likely did not go unnoticed in Iraq that the Security Council as of mid-October 1997 did not appear to be capable of maintaining its earlier cohesion concerning further sanctions for non-compliance. Security Council resolution 1134 (1997) contained "a watered-down threat to impose them in the future."[149] However, even here France, Russia, China, Egypt, and Kenya abstained. The game of cat and mouse continued. In resolution 1154 (1998), adopted unanimously, the Security Council stated that if Iraq did not comply in granting immediate, unconditional, and unrestricted access to inspection sites, it would face the "severest consequences."[150] In October 1998, Iraq formally ended all co-operation with UNSCOM. In December 1998, after further, fruitless back-and-forth between Iraq, UNSCOM, and the Security Council, the United States and the United Kingdom launched a bombing campaign dubbed "Operation Desert Fox." Although several Security Council members declared the operation to be unlawful, the United States and the United Kingdom maintained that it was validly based on the authority contained in resolution 678. It was said to have been revived as a result of Iraq's "material breaches" of the ceasefire conditions set out in resolution 687.[151] The Security Council as such neither endorsed nor rejected that line of reasoning.

The stalemate between Iraq and the United Nations continued. Neither the continuing sanctions nor Operation Desert Fox induced Iraq to renew its co-operation with the inspections regime. In light of UNSCOM's fate, the Security Council decided to replace it with a new inspection regime. Through resolution 1284 (1999), it established the U.N. Monitoring, Verification, and Inspection Commission (UNMOVIC). However, it was not until the United States, in 2002, began pressing for a military intervention in Iraq to enforce compliance with resolution 687[152] that Iraq indicated renewed willingness to co-operate with U.N. inspectors. The United States, supported by the United Kingdom, sought adoption of a resolution that would have stiffened the inspection regime and disclosure requirements imposed on Iraq. Most notably, under the proposed resolution, further "material breaches" by Iraq of its obligations would have authorized member states

---

148 See *e.g.* U.N. SC Res. 1115 (1997).

149 G.G. Goldstein, "The Middle East and the Persian Gulf," in Tessitore and Woolfson, *supra* note 102 at 44.

150 Note that a majority of Security Council members stated in the context of the adoption of this resolution that additional Security Council authorization would be needed to enforce the implementation of the inspections regime by military means. See U.N. Doc. S/PV 3858, *passim* (1998).

151 See U.N. Doc. S/PV 3955 at 5-7 (U.K.) and at 8-10 (U.S.). Note that the United States and United Kingdom had already relied on *inter alia* this argument to justify previous operations, such as those enforcing the no-fly zones.

152 See G.W. Bush, *President's Remarks at the United Nations General Assembly*, September 12, 2002, U.N. Doc. A/57/PV 2 at 6-9.

to take military enforcement measures. However, other members of the Security Council were reluctant to lay the tracks towards the use of military force. After intense negotiations, a compromise was enshrined in resolution 1441 (2002), adopted unanimously.[153]

Security Council Resolution 1441 (2002)
U.N. Doc. S/RES/1441, November 8, 2002

The Security Council,

Recalling all its previous relevant resolutions, in particular its resolutions 661 (1990) of 6 August 1990, 678 (1990) of 29 November 1990, 686 (1991) of 2 March 1991, 687 (1991) of 3 April 1991, 688 (1991) of 5 April 1991, 707 (1991) of 15 August 1991, 715 (1991) of 11 October 1991, 986 (1995) of 14 April 1995, and 1284 (1999) of 17 December 1999, and all the relevant statements of its President,

Recalling also its resolution 1382 (2001) of 29 November 2001 and its intention to implement it fully,

Recognizing the threat Iraq's noncompliance with Council resolutions and proliferation of weapons of mass destruction and long-range missiles poses to international peace and security,

Recalling that its resolution 678 (1990) authorized Member States to use all necessary means to uphold and implement its resolution 660 (1990) of 2 August 1990 and all relevant resolutions subsequent to Resolution 660 (1990) and to restore international peace and security in the area,

Further recalling that its resolution 687 (1991) imposed obligations on Iraq as a necessary step for achievement of its stated objective of restoring international peace and security in the area,

Deploring the fact that Iraq has not provided an accurate, full, final, and complete disclosure, as required by resolution 687 (1991), of all aspects of its programmes to develop weapons of mass destruction and ballistic missiles with a range greater than one hundred and fifty kilometres, and of all holdings of such weapons, their components and production facilities and locations, as well as all other nuclear programmes, including any which it claims are for purposes not related to nuclear-weapons-usable material, ...

Recalling that in its resolution 687 (1991) the Council declared that a ceasefire would be based on acceptance by Iraq of the provisions of that resolution, including the obligations on Iraq contained therein,

Determined to ensure full and immediate compliance by Iraq without conditions or restrictions with its obligations under resolution 687 (1991) and other relevant resolutions and recalling that the resolutions of the Council constitute the governing standard of Iraqi compliance ... .

---

153 At the relevant time, the non-permanent members of the Security Council were Bulgaria, Cameroon, Colombia, Guinea, Ireland, Mauritius, Mexico, Norway, Singapore, and the Syrian Arab Republic.

Acting under Chapter VII of the Charter of the United Nations,

1. *Decides* that Iraq has been and remains in material breach of its obligations under relevant resolutions, including resolution 687 (1991), in particular through Iraq's failure to cooperate with United Nations inspectors and the IAEA, and to complete the actions required under paragraphs 8 to 13 of resolution 687 (1991);

2. *Decides*, while acknowledging paragraph 1 above, to afford Iraq, by this resolution, a final opportunity to comply with its disarmament obligations under relevant resolutions of the Council; and accordingly decides to set up an enhanced inspection regime with the aim of bringing to full and verified completion the disarmament process established by resolution 687 (1991) and subsequent resolutions of the Council;

3. *Decides* that, in order to begin to comply with its disarmament obligations, in addition to submitting the required biannual declarations, the Government of Iraq shall provide to UNMOVIC, the IAEA, and the Council, not later than 30 days from the date of this resolution, a currently accurate, full, and complete declaration of all aspects of its programmes to develop chemical, biological, and nuclear weapons, ballistic missiles, and other delivery systems such as unmanned aerial vehicles and dispersal systems designed for use on aircraft, including any holdings and precise locations of such weapons, components, sub-components, stocks of agents, and related material and equipment, the locations and work of its research, development and production facilities, as well as all other chemical, biological, and nuclear programmes, including any which it claims are for purposes not related to weapon production or material;

4. *Decides* that false statements or omissions in the declarations submitted by Iraq pursuant to this resolution and failure by Iraq at any time to comply with, and cooperate fully in the implementation of, this resolution shall constitute a further material breach of Iraq's obligations and will be reported to the Council for assessment in accordance with paragraphs 11 and 12 below ... .

11. *Directs* the Executive Chairman of UNMOVIC and the Director General of the IAEA to report immediately to the Council any interference by Iraq with inspection activities, as well as any failure by Iraq to comply with its disarmament obligations, including its obligations regarding inspections under this resolution;

12. *Decides* to convene immediately upon receipt of a report in accordance with paragraphs 4 or 11 above, in order to consider the situation and the need for full compliance with all of the relevant Council resolutions in order to secure international peace and security;

13. *Recalls*, in that context, that the Council has repeatedly warned Iraq that it will face serious consequences as a result of its continued violations of its obligations;

14. *Decides* to remain seized of the matter.

NOTES

1) In the weeks following the adoption of Resolution 1441, UNMOVIC inspectors were unable to uncover clear evidence that Iraq had weapons of mass destruction or had resumed its weapons programs. The Security Council could not reach agreement on whether Iraq's conduct and its degree of compliance with the requirements set out in resolution 1441 warranted an armed intervention, and no further resolution explicitly

authorizing such intervention was adopted. The United States and Britain maintained that an additional resolution providing specific authorization of force was not required.

2) In March 2003, the United States led coalition forces that included troops from the United Kingdom, Australia, the Czech Republic, Poland, and Slovakia in an invasion of Iraq ("Operation Iraqi Freedom"). In a letter to the Security Council President, the United States legally justified this military intervention as follows.

U.S. Letter to the President of the U.N. Security Council, March 20, 2003
U.N. Doc. S/2003/351, 21 March 2003

Coalition forces have commenced military operations in Iraq. These operations are necessary in view of Iraq's continued material breaches of its disarmament obligations under relevant Security Council resolutions, including resolution 1441 (2002). The operations are substantial and will secure compliance with those obligations. In carrying out these operations, our forces will take all reasonable precautions to avoid civilian casualties.

The actions being taken are authorized under existing Council resolutions, including its resolutions 678 (1990) and 687 (1991). Resolution 687 (1991) imposed a series of obligations on Iraq, including, most importantly, extensive disarmament obligations, that were conditions of the ceasefire established under it. It has been long recognized and understood that a material breach of these obligations removes the basis of the ceasefire and revives the authority to use force under resolution 678 (1990). This has been the basis for coalition use of force in the past and has been accepted by the Council, as evidenced, for example, by the Secretary-General's public announcement in January 1993 following Iraq's material breach of resolution 687 (1991) that coalition forces had received a mandate from the Council to use force according to resolution 678 (1990).

Iraq continues to be in material breach of its disarmament obligations under resolution 687 (1991), as the Council affirmed in its resolution 1441 (2002). Acting under the authority of Chapter VII of the Charter of the United Nations, the Council unanimously decided that Iraq has been and remained in material breach of its obligations and recalled its repeated warnings to Iraq that it will face serious consequences as a result of its continued violations of its obligations. The resolution then provided Iraq a "final opportunity" to comply, but stated specifically that violations by Iraq of its obligations under resolution 1441 (2002) to present a currently accurate, full and complete declaration of all aspects of its weapons of mass destruction programmes and to comply with and cooperate fully in the implementation of the resolution would constitute a further material breach.

The Government of Iraq decided not to avail itself of its final opportunity under resolution 1441 (2002) and has clearly committed additional violations. In view of Iraq's material breaches, the basis for the ceasefire has been removed and use of force is authorized under resolution 678 (1990).

Iraq repeatedly has refused, over a protracted period of time, to respond to diplomatic overtures, economic sanctions and other peaceful means, designed to help bring about Iraqi compliance with its obligations to disarm and to permit full inspection of its weapons of mass destruction and related programmes. The actions that coalition forces are undertaking are an appropriate response. They are necessary steps to defend the United States and the international community from the threat posed by Iraq and to restore international peace and security in the area. Further delay would simply allow Iraq to continue its unlawful and threatening conduct.

It is the Government of Iraq that bears full responsibility for the serious consequences of its defiance of the Council's decisions.

I would be grateful if you could circulate the text of the present letter as a document of the Security Council.

(Signed) John D. Negroponte

Written Answer of the U.K. Attorney General to a Parliamentary Question on Iraq
U.K., H.L., *Parliamentary Debates*, vol. 646, col. WA3 (17 March 2003)

Authority to use force against Iraq exists from the combined effect of resolutions 678, 687 and 1441. All of these resolutions were adopted under Chapter VII of the U.N. Charter which allows the use of force for the express purpose of restoring international peace and security:

1. In resolution 678 the Security Council authorised force against Iraq, to eject it from Kuwait and to restore peace and security in the area.

2. In resolution 687, which set out the ceasefire conditions after Operation Desert Storm, the Security Council imposed continuing obligations on Iraq to eliminate its weapons of mass destruction in order to restore international peace and security in the area. Resolution 687 suspended but did not terminate the authority to use force under resolution 678.

3. A material breach of resolution 687 revives the authority to use force under resolution 678.

4. In resolution 1441 the Security Council determined that Iraq has been and remains in material breach of resolution 687, because it has not fully complied with its obligations to disarm under that resolution.

5. The Security Council in resolution 1441 gave Iraq "a final opportunity to comply with its disarmament obligations" and warned Iraq of the "serious consequences" if it did not.

6. The Security Council also decided in resolution 1441 that, if Iraq failed at any time to comply with and cooperate fully in the implementation of resolution 1441, that would constitute a further material breach.

7. It is plain that Iraq has failed so to comply and therefore Iraq was at the time of resolution 1441 and continues to be in material breach.

8. Thus, the authority to use force under resolution 678 has revived and so continues today.

9. Resolution 1441 would in terms have provided that a further decision of the Security Council to sanction force was required if that had been intended. Thus, all

that resolution 1441 requires is reporting to and discussion by the Security Council of
Iraq's failures, but not an express further decision to authorise force.

NOTES

1) Does the justification outlined in the U.S. letter (and echoed in similar letters from
Australia and the United Kingdom[154]) provide a legal basis for Operation Iraqi Freedom? In
answering this question, a number of further issues, set out in Notes 2 to 6 below, must be
considered.[155] Note that the justifications provided in the Australian and U.K. letters were
limited to the arguments related to the string of Security Council resolutions culminating
in resolution 1441. In that context, compare also the written answer to a parliamentary
question provided by the U.K. Attorney General, Lord Goldsmith, and set out above.

2) Was the ceasefire effected under resolution 687 a final settlement, or was it merely
a "suspension" of hostilities, subject to Iraq's compliance with the conditions set out in
the resolution?

3) Consider article 60 of the Vienna Convention on the Law of Treaties, reproduced in
the Documentary Supplement. Was the ceasefire arrangement under resolution 687 akin
to a treaty and thus subject to termination or suspension in the face of "material breach"
by one party? Who were the parties to the ceasefire arrangement under resolution 687?

4) Consider operative paragraph 2 of resolution 678. Does it provide the authority to
use force that was asserted by the United States and others?

5) Could it be argued that the practice of the Security Council and its member states
since the first military intervention in Iraq supports the legal arguments advanced by the
coalition states? Has a practice evolved pursuant to which member states are impliedly
authorized to enforce Security Council resolutions against states that are in material
breach of their obligations under such resolutions? Would such a development be
compatible with the U.N. Charter and its collective security system?[156]

6) Does resolution 1441 authorize the military intervention of 2003? Alternatively,
does it lend support to the legal justification offered by the coalition states?

7) Aside from the justification provided in the Australian, U.K., and U.S. letters to the
Security Council President, could the invasion of Iraq have been justified as self-defence?
Compare Section B.1 above on "The Right of Self-Defence." As to the removal of

---

154 Similar letters were sent by Australia and the United Kingdom. See Letter dated March 20, 2003 from
the Permanent Representative of Australia to the United Nations addressed to the President of the
Security Council, U.N. Doc. S/2003/352, 21 March 2003; Letter dated March 20, 2003 from the
Permanent Representative of the United Kingdom of Great Britain and Northern Ireland to the United
Nations addressed to the President of the Security Council, U.N. Doc. S/2003/350, 21 March 2003.

155 On these issues, see sources cited in note 156 and contributions to the symposium on "Future Implications
of the Iraq Conflict" (2003) 97 A.J.I.L. 543-642; C. Scott, "Iraq and the Serious Consequences of Word
Games: Language, Violence, and Responsibility in the Security Council" (2002) 3 German L.J. 2. See
also Legal Department of the Ministry of Foreign Affairs of the Russian Federation, "Legal Assessment
of the Use of Force Against Iraq," reproduced in (2003) 52 I.C.L.Q. 1059.

156 See *e.g.* C. Scott, "Interpreting Intervention" (2001) Can. Y.B. Int'l L. 333; Lobel and Ratner, *supra* note
115; C. Stahn, "Enforcement of the Collective Will After Iraq" (2003) 97 A.J.I.L. 804.

Saddam Hussein's government, are there any circumstances under which a state might be able to justify military action against another state to effect "regime change" as self-defence? What legal considerations enter into answering this question? Are the observations of the ICJ in paras. 257–269 of its decision in the *Nicaragua* case, reproduced above in Section A, still apposite?

8) Alternatively, could Operation Iraqi Freedom have been justified as a humanitarian intervention to liberate Iraqis from the abusive regime of Saddam Hussein? Compare Section B.3 above on "Humanitarian Intervention."

9) Could a subsequent approval by the Security Council have provided valid Chapter VII authorization of the intervention? Does silence or failure to condemn constitute approval?[157] See also above, Section B.3 on "Humanitarian Intervention," and below, Section D on "The United Nations and Regional Arrangements."

10) Is the U.N. collective security system adequate to addressing the security threats posed by international terrorism, rogue states, and weapons of mass destruction? For example, when faced with the possibility that weapons of mass destruction are in the hands of a rogue state that has defied all efforts at an amicable solution, are states entitled to take military steps to ensure their security if the Security Council fails to authorize the use of force?[158] Did the NATO bombing of Kosovo, albeit undertaken for humanitarian reasons, provide a precedent for this type of argument? In analogy to the Kosovo example, could it be argued that the Iraq invasion was, albeit perhaps for different reasons, at the very least "legitimate"? Compare materials above in Section B.3.[159]

11) Compare also the materials relating to the report of the High-level Panel on Threats, Challenges, and Change, above in Sections B.1 and B.3. Further to the excerpts reproduced, the report of the Panel observed:

> 204. The effectiveness of the global collective security system, as with any other legal order, depends ultimately not only on the legality of decisions but also on the common perception of their legitimacy ...
>
> 205. ... In particular, in deciding whether or not to authorize the use of force, the [Security] Council should systematically address a set of agreed guidelines, going directly not to whether force *can* legally be used but whether, as a matter of good conscience and good sense, it *should* be.

Would application of such guidelines (their key principles are reproduced above in Section B.3), assuming they can indeed be agreed upon, enhance the legitimacy of Security Council decisions? Why or why not? What if a situation were to arise in which, according to the guidelines, the use of military force would be appropriate. If the Security

---

157 Lobel and Ratner, *supra* note 115.

158 Note that the Security Council has adopted a general resolution on non-proliferation of weapons of mass destruction. *Inter alia*, it requires states to refrain from any sort of support of non-state actors seeking such weapons. See S.C. Res. 1540 (2004) U.N. Doc. S/RES/1540, 28 April 2004. (Adopted by a unanimous vote.)

159 See *e.g.* R. Wedgwood, "The Fall of Saddam Hussein: Security Council Mandates and Pre-emptive Self-Defense" (2003) 97 A.J.I.L. 576. But see also R. Falk, "What Future for the U.N. Charter System of War Prevention?" (2003) 97 A.J.I.L. 590.

Council nonetheless failed to pass a resolution authorizing the use of force, could individual states, or a group of states, now argue that it is legal, or at least "legitimate," for them (1) to use force to prevent a threat to their security that is not imminent but real (for example, the acquisition by a state, with hostile intent, of weapons of mass destruction); or (2) to use force in another state to combat an actual or imminent situation involving genocide and other large-scale killing, ethnic cleansing, or serious violations of humanitarian law?[160]

12) What were the original reasons for giving the Security Council sole authority over military measures that are beyond the scope of states' right to self-defence? Are they still valid today? Could the Security Council's functions be discharged by other collectives, such as the U.N. General Assembly (pursuant to the "Uniting for Peace" resolution), regional organizations, or groupings of democratic states?[161]

Responses to State-Sponsored Terrorism

The approach of the international community toward various aspects of international terrorism was reviewed in Chapter 9, Section A.6 on "Suppression of Transnational Crimes." There it was seen that the U.N. General Assembly and two specialized agencies, the International Civil Aviation Organization (ICAO) and the International Maritime Organization (IMO), have sponsored 10 multilateral conventions and two protocols against terrorism. These seek to prevent, if not to punish, those who: hijack aircraft or commit other unlawful offences against civil aviation including airports; attack internationally protected persons; take hostages; commit offences against nuclear material; criminally attack maritime vessels and fixed platforms on the continental shelf; and commit terrorist bombings. The thrust of these conventions and protocols is to secure the prosecution of the perpetrators of such crimes through widespread implementation. They obligate the states parties (1) to amend their domestic criminal law to provide for wide bases of jurisdiction over the offence, including universal jurisdiction, and (2) either to extradite an arrested alleged perpetrator or, if not, to submit the case to their own authorities for the purpose of prosecution.[162]

Since the attacks of September 11, 2001, terrorism has increasingly come to be seen as a matter of national and international security, rather than primarily a matter for international co-operation in criminal law matters. Thus, questions regarding the scope of states' right to self-defence and the role of the Security Council have assumed heightened importance. As discussed in previous sections of the chapter, if a state sponsors terrorist acts or aids terrorist groups in any way to further its or their goals against other states or their nationals, it would be in violation of article 2(4) of the Charter and of the 1970

---

160   Report of the High-level Panel on Threats, Challenges, and Change, *A More Secure World: Our Shared Responsibility*, U.N. Doc. A/59/565 (29 November 2004) at 57.

161   For a range of views see A. Buchanan and R.O. Keohane, "The Preventive Use of Force: A Cosmopolitan Institutional Perspective" (2004) 18 Ethics & Int'l. Aff. 1; I. Johnstone, "Security Council Deliberations: The Power of the Better Argument" (2003) 12 E.J.I.L. 437; V. Lowe, "The Iraq Crisis: What Now?" (2003) 52 I.C.L.Q. 859 at 867-69; Wedgwood, *supra* note 159.

162   See M. Lippman, "The New Terrorism and International Law" (2003) 10 Tulsa J. Comp. & Int'l L. 297.

Declaration on Friendly Relations, and an act of aggression under article 3(g) of the 1974 Definition of Aggression. A victim state could respond in self-defence and the Security Council could become seized of the matter.[163] For example, the Security Council determined that the Taliban regime in Afghanistan had allowed terrorist organizations, including Al-Qaida, to operate training camps in Afghanistan and was providing safe haven to Osama bin Laden. In several resolutions, the Security Council demanded that the Taliban stop sheltering terrorists and turn over Osama bin Laden. It also imposed sanctions on the Taliban regime to pressure it into compliance.[164] In addition, in resolution 1373 (2001), reproduced in the materials on "Attacks by Non-state Actors" in Section B.1 on the "Right of Self-Defence," the Council required that states take extensive measures to suppress terrorism. Some observers have asked whether it was within the Security Council's powers to adopt a resolution with such wide-ranging requirements.[165]

Yet another question is raised as to whether it is within the mandate of the Security Council under article 39 of the Charter and Chapter VII *in toto* to impose sanctions on a state that refuses to extradite alleged terrorists. Is this a matter of domestic affairs under article 2(7)? In the document that follows, the Security Council took this step following the refusal by Libya to extradite two alleged terrorists, who were accused of blowing up Pan Am flight 103 over Lockerbie, Scotland and killing 270 people, to either the United Kingdom or the United States, and also the refusal to extradite four persons to France for allegedly destroying UTA flight 772 over Chad. The decision to impose sanctions was expressly taken under Chapter VII. This unprecedented step has provoked disquiet among non-aligned states, who are concerned about the prominence of the Western states on the Security Council with its newly found relative convergence of powers of decision after the Cold War era and the fact that this use of sanctions was a radical departure from established practice.[166] The concern about departure from principle and practice was also evident in the Security Council itself where the issue had to be handled, some would say artificially, as a matter of international peace and security.

On January 21, 1992 the Security Council unanimously adopted resolution 731 condemning the destruction of the two flights, deploring the fact that Libya had not responded effectively to requests to co-operate fully in establishing responsibility for the terrorist acts and urging Libya to provide a full and effective response to these requests. The resolution did not actually use the term "extradition," but that was clearly its intent. It was stated that in complying with this resolution Libya would be contributing to the elimination of international terrorism. When Libya failed to comply, the Security Council adopted the following resolution.

---

163 Compare materials on the "Definition of Aggression" in Section A and on "Attacks by Non-state Actors" in Section B.1 on the "Right to Self-Defence."

164 See S.C. Res. 1214 (1998), UN SCOR, 53rd year, *Res. and Dec.*; U.N. Doc. S/INF/54 at 82 (adopted by a unanimous vote); S.C. Res. 1267 (1999), UN SCOR, 54th year, *Res. and Dec.*; U.N. Doc. S/INF/55 at 18 (adopted by a unanimous vote); S.C. Res. 1332 (2000), UN SCOR, 55th year, *Res. and Dec.*; U.N. Doc. S/INF/56 at 32 (adopted by a vote of 13 in favour and 2 abstentions (China and Malaysia)).

165 See *e.g.* P.C. Szasz, "The Security Council Starts Legislating" (2002) 96 A.J.I.L. 901. See also SC Res. 1526 (2004) U.N. Doc. S/RES/1526, 30 January 2004.

166 See P. Kirsch, "The Expanding Peacekeeping Role of the United Nations" (1992) 86 A.S.I.L. Proc. 135.

Security Council Resolution 748 (1992)[167]
U.N. Doc. S/RES/748, March 31, 1992

The Security Council,

Reaffirming its resolution 731 (1992) of 21 January 1992, ...

Deeply concerned that the Libyan Government has still not provided a full and effective response to the requests in its resolution 731 (1992) of 21 January 1992,

Convinced that the suppression of acts of international terrorism, including those in which States are directly or indirectly involved, is essential for the maintenance of international peace and security,

Recalling that, in the statement issued on 31 January 1992 on the occasion of the meeting of the Security Council at the level of heads of State and Government, the members of the Council expressed their deep concern over acts of international terrorism, and emphasized the need for the international community to deal effectively with all such acts,

Reaffirming that, in accordance with the principle in Article 2, paragraph 4, of the Charter of the United Nations, every State has the duty to refrain from organizing, instigating, assisting or participating in terrorist acts in another State or acquiescing in organized activities within its territory directed towards the commission of such acts, when such acts involve a threat or use of force,

Determining, in this context, that the failure by the Libyan Government to demonstrate by concrete actions its renunciation of terrorism and in particular its continued failure to respond fully and effectively to the requests in resolution 731 (1992) constitute a threat to international peace and security,

Determined to eliminate international terrorism, ...

Acting under Chapter VII of the Charter,

1. *Decides* that the Libyan Government must now comply without any further delay with paragraph 3 of resolution 731 (1992) regarding the requests contained in documents S/23306, S/23308 and S/23309;

2. *Decides also* that the Libyan Government must commit itself definitively to cease all forms of terrorist action and all assistance to terrorist groups and that it must promptly, by concrete actions, demonstrate its renunciation of terrorism;

3. *Decides that*, on 15 April 1992 all States shall adopt the measures set out below, which shall apply until the Security Council decides that the Libyan Government has complied with paragraphs 1 and 2 above;

4. *Decides also* that all States shall:

(a) Deny permission to any aircraft to take off from, land in or overfly their territory if it is destined to land in or has taken off from the territory of Libya, unless the particular flight has been approved on grounds of significant humanitarian need by the Committee established by paragraph 9 below;

---

167 Adopted by unanimous vote. For the texts of the various documents pertaining to the aerial incident at Lockerbie and in Niger see (1992) 31 I.L.M. 717.

(b) Prohibit, by their nationals or from their territory, the supply of any aircraft or aircraft components to Libya, the provision of engineering and maintenance servicing of Libyan aircraft or aircraft components, the certification of airworthiness for Libyan aircraft, the payment of new claims against existing insurance contracts and the provision of new direct insurance for Libyan aircraft;

5. *Decides further* that all States shall:

(a) Prohibit any provision to Libya by their nationals or from their territory of arms and related material of all types, including the sale or transfer of weapons and ammunition, military vehicles and equipment, paramilitary police equipment and spare parts for the aforementioned, as well as the provision of any types of equipment, supplies and grants of licensing arrangements, for the manufacture or maintenance of the aforementioned;

(b) Prohibit any provision to Libya by their nationals or from their territory of technical advice, assistance or training related to the provision, manufacture, maintenance, or use of the items in (a) above;

(c) Withdraw any of their officials or agents present in Libya to advise the Libyan authorities on military matters;

6. *Decides* that all States shall:

(a) Significantly reduce the number and the level of the staff at Libyan diplomatic missions and consular posts and restrict or control the movement within their territory of all such staff who remain; in the case of Libyan missions to international organizations, the host State may, as it deems necessary, consult the organization concerned on the measures required to implement this subparagraph;

(b) Prevent the operation of all Libyan Arab Airlines offices;

(c) Take all appropriate steps to deny entry to or expel Libyan nationals who have been denied entry to or expelled from other States because of their involvement in terrorist activities;

7. *Calls upon* all States, including States not members of the United Nations, and all international organizations, to act strictly in accordance with the provisions of the present resolution, notwithstanding the existence of any rights or obligations conferred or imposed by any international agreement or any contract entered into or any licence or permit granted prior to 15 April 1992;

8. *Requests* all States to report to the Secretary-General by 15 May 1992 on the measures they have instituted for meeting the obligations set out in paragraphs 3 to 7 above;

9. *Decides* to establish, in accordance with rule 28 of its provisional rules of procedure, a Committee of the Security Council consisting of all the members of the Council, to undertake the following tasks and to report on its work to the Council with its observations and recommendations:

(a) To examine the reports submitted pursuant to paragraph 8 above;

(b) To seek from all States further information regarding the action taken by them concerning the effective implementation of the measures imposed by paragraphs 3 to 7 above;

(c) To consider any information brought to its attention by States concerning violations of the measures imposed by paragraphs 3 to 7 above and in that context, to make recommendations to the Council on ways to increase their effectiveness;

(d) To recommend appropriate measures in response to violations of the measures imposed by paragraphs 3 to 7 above and provide information on a regular basis to the Secretary-General for general distribution to Member States;

(e) To consider and to decide upon expeditiously any application by States for the approval of flights on grounds of significant humanitarian need in accordance with paragraph 4 above;

(f) To give special attention to any communications in accordance with Article 50 of the Charter from any neighbouring or other State with special economic problems that might arise from the carrying out of the measures imposed by paragraphs 3 to 7 above;

10. *Calls upon* all States to cooperate fully with the Committee in the fulfilment of its task, including supplying such information as may be sought by the Committee in pursuance of the present resolution;

11. *Requests* the Secretary-General to provide all necessary assistance to the Committee and to make the necessary arrangements in the Secretariat for this purpose;

12. *Invites* the Secretary-General to continue his role as set out in paragraph 4 of resolution 731 (1992);

13. *Decides* that the Security Council shall, every 120 days or sooner should the situation so require, review the measures imposed by paragraphs 3 to 7 above in the light of the compliance by the Libyan Government with paragraphs 1 and 2 above taking into account, as appropriate, any reports provided by the Secretary-General on his role as set out in paragraph 4 of the resolution 731 (1992);

14. *Decides* to remain seized of the matter.

NOTES

1) The Security Council members, who voted unanimously, were China, France, the Russian Federation, the United Kingdom, and the United States (the permanent members with the veto power) and Austria, Belgium, Cape Verde, Ecuador, Hungary, India, Japan, Morocco, Venezuela, and Zimbabwe.

2) What were Libya's obligations under international law with respect to extradition? Libya, France, the United Kingdom, and the United States have ratified the 1971 Montreal Convention for the Suppression of Unlawful Acts Against the Safety of Civil Aviation,[168] article 7 of which provides:

> The Contracting State in the territory of which the alleged offender is found shall, if it does not extradite him, be obliged, without exception whatsoever and whether or not the offence was committed in its territory to submit the case to its competent authorities for the purpose of prosecution. Those authorities shall take their decision in the same manner as in the case of an ordinary offence of a serious nature under the law of that State.

In Chapter 9, Section B.2 on "Extradition," it was seen that there are various grounds for refusing extradition. Which grounds might be pertinent here? If Libya could not

---

168 Can. T.S. 1973 No. 6. All four states are also parties to the 1970 Hague Convention for the Suppression of Unlawful Seizure of Aircraft, Can. T.S. 1972 No. 23.

extradite under its domestic law, would it still comply with its treaty obligations under the Montreal Convention if it was prepared to prosecute in good faith? To do so, would it need the co-operation of France, the United Kingdom, and the United States in supplying evidence? Note the obligation in article 11 of the Montreal Convention that the parties "shall afford the greatest measure of assistance in connection with criminal proceedings brought in respect of the offenses." The same article goes on to state that "[t]he law of the State requested shall apply to all cases."

3) Was the refusal to extradite by Libya a threat to international peace and security as those terms have been interpreted in the past by the Security Council? Was collective enforcement action in this case constitutional under the Charter?

4) Libya refused to hand the two alleged offenders over to the requesting states because it asserted that they would not receive a fair trial in their national courts. Further, the ICJ at The Hague does not have criminal jurisdiction over individuals or states.

5) The impasse was broken when the U.N. Security Council agreed to suspend sanctions once Libya complied. In January 2001, one defendant, al-Megrahi, was found guilty and sentenced to life imprisonment. The other was acquitted. Subsequently Libya made arrangements to compensate the families of the victims. In April 1999, Libya agreed to send the two alleged offenders, Abdel Basset al-Megrahi and Al-Amin Khalifa Fhimah, former employees of Libyan Arab Airlines, to The Hague to be tried there under Scottish law by a panel of three Scottish judges. The venue for the trial was Camp Zeist, a former U.S. airbase in the Netherlands. By legislation the Dutch government turned Camp Zeist into a part of Scotland for the trial and the accused were extradited there from the Netherlands. The charges were murder and conspiracy to commit murder.

6) On April 14, 1992 the ICJ handed down a decision concerning the Lockerbie incident in which by a majority of 11 to 5 it dismissed an application by Libya for interim protection in its dispute with the United Kingdom and the United States. The Court had been asked by Libya to enjoin the two states from taking "any action calculated to coerce or compel Libya to surrender the accused individuals to any jurisdiction outside of Libya."[169] The Court, by entertaining Libya's request, indicated that because the U.N. Security Council had already spoken on the subject through its resolutions, the Court was not prevented from taking jurisdiction. The fundamental finding of the Court was that resolution 748 adopted under Chapter VII of the Charter had, in accordance with article 103 of the Charter, preference over any other treaty commitment of member states. Thus, provisional measures were not considered appropriate as they would have impaired the effects of resolution 748.[170]

---

169 *Aerial Incident at Lockerbie Case: Case Concerning Questions of Interpretation and Application of the 1971 Montreal Convention Arising from the Aerial Incident at Lockerbie* (*Libya v. United States*; *Libya v. United Kingdom*), [1992] I.C.J. Rep. 3.

170 See T. van Boven, "The Security Council: The New Frontier" (1992) 48 Rev. Int. Comm. Jurists 12 at 13; T. Franck, "The 'Powers of Appreciation': Who Is the Guardian of U.N. Legality" (1992) 86 A.J.I.L. 519; W.M. Reisman, "The Constitutional Crisis in the United Nations" (1993) 87 A.J.I.L. 83 at 86; and C. Tomuschat, "The Lockerbie Case before the International Court of Justice" (1992) 48 Rev. Int. Comm. Jurists 38 at 42. On the question raised by the case whether the ICJ has any judicial review power over decisions of other U.N. organs, and the Security Council in particular, see the discussion in chapter 6, Section D.4.

7) Further, on February 27, 1998, the ICJ rendered its decision on preliminary objections to the exercise of jurisdiction by the Court presented by the respondent, the United States.[171] The United States' first submission was that there was no legal dispute between the parties concerning the interpretation or application of the Montreal Convention. The United States argued, second, that the Libyan Application was inadmissible. Libya was requesting that the Court adjudge and declare that (1) Libya had fully complied with its Montreal Convention obligations; (2) that the United States had breached and was continuing to breach its Montreal Convention obligations toward Libya; and (3) that the United States was under a legal obligation to cease and desist from such breaches and from the use of any and all force or threats against Libya. The ICJ rejected by 13 votes to 2 the U.S. objection concerning the lack of a legal dispute; by 13 votes to 2 it found that on the basis of article 14(1) of the Montreal Convention it has jurisdiction to hear the dispute as to interpretation or application of the Convention; by 12 to 3 it rejected the contention that the case was inadmissible because of Security Council resolutions 748 and 883; by 12 to 3 it found the Libyan application admissible; and by 10 to 5 it declared that the objection that the claims of Libya became moot because resolutions 748 and 883 rendered them without object did not have an exclusively preliminary character. The merits of the case never went to trial. In August 2003, Libya officially admitted responsibility for the bombings; the following month the case was discontinued by joint requests of the parties.

8) The emphasis underlying resolution 748 is "collective security" against the terrorist threat. It is important to note that the responsibility of the Security Council in the maintenance of international peace and security and specifically the question of collective security was on the agenda of the 3046th Meeting of the Security Council, which was held for the first time at the level of Heads of State and Government on January 31, 1992. In a statement issued by the President of the Security Council on behalf of all those present it was stated, *inter alia*, that:

> The members of the Council reaffirm their commitment to the collective security system of the Charter to deal with threats to the peace and to reverse acts of aggression.
>
> The members of the Council express their deep concern over acts of international terrorism and emphasize the need for the international community to deal effectively with all such acts.

9) Note that on September 12, 2003, the Security Council voted to lift the sanctions against Libya. Libya, in turn, agreed to accept responsibility for the Lockerbie bombing, to renounce terrorism, to pay compensation to the victims' families, and to undertake to co-operate with any future Lockerbie investigation.[172]

---

171 *Case Concerning Questions of Interpretation and Application of the 1971 Montreal Convention Arising From the Aerial Incident at Lockerbie (Libya v. United States) Preliminary Objections* (1998) 37I I.L.M. 587.

172 See SC Res. 1506 (2003) U.N. Doc. S/RES/2003, 12 September 2003. Adopted by a vote of 13 in favour, with 2 abstentions (France, United States).

C. PEACEKEEPING ROLE OF THE UNITED NATIONS

The practice of sending U.N. Peacekeeping Forces or "Blue Berets" into crisis situations and interposing them between belligerents is well established,[173] but it was not envisaged in the Charter itself. Because peacekeeping operations go beyond the peaceful measures envisaged in Chapter VI of the U.N. Charter, but are not usually enforcement measures under Chapter VII, they have been dubbed "Chapter VI½" operations.[174] They were designed to keep a fragile peace and to stabilize a critical situation until a lasting solution could be found.[175] Examples of this kind of action are the forces that have been posted in Cyprus,[176] Lebanon,[177] the Middle East,[178] Cambodia,[179] and Yugoslavia.[180]

Such U.N. forces were rightly viewed as peacekeepers and not peacemakers or enforcers. Their placement requires the consent of the state in whose territory they are stationed[181] and their effectiveness needs continued Security Council support. In weighing the track record of the various peacekeeping operations Malcolm Shaw has expressed the opinion that they have met with "limited success in temporarily preventing major disturbances."[182] However, U.N. forces failed to avert the Arab–Israeli war in 1967 and the Turkish invasion of Cyprus in 1974. Shaw suggested that the withdrawal of the UNEF in the Middle East by the Secretary-General, after an Egyptian request, in effect may have precipitated the ensuing conflict.[183] Nevertheless, such operations clearly have an important role to play in preventing the escalation of conflicts.

---

173 In general, see H. Wisemann, *Peacekeeping: Appraisals and Proposals* (1983); R. Higgins, *United Nations Peacekeeping, 1946-67: Documents and Commentary* (1969-81) 4 vols.; United Nations, *The Blue Helmets*, 2d ed. (1990); and James, *Peacekeeping in International Politics* (1991).

174 Franck, *Recourse to Force*, *supra* note 2 at 39-40.

175 P. Kirsch, *supra* note 166.

176 Since GA Res. 186 of 1964, the U.N. Peacekeeping Force—Cyprus (UNFICYP) has been present because of the threat to international peace and security. See J. Stegenga, *The United Nations Force in Cyprus* (1968).

177 U.N. Interim Force in the Lebanon (UNIFIL) was created by GA Res. 425 (1978). See R. Thakur, *International Peacekeeping in Lebanon* (1987).

178 U.N. Emergency Force (UNEF) was established to monitor the Israel–Egypt disengagement in 1973, GA Res. 340 (1973) (dissolved since 1979) and the U.N. Disengagement Observer Force (UNDOF) was created to oversee the Israel–Syria disengagement, GA Res. 350 (1974). See *e.g.* Pogamy, *The Security Council and the Arab–Israeli Conflict* (1984).

179 U.N. Transitional Authority in Cambodia (UNTAC) was established in 1991 to restore and maintain peace in Cambodia and to ensure free and fair elections. See the *Final Act of the Paris Conference on Cambodia* (1992) 31 I.L.M. 174.

180 U.N. Protection Force (UNPROFOR) was established in 1992 to secure the functioning of the Sarajevo airport and the delivery of humanitarian assistance in Bosnia-Herzegovina. A collection of documents about the Yugoslav situation may be viewed in (1992) 31 I.L.M. 1421.

181 For, outside Chapter VII, the United Nations must respect the territorial sovereignty of member states: see U.N. Charter article 2(7) in the Documentary Supplement.

182 Shaw, *supra* note 3 at 1111.

183 *Ibid.*, n. 132.

In the late 1980s and early 1990s, with the Cold War left behind, the increased co-operation among the major powers saw peacekeeping come to the fore and the United Nations "conducting some missions that were unthinkable in the previous era."[184] In the Cold War period, 1945-1987, the Security Council created 13 peacekeeping or observer missions. These were preceded in the majority of cases "by cease-fire agreements and clearly delineated lines of authority."[185] At the end of the Cold War a new generation of operations was needed to deal with more fluid situations.[186] They typically required more robust actions by U.N. forces, who often had to act as peacemakers, in addition to filling more traditional roles as peacekeepers. In addition, the U.N. has increasingly been called upon to undertake peacebuilding activities—that is, to provide missions and personal aid to the reconstruction of civil society after a destructive conflict has ended. Many operations now involve such wide-ranging activities as confidence-building measures, power-sharing arrangements, electoral support, strengthening the rule of law, and economic and social development. The U.N. Department of Peacekeeping Operations was created in 1992 to support this increased demand for complex peacekeeping. Yet, for the ever-widening range of demands on peacekeeping activities, a significant complicating factor was and is the danger to international peace and security posed by internal rather than international armed conflicts.

Many of the new generation peacekeeping operations were successful. In El Salvador and Mozambique, for example, U.N. peacekeeping helped build stable peace. Other efforts failed, in some cases due to overly optimistic assessments of what U.N. peacekeeping could accomplish, in others due to the reluctance of states to commit the required resources and personnel, or to provide missions with sufficiently robust mandates. For example, the Security Council sent peacekeepers to conflict zones like Somalia, where neither a ceasefire nor the consent of all the parties in conflict had been secured. The killing of U.S. servicemen in the streets of Mogadishu in 1993 prompted the U.S. government to review its policy on peacekeeping.[187] Subsequent dramatic failures—most notably the 1995 massacre in Srebrenica (Bosnia and Herzegovina) and the 1994 genocide in Rwanda—led to a period of both retrenchment and reassessment of U.N. peacekeeping. In both the Srebrenica and Rwanda situations, limitations in troop strength and tight restrictions on the mandate to use force hampered the peacekeepers' ability to avert catastrophe.[188]

The Report of the Panel on U.N. Peace Operations (Brahimi Report), commissioned by Secretary-General Kofi Annan in 2000, set out a range of minimum requirements for successful U.N. peacekeeping missions, including rapid deployment capacity, better headquarters capacity for mission planning and support, clear and realistic mandates,

---

184   *Report of the Secretary-General on the Work of the Organization*, UN GAOR, 46th Sess., Supp. No. 1 at 3; U.N. Doc. A/46/1 (1991).

185   B. Menon, "Beyond Peacekeeping" in Tessitore and Woolfson, *supra* note 102 at 3.

186   S.R. Ratner, *The New UN Peacekeeping: Building Peace in Lands of Conflict After the Cold War* (1995) at 22-24.

187   United States, *Administration Policy on Reforming Multilateral Peace Operations* (1994) 33 I.L.M. 798.

188   Shaw, *supra* note 3 at 1139-45.

consent to the operation by the parties in conflict, and adequate resources.[189] Efforts at improvement notwithstanding, significant challenges to effective peacekeeping remain. The U.N. Department of Peacekeeping Operations describes the situation as follows:[190]

> The challenges that face UN peacekeeping in 2004 are immense. In the Democratic Republic of the Congo, for example, the UN is supporting a transitional government in a huge country with minimal infrastructure and little national cohesion. It is preparing Kosovo and the parties involved for talks on final status. It is building up its mission in Liberia and managing the downsizing of UN operations in Timor-Leste and Sierra Leone. At the same time, new crises have flared and new peace agreements have been signed. Several of the world's most capable militaries are heavily committed—mostly in Iraq and Afghanistan— while developing countries, which make up the UN's top 10 contributors to peacekeeping operations, have limited means.

> By July 2004, the Department of Peacekeeping Operations was managing 17 field operations (16 peacekeeping operations and one political mission) throughout the world, including a recently expanded operation in Cote d'Ivoire and two newly established missions in Burundi and Haiti. In addition, the United Nations was facing the prospects of at least one more new mission—in Sudan. As a result, the number of uniformed personnel deployed in peacekeeping operations was expected to grow from 51,000 in early 2004 to some 78,000 in the course of the year with the addition of 25,000 troops, 2,500 civilian police and 1,500 military observers. Some 42 senior officials—civilian, military and police—could be needed to manage those operations on the ground, along with 6,500 civilian personnel (added to some 9,700 already deployed as of early 2004) as well as necessary material resources such as vehicles and office and communications equipment. The peacekeeping budget may nearly double as a result: additional missions could require an estimated $2.38 billion above the currently proposed budget of $2.65 billion for 2004-2005. ...

> Key factors
> Certain factors are universally critical for the success of any UN peacekeeping operation, regardless of location. The international community must diagnose the problem correctly before prescribing peacekeeping as the treatment; there must be a peace to keep; and all key parties to the conflict must consent to stop fighting and to accept the UN role in helping them resolve their dispute. Members of the Security Council must agree on a clear and achievable mandate and the operation's desired outcome. In addition, deployment must proceed at the required pace.

> The international community has to be prepared to stay the course. It is therefore essential that Member States summon the political will to support the United Nations politically, financially and operationally to enable the Organization to be truly credible as a force for peace. Real peace takes time; building national capacities takes time; rebuilding trust takes time. International peacekeepers must perform the tasks with professionalism, competence and integrity.

---

189 Report of the Panel on UN Peace Operations, U.N. Doc. A/55/305-S/2000/809, 21 August 2000.

190 "What Are the Current Challenges to Successful Peacekeeping?" in *United Nations Peacekeeping—Meeting New Challenges* (2004), online: <http://www.un.org/Depts/dpko/dpko/faq/>.

Some key issues currently facing U.N. peacekeeping include:

- *Personnel:* Finding troop contingents for burgeoning peacekeeping operations—and increasing participation by "northern" countries—remains a major concern. However, a larger challenge is meeting demands for the recruitment of thousands of skilled police officers and civilian staff with expertise in justice, civil administration, economic development or other specialized fields. U.N. peacekeeping must also secure other capabilities such as tactical air support, field medical facilities and movement control operations—resources usually provided by willing Member States.

- Ideally, these personnel would have some knowledge of the language, culture and political situation of the country concerned. They must also be available for deployment on short notice. The U.N. has recently broadened the civilian police eligibility pool to include retired officers. In addition, it has placed a high priority on training and on building rosters of rapidly deployable, qualified staff.

- *The need to restore basic services and government:* In the past, international donors have been reluctant to pay for civil service salaries or basic office equipment in local administrations. Currently, however, there is a growing consensus on the need to shore up basic state services, including the judiciary, civil administration and public utilities and to return post-conflict societies to normalcy as quickly as possible.

- *Law and order:* The U.N. has included rule of law as a critical part of mission planning and has made considerable progress in establishing a capacity to support activities by police, judiciary and corrections in ongoing operations.

In post-conflict societies, a judicial system—legal frameworks, courts, judges and prosecutors, prisons—must be able to render independent and fair justice at an early stage. If the local police force has lost credibility with the population, it may be necessary to deploy a temporary international force or to undertake a comprehensive retraining programme. The situation may call for a tribunal dedicated to redressing past war crimes, or for a truth and reconciliation commission.

- *Elections and restoration of democracy:* Several peacekeeping missions have been mandated to conduct elections. Elections are not a quick fix, however, and the U.N. has learned the importance of creating the right conditions first, including an acceptable level of security, a legal framework, a transparent voter registration process and sometimes even a constitution, with the consensus of all actors involved.

- *Security:* An insecure environment hinders peacekeeping and peacebuilding. Successful peacekeeping often requires large numbers of troops, particularly in the initial period of the mission. Their presence can provide some stability and security until a credible local police force can be built up.

The safety and security of U.N. field personnel became an issue of great concern within the U.N. with the unprecedented attack on U.N. headquarters in Baghdad on 19 August 2003, causing Secretary-General Kofi Annan to order a review of the entire United Nations security system. Improvements are ongoing and require further support by Member States.

- Collective action: The United Nations, through the Security Council, has provided a forum for the countries of the world to decide together how to respond to threats to peace and security. The contentious diplomatic prelude to the Iraq war inspired the Secretary-General to appoint a high-level Panel on Threats, Challenges and Change tasked with examining the major threats and challenges the world faces in the field of peace and security and making recommendations on how to respond effectively through collective action.

The High-level Panel's report, entitled *A More Secure World: Our Shared Responsibility*, was received by the Secretary-General in December 2004. He used it as a basis for his own report to the U.N. General Assembly in March 2005 entitled *In Larger Freedom: Towards Development, Security, and Human Rights for All.* His vision of collective security, in which he called for specific actions and institutional developments, ultimately found muted acceptance at the 2005 World Summit of heads of states and governments held at the United Nations in September 2005.[191]

D. THE UNITED NATIONS AND REGIONAL ARRANGEMENTS

United Nations Charter
Articles 52-54
Reproduced in the Documentary Supplement

NOTES

1) Chapter VIII of the Charter addresses the relationship between the United Nations, notably its Security Council, and "regional arrangements or agencies." Article 52(1) affirms the role of such regional entities in the maintenance of international peace and security. Indeed, article 52(2) envisages that regional efforts at peaceful settlement of disputes precede recourse to the Security Council. At the same time, article 53(1) is clear that any "enforcement action" by regional organizations requires the authorization of the Security Council. However, article 51, in referring to states' right to "individual and collective self-defence," provides some scope for the resort to force by regional or other mutual defence arrangements. In addition, as Shaw has observed, "regional peace-keeping operations, in the traditional sense of being based on consent and eschewing the use of force save in self-defence, do not need the authorization of the Security Council."[192] The Security Council must be at all times kept fully informed of any activities undertaken or contemplated by regional entities for the maintenance of international peace and security (article 54).

---

191 The three reports are respectively available as U.N. Doc. A/59/565 (2004); U.N. Doc. A/59/205 (2005); and U.N. Doc. A/60/L.1 (2005).

192 Shaw, *supra* note 3 at 1155. On the negotiating history of Chapter VIII of the U.N. Charter, see Franck, *Recourse to Force, supra* note 2 at 157-58.

2) Over the years, a range of regional actions in the peace and security context have taken place that did not fit squarely within the parameters provided by the Charter. Indeed, international practice may have evolved such that at least prior authorization of the Security Council is not required for certain regional measures. There appears to be willingness to countenance actions that might be described as "muscular" peacekeeping, designed to halt humanitarian crises.[193]

For example, although there was no prior authorization, the Security Council subsequently gave its blessing to the use of force by the Economic Community of West African States (ECOWAS) in Liberia in the 1990s.[194] ECOWAS has 16 member states, including Liberia. When a bloody civil war broke out in Liberia, ECOWAS initially sought to mediate between the factions. In June 1990, Liberia's President requested that ECOWAS send a peacekeeping force to help re-establish order. In August 1990, in view of the state of anarchy that prevailed in Liberia, ECOWAS instead deployed—against Liberian wishes—a large and heavily armed monitoring group (ECOMOG) to enforce a ceasefire between the warring parties. It was not until January 1991 that the President of the U.N. Security Council issued a statement that commended ECOWAS' efforts to promote peace in Liberia.[195] The ECOWAS-monitored ceasefire and peace plan broke down during 1992 and fighting flared up again. ECOMOG became heavily embroiled in combat. In resolution 788 (1992), the Security Council finally determined that "the deterioration of the situation in Liberia constitutes a threat to international peace and security, particularly in West Africa as a whole," and went on to recall "the provisions of Chapter VIII of the Charter." It then welcomed ECOWAS' "continued commitment ... to and the efforts towards a peaceful resolution of the Liberian conflict," and decided, under Chapter VII, to impose a comprehensive arms embargo on Liberia.[196] In 1993, again commending ECOWAS for its efforts, the Security Council established a U.N. Observer Mission to assist ECOMOG in the implementation of a peace agreement that had been reached in the interim.[197]

3) Note that the Security Council similarly commended various actions, including the ousting of a military junta, undertaken by ECOMOG from 1997 onward to quell the civil war and attendant humanitarian crisis in Sierra Leone.[198]

193 See e.g. Franck, Recourse to Force, supra note 2 at 162.

194 For a detailed analysis, see I. Mgbeoji, Collective Insecurity: The Liberian Crisis, Unilateralism, and Global Order (2003); D. Wippman, "Enforcing the Peace: ECOWAS and the Liberian Civil War" in L.F. Damrosch, ed., Enforcing Restraint: Collective Intervention in Internal Conflicts (1993) at 157.

195 U.N. Doc. S/22110, Add. 3, 22 January 1991.

196 S.C. Res. 788 (1992), UN SCOR, 47th year, Res. and Dec.; U.N. Doc. S/INF/48 at 72. (Adopted by unanimous vote.)

197 See S.C. Res. 856 (1993), UN SCOR, 48th year, Res. and Dec.; U.N. Doc. S/INF/49 at 110. (Adopted by unanimous vote.)

198 For a summary, see Franck, Recourse to Force, supra note 2 at 159-62.

4) Do you agree with Lobel and Ratner's assessment that, in the Liberia case, the Security Council implicitly authorized the ECOWAS intervention?[199] What about Franck's conclusion that the Security Council's "*ex post facto* approval [of the Liberia and Sierra Leone interventions] effectively reinterprets the text of Article 53"?[200] What are the risks of this type of development?

5) Can broader legal conclusions regarding interventions by regional actors or "coalitions of the willing" be drawn from the examples of Liberia and Sierra Leone? Why have other interventions, such as those by NATO in Kosovo or by the U.S.-led coalition forces in Iraq in 2003 (Gulf War II), remained highly controversial? Can silence of the Security Council, or its failure to condemn an action, be interpreted as an authorization of the use of force?[201] See the discussion of the Kosovo intervention, above in Section B.3 on "Humanitarian Intervention," and the discussion of Gulf War II, above in Section B.4 on "Collective Measures Pursuant to the U.N. Charter."

6) Note that the Cuban Quarantine, discussed in Section B.1 of this chapter, was endorsed by an OAS resolution. The United States justified the quarantine not as (collective) self-defence, but as a regional peace and security measure under Chapter VIII of the Charter. According to the United States, since the quarantine was recommended but not ordered by the OAS, it did not constitute "enforcement action" within the meaning of article 53, thus not requiring Security Council authorization. However, the United States also suggested that the silence of the Security Council could be construed as a (subsequent) authorization of the measure.[202] Compare again the earlier discussions of the 1999 Kosovo and 2003 Iraq interventions.

---

199 Lobel and Ratner, *supra* note 115 at 132.

200 Franck, *Recourse to Force*, *supra* note 2 at 162.

201 See Lobel and Ratner, *supra* note 115.

202 See A. Chayes, "Law and the Quarantine of Cuba" (1963) 43 Foreign Aff. 550 at 556.

Online Index

An electronic index is available on the book's website. To access the index, go to:

<http://www.emp.ca/intlaw7>

Once at the website, click on the link Online Index and enter a keyword to search the entire text and footnotes. The website will return all references to the input keyword by page numbers in the book.